METHUEN'S
MANUALS OF MODERN PSYCHOLOGY
(*Founder Editor C. A. Mace 1946-68*)
General Editor H. J. Butcher

The Psychological Assessment of Mental and Physical Handicaps

The Psychological Assessment of Mental and Physical Handicaps

Edited by PETER MITTLER

METHUEN & CO LTD
11 New Fetter Lane London EC4

First published 1970
© 1970 *Methuen & Co Ltd*
Printed in Great Britain by
T & A Constable Ltd
Edinburgh

SBN 416 04570 7

Distributed in the USA
by Barnes & Noble Inc

Contents

1   Principles of Psychological Assessment
H. Gwynne Jones

PART ONE

Assessment of Adults: Types of Assessment

4 Vocational Guidance
Phillida Salmon

5 The Clinical Interview
R. R. Hetherington

6 Psychophysiological Techniques

Gordon S. Claridge

PART TWO

Assessment of Adults:
Clinical Applications

7 Acute Psychiatric Patients

P. Ley

8 Long-stay Psychiatric Patients
John E. Orme

A*

9   Neurological Deficits

Elizabeth K. Warrington

10   Subnormal Adults

H. C. Gunzburg

11 Geriatric Patients

Moyra K. Williams

PART THREE

Assessment of Children

14　Deaf and Partially Hearing Children
Michael Reed

15　Children with Physical Handicaps
Joan Reynell

17 Severely Subnormal Children

Rosemary Shakespeare

18 Maladjusted Children
Maurice Chazan

19 Culturally Handicapped Children
A. T. Ravenette

20 Language Disorders
P. J. Mittler

PART FOUR

Experimental Advances

Contributors

D. Bannister, B.A., Dip.Psych., Ph.D., M.R.C. External Scientific Staff, Bexley Hospital, Dartford, Kent.

T. M. Caine, M.A., Ph.D., Consultant Psychologist, Claybury Hospital, Woodford Green, Essex.

Maurice Chazan, M.A., Department of Education, University College of Swansea.

Gordon S. Claridge, B.A., Ph.D., Senior Lecturer in Clinical Psychology, Department of Psychological Medicine, University of Glasgow.

T. F. Fitzpatrick, B.A., M.Ed., Dip.Ed.Psych., Senior Research Associate, Department of Education, University of Manchester.

J. L. Gedye, M.A., M.B., B.Chir., Lecturer in the Department of Electrical Engineering Science, University of Essex.

R. D. Griffiths, B.A., M.Phil., Lecturer in Psychology, Institute of Psychiatry, Maudsley Hospital, University of London.

H. C. Gunzburg, M.A., D.Phil., Consultant Psychologist, Hospitals for the Subnormal, Birmingham Area.

R. R. Hetherington, B.Sc., Ph.D., F.B.Ps.S., Senior Lecturer in Clinical Psychology, Department of Psychiatry, University of Liverpool.

H. Gwynne Jones, B.Sc., Dip.Ed., Professor of Psychology, Department of Psychology, University of Leeds.

Winifred Langan, Dip.Psych., Ph.D., formerly Senior Educational Psychologist, Manchester Education Committee (now retired).

P. Ley, B.A., Ph.D., Dip.Psych., Lecturer in Clinical Psychology, Department of Psychiatry, University of Liverpool.

E. Miller, B.Sc., Lecturer in Psychology, Department of Psychology, University of Hull.

P. J. Mittler, M.A., Ph.D., Director, Hester Adrian Research Centre for the Study of Learning Processes in the Mentally Handicapped, University of Manchester.

John E. Orme, B.A., Ph.D., Consultant Psychologist, Middlewood Hospital, Sheffield.

A. T. Ravenette, B.A., Dip.Psych., Ph.D., Senior Educational Psychologist, London Borough of Newham.

Michael Reed, B.Sc., Inspector of Special Education, Inner London Education Authority.

Joan Reynell, B.Sc., Ph.D., Senior Lecturer in Educational Psychology, Institute of Child Health, University of London.

Mary Ritchie, B.Sc., Educational Psychologist, Gloucestershire Education Committee.

Phillida Salmon, M.A., Ph.D., Lecturer in Developmental Psychology, Department of Humanities and Social Sciences, University of Surrey.

R. Douglass Savage, B.A., Ph.D., Lecturer in Applied Psychology, Department of Psychological Medicine, University of Newcastle-upon-Tyne.

Rosemary Shakespeare, B.A., Dip.Psychol., Senior Clinical Psychologist, St Ebba's Hospital, Epsom, Surrey.

M. B. Shapiro, M.A., Ph.D., Reader in Psychology, Institute of Psychiatry, Maudsley Hospital, University of London.

Moya Tyson, B.A., B.Sc.(Econ.), Ph.D., Senior Educational Psychologist for Special Schools and Special Units, London Borough of Hounslow.

★ F. W. Warburton, M.A., Ph.D., Professor of Experimental Education, University of Manchester.

J. Ward, B.A., Dip.Psych., Dip.Child Psych., Lecturer in Education, Department of Education, University of Manchester.

Elizabeth K. Warrington, B.Sc., Ph.D., Principal Psychologist, The National Hospital for Nervous Diseases, Queen Square, London.

Moyra Williams, D.Phil., Principal Clinical Psychologist, Fulbourne and Addenbrooke's Hospitals, Cambridge.

Phillip Williams, M.A., B.Sc., Ph.D., Senior Lecturer in Education, Department of Education, University College of Swansea.

W. Mary Woodward, B.A., Ph.D., Senior Lecturer in Psychology, Department of Psychology, University College of Swansea.

★ deceased.

Acknowledgements

The editor and contributors would like to thank the following for permission to use figures and tables from the sources given below:

Pitman Medical Publishing Co. Ltd for Table 2.1 from R. W. Payne in *Handbook of Abnormal Psychology*, edited by H. J. Eysenck; *The British Journal of Educational Psychology* for Figure 2.1 and Table 12.2 by H. J. Eysenck and for Figure 16.1; *The British Journal of Social and Clinical Psychology* for Table 8.1; *Archives of Neurology* for Table 9.1 by L. B. Milner; The Johns Hopkins Press, Baltimore, for Table 9.2 from H. Hécaen in *Interhemispheric Relations and Cerebral Dominance*, edited by Mountcastle; Harper and Row, New York, for Figures 9.1 and 9.2 from *Human Brain and Psychological Process* by A. R. Luria and for Figure 11.3 from *Psychological Development Through the Life Span* by S. L. Pressey and R. G. Kuhlen; *Brain* for Figure 9.3 by M. Kinsbourne and E. Warrington, Figure 9.5 by J. McFie and O. Zangwill and Figure 9.6 by M. Piercy; Edward Arnold (Publishers) Ltd for Figure 9.4 from *The Parietal Lobes* by M. Critchley; *American Journal of Mental Deficiency* for table 10.1 by R. Heber; Penguin Books Ltd for Figures 11.1 and 11.2 from *The Psychology of Human Ageing* by D. B. Bromley; The Controller, Her Majesty's Stationery Office, for Tables 12.1 and 12.3 from *Children and their Primary Schools* (The Plowden Report) and for Tables 14.1A and 14.1B from *The Education of Deaf Children;* Manchester University Press for Table 14.2 from Murphy in *Educational Guidance and the Deaf Child*, edited by A. W. G. Ewing, and for Table 14.3 from *Educating Hearing Impaired Children in Normal Schools* by J. C. Johnson; William Heinemann Medical Books Ltd for Figures 14.2 and 14.3 from *The Deaf Child* by E. Whetnall and D. B. Fry; Lloyd-Luke (Medical Books) Ltd for Figure 15.2 from *Assessement of Cerebral Palsy*, Vol. II, by K. S. Holt and J. K. Reynell; McGraw-Hill Publishing Co. Ltd for the Diagnostic Framework Table in Chapter 16 from *The Mentally Retarded Child* by H. B. and N. M. Robinson (1965); University of Minnesota Press for Tables 20.1A and 20.1B from *Certain Language Skills in Children*, Institute of Child Welfare Monograph No. 26, by M. C. Templin (1957); *Speech Pathology and Therapy* for Table 20.2 by T. T. S. Ingram; The University of Illinois Press for Figure 20.1 from the *Illinois Test of Psycholinguistic Abilities* by S. A. McCarthy and J. J. Kirk; *Journal of Mental Deficiency Research* for Figure 20.2 by V. K. Tubbs.

'Après le mal, le remède; après la constatation des défaillances intellectuelles de toutes sortes, passons au traitement.'

From: BINET, A. (1911) *Les Idées Modernes sur les Enfants*
Paris: Flammarion. p. 140.

Introduction

Each day about four thousand people are given an individually administered psychological test in Great Britain alone. This is, of course, a speculative and probably inaccurate estimate, based on official returns of the number of full-time psychologists working in clinical and educational services; extrapolating even further, it is possible that one million individual tests are administered by psychologists in a year.

Whatever the accuracy of such an estimate, it is fair to say that psychological testing and assessment represent a substantial proportion of all applied psychology, and that it is certainly that branch of psychology with which the public comes into the most frequent contact, either directly or indirectly. A poll of a random sample of the population would probably reveal an 'image' of the psychologist as a person who spends much of his time 'testing people' for various purposes. Although this view might represent a stereotype, and although the methods and purposes of psychological testing have undoubtedly become more varied and sophisticated, there is every likelihood that this stereotype will remain, since the number of applied psychologists is increasing yearly, and the demand for their services rising even more sharply. At the beginning of 1969, there were some 350 full-time educational and about the same number of clinical psychologists, with perhaps another 100 engaged in full-time training.

In view of the substantial investment of time and training in psychological testing of all the various kinds of handicapped adults and children, it is surprising to find so little literature devoted to this subject. There are, of course, a number of standard texts which deal with psychometric aspects of test construction, reliability, validity, standardization, etc., but none of these fully covers the more clinical aspects of testing handicapped people. There are also several comprehensive books dealing with different handicaps, or with their educational implications, but only marginally with assessment methods and problems. But the student and practitioner of clinical or educational psychology remains short of comprehensive books dealing specifically with the assessment and diagnostic aspects of his work; this is particularly the case in Britain.

This book aims to fill such a gap. It is addressed to clinical and educational psychologists and to undergraduate and postgraduate students on courses concerned with clinical aspects of psychological testing. It is also relevant for the increasing number of workers who are concerned with the systematic assessment of the handicapped. This book is deliberately designed to overlap the boundaries and to blur the distinctions between disciplines that in Britain are described as clinical and educational psychology. This is indeed the principal justification for its length. It is recognized, of course, that these are distinct areas of professional specialization, each of which has its own contribution to make. But the two professions have much in common, even though the emphasis and some of the techniques may be different. It is hoped, therefore, that each profession may learn a little from this book about the problems and strategies of the other.

But assessment is not the prerogative of psychologists; other professions are increasingly concerned with the development of more effective and above all more reliable assessment methods. Obvious examples are to be found in all branches of medicine, where insistence on accurate assessment can be traced back to Galen, but many other professions are now devoting more systematic thought to the need for improved assessment methods. Physiotherapists, speech and occupational therapists, social workers and many others are thinking and writing on this subject, while teachers, particularly those in special education, are probably the biggest single professional group to whom assessment is of prime importance. The concept of handicap has broadened considerably in recent years. We recognize a greater number of handicaps, some of which are subtler and more complex in their effects than the more obvious disabilities. Concepts such as maladjustment, minimal brain damage and social disadvantage are examples of handicaps which are receiving much attention. It is also clear that people with an obvious and well-recognized illness or disability often suffer from additional disadvantages in their personal and social experiences; these too need skilled assessment, since successful treatment depends on the needs of the individual being considered in the context of his family and social background. Moreover, we think of 'handicap' on a continuum with the 'normal' and see handicap in normal people, and normality in the handicapped.

A critical question that psychologists need to resolve concerns the sharing of their assessment skills with other professions. Psychologists are under increasing pressure to allow at least some of their tests and instruments to be used by others; this is a highly controversial and complex issue, but one which demands more sustained thought on the part of psychologists than it has so far received. It is undeniable that the administration and interpretation of psychological tests demands a certain level of formal training, and that the unrestricted or at least unsupervised use of tests by non-psychologists might well be to the disadvantage of those being assessed, and lead to a general lowering of standards of testing. But other considerations are also relevant. Firstly, it can hardly be denied that there is a continuum of tests, at one end of which lie a number of highly specialized and complex instruments which clearly need to be restricted to trained psychologists, while at the other end of the scale lie many others which are simple to administer and interpret. Although such a distinction is already applied in the sale of tests, it is not clear how much agreement exists on where the line between them should be drawn, nor is there any recent information on the use of tests by people who might not be considered appropriately qualified by present standards.

Secondly, a distinction needs to be drawn between graduate psychologists and those with an additional postgraduate qualification in educational or clinical psychology. How many university departments in Britain offer a course on at least the elements of psychological assessment at undergraduate level, and how adequately do these provide a foundation in psychometric theory and test construction for later postgraduate work? The experience of tutors responsible for postgraduate courses seems to suggest that some graduates come to these courses rather poorly equipped with knowledge of basic psychometric theory and practice; inevitably, interest varies, as does the quality of teaching in the subject. Few could claim that graduate psychologists engaged on full-time research should not use psychological tests without further training or appropriate supervision, but many mistakes of research design or interpretation could be avoided if research psychologists were more cautious in their use of tests and techniques which require training and experience. The mere possession of a degree in psychology is no guarantee that tests will be responsibly and professionally used.

A third consideration is one of wider social need. The demand for better assessment instruments on the part of non-psychologists is insistent and justified by the urgency of the need. How long can psychologists resist this pressure, and how legitimate is their claim to the virtual monopoly of psychological tests? How long can this monopoly be maintained in view of the likelihood that some restricted tests are already in unofficial use by other professions?

One approach to this problem is for certain university departments and appropriate professional societies to provide intensive courses for non-psychologists who need to use tests. The biggest demand would undoubtedly come from teachers, and indeed there is already some limited provision of this kind for those doing advanced diplomas in the education of handicapped children and in educational guidance and counselling. But more teachers concerned with remedial education could be introduced to a wider range of diagnostic tests than they commonly use at present, and many others would welcome the opportunity to gain more specialized knowledge – e.g. speech therapists interested in learning about language tests. One consequence of such a proposal is that the first stages of diagnostic testing could then be carried out by teachers or other therapists; the psychologist would be called in for more specialized assessment and advisory work, and would be able to delegate more routine testing to those more closely involved with the day-to-day treatment of the individual – rather along the lines of the recommendations of the Seebohm report (1968) on the more effective use of professionally trained social workers. Similar developments are under consideration in medicine, and even in psychology there are already instances of technicians and testers administering routine tests, leaving the psychologist free to devote himself to the more difficult procedures.

Proposals to train non-psychologists in some aspects of testing are likely to be strongly opposed on the grounds of risks to professional standards. On the other hand, the shortage of psychologists is likely to continue, despite recent recommendations for changes in recruitment and training, and not even the most optimistic forecast could envisage that psychologists could ever hope to meet all the demand for their services. In view of this shortage, it seems reasonable to suggest that psychologists themselves should take the initiative in making certain tests and techniques available on a wider scale, while ensuring that relevant training was available.

While this book is aimed particularly at psychologists, it is also designed to interest others who are professionally concerned with assessment problems and with the treatment of the handicapped. Each chapter has been written by a specialist with extensive practical experience of assessment. An attempt has been made to present theoretical issues, especially in the first three chapters, while the final part of the book is devoted to a number of research developments which, though still largely at an experimental stage, are likely to affect assessment techniques in the future. It is not claimed that this section provides a representative sample of current research relevant to assessment, but the several themes are reflected elsewhere in the book. For example, the chapters by Shapiro and Tyson illustrate two contrasting, but complementary, approaches to a more detailed assessment than is provided by conventional tests, an assessment that is linked to the planning and execution of a remedial or treatment programme. Piagetian methods of clinical assessment as described and modified by Woodward represent an attempt to isolate and understand cognitive processes, rather than mere achievement, while the new British Intelligence Scale described by Warburton and his associates is perhaps the most ambitious example of a multi-factorial approach to intellectual testing developed so far. By contrast, Gedye and Miller's report of research in automated testing is a very new but important development in techniques. Finally, the chapters by Bannister and Caine report original work in the field of personality assessment which has significant implications for our understanding of non-cognitive factors, not only in mental disorders but in normal personality functioning.

The central portions of the book dealing with assessment problems and techniques in the various handicaps are intended to provide a guide both to practical matters and to the more theoretical or research-orientated aspects of the applied psychologist's work; successful and relevant assessment demands a combination of theoretical knowledge and practical skills. It also depends on a thorough knowledge of the developmental or clinical features of handicap, so that assessment may provide a firm foundation for treatment. In the last analysis it is by his usefulness to his patient that the psychologist himself will be assessed.

PETER MITTLER

Manchester
January 1969

Principles of psychological assessment

H. Gwynne Jones

I THE NATURE OF PSYCHOLOGICAL ASSESSMENT

To the author's surprise, the Oxford Dictionary definition of *assessment* refers only to its usage in connection with matters of taxation (Onions, 1959). More gratifying, perhaps, to a psychologist is the definition of an *assessor* as 'one who sits beside . . . an advisor to a judge . . . especially when skilled in technical points'. Sundberg and Tyler (1962), in an excellent discussion of the meaning of psychological assessment, point out that probably the first influential use of the term in psychology was in the book *Assessment of Men* (O.S.S. Staff, 1948)* and that it was then used in preference to *psychodiagnosis* in order to emphasize that the aim of the Office of Strategic Services was the evaluation of the *worth* of a man rather than the discovery of pathology. This usage has clear historical linkages with the dictionary definition, and even more obvious affinity with the use of the term in fields such as literary criticism, so sadly neglected by the lexicographers.

The aim of the academic or general psychologist is the description of human behaviour and experience in terms of a parsimonious set of defined concepts and general laws linking these concepts. The applied psychologist works within and is dependent upon the utility of this theoretical frame of reference, but his immediate concern is with real people in real-life situations and his aim the achievement of some practical goal in relation to these people. That goal usually involves some modification of the behaviour and experience of the people concerned. An element of mutual assessment is involved in any human social interaction and, inevitably, assessment by the psychologist of his patient or client must loom large in their transactions.

At its most general level, assessment means the formation of impressions and the making of judgements about others. At a more technical level, psychological assessment is defined by Sundberg and Tyler as 'the systematic collection, organization, and interpretation of information about a person and his situations', to which one might add 'and the prediction of his behaviour in new situations'. This definition refers to the technology and methodology concerned with precise measurement of behaviour, the formulation of hypotheses and their

---

* The more restricted term *mental measurement* was used much earlier to describe the use of standardized tests for the evaluation of psychological qualities, especially intellectual abilities.

testing with which this book is largely concerned. Particularly in this introductory chapter, however, there is also need to consider Sundberg and Tyler's higher level definition of assessment as 'the processes used for decision-making and for developing a working image or model of the person-situation'.

Decision-making is a fundamental aspect of all applied psychology. Most projects may be regarded as proceeding through a seven-stage course, each involving decision processes.

1 Specification of the problem

A 'case' is usually presented to a psychologist either directly by the client's own statement of his problem and the type of help he is seeking, or by referral from a colleague or social agency, such as a school or court. An element of evaluation or assessment immediately enters into the situation when the problem as presented is reviewed in the light of the psychologist's own particular theoretical frame of reference and professional experience. Very frequently, his view of the problem, even at this initial stage, differs greatly from that of his client and the referring agent. Already, he is faced with the decision as to whether the problem, as he sees it, is one with which he is competent to deal. Psychology has some relevance to most human affairs, but not all human affairs are best dealt with by a psychologist. Assuming, however, that the case is accepted, decisions then have to be taken as to the aims of any formal assessment procedures to be employed in the investigation of the case.

2 Routine collection of data

In psychological as in most other professional practice, many problems and cases tend to fall into easily recognized categories in relation to which useful routines of investigation have evolved. Often, items included in such a routine are checks on rare but possible complications with important implications. The need for an economic distribution of time and effort often tempts one to exclude such checks, but penalties for error as well as probabilities must be appropriately weighed in decision-making. A respected medical colleague of the writer goes so far as to conceal his own medical background when he becomes a patient. This is to avoid being given V.I.P. treatment and being spared unpleasant routine checks.

In the routines of psychological investigation, testing techniques usually play an important part and, when appropriately standardized and validated, can be both economical and efficient. However, the availability of a multitude of tests and the large claims made for them have led to a tendency for some applied psychologists to confine their investigations to the employment of a standard battery of tests covering a wide range of cognitive and orectic attributes of the individual. In the author's view this is regrettable. Even the most comprehensive test-battery of practicable dimensions will not include measures of all the variables which might well be relevant to the problem under investigation: it will certainly include much that is irrelevant. One danger of this approach is the temptation to over-interpret one's findings. It is not only possible but very easy to draw invalid inferences from valid tests. Some examples of this danger will be given later in this chapter and many in later chapters.

Even in relatively routine situations it is essential to make explicit decisions as to the goals of assessment and to select appropriate procedures. In the author's own field of clinical psychology he frequently decides, on grounds of maximizing the ratio of gain to effort, to withhold his fire until the later stages of investigation, relying upon his medical and social-worker colleagues for the initial stages of inquiry. For some types of patient and some types of problem, however, the patient's relative status in respect of certain psychological functions is so frequently relevant as to demand routine measurement. A child, for example, lives a great deal of his life in a formal educational environment and cannot escape the associated pressures which inevitably become involved in, say, his emotional maladjustment from whatever source it stems. Fairly precise assessment of his intellectual status and levels of scholastic attainment is then essential for a realistic appraisal of his difficulties. These variables are frequently only peripherally related to the problems presented by adult patients and, initially at least, may quite adequately be assessed, although less accurately, from life-history and interview data.

3 The evaluation of routine data and the specification of problems requiring further investigation

This stage represents the first major attempt to arrive at the conceptual model of the 'person-situation' referred to in our definition of the assessment process. For the routine stage, a standard template of such a model may be employed, but rarely does an individual case more than very roughly approximate to the trial shape. To force it into conformity is to ignore the multiplicity of factors which conjointly determine behaviour and the special weight which any one or more of these needs to be given in specific instances.

Thus, at this stage, all the available data concerning the client and his problem have to be carefully evaluated. For the psychologist, the frame of reference for this evaluation is provided by the set of concepts, theories and empirical generalizations of general psychology and its relevant specialized branches. More often than not, however, applied psychology is practised in the context of interdisciplinary collaboration, and different theoretical languages have to be integrated or at least reconciled and brought to focus on the particular practical problem. This is the stage when joint discussion is most fruitful, if not essential.

The case conference highlights the problems of communication which is a necessary and inevitable aspect of any process of assessment and which will be discussed later. At the conference, each specialist reports his own findings to date and contributes to the joint discussion and evaluation which usually results in the specification of problems and areas of uncertainty which require further investigation. Decisions are made as to the priorities and the allocation of these investigations among the disciplines concerned.

4 Specific investigations

For the psychologist, standardized tests may again prove valuable tools at this stage of assessment, but the tests employed tend to be of a more specific nature, both in terms of the range of psychological functions assessed and the standardization sample. The test at this stage is often used very much in the way of an experimental procedure to verify a specific hypothesis and its norms to provide control data. For example, at the initial routine stage of investigation, intellectual functions may be assessed by a 'global' test such as the W.A.I.S. or Stanford Binet with norms representative of a very broad sample of the population. At the present stage, however, emphasis may need to be placed on some more restricted aspect of intellectual ability, say speed of problem-solving, or the relationship between this and other specified aspects of functioning. Equally, the client's scores may need to be evaluated in relation to those of a specific sub-population, e.g. university students or even university students within a given faculty. Validation data of a particular kind may also be important, e.g. data concerning probability of success on a particular type of academic course.

These requirements, for the example described, are to a large extent met by a test or series of tests such as the *Nufferno* (Furneaux, 1956). But frequently at this degree of specificity, no standardized validated tests are available. For example, Jones (1960) describes the diagnostic assessment of a series of psychiatric patients, all displaying abnormalities within the single function of learning, but each on detailed analysis proving to be based on quite different, more basic and highly specific dysfunctions. It is difficult to conceive of a test of learning ability which would adequately cover and differentiate between all the relevant factors such as the mechanisms involved (e.g. short versus long-term storage), stages of the process (e.g. acquisition, retention and recall), material learned (e.g. verbal versus non-verbal) and the sensory modalities via which the information is processed. Even if an appropriate battery could be constructed, its use, even at this stage of assessment, would be grossly uneconomic. A decision to focus the investigation, initially at least, on some more limited aspect of functioning is likely to be more productive. Such a decision is essentially the statement of a hypothesis and the assessment procedures which follow are essentially of an experimental nature. This is particularly so when the hypothesis refers not to some static aspect of functioning but to dynamic interrelationships between variables, i.e. not of the form 'A is unable to carry out operations of type B', but of the form 'A is unable to carry out operations of type B in circumstances of type C'.

A major advantage of such an experimental approach to assessment problems is its self-corrective nature. Failure of validation necessarily leads to modification of the current hypothesis and hence to further experimental testing. The discipline of experimental work and its sceptical foundations also make it more likely that alternative explanations of findings are examined. Another important consequence of this approach is that it leads naturally to treatment or other modification procedures. The best form of validation is the achievement of experimental control via some manipulable independent variable. The extension of this control on a more permanent basis and into the patient's normal environment is the essential basis of 'behaviour therapy' and related approaches to behaviour modification. Examples of the experimental approach to applied psychology will be found throughout this book and the chapter by Shapiro is devoted entirely to the intensive assessment of the single case by these methods.

As has already been argued, the use of standardized tests is not incompatible with experimentally orientated assessment. However, to be used in this way, adequate information concerning the test's standardization, reliability, validity and internal structure must be available and the scores obtained interpreted in the light of this information and with a fair degree of psychometric sophistication. Much of this book is concerned with psychometric problems and a later section of this chapter deals with some technical aspects of testing.

The term 'test' is best restricted to assessment techniques yielding quantitative ratings or scores objectively derived from standard procedures. Many psychologists also make a great deal of use of devices and techniques, sometimes referred to as tests but which require subjective judgement of the raw data and result in assessments of a qualitative nature. These are better described as 'clinical instruments' and include the popular projective techniques such as the *Rorschach Ink-blots* and the *Thematic Apperception Technique* or *T.A.T.* (see Chapter 3). These are less amenable to experimental usage for the testing of predictions, but may be the source of hypotheses leading to predictions concerning the behaviour of the individual being assessed which can be tested in other situations. Indeed, the subjectivity of interpretation and the relatively low reliability and validity associated with these procedures makes such external checks essential.

A major criticism which may be made of many techniques of this nature is the excessive load which they are expected to bear. Cronbach and Gleser (1957), applying the concepts of information theory to psychometrics, point out the inevitable inverse relationship between *band-width*, the amount and complexity of information processed in a given time, and *fidelity*, the precision with which the information is transmitted. Maximum fidelity is always desirable, but particular assessment aims may require a broader band-width at the expense of some fidelity. This is often so during the earlier stages of an investigation, but at the present stage the ideal usually remains a test of high fidelity and low band-width, i.e. a highly valid measure of a specific attribute. Regarded in this light, the frequent claim that a technique such as the Rorschach provides an assessment of the *total personality*, is patently ridiculous.

For the tough-minded psychologist, however, the danger of abandoning this

B

type of technique is that he may, at the same time, neglect important content and dynamic aspects of his clients' problems. Techniques of conceptual analysis, such as those of Osgood and Kelly (see Chapter 26), can often provide useful alternatives. Although sensitive and flexible, they are essentially objective procedures, the reliability and validity of which can be assessed by orthodox means. Their adaptability enables their band-width to be adjusted according to the nature of the problem and they fit very well into an experimental framework. Apart from their usefulness for the assessment of individual differences in formal aspects of conceptual thinking, they have proved very valuable in the investigation of inter-personal relationships, the nature of individual self-concepts and aspects of change during various types of therapy.

5 Re-evaluation of assessment data and action decisions

In the preceding section an emphasis has been placed on objective methods of assessment and the experimental method. The latter never leads to certainty: an experiment can only demonstrate the falsity of a hypothesis or add some slight incremental gain to the confidence with which it is proposed. The experimenter is merely assessing the relative probabilities within a given very limited sub-set of a very large set of possibilities. Research is a continuing process with no end-point.

The applied psychologist or practitioner must, however, be prepared to make a judgement and to reach a conclusion from inconclusive data. Particularly when dealing with the problems of individuals, he is constantly aware of the restrictions of time, the complexity of the relevant variables and the difficulty of generalizing from the miniature situations of the laboratory to real life. At some stage the current hypotheses which are richest in relevant implications must become working hypotheses upon the basis of which he must be prepared to give an opinion or to decide upon appropriate action. Thus, what is advocated is an attempt to work in a scientific spirit, to be sceptical, to test assumptions and predictions whenever possible and to seek reasonable alternative hypotheses to explain the facts, but also acceptance of the responsibility of forming an opinion on less than adequate evidence and readiness to act on that opinion.

What is here described as the forming of an opinion is identical with the process of developing a working image or model of the person-situation referred to in Sundberg and Tyler's definition of assessment. This includes a great deal more than the abstract generalizations and hypotheses formally stated and formally tested during the investigation phase of assessment. From his very first contact the psychologist is aware of his client as a person in a particular social context. He is, however, a hypothetical person constructed by the psychologist, more an image than a model at this stage – and that image may have many features which reflect the assessor more than the assessed. The psychologist, by virtue of his specialist knowledge and training, should be very aware of the biases entering into inter-personal perception, but equally aware of the difficulty of controlling them, especially perhaps the particular biases which psychologica training itself imposes.

The formal processes of assessment are designed to be as free as possible from such bias although it inevitably enters into the selection of procedures. As assessment data accumulates it progressively modifies the image, but the stage now being discussed is the one at which all the data collected are systematically examined and *interpreted* in the light of all the information available concerning the person being assessed. In this way the psychologist's initial concept of his client, the image referred to, is refined into a hypothetical dynamic model of selected aspects of his make-up and their interactions with equally schematized representations of environmental situations relevant to his problems. Such an abstract model leaves out much of the person but provides a parsimonious basis for decision-making.

The efficiency of the evaluation and interpretation of test results and similar data is greatly enhanced by the application of statistical and related objective techniques, but in most psychological assessment a great deal also depends upon the assessor's own more subjective judgement, i.e. on his clinical skill. Meehl's (1954) influential book on *Clinical versus Statistical Prediction* gave focus and new impetus to a perennial controversy concerning the relative effectiveness of actuarial and clinical methods for assessment purposes, particularly when data from a variety of sources has to be integrated. Meehl reviewed a number of studies in which the two methods were compared in terms of their accuracy in predicting real-life criteria such as academic grades, success in various occupations, outcomes of therapy, etc. In none of these, nor indeed in many later similar investigations, was it possible to demonstrate that the clinical approach produced more accurate predictions even when additional data were available to the clinician. However, the complexities of many psychological problems make any sort of actuarial decision based on multivariate statistical prediction impracticable, as Meehl himself takes care to point out. In his own words it is frequently necessary to 'use our heads instead of a formula'. Also, as should be evident from this description of stages in the assessment process, a great deal of decision-making and other judgemental activity of a type quite different from that assessed in these investigations is required of the psychologist. Meehl's main conclusion, with which the writer certainly agrees, is that a great deal of skilled time is now spent in tasks which could be more efficiently carried out by clerical workers using routine statistical methods. The increasing availability of computers lends special force to this argument.

The action decisions and the actions taken following this phase of assessment may be the responsibility of the psychologist himself, the joint responsibility of an inter-disciplinary team, or the responsibility of a colleague in that team. The latter two possibilities again raise the problems of communication and the psychologist will anyway need to communicate at least some aspects of his findings to the client, and often to the referring agency. Frequently, in fact, the psychologist's task ends with the writing of a report including action recommendations.

Decisions and actions will, of course, be taken in relation to the original practical goal which will have become more clearly defined, possibly modified and incorporated into the assessment model. Inevitably, value judgements and ethical considerations are prominent at this stage but in fact enter into all aspects of assessment. Decision processes, communication problems and ethical questions are discussed separately in a later section of this chapter.

6 Treatment as assessment and the assessment of treatment

At the beginning of this chapter, stress was laid on the fact that applied psychology is concerned with the solution of problems and the resolution of difficulties experienced by human beings in real-life situations. Thus the goal of assessment is the devising and application of procedures designed to modify the client's reactions to situations or, by appropriate manipulation of the environment, to modify the actual situations, i.e. treatment in the broadest sense. As already argued, such treatment can and indeed should be considered as part of the assessment process. The crucial test of a model is whether the modification procedures it suggests do produce the predicted effects. Thus, the treatment situation is appropriately entered with the same experimental attitude as that adopted during assessment. The initial assessment model is likely to require considerable modification and may need to be abandoned in favour of another suggested by the observed treatment effects.

Quite apart from the concept of treatment as a form of assessment, it is important to apply objective methods of describing relevant changes in the client's modes of functioning in order to assess the efficacy of the modification procedures. Too frequently, criteria of improvement are vague, subjective and holistic. A thorough evaluation of all the possible effects of a particular treatment is scarcely possible, but an attempt should be made to measure changes along dimensions related to the specified aims of the therapist.

7 Research

In a sense, the experimental type of assessment advocated in this and a later chapter by Shapiro is a form of research carried out on a single case. This has a value, however, well beyond the individual case. Psychological problems are seldom unique and valid microcosmic generalizations are likely to apply to a large group of individuals. Thus, new standard techniques of testing what may become standard hypotheses can be gradually developed and appropriate control data collected. Research orientated applied work of this type has the dual advantage of enabling future work to be carried out with progressively greater economy of effort and of contributing to general theories of normal and abnormal psychology.

A great deal more also needs to be known about standard test and similar procedures used or advocated for use in various fields of applied psychology.

Appropriate data can only come from the 'field' and operational research concerned with such matters as the validation of assessment procedures or the evaluation of the effects of standard remedial techniques is a very proper function of the applied psychologist and one which derives from and contributes to his more 'clinical' activities.

Many applied psychologists will also retain a strong and active interest in research of a more 'pure' nature on topics related to their applied field. Advances in practice are very dependent upon advances in fundamental research and practical work, if allied with knowledge of the research literature, can be a most fruitful source of valuable hypotheses.

II DECISION MAKING IN ASSESSMENT

Formal decision theory (see Edwards and Tversky, 1967; Luce *et al.*, 1965) originated outside psychology and was developed by economists and others to provide a model of how decisions *should be*, rather than how they *are*, made. Initially, and to a great extent even now it is concerned with *economic* not *psychological* man. Its theorems were derived from assumptions which include the assumption that man behaves rationally with complete sensitivity to and knowledge of all the possible actions open to him and their outcomes (or the probabilities of different outcomes). Basically, therefore, decision theory is prescriptive rather than descriptive. The two main types of variables with which it is concerned are the *utility*, i.e. the gain or loss, or pay-off, of each possible outcome and the *probability* that each relevant event will occur. Its mathematical theorems are concerned with the manner in which probabilities and utilities interact to control decisions.

In recent years a great deal more psychological research has been concerned with the manner in which real-life human decision-making behaviour differs from the ideal. Both the prescriptive and the descriptive models have become highly elaborated and applied in a variety of fields. In general, it appears that the weakness of a real man as compared with economic man lies not so much in the rationality of his decision-making but in his processing of the information upon which the decisions are based. In particular, human beings appear to find it difficult to combine conflicting attributes of alternatives even in rather simple choice situations, and as soon as the choice becomes at all complicated the natural decisions deviate markedly but systematically from the optima. Despite the claims made for the human brain as a computer (based largely on its operation in perceptual situations), interactions between factors tend to be ignored and complex multidimensional problems tend to be simplified by collapsing them along a single simple evaluative dimension. The latter finding is reminiscent of the pervasive 'halo-effect' in assessment situations and Osgood's demonstration of the excessive semantic weight borne by the 'good-bad' dimension in human conceptualization.

These conclusions raise once more the problem of 'clinical versus statistical prediction' and it would seem wise for the psychologist to employ actuarial techniques whenever these are feasible and appropriate. Some decision theorists also advocate that, in complex judgement situations, the human observer should enter into a man/computer collaboration by subdividing his task into several more elementary judgements and formulating a set of combinatorial rules the application of which is delegated to a computer. In 'clinical' situations, however, many of the more elementary judgements and the weighting system adopted for their combination would need to be subjectively determined in the light of the 'goals' set by the clinician (Shepherd, 1964). Not the least advantage of such a procedure would be the necessity for the clinician to make his rationale explicit and therefore more open to analysis and self-criticism.

Formal decision theory in its prescriptive sense is clearly relevant to applied psychology as a guide to improving assessment strategies, but the descriptive study of decision-making in clinical situations should also contribute a great deal to the improvement of practice. Little has been done in this way as yet, but Cronbach and Gleser (1957) present a valuable and thoughtful account of the application of decision theory to the more formal testing aspects of assessment. Sundberg and Tyler sum up the main implications of this work as:

(1) That emphasis in assessment needs to be laid on the *utility of outcomes*, not on specific testing techniques. From this point of view, for certain assessment purposes a relatively crude method of investigation may be preferable to any of the available sophisticated psychometric instruments.

(2) That validity questions should be considered in terms of improvement on alternative procedures and not improvement on chance. This is related to the question of *incremental validity* as Meehl (1959) describes the analysis of the independent contribution of specific sources of assessment information. An example of this type of consideration is the discussion, earlier in this chapter, of the relative importance of routine intelligence testing in the assessment of child and adult psychiatric patients.

(3) That concern should be directed at the *total strategy or sequence of assessment* and critical consideration given to the utility of all aspects, psychometric and otherwise, of the entire procedure. For example, one strategy of decision-making, already mentioned, is to reduce the number of facts that require consideration at any one time. This suggests a sequential procedure in which alternatives are considered in the order of their decreasing subjective importance.

(4) That *examination of the goals* is fundamental in assessment and that the criterion for decision-making should be the maximization of movement towards these goals. Again, this is consistent with a sequential strategy involving the hierarchical organization of a series of sub-goals. This raises the problem of the precise definition of goals which in turn requires an effective 'job-analysis' of the situations facing the client. Job-analysis is a well-recognized aspect of vocational guidance and personnel selection, but in fields such as clinical psychology, equivalent situation descriptions are usually couched in extremely vague and subjective terms. Perhaps because of the inadequate definition of

goals in this field, no adequate job-analysis has ever been made of the work of the assessor or diagnostician nor of that of the therapist. Such an analysis would serve the important function, among others, of identifying the main decision points in the total process.

This very general and rather high-flown discussion of decision-making might be made more concrete by ending with a brief consideration of two fairly specific problems which constantly recur in psychological assessment and are frequently given less thought than they deserve. The first relates to statistical tests of significance. The 5% and 1% probability levels conventionally accepted as 'significant' in 'pure' research investigations may be quite inappropriate for certain assessment purposes. An experimental hypothesis is normally tested indirectly by testing the 'null' hypothesis, i.e. that the observed effects are due to chance factors, and probability theory allows the investigator to specify precisely the theoretical distribution of values to be expected from random sampling error. The experimental data are compared with this theoretical distribution and the test of significance then allows the null hypothesis to be accepted or rejected with varying degrees of confidence.

Two types of error are associated with this procedure: *type I* errors occur when the null hypothesis is rejected when correct and *type II* errors when the null hypothesis is accepted when incorrect. Decisions as to the balance to be aimed for between these two types of error is the responsibility of the investigator and should be based on their relative importance. In the traditional procedure, the test of significance is set up so as to fix the probability of type II errors at the conventional low values ($P<0.01$ or $P<0.05$) without consideration of the associated values of type I errors. This is essentially a decision-making strategy linked to the long-term aims of fundamental research and which, with replication and cross-validation procedures, ensures the reliability of the empirical data upon which theoretical systems are built.

In applied work, with its different aims, quite different strategies may be appropriate. For example, in an industrial situation, a psychological test may be used to select employees for a training scheme. The two types of error then concern the selection of individuals who fail to complete the training successfully and the rejection of those who would have been successful. In this type of situation it may be possible to allocate a money cost to each type of error and to strike the balance in terms of objective economic criteria. In other spheres, the costing can only be carried out by means of subjective value judgements concerning such matters as human satisfaction and effective living. Although this is a more difficult task, it is an inescapable one. Decision problems involving this type of judgement are common in clinical and educational psychology.

In clinical psychology particularly, decisions are frequently of a classificatory or diagnostic nature and are made on the basis of scores achieved on relevant diagnostic tests. It is then not sufficient to consider only the validation data concerning the test, the relevant *base rates*, i.e. the frequencies of the conditions in the parent population, must also be taken into account. Problems relating to base rates have been discussed in detail by Meehl and Rosen (1955) who point out, in line with the principle of incremental validity already mentioned, that the practical value of a test in a particular context depends upon the extent its use improves on the accuracy of predictions based on base rate tables alone. When conditions are rare in the population, the use of a test even of fairly high validity may actually reduce the proportion of correct decisions.

Consider the hypothetical case of a test of brain damage which, in a validation experiment, was administered to 100 unequivocally brain-damaged and 100 normal control subjects. In the traditional manner, a cut-off score on the test was selected so as to fix the type II errors (brain-damaged subjects allocated to the normal category, i.e. false negatives) at 5%. Fifteen per cent of the control subjects achieved scores below the cut-off (type I errors: false positives) so that the total misclassification was $\frac{20}{200}$, i.e. 10% as shown in the 2 × 2 table below:

		Test allocation		
		Brain-damaged	Non brain-damaged	
Criterion	Brain-damaged	95	5	100
Allocation	Non brain-damaged	15	85	100
		110	90	200

TABLE 1.1

If this test was used as a diagnostic instrument in a clinic where the records indicate that only 5% of the intake are in fact brain-damaged, the expected frequencies in the 2 × 2 table for 100 patients so tested are shown below. It can be seen from this that the total misclassification (14·25 + 0·25) is 14·5% whereas, if all the patients had been assumed to be non brain-damaged, the error rate would have only been 5% in accordance with the base-rates:

		Test allocation		
		Brain-damaged	Non brain-damaged	
Criterion	Brain-damaged	4·75	0·25	5
Allocation	Non brain-damaged	14·25	80·75	95
		19	81	100

TABLE 1.2

This paradoxical effect makes even the best of diagnostic tests relatively useless for screening large populations for the presence of very rare conditions, e.g. the examination of army recruits for potential psychosis. In general, such tests are most efficient when the incidence of the relative condition approximates to 50%. Examination of the second table, however, shows that the high misclassification arises from an excess of false positives. In a clinical situation of the type described this may be tolerable in terms of the relative costing of the two types of error. It might well be a sensible sequential assessment strategy to employ a test of this nature at an early stage in order to select individuals for further, more detailed, intensive investigation of a particular type.

In considering base-rates it is also important to ensure that these are appropriate to the specific assessment situation. In our hypothetical clinic, although only 5% of the patients are brain-damaged, it is quite likely that the physicians concerned only refer for this type of psychological assessment those about whom the suspicion of brain-damage has already been raised. The relevant base rates would then refer only to such 'doubtful' cases, among whom the ultimate firm diagnosis of brain damage might be quite common.

III THE COMMUNICATION OF ASSESSMENT INFORMATION

The formal psychological report plays an extremely important role in assessment. However well-conceived the assessment strategy might be, and however efficient the technique employed, the information obtained will serve no useful purpose unless its implications are grasped by whoever is involved in the actions which follow. Formal reports may be made only at the end of the whole sequence of assessment, or also at intermediate stages but, as already indicated, informal communications of various sorts between the psychologist, his client and various colleagues are inevitable and often of great importance throughout the assessment process. Reports take many forms, depending upon the setting in which they are made, the nature of the problems being investigated, the recipients and the psychologist's own theoretical orientation and other characteristics. Thus only very general comments and brief discussion are appropriate here.

According to the situation, formal reports may be addressed to other psychologists, colleagues in related disciplines, laymen of various types concerned with referring and disposal agencies or the client himself. In an important sense, too, the psychologist is himself the recipient of his own communications. The task of schematizing and making explicit one's inferences and conclusions does a great deal to clarify one's conceptual model of the person being assessed. Formal reports are also important for purposes of record-keeping, a long-term, more open type of communication of value in future transactions with the subject of the report and for research. This recording function of reports implies that they must be comprehensive and comprehensible to a variety of readers Thus, for example, if, with good reason, actual test results are not included in a report, they should be listed in detail and appended to the copy included in the records.

The psychologist's own conceptualization and thinking is expressed in his own
B*

technical language which to others may be incomprehensible jargon or mis-leading, which is worse. Many psychological terms figure in everyday language but with different connotations. One can only feel sympathy for the bafflement of the magistrate faced with the problem of trying to give due allowance to the alleged homosexual tendencies of a married defendant, father of six children, charged with rape. Even psychologists may have considerable difficulty in interpreting the reports of other psychologists of a quite different theoretical persuasion. The vast majority of reports should therefore be written in plain everyday language with concrete examples of behaviour characteristic of the traits ascribed to the subject and equally concrete illustrations of the predicted consequences of various possible courses of action. Probability statements, although based on technical statistical procedures, are readily expressed as odds, percentages or the use of terms such as 'rare' or 'frequent' qualified by 'extremely', 'moderately', or similar appropriate adjectives.

The writing of such a report is in many ways a work of translation which may contribute a great deal to one's understanding of the original version. If set as an academic task, it could be accomplished with relative ease by most psychologists but, in practice, involvement with jargon becomes very strong and it requires a deliberate adoption of a different intellectual orientation ('set' in jargon terms) to achieve detachment.

Fundamentally more difficult is the problem of communicating with a colleague, say a psychiatrist, about one's evaluation of a situation which also falls within his own legitimate range of expertise but which he examines through the spectacles of his own theoretical system, which may well overlap with one's own. This is not a straightforward matter of translation, as mutual appreciation of the differences between the models set up and the independent dimensions of each may be necessary for an adequate understanding of the problem being investigated. Some terms elude translation, as is well recognized in literary fields, and in these situations it is often necessary to learn something of each other's language. This is when informal communication becomes extremely important. Incidental interaction and discussion between members is by no means the least important activity within a clinic or other inter-disciplinary setting.

Few recommendations can be made concerning the lay-out and organization of a psychological report as different problems require different treatment. Very frequently, however, the original or later users of the report need to grasp its gist from a brief examination. It should never be over-long, very rarely more than two pages, and should make sense when both ends only are read. Thus it should open with a clear display of the name and other data to identify the person being assessed followed by a statement of the problem being investigated or the reason for referral. Similarly, all but the briefest of reports benefit from a terminal short summary of the findings followed by a clear list of recommendations concerning further action. When tests or other standard techniques have been employed these should be listed, usually with the scores achieved, separately from and preceding the main body of the report. It is essential that the aims or goals of the assessment are made clear and an outline given of the steps in the argument leading to the recommendations. One fruitful manner of reporting data, and indeed of planning an assessment investigation, is to list agreements and discrepancies, the former lending strength to assertions made and the latter posing subsidiary problems requiring further investigation. The limitations of the assessment procedures should be made clear and dogmatic assertions avoided but, whenever possible, the report should include a clear statement of an opinion modified if necessary by an indication of the degree of confidence with which it is held.

IV VALUE JUDGEMENTS AND ETHICAL CONSIDERATIONS

The earlier discussion of decision-making in assessment should have made clear the frequency and importance of the value judgements which have to be made. Sundberg and Tyler draw a distinction between two different types of decision related to two value systems. Decisions *about* the person being assessed are concerned with such matters as personnel selection, educational allocation and the assignment of patients to different types of treatment. In a broad sense, in contemporary society, the overall aim of the majority of these procedures is the welfare of the individuals concerned, but the majority of the detailed decisions are made in terms of *institutional values* related to economic efficiency and similar criteria. On the other hand, decisions *with* the client are about such matters as the career he will take up, the activities he will pursue and the relationships he will enter into or break. These involve *individual values* and in essence the psychologist's role is to assist his client to clarify his own value system, to become aware of his strengths and weaknesses and of the alternatives before him and to make up his own mind about these. Individual values, of course, also enter into many decisions about people.

Sundberg and Tyler's discussion is within the context of clinical psychology. If the same line of argument is extended to include the whole realm of applied psychology it becomes clear that decisions about people can be based on values akin to those described as institutional but involving much larger units of society or even organized society as a whole. Decisions concerning the treatment of offenders would fall into this category and exemplify decisions in which the individuals affected have little or no say. Applications of psychology in market research and similar fields are to a considerable extent concerned with discovering the unsatisfied and potential needs of consumers with the aim of supplying improved products. Certainly, however, they are also to some extent aimed at the discovery of weak points in the consumer and exploiting them.

Value judgements inevitably raise questions of ethics and these have to be faced by the applied psychologist whether his decisions are of an institutional or individual nature. Within the context of his personal ethical philosophy he has to be satisfied that he is not degrading or exploiting his client in order to satisfy his own economic or psychological needs. In recent years, too, attention has been increasingly drawn to the unjustified invasion of privacy which might result from the growing usage of personality questionnaires and other test procedures within industry and the public service.

The personal nature of the psychologist's ethical position is stressed partly because ethics is essentially a personal matter and partly because, in Britain, psychology is not fully organized on a professional basis and no standard formal code of ethics exists to which all psychologists must subscribe. Thus the author can only state his own point of view developed mainly during his work as a clinical psychologist. Essentially, this is based on respect for the humanity and individual personality of the patient, tolerance, sympathy and understanding. Whenever possible, decisions are made with the patient and this becomes particularly important when behaviour modification involving intrinsically offensive procedures as in aversive therapy is attempted. The patient who seeks, submits to and persists in this form of treatment is one who regards his therapist as a person who shows sufficient concern to be prepared to share what is inevitably an unpleasant and degrading but possibly therapeutically valuable experience. The writer would certainly be unwilling to participate in obnoxious aversive therapy, even if effective, if imposed on an individual by coercion or even forceful persuasion.

Despite these principles, it must be recognized that certain severely handicapped individuals such as the subnormal and some chronic psychotics have such grossly impoverished personalities that, although they continue to merit very real respect, they cannot participate in the decision-making under discussion. The writer believes very strongly that the psychologist must then be prepared to accept his responsibility as an agent of society much as a parent must accept responsibility for the guidance of his children and also recognize that the experiences which shape behaviour are not all gratifying in the short term.

Treatment situations highlight the ethical problems of applied psychology but equivalent problems are inherent in all types of assessment. Ethical value judgements have to be made both concerning the ends to be aimed for and the means by which it is hoped to achieve those ends.

V CONTROVERSIAL ISSUES IN APPLIED PSYCHOLOGY

Psychology is a developing profession, as yet in its infancy. The rate of change is accelerating but there are several perennial and fundamental issues which remain controversial and about which each individual applied psychologist must make a decision. Discussion of those issues of this nature which have relevance for the topic of this chapter may conveniently be divided in terms of the two areas of the role of the applied psychologist and his theoretical frame of reference. In many ways, however, this division is artificial as the two areas are intimately inter-related.

The role of the applied psychologist

To a considerable extent, professional roles are determined by the expectancies of employers and others but these expectancies are in turn dependent upon previous experience of what the profession offers and are often surprisingly flexible. To a large degree, any professional group creates its own role which reflects its basic aims and aspirations. In so far as these aims find practical expression in a way which appears to serve the ends of society and does not conflict with the vested interests of other professional groups, that role is accepted. In the past, individual psychologists have adopted highly idiosyncratic roles in particular settings and these have served as models for others to copy, but there are also more generalized roles, the more important of which may be considered in terms of choices between paired alternatives:

1 Scientist versus technician

In his work, the applied psychologist may, on request, apply techniques he has been specifically trained in, or even helped to develop, and then report his findings to a colleague in another profession who takes responsibility for action decisions. This is equivalent to the manner in which, say, a haematologist reports on blood tests to a physician who bears the ultimate clinical responsibility for the patient. Alternatively, the psychologist may focus not on techniques but on specific problems presented by the client and tackle them as an applied scientist.

The author's own adherence to the latter alternative will have become evident in earlier sections of this chapter. Nevertheless, he appreciates that this choice is more difficult than it appears at first sight. The psychologist's academic background and his awareness of the prestige associated with research, independence and originality favours option for the scientist's role. Nevertheless, a valuable contribution can be made by psychological technicians fulfilling a role much wider than that of a 'sergeant-tester' and which requires full psychological training. The scientist requires special skills and interests not shared by many admirable psychologists who perform excellently in the alternative role and need in no sense to feel guilty or inferior. It can even be argued that the more scientifically inclined are most effective when they apply their scientific skills in research (including research into the improvement and development of assessment techniques) but act as technicians in their professional dealings with individual clients. This is largely the approach of the haematologist already mentioned, as of pathologists, bacteriologists, hospital physicists and others who few would not regard as scientists but who carry out applied work in clinical settings.

2 Scientist versus artist

This option, which includes both the scientist and technician roles within the first alternative, is related to the 'clinical versus statistical prediction' problem already discussed at some length. There is clearly an art involved in the practice of applied psychology. The practitioner must obtain and maintain the co-operation and trust of his clients, administer his tests and techniques in a smooth and natural manner, and deal with all the complexities of a professional relationship. But, in his fundamental approach, he is faced with the choice between, if stated in the extreme, acting as an unbiased, objective, sceptical scientist who relies on measurement and refuses to speculate beyond the range of the data in which he can have confidence, and becoming an intuitive clinician who, enlightened by his theoretical beliefs, arrives at a subjective understanding of the client and his problem, communicates this understanding in a manner which makes it difficult to validate and recommends or takes action accordingly.

The temperament and personality of the psychologist will play an important part in this choice. Again, the writer's own leanings will have already become evident, but his awareness of the inevitable and important contribution of subjective judgements to assessment should be equally clear. It should also be pointed out that many psychologists who advocate an objective approach also argue that too much can be made of analogies with the physical sciences with consequent overstressing of the hypothetico-deductive method. For example, Bromley (1963), discussing methodology in clinical psychology, sees clinical decision-making as more akin to judicial procedures than to the tactics of physical science. He also argues that this judicial approach is equally scientific. The writer has considerable sympathy with this view, but at the same time considers the formulation of hypotheses and their predictive testing to be the very essence of science despite great differences in techniques and instrumentation between one science and another. The more explicit the hypotheses from which practical action springs, the less is the danger of gross error.

Those who favour an artistic and intuitive approach tend, for assessment purposes, to rely greatly on interview procedures and flexible clinical instruments, such as the projective techniques. This is so as to take full account of the holistic nature of the individual personality which, it is claimed, is disregarded by users of the more analytic, more objective procedures. Clearly all individuals are in an important sense unique and in many respects one can only deal with or 'know' another person in a holistic manner. Assessment and description are, however, quite impossible without some analysis into partial aspects of functioning, and the reciprocal relationship between band-width and fidelity has already been discussed. Analysis and particularization are clearly evident in the reports of all psychologists and it is difficult to see how the model which emerges from an assessment procedure can be other than abstract.

The roles which have been presented as alternatives are not mutually incompatible. An individual applied psychologist can and is likely to act as both a technician and a scientific investigator without neglecting his clinical arts. He is also likely to be something of a therapist and a researcher. No one can be equally competent in all these roles, but their very diversity provides the opportunity for the cultivation of individual bents.

Theoretical frames of reference

The applied psychologist also needs to make a choice concerning the nature of the theory of personality and psychopathology which is to guide his practice. Here again, he is mainly faced by the choice between two major alternatives, more genuinely incompatible in this instance but perhaps not entirely so when examined closely. This choice is related in some ways to the scientist/artist dichotomy in role-playing and contrasts the essentially behaviourist and essentially psychodynamic points of view. Psychoanalytic theory may be considered the prototype of the latter.

The author's prejudice favours the behaviourist outlook, but not in an uncritical way and in the form of a neo-behaviourism which retains little of Watson's early teaching and pays due regard to the findings of social and developmental psychology and the importance of cognitive mediating processes, including the concept of the self. Behaviourism is perhaps no longer an apt term: no applied psychologist can afford to neglect the subjective experience of his client. The 'schools' have outlived their usefulness and become integrated into the general empirically based theoretical system of contemporary experimental psychology. The outstanding advantage of this type of theory is that it constitutes a developing open system sharing the concepts and language of general biology and having close links with the other sciences. Although many of Freud's concepts have undoubtedly had an important influence on psychological theory and practice, psychoanalytic theory in general has the grave disadvantages of its dogmatic nature and mythological language which isolate it from the general field of biological and even medical science.

VI PSYCHOMETRICS: SOME TECHNICAL ASPECTS

The main technical concepts of psychometric assessment: test construction, standardization and norms, reliability and validity are discussed in detail in relation to particular contexts in later chapters of this book. This section of this chapter is devoted to selected topics of general relevance.

1 The nature of mental measurement

A psychological test may be defined as a device for the quantitative assessment of a psychological characteristic but it is important to realize the nature of the quantification which is involved. In particular, the term *mental measurement* which is often used, particularly in relation to the assessment of intelligence, may be misleading owing to confusion with the more sophisticated forms of physical measurement.

When we measure the length of a line with a ruler, we are carrying out an *extensive* measurement. This implies that our ruler could be checked against an actual physical object of standard length, say in the National Physical Laboratory. It also implies that we are measuring in terms of a scale with equal and additive units: an inch at any one part of our ruler is equal in length to an inch at any other part of the ruler. These requirements enable us to make such statements as, 'The difference in length between lines A and B (say 8″-6″) is equal to the difference between lines C and D (say 5″-3″)'. As our linear scale also has an absolute zero, we can also say that 'B is twice as long as D' ($\frac{6}{3} = 2$). This last type of ratio statement would not be permissible with, say, the Centigrade scale of temperature. As the Centigrade units are equal and additive $20°C - 18°C = 11°C - 9°C$, but, as the zero point is arbitrarily placed at the freezing point for water, 18°C is not twice as hot as 9°C. The absolute scale of temperature would have to be employed to make valid inferences concerning ratios.

Extensive measurement is not always possible, even in the physical sciences. *Intensive* measurement may then be resorted to as in Moh's Scale of Hardness. Moh arranged ten minerals in an ascending order of hardness from talc (1) to diamond (10). Each will scratch those placed below it and is scratched by those above it, rather like the pecking order in a community of hens. Any other mineral may be given a hardness rating by testing it against the standard minerals. This scale only allows statements of the form 'A is harder than B', and inferences of the type 'If A is harder than B, and B is harder than C, then A is harder than C'. No equality or ratio inferences are possible.

The essential differences between extensive and intensive measurement may be illustrated by the experiences of a squad of recruits joining a regiment. At their medical examinations, the doctor will measure their heights and record them in feet and inches. When they arrive on the parade ground, however, the drill sergeant will not refer to these records but will assemble them in ranks, 'tallest on the right and shortest on the left'. When this 'sizing off' is sufficiently pleasing to the sergeant's eye he will instruct the squad to 'number off from the right', and to remember these numbers. In doing this, the sergeant has carried out a form of intensive measurement and it would be quite in order to infer that, in any rank, any soldier is taller than those with higher numbers and shorter than those with lower numbers. It would be patently ridiculous to suggest that number five is twice as tall as number ten.

The differences between these two forms of measurement have been stressed because it can be argued that all psychological measurement is necessarily confined to intensive scales. However sophisticated an intelligence scale may seem, its units cannot be treated as equal and additive, and there is certainly no standard unit of intelligence at any National Psychological Laboratory. The only permissible quantitative statements are basically of the form 'Bill is brighter than Jack'. It would be quite unjustified to claim that a person of I.Q. 140 was twice as bright as someone of I.Q. 70, or even that the difference between I.Q.s 140 and 120 bears any particular relation to the difference between I.Q.s 90 and 70.

The argument presented in the last paragraph is a purist one. Others, such as Nunnally (1967), argue cogently that, apart from length and weight, even physical measurements are made indirectly via variables which correlate with the variable measured. Time may be measured by the swing of a pendulum or temperature by the height of a column of mercury. In other words, measuring scales are established by convention and when the convention is put to use it can be tested whether the data fits a model of a ratio, interval or ordinary scale. If there is a 'real' scale for an attribute, the conventional scale, based on a correlated attribute, is likely to mirror at least some monotonic transformation of the 'real' scale, and relationships expressed, as in most psychological experiments, by correlations and significances of mean differences, are affected very little by monotonic transformation of the variables. In fact, Nunnally opposes the concept of 'real' scales and points out that difficulties only arise when the fundamentalist view is adopted that it is meaningful to think in terms of 'real' scales and of actual measures as approximations of such 'real' scales. This is precisely why the author has presented the purist view, as psychologists less psychometrically sophisticated than Nunnally are very inclined to reify the scales utilized in their assessment procedures; this can lead to conceptual confusion.

2 Statistics and the interpretation of test scores

Psychological tests are used mainly to classify people or to predict behaviour in criterion situations. The accuracy with which these tasks may be performed depends upon the relevance of the test to the criterion, the appropriateness of the statistical procedures employed and the magnitude of the errors of measurement which inevitably occur in all testing. The psychologist who at any one time is concerned with a single individual needs to take particular care in allowing for errors of measurement. For example, of those individuals obtaining a median score on a test with a reliability coefficient of 0·9, some 10% would be more correctly placed above the 70th or below the 30th percentile. Thus a single obtained score must be considered only as an estimate representing a range of scores of varying probabilities which can be calculated from the standard error of measurement.

Often, however, the psychologist is concerned, not with a single score, but the relationship between two scores, particularly the implications of a discrepancy between them. For example, an intelligence test such as the W.A.I.S. yields two related but different measures, the 'Verbal' and 'Performance' I.Q.s, and differences between these two scores have been shown to be related to certain pathological conditions. Before he can assess the feasibility of a hypothesis based on these findings in connection with an individual case, the psychologist must ask himself the normative question: how frequently would a discrepancy as large as the one observed occur in the standardization population? Payne and Jones (1957), who discuss this and related problems, describe the appropriate test as that of the *abnormality* of a difference. Their solution is to form a 'critical ratio' (C.R.) from the observed difference (D) between the two scores (X, Y) and the mean difference $(\overline{D})$ and standard deviation of differences (σ_D) in the general population:

$$\text{C.R.} = \frac{D - \overline{D}}{\sigma_D} = \frac{D - \overline{D}}{\sqrt{\sigma_x{}^2 + \sigma^2{}_y - 2r_{xy}\sigma_x\sigma_y}}$$

If the raw X and Y scores are initially transformed into standard scores (Zx, Zy) which has other advantages, this expression simplifiies to:

$$\text{C.R.} = \frac{Z_x - Z_y}{\sqrt{2 - 2r_{xy}}}$$

What is important in this type of situation is that the psychologist asks the appropriate question and applies the statistical test appropriate to the question asked. In the example given, the discrepancy noted is assessed against discrepancies throughout the entire I.Q. range of the standardization sample. A psychologist engaged in counselling students in a highly selected grammar school population is likely to find that appreciably lower 'performance' than 'verbal' I.Q.s are quite common. His test should refer to his particular school population and the direction of the discrepancy should be taken into account.

Another test proposed by Payne and Jones is one of what they describe as the *reliability* of discrepancy. Other authors sometimes use the same term in a different sense. This test is designed to answer the quite different question as to whether an observed difference represents a genuine profile of abilities and not a chance difference resulting from errors of measurement. There is no question of rarity or 'abnormality' and indeed the correlation between the traits being assessed might be very low so that significance in the 'abnormality' sense could only be achieved when one or other of the individual scores was extremely high or extremely low. Here the individual is being treated as a microcosm with no reference to the macrocosm of people at large. Thus, in this instance the C.R. is set up entirely in terms of the standard errors of measurement without reference to the correlation between X and Y. In standard score form it becomes:

$$\text{C.R.} = \frac{Z_x - Z_y}{\sqrt{(1 - r_{xx}) + (1 - r_{yy})}}$$

In other instances, as when a particular type of assessment is repeated with certain expectation or prediction, a regression equation might be set up and the discrepancy beween the observed (Y) and predicted $(\hat{Y})$ scores assessed against the standard error of prediction by forming a critical ratio:

$$\text{C.R.} = \frac{Y - \hat{Y}}{\text{S.E. prediction}}$$

This test is commonly applied to check on suspected intellectual deterioration when some appropriate pre-morbid test score provides a basis for prediction. Regression techniques also have the advantage that, when several test scores are available, a *multiple* regression equation may be set up for prediction purposes provided that research data is available to provide the necessary correlation information. Given similar adequate research data, multivariate discriminant functions may be used for classification purposes. These and indeed the whole range of psychometric procedures are described very fully by Nunnally (1967).

In recent years various forms of profile analysis and profile comparison have become popular means of dealing with the classification problems arising out of the use of multidimensional test batteries such as Cattell's 16 P.F. Personality Inventory and the Minnesota Multiphasic Personality Inventory (M.M.P.I.). The term 'profile' is applied to the configuration of the plotted individual scores on a graph. Normative data is supplied in the form of the mean profiles for specified reference groups with which the profiles of individuals may be compared.

The recommended methods of conducting these comparisons range from visual inspection, rules of thumb and simple numerical devices to complicated mathematical procedures, involving the calculation of correlations and related measures. One of the major difficulties concerning the linear combination of scores is the loss of reliability which may occur. A single difference score is appreciably less reliable than the individual scores from which it derives and longer combinations which involve subtractions can become grossly unreliable.

Any profile contains three sources of information:

(1) its *level*, i.e. the mean score on the variables;

(2) its *dispersion*, which refers to the spread or scatter around the average (level) and is most appropriately measured by the standard deviation of scores for the person;

(3) its *shape*, or the pattern of rises and falls in the profile. This may be defined roughly by the rank order of scores.

Level, dispersion and shape are fairly independent of each other but not entirely. For example, an extreme level in either direction would necessarily limit dispersion.

If level and dispersion are not considered important, the degree of similarity between two profile shapes may be measured by correlating their scores *after* they have been standardized *within* each person, i.e. after the level has been made zero and the dispersion standard deviation made 1·0.

An elegant measure of profile similarity which takes into account all three sources of information is the distance measure (D) employed by Osgood and Suci in their semantic differential technique. A space is defined by plotting each variable at right angles to the others. D is then the distance between the points determined by each individual's scores and is calculated by a simple extension of Pythagoras' Theorem. Thus for two individuals, A and B, and variables 1 to K:

$$D^2 = (X_{A1} - X_{B1})^2 + (X_{A2} - X_{B2})^2 \ldots + (X_{AK} - X_{BK})^2$$

To the author's understanding, however, it seems that even D has the limitations inherent in profile comparison. A single profile is represented by a single point in the multidimensional space and the surface of a multidimensional sphere of which this point is the centre must then represent a vast number of points all equidistant from the original point but all representing different combinations of scores and, therefore, different profiles.

VII CONCLUDING COMMENTS

Many topics have been touched on in this chapter which will be treated in detail and in specific contexts in the remainder of the book. The aim has been to attempt a broad survey of the nature and implications of assessment, to analyse the process, indicate the main pitfalls and point to the technical and methodological aids available to the applied psychologist. Stress has been laid on the importance of decision-making strategies and the inevitability of value judgements. Much that might have been included has been omitted: for example, the potential value of automated testing devices linked to computers. The aim has been to provide a frame of reference for the reader within which the remaining chapters might find a natural place and become integrated.

All psychological research is relevant to psychological assessment but there is a clear need for a great deal more research specifically in assessment and directed to a study of both process and outcome. Techniques deriving from descriptive decision-theory show a great deal of promise and, by their emphasis on the utility concept, might do much, not only to indicate how effective orthodox assessment procedures really are, but also to streamline them.

REFERENCES

BROMLEY, D. B. (1963) Scientific method in psychology: a revaluation. *Proc. Ann. Conf. Brit. Psychol. Soc.*, 1963.

CRONBACH, L. J. and GLESER, G. C. (1957) *Psychological Tests and Personnel Decisions*. University of Illinois Press.

EDWARDS, W. and TVERSKY, A. (Eds.) (1967) *Decision Making*. Harmondsworth: Penguin Books.

FURNEAUX, W. D. (1956) *The Nufferno Manuals of Speed and Level Tests*. London: Institute of Psychiatry (distributed by N.F.E.R.).

JONES, H. G. (1960) Applied abnormal psychology: the experimental approach. *In* H. J. EYSENCK (Ed.) *Handbook of Abnormal Psychology*. London: Pitman.

LUCE, R. D., BUSH, R. R. and GALANTER, E. (Eds.) (1965) *Readings in Mathematical Psychology*. New York: Wiley.

MEEHL, P. E. (1954) *Clinical versus Statistical Prediction*. Minneapolis: University of Minnesota Press.

MEEHL, P. E. (1959) Some ruminations on the validation of clinical procedures. *Canad. J. Psychol.*, **13**, 102-128.

MEEHL, P. E. and ROSEN, A. (1955) Antecedent probability and the efficiency of psychometric signs, patterns or cutting scores. *Psychol. Bull.*, 52, 194-216.

NUNNALLY, J. C. (1967) *Psychometric Theory*. New York: McGraw-Hill.

OFFICE OF STRATEGIC SERVICES STAFF (1948) *Assessment of Men*. New York: Rinehart.

ONIONS, C. T. (Ed.) (1959) *The Shorter Oxford English Dictionary*, Third edition (revised). Oxford University Press.

PAYNE, R. W. and JONES, H. G. (1957) Statistics for the investigation of individual cases. *J. clin. Psychol.*, 13, 115-121.

SHEPHERD, R. N. (1964) On subjectively optimum selections among multi-attribute alternatives. *In* SHELLEY, M. W. and BRIAN, G. L. (Eds.) *Human Judgements and Optimality*. New York: Wiley.

SUNDBERG, N. D. and TYLER, L. E. (1962) *Clinical Psychology*. New York: Appleton-Century-Crofts.

PART ONE

Assessment of Adults:
Types of Assessment

·

2

Intellectual assessment

R. Douglass Savage

The interaction of theories about the nature of intelligence and the development of measures of intellectual assessment is a complex and fascinating affair. The development of tests has frequently outrun our understanding of the nature of intelligence. On the other hand, theoretical developments in the field of cognitive ability generally have much to offer future test construction.

This chapter will outline the major theoretical developments in psychology relevant to intellectual assessment techniques and their major uses and abuses in the applied field. Stress will be laid on the investigation of the measurement of individual differences and changes in intellectual functioning.

I MEASURING INTELLECTUAL ABILITY

Several major influences on or stages in the history of intellectual assessment can be seen. The earliest attempts to measure individual differences in intellect by Galton (1869, 1883), and McKeen Cattell (1890) were undoubtedly influenced by Traditional British Associationism in the philosophical writings of John Locke and J. S. Mill and the physiological psychology of Alexander Bain. Associationism suggested that all knowledge came through the senses, therefore intellect could be measured in terms of sensory abilities or functioning, whilst the physiologically based theories stressed the importance of the measurement of motor qualities. However, the famous investigations of sensory absolute and differential thresholds, reaction time, strength of hand grasp in Galton's Anthropometric Laboratory at University College London, and McKeen Cattell's tests of muscular strength, speed of movement, sensitivity to pain, etc., at Pennsylvania and Columbia Universities, though of great value and interest, were largely abortive in terms of the development of measures of individual difference in intelligence. Galton was, nevertheless, aware of the need for test item standardization and the many problems of measuring individual variation in abilities.

James McKeen Cattell, imbued like Galton with the Darwinian spirit, had also seen the significance of assessing individual differences. In an article in 1890, he first used in print the term 'mental tests', but the investigations of Sharp (1898-99) and Wissler (1901), though somewhat limited and mis-interpreted, helped this star of intellectual measurement to fade. It was the work of Binet and Henri (1896), Binet and Simon (1905), Binet (1909) and his American champion,

Terman (1916), that led to the development and ascendency of standardized mental tests involving more complex functions than those used by Galton and Cattell.

1 The search for *g*

Eysenck (1967) attributes the first stage of intelligence measurement proper to Spearman (1904) and Binet and Simon (1905), both of whom stressed the importance of a *general factor of intellectual ability*. Binet invented the concept of Mental Age and supplied a 30 item test constructed to measure intelligence (Binet and Simon, 1905), whilst Spearman (1904) outlined the application of correlational methods and developed factor analysis in relation to the construction of intelligence tests.

The object of Binet's first intelligence scale was to discriminate between normal and mentally deficient children by a more direct method, to supplement or replace the less certain physical, social and educational signs of retardation (Binet and Simon, 1905). Though Binet's scales give only a single measure of intellectual ability, his view of intelligence was comprehensive. He proposed 10 intellectual functions including memory, attention, comprehension, muscular force and judgement of visual space, and recognized the importance of common sense, initiative and ability to adapt. The 1908 and later Binet scales placed increasing importance on the differentiation among normal children and firmly established the mental age concept in intellectual assessment. The development and wide appeal of the American standardized Stanford-Binet Scale in 1916, the L and M revised edition by Terman and Merrill (1937) and the recent combined L-M form (Terman and Merrill, 1960) need only brief recall.

This work of Binet and his successors had a temendous effect both on the type of intellectual test developed and on research into the concepts of human ability. In the former, his influence was generally for the good; the Binet type tests have rather high levels of construct validity for the concept of intelligence and led to the development of measures of intelligence with real practical value. In many studies, the predictive validity of the Stanford-Binet has been found to be good in relation to academic and occupational success (Buros, 1949, 1953, 1959, 1965; Anastasi, 1961). However, though Binet was well aware of the need to dissect and understand the nature of human intellect, according to Peterson (1925) he never published a formal definition of intelligence; many of his followers, Terman included, paid little or no attention to this problem and showed little concern for psychological theory.

Theories regarding the nature of intelligence constituted a further stage in the development of cognitive assessment. Charles Spearman (1904, 1923, 1927) concerned himself with the nature of human abilities, producing a much more scholarly and mathematical approach to the problems than that of Binet. Although the theories and findings of Spearman tended to support the type of tests developed by Binet, he proposed a more refined method of measuring *g*. It was first necessary to determine the tasks which measured *g* rather than being dominated by specific factors, then to weight each task appropriately. Binet's and subsequent practice, including Wechsler's, of assembling a hodgepodge of problems without first testing for the presence of a general factor or a factor structure at all, and without appropriately weighting the items in terms of these factors, is quite alien to Spearman's approach.

However, Spearman was chiefly concerned with developing the mathematical models and techniques for studying human abilities. He laid the foundation for the application of modern factor analysis to psychological problems. His measures of intellectual ability never obtained the wide appeal and usage of the Binet scales. Regrettably, Spearman's influence in the U.S.A. has been even more limited than in the U.K. Nevertheless, the neglect in applied psychology, particularly in the clinical area, of his main proposition that intellectual scales should be factor based, has been greatly to its disadvantage. Not least, in the problem of comparing Intelligence Quotients from one measure with those from another and unravelling the components of intellectual change. It should be noted, however, that Guilford in his recent book *The Nature of Intelligence* (1967) refers frequently to the importance as well as the limitation of Spearman's psychological and factor theories. In particular, Guilford considered Spearman's concept of 'eduction' similar to his own concept of 'fundaments'. It follows from Spearman's two-factor theory that the aim of psychological testing should be to measure the amount of each individual's *g*. If this factor runs through all abilities, it furnishes the major if not only basis for prediction of the subject's performance from one situation to another.

One might consider to what extent the Intellectual measures claiming to measure *g* in fact do so, to what extent such tests have been employed clinically, and to what degree they have been clinically useful. I will discuss, particularly, the widely used Stanford-Binet revisions (1916, 1937, 1960), and the Raven's Progressive Matrices (1938-62), though the Cattell Culture Fair Intelligence Test (1933-63), and the Harris-Goodenough Drawing Test of Psychological Maturity (1926-63, a revision of the 1926 Goodenough Draw a Man Test) may be closely identified with measuring the elusive *g*.

The Stanford-Binet, despite its wide variety of types of item, has a large general factor accounting for much of its variance (McNemar, 1942; Jones, 1949; Hofstaetter, 1954). However, these investigators also distinguished group factors and variations in factor structure with age. This test cannot, then, be said to be a satisfactory attempt to measure *g*, for not only is about 50% of the variance attributable to other factors, but these factors cannot be separated in practice. The overall I.Q. though adequate for general classification purposes, cannot be broken down into its main components. Here lies its major clinical limitation. Furthermore, the Stanford-Binet, even in its latest 1960 edition, has insufficient headroom and normative data to be suitable for adult testing. Though its value with low grade mental deficiency must not be underestimated, one would still prefer to obtain assessments of various intellectual factors or components than merely obtain an overall I.Q. The use of the Stanford-Binet as a clinical interview on which to speculate about personality and various other patient factors is unnecessary, highly unscientific and extremely misleading. It can too frequently lead to an air of authority surrounding a purely 'intuitive' and highly unreliable set of statements on factors which the test was not designed to assess quantitatively. The historical importance of this measure and its use with children are more compelling attributes than its application with adult patients.

The Progressive Matrices (Raven, 1938-62), were more specifically designed to measure Spearman's g factor, and require chiefly the 'eduction of relations among abstract items'. Spearman himself (1939, 1946; Spearman and Jones, 1950) regarded the Progressive Matrices (1938) as a non-verbal test of g, 'the best of all'. Vernon and Parry (1939) regarded it as 'an almost pure g test'. Work by Vernon (1947a, 1947b, 1947c, 1950), Adcock (1948), Emmett (1949) and others has produced evidence showing negligible variance in the Progressive Matrices attributable to $k:m$ factor loadings and g accounting for 62% or more of the variance. Burt (1954), however, found a general factor accounting for only 41% of the total variance, with a significant second factor, and Tizard *et al.* (1950) did not identify their single factor finding with Spearman's g, but as a complex non-verbal practical factor unrelated to verbal intelligence. Burke (1958), after reviewing the literature, concluded, 'the evidence is not convincing that P.M. (1938) has validity as a pure measure of the Spearman construct of g and doubt may be raised whether such a construct can be measured independently of the modality through which it is expressed, the selectivity of the subjects and their sex, and possibly the presuppositions of the factor analyst'.

Though one may question the theoretical purity of the Raven's Progressive Matrices, they have been extensively used clinically in Great Britain and found to be promising in many respects when combined with the Mill Hill Vocabulary Scales (Raven 1943a-1958).

The Standard Progressive Matrices (1938-60) have been supplemented by the Advanced Progressive Matrices (1943-62). The Set 1 Progressive Matrices (1947) can be used in conjunction with Set 2, the 1962 Revision of the Advanced Progressive Matrices. The latter can be given untimed 'as a measure of intellectual capacity' or with a time limit as a 'measure of intellectual efficiency'. Bortner (1965), however, remains convinced that the validity and reliability of these 'scales' is equivocal. The matrices may be useful as a screening device where estimates of general intellectual level are required, but its use as a clinical instrument is extremely limited. As a general assessment measure it has been found useful in relation to deaf, cerebral palsied, speech and communication disorders (Burke, 1958; Buros, 1965) and in situations where it is difficult to administer the instructions for more complicated tests. The limited information in the manuals and the inability to measure various aspects of cognitive functioning severely hinder the clinical applications of this measure. Even when Mill Hill Vocabulary and Ravens Progressive Matrices are used, their value is reduced by the limited normative, reliability and error measurement data comparable to Field's

Wechsler Tables (1960). They have been used in clinical practice and research to compare psychiatric groups and get over-all I.Q. assessment (Davidson, 1939; Eysenck, H. J., 1943, 1944; Halstead, 1943, 1950; Eysenck, M., 1945; Himmelweit, 1945; Halstead and Slater, 1946; Foulds and Raven, 1950; Desai, 1952, 1955; Stacey and Gill, 1955; Foulds, 1956; Foulds and Dixon, 1962a, b).

The I.P.A.T. Culture Free Intelligence Test (Cattell and Cattell 1933-63) and the Goodenough Drawing Tests (1926-1963, Harris-Goodenough Revision) might on first sight also be thought to be designed to measure Spearman's *g*. *Generally speaking, however, the attempt to produce a pure* g *test has been unsuccessful and one doubts that such a measure is possible at least until there is some agreement on the definition of* g. *If available, it would almost certainly need to be complemented by measures of other factors to be of detailed clinical use.* Apart from the diagnosis of mental deficiency, it is individual variability in cognitive functioning that has been thought to have diagnostic potential, provided of course, it is statistically viable in terms of factor structure and error measurement.

2 Group factor tests and theories

The development of factor analysis as a tool has had a profound effect on theories of intelligence, though careful investigation reveals that its *direct* effect on developing measures of intelligence for *adult clinical*, as distinct from group, military or educational use, is much less than one suspects. In this factorial phase, dominated by the work of Thurstone (1926), Thomson (1939-56), Burt (1939), Holzinger (1937), Holzinger and Harman (1941), and Vernon (1960), a crucial landmark was Thurstone's work at the University of Chicago Psychometric Laboratory on 'Primary Mental Abilities'. Thurstone asked how many and what kind of factors were necessary to account for the observed correlations between tests of ability. In answering these questions, he made an outstanding contribution to the theory, methodology and empirical investigation of problems of individual difference measurement. He and his wife, Thelma, originally employed 60 tests, developing, administering and analysing without the aid of modern computer technology and eventually isolated several factors thought sufficiently stable over age for use with school children – Verbal Comprehension (V), Word Fluency (W), Number (N), Space (S), Rote Memory (M) and Induction or Reasoning (R) (Thurstone and Thurstone, 1941). A perceptual factor (P) and a deductive factor (D) were not originally regarded as sufficiently clear for general application.

The multifactorial intellectual theories of Thurstone (1938, 1947) and later American psychologists, particularly Guilford (1956, 1967) would appear at face value to have much to offer the test constructor. Clear, identifiable factors could be measured and individual variations within and between factor constructed tests analysed, particularly in relation to simple structure orthogonal factors. Indeed, the 1962-63 S.R.A. Primary Mental Abilities Tests by L. L. and Thelma G. Thurstone provide tables for comparing factor test scores for differential diagnosis of cognitive variability.

Consequently Thurstone's S.R.A. Primary Mental Abilities tests are of great interest though, unfortunately, their age limits (5-17) restrict their importance in adult intellectual measurement. Nevertheless, these measures are woefully under-used in British clinical practice, yet they have some distinct advantages over the W.I.S.C. and W.A.I.S., which show such a complex factor subtest structure.

The latest edition of the P.M.A. (1962-63) and the Technical Supplement suggest that profile analysis of the factor based scores has validity in relation to achievement in various areas, reliability and standard error of difference score tables are provided for differential diagnostic and predictive purposes. Milholland (1965), however, reviewing the test considers they have a long way to go and Anastasi (1961) regrets that though the early forms were based upon extensive research and presented an important breakthrough in test construction, rather than providing the needed refinement and empirical validation, the subsequent evolution of these tests has proceeded chiefly in the direction of abridgement and simplification. Inadequacies of normative data, reliability and validity procedures limit their clinical use.

The extension of the factorial principle of test construction from the S.R.A. P.M.A. to the adult field is seen in the General Aptitude Test Battery (G.A.T.B.) published by the United States Employment Services in 1947, revised 1952 and 1963. These measures are not as widely used in clinical circles as in vocational guidance but have some clinical potential in view of their factorial composition as well as their vocational value. Humphreys (1959) Comrey (1959) and Bechtoldt (1965) concluded that the test provides a fairly well constructed measure with wide empirical data and is as good as any other existing multifactorial battery; Carol (1965) recommended the G.A.T.B. as a research tool as do its makers. Work on ageing, for example, has shown that even when educational level is controlled, there are significant decrements in nearly all the factors measured by the G.A.T.B. Only verbal aptitude (V) seems to be impervious to the effects of ageing, a finding consistent with studies on many other measures (Payne, 1960). This measure may well have important clinical potential not only as in the work of Taylor (1963) on vocational guidance in psychiatric patients, but also as a factorial measure of abilities in general clinical practice and research.

Though one may recommend the Thurstone S.R.A. P.M.A. or the G.A.T.B. as one of the best 'single factor' groups of tests, one further word of caution is needed. Furneaux (1960) and Eysenck (1967) both stress the fact that these so-called 'single factor tests' are not so unitary as one would wish, but that 'speed' and 'accuracy' rather than content alone may account for some of the subtest differentiation. They suggest that the 'speed' factor, has been an undernourished dwarf, but is a potential giant in intellectual functioning theory. One can see that this may be particularly true in assessing the differential effects of mental illness on intellectual functioning. The Nufferno tests may be of use in this area (see p. 36).

The multifactorial approach of Thurstone and recent developments by Guilford are of vital technological importance to cognitive theory and intellectual test construction, as between 50 and 100 factors have now been identified. Guilford's theory (1965, 1967) classified the structure of intellect into *operations* which it can perform, different *contents* of these operations and different *products*, allowing for about 120 different mental abilities.

This is fascinating work and has led to the identification of many factors, but as Nunnally (1967) put it, 'an appalling number of separate factors'. The classification scheme alone leads only to finding more and more factors, it has little or nothing to say about possible relations among factors. McNemar (1964) and Vernon (1965) have made similar criticisms, whilst Eysenck (1967, p. 82) states that by ignoring the essential hierarchical nature of the data on intellect, 'Guilford has truly cut out the Dane from his production of Hamlet'. Guilford himself recognizes (1967, p. 464) that what is needed in addition to a classification scheme is a mathematical model for simplifying relations among the many factors following from the scheme. However, he argues against *g* as a key concept of these hierarchical models and points out in particular that *g* is not an invariant variable, but changes with almost every battery of tests that is analysed.

Burt (1949) and Vernon (1950a) are the most famous of the British psychologists who have proposed well known hierarchical systems to account for the structure of intellect. Burt divides the human mind into Spearman-type *g* intellectual factors and 'practical' or behavioural characteristics. These major properties are subdivided. Vernon's (1950) model also presents *g* followed by the major group factors *v:ed* and *k:m* (the latter 'practical' as in Burt's model), minor group and specific factors.

The malaise, however, may be uncovered. The speed and power concepts of Thorndike (1926), Eysenck (1953, 1967) and Furneaux (1960) may restore both *g* and hierarchies, and still pay tribute to the classification and identification work of Guilford. Indeed, Eysenck's model for the structure of Intellect (1953, 1967) has much in common with that of Guilford.

Operations, Eysenck calls mental processes, contents are 'test materials', but 'products' are replaced by 'quality' which includes the concepts of mental speed and power (after Thorndike, 1926). Eysenck's scheme retains an essential hierarchical structure with *g* central and involving mental speed as the major source of variation, averaged over all processes and materials with the 'Primary Mental Abilities' of Thurstone and Guilford emerging at a lower level of generality.

Furneaux (1952, 1956, 1960) produced strong arguments against regarding 'general intelligence' as a basic scientific concept. He points out that a *g* score derived from an intellectual measure results from the interaction of a number of fundamental processes. *Speed*, *accuracy* and *continuance* concepts in relation to *type* and *difficulty* of the problems in intelligence are given particular prominence in his logical atomistic approach to the study of test taking behaviour and test making. He states, 'Little useful information about intellectual functioning can be obtained from the use of conventional intelligence tests in the absence of an adequate theoretical and experimental analysis of the ways in which a person's responses, first to single problems and then to carefully defined sets of problems, can legitimately be scored'. To help pursue these problems, the *Nufferno Manual of Speed Tests* and the *Nufferno Manual of Level Tests* were published by the Institute of Psychiatry, London University, and distributed by the N.F.E.R. in 1956. These measures have been used in a variety of investigations since their initial development. Normative data on adult males 18-30, university students and school children are available and several studies report their use with

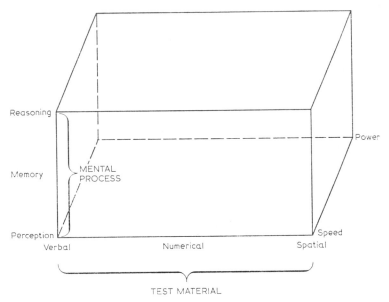

Figure 2.1.   *Model of the structure of Intellect*
(Eysenck, 1953, 1967)

abnormal groups. Shapiro and Nelson (1955), using Nufferno's Speed Tests with normals, schizophrenics, manic depressives and organics, found speed tests differentiated psychiatric from normal groups and correlated negatively with severe illness, whilst the level tests did not differentiate between the groups. Ogilvie (1954), Broadhurst (1957), Eysenck *et al.* (1957) and Payne and Hewlett (1960) substantiated the above findings. Error scores on the Nufferno speed and level tests have been found to be greater in extraverts than introverts (Furneaux, 1960).

The basic unit of analysis and concern in the Furneaux model for intellectual assessment and test construction is the *individual item*. The category of the item answer, R (correct), W (incorrect), A (abandoned), N (not attempted) must be noted and the three further parameters (i) mental speed, (ii) persistence or continuance and (iii) error checking must be taken into account. Consequently, the early concept and importance of mental speed in intellect is reinstated

(Thorndike, 1926; Eysenck, 1953) and non-cognitive (personality) factors such as persistence and carefulness in checking are incorporated as, for example, in Wechsler's theories and measures (1955, 1958). The personality factors here, unlike Wechsler's, are scored independently of other intellectual factors. Furneaux has demonstrated the fundamental nature of mental speed function by showing that when an individual's R latencies are plotted against difficulty level of the items concerned, a negatively accumulating curve is obtained; when time units are then logarithmically transformed *all plots become linear*. This may be interpreted to mean that the only or at least a major source of difference in intellectual ability between individuals is speed.

This important work needs further extension. It is interesting to note, however, that a factor of retardation, or slowness of mental speed, has been found in several studies involving psychotics and is postulated by Payne (1960), Payne and Hewlett (1960) and many others as an important diagnostic cognitive abnormality in mental illness. This slowness may be the result of several factors such as individual differences in some kind of search or scanning mechanisms, distractibility or blocking of the scanning process (Broadbent, 1958, 1964; Eysenck, 1967) or overinclusion leading to misinterpretation (Payne, 1960). The presence of wide individual variation, distractibility, blocking, overinclusion and the like in mentally ill patients is well established and may account for the success and limitations of many of our present cognitive measures in differential diagnosis. Similarly, wide individual and group differences in error scores have been reported by Poull and Montgomery (1929) and Porteus (1942) on delinquent and other children, Hildebrand (1953) and Furneaux (1956) on introverts and extraverts, Howell (1955) with psychotics, Eysenck (1957) and Furneaux (1960) with data from Ogilvie (1954). Broadhurst (1957) suggested that schizophrenics make significantly more errors than normals and neurotics. Brierley (1961) found neurotic groups differed in their speed and level on the Nufferno tests. Introverted neurotics had low speed, extraverted neurotics low accuracy.

However, we are also concerned with intellectual assessment as practitioners of psychology. These theories have not, unfortunately, led to widespread changes or developments in clinical practice. Theoretical confusion rarely breeds practical success. The everyday instruments used in assessing clinical intellectual levels of patients and analysing their problems have developed elsewhere to the loss of psychology and an even greater indictment of the poor relationships between applied and pure psychology. There would seem no doubt that our knowledge of the structure of intellect and its change could and should lead to new measures (money permitting) and approaches to the problem. What, however, of the multifactorial tests? We have some group tests, but few, if any, individual (clinical) measures with clear factor-structured items and subtests. The subtest-factor structure relationships on the W.A.I.S. are completely confusing (Savage and Britton, 1968) and impossible to differentiate in clinical use; the Binet is factorially indivisable in practice (Buros, 1965), the Matrices 'do or perhaps do not measure *g*' (Burke, 1958).

C

The most widely used multifactorial technique in adult clinical practice, the *Wechsler Adult Intelligence Scale* is based on Wechsler's theory of intelligence which deliberately prefers items and subtests to measure several factors. He states that 'intelligence, operationally defined, is the aggregate or global capacity of the individual to act purposefully, to think rationally and to deal effectively with his environment. It is aggregate or global because it is composed of elements or abilities which, though not entirely independent, are qualitatively differentiable.'

Excellent reviews of the Wechsler-Bellevue I and II, the W.A.I.S. and the Wechsler Intelligence Scale for Children have been published (Rabin, 1945; Rabin and Guertin, 1951; Guertin *et al.*, 1956, 1962, 1966; Littell, 1960). This section, therefore, will concentrate on the more recent Wechsler Adult Intelligence Scale.

The normative data of the W.A.I.S. is a great improvement on the previous Wechsler-Bellevue measures and up to the age 65 probably represents the best standardization sample used in psychometric test construction; age, sex, education, occupation, geographical region, urban versus rural residence and colour were controlled on the basis of the 1950 U.S. census. The details are provided in Wechsler (1955, 1958). This is almost certainly the most widely used measure of intellectual assessment in the clinical field and needs no detailed description. It is available in many languages including Danish, French, German, Italian and Japanese, as well as English.

The clinical use of the W.A.I.S. as an instrument for classifying general cognitive level in terms of a standardized score, the Full Scale Intelligence Quotient (F.S.I.Q.) probably has no present equal in the assessment of individual ability. Problems, however, do exist in relation to general intellectual assessment with the W.A.I.S., in particular where the classification of mental deficiency and examining the effects of age on cognitive functioning are concerned. There is accumulating evidence that the W.A.I.S. yields higher subnormal I.Q.s than the W.-B., W.I.S.C. or Stanford-Binet. Some researchers (Fisher, 1962) suggest the W.A.I.S. is less valid, while others, such as Webb (1964), regard it as more valid than alternative measures of mental defective assessment. Tarjan *et al.* (1960) found that release rate of male and female mental defectives was a function of F.S.I.Q. There does not appear to be any agreement, however, on the relationship between V.I.Q. and P.I.Q. to release from institution and outside work adjustment. V.I.Q. was considered a better predictor than P.I.Q. in males by Miller, Fisher and Dingram (1961), whilst Appell *et al.* (1962) found P.I.Q. highly related to job success in mental defectives.

In order to assess general intellectual levels in the aged, the normative data published by Doppelt and Wallace (1955) in America, Riegel and Riegel (1959) in Germany and by Bolton, Britton and Savage (1966) for a British population are of interest as they are almost identical, whilst those of Wechsler (1958), Cook and Hirt (1961) and Eisdorfer and Cohen (1961) in America and Beverfelt *et al.* (1964) in Norway were more deviant. Some of this data will be presented in section II. The problem of ageing and intellectual assessment on the W.A.I.S. is far from clear, much more research involving large representative samples is needed. Despite the many criticisms of the W.A.I.S. standardization and normative data over a wide age range, it can be considered an adequate English language measure of intellect (albeit American) and the classification categories are generally accepted. One cannot help, however, but comment on the comparative lack of British research in this area, the limited investigations of Field (1960), Maxwell (1960, 1961) and Bolton, Britton and Savage (1966) being the only major attempts to obtain British normative data. It has no doubt been felt that the original normative data is 'near enough' not to warrant the considerable expense and administrative problems of a genuine British standardization. In principle, one must feel this is a dangerous attitude.

Does the W.A.I.S. have a sound multifactorial theory behind it? Unfortunately, the answer is no. The intellectual categories of the W.A.I.S. divided into P.I.Q., V.I.Q. and their appropriate subscales do not correspond to their factorially analysed composition. In 1957, Cohen presented a factor analysis of the W.A.I.S. standardization data including the aged sample of Doppelt and Wallace (1955). Using Thurstone's Centroid Method, he rotated the data to a criterion of oblique simple structure and identified a verbal comprehension factor loading on I.C.V. and S subtests, a perceptual organization factor loading on BD, PA and OA, a memory factor and a specific PC factor. There was little change in factor structure on the W.A.I.S. with age, the only emphasis being a shift in the memory factor to increased importance. As Wechsler (1955, 1958) had intended, the different subtests were different measures of intelligence, not measures of different kinds of intelligence. The large common variance between subtests is important, as it makes subtest pattern analysis with the W.A.I.S. more difficult than had the subtests been factorially pure or unidimensional. An attempt to replicate Cohen's factorial studies and provide further evidence on aged and pathological groups was published by Berger *et al.* (1964). Analysis of the data showed a similarity of factor structure between the two studies with significant correlations between diagnostic groups (schizophrenics, neurotics, brain-damaged and aged normals) on the first three factors identified as verbal, performance and memory. The fourth factor, a specific DS factor, did not relate to diagnostic group, except for brain damaged and chronic schizophrenic. The aged groups showed similar factor structure on the first two factors, but an age related change in the factor structure appeared on 3 and 4 – in particular the memory factor 3 was not identified in the eldest group. When the factor structure in both the pathological and aged groups were considered, it was apparent that age changes outweighed those induced by pathology. Saunders (1959) used varimax orthogonal rotation and isolated 10 significant orthogonal factors by scoring the subtests as split-halfs to increase the factor space, but these factors did not correspond to the subtest categories.

Two studies carried out by Maxwell (1960, 1961) analysed the performance of subjects at different age levels. In the age range 18-54 two factors emerged in which all subtests clustered, but dominated by verbal items (V, S, C) and a performance factor with BD and OA weighting highly. In the older sample, three factors emerged, verbal-comprehension, perceptual organization and memory. This structure was found by Riegel (1960), Riegel and Riegel (1962), Green and Berkowitz (1964), Dennerll *et al.* (1964). Radcliffe (1966) suggested that age complicated rather than reduced the factor structure, but his samples were under 55. A more recent paper by Savage and Britton (1968) involving principal component and varimax factor analysis on an aged sample (70+) supports the earlier studies, indicating a decrease in factorial complexity with age. Only the general factor accounting for 68% of the variance was significant on the principal component analysis, the 'memory' factor variance spreading over the verbal and performance factors; the varimax rotation produced three significant factors – verbal, performance and memory.

Although the multifactorial structure of the W.A.I.S. still needs precise investigation and sorting, it is clear that dependent on the mathematical procedure used, a general factor, a verbal, a performance and a memory factor can be confidently extracted. It is obvious, therefore, that the influence of multifactorial theory on the W.A.I.S. has been *ad hoc*. The factor structure is related to the F.S.I.Q., V.I.Q., P.I.Q. and subtest scaled scores in a complex fashion.

One *may* obtain a more reliable and valid measure of intelligence by developing a form based on the principal factor structure findings in relation to the W.A.I.S. In the meantime, computer programmes are now available to give subject factor scores on significant factors which can be used to provide a *factor (structured) profile of the intellectual characteristics for individual patients*. Maxwell (1960) presented a factorial short form of the W.A.I.S. with provision for calculating subject factor scores. In this way, intellectual theoretical and test construction procedures can be meaningfully merged. The need for a sound factorially based individual intelligence test covering the whole adult age range and applicable to clinical assessment is still with us.

Having commented on the W.A.I.S. in relation to theories of intelligence, some of its practical properties need to be examined.

(i) *Reliability*. Wechsler (1958) himself presents split-half, test-retest and correlational data showing the W.A.I.S. V, P, and F.S.I.Q. to have higher reliability than the W.-B., and higher F.S.I.Q. than P.I.Q. reliability. These were confirmed by Bayley (1957), Armitage and Pearl (1958), Coons and Peacock (1959), Cook and Hirt (1961), Duncan and Barrett (1961) and Prado and Schnadt (1965). Similar findings have been reported in relation to the W.I.S.C. and W.A.I.S. I.Q., the latter being consistently higher. (Fisher, 1962; Webb, 1963). Broadly speaking, the F.S.I.Q. reliability coefficients range from 0·90 to 0·97, V.I.Q. and P.I.Q. between 0·84 and 0·96. Cook and Hirt's (1961) caution that clinical inferences based on V.I.Q. and P.I.Q. discrepancies of W.A.I.S. and W.B. are not equally interpretable seems sound. Further general studies on the test-retest reliability of the W.A.I.S. over various time and age ranges would not go amiss.

In view of the wide use of subtest scatter (discussed Section II), the reliability of the subtests is also of major significance. Wechsler (1955), Jones (1956), McNemar (1957), Field (1960), Fisher (1960) and Alimena (1961) have commented on the position and distinguished between 'reliability' and 'abnormality' of scores. A glance at the tables in Wechsler (1955) will confirm that a large proportion of test-retest variance on the subtests is attributable to error, and caution is urged when comparing subscale test-retest data. One would recommend a z-score calculation (Payne and Jones, 1957, 1966) or the Field (1960) tables when comparing test-retest and subtest scores.

(ii) *Validity*. The concurrent predictive validity of the W.A.I.S. has been widely studied. Duncan and Barrett (1961) found the W.-B. and W.A.I.S. V.I.Q., P.I.Q. and F.S.I.Q. correlated 0·83, 0·45 and 0·82 respectively. These data are consistent with Neuringer's (1963) well-controlled study which found 0·84, 0·44, and 0·77 correlations between W.-B. and W.A.I.S. V.I.Q., P.I.Q. and F.S.I.Q. respectively. Studies of W.A.I.S. and Stanford-Binet by Fisher *et al.* (1961), Brengelman and Kenny (1961), Giannell and Freeburne (1963) and Benson (1963) reported correlations between 0·74 and 0·86 for Full Scale I.Q. and between 0·60 and 0·78 for P.I.Q. and S.-B. Numerous other W.A.I.S. studies with Peabody Picture Vocabulary Test, the Shipley Test, Kent-Emergency Test, Raven's Progressive Matrices, W.I.S.C., Columbia Mental Maturity Scale, Goodenough Draw a Man Test, the Bender, Ammons Full Range Picture Vocabulary Test, Army Classification Tests and many more are reported in Guertin *et al.* (1962, 1966). Guertin concludes that 'as the W.A.I.S. is so frequently utilized as a criterion measure this testifies to the validity generally assumed to characterize it'.

The factor analytic studies discussed earlier have also cast some light on the content and construct validity of the W.A.I.S. There is little change in factor structure with age, except in the distribution of the memory factor variance. As Wechsler had intended, the different subtests are different measures of intelligence, not measures of different kinds of intelligence. The large common variance between subtests is important as it makes pattern analysis difficult. At the same time, a consistent picture of intelligence is presented which suggests adequate construct and content validity for the concept of intelligence as a global capacity.

(iii) *Short forms of the W.A.I.S.* Since the introduction of the W.A.I.S., there have been several publications of possible short form W.A.I.S. measures which have proved clinically valuable. Doppelt (1956) suggested a short form W.A.I.S. of four subtests based on analysis of the standardization data in terms of regression equations. However, Himmelstein (1957) found that simple prorating of the subtest scores was as effective as the regression equation method of calculating the scores suggested by Doppelt.

Later E. Maxwell (1957) presented correlation data for possible two, three, four and five subtest combinations for the 25-30 age group and Jones (1962) outlined the development of two, three, four, five and six subtest batteries.

A. E. Maxwell (1960), Nickols (1962) and Karras (1963) have proposed abbreviated scales consisting of selected subtests based on correlational or factor analyses and utilizing regression or prorating methods for obtaining verbal, performance and full-scale scores.

An alternative method of producing short forms of the W.A.I.S. was used by Wolfson and Bachelis (1960), Satz and Mogel (1962) and Pauker (1963), who produced abbreviated scales containing a proportion of items from all of the subtests in an attempt to sample the range of abilities included in the original full scale. However, these scales would seem to be rather more difficult to administer than forms using one or two complete subtests and the reduction in item spread raises difficulties with those capable of answering few items on each subtest.

In practice A. E. Maxwell's 5 subtest factor-based scale (1960) C, S, V, BD and OA is useful for the age range 18-54 and a recent short form by Britton and Savage (1966) for the aged can complement this. The short form for the aged consists of four subtests. Results compare favourably with those found for younger age groups with W.A.I.S. short forms reviewed in earlier studies. The Aged Short Form and Full W.A.I.S. V.I.Q., P.I.Q. and F.S.I.Q. correlated 0·96, 0·924 and 0·969 respectively. They indicate that an adequate cognitive assessment of aged subjects may be obtained, whilst avoiding many of the problems associated with the administration of the full-scale W.A.I.S. to the elderly. It is an easily administered, time saving, four subtest, short form of the W.A.I.S. using a simple prorating system, and the tables provided in the W.A.I.S. Manual (Wechsler, 1955) which seems to give an adequate assessment of cognitive functioning in an elderly population.

The W.A.I.S. original and short forms therefore, emerge as valid, reliable, well-standardized measures of the concept of intelligence as Wechsler intended it. Its success as a measure of intellectual *change* and of various *aspects* of intellectual functioning will be considered in detail in the appropriate parts of the following sections.

II INTELLECTUAL ASSESSMENT AND MENTAL ILLNESS

Psychologists have long concerned themselves with mental illness and regarded psychiatric diagnostic labels as of fundamental importance to the scientific analysis of both mental abnormality and intellectual ability. It is not intended to consider this literature in detail, as excellent reviews have been provided by Brody (1941-43), Hunt and Cofer (1944) and particularly comprehensive ones by Payne (1960) and Yates (1954, 1966). In general, civilian neurotics show slightly above average I.Q.s, army neurotics slightly below: whilst schizophrenics and affective psychotics show intelligence levels below the mean, with epileptics and paranoid conditions demonstrating above average cognitive ability (Payne, 1960). Where patients have been further classified into schizophrenic or affective psychoses sub-categories, interesting patterns have emerged.

Paranoid groups are substantially brighter than normal. Among the schizophrenic and affective groups, the level of intellectual functioning is associated with the diagnostic category. Recent work by Bolton, Britton and Savage (1966) on normal, neurotic, psychotic and organic groups of aged also illustrates the interrelationship between psychiatric diagnostic categories and intellectual functioning. However, the authors caution, as do Payne (1960) and Yates (1954, 1966) implicitly, that the relationship between intellectual level and psychiatric category is not a perfectly correlated one, and the practice of trying to identify or diagnose psychiatric syndromes from psychometric intellectual measures is an unjustified, invalid use of the techniques. It is still a too common occurrence in psychological reports.

Normative data on intellectual measures such as the W.A.I.S. and Progressive Matrices *should be used to make statements about the intellectual functioning* of a patient, *not* his psychiatric diagnostic label. The task of making a statement about the actual intellectual functioning level of a patient during the illness is decidedly simpler than the elusive problem of *Intellectual Deficit*, especially when adequate normative data on the measurement techniques are available. The assessment of cognitive change associated with mental illness is nevertheless a vital issue which has long plagued applied psychologists.

1 Intellectual level and change in neurotic disorders

Investigations show that neurotic disorders produce little intellectual impairment compared with other psychiatric disorders. However, several investigators (Babcock, 1930; Eysenck, 1947; Payne, 1960) have reported or reviewed studies showing apparent cognitive impairment in certain neurotic groups. Eysenck (1947) has also suggested that dysthymic groups (introverted neurotics, obsessive compulsives and neurotic depressives) have higher mean I.Q. than hysterics (extraverted neurotics) and psychopaths. Data presented by Payne (1960) from various sources tend to support this view. This apparently reliable finding is difficult to explain unless one accepts that hysterics who become patients are more severely neurotic than their dysthymic counterparts and that severe neuroticism can produce intellectual impairment. Recent work involving aged neurotics (Bolton, Britton and Savage, 1966; Bolton, 1967; Britton, 1967) has suggested that aged neurotics have significantly lower intellectual functioning levels than normals, but higher than psychotics and organics.

More detailed studies on the relationship between various aspects of intellectual functioning and neurosis would be relevant here. The deficit involved, if any, may affect certain aspects of functioning and not others. Analysis of the W.A.I.S. subtest scores has frequently been performed in this regard, though other psychometric investigations and experimental studies of anxiety and performance have important contributions to make to resolving these problems.

Wechsler (1955, 1958) originally suggested a W.A.I.S. subtest pattern associated with anxiety and neurosis. However, despite investigations by Lewinski (1945), Rashkis and Welch (1946), Heyer (1949), Warner (1950), Munroe (1952),

Cohen (1955), Bauer and Johnson (1957) and Ladd (1964) on the W.-B. and W.A.I.S., Guertin *et al.* (1962, 1966) concluded 'it would be nice if a highly reliable and valid sign could be discovered. So far it has not happened, but if it did, the discovered sign would probably identify only a small percentage of the subjects possessing a given trait or system'.

Some recent work has demonstrated that aged neurotics living in the community had significantly lower W.A.I.S. F.S.I.Q., V.I.Q. and P.I.Q. scores and significantly higher V/P discrepancies and W.A.I.S. Deterioration Quotients (Bolton, Britton and Savage, 1966) than normals. Neuroticism measured by a psychiatrist and the M.M.P.I. clinical scale was related negatively to intellectual functioning (Britton, Bergmann, Kay and Savage, 1967). Earlier studies on the W.-B. and M.M.P.I. (Brower, 1947; Winfield, 1953) found no relationships between cognitive and personality scores. L'Abate (1962), who worked with the W.A.I.S. and M.M.P.I. to evaluate the Wechsler (1958) Indices of Maladjustment, hypothesized that these should relate better to the M.M.P.I. scale scores than the direct W.A.I.S. subtest and I.Q.s to the M.M.P.I. scales. The results failed to support the hypotheses. The Wechsler Indices of Maladjustment had lower correlations with M.M.P.I. than the other W.A.I.S. variables. W.A.I.S. V.I.Q., P.I.Q. and F.S.I.Q. had been found to relate to severity of M.M.P.I. pathology by Dowlis and Buchanan (1961), but among others Richard *et al.* (1961), and Birren *et al.* (1963) have produced conflicting results. The situation is far from clear.

The evidence would suggest that neurosis and intellectual underfunctioning are generally related, but many problems need sorting out. Foulds (1951, 1956), Ogilvie (1954), Shapiro and Nelson (1955), Payne (1960), Furneaux (1960), Payne and Hewlett (1960) and others have demonstrated that speed of functioning or retardation is an important factor in intellectual behaviour when differentiating neurotic groups from normal and in differentiating types of neurotics with the Progressive Matrices, the Porteus Mazes, the Babcock-Levy and Nufferno tests. The latter are extremely useful in investigating cognitive speed and level (Furneaux, 1956, 1960).

Studies relating the W.A.I.S. subtests to anxiety measures on many groups of psychiatric patients, high and low anxiety groups, undergraduates, etc. by Mayner *et al.* (1955), Dana (1957), Goldstein and Faber (1957) and Matarazzo *et al.* (1957) have found no consistent relationship between the Taylor Manifest Anxiety Scale and the W.A.I.S. subtests. Siegman (1956) did find Taylor scale anxiety to be significantly associated with the timed W.A.I.S. subtests, a finding in line with the Furneaux hypothesis discussed in the last section. The problem of anxiety and cognitive performance is, however, also complicated by other factors as Kerrick (1955) and Mayner *et al.* (1955) produced dissimilar results. Jurjevich (1963) found that none of the W.A.I.S. anxiety indicators related to M.A.S. or Welch M.M.P.I. anxiety measures. Britton *et al.* (1967) found that psychiatric diagnosis of neuroticism and the M.M.P.I. scales, Hysteria, Depression and Hypochondriasis related negatively to V.I.Q., P.I.Q. W.A.I.S. scores, but the W.A.I.S. V./P. discrepancy only to psychiatric diagnosis, and W.A.I.S. D.Q. to psychiatric diagnosis and the M.M.P.I. depression and m/f scales only.

The influence of anxiety or neuroticism on performance including cognitive tests is almost certainly an inverted U-shaped curvilinear relationship (Eysenck, 1957; Savage, 1962 and others) relating to the level and method of measuring anxiety, the nature and difficulty of the test, the stressful or neutral nature of the test conditions and many other variables. Consequently, unless these variables can be assessed simultaneously in the clinical situation, the use of the W.A.I.S. subtest scores or other cognitive measures to assess neurosis rather than to assess cognitive functioning as such is unreliable and invalid.

At the same time, one is aware that neurosis or individual neurotics may have cognitive levels and variability of functioning assessable with psychometric techniques, particularly the W.A.I.S. and Nufferno tests, provided normative data, errors of measurement and the like are properly considered.

2 Intellectual level and change in psychotic illness

The psychotic disorders have received a considerable amount of attention from the clinical and research psychologists interested in cognitive functioning and its measurement. Some of the first investigations of general intellectual level in mental patients by Wells and Kelley (1920) and Schott (1931) used the Binet on psychotic patients – manic-depressive and schizophrenic – to report slightly lower levels of intellectual ability than normal in these groups. Payne (1960) presents several tables derived from numerous studies over about 20 years describing the situation in some detail. The table below is adapted from Payne (1960) to show the general situation.

Category	Mean I.Q.	No. of cases
Unspecified schizophrenic	97·53	928
Mixed schizophrenic	99·61	72
Paranoid schizophrenic	94·84	166
Simple schizophrenic	88·23	44
Catatonic schizophrenic	82·80	45
Hebephrenic schizophrenic	80·60	29
Paranoid non-schizophrenic	118·30	7
Manic-depressive (depressed)	103·30	18
Depressive	91·00	8
Manic	90·00	32
Involutional depression	99·90	7

TABLE 2.1

Intelligence quotients in affective and schizophrenic
psychotic sub-groups
(adapted from Payne, 1960)

C*

(a) *Affective Disorders*

The data suggest that involutional depression and the depressed phase of manic-depression does not produce or is not associated with intellectual impairment to any degree, whilst depressives and manics independently show cognitive levels below normal (Payne, 1960). More recent work by Granick (1963) and Friedman (1964) confirmed the view that depression has a minimal effect on a large variety of tests measuring intellectual impairment and slowness. They failed to differentiate the depressives from normal groups on their measures. However, on aged samples, Bolton *et al.* (1966), Bolton (1967), Bolton *et al.* (1967) found affective groups to be significantly poorer on W.A.I.S. intellectual scores, the Modified Word Learning Test and the Auditory Recall Test than normal aged groups and Britton *et al.* (1967) noted that aged subjects with high depressive scores on the M.M.P.I. clinical scale showed low W.A.I.S. V.I.Q., P.I.Q. and high D.Q. scores. A relationship between poor performance on the Modified Word Learning Test (Walton and Black, 1957, 1959) and depression had been noted.

It would appear that cognitive level in the psychotic affective disorders is generally below normal, but the evidence is not conclusive. It may be that certain aspects of cognitive performance are adversely affected and others less so. The learning of new verbal material (as in the M.W.L.T.) and performance on motor-perceptual speed tasks may be influenced much more negatively than general attainment level on intellectual tests. The crucial problem, however, is not so much the level of cognitive functioning during illness, but the relationship of this to pre-morbid intellectual level. Payne (1960) suggests that though affective psychotics may have similar illness cognitive levels to schizophrenics, their pre-morbid levels are higher. Testing patients before and/or after recovery should clarify this issue. More practically, an investigation of intellectual functioning during and after illness in view of the success of antidepressant drugs would be possible and most valuable in this area.

In 1931 Gardner concluded that 100 manic-depressives were worse than their colleagues at school, though no statistical analysis was performed. Twenty-five manic depressives given the Army G.C.T. by Mason (1956) on entering the services before illness developed were above average in intelligence. Whilst Davidson's (1939) study had shown that clinically improved manic-depressives showed higher Binet scores than during illness and those clinically worse produced lower I.Q.s. Manic-depressive, control and treatment groups (given E.C.T.) were compared by Callagan (1952) who found the W.-B., V.I.Q. and P.I.Q. scores improved in one week and five weeks after E.C.T. treatment, but not in the other groups. Intelligence assessment improved and correlated with psychiatric rating of clinical improvement in all cases.

The performance of manic-depressives and depressives on a comparison of vocabulary and Binet score, the Babcock tests of mental efficiency and the Shipley Hartford test suggested that intellectual deterioration occurred in these groups (Babcock, 1941; Wittman, 1933; Davidson, 1938, 1939; Rapaport *et al.*, 1945; Shapiro and Nelson, 1955). These results are consistent with those of

Bolton *et al.* (1967) using the similarly based M.W.L.T. with aged affective disordered groups. However, deterioration as measured by the W.A.I.S. D.Q., V./P., Hewson ratios, Reynell's Index and Allen's Index did not differentiate affectives from other groups in the aged. The earlier studies similarly could not distinguish between affective disorders and other abnormal groups (Payne, 1960) on cognitive deterioration measures.

(b) *Schizophrenia*

Schizophrenia is undoubtedly a heterogeneous syndrome psychiatrically, and cognitive functioning cannot be described under a single 'disease entity'. Generally speaking, schizophrenic illness level of intellectual performance is below average, similar to that of the affective psychotic disorders (Payne, 1960; Savage, 1964). Without remission, however, schizophrenia tends to produce progressive intellectual deterioration. Table 2.1 shows that the main clinical schizophrenic subgroups differ considerably in mean illness I.Q. levels. The first two groups, non-specified and mixed, probably relate to 'early' or 'acute' schizophrenia. The paranoid schizophrenics (like the paranoid non-schizo-phrenics) have substantially higher I.Q.s than the more severely ill, particularly the catatonic and hebephrenic groups. The severity of cognitive inpairment clinically assessed is of course a prime psychiatric symptom for diagnosing the more severe schizophrenic states and it must be remembered that many severely ill cannot be assessed by psychometric measures of intellect. The figures quoted, therefore, are probably on the high side.

Birren (1944) and Rapaport and Webb (1950) suggested that schizophrenic patients did not differ from the general population mean I.Q. before, but were significantly lower during illness, whilst Mason (1956) found schizophrenics to be below average before their illness as well as during. Recently Albee *et al.* (1963, 1964) have presented childhood and adult intellectual data on adult schizophrenia which demonstrated that (i) pre-morbid and illness I.Q. levels were not different, (ii) schizophrenics-to-be had lower I.Q.s than normal children in their own social classes, (iii) had lower I.Q. than their siblings as children and (iv) that deterioration is evident during childhood. This data and comparable studies by Foulds and Dixon (1962a, b) and Foulds, Dixon, McClelland and McClelland (1962) are most important as they came to the same conclusion that *cognitive deficit is progressive but complete before breakdown* and no further effect of illness was found over a two-year test-retest period not accountable for by age. Though Carp (1950) and Callagan (1952) found that insulin treatment did not significantly affect I.Q. level, Sodium Amytal adminis-tration was found to be associated with improved intellectual performance on the Binet and W.-B. by Layman (1940) and Mainord (1953). Unfortunately, more controlled studies by Ogilvie (1954) and Broadhurst (1957) failed to confirm the beneficial effect of Amytal on intellectual performance on the Nufferno tests.

Progressive deterioration in intellectual performance on the Binet was found by Payne (1960) in the Trapp and James (1937) study. The average I.Q. of schizophrenic patients dropped significantly and the drop in the I.Q. correlated significantly with length of illness. The paranoid group showed less decline, but it was still associated with length of illness. More recent work by Lubin *et al.* (1962), Hamlin and Jones (1963) and Wynne (1963) also found a significant decline in intellectual functioning in non-remitting schizophrenics. Schwartzman *et al.* in Yates (1966) also demonstrated cognitive decline over a two-year period in non-remitting schizophrenia and an improvement in recovered patients.

Indirect methods of measuring cognitive impairment have been severely criticized in reviews by Yates (1954, 1966), Payne (1960) and Savage (1964) as being empirically and theoretically unsound. However, the many studies of schizophrenic intellectual performance on these measures cannot be ignored. Despite criticism of its use, vocabulary has been found to deteriorate less than other measures of intelligence in relation to schizophrenia and other disorders (Yates, 1954, 1966; Payne, 1960). The position would appear to be that for most schizophrenics, intellectual deterioration is a slow process commencing long before hospitalization and often complete on entry. For other smaller groups, deterioration may continue after hospitalization, particularly after two years and progressing to an untestable level.

3 Intellectual level and change in brain-damaged adults

Brain damage and intellectual functioning are inextricably bound up with assessment problems in clinical psychology. One is continually faced with the diagnostic labels – query brain damage, brain damage suspected, intellectual deterioration, etc. Unfortunately, the nature of the inquiry from our medical colleagues has somewhat distracted psychologists and encouraged attempts to diagnose brain damage, using intellectual measures in this pursuit. The aim – neurological diagnosis by intellectual assessment, laudable as it may have seemed – was unfortunate. It no doubt distracted a large body of able talent and worthwhile investigation from developing better methods of intellectual assessment and at the same time added little to the problem of diagnosing brain damage *per se*. There are several inherent difficulties in the use of intellectual measures to diagnose brain damage which have been excellently discussed by Yates (1954, 1966) and Meyer (1960) among others. Briefly, the problems revolve round the concept of brain damage, the validity of intellectual assessment in relation to brain damage, and the measurement of intellectual level or impairment *per se* in individual patients or clinical groups. The view, stated earlier, that intellectual measures should be employed to assess intellectual functioning level and/or change in particular individual or groups of patients and in making valuable statements about this and, among other things, its predictive importance in relation to employment possibilities and limitations, rehabilitation training, remedial education, etc., is a much more valid and reliable use of these techniques than trying to place people in medical diagnostic groups. The medical profession already has techniques, some excellent, some not so reliable, to do this. *Intel-*

lectual or cognitive measures in general should be used to diagnose some of the effects or consequences of brain damage, not brain damage as such.

In constructing tests of brain damage the concept is often assumed to be unitary. But as Yates (1966) points out, 'it is essential to regard the effects of brain damage from an hierarchical viewpoint'. That is, brain damage will produce in any given individual (*a*) a general deterioration in all aspects of functioning but will also produce (*b*) differential (group) effects depending on the location, extent, etc., of the brain damage; and will produce (*c*) highly specific effects if it occurs in certain highly specified areas of the brain. In any individual case, it is essential to consider the evidence carefully from all three of these angles.

Comprehensive reviews of the empirical and theoretical literature on these problems have been presented by Yates (1954, 1966), Meyer (1960), Willett (1960), Smith (1962), Haynes and Sells (1963), Maher (1963), Talland (1963), Piercy (1964) and Savage (1964). In general, individual psychometric measures have not proved satisfactory in assessing brain damage and are unlikely to do so. The effects of brain damage on intellectual functioning will be manifest according to which hierarchical level is being tapped by a particular test. The problem of diagnosis is also aggravated by the assumptions that (i) neurological and psychiatric classificatory procedures are themselves valid when used as criteria of brain damage and (ii) that a test which defines between clear-cut brain-damaged and normal subjects will necessarily discriminate an individual and identify him as brain damaged when other measures have failed to do so.

Despite all the empirical and theoretical difficulties, many cognitively based measures have been developed to assess or diagnose brain damage. They suffer, however, from two basic flaws. They relate to no sound theory of cerebral functioning and assume that intellectual impairment is a distinctive feature of brain damage. In fact, relating cognitive functioning level or impairment to brain functioning theory is far from being a theoretical reality, cognitive impairment is common to several mental conditions and intellectual deterioration or dysfunction is not necessarily permanent as the brain damage concept often assumes.

(a) *Intellectual Impairment*
Early studies of the effects of cerebral injury on psychological test performance suggested that the ability to form new associations is highly susceptible to brain damage (Achilles, 1917; Wechsler, 1917; Wells, 1927; Lilliencrants, 1923). Thus most of the initial work developing cognitive tests as measures or indices of brain damage was influenced by the conclusions of Babcock (1930, 1933) that the *discrepancy between* (*a*) untimed responses which require old associations of a kind correlating highly with intellectual level and (*b*) responses on tests which emphasize time and the acquisition of new material are the *best* measures of deterioration and (*c*) that mental deterioration can be used to measure brain damage even though it related to other conditions. Babcock's work along with the investigations of Goldstein and Scheerer (1941) stressing the importance of

loss of abstract reasoning in brain-damaged patients had both beneficial and limiting effects on subsequent investigations and test development. Attempts to confirm the Babcock position have had little or no success. Brody (1942) found that all abilities except vocabulary severely declined but no other psychometric pattern for dementia emerged. Many studies have been reported on normal and functional mentally ill groups such as neurotics, manic-depressives, and schizo-phrenics and demonstrated the existence of deterioration in all of these groups (Wittman, 1933; Babcock and Levy, 1940; Babcock, 1941; Rapaport *et al.*, 1945; Nelson and Shapiro, 1955). Senile psychosis (Botwinick and Birren, 1951), epilepsy (Wittman, 1933; Barnes and Felterman, 1938), drug and alcohol addiction (Wittman, 1933; Hall, 1938; Partington, 1940) have also been investi-gated with inconclusive results. It is suggested by Payne (1960) that speed and age are important compounding influences in these investigations.

The Goldstein-Scheerer Test Battery (1941) stressing reasoning and sorting tasks was also proposed as a measure of deterioration in organic brain damage. This test also suffers the general deficiencies associated with inadequate norms, no evidence on reliability and the finding that abstract reasoning defect is not peculiar or limited to brain damage, but is also seen in schizophrenia (Boyd, 1949; Bolles and Goldstein, 1959). Later studies by Tooth (1947) and McFie and Piercy (1952) have failed to distinguish brain-damaged from other groups with this measure. Modern opinion on this test was summed up by Payne (1965), 'The Goldstein-Scheerer test battery is at present of very limited practical value. Although intended to assess brain damage, it cannot be used for this purpose because of its lack of a standardized scoring system and lack of norms.' The technique involved sorting tests which have been developed in relation to thought disorder measurement by Rapaport *et al.* (1945), Lovibond (1954), Semeonoff and Trist (1958) and Payne and Hewlett (1960) where it may be of much more value.

Another measure, the Shipley-Hartford Retreat Scale (Shipley, 1940; Shipley and Burlingame, 1941) claimed to be useful in discriminating organics from normal, neurotic and psychotic groups. Once again, however, standardization data are inadequate, age, sex and intelligence were not controlled and later research by Ross and McNaughton (1944), Aita *et al.* (1947), Manson and Grayson (1947), Kobler (1947), Margaret and Simpson (1948), Garfield and Fey (1948), Canter (1951) and Mason and Ganzler (1963) all failed to confirm the Shipley-Hartford as an acceptable measure of brain damage or in relation to intellectual deterioration.

The Hunt-Minnesota Test for organic damage (Hunt, 1943) has fared little better. Hunt's original study misclassified only one subject, but in Aita *et al.* (1947) 10% of their control group and only 2·2% of the brain-damaged had a T score of greater than the cut-off point of 90. Canter (1951), Malamud (1946), Meehl and Jeffrey (1946) and Juckem and Wold (1948) confirmed the high degree of misclassification of normals and abnormal subjects with this test. In practice, the Hunt-Minnesota has not lived up to its promise and has virtually no use as a test of brain damage.

The Wechsler Deterioration Indices (Wechsler 1944, 1958) are perhaps the most widely used measures of deterioration in clinical practice and frequently related to organic pathology. Wechsler (1958) stated, 'In general, the gradual falling off of ability in later age may be considered as an indication of normal decline; a marked and disabling loss, at any age, as a sign of definite impairment'. The major problem, however, is still the assessment of previous cognitive level. Wechsler noted (1958) that age curves of his subtests on the W.-B. and W.A.I.S. declined at different rates and proposed to measure deterioration by comparing 'slowly' declining abilities with those declining 'quickly', assuming that those not declining significantly with age were those least affected by the deterioration process and most likely to represent pre-illness levels of functioning. His Deterioration Quotient (D.Q.) for the W.A.I.S. was defined as

$$\text{D.Q.} = \frac{\text{Hold Tests} - \text{Don't Hold Tests}}{\text{Hold Tests}} \times 100$$

where Hold tests were Information, Vocabulary, Object Assembly and Picture Completion and Don't Hold Tests were Digit Span, Similarities, Digit Symbol and Block Design. A large D.Q., particularly over 20% was assumed to relate to brain damage. Many studies have investigated this possibility. Levi *et al.* (1945) found the D.Q. clinically useful, but Allen (1947, 1948) reported that only 54% of the brain-injured were so identified using the D.Q. cut-off point of 20%. He suggested an alternative, Allen's Index of deterioration.

$$(I+C)-(D+DS)<5$$

Results of studies comparing Wechsler's and Allen's Indices as effective classifiers of organic brain damage in relation to other pathological groups have been inconclusive; Blake and McCarthy (1948) favoured Wechsler's D.Q., Rogers (1950) Allen's Index. Further studies on the D.Q. by Kass (1949), Berkowitz (1953), Botwinick and Birren (1951) and Doerken and Greenbloom (1953) showed that the D.Q. failed to differentiate effectively between mental defectives, confirmed brain-damaged, senile psychotics and normals.

Hewson (1949) approached the problem by investigating 13 ratios based on the Wechsler subscales. The derivation of the scales has been severely criticized by Rabin and Guertin (1951). Nevertheless, the Hewson Ratios have attracted much interest. Gutman (1950) found them superior to the D.Q. and Allen Index in diagnosing organic brain damage, though he was not completely satisfied with the degree of success. Wheeler and Wilkins (1951), Everett (1956) and McKeever and Gerstein (1958) found considerable overlap and mis-classification in organic, schizophrenic and other groups. Adaptation of the Hewson Ratios to the W.A.I.S. by Woolf (1960) was reasonably successful, 64% organics correctly classified and 23% misclassified non-organics, not unlike the results of Bryan and Brown (1957). Smith (1962a) found organic ratios in 81·3% of a group of cerebral tumours and non-organic ratios in 73·5% of the psychogenic patients. Recent work by Bolton *et al.* (1966) and Bolton (1967) suggested that the Hewson Ratios gave the best identifications of organic disorder, when comparing them with W.B.-D.Q., W.A.I.S.-D.Q., Allen Index and the V./P. discrepancy using the W.A.I.S. on normal, neurotic, psychotic and organic aged samples, though their misclassification of normals was high.

Thus despite the uncertainty surrounding their construction, there is some evidence that the Hewson Ratios have some validity in differential diagnosis in organic disorders and senile dementia. Nevertheless as Bolton *et al.* (1966) caution the '*deterioration measures derived from the W.A.I.S. should be used in conjunction with normal data to make sound statements about intellectual impairment rather than as psychiatric diagnostic indices*'.

Several studies have attempted to validate certain W.-B. and W.A.I.S. subtest patterns in relation to brain damage. The criticisms and limitations of this method were discussed earlier and should be kept in mind. Nevertheless Wechsler's original observation that a V.I.Q./P.I.Q. discrepancy in favour of the former exists in organic patients was confirmed by Morrow and Mark (1955), Klove and Reitan (1958), Klove (1959), Norman and Daly (1959), Ladd (1964) and others on several types of organic disorder. Other studies, however, have criticized the assumption that a zero V./P. discrepancy is normal and Wechsler's view that 15 and 20 point V./P. discrepancies are clinically important cut-off points in relation to the diagnosis of organic involvement in intellectual impairment. Eisdorfer *et al.* (1959) questioned this in the aged sample and Bolton *et al.* (1966) presented normative data on the Wechsler Diagnostic Indices with the aged which suggests higher V./P. differences are necessary before organic disease can be inferred or suspected or diagnosed.

Field (1960) and Fisher (1960) have provided tables to assess the significance of V./P. discrepancies and Field emphasizes the distinction between the 'abnormality' of a difference and its 'reliability'. A 25-point V./P. discrepancy occurred in 1 in 100 subjects and might be considered 'abnormal' statistically. On the other hand, a V./P. discrepancy of 13 would occur 1:100 by chance because of errors of measurement. Therefore, a 13-point discrepancy or greater is not spurious, but 'real' differences are not unusual in the population until they reach 25 or more. The data of Fisher (1960) and Field (1960) plus those on the aged of Bolton *et al.* (1966) suggest that Wechsler's original cut-off points for abnormal or clinically significant intellectual deterioration and variability may have been on the low side. Nevertheless, the V./P. discrepancy is probably a better index of impairment than any of the others, and has been more frequently associated with brain damage in a positive manner (Balthazar *et al.*, 1961; Jenkins, 1961; Hirt and Cook, 1962; Mackie, 1963; Dennerll *et al.*, 1964) though not always (Fisher, 1961a, b; Bolton *et al.*, 1966).

The confused picture of attempts to diagnose brain damage from patterns of Wechsler subtests has been excellently presented by Guertin *et al.* in a series of reviews, especially in 1956, 1962, 1966. The general statistical difficulties of pattern analysis (Nunnally, 1967) and confusing empirical data (Guertin *et al.*, 1966; Yates, 1966) do not lead one to hope for much in this area. Even attempts to identify intellectual loss in relation to specific areas of lesion and well-known medical syndromes have not been particularly encouraging when general psychometric tests of intelligence were employed. The literature has been reviewed by Meyer (1960), McFie (1960), Guertin *et al.* (1962, 1966) and Piercy (1964). The investigations epitomized by the work of Hebb (1949, 1959), McFie and Piercy (1952), Ettlinger *et al.* (1955, 1956), Meyer and Yates (1955), Penfield and Milner (1958), Meyer (1959, 1960) and McFie (1960) suggest that specialization for particular intellectual functions appear to occur in both left and right hemispheres, but in the left hemisphere it is more extreme and covers a wider range of functions.

Within the hemispheres, posterior lesions produce greater intellectual deficit than anterior lesions, the posterior cortex being more highly differentiated than the anterior cortex. The frontal lobes can no longer be regarded as subserving the highest intellectual functions in adults, but may be more important in children. Lesions in the temporal lobes are associated with memory loss, the parietal area with motor-perceptual difficulties.

Although generalizations trying to relate intellectual impairment and cerebral damage are dangerous, research continues to indicate that patients with right cerebral damage do function differentially from those with left cerebral damage, and both from individuals with brain damage that is not limited to one hemisphere. In general, verbal capacity is better than performance in patients with right hemisphere lesions. However, the longer the patient has had the disorder, left or right hemisphere specific, the less intellectual differentiation between these two kinds of disorder. At present, it is relatively safe to assume that V.I.Q. > P.I.Q. is not just characteristic of cerebral pathology *sui generis*, but may be indicative of pathology in the right hemisphere or a more diffuse kind; the reverse pattern (P.I.Q. > V.I.Q.), though not typical of most cerebral disorders, differentially characterizes the left hemisphere disturbance.

Intellectual impairment indices may be perfectly reliable and valid for assessing certain aspects of cognitive functioning. They should be investigated and assessed as such, not as measures of brain damage. Attempts to validate them concurrently and predictively as measures of cerebral dysfunction have been unsuccessful in most cases, even the standardization data on the 'organic' indices being completely inadequate. In spite of the early hope for measures of deterioration as diagnostic indicators of brain damage, they cannot be said to have been successful. The basic confusion is in the concept and width of the term brain damage, and the fact that cognitive impairment is common to other clinical diagnostic groups. Faith still appears to persist that psychometric cognitive tests should be able to provide a diagnosis of brain damage, affective disorder and the like, but this faith is misinformed and unrealistic. Other approaches to the problems are now available and should be pursued.

(b) *Learning and Memory Tests*
The Modified Word Learning Test is a verbal learning test published by Walton and Black (1957); though obviously related to the historic work of Babcock and

others, it developed more specifically from the studies of Nelson (1953), Shapiro and Nelson (1955), Shapiro *et al.* (1956) and Inglis *et al.* (1956). It has been very successful compared with most measures developed to identify brain damage. Although I.Q., vocabulary level and age were found to exert some influence on scores on the test, they were not enough to affect organic group identification significantly and misclassification is minimal. Walton and Black (1959), Riddell (1962), Kendrick (1963), Bolton, Savage and Roth (1967) and others have confirmed the success of this test in identifying verbal learning loss associated with generalized cerebral damage, and low misclassification of other groups. The only significant study criticizing the M.W.L.T. was by Orme *et al.* (1964) who found it misclassified a large percentage of schizophrenics.

It can, nevertheless, be recommended for clinical use on adult and aged patients as one of the best measures for the behaviourally based diagnosis of generalized organic disorders. More research on other well-defined organic groups could be most useful with this test. The development of a complementary performance learning task is being undertaken by the present writer.

Early studies on memory dysfunction by Achilles (1917), Moore (1919), Lilliencrants (1923) and Wylie (1930) suggested that both recognition and recall are important factors in organic disorder. The Wechsler Memory Scale (Wechsler, 1945) has been long and widely used in clinical practice. Kral and Durost (1953) found immediate memory impaired in both senile dements and Korsakoff's psychoses. Kral (1962) distinguished 'benign' and 'malignant' memory loss, the latter involving loss of recent memory, a finding in sympathy with the inability to acquire new material noted by Walton and Black (1957) and many previous workers. The Auditory Recall Test (A.R.T.) of Inglis (1957, 1959) set out to measure this acquisition phase in memory. He successfully discriminated elderly psychiatric patients with memory disorder from others and Caird *et al.* (1962) confirmed these results. Kendrick (1963) and Bolton *et al.* (1967) showed that the A.R.T. and the M.W.L.T. or Synonym Learning Test were significantly correlated – unlike Riddell (1962), who had suggested they were measuring different things. His claim that the A.R.T. measures memory loss whilst the M.W.L.T. is more significantly related to 'organic' involvement has not been further substantiated. The specific relationships between these tests and brain damage are not easy to analyse; they are more often assumed than proven. The Issacs and Walker (1964) test similar to the A.R.T. has been developed, but does not appear much of an improvement.

The available evidence, however, suggests that performance on memory and verbal learning tests is significantly impaired by brain damage. This area deserves more extensive experimental and clinical investigation. The techniques appear soundly based, open to experimental investigation and theoretical development.

(c) *Perceptual and Motor-perceptual Diagnostic Tests*
Perceptual and motor-perceptual assessment techniques have been used to diagnose organic disorders for many years. Among the most well known are the

Bender Visual Motor Gestalt Test (1938–46), Benton Visual Retention Test (Benton, 1946-60), the Graham-Kendall Memory for Designs Test (Graham and Kendall, 1946), the Block Design Test (Shapiro, 1951, 1952, 1953), the Spiral After-Effect (Holland and Beach, 1958) and the more recent Minnesota Percepto-Diagnostic Test (Fuller and Laird, 1963; Fuller, 1967). Once again, however, the problem of misclassification and the fact that poor perceptual or motor-perceptual performance is associated with other than organic disorders has led to many difficulties.

The Graham-Kendall measures memory for designs, but even the original tables (1946) reveal 50% misclassification of organics. The test has, however, been further standardized (Kendall and Graham, 1948; Graham and Kendall, 1960; Kendall, 1962) to provide age and intelligence standardization: significant differences between brain-damaged and control groups were found, but using a cut-off point scoring system, considerable overlap with other diagnostic groups was seen. Nevertheless, the investigations of Brilliant *et al.* (1963) and Korman and Blumberg (1963) suggest that this is one of the most consistently successful motor-perceptual measures for identifying brain damage.

The Bender-Gestalt (Bender, 1938, 1946; Pascal and Suttell, 1951) has long been used in this area. It has not always been found highly successful in discriminating brain-damaged from schizophrenic groups (Olin and Reznikoff, 1958). However, many studies reviewed by Tolor (1956) and Billingslea (1963) and some by Brilliant and Gynther (1963), Korman and Blumberg (1963) and Orme *et al.* (1964) have found the test more successful in identifying brain-damaged subjects. The Benton Visual Retention Test (third ed. Benton, 1946, 1954, 1960) which has several forms of administration involving memory and copying designs has also claimed favourable discrimination of brain-damaged groups (Benton, 1946-60; Brilliant *et al.*, 1963).

As elsewhere, the problems with motor-perceptual measures involve definition of an acceptable level of successful classification or identification and misplacement. The figures to date suggest an error in group classification which does not give confidence for the individual clinical case. A sound study by Wheeler *et al.* (1963) using discriminant function analysis on large numbers of brain-damaged and non-brain-damaged subjects showed considerable decline in the accuracy of motor-perceptual measures in cross-validation with the Wechsler subtests, Halstead Category Test and Trail Making Tests.

Two measures based on theoretical views relating central nervous system inhibition build-up to brain damage have been used diagnostically (Shapiro, 1951, 1952, 1953; Eysenck, 1957; Holland and Beech, 1958). Shapiro's *Block Design Rotation Test* used a cut-off point of 6% rotation to identify 14 out of 19 brain-damaged subjects and misclassified one functional patient. The 1952 study of Shapiro *et al.*, however, suggested that an increase in C.N.S. inhibitory process in brain-damaged S.s was not necessary to account for their differential rotation, but rather that visual field and oculomotor defects were more important.

Recently, however, the Minnesota Percepto-Diagnostic Test developed by

Fuller and Laird (1963) and revised by Fuller (1967) has used the Shapiro type Rotation score with six figures from the Bender Gestalt. They have also presented normative data covering an extensive age range and demonstrated the test's usefulness in diagnosing brain-damaged from psychotic and other groups (Fuller and Laird, 1963; Uyeno, 1963; Fuller, 1967). In view of its standardization etc., it is most certainly a promising motor-perceptual test *per se* whose relationship to brain damage of various types and at various ages should be further investigated.

Finally, mention should be made of a perceptual-motor-learning test, the Elithorn Maze Test (Elithorn, 1955; Benton *et al.*, 1963); this most promising test is being increasingly used and normative data on adults (Elithorn, 1955) and aged adults (Davies, 1965) is available. A study involving verbal level I.Q., verbal learning (M.W.L.T.), performance level I.Q., motor-perceptual level (M.P.D.T.) and a motor-perceptual-learning task (the Elithorn Mazes) would be most valuable in differentiating the important diagnostic implications of level and learning in verbal and performance abilities in relation to brain damage effects on intellectual functioning.

It is obvious from this section that the relationships between the various aspects of intellectual functioning and the various concepts of brain damage are far from understood. Much research is needed in this area which is based on sound theoretical and empirical positions. The applications of the available intellectual assessment techniques to differential diagnosis in brain damage or other psychiatric groups is a debatable exercise. *The measures themselves are, however, improving as measures of aspects of intellectual functioning and can profitably be used as such in relation to medical diagnostic categories.*

As Piercy (1964) notes,

> studies of the intellectual consequences of cerebral lesions and theories of normal intelligence have not been closely associated. Neurologists and others have considered the relationship between aphasia and intelligence based on studies of normal people but not in terms of theories of intelligence. Similarly, psychologists concerned with the nature of normal intelligence have been largely uninfluenced by neurological symptomatology.

As indicated earlier, the psychiatric-psychological relationship has been similarly negligent.

Some evidence on the nature of intelligence has come from a comparison of the effects of cerebral lesions in children and adults which Piercy reviews excellently in relation to medical diagnostic categories. It would appear (Hebb, 1949, 1959) that a greater mass of cerebral tissue is necessary to *develop* a given intellectual ability than is needed to *sustain* that ability in later life. Thus a large lesion in adult life might have little effect on general intellectual level, but might severely affect intellectual development if it occurred in infancy. The similarities between Hebb's theory (1949, 1959) and Cattell's theory of 'fluid' and 'crystallized' intelligence (Cattell, 1963) are compelling and have important implications for research and development in intellectual assessment techniques. Savage and his colleagues, Bolton and Britton, have recently verified the importance of the concepts of 'fluid' and 'crystallized' intelligence in intellectual assessment in normal, neurotic, psychotic and organic aged subjects (Savage and Bolton, 1968; Savage and Britton, 1968). They also suggest a two factor theory for level and two types of impairment in intellect. The need to analyse the components of intellectual ability before attempting to relate them to cerebral lesions (or anything else for that matter) is essential; experimental procedures rather than the present psychometric techniques are essential in this area. At the same time the standardization procedures must be extended into experimental practice.

III   EXPERIMENTAL APPROACH TO INTELLECTUAL ASSESSMENT

As several eminent authors have pointed out, the factor analytic and psychometric approaches to intelligence testing, in gaining or trying for technical mathematical perfection, have become divorced from both psychological theory and experiment, and furthermore, from clinical problems and practice. The integration of intelligence testing with the main stream of academic psychology and a more determined experimental and laboratory approach to the problems involved is needed to complement psychometric techniques.

However, the application of experimental psychology to intellectual assessment is not extensive, despite reviews by Eysenck (1960, 1967), Jones (1960a, b), Zangwill (1964) and Guilford (1967) which suggest many possibilities. The developments in new techniques to investigate perception, learning, memory, motivation, language and communication have scarcely impinged on psychometric intellectual assessment and clinical problems in neurology and psychiatry. There is obviously much interesting work to be done in this area. Furthermore, the cognitive laboratory studies of today could become the clinical routine practice of tomorrow. Given finance and staff, detailed experimental investigations of the cognitive functions not tapped by present psychometric measures could be undertaken in everyday clinical practice.

Guilford (1967) suggests, and this will scarcely surprise applied psychologists, that 'He (the experimental psychologist) would probably be surprised to be told that his research makes contributions to the nature of intelligence. . . . He probably also suspects intelligence measurements of being less precise than those he ordinarily tries to obtain.' However, Binet himself was an experimental psychologist greatly influenced by laboratory techniques, and even modern psychometric tests include items covering the laboratory topics of memory, rote and serial learning, visual perception, space perception, thinking and so forth.

Investigations from the experimental psychology study of ageing can be used to illustrate the application of experimental psychology to intellectual assessment and clinical problem areas. Perceptual experiments involving pictures or designs under difficult conditions have shown older subjects to require longer or to make more errors than younger ones in arriving at correct identification. Perceptual learning on the Elithorn maze and Trail Making tests was found by Heron and Chown (1967) to be inferior in older subjects. This and other visual discrimination and learning experiments (Welford, 1964) have important implications for item selection in intellectual measures for normal and clinical use. Birren and Riegel (1962), for example, showed that the identification of verbal material by older subjects was less efficient than in younger.

Short-term and long-term memory are important components of intellectual ability. Experimental studies of short-term memory have shown that digit span techniques show little change with age (Gilbert, 1941), whilst problem-solving tasks in which different items of data had to be pieced together in time were related to increasing difficulty with age due to greater problems with short-term attention. The older subjects tended to forget one item while seeking another. Brown (1964), however, suggests that span of immediate memory is very much reduced by a shift in attention between perception and recall, effects which Welford (1958) shows increase with age. This data is consistent with the finding of Inglis (1960, 1962), Inglis and Caird (1963) and Mackay and Inglis (1963) in which older subjects presented with pairs of digits to both ears were less able to recall digits to the ear reported second.

It is now well known that learning is less readily achieved in older than younger subjects (Bromley, 1966) and that they find it difficult to eliminate errors already learned (Kay, 1954). The learning work is reviewed by Welford (1958), who suggests that the factors limiting learning by older people seem to be the same as in mental skills. This work confirms the importance of the Modified Word Learning, the Auditory recall, the Elithorn Maze and Minnesota Percepto-Diagnostic Tests approach of experimentally breaking down certain components of intellectual ability and devising sound psychometric measures for their assessment. The sensory-motor experimental work suggests the importance of 'speed' noted by Eysenck earlier. Miles (in Welford, 1964) suggested that older people are slower at making complex movements, whilst Singleton (1954-1955) found reaction time in complex situations to be longer in older subjects. Simple reaction times did not distinguish between the age groups. The information theory of Crossmann (1964) has been used to co-ordinate these results. In most cases speed and accuracy are compensatory, older subjects tend to concentrate on accuracy at the expense of speed. The amalgamation of Crossman's and Eysenck's theories which are not inconsistent with Cattell's or the psychometric findings of Birren *et al.* and Savage *et al.* have interesting possibilities for intellectual assessment method.

Many clinicians believe that personality characteristics affect intellectual performance and use intelligence tests to diagnose non-intellectual difficulties or abnormalities. Wechsler's tests and theory of intellectual functioning encourage such a position, but unfortunately do not separate out the non-intellectual components in the subtest or scale scores. The practice of directly diagnosing personality abnormalities from present intellectual tests is not recommended. However, experimental studies have shown relationships between intelligence, learning and personality. Personality factors in intelligence measurement must not be ignored. They must be accurately measured. Eysenck (1947) found that extraverts opt for speed, introverts for accuracy in laboratory tasks and Jensen (1964) confirmed this with the Progressive Matrices intelligence tests. Farley (1966) found a monotonic increase in solution time on the Nufferno tests related positively to introversion, whilst low accuracy characterized hysterics and low speed dysthymics in Brierley's (1961) study.

Neuroticism has been shown by many investigators to give a curvilinear relationship with task difficulty on many functions including intelligence tests (Lynn and Gordon, 1961; Farley, 1966). Teasing out the complex interrelationships between personality and intellectual functioning requires carefully controlled studies using sound measures of personality and 'purer' measures of intellectual (i.e. non-personality) assessment. The work on learning and personality has much to offer in terms of guide lines. As Jones (1960a) points out, efficiency of learning is a curvilinear function of drive strength, some intermediate level of drive being optimal, and optimal drive strength is an inverse function of the difficulty of the task. These laws are consistent with the major findings of the Iowa (Faber, 1954; Taylor, 1956; Spence, 1956) and Maudsley groups (Eysenck, 1957, 1960). Eysenck's (1962, 1967) views on the importance of extraversion and introversion in relation to conditionability and learning also have important implications for the assessment of intellectual functions in normal and abnormal subjects.

Psychoticism also affects learning and intellectual behaviour in a complex way requiring detailed experimental investigations. Reviewing the literature on learning and psychosis, Jones (1960) showed these studies to be few and generally inadequate. Nevertheless, it is clear that though psychotics are capable of learning it is somewhat impaired in relation to that of normals. The early work of Hull (1917), Simmins (1933) and Babcock (1930, 1933, 1941), and later by Nelson and Shapiro (1955) mentioned previously, testifies to impaired learning in psychotic groups on verbal functions. Perceptual learning functions have been found by Shakow (1932, 1946), Huston (1932) and others to improve with practice on some tasks, though impairment compared to normals was noted, except in paranoid patients. Extensive work by O'Connor, Tizard and Venables (O'Connor, 1957; Tizard and Venables, 1957), suggested that the build-up of reactive inhibition and motivation levels were crucial factors in explaining the impaired levels and slowness of learning in schizophrenic subjects and their difference from manic-depressives. The work by O'Connor (1957) also suggested paranoid and non-paranoid subjects differed in their learning curves. Campbell (1957) concluded that normal, depressive and schizophrenic groups show different learning curves rather than different levels on the same curve. Other evidence, however, suggests that the learning deficit may be secondary to abnormal motivation, distractibility, etc. (Shakow, 1946; Jones, 1960a). Recent investigations by Chapman and McGhie (1962, 1963, 1964) suggest the fundamental deficit in schizophrenia is the inability to process learning information efficiently. This is consistent with the impaired learning (Campbell, 1957), overinclusion (Payne; Payne and Hewlett, 1960), scanning defects (Shakow, 1946) and serial invalidation (Bannister, 1962) reports.

The importance of experimental studies can also be seen in the brain-damage area. Investigations of perceptual and learning abilities in brain-damaged subjects have been related by several investigators to the growth of reactive and conditioned inhibition (Eysenck, 1957, 1960; Holland and Beech, 1958). The spiral after effect, originally a laboratory experiment, has become a 'diagnostic psychometric technique', even though argument still rages about its usefulness. London and Bryan (1960) suggested that lack of understanding of the instructions and anxiety may have accounted for the poorer brain-damaged performance, whilst Pollack and Frank (1962) thought inability to alter set a prime factor. Reaction time experiments have been performed on schizophrenic and brain-damaged subjects. Recently Benton *et al.* (1962) found slowness in focal and diffuse brain-damaged subjects a function of whether the light stimulus was preceded by an identical or different stimulus to the same modality or a stimulus in a different modality. Sutton *et al.* (1961) on the other hand had found auditory retarded previous visual stimuli for schizophrenics and the reverse for brain-damaged subjects. Variations in the preparatory interval had no effect (Carson, 1962), but McDonald (1964) showed adaptability to varied interstimuli intervals by brain-damaged subjects. The standardization of laboratory motor-perceptual tasks has much to offer clinical practice.

Human material on learning in brain-damaged patients is somewhat complex due to the limited control over the focus and extent of lesions. Reese *et al.* (1953) reviewed the literature on quantitative and qualitative motor and learning responses in organic and non-organic patients in relation to differential diagnostic techniques. They concluded that patients with various intercranial pathologies showed marked deficiencies in learning, motor, automatic and discriminative conditioned responses. Motor reaction time was not found to be improved in temporal lobe patients by Morrell (1956), and sound alpha rhythm conditioning was markedly impaired.

Some investigators (Zangwill, 1946; McFie and Piercy, 1952; Battersby *et al.*, 1955) have indicated that the learning of various tasks is a function of the brain as a whole and impairment related to size of lesion not to sensory defects. Meyer (1955, 1959) has demonstrated impairment of auditory learning following temporal lobectomy of the dominant side and that this impairment was unrelated to the size of the injury. No such deficit was found in the non-dominant cases and no visual or tactile learning deficits appeared after either operation. Retention impairment was considered by McFie and Piercy (1952) to be similar to learning in relation to brain and lesion size. Though Guthrie *et al.* (1955) and Weider *et al.* (1955) did not confirm this with time memory, and generally bilateral temporal damage caused most impairment of retention. The acquisition rather than the memory phase as such seems more important (Hull, 1917; Eysenck and Halstead, 1945).

Learning and retention are undoubtedly involved in intellectual assessment techniques, as the investigations of Eysenck and Halstead (1945), Meyer and Yates (1955), Stake (1961), Duncanson (1964) and Jensen (1964) demonstrated. The importance of learning and memory in relation to ageing have also been stressed by Inglis (1957), Welford (1964), Bromley (1966), Heron and Chown (1967), Savage and Bolton (1968) and Savage and Britton (1968).

The opportunity and need for experimental study and the development of 'experimental psychometric' techniques of intellectual assessment is enormous. Personality and experimental psychology can also combine to benefit psychometric assessment techniques in the intellectual area.

The application of the theory and findings of Broadbent (1964) and his colleagues to clinical field problems, including cognitive assessment, is regrettably less frequent than might be desired. The applied experimental science approach to clinical psychology encouraged by Eysenck (1950, etc.), Shapiro (1957), Zangwill (1964, etc.), Savage (1966) and others will, one hopes, eventually lead to a more elaborate and extensive everyday clinical use of basic psychological theory and data from perception, learning, memory, physiological psychology, psychometrics, experimental social and personality fields.

It will be obvious to readers that much important work has been omitted from this chapter. One's only excuse is that it is a chapter, not a book. In particular, many aspects of cognitive functioning not normally present in intelligence measurement, but vital to a comprehensive understanding of the problem could not be included: cognitive theory generally, cognitive set, mathematical models of cognition, the neo-behaviourist approach to cognition, cognitive dissonance, problem solving, computer simulation of thought and thought disorder generally. Readers are referred to Van de Geer and Jaspers (1966), Wright and Kegan (1963), Osgood (1957), Luce *et al.* (1963) and Scheerer (1964), as well as later chapters in this book for information on some of these topics (Neisser, 1967).

The aim has been to suggest how present intellectual assessment techniques should be used in clinical practice – their strengths and limitations – and some theoretical and empirical lines along which future developments might beneficially progress. In practice, assessment batteries must eventually enable intellectual factors and personality characteristics to be independently quantified, but dependably related to one another; they must combine the best traditions of psychometrics and experimental psychology and must make a unique psychological contribution to solving individual clinical problems of diagnosis and prognosis.

REFERENCES

ACHILLES, EDITH M. (1917) Experimental studies in recall and recognition. *Arch. Psychol.*, **6**, No 44.

ADCOCK, C. (1948) A reanalysis of Slater's spatial judgement research. *Occup. Psychol.*, **22**, 213-216.

AITA, J. A., ARMITAGE, S. G., REITAN, R. M. and RABINOWITZ, A. (1947) The use of certain psychological tests in the evaluation of brain injury. *J. gen. Psychol.*, **37**, 25-44.

ALBEE, G. W., LANE, E. A., CORCORAN, C. and WERNEKE, A. (1963) Childhood and intercurrent intellectual performances of adult schizophrenics. *J. consult. Psychol.*, **27**, 364-466.

ALBEE, G. W., LANE, E. A. and REVTER, H. M. (1964) Childhood intelligence of future schizophrenics and neighborhood peers. *J. Psychol.*, **58**, 141-144.

ALIMENA, B. (1961) A note on norms for scatter analysis on the Wechsler intelligence scale. *J. clin. Psychol.*, **17**, 61.

ALLEN, R. M. (1947) The test performance of the brain injured. *J. clin. Psychol.*, **3**, 225-230.

ALLEN, R. M. (1948) A note on the use of the Wechsler-Bellevue Scale Mental Deterioration Index with brain injured patients. *J. clin. Psychol.*, **4**, 88-89.

ANASTASI, ANNE (1961) *Psychological Testing* (2nd ed.). New York: Macmillan.

APPELL, M. J., WILLIAMS, C. M. and FISHELL, K. N. (1962) Significant factors in placing mental retardates from a workshop situation. *Personnel and Guidance Journal*, **41**, 260-265.

ARMITAGE, S. G. and PEARL, D. (1958) WB changes over time. *J. clin. Psychol.*, **14**, 22-24.

BABCOCK, HARRIET (1930) An experiment in the measurement of Mental deterioration. *Arch. Psychol. N.Y.*, **18**, No. 117.

BABCOCK, HARRIET (1933) *Dementia Praecox, a Psychological Study*. New York: The Science Press.

BABCOCK, HARRIET (1941) The level-efficiency theory of intelligence. *J. Psychol.*, **11**, 261-270.

BABCOCK, HARRIET and LEVY, LYDIA (1941) *Manual of Directions for the Revised Examination of the Measurement of Efficiency of Mental Functioning*. Chicago: Stoelting.

BALTHAZAR, E. E., TODD, R. E., MORRISON, D. H. and ZIEBELL, P. W. (1961) Visuo-constructive and verbal responses in chronic brain damaged patients and familial retardates. *J. clin. Psychol.*, **17**, 293-296.

BANNISTER, D. (1962) Personal construct theory – a summary and experimental paradigm. *Acta Psychologica*, **2**, 104-120.

BARNES, M. R. and FELTERMAN, J. E. (1938) Mentality of dispensary epileptic patients. *Arch. Neurol. Psychiat. Chicago*, **40**, 903-910.

BATTERSKY, W. S., KRIEGER, H. P. and BENDER, M. B. (1955) Visual and tactile discrimination learning in patients with cerebral tumours. *Am. J. Psychol.* **68**, 562-574.

BAUER, R. W. and JOHNSON, D. E. (1957) The question of deterioration in alcoholism. *J. consult. Psychol.*, **21**, 296.

BAYLEY, NANCY (1957). Data on the growth of intelligence between 16 and 21 years as measured by the W.-B. scale. *J. genet. Psychol.*, **90**, 3-15.

BECHTOLDT, H. P. (1965) Review of the GATB, pp. 1023-1027, *in* BUROS, O. S. (Ed.) *Sixth Mental Measurements Yearbook*. New Jersey: The Gryphon Press.

BENDER, LAURETTA (1938) A visual-motor test and its clinical use. *Amer. J. Orthopsychiat.*, Monogr. No 3.

BENDER, LAURETTA (1946) *Instruction for the Use of the Visual Motor Gestalt Test*. New York: Amer. Orthopsychiat. Assn.

BENSON, R. R. (1963) The Binet vocabulary score as an estimate of intellectual functioning. *J. clin. Psychol.*, **19**, 134-135.

BENTON, A. L. (1946-60) *Visual Retention Test – 1946, revised 1954, 1960*. New York: Psychological Corporation.

BENTON, A. L., ELITHORN, A., FOGEL, M. L. and KERR, M. (1963) A perceptual maze test sensitive to brain damage. *J. Neurol. Neurosurg. Psychiat.* **26**, 540-544.

BENTON, A. L., SUTTON, S., KENNEDY, J. A. and BROKAW, J. R. (1962) The cross-modal retardation in reaction time of patients with cerebral disease. *J. Nerv. Ment. Dis.* **135**, 413-418.

BERGER, L., BERNSTEIN, A., KLEIN, E., COHEN, J. and LUCAS, G. (1964) Effects of ageing and pathology on the factorial structure of intelligence. *J. consult. Psychol.*, **28**, 363-368.

BERKOWITZ, B. (1953) The W.-B. performance of white males past the age of 50. *J. Gerontol.*, 8, 76-80.

BEVERFELT, E., RICHARD, N. and NORDVIE, R. (1964) Factor analysis of W.A.I.S. performance of elderly Norwegians. *J. Gerontol.*, **19**, 49-53.

BILLINGSLEA, Y. (1963). The Bender-Gestalt: a review and a perspective. *Psychol. Bull.*, **60**, 233-321.

BINET, A. (1909) *Les Idées modernes sur les enfants*. Paris: Flammarion.

BINET, A. and HENRI, V. (1896) La Psychologie Individuelle. *Année psychol.* **2**, 411-465.

BINET, A. and SIMON, TH. (1905) Méthodes Nouvelles pour le diagnostic du niveau intellectuel des anormaux. *Année psychol.*, **11**, 191-244.

BIRREN, J. E. (1944) Psychological examination of children who later became psychotic. *J. abnorm. soc. Psychol.*, **39**, 84-96.

BIRREN, J. E. (1964) *The Psychology of Ageing*. Englewood Cliffs, N.J.: Prentice-Hall.

BIRREN, J. E., BUTLER, H. N., GREENHOUSE, S. W., BOROLOFF, L. and YARROW, M. R. (1963) *Human Ageing: A Biological and Behavioral Study*. U.S. Department of Health, Education and Welfare, Bethesda, Maryland.

BIRREN, J. E. and REIGEL, K. F. (1962) *In* TIBBITS, C. and DONAHUE, W. (Eds.) *Social and Psychological Aspects of Ageing*. New York: Columbia Univ. Press.

BLAKE, R. R. and MCCARTHY, B. S. (1948) A comparative evaluation of the Wechsler-Bellevue Mental Deterioration Index of Allen in brain injured patients and normal subjects. *J. clin. Psychol.*, **4**, 415-418.

BOLLES, MARJORIE and GOLDSTEIN, K. (1939) A study of impairment of 'abstract behaviour' in schizophrenic patients. *Psychiat. Quart.*, **12**, 42-65.

BOLTON, N. (1967) *A psychometric investigation of the psychiatric syndromes of old age: measures of intelligence, learning, memory, extraversion and neuroticism.* Unpublished Ph.D. thesis, University of Newcastle upon Tyne.

BOLTON, N., BRITTON, P. G. and SAVAGE, R. D. (1966) Some normative data on the W.A.I.S. and its indices in an aged population. *J. clin. Psychol.,*22,184-188.

BOLTON, N., SAVAGE, R. D. and ROTH, M. (1967) The Modified Word Learning Test on an Aged Psychiatric Population. *Brit. J. Psychiat.,* 113, 1139-1140.

BORTNER, J. (1965) Review of Progressive Matrices, pp. 764-765 *in* BUROS, O.S. (Ed.) *Sixth Mental Measurements Yearbook.* New Jersey: The Gryphon Press.

BOTWINICK, J. and BIRREN, J. E. (1951) The measurement of intellectual decline in senile psychosis. *J. consult. Psychol.,* 15, 145-150.

BOYD, H. (1949) A provisional quantitative scoring with preliminary norms for the Goldstein-Scheerer Cube Test. *J. clin. Psychol.,* 5, 148-153.

BRENGELMAN, J. G. and KENNY, J. T. (1961) Comparison of Leiter W.A.I.S. and S.B. I.Q. in retardates. *J. clin. Psychol.,* 17, 235-238.

BRIERLEY, H. (1961) The speed and accuracy characteristics of neurotics. *Brit. J. Psychol.,* 52, 273-280.

BRILLIANT, PATRICIA, J. and GYNTHER, M. B. (1963) Relationships between performance on three tests for organicity and selected patient variables. *J. consult. Psychol.,* 27, 474-479.

BRITTON, P. G. (1967) *An investigation of cognitive and personality functions in a sample of the aged in the community.* Unpublished Ph.D. Thesis, University of Newcastle upon Tyne.

BRITTON, P. G., BERGMANN, K., KAY, D. W. K. and SAVAGE, R. D. (1967) Mental state, cognitive functioning, physical health and social class in the community aged. *J. Gerontol.,* 22, 517-521.

BRITTON, P. G. and SAVAGE, R. D. (1966) A short form of the W.A.I.S. for use with the aged. *Brit. J. Psychiat.,* 112, 417-418.

BROADBENT, D. E. (1958) *Perception and Cummunication.* Oxford: Pergamon Press.

BROADBENT, D. E. (1964) Vigilance in Experimental Psychology, Ed. by A. SUMMERFIELD. *Brit. med. Bull.,* 20, No. 1. pp. 17-20.

BROADHURST, ANNE (1957) *Some variables affecting speed of mental functioning in schizophrenics.* Unpublished Ph.D. Thesis, University of London. (*In* PAYNE, 1960).

BROADHURST, P. L. and BROADHURST, A. (1964) An analysis of the pursuit rotor learning of chronic psychotics. *Brit. J. Psychol.,* 55, 321-331.

BRODY, M. B. (1941-43) A survey of the results of intelligence tests on psychosis. *Brit. J. med. Psychol.,* 19, 215-261.

BRODY, M. B. (1942) A psychometric study of dementia. *J. ment. Sci.,* 88, 512-533.

BROMLEY, D. B. (1966) *The Psychology of Human Ageing.* Harmondsworth: Pelican, Penguin Books.

BROWER, D. (1947) The relation between intelligence and M.M.P.I. scores. *J. soc. Psychol.*, **25**, 243-245.

BROWN, J. (1964) Short Term Memory, *in* A. SUMMERFIELD (Ed.) *Experimental Psychology. Brit. med. Bull.*, **20**, 1, 8-11.

BRYAN, G. E. and BROWN, H. M. (1957) A method for differential diagnosis of brain damage in adolescents. *J. nerv. ment. Dis.*, **125**, 69-72.

BURKE, H. R. (1958) Raven's Progressive Matrices – a review and critical evaluation. *J. genet. Psychol.*, **93**, 199-228.

BUROS, O. K. (1949) *The Third Mental Measurements Yearbook.* New Jersey: The Gryphon Press.

BUROS, O. K. (1953) *The Fourth Mental Measurements Yearbook.* New Jersey: The Gryphon Press.

BUROS, O. K. (1959) *The Fifth Mental Measurements Yearbook.* New Jersey: The Gryphon Press.

BUROS, O. K. (1965) *The Sixth Mental Measurements Yearbook.* New Jersey: The Gryphon Press.

BURT, C. (1939) Factorial analysis. Lines of possible reconciliation. *Brit. J. Psychol.*, **30**, 84-93.

BURT, C. (1949) The structure of the mind: a review of the results of factor analysis. *Brit. J. educ. Psychol.*, **19**, 100-111, 176-199.

BURT, C. (1954) The differentiation of intellectual ability. *Brit. J. Educ. Psychol.*, **24**, 76-90.

CAIRD, W. T., SANDERSON, R. F. and INGLIS, J. (1962) Cross-validation of a learning test for use with elderly psychiatric patients. *J. ment. Sci.*, **108**, 368-370.

CALLAGAN, J. E. (1952) *The effect of electro-convulsive therapy on the test performances of hospitalised depressed patients.* Unpublished Ph.D. Thesis, University of London. (*In* PAYNE, 1960.)

CAMPBELL, D. (1957) *A study of some sensory-motor functions in psychiatric patients.* Unpublished Ph.D. Thesis, University of London.

CAMPBELL, D. (1960) The Psychological Effects of Cerebral Electric Shock, *in* EYSENCK, H. J. (Ed.) *Handbook of Abnormal Psychology.* London: Pitman.

CANTER, A. H. (1951) Direct and indirect measures of psychological deficit in multiple sclerosis, Part II. *J. gen. Psychol.*, **44**, 27-50.

CAROL, J. E. (1965) A review of the G.A.T.B., pp. 1027-1029, *in* BUROS, O. K. (Ed.) *Sixth Mental Measurements Yearbook.* New Jersey: Gryphon Press.

CARP, A. (1950) Performance on the Wechsler-Bellevue Scale and insulin shock therapy. *J. abnorm. soc. Psychol.*, **45**, 127-136.

CARSON, R. C. (1962) Proverb interpretation in acutely schizophrenic patients. *J. nerv. ment. Dis.*, **135**, 556-564.

CATTELL, R. B. (1963) Theory of fluid and crystallised intelligence: a critical experiment. *J. educ. Psychol.*, **54**, 1-22.

CATTELL, R. B. and A. K. S. (1933-63) *Culture Free (Fair) Intelligence Tests.* Illinois, Inst. Pers. Abil. Test.

CATTELL, R. B. and EBER, H. W. (1957) *Handbook for the Sixteen Personality Factor Questionnaire*, Forms A, B and C. Illinois, Inst. Pers. Abil. Test.

CATTELL, R. B. and EBER, H. W. (1962) *Handbook for the Sixteen Personality Factor Questionnaire*, Forms A, B and C. Illinois, Inst. Pers. Abil. Test.

CATTELL, MCKEEN, J. (1890) Mental tests and measurements. *Mind*, **15**, 373-380.

CHAPMAN, J. and MCGHIE, A. (1962) A comparative study of disordered attention in schizophrenia. *J. ment. Science*, **108**, 487-500.

CHAPMAN, J. and MCGHIE, A. (1963) An approach to the psychotherapy of cognitive dysfunction. *Brit. J. med. Psychol.*, **36**, 253-60.

CHAPMAN, J. and MCGHIE, A. (1964) Echopraxia in schizophrenia. *Brit. J. Psychiat.*, **110**, 365-74.

COHEN, J. (1955) The efficacy of diagnostic pattern analysis with the W.-B. *J. consult. Psychol.*, **19**, 303-306.

COHEN, J. (1957) The factorial structure of the W.A.I.S. between early adulthood and old age. *J. consult. Psychol.*, **21**, 283-290.

COMREY, A. L. (1959) The G.A.T.B., pp. 695-697, *in* BUROS, O. K. (Ed.) *Fifth Mental Measurements Yearbook*. New Jersey: The Gryphon Press.

COOK, R. A. and HIRT, M. L. (1961) V.I.Q. and P.I.Q. discrepancies on the W.A.I.S. and W.-B. Form I. *J. clin. Psychol.*, **17**, 382-383.

COONS, W. H. and PEACOCK, E. P. (1959) Interexaminer reliability of the W.A.I.S. with mental hospital patients. *OPA Quarterly*, July, 1959.

CRONBACH, J. L. and GLESER, G. (1953) Assessing similarities between profiles. *Psychol. Bull.*, **50**, 456-473.

CROSSMAN, E. R. F. W. (1964) Information Processes in Human Skill *in* A. SUMMERFIELD (Ed.) *Experimental Psychology*. *Brit. med. Bull.*, **20**, 32-37.

DANA, R. H. (1957) A comparison of four verbal subtests on the W.-B. Form I and the W.A.I.S. *J. clin. Psychol.*, **13**, 70-71.

DAVIDSON, M. (1938) A study of schizophrenic performance on the Stanford-Binet scale. *Brit. J. med. Psychol.*, **17**, 93-97.

DAVIDSON, M. (1939) Studies in the application of mental tests to psychotic patients. *Brit. J. med. Psychol.*, **18**, 44-52.

DAVIES, ANN D. M. (1965) The perceptual maze test in a normal population. *Percept. mot. Skills*, **20**, 287-293.

DENNERLL, R. D., BROEDER, U. and SOKOLOV, S. L. (1964) W.I.S.C. and W.A.I.S. in children and adults with epilepsy. *J. clin. Psychol.*, **20**, 236-240.

DESAI, M. M. (1952) The test-retest reliability of the Progressive Matrices Test. *Brit. J. med. Psychol.*, **25**, 48-53.

DESAI, M. M. (1955) The relationship of the Wechsler-Bellevue Verbal scale and the Progressive Matrices Test. *J. consult. Psychol.*, **18**, 60.

DOCUMENTA GEIGY (1966) *Scientific Tables* (Sixth Ed.), Edited by KONRAD DIEM. Manchester: Geigy Pharmaceutical Co.

DOERKEN, R. J. and GREENBLOOM, GRACE, C. (1953) Psychological investigations of senile dementia: II: The W.-B. Adult Intelligence Scale. *Geriatrics*, **8**, 324-333.

DOPPELT, J. E. (1956) Estimating the full scale score on the Wechsler Adult Intelligence Scale from scores on four subtests. *J. consult. Psychol.*, **20**, 63-66.

DOPPELT, J. E. and WALLACE, W. L. (1955) Standardisation of the Wechsler Adult Intelligence Scale for older persons. *J. abn. soc. Psychol.*, **51**, 312-330.

DOWLIS, J. L. and BUCHANAN, C. E. (1961) Some relationship between intellectual efficiency and the severity of psychiatric illness. *J. Psychol.*, **51**, 371-381.

DUNCAN, D. R. and BARRETT, A. M. (1961) A longitudinal comparison of intelligence involving the W.-B. and W.A.I.S. *J. clin. Psychol.*, **17**, 318-319.

DUNCANSON, J. P. (1964) The relationship between introversion-extraversion, neuroticism and performance in school examinations. *Brit. J. educ. Psychol.*, **34**, 187-196.

EISDORFER, C., BUSSE, E. W. and COHEN, L. D. (1959) The W.A.I.S. performance of an aged sample: the relationship between verbal and performance I.Q.s. *J. Gerontol.*, **14**, 197-201.

EISDORFER, C. and COHEN, L. D. (1961) The generality of the W.A.I.S. standardisation for the aged: a regional comparison. *J. abnorm. soc. Psychol.*, **62**, 520-527.

ELITHORN, A. (1955) A preliminary report on a perceptual maze test sensitive to brain damage. *J. Neurol. Neurosurg. Psychiat.*, **18**, 287-292.

EMMETT, W. G. (1949) Evidence of a space factor at 11+ and earlier! *Brit. J. Psychol.* (Stat. Sec.), **2**, 3-16.

ETTLINGER, G., JACKSON, C. V. and ZANGWILL, O. L. (1955) Dysphasia following right temporal lobectomy in a right-handed man. *J. Neurol. Neurosurg. Psychiat.*, **18**, 214-217.

ETTLINGER, G., JACKSON, C. V. and ZANGWILL, O. L. (1956) Cerebral dominance in sinistrals. *Brain*, **79**, 569-588.

EVERETT, E. G. (1956) A comparative study of paretics, hebephrenics and paranoid schizophrenics on a battery of psychological tests. *Dissert. Abstr.*, **6**, 152.

EYSENCK, H. J. (1943) Neurosis and Intelligence. *Lancet*, **245**, 362-363.

EYSENCK, H. J. (1944) The effect of incentives on neurotics and the variability of neurotics as compared with normals. *Brit. J. Med. Psychol.*, **20**, 100-103.

EYSENCK, H. J. (1947) *Dimensions of Personality*. London: Routledge and Kegan Paul.

EYSENCK, H. J. (1950) Function and training of the clinical psychologist. *J. ment. Sci.*, **96**, 710-725.

EYSENCK, H. J. (1953) *Uses and Abuses of Psychology*. Harmondsworth: Penguin.

EYSENCK, H. J. (1957) *Dynamics of Anxiety and Hysteria*. London: Routledge and Kegan Paul.

EYSENCK, H. J. (Ed.) (1960) *Handbook of Abnormal Psychology*. London: Pitman.

EYSENCK, H. J. (1962) Personality and Conditioning. *Brit. J. Psychol.*, **53**, 299-305.

EYSENCK, H. J. (1967) Intelligence Assessment: a theoretical and experimental approach. *Brit. J. Educ. Psychol.*, **37**, 81-98.

EYSENCK, H. J., GRAINGER, G. W. and BRENGELMANN, J. C. (1957) *Perceptual Processes and Mental Illness.* Maudsley Monogr. No. 2. London: Institute of Psychiatry.

EYSENCK, H. J. and HALSTEAD, H. (1945) The memory function. *Amer. J. Psychiat.*, **102**, 174-180.

EYSENCK, MARGARET, D. (1945) A study of certain qualitative aspects of problem solving behaviour in senile dementia patients. *J. ment. Sci.*, **91**, 337-345.

FABER, I. E. (1954) Anxiety as a drive state, *in* M. R. JONES (Ed.). *Nebraska Symposium on Motivation.* Lincoln: University of Nebraska Press.

FARLEY, F. H. (1966) Individual differences in solution time in error-free problem-solving. *Brit. J. soc. clin. Psychol.*, **5**.

FIELD, J. G. (1960) Two types of tables for use with Wechsler's Intelligence scales. *J. clin. Psychol.*, **16**, 3-7.

FISHER, G. M. (1960) A corrected table for determining the significance of the difference between verbal and performance I.Q.s on the W.A.I.S. and W.-B. *J. clin. Psychol.*, **16**, 7-8.

FISHER, G. M. (1961a) A comparison of the performance of endogenous and exogenous mental retardates on the W.A.I.S. *J. ment. Defic. Res.*, **5**, 111-114.

FISHER, G. M. (1961b) Discrepancy in V.I.Q. and P.I.Q. in adolescent socio-paths. *J. clin. Psychol.*, **17**, 60.

FISHER, G. M. (1962) Further evidence on the invalidity of the W.A.I.S. for the assessment of intelligence of mental retardates. *J. ment. Defic. Res.*, **6**, 41-43.

FISHER, G. M., RISLEY, T. and SILVERSTEIN, A. B. (1961) Sex differences in the performance of mental retardates on the W.A.I.S. *J. clin. Psychol.*, **27**, 170.

FOULDS, G. A. (1951) Temperamental differences in maze performance. Part I: Characteristic differences among psychoneurotics. *Brit. J. Psychol.*, **42**, 209-217.

FOULDS, G. A. (1956) The ratio of general intellectual ability to vocabulary among psychoneurotics. *Intern. J. soc. Psychiat.*, **1**, 5-12.

FOULDS, G. A. and DIXON, P. (1962a) The nature of intellectual deficit in schizophrenia. Part I: A comparison of schizophrenics and neurotics. *Brit. J. soc. clin. Psychol.*, **1**, 86-98.

FOULDS, G. A. and DIXON, P. (1962b) The nature of intellectual deficit in schizophrenia. Part III: A longitudinal study of subgroups. *Brit. J. soc. clin. Psychol.*, **1**, 199-207.

FOULDS, G. A., DIXON, P., MCCLELLAND, M. and MCCLELLAND, J. (1962) The nature of intellectual deficit in schizophrenia. Part II: A cross-sectional study of paranoid, catatonic, hebephrenic and simple schizophrenics. *Brit. J. soc. clin. Psychol.*, **1**, 141-149.

FOULDS, G. A. and RAVEN, J. C. (1950) An experimental survey with Progressive Matrices (1947), Sets I and II. *Brit. J. educ. Psychol.*, **20**, 104-110.

FRIEDMAN, A. S. (1964) Minimal effects of severe depression on cognitive functioning. *J. abnorm. soc. Psychol.*, **69**, 237-243.

FULLER, G. B. (1967) *Revised Minnesota Percepto-Diagnostic Test*. New York: Psychological Corporation.

FULLER, G. B. and LAIRD, J. J. (1963) The Minnesota Percepto-Diagnostic Test. *J. clin. Psychol.*, **19**, 3-34.

FURNEAUX, W. D. (1952) Some speed, error and difficulty relationships within a problem-solving situation. *Nature*, **170**, 37.

FURNEAUX, W. D. (1956) *The Nufferno Manuals of Speed and Level Tests*. Published by Institute of Psychiatry, London University. Distributed by National Found. Edn. Research, Slough.

FURNEAUX, W. D. (1960) Intellectual Abilities and Problem-solving behaviour. *In* EYSENCK, H. J. (Ed.) *Handbook of Abnormal Psychology*. London: Pitman.

GALTON, F. (1869) *Hereditary Genius: An Inquiry into its Laws and Consequences*. London: Macmillan.

GALTON, F. (1883) *Inquiries into Human Faculty and its Development*. London: Macmillan.

GARDNER, C. E. (1931) The learning ability of schizophrenics. *Amer. J. Psychiat.*, **11**, 247-252.

GARFIELD, S. L. and FEY, W. L. (1948) A comparison of the Wechsler-Bellevue and the Shipley-Hartford Scales as measures of mental impairment. *J. consult. Psychol.*, **12**, 259-264.

GIANNELL, A. and FREEBURNE, C. M. (1963) The comparative validity of the W.A.I.S. and the S.B. with college freshmen. *J. Educ. Meas.*, **23**, 557-567.

GIBBINS, K. and SAVAGE, R. D. (1965) Study habits, intelligence, personality and academic achievement. *Durh. Res. Rev.*, **16**, 8-12.

GILBERT, J. G. (1941) *J. abnorm. Soc. Psychol.*, **36**, 73, cited from WELFORD, A.T., The study of ageing, p. 67. *Brit. Med. Bull.*, 1964, **20**, 165-69.

GOLDSTEIN, L. D. and FABER, I. E. (1957) On the relation between A-scale scores and D.S. performance. *J. consult. Psychol.*, **21**, 152-154.

GOLDSTEIN, K. and SCHEERER, M. (1941) Abstract and concrete behaviour. An experimental study with special tests. *Psychol. Monogr.*, **53**, No. 2.

GOODENOUGH, F. L. and HARRIS, D. B. (1926-63) *Goodenough-Harris Drawing Test*. Harcourt, Brace and World.

GRAHAM, FRANCES K. and KENDALL, BARBARA S. (1946) Performance of brain damaged cases on a memory-for-designs test. *J. abnorm. Soc. Psychol.*, **41**, 303-314.

GRAHAM, FRANCES K. and KENDALL, BARBARA S. (1960) *Memory for Designs Test*. Psychological Test Specialists.

GRANICK, G. (1963) Comparative analysis of psychotic depressives with matched normals on some untimed verbal intelligence tests. *J. consult. Psychol.*, **27**, 439-443.

GREEN, R. F. and BERKOWITZ, B. (1964) Changes in intellect with age: factorial analysis of W.-B. scores. *J. genet. Psychol.*, **104**, 3-18.

GUERTIN, W. H., FRANK, G. H. and RABIN, A. I. (1956) Research with the W.-B. Intelligence Scale 1950-1955. *Psychol. Bull.*, **53**, 235-257.

D

GUERTIN, W. H., LADD, C. E., FRANK, G. H., RABIN, A. E. and HIESTER, D. S. (1966) Research with the Wechsler Intelligence Scales for Adults, 1960-65. *Psychol. Bull.*, **5**, 385-409.

GUERTIN, W. H., RABIN, A. I., FRANK, G. H. and LADD, C. E. (1962) Research with the Wechsler Intelligence Scales for Adults, 1955-60. *Psychol. Bull.*, **59**, 1-26.

GUILFORD, J. P. (1956) The structure of intellect. *Psychol. Bull.*, **53**, 267-293.

GUILFORD, J. P. (1965) Motivation in an informational psychology. *In* D. LAVINE (Ed.) *Nebraska Symposium on Motivation.* Lincoln: University of Nebraska.

GUILFORD, J. P. (1967) *The Nature of Intelligence.* New York: McGraw Hill.

GUTHRIE, T. C., WEIDER, A., GOODELL, H., BERLIN, L. and WOLFF, H. (1955) Studies on human cerebral function: the capacity for retention as measured by the ability to estimate on seconds. *Trans. Amer. Neurol. Ass.*, **80**, 201-202.

GUTMAN, B. (1950) The application of the Wechsler-Bellevue scale in the diagnosis of organic brain disorders. *J. clin. Psychol.*, **6**, 195-198.

HALL, MARGARET, E. (1938) Mental and physical efficiency of women drug addicts. *J. abnorm. Soc. Psychol.*, **33**, 332-345.

HALSTEAD, H. (1943) An analysis of the Matrix (Progressive Matrices) Test results on 700 neurotic (military) subjects and a comparison with Shipley Vocabulary Test. *J. ment. Sci.*, **89**, 202-215.

HALSTEAD, H. (1950) Abilities of male mental hospital patients. *J. ment. Sci.*, **96**, 726-733.

HALSTEAD, H. and SLATER, P. (1946) An experiment in the vocational adjustments of neurotic patients. *J. ment. Sci.*, **92**, 509-515.

HAMLIN, R. M. and JONES, R. E. (1963) Vocabulary deficit in improved and unimproved schizophrenic subjects. *J. nerv. ment. Dis.*, **136**, 360-364.

HAYNES, J. R. and SELLS, S. B. (1963) Assessment of organic brain damage by psychological tests. *Psychol. Bull.*, **60**, 316-325.

HEBB, D. O. (1949) *The Organisation of Behaviour.* London: Wiley.

HEBB, D. O. (1959) Intelligence, brain function and the theory of mind. *Brain*, **82**, 260-275.

HERON, A. and CHOWN, SHEILA (1967) *Age and Function.* London: J. & A. Churchill.

HEWSON, LOUISE R. (1949) The W.-B. scale and the substitution test as aids in neuropsychiatric diagnosis. *J. nerv. ment. Dis.*, **109**, 158-183.

HEYER, A. W. (1949) Scatter Analysis techniques applied to anxiety neurotics from a restricted culture education environment. *J. Gen. Psychol.*, **40**, 155-166.

HILDEBRAND, H. P. (1953) *A Factorial study of introversion-extraversion by means of objective tests.* Unpublished Ph.D. Thesis, University of London.

HIMMELSTEIN, P. (1957) A comparison of two methods of estimating full scale I.Q. from an abbreviated W.A.I.S. *J. consult. Psychol.*, **21**, 246.

HIMMELWEIT, HILDE T. (1945) The intelligence-vocabulary ratio as a measure of temperament. *J. Personality*, **14**, 93-105.

HIRT, M. L. and COOK, R. A. (1962) Use of a multiple regression equation to estimate organic impairment from Wechsler scale scores. *J. clin. Psychol.*, 18, 80-81.

HOFSTAETTER, P. R. (1954) The changing composition of 'Intelligence' – a study of the t-Technique. *J. genet. Psychol.*, 85, 159-164.

HOLLAND, H. C. and BEECH, A. R. (1958) The spiral after-effect as a test of Brain Damage. *J. ment. Sci.*, 104, 466-471.

HOLZINGER, J. K. (1937) *Student Manual for Factor Analysis*. Chicago U.P.

HOLZINGER, J. K. and HARMAN, H. H. (1941) *Factor Analysis*. Chicago: Chicago Univ. Press.

HOWELL, R. J. (1955) Sex differences and educational influence on a mental deterioration scale. *J. Gerontol.*, 10, 190-193.

HULL, C. L. (1917) The formation and retention of associations among the insane. *Amer. J. Psychol.*, 28, 419-435.

HUMPHREYS, L. G. (1959) The G.A.T.B., pp. 698-700, *in* BUROS, O. K. (Ed.) *Fifth Mental Measurements Yearbook*. New Jersey: The Gryphon Press.

HUNT, H. F. (1943) A practical clinical test for organic brain damage. *J. appl. Psychol.*, 27, 355-386.

HUNT, J. MCV. and COFER, C. N. (1944) Psychological deficit. *In* J. MCV. HUNT (Ed.) *Personality & the Behaviour Disorders* (Vol. II). New York: Ronald Press.

HUSTON, P. E. (1932) Eye-hand co-ordination in schizophrenic patients and normals as measured by the pursuitmeter. *Psychol. Bull.*, 29, 662.

INGLIS, J. (1957) An experimental study of learning and memory function in elderly psychiatric patients. *J. ment. Sci.*, 103, 796-803.

INGLIS, J. (1959) A paired-associate learning test for use with elderly psychiatric patients. *J. ment. Sci.*, 105, 440-443.

INGLIS, J. (1960) Dichotic stimulation and memory disorder. *Nature*, 194, 186, 181-182.

INGLIS, J. (1962) Effect of age on responses to dichotic stimulation. *Nature*, 194, 1101.

INGLIS, J. and CAIRD, W. K. (1963) Age differences in successive responses to stimulation. *Can. J. Psychol.*, 17, 98-105.

INGLIS, J., SHAPIRO, M. B. and POST, F. (1956) Memory function in psychiatric patients over 60: the role of memory tests in discriminating between 'functional' and 'organic' groups. *J. ment. Sci.*, 102, 589-598.

ISSACS, B. and WALKER, F. A. (1964) A simplified paired-associate test for elderly hospital patients. *Brit. J. Psychiat.*, 110, 80-83.

JENKINS, C. D. (1961) The relation of electro-encephalographic showing to the impairment of selective intellectual functions. *Dissertation Abstracts*, 21, 2005.

JENSEN, A. R. (1964) *Individual Differences in Learning: Interference Factors*. J. S. Dept. of Health, Education and Welfare, co-op Project No. 1867.

JONES, H. GWYNNE (1956) The evaluation of the significance of differences between scaled scores on the W.A.I.S.: the perpetuation of a fallacy. *J. consult. Psychol.*, 20, 319-320.

JONES, H. GWYNNE (1960a) Learning and abnormal behaviour. *In* EYSENCK, H. J. (Ed.) *Handbook of Abnormal Psychology*. London: Pitman.

JONES, H. GWYNNE (1960b) Applied Abnormal Psychology: the experimental approach. *In* EYSENCK, H. J. (Ed.) *Handbook of Abnormal Psychology*. London: Pitman.

JONES, L. V. (1949) A factor analysis of the Stanford-Binet at Four Age Levels. *Psychometrika*, **14**, 299-331.

JONES, R. L. (1962) Analytically developed short forms of the W.A.I.S. *J. consult. Psychol.*, **26**, 289.

JUCKEM, H. J. and WOLD, J. A. (1948) A study of the Hunt-Minnesota Test for organic brain damage at the upper levels of vocabulary. *J. consult. Psychol.*, **12**, 53-57.

JURJEVICH, R. (1963) An analysis of the altitude I.Q.s of delinquent girls. *J. gen. Psychol.*, **69**, 221-226.

KARRAS, A. (1963) Predicting full scale W.A.I.S. I.Q.s from W.A.I.S. subtests in a psychiatric population. *J. clin. Psychol.*, **19**, 100.

KASS, W. (1949) Wechsler's mental deterioration index in the diagnosis of organic brain damage. *Trans. Kans. Acad. Sci.*, **52**, 66-70.

KAY, H. (1954) Cited in A. T. WELFORD, *The study of Ageing*, 1964. *Brit. med. Bull.*, **20**, 1, 65-69.

KENDALL, BARBARA S. (1962) Memory for designs performance in the seventh and eighth decades of life. *Percept. mot. Skills.*, **14**, 399-405.

KENDALL, BARBARA S. and GRAHAM, FRANCES K. (1948) Further standardization of the memory for designs test on children and adults. *J. consult. Psychol.*, **12**, 349-354.

KENDRICK, D. C. (1963) The Walton-Black Modified New Word Learning Test: a Tribute to Donald Walton. *Bull. Brit. Psychol. Soc.*, **16**, 51.

KERRICK, JEAN S. (1955) Some correlates of the Taylor Manifest Anxiety Scale. *J. abnorm. soc. Psychol.*, **50**, 75-77.

KLOVE, H. (1959) Relationship of differential electro-encephalographic patterns to distribution of W.-B. scores. *Neurology*, **9**, 871-876.

KLOVE, H. and REITAN, R. M. (1958) The effects of dysphasia and spatial distortion on W.-B. results. *A.M.A. Arch. Neurol. Psychiat.*, **80**, 708-713.

KOBLER, F. J. (1947) The measurement of improvement among neuropsychiatric patients in an army convalescent facility. *J. clin. Psychol.*, **3**, 121-128.

KORMAN, M. and BLUMBERG, S. (1963) Comparative efficiency of some tests of cerebral damage. *J. consult. Psychol.*, **27**, 303-309.

KRAL, V. A. (1962) Senescent forgetfulness: benign and malignant. *Canad. med. Assoc. J.*, **86**, 258-260.

KRAL, V. A. and DUROST, H. B. (1953) A comparative study of the amnestic syndrome in various organic conditions. *Amer. J. Psychiat.*, **110**, 41-47.

L'ABATE, L. (1962) The relationship between W.A.I.S. derived indices of maladjustment and M.M.P.I. in deviant groups. *J. consult. Psychol.*, **26**, 441-445.

LADD, C. E. (1964) W.A.I.S. performances of brain damaged and neurotic patients. *J. clin. Psychol.*, **20**, 114-117.

LANE, E. A. and ALBEE, G. W. (1963) Childhood intellectual development of adult schizophrenics. *J. abnorm. soc. Psychol.*, **67**, 186-89.

LANE, A. E. and ALBEE, G. W. (1964) Early childhood intellectual differences between schizophrenic adults and their siblings. *J. abnorm. soc. Psychol.*, **68**, 193-195.

LAYMAN, J. W. (1940) A quantitative study of certain changes in schizophrenic patients under the influence of sodium amytal. *J. gen. Psychol.*, **22**, 67-68.

LEVI, J., OPPENHEIM, S. and WECHSLER, D. (1945) Clinical use of the mental deterioration index of the Wechsler-Bellevue Scales. *J. abnorm. soc. Psychol.*, **40**, 415-417.

LEWINSKI, R. J. (1945) The psychometric pattern: anxiety neurosis. *J. clin. Psychol.*, **1**, 214-221.

LILLIENCRANTS, J. (1923) Memory defects in organic psychosis. *Psychol. Monogr.*, **32**, No. 143.

LITTELL, W. M. (1960) The Wechsler Intelligence Scale for Children – a review of a decade of research. *Psychol. Bull.*, **57**, 132-162, and in R. D. SAVAGE (Ed.) (1966) *Readings in Clinical Psychology*. Oxford: Pergamon Press.

LONDON, P. and BRYAN, J. H. (1960) Theory and Research on the clinical use of Archimedes spiral. *J. gen. Psychol.*, **62**, 113-125.

LOVIBOND, S. H. (1954) The object sorting test and conceptual thinking in schizophrenics. *Aust. J. Psychol.*, **6**, 52-70.

LUBIN, A., GIESEKING, C. F. and WILLIAMS, L. (1962) Direct measurement of cognitive deficit in schizophrenia. *J. consult. Psychol.*, **26**, 139-143.

LUCE, R. D., BUSH, R. R. and GALANTER, E. (Eds.) (1963) *Handbook of Mathematical Psychology*. New York: Wiley.

LYNN, R. and GORDON, I. E. (1961) The relation of neuroticism and extraversion to intelligence and educational attainment. *Brit. J. Psychol.*, **31**, 194-203.

MCDONALD, R. D. (1964) Effect of brain damage on adaptability. *J. nerv. ment. Dis.*, **138**, 241-47.

MCFIE, J. (1960) Psychological testing in clinical neurology. *J. nerv. ment. Dis.*, **131**, 383-393.

MCFIE, J. and PIERCY, M. F. (1952) Intellectual impairment with localised lesions. *Brain*, **75**, 292-311.

MACKAY, H. A. and INGLIS, J. (1963) The effect of age on a short term auditory storage process. *Gerontologia*, **8**, 193-200.

MCKEEVER, W. F. and GERSTEIN, A. I. (1958) Validity of the Hewson ratios: investigation of a fundamental methodological consideration. *J. consult. Psychol.*, **22**, 150.

MACKIE, J. B. (1963) A comparative study of brain damaged and normal individuals on tests of intelligence, perception and rigidity. *Dissert. Abstr.*, **24**, 1700-1701.

MCNEMAR, Q. (1942) *The Revision of the Stanford-Binet Scale.* Boston: Houghton Mifflin.

MCNEMAR, Q. (1950) On abbreviated Wechsler-Bellevue Scales, *J. consult. Psychol.*, **14**, 79-81.

MCNEMAR, Q. (1957) On W.A.I.S. difference scores. *J. consult. Psychol.*, **21**, 239-240.

MCNEMAR, Q. (1962) *Psychological Statisics.* New York: Wiley.

MCNEMAR, Q. (1964) Lost: our intelligence? Why? *Amer. Psychol.*, **19**, 871-882.

MAHER, B. A. (1963) Intelligence and Brain Damage. In ELLIS, N. R. (Ed.) *Handbook of Mental Deficiency.* New York: McGraw Hill.

MAINORD, W. A. (1953) Some effects of sodium amytal on deteriorated schizophrenics. *J. consult. Psychol.*, **17**, 54-57.

MALAMUD, R. F. (1946) Validity of the Hunt-Minnesota Test for Organic Brain Damage. *J. appl. Psychol.*, **30**, 271-275.

MATARAZZO, J. D., ULETT, G. A. and SASLOW, G. (1957) Human image performances as a function of increasing levels of anxiety. *J. gen. Psychol.*, **53**, 79-96.

MANSON, M. P. and GRAYSON, H. M. (1947) The Shipley-Hartford Retreat Scale as a measure of intellectual impairment for military prisoners. *J. appl. Psychol.*, **31**, 67-81.

MARGARET, ANN and SIMPSON, MARY M. (1948) Two measures of deterioration in psychiatric patients. *J. consult. Psychol.*, **12**, 365-370.

MASON, C. F. (1956) Pre-illness intelligence of mental hospital patients. *J. consult. Psychol.*, **20**, 297-300.

MASON, C. F. and GANZLER, H. (1963) Adult age norms for the Shipley Scale. *Newsletter for Research in Psychology*, **5**, 30.

MAXWELL, A. E. (1957) Validities of abbreviated W.A.I.S. Scales. *J. consult. Psychol.*, **21**, 121-126.

MAXWELL, A. E. (1960) Obtaining factor scores on the Wechsler Adult Intelligence Scale. *J. ment. Sci.*, **106**, 1060-1062.

MAXWELL, A. E. (1961) Trends in cognitive ability in the older age ranges. *J. abn. soc. Psychol.*, **63**, 2, 449-452.

MAYNER, M. S., SERSEN, E. and TRESSELT, M. E. (1955) The Taylor Manifest Anxiety scale and intelligence. *J. consult. Psychol.*, **19**, 401-403.

MEEHL, P. E. and JEFFREY, M. (1946) The Hunt-Minnesota Test for Organic Brain Damage in cases of functional depression. *J. appl. Psychol.*, **30**, 276-287.

MEYER, V. (1959) Cognitive changes following temporal lobectomy for the relief of temporal lobe epilepsy. *Arch. Neurol. Psychiat. Chicago*, **81**, 299-309.

MEYER, V. (1960) Psychological Effects of Brain Damage. *In* EYSENCK, H. J. (Ed.) *Handbook of Abnormal Psychology.* London: Pitman.

MEYER, V. and YATES, A. J. (1955) Intellectual changes following temporal lobectomy for psychomotor epilepsy. *J. neurol. Neurosurg. Psychiat.*, **18**, 44-52.

MILHOLLAND, J. (1965) The culture fair intelligence test. *In* BUROS, O. K. (Ed.) *Sixth Mental Measurements Year Book,* New Jersey: The Gryphon Press.

MILLER, D. R., FISHER, G. M. and DINGRAM, H. F. (1961) A note on differential utility of W.A.I.S. verbal and P.I.Q.s. *Amer. J. mental Defic.*, **65**, 482-485.

MOORE, T. V. (1919) The correlation between memory and perception in the presence of diffuse cortical degeneration. *Psychol. Monogr.*, **27**, No. 120.

MORRELL, L. (1956) Interseizure disturbances in focal epilepsy. *Neurology*, **6**, 327-334.

MORROW, R. S. and MARK, J. C. (1955) The correlation of intelligence and neurological findings on twenty-two patients autopsicd for brain damage. *J. consult. Psychol.*, **19**, 283-289.

MUNROE, J. J. (1952) The effects of emotional adjustment and intelligence upon Bellevue scatter. *J. consult. Psychol.*, **16**, 110-114.

NEISSER, U. (1967) *Cognitive Psychology*. New York: Appleton-Century-Crofts.

NELSON, E. H. (1953) *An experimental investigation of intellectual speed and power in mental disorders*. Unpublished Ph.D. Thesis, University of London.

NEURINGER, C. (1963) The form equivalence between the W.-B. intelligence scale form I and the W.A.I.S. *J. educ. & psychol. Measur.*, **23**, 755-764.

NICKOLS, J. E. JR. (1962) Brief forms of the Wechsler Intelligence Scales for Research. *J. clin. Psychol.*, **18**, 167.

NORMAN, R. D. and DALY, M. F. (1959) Senescent changes in intellectual ability among superior older women. *J. Gerontol.*, **14**, 457-464.

NUNNALLY, J. (1962) The analysis of profile data. *Psychol. Bull.*, **59**, 311-319.

NUNNALLY, J. (1967) *Psychometric Theory*. New York: McGraw Hill.

O'CONNOR, N. (1957) Reminiscence and work decrement in catatonic and paranoid schizophrenics. *Brit. J. Psychol.*, **30**, 188-193.

OGILVIE, B. C. (1954) *A study of intellectual slowness in schizophrenia*. University of London Library: Unpublished Ph.D. Thesis.

OLIN, T. D. and REZNIKOFF, M. (1958) A comparison of copied and recalled reproductions of the Bender-Gestalt designs. *J. proj. Tech.*, **22**, 320-327.

ORME, J. E., LEE, D. and SMITH, M. P. (1964) Psychological assessment of brain damaged and intellectual impairment in elderly psychiatric patients. *Brit. J. soc. clin. Psychol.*, **3**, 161-167.

OSGOOD, C. E. (1957) *Contemporary Approaches to Cognition*. Cambridge, Mass.: Harv. Univ. Press.

OSGOOD, C. E. and SUCI, G. J. (1952) A measure of relation determined by both mean differences and profile information. *Psychol. Bull.*, **49**, 251-262.

PARTINGTON, J. E. (1940) The comparative mental efficiency of a drug addict group. *J. appl. Psychol.*, **24**, 48-57.

PASCAL, G. R. and SUTTELL, BARBARA, J. (1951). *The Bender-Gestalt Test*. New York: Grune & Stratton.

PAUKER, J. K. (1963) A split-half abbreviation of the W.A.I.S. *J. clin Psychol.*, **19**, 98-100.

PAYNE, R. W. (1960) Cognitive Abnormalities. *In* EYSENCK, H. J. (Ed.). *Handbook of Abnormal Psychology*. London: Pitman.

PAYNE, R. W. (1965) A review of the Goldstein-Scheerer. *In* BUROS, O. K. (Ed.) *Sixth Mental Measurements Year Book*. New Jersey: The Gryphon Press.

PAYNE, R. W. and HEWLETT, J. H. G. (1960). Thought disorder in psychotic patients. *In* EYSENCK, H. J. (Ed.) *Experiments in Personality*. London: Routledge and Kegan Paul.

PAYNE, R. W. and JONES, H. GWYNNE (1957) Statistics for the investigations of individual cases. *J. clin. Psychol.*, **13**, 115-121, and in R. D. SAVAGE (Ed.) (1966) *Readings in Clinical Psychology*. Oxford: Pergamon Press.

PENFIELD, W. and MILNER, B. (1958) The memory deficit produced by bilateral lesions in the hippocampal zone. *Arch. Neurol. Psychiat.*, **79**, 475-497.

PETERSON, J. (1925) *Early Conceptions and Tests of Intelligence*. New York: Harcourt, Brace and World.

PIERCY, M. (1964) The effects of cerebral lesions on intellectual function: a review of current and research trends. *Brit. J. Psychiat.*, **110**, 310-352.

POLLACK, M. and FRANK, M. (1962) Disordered perception of simultaneous stimulation of face and hand, a review and a theory. *In* WORTIS, J. (Ed.) *Recent Advances in Biological Psychiatry*, IV. New York: Plenum Press.

PORTEUS, S. D. (1942) *Qualitative Performance in the Maze Test*. New York: Smith.

POULL, L. E. and MONTGOMERY, R. P. (1929) The Porteus Maze Test as a discriminative measure in delinquency. *J. appl. Psychol.*, **13**, 145-151.

PRADO, W. M. and SCHNADT, F. (1965) Differences in W.A.I.S. – W.-B. functioning of three psychiatric groups. *J. clin. Psychol.*, **21**, 184-186.

RABIN, A. I. (1945) The use of the W.-B. scales with normal and abnormal persons *Psychol. Bull.*, **42**, 410-422.

RABIN, A. I. and GUERTIN, W. H. (1951) Research with the W.-B. test. *Psychol. Bull.*, **48**, 211-248.

RADCLIFFE, J. A. (1966) W.A.I.S. factorial structure and factor scores for age 18-54. *Australian J. Psychol.*, **18**, 228-238.

RAPAPORT, D., GILL, M. and SCHAFER, R. (1945) *Diagnostic Psychological Testing*, Vol. I. Chicago: Year Book.

RAPAPORT, S. R. and WEBB, W. (1950) An attempt to study intellectual deterioration by premorbid and psychotic testing. *J. consult. Psychol.*, **14**, 95-98.

RASHKIS, H. A. and WELCH, G. S. (1946) Detection of anxiety by use of the Wechsler Scale. *J. clin. Psychol.*, **2**, 354-357.

RAVEN, J. C. (1938) *Standard Progressive Matrices*. London: H. K. Lewis.

RAVEN, J. C. (1943) *Advanced Progressive Matrices Set 1*. London: H. K. Lewis.

RAVEN, J. C. (1943a) *Mill Hill Vocabulary Scales*. London: H. K. Lewis.

RAVEN, J. C. (1947) *Progressive Matrices Set 1*. London: H. K. Lewis.

RAVEN, J. C. (1956) *Standard Progressive Matrices* – Revision. London: H. K. Lewis.

RAVEN, J. C. (1958) *Mill Hill Vocabulary Scales* – 2nd Ed. Manual. London: H. K. Lewis.

RAVEN J. C. (1962) Revision of Advanced Progressive Matrices *Set 2*. London: H. K. Lewis.

REESE, W. G., DOSS, R. and GANTT, W. H. (1953) Automatic responses in differential diagnosis of organic and psychogenic psychoses. *A.M.A. Arch. Neurol. Psychiat.*, **70**, 778-793.

RICHARD, SUSANNE, LIVSON, FLORINE and PETERSON, P. G. (1961) *Ageing and Personality: A Study of Eighty-seven Older Men*. New York: Wiley.

RIDDELL, S. A. (1962) The relationship between tests of organic involvement, memory impairment and diagnosis in elderly psychiatric patients. *Brit. J. soc. clin. Psychol.*, **1**, 228-231.

RIEGEL, R. M. (1960) Factorenanalysen des Hamburg-Wechsler Intelligence Tests. *Sonderdruck aus diagnostica*, **6**, 41-66.

RIEGEL, R. M. and RIEGEL, K. F. (1959) Standardisierung des Hamburg-Wechsler Intelligence Tests (HAWIE) fur die Altersstufen uber 50 Jahre. *Sonderdruck aus Diagnostica*, 97-128.

RIEGEL, R. M. and RIEGEL, K. F. (1962) A comparison and reinterpretation of factor structure of the W.-B., the W.A.I.S. and the HAWIE on aged persons. *J. consult. Psychol.*, **26**, 31-37.

ROGERS, L. S. (1950) A note on Allen's Index of deterioration. *J. clin. Psychol.*, **6**, 203.

ROSS, W. D. and MCNAUGHTON, F. L. (1944) Head injury: a study of patients with chronic post-traumatic complaints. *Arch. Neurol. Psychiat.*, Chicago. **52**, 255-269.

SAUNDERS, D. R. (1959) On the dimensionality of the W.A.I.S. battery for two groups of normal aged. *Psychol. Rep.*, **5**, 529-541.

SATZ, P. and MOGEL, S. (1962) An abbreviation of the W.A.I.S. for clinical use. *J. clin. Psychol.*, **18**, 77-79.

SAVAGE, R. D. (1964) Intellect and Mental Illness. *Univ. Durham Research Review*, **15**, 145-151.

SAVAGE, R. D. (1966) *Readings in Clinical Psychology*. Oxford: Pergamon Press.

SAVAGE, R. D. and BOLTON, N. (1968) A factor analysis of learning impairment and intellectual deterioration in the elderly. *J. Genet Psychol.*, **113**, 177-182.

SAVAGE, R. D. and BRITTON, P. G. (1968) The factorial structure of the W.A.I.S. on an aged community sample. *J. Gerontol.* **23**, 2, 183-186.

SCHEERER, C. (Ed.) (1964) *Cognition: Theory, Research and Promise*. New York: Harper & Row.

SCHOTT, E. L. (1931) Superior intelligence in patients with nervous and mental illnesses. *J. abnorm. soc. Psychol.*, **26**, 94.

SEMEONOFF, B. and TRIST, E. (1958) *Diagnostic Performance Tests*. London: National Foundation for Education Research and Tavistock.

SHAKOW, D. (1932) A study of certain aspects of motor coordination in schizophrenia with the prod meter. *Psychol. Bull.*, **29**, 661.

SHAKOW, D. (1946) The nature of deterioration in schizophrenic conditions. *Nerv. ment. Dis. Monogr.*, No. 70.

D*

SHAPIRO, M. B. (1951) Experimental studies of a perceptual anomaly. I: Initial experiments. *J. ment. Sci.*, **97**, 90-110.

SHAPIRO, M. B. (1952) Experimental studies of a perceptual anomaly. II: Confirmatory and explanatory experiments. *J. ment. Sci.*, **98**, 605-617.

SHAPIRO, M. B. (1953) Experimental studies of a perceptual anomaly. III: The testing of an exploratory theory. *J. ment. Sci.*, **99**, 394-409.

SHAPIRO, M. B. (1957) Experimental method in the psychological description of the individual patient. *Intern. J. soc. Psychiat.*, **3**, 89-103.

SHAPIRO, M. B. and NELSON, E. H. (1955) An investigation of the nature of cognitive impairment in cooperative psychiatric patients. *Brit. J. med. Psychol.*, **28**, 239-256.

SHAPIRO, M. B., POST, F., LOFVING, B. and INGLIS, J. (1956) Memory function in psychiatric patients over 60: some methodological and diagnostic implications. *J. ment. Sci.*, **102**, 427.

SHARP, S. E. (1898-99) Individual psychology: a study in psychological method. *Amer. J. Psychol.*, **10**, 329-391.

SHIPLEY, W. C. (1940) A self-administering scale for measuring intellectual impairment and deterioration. *J. Psychol.*, **9**, 371-377.

SHIPLEY, W. C. and BURLINGAME, C. C. (1941) A convenient self administering scale for measuring intellectual impairment in psychotics. *Amer. J. Psychiat.*, **97**, 1313-1323.

SIEGMAN, A. W. (1956) The effect of manifest anxiety on a concept formation task, a non-directed learning task and timed and untimed intelligence tests. *J. cons. Psychol.*, **20**, 176-178.

SIMMINS, CONSTANCE (1933) Studies in experimental psychiatry. IV: Deterioration of 'g' in psychotic patients. *J. ment. Sci.*, **79**, 704-734.

SINGLETON, W. T. (1954, 1955) Cited from WELFORD, A. T. (1964) The Study of Ageing. *Brit. med Bull.*, **20**, 65-69.

SMITH, A. (1962) Ambiguities in concepts and studies of 'brain damage' and 'organicity'. *J. nerv. ment. Dis.*, **135**, 311-326.

SMITH, A. (1962a) Psychodiagnosis of patients with brain tumours: the validity of Hewson's ratios in neurological and mental hospital populations. *J. nerv. ment. Dis.*, **135**, 513-533.

SPEARMAN, C. (1904) General Intelligence objectively determined and measured. *Amer. J. Psychol.*, **15**, 201-293.

SPEARMAN, C. (1923) *The Nature of Intelligence and the Principles of Cognition.* London: Macmillan.

SPEARMAN, C. (1927) *The Abilities of Man.* London: Methuen.

SPEARMAN, C. (1939) Intelligence Tests. *Eugen. Rev.*, **30**, 249-254.

SPEARMAN, C. (1946) Theory of a general factor. *Brit. J. Psychol.*, **36**, 117-131.

SPEARMAN, C. and JONES, L. L. W. (1950) *Human Ability.* London: Macmillan.

SPENCE, K. W. (1956) *Behaviour Theory and Conditioning.* London: Oxford University Press.

STACEY, C. R. and GILL, M. R. (1955) The relationship between Raven's Colored Progressive Matrices and two tests of general intelligence for 172 subnormal adult subjects. *J. clin. Psychol.*, **11**, 86-87.

STAKE, R. E. (1961) Learning parameters, aptitudes and achievements. *Psychometric Monogr.* No. 9.

SUMMERFIELD, A. (Ed.) (1964) Experimental psychology. *British med. Bull.*, **20.**

SUTTON, S., HAKEREM, G., ZUBIN, J. and PORTNOY, M. (1961) The effect of shift of sensory modality on serial reaction time: a comparison of schizophrenics and normals. *Amer. J. Psychol.*, **74**, 224-231.

TALLAND, G. A. (1963) Psychologies concern with brain damage. *J. nerv. ment. Dis.*, **136**, 344-351.

TARJAN, G., DINGMAN, H. F., EYMAN, R. K. and BROWN, S. J. (1960) Effectiveness of hospital release programs. *Amer. J. ment. Defic.*, **64**, 609-617.

TAYLOR, F. R. (1963) The general aptitude test battery as a predictor of vocational readjustment in psychiatric patients. *J. clin. Psychol.*, **19**, 130.

TAYLOR, JANET (1956) Drive theory and manifest anxiety. *Psychol. Bull.*, **53**, 303-320.

TERMAN, L. M. (1916) *The Measurement of Intelligence*. Boston: Houghton Mifflin.

TERMAN, L. M. and MERRILL, M. R. (1937) *Measuring Intelligence*. Boston: Houghton Mifflin.

TERMAN, L. M. and MERRILL, M. R. (1960) *Stanford-Binet Intelligence Scale*. Boston: Houghton Mifflin (1961); London: G. G. Harrap.

THOMSON, G. (1939-56) *The Factorial Analysis of Human Ability*, 1st Ed. 1939, 5th Ed. reprint 1956. London: University of London Press.

THORNDIKE, E. L. (1926) *The Measurement of Intelligence*. New York: Teacher's College, Columbia University.

THURSTONE, L. L. (1926) *The Nature of Intelligence*. New York: Harcourt, Brace and World.

THURSTONE, L. L. (1938) Primary mental abilities. *Psychometr. Monogr.* No. 1.

THURSTONE, L. L. (1947) *Multiple Factor Analysis*. Chicago: University of Chicago Press.

THURSTONE, L. L. and THURSTONE, THELMA (1941) Factorial studies of intelligence. *Psychometr. Monogr.* No. 2.

THURSTONE, T. G. and THURSTONE, THELMA (1962-63) *SRA Primary Mental Abilities*. Science Research Associates.

TIZARD, J., O'CONNOR, N. and CRAWFORD, J. M. (1950) The abilities of adolescent and high-grade male defectives. *J. ment. Sci.*, **96**, 889-907.

TIZARD, J. and VENABLES, P. H. (1957) The influence of extraneous stimulation on the reaction time of schizophrenics. *Brit. J. Psychol.*, **48**, 299-305.

TOLOR, A. (1956) A comparison of the Bender-Gestalt test and the Digit Span Test as measures of recall. *J. consult. Psychol.*, **20**, 305-309.

TOOTH, G. (1947) On the use of mental tests for the measurement of disability after head injury. With a comparison between the results of these tests in patients after head injury and psychoneurotics. *J. Neurol. Neurosurg. Psychiat.*, **10**, I-II.

TRAPP, C. E. and JAMES, EDITH B. (1937) Comparative intelligence ratings in four types of dementia praecox. *J. nerv. ment. Dis.*, **86**, 399-404.

U.S.E.S. (1947, 1952, 1963) *General Aptitude Test Battery* (G.A.T.B.). United States Employment Services.

UYENO, E. (1963) Differentiating psychotics from organics on the Minnesota Percepto-Diagnostic Test. *J. consult. Psychol.*, **27**, 462.

VAN DE GEER, J. and JASPERS, J. M. F. (1966) Cognitive functions. *Ann. Rev. Psychol.*, **17**, 145-176.

VENABLES, P. H. and TIZARD, J. (1956) Performance of functional psychotics on a repetitive task. *J. abnorm. soc. Psychol.*, **53**, 23-26.

VERNON, P. E. (1947a) Psychological tests in the Royal Navy, Army and A.T.S. *Occup. Psychol.*, **21**, 53-74.

VERNON, P. E. (1947b) Research on personnel selection in the Royal Navy and the British Army. *Amer. Psychol.*, **2**, 35-51.

VERNON, P. E. (1947c) The variations of intelligence with occupation, age and locality. *Brit. J. Psychol.* (Stat. Sect.), **1**, 52-63.

VERNON, P. E. (1950) An application of factorial analysis to the study of test items. *Brit. J. Psychol.* (Stat. Sect.), **3**, 1-13.

VERNON, P. E. (1950a) *The Structure of Human Abilities.* London: Methuen. 2nd Ed. (1960.)

VERNON, P. E. (1965) Ability factors and environmental influences. *Amer. Psychol.*, **20**, 273.

VERNON, P. E. and PARRY, J. B. (1949) *Personnel Selection in the British Forces.* London: University of London Press.

WALTON, D. and BLACK, D. (1957) The Modified Word Learning Test. The validity of a psychological test of brain damage. *J. ment. Sci.*, **30**, 270-279. *Also in* SAVAGE, R. D. (1966) *Readings in Clinical Psychology.* Oxford: Pergamon Press.

WALTON, D. and BLACK, D. A. (1959) The predictive validity of a psychological test of brain damage. *J. ment. Sci.*, **105**, 440.

WARNER, J. S. (1950) The Wechsler-Bellevue psychometric pattern on anxiety neurosis. *J. cons. Psychol.*, **14**, 297-304.

WEBB, A. P. (1963) A longitudinal comparison of the W.I.S.C. and W.A.I.S. with educable mentally retarded Negroes. *J. clin. Psychol.*, **19**, 101-102.

WEBB, A. P. (1964) Some issues relating the validity of the W.A.I.S. in assessing mental retardation. *California J. Educ. Res.* **15**, 130-135.

WECHSLER, D. (1917) *A study of retention in Korsakoff's psychosis.* Unpublished Ph.D. Thesis, University of Columbia.

WECHSLER, D. (1944) *The Measurement of Adult Intelligence.* Baltimore: Williams and Wilkins.

WECHSLER, D. (1945) A standardized memory scale for clinical use. *J. Psychol.*, **19**, 87-95.

WECHSLER, D. (1955) *The Manual for the W.A.I.S.* New York: Psychological Corporation Ltd.

WECHSLER, D. (1958) *The Measurement and Appraisal of Adult Intelligence* (4th Ed.) Baltimore: Williams and Wilkins.

WEIDER, D., GUTHRIE, T. C., BERLIN, L. and WOLFF, H. (1955) Studies of human cerebral functions: the capacity of orientation as measured by the estimation of a miture. *Trans. Amer. Neurol. Ass.*, **80**, 226-228.

WELFORD, A. T. (1958) *Ageing and Human Skill.* Oxford University Press.

WELFORD, A. T. (1964) The Study of Ageing. *In* SUMMERFIELD, A. (Ed.) Experimental Psychology. *Brit. Med. Bull.*, **20**, 65-69.

WELLS, E. L. (1927) *Mental Tests in Clinical Practice.* New York: World Books.

WELLS, E. L. and KELLEY, C. M. (1920) Intelligence and psychosis. *Amer. J. Insan.*, **77**, 17-45.

WHEELER, L., BURKE, C. J. and REITAN, R. M. (1963) An application of discriminant functions to the problem of predicting brain damage using behavioural variables. *Percept. mot. Skills*, **16**, 417-40.

WHEELER, W. M. and WILKINS, W. L. (1951) The validity of the Hewson ratios. *J. consult. Psychol.*, **15**, 163-166.

WILLETT, R. (1960) The effects of psychosurgical procedures on behaviour. *In* EYSENCK, H. J. (Ed.) *Handbook of Abnormal Psychology.* London: Pitman.

WINFIELD, D. L. (1953) The relationship between the I.Q. score and the M.M.P.I. *J. Soc. Psychol.*, **38**, 299-300.

WISSLER, C. (1901) The correlation of mental and physical tests. *Psychol. Rev. Monogr. Suppl.*, **3**, 16.

WITTMAN, PHYLLIS (1933) The Babcock test in state hospital practice. *J. abnorm. soc. Psychol.*, **28**, 70-83.

WOLFSON, W. and BACHELIS, L. (1960) An abbreviated form of the W.A.I.S. verbal scale. *J. clin. Psychol.*, **16**, 421.

WOOLF, B. B. (1960) The application of the Hewson ratios as an aid in differential diagnosis of cerebral pathology. *J. nerv. ment. Dis.*, **130**, 98-109.

WRIGHT, J. C. and KEGAN, J. (Eds.) (1963) Basic cognitive process in children. *Monogr. Soc. Res. Child Developm.*, **28**.

WYLIE, MARGARET (1930) An experimental study of recognition and recall in abnormal mental cases. *Psychol. Monogr.*, **39**, No. 180.

WYNNE, R. D. (1963) The influence of hospitalization on the verbal behaviour of chronic schizophrenics. *Brit. J. Psychiat.*, **109**, 380-389.

YATES, A. J. (1954) Validity of some psychological tests of brain damage. *Psychol. Bull.*, **51**, 359-379.

YATES, A. J. (1966) Psychological deficit. *Ann. Rev. Psychol.*, **17**, 111-114.

ZANGWILL, O. L. (1946) Some qualitative observations on verbal memory in cases of cerebral lesions. *Brit. J. Psychol.*, **37**, 8-18.

ZANGWILL, O. L. (1964) Neurological Studies of Human Behaviour. *In* SUMMERFIELD, A. (Ed.) Experimental Psychology. *Brit. med. Bull.*, **20**, 43-48.

3

Personality assessment

R. D. Griffiths

I INTRODUCTION

1 A definition of personality

Personality, in the course of the present review, is defined as the more or less stable organization of a person's emotional, conative, intellectual and conceptual, and physiological behaviour which determines to a large extent his adjustments to environmental situations (cf. Allport, 1949; Eysenck, 1965). Some aspects of this definition merit discussion.

Personality is described as 'more or less stable'. Stability and consistency over time is an important characteristic of the concept of personality (Wepman and Heine, 1964). The repetition of a behavioural act is a necessary antecedent to the consideration of that act as a personality characteristic. Unreliably observed behaviour is important only as a source of error in observation and measurement, unless one is concerned with variability itself as a characteristic. Stability and consistency are not, however, expected to be perfect. Allowance is made for some degree of change as part of development (Bayley, 1949; Bloom, 1965) or as the outcome of such interference as therapy procedures (Rogers and Dymond, 1954; Willett, 1960).

Organization is also an important aspect of personality. Research and assessment have focused on the detection of consistencies between behavioural acts, and such reviewers as Allport (1949) consider the 'presence of orderly arrangement as an outstanding phenomenon of mental life'. Theories and models of personality share the tendency to search for behavioural consistencies and to postulate various dispositions to explain such relationships (Christie and Lindauer, 1963). Models and theories are also abstractions based on inferences from behavioural observation; personality characteristics, such as traits, are theoretical concepts rather than concrete entities (Kelly, 1955; Eysenck, 1965). As theories and models, the various personality systems share the general characteristics of these abstract concepts.

As Kelly has indicated, the ultimate truth or untruth of theories often cannot be ascertained, and investigations are invariably limited to considering the truth of hypotheses derived from theoretical systems. There is general agreement that the criterion used to decide the value of a theory is its utility (Kelly, 1955; Wepman and Heine, 1964; Eysenck, 1965), which can be subdivided into the number of testable hypotheses which are generated, and possibly the degree of comprehensive application and relevance of these hypotheses. Personality theories, as theories, can also be judged according to these criteria – and the relevance of this view to the applied psychologist will be obvious. In brief, the value of a theory will depend on the use he can find for it in suggesting relationships between variables, prediction of behaviour etc.

Five aspects of behaviour have been outlined as being of relevance. The emotional and conative aspects of behaviour are mentioned in most other definitions. The intellectual and conceptual are regarded as aspects of cognitive behaviour; 'intellectual' is used here to refer to the form and structure of cognitive behaviour and 'conceptual' to the content (Kelly, 1955). The inclusion of this latter area is considered desirable because of the work demonstrating the importance of conceptual behaviour – for example, in terms of the non-conceptual correlates (Bannister, 1962; Fransella and Bannister, 1967). The consideration of physiological behaviour is primarily concerned with measurements of peripheral physiological changes – these are considered more relevant in the present volume than, for example, assessment of body build characteristics (cf. Eysenck, 1965) because of their considerable usefulness and relevance to applied psychologists (see Chapter 6).

Personality is indicated to determine the individual's adjustments 'to a large extent'. This delimitation is an indication of the assumption that behaviour, whilst determined to a large extent by personality, is also influenced to varying degrees by environmental factors (cf. Bloom, 1965). It is probable that in many situations, e.g. in the presence of an extreme fear stimulus, personality differences may account for little of the behaviour as compared with environmental determinants. In the latter part of the definition the plural 'environmental situations' is used because of the considerable evidence that the environment is as complex and variable as the individual. Many definitions of personality are phrased in such a way as to indicate that the environment is to be considered as a constant, thus not excluding the importance of environmental determinants (Cattell, 1965; cf. Wepman and Heine, 1964).

It is also assumed in the present review that personality cannot be regarded as an entity which is dependent on existence in a social situation. Personality is regarded as biophysical rather than biosocial (Allport, 1949; Vernon, 1964b; Eysenck, 1965) – extreme instances of the biophysical point of view being that many personality characteristics are derived from physiological variables. The reader is referred to the recent discussion by Vernon (1964) of different approaches to personality, and also to his discussion of the 'personality system' which is a model incorporating both personal and situational variables.

Personality is also to be differentiated from character and temperament. The term 'character' has been used in a number of ways. Allport (1949) uses the term to signify personality characteristics which are being evaluated according to a set of cultural norms. Eysenck (1965) uses the term to signify 'the system of conative behaviour (will)' – used in this sense, it is regarded in the present context as a narrower concept than personality. Similarly temperament is used by

Eysenck to refer to emotional responsiveness, and is consequently part of the more general concept of personality in the present discussion. The term 'temperament' is also traditionally used to refer to variables with a high level of hereditary and constitutional determination.

2 Behaviour as the basic datum

The basic data for the assessment of personality are observations of behaviour. Though this may seem too obvious to mention, agreement on this point is less than universal. Eysenck (1965) has stressed the distinction between those studying behavioural acts and those studying dynamic concepts, and quotes the definitions of personality provided by Watson (1930) and Prince (1924) to demonstrate his point. As he continues to point out, however, inspection of the use of dynamic traits reveals that they are really abstract concepts derived from and consequently used to explain behavioural acts, i.e. the dynamic trait approach is also ultimately based on behavioural observation. The difficulty involved here is that 'dynamic' psychologists often appear to assume a deductive strategy which assumes the existence of certain concepts, rather than an inductive approach to generate hypotheses about possible determinants (cf. Ellis, 1950).

Though observation of behaviour is the basic datum, personality is not regarded as being behaviour and nothing else. Though the basic datum is 'the response of a person to a stimulus situation' (Wepman and Heine, 1964), the concept of personality is derived from inferences made from these observations.

Behavioural observation in the present review is used in a general sense to include such measures as self-report, actual observations and records of behaviour, and physiological changes. Though verbal and self-report are acceptable as behavioural facts, this does not imply necessary acceptance of the validity of these reports – an alternative strategy is to look for behaviour correlates of these reports (cf. Bordin, 1943).

3 The development of an economic and valid descriptive system

It is important to try to reduce a wide range of behaviour to a smaller number of variables which are independent (or, at least, primarily so), meaningful and comprehensive in their coverage. Though behaviour is the basic datum, personality theorists usually proceed beyond this level – as has been indicated above. If this were not so, personality would presumably be defined, in a specifist manner, as 'made up of thousands of independent and specific habits'. Observation is not enough *per se*, and scientific analysis cannot exist without abstractions derived from common properties. As Allport (1949) has indicated, the progress of science depends in large part upon its ability to identify elements which, in combinations empirically demonstrated to exist in nature, constitute the phenomenon that the science has set out to examine. The elements are the abstractions or concepts which are component parts of our theories. In personality assessment, the most common elements are habit, and various 'trait' and 'type' concepts. Two characteristics of these elements are important.

The first is that they are empirically derived, whether by clinical judgement or more sophisticated measures. The second characteristic is derived from their role as components in theories – that continued use depends largely on how useful they prove themselves to be. This is again essentially an empirical problem – and especially for the applied psychologist. One criterion might be, for example, the usefulness of a concept such as suggestibility or reciprocal inhibition in the prediction of behaviour in an unobserved situation.

Other desirable qualities in sets of such elements are that they should be relatively small in number (Eysenck, 1965; Cattell, 1965) in order to provide economy. Any system of such elements should also be closely associated with precise empirical observation, and delineated by operational definitions and criteria in any given situation. Independence of elements is desirable as an aid to economy, but not a necessity in situations where constructs may overlap in reality, or where single measures either account for only parts of a situation or are unreliable indices for prediction when measured in isolation (Cattell, 1965; Cohen, 1966).

Theories and models are constructed in order to provide explanations of the behaviour of the intact, fully functioning and complex human being in his environment and, of greater immediate importance, in order to be able to make predictions about future behaviour in unobserved situations. Prediction is an important aim for the applied psychologist though it obviously cannot be divorced from the understanding of basic determinants of observed behaviour.

4 The role and functions of the applied psychologist

Since the present volume is intended to be of use to the applied psychologist, it might be of interest to attempt to define his role and to state some general comments about the uses of personality assessment as related to the psychologist's work. Shapiro (1963) has defined the role of the clinical psychologist as involving 'the application of the methods and findings of the science of psychology to the diagnosis and description, treatment and management of psychological disorder'. Generalization of this definition yields a definition of the role of the applied psychologist, i.e. his role involves the application of the findings and techniques of the science of psychology to the practical routine problems of the institution (educational, industrial, etc.) within which he works.

As Shapiro has indicated (1957), it would seem useful, in defining the psychologist's role, to exclude any functions which he might share with other professions or with the intelligent layman. In this respect Shapiro's emphasis, and that of the present author, falls on the psychologist's scientific training and his application of these skills to problems involving psychological variables. The scientific bias involves the application of certain well-accepted scientific standards to his work, e.g. objectivity (c.f. Bass and Berg, 1959), and criteria of validity and reliability which are used to select or reject his methods and instruments. The definition does not, and should not, exclude the use of subjective judgement by the psychologist (and the willingness to offer opinions to his colleagues), but it does indicate that he does not depend exclusively upon such procedures, and that when he does offer opinion it should represent a distillation of what scientific psychology has to offer with reference to any particular problem. The present view of clinical psychology differs from that of Vernon (1964b), who in many ways seems to do clinical psychology a disservice by identifying the clinical psychologist with the application of intuitive judgement and 'depth' concepts.

One important function of the applied psychologist, directly or indirectly, is the problem of prediction. Most, if not all, applied psychologists are involved in prediction (e.g. of school or work success, clinical states, etc.) in some form or other. Descriptive assessment, whether of cognitive or any other personality characteristic, or in the form of an experimental analysis of an individual's functioning, is of limited usefulness *per se* unless it has implications for the individual's future behaviour. Similarly, modification procedures involve assumptions that when certain variables are manipulated or changed, certain changes will also occur in relevant aspects of the individual's behaviour – here there is an implicit prediction of the effects of certain changes. Prediction is also linked with the possibility of control.

Personality assessment is generally claimed to be relevant because of its relevance to the function of prediction. Rarely is assessment of personality characteristics undertaken purely for its own sake. For the applied psychologist such assessment is invariably carried out because of its reputed, or preferably its empirically demonstrated, relevance to a behavioural situation which is of relevance, e.g. assessment of an individual's cognitive functioning, or his anxiety level or his achievement motivation because of the relevance of these variables to a forthcoming examination at school, or a new job which is to be undertaken. Even in instances where personality assessment is requested, apparently for its own sake, requests (e.g. 'How aggressive (intelligent, persistent, suggestible, etc.) is this individual?') are usually readily translatable into problems of behavioural prediction. And when such requests are translated, the number of situations in which a psychologist or his colleagues are interested will usually be small in number. Hence the importance of the utility of personality theories for the applied psychologist – and hence the set of criteria which he will invariably apply to theories. Though the discussion of personality undertaken during this review will be a general one, the implications and applications of personality assessment to prediction will be given considerable weight because of the audience to whom this volume is primarily addressed, i.e. applied psychologists.

To conclude this brief discussion of the applied psychologist's role, it might be useful to note certain similarities between himself and his 'pure scientist' colleague. Both 'pure and 'applied' psychologists are concerned with the identification of variables (and the interrelationships between these variables) which are relevant to human behaviour and basic aspects of human functioning. The 'pure' scientist is limited to this role, but the 'applied' scientist is concerned with the application of his findings and techniques to routine problems. This difference engenders a different view of things, and differing set of criteria, i.e. the applied psychologist will be interested in the implications and applications of any findings to his work. Foulds (1965), for example, concludes that classification for research and clinical purposes may entail different procedures and instruments. One such difference might be that test reliabilities accepted by researchers studying groups may not be acceptable for applied psychologists investigating individuals (cf. Jensen, 1959). Eysenck (1965) has also stressed differences in aim – 'The scientist looks for pure factors and unequivocal tests; the applied psychologist may look for mixed factors and complex tests to provide better predictions of complex variables'. With reference to personality theories and models, both 'applied' and 'pure' scientists are concerned with the aspects of utility which have already been outlined, but there are differences in the immediacy of problems and also the content.

In summary, the argument for the basic relevance of personality theory to applied psychology is as follows. Personality theory – whether it be psychoanalytic theory or factor analytic theory or any other sort of theory – is concerned with the identification of elements or dimensions of similarity within the wide range of behaviour. The sets of elements which are described should be relatively small in number, empirically derived and comprehensive in terms of their relevance to various behaviours. Furthermore, these elements are invariably linked to theoretical constructs and systems (but see Skinner, 1950, for a critique of the value of abstract theoretical concepts) which might be psychological (e.g. the Oedipus complex) or physiological (autonomic lability, inhibition-excitation balance) or mixtures of both approaches.

Personality theory and assessment is relevant in two ways to the problems of prediction (and control) which the applied psychologist has to contend with. It provides an economic system of description so that a wide range of behaviour is reduced to a smaller set of variables. And it provides measures of these variables which are relevant to behaviour in situations which are of interest (school performance, job success, marital adjustment, etc.). Such relevance can exist at a number of levels, e.g. the level of opinion and belief of the clinician; the level of empirically demonstrated relationship; or at a theoretical and abstract level. Such levels of relevance are obviously not mutually exclusive and might in many instances be parts of a sequential procedure, e.g. a clinician proposes a hypothesis about the relevance of a construct to a criterion behaviour situation on the basis of his observations or intuitions; the testing of predictions derived from his hypothesis yields empirical data; a theory may then be proposed, or an existing theory applied, to account for observed relationships and to suggest further investigation.

II STRATEGIES AND APPROACHES TO THE DERIVATION OF A SYSTEM OF PERSONALITY DESCRIPTION

Hall and Lindzey (1957) have traced the roots of personality theory to (1) the clinical observation tradition, (2) Gestalt psychology, (3) experimental psychology and learning theory and (4) the psychometric tradition. There are three main strategies which are used in personality assessment. The first, both historically and in terms of current usage, is the clinical approach. A second major approach, associated with the experimentalist rather than the clinician, is factor analysis (Thurstone, 1931; Burt, 1940, 1949; Eysenck, 1952, 1965; Cattell, 1952, 1965; Vernon, 1964a). A third approach, which is to be designated the construct-empirical, combines the clinical basis of one approach and the empirical bias of the second.

1 The clinical approach

Clinical method involves assessment procedures which depend upon the subjective decision and judgement of trained practitioners. The main technique is the interview, i.e. verbal interchange with a subject. The clinician has been described by Sarbin, Taft and Bailey (1960) as follows: 'His intentions are idiographic; he is interested in the whole personality, in understanding rather than predicting; in the unique; in configurations of traits; in intentions; and the test of knowledge is internal consistency, affective congruence and logical coherence'.

Unfortunately, clinical judgement has been demonstrated to be of variable, and frequently very low, reliability. There is considerable evidence of disagreement (Ash, 1949; Schmidt and Fonda, 1956; Kreitman *et al.*, 1961; Hunt and Jones, 1962), though the design of many of these studies is such that high reliability is virtually impossible and probably an underestimation of what the true level might be (cf. Foulds, 1965).

Hunt and Jones (1962) conclude that it has become increasingly obvious that 'the subjective decisions of clinicians . . . are influenced by factors other than the patient's behaviour'. Indeed, clinicians are essentially unstandardized measuring instruments, and vary in as many ways as their subjects. Group discrepancies in judgement are also demonstrated (Pomeroy and Cogan, 1955), and training provides no guarantee of increased reliability (Arnhoff, 1954). Uncontrolled judgement is also known to be influenced by extraneous factors such as experiences prior to making judgements, and temporal or spatial order of judgements (Hunt and Flannery, 1938; Hunt and Jones, 1962; Shapiro, 1963, 1967b). Ambiguous terminology is common, and reliability is improved by explicit definition and description of cues (Hamburg *et al.*, 1958; Knowles, 1963). There has also been a tendency amongst some clinicians, notably analytic schools, to confuse observation and interpretation (Ellis, 1950; Brody, Newman and Redlich, 1951).

Recent surveys (Kelly and Fiske, 1951; Meehl, 1954; Vernon, 1964b) suggest that actuarial assessment, and precise measures of limited aspects of behaviour, can be considerably more accurate than clinical prediction. A difficulty here is that clinical method, though unreliable, is to a large extent indispensable because of its flexibility and, more so, because of the dearth of actuarial studies and their limitation to recurrent situations (Hunt and Jones, 1962; Vernon, 1964b). It has been clearly demonstrated, however, that the confidence held in such clinical methods as the interview is not really justified (Kelly and Fiske, 1951).

Recent work is also consistent with the hypothesis that reliabilities can be increased considerably by certain modifications. Shapiro (1963) has stressed the distinction between subjective and uncontrolled observation, and suggests that judgements made under controlled and reproducible conditions can be highly reliable. This hypothesis is confirmed by recent work on standardized interviews (Wing, 1966; Wing *et al.*, 1967). Similar improvements in technique are necessary if clinical judgement is to be used extensively in personality assessment. Furthermore, although clinical method must be accepted as a necessary procedure (Bruner, 1960), and one which does not necessarily produce unreliable results (Shapiro, 1963), it will probably constitute a part, rather than the whole, of the procedure of developing personality theories.

2 The construct-empirical approach

This set of strategies contains elements of both clinical decision and the empirical-psychometric approach. It involves the construction of tests to measure constructs derived from theory or popular opinion. Subjective judgement is involved in formulating theories from which eventual measures are derived, in deciding what scales or measures to construct and in selecting items for these scales, but when such scales or measures are constructed they can then be subjected to strict empirical and statistical analysis. The scales, as has been indicated, are used to provide measures of constructs from theoretical systems such as the Murray (1938) need system or Kraepelinian classificatory system, or even concepts drawn from popular opinion. Examples of this approach are the Humm-Wadsworth Temperament scale (1935), the M.M.P.I. (Hathaway and McKinley, 1943), the Edwards Personal Preference Schedule (1953-59) and the Bernreuter Inventory (1933).

The difficulties involved in this approach are many. The unreliability of clinical decision has been indicated in the previous section. In constructing scales, choosing items, etc., there is no guarantee that two or more persons will agree. Empirical and statistical checking does provide, however, a safeguard. For example, Flanagan's analysis of the Bernreuter (1935) indicated that the four scales could be represented adequately by two, which he related to self-confidence and sociability. Payne (1955, 1960) failed to find a common factor among tests of dissociation, as did Kenny and Ginsberg (1958) among tests of intolerance of ambiguity. Comrey (1957, 1958) has demonstrated low item correlations within M.M.P.I. scales, and high correlations between scales are also evident. The M.M.P.I. provides measures of a respondent's similarity to a clinical group, and should not be used either as a measure of a psychological trait or to provide an index of the severity of illness (Cohen, 1966). That it succeeds in fulfilling this function adequately can also be doubted in view of the low reliability of the individual scales (cf. Britton and Savage, in Savage, 1966), and the item and scale correlations reported by Comrey.

It should be noted, however, that the validity of theoretical systems from which tests are derived does not determine the empirical usefulness of these tests. For example, whether the Murray system of needs is valid or not, some of the Edwards Personal Preference Schedule scales would seem to have potential value in terms of demonstrated extra test correlates (Bernadin and Jessor, 1957; Bendig, 1958; Merrill and Murphy, 1959). Assuming that such correlates are known and the test is satisfactory in other respects (reliability, etc.), then the test is potentially useful. Berg (1967) has argued that any measures which can be shown to differentiate groups are potentially useful independently of their content. In fact, apparently irrelevant items are more useful in such situations than items whose significance is obvious to a respondent. Though empirical differentiation is undoubtedly useful, it is generally agreed, however, that more progress can be expected using measures derived from a rational and logical framework of theory (Cattell, 1956; Eysenck, 1965; Foulds, 1965).

3 Factor analysis

Factor analysis is derived from the application of a number of mathematical techniques to detect similarities and unities in behavioural data (Thurstone, 1931; Burt, 1949; Cattell, 1952, 1965; Eysenck, 1965). The approach is indicated by Eysenck (1965) to have two functions. The first is as an instrument for the analysis of uncovered territory – more specifically, to demonstrate dimensions of similarity. Cattell (1950) defines this aim as 'the search for dimensions of personality, i.e. for the number of truly independent directions in which personality needs to be measured in order completely to describe it'. Analysis of correlation constitutes the basis of the method.

A second function, and one preferred by Eysenck, is the use of factor analysis for testing hypotheses – within the framework of the hypothetico-deductive method. Various hypotheses can be accepted or refuted by the outcome of experiment, e.g. the refutation of a general factor in tests of dissociation by Payne (1960), and of a factor of intolerance of ambiguity by Kenny and Ginsberg (1958).

The analysis of behavioural data by statistical correlation techniques has the same goal (i.e. the discovery of organization), and in general outline the same strategy, as the clinical approach, but differs in accuracy and also in the explicitness of the methods (Meehl, 1954; Miller, 1959; Cattell, 1965).

Cattell (1965) has outlined the three sources of observation used as the basis for factor analysis, viz. questionnaires, objective test performance (including physiological measures) and life-history data (including ratings). The accuracy of the original observational measures, and the choice of behaviour to be measured, is important (Eysenck, 1965) for a factorial structure cannot really be stronger than the foundation upon which it is built. High reliability, for example, is desirable and Eysenck has criticized Cattell for using many, and presumably shorter and less reliable, tests in his analyses. Differences in the generality or comprehensiveness of factors can vary considerably with different test batteries, e.g. there are discrepancies of this sort between Cattell's O and Q data (Coan, 1964; Cattell, 1965). Specificity in factorial structures has also beeen discussed by Vernon (1964a) in his consideration of cognitive tests. This variation indicates the degree of caution necessary in generalizing from any one single study. Factor analysis cannot rise above the shortcomings of the tests and measures on which it is based (Miller, 1959). The differences between studies, though these may be limited to generality of factors rather than the actual factors themselves (though this is not necessarily so since different factors are certainly involved in the many diverse situations which can exist), has important implications for the applied psychologist. That is, he can never really assume that a factorial description of another situation or set of measures will be identical with that which may best describe a given situation in which he is interested. If he is to use this approach, further empirical investigation will be necessary. Further aspects of factor analysis can be illustrated by discussing two of its most active users, Eysenck and Cattell.

A comparison of these two suggests a number of important similarities and differences. Eysenck (1965) works with the two main dimensions of neuroticism and extraversion (more recently also psychoticism), whereas Cattell (1965) works with a larger number of less general first-order factors. The latter has concluded that 'almost certainly there are 2 or 3 dozen factors of general importance', and has identified 16 in the questionnaire area, and about 20 in objective tests. The difference between the two seems to represent a difference of approach between British and American workers.

British workers (cf. Spearman) have tended to extract the most comprehensive factors first and to keep factors independent. Americans (cf. Thurstone, 1931) have extracted smaller factors and allowed these to be correlated. The two approaches are not, however, incompatible because it is now known that further analysis of the narrow first-order factors yields the more general second-order factors. The controversy is to a certain extent resolved in this way. Analysis of Cattell's first-order factors in the questionnaire realm, for example, has yielded four second order factors of which two are identifiable as extraversion and anxiety or neuroticism (Eysenck, 1959, 1965; Cattell and Scheier, 1961; Pawlik and Cattell, 1964; Adcock, 1965; Cohen, 1966). Thus the apparent inconsistency is resolved in that the results are convertible into each other.

Eysenck continues to use second-order factors because of their stability and consistent demonstration in a large number of studies. He indicates that primary factors are difficult to reproduce, and notes the discrepancies between the primaries of Guilford and Cattell though both are derived from similar behavioural observations. In a similar manner Mitchell (1963), demonstrated correlations of a low order between the scales of the 16 P.F. (Cattell, 1950) and Gough's California Personality Inventory (1957), indicating that first-order dimensions have little in common. The second-order factors are, however, highly congruent.

Cattell attempts to justify working at the primary level in several ways. First of all he claims that there is considerable evidence of ability to match primaries across media of observation, different age and pathological groups and in inter and intra individual studies. Other reviewers are not, however, as confident of his success in matching (Becker, 1960; Lorr, 1965). Cattell's conclusions about the identity of factors is not accepted by some other reviewers (Thorndike, 1950; Eysenck, 1965). Cattell's reply to Guilford (1959) and Peterson (1960), who have pointed out differences between media, is that simple structure oblique and arbitrary orthogonal factors cannot be expected to be completely concordant.

Cattell also claims that, as compared with first-order factors, there is considerable loss of predictive information by the analysis of second-order factors. Evidence is provided, for example, for the differentiation of normals and neurotics on a number of primaries (Cattell and Scheier, 1961; Adcock, 1965). However, the individual use of his factor scales is limited by such characteristics as low-scale reliabilities, and the general superiority of the narrower over the more general analysis has yet to be demonstrated conclusively. The reader is referred to Cohen (1966) and Adcock (1965) for further details of the comparison between Eysenck and Cattell – and to the latter writers themselves for further description of their factor structures.

Recent reviews would seem to indicate that neither Eysenck's M.P.I. (or the more recent E.P.I.) nor Cattell's 16 Personality Factor Battery can be considered satisfactory measures for use in practical and applied situations – especially where decisions about single cases are involved (Bolton and Savage, 1966, in Savage, 1966; Lorr, 1965; Becker, 1961; Levonian, 1961).

An additional problem for factor analysis is that discussed by Allport (1949), and more recently by Shapiro (1962, 1963). This involves the legitimacy of extrapolation from inter individual comparison to intra individual comparisons. In brief, is it possible to assume that intra individual behaviour may be resolved to the same factors and same factorial structures? Coan (1964) suggests that inferences from one to the other are valid in some cases, but possibly not in others. The extent of such correspondence has yet to be demonstrated. Coan suggests that some weak support for his assumption comes from the apparent similarity between Cattell's inter and intra subject analyses (Luborsky, 1953; Shotwell, Hurly and Cattell, 1961; Cohen, 1966).

A further difficulty in factor analysis is the problem of determining the identity and psychological significance of factors. For factors are abstractions rather than distinct entities. A common method of identification has been the examination of the items which cluster to constitute a factor. The assumption is that concomitance indicates some underlying property, and that properties are known by the behaviour where they occur. Subjective judgement can be extremely unreliable, as is evidenced by the disagreements in identifying factors noted by Eysenck (1965). A considerable improvement upon this is external validation of factors by experimental investigation, i.e. hypotheses about the nature of factors are tested by experimental investigation (Eysenck, 1965; Eysenck and Rachman, 1965). It should be noted, however, that the naming of factors is, strictly speaking, extraneous to the original analysis; identification of factors might be erroneous, but this does not affect the correctness of the original analysis.

Cattell (1965) has commented upon the concordance between factorial results and popular opinion in many instances, and Hathaway (1965) concludes that factor analysis could not produce truly new dimensions. Hathaway suggests that if factors do not 'make sense' they cannot be used, and they do not 'make sense' unless they are already recognized in the people they represent. It might be noted, however, that a factor might (at least in theory) be empirically useful in prediction (assuming that measures have been derived) but unidentified; secondly, that the discovery of completely new dimensions is not a necessary criterion for usefulness – the accuracy of factor analysis in providing quantification of existing dimensions is sufficient justification for its use; and thirdly that factor analysis has also been useful in contraindicating the existence of constructs suggested by clinical or popular opinion (Kenny and Ginsberg, 1958; Payne, 1960).

A general conclusion would be that factor analysis has important uses, though also a number of shortcomings and unresolved problems. It cannot provide an easy and automatic solution to the analysis and structure of personality, but is an important tool in securing these aims. As Eysenck (1965) concludes, 'Neither factorial nor experimental methods alone hold the key to the riddle of personality organization; both are needed in equal measure, and each will be found to supplement the other'.

III A FRAMEWORK OF PERSONALITY DESCRIPTION

A hierarchical view of personality

A hierarchical or pyramidal view of personality organization is one which is espoused by a number of reviewers (Vernon, 1964a; Coan, 1964; Eysenck, 1965), and is a view which would seem to have considerable conceptual usefulness. As has been indicated, the basic data for personality assessment are behaviour observations.

These observations provide the elements at the base of the hierarchical model. Specific responses, which occur on one occasion but possibly not again, are not as important as habitual responses or behaviour. Habitual responses, or habits, constitute the first level of the hierarchy. The unreliably observed specific responses are not a focus of interest. When habitual responses are demonstrated (by clinical observation or more precise statistical methods) to correlate, the existence of higher order constructs, i.e. traits, is inferred (persistence, shyness, dominance, etc.). Finally traits have been found to intercorrelate to constitute a further level of analysis – the type, in Eysenck's (1965) terminology. This hierarchical system is discussed by Eysenck (1965) who also provides examples of its usefulness (e.g. see his discussion of introversion, and also of aspects of sociability). Vernon (1964a) has applied the model to cognitive behaviour, and attributes the earlier formulation of the model to Burt (1949). The various levels of analysis are compared by Eysenck to factors in factor analysis, e.g. both kinds of concept have a basis in the detection of correlation.

The model is clearly to be regarded as a useful abstraction, and its components can vary from one situation to another, e.g. there is considerable specificity of structure in factor analysis, with variation both in the factor composition and the generality of factors (Guilford, 1958; Coan, 1964). Factors or constructs obtained – which need not necessarily be derived formally from factor analysis, but are by preference to be empirically demonstrated in this way rather than by the more unreliable clinical methods – do not have a fixed relationship to any level of the hierarchy, and may vary with a number of variables such as differences in observation media or tests (Vernon, 1964a; Cattell, 1965).

Two concepts important in such a model are the *trait* and the *type*.

(a) *Trait*

Traits are abstractions which are inferred (Allport, 1949) from observations of consistencies in habitual responses. Behaviour defining a trait is considered to be related to a continuum which is differentiable from other such criteria. Cattell (1965) defines a trait as 'a relatively permanent and broad reaction tendency', and subdivides traits into abilities, temperamental and dynamic constructs.

A trait must be considered phenotypic in that its existence is inferred from correlations of surface variables (Coan, 1964); it may also be genotypic. When traits are demonstrated (and similarly types), this is often followed by inferences as to the cause of consistencies. Unity in an abstracted trait is no proof of unity in underlying factors. It is probable that many traits have a multifactorial basis.

Traits are obviously not of necessity derived from factor analysis – inferences about consistencies are derived just as easily, but probably not as accurately, by clinical judgement. Inaccuracies in clinical inference have been demonstrated by failure to demonstrate correlation amongst measures which were originally believed to define a given trait (Kenny and Ginsberg, 1958; Payne, 1960).

Trait is usually differentiated from attitude (Allport, 1949; Foulds, 1965) by the more well defined and specific object of reference of the latter, and the usual association between the latter and acceptance or rejection. Allport (1949) also stresses the distinction between the common trait (in terms of which individuals may be compared) and the individual trait (which is specific to a given person). But analysis indicates that even though common trait measures might be, as he indicates, differently organized in different individuals, this does not preclude their use in such situations as individual comparison or prediction. His discussion of individual traits (e.g. that a given trait of honesty might be the outcome in different people of different combinations of anxiety, ambition, etc.) in fact makes use of common properties to define unique traits.

(b) *Type*

A correlation of traits (persistence, suggestibility, dominance, etc.) defines a type. Foulds (1965) defines a type as 'a constellation of traits or attitudes which can be distinguished from other such constellations'. Eysenck (1965) stresses that traits and types are similar to the extent that both are derived from the analysis of consistencies, but differ in their degree of generality. In factor analysis types correspond to second order factors and traits to first-order factors. Examples are Eysenck's concepts of extraversion and neuroticism and Cattell's corresponding concepts of exvia-invia and anxiety (Adcock, 1965). Differences between Eysenck and Cattell in preferred levels of analysis have already been noted.

V SOME GENERAL PROBLEMS

The following section is devoted to a discussion of some general problems in the assessment of personality.

1 Holistic (gestalt) versus atomistic approaches to personality assessment

There is now considerable evidence which makes it possible to state a number of conclusions in the controversy between the holistic and atomistic approaches to personality (cf. Eysenck, 1952, 1965).

There is clear evidence that confidence in holistic techniques such as the interview or projective tests is not justified (Kelly and Fiske, 1951; Meehl, 1954). Recent evidence is consistent with greater usefulness of measures of narrower variables as compared with broader or 'depth' assessment (Vernon, 1964b). In prediction, reliable measures of small sets of variables which are correlated with a criterion are superior to more comprehensive assessments which inevitably include information of unknown validity (Stuit, 1947; O.S.S., 1948; Himmelweit and Summerfield, 1951; Meehl, 1954). Increments in information available can produce decrements in predictive accuracy. Further research is necessary to establish whether these findings are peculiar to certain kinds of situation, and to establish optimum levels of information.

Recent work has also demonstrated the plausibility of taking a number of specific measures and combining various scores into one predictive index, i.e. a combination of atomistic and holistic approaches. Such a technique is being developed by Cattell (1965) in his 'specification equation': here measures of an individual's characteristics are weighted according to empirically determined relationships to a criterion, and combined into a general prediction formula. Considerable work is necessary before such equations are generally available for prediction of behaviour in a number of criterion situations (nevertheless cf.

Cattell, Sealy and Sweeney, 1967), but the integration of specific aspects of information to provide a general predictive index does seem to be a promising strategy. The usefulness of multiple variable batteries is also discussed by Tiffin and McCormick (1966). The aim of this work is consistent with the gestalt claim that 'partial approaches are likely to lead to partial understanding' (cf. Eysenck, 1965).

2 Specificity and generality of behaviour

The degree of specificity or generality in behaviour is important for personality assessment, both practically and theoretically. Specificity refers to the observation that an individual who behaves in a given way in one situation (honest, sociable, aggressive, anxious, etc.) does not do so in others, and generality refers to behavioural consistency over time and place. There is a body of evidence indicating that human behaviour is not as consistent as it is often assumed to be.

On the basis of measures of 'honesty, persistence and cooperativeness' in a large group of children and in a number of situations, Hartshorne and May (1928, 1929) conclude that these characteristics must be regarded as 'groups of specific' habits rather than 'general traits'. These conclusions were based on the low correlations between various tests. Similarly Dudycha (1936) demonstrated the specificity of punctuality in a student population, and more recently studies reported in a symposium on vigilance indicate a high degree of specificity in vigilance performance under experimentally controlled conditions (Buckner and Mcgrath, 1963). Vigilance researchers also report failure to establish any relationships between independently measured personality characteristics and performance on vigilance tasks. In social psychology, sociometric measures are known to vary with different group compositions (Cannon, 1958).

There is also considerable evidence for specificity in factor analytic research. Previous discussion has indicated the difference in factorial structures which occur between different populations and test batteries, e.g. differences in the generality of factors (Coan, 1964; Eysenck, 1965). In his discussion of cognitive organization Vernon (1964a) indicates that any specific factor can be made into a group factor by selection of appropriate tests. The factorial structure of behavioral areas can also change as a function of practice effects (Fleishman and Hempel, 1954). There is also considerable specificity in the effects of learning (Thorndike and Woodworth, 1901; Guilford, 1958). Bloom (1965) has recently concluded that there is a considerable degree of specificity of effect in the environment (cf. Newman, Freeman and Holzinger, 1937).

Though there is considerable evidence for specificity in human behaviour, the evidence is not to be accepted uncritically. The Hartshorne and May studies have been criticized, for example, because the subjects were children and the focus was upon behaviours which might not be representative of the characteristics of behaviour generally. Though correlations were low, they were consistently positive, and one of the researchers, in fact, concludes that there was enough evidence to justify a trait of honesty (Maller, 1934). Correlations were also considerably higher when tests were grouped according to their similarity. Burton (1963) has re-analysed correlations among the more reliable of the honesty measures, and concludes that the low order of correlations is chiefly due to low reliability of measures. Using six tests with reliabilities over 0·7, he applied the principal component method and demonstrated that almost half of the variance is explicable by one single general factor with test loadings from 0·53 to 0·76. This suggests a general honesty trait after all.

Allport (1949) has also criticized the Hartshorne-May studies because of the extrapolation from group trends to individual trends. He indicates that low correlations between habits of behaviour mean at the most that individuals are not consistent in the same way – but each individual may be highly consistent within himself. It has also been suggested that, in such a study as that of Dudycha, the apparent degree of specificity is exaggerated by the use of statistical measures which accentuate slight variations in behaviour. χ^2 analysis suggests that there is more consistency than the more sensitive Pearson coefficient.

The relative strength of traits is also suggested by Allport to be important. Individuals at the extremes of the distribution of a trait are more consistent than those who cluster about the mean, and the former may account for as many as 40% of a total group. When the 40% at the extremes of Dudycha's punctuality measures were studied, a very high degree of consistency was found. There was also significantly more consistency in earliness than lateness, i.e. there may well be consistency differences between traits.

In conclusion, the controversy really develops into a question of the empirical demonstration of the relative degree of generality or specificity in a given situation (Eysenck, 1965). Specificity or generality seem to vary with different behaviours, the strength of traits, the reliabilities and sensitivity of measures used and similarity or differences in stimulus conditions. In applied situations, an assessment of the relative degree of generality or specificity may be crucially important. As Shapiro (1963, 1966) has indicated, specificity of behaviour can co-exist with generality of processes.

3 Situational and environmental determinants of behaviour

The focus of our attention up to this point has been on personality variables as determinants of behaviour. However, behaviour is clearly a function of both personality and environment (cf. Mackinnon, 1944), and environment may be a very potent force. Bloom (1965), for example, suggests that 'much of what has been termed individual variation may be explained in terms of environmental variation' – this comment is also relevant to the degree of specificity of behaviour discussed above. Similarly, Cattell (1965) concludes that lack of allowance for the situation is one of the main causes for misjudging personality. The Hartshorne and May studies, in fact, also demonstrated higher correlations between behaviours in similar test situations, and the greater degree of success in armed forces' application of assessment methods might be related to the greater consistency in environment as compared with civilian life (Ellis, 1946; Ellis and Conrad, 1948; Eysenck, 1965).

The complicated relationships between environment and behaviour characteristics are also demonstrated by the correlations (for example, between physical environmental factors and height or weight as contrasted with social and educational environmental factors and intelligence or scholastic achievement) reported by Newman, Freeman and Holzinger (1937; see also Bloom, 1965). In another field, experimental psychology, the Yerkes-Dodson hypothesis (Broadhurst, 1960; Jones, 1960) indicates that performance level is a function of both drive level and task difficulty – the latter being primarily an environmental variable. Farber and Spence (1953), for example, demonstrated that high anxiety subjects (inferred to be a high drive group) were superior to a low anxiety group on a simple eyelid conditioning experiment, but inferior on a more complex finger maze task. They conclude that 'performance is a function of drive level and the specific characteristics of a given task'.

Environmental stimulation also frequently consists of other people. Considerable evidence indicating interaction effects between people in therapy situations is reviewed by Rottschafer and Renzaglia (1962), Luborsky and Strupp (1962), Kemp (1964), Carson *et al.* (1964) and Moos and Clemes (1967). Endler, Hunt and Rosenstein (1962) have also demonstrated that both individuals and settings contribute significantly to overall behavioural variance in anxiety, and behavioural differences correlated with situational factors are further reported by Raush, Dittman and Taylor (1959), Thistlewaite (1959), and Soskin and John (1963). Responses in projective tests are clearly functions of diverse aspects of the testing situation (Masling, 1960).

A general problem in research into person-environment interactions arises from the description of the environment. Bloom (1965) has stressed the crudity of measurement, and has indicated the need for further research within what seem to be the four main approaches to quantification and description of situations. These four approaches are (1) the use of such indices as social class, geographical area, etc.; (2) the concept of role, i.e. as a method of detecting the forces which impinge on an individual by virtue of a social position (Sarbin, 1954; Stern and Stein, 1956; Cattell, 1963); (3) analysis via the Murray interactive system of personal 'need' and environmental 'press' Thistlewaite, 1959; Moos and Houts, 1967; Moos and Clemes, 1967). Last of all is the factor analytic approach, with the aim of discovering dimensions for describing the environment in a manner similar to that used in describing people. Cattell (1965) hopes to include environmental components in his specification equations. Examples of applications of these techniques in industrial settings are discussed by Sells (1966).

Refinement of environmental measures is also important because of their inclusion as parts of criterion situations when assessment techniques are being validated – different aspects of such criterion situations might be important and yet unrelated (Wallace and Weitz, 1955). Cattell (1965) recommends the setting up of a two file system (person/situation) in industrial selection, and Bloom (1965) confidently predicts that combinations of environmental and personal measures will produce predictive procedures with validity coefficients near unity.

4 Individual differences in perception and conceptualization

Individual differences in perception and conceptualization have been explored quite considerably in recent years, and findings are of relevance to applied psychologists as correlates (and consequently as possible predictors) of behaviour. The major protagonist of this approach is probably Kelly (1955; Bannister, 1962), whose hypothesis about cognitive determination of behaviour is indicated by his main postulate that 'the individual's processes are channelized by the way in which he anticipates events'. There is considerable evidence of perceptual and conceptual correlates of behaviour.

Cohen, for example (Hovland and Janis, 1959), has demonstrated many behavioural correlates of self-esteem, and further evidence of relationships between self-attitudes and behaviour is provided by Lavin (1965), Martire (1956) and the Rogerian researchers (Sheerer, 1949; Stock, 1949; Suinn, 1961). More recently, Fransella and Bannister (1967) have demonstrated the high level of prediction of behaviour made possible by measures of personal construct systems, e.g. evaluative constructs. Bordin (1943; Bass and Berg, 1959) has attempted to account for the validity of interest scales in terms of the tapping of a self-concept system which has a determinative effect on behaviour.

There are instances, however, of apparent discrepancies between measures of conceptualization (including interests and attitudes) and behaviour (Walster, 1963; Cook and Sellitz, 1964; Moore, 1965; Fishbein, 1966) which indicate that caution is necessary in uncritical acceptance of Allport's (1949) comment that man's stated intention and preference is an important indicator of his behaviour. In spite of this evidence, however, results such as those of Fransella and Bannister (1967) do indicate that further research into conceptual and perceptual variables is needed, and that these measures might provide important aids in predictive situations.

5 Observation and prediction

A number of conclusions might now be stated on the use of observations of behaviour for prediction. Wherever possible, observations should be made of variables which are empirically demonstrated to be related to criterion situations rather than assumed to be related on clinical or dynamic grounds (Meehl, 1954, 1960). Actuarial prediction, even of quite narrow characteristics, can be of considerable usefulness (Kelly and Fiske, 1951; Vernon, 1964b), though the application of these methods is currently limited because of scarcity of empirical work and tests available (Vernon, 1964b; Hunt and Jones, 1962).

Prediction based on single variables can be accurate enough to be useful (Meehl, 1954; Rutter, 1965; Fransella and Bannister, 1967). Increasing information available is of little use unless the additional information is related to the criterion (Stuit, 1947; O.S.S., 1948). Choice of behavioural measure, criterion measure (Sells, 1966) and form of statistical analysis (Allport, 1949; cf. Thomas, Birch and Chess, 1964) must be carefully made.

Wherever possible, batteries of multiple measures are desirable – because one single measure may account for only part of a behavioural criterion (cf. Lavin, 1965) and be of no importance in others, and because of possible unreliabilities in single measures. In these respects such developments as Cattell's specification equations (1965), and the use of multiple test batteries recommended by Tiffin and McCormick (1966) and demonstrated by Ghiselli (1960, 1963), are likely to be extremely useful. Lavin's (1965) summary of educational achievement suggests, however, that in some cases single measures such as intelligence tests may provide an accuracy of prediction which is not increased by further indices (on the other hand cf. Cattell, Sealy and Sweeney, 1967).

In many cases the personality correlates of behaviour in which a psychologist is interested may not be established, or may not appear to exist at all (Buckner and McGrath, 1963). In such cases, it might be useful to attempt to simulate the situations involving criterion behaviours. This could be one aspect of the intensive single case study approach which is suggested by Shapiro (1957, 1961, 1963), partly because of the absence of acceptable and useful tests and the specificity of behaviour. It might also be indicated that requests from colleagues for personality assessment can invariably be translated into problems of behavioural prediction – thus, if useful tests do not exist for the assessment of, for example, anxiety or sociability or persistence, an attempt might be made to study these parameters (with appropriate operational definition) in relevant but simulated conditions; observations of behaviour under these conditions then become predictions of the same behavioural characteristic in the criterion situation. Behaviour in one situation becomes a prediction of behaviour in a similar situation (Guthrie, 1944; Chapple and Donald, 1946). In such cases, the problem becomes primarily one of the simulation of the criterion situation, though it might be desirable to work within a framework of studing the basic processes and psychological variables which are involved. The strategy of simulation is also conceived as a direct attack on the problem of specificity. The intensive study of the single case advocated by Shapiro (see Chapter 21) is ideally suited to this approach because of the stress on content validity and criterion behaviour.

Since a considerable amount of prediction of behaviour will involve social situations, a review of the findings and techniques of social psychology might well be undertaken to ascertain the amount of help that could be derived from this area in, for example, simulation. Examples of possibly useful techniques might be specific observational methods (Bass, 1951; Bass and Berg, 1959) and sociometric instruments (Moreno, 1934; Cannon, 1958; Bloom, 1965). Since it

E

can be argued that an individual responds to a perceived environment rather than a 'real' environment (Bannister, 1962), indices of similarity in conceptions of simulated and criterion situations might be developed as measures of the success of simulation.

6 The analysis of success in measurement and prediction

It might be useful to discuss at this point some aspects of the analysis of success in prediction. Recently, conventional statistics used to measure validity and reliability have been shown to have a number of disadvantages. The main traditional measure has been the correlation coefficient, or derivations of it. Mention has already been made of the distorting effect of statistical methods in the analysis of specificity (Allport, 1949). Similarly Taylor and Russell (1939) indicate that the magnitude of correlations is not an adequate representation of the relationship between, for example, a test and a criterion. Examples are quoted to demonstrate that commonly used indices suggest that tests are of little use. Taylor and Russell (1939) suggest that acceptance of these measures may produce unrealistic pessimism about the usefulness of tests in clinic, school or industry.

Taylor and Russell continue to propose an alternative and more realistic method of analysis. A test is considered acceptable if, on the whole, the proportion of successful placements is higher with a test than without it. In the consideration of personality measures, 'placement' must be interpreted as prediction of a predetermined category of behavioural acts, e.g. behaving, or not behaving, in a way which might be labelled, for example, as 'anxious' or 'sociable' or 'dominating'. Taylor and Russell indicate that a test will probably be valuable in such situations provided there is some relationship between score and criterion.

The usefulness of the test is also affected by the selection ratio (the proportion of those assessed who can be accepted) and the base rate involved (the proportion of unselected populations which fall within a category which the test is used to detect or predict.) Low selection ratios produce increased test usefulness, and it can be demonstrated that even tests having low validity coefficients can prove to be very useful. Tables for the calculation of the indices of test usefulness are provided by Taylor and Russell, and reproduced by Tiffin and McCormick (1966). A criterion which must be satisfied in order to use these tables is that there should be a linear relationship between test score and criterion. Tiffin and Vincent (1960) have also investigated the concordance between empirical results and theoretical expectancies derived from Taylor and Russell; they suggest that in most cases the correlation is sufficiently linear to allow the use of the Taylor-Russell tables. Work by McCollum and Savard (1957), which is summarized by Tiffin and McCormick, has demonstrated the usefulness of using a direct method of analysis which gives essentially the same results without the use of tables. The use of individual expectancy charts is also discussed by Tiffin and McCormick, and the reader is referred to this source for further information of methods which are clearly relevant to the use of personality tests in behavioural prediction.

The work of Ghiselli (1960, 1963) on the use of multiple predictors also deserves considerable attention.

Cronbach and Gleser (1957) also reach a number of conclusions which are relevant to the assessment of procedures used for measurement and prediction. Their main thesis is the role of the test as an aid to decision making. They suggest that, in applied and practical situations, a precise quantitative estimate is not always necessary. What is important is whether the test is useful in making a choice between two or more alternatives, i.e. accuracy in allocation is a better criterion than the capacity of an observational method to reduce uncertainty about the true value of a variable. Assessments of the value of a given method should involve comparisons with alternative methods rather than with chance.

Cronbach and Gleser also make a distinction between terminal decisions and sequential decision processes, and suggest that unreliable methods are more likely to be acceptable in sequential processes, i.e. where there is opportunity for further checks and correction of error. Though these conclusions are generally relevant to personality assessments, as yet there has been limited application.

One further example of a method useful in prediction situations is the application of Bayesian theory to decision problems. One aim here is to control the kinds of error which occur, and to reduce the more serious kinds of error, e.g. in attempting to decide whether person X is to be considered as potentially aggressive or not, it would be more serious to make a false negative error than a false positive error. The method is outlined by Maxwell (1961) and has been applied successfully in a diagnostic situation by Kendrick (1965).

In analyses of sucess in prediction situations, it is important to note that lack of success can occur because of unreliability in a criterion (e.g. psychiatric diagnosis) rather than in a predictor measure. A test measure may predict some aspects of a criterion but not others (Sells, 1966). Because of the wide variety of criteria, tests are to be regarded as having multiple validities and reliabilities.

It is also important to note that measures might be less useful in individual use than group use – high reliability continues to be a necessary prerequisite, for example, for the use of tests in individual decision making (Jensen, 1959), though low reliabilities are sometimes acceptable when large groups are involved and in research situations.

V PERSONALITY AND COGNITIVE FUNCTIONING

Though it is currently common practice to differentiate cognitive from non-cognitive functioning and to refer to the non-cognitive factors as 'personality', it should be remembered that intelligence and cognitive functioning are really very important aspects of the integrated personality. The structure of cognitive functioning has been analysed extensively by factor analysts, and large numbers of tests are available to measure general intelligence, and also the various group and specific factors (Vernon, 1964a).

Measures of intelligence have also been used with considerable success to predict academic success and job success. Intelligence is not, however, sufficient to account for all the variance in these criterion situations. Lavin (1965) concludes, on the basis of his survey, that cognitive ability accounts for 35 to 40% of the variance in academic achievement. About 50% of the variance remains unaccounted for. Cattell, Sealy and Sweeney (1967) have recently demonstrated the usefulness of adding personality and motivational measures to the intelligence measures. These three areas are shown to account for 75% of the variance in academic achievement, with each single area accounting for about 25%. This demonstrates the improvement in the level of prediction when other measures are used in conjunction with cognitive assessment. Similarly, Furneaux (1962) has demonstrated the usefulness of combining cognitive and non-cognitive measures (neuroticism and extraversion) in predicting academic achievement in a university population.

In two very important and provocative papers, Eysenck and White (1964) and Eysenck (1967) have cautioned that, though cognitive and non-cognitive aspects of personality may be considered as independent, it is clearly erroneous to extrapolate from statistical independence to lack of interaction. In an analysis of Lienert's data, Eysenck and White (1964) demonstrated the more clearly marked structure of cognitive abilities in a stable group as compared with a neurotic group. Three significant factors were derived from the stable group, and two in the neurotic group. Eysenck (1967) recommends a combination of psychometric assessment and experimental analysis, and reviews studies which demonstrate the interaction between intellectual and non-cognitive areas.

Amongst other studies, Eysenck quotes both his own and colleagues' work indicating differential vocabulary-intelligence ratios between introverts and extraverts (Himmelweit, 1945; Eysenck, 1947). Other differences between introverts and extraverts, and stable or unstable groups, are differential preferences for speed and accuracy (Eysenck, 1947; Jensen, 1964; Farley, 1966), the tendency for extraverts to slow down near the end of prolonged tasks (Eysenck, 1959) and differences between introverts and extraverts in long and short-term recall (Eysenck, 1967). Farley has also recently demonstrated a curvilinear relationship between neuroticism and cognitive test performance. Other investigators have also indicated interactions between cognitive and non-cognitive variables.

Cattell (1965), using oblique factors in his personality analysis, has noted correlations between intelligence and various stability traits. The tendency for highly intelligent groups to be more stable generally is also demonstrated by Terman and Oden (1959). Foulds (1951, 1952) has reported on the differential effects of distraction on hysterics and dysthymics completing maze tasks. Furneaux (1960) has analysed cognitive functioning into the separate factors of speed, persistence and an error checking mechanism. As Eysenck (1967) indicates the two latter factors may be regarded as being non-cognitive. Some of the clinical implications of Furneaux's work are discussed by Shapiro (1967a). Intelligence measures have been demonstrated to have considerable predictive usefulness in a study of autistic children followed up over ten years or more (Rutter, 1965).

Of additional interest in the clinical field is the analysis of cognitive defects in psychotics by McGhie and his colleagues (McGhie, 1967), and the suggestion that these defects might eventually be shown to account for many of the clinical observations of behavioural abnormalities in these groups.

Enough has been said to justify two conclusions. The first is that cognitive functioning is an important area of personality, and should be considered as such. The second is that there is evidence for considerable interaction between cognitive and non-cognitive variables in personality. Further investigations of interactions is likely to make an important contribution to increased understanding of the functioning of the integrated personality.

VI THE DEVELOPMENT OF PERSONALITY

Though the focus of this review is upon aspects of adult personality, the investigation of stability and change of characteristics from birth to maturity is of considerable importance to the applied psychologist. The empirical study of stability is relevant to the problem of length of time before maturity when the level or degree of mature characteristics can be accurately predicted. Are characteristics such as intelligence, aggressiveness or sociability stable from the earlier years, or is there instability to the extent that any test result cannot be regarded to have generality over more than a limited period?

Thomas, Birch and Chess (1964) have outlined the more prominent theories of development (cf. also Bloom, 1965), but stress the scarcity of empirical data. Their conclusion is that no adequate theories are available, and an inductive hypothesis-producing rather than a deductive hypothesis testing approach is recommended. The usefulness of longitudinal data for prediction purposes is also noted by Bloom (1965). He notes that developmental data make it possible to consider initial measurement for a given individual along with the correlation between early and later measures; the standard error of estimate is then used to determine the limits within which the second measurement should fluctuate. Bloom's own conclusion is that the standard error is smaller as measures approximate to the criterion level. This is demonstrated by reference to studies of intelligence and other studies.

It has been demonstrated (Thurstone, 1955; Bloom, 1965) that, in terms of intelligence measured at 17, about 50% of development occurs between conception and 4 years; 30% between 4 and 8, and a further 20% between 8 and 17. Differences in rate of development between different aspects of cognitive ability are also indicated (e.g. perceptual, space and reasoning abilities, memory, etc.). Investigations of intelligence generally indicate that measures during the first five years cannot be considered a basis for long-term decisions about an individual (Anderson, 1939; Bayley, 1949; Bloom, 1965). Bloom has also postulated a hypothesis that the effects of the environment upon a given characteristic depend in part on the stage of development. Terman and Oden (1959) have demonstrated, in contrast to studies of intelligence indicating early instability (though it must be recognized that their measures were begun at later age levels), the stability of intellectual functioning in a highly intelligent sample. There is also evidence that growth of intelligence may continue through adult life, though there are differences which might be related to such factors as occupation (Burke, 1958; Bloom, 1965) or sudden change in environment (Tozer and Larwood, 1958). Further empirical information on development is also available.

Thomas, Birch and Chess (1964) demonstrate the high level of stability in formal aspects of functioning such as activity level, rhythmicity, distractibility, persistence and adaptability from birth to 2 years. This indicates a high level of behavioural individuality at a very early age. Kagan and Moss (1962), in a study of early behaviour and theoretically related later behaviour between the 6-10 year level and adulthood, also demonstrate positive but variable correlations between such characteristics as spontaneity, dependence, passivity, and sex-typed behaviour. Significant differences occur between stability in different characteristics, and there are differences between sexes. Further empirical evidence of positive, but variable, stability is provided by Gesell *et al.* (1939), McKinnon (1942), Neilson (1948), Sontag *et al.* (1958), Escalona and Heider (1959), Peck and Havinghurst (1960) and Witkin *et al.* (1962).

This list is by no means exhaustive of all studies. Many of the studies cannot be accepted uncritically because of such errors as rating contamination, lack of reliability or validity indices, etc. (Thomas, *et al.*, 1964). Cattell (Bass and Berg, 1959) and his colleagues have also carried out research to investigate factorial organization at different age levels. They claim, for example, that at 4 years such factors as cyclothymia-schizothymia and dominance-submissiveness are clearly detectable. Academic achievement is also reasonably stable and consequently predictable during school years (Payne, 1963; Bloom, 1965).

Longitudinal studies are also important because of their implications for research into the determinants of various characteristics, e.g. the findings reported by Thomas *et al.* (1964) clearly indicate a strong hereditary component in personality variables. The (non-longitudinal) various twin-comparisons of intelligence are also well known (Newman, Freeman and Holzinger, 1937; Burt, 1958; Husen, 1959). Shields (1962) has recently demonstrated evidence consistent with an inherited basis for Eysenck's dimensions, and Cattell's school has reported differential hereditary determination of Cattell's factors (Cattell, Stice and Kristy, 1957). The work of Pasamanick on correlations between pre- and para-natal factors and subsequent intelligence defects, reading abnormalities, etc., are also of interest to the aetiology (and also the predictability) of certain functions (Kawi and Pasamanick, 1959; Knobloch and Pasamanick, 1960; Lilienfeld and Pasamanick, 1960). Environmental influences are discussed by Bloom (1965) and demonstrated by such studies as those reported by Newman, Freeman and Holzinger (1937).

Studies in general indicate a high degree of individuality at an early age, and varying but in some cases quite high stability over a number of years. Observations of behaviour made during the first five years or so tend, however, to be highly unreliable predictors of the corresponding adult behaviours. Prediction becomes more accurate with greater proximity to the criterion age and early measures clearly cannot be used for long-term decisions. There also seem to be differences in stability between characteristics, and there is an interaction effect between characteristic and sex. Hereditary influences are indicated to be very important for both cognitive and non-cognitive characteristics though differences between characteristics again seem to exist.

To complete the review of personality research, a brief and critical survey of the most common assessment techniques is provided.

VII QUESTIONNAIRES AND INVENTORIES

Considerable use of 'paper and pencil' tests has been made by psychologists. Such methods have, in theory, a number of advantages. Amongst these is the degree of objectivity involved in the standardization of administration, scoring and interpretation (Bass and Berg, 1959). Quantification and statistical analysis, whilst obviously not ensuring acceptable validity or reliability, do facilitate the assessment of these test characteristics. Questionnaires can be regarded as standardized interviews, and the lack of comprehensiveness of questionnaires as compared with the interview is certainly not a necessary disadvantage. Reliable measures of specific characteristics have been demonstrated on a number of occasions to be far more useful than more general assessments (Kelly and Fiske, 1951; Meehl, 1954; Vernon, 1964b). In addition, questionnaires are invariably more economical to use.

Questionnaires and inventories are commonly used to provide three kinds of measures. The first is an index of the strength of a psychological characteristic derived from factor analysis, e.g. Eysenck's M.P.I. (1959) and Cattell's 16 P.F. test (1950). The construct validation (Cronbach and Meehl, 1955) of these tests must, in general use, be supplemented by further information such as external validation (e.g. Kelvin, Lucas and Ojha, 1965) and item analyses (Levonian, 1961; Lorr, 1965). Their usefulness in empirical situations depends, in fact, on the extension of research beyond construct or factorial validation.

The second kind of measure is an index of the similarity of the respondent to defined criterion groups, e.g. the M.M.P.I. (Hathaway and McKinley, 1943). With such a test as the M.M.P.I., the group similarity index is the sole legitimate measure – test scores do not measure a unitary psychological characteristic, the degree of illness or prognosis (Payne, 1958). The usefulness of such tests depends to a large extent on the reliability and validity of the original criterion measure, e.g. psychiatric groups. In a test which provides scores on a number of scales, the independence of scales should be empirically demonstrated rather than uncritically accepted – the M.M.P.I. scales are clearly not independent (Britton and Savage, in Savage, 1966).

The third kind of measure is of a construct developed from general opinion or a particular theory, e.g. the Bernreuter questionnaire or the Edwards Personal

Preference Schedule (Edwards, 1954). In the construction of such tests there is a danger of the unreliability of subjective judgement, but subsequent correction of errors is possible (e.g. Flanagan, 1935). Such tests can also have empirical validity which is independent of the original theoretical systems from which they were derived (in the case of the Edwards scale cf. Bernadin and Jessor, 1957; Bendig, 1958). Strictly speaking, questionnaires usually have multiple validities and reliabilities, and might be useful in some situations but not others. Validity coefficients, for example, are subject to considerable variability (Vernon, 1964b). Face validation can never be regarded as a substitute for empirical demonstration of usefulness (Christie and Lindauer, 1963).

Though considerable research into questionnaires has been carried out, Kornhauser's (1945) demonstration of psychologists' dissatisfaction with them is still probably true. There are several reasons for this.

Most questionnaires are inadequately validated for the practical uses made of them by psychologists in applied settings. Cattell's (1959) conclusion about inadequate external validation of factored batteries continues to be true for the large number of situations where clinical psychologists, for example, might need these measures. Clinical assessment of the probable relevance of results is never a substitute for empirically demonstrated relationships. Tests having descriptive usefulness cannot be assumed to have predictive usefulness (Payne, 1958; Kelvin, Lucas and Ojha, 1965). An additional problem is that low levels of reliability or validity, whilst acceptable in group studies, constitute barriers to the use of tests with individuals (Jensen, 1959). The problem of generality and specificity of behaviour is an additional complication which has not really been related to the implication of test scores.

There must also be considerable concern over method contamination in questionnaires, i.e. the influence of measurement by questionnaire on results. Cattell (1965), in fact, regards questionnaires as 'conspective' (i.e. giving the same results to all testers) rather than objective instruments – because of the possible inaccuracies of self-report. Items in questionnaires have been demonstrated to be susceptible to considerable misinterpretation (Landis and Katz, 1934; Eisenberg, 1941; Benton, 1953), and the form of items is also important (Smith, 1932; Sletto, 1936; Fiske, 1957) as a partial determinant of responses.

An additional problem which has attracted considerable attention is that of response sets, i.e. the demonstration that test responses are influenced by individual idiosyncrasies which are independent of the content of the items (Cronbach, 1946, 1950). Research has been directed primarily at social desirability (Edwards, 1957) and acquiescence (Jackson and Messick, in Berg, 1967). The reader is referred to the recent volume edited by Berg (1967) for a summary of the evidence. Edwards (1959, 1967) for example, has provided considerable, and rather disturbing, evidence of high correlations between social desirability values of items and the probablity of their endorsement on a number of scales, though the implications of such findings are equivocal (Costello, 1966). A number of conclusions about response sets might be briefly stated.

First of all, there is no conclusive evidence that response sets are general personality traits – there is a general failure to demonstrate extra test correlates (Eysenck, 1965; McGee in Berg, 1967). Recent research indicates, in addition, that social desirability and acquiescence are multifactorial, i.e. there are different kinds of social desirability or acquiescence (Hathaway, 1965; Messick, in Berg, 1967). Response sets are, at least in part, determined by the characteristics of test items (cf. Berg, 1967). There is evidence that these sets can be reduced by careful test construction, and also detected in test profiles. Edwards has pioneered the development of pair comparison items with equivalence of social desirability between paired items (1957, 1959), though there is evidence that his efforts to control this factor on his Personal Preference Schedule has not been successful (Corah *et al.*, 1958). Other techniques, summarized by Jackson (Berg, 1967), have involved balance of items within tests (e.g. Bennett and Slater, 1945), and the inclusion within tests of scales for the detection of response biases (Hathaway 1965).

The detection and control of such influences is extremely important in the use of tests with single cases, though Hathaway (1965) has suggested that response sets might contribute to the usefulness of a scale, i.e. response sets cannot always be considered as contributing to error. Though, as Christie and Lindauer (1963) have stressed, test scores are in varying degrees functions of item content, various response sets, and possibly interactions among these variables, these considerations do not exclude a test from use. The crucial determinant is the demonstration of relevant extra-test behavioural correlates by empirical research. Unfortunately, this latter information is remarkably uncommon!

Further progress in the use of questionnaires in applied settings can be expected when the findings and views of Taylor and Russell (1939) and Cronbach and Gleser (1957) find wider application. The implication of these findings is that the provision of precise quantitative measures, though desirable, are not necessary pre-requisites for use. The capacity of a test to provide a dichotomous answer may well be sufficient, e.g. a yes/no reply in a prediction situation. The application of such approaches as Bayesian theory (Maxwell, 1961) may also contribute to the use of multiple measures in order to maximize the efficiency of decisions.

A realistic general conclusion on the usefulness of questionnaires is stated by Eysenck (1965) – 'Questionnaires are a necessary but not sufficient means of arriving at a complete and adequate picture of an individual's main traits and personality variables'. Many (and probably all) of the difficulties involved in the use of questionnaires are found in other techniques such as the interview or projective test, and probably to a much greater extent.

VIII RATINGS AND RATING SCALES

Rating scales are essentially a means of recording (in quantified form) the impression which an individual makes on others in terms of specified aspects of his behaviour. Jenkins *et al.* (1959) have specified the aims of scales as quantification,

E*

the provision of means of comparison and data for use in prediction. Rating scales are basically of two types, viz. numerical and ranking methods, though further subdivisions are possible (Guilford, 1959; Costello, 1966). Ratings are frequently used as validation criteria for other techniques. This is in many ways undesirable as ratings are known to be susceptible to considerable distortion.

Ratings have been shown to be subject to a number of systematic biasing effects, e.g. proximity errors, these being contamination between measures taken at the same time; halo effects (Vernon, 1938, 1964b); order effects, i.e. judgements can be influenced by context and sequence (Campbell *et al.*, 1957; Hunt and Jones, 1962; Shapiro, 1963, 1967b), and unequal subjective units in scaling (Guilford, 1959). Ratings may also be affected by the rater's own characteristics (Landis, 1936; Sears, 1936), and consistent differences have been reported between such groups as nurses and doctors (Pomeroy and Cogan, 1955). Ratings can also be affected by extraneous ratee characteristics (Hanna, 1950; McKeachie, 1952). Ratings of overt behaviour are generally believed to be more reliable than ratings of abstract variables, but this is not necessarily true (Newcomb, 1931; Frenkel-Brunswik, 1942; Hamburg *et al.*, 1958).

In his comparison of different modes of personality assessment, Cattell (1965) concludes that, taking into account customary usage, ratings are probably inferior to questionnaire measurement. Though ratings are known to be potentially unreliable, a number of strategies have been recommended to reduce possible distortion.

The definitions of traits, and the degrees of these traits, should be explictly stated (otherwise cf. Loehlin, 1961). Training of raters is desirable (King, Erhmann and Johnson, 1952), though not guaranteed to produce increased reliability (Arnhoff, 1954). Information about distorting effects can also be useful to combat these effects (cf. Sears, 1936). Standardization of conditions where ratings are made is also desirable, and time sampling is also a technique which seems to have considerable potential usefulness (Vernon, 1953). Costello (1966) has also provided a useful summary of the requirements necessary for scale construction and use which were formerly outlined by Lorr, Klett and McNair (1963). Vernon's (1953) recommendation of 'engineered diagnostic situations' is also worthy of note.

A number of studies have demonstrated that the distortions inherent in uncontrolled rating can be controlled to a degree where results compare favourably with objective techniques (Hamburg *et al.*, 1958; Wing, 1966; Wing *et al.*, 1967). Checks on reliability and validity are necessary when these techniques are used in research, or as validation criteria (cf. Thomas, Birch and Chess, 1964). It is of interest to note that both Eysenck (1965) and Cattell (1965) conclude that factorial studies of ratings and questionnaires suggest a very similar factor structure, especially at the second-order factor level. There are also, however, discrepancies in such variables as the generality of factors between these areas (Coan, 1964).

IX PROJECTIVE TECHNIQUES

Projective techniques are designed to encourage a wide range of complex responses which are believed to be determined primarily by the feelings and attitudes of the respondent and hence reveal something of his underlying dynamics and personality characteristics (cf. Gleser, 1963). The distinguishing characteristics of these techniques have been outlined by Anastasi (1961) and Vernon (1964b), and subdivisions have been suggested by Lindzey (1959). Some of the assumptions underlying the use of these tests, e.g. that they 'tap the durable essence of personality equally in different individuals' have been summarized by MacFarlane and Tuddenham (1951). Rosenzweig (1951) has discussed the differences between the philosophy of the projectivist and that of the psychometrist and experimentalist.

The concept of projection has been analysed and differentiated by Murstein and Pryer (1959). These authors conclude that there are a number of different varieties of projection, and that in any testing situation it may be impossible to differentiate one from another. The experimental work mentioned by Murstein and Pryer does not seem to have contributed a great deal to our understanding of the concept, though there are significant exceptions to this conclusion (Sears, 1936).

Recently it has been indicated that projective tests do not tap perception but, strictly speaking, provide indices of verbal reports of perception (Zubin, Eron and Schumer, 1965). Individual responses in projective test situations are known to be affected significantly by such variables as verbal cues (Sandler, 1959; Greenspoon and Thompson, 1959; Gross, 1965), or expectations and tester characteristics (Bernstein, 1956; Henry and Rotter, 1956; Masling, 1960). Zubin, Eron and Schumer recommend that further research should be undertaken within a framework of perceptual theory, and suggest the application of a model of perceptual behaviour proposed by Graham in Stevens' handbook. The responses observed in projective tests are, in terms of this model, functions of a number of independent variables, e.g. the present stimulus (cf. Baughman, 1958; Murstein, 1966), time of exposure of stimulus (Smith and Raygor, 1956), temporary and permanent states of the organism, past experience (Rabin, Nelson and Clark, 1954) and personality characteristics. In research and routine practice, it is necessary to exhaust the effects of all parameters in the first part of the equation before invoking personality characteristics. To assume that personality characteristics alone are involved is a gross oversimplification.

In the meantime, there are many problems to overcome with currently used techniques. Reviews indicate that the reliability and validity of projective techniques are generally unsatisfactory (Jensen, 1959; Eysenck, 1959). As Jensen indicates, the confidence limits of the reliability coefficient of projective tests are difficult to define because of the lack of standardization. Because of the uncontrolled nature of these tests, any reliability or validity coefficient is limited to the conditions under which it is derived; each technique might have a wide range of reliabilities and validities.

There is a general lack of normative data, though there are promising moves in this direction (Ledwith, cf. Gleser, 1963). Eysenck has drawn attention (1959) to the unsatisfactory nature of most validation research. And acceptable studies indicate inadequate predictive and concurrent validity (Eron, 1950; Kelly and Fiske, 1951; Barry, Blyth and Albrecht, 1952; Holtzman and Sells, 1954; Rieman, 1953). The significance of such generally used measures as Rorschach scores is highly questionable, and there is lack of information about empirical correlates or, alternatively, considerable disproof of the significance claimed for these scores (Bradway and Heisler, 1953). Methods of scoring are also inadequate, and may have considerable influence upon the nature of conclusions (Cronbach 1949). The demonstration that test responses are affected by many aspects of the test situation is also extremely important because of the uncontrolled nature of test administration. Standardized and forced-choice projective tests give generally higher reliability (Holtzman, 1959; Cattell, 1965), but are inconsistent with the traditional freedom of response encouraged by projectivists. There is also considerable evidence that many of the assumptions underlying projective tests, e.g. the linearity of relationship between a need and its expression in perception, are either incorrect or oversimplified (Sears, 1951; Getzels and Walsh, 1958; Leiman and Epstein, 1961).

Though currently used techniques do not satisfy the criteria necessary for use, there is, however, considerable indication that development within a framework such as that outlined by Zubin, Eron and Schumer (1965) might be very rewarding. Perception as a medium for personality assessment may have potential value both in single case assessment (Beech, 1959; Schmidt and Brown, 1965) and research into basic psychological functioning (Sears, 1951; Leiman and Epstein, 1961).

X BEHAVIOUR TESTS

Behaviour tests involve observations of behaviour in situations where the testee is not aware of the significance of his behaviour to the tester (Cattell, 1965). Behaviour tests may vary from relatively simple perceptual or psychomotor tests (rail-walking, vigilance tasks, etc.) to observations of groups in quasi-realistic problem solving (Vernon, 1953). These tests are regarded by Cattell (1965) as being truly objective and uncontaminated indices of personality functioning.

Early workers with behaviour tests were frequently frustrated by negative findings, e.g. low correlations between tests meant to measure the same characteristic or between test and relevant extra-test behaviour (Vernon, 1953). *Ad hoc* usage of tests as measures of traits such as suggestibility (Brown, 1916) or persistence was obviously unreliable and subject to a considerable degree of error.

A logical and rational basis to objective tests was really provided by factor analysis, especially by aspects of the work of Cattell and Eysenck. Cattell (1965) has demonstrated the heavy loadings of many objective tests on a number of his factors, and Eysenck has demonstrated the usefulness of these tests in normal-neurotic discrimination (Eysenck, Brengelmann and Granger, 1957). Independent reviewers have concluded that there is essential agreement between the results of these investigators though there are differences in the generality of factors when objective tests are compared with other areas (Coan, 1964; Adcock, 1965). Cattell has constructed the 'Objective Analytic Personality Battery' (1956) to provide a set of measures of relevant traits. Eysenck (1947) has also demonstrated the usefulness of various measures in measuring aspects of such traits as suggestibility (body sway, the Chevreul pendulum, etc.). There is also evidence of the predictive usefulness of objective test measures (O'Connor and Tizard, 1951).

Considerable care is necessary, however, in the use of these tests. Careful control of conditions is necessary because of possible effects of differences in motivation or instructions. Cattell (1965) has stressed the considerable time taken up by his own objective test battery. Though such batteries might be useful in group situations, their usefulness in single case assessment (sufficiently high reliability, etc.) is yet to be demonstrated. Correlations with extra test behaviour are frequently too low to justify use (Gardner, 1940, in Vernon, 1953). Further complication is involved in the repetition of tests, because of changes in factorial composition with practice (Fleishman and Hempel, 1954; Guilford, 1958). For these reasons, the use of objective tests in individual assessment is at present rather limited.

Another use of behaviour tests involves the simulation of criterion situations, e.g. War Office Selection Board group observation techniques, or such observations as are reported by Hartshorne and May (1928). Burt (1939; cf. Vernon, 1953) has also demonstrated the usefulness of such techniques. Vernon (1953) suggests that a combination of realistic conditions, time sampling and improved rating procedures might be expected to produce a general improvement in prediction (see Vernon's reference to Thomas, 1929, and Murphy, 1937). Two important problems concern the realism of these situations for the testees (i.e. there is a problem of simulation), and the related problem of the generality of results outside the testing situation. Wherever such techniques are used, empirical proof of their usefulness is obviously necessary.

XI THE INTERVIEW

Since the interview is discussed in Chapter 5, the present consideration will be limited to some general comments relevant to the use of the interview for the assessment of personality variables. The interview is probably the most widespread single technique used for assessment, selection and guidance (Spriegel and James, 1958), and enjoys considerable repute which is not fully deserved (cf. Kelly and Fiske, 1951).

The evidence demonstrating the possible unreliability of interview assessment is highly relevant to the use of this technique for personality assessment (Ash,

1949; Vernon, 1953; Luborsky, 1954; Kreitman *et al.*, 1961), though it must be admitted that studies such as those of Ash are not above very serious criticism and probably overestimate disagreement between interviewers (Foulds, 1965). Other studies indicate that the interview can be highly reliable and valid (Vernon and Parry, 1949; Hanna, 1950; Hunt, Herrmann and Noble, 1957; Burroughs, 1958) – though these results seem far less frequent than those which stress limitations because of low reliabilities. The kinds of decisions or assessments are also of importance, e.g. the more specific the area of decision, the greater the disagreement (Schmidt and Fonda, 1956; Kreitman *et al.*, 1961; Hunt and Jones, 1962).

There is also evidence of the possibility of considerable method contamination in interview assessment. The results of interview assessment can be functions of both interviewer and interviewee, and interactions between the two. Distortion through interviewer bias has been demonstrated by Rice (1929) and Kelley (1950). The recording of interview material is often grossly inaccurate (Payne, 1949, in Maccoby and Maccoby, 1954), and methods of questioning can produce distortion (e.g. Smith, 1932). Extraneous interviewee characteristics can influence judgements of relevant characteristics (Hanna, 1950; Haire and Grunes, 1950; Giedt, 1955; Masling, 1960). Interviewers can also affect their subjects in consistent directions (Goldman-Eisler, 1951, 1952, 1954). These sources of unreliability are all the more important because, in an interview situation, they are often uncontrolled and unknown.

There is recent evidence, however, that controlled and standard interview techniques can increase accuracy and reliability to levels which compare well with the best objective devices. Standardization involves a definition of aims, criteria for judgement and cues, standard recording techniques, etc., and reliabilities beyond 0·8 and 0·9 have recently been demonstrated (Wing, 1966; Wing *et al.*, 1967). These techniques are restricted in range and lack the flexibility which is characteristic of the interview generally, but further development along these lines is obviously desirable. Recent reviewers (Ulrich and Trumbo, 1965) have also suggested that the interview can be more useful if it is recognized that it is better suited to some goals than others. Limitation and specification of aims is probably desirable for both interviews and projective techniques. In predictive situations the usefulness of the interview must be compared with other alternatives (Cronbach and Gleser, 1957), and in many cases narrower and more objective devices might be considerably more useful than more comprehensive techniques (Himmelweit and Summerfield, 1951; Kelly and Fiske, 1951; Luborsky, 1954).

XII PHYSIOLOGICAL MEASUREMENT

Though physiological measurement has not, as yet, been developed to the point where it has become a routine clinical method in any of the applied fields, there is considerable indication that such development might make a fruitful contribution both to the assessment and measurement of personality and the understanding of basic aspects of human functioning.

The potential value of such measurement is stressed by Eysenck (1965), who also reviews a range of studies indicating physiological differences between clinical groups (Jost, 1941; Wenger, 1941, 1948; Sherman and Jost, 1942, and Wenger *et al.*, 1957). More recently, Eysenck has attempted to provide evidence to support his hypotheses about the physiological basis of his main personality dimensions, e.g. neuroticism being related to autonomic overresponsiveness (Eysenck and Rachman, 1965). Cattell and Guilford have also shown considerable interest in the physiological correlates of their personality dimensions.

Of considerable relevance to personality theorists is research into the generality or specificity of autonomic reaction. The almost traditional division of the autonomic nervous system into two branches commonly known as the sympathetic and para-sympathetic (Eppinger and Hess, 1910; Cannon, 1920) must now be adjusted to comply with Lacey's demonstration of autonomic response specificity. Lacey's principle of autonomic specificity states that 'for a given set of autonomic functions individuals tend to respond with a pattern of autonomic activation in which maximum activation occurs in the same physiological function, whatever the stress' and he has provided considerable evidence to support the hypothesis (Lacey, 1950, 1958; Lacey and Lehn, 1952; Lacey *et al.*, 1953, 1962; Lacey and Lacey, 1958). Specificity of response is not universally reported, however, and there are also reports of consistencies between different aspects of response to the same stress situation (Sainsbury and Gibson, 1954; Sternbach, 1960; Wenger, Clemens *et al.*, 1961). Results can also be, at least in part, artifacts of the method of analysis (Schnore, 1959). It seems likely that, as Eysenck (1965) indicates, the eventual resolution of the controversy will be an empirical demonstration of the relative degrees of specificity and generality, i.e. there is probably a continuum from extreme specificity to extreme generality. Lacey's work does demonstrate the dangers of using single measures of general characteristics (e.g. G.S.R. correlations in Lacey and Lacey, 1958).

Malmo (1962) has reported a number of studies which suggest the aetiological role of physiological variables in symptom determination and has demonstrated correlations between physiological sensitivities and symptoms having psychological components. For example, psychological tension has been related to consistent changes in muscle tension in experimentally induced stress situations. Problems in the use of physiological measures for general assessment are also discussed by Martin (1960) – e.g. the physiological measure as an index of emotion. Lacey *et al.* (1962) have proposed a theory linking specified psychological and physiological variables.

Further research, related to the possible use of physiological measures in personality assessment, indicates the plausibility of the use of such measures as indices of the effects of therapy procedures (Dittes, 1957; Clark, 1963) – though considerable care is necessary in inferences made from physiological to psychological variables (Lacey, 1958). There is also some evidence which indicates the greater sensitivity of physiological indices (Moore, 1965). The problem of generalization of findings outside the measurement situation is not, however, resolved (Malmo, 1962; Venables, 1967). Two further areas of the research into relationships between physiological and psychological variables are (1) the work into psychophysiological aspects of schizophrenics (Venables, 1967) and (2) the clinical use of physiological measures of sedation thresholds (Shagass, 1954; Shagass, Mihalik and Jones, 1957).

In conclusion, considerable evidence is available to demonstrate the potential usefulness of physiological measures as measures of personality. Further work will be necessary, however, before these measures can be introduced as routine assessment procedures.

XIII SUMMARY AND CONCLUSIONS

The six main areas of personality assessment have been reviewed briefly. It seems evident that each can make a contribution to personality research. It also seems evident that more work is necessary before the potential usefulness is realized, though the avenues and framework for further development seem fairly clear in some cases, e.g. in the projective field (Zubin, Eron and Schumer, 1965). No one area is likely to provide a key to personality (Eysenck, 1965), and further work is necessary to integrate the contribution which emerges from each area.

The hypothesis proposed in the introductory section was that the use of personality assessment in applied situations usually involves problems of prediction. For example, personality assessment might be important to the extent that certain characteristics are believed or known to be involved in an unobserved criterion situation, and the psychologist has been requested to make predictions about behaviour in that situation. Alternatively, requests for personality assessment are usually translatable into problems of the prediction of behaviour in specified situations, e.g. is this individual aggressive? Investigation of personality characteristics is unlikely to be undertaken *in vacuo*; assessments are invariably considered to have some relevance and usefulness outside the immediate measurement situation.

A technique such as factor analysis is useful in providing an empirical and rational framework for measurement in such situations as are met by the applied psychologist. An ideal strategy in such situations is the determination of the characteristics which are relevant, and the measurement of these characteristics with the most suitable techniques available.

Research, and common sense, indicate that there is a considerable degree of specificity in that different characteristics are involved in different situations, so that the need for accuracy necessitates a detailed assessment of each prediction situation in order to determine the important characteristics and their relative strength. Considering the many situations which usually confront an applied psychologist in his work, there are obviously limitations which would make the detailed analysis of every problem difficult or impossible. Yet the problem might not be as complex as is indicated at first glance, since each psychologist is usually faced with a finite number of recurrent prediction problems and some will be far commoner and more important than others. Attention might be directed at first to the commoner problems. An analysis of each situation would have as its aim the routinization of assessment within a framework of the relationship of each measure to the criterion. An example of the routinization of such a problem is provided by the work of Kendrick (1965). Though considerable work is involved in the initial investigation, there is a subsequent saving of time and effort.

The investigation of such recurrent problems does not necessitate the use of complex statistical analysis (e.g. Cattell, 1965). The application of simpler techniques such as the Bayesian approach (Maxwell, 1961) may be adequate when relevant characteristics have been identified. Progress in these directions may also be helped by further analysis of the environment (Bloom, 1965), so that the eventual model of prediction takes into account the interaction of a multidimensional person with a multidimensional situation.

This procedure is, at the moment, an aim rather than a reality. In spite of this, the rewards of successful prediction are potentially so valuable that the goal more than justifies the necessary effort.

REFERENCES

ADCOCK, C. J. (1965) A comparison of the concepts of Eysenck and Cattell. *Brit. J. Educ. Psychol.*, **35**, 90-97.

ALLPORT, G. W. (1949) *Personality: A Psychological Interpretation.* London: Constable.

ANASTASI, A. (1961) *Psychological Testing.* New York: Macmillan.

ANDERSON, L. D. (1939) The predictive value of infancy tests in relation to intelligence at five years. *Child Develop.*, **10**, 203-212.

ARNHOFF, F. N. (1954) Some factors influencing the unreliability of clinical judgement. *Journal of clin. Psychol.*, **10**, 272-275.

ASH, P. (1949) The reliability of psychiatric diagnosis. *J. abn. soc. Psychol.*, **44**, 272-276.

BALES, R. F. (1950) *Interaction Process Analysis.* Cambridge, Mass.: Addison-Wesley.

BANNISTER, D. (1962) Personal construct theory: A summary and experimental paradigm. *Acta Psychol.*, **20**, 104-120.

BARRY, J. R., BLYTH, D. D. and ALBRECHT, R., (1952) The relationships between Rorschach score and adjustment level. *J. consult. Psychol.*, **16**, 30-36.

BASS, B. M. (1951) Situational tests. ii. Variables of the leaderless group discussion. *Educ. psychol. Meas.*, **11**, 196-207.

BASS, B. M. and BERG, I. A. (1959) *Objective Approaches to Personality Assessment.* New Jersey: Van Nostrand.

BAUGHMAN, E. E. (1958) The role of the stimulus in Rorschach Responses. *Psychol. Bull.*, **55**, 121-147.

BAYLEY, N. (1949) Consistency and variability in the growth of intelligence from birth to 18 years. *J. genet. Psychol.*, **75**, 165-196.

BECKER, W. C. (1960) The matching of behaviour rating and questionnaire personality factors. *Psychol. Bull.*, **57**, 201-212.

BECKER, W. C. (1961) A comparison of the factor structure and other properties of the 16 P.F. and Guilford-Martin Personality Inventories. *Educ. psychol. Meas.*, **21**, 393-404.

BEECH, H. R. (1959) An experimental investigation of sexual symbolism in anorexia nervosa, employing a subliminal stimulation technique: preliminary report. *Psychosom. Med.*, **21**, 4, 277-280.

BENDIG, A. W. (1958) A comparison of the validity of two temperament scales in predicting academic achievement. *J. educ. Res.*, **51**, 605-609.

BENNETT, E. and SLATER, P. (1945) Some tests for the discrimination of neurotic from normal subjects. *Brit. J. med. Psychol.*, **20**, 271-282.

BENTON, A. L. (1953) The interpretation of questionnaire items in a personality schedule. *Arch. Psychol.*, No. 190, New York.

BERG, I. A. (Ed.) (1967) Response Set in Personality Assessment. Chicago: Aldine Publishing Co.

BERNADIN, A. C. and JESSOR, R. A. (1957) A construct validation of the E.P.P.S. with respect to dependency. *J. consult. Psychol.*, **21**, 63-67.

BERNREUTER, R. G. (1933) The theory and construction of the personality inventory. *J. social. Psychol.*, **4**, 387-405.

BERNSTEIN, L. (1956) The examiner as an inhibiting factor in clinical testing, *J. consult. Psychol.*, **20**, 287-290.

BLOOM, B. S. (1965) *Stability and change in Human Characteristics*. New York: Wiley.

BORDIN, E. S. (1943) A theory of vocational interests as dynamic phenomena. *Educ. psychol. Meas.*, **3**, 49-66.

BRADWAY, K. and HEISLER, V. (1953) The relation between diagnoses and certain types of estreme deviations and content in the Rorschach. *J. project. Tech.*, **17**, 70-74.

BROADHURST, P. (1960) Abnormal animal behaviour. *In* EYSENCK, H. J. (Ed.) *Handbook of Abnormal Psychology*. London: Pitman.

BRODY, E. B., NEWMAN, R. and REDLICH, F. C. (1951) Sound recordings and the problem of evidence in psychiatry. *Science*, **113**, 379-380.

BROWN, W. (1916) Individual and sex differences in suggestibility. *Univ. Calif. Publ. Psychol.*, **2**, No. 6.

BRUNER, J. S. (1960) *The Process of Education*. Cambridge, Mass.: Harvard Univ. Press.

BUCKNER, D. N. and MCGRATH, J. J. (1963) *Vigilance: a Symposium*. New York: McGraw-Hill.

BURKE, H. R. (1958) Raven's Progressive Matrices – a review and critical evaluation. *J. genet. Psychol.*, **93**, 199-228.

BURROUGHS, G. E. R. (1958) A study of the interview in the selection of students for teaching. *Brit. J. educ. Psychol.*, **28**, 37-46.

BURT, C. L. (1939) The factorial analysis of emotional traits. *Character and Personality*, **7**, 238.

BURT, C. (1940) *The Factors of the Mind*. University of London Press.

BURT, C. (1949) The structure of the mind: a review of the results of factor analysis. *Brit. J. educ. Psychol.*, **19**, 100-111, 176-199.

BURT, C. (1958) The inheritance of mental ability. *Amer. Psychol.*, **13**, 1-15.

BURTON, R. V. (1963) The generality of honesty reconsidered. *Psychol. Rev.*, **70**, 481-499.

CAMPBELL, D. T., HUNT, W. R. and LEWIS, N. A. (1957) The effects of assimilation and contrast in judgments of clinical material. *Amer. J. Psychol.*, **70**, 347.

CANNON, R. L. (1958) The stability of sociometric scores of high school students. *J. educ. Res.*, **52**, 43-48.

CANNON, W. B. (1920) *Bodily Changes in Pain, Hunger, Fear, and Rage*. New York: Appleton-Century-Crofts.

CARSON, R. C., HARDEN, J. A. and SHOWS, W. D. (1964) The A-B distinction and behaviour in a quasi therapeutic situation. *J. consult. Psychol.*, **28**, 426-433.

CATTELL, R. B. and STICE, G. (1949) *The Sixteen Personality Factor Questionnaire*. Champaign, Ill.: Inst. Personality and Ability Testing Manual, 1950.

CATTELL, R. B. (1950) *Personality*. New York: McGraw-Hill.

CATTELL, R. B. (1952) *Factor Analysis*. New York: Harper and Row.

CATTELL, R. B. (1956) *The objective Analytic Personality Factor Battery*. I.P.A.T., 1604, Coronado Drive, Champaign, Ill.

CATTELL, R. B. (1959) Foundations of personality measurement theory in multivariate experiment *in* BASS, B. M. and BERG, I. A. (Eds.) *Objective Approaches to Personality Assessment*. Princeton, New Jersey: van Nostrand.

CATTELL, R. B. (1963) Personality, role, mood and situation perception: a unifying theory of modulators. *Psychol. Rev.*, **70**, 1-18.

CATTELL, R. B. (1965) *The Scientific Analysis of Personality*. Penguin Books.

CATTELL, R. B., SEALY, A. P. and SWEENEY, A. B. (1967) What can Personality and motivation source trait measurements add to the prediction of school achievement? *Brit. J. educ. Psychol.*, **36**, 280-295.

CATTELL, R. B., STICE, G. F. and KRISTY, N. F. (1957) A first approximation to nature nurture ratios in 11 primary personality factors in objective tests. *J. abn. soc. Psychol.*, **54**, 143-159.

CATTELL, R. B. and SCHEIER, I. H. (1961) *The Meaning and Measurement of Neuroticism and Anxiety*. New York: The Ronald Press Co.

CHAPPLE, E. D. and DONALD, G. (1946) A method for evaluating supervisor personnel. *Harvard Bus. Review*, **24**, 197-214.

CHRISTIE, R. and LINDAUER, F. (1963) Personality Structure. *In Annual Rev. Psychol.*, 14. Palo Alto, California: Annual Reviews.

CLARK, D. F. (1963) Treatment of a monosymptomatic phobia by systematic desensitization. *Behav. Res. Ther.*, 1, 89-104.

COAN, R. W. (1964) Facts, factors and artifacts: the question for psychological meaning. *Psychol. Rev.*, 71, 123-140.

COHEN, A. R. (1959) Some implications of self esteem for social influence. *In* HOVLAND, C. I. and JANIS, I. L. (Eds.) *Personality and Persuasibility*. New Haven, Conn.: Yale Univ. Press.

COHEN, J. (1966) The impact of multivariate research in clinical psychology. *In* CATTELL, R. B. (Ed.) *Handbook of Multivariate Experimental Psychology*. Chicago: Rand Mcnally and Co.

COMREY, A. L. (1957) A number of papers on the analysis of some M.M.P.I. scales. *Educ. psychol. Meas.*, 17, 568-577, 578-585, 586-592.

COMREY, A. L. (1958) Reports of further analyses of M.M.P.I. scales. *Educ. psychol. Meas.*, 18, 91-98, 99-101, 293-300.

COOK, S. W. and SELLITZ, C. (1964) A multiple indicator approach to attitude measurement. *Psychol. Bull.*, 62, 36-55.

CORAH, M. L. *et al.* (1958) Social desirability as a variable in the E.P.P.S. *J. consult. Psychol.*, 22, 70-72.

COSTELLO, C. G. (1966) *Psychology for Psychiatrists*. Oxford: Pergamon.

CRONBACH, L. J. (1946) Response sets and test validity. *Educ. psychol. Meas.*, 6, 475-494.

CRONBACH, L. J. (1949) Statistical methods applied to Rorschach Scores – a review. *Psychol. Bull.*, 46, 393-429.

CRONBACH, L. J. (1950) Further evidence on response sets and test design. *Educ. psychol. Meas.*, 10, 3-31.

CRONBACH, L. J. and GLESER, G. C. (1957) *Psychological Testing and Personnel Decisions*. Urbana: University of Illinois Press.

CRONBACH, L. J. and MEEHL, P. E. (1955) Construct validity in psychological tests., *Psychol. Bull.*, 52, 281-302.

DITTES, J. E. (1957) Extinction during psychotherapy of G.S.R. accompanying 'embarrassing' statements. *J. abnorm. soc. Psychol.*, 54, 187-191.

DUDYCHA, G. J. (1936) An objective study of punctuality in relation to personality and achievement. *Arch. Psychol.*, No. 204.

EDWARDS, A. L. (1954) *The Edwards Personal Preference Schedule*. New York: Psychol. Corp.

EDWARDS, A. L. (1957) *The Social Desirability Variable in Personality Assessment and Research*. New York: Dryden.

EDWARDS, A. L. (1959) Social desirability and personality test construction. In BASS, B. M. and BERG, I. A. (Eds.) *Objective Approaches to Personality Assessment*. New York: Van Nostrand.

EDWARDS, A. L. (1967) Section of BERG I. A. (Ed.) *Response Set in Personality Assessment*. New York: Aldine Press.

EISENBERG, P. (1941) Individual interpretation of psychoneurotic inventory items. *J. gen. Psychol.*, **25**, 19-40.

ELLIS, A. (1946) The validity of personality questionnaires. *Psychol. Bull.*, **43**, 385-440.

ELLIS, A. and CONRAD, H. S. (1948) The validity of personality inventories in military practice. *Psychol. Bull.*, **45**, 385-426.

ELLIS, A. (1950) An introduction to the principles of scientific psychoanalysis. *Genet. Psychol. Mon.*, **41**, 174-212.

ENDLER, N. S., HUNT, J. MCV. and ROSENSTEIN, A. J. (1962) An S-R Inventory of anxiousness. *Psychol. Monographs*, **76**, 1-33.

EPPINGER, H. and HESS, L. (1910) *Die Vagotonie*. (Discussed in WENGER, M. A., *Psychosom. Med.*, 1941).

ERON, L. D. (1950) A normative study of the thematic apperception test. *Psychol. Mon.*, **64**, 1-48.

ESCALONA, S. and HEIDER, G. M. (1959) *Prediction and Outcome*. New York: Basic Books.

EYSENCK, H. J. (1947) *Dimensions of Personality*. London: Routledge and Kegan Paul.

EYSENCK, H. J. (1952) *The Scientific Study of Personality*. London: Routledge and Kegan Paul.

EYSENCK, H. J., BRENGELMANN, J. C. and GRANGER, G. W. (1957) *Perceptual Processes and Mental Illness*. London: Chapman and Hall.

EYSENCK, H. J. (1959) Personality Tests: 1950-55. In FLEMING, G. W. and WALK, A. (Eds.) *Recent Progress in Psychiatry*, Vol. III.

EYSENCK, H. J. and WHITE, P. O. (1964) Personality and the measurement of intelligence. *Brit. J. educ. Psychol.*, **34**, 2, 197-202.

EYSENCK, H. J. and RACHMAN, S. R. (1965) *The Causes and Cures of Neurosis*. London: Routledge and Kegan Paul.

EYSENCK, H. J. (1965) *The Structure of Human Personality*. London: Methuen and Co. Ltd.

EYSENCK, H. J. (1966) Personality and experimental psychology. *Bull. Brit. Psychol. Soc.*, **62**, 1-28.

EYSENCK, H. J. (1967) Intelligence assessment: A theoretical and experimental approach. *Brit. J. educ. Psychol.*, **37**, 99-110.

FARBER, I. E. and SPENCE, K. W. (1953) Complex learning and conditioning as a function of anxiety. *J. expt. Psychol.*, **45**, 120-125.

FARLEY, F. H. (1966) Individual differences in solution time in error free problem solving. *Brit. J. soc. clin. Psychol.*, **5**, 306-310.

FISHBEIN, M. (1966) The relationships between beliefs, attitudes and behaviour. In FELDMAN, S. (Ed.) *Cognitive Consistency*. New York and London: Academic Press. See also chapter by WEICK, K. E., on Task Acceptance Dilemma: A site for research on cognition, pp. 227-257.

FISKE, D. W. (1957) An intensive study of variability scores. *Educ. psychol. Meas.*, **17**, 453-465.

FISKE, D. W. (1957) The constraints in intra individual variability in test response. *Educ. psychol. Meas.*, **17**, 317-337.

FLANAGAN, J. C. (1935) *Factor Analysis in the Study of Personality*. Stanford, California: Stanford Univ. Press.

FLEISHMAN, E. A. and HEMPEL, W. E. (1954) Changes in the factor structure of a psychomotor task as a function of practice. *Psychometrika*, **19**, 239-252.

FOULDS, G. A. (1951) Temperamental differences in maze performance. I: Characteristic differences among psychoneurotics. *Brit. J. Psychol.*, **42**, 209-217.

FOULDS, G. A. (1952) Temp. differences in maze performance. II: The effect of distraction and electroconvulsive therapy on psychomotor retardation. *Brit. J. Psychol.*, **43**, 33-41.

FOULDS, G. A. (1965) *Personality and Personal Illness*. London: Tavistock.

FRANSELLA, F. and BANNISTER, D. (1967) A validation of Repertory Grid Technique as a measure of political construing. *Acta Psychol.*, **26**, 97-106.

FRENKEL-BRUNSWIK, E. (1942) Motivation and behaviour. *Genet. Psychol. Monogr.*, **26**, 121-265.

FURNEAUX, W. D. (1960) Intellectual abilities and problem-solving behaviour. *In* EYSENCK, H. J. (Ed.) *Handbook of Abnormal Psychology*. London: Pitman.

FURNEAUX, W. D. (1962) The psychologist and the university. *Univ. Quart.*, **17**, 33-47.

GESELL, A. *et al.* (1939) *Biographies of Child Development*. New York: Harper.

GETZELS, J. W. and WALSH, J. J. (1958) The method of paired direct and projective questionnaires in the study of attitude structure and socialization. *Psychol. Monogr.*, **72**, No. 454.

GHISELLI, E. E. (1960) The prediction of predictability. *Educ. Psychol. Meas.*, **20**, 1-8.

GHISELLI, E. E. (1963) Moderating effects and differential validity and reliability. *J. appl. Psychol.*, **47**, 81-86.

GIEDT, F. H. (1955) A comparison of visual content and auditory cues in interviewing. *J. consult. Psychol.*, **19**, 407-416.

GLESER, G. (1963) Projective methodologies. *Ann. Rev. Psychol.*, **14**. Palo Alto, California: Annual Reviews Inc.

GOLDMAN-EISLER, F. (1951) The measurement of time sequences in conversational behaviour. *Brit. J. Psychol.*, **42**, 355-362.

GOLDMAN-EISLER, F. (1952) Individual differences between interviewers and their effects on interviewees conversational behaviour. *J. ment. Sci.*, **98**, 660-671.

GOLDMAN-EISLER, F. (1954) A study of individual differences and of interaction in the behaviour of some aspects of languages in the interview. *J. ment. Sci.*, **100**, 177-197.

GREENSPOON, J. and THOMPSON, L. (1959) Generalization of a reinforced verbal response. Paper at Midwestern Psych. Assoc. Convention. Chicago, Ill.

GROSS, L. E. (1965) The effects of verbal and non-verbal reinforcement in the Rorschach. *J. consult. Psychol.*, **23**, 66-68.

GUILFORD, J. P. (1958) Psychological measurement. *In* SEWARD, G. S. and SEWARD, J. P. (Eds.) *Current Psychological Issues. Essays in honour of R. S. Woodworth*. New York: Holt.

GUILFORD, J. P. (1959) *Personality*. New York: McGraw Hill.

GUTHRIE, E. R. (1944) Personality in terms of associative learning. *In* HUNT, J. MCV., *Personality and Behaviour Disorders*. New York: Ronald Press.

HAIRE, M. and GRUNES, W. F. (1950) Perceptual defences: processes protecting an organized perception of another personality. *Hum. Rel.*, **3**, 403-412.

HALL, C. S. and LINDZEY, G. (1957) *Theories of Personality*: New York: Wiley.

HAMBURG, D. A., SABSHIN, M. and BOARD, F. A. *et al.* (1958) The classification and rating of emotional experience. *Arch. Neurol. Psych.*, **79**, 415.

HANNA, J. V. (1950) Estimating intelligence by interview. *Educ. psychol. Meas.*, **10**, 420-430.

HARTSHORNE, H. and MAY, M. A. (1928) *Studies in the Nature of Character; Studies in Deceit*, Vol. I. New York: Macmillan.

HARTSHORNE, H., MAY, M. A. and MALLER, J. B. (1929) *Studies in Service and Self Control*. New York: Macmillan.

HARTSHORNE, H. and SHUTTLEWORTH, F. K. (1930) *Studies in the Organization of Character*. New York: Macmillan.

HATHAWAY, S. R. and MCKINLEY, J. C. (1943) *The Minnesota Multiphasic Personality Inventory*. New York: The Psychological Corporation.

HATHAWAY, S. R. (1965) Personality inventories. *In* WOLMAN, B. B. (Ed.) *Handbook of Clinical Psychology*. New York: McGraw-Hill.

HENRY, E. M. and ROTTER, J. B. (1956) Situational influences on Rorschach responses. *J. consult. Psychol.*, **20**, 457-462.

HIMMELWEIT, H. T. (1945) The intelligence-vocabulary ratio as a measure of temperament. *J. Personality*, **14**, 93-105.

HIMMELWEIT, H. T. (1950) Student selection – an experimental investigation. *Brit. J. Sociol.*, **1**, 328.

HIMMELWEIT, H. T. and SUMMERFIELD, A. (1951) Student selection – an experimental investigation. *Brit. J. Sociol.*, **2**, 59-75.

HOLTZMAN, W. H. and SELLS, S. B. (1954) Prediction of flying success by clinical analysis of test protocols. *J. abn. soc. Psychol.*, **49**, 485-490.

HOLTZMAN, W. H. (1959) Objective scoring of projective techniques. *In* BASS M. and BERG, I. A. (Eds.) *Objective Approaches to Personality Assessment*. New Jersey: Van Nostrand.

HOVLAND, C. I. and JANIS, I. L. (Eds.) (1959) *Personality and Persuasibility* New Haven, Conn.: Yale Univ. Press.

HUMM, D. G. and WADSWORTH, G. W. (1935) The Humm-Wadsworth Scale. *Amer. J. Psychiat.*, **92**, 163-200.

HUNT, W. A. and FLANNERY, J. (1938) Variability in affective judgment. *Amer. J. Psychol.*, **51**, 507-513.

HUNT, W. A., HERRMANN, R. C. and NOBLE, H. (1957) The specificity of the psychiatric interview. *J. clin. Psychol.*, 13, 49-53.

HUNT, W. A. and JONES, W. F. (1962) Experimental investigation of Clinical judgment. *In* BACHRACH, A. J. (Ed.) *Experimental Foundations of Clinical Psychology.* New York: Basic Books.

HUSEN, T. (1959) *Psychological Twin Research.* Stockholm: Almquist and Wicksell.

JENKINS, R. L., STAUFFACHER, J. and HESTER, R. (1959) A symptom rating scale for use with psychotic patients. *Arch. gen. Psychiat.*, 1, 197.

JENSEN, A. R. (1959) The reliability of projective techniques: a review of the literature. *Acta Psychol.*, 16, 3-31.

JENSEN, A. R. (1964) The Rorschach technique: a re-evaluation. *Acta Psychol.*, 22, 60-77.

JONES, H. G. (1960) Learning and abnormal behaviour. *In* EYSENCK, H. J. (Ed.) *Handbook of Abnormal Psychology.* London: Pitman.

JOST, H. (1941) Some physiological changes during frustration. *Child Devel.*, 12, 9-15.

KAGAN, J. and MOSS, H. A. (1962) *Birth to Maturity. A Study in Psychological Development.* New York and London: John Wiley.

KAWI, A. A. and PASAMANICK, B. (1959) Prenatal and paranatal factors in the development of childhood reading disorders. *Monogr. Soc. Res. Child. Develop.*, 24, 14.

KELLEY, H. H. (1950) The warm-cold variable in first impressions of persons. *J. Personal.*, 18, 431-439.

KELLY, E. L. and FISKE, D. V. (1951) *Prediction of Performance in Clinical Psychology.* Ann Arbor: Michigan Univ. Press.

KELLY, G. A. (1955) *A Theory of Personality: The Psychology of Personal Constructs.* New York: W. W. Norton.

KELVIN, R. P., LUCAS, C. J. and OJHA, A. B. (1965) The relation between personality, mental health and academic performance in university students. *Brit. J. soc. clin. Psychol.*, 4, 244-253.

KEMP, D. E. (1964) Correlates of the Whitehorn-Betz A-B scale in an experimental therapeutic situation. Paper delivered to American Psychological Association, Los Angeles.

KENDRICK, D. C. (1965) Speed and learning in the diagnosis of diffuse brain damage in elderly subjects: a Bayesian statistical approach. *Brit. J. soc. clin. Psychol.*, 4, 141-148.

KENNY, D. T. and GINSBERG, R. (1958) The specificity of intolerance of ambiguity measures. *J. abn. soc. Psychol.*, 56, 300-304.

KING, G. F., ERHMANN, J. C. and JOHNSON, D. M. (1952) Experimental analysis of the reliability of observations of social behaviour. *J. soc. Psychol.*, 35, 151-160.

KNOBLOCH, H. and PASAMANICK, B. (1960) The developmental behavioural approach to the neurologic examination in infancy. *Child Develop.*, 33, 181-198.

KNOWLES, J. B. (1963) Rating methods and measurement of behaviour. *In* SAINSBURY, P. and KREITMAN, R. (Eds.) *Methods of Psychiatric Research.* London: Oxford Univ. Press.

KORNHAUSER, A. (1945) Replies to psychologists to a short questionnaire on mental test development, personality inventories, and the Rorschach Test. *Educ. psychol., Meas.,* 5, 3-15.

KREITMAN, N., SAINSBURY, P. *et al.* (1961) The reliability of psychiatric assessment: an analysis. *J. ment. Sci.,* 107, 450, 887-908.

LACEY, J. I. (1950) Individual differences in somatic response patterns. *J. comp. physiol. Psychol.,* 43, 338-350.

LACEY, J. I. and LEHN, R. V. (1952) Differential emphasis on somatic response to stress. *Psychosom. Med.,* 14, 71-78.

LACEY, J. I., BATEMAN, D. E. and LEHN, R. V. (1953) Autonomic Response Specificity: an experimental study. *Psychosom. Med.,* 15, 8-12.

LACEY, J. I. and LACEY, B. C. (1958) Verification and extension of the principle of autonomic response stereotypy. *Amer. J. Psychol.,* 71, 50-73.

LACEY, J. I. (1958) Psychological approaches to the evaluation of psycho-therapeutic process and outcome. *In* WASH, D. C., *Research in Psychotherapy.* Amer. Psychol. Assn. 205.

LACEY, J. I., KAGAN, J., LACEY, B. C. and MOSS H. A. (1962) The Visceral Level: situational determinants and behavioural correlates of autonomic response patterns. *In* KNAPP, P. (Ed.) *Expressions of the Emotions in Man.* New York: International University Press.

LANDIS, C. and KATZ, S. E. (1934) The validity of certain measures which purport to measure neurotic tendencies. *J. Appl. Psychol.,* 18, 343-356.

LANDIS, C. (1936) Questionnaires and the study of personality. *J. nerv. ment. Dis.,* 83, 125-134.

LAVIN, D. E. (1965) *The Prediction of Academic Performance: A Theoretical Analysis and Review of Research.* New York: Russell Sage Foundation.

LEIMAN, A. H. and EPSTEIN, S. (1961) Thematic sexual responses as related to sexual drive and guilt. *J. abn. soc. Psychol.,* 63, 169-175.

LEVONIAN, E. (1961) Personality measurement with items selected from the 16 P.F. Questionnaire. *Educ. psychol. Meas.,* 21, 937-946.

LEVONIAN, E. (1961) A statistical analysis of the 16 P.F. Questionnaire. *Educ. psychol. Meas.,* 21, 589-596.

LILIENFELD, A. M. and PASAMANICK, B. (1960) The association of maternal and foetal factors with the development of mental deficiency. *Amer. J. ment. Defic.,* 60, 557-569.

LINDZEY, G. (1959) On the classification of projective techniques. *Psychol. Bull.,* 56, 159-168.

LOEHLIN, J. C. (1961) Word meanings and self description. *J. abn. soc. Psychol.,* 62, 28-34.

LORR, M. (1965) A review of the 16 P.F. scale. *In* BUROS, OSCAR K. (Ed.) *Sixth Mental Measurements Yearbook.* New Jersey: The Gryphon Press.

LORR, M., KLETT, C. J. and MCNAIR, D. M. (1963) *Syndromes of Psychosis*. New York: Pergamon.

LUBORSKY, L. B. (1953) Intraindividual repetitive measurements in understanding therapeutic change. *In* MOWRER, O. H. (Ed.) *Psychotherapy: Theory and Research*. New York: Ronald Press.

LUBORSKY, L. B. (1954) Selecting psychiatric residents: survey of the Topeka Research. *Bull. Menn. Clinic*, 18, No. 6.

LUBORSKY, L. B. and STRUPP, H. H. (1962) Research problems in psychotherapy: a three year follow-up. *In* STRUPP and LUBORSKY (Eds.) *Research in Psychotherapy*, Vol. 2. Washington D.C.: Amer. Psychol. Assoc.

MACCOBY, E. and MACCOBY, N. (1954) The interview: a tool of Social Science. *In* LINDZEY, G. (Ed.) *Handbook of Social Psychology*. New York: Addison Wesley.

MCCOLLUM, I. N. and SAVARD, D. A. (1957) A simplified method of computing the effectiveness of tests in selection. *J. appl. Psychol.*, 41, 243-246.

MACFARLANE, J. W. and TUDDENHAM, R. D. (1951) Problems in the validation of projective techniques. *In* ANDERSON, H. and ANDERSON, G. L. (Eds.) *An Introduction to Projective Techniques*. New York: Prentice Hall.

MCGHIE, A. (1967) Psychological studies of schizophrenia. *Brit. J. med. Psychol.*, 39, 281-288.

MCKEACHIE, W. J. (1952) Lipstick as a determiner of first impressions of personality: an experiment for a general psychology course. *J. soc. Psychol.*, 36, 241-244.

MACKINNON, D. W. (1944) The structure of personality. *In* HUNT, J. MCV. (Ed.) *Personality and Behaviour Disorders*, Vol 1. New York: Ronald Press.

MCKINNON, K. M. (1942) Consistency and change in behaviour manifestations. *Child Develop.*, Monog. No. 30.

MALLER, J. B. (1934) General and specific factors in character. *J. soc. Psychol.*, 5, 97-101.

MALMO, R. R. (1962) Activation. *In* BACHRACH, A. (Ed.) *Experimental Foundations of Clinical Psychology*. New York: Basic Books.

MARTIN, I. (1960) Somatic reactivity. *In* EYSENCK, H. J. (Ed.) *Handbook of Abnormal Psychology*. London: Pitman.

MARTIRE, J. G. (1956) Relationships between the self concept and differences in the strength and generality of achievement motivation. *J. Personality*, 24, 364-375.

MASLING, J. (1960) The influence of situational and interpersonal variables in projective testing. *Psychol. Bull.*, 57, 65-85.

MAXWELL, A. E. (1961) *Analysing Qualitative Data*. London: Methuen.

MEEHL, P. E. (1954) *Clinical versus Statistical Prediction*. Minneapolis: Univ. of Minnesota Press.

MEEHL, P. E. (1960) The cognitive activity of the clinician. *Amer. Psychol.*, 15, 19-27.

MERRILL, R. M. and MURPHY, D. T. (1959) Personality factors and academic achievement in college. *J. Counsel. Psychol.*, **6**, 207-210.

MILLER, J. G. (1959) Future impact of psychological theory on personality assessments. *In* BASS, B., and BERG, I. A. (Eds.) *Objective Approaches to Personality Assessment*. New Jersey: Van Nostrand.

MITCHELL, J. V. (1963) A comparison of first and second order dimensions of the 16 P.F. and California personality inventories. *J. soc. Psychol.*, **61**, 151-166.

MOORE, N. (1965) Behaviour therapy in bronchial asthma. (A controlled study of some factors.) D.P.M. dissertation, Univ. of London.

MOOS, R. H. and CLEMES, S. R. (1967) The multivariate study of the patient-therapist system. *J. consult. Psychol.*, **31**, 119-130.

MOOS, R. H. and HOUTS, P. S. (1967) The assessment of social atmospheres in psychiatric wards. Paper to Western Psychological Assoc. Convention, San Francisco.

MORENO, J. (1934) *Who Shall Survive?* Washington: Nervous and Mental disease Publishing Co.

MURRAY, H. A. (1938) *Explorations in Personality*. New York: Oxford.

MURSTEIN, B. I. and PRYER, R. S. (1959) The concept of projection: a review. *Psychol. Bull.*, **56**, 353-374.

MURSTEIN, D. I. (1966) *The Handbook of Projective Techniques*. New York: Basic Books.

NEILSON, P. (1948) Shirley's babies after 15 years: a personality study. *J. Genet. Psychol.*, **73**, 175-186.

NEWCOMB, F. M. (1931) An experiment designed to test the validity of a rating technique. *J. educ. Psychol.*, **22**, 279-289.

NEWMAN, H. H., FREEMAN, F. N. and HOLZINGER, K. J. (1937) *Twins: a Study of Heredity and Environment*. Chicago: Univ. of Chicago Press.

O'CONNOR, N. and TIZARD, J. (1951) Predicting the occupational adequacy of certified mental defectives. *Occup. Psychol.*, **25**, 205-211.

O.S.S. Assessment Staff (1948) *Assessment of Men*. New York: Rinehart.

PAWLIK, K. and CATTELL, R. B. (1964) Third order factors in objective personality tests. *Brit. J. Psychol.*, **55**, 1-19.

PAYNE, A. (1963) *The selection and treatment of data for certain curriculum decision problems: a methodological study*. Unpublished Ph.D. dissertation, Univ. of Chicago.

PAYNE, R. W. (1955) Experimentelle Untersuchung zum Spaltungsbegrieff von Kretschmer. *Z exp. u. angew. Psychol.*, **3**, 65-97.

PAYNE, R. W. (1958) Diagnostic and personality testing in clinical psychology. *Amer. J. Psychiatry*, **115**, 25-29.

PAYNE, R. W. (1960) Cognitive abnormalities. *In* EYSENCK, H. J. (Ed.) *Handbook of Abnormal Psychology*. London: Pitman.

PECK, R. F. and HAVINGHURST, R. J. (1960) *The Psychology of Character Development*. New York: Wiley.

PETERSON, D. R. (1960) The age generality of personality factors derived from ratings. *Educ. psychol. Meas.*, **20**, 461-474.

POMEROY, S. and COGAN, W. S. (1955) The reliability of the Wittenborn scale for rating currently discernible psychiatric pathology. *J. clin. Psychol.*, **11**, 411.

PRINCE, M. (1924) *The Dissociation of a Personality*. London and New York: Longmans.

RABIN, A., NELSON, W. and CLARK, M. (1954) Rorschach content as a function of perceptual experience and sex of examiner. *J. clin. Psychol.*, **10**, 188-190.

RAUSH, H. L., DITTMAN, A. T. and TAYLOR, T. J. (1959) Person, setting and change in social interaction. *Hum. Rels.*, **12**, 361-378.

RICE, S. A. (1929) Contagious bias in the interview. *Amer. J. Sociol.*, **35**, 420-423.

RIEMAN, G. R. (1953) The effectiveness of Rorschach elements in the discrimination between neurotic and ambulatory schizophrenic subjects. *J. consult. Psychol.*, **17**, 25-31.

ROGERS, C. R. and DYMOND, R. F. (Ed.) (1954) *Psychotherapy and Personality Change*. Chicago: University of Chicago Press.

ROSENZWEIG, S. (1951) Idiodynamics in personality theory with special reference to projective methods. *Psychol. Review*, **58**, 213-223.

ROTTSCHAFER, R. N. and RENZAGLIA, G. A. (1962) The relation of dependent like behaviour to counselor style and induced set. *J. consult. Psychol.*, **26**, 172.

RUTTER, M. (1965) The influence of organic and emotional factors on the origins, nature and outcome of childhood psychosis. *Devel. Med. and Child Neurol.*, **7**, 518-528.

SAINSBURY, P. and GIBSON, J. G. (1954) The symptoms of anxiety and tension, and accompanying physiological changes in the muscular system. *J. Neurol. Neurosurg. Psychiat.*, **17**, 216-224.

SANDLER, J. (1959) *The effect of negative verbal cues on behaviour*. Unpublished Ph.D. thesis, Florida State Univ.

SARBIN, T. R. (1954) Role Theory. *In* LINDZEY, G. (Ed.) *Handbook of Social Psychology*, Vol. 1. Reading, Mass.: Addison-Wesley.

SARBIN, T. R., TAFT, R. and BAILEY, D. E. (1960) *Clinical Inference and Cognitive Theory*. New York: Holt, Rinehart and Winston.

SAVAGE, R. D. (Ed.) (1966) *Readings in Clinical Psychology*. Oxford: Pergamon.

SCHMIDT, E. and BROWN, P. (1965) The experimental testing of two psychoanalytic hypotheses. *Brit. J. med. Psychol.*, **38**, 177-180.

SCHMIDT, H. O. and FONDA, C. P. (1956) The reliability of psychiatric diagnosis: a new look. *J. abn. soc. Psychol.*, **52**, 262-267.

SCHNORE, M. M. (1959) Individual patterns of physiological activity as a function of task difference and degree of arousal. *J. expt. Psychol.*, **58**, 117-128.

SEARS, R. R. (1936) Experimental studies of projection. 1: Attribution of traits. *J. soc. Psychol.*, **7**, 151-163.

SEARS, R. R. (1951) A theoretical framework for personality and social behaviour. *Amer. Psychol.*, **6**, 476-483.

SELLS, R. B. (1966) Multivariate technology in industrial and military personnel psychology. *In* CATTELL, R. B. (Ed.) *Handbook of Multivariate experimental Psychology*. Chicago: Rand McNally.

SHAGASS, C. (1954) The sedation threshold. A method for estimating tension in psychiatric patients. *Electroenceph. and Clinical Neurophysiol.*, **6**, No. 2.

SHAGASS, C., MIHALIK, J. and JONES, A. L. (1957) Clinical psychiatric studies using the sedation threshold. *J. psychosom. Res.*, Vol. 2, 45-55.

SHAPIRO, M. B. (1957) Experimental method in the psychological description of the individual psychiatric patient. *Int. J. soc. Psychiat.*, **III**, 89-102.

SHAPIRO, M. B. (1961) The single case in fundamental clinical psychological research. *Brit. J. med. Psychol.*, **34**, 355-362.

SHAPIRO, M. B. (1962) A clinical approach to fundamental research with specific reference to the single case. *In* SAINSBURY, P. and KREITMAN, N. (Eds.) *Basic Research Techniques in Psychiatry*. London: Oxford Univ. Press.

SHAPIRO, M. B. (1963) *Notes on Introductory Lectures on Clinical Method*. (Unpublished.) Copyright, Institute of Psychiatry, London.

SHAPIRO, M. B. (1966) The generality of psychological processes and specificity of outcomes. *Percept. motor Skills*, **23**, 16.

SHAPIRO, M. B. (1967a) Clinical psychology as an applied science. *Brit. J. Psychiat.*, **113**, 1039-1042.

SHAPIRO, M. B. (1967b) The psychology of pleasantness and unpleasantness *Bull. British Psychol. Society*, April.

SHEERER, E. T. (1949) An analysis of relationships between acceptance of and respect for self and acceptance of and respect for others in 10 counselling cases. *J. consult. Psychol.*, **13**, 169-175.

SHERMAN, M. and JOST, H. (1942) Frustration reactions of normal and neurotic persons. *J. Psychol.*, **13**, 3-19.

SHIELDS, J. (1962) *Monozygotic Twins brought up apart and brought up together. An Investigation of the Genetic and Environmental Causes of Variation in Personality*. London: Oxford Univ. Press.

SHOTWELL, A. M., HURLY, J. R. and CATTELL, R. B. (1961) The motivational structure of a hospitalized mental defective. *J. abn. soc. Psychol.*, **62**, 422-426.

SKINNER, B. F. (1950) Are theories of learning necessary? *Psychol. Review*, **57**, 193-216.

SLETTO, R. F. (1936) A critical study of the criterion of internal consistency in personality scale construction. *Amer. Sociol. Rev.*, **1**, 61-68.

SMITH, D. E. P. and RAYGOR, A. L. (1956) Verbal satiation and personality. *J. abn. soc. Psychol.*, **52**, 323-326.

SMITH, R. B. (1932) Development of an inventory for the measurement of inferiority feelings at the high school level. *Arch. Psychol.*, **22**, No. 144.

SONTAG, L. W., BAKER, C. T. and NELSON, V. L. (1958) Mental growth and personality development: a longitudinal study. *Mon. Soc. Res., Child Develop.*, **23**, No. 68, 1-143.

SOSKIN, W. and JOHN, V. (1963) The stream of spontaneous talk. *In* BARKER, R. (Ed.) *The Stream of Behaviour*. New York: Appleton-Century-Crofts.

SPRIEGEL, W. R. and JAMES, V. A. (1958) Trends in recruitment and selection practices. *Personnel*, **35**, 42-48.

STERN, G. G., STEIN, M. I. and BLOOM, B. S. (1956) *Methods in Personality Assessment*. Glencoe, Illinois: Free Press.

STERNBACH, R. A. (1960) Some relationships amongst various 'Dimensions' of autonomic activity. *Psychosom. Med.*, **22**, 430-434.

STOCK, D. (1949) An investigation into the interrelations between the self concept and feelings directed towards other persons. *J. consult. Psychol.*, **13**, 176-180.

STUIT, D. B. (1947) *Personnel Research and Test Development in the Bureau of Naval Research*. Princeton: Princeton Univ. Press.

SUINN, R. M. (1961) The relationship between self-acceptance and acceptance of others: a learning theory analysis. *J. abn. soc. Psychol.*, **63**, 37-42.

TAYLOR, H. G. and RUSSELL, J. T. (1939) The relationship of validity co-efficients to the practical effectiveness of tests in selection. *J. appl. Psychol.*, **23**, 569-578.

TERMAN, L. M. and ODEN M. H. (1959) *Genetic Studies of Genius: the Gifted Group at Mid Life*. Stanford: Stanford Univ. Press.

THISTLEWAITE, L. (1959) College Press and Student Achievement. *J. educ. Psychol.*, **50**, 183-191.

THOMAS, A., BIRCH, H. G. and CHESS, S. (1964) *Behavioural Individuality in Early Childhood*. London: University of London Press.

THORNDIKE, R. L. and WOODWORTH, R. S. (1901) The influence of improvement in one mental function upon the efficiency of other functions. *Psychol. Rev.*, **8**, 247-261.

THORNDIKE, R. L. (1950) Individual differences. *Ann. Rev. Psychol.*, **1**, 87-104.

THURSTONE, L. L. (1931) Multiple Factor Analysis. *Psychol. Rev.*, **38**, 406-427.

THURSTONE, L. L. (1955) *The Differential Growth of Mental Abilities*. Chapel Hill, N. Carolina: Univ. of Carolina Psychometric Laboratory, No. 14.

TIFFIN, J. and MCCORMICK, E. J. (1966) *Industrial Psychology*, Third Edition. London: Allen and Unwin.

TIFFIN, J. and VINCENT, N. L. (1960) Comparison of empirical and theoretical expectancies. *Personnel Psychol.*, **13**, 59-64.

TOZER, A. H. D. and LARWOOD, H. J. C. (1958) The changes in intelligence test scores of students between the beginning and end of their university courses. *Brit. J. educ. Psychol.*, **28**, 120-128.

ULRICH, L. and TRUMBO, D. (1965) The selection interview since 1949. *Psychol. Bull.*, **63**, 100-116.

VENABLES, P. H. (1967) Psychophysiological aspects of schizophrenia. *Brit. J. med. Psychol.*, **39**, 289-297.

VERNON, P. E. (1938) The assessment of psychological qualities by verbal methods. *Industrial Health Res. Bd. Rep.*, *No.* 83. London: H.M.S.O.

VERNON, P. E. and PARRY, J. B. (1949) *Personnel Selection in the British Forces.* London: Univ. of London Press.

VERNON, P. E. (1953) *Personality Tests and Assessments.* London: Methuen.

VERNON, P. E. (1964a) *The Structure of Human Abilities.* London: Methuen.

VERNON, P. E. (1964b) *Personality Assessment: A Critical Survey.* London: Methuen.

WALLACE, S. R. JNR., and WEITZ, J. (1955) Industrial psychology. *Ann. Rev. of Psychol.*, **6**, Palo Alto, California. Ann. Reviews.

WALSTER, E. (1963) *Post decisional re-evaluation of alternatives: regret and dissonance reduction.* Unpublished Ph.D., Stanford Univ.

WATSON, J. B. (1930) *Behaviourism.* London: Kegan Paul.

WENGER, M. A. (1941) The measurement of individual differences in autonomic balance. *Psychosom. Med.*, **3**, 427-434.

WENGER, M. A. (1948) Studies of autonomic balance in Army Air Forces Personnel. *Comp. Psychol. Mon.*, **19**, I-III.

WENGER, M. A., ENGEL, B. T. and CLEMENS, T. L. (1957) Studies of autonomic response patterns: rationale and methods. *Behavioural Science*, 2, No. 3.

WENGER, M. A., CLEMENS, T. L., COLEMAN, D. R. CULLEN, T. D. and ENGEL, B. T. (1961) Autonomic response specificity. *Psychosom. Med.*, **23**, No. 3, 185-193.

WEPMAN, J. M. and HEINE, R. W. (1964) *Concepts of Personality.* London: Methuen.

WILLETT, R. (1960) The effects of psychosurgical procedures on behaviour. *In* EYSENCK, H. J. (Ed.) *Handbook of Abnormal Psychology.* London: Pitman.

WING, J. K. (1966) The measurement of psychiatric diagnosis. *Proc. Royal Soc. Med.*, **59**, 1030-1032.

WING, J. K. *et al.* (1967) The reliability of a procedure for measuring and classifying present psychiatric state. *Brit. J. Psychiat.*, **113**, 499-515.

WITKIN, H. A. *et al.* (1962) *Psychological Differentiation: Studies of Development.* New York: Wiley.

ZUBIN, J., ERON, L. D. and SCHUMER, F. (1965) *An Experimental Approach to Projective Techniques.* New York: Wiley.

4

Vocational Guidance

Phillida Salmon

I INTRODUCTION

It would probably be difficult to exaggerate the psychological importance of work. Work absorbs the greater part of our waking hours, it provides the wherewithal for living, and it brings us into contact with activities, ideas, organizations and people having a reference far beyond our immediate personal lives. Perhaps most important of all, it carries a widely recognized social identity. Because of this, work needs to be integrated with other crucial aspects of a person's life, which also contribute to his identity. For instance, instead of enriching one's sense of self, a job which is beyond one's capacities will be a continuous source of threat; one which is well below them will fall short of its potential significance. Again, work which is greatly above or beneath one's own aspirations cannot provide the same degree of fulfilment as work which is more in line with one's hopes and ambitions. With regard to the more subtle factors of the personal work setting, workmates who are felt to be broadly similar to oneself can reinforce one's sense of identity in work, while the experience of working among people who seem alien to oneself is liable to produce a sense that the job is somehow at odds with one's life.

For psychiatric patients, work all too often holds problems. Sometimes the problem is the most basic one of all – the lack of any kind of job. Much more frequently, however, the patient does have a job, but in some major way it seems ill suited to him. Why should this be so? In a few cases, certainly, a difficult work situation seems to have triggered off, or even caused, the psychiatric breakdown; but in the vast majority of cases, the patient's illness does not seem to be connected with his work. Yet people with neurotic or acute psychotic illnesses are very often maladjusted at work.* It can, of course, be argued that in so far as psychiatrically ill people have failed to come to terms with themselves and those around them, this failure is as likely to show up in the work situation as in any other context. If this is so, the vocational problem is merely one aspect of a more general problem, and can be expected to clear up when the patient has recovered from his psychiatric illness. This argument does not, however, accord well with clinical experience. Even after successful treatment a specific vocational problem still remains for many neurotic and psychotic patients. If the patient has no

---

* This chapter is concerned only with relatively short-term psychiatric cases; the problems of chronic psychiatric patients are dealt with elsewhere in this book (Orme, Chapter 8).

job to go to it is apparently because he has never found the right job; if he currently has a job, then again it seems to be the wrong job for him. Such patients seem simply to have made the wrong vocational choices.

Choosing the right occupation is not an easy task for anyone; but there are a number of reasons why an individual with serious personal problems should be particularly liable to fail. From the vocational point of view, educational factors such as formal qualifications, areas of specialization and length of schooling are highly relevant, since they rule out some choices while facilitating others. The problems of many adult psychiatric patients date back to childhood, and in practice this often means that they have suffered breaks in schooling, or have failed, because of poor adjustment to school, to achieve educational qualifications consonant with their abilities. This is likely to impose severe limits on their freedom of occupational choice, and in particular to condemn them to jobs well below their true capacity. A different reason for inappropriate occupational choices lies in the fact that many jobs which can ultimately offer a high level of personal fulfilment demand, in the short term, a greater capacity to tolerate frustration than people already under stress can achieve. For the individual who badly needs currently satisfying experience, and is unable to 'defer gratification', jobs which involve the long hard grind of a five-year apprenticeship, for instance, are unlikely to prove suitable.

In many cases, choosing the wrong occupation seems to derive from an excessively high, or excessively low, level of aspiration. A person who finds himself continually blocked or frustrated in his personal and family life is likely to look to his work to provide an outlet for all his unsatisfied hopes and aspirations. His need to find maximum fulfilment occupationally may lead him to select jobs which offer high social prestige or personal autonomy, but which demand far greater intellectual attainment or better personality integration than he possesses, or is likely to achieve. Conversely, while some people choose jobs to compensate them for personal failures, others have so strong a sense of failure that this dominates their occupational choices. Many neurotic choices of job seem to have derived from an unduly passive and timid outlook, which represents 'the fear of failure' rather than 'the hope of success'. This is likely to result in the selection of a job well below the individual's capacity, offering little in the way of personal fulfilment. The sense of failure underlying such choices may itself have been heavily reinforced by a past experience of failure in a particular work setting. Although most people are able to take this almost inevitable experience in their stride, and even use it to gain insight into particular job demands in relation to their own needs and capacities, the experience is likely to undermine more vulnerable individuals, leaving them with a crippling sense of personal inadequacy.

Psychiatric patients are, therefore, very likely to have occupational problems, and vocational guidance is frequently needed. In the psychiatric hospital, although other hospital departments and external agencies are involved in the problem, the main responsibility for vocational guidance is the psychologist's, and for both in-patients and out-patients it is to him that the problem is initially referred by the psychiatrist. First of all, therefore, the psychologist needs some way of categorizing its various aspects. Several classification schemes exist, all serving to analyse the patient's occupational needs and potentialities and the relevant occupational fields into their components, for the purpose of assessing and co-ordinating necessary information.

II VOCATIONAL CATEGORIZATION SCHEMES

All vocational categorization systems consist basically of two major categories – information about people, and information about jobs. There are usually, however, several sub-categories of the first of these – information about people. No attempt can be made here to provide an exhaustive account of existing classification schemes; but two such schemes may be mentioned as examples.

1 The Vernon-Parry Scheme

This is the initial classifying procedure which was used by Vernon and Parry (1949) in the guidance and selection of British Forces personnel for education and industry. This procedure consisted of the following five stages:

1. The provision of essential information about possible jobs to the candidate.
2. The collection of relevant biographical data about him from records and inquiries.
3. The consideration of sociological factors in his situation.
4. The measurement of his aptitudes and abilities by means of standardized tests.
5. The assessment of his personal qualities by interview.

2 The Rodger Seven-Point Plan

In contrast with this scheme, Rodger (1951) provided a classifying system which is more orientated to guidance than to placement, and which consequently focuses in rather greater detail on the characteristics of the person. The points in his Seven-Point Plan are the following:

1. The physical and medical requirements of the job.
2. The educational qualifications of the subject.
3. His general intelligence level.
4. His special aptitudes.
5. His interests.
6. His disposition or temperamental qualities.
7. His other relevant circumstances (e.g. financial).

It will be seen that Rodger's scheme fills out the details of several areas included by Vernon and Parry.

3 Proposed scheme for psychiatric patients

No new classification scheme appears to have supplanted the general approach underlying both these systems, and many existing procedures are based on Rodger's Seven-Point Plan. Nevertheless, for vocational guidance of psychiatric patients, such schemes as these can be argued to take too little account of specifically motivational factors. For many people, and particularly for those with psychiatric problems, a job may prove impossible, though the work itself is congenial, because of purely personal factors in the work setting. The fact that the job entails being one of a group, or demands quick decisions, or requires a varying pace of work – these and numerous other subtle factors, which go beyond the broad categories of 'interest', can make or mar the success of many individuals in their jobs.

A classification system which takes account of these subtle motivational factors, but which is sufficiently economical to suit the limited time normally available to psychologists in a psychiatric setting, seems essentially to require four major areas of investigation. These are:

1. The patient's capacities and skills.
2. His specifically vocational interests.
3. His needs for particular kinds of work settings.
4. The relevant kinds of job opening.

III VOCATIONAL ASSESSMENT

Preliminary investigation

A preliminary investigation normally needs to be made before these four areas can be assessed. This concerns the question whether the vocational problem is a genuine one. Despite the frequency of real vocational difficulties among psychiatric patients, there are occasionally cases where the patient seems occupationally well adjusted, but where, in his general dissatisfaction, he has fixed upon his work as the focus of his problem. Similarly, in cases where the patient's difficulties are unclear, or do not point to any obvious line of help, the psychiatrist himself may focus on any current job difficulty as being primary, since this has the apparent advantage of resolving the uncertainty into a practical problem, for which facilities for help are available.

When this situation occurs, vocational difficulties have become a kind of substitute symptom. Even so, guidance may be helpful. If the patient sees his problems in occupational terms, discussion with him of his vocational assets and difficulties may lead to insights which will help him with problems in other areas. As in the case of a young psychotic out-patient referred for both personal and vocational assessment, job discussion may be the only way of reaching him. This man, who had many paranoid delusions, was extremely disturbed but quite lacking in insight; he persistently refused all help except vocational advice. Psychotherapy, given in the guise of occupational discussion, eventually proved very successful. Nevertheless, the approach to a person who has specific work problems is clearly different from that suitable for a person whose apparent job difficulties are simply an overspill from other problems, and who may in reality be perfectly well adjusted to his current work.

For these reasons, specifically vocational testing should be preceded by a more general investigation. A perusal of the patient's case notes, and a full discussion with the referring psychiatrist and with the patient himself – usually supplemented by personality testing – will establish the context within which vocational assessment should proceed.

1   Assessment of vocational capacities

In the categorization scheme suggested here, the first area to be assessed is that of the patient's capacities and skills. This can usefully begin with an interview inquiry, to obtain some relevant biographical information, since educational history and jobs filled constitute fairly good operational criteria of capacity. In addition, facts about the patient's financial position and family responsibilities – relevant to his eligibility for educational and training schemes – can be obtained. This method of beginning provides an informal, natural introduction to the investigation.

(a) *Intelligence Testing*

For most purposes, in addition to aptitude indices, it is useful to obtain an independent measure of the patient's intelligence. Minimum levels of intelligence have been established for certain specific levels of educational attainment and job success. For example, following such studies as that done by Schonell *et al.* (1962), an I.Q. of 115 or above can probably be assumed to be necessary for university entrance, except in exceptional circumstances. Similarly, a study by Ungar and Burr (1931) has indicated minimum mental ages required for holding down a number of semi-skilled and unskilled jobs. Ghiselli and Brown (1948), in their review of 185 studies concerned with the validity of intelligence tests in the selection of workers, found a high variation in the validity coefficients obtained, but concluded that, for certain occupational levels, such tests were probably useful in selection. Whereas their validity tended to be low for semi-skilled and unskilled levels of work, it was high in the case of clerical workers, and moderately so for skilled workers, supervisors and salesmen. Patchy though such predictive studies have been across the whole occupational range, they are probably sufficiently numerous to justify the measurement of intelligence.

In addition, specific features of the patient's response to an intelligence test may suggest special abilities or disabilities to be investigated further by aptitude testing. A very large Verbal/Performance discrepancy on the W.A.I.S., for example, a relatively poor Block Design score, or a much higher score on the Synonyms than the Definitions test of the Mill Hill Vocabulary Scale – all these would suggest differential levels, which, whether due to interest, educational, or organic factors, would need to be assessed, for their vocational significance, by means of aptitude testing. Such findings on their own, however, should not be used as the basis for vocational decisions. For instance, it would certainly be wrong to draw conclusions about vocational abilities or disabilities from a patient's profile on the W.A.I.S., since subtest score differences have not been measured against occupational criteria.

(b) *Aptitude Testing*
Vocational guidance, unlike vocational selection, is essentially an open-ended process concerned with many occupational possibilities, rather than with one job whose characteristics are already known. This means that, in testing aptitudes, standard batteries referring to a wide range of jobs are more appropriate than either factorially pure single aptitude measures or custom-built tests relating to one particular occupation. Aptitude batteries provide information about a number of vocationally significant aptitudes, in the form of a profile of aptitude scores; this shows the subject's abilities and disabilities for different occupational areas. Of such batteries, the two most widely used, and probably the best, are the U.S.E.S. General Aptitude Test Battery, and the Differential Aptitude Tests developed by the Psychological Corporation.

   (i) *General Aptitude Test Battery*. The G.A.T.B., which takes about two and a quarter hours to administer in full (and is normally given over at least two sessions), involves twelve tests, eight of which are paper-and-pencil tests, the remaining four involving simple apparatus. From these tests, the following nine aptitude measures are derived:
   General Intelligence (G)
   Verbal Aptitude (V)
   Numerical Aptitude (N)
   Spatial Aptitude (S)
   Form Perception (P)
   Clerical Perception (Q)
   Motor Co-ordination (K)
   Manual Dexterity (M)
   Finger Dexterity (F)

All the tests are preceded by practice items, to familiarize the subject with the requirements. They consist essentially of a large number of relatively simple tasks, done under conditions of speed. Raw scores are translated into standard scores having a mean of 100 and a standard deviation of 20. The scores thus obtained can then be compared with those of the relevant Occupational Ability Patterns, indicating minimal levels for a number of occupations. The battery is designed for use with unselected populations aged sixteen and upwards. Clinical experience confirms that it is suitable for patients of well below average intelligence, although certain minimum literacy standards are required, and, in practice, an I.Q. of 80 probably represents the lower limit of intelligence needed.

   (ii) *Differential Aptitude Tests*. The D.A.T. involves a rather longer administration time than the G.A.T.B. – a little over three hours. The manual does, however, suggest that the full battery should be broken into sections rather than being given at a single session. Whereas the G.A.T.B. entails twelve subtests, yielding nine measures, the D.A.T. consists of eight subtests, each yielding its own aptitude measure. Of these eight, five are comparable with the G.A.T.B. aptitudes: Verbal Reasoning (G.A.T.B. V), Numerical Abilities (G.A.T.B. N), Space Relations (G.A.T.B. S), Abstract Reasoning (G.A.T.B. G), and Clerical Speed and Accuracy (G.A.T.B. Q). The remaining three D.A.T. aptitudes – Mechanical Reasoning, Language Usage (Spelling), and Language Usage (Sentences) – cannot be directly translated into those of the G.A.T.B. Super and Crites (1965) suggest that these three measures are composite rather than pure, Mechanical Reasoning involving experience as well as aptitude, and the Language Usage measures entailing achievement. Four of the G.A.T.B. measures – P, K, M and F – are not represented in the D.A.T. battery.

Unlike the G.A.T.B., the D.A.T. does not require apparatus, but consists entirely of pencil and-paper tests. Its general layout is broadly comparable, practice items preceding each test; but the tasks themselves probably seem rather more occupationally relevant to the subject, and less purely academic – this is particularly the case with Mechanical Reasoning. There is also, of course, considerably less emphasis on speed, since the subtests on the whole are much longer than those in the G.A.T.B. Raw scores are translated into percentile scores according to sex, and high school grade; it is therefore necessary, in testing British adults, to make a rough approximation to high school grade in terms of the number of years of schooling completed. The manual provides educational and occupational norms for the various percentile levels on the eight aptitude measures.

In general, the G.A.T.B. is probably preferable, for vocational guidance, to the D.A.T. Its standardization is based on strictly occupational criteria, such as output record, supervisors' ratings, and in some cases training performance; whereas that of the D.A.T. rests mainly on educational achievement criteria, such as school grades. This important difference certainly operates in favour of the G.A.T.B., as far as the occupational relevance of the two batteries is concerned. In addition, the G.A.T.B. norms include a much wider range of skilled and semi-skilled occupations than those of the D.A.T. On the other hand, for psychiatric patients the heavy emphasis on speed of the G.A.T.B. can be a serious disadvantage. It is difficult to avoid a sense of pressure and stress in giving the test, and this may so disorganize the performance of an already anxious patient that it does not represent a true measure of his ability. The argument that performing under time stress is an essential aspect of work capacity does not seem to accord with the fact that most jobs are unpaced. Another advantage of the D.A.T. over the G.A.T.B., from the point of view of testing psychiatric patients, is the fact that its general content seems less obviously academic. Many a person with psychiatric problems has a history of failure at school, and this is only too likely to produce a sense of hopeless inadequacy when he is once again confronted with the kind of educational task at which he failed so miserably as a child.

Both batteries do, unfortunately, have certain obvious limitations in use with British subjects, in that their standardizing populations were American. While their test norms *may* be equally applicable here, experience strongly suggests that, for instance, those of the G.A.T.B. M and F measures are too high. Secondly, caution needs to be exercised in translating the occupations named into British terms, as, for example, in the case of 'psychiatric attendant', where the same label represents rather different occupations in the two countries. Problems such as these will remain until aptitude batteries have been standardized on British populations.

In a few cases, tests of attainment also need to be given, as, for example, the Schonell tests of reading, spelling and arithmetic. These are particularly relevant for people of low educational attainment, and those who have special educational disabilities, especially when some form of remedial teaching is available for them.

2 Assessment of vocational interests

A knowledge of an individual's vocationally relevant interests is just as vital to counselling as is information about his vocational aptitudes. The intrinsic interest which a particular occupation holds for a particular person normally provides a large part of his motivation for selecting it, and once in the job, largely sustains his involvement in it, and contributes to his occupational satisfaction. Though interest frequently coincides with aptitude, this is by no means necessarily so, and it often fails to do so in the case of maladjusted people. Nor are people always aware of their own vocational interests. Particularly where an individual is inexperienced or relatively lacking in ability, his own directly expressed preferences are likely to be misleading, in so far as they may be only slightly correlated with *measures* of his interest which themselves have good predictive validity (Strong, 1955). It is therefore necessary, in most cases, to obtain an independent index of vocational interests.

Vocational interest testing is not, however, equally appropriate at every occupational level. Although intrinsic interest factors have been found to be closely related to both job choice and job satisfaction for the upper half of the occupational ladder – professional, managerial, business, and skilled occupations – they are evidently less important in making or marring vocational adjustment over the lower occupational range. In semi-skilled and labouring work, strictly vocational interest seems to be replaced, as a determining factor, by practical and financial aspects of the job and by considerations of personal standing (Centers, 1948). This difference has been built into existing measures of vocational interest, in that these are designed for the upper occupational range, and are therefore not suitable for subjects at the semi-skilled or unskilled occupational levels.

As with aptitude tests, measures of vocational interests have been devised according to two rather different principles – empirical differentiation of occupational groups, on the one hand, and measurement of relatively pure interest factors on the other. The Strong Vocational Interest Blank represents the first type of approach. Like the G.A.T.B., it was constructed by testing differences in interests between criterion groups of people successfully engaged in various occupations. Such group differences were then incorporated into keys for each occupation tested, by means of which a subject can be compared for the degree of similarity between his own interests and those of each occupational group. In contrast with this method of test construction, the Kuder Preference Record (Vocational) was derived from an *a priori* system of structuring vocationally relevant interests. This test, which was intended to assess relative strength in certain broad categories of interests, was based, not on tested occupational differences, but on purely internal content considerations of consistency, reliability and independence of scales. Where the Strong V.I.B. yields a number of comparisons between the subject and different occupational groups, the Kuder-Vocational provides a profile of scores, representing a within-individual comparison of relative degrees of interest in different vocationally relevant areas. These two tests have been studied more extensively than any of the other measures of vocational interest, and they are probably also the most widely used, although, like aptitude batteries, they have not been standardized for British conditions.

(1) *Strong Vocational Interest Blank.* The Strong V.I.B. is suitable for subjects of about 17 and upwards, but requires a well above average level of intelligence and education, because of a somewhat difficult vocabulary. It consists of 400 items, concerned with directly occupational activities, and also with questions such as leisure interests, school subjects and personal characteristics. To most of the items, the subject records a Like, Indifferent to, or Dislike response; to the remainder, his responses are in the form of ranking preferences, comparing of items, and rating certain of his own abilities. The test, which is entirely self-administered, normally takes approximately one hour to complete. Full scoring entails applying over 40 different keys to the record of a male subject, and over 20 to that of a female subject; since a single key requires about 15 minutes to apply by hand, machine scoring is essential. The subject's scores on each key are converted, via a standard score for one of two reference groups, into letter ratings, in order to facilitate quick interpretation. Since it is difficult to grasp the implications of a large number of separate ratings, Strong has provided a categorization of the occupations tested, in terms of factorially similar groups. Alternatively, a scheme devised by Darley (1941) enables the scores to be analysed into predominant interest patterns.

The greatest asset of the Strong V.I.B., as compared with other measures of vocational interest, is probably its large number of extensively validated occupational norms. The interests which it measures have been found to be highly stable, and to have moderate or good predictive validity, both for occupational choices, and for job satisfaction (Super and Crites, 1965). Additionally, because

F*

the test is based on empirical measurement of occupational group differences, it succeeds in turning to advantage two features which frequently undermine the validity of inventory-type measures – relative unfamiliarity with certain test items, and response bias on the part of the subject. Many occupational groups tested were found to differ in either or both of these features, and this difference has accordingly been built into the norms.

For vocational guidance in a psychiatric setting, the Strong V.I.B. has, however, certain drawbacks. Its requirements of a relatively high intellectual and educational level preclude its being given to certain patients who, though not quite up to its demands, do nevertheless come within the skilled occupational range, and are therefore in the category of those for whom vocational interest testing is relevant. Secondly, the test has comparatively little differentiating capacity among the occupationally significant interests of girl and women subjects. This is not merely because there are fewer female than male occupational norms as yet available in the test; it is also a function of the lack of independence between the different scales for women (Crissy and Daniel, 1939). Finally, the necessity for machine scoring, though possibly more easily arranged in the American clinical setting, is likely to involve many practical difficulties in this country, and probably represents the main reason why the test is not more widely used here.

(ii) *Kuder Preference Record (Vocational)*. The Kuder-Vocational test, which was designed for American high school students, as well as college students and adults, can be used with subjects of a rather lower intelligence and educational level than the Strong V.I.B. – an average level probably being the minimum. Slightly younger subjects can also be tested with it, although this is not normally desirable, since interests fluctuate a great deal during adolescence. The test is less varied in its format than the Strong, consisting simply of a series of 168 triads of items, each describing a possible activity. The subject is required to record, for each triad, his first ('like most') and last ('like least') choices. Responses are recorded by punching holes through a series of circles on the answer pad. The complete task normally requires about three quarters of an hour. In marked contrast with that of the Strong, the scoring system for the Kuder-Vocational is extremely quick, consisting of a simple count of punched holes appearing within eleven chains of circles on the backs of successive pages of the answer pad. Each count represents the subject's score on one of eleven scales, of which the first is a Verification Scale – a check on carelessness in recording responses or a highly atypical set of responses – and the remaining ten are measures of different types of interest: outdoor, mechanical, computational, scientific, persuasive, artistic, literary, musical, social service and clerical. Providing that the subject's Verification score is within the limits given in the manual, his scores on the ten interest scales are converted into percentile scores, according to separate norms for sex and two age groups. In many cases, the whole sequence of test-taking, obtaining raw scores, and entering these on the Profile Sheet can be left to the subject himself, after initial instructions.

The most obvious advantage of the Kuder-Vocational over the Strong V.I.B. lies in the ease and rapidity of its scoring system. This not only avoids the practical difficulties of special apparatus, computer programming arrangements and expenses; it also adds considerably to the meaningfulness of the test to many subjects, who experience much greater interest and involvement in the situation through being responsible for carrying the measurement process through to its final stages. In a psychiatric setting, this feature of the test is probably particularly important, since patients often have unduly passive attitudes towards their own performance. A further advantage of this measure is its relatively wide applicability, which is ensured both by a reasonably easy vocabulary level, and by a list of definitions of difficult words and phrases within the test booklet.

On the other hand, the Kuder-Vocational lacks the direct vocational relevance of the Strong. Since it was designed as a measure of relatively pure interests, its occupational significance is probably limited to jobs where the activities involved are fairly homogeneous. Although the test manual does present some occupational norms, these are less well standardized than those of the Strong. The Kuder-Vocational is therefore probably better suited to counselling in terms of general vocational direction, than to specifically occupational advice. In addition, the test is probably a less reliable measure than the Strong, particularly in a psychiatric setting. This is partly because the scales which it provides are less stable over time than are those of the Strong (Rosenberg, 1953). Quite apart from this, however, the activities which make up the test content, though not always referring to occupational categories, have a relatively obvious vocational concern, and with sophisticated subjects this can lead to distortion in the direction of social desirability – the Social Service scale being particularly susceptible to this tendency (Piotrowski, 1946). In a context where a subject is aware that his response may have a direct effect on his situation – as in the case of a psychiatric in-patient – this type of distortion can undermine the accuracy of the test as a measure of genuine vocational interests.

One other question is of particular concern when either the Strong or the Kuder is used with psychiatric patients. This is the problem of the undue influence which personal maladjustment can sometimes exert on vocational interest scores. While occupationally relevant preferences can be reasonably argued to represent one aspect of the person's overall adjustment, and it would obviously be artificial to view them as entirely separate, nevertheless, in certain cases, psychiatric features may overinfluence direction of interests, while in others they may intrude so as to obscure genuine interests. Among a considerable number of studies with similar findings, a recent investigation by Brandt and Hood (1967) showed that, as far as predicting current occupation was concerned, the Strong was a much less useful instrument for personally disturbed individuals than for more stable ones. The Kuder seems particularly susceptible to the elevation, among psychiatrically disturbed people, of the 'aesthetic' triad of interest scales – Literary, Artistic and Musical (Patterson, 1957). Whether such elevated scores represent 'true' interests in these vocational areas, or whether they are merely a function of temporary personality disturbance – perhaps resulting in social withdrawal, an overwhelming need for personal recognition, or some other passing motivational state – for practical purposes they are often misleading to the patient himself, and occupationally valueless to the counselling psychologist, unless they happen to coincide with genuine ability and attainment in these areas.

3   Assessment of personal needs

To a greater or lesser extent, personal factors of the work situation are likely to affect the occupational satisfaction, and ultimately the occupational success, of every individual. Relatively subtle aspects of the job – such as the 'image' which it possesses, the typical education and socio-economic background of those who work at it, whether its level, prestige or content are in line with parental pressures and expectations, or those of peers, and the degree to which it provides day-to-day variability, autonomy or social contact – these aspects may often be more vital in determining whether a job is congenial than are the intrinsic qualities of the work which it entails. Such factors are likely to be particularly important to job *dissatisfaction*; and among psychiatric patients who have already failed in a specific work setting, it is factors such as these which often seem to have been responsible.

Measuring this type of variable is certainly desirable in any kind of vocational guidance, but it seems essential when the subject is a psychiatric patient. Not only is a personally vulnerable individual more likely to break down in a work setting which he finds uncongenial; but, in many cases, psychiatric problems themselves entail specific needs for particular kinds of context. For instance, many patients who are prone to schizophrenic breakdown have, even in remission, highly rigid and unadaptable personalities, requiring occupational settings which are clearly structured, and do not demand much initiative or adaptability on the part of the worker himself. Psychopathic personalities, on the other hand, are often quite unable to settle to repetitive or routine jobs, and have a marked personal need for work which, even though not highly skilled in itself, offers the immediate rewards of variety or personal autonomy. Again, people who are prone to obsessional symptoms tend to need occupational settings where work requirements are well defined, the pace is not too rapid, and it is possible to achieve a high standard of work by steady and careful application.

(i) *Repertory Grid technique.* General needs relating to diagnostic categories can normally be assessed from a knowledge of the patient's psychiatric history, his interview presentation, and the personality testing which in most cases precedes specifically vocational measurement. Additionally, however, one needs to know the personal requirements which derive from each person's unique outlook, quite apart from any psychiatric diagnostic category to which he belongs. Such requirements, which are necessarily idiosyncratic, may be illustrated by the case of a young woman hospitalized following a hypomanic episode, and presented, according to her own request, for vocational guidance. As her history was a very unusual one, in that from early adolesencce she had dressed in masculine clothes, and had kept company with boys and men as far as possible, it seemed relevant to assess her general conception of her sex-role and social identity. Detailed investigation of her construing of herself and of men and women in general, by means of Repertory Grid technique, revealed that the world of women, and of herself as a woman, was almost totally devoid of meaning to her, while that of men, and of herself as a man, was highly structured, and held a rich and complex significance for her. This finding was endorsed by the fact that on the Slater and Slater Selective Vocabulary Scale, she obtained a very high score on masculine words (33) in proportion to her score on feminine ones (15). This patient's elaborate cross-sexual identification was clearly a very important motivational factor in her expressed aspiration to become a motor mechanic.

For investigating highly specific needs such as these, deriving from the particular dimensions of meaning relevant for one individual, Repertory Grid technique is ideally suited.* Both elements and constructs can be elicited from the patient, thus ensuring personal relevance and significance of the test content. In practice, this normally entails asking the patient to think of a number of jobs he knows something about, including, for instance, jobs he has done and liked, those he has done but disliked, those he thinks he would like to do, those he would not like to do, and so on. Each job name can then be written on a separate card, and triads of cards presented to the subject, who is asked to think of some way in which two of them are alike, and, by the same token, different from the third. After a number of constructs have been elicited in this way, some or all of these can be presented to the patient, who is asked to rate or rank order the whole set of elements on them, and normally, in addition, on one which can be supplied as an index of overall personal liking, such as 'Jobs I would like – jobs I would dislike'. Scoring takes the form of assessing the statistical relationships between the various construct categories, relationships with the personal liking category being particularly important. These relationships suggest the dimensions which are strongly positively and negatively evaluated by the patient, and which would therefore be relevant in determining to what extent any job would be congenial to him.

Useful though such an assessment procedure may be in ensuring the subjective significance for the individual patient of the measuring index, the fact that each assessment entails a new, *ad hoc* instrument has a major disadvantage, in that findings cannot be related to any occupational norms. The psychologist interpreting results obtained by this method must inevitably resort to guesswork, which will be as good, or as bad, as his knowledge of fairly intimate and detailed

* For a more detailed description of Repertory Grid technique, see Chapter 26, BANNISTER, D. and MAIR, J. M. M. (1968) *The Evaluation of Personal Constructs*. London and New York: Academic Press.

aspects of different jobs is broad or limited. When specifically occupational conclusions are required, therefore, as opposed to more general vocational recommendations, a standard measuring approach is probably more appropriate. This is likely to sacrifice some degree of personal meaningfulness, but results can be more easily and systematically integrated with directly occupational information.

(ii) *Daws's Occupational Satisfactions Scheme*. A classification scheme of personal job needs, which seems to include many themes emerging in discussion with psychiatric patients, has been drawn up by Daws (1965). This scheme was based on survey data from semi-structured interview discussion of anticipated job satisfactions and experience, with English schoolboys approaching school-leaving age. It was designed to permit a two-way classification – (*a*) motivational analysis of jobs and (*b*) analysis of the individual needs of subjects (Daws, 1968).

The scheme is entitled *The Occupational Satisfactions Sought by Fifth Form Pupils*, and consists of the following categories:

1. *Material*
   (*a*) Income
   (*b*) Security
   (*c*) Prospects
   (*d*) Intra-firm
   (*e*) Temporal-Spatial

2. *Status*
   (*a*) Community Status
   (*b*) Intra-firm or Professional
   (*c*) Approval of 'Significant Others'
   (*d*) Personally valued Occupational Role

3. *Skill*
   (*a*) Mastery, Exercise and Knowledge
   (*b*) End Product
   (*c*) Autonomy and Self Determination
   (*d*) Responsibility
   (*e*) Power and Influence

4. *Dominant Value* or *Cathexis*

5. *Associational*
   'Meeting People' { (*a*) Work Associates
                      (*b*) Service or 'Target' groups

6. *Perceptual*
   (*a*) Variety
   (*b*) Outdoors
   (*c*) Travel

This classification, which *a priori* seems relevant to the needs of a wide range of people, might form the basis for a standard measuring instrument (such as a Repertory Grid technique with constructs supplied as indices of the satisfactions listed). As yet, however, no specific methods of measurement have been integrated into the scheme. Similarly, information has not yet been collected about the occupations in which specific satisfactions were available or precluded. The fact that so far the internal structure of the scheme remains unchecked against the actual responses of a standardizing population, while its relevance to particular occupations or groups of occupations is also not yet established, means that, at present, its usefulness probably lies in providing a framework within which personal needs can be assessed informally, in general discussion with the patient. A more systematic measuring device is represented by the Kuder Preference Record (Personal).

(iii) *Kuder Preference Record (Personal).* The Kuder-Personal was designed as a measure of the subject's characteristic reactions to situations and activities which, though not specifically occupational, are nevertheless relevant to many job requirements. Since most of the situations and activities involved are interpersonal, the technique lies somewhere between a personality test and an interest test. Its construction was similar to that of the Kuder-Vocational, being based on criteria of internal reliability, consistency and independence of scales. Its standardizing population, however, and its range of applicability are considerably wider than those of the Vocational Form, as they include the semi-skilled occupational level. Like the Kuder-Vocational, the Kuder-Personal yields information in the form of a within-individual comparison of relatively strong and weak areas of preference. There are five such areas, represented by the following scales:

Preference for being active in groups
Preference for familiar and stable situations
Preference for working with ideas
Preference for avoiding conflict
Preference for directing or influencing others

The format of the test is very like that of the Kuder-Vocational. It consists of a list of triads of activities, to each of which the subject records his first and last preference choices, by the same method of punching a pin through circles on the answer pad. For most subjects, the test takes about three-quarters of an hour. As with the Kuder-Vocational, the subject can frequently be entrusted with the complete sequence of self-administration of the test, calculation of raw scores by counting chains of holes within linked circles on the back of the answer pad, and conversion of these into percentiles on the Profile Sheet, which provides separate norms for males and females, and for different age groups. Like the Vocational Form, the test yields a Verification score, to detect carelessness or highly idiosyncratic responses. Provided that this score is within normal limits, interpretation in occupational terms takes the form of comparing the subject's high and low Scale scores with those of certain occupations shown in the test manual; these are grouped according to high scores on the nine Scales of the Vocational Form, so that, ideally, the subject's response should have been measured on this test also.

As far as the reliability of the test is concerned, evidence suggests that scores on the scales are reasonably stable for most individuals (1953 Test Manual). The occupational validity of the measure also appears promising, in that, for the occupations on which it has been assessed, its Scales are associated in the expected way with both job choice and job satisfaction (Manual). Unfortunately, however, few occupations have as yet been empirically studied, so that most of the occupations listed in the test manual are classified according to *a priori* principles of occupational similarity. This means that any strictly occupational conclusions based on such evidence must necessarily be tentative. Another disadvantage of the test is that it is apparently vulnerable to faking (Super and Crites, 1965), but has no scale for detecting this.

The Kuder-Personal does, however, seem to meet a need which is particularly important in the vocational requirements of psychiatric patients. An individual's positive liking for one of the kinds of situation measured by the test seems often to have contributed a great deal to his satisfaction in a previous occupation. Still more frequently, however, it is his *inability* to adjust to one kind of situation which seems to underlie his occupational frustration and unhappiness. It seems likely, from clinical experience, that negative results, in the form of *low* scores on any of the test Scales, may be more significant vocationally than positive preferences.

4   Assessment of relevant job openings

With regard to the final category of information – assessment of relevant job openings – it is sometimes argued that vocational guidance should proceed as far as recommendation about general vocational direction, but stop short at naming actual occupations, since job placement is the function of other professional departments – the P.S.W., the D.R.O. or the Labour Exchange. If, however, the discussion of specifically occupational possibilities with the patient is left to another department, two difficulties are likely to arise. The first is due to the unmarriageability of psychological information about the patient, and the job categories normally used by social workers and employment personnel. 'Low average intelligence, good form perception, poor clerical aptitude, an interest in persuasive work and a dislike of familiar and stable situations' – this kind of *psychologically* meaningful information conveys virtually nothing in terms of the *occupational* classification used by the local Labour Exchange. Such information needs to be translated into specifically occupational categories before it can be used by other professional departments. The second difficulty entailed in omitting directly occupational categories from vocational guidance is that, unless guidance has been planned from the outset from a knowledge of practical possibilities, it will be impossible to head the patient off from lines which are not feasible because of such factors as a lack of training facilities, age limits, years of low pay, or the local absence of that type of job.

In assessing relevant job openings, precedures are likely to be considerably less systematic, and less standard from one setting to another, than those for the other three kinds of assessment. This is partly because the basic practical details of some occupations are not easily accessible, while those of others must be obtained from very disparate sources before being collated and compared. The lack of standard procedures also derives from the fact that the relevant occupational ranges to be covered will differ according to the geographical and socio-economic setting in which vocational counselling is given.

(i) *Occupational classifications.* The first need, in this type of assessment, is for a system of occupational classification which can be meaningfully related to the three types of information obtained about the person – his skills and capacities, his occupational interests and his personal requirements. Such a classifying system is needed, over and above the occupational information provided by the various tests of the person. Although both aptitude and interest tests give norms for various occupations, these occupations do not necessarily – and indeed, seldom do – coincide with each other. This means that often there can be no cross-reference as to the occupations relevant to performance on *both* types of test. Additionally, the lower levels of the occupational range, though accounting for a larger proportion of available jobs than the upper levels, tend not to be included within the norms of many tests.

Most existing systems of classifying occupations are unsuitable for this type of assessment, in that they are not based on psychological differences. The scheme used in British Employment Exchanges – the Registrar General's Classification of Occupations – categorizes jobs in terms of their socio-economic level. The American Dictionary of Occupational Titles is somewhat more psychologically orientated, being based mainly on levels of skill. The Minnesota Occupational Rating Scales take this type of categorization a stage further, and classify occupations according to the similarity of the pattern of abilities which they require; this scheme consists of 214 such patterns. An explicitly psychological classification, which entails considerably fewer units than this, and takes both abilities and interests into account, is the system proposed by Ann Roe (1956).

(ii) *Roe's occupational classification.* Roe's scheme is based on a comprehensive overview of studies concerned with the psychological aspects of occupations. Using two dimensions – primary focus of activity, and level of responsibility, capacity or skill – Roe structures the complete occupational range according to findings of the similarity of different jobs in terms of these dimensions.

Within this classifying system, primary focus of activity – or *Group*, as Roe labels this dimension – has the following eight subdivisions:

Service
Business contact

Organization
Technology
Outdoor
Science
General cultural
Arts and entertainment

It will be seen that several of these subdivisions closely parallel areas of interest measured by such tests as the Kuder-Vocational, as in the case of Service (Kuder Social Service), Outdoor (Kuder Outdoor) and Science (Kuder Scientific). Other subdivisions make distinctions which seem meaningful in terms of personal needs – for instance, the distinction between Business contact and Organization, representing directly interpersonal activities as compared with relatively impersonal occupational concerns.

The other dimension of Roe's scheme, level of responsibility, capacity, or skill – named *Level* – is subdivided into six categories. These are:

Professional and managerial 1 (High independent responsibility)
Professional and managerial 2 (Less independent responsibility)
Semi-professional and small business
Skilled
Semi-skilled
Unskilled

Although the categories used by tests of abilities and aptitudes are not directly comparable with these subdivisions, the information which such tests convey is clearly relevant to Roe's Level dimension. Intelligence Quotients and aptitude levels indicate the upper limit to which the subject can – in theory – aspire; factors such as his socio-economic class, his financial responsibilities and his educational qualifications establish the assets and the barriers which he would be likely to meet – in practice – in attempting to attain that limit.

In relation to the requirements of vocational guidance, Roe's classification system seems a very appropriate one. In the first place, it is structured in terms of psychologically meaningful dimensions, and is therefore broadly comparable with categories of information derived from psychological measurement of the subject. Secondly, the system appears potentially comprehensive, as far as the range of occupations is concerned. This means that, as findings relating to the psychological demands of particular occupations become available, these occupations can be entered into the appropriate cell of the 48-cell matrix (eight Group categories, by six Level categories). Not being a closed system, the scheme can also, in theory, incorporate new occupations, not yet in existence, as these develop.

The classification appears particularly helpful in occupational guidance with psychiatric patients. This is because it structures the lower range of the occupational ladder – semi-skilled and unskilled work – in terms of psychologically meaningful dimensions. Patients whose ability and attainment are too low for them to be able to achieve a skilled work level, very often have strong personal needs and vulnerabilities necessitating certain kinds of job role or setting. For instance, one patient whose intellectual endowment is slight may nevertheless be entirely dominated by his desire to contribute occupationally to the welfare of others. While jobs such as these given in the norms of formal interest tests – *teacher*, *doctor*, or *nurse* – would be out of the question for him, those shown in Levels 5 and 6 of the Service group in Roe's scheme – *waiter*, *hospital attendant*, *lift-operator* – might well be relevant. Similarly, another patient might be strongly motivated to achieve the prestige of a 'scientific' job, without having the ability to become a *scientist*, or even a *laboratory technician*. In this case, *veterinary attendant*, in Level 5 of Roe's Science group, or *non-technical helper in a scientific organization*, in Level 6, might satisfy his need without demanding an impossibly high level of achievement from him. Since people with psychiatric problems often show interests and personal needs which are somewhat out of accord with their abilities and attainment, Roe's coverage of the full occupational range in terms of a motivationally important interest dimension, is extremely valuable in a psychiatric setting.

(iii) *Informal techniques of collecting occupational information.* The assessment of relevant job openings not only entails a pinpointing of the particular occupations which seem most appropriate for the subject. It also involves the accumulation of practical information about the general availability, conditions and entry requirements of a wide range of occupations. This is where techniques are likely to vary considerably from one psychologist to another.

Official sources of practical information about occupations are of three main kinds. The first is represented by semi-Government bodies such as the Central Youth Employment Executive. This organization has issued a large number of booklets, published by H.M.S.O., each concerned with the main features of a particular occupation as a career. Although some semi-skilled jobs (such as laundry and dry-cleaning) are included in the range covered by the booklets, these are mostly concerned with occupations of at least a skilled level. They give a general description of the work entailed in the occupation and its various specializations, its personal and educational requirements, its pay and general conditions, and, in relevant cases, a list of training establishments or organizations to write to for further information. These booklets are useful in providing a good deal of practical information about quite a wide range of occupations. They are factual, simply written, and attractively presented, often including photographs. Their main disadvantage, from the point of view of vocational guidance with psychiatric patients, is that, being explicitly orientated to school-leavers, they give no indication as to possibilities of entry, years of training, pay, or promotion prospects for older people. In addition, they are limited, in the main, to the upper occupational range.

Another source of official information relevant to occupational choices consists of the various educational bodies who issue pamphlets or books on educational courses, colleges and grants. These publications are, of course, relevant only for individuals considering further training of some kind, and hence, again, only the upper occupational range is likely to be catered for by this type of information. An example of this type of publication is a pamphlet issued in 1967 by the National Union of Teachers, entitled 'University and College Entrance – the Basic Facts'. This provides a comprehensive and up-to-date list of universities and colleges in this country, the type of educational course which each offers, together with its entry requirements, and the various educational grants available to students. A pamphlet which covers a generally less advanced educational range is 'Adult Education', published annually by the National Institute of Adult Education. This is particularly helpful in advising subjects who are unable to take full-time university courses, but who wish to obtain further vocational or non-vocational education, such as is provided in courses run by Local Authorities, the W.E.A., or university extra-mural departments. Also prominent among bodies producing this kind of publication from time to time is the Advisory Centre for Education.

The third official source of information about occupations is made up of all those individual professional and commercial bodies which produce publications about jobs in their own field. These range from relatively dispassionate and factual accounts – as, for instance, the 'Careers in Psychology' pamphlet produced by the British Psychological Society, or the booklet published by the B.B.C. describing a variety of technical jobs available in its engineering division – to the frankly propagandist literature put out by some commercial firms, as in the case of certain large London stores. Obviously the value of such publications is very variable, as far as providing reliable and detailed information about jobs is concerned, but in some specific cases they may be helpful.

Officially issued information needs to be supplemented by various informal strategies for gathering occupationally relevant facts. Visits to official employment and training bodies such as the local Labour Exchange, the Ministry of Labour Industrial Rehabilitation Unit, and the Government Training Centre, will help to assess local employment conditions and training, or retraining, courses available to people with psychiatric disabilities. Personal contact with the local Technical College can also be helpful, in checking details of courses offered. Such contact additionally establishes good relations, which can sometimes pay dividends later, as in the case of an 18-year-old schizophrenic boy, ex-grammar school but without the necessary qualifications, who was accepted for a Clerical and Office Methods course by the Principal of the local College of Technology. A rather different approach to the collection of occupationally relevant facts is to use job advertisements themselves as operational criteria of job demands and conditions. Newspaper cuttings of advertisements can be pasted into a large scrapbook categorized within some such scheme as Roe's classification system. This method seems particularly useful for semi-skilled and unskilled occupations, for which it is difficult to obtain information about age limits, pay, conditions, training and prospects in any systematized form.

IV COMMUNICATION OF RESULTS AND RECOMMENDATIONS

It is relatively rare to find a vocational guidance situation where the results of all types of test point in the same occupational direction. Because of this, questions are likely to arise, at the stage of co-ordinating results and making recommendations, as to the relative weights which should be given to different and conflicting test results. In general, *negative* results, in the form of low scores, have a clearer and more immediate significance than have positive ones, in that they exclude certain occupational possibilities altogether. Thus, a person whose spatial aptitude level is below 80 can safely be assumed to be unfitted for work as a mechanical engineer, regardless of his high level of interest in mechanical vocational areas. The categorization system proposed here for vocational assessment in a psychiatric setting has, in fact, been based on a view of four relevant variables as successively delimiting the occupational area within which the patient is likely to succeed. From this point of view, the patient's capacities come first, since they are the major limiting factors – then his broad interests (which must be interpreted within the confines of areas open to his capacities) – then his specific needs for particular kinds of job setting (within the fields of work suited to his capacities and interests) – and finally, the practicability and availability of the openings established as suited to these three aspects of the person. Thus, the investigation represents a serial screening process, in which each stage narrows down the relevant information to be obtained from the succeeding stage. This point of view has implications for the co-ordinating and communicating of the results of the investigation, in that, again, low scores should be considerably stressed, and interpretation of results at each stage should be made in the light of those obtained from earlier stages.

The considerations governing the formal reporting of test results and recommendations to the referring psychiatrist are likely to be much the same as those involved in other kinds of psychiatric referral. In general, recommendations should be phrased in non-technical language, so that the psychiatrist can grasp their significance and make use of them in his communication with other departments and organizations.

There is, however, a difference between vocational guidance and other kinds of psychological assessment which has considerable significance for the communication between psychologist and patient. Whereas requests for diagnostic or personality assessment are made by the psychiatrist, who formulates the need for such assessment without consulting the patient about it, in the case of vocational guidance the request nearly always originates with the patient himself. This difference has several implications. In the first place, the patient is likely to be considerably more interested in the measurement procedures and their results than he is in those of other types of assessment. Secondly, unlike situations of diagnostic assessment – where the patient may be looked on as a 'case', and his remarks as symptoms rather than as conveying directly relevant information – in the case of vocational testing, his subjective views about the problem are vital, and must be taken into account in coming to any conclusions. Finally, since the aim of vocational guidance is essentially to help the patient to gain a greater understanding of himself so that he may make a personally relevant occupational choice, he must be taken into the psychologist's confidence as far as the results of assessment are concerned. The psychologist is thus involved in direct communication with the patient. This feature of vocational assessment is, of course, in marked contrast with normal practice as regards reporting results derived from other types of psychological assessment of psychiatric patients.

In making vocational recommendations to the patient, therefore, it is usually appropriate to explain the basis for them in terms of actual test results. Although it is probably unwise to tell the patient an I.Q. level which has been obtained for him (because of lay conceptions of the 'absolute' nature of such measures), in many cases it will help him to understand his own capacities and disabilities if he is shown the profile of his aptitude scores. Similarly, patients usually find the profile of vocational and personal interest levels highly meaningful; and it is often helpful to the psychologist to have their comments on such scores. Needless to say, however, such results should not be presented to any patient without some simple account to him of the way in which the tests were constructed, the significance of percentile scores, and so on. Obviously, too, discretion must be exercised in showing actual results to patients, and, for example, this would not be appropriate for a person whose level of aspiration and self-expectation greatly exceeded his own measured abilities. Even if actual scores are not presented, however, a reasonably frank discussion with the patient of his own measured potentialities, interests and needs, is likely to help him to make appropriate vocational choices.

It is, indeed, these features which make vocational guidance rather different from other types of clinical psychological procedures. The fact that the problem is formulated by the patient himself, that the psychologist is working within the same broad conceptual framework as the person he is concerned to assess, and that, following the assessment, the results must be communicated to that person in terms which are meaningful to him – it is these aspects of vocational guidance which give it a distinctive, and in many ways an exceptionally rewarding function among psychological assessment procedures in the psychiatric setting.

REFERENCES

BRANDT, J. E. and HOOD, A. B. (1967) Predictive validity of the S.V.I.B. as related to personality adjustment. *Proc. 75th Annual Convention A.P.A.*

CENTERS, R. (1948) Motivational aspects of occupation satisfaction. *J. soc. Psychol.*, **28**, 187-217.

CRISSY, W. J. E. and DANIEL, W. J. (1939) Vocational interest factors in women. *J. appl. Psychol.*, **23**, 488-494.

DARLEY, J. G. (1941) *Clinical Aspects and Interpretation of the Strong Vocational Interest Blank*. New York: Psychological Corporation.

DAWS, P. (1965) *The occupational satisfactions sought by fifth form pupils*. Unpublished paper, Vocational Guidance Research Unit, Univ. of Leeds.

DAWS, P. (1968) Personal communication.

GHISELLI, E. E. and BROWN, C. W. (1948) The effectiveness of intelligence tests in the selection of workers. *J. appl. Psychol.*, **32**, 575-580.

PATTERSON, C. H. (1957) Interest tests and the emotionally disturbed client. *Educ. psychol. Meas.*, **17**, 264-280.

PIOTROWSKI, Z. A. (1946) Differences between cases giving valid and invalid inventory responses. *Ann. N.Y. Acad. Sci.*, **46**, 633-638.

RODGER, A. (1951) *The Seven-Point Plan*. Paper No. 1. London: National Institute of Industrial Psychology.

ROE, A. (1956) *The Psychology of Occupations*. New York: Wiley.

ROSENBERG, N. (1953) Stability and maturation of Kuder interest patterns during high school. *Educ. psychol. Meas.*, **13**, 449-458.

SCHONELL, F. J. et al. (1962) *Promise and Performance*. London: University of London Press.

STRONG, E. K. (1955) *Vocational Interests 18 years after College*. Minneapolis: Univ. of Minnesota Press.

SUPER, D. E. and CRITES, J. O. (1965) *Appraising Vocational Fitness*. New York, Evanston; London: Harper and Row.

UNGAR, E. W. and BURR, E. T. (1931) *Minimum Age Levels of Accomplishment*. Albany: State Univ. of New York Press.

VERNON, P. E. and PARRY, J. B. (1949) *Personnel Selection in the British Forces*. London: University of London Press.

5

The clinical interview

R. R. Hetherington

I WHAT IS A CLINICAL INTERVIEW?

The *Shorter Oxford English Dictionary* defines an interview as 'a meeting of persons face to face, especially for the purpose of formal conference on some point'. Matarazzo (1965) defines the interview as 'a form of conversation wherein two people, and recently more than two, engage in verbal and non-verbal interaction for the purpose of accomplishing a previously defined goal'. Maccoby and Maccoby (1954) are more specific about the kind of interaction, when they define the interview as 'a face-to-face verbal interchange, in which one person, the interviewer, attempts to elicit information or expressions of opinion or belief from another person. . . . In the interview, the verbal expressions of the respondent must be directed towards the interviewer in response to the interviewer's questions or comments'. Khan and Cannell (1958) see the interview as necessarily being restricted in scope and 'focused on some specific content area, with consequent elimination of extraneous material'. They say that an important feature of the interview is that it is 'a pattern of interaction in which the role relationship of interviewer and respondent is highly specialized'.

These three definitions together cover the main features of the clinical interview which are:

(*a*) That it must be a face-to-face meeting between two or more people who must be able to see, hear and understand one another.

(*b*) That it must be conducted for some specific purpose which is known by the interviewer, and usually by the respondent as well.

(*c*) That the range of topics for discussion is deliberately restricted and controlled by the interviewer who attempts to elicit information to expressions of opinion from the respondent.

(*d*) That specific roles are adopted by both interviewer and respondent.

There are many excellent reviews of the history of the interview, the best of which is, perhaps, that of Matarazzo (1965), who in his long chapter on the interview gives a large number of references to historical studies.

II USES TO WHICH THE CLINICAL INTERVIEW HAS BEEN PUT

These may be classified under three heads: fact-finding; diagnostic and personality assessment; and therapeutic. Any such classification is bound to be artificial since each category overlaps the other two. Any interview tends to be therapeutic in the sense that the respondent may benefit in some way from his encounter with the interviewer. Diagnostic and personality assessment interviews involve a great deal of fact-finding, and fact-finding interviews yield pointers to diagnosis and personality.

However, the classification is probably useful as it defines the goal of the interview in question. The fact-finding interview is designed to elicit matters of fact rather than of opinion. This information is something the respondent possesses and which need not be about him or concern him directly. Such interviews may be not only with the patient but also with relatives or friends of the patient. The diagnostic or personality assessment interview is usually directed to eliciting data from, and about, the patient himself. The therapeutic interview seeks to change the patient in some way, to modify his attitudes, opinions and behaviour, rather than just to learn about them. In practice, the clinical interview may be partly fact-finding, will certainly be diagnostic and may prove to be therapeutic as well.

III   RESEARCH ON INTERVIEWING

There are two good reviews of research on interviews: on the *structural and formal aspects* by Matarazzo (1962) and on the *content aspects* by Maccoby and Maccoby (1954). The article by Matarazzo describes research which shows, for example, that the more an interviewer remains silent during an interview the more the respondent remains silent. There is apparently no tendency for the latter to try and fill the gaps. Indeed, a decrease in activity of any kind, such as gestures, on the part of the interviewer leads to a decrease in the respondent's activity also, except in the case of schizophrenics, who show an increase. Although there are wide individual differences in interaction behaviour among various subjects, the interaction behaviour for any given subject is highly stable (reliable and unique for him), irrespective of who is interviewing him and with no control of the topics discussed. If this is so, then measures of *how* a respondent reacts may be just as important as what he says.

The paper by Maccoby and Maccoby (1954) is concerned with the interview as a tool of research, and is therefore relevant to fact-finding and diagnostic interviews. This is a useful article, since it not only deals with the mechanics of interviewing but discusses the important topic of role relations within the interview. We shall be quoting extensively from this paper in later sections of this chapter.

1   Fact-finding interviews

These should be reliable and valid provided that communication between the interviewer and respondent is adequate, that the latter is sufficiently motivated, and that the interviewer records his data accurately. Bias is not unknown, as an early study by Rice (1929) shows. In this paper he reports that two interviewers set out to discover why people were applying for relief. One was a socialist and he concluded that 39% were seeking application because of poor industrial conditions, and in 22% the main cause was drink. The other investigator was a temperance enthusiast and his comparable figures were 7% and 62% respectively.

Maccoby and Maccoby (1954) insist that the interview cannot be dispensed with in the exploratory and planning stages of some kinds of research.

2 Diagnostic and personality assessment interviews

In these types of interview questions of reliability and validity loom large. These matters have been dealt with in some detail by Vernon (1953). He sums up the situation as follows:

> We may conclude that many interviews given by untrained and also some highly trained persons are of little or no value for the practical assessment of personality . . . it would be better indeed if the interview was confined to assessing certain traits which cannot readily be covered by other methods, that is – treated as one test whose results are combined with other tests.

Maccoby and Maccoby (1954) conclude that 'validity studies all suggest that when people are interviewed directly concerning behaviour about which there is a strong expectation of social approval and disapproval . . . respondents tend to err in the direction of idealizing their behaviour'.

Many studies have shown the poor predictive value of interviews (Kelly and Fiske, 1950; Mechl, 1954). The use of the interview for psychiatric diagnosis has been heavily criticized (Ash, 1949; Eysenck, 1952, 1960a), although many writers concede that this might be due to the deficiencies of nosological systems as much as to interview methods themselves. Foulds (1965) points out that whereas the *inadequacy* of psychiatric classification is indeed recognized by all concerned, its *unsuitability* has not been so recognized. By using a highly structured interview, almost amounting to a questionnaire, Foulds (1965) claims greatly to have increased the reliability of diagnosis by means of the interview.

3 Psychotherapeutic interviews

The efficacy of psychotherapy, and therefore of the interviews by which such therapy is undertaken, has been thoroughly reviewed by Eysenck (1960b). He comes to the conclusion that there is no scientific evidence that psychotherapy has ever done anyone any good. This, however, has not been the last word on the subject, and Vernon (1964), after a further careful review of the literature, states:

> It is quite untrue that psychotherapy and counselling have no effects, though they may measure up poorly against conventional criteria. The nature of the effects to be expected needs to be analysed, and great care devoted to the development of appropriate measures and design of valid experiments.

A recent study by Kellner (1968) confirms this. He says that in order to test a method of psychotherapy it is important to select an homogeneous group, and that in these circumstances, differences in outcome between treated subjects and untreated controls can be demonstrated. The chief factors involved are the amenability of the patient, the measures of change used and the therapeutic method employed.

4 Accuracy of reporting the interview

Some research has also been undertaken on the accuracy of reports based on interviews. S. L. Payne (1949) reports, in a comparison of mechanically recorded interviews with interviewer reports written from memory immediately after the interview, that 25% of the statements attributed by the interviewer to the respondent are clearly wrong. Covner (1944) reports a greater accuracy in a similar study 75-95%; but showed great condensation of the material: 30% only of the material was recorded, much of the omitted data being of apparent importance. Ruesch and Prestwood (1949) point out that tape-recordings of interviews convey feelings in a way that printed transcriptions can never do. The problems in this area are usefully discussed by Davitz (1964).

IV   THE ROLE OF THE CLINICAL PSYCHOLOGIST AND ITS BEARING ON THE CLINICAL INTERVIEW

In order to discuss the use of the interview in clinical work, it seems important first to discuss the role of the psychologist in a medical setting. The use he makes of the interview must depend heavily on the role he adopts, or is willing to play. Few would disagree with Eysenck (1955) when he writes:

> The psychologist will be useful precisely to the extent that he can bring his training in scientific method and his knowledge of psychological principles to bear on the problems presented to him, in this case, the problem of the individual patient.

Nevertheless, the phrase 'the problems presented to him' needs clarification, as it implies at least two possible roles which might be played by the psychologist. R. W. Payne (1953) sees the role of the psychologist as a scientific medical auxiliary 'comparable to that existing in the hospital between the physician and the biochemist'. Such an auxiliary, says Payne, 'applies his scientific knowledge and method to answer specific questions put to him by the physician in the course of clinical practice'. He deplores 'the absence of any general scientifically tested theory about the causes and treatment of psychological abnormalities'. It seems that Payne considers that if there *were* any such general theory he would be happy to spend his time applying it to questions put to him by the psychiatrist. It has been suggested (Eysenck, 1957) that psychologists and psychiatrists might co-operate on the basis of absolute equality, with the latter having responsibility for the physical health of the patient. Presumably, in this case, the psychologist would ask, as well as try to answer, some of the questions. In this case his scientific role would cease to be so clearly an auxiliary one.

This view of the psychologist as a scientist working within a hypothetico-deductive framework has not been universally assented to. Foulds (1948) writes:

> The 'scientific' psychologist whose attention is fixed on the manipulation of figures rather than on the subject of the experiment is recklessly anticipating the day when it may safely be assumed that the psychologist need know nothing of human nature.

And Geiger (1962) writes:

> The subject of social science, its object of study, is the behaviour of human beings. Every science starts out with description. After a while, when a body of descriptive literature has been accumulated, the parent of all the present sciences got its start, and that is the way all the other sciences began, if only to prove they were truly 'scientific'. It was natural therefore for the social sciences to want to develop a body of data which would enable them to make predictions. . . . In time the scientific image of man became the sort of man whose behaviour you could predict. That was the way science worked, and if you wanted scientific knowledge of man you cut him down to scientific size. You dealt with what you could measure, predict, and manipulate in human beings. You studied man as a 'thing' because science knows how to study things. . . . This can no longer be said about the science of psychology. Oddly enough, from being the most slavishly imitative of the sciences in its idea of 'method' (imitative of the 'thing' sciences), psychology has rather suddenly become a pioneer in the development of a new attitude towards man. The cause . . . is probably the impact of psychotherapy on academic psychology. . . . The therapist deals with sick and suffering human beings. He begins, no doubt, with theories, but somewhere in the process the human being in the therapist takes over . . . he experiences compassion. . . . Psychology has recovered its soul, the subject of its study. There is no longer a 'thing'.

The restriction of the psychologist's role to that of a scientist of the hypothetico-deductive kind would certainly seem to preclude the use by the psychologist of many of the skills traditionally associated with the psychiatrist, among which of course is the skill of interviewing.

In an effort to differentiate his role from that of the psychiatrist, the psychologist is apt to emphasize his scientific rather than his clinical interests. An intriguing discussion about the differences between clinical and scientific or research attitudes is to be found in Lewis (1930), who suggests that it is not easy for a person to adopt the two kinds of attitude at the same time. Some psychiatrists too, seem anxious to establish a clear line of demarcation between the psychiatric and psychological roles, the former being 'clinical' and the latter 'scientific'. This dichotomy is probably more artificial than real, since clinical medicine is becoming more scientific, and as Newman (1957) points out, is tending to produce a 'flight from the patient' into the laboratory. In any case, a large part of every psychiatrist's work consists in stimulating the patient and observing his motor or verbal behaviour, a technique which is not exclusively medical since it is used by anyone who interviews anyone else. Indeed, by virtue of his general knowledge of individual and social psychology, the clinical psychologist should be at least as well, if not better trained to observe and record these data than his colleagues in other disciplines (Hetherington, 1964). This point was well made by Klein (1951) in his textbook on abnormal psychology and is as relevant today as it was some fifteen years ago:

> . . . there is considerable overlap of functions among the specialties. . . . This is apparent when we consider the work of the clinical psychologist. This field is an outgrowth of early efforts to apply psychological methods and principles to problems of school failure. In the course of years it became increasingly evident that such problems are bound up with a multiplicity of factors: mental defect, inadequate preparation in particular subjects, sensory deficiencies, poor nutrition, poor teaching methods, inadequate motivation, feelings of inferiority, lack of emotional security, personality clashes between parent and child, child and teacher, child and playmates. Quite obviously factors of this sort also interest the psychiatrist. . . . Trying to find an absolute sharp line of cleavage between the respective spheres of activity is like trying to find a line between the various medical specialties and arguing that an eye expert ought not to take a patient's pulse or measure blood pressure.

The role of the clinical psychologist need not, in fact, be restricted to that of a scientific medical auxiliary answering questions mostly posed by other people. It could equally well be seen as that of a professional member of a therapeutic team whose task it is to come to as full an *understanding* as possible of the psychological features of the patient and his problems. If the latter role is the preferred one, then the need for an interview as an assessment technique is clear.

A full understanding of the patient's problems is unlikely to be achieved by a detached, objective appraisal of selected aspects of the case. Some data do not become available until the patient has achieved sufficient confidence in the interviewer to be able to speak freely about his worries and preoccupations. Foulds (1948) has pointed out that patients may respond at different levels:

> The question arises as to whether the tests reveal the personality behind the defence dynamisms or whether they merely give the opportunity for the display of the persona, the type of personality by which the subject may wish to be known. There may conceivably be three levels of the personality which we should seek to interrelate: the persona, the 'public reputation' and the hypothetical covert personality.

This question may apply *a fortiori* to interviewing, and Oldfield (1941) makes it explicit that it does:

> The situation is more or less alarming to the patient and the relation of the psychologist to the patient is almost inevitably one of superior to inferior. The result of both these factors is to tend to fix upon the patient attitudes foreign to his normal personality. Unless this state can be dissolved, it is

impossible even for the most skilled conversationalist to evoke attitudes sufficiently well defined and natural to allow judgements to be based on them. (This passage has been modified by substituting the word 'patient' for 'candidate' and 'psychologist' for 'interviewer'.)

This question of communication is vital, and if the psychologist is to take any responsibility for formulating the nature and pattern of the patient's psychological problems, he must use techniques which foster mutual confidence and trust between himself and the patient, and which give an opportunity for the patient to express important data about himself. Such techniques must include the clinical psychological interview. Only when a preliminary stage of understanding has been reached can the psychologist begin to formulate those problems which can fruitfully be investigated by means other than the interview. This point has been made earlier in this chapter in relation to the use of the interview in the early stages of research (Maccoby and Maccoby, 1954).

If this role of the psychologist is accepted, then it will appear that much of the discussion about the usefulness of the interview is beside the point. If the interview is accepted as a proper means of reaching an understanding of the patient and his problems, rather than as a tool for prediction or diagnosis, then the traditional lines of criticism are seen to be irrelevant.

V THE AIMS OF THE CLINICAL PSYCHOLOGICAL INTERVIEW

The primary aim of the clinical psychological interview is to obtain as full an understanding as possible of the patient and his problems. This term 'understanding' has been deliberately chosen to cover a wide field. The psychologist must try to achieve some knowledge of the patient's personality, what sort of person he is, what his capacities and interests are, and his attitude to himself and his problems, and to other people.

There is clearly no call for duplication of this sort of interview with those of the psychiatrist or social worker. Factual data which are already available need not be obtained all over again. Thus details about the patient's age, occupation, home background and educational history, if available, should already be noted in the patient's file. If not, they must be obtained along with other data during the interview. The psychiatric interview is concerned to elicit signs and symptoms from which the doctor can make a diagnosis which will lead to treatment and disposal of the patient. His basic question is: 'What is wrong with this patient?' The psychiatric social worker is concerned to gather data about the patient's home and occupational environment. Her basic question is: 'What sort of environment does the patient come from?' The clinical psychologist's interview is designed to answer the questions: 'What sort of person is the patient? What does he think and feel about himself and his problems?' These three kinds of interview have differing aims which make them quite distinct. Nevertheless, these descriptions of the aims are oversimplified, and suggest less overlapping than there really is. The psychiatrist, for example, is also interested in what sort of person the patient is, just as the clinical psychologist will probably make a special note of pathognomonic behaviour patterns.

Role relationship factors

Under this heading we shall be considering all those factors, both physical and psychological, which might have an effect on the interpersonal relationships of the interviewer and respondent. Possible role relationships between the psychologist and his client or patient have been discussed by Hetherington (1964). We shall assume that the role sought by the psychologist is that of a non-directive professional. In this case the relationship is bound to be asymmetrical, as Oldfield (1941) points out. The patient tells the psychologist about his worries and problems but the psychologist does not reciprocate. The doctor never says, 'I have headaches too' (Barton Hall, 1960), nor does the psychologist reveal his own anxieties. This rule, as we shall see later, affects the form and content of the questions asked. Apart from this, however, every attempt should be made to minimize status barriers and to achieve an easy, informal relationship.

(a) *The Physical Setting*

The physical setting is too often ignored, or too little attention is paid to it. There may, of course, be nothing that can be done about it, through sheer lack of space in which to arrange the table or desk and chairs in any suitable way. But if the stage can be set, as it were, and the properties chosen, certain details are important. The *window* should not be directly behind the psychologist's head so that his face is in shadow and difficult to see. Lighting should be arranged so that psychologist and patient are illuminated equally well. Facial expression, posture and gesture are important means of communication, no less for the patient as for the psychologist, and they should be equally easy to observe in both.

This may be best arranged by having the *desk* or *table* at an angle of 45° to the window. The *chairs* are often better placed so that the patient is not seated directly opposite the psychologist, thus only being able to avoid the latter's gaze by turning his head. If the patient is seated at the top of the table adjacent to that of the psychologist, he can look at the latter when he pleases, by turning his head through 45°. The chairs should not differ in comfort or size, or such difference should be in favour of the patient's chair. If tea or coffee is provided during the interview, both should be served with crockery of the same kind. (Some hospitals keep patients' and staff crockery separate and distinguishable.) These are all simple and straightforward measures to reduce status barriers between the psychologist and the patient.

(b) *Attitude of the Psychologist*

The psychologist may well refuse to wear a white coat, as this will confuse his role with that of the doctor, and is likely unduly to enhance status differences.

The general friendliness and permissiveness of the proceedings can be increased by the simple act of the psychologist's fetching the patient from the ward or waiting-room himself, and not having a nurse do so. Many writers emphasize the need for sincerity and for trying to *feel* the emotions implied by friendly actions. It is not enough to act a part or play a role, as feelings seem to be directly perceived in a rather primitive way, as has been pointed out by Koffka (1928), Raven (1952) and Scheler (1954), whose arguments have been summarized by Hetherington (1961). The psychologist's general bearing should be of unhurried welcome and interest in the patient *as a person*, and not just as a case. This point has been made by several writers. Patients often feel resentful at being categorized. William James (1902), in a famous passage, expresses this in characteristic language:

> The first thing the intellect does with an object is to class it along with something else. But any object which is infinitely important to us and awakens our devotion, feels to us also as if it must be *sui generis* and unique. Probably a crab would be filled with a sense of personal outrage if it could hear us class it without ado or apology as a crustacean, and thus dispose of it. 'I am no such thing,' it would say, 'I am *myself, myself* alone.'

Maslow (1962) has made this point more recently. One illustration he gives of this 'resistance to being rubricized', tells how 'a psychiatrist terminated a very brief and hurried first interview with a prospective patient by saying: "Your troubles are roughly those characteristic of your age group".' The potential patient became very angry and later reported being 'brushed off' and insulted. She felt as if she had been treated as a child, 'I am *not* a specimen. I'm *me*, not anybody else.' The patient resents the categorizing of *him*, although his illness, once separated from him, could more tolerably be diagnosed. Cohen (1959) nicely describes this separation in the case of physical illness:

> The patient who comes for a medical examination . . . finds himself in the curious position of having to provide details about his ailment as if he himself were perfectly healthy but that he unfortunately possesses a defective piece of bodily equipment . . . his doctor is not so much interested in him as in his malady. He examines the patient's body *as if, indeed, the patient were not there.*

This is, of course, not so easy to achieve in the case of mental illness when it is the patient *himself*, rather than his body who is ill. In any case, as Cohen points out, 'The psychologist, as such, is not concerned with the sickness itself . . . but with the patient's response to his illness'. When interest in, and rapport with, the patient as a *person* is achieved, then rubricizing becomes impossible and the patient is in no danger of feeling insulted.

This need to meet and accept the patient as he is, in and for himself, without classification or diagnosis, implies that his behaviour, views and opinions must also be accepted. Therefore it is important that the interviewer should not appear shocked, affronted, embarrassed or angry at anything the patient says. Not only would such reactions on the psychologist's part imply non-acceptance of the patient, but it would also influence the direction and content of his conversation by the well known mechanism of verbal conditioning (Gelder, 1968). Such

G

direction and content of the patient's conversation can equally well be influenced by the psychologist's approbation and approval. Maccoby and Maccoby (1954) insist that 'it is a cardinal principle of interviewing that the interviewer must attempt not to reveal his own attitudes on the subject matter of study: he must not show shock or disapproval over anything the respondent says, or nod enthusiastically when the respondent supports the interviewer's own point of view'.

Remarks like 'How right you are!' or 'Oh, I do agree!' can influence the patient's answers one way just as surely as remarks like 'You don't think *that*, do you!' or 'What an extraordinary idea!' can influence them in the other direction.

(c) *Attitude of the Patient*

It may be assumed that most patients will come to the psychological interview apprehensive and anxious. This may arise partly because of the stereotype they have already formed of the psychologist, his status and his functions.

Maccoby and Maccoby (1954) make two important observations in this connection:

> The content of the communication will be affected by the status relationships: the person of lower status will be motivated to present himself in a favourable light to someone who might be in a position to influence his future. At the same time there may be elements of hostility based on the resentment of authority. . . .
>
> An essential element of the interviewer's role is that he should not be in a position to control sanctions affecting the respondent. He should be *outside* the power hierarchy in which the respondent finds himself.

Anxiety, however, is an inevitable corollary of being ill; ill people usually fear the worst. Some patients may be quite unwilling to see the psychologist, although most will have in fact agreed to do so more or less willingly. If the psychologist has been able to find a comfortable place in the therapeutic team, patients will expect to see him, and wish to do so. If, however, the psychologist is an occasional visitor to the ward or clinic, he may be viewed with suspicion and his visit will itself create anxieties (Hetherington, 1956). If a patient flatly refuses to talk about himself and his problems, it is unwise to continue, and better to divert the conversation to mundane, neutral, topics until the patient voluntarily returns to the subject of himself, or terminates the interview.

The patient's motivation in submitting to an interview is usually, then, his anxieties about himself, and these may be removed prematurely by too much reassurance without basis, by sedation or by hospitalization (Meares, 1957). On the other hand, too much anxiety may prevent the patient from co-operating in the interview at all. In practice, the problem of the psychologist is to reduce the patient's anxiety level, not to increase it even if it were considered ethically permissible to do so. The patient's motivation can often be increased if care is taken to make the questions and topics discussed appear relevant to his problems and anxieties. In this way the interviewer's desire to help the patient is indicated, rather than a suggestion that the psychologist is seeking information for his own purposes.

VI OBTAINING THE DATA

1 Structured or unstructured interviews

Directly the question of whether or not to structure an interview is raised, problems of 'stimulus equivalence' arise. A given standard interview question may in fact *mean* something different to different respondents, however carefully it is phrased. Its meaning will depend on a number of factors which cannot be controlled: the level of information possessed by the respondent, the degree to which concepts, language and cultural background are shared by the interviewer and respondent, how the latter perceives the interview situation, the role he has allotted to the interviewer and his consequent view of his own role. It might be better to concentrate on trying to get the meaning of the question across to the respondent rather than to stick to some standard form of words. (The same problem arises with test instructions – it is the *message* not the actual words which is important.)

The structuring of the interview might then refer to the *topics* introduced rather than the actual questions asked. What is asked about may be more important than the exact way of asking. (Nevertheless the phrasing of questions is important as we shall see in the next section.) We have given a possible structured topic interview, with sample stimulus and pursuit questions, in an appendix to this chapter.

It may not be wise to prolong the interview for more than one hour, and a second session may be necessary thoroughly to cover all the topics. Highly structured interviews based on standard questions may be more *reliable* in that similar results may be obtained by different interviewers or on different occasions; but less structured topic-interviews may be more *valid* in that the real problems of the patient are more likely to emerge.

2 Phrasing the questions

If questions are to be asked, and any interview, however unstructured, involves asking questions; there are certain rules which it is well to remember. What follows is largely based on Maccoby and Maccoby (1954).

(*a*) Avoid words and phrases with a double meaning.

(*b*) Avoid long, multiple questions which allow the respondent to answer part while avoiding the rest.

(*c*) Specify exactly the time, place and context which you want the respondent to assume (e.g. when you were in your teens . . ., during last week . . ., or since you became ill. . . .). This is especially important in the case of the last example as patients often consider they feel and act quite differently when they are ill compared to when they are not.

(*d*) Either make explicit all the alternatives the respondent should have in mind when he answers (i.e. he is being asked to *recognize* the answer), or make none of them explicit (i.e. he is being asked to *recall* the answer). (e.g. Do not say 'Do you get depressed when you are tired?' but either 'When do you get depressed?' or 'Do you get depressed when you are tired, or when things go wrong, or when other people frustrate you, or for no apparent reason', etc.) But see note (*b*) above about avoiding long questions. In general, recall is more accurate than recognition, but more difficult. Leading questions which only present one alternative for recognition are especially dangerous.

(*e*) When the interview concerns a subject with which the respondent may not be very familiar or one in which he may not have the technical vocabulary, it is sometimes desirable to preface questions with an explanatory paragraph or an illustration which will set the stage for the question the interviewer wants to ask. The question itself may then still be kept brief.

(*f*) When an interviewer deals with sensitive topics, attention must be given to wording questions in such a way as to minimize the patient's natural desire to present himself in a good light. (e.g. Do not say: 'Do you masturbate?' but rather 'When did you start masturbating?' Or 'Are you quarrelsome?' is better put in the form 'Do you get into quarrels much?')

When the information required is in areas about which the patient is sensitive or likely to feel embarrassed, ashamed or guilty, the advisability of using indirect methods has to be considered. These often consist of asking questions about some hypothetical character. When this is done, there may well be some doubt as to the extent to which the patient has identified himself with the character concerned.

3 Ethical problems

This raises the problem about the ethics of apparently asking questions in one field or about one topic when really information is being gathered about some other matter altogether. In other words: is it permissible to trick a patient into revealing data about himself which he might prefer to keep secret?

This seems to be a matter directly related to the role relationships of the psychologist and patient. If the interview is seen as a battle between the two, one probing the other's defences, tricking him into revealing data, then the ethical questions are relevant. If, on the other hand, there is a mutual agreement that one is trying to help the other, and that *together* some information will be gathered which will be used to further the patient's interests, there can be no question of tricking or trapping the patient. A patient in these circumstances may readily agree to co-operate in some projective technique, knowing that in doing so he may reveal aspects of himself, of which perhaps even he is unaware. It is certainly doubtful whether a psychologist is ever justified in presenting a projective test as a 'test of imagination' (Murray, 1943), when in fact it is a probe into unconscious attitudes, which leaves the patient 'happily unaware that he has presented the psychologist with what amounts to an X-ray picture of his inner self'.

VII   RECORDING THE DATA

Interview data may be written down from memory by the interviewer immediately after the interview is finished, or it may be taken down verbatim, or it can be recorded on tape.

Notes made from memory afterwards are subject to all the falsification, condensation, transposition and modification so fully described by Bartlett (1932). The studies by S. L. Payne (1949) and Covner (1944) quoted earlier in this chapter revealed the danger of recording from memory. This should never be done in serious work. The arguments advanced in its favour are that the patient speaks more freely if he feels he is not being recorded verbatim, and that the respondent is more relaxed and natural under these circumstances. In practice, when the role relationships are adequate, the patient expects the psychologist to record what he says because he is as keen as the latter that the record should be accurate. Frequently the patient will pause to allow the psychologist to catch up with his notes. It is, in fact, an indication of the seriousness of the proceedings, that notes should have to be taken.

Notes made during the interview are best made in shorthand. However, few psychologists can do this, so a compromise is condensed writing – which can be according to a definite system like Dutton's 'speedwords', or according to some system evolved by the interviewer. The preceding passage, for example, might be rendered thus:

Nts md dg the int. are best md in shtd. Howev. few Ψists can do ths, so a comp is condsd writg. wh cn be acdg to sm syst. evld by the inter.

With a little practice this can be fast enough for most occasions.

A tape-recording of the interview is clearly the best as tones of voice, inflexions, pauses and so on are also recorded (Ruesch and Prestwood, 1949). However, this leads to expensive problems of buying and filing tapes, and an immense labour of transcribing and editing later. Were there unlimited resources of money and secretarial help, video-tape recordings are the ideal. These however, also raise ethical problems. It would be intolerable to tape-record or video-tape record an interview without the prior knowledge and consent of the patient, just as the use of one-way screens is quite inadmissible without the patient's permission. Patients, while readily agreeing to notes being taken at the time, are often less willing to have a tape-recording made.

VIII   REPORTING THE DATA

As full a report of the interview as possible should be made initially. In any case what the patient says should be taken down verbatim with an indication of pauses, hesitations and unusual tone of voice. Notes should also be made of the chief stimulus and pursuit questions of the interviewer. All his interventions should be noted, even if only by a query (?) in the text. For example:

> I never like going out during the day (?) Because I don't like meeting people. (?) It's . . . well it's having to talk to them . . . not knowing what to say. . . . (When do you go out then?). . . . Well, I go out after dark sometimes, then people don't recognize me. (?) I mean there are fewer people about anyway.

The queries (?) are interventions by the psychologist such as 'Yes?', 'Go on', 'Tell me more', etc., and the stimulus or pursuit questions are recorded in brackets. Otherwise all recorded statements are those made by the patient. The dots refer to pauses.

The next question is how much of this needs to be included in the final report submitted to the referring doctor or agency. This in turn will depend on the type of referral: what has actually been asked for. Referrals vary from 'I.Q. please' to 'Have a look at Mrs Smith and tell me what you think of her'.

In general it is preferable to give an outline of the patient's psychological problems and difficulties both as they appear to him and as they emerge from a consideration of the interview data, the test results, and any further information in the case history. In many cases the report itself may only be an *aide memoire* for the doctor or referring agency, and the bulk of the information will be given in the case conference about the patient. When this happens, only a brief summary of the main findings of the interview need be given. When a fuller report is called for, those data which help to outline the main problems will need to be quoted.

Even in referrals of the 'I.Q. please' type, data about the patient's motivation, co-operation and mood may be necessary and relevant and will have to be reported. An important statement on the preparation of case reports has recently been made by the British Psychological Society (1969).

If a case conference is undertaken, it is often an advantage for the psychologist not to have seen the case history, or at any rate not to know the data collected by the doctor or social worker. When the reports of all three are compared at the case conference, interesting inconsistencies in the patient's various accounts of himself may be revealing. In some therapeutic teams lack of such inconsistencies is viewed with disappointment.

IX APPENDIX

A POSSIBLE STRUCTURED PSYCHOLOGICAL INTERVIEW

Suggested topics with stimulus and pursuit questions
These are *not* to be regarded as standard questions. They merely indicate the nature and range of each topic.

A. INTERESTS, LIKES AND DISLIKES

  1. *How do you spend your leisure time?*
    (a) What do you like doing best?
    (b) What do you like doing least?
    (c) What sort of things do you do at the weekends?
    (d) How do you spend the long winter evenings?
    (e) What are your hobbies?
    (f) What sports do you pursue?

  2. *Do you like your work?*
    (a) Did you choose your job or did circumstances force you into it?
    (b) What *is* your job?
    (c) Do you find yourself thinking about it or working 'after hours'?

B. RELATIONS TO OTHERS

  1. *How do you get on with your relatives?*
    (a) How many brothers and sisters have you? (note number, sex and ages).
    (b) How do you get on with them?
    (c) Was there any favouritism when you were all young?
    (d) How do you get on with your father?
        did
    (e) How do you get on with your mother?
        did
    (f) How do your parents get on with one another?
        did
    (g) Are you married? (Divorced? Separated? Widowed?)
    (h) How do you get on with your husband?
                wife?
    (i) Is he older or younger than you?
       she
    (j) How many children have you (note ages and sex).
    (k) How do you get on with them?
    (l) How do you get on with your 'in-laws'?
    (m) Have you had any love-affairs which have upset you? (Pre-marital? Extra-marital?)

  2. *How do you get on with others?*
    (a) Your colleagues at work?
    (b) Your friends?
    (c) Casual acquaintances?

  3. *How do others get on with you?*
    (a) Do you think you are popular?
    (b) Do you get into quarrels much?
    (c) Do you seek other people's company?

4. *Do you like being with others?*
   (a) Do you mind being the centre of attention?
   (b) Do you mind being in large crowds?
   (c) Do you prefer to be alone sometimes?

5. *Do you mind taking responsibility?*
   (a) Do you prefer to carry out a task alone?
   (b) Do you mind telling others what to do?
   (c) Do you object to taking orders from others?

C. ATTITUDE TO PAST AND FUTURE

1. *What do you think of your past?*
   (a) Looking back, have you had a happy life, on the whole?
   (b) Have you any regrets?
   (c) Do you look back on the past with pleasure?

2. *What do you hope for the future?*
   (a) Do you plan ahead?
   (b) Do you eagerly anticipate the future?
   (c) Do you dread the future?

D. ATTITUDE TO ILLNESS

(a) Looking back to the time before you were ill, can you tell me the main events that have taken place from then until now?

(The task here is to get the patient to give his own account of his illness and its development with as little prompting as possible. If he says he is not ill, ask why he thinks he is in hospital or has attended the clinic.)

REFERENCES

ASH, P. (1949) The reliability of psychiatric diagnosis. *J. abn. soc. Psychol.*, **44**, 272-276.

BARTLETT, F. C. (1932) *Remembering*. Cambridge: Camb. Univ. Press.

BRITISH PSYCHOLOGICAL SOCIETY (1969) The Diploma in Clinical Psychology: a statement from the Society's Board of Examiners. *Bull. Br. Psych. Soc.*, **22**, 113-115.

COHEN, J. (1959) The relationship of psychology to medicine. *Imprensa Medica*, **23**, 1-9.

COVNER, B. J. (1944) Studies in phonographic recordings of verbal material. III: The completeness and accuracy of counselling interview reports. *J. gen. Psychol.*, **30**, 181-203.

DAVITZ, J. R. (Ed.) (1964) *The Communication of Emotional Meaning*. New York: McGraw-Hill.

EYSENCK, H. J. (1952) *The Scientific Study of Personality*. London: Kegan Paul.

EYSENCK, H. J. (1955) *Psychology and the Foundations of Psychiatry*, Inaugural Lecture, London Univ. London: H. K. Lewis.

EYSENCK, H. J. (1957) *The Dynamics of Anxiety and Hysteria*. London: Kegan Paul.

EYSENCK, H. J. (1960a) Classification and the problem of diagnosis. *In* EYSENCK, H. J. (Ed.) *Handbook of Abnormal Psychology*. London: Pitman.

EYSENCK, H. J. (1960b) The effects of psychotherapy. *In* EYSENCK, H. J. (Ed.) *Handbook of Abnormal Psychology*. London: Pitman.

FOULDS, G. A. (1948) The importance of an agreed subjective criterion in the interpretation of certain questionnaire and projection tests. *J. Pers.*, **17**, 221-231.

FOULDS, G. A. (1965) *Personality and Personal Illness*. London: Tavistock.

GEIGER, H. (1962) Science and Peace. *J. hum. Psychol.*, **2**, 72-79.

GELDER, M. G. (1968) Verbal conditioning as a measure of interpersonal influence in psychiatric interviews. *Br. J. soc. clin. Psychol.*, **7**, 194-209.

HALL, S. BARTON (1960) Personal communication.

HETHERINGTON, R. R. (1956) The clinical psychologist in the mental hospital. *Br. med. J.*, **2**, 708-709.

HETHERINGTON, R. R. (1961) Personal relationships in clinical psychology. *Br. J. med. Psychol.*, **34**, 143-150.

HETHERINGTON, R. R. (1964) The psychologist's role in society. *Bull. Br. Psychol. Soc.*, **17**, 9-12.

JAMES, WILLIAM (1902) *The Varieties of Religious Experience*. London: Longmans.

KAHN, R. L. and CANNELL, C. F. (1958) *The Dynamics of Interviewing*. New York: Wiley.

KELLNER, R. (1968) The evidence in favour of psychotherapy. *Br. J. med. Psychol.*, **41**, 341-358.

KELLY, E. L. and FISKE, D. W. (1950) The prediction of success in the V.A. training programme in clinical psychology. *Amer. Psychol.*, **5**, 395-406.

KLEIN, D. B. (1951) *Abnormal Psychology*. New York: Holt.

KOFFKA, K. (1928) *The Growth of the Mind*. London: Kegan Paul.

LEWIS, SIR THOMAS (1930) Research in medicine: its position and its needs. *Br. med. J.*, **1**, 479-483.

MACCOBY, E. E. and MACCOBY, N. (1954) The interview: a tool of social science. *In* LINDZEY, G. (Ed.) *Handbook of Social Psychology*. Cambridge, Mass.: Addison-Wesley.

MASLOW, A. H. (1962) *Toward a Psychology of Being*. London: Van Nostrand.

MATARAZZO, J. D. (1962) Prescribed behaviour therapy: suggestions from interview research. *In* BACHRACH, A. J. (Ed.) *Experimental Foundations of Clinical Psychology*. New York: Basic Books.

MATARAZZO, J. D. (1965) The interview. *In* WOLMAN, B. B. (Ed.) *Handbook of Clinical Psychology*. New York: McGraw-Hill.

MEARES, A. (1957) *The Medical Interview*. Springfield, Ill.: Thomas.

G*

MEEHL, P. E. (1954) *Clinical vs. Statistical Prediction.* Minneapolis: Univ. Minneapolis Press.

MURRAY, H. A. (1943) *Thematic Apperception Test, Manual.* Camb. Mass.: Harvard Univ. Press.

NEWMAN, C. (1957) *The Evolution of Medical Education in the Nineteenth Century.* London: O.U.P.

OLDFIELD, R. C. (1941) *The Psychology of the Interview.* London: Methuen.

PAYNE, R. W. (1953) The role of the psychologist at the Institute of Psychiatry. *Revue Psychol. appl.,* **3**, 150-160.

PAYNE, S. L. (1949) Interview memory faults. *Publ. Opin. Quart.,* **13**, 684-685.

RAVEN, J. C. (1952) *Human Nature.* London: H. K. Lewis.

RICE, S. A. (1929) A contagious bias in the interview. *Amer. J. Sociol.,* **35**, 420-423.

RUESCH, J. and PRESTWOOD, A. R. (1949) Anxiety: its initiation, communication and interpersonal management. *Arch. Neurol. Psychiat.,* **62**, 527-550.

SCHELER, M. (1954) *The Nature of Sympathy.* London: Kegan Paul.

VERNON, P. E. (1953) *Personality Tests and Assessments.* London: Methuen.

VERNON, P. E. (1964) *Personality Assessment: a Critical Survey.* London: Methuen.

6

Psychophysiological techniques

Gordon S. Claridge

I THE PSYCHOPHYSIOLOGICAL APPROACH

Ten years ago the editor of a book such as this is unlikely to have commissioned a chapter on psychophysiological techniques. Even as an academic pursuit psychophysiology still occupies a somewhat precarious position among the behavioural sciences, sitting as it does awkwardly straddling orthodox physiology and classical psychology. As an applied discipline it can scarcely be said to exist at all; few, if any, of the procedures to be described here being in daily clinical use. If they are in use it is on a purely experimental basis, either as part of the general search for more objective diagnostic tests or applied to specific problems where the advantages of the psychophysiological approach have been demonstrated. The aim of this chapter will be to outline some of the more promising techniques available and to give the reader an idea of how they can be used in a clinical setting. First, however, let us look briefly at their historical and theoretical background and then try and define the present scope of psychophysiology.

The recent emergence of a clinical psychophysiology – to coin such a clumsy term – is a curious repetition of events. At the end of the last century there was a strong belief by a few men that the future of psychiatric diagnosis lay in the discovery of measurable somatic and behavioural correlates of personality. Pursuit of this belief led to active collaboration between the clinician and the experimentalist, objective study of the psychiatric patient forming an integral part of the newly emerging science of psychology. Notable contributions to this movement in abnormal psychology were made by Kraepelin in Wundt's laboratory and by the French physician, Ch. Féré, who collaborated with Binet in research on the psychogalvanic reflex or 'Féré effect', as it is still sometimes called. The efforts of these early pioneers failed, partly for technical and partly for ideological reasons. Psychiatry took a new direction and attempts to establish an objective basis for psychopathology had to await later developments in the basic sciences.

Three such developments have contributed to the recent revival of a psychophysiological approach to mental disorder. The first is the advance that has been made in the design and construction of the precision apparatus necessary for accurate work in this area. The second is the rapid change that has occurred in neurophysiology, which is now able to give a more adequate account of the neural mechanisms of behaviour. This has strengthened the theoretical basis of psychophysiology, giving, for example, impetus to arousal theories that try to link important psychological processes, such as drive and emotion, with central events in the brain (Duffy, 1934; Hebb, 1955). The third reason is that experimentalists are showing a greater concern for individual differences in psychophysiological response and their possible relationship with personality variables. One example is the formulation of anxiety as a state of heightened physiological arousal acting as a mediating process in the acquisition of neurotic symptoms (Malmo, 1957). Another, with rather broader implications for personality theory, can be traced to the influence of Russian physiology, particularly the old Pavlovian notion of 'nervous types', the idea that differences in personality arise from variations in the strength and equilibrium of central nervous processes of excitation and inhibition. The concept of nervous types has received considerable attention from contemporary Russian psychologists (Gray, 1964), as well as having a major influence on Western personality theory (Eysenck, 1957). Eysenck's own contribution in this respect is well known and has consisted of trying to link descriptive personality dimensions, such as extraversion, with underlying variations in cortical excitation and inhibition. Although Eysenck has preferred to analyse individual differences using a Pavlovian model of nervous activity, there is now an increasing convergence of Russian and Western ideas. The Russian concept of excitation-inhibition and the Western notion of arousal are clearly very similar and recently there have been several attempts to translate the Pavlovian-Eysenckian model into the more familiar terminology of arousal theory (Claridge, 1967; Gray, 1967; Eysenck, 1967).

An important offshoot of these technical and theoretical advances in the basic sciences is that those working in the clinical field have been stimulated to take a greater interest in the psychophysiology of the psychiatric patient. This development is a logical extension of the study of individual differences among normal personalities. Early on Pavlov (1941) applied his model of nervous types to mental illness, while it is an assumption of theories like Eysenck's that the functional psychiatric disorders simply represent the extremes of a number of continuously variable dimensions of behaviour. Study of the psychiatric patient thus allows the experimenter to examine normal psychophysiological processes in an exaggerated form. Put the other way round, it means that it should be possible to standardize objective psychophysiological tests that differentiate the major psychiatric disorders or develop precise techniques which allow the clinician to quantify defined features of personality disturbance. Duffy (1962), writing from her own position within arousal theory, has gathered together a good deal of scattered empirical evidence which would support this conclusion; while a recent investigation by Claridge (1967) has demonstrated that, when psychiatric disorder is studied from a defined theoretical viewpoint, the results fall very much in line with current psychophysiological models of abnormal behaviour.

It is clear even from this brief account that the re-emergence of clinical psychophysiology is due to many disparate, if converging, influences. Its mongrel background makes its exact boundaries hard to delimit. Broadly defined in the tradition of its early pioneers, psychophysiology would embrace the investigation of any relatively simple somatic or behavioural response which was thought to give a clue about the physiological basis of introspective data. Contemporary psychophysiologists have defined their field of interest rather more narrowly than this. They have tended to confine themselves to the study of accepted physiological parameters, such as autonomic responses, using these as direct peripheral indicators of brain activity and its mental correlates. A typical experiment would involve relating, say, changes in skin resistance to introspective reports of anxiety in an individual subjected to a variety of psychological stresses. The application of this procedure to personality would consist of studying individual differences in skin resistance and correlating these with some measure of anxiety-proneness.

This more restricted view of the field does not, however, take into account the fact that the evolution of the psychophysiological approach to behaviour owed a good deal to experimental techniques that have traditionally been regarded as the legitimate concern of the psychological or psychophysical laboratory. Many nineteenth-century workers were interested, for example, in the ergograph fatigue curves and visual after-images of their subjects and used these procedures alongside autonomic measures in their studies of the somatic correlates of mental disease. The contribution of Russian physiology has also rested heavily on techniques that some would not regard as strictly psychophysiological. It has, of course, made considerable use of conditioning procedures and, more recently, of sensory threshold and similar measures. Since Eysenck has followed the Pavlovian theoretical model of brain activity, he too has been led to test his theory using techniques derived from the conventional psychological laboratory, rather than from physiology. These have included learning, vigilance, and complex motor tasks, as well as various measures of perceptual response. At the other end of the spectrum we find a number of refined EEG techniques, such as the measurement of discrete cortical responses. These are derived from neurophysiology and are now making it possible to study precise aspects of brain activity in the intact organism. The use of such procedures in behavioural research is still relatively uncommon, but already they are helping to push the boundaries of psychophysiology further and further into the nervous system.

The techniques of psychophysiology can therefore be said to range from the procedures of classical experimental psychology, at one end, to those of neurophysiology, at the other*. For this reason the definition of psychophysiology adopted here will be a relatively wide one, though emphasis will naturally be placed on those techniques having a physiological 'flavour'. Occasional mention

---

* The interest of psychophysiology can also be said to encompass other kinds of data, such as those on the endocrine response to stress, which have been well-documented (e.g. Basowitz *et al.*, 1954). However, as psychophysiological techniques, biochemical assay procedures were not considered suitable for inclusion here. Interested readers will find a general discussion of the role of neurohumoral factors in behaviour in Duffy (1962).

will also be made, however, of some other correlates of conventional psycho-physiological measures, particularly where these have made, or promise to make, a significant contribution to the theory underlying current work in the field. This may help the reader to view the main techniques described within the broader context of a general biological approach to behaviour. Finally, befitting a book of this kind, attention will be drawn wherever possible to the clinical aspects of psychophysiology.

II TYPES OF TECHNIQUE

From what has been said already it is clear that the aim of all psychophysiological measurement is to try and assess the ongoing state of the central nervous system. Since almost all psychophysiological research on humans is carried out in the intact organism, measurement is inevitably indirect in one way or another. This may be because the response or responses being studied involve a system physically peripheral to the brain, such as the autonomic nervous system, or because external recordings from the brain itself provide only a crude indicator of C.N.S. activity. Alternatively, it may be because the phenomenon under investigation is a molar behavioural one too far removed from the underlying physiology for its exact neural basis to be known. In order to get as close as possible to the central nervous system, psychophysiologists have naturally concentrated their attention on strictly physiological parameters that can be recorded directly from the body surface. These will be discussed here under two headings: somatic measures and EEG measures. Afterwards a number of techniques using drugs will be described. These will be discussed separately because, although some drug techniques also make use of physiological recordings from the subject, this is usually incidental to the main purpose of the procedure and is only one of a number of methods available for assessing the drug effect.

Technical details of measuring physiological responses will only be briefly outlined here. Any reader contemplating using these procedures is advised to consult the recently published *Manual of Psychophysiological Methods* edited by Venables and Martin (1967). This book contains an excellent introduction to the principles and practice of measurement in this area as well as details of commercial equipment available. A good general introduction to psycho-physiology and reprints of classic papers in the field can be found in Sternbach (1966).

1 Measures of somatic response*

(a) *General Considerations*
Because of their role in the expression of emotional arousal, changes in the autonomic system and in skeletal muscle activity have become an obvious target

---

* The general term 'somatic' is used here to cover measures both of involuntary autonomic response and skeletal muscle response.

for investigation by psychophysiologists. Measurement of these systems provides a convenient way of monitoring the organism's internal state of activation in a large number of experimental situations. Typical experiments include taking physiological recordings during the performance of psychological tasks (Corcoran, 1964), as a means of quantifying the response to experimental stresses (Sternbach, 1960a), and in the investigation of individual differences among psychiatric patients (Malmo and Shagass, 1949, 1952). In all of these situations the technical procedure is basically the same. All somatic responses either occur naturally as electrical signals or can be readily converted into this form by means of suitable devices (transducers) arranged so that they pick up changes in the particular system being studied. These signals are then amplified and sampled at regular intervals or continuously recorded, usually in visual form on a moving paper chart. An additional facility that is sometimes included is the storage of data on magnetic tape. The data are then in a suitable form for direct computer analysis without going through the intermediate phase of measurement from visual charts. Ideally the investigation of somatic activity would include the monitoring of all response systems simultaneously, but this is rarely possible and the experimenter has to be content to study only a selected few. Those most usually chosen are skin resistance (or potential), muscle tension and various aspects of cardiovascular activity, especially heart rate. Although the complete somatic pattern cannot be studied, most workers would agree that as many different response systems as possible should be sampled. This is because of the tendency found in some people to show idiosyncratic patterns of activity, a phenomenon known as 'response specificity' (Lacey *et al.*, 1953; Lacey and Lacey, 1958). Thus, some individuals may show their maximum reactivity in their heart rate, others in their blood pressure, yet others in their skin resistance. Clearly if only one type of response is measured some of the individual variation in general reactivity may not be seen. This difficulty is less likely to arise where a wide range of reactivity is known to be present in the group studied. In a group of neurotic patients, for example, a single measure such as heart rate may be adequate to establish differences between subtypes within the sample (e.g. Claridge and Herrington, 1963b). Thus, there is a general tendency for people to differ in their overall arousability, but over and above this there are individual fluctuations in their reaction profiles, due to response specificity.

The number and kind of response systems chosen for study will depend on various factors, some of which are entirely practical. Certain autonomic responses are more difficult (or more expensive) to measure than others. The accurate measurement of pupil response falls into this category. Others, such as salivary flow, are relatively insensitive and unsuitable for continuous recording or investigation of subtle variations in arousal. Another practical consideration is the physical restriction placed on the subject due to multiple recordings from numerous electrodes. A subject who is too 'wired up' may find it difficult, if not impossible, to carry out some psychological tasks that may form an additional part of the investigation. If the subject is a psychiatric patient, particularly a disturbed child, he may find some part of, or even the whole, procedure intolerable. It may provoke anxiety even in the normal individual, an arousing effect that has to be carefully controlled for with an adequate preparation period before actual recording begins. Some of these problems can be partly overcome by adopting telemetering methods which allow physiological measures to be made from the freely moving subject (see Wolff, 1967). Telemetering is expensive, however, and introduces its own problems. The main one is the difficulty of interpreting the record of somatic activity, of distinguishing between responses that are of psychological significance and those that are due to some incidental cause, such as pure movement artifact under electrodes, or to a genuine physiological change of peripheral rather than central origin.

The problem of interpretation is a general one to be faced in all psychophysiological research in this area and a common pitfall for workers entering the field. It is best illustrated by considering the cardiovascular system, some feature of which is often used as an index of psychophysiological arousal. The cardiovascular system is influenced by a number of finely tuned homeostatic mechanisms which allow it to readjust constantly to variations in the physical state of the organism. These variations may be due to chronic causes, such as age, weight, and diet or to acute causes such as immediate changes in posture or physical exertion. Both kinds of peripheral effect will complicate the application of cardiovascular measures in psychophysiological research. In fact, the interpretation of somatic data in general as indices of central arousal is hazardous once one goes beyond the young physically healthy subject lying at rest in a sound-proofed air-conditioned room. The hazard will be constantly present in the clinical setting. The psychiatric patient may be physically as well as mentally unhealthy and fall outside the age range of most subjects used in academic research. In addition he will almost certainly have received some form of drug therapy, the after-effects of which may persist for an indeterminate length of time. If he is actually on drugs at the time of testing, then the investigator has, to say the least, been extremely careless. Of course, this does not apply where the purpose of the experiment is actually to study a drug effect. Even here, however, the experimenter must be aware of the precise action of the drug on peripheral mechanisms in the body, in order to avoid false conclusions about its supposed effect on central psychological processes. The aspiring psychophysiologist is therefore well-advised to make himself familiar with appropriate parts of basic texts on the physiological (Keele and Neil, 1961) and pharmacological (Goodman and Gilman, 1965) basis of the techniques he is using. This will help him to be aware of, and control for, some of the more obvious sources of error in the interpretation of his data.

Whatever somatic system or systems are chosen for study, the same care is necessary in standardizing the conditions of measurement. Variables to be controlled include the physical environment in which measurements are taken, preparation of the subject (e.g. siting of electrodes), and the recording procedure itself. Given careful control of these variables comparisons can be made on two parameters of somatic activity, which should be clearly distinguished from each other. One is the *level* of activity, which reflects the general tonus of the system being studied and which shows a slow drift over time. The second is the *response* of the system, either to an applied stimulus or due to intrinsic fluctuations within itself. Responses occur superimposed on the background level and change over a much shorter time course. The most familiar example of this kind of reaction is the galvanic skin response.

Response and level are not always independent of each other, in the sense that the size of a discrete somatic response may vary inversely with the basal level from which it occurs. This relationship has become known as the so-called 'law of initial values' (Wilder, 1957) and various mathematical corrections have been suggested to try and obtain measures of responsivity independent of level (Lacey, 1956; Heath and Oken, 1962; Benjamin, 1963). None of these methods is entirely satisfactory, but data should always be inspected for possible operation of the law of initial values and, if necessary, corrected for dependence of change scores on level. Otherwise false conclusions may be drawn. For example, a subject showing a tiny somatic response to an imposed stress may be wrongly assumed to be under-reactive. In fact, he may be so anxious that the general tonus of the system being studied is too high for further large increases to occur.

The exact details of procedure and choice of parameters to be studied will, of course, depend on the aim of the investigation undertaken and the facilities available. With regard to the latter point, one final comment is worth making. For those entering the field with a limited budget it is certainly preferable to buy a small quantity of commercial apparatus and concentrate attention on one or two measures, such as skin resistance and heart rate, than to try comprehensive polygraphic recording with improvised equipment. Suitably designed commercial apparatus is gradually being made available in Great Britain and should help to make for greater accuracy of measurement in the field and for greater comparability of results from different laboratories or clinics.

(b) *Clinical Application*

In the limited space available it would be impossible to review the many studies of somatic response having a broadly clinical flavour. The reader is therefore referred to easily available reviews of the relevant literature. The studies of interest fall roughly into two categories: those concerned with the statistical analysis of large quantities of somatic data and those concerned with the comparison of clinical groups on a few measures. Studies of the first kind have been extensively reviewed by Eysenck (1953), while Martin (1960) has examined studies of the second kind carried out up to 1960. In her book referred to earlier, Duffy (1962) has also looked at the available evidence from the viewpoint of her own activation theory. The discussion here will be confined to those studies that are of recent origin, are theoretically of some significance, or help to illustrate the value of somatic research in the clinical field.

Although there have been numerous studies of somatic response in the

psychiatric patient, their technical and theoretical sophistication has varied enormously. A major problem has been the lack of regard for the obvious heterogeneity of psychiatric illness and a failure to select patients according to well-defined criteria. Studies in many early (and some contemporary!) laboratories were carried out on mixed groups of undifferentiated neurotics or psychotics, or even just on 'psychiatric patients'. Not surprisingly, the results of such studies have been inconclusive. More promising findings have emerged from those investigations which have been carried out from a definite theoretical viewpoint, or at least with an awareness of the need for careful selection of the patient material. An outstanding recent example is a group of experiments reported by Lader and his colleague, Lorna Wing, and brought together in monograph form (Lader and Wing, 1966). The primary aim of their investigation was to study the somatic correlates of anxiety in neurotic patients. The basic procedure was developed in an initial series of experiments on normal subjects and involved simultaneous polygraphic recording of skin resistance, pulse volume, pulse interbeat interval, and muscle tension. Several measures of physiological response were derived from the data. The most important of these was the rate of habituation to randomly presented tones, i.e. the rate at which somatic responses to the tone diminished on repeated presentation. The prediction was then made that habituation would be slower (that is arousal would be higher) in neurotic patients with anxiety. This was shown to be true for both the habituation score and for a composite measure of arousal derived from the skin conductance data.*
The latter index, called the D-score, was made up of the habituation score itself, the change in basal conductance throughout the experiment, and the number of spontaneous fluctuations in conductance. The D-score significantly differentiated anxiety states and normals and correlated significantly with a clinical rating of overt anxiety. Lader and Wing then went on to assess the effect of drug therapy in the same group of anxiety neurotics. Using a double-blind, cross-over design they compared the effect of amylobarbitone sodium with a placebo. They demonstrated that a week of treatment on the active drug produced a parallel reduction in clinically rated anxiety and in physiological reactivity.

The results reported by Lader and Wing are very much in line with current arousal conceptions of anxiety. They also supplement the findings of earlier studies contrasting dysthymic neurotics with those diagnosed as hysteric. These two subtypes of neurosis are found to occupy opposite poles of a continuum, at least on some parameters of somatic response. Thus, van der Merwe (1948) compared the peripheral vasomotor activity of hysterics and dysthymics and demonstrated that on one factor, called 'emotional tension', the two neurotic groups were ranged on either side of normal. In a more recent study Claridge and Herrington (1963b) measured the heart rate of normal, hysteric and dysthymic subjects during performance of an auditory vigilance task. The average heart rate of normals was significantly lower than that of dysthymics, but higher than that

---

* In accordance with normal practice, resistance measures were converted to their reciprocal, conductance.

of hysterics. The performance of the three groups on the vigilance task itself was theoretically consistent with this finding. Hysterics, in keeping with their low level of autonomic arousal, performed poorly compared with normals who, in turn, were inferior to dysthymics. These results support the view held by a number of workers, including Eysenck, that it is useful, as a starting-point at any rate, to distinguish between two broad subtypes of neurosis, hysteria and dysthymia. Consideration of this fact could usefully serve as a guide-line for patient selection and may lead to less equivocal findings in future studies of somatic response in psychoneurosis.

Turning now to the functional psychoses, the interpretation of peripheral somatic responses in these conditions is generally much more difficult than in the case of neurosis, where states like anxiety can be related fairly easily to simple concepts of arousal. In psychosis not only is the central dysfunction more intricate, but somatic activity may also be disturbed due to purely peripheral causes. Correlation of somatic and central events is therefore doubly hazardous. Furthermore, the clinical variability of the psychoses makes the selection of homogeneous groups of patients a major problem. Variables to be controlled include the treatment history and the type and chronicity of the illness. With regard to chronicity it is important to realize that the psychoses are changing illnesses and marked shifts in psychophysiological status almost certainly occur as the psychotic patient progresses from the acute to the chronic phase. The study of undifferentiated groups of psychotic patients is therefore unlikely to reveal anything of value. To illustrate how some of these problems can be overcome by careful experimentation let us examine one notable example where the measurement of somatic response has made it possible to quantify important features of psychosis.

The work referred to is that reported by Venables and his colleagues (Venables, 1964). Venables has been particularly interested in the measurement of skin potential which, unlike skin resistance, involves recording the existing electrical potential of the skin, rather than its resistance to an applied current. Over a period of several years, Venables has examined skin potential activity in chronic schizophrenic patients, relating it both to the subtype of illness and to other measures of arousal. In keeping with the nature of schizophrenia results have been complex, but important findings have nevertheless emerged. A central feature of Venables' research has been his attempt to relate arousal level to defined parameters of schizophrenia, such as activity-withdrawal and the paranoid/non-paranoid dichotomy. Venables and Wing (1962) were able to show that greater degrees of behavioural withdrawal were associated with higher levels of autonomic arousal, as measured by skin potential. However, further breakdown of schizophrenia into subtypes indicated that this was not true of all patients. A group of paranoid patients showing coherent delusions was isolated in whom the relationship between withdrawal and physiological arousal was opposite to that found in other psychotic patients. In this small group of coherently deluded psychotics the more active patients were more aroused, possibly indicating a different psychophysiological mechanism for their illnesses than that underlying the illnesses of more disorganized schizophrenics.

Venables has also made use of other, perceptual, indices of arousal, the two-flash threshold and, more recently, the two-click threshold (Venables, 1967). Both of these procedures are basically similar. They are measured by finding the point at which two brief light flashes or clicks, presented in quick succession, can just be discriminated. Discrimination is normally better, that is the threshold is lower, in states of high arousal. In one important study Venables (1963) compared the relationship between the two-flash threshold and his other arousal measure, skin potential, in different experimental groups. He demonstrated that the two measures were correlated in opposite directions in normal subjects compared with chronic schizophrenics. Again, however, coherently deluded paranoid patients differed from other schizophrenics, the relationship between the two measures in this group being similar to that found in normal subjects. At present these results are difficult to account for though they do suggest that in psychosis it is the relationship between different components of arousal that is abnormal, rather than the absolute change in arousal as a whole. This conclusion is supported by the results of other studies of schizophrenia to be mentioned later. It also provides one rational way, at least, in which future research in this area could approach the psychophysiological analysis of functional psychosis.

So far we have looked mainly at the potential value of somatic techniques in diagnosis. The procedures described also promise to be useful in other areas of clinical psychophysiology. Brief mention has already been made of their use in the evaluation of drug treatment in anxiety states (Lader and Wing, 1966). In another part of their research, also reported in their monograph, Lader and Wing extended the study of drugs to a comparative bioassay of amylobarbitone sodium against chlordiazepoxide (Librium). The purpose of this experiment was to compare the relative effectiveness of these two drugs at different dose levels. This was done by taking the composite measure of arousal (D-score) referred to earlier and using it as an objective measure of the physiological effect of each drug. By this means it was possible to find a dose of chlordiazepoxide which was equivalent in its effect to a standard dose of amylobarbitone sodium. Matched doses of the two drugs could then be assessed for their relative clinical effectiveness. Such a quantitative approach to chemotherapy could, if extended to other drugs and other psychiatric conditions, bring about a very desirable improvement on present subjective methods of matching dose levels in drug trials and of evaluating physical methods of treatment.

Another important application of somatic techniques is in conjunction with behaviour therapy. During desensitization, for example, changes in autonomic responsivity can provide a precise measure of the reduction in anxiety provoked by phobic stimuli (Clark, 1963; Hoenig and Reed, 1966). This allows the therapist to assess the progress of treatment objectively. Before treatment begins the initial autonomic reactivity of the phobic patient may also be of interest, for two reasons. First, it may give a guide to the patient's overall level of arousability and help the behaviour therapist formulate his treatment schedule, for example by indicating whether the additional use of drugs would facilitate the deconditioning process. Secondly, it may make it easier for the therapist to explore the precise situations in which the patient feels anxiety and so allow him to produce carefully graded hierarchies for reciprocal inhibition (Wolpe, 1960). For these purposes the galvanic skin response is probably the most convenient and sensitive index to use (Seager and Brown, 1967). Other more specific applications of somatic techniques to behaviour therapy are also worth noting. Malmo *et al.* (1960), for example, report on the use of electromyography in the treatment of hysterical deafness. They recorded forearm muscle tension as a sign of response to auditory stimuli used in a procedure designed to condition the patient to hear. A rather different application is that described by Freund (1963), who has used plethysmography to measure changes in penis volume as an index of sexual orientation. This technique could prove of value as an adjunct to the assessment of patients with sexual disorders undergoing aversion therapy.

These, then, are some of the ways in which the study of somatic response can help the psychologist quantify important features of behaviour in the clinical setting. At present, clinical application of the techniques described is confined to a few research centres, but with increasing technical and theoretical advance they are likely to be used routinely on a much larger scale in the future. If so, they will form an important addition to the assessment procedures of the clinical psychologist.

2 EEG techniques

As we have seen, the rationale for using the procedures described above is that changes in peripheral somatic response are assumed to reflect alterations in central arousal processes. The study of the electrical activity of the brain itself is a logical extension of this idea, since in theory, at least, it allows the psychophysiologist to get closer to the physiological substrate of the behaviour he is trying to explain. It is in this area of investigation that psychophysiology merges with that part of neurophysiology which is concerned with the study of the central nervous system in the intact organism. The recent emergence of this 'behavioural' neurophysiology has brought with it a number of new techniques which will be referred to briefly later on. To begin with, however, we shall be concerned with more conventional EEG procedures that have been adopted by the psychophysiologist. Needless to say, most of the general comments made in the previous section concerning the need for technical accuracy and sound background knowledge apply equally, if not more so, to EEG work. For technical advice the reader is referred to Margerison *et al.* (1967). An excellent general introduction to the relevant neurophysiology is given by Brazier (1960b), while an early, but still valuable, account of the EEG in relation to behaviour disorder can be found in Lindsley (1944). Elsewhere, Lindsley (1960) has looked at the EEG from the standpoint of the psychophysiology of arousal and attention.

The interest of psychophysiologists in the EEG should be clearly distinguished from its present clinical use in diagnosis, either psychiatric or neurological. The neurologist is concerned with the detection of gross abnormalities of wave-form or rhythm indicative of brain pathology and in this respect the EEG has achieved some status as an aid to diagnosis. On the other hand, clinical use of the EEG in psychiatric practice has been less successful. Although such features as dys-rhythmia and the predominance of certain EEG frequencies have sometimes been reported in various functional clinical conditions (Kennard, 1953), these have usually proved too inconsistent or too non-specific to be of either practical or theoretical value. The visual interpretation of multi-channel EEG recordings in psychiatric disorders therefore holds little promise as an assessment procedure. One reason for this failure of the 'clinical' EEG is now fairly obvious. Ordinary EEG tracings taken from the skull surface provide at best only a very crude indicator of brain function, representing as they do the composite activity of large areas of cortex remote from the recording electrodes. Only if brain activity is grossly disturbed by organic pathology will significant EEG signs appear on visual inspection of the record, and even here not always reliably. It is not surprising that in the neurologically normal individual subtle variations in psychological state will not be matched by easily recognizable changes in the total EEG pattern.

In psychophysiology the EEG occupies a different position. Its status is similar to that of the somatic measures described in the previous section, that is it provides yet another way of monitoring the physiological correlates of behaviour occurring under simple well-defined conditions. Thus, it is common practice for EEG recordings to be included in polygraphic studies of the autonomic system. One or more channels of the polygraph may be taken up with recordings from a site or several sites on the scalp. This procedure allows the investigator to correlate alterations in somatic response with simultaneous fluctuations in brain activity. This more restricted use of the EEG has led the psychophysiologist to confine his attention to a few limited parameters of brain activity. These parameters have been chosen because they are well-recognizable features of the EEG and are theoretically of some significance. Interest has centred particularly upon measures that appear to reflect fluctuations in consciousness or attention. It is well established that states of relaxation are in general accompanied by a predominance of brain waves in the *alpha* range, that is those falling between frequencies of 8 and 13 cps. During sudden alerting or in states of high arousal these are replaced by faster low voltage *beta* waves in the range 18-30 cps. The chronic level of arousal or shifts in arousal under different conditions of stimulation can thus be quantified by measuring the frequency, amplitude, or a combination of both of these components of EEG activity. Commonly used frequency measures are those based on an estimation of the relative presence or absence of alpha rhythm in the record. One such measure is the *alpha index* or *per cent time alpha*. As the name implies, this is a measure of the amount of alpha present in a selected portion of the EEG record, expressed as a percentage of the total time sampled.

Its numerical value is, of course, inversely related to the degree of activation. In practice the measurement of alpha index is facilitated by incorporating an electronic filter in the circuit of the recording apparatus so that all rhythms outside the alpha band are filtered out.

A closely related frequency measure, sometimes used to study the reactivity of the EEG rather than its ongoing level, is the alpha-blocking response. This is usually expressed as the time taken for alpha rhythm to return to the record following a previous short period of stimulation with, say, a bright light. In practice, of course, the latency period following cessation of the stimulus is usually characterized by a gradual build-up in the amplitude and frequency of alpha rhythm. Various criteria for the return of alpha rhythm may be adopted, such as the time taken to the first alpha burst or the time to the point where alpha index is similar to that present in the pre-stimulus record. Some of these methods have been compared by Claridge and Herrington (1963a).

Techniques based on the amplitude of the EEG have been less commonly used, though a notable exception is that described by Goldstein and his colleagues (Goldstein *et al.*, 1965; Sugarman *et al.*, 1964). Their method involves integrating EEG amplitude over time, the integrator output being independent of wave-form frequency. It is thus an electronic form of planimetry of the EEG record, providing an index of total energy output over specified periods of time. This procedure is of special interest here because Goldstein and Sugarman have used it to demonstrate differences between normal and schizophrenic subjects. On one measure in particular, that of variability of electrical energy in the EEG, schizophrenics differed markedly from normals, showing an abnormal degree of cortical stability. Venables (1966) has discussed the significance of this finding in relation to other recent research on the psychophysiology of schizophrenia.

Among the advantages of adding EEG recording to polygraphic measurement of somatic responses, two may be mentioned here. First, it has often been assumed that the autonomic and cortical changes occurring during physiological arousal parallel each other in a simple linear fashion. Thus, increasing anxiety appears to produce a shift towards greater sympathetic reactivity of the autonomic nervous system and the appearance of activated EEG patterns, characterized by reduced alpha index and increased frequency of the dominant rhythms. The evidence now throws considerable doubt on this simple unitary view of arousal and suggests that EEG and somatic measures cannot be regarded as interchangeable indices of a single arousal process. The relationship between such measures may not always be the same but may depend critically on a number of factors, such as the group of individuals studied and/or the conditions under which recordings are made. Studies of normal subjects have shown autonomic and EEG measures to be entirely unrelated (Sternbach, 1960b), related in a curvilinear fashion (Stennett, 1957) and correlated in opposite directions at high and low levels of arousal (Darrow *et al.*, 1946). In a rather different investigation reported by Claridge (1967) autonomic, EEG, and other psychophysiological data collected on normal and neurotic subjects were factor analysed. Of two correlated factors extracted one was mainly accounted for by the EEG measures, the other having high loadings on autonomic indices. It was concluded that the classical autonomic and EEG signs of activation may only occur consistently together in certain individuals, specifically those falling along the descriptive personality dimension of dysthymia-hysteria, and even here only under particular experimental conditions. In other individuals, especially acute psychotic patients, various measures of arousal may be related in a quite different way. Although in the research referred to no strictly physiological data were available to test this view of psychosis, a recent study by Titaeva (1962) has demonstrated that in schizophrenia autonomic and EEG measures become 'dissociated', signs of high cortical arousal being accompanied by low sympathetic reactivity, and vice versa. There are, therefore, good theoretical grounds for looking, not at a single psychophysiological measure or type of measure, but at how different components of arousal relate to each other in different personalities or psychiatric conditions. The comparison of EEG with autonomic indices is one example of this approach. Another has already been referred to, namely Venables' comparison of the skin potential and two-flash threshold in psychotic and normal subjects. A further example, involving two quite different measures, will be described in the next section.

Apart from theoretical considerations, there are also practical advantages in making use of EEG techniques in psychophysiology. For certain applications peripheral somatic responses may be a too insensitive indicator of physiological change and it may, therefore, be more appropriate to examine variations in one of the EEG parameters described earlier. An example of such an application will help to illustrate the point. This particular example is perhaps also of interest because it is taken from the clinical field.

Over a number of years evidence has been gathered on a large number of psychiatric patients that a measure of the Archimedes spiral after-effect will discriminate between dysthymic neurotics, on the one hand, and those with hysterico-psychopathic disorders on the other (Claridge, 1967). Following fixation of a rotating spiral dysthymic patients experience significantly longer after-effects than either normal subjects or hysterico-psychopaths. The measurement of this after-effect is inevitably subjective and dependent upon the individual's judgement of when the visual illusion of movement has stopped. In order to try and develop a more objective index of the effect it was decided to examine its EEG correlates (Claridge and Herrington, 1963a). Subjects were instructed to fixate the centre of a rotating Archimedes spiral. When the spiral disc was stopped they were asked to close their eyes instead of continuing to fixate it. It was found that on eye closure an alpha-blocking response of the kind described earlier occurred. That is to say, previous fixation of the rotating spiral delayed the return of the normal alpha rhythm. In a mixed group of neurotic and normal subjects the length of this delay was significantly correlated with the subjective spiral after-effect assessed on a separate occasion by the usual method. Group differences in alpha blocking, though not significant, paralleled those for the spiral after-effect, dysthymics showing more alpha blocking than either normals or hysterico-psychopaths.

The measurement of a simple parameter was well suited to the application just described. However, to extract more detailed information from the EEG special techniques are required. The introduction of computer analysis and averaging procedures into behavioural neurophysiology is now making it possible to quantify the background EEG in the human subject as well as to isolate discrete wave-forms representing the brain's response to stimulation (Brazier, 1960a; Margerison *et al.*, 1967). Thus by averaging the EEG response to a large number of identical stimuli presented successively it is possible to detect a characteristic wave-form called the cortical evoked response. Normally, simple stimuli such as light flashes or tones are used, though other more complex stimuli have also been investigated. Variations in the characteristics of the cortical evoked response in psychiatric patients have been studied by a number of workers, though it is as yet too early to assess the significance of their findings (Shagass and Schwartz, 1962; Speck *et al.*, 1966).

Another precise EEG phenomenon which promises to become of increasing interest to psychophysiologists is the 'contingent negative variation' (C.N.V.) described by Grey Walter (Walter *et al.*, 1964). Also called by him the 'expectancy wave', this is a slow wave-form first noticed by Walter during conditioning studies in which the EEG responses to paired stimuli were being averaged. The C.N.V. typically occurs as a potential change to a signal which warns the subject to expect a second stimulus to which he has to make a response or pay attention. Its persistence or suppression is said to vary according to the subject's psychiatric state, his readiness to respond and the significance of the stimuli presented (McCallum, 1967). It therefore appears to be a genuine and stable neurophysiological correlate of certain features of higher mental activity. Like the cortical evoked response, the C.N.V. requires further intensive investigation before its potential value in the clinical field can be judged.

The advanced EEG procedures just mentioned take even the research psychophysiologist to the very edges of his discipline and they are likely to be of immediate practical interest to few clinical workers. Their main significance at present is that they point the way for future developments in psychophysiology. A good deal of collaborative basic research still needs to be done in the area, involving both behaviourally orientated neurophysiologists and psychologists with a physiological bent. Psychophysiology has already made considerable progress both factually and theoretically. Its next obvious step is to push investigations of its own molar concepts to their logical place in the brain itself.

3 Drug techniques

The techniques to be described in this section differ from those considered so far in that they have entered psychophysiology not from the basic sciences of psychology and physiology but from experimental psychiatry. Because of their history they are the most clinical of the procedures described here, all having been devised as an aid to psychiatric diagnosis. They all rest on the underlying assumption that variations in mental state will be reflected in the physiological response to acute administration of one drug or another. The techniques concerned can be clearly divided into two types: those involving fixed doses of drugs that primarily affect the autonomic nervous system and those in which tolerance thresholds for centrally acting drugs are estimated. Each of these will be considered in turn.

(a) *Autonomic Drug Procedures*

In a search for greater objectivity of diagnosis a number of psychiatrists have devised tests which make use of the effects of certain drugs on the autonomic nervous system. The rationale for all of these tests is basically the same. All of the drugs in question will, when given by injection, induce a profound shift in autonomic balance. This shift will take the form of an immediate response to the drug by one division of the autonomic system, followed by a compensatory reaction by its opposing half in order to restore autonomic equilibrium. The profiles of response to all autonomic drugs show wide individual variations that have been related to differences in psychiatric state.

In devising a test of this sort any of a number of autonomic parameters could, in principle, be studied though in practice the cardiovascular system, and almost always blood pressure, has been chosen. As for the choice of drug, there are four possibilities, namely, drugs that either activate or block the sympathetic half of the autonomic nervous system (sympathomimetics and sympatholytics) or those that activate or block its parasympathetic division (parasympathomimetics and parasympatholytics). All of these variations have been tried, though some more commonly than others (Cyvin *et al.*, 1956). The most widely used drug has been Mecholyl, an acetylcholine-like substance having a parasympathomimetic action on the cardiovascular system. Its effect is to cause increased peripheral vasodilation and decreased cardiac output, resulting in a fall in blood pressure which is then restored to normal through reflex homeostatic mechanisms.

The effect of Mecholyl on the blood pressure of psychiatric patients has been studied by a number of workers, but especially by Funkenstein and his colleagues (Funkenstein *et al.*, 1949) and the procedure has become widely known as the Funkenstein test. In its complete form the Funkenstein test consists of two parts, in which the response to adrenaline is also measured. Most people, however, have concentrated only on the Mecholyl half. In their original report Funkenstein and his colleagues distinguished seven types of reaction to Mecholyl, classified in terms of the relative drop and kind of recovery shown by the blood pressure following injection. A simpler classification based on three reaction types was later introduced by Gellhorn (1953) whose interest in the test derives from his conviction that it measures posterior hypothalamic (sympathetic) reactivity. A full account of the physiological and clinical data adduced to support this view can be found in Gellhorn and Loofbourrow (1963).

In the clinical field the main claims made for the Mecholyl test concern the altered response to the drug in psychotic depressive patients and the ability of the technique to predict the outcome of ECT. Reviews of its success in these two respects have been made by Feinberg (1958), Thorpe (1962), and, most comprehensively, by Rose (1962). In general, the main conclusion to be reached is that no autonomic drug technique has lived up to expectation as a clinical tool, though many studies of such procedures have been found wanting on methodological grounds. Their clinical value has usually been enhanced when improvements to the procedure and scoring of the tests have been introduced, as in a recent study by Ingram and Brovins (1966).

At present the main contribution of autonomic drug techniques seems to be in the research field, using them together with other psychophysiological procedures for exploring the autonomic correlates of arousal. Used in basic parametric work of this sort, there is good evidence that they are of value, as suggested by the results of a series of studies brought together in Claridge (1967). The experiments described there were concerned with the investigation of blood pressure response in neurotic and normal subjects given Mecholyl or a sympatholytic drug, phentolamine (Rogitine). In both cases it emerged that a general factor of sympathetic arousability was being measured. This autonomic component of arousal was found to be one of the two correlated factors referred to earlier which appear to determine the descriptive personality dimension of dysthymia-hysteria.

Another autonomic test used in that research is also worth considering briefly here because, while not a drug technique, it belongs most appropriately with the other procedures of experimental psychiatry. The technique referred to is the cold pressor test, which measures the cardiovascular response to immersion of the hand in ice-cold water. The effect of this sympathetic stimulation is to cause an immediate rise in blood pressure followed by a gradual restoration of autonomic equilibrium. As with autonomic drugs, a wide variation in sympathetic response is found. Introduced as a standard test of cardiovascular reactivity (Hines and Brown, 1936), the procedure has been studied by a few workers in the psychiatric field (Glaser, 1952; Igersheimer, 1953). Because of its simplicity and the fact that no injection is required, the cold pressor test deserves more attention than it has so far received from clinical psychophysiologists.

One final comment should be made about the techniques described in this section. Unlike most of the work carried out by psychologists on the autonomic nervous system, the procedures referred to here all involve fairly massive physiological assault on the organism. From a theoretical viewpoint this has certain advantages. The more usual polygraphic studies of somatic response, however carefully controlled, are always subject to the influence of subtle psychological factors in the test situation that may be difficult to disentangle from the effect of the experimental variables being investigated. Reliable individual differences may therefore be difficult to demonstrate. This is less true when severe physical, especially pharmacological, stressors are used since their effects are likely to swamp such extraneous influences as are present. This theoretical gain is perhaps outweighed by two practical disadvantages. One is the discomfort to the patient or subject. The other is that drug effects are inevitably complicated and require careful interpretation if false conclusions are not to be drawn from them. Whether it is considered worthwhile trying to set aside or minimize these disadvantages will naturally depend on the nature of the investigation being undertaken.

(b) *Drug Threshold Procedures*

A group of diagnostic drug procedures that differ somewhat from those described in the previous section involves the estimation of the individual's tolerance of certain centrally acting drugs. The rationale behind tests of this kind is that the variability in the tolerance of such drugs is partly due to personality differences. The basic procedure for determining drug thresholds is, in principle, very simple. The selected drug is administered progressively by slow intravenous injection until some predetermined change in the individual's behaviour or physiological state occurs. At this point it is assumed that he has reached his tolerance level for the drug and the threshold can then be expressed quantitatively in terms of the amount of drug injected.

The measurement of drug tolerance in this way and its application in the clinical field were pioneered by Shagass and his colleagues, who introduced the technique of 'sedation threshold' (Shagass, 1954, 1957). As originally defined by Shagass, the sedation threshold was an index of the tolerance of the barbiturate drug, amylobarbitone sodium, and was measured by determining the amount of this drug required to induce certain changes in the EEG. As an additional criterion of the drug effect the onset of slurring of speech was also noted. Subsequent variations on this procedure have been concerned either with the investigation of other drugs or with trying to find simpler or more reliable criteria for drug thresholds.

Of the drugs investigated sedatives have almost always been chosen, though in a recent departure from this practice Rossi successfully used the 'stimulation threshold' for methamphetamine as a diagnostic procedure in depression (Giberti and Rossi, 1962). However, the estimation of sedative, rather than stimulant, thresholds has the obvious practical advantage that it is less unpleasant for the patient. Among the sedative drugs the choice has usually been between amylobarbitone sodium, and the shorter acting barbiturate, thiopentone sodium. The latter is sometimes preferred because the patient is less inconvenienced by the after-effects of the injection.

A number of workers have suggested alternative criteria for determining the onset of barbiturate thresholds. Shagass himself introduced a simpler version of the sedation threshold, called the 'sleep threshold', defined simply as the amount of drug required to induce unresponsiveness to verbal prompting (Shagass and Kerenyi, 1958). Fink (1958) used the appearance of lateral gaze nystagmus as a criterion, while Perez-Reyes *et al.* (1962) have described a method for determining what they have called the 'GSR-inhibition threshold'. This involves measuring the amount of thiopentone required to eliminate the GSR to auditory stimuli applied at intervals during the injection. A simple behavioural method for estimating the amylobarbitone threshold was introduced by Claridge and Herrington (1960) and has since been used extensively by them. Here the subject is asked to double digits played at regular intervals over a tape-recorder and the threshold is taken as the amount of drug injected up to the point where correct responses are being made to only fifty per cent of the digits. Another modification introduced by Claridge and Herrington was the use of a continuous infusion procedure to replace the practice adopted by all other workers of injecting the drug in 'bursts' every forty seconds or so. Continuous infusion helps to eliminate the fluctuations in consciousness that otherwise make it difficult to detect clear-cut end-points, whatever criterion for the threshold is used. This modification is recommended as a standard injection procedure for anyone using techniques of this kind.

Turning now to the place of drug threshold procedures in psychiatric assessment, much of the work carried out to date has already been detailed elsewhere (Claridge, 1967) and only the main areas of application will be noted here. The most extensive comparison of sedation threshold in different psychiatric conditions has been made by Shagass and reported in a key paper by Shagass and Jones (1958). Shagass' results may be summarized under three headings: the sedation threshold in neurosis, in depression, and in schizophrenia.

In neurosis patients falling within the general category of dysthymia are known to have significantly higher sedation thresholds, that is they tolerate larger doses of sedative drugs, than hysterical and psychopathic patients. This finding has been confirmed by Claridge and Herrington (1960) and supports the hypothesis that dysthymics are characterized by higher levels of arousability than hysterics and are therefore more resistant to sedation. In a subsequent analysis of a larger amount of data on neurotic patients Claridge (1967) demonstrated that the sedation threshold was highly loaded on one of the two components of arousal determining dysthymia-hysteria. It was, for example, significantly correlated with a number of measures of sympathetic reactivity derived from the autonomic drug tests outlined in the previous section.

In depression a number of workers have supported Shagass's original report that psychotic depressives have low and neurotic depressives high sedation thresholds (Boudreau, 1958; Nymgaard, 1959; Perris and Brattemo, 1963; Perez-Reyes and Cochrane, 1967). In keeping with these results, Shagass and Jones state that the sedation threshold will predict the outcome of ECT, the likelihood of a favourable response to this treatment diminishing as the threshold rises. Gellhorn has interpreted these results in support of the view that ECT has its main effect on the central mechanisms of sympathetic reactivity, which may be defective in psychotic depression (Gellhorn and Loofbourrow, 1963).

Results with the sedation threshold in schizophrenia are more complicated. In general early schizophrenics show low sedation thresholds though, according to Shagass and Jones, the threshold steadily rises again later, levelling off at about two years. Despite this average trend, some early schizophrenics show high thresholds within the range of dysthymic neurotics. The more significant feature of the behaviour of schizophrenics concerns, not the absolute values of the sedation threshold but its relationship with other psychophysiological measures. This has been shown to be opposite from that found in non-psychotic patients. Thus, it has been demonstrated that in acute schizophrenia the sedation threshold correlates significantly and negatively with the spiral after-effect, whereas in neurosis the correlation is positive and significant (Krishnamoorti and Shagass, 1964; Herrington and Claridge, 1965). Furthermore, in schizophrenics who show a good response to treatment the correlation between the sedation threshold and spiral after-effect once more becomes positive and not significantly different from that found in neurotic patients. Elsewhere (Claridge, 1967) it has been suggested that acute schizophrenia involves a complex but orderly change in, or 'dissociation' of, different components of central nervous activity, rather than, for example, a simple upward or downward shift in arousal. This dissociation of C.N.S. function can take several forms that parallel the clinical features of the illness, such as the subtype of schizophrenia and the presence or absence of thought disorder.

Like other psychophysiological measures, drug threshold techniques are barely established as routine assessment procedures. They do, however, show considerable promise, especially when looked at in relation to other psychophysiological and behavioural measures. For investigating individual differences they have certain advantages over more peripheral somatic techniques, providing a more direct index of central arousability. The sedation threshold, for example, appears to measure, in the absence of gross pathological change, a fairly stable biological characteristic of the individual and, as a recent study of normal twins has shown (Claridge and Ross, unpublished), it has strong genetic determinants. Where shifts in the sedation threshold do occur these often reflect changes in the clinical state, a fact that can be exploited when assessing the patient's response to physical forms of treatment.

The disadvantages of drug threshold procedures should also be noted. For the psychologist their major drawback is that medical help is required to administer them, though in a closely knit clinical team this is rarely a problem. Discomfort for the patient might also be mentioned though again this is less of a difficulty than it appears at first sight, at least where sedative drugs are concerned. In our own experience patients rarely complain and indeed many have reported that the sedation threshold has a pleasantly therapeutic effect! Of course, it should go without saying that any drug technique must only be used after careful physical examination of the patient. Quite apart from the obvious medical reasons for this precaution, there are also good scientific grounds for not using the sedation threshold, or for that matter any other psychophysiological procedure, as a personality test in physically unwell patients. The assumption underlying all measurement in this field is that psychological events account for a significant proportion of the variability in the physiological parameters studied.

This assumption is not met in the physically ill individual because many of the physiological systems measured, such as the autonomic nervous system, may also be the vehicles for organic pathology. It is clearly meaningless to put psychological interpretations on somatic changes that may be entirely due to, or at the very least considerably contaminated by, a known physical disease. In the case of 'passive' recording of, say, the autonomic nervous system the results will almost certainly be worthless. In the case of drug procedures they will expose the patient to unjustifiable hazard.

III CONCLUSIONS

This chapter has served to define an approach to psychological assessment rather than to detail procedures that are in current clinical use or that can be easily adopted by the practitioner. Indeed few readers may feel driven to apply the techniques described because their use requires a reorientation towards psychological measurement that many workers may find indigestible. It is therefore perhaps worth closing this chapter with a few comments about the present and future status of clinical psychophysiology in relation to other forms of assessment.

In addition to its place in basic research, the psychophysiological approach to behaviour has, as we have seen, two contributions to make in the clinical setting. The first is to diagnosis and the second is to the assessment of changes in the individual patient. In both cases the psychophysiologist is concerned more with the *processes* underlying behaviour than with the *content* of the behaviour itself. He is, for example, more interested in *how* anxious the patient is than in *what* he is anxious about. In this respect psychophysiological techniques differ fundamentally from many other contemporary personality assessment procedures and it is this different orientation that some clinicians may find hard to accept. Few, however, would deny that both features of behaviour are important, though it is an unwelcome fact that to date the process of psychopathology has been relatively more neglected than its content. The future of assessment in non-medical personality disorders – and here I would include the functional psychoses – appears to lie in a combination of both approaches or in the selection of that approach which is most logically suited to each individual clinical problem. Thus, in behaviour therapy or psychotherapy a knowledge of the patient's particular worries is essential; though, as we have seen, treatment may be facilitated if the therapist also has available an objective index of the purely somatic aspects of the patient's anxiety or, in other words, of the process underlying his psychological complaint. In other individuals, or in other conditions, the content of behaviour may be of less relevance. If, for example, it were possible to define accurately the physiological processes underlying schizophrenia then the content of the individual patient's delusions would assume less importance in diagnosis and treatment. Indeed, this is true even at the present time in many neurotic and psychotic patients given purely physical forms of treatment. In such cases the drugs or other treatment prescribed are assumed to have their beneficial effect by acting on the processes underlying the disorder. It is therefore logical to select patients for treatment and assess their progress by means of techniques that measure these very same processes. The assessment procedures described here are ideally suited to this purpose.

One final point should be made about the place of psychophysiological procedures in the diagnosis or classification of psychiatric disorders. We have seen that there are few if any 'tests' available in this area, in the sense that no single procedure is diagnostic of any particular psychiatric condition. The truth is that such a situation is unlikely ever to exist in clinical psychology. It is more probable that the psychophysiologist's future contribution to diagnosis will lie in the careful description of the psychiatric patient in terms of a number of parameters which define significant features of the psychopathological process in different personality disorders. A start has been made in this direction, though many practical and theoretical problems remain. Perhaps the most immediate practical problem is the shortage of psychologists prepared to carry the techniques of psychophysiology and its allied disciplines into the psychiatric clinic. It is only by doing this on a large scale that what at present appear somewhat esoteric research tools can take their place among the everyday assessment procedures of the future. One reason why we now have precise techniques for measuring intelligence and cognitive defect is that psychology has devoted a good deal of time, effort, and expense to their construction and standardization on large populations of normal and abnormal individuals. To try and reach a similar position in the assessment of personality and its abnormalities is a daunting task but one that will have to be taken up sooner or later if clinical psychology is to make more than a meagre contribution to the examination of the psychiatrically ill patient.

REFERENCES

BASOWITZ, H., PERSKY, H., KORCHIN, S. J. and GRINKER, R. R. (1954) *Anxiety and Stress*. New York: McGraw-Hill.

BENJAMIN, L. S. (1963) Statistical treatment of the law of initial values (LIV) in autonomic research: a review and recommendation. *Psychosom. Med.*, **25**, 556-566.

BOUDREAU, D. (1958) Evaluation of the sedation threshold test. *Arch. Neurol. Psychiat. (Chic.)*, **80**, 771-775.

BRAZIER, M. A. B. (1960a) Some uses of computers in experimental neurology. *Exp. Neurol.*, **2**, 123-143.

BRAZIER, M. A. B. (1960b) *The Electrical Activity of the Nervous System*. London: Pitman.

CLARIDGE, G. S. (1967) *Personality and Arousal*. Oxford: Pergamon.

CLARIDGE, G. S. and HERRINGTON, R. N. (1960) Sedation threshold, personality and the theory of neurosis. *J. ment. Sci.*, **106**, 1568-1583.

CLARIDGE, G. S. and HERRINGTON, R. N. (1963a) An EEG correlate of the Archimedes spiral after-effect and its relationship with personality. *Behav. Res. Ther.*, **1**, 217-229.

CLARIDGE, G. S. and HERRINGTON, R. N. (1963b) Excitation-inhibition and the theory of neurosis: a study of the sedation threshold. *In* EYSENCK, H. J. (Ed.) *Experiments with Drugs*. Oxford: Pergamon.

CLARK, D. F. (1963) Treatment of monosymptomatic phobia by systematic desensitization. *Behav. Res. Ther.*, **1**, 63-68.

CORCORAN, D. W. J. (1964) Changes in heart rate and performance as a result of loss of sleep. *Brit. J. Psychol*, **55**, 307-314.

CYVIN, K., JÖRSTAD, J. and RETTERSTÖL, N. (1956) Sympathomimetics as diagnostic tests in psychiatry. *Acta psychiat. et neurol. scand.*, **106**, 206-220.

DARROW, C. W., PATHMAN, J. and KRONENBERG, G. (1946) Level of autonomic activity and electroencephalogram. *J. exp. Psychol.*, **36**, 355-365.

DUFFY, E. (1934) Emotion: an example of the need for reorientation in psychology. *Psychol. Rev.*, **41**, 239-243.

DUFFY, E. (1962) *Activation and Behaviour*. New York: Wiley.

EYSENCK, H. J. (1953) *The Structure of Human Personality*. London: Methuen.

EYSENCK, H. J. (1957) *Dynamics of Anxiety and Hysteria*. London: Routledge & Kegan Paul.

EYSENCK, H. J. (1967) *The Biological Basis of Personality*. Springfield, Ill.: Charles C. Thomas.

FEINBERG, I. (1958) Current status of the Funkenstein Test. A review of the literature through December 1957. *Arch. Neurol. Psychiat. (Chic.)*, **80**, 488-501.

FINK, M. (1958) Lateral gaze nystagmus as an index of the sedation threshold. *Electroenceph. clin. Neurophysiol.*, **10**, 162-163.

FREUND, K. (1963) A laboratory method for diagnosing predominance of homo- or hetero-erotic interest in the male. *Behav. Res. Ther.*, **1**, 85-93.

FUNKENSTEIN, D. H., GREENBLATT, M. and SOLOMON, H. C. (1949) Psychophysiological study of mentally ill patients. I: The status of the peripheral autonomic nervous system as determined by the reaction to epinephrine and mecholyl. *Amer. J. Psychiat.*, **106**, 16-28.

GELLHORN, E. (1953) *Physiological Foundations of Neurology and Psychiatry*. Minneapolis: Univ. Minnesota Press.

GELLHORN, E. and LOOFBOURROW, G. N. (1963) *Emotions and Emotional Disorders*. New York: Harper.

GIBERTI, F. and ROSSI, R. (1962) Proposal of a psychopharmacological test ('stimulation threshold') for differentiating neurotic from psychotic depressions. *Psychopharmacologia (Berl.)*, **3**, 128-131.

GLASER, G. H. (1952) The effects of frontal topectomy on autonomic nervous system stability in schizophrenia. *J. nerv. ment. Dis.*, **115**, 189-202.

GOLDSTEIN, L., SUGARMAN, A. A., STOLBERG, H., MURPHEE, H. B. and PFEIFFER, C. C. (1965) Electro-cerebral activity in schizophrenics and non-

H

psychotic subjects: quantitative EEG amplitude analysis. *Electroenceph. clin. Neurophysiol.*, **19**, 350-361.

GOODMAN, L. S. and GILMAN, A. (1965) *The Pharmacological Basis of Therapeutics*. New York: Macmillan.

GRAY, J. A. (1964) *Pavlov's Typology*. Oxford: Pergamon.

GRAY, J. A. (1967) Strength of the nervous system, introversion-extraversion, conditionability and arousal. *Behav. Res. Ther.*, **5**, 151-169.

HEATH, H. A. and OKEN, D. (1962) Change scores as related to initial and final levels. *Ann. N.Y. Acad. Sci.*, **98**, 1242-1256.

HEBB, D. O. (1955) Drives and the CNS (conceptual nervous system). *Psychol. Rev.*, **62**, 243-254.

HERRINGTON, R. N. and CLARIDGE, G. S. (1965) Sedation threshold and Archimedes' spiral after-effect in early psychosis. *J. psychiat. Res.*, **3**, 159-170.

HINES, E. A. and BROWN, G. E. (1936) The cold pressor test for measuring the reactibility of the blood pressure: data concerning 571 normal and hypertensive subjects. *Amer. Heart J.*, **11**, 1-9.

HOENIG, J. and REED, G. F. (1966) The objective assessment of desensitization. *Brit. J. Psychiat.*, **112**, 1279-1283.

IGERSHEIMER, W. W. (1953) Cold pressor test in functional psychiatric syndromes. *Arch. Neurol. Psychiat. (Chic.)*, **70**, 794-801.

INGRAM C. G. and BROVINS, W. G. (1966) The reproducibility of the Mecholyl test. *Brit. J. Psychiat.*, **112**, 167-171.

KEELE, C. A. and NEIL, E. (1961) *Samson Wright's Applied Physiology*. London: Oxford Univ. Press.

KENNARD, M. A. (1953) The electroencephalogram in psychological disorders: a review. *Psychosom. Med.*, **15**, 95-115.

KRISHNAMOORTI, S. R. and SHAGASS, C. (1964) Some psychological test correlates of sedation threshold. *In* WORTIS, J. (Ed.) *Recent Advances in Biological Psychiatry*, Vol. VI. New York: Plenum.

LACEY, J. I. (1956) The evaluation of autonomic responses: toward a general solution. *Ann. N.Y. Acad. Sci.*, **67**, 125-164.

LACEY, J. I., BATEMAN, D. E. and VAN LEHN, R. (1953). Autonomic response specificity. An experimental study. *Psychosom. Med.*, **15**, 8-21.

LACEY, J. I. and LACEY, B. C. (1958) Verification and extension of the principle of autonomic response stereotype. *Amer. J. Psychol.*, **71**, 50-73.

LADER, M. H. and WING, LORNA (1966) *Physiological Measures, Sedative Drugs, and Morbid Anxiety*. Maudsley Monographs No. 14. London: Oxford University Press.

LINDSLEY, D. B. (1944) Electroencephalography. *In* HUNT, J. MCV. (Ed.) *Personality and the Behaviour Disorders*. New York: Ronald.

LINDSLEY, D. B. (1960) Attention, consciousness, sleep and wakefulness. *In* FIELD, J. *et al*. (Eds.) *Handbook of Physiology*. Section I: *Neurophysiology*, Washington: American Physiological Society.

MALMO, R. B. (1957) Anxiety and behavioural arousal. *Psychol. Rev.*, **64**, 276-287.

MALMO, R. B., DAVIS, J. F. and BARZA, S. (1960) Total hysterical deafness: an experimental case study. *In* EYSENCK, H. J. (Ed.) *Behaviour Therapy and the Neuroses*. Oxford: Pergamon.

MALMO, R. B. and SHAGASS, C. (1949) Physiologic studies of reaction to stress in anxiety and early schizophrenia. *Psychosom. Med.*, **11**, 9-24.

MALMO, R. B. and SHAGASS, C. (1952) Studies of blood pressure in psychiatric patients under stress. *Psychosom. Med.*, **14**, 82-93.

MARGERISON, J. H., ST JOHN-LOE, P. and BINNIE, C. D. (1967) Electroencephalography. *In* VENABLES, P. H. and MARTIN, I. (Eds.) *Manual of Psychophysiological Methods*. Amsterdam: North-Holland Publishing Co.

MARTIN, I. (1960) Somatic reactivity. *In* EYSENCK, H. J. (Ed.) *Handbook of Abnormal Psychology*. London: Pitman.

MCCALLUM, C. (1967) New waves in the brain. *New Scientist*, **36**, 592-594.

NYMGAARD, K. (1959) Studies on the sedation threshold. A: Reproducibility and effect of drugs. B: Sedation threshold in neurotic and psychotic depression. *Arch. gen. Psychiat. (Chic.)*, **1**, 530-536.

PAVLOV, I. P. (1941) *Lectures on Conditioned Reflexes*. Vol. II: *Conditioned Reflexes and Psychiatry*. Translated and edited by GANTT, W. H. New York: International Publishers.

PEREZ-REYES, M., SHANDS, H. C. and JOHNSON, G. (1962) Galvanic skin reflex inhibition threshold: a new psychophysiologic technique. *Psychosom. Med.*, **24**, 274-277.

PEREZ-REYES, M. and COCHRANE, C. (1967) Differences in sodium thiopental susceptibility of depressed patients as evidenced by the galvanic skin reflex inhibition threshold. *J. psychiat. Res.*, **5**, 335-347.

PERRIS, C. and BRATTEMO, C-E. (1963) The sedation threshold as a method of evaluating anti-depressive treatments. *Acta psychiat. scand.*, **39**, Suppl. 169, 111-119.

ROSE, J. T. (1962) The Funkenstein Test – a review of the literature. *Acta psychiat. scand.*, **38**, 124-153.

SEAGER, C. P. and BROWN, B. H. (1967) An indicator of tension during reciprocal inhibition. *Brit. J. Psychiat.*, **113**, 1129-1132.

SHAGASS, C. (1954) The sedation threshold. A method for estimating tension in psychiatric patients. *Electroenceph. clin. Neurophysiol.*, **6**, 221-233.

SHAGASS, C. (1957) A measurable neurophysiological factor of psychiatric significance. *Electroenceph. clin. Neurophysiol.*, **9**, 101-108.

SHAGASS, C. and JONES, A. L. (1958) A neurophysiological test for psychiatric diagnosis: results in 750 patients. *Amer. J. Psychiat.*, **114**, 1002-1009.

SHAGASS, C. and KERENYI, A. B. (1958) The 'sleep' threshold. A simple form of the sedation threshold for clinical use. *Canad. Psychiat. J.*, **1**, 101-109.

SHAGASS, C. and SCHWARTZ, M. (1962) Excitability of the cerebral cortex in psychiatric disorders *In* ROESSLER R. and GREENFIELD, N. S. (Eds.)

Physiological Correlates of Psychological Disorder. Madison: Univ. Wisconsin Press.

SPECK, L. B., DIM, B. and MERCER, M. (1966) Visual evoked responses of psychiatric patients. *Arch. gen. Psychiat.*, **15**, 59-63.

STENNETT, R. G. (1957) The relationship of alpha amplitude to the level of palmar conductance. *Electroenceph. clin. Neurophysiol.*, **9**, 131-138.

STERNBACH, R. A. (1960a) A comparative analysis of autonomic responses in startle. *Psychosom. Med.*, **22**, 204-210.

STERNBACH, R. A. (1960b) Two independent indices of activation. *Electroenceph. clin. Neurophysiol.*, **12**, 609-611.

STERNBACH, R. A. (1966) *Principles of Psychophysiology*. New York: Academic Press.

SUGARMAN, A. A., GOLDSTEIN, L., MURPHEE, H. B., PFEIFFER, C. C. and JENNEY, E. H. (1964) EEG and behavioural changes in schizophrenia. *Arch. gen. Psychiat.*, **10**, 340-344.

THORPE, J. G. (1962) The current status of prognostic test indicators for electro-convulsive therapy. *Psychosom. Med.*, **24**, 554-568.

TITAEVA, M. A. (1962) EEG investigations of the reactivity of the central nervous system in patients with a catatonic form of schizophrenia. *In* ROKHLIN, L. L. (Ed.) *Problemy Schizophrenii*, Vol. 2. Moscow: Ministry of Health, The RSFFR.

VAN DER MERWE, A. B. (1948) The diagnostic value of peripheral vasomotor reactions in the psychoneuroses. *Psychosom. Med.*, **10**, 347-354.

VENABLES, P. H. (1963) The relationship between level of skin potential and fusion of paired light flashes in schizophrenic and normal subjects. *J. psychiat. Res.*, **1**, 279-287.

VENABLES, P. H. (1964) Input dysfunction in schizophrenia. *In* MAHER, B. A. (Ed.) *Progress in Experimental Personality Research*. New York: Academic Press.

VENABLES, P. H. (1966) Psychophysiological aspects of schizophrenia. *Brit. J. med. Psychol.*, **39**, 289-297.

VENABLES, P. H. (1967) The relation of two flash and two click thresholds to withdrawal in paranoid and non-paranoid schizophrenics. *Brit. J. soc. clin. Psychol.*, **6**, 60-62.

VENABLES, P. H. and MARTIN, I. (Eds.) (1967) *Manual of Psychophysiological Methods*. Amsterdam: North-Holland Publishing Co.

VENABLES, P. H. and WING, J. K. (1962) Level of arousal and the subclassification of schizophrenia. *Arch. gen. Psychiat. (Chic.)*, **7**, 114-119.

WALTER, W. GREY, COOPER, R., ALDRIDGE, V. J., MCCALLUM, W. C. and WINTER, A. L. (1964) Contingent negative variation: an electric sign of sensori-motor association and expectancy in the human brain. *Nature (London)*, **203**, 380-384.

WILDER, J. (1957) The law of initial values in neurology and psychiatry. *J. nerv. ment. Dis.*, **125**, 73-86.

WOLFF, H. S. (1967) Telemetry of psychophysiological variables. *In* VENABLES P. H. and MARTIN, I. (Eds.) *Manual of Psychophysiological Methods.* Amsterdam: North-Holland Publishing Co.

WOLPE, J. (1960) Reciprocal inhibition as the main basis of psychotherapeutic effects. *In* EYSENCK, H. J. (Ed.) *Behaviour Therapy and the Neuroses.* Oxford: Pergamon.

PART TWO

Assessment of Adults:
Clinical Applications

7

Acute psychiatric patients

P. Ley

I INTRODUCTION

Clinical psychologists working with acute psychiatric patients have a variety of problems referred to them. These can be grouped, without too much injustice, into five main categories:

1. Differential diagnosis.
2. Assessment of suitability for treatment.
3. Personality descriptions.
4. Assessment of the effects of treatment.
5. Vocational guidance.

This chapter will be concerned with the first three categories. Vocational guidance is dealt with elsewhere, and the assessment of the effects of treatment presents, in principle, no great problems. The patient is measured on relevant variables before and after treatment and change is assessed. Unless a control group is used a sophisticated design will be necessary, so that the patient can be used as his own control, but this is not difficult. More problematic is the finding of relevant variables. In the past, many of the available tests seemed at best only indirectly relevant, but with the development of the Personal Question-naire and its derivatives (Shapiro, 1961; Ingham, 1965; Kellner, 1967), and other individual measures such as the repertory grid (Slater, 1965), problems in this area have been reduced. It will be argued later that the experimental investigation of individual cases is a valuable enterprise for psychologists to undertake, and the assessment of the effects of treatment falls nicely into this framework.

Much of the later discussion will have general implications for the assessment of suitability for treatment, but one specific problem which seems to be increasingly referred to psychologists is, 'Is this patient suitable for behaviour therapy?' In view of its topicality it is worth mentioning some of the available evidence relevant to answering this question. Lazarus (1963) found low E scores to be associated with poor response to behaviour therapy, while Young (1963) found that high E scores were associated with higher probability of relapse after treatment for enuresis. On the other hand, Schmidt *et al.* (1965) found that E score was not related to success or failure, nor were age, intelligence, I.Q. and duration of symptom. High N scores, high MAS scores and being female were negatively related to response to behaviour therapy, as was having had many psychiatric treatments. Lazarus also found that high N scores made for poor response. The patient's motivation is also believed to be important, and Freund (1960) demonstrated a clear difference in success of aversion therapy for homosexuality between patients sent by the courts and patients who came voluntarily. Characteristics of the therapist may also be of importance. At least Schmidt *et al.* found significant differences between therapists, as did Koenig and Masters (1965). In this last investigation different treatments and different therapists were used in an attempt to reduce frequency of smoking. Each therapist used each treatment with some patients. No significance differences between treatments emerged, but there were significant differences between therapists. Type of disorder also seems to be related to response to treatment. Enuresis responds well (Jones, 1960a), as do phobias (Marks and Gelder, 1965), but possibly not severe agoraphobia (Gelder and Marks, 1966), while the effectiveness of aversion therapy in sexual deviations is questionable (Feldman, 1966). It is not clear from the literature that suitability for behaviour therapy can be assessed with any confidence, and it is probably better to answer the question by finding a method of treatment suitable for the patient and seeing if it works. At this stage in the development of behaviour therapy, an experimental approach which allows significant factors in the therapeutic situation to be assessed is more important than guessing at whether the patient is suitable or not.

To return to diagnostic problems in acute psychiatric patients, most clinical psychologists, whatever their disagreements about techniques and theories, would agree that what they do should be for the patient's benefit. The question is which of the things they do is most beneficial to patients. Is diagnostic testing the most useful of the clinical psychologist's activities?

II THE VALUE OF DIAGNOSTIC TESTING

Doubts as to the value of diagnosis and diagnostic testing are widespread. In a recent review Phares (1967) expresses his scepticism as follows:

> Each new generation of clinicians must learn the three basic lessons of psychiatry:
> (1) People within the same diagnostic category are notoriously dissimilar from one another.
> (2) Psychiatrists have never been able to agree amongst themselves as to who belongs in which category.
> (3) Categorization of patients has little to do with their treatment or disposition.

Similar sentiments have been expressed by other authors, too numerous to mention. Payne (1958) has spelled out the implications of the unreliability of diagnosis for diagnostic testing in some detail. His conclusion is alarming:

> The diagnostic test score is thus completely useless. . . . It can be used validly to predict which label the psychiatrist who took part in the validity

study would have assigned to the patient. . . . However, it cannot be used validly to predict any of the consequences of the label.

The argument leading to this conclusion that the only value of a diagnostic test score is some indication of the probability that the psychiatrist who diagnosed the standardization population would diagnose the case under consideration in such and such a way, runs as follows.

In the construction of a diagnostic test, groups of patients diagnosed by a psychiatrist as belonging to different categories are collected. They are given the test and normative data are collected and cut-offs chosen. Tests constructed in this way seldom, if ever, correlate more than 0·70 with psychiatric diagnosis. Psychiatric diagnosis has a reliability of 0·70 at the most, and validity is seldom higher than reliability. Thus we have one variable (our test) which correlates 0·70 or less with a second variable psychiatric diagnosis, which correlates 0·70 or less with a third variable, prognosis and response to treatment.

There are a number of reasons for wishing to arrive at a diagnosis and classify patients:

(1) administrative purposes;
(2) indication of likely aetiology;
(3) choice of treatment;
(4) prognosis;
(5) research purposes.

The aetiology of most psychiatric conditions remains unknown, and classification for administrative purposes is a fairly trivial activity, the psychologist is presumably intending the test result to be of value in helping the psychiatrist make a correct prognosis and choose the correct treatment.

However, if the relationships between test and diagnosis, and diagnosis and response to treatment and prognosis are as outlined above, i.e. the correlations are 0·70 or less, then there is no reason for supposing that the test will tell us anything about response to treatment or prognosis or the other things in which one is interested. In a different form, the argument runs as follows.

Some patients are classified by the test as being diagnosed in a certain way by the psychiatrist. Some patients diagnosed in that way by the psychiatrist show certain significant characteristics. In symbolic form: Some A is B, and some B is C. We obviously cannot necessarily conclude that some A is C, that patients classified by the test will show the significant characteristics, unless we can show that so much A is B, and so much B is C, that there is necessarily overlap between those Bs who are A, and those Bs who are C. If the correlations between A and B, and B and C are 0·70 or less, then the condition of so much B being A and so much B being C, that there is necessarily overlap does not hold. For those who feel that the use of correlation coefficients in this sort of situation is a dubious procedure, the same argument can be put in terms of percentages. Suppose that our test score correctly identifies 50% of patients diagnosed by the psychiatrist as being in a certain category, and that of the patients diagnosed by the psychiatrist as being in that category 50% show a favourable response to a given treatment, it can be seen that there is no necessary overlap between the patients the test identifies and the patients who respond to the treatment. There will only necessarily be overlap if the sum of the percentage of patients correctly classified by the test and the percentage responding to treatment is more than 100%.

Note that the argument does not say that there will be no overlap in the usual case. There may or may not be a relation between test scores and the variables in which psychologist is interested. The only way to find out is to investigate directly the relationship between test scores, response to treatment, prognosis, etc. However, if one does this, then finding the relationship between test scores and diagnosis becomes a pointless exercise, as the information of real interest will have been obtained already.

In sum, the argument maintains that with the low validity of diagnostic tests, the low reliability of psychiatric diagnosis, and the low validity of psychiatric diagnosis, diagnostic testing may well be of little or no value. The validity of various tests which may be used for diagnostic purposes is reviewed elsewhere in this volume, so review would be redundant. The next two sections will survey some of the evidence bearing on the reliability and validity of psychiatric diagnosis.

III RELIABILITY OF PSYCHIATRIC DIAGNOSIS

Psychiatric diagnosis has had a mixed press from the point of view of reliability. Its detractors include Ash (1949), Eysenck (1952, 1960), Mehlman (1952), Payne (1958), Scott (1958) and Pasamanick et al. (1959), while Hunt et al. (1953, 1962), Foulds (1955, 1965), Schmidt and Fonda (1956), Kreitman (1961), Wilson and Meyer (1962) and Matarazzo (1965) have been amongst those who have defended its reliability. Investigations of the reliability of diagnosis have taken a number of forms. The two major methods have been: (1) investigations of the relative frequency of use of different diagnostic categories by different psychiatrists working with presumably similar patients, and (2) investigations of agreement on diagnosis by two or more psychiatrists seeing the patient simultaneously, or after a short time-interval.

The first type of investigation is obviously crude, in the sense that it is difficult to isolate variables making for any unreliability found. Specific investigations have also been criticized on methodological grounds by Kreitman (1961) and Matarazzo (1965). This type of investigation is also of little use in assessing the degree of reliability of psychiatric diagnosis as a criterion in validating tests, but for what it is worth, the results are as follows:

Boisen (1938), Stouffer (1949, cited by Eysenck, 1952), Mehlman (1952) and Pasamanick et al. (1959) all report large variations in the frequencies of diagnoses assigned to apparently similar patients by different psychiatrists. Goldfarb (1959) reports similar variations amongst clinical psychologists. One study (Wilson and Meyer, 1962) goes against the trend and reports strikingly similar frequencies of use of diagnostic categories. On balance, these investigations suggest that psychiatric diagnosis is far from being perfectly reliable.

The second method of assessment – two or more psychiatrists seeing the same patients – has produced results of more direct relevance to the present problem. Ash (1949) investigated agreement by two or three psychiatrists on the same patients. With regard to five major categories (psychosis, neurosis, mental deficiency, psychopathic personality and normal range), there was agreement on 51% of the patients by two psychiatrists, and 46% by three. On specific diagnosis (apparently about 55 specific categories were used) there was agreement between two psychiatrists in 49% of cases, and amongst three psychiatrists in 20% of cases. It should be noted that 75% of the diagnoses made were in the 'normal range' category, so the population is not typical of the usual psychiatric population.

Hunt *et al.* (1953), working with naval personnel, found 93·7% agreement on a diagnosis of unfitness for service, but agreement on major diagnostic category was only 54%, and on specific diagnosis category 33%. There were three major categories and 32 specific categories.

A higher degree of diagnostic concordance was found by Schmidt and Fonda (1956). For the three major categories (organic, psychotic, character) there was 84% agreement, and for eleven specific categories there was 55% agreement. Agreement on specific diagnoses within major categories showed wide variation. Agreement within the organic category was 74%, within the psychotic category 47%, and within the character category 24%.

Norris (1959) reports on the degree of diagnostic concordance between an observation unit and mental hospitals. Over twelve diagnostic categories and a mixed category she found 58% agreement. There was agreement on a diagnosis of schizophrenia in 68% of cases, on a diagnosis of manic depression in 69% of cases, on diagnoses of psychosis due to a specified organic cause, but excluding cerebro-vascular psychosis, in 80% of cases, and on a diagnosis of psychoneurosis in 56% of cases.

An investigation by Kreitman *et al.* (1961) reports agreement between two psychiatrists as 78% for three major categories, and 63% for eleven specific categories. Within categories agreement on specific diagnosis was 75% for organic disorders, 61% for functional psychoses and 28% for neuroses.

Beck *et al.* (1962) found 70% agreement on major categories, and 54% on specific categories. This investigation yielded 53% agreement on a diagnosis of schizophrenia, 40% on involutional reaction, 63% on neurotic depression, 55% on anxiety reaction, 54% on sociopathic disturbance, and 38% on personality trait disturbance.

Sandifer *et al.* (1964) report a concordance rate of 57% for eleven categories, with 74% agreement on assignment to the major category of characterological disorder, 71% agreement on assignment to the psychotic category and 79% agreement on assignment to the organic category.

Finally, a further study by Sandifer *et al.* (1968) investigated agreement on diagnosis by three groups of psychiatrists, two British and one American. Agreement on assignment of patients to twelve diagnostic categories was 73% for a group of Scottish psychiatrists, 64% for a group of London psychiatrists and 58% for the American psychiatrists. These differences are probably due, at least in part, to differences in the extent of usage in the categories. Thus, 90% of the cases were in the five most frequently used categories in the case of the Scottish psychiatrists, in the six most frequently used categories in the case of the London psychiatrists, and in the seven most frequently used categories in the case of the Americans. Concordance on a diagnosis of schizophrenia was 62%, and on manic depression 63% for the American psychiatrists; while for the combined British sample the concordance for schizophrenia was 57%, and for manic depression, 58%.

Because of the use of different categories and differing methods of reporting results, any tabular summary of these investigations would be very complex and laden with qualifying footnotes. However, one broad trend seems to emerge clearly. The greater the number of categories used, i.e. the more specific the diagnosis, the smaller will be the degree of agreement found.

Agreement on whether the patient is in the organic, psychotic or characterological categories appears to be high. Inter-psychiatrist agreement on assignment to the organic category is between 85 and 92%; to the psychotic category, between 59 and 89%; and to the characterological category 71 and 74%.

The more specific categories, schizophrenia, affective psychosis, psychoneurosis, personality disorder, produce less agreement. Assignment to the category schizophrenia produces agreement of between 51 and 74%; to the category affective psychosis between 40 and 75%; to the category psychoneurosis between 24 and 56%; and to the category personality disorder 44 and 74%.

Even more specific diagnosis, i.e. what sort of schizophrenia, affective psychosis, neurosis or personality disorder, produces still less agreement. Specific diagnosis within the affective psychosis category produces agreement between 22 and 57%, in the psychoneurosis category, between 12 and 54%, and in the personality disorder category 6 to 55%.

The type of organic disorder can however be specified with between 74 and 80% agreement.

It is also worth noting that there appears to be no basis for the belief that the patients on whom two psychiatrists agree are in fact 'true' cases. If this was so, one would expect little drop in the degree of agreement when more than two psychiatrists diagnose the same patient. As mentioned already, Ash (1949) found that concordance was less for three psychiatrists than for two. There was 49% agreement on specific category for two psychiatrists, and 20% for three. Sandifer *et al.* (1968) found that the percentage of patients on whom there was complete agreement was 47% for the four Scottish psychiatrists, 20% for the four London psychiatrists, and 10% for the six to ten U.S.A. psychiatrists.

These figures suggest that concordance will drop as more psychiatrists see the patient.

A number of possible reasons can be advanced for explaining the low degree of agreement found. It could be due to one or more of the following: poor agreement on the definition of the label; poor agreement on the basic data, i.e. signs and symptoms; or poor agreement on the rules to follow in travelling from the basic data to the diagnostic label.

There appears to be some disagreement as to the definition of categories. For example, Timbury and Mowbray (1964) report differences in textbook descriptions of schizophrenia, and in a study of Scottish psychiatrists found considerable differences between psychiatrists in their stated methods and standards used for diagnosing schizophrenia. Willis and Bannister (1965) found agreement on the importance of major symptoms and treatment possibilities, but found that their psychiatrists showed no tendency to group either treatments or symptoms in any agreed fashion. A third investigation by Sandifer *et al.* (1966) investigated agreement on 20 diagnostic stereotypes amongst 16 experienced psychiatrists. Eighty-five per cent of the individual psychiatrists' stereotypes were more like the indicated joint stereotype than other stereotypes. There was more agreement on some categories than others, and stereotypes on which there was high interjudge agreement were more reliable on re-test for individual psychiatrists.

There is also evidence to show that observers seeing a patient at the same time will disagree as to the presence or absence of various symptoms. Rosenzweig *et al.* (1961) had three psychiatrists present while one of them interviewed a patient. The psychiatrists were asked to report on the presence or absence, or, in some cases, degree of 89 symptoms and signs. There was above chance agreement on 31 items.

If different psychiatrists see the same patient with a short time-interval in between, there is also disagreement on the presence or absence of symptoms. Kreitman *et al.* (1961) found a range of percentage agreement on the presence of certain major symptoms from 0 to 85 with a median of 39·5%.

Thus the first two possible reasons for imperfect concordance find some support. To some extent there is disagreement on the definition of categories, and there is disagreement on whether or not patients show certain symptoms. There is little data on whether or not psychiatrists agree on the rules to be followed in converting observations of patient characteristics into a diagnostic label. Nathan (1967) thinks that there is a major cause of disagreement in this area, and advocates a systems analysis approach to psychiatric decision-making. It should be noted that this is more than the usual pious exhortation. Nathan actually takes his proposal seriously and provides a comprehensive system of flow charts to enable psychiatrists to use this approach.

Recently, Wing *et al.* (1967) have proposed a highly structured interview for use by psychiatrists. Use of their procedure appears to overcome many of the difficulties caused by unreliable assessment of symptoms. Their greatest reported disagreement was in their attempt to rate the presence or absence of a number of anxiety symptoms. Even here there was only 28·7% disagreement. When individual items are combined into scales, very high reliabilities are reported. Use of the system to diagnose patients resulted in an overall level of agreement of 85% in the assignment of patients to ten diagnostic categories. This compares with 55% for eleven categories (Schmidt and Fonda, 1956); 58% for twelve categories (Norris, 1959); 63% for eleven categories (Kreitman *et al.* 1961); and 57% for eleven categories (Sandifer *et al.* 1964).

It should be emphasized that Wing *et al.* use a highly structured interview with detailed instructions for supplementary questions and cross-examination, and their success should give no encouragement to those who do not use such a procedure.

IV   VALIDITY OF PSYCHIATRIC DIAGNOSIS

It was suggested earlier that the main functions of a psychiatric diagnosis in our present state of knowledge are:

(1) to indicate a suitable treatment;
(2) to aid in prognosis;
(3) to categorize patients for research purposes.

It can also be argued that another aspect of the validity of psychiatric diagnosis is its ability to predict later diagnoses given to a patient when more is known about him. In a sense it would be expected that diagnosis would be more accurate when more is known about the patient. Each of these facets of the validity of diagnosis will be considered below.

1 Long-term stability of diagnosis

If a later diagnosis is more accurate than an earlier diagnosis, then a comparison of changes in diagnosis during a patient's hospital career should give some indication of the validity of the first diagnosis. Results in this area are not encouraging. Masserman and Carmichael's (1938) investigation showed that 40% of diagnoses needed to be changed. Barbigan *et al.* (1965) report that 16% of diagnoses were different on second admission, 28% on third admission, 51% on fourth admission, and 55% on fifth or subsequent admission. However, these figures compare favourably with the figures reported by Cooper (1967). He reports that only 20% of a group of 293 patients kept the same diagnosis over four admissions to hospital in a two-year period. If the diagnostic categories were made broader, the figure rose to 37%. Cooper reclassified 200 of these patients into eight categories and found that 54% kept the same diagnosis. (He also rediagnosed them himself, using a set of specific criteria, and increased the figure still further to 81%, but this might well be taken as a figure indicating the reliability of his standard diagnosis check list.) One obvious possible reason for change in diagnosis was that the patient's clinical picture had actually changed, but Cooper was able to find evidence of this in only 16% of the patients.

There are a large number of investigations using more homogeneous groups of patients. Walton (1958) found that 73% of a group of psychiatric patients over 65 years of age were given the same diagnosis, organic or functional, two years after their first diagnosis, and Winokur and Pitts (1964) report that of a group of 75 patients diagnosed on admission as reactive depression, 16% were so diagnosed on discharge. Sixty per cent had their diagnosis changed to endogenous depression, and the remainder were in other categories. In a follow-up of patients diagnosed as suffering from schizophrenia, schizo-affective psychosis, or affective psychosis, Clark and Mallett (1963) found that 84% of patients retained the same diagnosis. In their review of the literature they mention the investigations of Holmboe and Astrup (1957) and Astrup *et al.* (1959). In the first of these, a follow-up of 255 acute schizophrenics, none of the patients received a different diagnosis, while in the second 270 patients with acute affective psychosis were followed up, and in 6% of cases, the diagnosis had to be changed. Another study by Guze and Perley (1963), using a stricter than usual set of criteria for the diagnosis of hysteria, found that about 90% of a group of selected female hysterics retained the same diagnosis at follow-up.

Once again the studies are not strictly comparable. Sometimes the same psychiatrists make all the diagnoses, sometimes different psychiatrists are involved initially and at follow-up. Cooper (1967) provides evidence that if the same psychiatrist diagnoses on the different occasions there will be significantly higher consistency. There are also differences in the selection of patients for follow-up. Masserman and Carmichael (1938), Barbigan *et al.* (1965) and Cooper (1967) reported on unselected groups of patients, whereas the other investigations focus on specific groups of patients.

However, it appears that if a group of patients is carefully selected as being in a certain diagnostic category, the diagnosis will be relatively stable. If the patients are an unselected group, then diagnosis will show frequent change at follow-up and/or on re-admission.

2 Diagnostic label and treatment

There appears to be only one investigation of the association between diagnosis and treatment in a large mixed group of patients. This is reported by Bannister, Salmon and Lieberman (1964). These investigators found that there was a significant association between diagnosis and treatment but, although significant, the association was a low one. At best treatment could be predicted from diagnosis with 51% accuracy. This is a big improvement over the 20% chance expectation, but is still low. Thus in a mixed group of patients diagnosis is not strongly related to treatment.

In certain specific diagnostic groups there is of course evidence of a strong association between diagnosis and response to treatment. The best documented of these is the distinction between neurotic and endogenous depression and response to ECT. Roth (1959), Parnell and Skottowe (1962), Rose (1963), Carney *et al.* (1965) and Mendels (1965) provide evidence that ECT leads to significantly more improvement in endogenous than in neurotic depression. Despite the usefulness of the distinction in relation to ECT it may be of less value in predicting response to drugs (Kiloh and Garside, 1963; Kessel and Holt, 1965).

It can be concluded, therefore, that diagnostic labels have a low but significant relation to the treatment a patient is likely to receive, and that in some instances diagnostic labels have a high relationship to response to specific treatments.

3 Diagnostic label, length of hospitalization and other prognostic variables

One would expect that there would be large differences between the broad categories – organic, neurotic and psychotic – in terms of prognostic variables. There is not a great deal of published evidence on this topic but this is probably because it is felt that the differences are so obvious. There is, however, evidence of significant degrees of agreement between psychiatrists and between clinical psychologists on the favourableness or otherwise of prognosis in functional psychoses (Stone, 1967). Furthermore, Stone was able to demonstrate a correlation between a scale of favourableness of prognosis and published data on improvement rates in different categories. Thus prognostic statements about functional psychotics have some reliability and validity.

There is also evidence that diagnosis has some relationship to length of stay in hospital, and likelihood of re-admission. For example, in a study of a large group of unselected patients Parnell and Skottowe (1962) found that diagnosis was more strongly associated with length of hospitalization than age, marital status or body build, but that a combination of these three factors was a better predictor of length of stay than diagnosis alone. In terms of association with length of stay there was no difference between reactive and endogenous depressions, but there was a great difference between a diagnosis of endogenous depression and schizophrenia. This fits in well with clinical opinion and other evidence is consistent with it. For example, Clarke and Mallett (1963) found a strong association between the affective psychosis/schizophrenia dichotomy and chances of re-admission to hospital in a three-year follow-up period.

Within the group of patients diagnosed as schizophrenic, the process reactive distinction appears to be of some value. Associations between this classification and prognostic variables have been reported by Farina and Webb (1956), Seidel (1960), Chapman *et al.* (1961), Farina *et al.* (1962), Farina *et al.* (1963), Stephens and Astrup (1963) and Garfield and Sundland (1966). Patients can be categorized as process or reactive with a fair degree of agreement between independent assessors. Kantor *et al.* (1953) report 75% agreement; King (1958) reports 77% agreement; and Johannsen *et al.* (1963), 88%. These figures are very respectable considering that the patients are being categorized on what is probably a continuous dimension, and although different sets of criteria and scales were used in the prognostic studies, all available sets of criteria appear to have high inter-correlations, e.g. Johannsen *et al.* (1963), Solomon and Zlotowski (1964).

4 Diagnostic label and research findings

Within groups of patients labelled as schizophrenics, it is now fairly clear that three dimensions are useful in describing patients for research purposes. These are paranoid/non paranoid, process-reactive and acute-chronic. The fact that the process-reactive dimension can be used reliably has already been noted. In the case of the paranoid/non-paranoid dimension, Orgel (1957) provides criteria which can be used by different observers with very high inter-rater agreement. The problem in the case of the acute-chronic dimension is largely that of determining a cut-off for chronicity. Different investigators choose different lengths of hospitalization. For example, Venables (1964) recommends a cut-off of two years, while Johannsen *et al.* (1963) use a shorter time. It should be fairly simple to get some agreement on a cut-off point, if indeed it is felt that one is necessary. Brown (1960) reviews a wealth of information on length of hospital stay in schizophrenia, and using this an agreed cut-off could be determined.

Evidence on the usefulness of the acute-chronic distinction organizing research on schizophrenia is provided in a number of reviews, notably Venables (1964). Venables also provides some evidence on the value of the paranoid/non-paranoid distinction, as does Silverman (1964). One of the best reviews in this connection is, of course, that of Shakow (1963), who summarizes studies involving comparisons between paranoid and non-paranoid patients. On the 58 measures involved in the investigations, the paranoids are nearer normals on 31 while the non-paranoids are nearer normals on only seven.

The process-reactive distinction is considered by Silverman (1964), but there are a number of reviews available which concentrate on it. Heron (1962) summarizes a vast amount of evidence, as does Higgins (1964), while Higgins and Peterson (1966), provide a critique of the usefulness of the concept.

It appears from the work of Johannsen *et al.* (1963) that the three dimensions, process-reactive, acute-chronic and paranoid/non-paranoid, are relatively independent, and these dimensions may well be the best way of categorizing schizophrenics for research purposes.

In the case of the neuroses, the most fruitful classification to date has been the hysteric-dysthymic distinction. Eysenck (1957), and various contributors to Eysenck (1960), have reviewed much of the available evidence.

All of these methods of categorizing patients have been used in large numbers of investigations, and all have been associated with large numbers of significant results. Other classifications of patients have also been used, but these have either been less frequently used or less productive.

V PAYNE'S ARGUMENT RECONSIDERED

The evidence reviewed above suggests that Payne's argument is almost certainly true of specific diagnostic categories. Agreement on specific type of neurosis, it will be recalled, was in the region of 12 to 54%. To devise diagnostic tests to distinguish one type of neurotic from another would seem to be quite pointless. It would appear that the current categorical model is virtually unworkable in this field. The same may well be true of subtypes of schizophrenia. Unfortunately, the evidence available does not allow statements about the reliability of assignment to specific subtypes, but one study using Lorr's In-Patient Multidimensional Psychiatric Rating Scales found that 62% of schizophrenics could not be reliably assigned to one of Lorr's acute psychotic types (Klett and McNair, 1966). Assignment to a type or to the unclassifiable group was done with 72% agreement between judges, but only 38% of patients were assigned to a type by both judges. It is probable that in the case of neurosis and schizophrenia, if not in all cases, a dimensional approach may be more profitable than a categorical one. This thought is not original. Wittenborn (1950, 1951) and Eysenck (1960), amongst many others, have made the suggestion quite forcibly. However, the dimensionalists, to date, seem to have been almost solely concerned with showing a certain degree of correspondence between their description of patients and traditional categorical ones. Presumably, the real problem in choosing between the two approaches in the clinical situation is whether or not a dimensional approach is better in predicting variables of interest than a categorical one. There is a need for investigation of the relative effectiveness of the available ways of describing patients in predicting outcome variables.

The major categories – psychosis, organic states and characterological (including neurosis and personality disorder) – are used with a high degree of agreement by different psychiatrists. But this is not perfect, and within categories there is no great degree of homogeneity. More useful are the medium level categories – schizophrenia, affective psychosis, etc. – but these are less reliably used. At this level, agreement is in the range 40-75%. Diagnostic tests might possibly have high enough validities to ensure that there would be some overlap between test diagnosis and the important correlates of the diagnostic label in these cases, but it would clearly be wiser to correlate the tests directly with variables of interest rather than use an intermediary of this degree of reliability and validity. The conclusion is that Payne's argument is essentially correct, and that standardizing tests against diagnosis is not the most profitable type of endeavour. It is fortunately likely that when the attempt is made to correlate tests with prognosis many existing tests standardized by the traditional method will prove to be of value. For example, Inglis (1959) was able to show that in the investigation of Walton (1958), the Modified Word Learning Test was a significantly better predictor of outcome than the initial psychiatric diagnosis, and this may well be true of other tests.

VI THE BASE RATE PROBLEM

Another objection to the categorization of patients by use of tests has come from a different direction. This objection is based on the fact that in some circumstances the use of diagnostic tests will result in more errors than the use of no tests at all. In some circumstances the use of base rates will lead to more accurate classification than the use of tests. Excellent discussion of the basis of this statement is given in Meehl and Rosen (1955), Maxwell (1961) and Dawes (1962), so the present discussion will be brief. The two main formulae of interest when considering the usefulness of a test in relation to the base rates are the formula for arriving at the proportion of the total correctly classified, and the formula for estimating the probability that a patient having a score signifying a given diagnosis actually has that diagnosis.

The formula for obtaining the proportion correctly classified is as follows:

(1) $$P\,(\text{correct}) = (PTd_1/d_1 \times Pd_1) + (PTd_2/d_2 \times Pd_2)$$
where:

$P\,(\text{correct})$ is the proportion correctly classified;

PTd_1/d_1 is the proportion of patients with a given diagnosis who obtain a score on the test indicating that diagnosis;

Pd_1 is the proportion of patients with that diagnosis in the population in which the test is to be used;

PTd_2/d_2 is the proportion of patients who do not have the diagnosis who obtain scores on the test indicating that they do not have the diagnosis; and

Pd_2 is the proportion of patients in the population on which the test is to be used who do not have the diagnosis in question, i.e. $Pd_2 = 1 - Pd_1$.

The formula can be extended for use with more than two groups, but in the form given it is useful with many diagnostic tests which seek to classify patients as brain-damaged/not brain-damaged, neurotic/not neurotic and so on. Two examples of the use of the formula are given below.

Suppose that a test is available which correctly identifies 60% of schizophrenics (PTd_1/d_1), and correctly calls 90% of non-schizophrenics non-schizophrenic (PTd_2/d_2). On the face of it, this might well seem a useful test and in some circumstances it would be. If it were used on a population where 60% were schizophrenic (Pd_1), then using no test at all, the best bet would be that a patient was schizophrenic, and this diagnosis would be wrong in 40% of cases. Using the test, the formula leads us to expect that the proportion correctly classified will be:

$$(0\cdot60 \times 0\cdot60) + (0\cdot90 \times 0\cdot40) = 0\cdot72.$$

Thus the use of the test has reduced diagnostic errors from 40% to 28%. However, if the test were used on all patients at an out-patient clinic where the base rate for schizophrenia was 10%, the result would be different. Using no test and calling every patient non-schizophrenic would lead to 10% errors in diagnosis, but using the test we would expect the proportion correctly classified to be:

$$(0.60 \times 0.10) + (0.90 \times 0.90) = 0.87.$$

The use of the test has increased the errors made from 10% to 13%, and it is generally true that the more the base rates depart from 0.50 the less use any test will be.

The second formula gives the proportion of patients obtaining a score signifying a given diagnosis who actually have that diagnosis. The standardization data will not tell us this, they give only the proportion of patients with the diagnosis who will obtain the score. In practical use of tests it is the proportion of those with the score who have the diagnosis which is of interest. The formula is:

(2) $$Pd_1/T_1 = \frac{PTd_1/d_1 \times Pd_1}{(PTd_1/d_1 \times Pd_1) + (PTd_1/d_2 \times Pd_2)}$$

where:

Pd_1/T_1 is the proportion of those with the test score who have the diagnosis;

PTd_1/d_2 is the proportion of patients who do *not* have the diagnosis who obtain a test score signifying the diagnosis;

and the other terms are as defined in Formula (1).

Use of the formula in the first example above, where 60% of the patients on whom the test was to be used were schizophrenic, leads to the expectation that Pd_1/T_1 will be:

$$\frac{0.60 \times 0.60}{(0.60 \times 0.60) + (0.10 \times 0.40)} = 0.90.$$

Thus 90% of the patients obtaining a schizophrenic score will in fact be schizophrenic. In the second example, where only 10% were schizophrenic, the formula gives Pd_1/T_1 as:

$$\frac{0.60 \times 0.10}{(0.60 \times 0.10) + (0.10 \times 0.90)} = 0.40.$$

In this case the majority of patients obtaining the schizophrenic scores will be non-schizophrenics; only 40% will in fact be schizophrenics.

This last formula is also of value in cases where a score falls in the area of misclassification as given in the standardization data. Suppose a patient obtains a score worse than that of 60% of non-schizophrenics, while 30% of schizophrenics do better, use of the formula will often help in making a decision. It is necessary only to treat the patient's score as though it was a cut-off on a diagnostic test. The formula can then be applied. Supposing the base rate for schizophrenia is 70%, the probability that the patient is a schizophrenic is:

$$\frac{0.70 \times 0.70}{(0.70 \times 0.70) + (0.40 \times 0.30)} = 0.80.$$

If the base rate is 5% schizophrenics, the probability that the patient is a schizophrenic is:

$$\frac{0.70 \times 0.05}{(0.70 \times 0.05) + (0.40 \times 0.95)} = 0.085.$$

In the first case the best bet is that the patient is schizophrenic, while in the second the best bet is that the patient is not schizophrenic.

Other aspects of the application of Bayes Theorem in clinical psychology can be found in the sources cited at the beginning of this section. Enough has been said to show that in some circumstances valid, reliable tests may increase the number of errors made. Sometimes any test is worse than none, and this is more likely to be true in diagnosing common or rare conditions.

VII APPROACHES TO DEALING WITH PROBLEMS PRESENTED

In view of the unsatisfactory state of diagnosis and diagnostic testing, it is not surprising that many psychologists have adopted approaches other than the diagnostic one when dealing with patients. The three main ones are:

(1) trait descriptions;
(2) attempts to understand the patient; and
(3) experimental investigations of individual patients.

Combinations of these may, of course, be used by the same psychologist on the same or different patients.

1 Trait descriptions of patients

This approach avoids the diagnostic problem by concentrating on the description of patients in terms of continuous traits. Thus the problem 'Is this patient schizophrenic?' will be treated as an investigation into whether the patient is thought disordered. The patient will be deemed to be thought disordered if he produces a performance on a test of thinking which is statistically rare in normals, and in a pathological direction. Or the psychologist might measure the patient on a number of personality characteristics. It is quite likely that the psychologist will pass an opinion on whether the patient is schizophrenic or not, but essentially he has been trying to find abnormal performances on measures of continuous traits.

A wide variety of measures of personality traits are available (for a review see the chapter by Griffiths in this volume). Of special clinical interest are measures of anxiety and depression, and measures of these are available in many forms, e.g. I.P.A.T., Anxiety Scale, 8 Parallel Form Anxiety Scale, Hamilton's Anxiety Rating Scale (Hamilton, 1959); Beck Rating Scale for depression (Beck *et al.*, 1961; Metcalfe and Goldman, 1965) and the Hamilton Rating Scale for depression (Hamilton, 1960, 1967). A psychologist might well use one or more of these in dealing with a diagnostic problem, but it is unlikely that any psychologist would call them tests of endogenous depression or anxiety neurosis. The aim of using trait measures is to provide information which might help in diagnosis. If the psychologist passes an opinion on the likely diagnosis and is found to be wrong, the description of the patient in terms of these traits would still be valid.

The problem with this approach is that it can be shown to land the user in Payne's dilemma. Suppose that a psychologist describes a patient as being very extraverted on the basis of the E.P.I., and communicates this information to a psychiatrist, it is obviously possible that the psychiatrist's conception of extraversion does not correlate perfectly with the concept of extraversion measured by the test. The psychiatrist is likely to have views on the significant correlates of extraversion in the type of patient he is dealing with. The report will therefore lead the psychiatrist to expect the patient to show the correlates of his (the psychiatrist's) concept of extraversion. Whether the patient does or does not will depend on (a) the correlation between the test and the psychiatrist's idea of extraversion and (b) the correlation between the psychiatrist's idea of extraversion and the things it signifies. If these correlations are low then there may well be no relationship between test scores and the psychiatrist's expectations for his patient. This is exactly the situation found in relation to diagnostic tests.

The moral is clear. Just as a diagnostic test should be directly validated against the criteria of real interest, so should measures of traits. To take an example, the usefulness of the Grid Test of Thought Disorder (Bannister and Fransella, 1966) remains unknown in clinical practice until there is data on the correlates of thought disorder scores. Data are available on the correlation of scores with psychiatrically judged thought disorder, but there are no data on the relationship of scores to improvement, length of hospitalization, response to treatment, etc.

Payne's argument applies to trait descriptions just as much as to diagnostic tests. The trait we have most faith in has, in fact, been validated directly against a variety of criteria. Intelligence tests are widely used and often useful.

2 Understanding the patient – the clinical approach

Some psychologists would object to trait descriptions on other grounds. They would see them as atomistic and sterile. They would argue that what is required is an understanding of the patient as a total personality. Even when they show an interest in diagnosis their real concern is elsewhere (e.g. Harrower, 1965). There is much that is commendable in this approach. It has the merits of flexibility and is a genuine attempt to get to grips with the patient's problems. The aim is to understand the patient so that meaningful decisions can be made about him or by him. The approach is characterized by a respect for intuition and often for projective techniques. Other features of this approach have been summarized by Vernon (1964). Leaving aside the validity of intuition and projective techniques, the chief criticism of the clinical approach is that it has not proved conspicuously successful.

Even an understanding of the patient's total personality has to be communicated to others if it is to be useful. Often the patient will have to be described in terms of traits of one sort or another. The results of investigations in this field are somewhat disheartening. Horowitz (1962) reports a study comparing clinical assessments of patients by clinicians, who had biographical and projective techniques data on patients, with base rate assessments. The base rate assessments were as accurate in predicting therapists' ratings as the clinicians. The implication of this investigation is that people with no specific data on a patient can describe him as accurately as those with a large amount of clinical data. Other evidence casting doubt on clinically derived descriptions of traits is provided by Little and Schneidman (1959) and Goldberg and Werts (1966), amongst others. One of the best investigations is that of Raines and Rohrer (1955), who found that clinicians tended to have individual preferences in their ways of describing patients. Thus one clinician will have a tendency to find anxiety and projection in his patients much more often than other clinicians seeing the same patients. These preferences for finding certain sorts of defence mechanism and traits in patients were later shown to be related to the clinician's own personality (Raines and Rohrer, 1960). The investigators suggest a projection hypothesis to explain their findings. It should be noted that in the investigation relating clinicians' personality to descriptive predilections, the clinicians were all experienced and had been trained in the same institution.

It might be argued that accuracy of trait descriptions is not the best test of understanding of a patient. If the patient is seen as a dynamic whole it may be difficult for the clinician to describe him on static traits. For this reason several authors have suggested accuracy of prediction as a better criterion. Here again the results are disappointing. Included amongst the things that clinicians cannot predict are which patients will stay for how long in psychotherapy (Affleck and Garfield, 1961), and what schedule of psychotherapy will be most beneficial to their patients (McNair and Lorr, 1960). Both of these are things that most clinicians would consider important. One might suppose, however, that in many situations the clinician's greater understanding and flexibility of approach would make him a better predictor than alternative methods. Meehl (1954) found clinical prediction to be, at best, no better than actuarial prediction, and a recent review by Sawyer (1966) describes 45 investigations comparing clinical versus mechanical combination of data in making predictions. Sawyer's review is valuable in that it also divides the data by source – whether it was collected mechanically or clinically. In all 75 comparisons were involved and in none of these did clinical integration of data prove significantly superior to mechanical integration. In 28 cases the mechanical combination was significantly superior to the clinical. Not all of the studies reviewed are strictly relevant to the clinical field, but the conclusion would seem to be that the clinician has a role as a data collector in some instances, but that mechanical integration should be used, except in instances where the two methods have been shown to be of equal value, when the method of integration should be chosen on the basis of cost. It has been found that sometimes the clinician is cheaper (Johnston and McNeal 1967).

Many clinicians appear to feel that research findings such as these do not apply to them. Their clinical experience tells them that they are accurate. A possible explanation of their feeling of accuracy is the 'Barnum effect' (Forer, 1949; Meehl, 1956). There are a large number of statements which are likely to be true of any patient, and if the clinician uses these his colleagues will be likely to agree with him. It will be recalled that Horowitz (1962) was able to show that base rate descriptions were as accurate as those of clinicians who had seen the patient.

Another objection to research findings is that often the clinicians used in research are not very experienced. However, the hypothesis that experience will increase accuracy is not clearly confirmed by the evidence available. Taft (1955) found no clear evidence that it was correlated with accuracy, and Sarbin, Taft and Bailey (1960) review evidence to suggest that psychologists are no better than non-psychologists in their judgement of people, and that more experienced psychologists are no better than less experienced psychologists. Since their review other evidence has become available, none of which contradicts their conclusion. Goldberg (1959) found experienced clinicians to be no better than less experienced clinicians, and non-clinicians (typists, etc.) to be as good as either. Hiler and Nesvig (1965) found psychologists no better than non-psychologists, and Stricker (1967) found student clinicians better than experienced clinicians. It may be that when clinicians are confident of their judgements, they are more likely to be right, but again the evidence is equivocal.

In one investigation (Holsopple and Phelan, 1954) it was found that when clinicians were 'very sure' that they were right, they were right only 25% of the time; when they were 'relatively sure' they were right 40% of the time; but when they were 'not sure' they were right 42% of the time. Thus there was a negative association between the clinician's confidence that he really knew the case and the accuracy of his judgements. Similar findings are reported by Phelan (1960); and Oskamp (1965) demonstrated that clinicians became more confident of their accuracy as they obtained more information about a case, but that this increase in confidence was not matched by a corresponding increase in accuracy.

Individual investigations described above can be questioned, but their cumulative impact is too great for them to be ignored. Probably the clinician's mistake is that he treats his hypotheses as facts. Perhaps if he tested them and rejected those which are not borne out he would put up a better performance. Clinicians say that they are continually testing hypotheses by making predictions about what they will find, but this is usually very much an intra-clinician method and the hypotheses may be mere self-fulfilling prophecies. The work of Raines and Rohrer (1960), and the evidence on the conditioning of verbal behaviour (Holz and Azrin, 1966), suggest that more objective tests of hypotheses are desirable. It appears that selective use of reinforcement can influence the patient's verbalizations in clinical interview and psychotherapeutic situations (Krasner, 1965), and also influence the patient's responses to projective tests (Dinoff, 1960; Gross, 1959; Magnussen, 1960; Simkins, 1960). If these findings are reliable it is essential that the clinician should use other techniques to test his hypotheses about patients. One obvious solution is that he should attempt experimental investigations of his patients.

3 The experimental investigation of individual patients

This approach has been described by Shapiro (1957, 1967) and Jones (1960b). In view of Shapiro's contribution to this volume, an extensive description of the approach would be redundant. Briefly, the approach involves setting up hypotheses to explain some abnormality observed in the patient and making objective tests of these hypotheses. The investigation should ideally lead to a model which can be used to predict and control the patient's behaviour. If successful, the investigator will be able to specify the situations in which the abnormality will be rectified and a remedial experiment attempted. In some important ways advocates of this approach have similar aims to clinicians. Both believe that it is desirable to study individual cases, and both are concerned with the explanation of the patient's behaviour, rather than merely categorizing him. The main differences are differences in type of explanation favoured and methods of testing them.

The usual criticisms of the approach are: (1) that the results of such investigations are often trivial; (2) that the method is time-consuming; (3) that the method is unsuited to investigating the historical antecedents of the patient's problem; (4) that the explanatory models are mechanistic, behaviouristic or non-dynamic.

Triviality is a matter of opinion. Anyone unfamiliar with the sorts of investigation carried out can find examples in Jones (1960b). However, even if it is thought that the investigations carried out have led to findings of little consequence, there is obviously nothing inherent in the approach to lead one to suppose that the results will necessarily be trivial. At best this is a criticism of the uses of the method to date, rather than a criticism of the experimental investigation of individual patients.

The second criticism, that the method is time-consuming, is valid only in so far as one thinks that: (1) the method will not produce findings of sufficient value, and (2) that there are more valuable things for clinical psychologists to do. It is not self-evident that a series of investigations to explain a discrepancy in test results is of less value than seeing ten patients instead and trying to provide useful information about them from studying their drawings of a person, or what they say they see in ink blots. Triviality and excessive consumption of time lie in the eye of the beholder.

There is more substance in the third criticism. Often some workable theory of the historical antecedents of the patient's condition is of value. Sometimes possible competing theories will lead to differing predictions about the present, but this is not always so. In cases where there is difficulty in choosing between conflicting hypotheses about the past, scientific method is inapplicable. Bromley (1968) has suggested that appropriate criteria may be found in the method of quasi-judicial inquiry. At least there are available criteria for testing the likely truth of statements about the past. However, from the point of view of being able to predict and control the patient's behaviour knowledge of historical antecedents may be unnecessary.

A fourth criticism is usually meant to imply that experimental investigations may well be suited to investigations of differences between verbal and performance I.Q.s, but cannot be used to test more dynamic hypotheses about the patient. It might be harder but it should not be impossible. Techniques based on the semantic differential and repertory grid should, on the face of it, be very suitable for testing hypotheses about interpersonal relationships and the like. In any case there are already on record successful investigations of more dynamic aspects of behaviour than verbal-performance discrepancies (Metcalfe, 1956; Beech, 1957; Fransella and Adams, 1966).

The advantages of this method lie mainly in the fact that the psychologist has to formulate his hypotheses about patients more clearly, and, more important, test them. In the usual clinical approach, public tests of hypotheses are missing, and it is likely that even clinical psychologists are subject to selective perception and memory like the rest of the human race. It is unlikely that the traditional clinical approach would be impaired by the incorporation of experimental investigations.

4 The need for rational tests

Eysenck (1957) has suggested that it is possible to divide tests into three categories. Notional tests are those which lack demonstrated validity. Empirical tests are those which have demonstrated validity but no theoretical rationale. Rational tests have demonstrated validity and a theoretical rationale. It is clear that psychologists should be aiming at making all tests rational in this sense. But, from the point of view of the practising clinical psychologist, certain sorts of theoretical rationale are more important than others. While it is desirable to have data on the factorial structure of the W.A.I.S. and its subtests (Cohen 1957; Saunders, 1960a, b), knowledge of this factorial structure has few, if any implications for the control of the patient's behaviour. It is difficult to see how knowledge of factorial structure can suggest ways of improving performance on intelligence test subtests. For example, poor performance on the W.A.I.S. Similarities Subtest might possibly be explained on factor analytic grounds as resulting from defective verbal ability. This is clearly too holistic an explanation to have remedial implications. To improve the patient's performance, a model which explains the mechanics of similarities performance is necessary. To take an example, a patient who had received a head injury had a significantly poor performance on the W.A.I.S. Similarities Test. This seemed explicable, in part, in terms of a model rather similar to that suggested by Underwood (1952). The assumptions made were as follows. Each word in the pair sets off a stream of associations. Where an associate occurs in both streams, that associate will be given as the answer. If more than one associate is common to both streams, the strongest one will be given. The stronger the associate, the earlier it will occur in the stream. To test the model the patient was asked to give as many associates as he could to a large number of words. When this had been done it was possible to construct similarities items by choosing words from those to which associations were known, in such a way as to be able to predict the answer the patient would give. It was also possible to construct items in which the patient would see no similarity. Twelve similarities items were constructed and in eleven out of the twelve the predictions were fulfilled.

It is not suggested that this is the best conceivable model for similarities performance, but at least it suggests three likely reasons for poor performance. First, it could be due to a low number of associates to each word; in general it is reasonable to assume that the lower the number of associates the lower the chance of one common to each pair. Where this is the reason for poor performance the patient will say that the objects are not alike. Secondly, poor performance could be due to strong inappropriate common associates; and thirdly, it could be due to a defect in matching the two streams. The usefulness of such a model is increased by the available knowledge on increasing the availability of responses (Berlyne, 1965). In the patient's case it seemed that his inferior performance was due to his producing a very small number of associates to each word, but in the case of thought-disordered schizophrenics the second explanation might be more likely. Obviously the investigation must then proceed to try to explain the poverty of associations, but enough has been said to show that a mechanical model is likely to be of more use than a factor analytic one.

In similar vein there is need for explanations of why organics do badly on visual memory and auditory learning tests, why schizophrenics cannot explain proverbs and so on. Psychologists should not be content with 'explaining' poor visual memory in terms of brain damage, and thought disorder in terms of schizophrenia. Bindra (1959) makes this point forcibly. He points out, for example, that the finding of syphilitic brain damage in the general paretic does not explain why he behaves as he does. Other 'explanations' seem similar to attempts to explain the patient's behaviour by pointing to the diagnosis. For example, Payne (1960) and Venables (1964) suggest that many schizophrenic abnormalities can be explained in terms of a defective filter. This sort of theory is not very useful unless one can go to the shop and buy a replacement filter for the patient. Much more useful is the kind of explanation of thought disorder advanced by Bannister (1960, 1962, 1965). This theory has many more practical implications. It even suggests how to make normals thought-disordered.

The point of this long digression is to suggest that experimental investigations of individual patients will help in the development of understanding of the mechanics of test solution and thus lead to the development of rational tests. Further, as the aim of these investigations is to bring the behaviour of the patient under experimental control, it is likely that they will lead to the development of theories with remedial implications. Both of these are desirable objectives.

VIII IMPLICATIONS FOR CLINICAL PSYCHOLOGY PRACTICE

The evidence reviewed above does not, of course, prove that all diagnostic testing is a waste of time. However, it certainly suggests that in many, if not most, areas it is of unproven value. Tests of brain damage, showing sufficiently high validity in terms of predicting criterion, should be of value in view of the high reliability of the criterion, and it has already been mentioned that the Modified Word Learning Test emerged well as a predictor of outcome in one study. In terms of trait measurement, the assessment of intellectual level should be valuable. At least there is a wealth of data on the correlates of intelligence tests. Other traits, especially neuroticism, anxiety and depression, can also be measured reliably, but more data are required on the prognostic correlates of these traits before they can be used with confidence.

It would be naïve to suppose that the validation of prognostic tests is without its difficulties. Most of these centre round the use of improvement as a criterion. The reliability of global ratings of improvement is often disappointing. For example, Miles *et al.* (1951) found only 20% complete agreement between raters on a six-point scale. It is probable, however, that global improvement is not the best criterion, and that improvement in distinct areas should be measured. Here the results are slightly more encouraging. Morton (1955) found that ratings of level of adjustment in twelve separate areas produced inter-rater reliabilities in the range 0·79-0·91. The reliabilities for rating of improvement in these areas were somewhat lower (0·59-0·78), improvement being assessed as change from initial interview to terminal interview. Another problem in ratings of improvement is that psychiatrists and psychotherapists appear to have slightly different criteria from laymen. At least Storrow (1960) found two clusters in ratings of improvement. The ratings of patients and their relatives were in one cluster, while the ratings of the therapists and psychiatrists were in a separate cluster. Fulkerson and Barry (1961) provide a detailed review of other investigations on this topic.

An encouraging finding is that three of the criteria commonly used in prognostic studies have significant inter-correlations. Length of hospitalization has been shown to correlate with ratings of improvement (Pascal *et al.*, 1953; Ullman, 1957), and with chances of re-admission (Crandall *et al.*, 1954). The shorter the time a patient spends in hospital the lower his chances will be of re-admission and the higher the rating of adjustment will be at follow-up.

A variety of non-test indicators has been shown to correlate with outcome in schizophrenia. Zubin (1959) provides a useful score card of these, and there appear to be plenty of promising leads in the case of other conditions, although most of these require cross-validation, and many of their correlations with outcome are low (Windle, 1952; Fulkerson and Barry, 1961; Zubin *et al.*, 1961). At present it is not possible to point with confidence to any measures which consistently show a high degree of association with outcome. Even the process-reactive dimension, which has consistently been correlated with outcome, usually produces correlations of less than 0·50.

The problem is complicated further by the fact that prediction of outcome without tests is likely to have some validity. It will therefore be necessary to show that psychological tests have incremental validity -- that their use improves on the accuracy of prediction obtained without their use, and there are indications that in some areas predictions can already be made with a high degree of accuracy without tests. For example, Clow (1953) found that a majority opinion taken at a case conference predicted with 73% accuracy which, of a group of female schizophrenics, would be rated as improved and which unimproved at follow-up. It is also possible to predict response to ECT in depression with a high degree of accuracy. On Carney *et al.*'s (1965) figures, 83% of endogenous depressions given ECT will be improved at three months follow-up, while only 19% of neurotic depressions will be improved. In their study diagnosis predicted response to ETC with about 82% accuracy, while a weighted check-list of symptoms was 87% accurate. They also quote two studies using the Hobson Scale. In one of these the scale was 78% accurate and in the other 79% accurate. Mendels (1965) also used the Hobson Scale and found it 78% accurate at one month and 72% accurate at three months. It will be interesting to see if psychological tests can add to these figures.

Even granted psychological tests with incremental validity, their usefulness (and that of any other predictor) will depend on the base rates in the population in which they are used. Fortunately, many improvement rates do not depart greatly from 0·50. Zubin (1959) quotes an improvement rate of 40-50% for schizophrenics, Eysenck (1960) an improvement rate of 60-70% for neurotics, and in Carney *et al.*'s sample, just over 40% of depressed patients responded well to ECT.

In addition to the development of prognostic tests, it was suggested that clinical psychologists should concern themselves with individual cases in an experimental way, and it was implied that this endeavour might well lead to, amongst other things, a better understanding of the mechanics of test perfor-mance. The value of such better understanding is obvious. It is probable that the poor performance of a psychotic on an auditory learning test is due to different causes than the poor performance of an organic. With knowledge of the mechanisms involved it might well be possible to differentiate psychotic poor performance from organic poor performance, and so on. The further advantage of investigations of individuals is that it should lead to research hypotheses about important features of patients. After all, it is generally conceded that clinical investigation is an excellent source of hypotheses even if it is a bad way of testing them. Addition of experimental method to the usual procedure would improve clinical investigation while retaining its value as a hypothesis generator.

In all likelihood many clinical psychologists will not be convinced by the arguments advanced above and will continue to believe that traditional diagnostic labelling is a profitable exercise. For them there is encouragement in the fact that several measures show a high degree of agreement with traditional nosology. The S.S.I. has been shown in a number of investigations to correlate fairly well with diagnosis (Foulds, 1965), and the Wittenborn Rating Scales also agree with diagnosis. For example, Machir (1963) reports 75% agreement between Wittenborn-based diagnoses and psychiatric ones. An investigation using the I.P.A.T. Neuroticism Scale Questionnaire reports a misclassification of 13·9% in the diagnosis of neurosis (Kear-Colwell, 1965), and the list could be extended. For those who want even more nosological categories, Thorne (1964) presents a system for the classification of clinically significant psychological states intermediate between normality and psychiatric disorders.

The traditional approach is still going strong, but it is hard to disagree with Payne (1958), Arthur (1966) and Cole and Magnussen (1966), that clinical psychologists should be less concerned with attaching diagnostic labels than predicting important aspects of outcome.

REFERENCES

AFFLECK, D. C. and GARFIELD, S. L. (1961) Predictive judgments of therapists and duration of stay in psychotherapy. *J. clin. Psychol.*, **17**, 134-137.

ARTHUR, A. Z. (1966) A decision making approach to psychological assessment in the clinic. *J. consult. Psychol.*, **30**, 435-438.

ASH, P. (1949) The reliability of psychiatric diagnosis. *J. abnorm. soc. Psychol.*, **44**, 272-277.

ASTRUP, C., FOSSUM, A. and HOLMBOE, R. (1959) A follow-up study of 270 patients with acute affective psychosis. *Acta psychiat. neur. Scand.*, **34**, Suppl. 135.

BANNISTER, D. (1960) Conceptual structure in thought disordered schizophrenics. *J. ment. Sci.*, **106**, 1230-1249.

BANNISTER, D. (1962) The nature and measurement of schizophrenic thought disorder. *J. ment. Sci.*, **108**, 825-842.

BANNISTER, D. (1965) The genesis of schizophrenic thought disorder: retest of the serial invalidation hypothesis. *Brit. J. Psychiat.*, **111**, 377-382.

BANNISTER, D. and FRANSELLA, F. (1966) A grid test of schizophrenic thought disorder. *Brit. J. soc. clin. Psychol.*, **5**, 95-102.

BANNISTER, D., SALMON, P. and LEIBERMAN, D. M. (1964) Diagnosis – treatment relationships in psychiatry: a statistical analysis. *Brit. J. Psychiat.*, **110**, 726-732.

BARBIGAN, M. M., GARDNER, E., MILES, M. C. and ROMANO, J. (1965) Diagnostic consistency and change in a follow-up study of 1215 patients. *Amer. J. Psychiat.*, **121**, 895-901.

BECK, A. T. (1962) Reliability of psychiatric diagnosis. I: A critique of systematic studies. *Amer. J. Psychiat.*, **119**, 210-216.

BECK, A. T., WARD, C. M., MENDELSON, M., MOCK, J. and ERBAUGH, J. (1961) An inventory for measuring depression. *Arch. gen. Psychiat.*, **6**, 561-571.

BECK, A. T., WARD, C. M., MENDELSON, M., MOCK, J. E. and ERBAUGH, J. K. (1962) Reliability of psychiatric diagnosis. II: A study of consistency of clinical judgments and ratings. *Amer. J. Psychiat.*, **119**, 351-357.

BEECH, H. R. (1957) Cited by JONES, H. G. (1960b).

BERLYNE, D. E. (1965) *Structure and Direction in Thinking.* New York: Wiley.

BINDRA, D. (1959) *Motivation: A Systematic Reinterpretation.* New York: Ronald.

BOISEN, A. (1938) Types of dementia praecox. *Psychiatry*, **1**, 233-236.

BROMLEY, D. B. (1968) Conceptual analysis in the study of personality and adjustment. *Bull. Brit. Psychol. Soc.*, **21**, 155-160.

BROWN, G. W. (1960) Length of hospital stay and schizophrenia: a review of statistical studies. *Acta psychiat. neurol. Scand.*, **35**, 414-430.

CARNEY, M. W. P., ROTH, A. and GARSIDE, R. F. (1965) The diagnosis of depressive syndromes and the prediction of ECT response. *Brit. J. Psychiat.*, **111**, 659-674.

CHAPMAN, L. J., DAY, D. and BURSTEIN, A. (1961) The process-reactive distinction and prognosis in schizophrenia. *J. nerv. ment. Dis.*, **133**, 383-391.

CLARK, J. A. and MALLETT, B. L. (1963) A follow-up study of schizophrenia and depression in young adults. *Brit. J. Psychiat.*, **109**, 491-499.

CLOW, H. E. (1953) The use of a prognostic index of capacity for social adjustment in psychiatric disorders. *In* HOCH, P. H. and ZUBIN, J. (Eds.) *Current Problems in Psychiatric Diagnosis.* New York: Grune & Stratton.

COHEN, J. (1957) The factorial structure of the W.A.I.S. between early adulthood and old age. *J. consult. Psychol.*, **21**, 283-290.

COLE, J. K. and MAGNUSSEN, M. G. (1966) Where the action is. *J. consult. Psychol.*, **30**, 539-543.

COOPER, J. E. (1967) Diagnostic change in a longitudinal study of psychiatric patients. *Brit. J. Psychiat.*, **113**, 129-142.

CRANDALL, A., ZUBIN, J., METTLER, F. A. and LOGAN, N. D. (1954) The prognostic value of 'mobility' during the first two years of hospitalization for mental disorder. *Psychiat. Quart.*, **28**, 185-210.

DAWES, R. M. (1962) A note on base rates and psychometric efficiency. *J. consult. Psychol.*, **26**, 422-424.

DINOFF, M. (1960) Subject awareness of examiner influence in a testing situation. *J. consult. Psychol.*, **24**, 465.

DOLLIN, A., and REZNIKOFF, M. (1966) Diagnostic referral questions in psychological testing: changing concepts. *Psychc Rep.*, **19**, 610.

I

EYSENCK, H. J. (1952) *The Scientific Study of Personality*. London: Routledge and Kegan Paul.

EYSENCK, H. J. (1957) *The Dynamics of Anxiety and Hysteria*. London: Routledge and Kegan Paul.

EYSENCK, H. J. (1960a) Classification and the problem of diagnosis. *In* EYSENCK, H. J. (Ed.) *Handbook of Abnormal Psychology*. London: Pitman.

EYSENCK, H. J. (1960b) *Handbook of Abnormal Psychology*. London: Pitman.

EYSENCK, H. J. (1960c) The effects of psychotherapy. *In* EYSENCK, H. J. (Ed.) *Handbook of Abnormal Psychology*. London: Pitman.

FARINA, A., and WEBB, W. W. (1956) Premorbid adjustment and subsequent discharge. *J. nerv. ment. Dis.*, **124**, 612-613.

FARINA, A., GARMEZY, N. and BARRY, M. (1963) Relationship of marital status to incidence and prognosis of schizophrenia. *J. abnorm. soc. Psychol.*, **67**, 624-630.

FARINA, A., GARMEZY, N., ZALUSKY, M. and BECKER, J. (1962) Premorbid behaviour and prognosis in female schizophrenic patients. *J. consult. Psychol.*, **26**, 56-60.

FELDMAN, M. P. (1966) Aversion therapy for sexual deviations: a critical review. *Psychol. Bull.*, **65**, 65-79.

FORER, B. R. (1949) The fallacy of personal validations: a classroom demonstration of gullibility. *J. abnorm. soc. Psychol.*, **44**, 118-123.

FOULDS, G. (1955) The reliability of psychiatric and the validity of psychological diagnosis. *J. ment. Sci.*, **101**, 851-862.

FOULDS, G. (1965) *Personality and Personal Illness*. London: Tavistock Publications.

FRANSELLA, F. and ADAMS, B. (1966) An illustration of the use of repertory grid technique in a clinical setting. *Brit. J. soc. clin. Psychol.*, **5**, 51-62.

FREUND, K. (1960) Problems in the treatment of homosexuality. *In* EYSENCK, H. J. (Ed.), *Behaviour Therapy and the Neuroses*. Oxford: Pergamon Press.

FULKERSON, S. C. and BARRY, J. R. (1961) Methodology and research on the prognostic use of psychological tests. *Psychol. Bull.*, **58**, 177-204.

GARFIELD, S. L. and SUNDLAND, D. M. (1966) Prognostic scales in schizophrenia. *J. consult. Psychol.*, **30**, 18-24.

GELDER, M. G. and MARKS, I. M. (1966) Severe agoraphobia: a controlled prospective trial of behaviour therapy. *Brit. J. Psychiat.*, **112**, 309-320.

GOLDBERG, L. R. (1959) The effectiveness of clinicians' judgments: the diagnosis of organic brain damage from the Bender Gestalt test. *J. consult. Psychol.*, **23**, 25-33.

GOLDBERG, L. R. and WERTS, C. E. (1966) The reliability of clinicians' judgments: a multi-trait, multi-method approach. *J. consult. Psychol.*, **30**, 199-206.

GOLDFARB, A. (1959) Reliability of diagnostic judgments made by psychologists. *J. clin. Psychol.*, **15**, 392-296.

GROSS, L. R. (1959) Effects of verbal and non-verbal reinforcement in the Rorschach. *J. consult. Psychol.*, **23**, 66-68.

GUZE, S. B. and PERLEY, M. J. (1963) Observations on the natural history of hysteria. *Amer. J. Psychiat.*, **119**, 960-965.

HAMILTON, M. (1959) The assessment of anxiety states by rating. *Brit. J. med. Psychol.*, **32**, 50-59.

HAMILTON, M. (1960) A rating scale for depression. *J. Neurol. Neurosurg. Psychiat.*, **23**, 56-62.

HAMILTON, M. (1967) Development of a rating scale for primary depressive illness. *Brit. J. soc. clin. Psychol.*, **6**, 278-296.

HARROWER, M. (1965) Differential diagnosis. *In* WOLMAN, B. B. (Ed.) *Handbook of Clinical Psychology*. New York: McGraw-Hill.

HERON, W. G. (1962) The process-reactive classification of schizophrenia. *Psychol. Bull.*, **59**, 329-343.

HIGGINS, J. (1964) The concept of process reactive schizophrenia: criteria and related research. *J. nerv. ment. Dis.*, **138**, 9-25.

HIGGINS, J. and PETERSON, J. C. (1966) Concept of process-reactive schizophrenia: a critique. *Psychol. Bull.*, **66**, 210-206.

HILER, E. W. and NESVIG, D. (1965) An evaluation of criteria used by clinicians to infer pathology from figure drawings. *J. consult. Psychol.*, **29**, 520-529.

HOLMBOE, R. and ASTRUP, C. (1957) A follow-up study of 255 patients with acute schizophrenia and schizophreniform psychoses. *Acta psychiat. neur. Scand.*, **32**, Suppl. 115.

HOLSOPPLE, J. Q. and PHELAN, J. G. (1954) The skills of clinicians in the analysis of projective tests. *J. clin. Psychol.*, **10**, 307-320.

HOLZ, W. C. and AZRIN, N. H. (1966) Conditioning human verbal behaviour. *In* HONIG, W. K. (Ed.) *Operant Behaviour: Areas of Research and Application*. New York: Appleton-Century-Crofts.

HOROWITZ, M. F. (1962) A study of clinicians' judgments from projective test protocols. *J. consult. Psychol.*, **26**, 251-256.

HUNT, W. A. and JONES, N. F. (1962) The experimental investigation of clinical judgment. *In* BACHRACH, A. J. (Ed.) *Experimental Foundations of Clinical Psychology*. New York: Basic Books Inc.

HUNT, W. A., WITTSON, C. L. and HUNT, E. B. (1952) The relationship between definiteness of psychiatric diagnosis and severity of disability. *J. clin. Psychol.*, **8**, 314-315.

HUNT, W. A., WITTSON, C. L. and HUNT, E. B. (1953) Theoretical and practical analysis of the diagnostic process. *In* HOCH, P. H. and ZUBIN, J. (Eds.) *Current Problems in Psychiatric Diagnosis*. New York: Grune & Stratton.

INGHAM, J. G. (1965) A method for observing symptoms and attitudes. *Brit. J. soc. clin. Psychol.*, **4**, 131-140.

INGLIS, J. (1959) On the prognostic value of the Modified Word Learning Test in psychiatric patients over 65. *J. ment. Sci.*, **105**, 1100-1101.

JOHANNSEN, W. J., FRIEDMAN, S. H., LEITSCHUH, T. M. and AMMONS, H. (1963) A study of certain schizophrenic dimensions and their relationship to double alternation learning. *J. consult. Psychol.*, **27**, 375-382.

JOHNSTON, R. and MCNEAL, B. F. (1967) Statistical versus clinical prediction: length of neuro-psychiatric hospital stay. *J. abnorm. Psychol.*, **72**, 335-340.

JONES, H. G. (1960a) The behavioural treatment of enuresis nocturna. *In* EYSENCK, H. J. (Ed.) *Behaviour Therapy and the Neuroses*. Oxford: Pergamon Press.

JONES, H. G. (1960b) Applied abnormal psychology: the experimental approach. *In* EYSENCK, H. J. (Ed.) *Handbook of Abnormal Psychology*. London: Pitman.

KANTOR, R., WALLNER, J. and WINDLER, C. (1953) Process and reactive schizophrenia. *J. consul. Psychol.*, **17**, 157-162.

KEAR-COLWELL, J. J. (1965) Studies of the IPAT Neuroticism Scale Questionnaire (NSQ). *Brit. J. Soc. clin. Psychol.*, **4**, 214-223.

KELLNER, R. (1967) *The assessment of changes in the symptoms of neurotic adults.* Ph.D. Thesis, University of Liverpool.

KESSELL, A. and HOLT, N. F. (1965) Depression – an analysis and a follow-up study. *Brit. J. Psychiat.*, **111**, 1143-1153.

KILOH, L. G. and GARSIDE, R. F. (1963) The independence of neurotic depression and endogenous depression. *Brit. J. Psychiat.*, **109**, 451-463.

KING, G. (1958) Differential autonomic responsiveness in the process-reactive classification of schizophrenia. *J. abnorm. soc. Psychol.*, **56**, 160-164.

KLETT, J. C. and MCNAIR, D. M. (1966) Reliability of the acute psychotic types. *In* LORR, M. (Ed.) *Explorations in Typing Psychotics*. Oxford: Pergamon Press.

KOENIG, K. P. and MASTERS, J. (1965) Experimental treatment of habitual smoking. *Behav. Res. Therap.*, **3**, 235-243.

KRASNER, L. (1965) Verbal conditioning and psychotherapy. *In* KRASNER, L. and ULLMAN, L. P. (Eds.) *Research in Behaviour Modification*. New York: Holt, Rinehart & Winston.

KREITMAN, N. (1961) The reliability of psychiatric diagnosis. *J. ment. Sci.*, **107**, 876-886.

KREITMAN, N., SAINSBURY, P., MORRISSEY, J., TOWERS, J. and SCRIVENER, J. (1961) The reliability of psychiatric assessment: an analysis. *J. ment. Sci.*, **107**, 887-908.

LAZARUS, A. (1963) The results of behaviour therapy in 126 cases of severe neurosis. *Behav. Res. Ther.*, **1**, 65-78.

LITTLE, K. B. and SCHNEIDMAN, E. S. (1959) Congruencies amongst interpretations of psychological test and anamnestic data. *Psychol. Monogr.*, **73**, Whole No. 476.

MACHIR, D. F. (1963) Rater reliability and prediction of diagnosis with the Wittenborn Psychiatric Rating Scales. *J. consult. Psychol.*, **27**, 546.

MCNAIR, D. M. and LORR, M. (1960) Therapists' judgments of appropriateness of psychotherapy schedules. *J. consult. Psychol.*, **24**, 500-506.

MAGNUSSEN, M. G. (1960) Verbal and non-verbal reinforcers in the Rorschach situation. *J. clin. Psychol.*, **16**, 167-168.

MARKS, I. M. and GELDER, M. G. (1965) A controlled retrospective study of behaviour therapy in phobic patients. *Brit. J. Psychiat.*, **111**, 561-573.

MASSERMAN, J. and CARMICHAEL, H. (1938) Diagnosis and prognosis in psychiatry. *J. ment. Sci.*, **84**, 893-946.

MATARAZZO, J. D. (1965) The interview. *In* WOLMAN, B. B. (Ed.) *Handbook of Clinical Psychology*. New York: McGraw-Hill.

MAXWELL, A. E. (1961) *Analysing Qualitative Data*. London: Methuen.

MEEHL, P. E. (1954) *Clinical versus Statistical Prediction*. Minneapolis: University of Minn. Press.

MEEHL, P. E. (1956) Wanted – a good cook book. *Amer. Psychologist*, **11**, 263-272.

MEEHL, P. E. and ROSEN, A. (1955) Antecedent probability and the efficiency of psychometric signs, patterns, or cutting scores. *Psychol. Bull.*, **52**, 194-216.

MEHLMAN, B. (1952) The reliability of psychiatric diagnosis. *J. abnorm. soc. Psychol.*, **47**, 577-578.

MENDELS, J. (1965) Electro-convulsive therapy and depression. *Brit. J. Psychiat.*, **111**, 675-690.

METCALFE, M. (1956) Demonstration of a psychosomatic relationship. *Brit. J. med. Psychol.*, **29**, 63-66.

METCALFE, M. and GOLDMAN, E. (1965) Validation of an inventory for measuring depression. *Brit. J. Psychiat.*, **111**, 240-242.

MILES, H. W., BARRABEE, E. L. and FINESINGER, J. E. (1951) Evaluation of psychotherapy with a follow-up study of 62 cases of anxiety neurosis. *Psycho som. Med.* **13**, 83-105.

MORTON, R. B. (1955) An experiment in brief psychotherapy. *Psychol. Monogr.*, **67**. Whole No. 386.

NATHAN, P. E. (1967) *Cues, Decisions and Diagnoses*. London: Academic Press.

NORRIS, V. (1959) *Mental Illness in London*. Maudsley Monograph No. 6. London: Chapman & Hall.

ORGEL, S. A. (1957) Differential classification of hebephrenic and paranoid schizophrenics from case material. *J. clin. Psychol.*, **13**, 159-161.

OSKAMP, S. (1965) Over-confidence in case study judgments. *J. consult. Psychol.*, **29**, 261-265.

PARNELL, R. W. and SKOTTOWE, I. (1962) The significance of somatotype and other signs in psychiatric prognosis and treatment. *Proc. Roy. Soc. Med.*, **55**, 707-716.

PASAMANICK, B., DINTZ, S. and LEFTON, M. (1959) Psychiatric orientation and its relation to diagnosis and treatment in a mental hospital. *Amer. J. Psychiat.*, **116**, 127-132.

PASCAL, G. R., SWENSEN, C. H., FELDMAN, D. A., COLE, M. E. and BAYARD, J. (1953) Prognostic criteria in the case histories of hospitalized mental patients. *J. consult. Psychol.*, **17**, 163-171.

PAYNE, R. W. (1958) Diagnostic and personality testing in clinical psychology. *Amer. J. Psychiat.*, **115**, 25-29.

PAYNE, R. W. (1960) Cognitive abnormalities. *In* EYSENCK, H. J. (Ed.) *Handbook of Abnormal Psychology*. London: Pitman.

PHARES, E. J. (1967) The deviant personality. *In* HELSON, H. and BEVAN, W. (Eds.) *Contemporary Approaches to Psychology.* New York: Van Nostrand.

PHELAN, J. G. (1960) The subjective feeling of certainty of diagnostic judgments of clinical psychologists. *J. clin. Psychol.*, **16**, 101-104.

RAINES, G. N. and ROHRER, J. H. (1955) The operational matrix of psychiatric practice. I: Consistency and variability in interview impressions of different psychiatrists. *Amer. J. Psychiat.*, **111**, 721-733.

RAINES, G. N. and ROHRER, J. H. (1960) The operational matrix of psychiatric practice. II: Variability in psychiatric impressions and the projection hypothesis. *Amer. J. Psychiat.*, **117**, 133-139.

ROSE, J. T. (1963) Reactive and endogenous depressions – response to ECT. *Brit. J. Psychiat.*, **109**, 213-217.

ROSENZWEIG, N., VANDENBER, S. G., MOORE, K. and DUKAY, A. (1961) A study of the reliability of the mental status examination. *Amer. J. Psychiat.*, **117**, 1102-1108.

ROTH, M. (1959) The phenomenology of depressive states. *Canad. psychiat. Ass. J.*, **4**, 532-554.

SANDIFER, M. G. JR., PETTUS, C. and QUADE, D. (1964) A study of psychiatric diagnosis. *J. nerv. ment. Dis.*, **139**, 350-356.

SANDIFER, M. G., GREEN, L. M. and CARR-MARRIS, E. (1966) The construction and comparison of psychiatric diagnostic stereotypes. *Behav. Sci.*, **11**, 471-477.

SANDIFER, M. G., MORDERN, A., TIMBURY, G. C. and GREEN, L. M. (1968) Psychiatric diagnosis: a comparative study in North Carolina, London and Glasgow. *Brit. J. Psychiat.*, **114**, 1-9.

SARBIN, T. R., TAFT, R. and BAILEY, D. E. (1960) *Clinical Inference and Cognitive Theory.* New York: Holt, Rinehart & Winston.

SAUNDERS, D. R. (1960a) A factor analysis of the I and A items of the W.A.I.S. *Psychol. Rep.*, **6**, 367-383.

SAUNDERS, D. R. (1960b) A factor analysis of the PC items of the W.A.I.S. *J. clin. Psychol.*, **16**, 146-149.

SAWYER, J. (1966) Measurement and prediction, clinical and statistical. *Psychol. Bull.*, **66**, 178-200.

SCHMIDT, E., CASTELL, D. and BROWN, P. (1965) A retrospective study of 42 cases of behaviour therapy. *Behav. Res. Therap.*, **3**, 9-19.

SCHMIDT, H. and FONDA, C. (1956) The reliability of psychiatric diagnosis: a new look. *J. abnorm. soc. Psychol.*, **52**, 262-267.

SCOTT, J. (1958) Research definitions of mental health and mental illness. *Psychol. Bull.*, **55**, 29-45.

SEIDEL, C. (1960) The relationship between Klopfer's Rorschach prognostic rating scale and Phillips' case history prognostic rating scale. *J. consult. Psychol.*, **24**, 46-49.

SHAKOW, D. (1963) Psychological deficit in schizophrenia. *Behav. Sci.*, **8**, 275-305.

SHAPIRO, M. B. (1957) Experimental method in the psychological description of the individual psychiatric patient. *Int. J. soc. Psychiat.*, **3**, 89-103.

SHAPIRO, M. B. (1961) *The personal questionnaire. A method of measuring changes in the symptoms of an individual psychiatric patient.* Institute of Psychiatry, London.

SHAPIRO, M. B. (1967) Clinical psychology as an applied science. *Brit. J. Psychiat.*, **113**, 1039-1042.

SILVERMAN, J. (1964) The problem of attention in research and theory in schizophrenia. *Psychol. Rev.*, **71**, 352-379.

SIMKINS, L. (1960) Examiner reinforcement and situational variables in a projective testing situation. *J. consult. Psychol.*, **24**, 541-547.

SLATER, P. (1965) The use of the repetory grid in the individual case. *Brit. J. Psychiat.*, **111**, 965-976.

SOLOMON, L. and ZLOTOWSKI, M. (1964) The relationship between the Elgin and Phillips measures of process-reactive schizophrenia. *J. nerv. ment. Dis.*, **138**, 32-37.

STEPHENS, J. M. and ASTRUP, C. (1963) Prognosis in process and non-process schizophrenics. *Amer. J. Psychiat.*, **119**, 945-953.

STONE, L. A. (1967) Psychiatrists' prognostic judgments regarding functional psychotic disorders: a prognostic scale. *Behav. Sci.*, **11**, 115-120.

STORROW, H. A. (1960) The measurement of outcome in psychotherapy. *Arch. gen. Psychiat.*, **2**, 142-146.

STOUFFER, S. A. (1949) Cited by EYSENCK, H. J. (1952).

STRICKER, G. (1967) Actuarial, naive clinical and sophisticated clinical prediction of pathology from figure drawings. *J. consult. Psychol.*, **31**, 492-494.

TAFT, R. (1955) The ability to judge people. *Psychol. Bull.*, **52**, 1-23.

THORNE, F. C. (1964) Diagnostic classification and nomenclature for psychological states. *J. clin. Psychol.*, **20**, 1-60.

THORPE, J. G. (1962) The current status of prognostic test indicators for electro-convulsive therapy. *Psychosom. Med.*, **24**, 554-567.

TIMBURY, G. C. and MOWBRAY, R. M. (1964) The diagnosis of schizophrenia by Scottish psychiatrists. *Brit. J. Psychiat.*, **110**, 174-180.

ULLMAN, L. P. (1957) Selection of neuropsychiatric patients for group psychotherapy. *J. consult. Psychol.*, **21**, 277-280.

UNDERWOOD, B. J. (1952) An orientation for research on thinking. *Psychol. Rev.*, **59**, 209-220.

VENABLES, P. H. (1964) Input dysfunction in schizophrenia. *In* MAHER, B. A. (Ed.) *Progress in Experimental Personality Research*, Vol. 1. New York: Academic Press.

VERNON, P. E. (1964) *Personality Assessment: A Critical Survey.* London: Methuen.

WALTON, D. (1958) The diagnostic and predictive accuracy of the Modified Word Learning Test in psychiatric patients over 65. *J. ment. Sci.*, **104**, 1119-1122.

WILLIS, J. H. and BANNISTER, D. (1965) The diagnosis and treatment of schizophrenia. *Brit. J. Psychiat.*, 111, 1165-1171.

WILSON, M. S. and MEYER, E. (1962) Diagnostic consistency in a psychiatric liaison centre. *Amer. J. Psychiat.*, 119, 207-209.

WINDLE, C. (1952) Psychological tests in psychopathological prognosis. *Psychol. Bull.*, 49, 451-482.

WING, J. K., BIRLEY, J. L. T., COOPER, J. E., GRAHAM, P. and ISAACS, A. D. (1967) Reliability of a procedure for measuring and classifying present psychiatric state. *Brit. J. Psychiat.*, 113, 499-515.

WINOKUR, G. and PITTS, F. N. (1964) Affective disorder. I: Is reactive depression an entity? *J. nerv. ment. Dis.*, 138, 541-547.

WITTENBORN, J. R. (1950) A new procedure for evaluating mental hospital patients. *J. consult. Psychol.*, 14, 500-501.

WITTENBORN, J. R. (1951) Symptom patterns in a group of mental hospital patients. *J. consult. Psychol.*, 15, 290-302.

YOUNG, G. C. (1963) Cited by EYSENCK, H. J. and RACHMAN, S., *The Causes and Cures of Neurosis*. London: Routledge and Kegan Paul (1965).

ZIGLER, E. and PHILLIPS, L. (1961) Psychiatric diagnosis: A critique. *J. abn. soc. Psychol.*, 63, 607-618.

ZUBIN, J. (1959) Role of prognostic indicators in the evaluation of therapy. *In* COLE, J. O. and GERARD, R. W. (Eds.) *Psychopharmacology: Problems in Evaluation*. Washington, D.C.: National Academy of Sciences.

ZUBIN, J., SUTTON, S., SALZINGER, K., BURDOCK, E. I. and PEREZ, D. (1961) A biometric approach to prognosis in schizophrenia. *In* HOCH, P. H. and ZUBIN, J. (Eds.) *Comparative Epidemiology in the Mental Disorders*. New York: Grune and Stratton.

8

Long-stay psychiatric patients

John E. Orme

I INTRODUCTION

Clinical psychologists tend to be mainly concerned with acutely ill patients or with patients who have not lived for long periods inside the psychiatric hospital. Whether the psychologist is engaged in diagnostic, research or therapeutic activities, it is unusual for him to spend much time with chronic long-stay patients. Yet this population will usually form a major proportion of the patients in the psychiatric hospital. Often, the psychologist will find that request for his help with such patients is itself a reflection of renewed psychiatric interest in the question, either with regard to a particular patient or as part of an attempt to re-energize this section of the hospital. The request for help varies, but usually takes the form of asking for guidance concerning a long-stay schizophrenic patient. He may be asked for an all-round assessment regarding such a patient's general status and whether he might be expected to benefit from a particular rehabilitation procedure, either within the hospital or leading to actual discharge and outside work. The psychologist may react to such requests for guidance with the feeling that his usual assembly of interview and assessment techniques are inapplicable. This is a reaction that has some basis in reality as assessment procedures rarely include adequate, normative data on the performance of either acute or chronic psychotics. In this respect it is interesting to recall the work of Rapaport (1946), who reported diagnostic performance characteristics on various well-known intellectual and personality tests for the whole range of major diagnostic classes including chronic schizophrenics. Rapaport's work has subsequently met with much criticism, particularly on the grounds of small samples and inadequate statistics. Nevertheless, the psychologist who tries to avoid any involvement in psychiatric nosology and its problems runs the risk of being ineffective.

There is undoubtedly an absence of any large body of systematized data to which the clinical psychologist can refer in the assessment of the long-stay patient. Many standard procedures that might be considered useful with acute and newly admitted patients are clearly impractical. This is because many long-stay patients are unable, for one reason or another, to complete such procedures at all, or to complete them in a reliable and valid manner. Furthermore, research work by psychologists on schizophrenia does not often involve chronically ill patients. Even when it does, the findings, interesting though they might be, have

I* 237

little to offer at present in the way of precise techniques and normative data in the investigation of the individual case.

This survey will, of necessity, list studies that may contribute to an assessment programme. At a practical level, the work of psychiatrists often has as much to offer as that of the psychologist, particularly in the use or rating scales and rehabilitation procedures. It must be emphasized that in work with the long-stay patient there is little opportunity for working as a technician carrying out routine procedures. The clinical psychologist will have to be skilful in applying his general knowledge of psychology and the assessment of any individual involves more than a mechanical interpretation of test scores.

II CHARACTERISTICS OF LONG-STAY POPULATIONS

1 Changes in long-stay populations

Any account of assessment in this field must describe the constitution of the long-stay population, the many recent innovations affecting it and the likely directions of future change. Within the last twenty years, important developments have occurred in psychiatric practice, affecting the proportions and status of long-stay patients. The use of physical methods of treatment, particularly ECT, the tranquilizers and the anti-depressants, must be mentioned. At the same time, the change in status of the mental hospital from a lunatic asylum to a therapeutic community itself includes a series of changes. Such changes range from obvious practices like the unlocking of ward doors to a whole change in opinion, both at a public level and also with regard to the attitude of the staff involved with psychiatric patients (see, for example, Mandelbrote, 1964).

Formerly, the mental hospital tended to be a place largely of custodial care, but the emphasis now is on preventing patients becoming long-term inmates. Many chronic patients have been discharged, or are more satisfactorily occupied in the hospital. Fewer new patients are becoming chronic. Indeed, many psychotics, as well as non-psychotics, are treated on an out-patient basis, and are never admitted to hospital. Yet it is not entirely certain to which factor, or interactions of factors, these improvements may be attributed. One study of long-term (two-year) treatment of chronic schizophrenia, found psychotherapy alone contributed little or nothing to improvement (Grinspoon *et al.*, 1967). These workers suggested Phenothiazine therapy reduced florid symptomatology, but even those who improved dramatically, remained basically schizophrenic. Two other studies (Hughes and Little, 1967; Letemandia and Harris, 1967) found that the regular use of Phenothiazines to maintain improvement in chronic schizophrenics was only justified in a small minority of cases.

It might be that enlightened social measures are at least as important in the improvements in the mental hospital. But the adoption of open wards and a 'therapeutic community' programme do not necessarily produce the striking results that are sometimes claimed. Letemandia *et al.* (1967), for example, studied a population of chronic schizophrenics through the institution of administrative changes. They concluded that the rationale for such procedures must largely rest on general humanitarian grounds rather than on any marked therapeutic change. Although it is not possible to generalize from such studies, it is clear that one should resist accepting changes and methods as therapeutic simply because they appear to be the right thing to do.

What undoubtedly does now happen in the mental hospital is that the newly admitted patient receives attention with the aim of returning him to the community as soon as is reasonably possible. This contrast with the past has been cryptically summarized as changing the locked-door principle for the revolving-door principle. But even if the patient requires subsequent re-admissions, it is considered that this is better than becoming a long-stay patient. Apart from being cheaper from the point of view of hospital economics, the patient and his family are less likely to suffer separations from the community which are damaging in several ways.

For the future, the running down of the long-stay population is expected to continue, but there is some disagreement on how far this decline can be carried. Variations occur in the types and sizes of populations served by the various local mental hospitals. It is uncertain how far the growth of psychiatric units attached to general hospitals will affect the type of patient dealt with by the mental hospital. Some have suggested the latter be reserved for the remaining residue of chronic cases. But it has also been suggested that the mental hospital should specialize its services. Such large hospitals have the economic and staffing resources to improve much-needed research into chronic mental illness and to develop special units for different kinds of patients. It is generally agreed that the present tendency to deal with patients in an amorphous mass, regardless of diagnosis and treatment needs, should be abolished. At present, chronic patients need far more specialist attention than they receive. Present systems are usually geared to admission procedures and long-stay patients receive scant attention. The disadvantages inherent in the large size of the mental hospital can be dealt with perhaps by dividing it into a number of semi-autonomous units.

2 Diagnostic patterns in long-stay populations

These preliminary remarks, which summarize what must be known by many, are, of course, necessary to any account of psychological work with long-stay patients. It makes clear that long-stay patients vary from one hospital to another and from one time to another, for reasons that may be social as much as psychiatric. Any psychiatric diagnosis will be found among a long-stay population. These diagnoses will include severe neuroses and affective disorders who do not respond to treatment or otherwise recover. There will be various organic conditions with behaviour disturbances, ranging from epilepsy, and the presenile dementias to relative rarities such as Huntington's Chorea and Wilson's Disease. But there is little doubt that the bulk of long-stay patients suffer from schizophrenic disorders (see Brooke, 1967). Sommer and Witney (1961) found that most of the patients who became chronic were simple and catatonic schizophrenics. Twice as many paranoid schizophrenics were discharged as any other categories of schizophrenia.

Even so, it is important to point out that only a decreasing minority of acute schizophrenics become long-term hospital cases. For example, a survey of one hospital (Orwin, 1967) showed that only 3·8% of schizophrenics became long-stay patients over the ten-year period studied. Furthermore, only 2·7% really needed to remain in hospital, and the survey further indicated that even this figure might be reduced if more medical and nursing staff were available. This minority must in some way be different from the other schizophrenic admissions to hospital and this difference might well be attributable to factors other than the illness itself. Institutionalization, as urged by Russell Barton (1966), may have a more severe effect on some patients than others, though there is still controversy whether the behaviour of the chronic schizophrenic reflects the effects of institutionalization rather than his illness. Attention has also to be paid to the present and previous psychological and social background of the patient.

It is relevant to consider studies of prognostic scales in schizophrenia. A fairly common finding is that of Garfield and Sundland (1966) who, comparing female schizophrenics (41 chronics and 24 acute), found that one main difference between the two groups was simply that the chronic were more likely to be unmarried. Such a finding might indicate that acute subjects had a better level of premorbid adjustment enabling them to marry, but equally show that being married exerted a social pressure in the form of a need to return to a home and family, or even of having a home to which they could return. Fulton and Lorei (1967) make similar comments and, indeed, it is possible that simple life-history data such as this may show up better as a prognostic guide than apparently more sophisticated measures. A factor analytic study (Elosuo, 1967) of the rehabilitation of chronic schizophrenics found that although male patients reached a better level of working than female patients, they appeared to be more institutionalized and more difficult to place outside the hospital. Advancing age naturally increased this difficulty, as did lower social class membership. Again, it was found that marriage or the existence of a home and relatives with a positive attitude were favourable factors in rehabilitation. Rehabilitation was most difficult in those patients where autism, passivity, hallucinations, delusions and negativism were prominent.

It is important for the psychologist assessing the long-stay patient to obtain such data in any given case. An estimate has to be made of the importance of social factors, since these may be of primary importance in length of stay and in disposal. Occupational potential is one of the most critical of these factors.

III   INTELLECTUAL STATUS AND INTELLECTUAL EFFICIENCY

1 Intellectual deficit in chronic schizophrenia

There is little doubt that a full assessment of intellectual status and efficiency is most important in the long-stay patient. Remembering that the latter is largely a case of chronic schizophrenia, an index of intellectual functioning will inform, as well as anything, about a particular patient's capacity to behave normally in social and occupational situations. In schizophrenia, of course, the question of intellectual impairment has long been an important question. A number of recent studies (e.g. Foulds and Dixon, 1962; Foulds *et al.*, 1962; Cook and Smith, 1965) have thrown doubt on the existence of progressive intellectual deterioration in schizophrenia. Nevertheless, such studies still show that the chronic schizophrenic does not recover from a marked degree of intellectual impairment that first occurs in the initial phases of his illness. There are a number of published reports showing that in any group of chronic schizophrenics marked intellectual impairment is present. The following are typical findings.

Shapiro and Nelson (1955) used the Babcock index of efficiency which is obtained from contrasting vocabulary with non-verbal tests. The amount of impairment found in 14 chronic schizophrenics was almost as great as that in an organic group. Foulds and Dixon (1962) studied 270 schizophrenics (acute and chronic) and 280 neurotics. They showed that Standard Progressive Matrices performances indicated that all groups of schizophrenics showed intellectual deterioration. Nevertheless, they concluded (Foulds *et al.*, 1962) that length of hospitalization had little effect once normal ageing decline in performance was allowed for. Catatonics were more impaired than paranoids, and hebephrenics the most impaired of all. This study concluded that the impression of progressive dementia given by many chronic patients was due to other factors than intellectual test performance decline. Cook and Smith (1965) using the Coloured Progressive Matrices, again found no evidence for a progressive intellectual decline in chronic schizophrenics, although there was little doubt that serious intellectual impairment was present. Nevertheless, a study by Orme *et al.* (1964) of intellectual impairment in various psychiatric groups showed marked differences in the degree of impairment between chronic and acute schizophrenics. Although the performance on the Coloured Progressive Matrices was not strikingly poorer with the chronics than the acutes, there were striking differences on other performances. In fact, this study had initially been investigating the usefulness of two techniques for indicating brain damage. These techniques were the Modified Word Learning test (Walton and Black, 1957) and a Memory for Designs task (Orme, 1962). Brain-damaged subjects were effectively differentiated from groups of anxiety state, hysterics, psychopaths, melancholics and acute schizophrenics by these two tasks. The chronic schizophrenics, however, performed more like the organic group and could not be satisfactorily differentiated from them on these tasks (see Table 8.1).

Such a result raises questions concerning the nature of marked intellectual impairment in chronic schizophrenia. It is possible that the minority of schizophrenics who become chronic long-stay patients show such a degree of impairment because of organic processes of some kind. But from the point of view of individual assessments, there seems little doubt that the amount of intellectual impairment present is often quite incapacitating, whatever its origin. This point is further underlined when it is remembered that results such as these are obtained from the most accessible and co-operative sample of the chronic schizophrenic population.

	Organics	Chronic schizo-phrenics	Acute schizo-phrenics	Anxious and depressed neurotics	Hysterics	Psycho-paths	Melar choli
1 Word learning incomplete after five trials	81	70	33	18	30	10	23
2. Design recall distortion score more than three	83	74	21	14	25	3	40
3. Patients with both 1 and 2	66	57	8	4	10	0	10
4. MHVS-CPM discrepancy score more than +7	32	39	25	4	5	0	10

TABLE 8.1

Percentage of patients in 6 diagnostic groups showing certain performance characteristics (Orme *et al.*, 1964)

2 The untestable chronic patient

A number of investigators have attempted to study the problem of the untestable chronic schizophrenic. The main object of such studies is to see whether the untestable are similar to the testable apart from the question of interview co-operation. Klein and Spohn (1964) studied 95 male chronic schizophrenics, starting with their response to the W.A.I.S. and Rorscharch. Sixty-eight patients were considered fully testable, 13 untestable and confused, 14 untestable with a definite refusal. The last group were paranoids. The confused group seemed quite different from the other two groups in their general ward behaviour. They had very poor quality communications and social behaviour. It is evident from studies such as this that there are two main groups of untestable patients. First, the paranoid group, who may, in fact, be able to function quite well were it not for their paranoid ideas. Nevertheless, such gross interference with behaviour in the important sphere of social interaction is itself of major importance in individual assessment. The second group of untestable patients are untestable because their behaviour is, in fact, generally disorganized to the extent that normal social instruction and test performance is just not possible. Once again, the particular way in which the lack of testability shows itself can, in fact, be of importance in assessment of the individual case.

When it is appreciated that the functioning level of many long-stay patients is so low, attention might profitably be directed to estimating performances on tasks of a very simple order. Tasks, in fact, that recall assessment of behaviour in the severely subnormal. Such assessments would involve the observation of behaviour in personal spheres such as dressing, washing, feeding, and at a slightly more complex level, social behaviour as noted in conversational inter-change and the capacity to carry out simple instructions. The latter might be made on ward and O.T. behaviour, and also in a specific response to the psychologist's interview. In the course of the latter, such observations can be made and the patient can be asked to carry out simple tasks. Obviously, with chronic patients who are too incapacitated to carry out standard intellectual tasks, the psychologist will have to resort to such measures, but they are relevant also for patients who carry out formal tests.

3 Measurement of intellectual deficit in chronic schizophrenia

It follows from the foregoing that a major requirement with long-stay patient assessment is the measurement of intellectual status. Such assessment is best made by the use of standard techniques with appropriate age norms. The Wechsler scale will provide this data, not so much in the overall full-scale I.Q. but in the scatter of functioning within the scale. Although specific patterns of performance have not been satisfactorily validated for various clinical groups, certain features are common enough to be useful in chronic schizophrenics. The performance I.Q. will tend to be lower than the verbal I.Q. The statistical significance of the discrepancy between the performance and verbal I.Q.s can be estimated using appropriate tables (Field, 1960). Such a discrepancy indicates intellectual inefficiency, broadly contrasting present intellectual productivity with past (and premorbid) intellectual attainments. Even so, verbal behaviour might be seriously disturbed, resulting in an equally poor performance on the verbal subtests. The psychologist will have to exercise his clinical experience to extract as much information from his findings as possible. With some perform-ances, the pathology is obvious. With others, one will have to judge that the performances obtained (verbal as well as non-verbal) fall seriously short of what would have been expected from the patient's educational and social history.

In addition to standard intellectual measures such as the Wechsler scale, more specific techniques can be used to estimate the level of intellectual efficiency. Care is needed to use techniques with an appropriate amount of normative data available. It is no use giving a sorting or conceptual test, standardized only on bright, young adults, to middle-aged chronic schizophrenics whose premorbid level of ability was, at the best, only in the average range. Some of the most applicable techniques are those used in the field of brain damage. Such techniques involve memory testing using design reproduction (e.g. the Benton Visual Retention Test). With such techniques, a fairly simple geometrical design is exposed for a certain interval (5 or 10 seconds) and is then drawn from memory by the subject. Errors of various kinds made by the subject are then scored according to the manual of which particular technique is being used. Clearly, with such techniques, scoring has to be reliable and adequate norms be available for interpretation.

A widely used verbal learning technique is the Modified Word Learning Test (Walton and Black, 1957). Here ten words are selected which appear to be unknown by the subject, according to his performance on a standard vocabulary test. Severe impairment, often organically based, is indicated by the subject being unable to learn the meanings of at least six of these words after five trials. Another useful verbal learning measure of impairment is provided by paired associate learning as described by Inglis (1959). Here the subject has to learn the associate words for three stimulus words within a certain number of trials.

Such techniques clearly pick up what degree of intellectual inefficiency is present compared with normal expectancies. The main problem here is the recurrent difficulty in interpreting the similarity of performance to frankly brain-damaged subjects. The writer in practice, uses the series of techniques described in Orme *et al.* (1964). The Coloured Progressive Matrices and Mill Hill Vocabulary Scales are used as measures of non-verbal and verbal intellectual performance. A discrepancy table is provided for estimating the significance of the commonly occurring low non-verbal performance. The intellectual level indicated by the Coloured Matrices performance can be estimated from the table given in another paper (Orme, 1966a). The measures used specifically for an estimate of memory and learning impairment are the reproduction of Bender designs and the Modified Word Learning Test.

It will be found that in many long-stay chronic patients, the degree of intellectual inefficiency and impairment is so great as to be a basic factor in the total assessment of the patient. Marked intellectual deficit clearly implies a poor prognosis for any radical improvement in social and occupational behaviour. Furthermore, marked intellectual deficit precludes the use of many other techniques that might have been used in assessment.

Al-Issa (1964b) and Al-Issa and Robertson (1964) used measures of Guilford's cognitive factors involving creativity and divergent thinking in chronic schizophrenics. They found that lower scores in divergent thinking were associated with the presence of thought disorder. Higher scores were related to more skilled work in hospital occupations. There is controversy, of course, as to whether creativity (as measured in tests) is distinct from general intelligence (Burt, 1962), but the findings here only tend to support the results noted earlier that intellectual deficit is common in chronic schizophrenia.

4 Language disturbance

It was noted earlier that one reason why a vocabulary test performance cannot safely be assumed to reflect a schizophrenic's premorbid level of ability is that his verbal productions are often clearly affected by his illness. In fact, observations on the schizophrenic's verbal behaviour are a fairly reliable indicator of the general severity of his illness. Williams (1965) has summarized the main types of language disturbance that occur in schizophrenia which range from gross limitation of utterance, even mutism, through perseverative or echolalic speech, to neologisms and word salads. Such disturbances can be noted at interview but can be studied quantitatively. With Rochford, Williams investigated (Rochford and Williams, 1964) the language disorder of a group of chronic schizophrenics and compared this with disturbances in senile dementia and with focal lesions. On an object-naming task, the schizophrenics showed negativism rather than the true failure of comprehension seen in senile dementia. Unlike children and organic states, the failures of the schizophrenics were not related to the frequency of word usage.

The point here is that a sequence of objects (or their pictures) can be arranged according to the frequency with which their names occur in ordinary word usage. Organically based disorders involve language dysfunction in naming such objects with regard to their order of difficulty. With schizophrenics failures on the task are not necessarily related to their frequency of usage or order of difficulty.

Word association disturbances, of course, are also commonly reported in schizophrenia. There is some evidence that schizophrenics' responses in particular tend to include both distant reactions and clang associations which are relatively uncommon in other disorders. It might be that the thought disorder seen, for example, in overinclusive thinking (to be discussed later), is a result of irrelevant associations. One study (Higgins *et al.*, 1965) studied word associations using Palermo and Jenkins' (1964) norms in a group of 47 male schizophrenics. The length of hospitalization ranged from eight days to 21 years and the findings consistently indicated that associative disturbance became greater with increasing chronicity of illness. Such a finding tends to support the clinical view of a progressive disorder. As noted previously, measures of intellectual deficit do not generally support such a view. It might be argued that the associative disturbance in chronic schizophrenia reflects institutionalization or that the disturbance is peculiarly schizophrenic, unlike general intellectual deficit.

IV PERSONALITY ASSESSMENT

1 The use of standard personality measures

Personality measures of various kinds, such as projective techniques and personality inventories, will clearly be ineffective or even invalid with many long-term patients. Furthermore, it would be advisable to estimate the results of many studies in the field as being the product of intellectual impairment rather than of some variable thought to be peculiarly schizophrenic. Such caution has to be applied to a whole range of research work with schizophrenics, particularly chronic long-stay cases. Generally, such studies only allow for intellectual variations by the use of a verbal test, usually vocabulary. Such measures are unlikely to reveal anything like the full extent of the impairment shown by the schizophrenics. It is this impairment that might well be the origin of the schizophrenic's apparently specific peculiarity on various perceptual and psychomotor tasks. As noted, any response, or lack of it by the chronic patient, can be used in estimating his general level of behavioural response. This applies to any kind of task, even the more or less negative responses to standard personality tasks. But it does need emphasizing that, with such a population, a normal range of scorable performance is not to be expected.

Among any groups of long-stay patients, a number will appear to be functioning reasonably well from an intellectual point of view. Such patients can be given the usual range of personality techniques employed by the clinical psychologist and the results examined in the usual manner. It is still worth noting that it is doubtful if any techniques exist which demonstrate either the existence or the degree of schizophrenia. But, from a practical point of view, the amount of personality disturbance in a more general sense can be estimated. This can be done by using combinations of techniques, inventories such as the M.M.P.I., and projectives such as the Rorschach.

It is interesting in this respect to note the Rorscharch findings in chronic schizophrenia. It is possible to give the Rorschach test to many chronic schizophrenics who cannot complete tasks such as inventories. Yet very often, the kind of result obtained with the Rorschach perhaps only reflects the picture of severe intellectual impairment obtained with cognitive assessments. Neiger *et al.* (1962), using Piotrowski's Rorschach signs for organic pathology, found that about half of their chronic schizophrenics gave scores in the organic range. Either an organic basis has to be postulated for the condition, or these chronic patients are showing a severe personality disturbance resulting in organic-like performances. The Holtzman ink-blot technique has certain advantages over the Rorschach method in scoring and evaluation. It is of interest to note that performance norms are available with this method for a group of 140 chronic schizophrenics (Holtzman *et al.*, 1961).

One study reports the performance of chronic schizophrenics with the Cattell 16 PF inventory (Gleser and Gottschalk, 1967). A sample of 36 male and 46 female patients with a median hospitalization of eleven years (range six months to 25 years) resulted in completed performances from 34 males and 35 females. The more severely disturbed patients (mostly males) gave lower scores than normal for intelligence (factor B), emotional stability (factor C), enthusiasm (F), conscientiousness (G) and venturesomeness (H). It is of interest that this study highlights the intellectual deficit, and general lack of stability of the chronic schizophrenic rather than any clear suggestion of a schizophrenic personality profile.

Al-Issa (1964b) reported data on the Eysenck Personality Inventory (E.P.I.) in chronic schizophrenia. Thirty-four chronic patients with an average age of 46·8 years and mean hospitalization of 14·2 years were studied. This group of patients were all in stable employment and under consideration for community resettlement. As they were thus relatively normal, it is perhaps not surprising that they returned an average neuroticism score as low as 16·8. Within the group, increased extraversion (largely social extraversion with this measure) went with a reduction in excessive speech. It is evident that such measures as this might be helpful in estimating the emotional instability (a better term than neuroticism) and sociability of the chronic patient. But it has to be remembered that many chronic patients will not complete such inventories and in any case these measures do not necessarily supply any direct information concerning the more specifically schizophrenic aspects of a patient's illness.

Leipold and Knutson (1964) studied the relationship of hospitalization to various personality measures in 114 patients evenly divided for sex. The sample were divided into three groups, one of new admissions, one with five to ten years hospitalization, and one with ten or more years hospitalization. Personality measures used were of extraversion-introversion (E.P.I.), of anxiety (Taylor Manifest Anxiety Scale), and of social factors (Marlow Crowne Social Desirability Scale). This study found that increasing hospitalization was associated with decreasing anxiety and a greater need for social approval. No differences were found between hospitalization as such and extraversion-introversion.

2 The quest for a measure of schizophrenia

Attempts to measure schizophrenia (or certain aspects of schizophrenia) in recent years have resulted in findings or techniques that, at the best, only identify a proportion of schizophrenics. In this respect might be mentioned the work of Payne on over-inclusion (Payne, 1961), McGhie on attention (Chapman and McGhie 1962), and Bannister's measures of thought disorder, using Kelly's repertory grid technique (Bannister, 1963). Usually the results are positive for only the paranoid or the non-paranoid group. But to be fair, it must be pointed out that these techniques may only be seeking to identify some particular feature, such as thought disorder, not perhaps common or pronounced in all schizophrenics. Even so, it remains possible that such findings are only registering the effects of normally occurring personality variables in schizophrenia (such as extraversion-introversion), intellectual deficit, and an interaction between these two (Orme *et al.*, 1968). Nevertheless, these techniques might prove to be of use in the practical assessment of chronic schizophrenics. For example, Norman Cameron's concept of over inclusive thinking was defined as the inability to retain conceptual boundaries. As a consequence, the schizophrenic included ideas in his concepts which in normal thinking would be regarded as only distantly relevant, or even irrelevant. In Payne's work, such over-inclusive thinking is regarded as an aspect of a general attention defect, based perhaps in the breakdown of some cerebral filter mechanism. Three measures have been considered by him to be the best methods of assessment of over-inclusive thinking. First, the number of irrelevant ways of sorting used in an object classification test. Second, the average number of words used to explain proverbs in the Benjamin Proverbs Test. Third, the average number of objects placed in a group with the Goldstein Object Sorting Test. Payne and his associates have found over-inclusive thinking, as so measured, to be related to delusional ideas and hence, to paranoid, rather than non-paranoid schizophrenics. But

Payne *et al.* (1963) found chronic schizophrenics to be less over-inclusive than acute schizophrenics and only a little more over-inclusive than normals. This finding is similar to that of Tutko and Spence (1962) who found reactive schizophrenics were more over-inclusive than process schizophrenics and organics. Payne therefore suggests the presence of over-inclusion might be a sign of good prognosis. It might be that over-inclusiveness is associated with a relatively benign form of schizophrenia. More ominous forms of schizophrenia, liable to become chronic, may present with different symptomatology.

Of relevance here are the studies of cognitive disorder in schizophrenia by Foulds *et al.* (1967). Here the object classification and proverb tests of over-inclusive thinking were given to 48 schizophrenics, who varied from acute to chronic, and paranoid to non-paranoid. Also given was the Bannister-Fransella (1966) test of intensity and consistency of constructs derived from the repertory grid technique. These studies raised a number of doubts concerning the validity of the measures, especially in chronic schizophrenics. Particularly evident was a lack of association with thought disorder as rated by psychiatrists. One other problem posed by these studies is the extent to which groups of chronic schizophrenics are comparable from one study to another.

Payne's studies of over-inclusive thinking also found a factor of retardation was important in describing the behaviour of schizophrenics and depressives. Such a factor was orthogonal and unrelated to the over-inclusive factor which tended to identify the paranoid schizophrenics. The non-paranoid schizophrenics were identified by the retardation factor but not differentiated from the depressives in whom retardation may be an important feature. Nevertheless, many studies of schizophrenics, especially chronics, have stressed how slow they are in response (see for example King, 1954). Even if such slowness is partly due to factors other than schizophrenia, it is clearly an important aspect of the patient's behaviour.

3 Nosological studies and chronic schizophrenia

It might be worth noting here certain psychometric studies of nosology which are of interest in chronic psychiatric populations. Most studies in the taxonomy of mental illness are concerned with neurotics and normals. If psychotics are used, they are usually acute, newly admitted patients (see Vernon, 1964, for a useful summary). Such sampling will naturally affect the findings, especially factorial ones, and in this respect it is doubtful if unitary concepts like Eysenck's psychoticism factor will be of much value in investigating the chronic patient. As noted, studies of schizophrenia tend to report findings only applicable to a proportion of schizophrenics. In particular, the distinction between the paranoid and non-paranoid occur throughout reviews such as Silverman's (1964) and of large-scale studies such as Gerard (1964). Less frequently occurring are the distinctions between the overlapping dichotomies of acute and chronic, reactive and process schizophrenia.

The literature tends to support the view that the acute-chronic distinction in schizophrenia is related to the reactive-process distinction. It would also appear that the chronic (and process) schizophrenics are those who have a poorer pre-morbid level of adjustment (see Higgins and Peterson, 1966, for a review). To review such studies is to raise again the questions of how important, possibly interacting, are the factors of organic processes, severity of illness and length of hospitalization in accounting for the characteristics of the chronic schizophrenic. Yet such reviews tend to suggest the paranoid/non-paranoid distinction is not closely related with these factors. Possibly, as the writer has suggested (Orme, 1966b), the paranoid/non-paranoid distinction is only the manifestation of extraversion-introversion in schizophrenia. How much of a chronic schizo-phrenic's characteristics are due to his illness and how much to institutionaliza-tion remains a controversial issue whose solution will affect the data of the present account. One difficulty of course, in studying the problem of lengthy illness versus lengthy institutionalization, is in finding a suitable control group to compare with a chronic schizophrenic group. Silverman *et al.* (1966) suggests short-term and long-term prisoners form appropriate comparison groups to acute and chronic schizophrenics in terms of institutionalization. In a study of such groups they report some (but not all) of the perceptual characteristics of chronic schizophrenics were, in fact, present in long-term prisoners.

Factor analytic studies of behaviour ratings result in closer approximation to psychiatric textbook descriptions than studies of psychological concepts and hypotheses. For example, Lorr *et al.* (1955) rated 423 hospitalized psychotics on various aspects of ward and interview behaviour. Factor analysis resulted in eleven oblique first-order factors which produced three second-order factors. First-order factors included clearly schizophrenic ones of withdrawal, conceptual disorganization (thought disorder), motor disturbance (catatonia), paranoid suspicion, grandiose expansiveness (paranoia). Of the three second-order factors, one was identified with catatonic schizophrenia and one with hebephrenic schizophrenia. More recently (Lorr *et al.*, 1963; Lorr *et al.*, 1967), other findings have been described, not at all divorced from the reality of clinical practice. Using the I.M.R.S. (In Patient Multidimensional Rating Scale), five dimensions of disorganized hyperactivity, schizophrenic disorganization, paranoid process, anxious depression, and hostile paranoia have been reported. Studies like these support earlier findings of Moore (1933) Wittenborn (1951), and Degan (1952) in identifying and measuring something like the entities arrived at clinically by the psychiatrist. The use of concepts of classification that differ from those of the clinical psychiatrist can only be justified if such concepts are readily shown to have more relevance than the clinician's concepts.

To some extent, rating scales and inventories have not been specifically aimed at the investigation of the chronic patient. Harris *et al.* (1967) have published a scale specifically aimed at the assessment of the chronic patient and one that is also sensitive to therapeutic changes. The scale rates what are called phenomeno-logical items (speech, mood, delusions, hallucinations, temporal orientation and general information) and behavioural items. The latter involve feeding, toilet habits and occupation.

Klein and Spohn (1964) studied 104 chronic schizophrenics with a mean age of 42 years, average hospitalization 13 years, and mean full-scale Wechsler I.Q. 83. A factor analysis of behavioural observations on these patients gave a five-factor solution which was linked to three dimensions of patient behaviour. The first dimension was an index of general mental health as shown particularly by obtaining a higher I.Q., a relative lack of apparent pathology, and less hospitalization. The second dimension appeared to tap pathological ward adjustment as shown particularly in withdrawal and passivity. The third dimension was most associated with the mere rate of social interaction. The authors point out that this last dimension was irrelevant to measures of mental health or pathology. As such, the degree of interaction did not here prove useful in measuring the degree of psychiatric illness. This result perhaps recalls the finding noted earlier, that extraversion-introversion was not related to the length of hospitalization.

Overall *et al.* (1961) studied a group of chronic schizophrenics over a six-month period. The Lorr Multidimensional Scale for rating psychiatric patients was used and factored for changes in score on the 42 items of the scale over this period. Six factors were obtained, of which the most important was one identified by mental disorganization. One is again perhaps coming back to the basic question of intellectual deficit and its causes.

V PROGNOSIS AND REHABILITATION

1 Individual differences

Robertson (1962), studying chronic schizophrenics undergoing treatment in a rehabilitation unit, noted that patients varied a great deal in the amount of perceptual-motor impairment on simple, essential tasks such as shoe cleaning and polishing, the use of ties and laces, eating and drinking performance. Comparing an efficient group of 12 with an inefficient group of 12, Robertson found the only association between efficiency and psychiatric symptoms was that the inefficient group showed more motor disturbance and were more incontinent. Robertson suggested that the perceptual-motor disturbance resembled the effects of certain drugs and of anoxia, and that the underlying cause might be in the varying biochemistry of a schizophrenic. Once again we are faced with the basic question of general intellectual inefficiency and the problems of causation that such inefficiency poses.

Wing (1962) rated symptoms in chronic schizophrenics obtained at interview. Emotional blunting, poverty of speech, incoherence of speech, delusions and hallucinations were rated on a five-point scale (1, no disorder; 2, minimal; 3, moderate; 4, severe; 5, very severe). From this material, patients are divided into three groups: (1) the moderately ill with a rating of three or less in each category; (2) the severely ill with florid symptoms (rating of four or five on either speech incoherence or delusions); (3) severely ill without florid symptoms (all remaining patients). Wing considers these groups to be clinically well-recognizable but without any relationship to length of hospitalization. The severely ill without florid symptoms, however, showed far less desire to leave hospital. Wing points out, as have many writers, the dual difficulty in the way of rehabilitation for the chronic schizophrenic patient. As well as the clearly schizophrenic symptomatology, there are the handicaps he has acquired as a result of a prolonged stay in hospital. Yet there is some evidence that those schizophrenics whose illness is of long duration might do better at industrial rehabilitation than those whose illness is of short duration (Early, 1963; Gittleson, 1966). Such findings perhaps support the belief that chronic schizophrenics are more amenable than acute patients. Compared with the acute psychotic, the chronic psychotic is likely to be more apathetic and to have settled for a more or less psychotic existence. He is less orientated to the social conformity demanded by life outside the hospital. It is, of course, a common observation of chronic schizophrenics that symptoms such as delusional ideas may exist side by side with more acceptable behaviour. A schizophrenic who fairly readily helps in domestic tasks will claim relationship with royalty or the aristocracy and yet not voice any complaint about the lowly nature of her work. Such amenability is perhaps an example of Bleuler's double orientation in the schizophrenic.

More specifically, such amenability might be related to the absence of overt anxiety. Lang and Buss (1965) discuss the evidence for this proposition and the implications it might have for drive state and conditionability. They also discuss the data on psychophysiological responsiveness. The literature tends to suggest that chronic schizophrenics (especially non-paranoids) show reduced latency and/or amplitude of response. These features are associated at a behavioural level with withdrawal. But as the chronic schizophrenic's levels of muscular tension and cardiovascular activity remain high, a theory of underarousal cannot be maintained. Chronic patients may be physiologically hyperaroused although the frequency and amplitude of overt behaviour is greatly reduced.

2 Rehabilitation methods

Hamilton and Salmon (1962) studied various activity programmes for chronic schizophrenics. They did not find that financial reward of various kinds led to greater output, as is usually assumed for the normal in our society. They were more impressed with the total effect of what could be called the 'workshop climate'. This climate was a composite of industrial work, male supervision, time keeping, payment, and working in the company of other men on a socially approved task. It must, of course, be added that in this respect the chronic schizophrenics are only performing like ordinary industrial workers. Studies as long ago as those at the Hawthorne works clearly showed there is more to productivity than financial reward. The chronic schizophrenic, like the ordinary worker, responds to a complex of factors difficult to disentangle. As has already been pointed out, it is not easy to decide if any single factor is overwhelmingly important in producing the improved outlook for psychiatric patients over the last 20 to 30 years.

Martin (1965) describes a scheme for rehabilitating long-stay patients by the use of a three-ward system. On the first ward, a permissive community atmosphere was encouraged to replace the existing, institutional, rigid atmosphere. An emphasis was placed on patients taking increased responsibility in looking after themselves and in occupational tasks. Those patients who showed a good response to the first ward were then moved on to the second ward. Here individual responsibility was further increased and linked with a rehabilitation course run by the Occupational Therapy Department. The third ward was a hostel ward where all the patients were in regular employment and where the ward was the home to which they returned. Most observers agree that, for chronic patients, the hospital demands far less in the way of social behaviour than the outside community. Rehabilitation procedures (and as we shall see, behaviour therapy methods) naturally aim at increasing the patient's behavioural repertoire by workable gradients. In this respect it is worth noting that long-stay wards tend to be made up of patients of similar management problems. Thus, the more withdrawn and deteriorated patients are to be found together. One result of this practice is that mutual social stimulation is minimal. It can be argued that chronic withdrawn patients can only participate more effectively if given the appropriate stimulation by grouping the patients in an heterogeneous rather than homogeneous manner in this respect (Spohn and Wolk, 1966).

VI BEHAVIOUR MODIFICATION, OPERANT CONDITIONING AND PSYCHOTHERAPY

Terms like behaviour modification and operant conditioning are of fairly recent origin and are used to cover a considerable variety of techniques. The common link is with learning theories and a fundamental assumption is that mental disorder can be adequately treated by dealing with its signs and symptoms. From the behaviourist point of view, the disturbed behaviour is the illness. However, there is no unified learning theory generally accepted in psychology. Furthermore although it is relatively easy to provide a learning theory rationale for the aetiology and treatment of monosymptomatic disorders, there are obvious difficulties in tackling the more generalized illnesses which are far commoner. The learning theorist has himself, accordingly come to be more realistic. Instead of trying to cure schizophrenia as such, the behaviour therapist now tries to modify some of a schizophrenic's more socially unacceptable symptoms.

1 Some theoretical standpoints

It is interesting to note theoretical propositions relevant to the field of chronic schizophrenia. Pavlov's views seem to identify schizophrenia as an organic condition. He considered a weakened nervous system to be a basic cause of schizophrenia. The so-called paradoxical and ultra-paradoxical effects were by-products of this weakness where weak stimuli evoke stronger responses than strong stimuli and positive stimuli evoked negative responses. Pavlov felt that intense and prolonged stimulation of the nerve cells induced such protective inhibitions which were to be distinguished from normal active inhibitory processes. Such protective inhibitions led to schizophrenia and directly accounted for the schizophrenic's slowness and poor response to conditioning. Other schizophrenic symptoms were due to the effect of these protective inhibitions in the cortex and other parts of the brain. For example, inhibition in one brain area, by positive induction, would lead to excitation in other areas. If this happened in non-cortical areas, it could account for the violent outbursts sometimes seen in schizophrenics. Pavlov accordingly suggested the use of prolonged sleep which would strengthen the protective inhibitions and allow cortical cells to recover. Subsequent to Pavlov, Russian workers found that although schizophrenics are difficult to condition, this feature is more evident in catatonics and less in paranoids (Lynn, 1963). Lundin (1961) considered schizophrenia to be an end-product of a learnt avoidance of human contact – such a concept, although bold, needs evidence for support.

2 Operant methods and socialization

Operant conditioning has been particularly applied to psychotic behaviour. For example, with a schizophrenic whose speech is socially unacceptable because of the frequent use of neologisms, such speech is ignored by the therapist who only responds to normal speech utterances. Such a process aims to punish and extinguish the verbally deviant behaviour. Acceptable speech is rewarded. But to carry out such a scheme, someone has to spend a lot of time with the patient, which may, to the latter, be as significant a factor as any.

An example of a procedure involving more than one patient is that described by Ayllon and Haughton (1962). In a ward largely consisting of chronic schizophrenics, over half had a history of refusing to eat, despite the use of special techniques such as spoon feeding, tube feeding, intravenous feeding and electric shock. All feeding aids were stopped and the patient left alone at meal times when they had to go into the dining-room to eat. As a next step, the patient could not eat unless she entered the dining-room within half an hour of being called. After this time, the doors were locked and the patient missed the meal. This procedure was considered to establish successful self-feeding in the social situation of the dining room. After the eating behaviour was thus controlled, the patients had to drop a coin in a slot to enter the dining-room. At the same time, access to the dining room was restricted to five minutes within being called. Such shaping procedures are examples of how operant conditioning procedures can be used to control psychotic behaviour.

It is interesting to note the striking similarities between such operant procedures and rehabilitation schemes. These similarities may only indicate that the behaviour therapist is doing explicitly what other workers have done implicitly.

On the other hand, the importance of human relationships may have been under-estimated by the behaviour therapist. These issues cannot be discussed at length here, but the clinical psychologist ought to be aware of contrasting interpretations of behaviour changes. With chronic schizophrenics who may have gone years without any personal attention, the innovation of any programme that seeks their co-operation must represent a dramatic turn of events in their lives.

As a contrast to the learning theory approach, attention should be paid to the work on chronic schizophrenia carried out by a mixed psychiatric – psychological team (Freeman *et al.*, 1958). This was a long-term, intensive study of the effects of a broadly based psychoanalytic treatment on a group of chronic schizophrenics. Beneficial changes were obtained in severely disturbed patients.

Many of their techniques however, commenced at a very basic level. From an analytic point of view, the chronic schizophrenic may show, to a marked extent, the loss of ego boundaries thought to be the primary disturbance in schizophrenia. In such patients, the concept of personal identity and self-organizing behaviour has to be rebuilt. Nevertheless, many workers feel that the limited results of prolonged psychotherapy with chronic schizophrenics make the subject one of only academic interest.

One recurrent problem in dealing with psychotic patients is that of arriving at a motivation principle to which such patients respond. They may, in fact, respond to many ordinary social reinforcements. The persistence of deviant behaviour in chronic patients has been thought, by some, to be a product of the differential reinforcement by the hospital environment, rather than to primarily psychotic processes. This point again raises the question of how far the effects of hospitalization account for any long-term patient's behaviour. Whatever the cause, the motivation of some patient's behaviour by ordinary goals may be absent. In such cases, the behaviour therapist will have to find adequate reinforcers which can later render the patient's behaviour socially acceptable (see Buss and Lang, 1965). The chronic schizophrenic may not initially respond to social rewards (such as pleasing the psychologist) but might to more tangible, biological rewards (cigarettes, money, pleasant stimuli) or punishments (electric shock, white noise).

One such account (Sherman, 1965) describes the use of sweets and tobacco in producing speech in each of three long-stay psychotics who had been mute for many years. In judging the effectiveness and relevance of these procedures, the relative paucity of response after very many sessions must be noted.

VII   SUMMARY AND CONCLUDING REMARKS

If one is dealing with a chronic patient who can adequately respond, the psychologists' methods of assessment will vary little from those he uses with acute patients. Even so, he would be advised in such cases to try and decide why the subject has been a long-stay patient. Has he, for known or unknown reasons, now shown a general improvement in his condition, or has his stay in hospital been largely fortuitous. He may have occupied a useful niche in the hospital's society, and only been dislodged by the innovation of some new hospital programme. Alternatively, it may be that he manifests behaviour difficulties of a serious kind outside the hospital, but functions reasonably well in the hospital. If so, the psychologist should examine this problem and make some attempt to assess and guide.

More generally, the psychologist will find that the chronic patient, usually a schizophrenic, will require an assessment orientation of a different kind to that normally applied. A dearth of ordinary responsiveness with regard to his rate of work and its level, will necessitate the psychologist using a rather different framework to that which he uses with acute patients. Yet, if he keeps in mind the fact that all observations of a patient are potentially valuable, he will find that his basic psychological equipment can lead to an informative picture. Even so, it must be acknowledged that techniques at present available can, on the whole, only form an interim method of assessment.

The emphasis throughout has been on the writer's belief that an intensive exploration of the patient's intellectual status and intellectual efficiency will provide the hard core of his assessment findings. Using the standard techniques where age norms are available, the psychologist can attempt to answer three questions which are of basic importance. (1) What can be estimated of the patient's premorbid, or prehospitalization level of intellectual functioning? (2) What is his present range of behaviour and intellectual functioning, not only with regard to level but with regard to speed, and to consistency? He may, for example, perform reasonably well in the test situation, but be very slow, or unable to work at this level without individual attention. (3) Do the psychologist's findings match descriptions of the patient's usual behaviour?

Various techniques to measure aspects of schizophrenic functioning have been discussed but it seems clear that at present their use with chronic schizophrenics is only of limited value. Possibly those techniques involving language function and word association would be useful but far more normative data is required. A recurrent problem here is in how similar are the chronic schizophrenic groups reported in various studies. Perhaps a choice from among the various rating scales available would form the most valid addition to the use of standard intelligence measures. Certainly, some record of the patient's usual behaviour should be obtained with details about his motivations, strength of drive, and affectiveness of social interactions. If nothing else, the patient's response in certain basic areas of functioning can be rated.

A full assessment of intellectual status and behavioural response not only gives an informative picture of the patient but also indicates degree of success likely in any rehabilitation or therapeutic procedures. At the very least, a useful basis is established which helps to estimate later changes in the patient's condition.

Most of the present account has concerned the problems of the chronic schizophrenic. Although such patients make up the bulk of the long-stay population, there are other diagnostic categories, as noted at the beginning. Where these are of non-organic conditions (chronic neurotics, personality disorders and depressives), the assessment procedure will still be similar to that described for schizophrenics. This is also true of the organic conditions although, if the disorder is one involving increasing incapacity, there may be little opportunity for therapeutic or rehabilitatory development. Occasionally, among long-stay patients there occur diagnostic problems which seem impossible to solve. Such patients do not appear to fit any diagnostic category although the severity of illness cannot be questioned. Such cases only illuminate the whole problem of work in this field as it remains a basic issue why a minority of patients become chronic long-stay cases. Even if they are satisfactorily labelled schizophrenic or depressive, this does not usually explain the problem of why they have not responded to treatment earlier or remitted in some way. To a great extent, work with long-stay patients offers a challenge to psychologists that has been largely ignored. A parallel might be drawn with the fields of subnormality and ageing where until recently, the problems were ignored or dismissed. The long-term patient presents many basic problems which urgently require investigation. Only with such investigations will a more adequate frame of reference for assessment procedures emerge.

REFERENCES

AL-ISSA, I. (1964a) The Eysenck Personality Inventory in chronic schizophrenia. *Brit. J. Psychiat.*, **110**, 397-400.

AL-ISSA, I. (1964b) Creativity and its relationship to age, vocabulary and personality of schizophrenics. *Brit. J. Psychiat.*, **110**, 74-79.

AL-ISSA, I. and ROBERTSON, J. P. S. (1964) Divergent thinking abilities in chronic schizophrenia. *J. clin. Psychol.*, **20**, 433-435.

AYLLON, T. and HAUGHTON, E. (1962) Control of the behaviour of schizophrenic patients to food. *J. exp. Anal. Behav.*, **5**, 343-352.

BANNISTER, D. (1963) The genesis of thought disorder: a serial invalidation hypothesis. *Brit. J. Psychiat.*, **109**, 680-686.

BANNISTER, D. and FRANSELLA, F. (1966) A grid test of schizophrenic thought disorder. *Brit. J. soc. Clin. Psychol.*, **5**, 95-102.

BARTON, R. (1966) *Institutional Neurosis*, (2nd Ed.). Bristol: Wright.

BROOKE, E. M. (1967) *A Census of Patients in Psychiatric Beds 1963*. London: H.M.S.O.

BURT, C. (1962) The psychology of creative ability. *Brit. J. educ. Psychol.*, **32**, 292-298.

BUSS, A. H. and LANG, P. J. (1965) Psychological deficit in schizophrenia. I: Affect, reinforcement and concept attainment. *J. abnorm. Psychol.*, **70**, 2-24.

CHAPMAN, J. and MCGHIE (1962) A comparative study of disorder attention in schizophrenia. *J. ment. Sci.*, **108**, 487-500.

COOK, D. and SMITH, M. R. (1965) A note on intellectual deficit in schizophrenia. *Brit. J. soc. clin. Psychol.*, **4**, 152-153.

DEGAN, J. W. (1952) Dimensions of functional psychosis. *Psychometr. Monogr.* **6**, 1-41.

EARLY, D. F. (1963) The Industrial Therapy Organization (Bristol). The first two years. *Lancet*, **1**, 435-436.

ELOSUO, R. (1967) On the rehabilitation of schizophrenics. *Acta psychiat. Scand.*, **43**, 169-195.

FIELD, J. G. (1960) Two types of tables for use with Wechsler's Intelligence Scales. *J. clin. Psychol.*, **16**, 3-7.

FOULDS, G. A. and DIXON, P. (1962) The nature of intellectual deficit in schizophrenia. I: A comparison of schizophrenics and neurotics. *Brit. J. soc. clin. Psychol.*, **1**, 7-19.

FOULDS, G. A., DIXON, P., MCCLELLAND, M. and MCCLELLAND, W. J. (1962) The nature of intellectual deficit in schizophrenia. Part II: A cross-sectional study of paranoid, catatonic, hebephrenic and simple schizophrenics. *Brit. J. soc. clin. Psychol.*, **1**, 141-149.

FOULDS, G. A. and DIXON, P. M. (1962) The nature of intellectual deficit in schizophrenia. III: A longitudinal study of the sub-groups. *Brit. J. soc. clin. Psychol.*, **1**, 199-207.

FOULDS, G. A., HOPE, K., MCPHERSON, F. M. and MAYO, P. R. (1967) Cognitive disorder among the schizophrenias, I and II. *Brit. J. Psychiat.*, **113**, 1316-1374.

FREEMAN, T., CAMERON, J. and MCGHIE, A. (1958) *Chronic Schizophrenia.* London: Tavistock Publications.

FULTON, J. R. and LOREI, T. W. (1967) Predicting length of psychiatric hospitalization from history records. *J. clin. Psychol.*, **23**, 218-221.

GARFIELD, S. L. and SUNDLAND, D. M. (1966) Prognostic scales in schizophrenia. *J. consult. Psychol.*, **30**, 18-24.

GERARD, R. W. (1964) The nosology of schizophrenia: a co-operative study. *Behavioural Science*, **9**, 311-333.

GITTLESON, N. L. (1966) The schizophrenic rehabilitee. *Brit. J. Psychiat.*, **112**, 201-202.

GLESER, G. C. and GOTTSCHALK, L. A. (1967) Personality characteristics of chronic schizophrenics in relationship to sex and current functioning. *J. clin. Psychol.*, **23**, 349-954.

GRINSPOON, L., EWALT, J. R. and SHADER, R. (1967) Long-term treatment of chronic schizophrenia. *Int. J. Psychiat.*, **4**, 116-128.

HAMILTON, V. and SALMON, P. (1962) Psychological changes in chronic schizophrenics following differential activity programmes. *J. ment. Sci.*, **108**, 505-520.

HARRIS, A. D., LETEMANDIA, F. J. J. and WILLIAMS, P. J. A. (1967) A rating scale of the mental state for use in the chronic population of the psychiatric hospital. *Brit. J. Psychiat.*, **113**, 941-949.

HIGGINS, J. and PETERSON, J. C. (1966) Concept of process-reactive schizophrenia: a critique. *Psychol. Bull.*, **66**, 201-206.

HIGGINS, J., MENDICKS, S. A. and PHILIP, F. J. (1965) Associative disturbance as a function of chronicity in schizophrenia. *J. abnorm. Psychol.*, **70** 451-452.

HOLTZMAN, W. H., THORPE, J. S., SWARTZ, J. D. and HERRON, E. W. (1961) *Inkblot Perception and Personality. Holtzman Inkblot Technique.* Austin, Texas: University of Texas Press.

HUGHES, J. S. and CRAWFORD LITTLE, J. (1967) An appraisal of the continuing practice of persisting tranquilizing drugs for long-stay psychiatric patients. *Brit. J. Psychiat.*, **113**, 367-873.

INGLIS, J. (1959) A paired associate learning test for use with elderly psychiatric patients. *J. ment. Sci.*, **105**, 440-442.

KING, H. E. (1954) *Psychomotor Aspects of Mental Disease.* Cambridge, Mass.: Harvard University Press.

KLEIN, E. B. and SPOHN, H. E. (1964) Behaviour dimensions of chronic schizophrenia. *Psychol. Rep.*, **11**, 777-783.

LANG, P. J. and BUSS, A. H. (1965) Psychological deficit in schizophrenia. II: Interference and activation. *J. abnorm. Psychol.*, **70**, 77-106.

LEIPOLD, W. D. and KNUTSON, C. S. (1964) Differences in social desirability, anxiety and introversion-extraversion with varying lengths of hospitalization. *Psychol. Rep.*, **15**, 723-726.

LETEMANDIA, F. J. J. and HARRIS, A. D. (1967) Chlorpromazine and the untreated chronic schizophrenic. *Brit. J. Psychiat.*, **113**, 950-958.

LETEMANDIA, F. J. J., HARRIS, A. D. and WILLEMS, P. J. A. (1967) The clinical effects on a population of chronic schizophrenia patients of administrative changes in hospital. *Brit. J. Psychiat.*, **113**, 959-972.

LORR, M., JENKINS, R. and O'CONNOR, J. P. (1955) Factors descriptive of psychopathology and behaviour of hospitalized psychotics. *J. abnorm. soc. Psychol.*, **50**, 78-86.

LORR, M., KLETT, C. J. and CAVE, R. (1967) Higher-level psychotic syndromes. *J. abnorm. Psychol.*, **72**, 74-77.

LORR, M., KLETT, C. J. and MCNAIR, D. (1963) *Syndromes of Psychosis.* New York: Macmillan.

LUNDIN, R. W. (1961) *Personality, an Experimental Approach.* New York: Macmillan.

LYNN, R. (1963) Russian theory and research on schizophrenia. *Psychol. Bull.* **60**, 486-498.

MANDELBROTE, B. M. (1964) Mental illness in hospital and community developments and outcome. *In* MCLACHLAN, G. (Ed.) *Problems and Progress in Medical Care.* Oxford University Press: Nuffield Provincial Hospitals Trust.

MARTIN, D. V. (1965) A graded rehabilitation scheme for long-stay patients. *In* FREEMAN, H. (Ed.) *Psychiatric Hospital Care.* London: Ballière, Tindall and Cassell.

MOORE, T. V. (1933) The essential psychoses and their fundamental syndromes. *Stud. Psychol. Psychiat.*, **3**, 1-128.

NEIGER, S. S., SLEMON, A. G. and QUIRK, D. A. (1962) The performance of chronic schizophrenic patients on Piotrowski's Rorschach Sign List for organic CNS pathology. *J. proj. Tech.*, **26**, 419-428.

ORME, J. E. (1962) Bender design recall and brain damage. *Dis. Nerv. Syst.*, **23**, 229-330.

ORME, J. E. (1966a) Hypothetically true norms for the progressive matrices tests. *Human Development*, **9**, 222-230.

ORME, J. E. (1966b) Time estimation and the nosology of schizophrenia. *Brit. J. Psychiat.*, **112**, 37-39.

ORME, J. E., LEE, D. and SMITH, M. R. (1964) Psychological assessments of brain damage and intellectual impairment in psychiatric patients. *Brit. J. soc. clin. Psychol.*, **31**, 161-167.

ORME, J. E., SMITH, M. R. and BERRY, C. (1968) Perceptual abnormality in schizophrenia. *Brit. J. soc. clin. Psychol.*, **7**, 13-15.

ORWIN, A. (1967) The mental hospital: a pattern for the future. *Brit. J. Psychiat.*, **113**, 857-864.

OVERALL, J. E., GORHAM, D. R. and SHAWVER, J. R. (1961) Basic dimensions of change in the symptomatology of chronic schizophrenia. *J. abnorm. soc. Psychol.*, **63**, 597-602.

PALERMO, D. S. and JENKINS, J. J. (1964) *Word Association Norms: Grade School Through College.* Minneapolis: Univ. Minnesota Press.

PAYNE, R. W. (1961) Cognitive abnormalities. *In* EYSENCK, H. J. (Ed.) *Handbook of Abnormal Psychology.* London: Pitman.

PAYNE, R. W., FRIEDLANDER, D., LAVERTY, S. G. and HADEN, P. (1963) Overinclusive thought disorder in chronic schizophrenia and its response to "Proketazine". *Brit. J. Psychiat.*, **109**, 523-530.

RAPAPORT, D. (1946) *Diagnostic Psychological Testing.* Chicago: Year Book Publishing Inc.

ROBERTSON, J. P. S. (1962) Perceptual-motor disorders in chronic schizophrenia. *Brit. J. soc. clin. Psychol.*, **1**, 1-6.

ROCHFORD, G. and WILLIAMS, M. (1964) The measurement of language disorders. *Speech Path. & Ther.*, **7**, 3-21.

SHAPIRO, M. B. and NELSON, E. H. (1955) An investigation of the nature of cognitive impairment in co-operative psychiatric patients. *Brit. J. med. Psychol.*, **28**, 239-256.

SHERMAN, J. A. (1965) Use of reinforcement and imitation to reinstate verbal behaviour in mute psychotics. *J. abnorm. Psychol.*, **70**, 155-164.

SILVERMAN, J. (1964) The problem of attention in research and theory in schizophrenia. *Psychol. Rev.*, **71**, 352-379.

SILVERMAN, J., BERG, P. S. D. and KANTOR, R. (1966) Some perceptual correlates of institutionalization. *J. nerv. ment. Dis.*, **141**, 651-657.

SOMMER, R. and WITNEY, G. (1961) The chain of chronicity. *Amer. J. Psychiat.*, **118**, 111-117.

SPOHN, H. E. and WOLK, W. P. (1966) Social participation in homogenous and heterogenous groups of chronic schizophrenics. *J. abnorm. Psychol.*, **71**, 147-150.

TUTKO, T. A. and SPENCE, J. T. (1962) The performance of process and reactive schizophrenics and brain injured subjects on a conceptual task. *J. abnorm. soc. Psychol.*, **65**, 387-394.

VERNON, P. E. (1964) *Personality Assessment. A Critical Survey.* London: Methuen.

WALTON, D. and BLACK, D. A. (1957) The validity of a psychological test of brain damage. *Brit. J. med. Psychol.*, **30**, 270-279.

WILLIAMS, M. (1965) *Mental Testing in Clinical Practice.* Pergamon: London.

WING, J. K. (1962) Institutionalism in mental hospitals. *Brit. J. soc. clin. Psychol.*, **1**, 38-51.

WITTENBORN, J. R. (1951) Symptom patterns in a group of mental hospital patients. *J. consult. Psychol.*, **15**, 290-302.

9

Neurological deficits

Elizabeth K. Warrington

1 INTRODUCTION

The aim of this chapter is to describe some of the cognitive deficits that occur in patients with localized cerebral lesions and to show that there is a high degree of cerebral organization of psychological functions. It was not so long ago that many psychologists viewed the brain as a functionally undifferentiated mass with the possible exception of special centres for language. Though there are still a few diehards for this point of view, most neuro-psychologists would accept that at least the basic skills such as perception, movement and language are separately organized within the cortex. Broca is credited with the first report of an anatomical correlate of psychological function; in 1861 he claimed that the centre for articulate speech is located in the third left frontal convolution. Thereafter, evidence of specific defects in psychological function resulting from circum-scribed lesions of the brain was so prolific that the neurologists of the turn of the century were labelled diagram-makers with little more credibility than the phrenologists. Since many further investigations failed to support the initial claims, the opinion gained ground that there was little if any functional organization within the cortex. This controversy is to some extent due to faulty classification, and if more attention had been given to the distinction between unitary functions and unitary accomplishments, much of this difficulty might have been avoided. For example, the skill of writing may be disturbed in a variety of ways by a variety of factors; the net result may be superficially the same, but the underlying lesion and the consequent disturbance in function may vary.

In the present chapter an attempt will be made to combine the classical neurological approach of classification in terms of symptom complexes (syndromes) with a more analytical approach fostered by experimental psychology. In particular, an attempt will be made to explore the nature of psychological deficits by experiment rather than merely to provide a descriptive account of the symptomatology of cerebral lesions. In this way, it is believed, clinical observations may provide a fruitful source of hypotheses which can then be tested.

The classification used in this chapter is intended to reflect the need for a functional classification rather than one based on symptom complexes. Methods of assessing neurological deficits are described, and wherever possible statements of inference are substantiated by reference to recent experimental and systematic studies; otherwise the relevant neurological source is given. This is already a vast field which is expanding rapidly, and it has therefore been necessary to be selective. Selection has been guided by two considerations. First, by whether the subject has been recently reviewed elsewhere – for example, language deficits, which have been discussed in less detail than their importance merits. Secondly, practical considerations of diagnostic testing have been taken into account; findings which have direct bearing on differential diagnosis have been given more attention than findings which contribute more to theoretical issues. Finally, this chapter is written from the standpoint that there is a high degree of cerebral functional organization which is stressed at the expense of more holistic approaches. The assessment of dementia, perhaps the most important differential diagnosis the clinical psychologist must be equipped to undertake, is not included. However, if dementia is considered as a number of more specific disabilities occurring concurrently, knowledge of the variety of focal deficits, together with a reasonable framework for assessing them, should indirectly result in the more accurate assessment of diffuse cerebral disease.

II INTELLECTUAL DEFICITS

An individual's level of intellectual functioning on a wide variety of mental tests has been repeatedly shown to be highly correlated. Spearman's two-factor theory of intelligence, which proposed a general factor (g) and a factor specific to each test, is consistent with this finding. In examing data from neurological material one might expect to find either that the extent of a cerebral lesion correlated with loss of general intelligence, or, alternatively, that some particular localization implicated general intellectual loss. However, there is little evidence to support either of these possibilities. The search for 'indices of brain damage' makes the assumption that the extent of a brain lesion will be reflected in impairment on mental tests. This search has, on the whole, been unsuccessful (especially with regard to the detection of localized brain lesions). Yates (1954) and Piercy (1959, 1964) have contributed good reviews of this subject which will not, therefore, be given more discussion in this chapter, which is intended to draw attention to focal deficits.

1 Frontal deficits

The question of whether or not any specific region of the brain is especially concerned with tasks making most demand on intelligence has received little attention since the time when the frontal lobes were thought to be responsible for the highest and most complex forms of intellectual function. This frontal lobe deficit was described in terms of a failure of 'synthetical thought process' (Starr, 1884), a failure in 'serialization and synthesizing' ability (Bianchi, 1922), a loss in the capacity for 'abstraction', a deficit of purposive thinking (Grünthal, 1935). These concepts are broad and imprecisely defined. This may account for an equal number of negative studies which claim to show that no intellectual changes can be detected in frontal lobe lesions (Förster, 1918; Kleist, 1934). Indeed, Hebb (1945) went so far as to say that no one had proved that any single form of human behaviour was dependent on the frontal lobes. Weinstein and Teuber (1957) found that tests of higher intellectual function claimed by others to show a frontal deficit demonstrated a greater deficit in left parietal lesions (in gunshot wound cases) while frontal lobe lesions did not show any intellectual deficit *per se*.

However, recent experimental and clinical studies show that even though the frontal lobes may not be the seat of intelligence, neither are they silent areas in which a lesion may not be detected. Certain tests and procedures have undoubted value in clinical diagnosis even though no satisfactory theoretical explanation of the deficits has yet been achieved.

Milner (1963) used the Wisconsin Card Sorting Test in which the subject was required to sort cards which show stimuli differing in colour, form and number, first according to colour, the subject being told 'correct' or 'incorrect' for each response. After ten correct responses, the category rewarded was changed without warning to form, and again after ten correct responses to number. She found that there was a marked deficit on this task in patients with dorsolateral frontal lesions, though not in those with orbito-frontal lesions or with lesions in other lobes of the brain.

Weigl's Colour-form Sorting Test is a simpler task based on the same principle. McFie and Piercy (1952) reported 74 patients with localized lesions and found that failure on this task was most common in patients with anterior left-hemisphere lesions. One striking feature to which Milner drew attention was the dissociation between the ability to verbalize the requirements of the test and to carry them out. This has often been observed with Weigl's Sorting Test when a patient may comment that the pieces can be sorted by colour and shape, but fails to carry this out.

Luria (1964, 1966) has contributed valuable detailed descriptions of frontal lobe symptomatology, which he discusses in terms of a failure of temporal synthesis and, more specifically, a loss of the capacity to regulate action by verbal command. Certain behaviour patterns which he has described are of some interest:

(a) *Perseveration*
Luria (1966) distinguishes between two forms of perseveration – continuation or repetition of one task and continuation or repetition when the task has been changed. For example, a patient asked to draw a circle may continue to draw it over and over again (see Fig. 9.1) or, alternatively, having drawn a circle, he will continue to draw a circle when he is required to draw a square (Fig. 9.2).

(b) *Motor Response to Verbal Instructions*
Patients may have difficulty in carrying out a task requiring the recoding of the immediate stimulus to action. For example, if the patient is required to tap twice

when the examiner taps once and to tap once when the examiner taps twice, Luria and Homskaya (1964) report that frontal lobe patients have particular difficulty on this type of task.

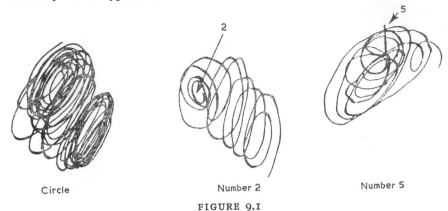

| Circle | Number 2 | Number 5 |

FIGURE 9.1

Perseveration of movements during performance of single tasks by a patient with a massive lesion of the frontal lobes (Luria, 1966).

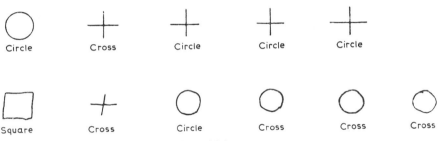

Patient P Intracerebral tumour of left frontal lobe

FIGURE 9.2

Perseveration of actions during performance of single tasks by a patient with a lesion of the frontal lobes (Luria, 1966).

(c) *Motor Control*

Luria (1966) reports that patients with frontal lobe lesions may be able to perform single movements correctly, but fail in performing these same movements when they have to be done in a sequence. This may be observed in a simple task requiring the patient to begin with one hand clenched and the other hand flat, and then to reverse the positions of the two hands in a continuous sequence.

Stevenson (1967), in an experimental study of the serial organization of behaviour, provides evidence of a frontal lobe deficit on a simple sequence problem in which the subject has to predict the position (e.g. left or right) of a hidden object. Two sequences were used: either L.R.L.R. (single alternation) or L.L.R.R.L.L.R.R. (double alternation). The only information the subject has for solving the problem is provided by the previous responses. He found that patients with unilateral frontal lobe lesions performed significantly worse than those with cerebral lesions outside the frontal lobes. Right frontal patients were as impaired as left frontal patients on these tests.

III THE AMNESIC SYNDROME

The amnesic syndrome consists of the impairment of memory for recent and past events, together with marked impairment of learning new material. This syndrome occurs in all degrees of severity, from an almost total loss of memory for day-to-day events accompanied by an equally profound inability to learn, to relatively mild conditions where a patient is able to function relatively normally in spite of an unreliable memory for recent events and a slowness in his learning ability. The amnesic syndrome may be distinguished from confusional states by clarity of consciousness and intact perception, and from dementia by intact intellectual capacity.

A number of conditions may give rise to an amnesic syndrome. However (with the exception of confabulation, which is not invariably shown), the syndrome presents itself remarkably constantly, and recent anatomical data suggest that common structures of the brain are implicated (Brierley, 1966). Alcoholic Korsakoff psychosis, bi-temporal lesions, encephalitis and severe head injury may all give rise to an amnesic syndrome. The common factor is damage to deep cortical and subcortical structures, particularly the mesial aspects of the temporal lobes, hippocampus and mammillary bodies.

1 Assessment of memory

No entirely satisfactory clinical test of memory is available (see Chapter 11 by M. Williams). Wechsler's Memory Scale has the advantage of a standardized test but the disadvantage of combining scores on subtests of rather different types of function. For example, digit span, a test of short-term memory, is included with tests of immediate retention, and memory for events of early life combined with memory for more recent happenings. Orientation for time and place and new learning are included.

In the assessment of amnesia it is important to compare early memories with recent memory. No standardized test of very long-term memory is available, and it is necessary to rely **on** detailed questioning directed towards both personal events and public events. Questioning about public events should be adapted to the patient's educational level. It is only of significance when there is a clear-cut discrepancy between memory of events during the preceding months and sometimes years, and those happenings associated with an earlier period.

Impairment of learning is a cardinal feature of the amnesic syndrome. Though tests of learning are available (Wechsler Memory Scale) it is often advantageous to adjust the task difficulty to the patient's span of apprehension. Digit span and other tasks of short-term memory are *not* impaired in amnesic cases. However, there is a dramatic breakdown in performance in learning material which exceeds the span by one or two items. Learning the digit span plus two is a convenient test. Zangwill (1943, 1946) recommends sentence learning, and notes that amnesic patients will be able to repeat a relatively long sentence correctly at their first attempt, but fail to learn a sentence longer than can be done at the first attempt. Babcock (1930) devised a sentence learning test of graded difficulty.

Warrington and Weiskrantz (1968a) have devised a method of assessing learning and retention which has the advantage of being a relatively 'easy' test which provokes less anxiety than more conventional learning tests. Subjects are shown a graduated series of fragmented drawings and words, the first being very incomplete and the fifth being a complete representation of the object or word. The most incomplete drawing is presented first and then succeeding versions until there is correct recognition or identification. A recognition error score is established on the first trial and the series is immediately repeated and the reduction in errors noted. Amnesic subjects were found to show a measurable degree of learning and retention on this task, though of course they were impaired compared with normal subjects. The test therefore commends itself as a means of measuring quantitatively both the severity of memory impairment and any change in the degree of defect.

Immediate memory and retention are markedly impaired for both verbal and non-verbal material. The Wechsler Memory Scale includes two subtests of immediate memory for material which normally exceeds the span, memory for a short story and memory for visual designs. A useful extension of these two tasks is to test recall after a short interval in which there has been some intervening activity. Patients with generalized intellectual deficits may give somewhat impaired performance on the immediate retention test but little further forgetting with retesting after a short delay, while it is characteristic of the amnesic that there is a marked deterioration on delayed recall as compared with immediate recall. With severe amnesic patients this interval may be as short as a few minutes.

Zangwill (1941) has drawn attention to a peculiarity of recognition in amnesic subjects. He described errors of 'paramnesic reduplication' in which the amnesic will recognize something which he has seen before as similar but not identical to the original, resulting in a failure to do recognition tasks with any accuracy. Warrington and Weiskrantz (1968b) report findings which support this view that the normal relationship of recall and recognition is not present in amnesic subjects.

Florid confabulation, though a classical and not infrequent phenomenon in Korsakoff states, may be absent in severe amnesic states, particularly in chronic states (Talland, 1965) and in patients with bitemporal lesions (Milner, 1966).

IV SYMBOLIC FUNCTIONS

Symbolic processes are unique to the human species and therefore understanding of human behaviour must take these processes into account. While learning and memory and, indeed, executive and perceptual skills can be studied in sub-human species, the generality of the findings to the human where there is an interaction of symbolic processes and the more basic skills is limited. The evolution of these higher processes is reflected in a fundamentally different organization of cortical function in man. Our present level of understanding of this interaction of symbolic processes and skills such as perception in terms of cortical organization is still limited.

Studies of patients in whom a section of the corpus callosum has been carried out for the control of epilepsy are relevant to this problem, but as yet, with the exception of a few individual case reports (Kaplan and Geschwind, 1962; Sperry *et al.*, 1965) most of the systematic studies are with animals. This subject has been recently viewed by Ettlinger (1965) and will not be considered further here. There is nevertheless a substantial body of data both at a clinical and experimental level concerning the functional organization of symbolic processes. It is beyond the scope of this chapter to give more than a brief outline of the field; the classification used is pragmatic and is not intended to imply a theoretical orientation. It is convenient for the purposes of describing neurological deficits to consider symbolic processes under four headings: Language, Reading, Writing and the Gerstmann Syndrome.

1 Language deficits

The first indication of functional specialization of mental process within the cortex was the discovery of the connection between aphasia and left-hemisphere lesions.

The problem of cerebral dominance has been reviewed in a monograph by Zangwill (1960), and the recent studies of Milner *et al.* (1964) give a clear picture of the relationship of handedness and the cerebral organization of language. Her results for 123 patients studied consecutively by the Wada technique of intracarotid injection of sodium amytal are summarized in Table 9.1.

Handedness	No. of cases	Speech representation		
		Left	Bilateral	Right
Right	48	90%	0%	10%
Left or ambidextrous				
without early left brain damage	44	64%	16%	20%
with early left brain damage	27	22%	11%	67%

TABLE 9.1

Handedness and speech lateralization
(Milner *et al.*, 1964)

She concludes that these findings support the evidence drawn from clinical case material that the cerebral organization of language is less predictable in left-handed and ambidextrous persons than in right-handers.

Since Broca's original case descriptions there has grown a large literature on language disorders. Yet the clinical syndromes are at present so varied and diverse that no entirely satisfactory classification has been achieved. In recent years there has been a number of extensive reviews (Critchley, 1964; Brain, 1966) which well describe the achievements and shortcomings in understanding the cortical basis of language. The present account is highly selective and emphasis will be placed on those aspects of the problem which are thought to be of diagnostic value.

Speech is a highly complex activity involving a number of functions all of which must be intact for it to be normal. Aphasic disturbances take many different forms and these differences are to some extent reflected by anatomical considerations. It is therefore an impossible task to give a single criterion for the presence of dysphasia. This is taken into account in the 'dysphasia batteries' now available, where different types of verbal task are included (Eisenson, 1954; Schuell, 1960). However, their clinical usefulness is limited because they fail to discriminate between normal subjects and patients with a mild disturbance of language, and make no allowance for the original level of verbal skills in the individual. Furthermore, these tests were standardized on a group of dysphasic subjects selected by virtue of the presence of dysphasia on clinical examination, using the same signs and tests which were subsequently to be measured. This methodological tautology could be circumvented by examining patients with localized lesions involving all cortical sectors on a variety of tests which emphasize different aspects of speech. Though this has not yet been done on an extensive scale, the evidence of systematic studies will be referred to.

A subdivision of dysphasic disorders into receptive, expressive and nominal difficulties is perhaps the most usual classification. However, this is an obvious oversimplification which can only be used with a number of qualifications.

(a) *Nominal Dysphasia*

Nominal dysphasia, or amnestic aphasia, is the inability to name objects. It is characteristic that patients can describe the object or give its use and also recognize or pick out the correct name from a selection. A patient with nominal dysphasia can often use these names in his spontaneous speech. Rochfort and Williams (1962) have shown that the frequency of the word in the language is related to performance, low-frequency names presenting more difficulty than high-frequency names. They have compared age of acquisition of words with dysphasic errors and found that the high-frequency words were those first learned by young children and the last lost in dysphasia. Hécaen and Angelergues (1964) found that the highest incidence of nominal dysphasia was in left temporal lobe lesions.

(b) *Expressive Dysphasia*

Any disturbance in spoken speech may be considered under the term expressive dysphasia. Dissatisfaction with expressive dysphasia as a meaningful category of language impairment has long been noted. Since the days when language disorders were first studied by neurologists, attention has been drawn to two distinct types of breakdown in expressive speech functions. Those characterized by articulatory difficulties, lack of fluency, agrammatism, telegraphic speech, may be contrasted with those characterized by circumlocutory speech, imprecision, semantic errors and increased fluency or pressure of speech. This fluent versus non-fluent subdivision of expressive disorders was first noted by Jackson (1868) and has been referred to many times since (Wernicke, 1908; Schiller, 1947; Conrad, 1954; Goodglass, Quadfasel and Timberlake, 1964). Hécaen and Angelergues (1964) make a distinction between articulatory disturbances and impairment of speech fluency, and found that articulatory difficulties are associated with anterior lesions, while impairment of speech fluency was more frequent with temporal lobe lesions. Benson (1967) has reported a quantitative study in which differences in verbal output of individual aphasics are related to localization of the lesion. He examined ten features of dysphasic speech: rate of speaking, prosody, pronunciation, phrase length, effort, pauses, press of speech, perseveration, word use and paraphasia. He noted that certain of these characteristics occurred together naturally so that two distinct clusters of clinical features were outlined, associated with lesions anterior and posterior to the Rolandic fissure respectively. The anterior lesion group had speech characterized by a low verbal output, dysprosody, dysarthria and predominant use of substantives, while the posterior group was normal or near normal in all these features but often had paraphasia, press of speech, and a distinct lack of substantives. Milner (1962) has used Thurstone's word fluency test and found that the left frontal group was significantly impaired compared with a left temporal group, while on a task of verbal learning and retention the position is reversed, the left temporal group being significantly worse than the left frontal group.

(c) *Receptive Dysphasia*

Understanding of spoken speech may be impaired selectively or, as is more usual, in the setting of more widespread language dysfunction; there is defective appreciation of meanings of words and, in particular, of meanings conveyed by their grammatical relations in a sentence. Performance is determined by the task difficulty. Single instructions may be understood, while double instructions may lead to failure on part of the task or confusion between them. De Renzi and Vignolo (1962) have devised and standardized a test of understanding of spoken speech, the Token test, which is helpful in clinical diagnosis. Tokens of two different shapes, two different sizes and five different colours are arranged on the table in front of the patient, who is then given oral commands expressed in progressively more and more complex, non-redundant messages. This test has

K*

the advantage of revealing slight disturbances in the understanding of speech without involving other intellectual functions besides language.

2 Reading and writing

It is now well documented that disorders of reading and writing may occur both in the setting of generalized language impairment and as relatively specific and isolated defects. Though the latter are, perhaps, of greater theoretical interest from the diagnostic point of view, too little attention has been given to the assessment of reading, writing and spelling. These functions are over-learned and standardized in the population, yet probably represent the highest language skills (they are acquired latest by a child) and are vulnerable in the breakdown of language processes. It is relatively easy, compared with the difficulties of assessing changes in, say, speech fluency, to obtain objective records. Traditionally, reading and writing skills have to some extent been regarded as unitary functions. However, a closer examination shows quite clearly that they can be disturbed in a variety of ways by a variety of factors.

There are two main categories of reading disturbances, each of which can be further subdivided: those resulting from language or linguistic factors and those which may be regarded as a form of recognition defect. Both types of difficulty may affect the reading of individual letters (literal dyslexia), or the reading of words and connected passages (verbal dyslexia).

(a) *Literal Dyslexia*
The inability to read individual letters may occur as a language impairment analogous to nominal dysphasia. Typically the patient is unable to name individual letters, but can point out or recognize a letter in a choice situation. These patients may be able to read words, though not the individual letters of the word; there is always some accompanying degree of verbal dyslexia. Posterior left temporal lesions most frequently give rise to this type of dyslexia.

Literal dyslexia may also be present as a recognition or agnostic defect. Not only is the patient unable to name letters, but is also unable to point to named letters. Ettlinger and Hurwitz (1962) have reported such a case and discuss this syndrome. The left parietal area is usually implicated.

(b) *Verbal Dyslexia*
The inability to read words and sentences may occur in the context of a motor dysphasia. The patient may not be able to pronounce the word but is well aware of its meaning. The milder manifestations of this difficulty present as halting, jerky reading with occasional slurring or mispronunciation of a syllable. This type of reading disturbance is most common with left anterior lesions.

Expressive dysphasia characterized by imprecise fluent and inaccurate speech (see above) is frequently accompanied by a verbal dyslexia. Reading of individual words is relatively well preserved, while the reading of sentences and passages is inaccurate. Typically, connecting words and relational words are omitted or misread. Semantic errors are frequent. Left temporal and left temporo-parietal lesions give rise to this form of dyslexia.

Impairment of receptive speech functions is also mirrored by a reading disorder. Paraphasic errors occur, but more important is the failure to understand what is read. Written instructions, even if correctly read, may not be carried out. For a fuller account of verbal dyslexia and for discussion of the interaction of linguistic factors reference should be made to Luria (1964).

Finally, verbal alexia occurs as a perceptual or recognition defect. Patients may easily recognize individual letters, but cannot grasp whole words; when confronted with whole words they must resort to putting them together letter by letter before they are able to identify them. Familiar as well as relatively unfamiliar words are read in this piecemeal fashion. Short words are read more accurately than long words, as less stress is placed on the mediating verbal process. In the mildest form the reading process is for the most part accurate, but very slow and laborious.

Kinsbourne and Warrington (1962a) in a tachistoscopic study of simultaneous form perception in patients with verbal alexia were able to show that thresholds for single letter perception were normal, while the threshold for two letters was markedly raised. Furthermore, with successive presentation of letters the longer the interval between the two letters the greater the likelihood of both being reported. This type of dyslexia is associated with a posterior left-hemisphere lesion probably involving the occipital lobe (Hécaen, Ajuriaguerra and David, 1952; Kinsbourne and Warrington, 1963a).

(c) *Writing and Spelling*

The writing process may be regarded as a complex function comprising spelling (requiring correct choice and sequence of letters) and script (demanding the correct formation of letters). Impairment of each may break down independently and should therefore be separately assessed. Spelling can be studied in isolation from script if performed orally. Clinical studies have emphasized a predominant type of spelling error in aphasics, namely letter substitution errors (Weisenburg and McBride, 1935).

Kinsbourne and Warrington (1964) carried out a systematic analysis of spelling errors in four groups of subjects, dysphasic patients, patients with finger agnosia (see Gerstmann syndrome, p. 272), patients with right-hemisphere lesions and patients with extracerebral lesions. Oral spelling was tested by means of a standard spelling test and it was found that aphasic patients and patients with finger agnosia each showed a distinctive pattern of spelling errors. Aphasic misspellings included a high proportion of extraneous letters, that is letter substitutions, while patients with finger agnosia produced a high proportion of errors relating to letter order. The two control groups, patients with right-hemisphere lesions and extra-cerebral lesions, showed an intermediate pattern of error scores and did not differ significantly from one another. The association of aphasic speech and letter substitution errors was thought to reflect the underlying disorder of language functions, while the association between finger agnostic and order errors to reflect an underlying difficulty in processing information in terms of a sequence (see Gerstmann syndrome).

Writing or script as distinct from spelling must also be considered as a complex function which may be impaired for different reasons. With apraxic defects, the impairment of voluntary movements if sufficiently severe will affect a relatively automatized task such as writing. One also observes an ideational impairment, a true dysgraphia, in which a patient has forgotten how to form a particular letter yet there is apparently no difficulty with other forms of voluntary or skilled movement. In the assessment of script it is helpful to compare the ability to copy script with spontaneous script. Patients with a more generalized apraxic defect fail on both tasks, while patients with a true dysgraphia are able to copy letters and words which they are unable to write spontaneously. Right and left parietal lobe lesions may give rise to impairment of script when it is associated with other apraxic deficits; a pure dysgraphia, however, is associated with a left parietal lesion (Critchley, 1953).

3 The Gerstmann syndrome

The combination of finger agnosia, dyscalculia, right-left disorientation and dysgraphia was first described as a 'syndrome' by Gerstmann (1927) who thought there was an underlying unitary disturbance of cerebral function having localizing significance. The status of the Gerstmann syndrome has been challenged both from the point of view of anatomical correlations and the functional relationships between the four elements (Benton, 1955); nevertheless these four symptoms do occur as focal signs in patients with cerebral lesions and each will be discussed briefly.

(a) *Finger Agnosia*

Finger agnosia may be defined as the inability to recognize the individual fingers. Traditionally, patients are asked to point to named fingers or to name an indicated finger. This procedure may be confounded by other disorders in the language or spatial sphere; for example, a patient with expressive or receptive dysphasia might fail on this task. Unless one is using the concept of finger agnosia in a purely descriptive sense, it is necessary to establish an impairment of finger recognition which is not secondary (subordinate) to any other psychological deficit. Kinsbourne and Warrington (1962b) described a number of tests for finger agnosia (in which the verbal and praxic component of the task was minimal) based on the hypothesis that underlying finger agnosia is the 'inability to appreciate the relative serial positions of the fingers'. Clinically, the most useful of these tasks is the 'in between test' (Fig. 9.3). Two of the fingers are simultaneously touched and the patient is asked to state the number of fingers between the ones touched. Thus, the answer may be 0, 1, 2 or 3. The task is first done with the eyes open, to establish that with visual cues the patient understands the task, and then it is repeated with the eyes closed. A failure on this stage of the procedure has been shown to be correlated with more conventional tests of finger agnosia, but not with dysphasia. In a normative study with children, Kinsbourne and Warrington (1963b) established, using a criterion of six out of eight correct responses, that 50% of the sample passed this test at six and a half, and at seven and a half there was a 95% pass rate.

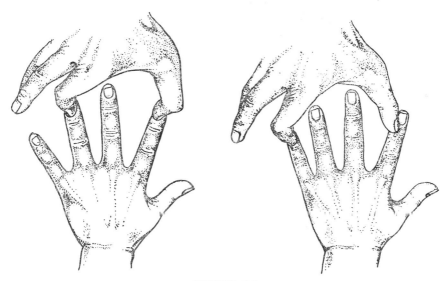

FIGURE 9.3

'In Between Test' for finger agnosia (Kinsbourne and Warrington, 1962b).

Lunn (1948) reviewed all the published cases of finger agnosia and after excluding cases with widespread lesions and subjects with mixed handedness found no case of finger agnosia with a right-hemisphere lesion. Hécaen (1962) reports that in an unselected series of unilateral right-handed cases, 20% with left-sided lesions and 3% with right-sided lesions presented with bilateral somatognosic disturbances, of which finger agnosia was the most common feature. Clinical evidence suggests that the left parietal area may be critical to the functions underlying finger recognition, though as yet a definitive study using well-localized lesions within each hemisphere has not been carried out.

(b) *Dyscalculia*

Dyscalculia is the loss of ability to carry out numerical calculations. Again, the assessment of dyscalculia is complicated by factors extraneous to the process of calculation, and even allowing for this, there is reason to believe that calculation itself is a complex process which may result from more than one kind of functional loss. Hécaen (1962) distinguishes three different aspects of acalculia: '(i) acalculia from figure or number alexia, (ii) acalculia of the spatial type and (iii) acalculia in the restricted sense of loss of ability to perform arithmetical sums'. Clinical experience suggests that this latter category may also be subdivided. It appears that there are patients who are unable to understand the nature of the arithmetical manipulation involved in a problem, that is, they do not know whether to multiply or divide to arrive at the right answer, yet can carry out the mechanical aspect of the task satisfactorily. The converse is also observed; the patient is unable to manipulate numbers accurately, yet understands the problem and the steps involved. The relative incidence of the three forms of dyscalculia described above have been recorded by Hécaen (see Table 9.2).

	Right-sided lesions	Left-sided lesions
(i) Dyscalculia of the spatial type	35/193	4/191
(ii) Figure alexia	3/146	53/143
(iii) Anarithmetria	25/124	91/105

TABLE 9.2
Relative incidence of three forms of dyscalculia
(Hécaen, 1962)

The arithmetic subtest of the W.A.I.S. has perhaps been the most frequently employed tool to assess arithmetical abilities. Tests of graded difficulty such as this, in which general intellectual level is to a large extent determining the score, are not satisfactory to demonstrate the presence of a specific disability. The assessment of dyscalculia still depends on clinical judgement. A patient unable to do simple mechanical additions and subtractions, without sufficient dementia or dysphasia to account for it, may be accepted as having a focal disability implicating the left parietal cortex.

(c) *Right-left Disorientation*

This is characterized by an inability to carry out instructions involving right and left. In the clinical setting right-left disorientation is best thought of as the extreme case of what is experienced by many normal people in responding quickly to the instruction, 'Go left' or 'Go right'. Benton (1959) has carried out the most extensive investigation of right-left orientation both in normal children and in patients with cerebral disease. He stresses the dependency of right-left orientation on the language processes. It is, however, worth noting that right-left disorientation can occur in the absence of dysphasia (Kinsbourne and Warrington, 1962b), though it is most plausible to accept that language is intrinsically concerned in some forms of the disorder. The disability itself can be accepted as a sign of left-hemisphere dysfunction, but is of little value for more precise localization within the left hemisphere.

(d) *Dysgraphia*

Dysgraphia, the disorder of writing, has been discussed above in the section on language disorders. Attention was drawn to the multiplicity of causal factors in such a complex task. It has been shown that one relatively specific type of spelling error, i.e. the order type (oral or written), was associated with finger agnosia. Kinsbourne and Warrington (1964) argued from this finding that there may be a unitary functional disorder underlying the four components of the Gerstmann syndrome. Finger agnosia was regarded as a difficulty in classifying the fingers in terms of their relative positions, and 'order' errors in spelling were character-istic of patients with finger agnosia. The common factor underlying the Gerst-mann syndrome could then be thought of as a difficulty in monitoring responses in terms of serial order. This would be consistent with Lashley's (1951) hypo-thesis that the classifying of stimuli (both verbal and non-verbal) in terms of their relative positions in space and time represents a distinctive mode of cerebral functioning.

The conjunction of finger agnosia, dyscalculia, right-left disorientation and dysgraphia as a syndrome is controversial. However, if the concept of the Gerstmann syndrome were re-examined, taking into account certain distinctive features of each of the elements, one might find that the problem could be resolved.

V EXECUTIVE DEFECTS

Apraxia is a term used to describe a defect of motor control or motor movement which cannot be explained in terms of paresis or sensory loss. A number of forms of apraxia have been identified, with a corresponding complexity of terminology: ideational apraxia, ideomotor apraxia, dressing apraxia and constructional apraxia. The terms constructional apraxia and visuo-spatial agnosia are used to describe the same symptom complex and the choice of terminology is often determined merely by the theoretical orientation of the author. Constructional apraxia, the failure to copy drawings or construct models, will be discussed later in the section on visuo-spatial defects.

The inability to use objects and tools, especially when a particular sequence of manipulations is necessary, is termed *ideational apraxia*. This may be examined by asking the patient to light a cigarette or cut with scissors. Typically, the patient may try to strike a match on the packet of cigarettes or light the box instead of the cigarette. *Ideomotor apraxia* is conventionally identified when a patient is unable to execute gestures or copy movements to command. This difficulty can be elicited by asking the patient to mime some simple task, such as pouring a glass of water, or more simply to copy finger positions such as extension or flexion of two of the fingers. *Dressing apraxia* is identified when a patient is observed to have difficulty in carrying out the movements required for dressing and is most commonly observed in difficulty with buttons or laces. However, it is most unlikely that dressing apraxia represents an isolated form of apraxia, and it is more plausible to regard this difficulty as secondary to either constructional apraxia or unilateral neglect.

Ajuriaguerra, Hécaen and Angelergues (1960) reported the first and most detailed study in which the incidence of these three forms of apraxia occurs in unilateral retrorolandic lesions. Both ideational and ideomotor apraxia are associated with left-hemisphere lesions, while dressing apraxia is more common in right-hemisphere lesions. Goodglass and Kaplan (1963) report an interesting study of gesture and pantomime in a group of aphasic patients. Their findings are consistent with those of Hécaen in so far as patients with left-hemisphere lesions were more impaired than those with right-hemisphere lesions, and there was no correlation between the severity of dysphasia and degree of impairment on tasks of gesture and pantomime. They draw attention to a previously un-recorded phenomenon: 'Body-Part as Object'. They observed that in response to the instruction to carry out an action with a pretended object, in the absence of the real object, the patient may use his own hands or fingers as the object. For example, in demonstrating the use of a toothbrush, he may rub his teeth with his index finger.

Wyke (1967, 1968) has carried out an experimental investigation of a number of basic executive skills, including the rapidity of arm movements and precision of arm–hand movements. Patients with right-hemisphere lesions were found to have a unilateral defect affecting the left hand while patients with left-hemisphere lesions showed a bilateral defect, worse in the hand and arm contralateral to the lesion. These findings, based on detailed and accurate measurements, support the view that lesions of the left hemisphere result in some higher-order executive defect which cannot be accounted for solely by motor inco-ordination or loss of power.

VI   VISUAL PERCEPTUAL DEFICITS

This account of perceptual defects will be restricted to the visual modality which has received most attention in recent years and is probably better understood than auditory and somæsthetic perception. Furthermore, from the point of view of clinical diagnosis, defects of visual perception are not only more frequent but also present fewer problems in assessment.

The understanding of visual perceptual deficits is often confounded by a failure to distinguish between recognition defects and perceptual defects. An agnostic defect is traditionally defined as a failure of recognition which cannot be accounted for by poor vision or a more generalized intellectual impairment. Neurologists subdivide the agnosias into agnosia for objects, colours and faces on the basis that there is no necessary association of these conditions. Impairment of picture interpretation has been regarded also as an agnostic defect for which Wolpert (1924) coined the term 'simultanagnosia'. However, picture recognition is a qualitatively different type of task than the other agnosias in so far as a picture is to a greater or lesser extent an abstraction of the real object and the perceptual similarity of the representation to the real object can be very variable. Perception of objects, colours, faces and pictures will be described in this section and attention drawn to certain fundamental differences in these functions.

1 Object agnosia

Agnosia for objects is identified when there is a failure of recognition. That is, not only is there a failure to name the objects, but also a failure to recognize the correct name or to indicate the appropriate use or some other descriptive attribute. A patient with object agnosia may describe a use appropriate to an incorrect recognition. Very few satisfactory cases of object agnosia have been reported but Hécaen and Ajuriaguerra (1956) have reported a convincing one following a left occipital lobectomy. Nevertheless, minor forms of this defect may be detected by group comparisons in systematic investigations of patients with unilateral lesions. Kok (1964) has reported a defect in tachistoscopic object-recognition in cases with left posterior lesions, in a choice situation where no naming is required.

2 Colour agnosia

Colour agnosia is defined as the inability to name colours or recognize named colours in the absence of any impairment of colour sense. The Holmgren wool-sorting test is the best available tool for examining colour recognition. Patients are able to sort the colours into correct categories of colour, succeed in matching pairs of colours and are able to arrange them in a series according to brightness or saturation. The defect is only manifest when an association of the colour to either a verbal label or conventional use, such as in traffic lights, is involved. Hécaen (1962) has observed 15 patients with colour agnosia, 9 of whom had posterior left-hemisphere lesions, 4 bilateral lesions and 2 right-sided lesions. De Renzi and Spinnler (1967) have investigated a large series of patients with unilateral lesions on a number of tasks involving perception, identification and cognition of colours. They discuss their findings with reference to aphasia and visual field defects. The association of right hemianopia, alexia and colour agnosia forms the classical syndrome of left occipital lobe lesions, but here the association is likely to be due to anatomical contiguity rather than an underlying unitary functional deficit.

3 Prosopagnosia

Agnosia for faces has been described as a distinctive and separate perceptual defect. Patients are unable to recognize people well-known to them by vision alone. Hécaen and Angelergues (1962) found it to be more common in cases with right-hemisphere lesions than with left-hemisphere lesions. This observation has now been confirmed in experimental investigations. De Renzi and Spinnler

(1966a) tested the recognition of a previously unknown face from immediate memory and found that the right-hemisphere group was significantly worse than the left-hemisphere group. Warrington and James (1967a) confirmed this finding and also drew attention to their result that in comparing recognition of well-known people's faces and recognition of previously unknown faces from immediate memory there was virtually zero correlation between the two tasks. They argued that the one task involves long-term memory for one category of information, namely, faces, and in the other a perceptual component is prominent. This result underlines the need to analyse the functional processes involved in testing procedures in the analysis of neurological deficits.

4 Perception of pictures and unfamiliar visual patterns

Individual case descriptions of impaired picture recognition in patients with right-hemisphere lesions received little attention until Milner and her group in Montreal drew attention to defective performance in a wide variety of visual perceptual tasks associated with right temporal lobectomy. There has been a series of recent papers (Milner, 1958; Kimura, 1963; Lansdell, 1968) which has claimed that the perception of unfamiliar and non-verbal visual material is impaired in patients with right temporal lesions. However, observation of patients with large right-hemisphere lesions led Warrington and James (1967b) to investigate the perception of visual material in which the perceptual dimension of the task was varied. They observed that if pictorial representations of objects were unclear or incomplete gross errors of recognition occurred. In more severe cases clear line drawings will not be recognized or may be misidentified; such errors may be observed on two subtests of the W.A.I.S., Picture Completion and Picture Arrangement. Oldfield and Wingfield (1965) have assembled a set of pictures in which objects of decreasing word frequency are clearly represented; this has proved a useful clinical test of picture recognition. Ettlinger (1960) found that patients with right-hemisphere lesions were significantly impaired compared with left-hemisphere lesions on a task of picture interpretation. Warrington and James (1967b) have shown in a systematic investigation that patients with right parietal lesions have a deficit on perception of fragmented pictures and letters which are graded in difficulty only in a perceptual dimension, while the right temporal cases were not significantly impaired on these tasks.

In the assessment of defects of visual perception it is helpful to distinguish between recognition defects and impaired perception. Lissauer (1890) distinguished two factors in perception, the act of conscious perception of a sensory impression and the act of linkage of the content of perception with images; a failure in the former he called an apperceptive defect and a failure of the latter an associative defect. These perceptual defects found in right-hemisphere lesions are similar to those described in neurological literature as apperceptive disorders, and visual object agnosia and colour agnosia may be thought of as associative disorders. One can therefore resolve these apparently conflicting data by considering the possibility that apperceptive and associative disorders of recognition are not a continuum, but represent a two-stage process. On this view there is a differentiation of function between hemispheres within the total perceptual recognition process. The right hemisphere is critical for the processing of visual sensory data and the left hemisphere for recoding visual information in terms of linkages with verbal symbols.

VII VISUO-SPATIAL DEFICITS

1 Visuo-spatial agnosia

The characteristic features of this syndrome consist of failure to appreciate spatial relationships and a failure to execute simple constructional tasks under visual control. Clinically, one observes a failure on tasks involving spatial analysis and difficulty in copying drawings or constructing patterns with bricks or sticks (see Fig. 9.4). Since the early case reports describing visuo-spatial agnosia,

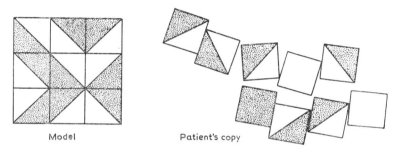

Model   Patient's copy

FIGURE 9.4
Copy of block design (Critchley, 1953).

discussion has centred on the nature of the disability, whether it is primarily an executive disorder of complex movements or a perceptual deficit that interferes with the appreciation of the spatial properties of visual stimuli. As the observations of the symptom complex have multiplied, so has the terminology. Constructional apraxia is regarded by some neurologists as a term synonymous with visuo-spatial agnosia, while others take the view that there are essential differences between impaired performance with right- and left-hemisphere lesions and retain both terms. In order to avoid confusion, rather than describe this labyrinth of clinical terms, deficits resulting from right and left parietal lobe lesions will be compared and attention drawn to certain qualitative differences that are emerging.

It was an early observation that different types of error, or faulty performance, occur in tasks of drawing or construction, and more recently a relationship has been observed between the predominant type of error and laterality of lesion. McFie and Zangwill (1960) have reported the fullest clinical description of these differences. They describe the drawings of right-sided cases as scattered and fragmented, as showing a loss of spatial relations and faulty orientation, while left-sided lesions result in coherent but simplified versions of the model, crude in outline and lacking in detail, but in which accurate spatial relationships are preserved. The right-sided cases were observed to draw energetically, and they often added more strokes in an effort to make the picture correct, while the left-sided cases drew slowly, putting the few parts in with difficulty (Fig. 9.5).

FIGURE 9.5

Attempts at constructing a four-pointed star with matchsticks by right- and left-hemisphere cases (McFie and Zangwill, 1960).

The first systematic comparison of left- and right-sided cases was carried out by Piercy, Hécaen and Ajuriaguerra (1960). First, they compared copies of drawings with spontaneous drawings and found that having a model to copy improves the performance of patients with left-hemisphere lesions, but makes little or no difference to right-sided cases. Secondly, they drew attention, in the right-hemisphere cases, to the poor orientation of the drawing on the paper, frequently diagonally placed (see Fig. 9.6). This tendency was most obvious in the drawings of a house and a cube, and it was suggested that figures in which diagonal lines are necessary to represent a three-dimensional object on a two-dimensional surface are vulnerable to this error.

Arrigoni and De Renzi (1964) have reported a difference in the incidence of two types of errors in right- and left-hemisphere cases. Left-sided cases more frequently oversimplified in copying a cube; five of them copied it as a simple square, while none of the right-sided cases did this. In copying complex figures

(Benton Visual Memory Scale) made up of more than one part, patients with right-hemisphere lesions were observed to make gross alterations in the spatial arrangements between the parts. Warrington, James and Kinsbourne (1966) carried out an investigation of drawing disability in which their aim was to quantify the deficit, both in the overall performance and in certain qualitative

Left hemisphere cases   Right hemisphere cases

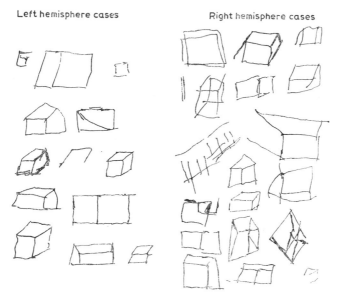

FIGURE 9.6
Copies of a cube (Piercy *et al.*, 1960).

aspects. The following differences in the drawings of right- and left-hemisphere lesions were observed:

(i) The left-hemisphere group incorporated significantly more right angles in copying a cube than the right-hemisphere group.

(ii) In copying a four-pointed star the right-hemisphere group tended to make the angles more acute than the model and the left-hemisphere group to make the angles more obtuse than the model.

(iii) There was a higher incidence of asymmetrical copies of simple geometrical figures in the right-hemisphere group.

(iv) The left-hemisphere group incorporated fewer details in their drawing (not copied) of a house. There was a tendency to draw the bare outline, omitting such details as windows, doors, chimney, etc.

It is beyond the scope of this chapter to discuss the implications in terms of theories of cortical organization. This is dealt with in detail by Warrington (1968). The point of view held by the author is that the two hemispheres may make separate and different contributions to the complex task of drawing or constructing in space, and disorder of either would lead to impaired overall performance. The right hemisphere supplies a perceptual and the left hemisphere an executive component to the task.

Critchley (1953) has summarized the anatomical findings in cases of visuo-spatial impairment published prior to 1953, and notes that it may be present with right parietal lesions, left parietal lesions or bilateral parietal lesions. Hécaen *et al.* (1956) reported 17 cases with surgical removal in the parietal or parieto-temporo-occipital areas of the non-dominant hemisphere. Eight of the 15 cases with right-hemisphere excisions had spatial defects. The only evidence of localization based on an unselected series of cases is that of Piercy, Hécaen and Ajuriaguerra (1960). It was found that lesions giving rise to visuo-spatial disorders are considerably more restricted in their site in the case of right-hemisphere lesions.

2 Visual disorientation

Holmes (1918) first described the clinical syndrome of visual disorientation, which he defined as the inability to localize the position and distance of objects in space by sight alone. A patient is unable to point with any accuracy to a single object (with either hand). He described a number of other disabilities which he regarded as secondary to the primary disorder, including disordered eye movements, impairment of reading a connected passage and counting scattered objects. Furthermore, performance on more complex visuo-spatial tasks will inevitably be impaired. He interpreted the basic defect in terms of a disturbance of the local sign functions of the retina. It has been shown that visual disorientation can occur in either half visual field contralateral to the lesion (Cole, Schutta and Warrington, 1962), or in both visual fields with a bilateral occipital lesion (Holmes, 1918). Visuo-spatial disorders from a unilateral lesion of the right parietal area are not restricted to the contralateral visual field. It was therefore suggested (Warrington and James, 1967c) that there are areas within the occipital lobes which contribute to the absolute localization of a single object in space whereas the integration of successive or 'simultaneous' spatial stimuli, which determines the spatial relations of two or more objects, is impaired by unilateral lesions within the right parietal area.

3 Visual neglect (unilateral spatial agnosia)

This may be observed in a patient's drawings, copies of drawings, block constructions or description of pictures; typically one part of the drawing is omitted, or part of the picture is not observed (see Fig. 9.7). Hécaen (1962) has reported 59 cases of unilateral spatial agnosia; of these 51 had right-sided lesions, 4 left-sided lesions and 4 bilateral lesions. This finding confirms the many case reports in the neurological literature that unilateral spatial agnosia most frequently occurs in association with right parietal lesions.

Kinsbourne and Warrington (1962c) described a phenomenon of paralexic reading in six patients with right-hemisphere lesions and no evidence of any impairment of language functions. These patients were observed to consistently misread the first part of the word. For example: level – novel; peeping – looking; eight – tight; milk – chalk, etc. No other type of error was observed in the six cases reported, and these errors were so frequent as to make accurate reading impossible. Neglect of extra-personal space was observed in all these cases and the apparent impairment of reading was regarded as secondary to the unilateral spatial neglect.

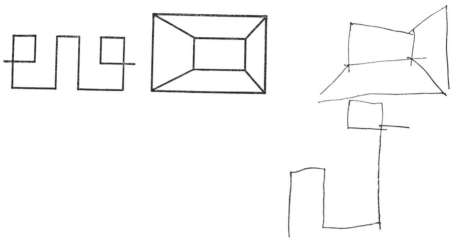

FIGURE 9.7

Example of unilateral visual neglect in copying geometrical figures.

VIII SUMMARY

The assessment of neurological deficits is in a transitional stage between relying upon qualitative and descriptive observations and the use of standardized test procedures. As yet, tests which are both appropriate to the assessment of neuro-logical conditions and which have been standardized on a suitable population are not available. This dearth is obvious from the foregoing account of neurolo-gical deficits: wherever possible, reference has been made to systematic and experimental investigations, but these rarely include adequate norms for the population, taking intellectual level and age into account. The purpose of these research studies has been to elucidate problems of cerebral organization rather than to provide clinical tools. Nevertheless, in the course of experimental investigations new test procedures have been evolved and these can often be directly applicable to the clinical situation. Moreover, with the better under-standing derived from experimental procedures, the inferences drawn from a particular pattern of functional disorder observed in a single clinical case can be more confidently drawn. An instance where a test procedure evolved for experimental purposes has lent itself to adaptation as a clinical tool is the perception of incomplete and sketchily-drawn pictorial material (described above) for the detection of posterior right-hemisphere lesions. Again, given the problem of the lateralization of a brain lesion, certain deficits are known to be exclusively, or at least predominantly, related to lesions of the left hemisphere; among these are aphasia and related disorders of language and communication. The position regarding right-hemisphere lesions is possibly less clear-cut but there are strong indications that certain perceptual – and in particular visuo-spatial – defects are associated with right-hemisphere lesions. Localization within the hemisphere must always proceed with caution, but there is evidence that a number of the syndromes described above have a more precise anatomical basis.

As will be seen we take our departure in this type of clinical assessment not so much from traditional cognitive categories (e.g. learning, memory) as from the forms of breakdown at the psychological level recognized in clinical neurology. The clinical psychologist working in the neurological field attempts to assess these defects more precisely and analytically, particularly where they present in sub-clinical form. In so doing he will hope to provide a clinical diagnostic service as well as contributing to a sound physiological basis for cognitive psychology.

I am most grateful to Dr R. T. C. Pratt, Professor O. L. Zangwill and Mrs S. M. Whitaker for their helpful advice in the preparation of this chapter.

REFERENCES

AJURIAGUERRA, J. DE, HÉCAEN, H. and ANGELERGUES, R. (1960) Les apraxies variétés cliniques et lateralisation lésionelle. *Rev. Neurol.*, **102**, 28-57.

ARRIGONI, G. and DE RENZI, E. (1964) Constructional apraxia and hemispheric locus of lesion. *Cortex*, **1**, 170-197.

BABCOCK, H. (1930) An experiment in the measurement of mental deterioration. *Arch. Psychol.*, Monograph 117.

BENSON, F. (1967) Fluency in aphasia: correlation with radioactive scan localization, *Cortex*, **3**, 373-394.

BENTON, A. L. (1955) The fiction of the Gerstmann syndrome. *J. Neurol. Neurosurg. Psychiat.*, **24**, 176-181.

BENTON, A. L. (1959) *Right-left Discrimination and Finger Localization*. New York: Hoeber.

BIANCHI, L. (1922) *Mechanism of the Brain and the Function of the Frontal Lobe*. Edinburgh: Livingstone.

BRAIN, R. (1966) *Speech Disorders* (2nd Ed.) London: Butterworths.

BRIERLEY, J. B. (1966) Neuropathology of amnesic states. *In* WHITTY, C. W. M. and ZANGWILL, O. L. (Eds.) *Amnesia*. London: Butterworths.

COLE, M., SCHUTTA, H. S. and WARRINGTON, E. K. (1962) Visual disorientation in homonymous half-fields. *Neurology*, **12**, 257-263.

CONRAD, K. (1954) New problems of aphasia. *Brain*, **77**, 491-509.

CRITCHLEY, M. (1953) *The Parietal Lobes*. London: Arnold.

CRITCHLEY, M. (1964) *In* REUCK, A. V. S. DE and O'CONNOR, M. (Eds.). *Disorders of Language*. London: Ciba.

DE RENZI, E. and SPINNLER, H. (1966a) Facial recognition in brain-damaged patients. *Neurology*, **16**, 145-152.

DE RENZI, E. and SPINNLER, H. (1966b.) Visual recognition in patients with unilateral cerebral disease. *J. nerv. ment. Dis.*, **142**, 515-525.

DE RENZI, E. and SPINNLER, H. (1967) Impaired performance on colour tasks in patients with hemispheric damage. *Cortex*, **3**, 194-216.

DE RENZI, E. and VIGNOLO, L. A. (1962) The token test. A sensitive test to detect receptive disturbances in aphasics. *Brain*, **85**, 665-678.

EISENSON, J. (1954) *Examining for Aphasia*. New York: Psychological Corp.

ETTLINGER, G. (1960) The description and interpretation of pictures in cases of brain lesion. *J. ment. Sci.*, **106**, 1337-1346.

ETTLINGER, G. (Ed.) (1965) *Functions of the Corpus Callosum*. London: Ciba.

ETTLINGER, G. and HURWITZ, L. (1962) The description and interpretation of pictures in cases of brain lesion. *J. ment. Sci.*, **106**, 1337-1346.

FÖRSTER, O. (1918) Psychische Folgen der Hirnverletzung. *Neurologisches Zentralblatt*, **16**, 418-419.

GERSTMANN, J. (1927) Fingeragnosie und isolierte Agraphie. Ein neues Syndrom. *Z. ges Neurol. Psychiat.*, **108**, 152-177.

GOODGLASS, H. and KAPLAN, E. (1963) Disturbance of gesture and pantomime in aphasia. *Brain*, **86**, 703-720.

GOODGLASS, H., QUADFASEL, F. A. and TIMBERLAKE, W. H. (1964) Phrase length and the type and severity of aphasia. *Cortex*, **1**, 133-153.

GRÜNTHAL, E. (1935) Über die Diagnose der traumatischen Hirnschädigung. *Zentralblatt Neurologie and Psychiatrie*, **76**, 717.

HEBB, D. O. (1945) Man's frontal lobes: a critical review. *Arch. Neurol. Psychiat.*, **54**, 10-24.

HÉCAEN, H. (1962) Clinical symptomatology in right and left hemisphere lesions. *In* MOUNTCASTLE, U. (Ed.) *Interhemispheric Relations and Cerebral Dominance*. Baltimore: Johns Hopkins Press.

HÉCAEN, H. and AJURIAGUERRA, J. DE (1956) Agnosie visuelle pour les objets inanimés par lésion unilatéral gauche. *Rev. Neurol.*, **94**, 222-233.

HÉCAEN, H., AJURIAGUERRA, J. DE and DAVID, M. (1952) Les deficits fonctionnels après lobectomie occipitale. *Mschr. Psychiat. Neurol.*, **123**, 239.

HÉCAEN, H. and ANGELERGUES, R. (1962) Agnosia for faces (Prosopagnosia). *Arch. Neurol.*, **7**, 92-100.

HÉCAEN, H. and ANGELERGUES, R. (1964) Localisation of symptoms in aphasia. *In* REUCK, A. V. S. DE and O'CONNOR, M. (Eds.) *Disorders of Language*. London: Ciba.

HÉCAEN, H., PENFIELD, W., BERTRAND, C. and MALMO, R. (1956) The syndrome of apractognosia due to lesions of the minor cerebral hemisphere. *Arch. Neurol. Psychiat.*, 75, 400-434.

HOLMES, G. (1918) Disturbances of visual orientation. *Brit. J. Ophthal.*, 2, 449-468.

JACKSON, H. (1868) On the physiology of language. Reprinted from *Medical Times & Gazette. Brain* (1915), 38, 59-64.

KAPLAN, E. and GESCHWIND, N. (1962) A human cerebral disconnection syndrome. *Neurology*, 12, 675-685.

KIMURA, D. (1963) Right temporal lobe damage: perception of unfamiliar stimuli after damage. *Arch. Neurol.*, 8, 264-271.

KINSBOURNE, M. and WARRINGTON, E. K. (1962a) A disorder of simultaneous form perception. *Brain*, 85, 461-486.

KINSBOURNE, M. and WARRINGTON, E. K. (1962b). A study of finger agnosia. *Brain*, 85, 47-66.

KINSBOURNE, M. and WARRINGTON, E. K. (1962c) A variety of reading disability associated with right-hemisphere lesions. *J. Neurol. Neurosurg. Psychiat.*, 25, 339-344.

KINSBOURNE, M. and WARRINGTON, E. K. (1963a) The localizing significance of limited simultaneous form perception. *Brain*, 85, 697-702.

KINSBOURNE, M. and WARRINGTON, E. K. (1963b) The development of finger differentiation. *Quart. J. exp. Psychol.*, 15, 132-137.

KINSBOURNE, M. and WARRINGTON, E. K. (1964) Disorders of spelling. *J. Neurol. Neurosurg. Psychiat.*, 27, 224-228.

KLEIST, K. (1934) *Gehirn Pathologie*. Leipzig: Barth.

KOK, E. P. (1964) Modifications of speed of perception of pictures of objects in optic aphasia. *Cortex*, 1, 328-343.

LANSDELL, H. (1968) Effect of extent of temporal lobe ablation on two lateralized deficits. *Physiology and Behaviour*, 3, 271-273.

LASHLEY, K. (1951) *In* JEFFRESS, L. A. (Ed.) *Cerebral Mechanisms in Behaviour*. New York: Wiley.

LISSAUER, H. (1890) Ein Fall von Seelenblindheit nebst einem Beitrage zur Theorie derselben. *Arch. Psychiat. Nervenkr.*, 21, 222-270.

LUNN, V. (1948) *Om Legemsbevidstheden. Belyst Ved Nogle Forstyvvelser of den Normale Oplevelses maade*. Copenhagen: Munksgaard.

LURIA, A. R. (1964) Factors and forms of aphasia. *In* REUCK, A. V. S. DE and O'CONNOR, M. (Eds.) *Disorders of Language*. London: Ciba.

LURIA, A. R. (1966) *Human Brain and Psychological Process*. New York and London: Harper and Row.

LURIA, A. R. and HOMSKAYA, E. D. (1964) Disturbance in the regulative role of speech with frontal lobe lesions. *In* WARREN, J. M. and AKERT, K. (Eds.) *The Frontal Granular Cortex and Behaviour*. New York: McGraw-Hill.

MCFIE, J. and PIERCY, M. (1952) The relation of laterality of lesion to performance on Weigl's sorting test. *J. ment. Sci.*, 98, 299-305.

MCFIE, J. and ZANGWILL, O. L. (1960) Visual constructive disabilities associated with lesions of the left cerebral hemisphere. *Brain*, **83**, 243-260.

MILNER, B. (1958) Psychological defects produced by temporal lobe excision. *Proc. Ass. Res. nerv. Dis.*, **36**, 244-257.

MILNER, B. (1962) Laterality effects in audition. *In* MOUNTCASTLE, V. B. (Ed.) *Interhemispheric Relations and Cerebral Dominance*. Baltimore: Johns Hopkins Press.

MILNER, B. (1963) Effects of different brain lesions on card sorting. *Arch. Neurol.*, **9**, 90-100.

MILNER, B. (1966) Amnesia following operation on the temporal lobes. *In* WHITTY, C. W. M. and ZANGWILL, O. L. (Eds.) *Amnesia*. London: Butterworths.

MILNER, B., BRANCH, C. and RASMUSSEN, T. (1964) Observations on Cerebral Dominance. *In* REUCK, A. V. S. DE and O'CONNOR, M. (Eds.) *Disorders of Language*. London: Ciba.

OLDFIELD, R. C. and WINGFIELD, A. (1965) Response latencies in naming objects. *Quart. J. exp. Psychol.*, **17**, 273-281.

PIERCY, M. (1959) Testing for intellectual impairment. *J. ment. Sci.*, **105**, 489-495.

PIERCY, M. (1964) The effects of cerebral lesions on intellectual function: a review of current research trends. *Brit. J. Psychiat.*, **110**, 310-352.

PIERCY, M., HÉCAEN, H. and AJURIAGUERRA, J. DE (1960) Constructional apraxia associated with unilateral lesions – left- and right-sided cases compared. *Brain*, **83**, 225-242.

ROCHFORT, G. and WILLIAMS, M. (1962) Studies in the development and breakdown in the use of names. *J. Neurol. Neurosurg. Psychiat.*, **25**, 222-233.

SCHILLER, F. (1947) Aphasia studied in patients with missile wounds. *J. Neurol. Neurosurg. Psychiat.*, **10**, 183-197.

SCHUELL, H. (1960) *Differential Diagnosis of Aphasia with the Minnesota Test*. Minneapolis: University of Minnesota Press.

SPERRY, R. W., GAZZANIGA, M. S. and BOGEN, J. E. (1965) Observations on visual perception after disconnection of the cerebral hemispheres in man. *Brain*, **88**, 221-236.

STARR, M. A. (1884) Cortical lesions of the brain. *Amer. J. med. Sci.*, **87**, 366-391.

STEVENSON, J. F. (1967) M.Sc. Thesis (unpublished). University of Cambridge.

TALLAND, G. A. (1965) *Deranged Memory*. New York and London: Academic Press.

WARRINGTON, E. K. (1968) Constructional apraxia. *In Handbook of Clinical Neurology*. Amsterdam: North Holland (in press).

WARRINGTON, E. K., JAMES, M. and KINSBOURNE, M. (1966) Drawing disability in relation to laterality of cerebral lesion. *Brain*, **89**, 53-82.

WARRINGTON, E. K. and JAMES, M. (1967a) An experimental investigation of facial recognition in patients with unilateral cerebral lesions. *Cortex*, **3**, 317-326.

WARRINGTON, E. K. and JAMES, M. (1967b) Disorders of visual perception in patients with localized cerebral lesions. *Neuropsychologia*, 5, 253-266.

WARRINGTON, E. K. and JAMES, M. (1967c) Tachistoscopic number estimation in patients with unilateral cerebral lesions. *J. Neurol. Neurosurg. Psychiat.*, 30, 468-474.

WARRINGTON, E. K. and WEISKRANTZ, L. (1968a) New method of testing long-term retention with special reference to amnesic patients. *Nature*, 217, 972-974.

WARRINGTON, E. K. and WEISKRANTZ, L. (1968b) A study of learning and retention in amnesic patients. *Neuropsychologia* (in press).

WEINSTEIN, S. and TEUBER, H. L. (1957) Effects of penetrating brain injury on intelligence test scores. *Science*, 125, 1036-1037.

WEISENBURG, T. H. and MCBRIDE, K. E. (1935) *Aphasia: A Clinical and Psychological Study*. New York: Commonwealth Press.

WERNICKE, C. (1908) The symptom complex of aphasia. *In* CHURCH, E. D. (Ed.) *Modern Clinical Medicine*. New York: Appleton.

WOLPERT, I. (1924) Die Simultanagnosie-Störung der Gesamtauffassung. *Z. ges Neurol. Psychiat.*, 93, 397-415.

WYKE, M. (1967) Postural arm drift associated with brain lesions in man. *Arch. Neurol.*, 15, 329-334.

WYKE, M. (1968) The effect of brain lesions in the performance of an arm-hand precision task. *Neuropsychologia*, 6, 125-134.

YATES, A. J. (1954) The validity of some psychological tests of brain damage. *Psychol. Bull.*, 51, 359-379.

ZANGWILL, O. L. (1941) On a peculiarity of recognition in three cases of Korsakoff's psychosis. *Brit. J. Psychol.*, 31, 230-248.

ZANGWILL, O. L. (1943) Clinical tests of memory impairment. *Proc. Roy. Soc. Med.*, 36, 576-580.

ZANGWILL, O. L. (1946) Some qualitative observations on verbal memory in cases of cerebral lesions. *Brit. J. Psychol.*, 37, 8-19.

ZANGWILL, O. L. (1960) *Cerebral Dominance and its Relation to Psychological Function*. Edinburgh and London: Oliver and Boyd.

Subnormal adults

H. C. Gunzburg

I INTRODUCTION

There are probably 1 million people in the U.K. and some 4-5 millions in the U.S.A. who are intellectually below average from the intelligence test point of view. These figures represent about 2% of the population and indicate a problem of some importance. Yet, only some 150,000 people in the U.K. were either attending special Training Centres, living in hospitals and institutions or were on waiting-lists for admission to one or the other facility. Well over 20,000 children attended Junior Training Centres and Hospital Schools, and some 54,000 children attended special schools or special classes on account of their intellectual weaknesses. Though these people represent a considerable expenditure in manpower and finance there remain many who manage to exist in the community without requiring constant assistance, despite intellectual handicap.

Intellectual subnormality makes people more vulnerable and predisposes them to succumb more readily to difficulties than would people of normal intelligence. Yet, it does not necessarily and in all cases *cause* the social *incompetence* which requires society to take action resulting in attendance at or living in special institutions. Though very profound mental handicap (under I.Q. 25) will always make a person socially incompetent because he needs constant nursing care, people only a little further up the I.Q. scale (I.Q. 25-50) are already able to contribute financially to their maintenance and may require comparatively little supervision. Intellectual subnormality becomes a less relevant criterion of unemployability and of the need for constant support once the I.Q. 50 mark has been passed; indeed, the paradoxical situation occurs that there is often need to institutionalize people with relatively high I.Q.s whilst mentally handicapped people with lower I.Q.s are able to live and work in the open community.

A recent survey of a 30% sample of adult admissions to subnormality hospitals (Castell and Mittler, 1965), indicated that the mean Wechsler Full Scale I.Q. of people classified as subnormal was 71·4 ± 12·3, whilst the mean I.Q. of people classified as severely subnormal was 60·4 ± 8·1. These intelligence levels probably reflect difficulties in social adaptation but not that social adjustment is impossible. The great number of people who can live relatively independent lives despite intellectual handicaps points to the need for developing assessment, education and training methods to encourage the acquisition and mastery of social techniques and skills in the comparatively small number of intellectually handicapped people who experience serious adjustment difficulties. In this work the psychologist could play a more effective role once his contribution exceeds mere psychometrics, and he concerns himself with the diagnostic assessment of weaknesses and strengths relevant to social adjustment and with the development of teaching and training techniques to alleviate the consequences of the mental handicap (Gunzburg, 1960; Clarke and Clarke, 1965).

1   The mentally handicapped person

Even a cursory perusal of medical textbooks (Tredgold and Soddy, 1963; Hilliard and Kirman, 1965) makes it clear that definite aetiological diagnoses can be given only in comparatively few cases and that these generally refer to the profoundly and severely mentally handicapped person who very much needs nursing care. A recent survey of 1,639 patients (Leck *et al.*, 1967) showed that in over 70% of the cases no recognized cause for their subnormality could be established; similarly, Berg (1965) found it impossible to establish definite causes of subnormality in two-thirds of 800 children with I.Q.s below 50.

It has also become clear that much subnormality can be ascribed to environmental factors, either producing generally poor genetic endowment or worsening an initially not very healthy situation. President Kennedy's Panel on Mental Retardation (1962) stated bluntly that the same conditions which spawn many health and social problems generate the problem of mental handicap. The Panel also claimed that if our present knowledge were fully applied and appropriate action taken, preventive measures would 'eliminate perhaps half or more of all new cases' of mental handicap. This emphasizes the fact that many aspects of mental subnormality are 'man made' in the sense of being the result of a combination of a multitude of environmental factors which may affect particularly vulnerable organisms. Environmental manipulation may partly undo the damage caused by environment. Adequate education, training and appropriate placement in the open community can succeed in restoring some of the relevant abilities which might otherwise never become available for practical use.

Psychological research workers have recently been interested in pinpointing the weaknesses of the mentally subnormal person which make it difficult for him to respond to the demands of the environment. Luria and his co-workers (1963) point to the difficulties the mentally handicapped have – owing to pronounced pathological changes in the brain – in establishing connections between verbal instruction and the manipulation of tasks. They point out that, in a clash between conceptual generalization and situational generalization, the latter, being a more primitive system, usually wins – hence the great learning difficulties of the severely subnormal. Particular difficulties are found in a lack of association between the verbal system and the one governing motor behaviour; it becomes important that the limited vocabulary of the severely mentally handicapped (Lyle, 1959, 1960; Mein and O'Connor, 1960) should be improved to give him 'coding ability' to help him to direct his behaviour (O'Connor and Hermelin, 1963).

The severely subnormal child and adult must be thoroughly bewildered in a world which they cannot grasp because of their 'decoding' difficulties. Earl (1961) suggested that the severely subnormal are characterized by a pronounced weakness of 'drive' which reduces their ability to strive towards a goal, to persist in effort or withstand frustration. In fact, learning difficulties as mentioned by various workers make ordinary social and employment situations hard to tackle, whilst the weakness of 'drive' reduces their ability to deal with any obstacles. This may easily result in 'catastrophic reactions' when a mentally subnormal, faced with tasks that are too difficult, seeks refuge in curious defence patterns of behaviour, such as perseverative and distractible behaviour (Goldstein, 1943). It is easy to conceive of a history of constant frustration and disappointment engendered by innate deficiencies and aggravated by the unhappy experience of an unsuccessful childhood and school life (Zigler, 1962). Adverse early events in the paranatal history have been shown to be related later to learning problems, mental retardation and reading problems (Jordan, 1964). In consequence, the mentally subnormal is less and less inclined to try, and tends to give up at the slightest excuse. Indeed, the typical answer to questions in a test situation is, 'I don't know', which does not necessarily reflect ignorance but utter lack of confidence. How to motivate the subnormal to marshal and apply his meagre mental abilities has been the key question in mental deficiency, since it became clear that intellectual subnormality did not of itself provide an explanation for the defective's inadequate social behaviour. Indeed it can be said that the past overemphasis on sub-average intellectual functioning and on I.Q. measurements has contributed quite considerably to the slow progress made in the subnormal's education and training. Regarded primarily as a 'cognitive deficit' rather than as a person who might be subject to the same feelings as normal people, and might also be emotionally maladjusted and deprived, there has been little attempt so far to guide him consistently and purposively towards definite goals. The psychometric assessment indicating functioning at the time of testing and usually biased in favour of academic ability, provides little indication of a 'social potential' or the feasibility of being able to reach certain selected targets of social competence *despite* low cognitive ability. It is in this area that the psychologist could make a most useful and direct contribution to the practical work of institutions, hospitals and training centres.

2   The role of the psychologist

A mentally subnormal person has been defined as showing sub-average general intellectual functioning which is associated with impairment in adaptive behaviour (Heber, 1959). In infancy and early childhood, this impairment tends to show in an inadequate rate of maturation of the sensory-motor development (such as sitting, crawling, etc.) and in later childhood it is observed in academic learning difficulties. Once adulthood is approached impairment in adaptive behaviour is shown by inadequacy to maintain oneself independently in the community and in employment, and in difficulties of adjusting to the social demands of the community. Inadequate social adjustment is related to low intellectual ability in the mentally subnormal, but a low I.Q. is not necessarily prognostic of social incompetence. There is now an abundance of research available – as summarized by Clarke and Clarke (1965) and Gunzburg (1968) – that I.Q.s even as low as 35 do not preclude successful functioning in the open community. Several studies of the individual careers of mental defectives provide much evidence of the multiplicity of factors responsible for social success and failure (Baller, 1936; Abel and Kinder, 1942; Charles, 1953; Saenger, 1957; Masland, Sarason and Gladwin, 1958; Edgerton, 1967).

Psychological assessments should therefore contribute to an understanding of why a mentally subnormal person does not function *socially*, and whether it is possible to pinpoint particular weaknesses and deficiencies so that remedial action can be taken. It has been shown that the number of mentally subnormal persons in need of assistance drops sharply once they are past the academic obstacle race of school education, and that they can often satisfy the demands of life and work better than those of their teachers. If a person is socially inadequate, the ready-made explanation of 'low I.Q.' is unacceptable (unless it is a profoundly handicapped subnormal) and it will be necessary to look for additional reasons which might contribute to his difficulties in adapting himself to the (perhaps quite modest) demands of society.

The second part of the psychologist's contribution will be concerned with the direct application of assessment results and psychological theory to deal with the various factors which affect acceptable functioning. This refers to the introduction and application of many new approaches, such as programmed learning, conditioning and other behaviour-shaping techniques which are based on psychological theory and could help the subnormal to become socially more effective (Gunzburg, 1956; Pfeiffer, 1966; Baumeister, 1967; Clark, 1968).

II   ASPECTS OF ASSESSMENT, EVALUATION AND PREDICTION

1   Classification

Dissatisfaction with the meagre results of psychometric testing and the misuse to which intelligence test figures have been put, has led to more cautious treatment of test scores and attempts at clinical interpretation of 'qualitative' features of test results. It is now recognized that it is preferable to use the test result only for broad classification and labelling purposes; recommended terminology refers to I.Q. *ranges* and is based on Standard Deviations (see Table 10.1).

These labels refer *only* to intelligence testing, which is the most convenient and most widely used assessment method at present available. It does not refer, for example, to degrees of social competence and it is a common occurrence that persons classified in one particular category on intellectual grounds are in a 'higher' or 'lower' group relating to social behaviour. Except for the Vineland Scale of Social Maturity (Doll, 1953), no social assessment instrument is available which could be used in a similar way, and unfortunately no generally accepted procedure of social classification has yet been established. As a result, far too much emphasis is based on the assumed implications of intellectual assessment without the advantage of a cross-check offered by an objective assessment of social behaviour.

	Wechsler type of test *I.Q. range*	*Stanford-Binet type of test* *I.Q. range*
'Borderline'	70–84	68–83
'Mild'	55–69	52–67
'Moderate'	40–54	36–51
'Severe'	25–39	20–35
'Profound'	>25	>20

TABLE 10.1

Classification terms based on intellectual assessments only
(Adapted from Heber, 1959)

2   The 'quality' of intellectual functioning

Many attempts have been made to analyse the intelligence test results to account for individual differences and to use such analysis for predictive and diagnostic purposes. Though such analyses are not generally accepted, they provide much corroborative evidence for the psychologist attempting to give a report on a *person* rather than on his *test results*. Some useful information can also be derived from studying behaviour on particular tests and the factors which might influence the validity of the test. Though it is now generally accepted that the test result only reflects intellectual functioning at the time of testing, it is obviously of very great importance to estimate as reliably as possible the intellectual resources which could be available to a particular person. Various methods have been used for this purpose.

(a)   *Altitude Quotient*
Jastak (1949) maintains that a person diagnosed as intellectually defective on the basis of a global I.Q. may in fact have a higher, though unused, potential. According to Jastak, it is only justifiable to label a person as mentally defective if he fails to score higher than the lowest two or three percentiles on a large number of tests representing different aspects of intellectual functioning. Persons who do not meet this criterion and show good or average ability in one or more specific tests are not genuine mental defectives.

Jastak, adopting Thorndike's concept of altitude, proposes a clinical assessment
L

method which contrasts an altitude quotient with the intelligence quotient. The altitude quotient, which is obtained by taking the peaks of a person's performance, would indicate the *optimum* performance level of a person, while the intelligence quotient refers to *actual* functioning, which may be lowered by interference from educational, emotional and other handicaps.

As anyone familiar with Wechsler psychograms will know, irregular performances in the various subtests are quite common, and are most probably due to unreliability of these short tests. Moreover, some of the subtests, such as Object Assembly, Picture Completion, Comprehension, have been shown to be relatively easy for mental defectives (Baroff, 1959; Fisher, 1960) and relatively good performances in these tests are probably of less clinical significance than peak performances in subtests such as Similarities or Block Design. Where this occurs it should encourage the search for other indications of higher intellectual ability.

Whilst the uneven profile in a test of intellectual ability may suggest inadequately used mental resources or pseudo-mental subnormality, uneven development in different aspects of functioning, e.g. psycho-motor efficiency, spatial organization and educational achievements, is probably typical for the mentally subnormal; in such an assessment it may be the even development which is indicative of pseudo-deficiency (Hurtig *et al.*, 1962; Zazzo, 1960a, b).

Many clinicians, dissatisfied with the incompatibility of low I.Q. scores with relatively good life performances, feel that an analysis of test profiles with a view to establishing glimpses of higher intellectual ability, provides useful corroborative evidence, but little research work is available to substantiate the validity of such pattern analysis. On the other hand, there is little doubt that a careful study of trends and inconsistencies within the formal test performance will provide useful pointers far in excess of the classification label provided by the global I.Q.

(b) *Verbal and Performance Bias*

Many psychologists and psychiatrists use the frequently found verbal/performance bias for predictive purposes. The published evidence does not fully support clinical impressions; not only are criteria of bias and its significance not adequately defined but 'success' and 'failure' in social adaptation are also vague terms (Wechsler, 1958; Graham and Kamano, 1958; Warren and Kraus, 1961; Manne *et al.*, 1962).

Generally speaking, adult subnormals do better in non-verbal than verbal tests. This may be the result of the poor socio-economic background of most familial or 'garden-variety' defectives which stultifies verbal-linguistic-abstract development; it may also be a genuine deficiency typical for people with low intelligence. Whatever the reason, performance higher than verbal I.Q. on a Wechsler type test is common in mental deficiency, whilst the reverse is considerably less frequent. Table 10.2 sets out the results for a large number of people admitted to a hospital for the mentally subnormal, aged between 16 and

30 years and obtaining a Wechsler Full Scale I.Q. above 50. A bias was defined as a difference of 13 I.Q. points or more.

Fitzpatrick (1956) showed that among subnormal people considered by hospital authorities for work outside the institution, there was a preponderance of performance biases, but if the performance bias (on the W.-B. test) exceeded 20 points it tended to be a poor prognostic sign of adjustment. However, Roberts (1945) found a non-verbal bias of 10-29 points 'an excellent indication of parole possibilities for older patients'. Ferguson (1958) and Windle (1962) also report similar findings, yet Tizard and O'Connor, who in an earlier publication (1950) had reviewed the relationship of psychometric patterns and social adjustment, quite rightly considered that the 'pattern hypothesis' had not been satisfactorily established.

	Men		Women		Total	
	N	%	N	%	N	%
Performance bias (13 pts +)	147	37·9	35	18·0	182	31·4
Verbal bias (13 pts +)	29	7·5	21	10·8	50	8·6
No bias (12 pts or less)	211	54·6	138	71·2	349	60·0
	387	100	194	100	581	100

TABLE 10. 2

Performance—and Verbal Bias in a population of mentally subnormal adults.

Earl (1940, 1961) and Gunzburg (1959) used a test battery of two non-verbal tests (Form board and Block Design) and two verbal tests (Vocabulary and Absurdities) and attempted to validate type of bias and absence of bias against later community adjustment. These studies are weakened by the impossibility of satisfactorily defining success or failure. Conclusions were that unbiased and performance-biased psychograms correlated highly with probable success, whilst irregular and verbal biases were indicative of failure. If the same data are only used to predict discharge from the institution – a more objective criterion of prognosis than social failure and success – this type of analysis can predict to a statistically significant degree, as Windle (1962) has shown. It is worth while to recall in this connection that it has been found (Gallagher, 1947; Taylor, 1959) that organic damage of various types (the brain injured, exogenous types) leads to distinct difficulties in executing performance tests. Organic pathology and even minimal neurological damage has been shown to be associated with unstable behaviour; thus, verbal bias (representing as it were a lowering of the expected usual performance ability) may well point to pronounced adjustment difficulties.

3 Assessment of social competence

Despite the emphasis put on the mental defective's inadequate social behaviour, it is surprising how little has been done so far either to assess or to correct it systematically. This is partly due to the dominant role of I.Q. assessment, partly to the difficulties experienced in defining and measuring such an elusive concept as 'social competence' which depends as much on circumstances as on the person himself.

The earliest, best known and most widely used assessment scale of social competence is that by E. A. Doll, known as the Vineland Social Maturity Scale (1953). Following the method used by intelligence test designers, Doll selected a large number of social skills, such as ability to wash self, moving about freely in the neighbourhood, being entrusted with small errands, and established for each skill the age at which that skill could be said to have matured. This results in a Social Age (S.A.) analogous to Mental Age and as in the case of intelligence tests a Social Age equal to Chronological Age indicates average normal achievement whilst an S.A. below C.A. indicates social backwardness and is typical for mental handicap.

Social competence obviously depends to some extent on intelligence; correlation coefficients between S.A. and M.A. ranging from 0·50 to 0·90 in normal populations have been quoted (Doll, 1953).

On the other hand, elementary skills are encouraged by adequate motor development and stimulating experiences; in such cases Social Age tends to be higher than Mental Age (Doll, 1953; Goulet and Barclay, 1962). It is unjustified to predict social ability level simply on the basis of M.A., because intensive training, opportunities for practice and age, as well as a less demanding community life, could well combine to let a mentally handicapped person function reasonably well in ordinary day-to-day situations, far above the level suggested by the intelligence test result (Goulet and Barclay, 1962; Barclay *et al.*, 1964).

The Vineland classifies people in relation to a scale of normal development and it is thus possible to estimate the width of the gap which separates an individual mentally handicapped person from his normal contemporaries. That gap tends to increase with age because the more advanced social skills require higher mental ability than the mentally handicapped has at his disposal. It has also been shown (Kellmer Pringle, 1966) that the discrepancies between S.A. and M.A. indicate certain types of emotional maladjustments, though not much research on this aspect has been published in the field of mental handicap (Lurie *et al.*, 1942).

It is unsatisfactory to confine psychological probing to the comparison of a person's social competence with that of normal people because this usually only confirms knowledge already obtained through an intelligence test. It is, however, very important to determine the level of social competence in relation to the mental handicap. After all, a mentally subnormal person could be 'underfunctioning' and 'backward' in relation to his admittedly meagre abilities, just as any mentally normal person can fail to make adequate use of his intellectual resources. The task of establishing the presence or absence of social backwardness in persons who are, by normal standards, socially backward anyway but who show very different degrees of social competence considering their mental handicap, is not an easy one. If one were to relate social efficiency to Mental Age, it would lead to 'under-expectation'. Comparing social efficiency with the achievements of various age groups of 'normal' children – as in the Vineland Scale – provides no guidance as to what could reasonably be expected. It will thus be necessary to obtain a clear general picture of social achievement levels of mentally handicapped people of various ages and intellectual status in order to evaluate an individual child's or adult's standing in particular aspects of social functioning (Cain, Levine and Elzey, 1963). This will enable the assessor to *establish objectively* whether achievements are average for a mentally subnormal, superior or below average and to initiate remedial action if appropriate.

Such information can be obtained by comparing an individual handicapped person with a large group of mentally handicapped people of similar age. One method of obtaining and evaluating information will be described. The *Progress Assessment Chart* method is essentially an inventory of 'social skills', knowledge of which will ease the mentally handicapped's adjustment to community demands. As in the P-P-A-C (Primary P-A-C for young children) and P-A-C 1 (for children, see Chapter 17), in the P-A-C 2 (for mentally handicapped adolescents and adults) a circle diagram permits arrangement of 'skills' in order of increasing difficulty from the centre to the periphery. Unlike the P-P-A-C and P-A-C 1, the order of the skills is not determined by reference to available research but is based on the empirical evidence of previous work (Gunzburg, 1960), though there is corroborative evidence (Matthew, 1964) that the arrangement is by and large valid.

The numbered spaces in the diagram referring to specific skills are heavily shaded by the examiner (see Fig. 17.1) if he has satisfied himself that the subject is competent – i.e. satisfied the criteria laid down for the particular item. After completion, the P-A-C 2 diagram indicates by the irregularly distributed gaps an individual person's deficiencies in social knowledge and competence and thus suggests an itemized teaching programme for further action. Whilst the P-A-C assessment provides a qualitative appraisal of social functioning and dysfunctioning, it is not a quantitative measure of achievement. If this is calculated as a global figure, the advantage of separately assessing distinct aspects of social development would be lost. However, norms for each of the four subsections, and relating to the average achievement levels of mentally handicapped adults (C.A. 16-25) of various I.Q. levels, are contained in the P-E-I 2 (Progress Evaluation Index 2 – Fig. 10.1) which is similar to the P-E-I 1 to be used in conjunction with the P-A-C 1.

The average achievement levels of specified I.Q. groups are indicated in the P-E-I by the light shading (e.g. in subsection Communication 13 skills represent the average achievement of young people in I.Q. group 55 to 69 and 20 skills in the I.Q. group 70 to 84). It is an easy matter to compare the actual achievements of an individual subject as scored on the P-A-C 2 and to establish objectively whether there is genuine backwardness and in what particular aspect, since he can now be seen against the background of achievements of young people of comparable age and intelligence.

This method has been described at some length because it has been designed specifically for the mentally handicapped and provides a detailed source of highly relevant information. It does not attempt to establish 'social intelligence' but suggests that there might be an *unrealized potential* if actual social functioning

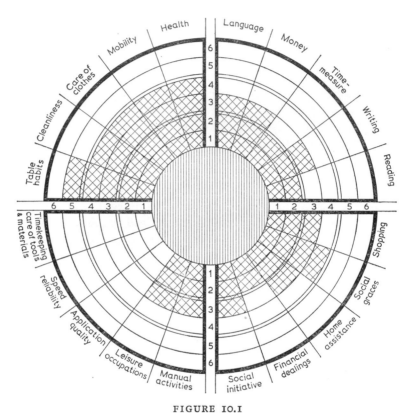

FIGURE 10.1

P-E-I 2 diagram indicating average attainment levels of I.Q. group 55–69.

is below that of other mentally handicapped people of comparable intelligence and age. The method emphasizes the need for systematic observation as the basis for remedial action and should pose the question, 'Why is this person socially backward when the majority of similarly handicapped people have been able to achieve a higher level of competence?' Unless there are good reasons for 'backwardness', such evaluation leading to an awareness of the existence of a specific problem may well encourage more direct and urgent teaching and training because such knowledge should be within the mentally handicapped person's capability.

4 Prognosis in adult mental subnormality

One of the main purposes of prognostic assessment is to establish the extent to which a subnormal will be able to marshal his meagre mental abilities to adjust to the demands of life and work in the open community. There is much evidence in the form of follow-up reports (Baller, 1936; Kennedy, 1948, 1962; Charles, 1953) that people who when children were considered severely subnormal, made adequate adjustments in adulthood. This area has been summarized by Clarke and Clarke (1965).

Many of the adult subnormals who draw attention to themselves by petty crimes, unsatisfactory employment records and general social inadequacy have sufficient mental resources to make it difficult to accept a low I.Q. as an explanation of their failure. It has been shown over and over again that even people with I.Q.s well below 50 are sometimes able to give satisfaction in employment and may lead a routine life; thus, subnormals with I.Q.s in the 70s would apparently have a considerable advantage over even more poorly endowed people. Nevertheless, their history of incompetent behaviour often forces society to put them out of circulation for their own protection as well as that of society. This is done in the hope that the temporary segregation in institution or hospital from the community at large will help the subnormal to find his bearings, to mature and 'learn his lesson' and to be more capable on his discharge.

It is extremely difficult for the authorities to judge when this type of indirect treatment of social inadequacy should be ended, either because as much has been achieved as can be expected, or because it is felt that continuation of the 'treatment' would lead to deterioration and consequently to failure. In those cases it will be necessary to decide when the probabilities for 'success' outside the institution or hospital are high enough to justify taking a calculated risk.

The psychologist is often asked in such a situation to predict the subnormal's reactions and further career when no longer under direct supervision, and to give a social prognosis which is based on more than guesswork. Such a demand can scarcely be met successfully because the psychologist has not only to assess the various factors in the subnormal which determine future behaviour but has also to guess at the impact of the environment and factors which the subnormal will encounter. Psychological evaluation of the various facets of a person's make-up is inadequate enough, even though the psychologist may spend hours over it, but the assessment of a completely unknown quantity – the environment with its multitude of different factors, is impossible. Since a subnormal is quite markedly at the mercy of environmental happenings and little able or willing to direct his destiny, a prediction of his behaviour in unknown circumstances is extremely hazardous.

(a) *I.Q. as a predictor of social prognosis*
It is widely assumed that intelligence as measured by a standardized I.Q. test is probably the best single factor in prognostic pronouncements. Yet there is now overwhelming evidence of the comparatively low correlation between

intelligence and later community adjustment which makes it quite hazardous to use an I.Q. by itself as the sole prognostic criterion (these studies are considered in detail by Sarason, 1953; Masland *et al.*, 1958; Windle, 1962).

It is, for example, likely that mildly subnormal people come to the attention of the authorities only when they display pronounced personality defects which interfere with their community adjustment, despite their relatively high and quite adequate intellectual ability. Thus while the higher I.Q. level in hospitalized/institutionalized people will attract attention and these people will often qualify sooner for discharge and early placement, since they are obviously people with a higher degree of employability (O'Connor and Tizard, 1951, 1956), they are also very likely the unstable, even psychopathic personalities who fail to conform with community demands and break down quite easily.

On the other hand, the less able subnormal with fairly low intellectual resources will find social demands difficult and will require assistance of some kind. He is less conspicuous in an institutional environment than the more alert mildly retarded, and decisions regarding his discharge tend to come less readily, yet, in the end, he may show a certain stability and imperturbability which make him a 'success' in the community.

Moreover, though the belief in the 'constancy of the I.Q.' is no longer held in defence of inactivity on the educational/therapeutic front it still bedevils rehabilitation efforts in adolescence and adulthood. Recent work by psychologists has, however, shown that the influence of maturation and environment makes it inadvisable to accept the I.Q. score in making long-term administrative decisions in individual cases.

There are now several studies (Minogue, 1926; Chipman, 1929; Prouty, 1929; Hoakley, 1932; Walton and Begg, 1957; Alper and Horne, 1959) which indicate clearly that increases in mental age take place after the age of 16. Some of these observations may largely be due to the old-fashioned method of computing the M.A. of adults by using 16 as the chronological norm. This is borne out by studies using the Wechsler type of tests where a different computation method is employed. In these cases there appears to be no evidence for increase of intelligence among subnormal adults (Clarke and Clarke, 1953, 1954; Mundy, 1957). Yet, once a more careful analysis of the test results is carried out, interesting facts emerge leading to a better understanding of the situation. Clarke and Clarke (1954) indicate that the I.Q.s assessed in adulthood may under certain circumstances be fairly stationary, but may 'increase' in predictable cases. The research investigated 'I.Q. constancy' of 59 people in the age range 14 to 50 (mean age $23 \cdot 5 \pm 8 \cdot 1$) and with an I.Q. range 35 to 98 (mean I.Q. $66 \cdot 2 \pm 14 \cdot 0$). There were large I.Q. increases in some people who were retested after approximately 27 months. An independent assessor then separated the sample into two groups according to a list of 12 objective criteria of 'early adverse environmental circumstances' (i.e. neglect, cruelty, N.S.P.C.C. intervention), and separated those people from established bad home background from those with no such handicap. The difference in I.Q. gain between the groups was significant at the 0·1% level and the investigators concluded that the I.Q. increments were the result of 'being removed from a very adverse environment'. Thus it is possible to consider these changes as a kind of recuperating and regaining of lost mental efficiency. In further work the researchers investigated the after-careers of their original 59 patients (Clarke *et al.*, 1958) and pointed out that mentally handicapped people who had come from the worst social conditions and had recovered intellectually had a considerably more successful social history than those in the other group.

A research on parallel lines by Roswell-Harris (1958), but using the Bowlby criteria of deprivation, confirmed independently that in a group of 100 young men retested after an interval of four years there was a mean significant increase for the whole group. It was, however, established that among the 73 young men who showed I.Q. increases on retest, those who had been considered to have been deprived of normal family life 'had made significantly larger increases in I.Q. than the young men who had not been deprived of normal family life'. It was also shown that there was a significant relationship between improvement in social knowledge and deprivation, so that 'the feebleminded young man . . . is more likely to show an increase of I.Q. and benefit from treatment and training . . . if he has also been deprived of normal family life during childhood'.

These are findings of far-reaching importance. The influence of environment on the intellectual functioning of mentally handicapped children had already been pointed out in a series of well-known studies originating at the University of Iowa (Skeels and Dye, 1939; Skodak and Skeels, 1949) and average I.Q. increases and decreases in the region of 27 points owing to environmental factors had been demonstrated. Recently similar changes due to environmental manipulation were shown by Lyle (1959, 1960) and Tizard (1964). The Clarke studies showed that environmental factors were also influential in adulthood. The changes in adult I.Q. are most likely not due to maturation or even environmental stimulation (no particular 'treatment' was carried out at Clarke's institution) but reflect the very common 'under functioning' in intellectual and social behaviour. Whilst there is obviously a group which is functioning to the best of its limited ability (and which generally will show a 'constant I.Q.' score) there are others where test scores reflect inadequate achievements and application *at the time of testing*, but are liable to change for the better once emotional disturbances and adverse environmental factors are no longer effective.

In this connection it is appropriate to refer to pseudomental deficiency (Cassel, 1949; Clarke and Clarke, 1955) which apparently offers an explanation why people at a later stage show acceptable mental functioning, though they had been diagnosed mental defectives in their childhood. As Clarke and Clarke (1955) point out, the diagnosis of pseudomental deficiency does not involve a diagnostic error in the first place (Doll, 1941; Porteus, 1941). Because of the impermanence of mental arrest – mostly in the mildly and moderately retarded

L*

– so-called pseudomental deficiency is not so much mistaken diagnosis but mistaken prognosis.

(b) *Prognosis on educational achievement*

It is an unproved assumption that literacy in its widest sense will help the subnormal to adjust more readily to the demands of society. Much emphasis is placed on teaching academic skills to a 'non-academic mind', simply because an adequate mastery of reading, writing and arithmetic is essential for a normal child's further career. The case for a different type of education and the concomitant type of assessment will be discussed later, but it is important to evaluate the relevance of educational test assessment for the purpose of prognosis.

There is no doubt that achievement in academic skills is normally highly correlated with intelligence test scores, yet within the subnormality range exceptions are frequent enough to warn against misleading generalizations.

Mechanical reading ability, for which an achievement index in form of reading age (R.A.) is most frequently quoted, represents by and large a skill which can be attained fairly easily by even severely retarded people and may never be acquired by some mildly retarded persons. Gunzburg (1968) showed that more than half of his mildly retarded group (I.Q. 55-69) reach a reading level above 7 years. Since such measures nearly always test only the ability to 'bark at print' without comprehension of the reading matter, R.A. can be safely disregarded as suggesting the level of intellectual functioning.

In fact, the few available investigations (Town, 1931; Krishef, 1959; Shafter, 1957) all agree that educational level, however measured, does not relate to social and vocational adjustments.

(c) *Personality factors*

Though the elusive concept of personality is very frequently mentioned as decisive for final adjustment to the community, there is a scarcity of studies using the objective criteria of a specified personality test. Practically all personality tests require a considerable degree of literacy and comprehension to express feelings or to respond to the demands of a projective technique. In consequence most of these approaches fail dismally with the defective who is poor in expressing himself and the assessor is left with a 'flat' record indicative only of the subject's low mentality.

The Rorschach Test was used by Solomon (1955) to predict the subject's behaviour outside the institution. He was able to show that subnormals who gave human content responses (H) were successful in their placement. Other signs, such as W, D, F, P responses did not differentiate successfully between the groups, as shown by Windle (1962).

Johnson's (1953) study, though dealing with children, might be mentioned here because she used Klopfer's Rorschach Prognostic Rating Scale, which is meant to be a measure of 'ego strength' and found a highly significant statistical difference between two groups of children where the prognosis of improvement respectively non improvement was born out by later events.

III THE APPLICATION OF PSYCHOLOGICAL RESEARCH TO THE TREATMENT, TRAINING AND EDUCATION OF THE ADULT SUBNORMAL

Encouraged by the detailed knowledge gained from specialized assessment procedures and by psychological theory supported by laboratory experiments, psychologists are nowadays taking an active part in guiding mentally handicapped people. The characteristic features of these attempts are the often very detailed documentation and assessment techniques used to determine the efficiency of various programmes and approaches. Investigations which have helped considerably to change the traditional outlook and approach to important problems can conveniently be discussed under the headings of Self-help, Communication, Socialization and Occupation.

1 Self-help

This area, comprising primarily skills relating to eating, going to the lavatory, dressing and washing, is of importance in the training of very severely handicapped people. There are still many of them, either at home or in hospital wards, who represent formidable nursing problems because they have not been able to acquire even the most elementary self-help skills. This may be due to extremely low intellectual abilities but also to pronounced behaviour disturbances. Psychologists have in recent years devoted attention to training of this kind, influenced partly by Pavlovian concepts and partly by Skinner's approach. Skinner (1965) himself showed how a 40-year-old microcephalic idiot was taught to make form discriminations and to trace letters by programmed instruction. Others applied this method to self-help skills in cases where traditional methods had failed (Ellis, 1963; Watson, 1967). Investigations extended the application of the technique to behaviour which interfered with the acquisition of self-help skills (Ayllon and Michael, 1959; Lindsley, 1960; Wolf *et al.*, 1964; Hundziak *et al.*, 1965).

The results reported are promising, but it must be remembered that 'success' may not necessarily be due to the technique itself, but may be the consequence of more interested staff being available and more attention being given to the problem than before. Yet, even so, these psychological approaches certainly succeed in demonstrating the feasibility of increasing self-sufficiency even in profoundly retarded people.

2 Communication

This area covers a wide range of communication skills whether they be language or writing, reading or being able to carry out number work. It is the main area of scholastic endeavour and comprises those skills which are most vulnerable to intellectual short-comings. Whilst no high proficiency can be expected in the application of these skills, it is quite within the capabilities of the moderate, mild and borderline retarded to acquire some measure of technical facility – for example in the ability to read words correctly without understanding their meaning; in 'telling the time' to state the correct time without being able to regulate behaviour accordingly. Even though such achievements are modest and their significance must not be over-rated, they give the adult some measure of self-confidence and help him to feel more 'at home' in a world which may otherwise be strange and frightening (Gunzburg, 1968).

Much psychological work has been carried out in this area, though by its very nature these, largely educational interests, seem to focus principally on the child with some intellectual ability.

The main medium of 'language skill' – all-important as it is – has received comparatively little attention, even in language development work relating to educationally subnormal children. Bernstein (1960, 1962) discussed the barriers created by the inadequate use and understanding of language by the subnormal and Mein and O'Connor (1960) studied the vocabularies of severely subnormal people in hospitals. Gunzburg (1964) using the Illinois Test of Psycholinguistic Abilities, standardized on very young children, showed that the range of this battery was not too easy even for moderately and mildly retarded adult people. Many studies use the traditional vocabulary tests, particularly the Peabody Picture Vocabulary Tests, but beyond a statement of the position little work dealing with improvement of the language abilities of the adult subnormal has been reported.

Attention has tended to concentrate on the improvement of technical reading skills. O'Connor and Hermelin (1963) demonstrated that 'discrimination between the learned written word and other similar ones can be taught (and) a "discrimination set" transferred to other instances'. Much of the more recent work is based on programmed learning techniques and uses teaching machines (Brown, 1965; Brown and Bookbinder, 1965; Haskell, 1966). Studies are now available (Stolurow, 1960, 1961, 1963; Silberman, 1962; Watson, 1964; Haskell, 1966) which show that the use of carefully controlled teaching programmes and machines is effective and could support the teacher's efforts. There are many practical problems, not least that of having to design programmes specifically for the use of the mentally retarded because the available material is unsuitable (Gunzburg, 1966). The teaching of writing has received even less attention probably because the severely subnormal will have little use for this mode of communication.

On the other hand, the ability to handle number concepts, particularly money operations, is of vital importance in community adjustment, even though it tends to be overlooked in favour of teaching the more impressive, even if less helpful, skill of reading. The complacency with which teachers and parents pointed to the child's ability of 'counting to 20, 50 or 100' received a severe jolt when psychologists, inspired by the work of Piaget (1952), began to investigate the defective's number concepts. M. Woodward published a series of studies (1959, 1961, 1962a) dealing mainly with children, but there is no reason to assume that her findings do not apply equally to young severely subnormal adults. Her findings are important for the successful planning and execution of a programme which includes form and number perception. Woodward gave various practical suggestions, based on her investigations into the development of a number concepts (1962b) and Locking (1966) proposed a system of teaching number concepts, which is allied to Stevens' (1951) theory of measurement.

Generally speaking, the comparative negligence with which the area of Communication skills has been treated in the childhood stage is even more conspicuous in the adult field. Mittler in his postscript to Marshall's (1967) study pointed out that children leaving Junior Training Schools at approximately 16 had attainments corresponding on average to those of children between 5 and 6 years, although their emotional and physical needs and their work capacity were likely to be far above this level. Tizard (1964) drew attention to the extreme lack of simple educational knowledge such as knowledge of one's age and recognition of coins displayed by adult severely subnormal people who had been 'educated' in their childhood. Gunzburg (1968) gives detailed information on the social and educational achievements of young adults (C.A. 16-25) grouped in the categories of mildly, moderately and severely retarded.

Communication skills are more dependent on intellectual ability than skills in the other three areas of Self-help, Socialization and Occupation. This has been shown by Marshall (1967), who obtained a correlation coefficient of $r=0.61$ between the Communication section of the P-A-C 1 and an intelligence assessment, but correlation coefficients of only 0.42, 0.41, 0.37, between the Self-help, Socialization and Occupation sections of the P-A-C 1 and intelligence. The Manual of the P-A-C (Gunzburg, 1969) shows similar correlations between the P-A-C 2 and the Wechsler Full I.Q. The correlation between Communication and the W.A.I.S. is 0.80, whilst the other three correlations coefficients are 0.39, 0.49, 0.28, between the Self-help, Socialization and Occupation sections.

3   Socialization

Next to communication, the skills which are least developed in the subnormal adult are those relating to social integration. As far as the severely subnormal are concerned, this is partly explained by the protective segregation policy which parents and teachers seem to pursue if they wish to shelter the S.S.N. child against unkindness and excessive demands. In consequence, the child misses the experience of having to learn to play and to live with other normal children. To some extent this applies also to the less handicapped child, whose reactions to society are, however, primarily influenced by a dim awareness of not being able to live up to demands. This weak drive (Earl, 1961), the inadequate support received from a poor home environment (Clarke and Clarke, 1965) and the modest mental ability available for tackling a vast number of difficult situations in an increasingly more complex industrialized society, lead to various forms of social and emotional maladjustment. Indeed, psychological advice is most frequently sought in this area because many situations which require drastic action by society in the form of imprisonment or institutionalization would be avoidable if the personality problems of the subnormal could be handled more successfully. Whilst considerable advances have been made in finding suitable employment for the severely and the less severely retarded, and a number of Occupation Centres and Hospital Workshops are trying to give training for life in the open community, comparatively little has been done to assist the severely handicapped as a person, rather than merely as a worker. Yet, his work effort and his social survival depend much on his ability to get on with other people, to adjust to their demands and to conform to their standards.

Many problems arise from the subnormal's misjudgements and inability to appreciate relative values. This may be due to class difference in language development (Bernstein, 1960, 1962), to different moral values (Brennan, 1963), to difficulties in appreciating other people's views (Clark, 1960), but, whatever the reason, such barely appreciated factors certainly put a very effective stop to satisfactory rehabilitation.

Various psychologists indicated how much improvements and responses to learning situations depended on social approval. Clark (1960), using a sociometric approach in conjunction with a rating scale, was successful in inducing more realistic and acceptable judgements in subnormal adults. Kaldeck (1958) and Snyder and Sechrest (1959) have described group psychotherapy work with adolescent and adult mental defectives.

Studies relating to behaviour modifications due to psychotherapeutic efforts have not been very numerous or convincing due to methodological shortcomings. They mostly report successes and great improvements, but there is obviously a 'publication bias' since 'failures' are scarcely ever published. (Vail, 1955). Moreover, most of these attempts take place in unstimulating and custodial institution settings and responsiveness to the friendly interest of the unusual psychotherapeutic situation is nearly certain. How far the particular psychotherapeutic approach itself is genuinely effective, as distinct from an ordinary friendly person to person attitude, is difficult to judge. The literature on this subject has been discussed and summarized by various authors (Stacey and De Martino, 1957; Gunzburg, 1958; Robinson and Robinson, 1965).

Studies of adolescents and adults with the Rorschach test have been quite numerous (e.g. Abel *et al.*, 1943-44; Sarason and Sarason, 1946; Jolles, 1947; Solomon, 1955) and have indicated a large number of aspects having a bearing on personality functioning. Similarly, the T.A.T. has been used (Bergman and Fisher, 1953; Lubin, 1955; Jordan and de Charms, 1959) and Rosenzweig's Picture Frustration Test (Foreman, 1962). The Draw-a-Person Test, used as a projective technique rather than a measure of intellectual ability, has come in for some attention (Earl, 1933; Gunzburg, 1955a, b) but yields only limited information, though it may well prove an important test in the subnormality field. Other tests, even though primarily designed to give information on intellectual functioning, may also yield incidental information on personality and social functioning. A test such as the well-known Block Design Test has been used in its original version (Kohs, 1923) to demonstrate the relationship between performance ability and social adjustment (Wile and Davis, 1930; Sarason and Potter, 1947; Earl, 1961) and the Porteus Maze Test (1950, 1959) is claimed to assess planning ability, foresight and impulsiveness. It has been used for identifying successful occupational placements (Tobias and Gorelick, 1962), delinquents (Wright, 1944; Grajales, 1948; Docter and Winder, 1954) socially well-adjusted individuals (Karpeles, 1932) and behaviourally retarded subjects. The Bender Visual Motor Gestalt Test was found by Wagner and Hawver (1965) to correlate highly (0·89) with workshop success in a group of 27 severely subnormal subjects aged 21-34, whilst the Stanford-Binet Test results correlated only 0·63.

4 Occupation

The most decisive advance in recent years has been the recognition of the mentally handicapped's ability to work in an industrial setting to an employer's satisfaction. From the very beginning of custodial care, the mental defective had been encouraged to assist in the running of the colonies and institutions set aside for him. Yet, so divorced from the community at large were they, that until quite recently trades such as mat or brushmaking were pursued there irrespective of the industrial revolution having long ago taken place outside the institution walls.

Some of the earliest studies of trainability and employability of defectives were carried out by O'Connor and Tizard (1956), Clarke and Hermelin (1955) and Gunzburg (1960) in this country. Most of the contemporary work in the U.S.A. has been collected and reprinted in a volume edited by Stahlecker (1967).

The type of presentation of the job in hand, its breakdown into simple component operations, has far-reaching consequences on the successful work performance of even very severely subnormal people. Investigations into the trainability of imbeciles were carried out by Clarke and Clarke (1965).

Various conclusions of general and practical usefulness resulted from this work. The severely subnormal adult is, neither in speed nor dexterity, significantly inferior to subnormal people with considerably higher I.Q. levels (Loos and Tizard, 1955). The main distinction between the performance of the severely subnormal person and others of higher or even normal intelligence is the *time taken in learning* (Clarke and Hermelin, 1955). Though the initial level of execution is usually extremely low, very impressive results can be achieved by adhering to certain principles, which, whilst established under psychological laboratory conditions, are nevertheless of general validity:

(*a*) suitable incentives
(*b*) breakdown of work

(c) correct movements
(d) short repeated learning sessions
(e) need for over learning
(f) verbal reinforcement
(g) initial aiming at accuracy rather than speed
(h) suitable layout of material to minimize errors.

Though generally speaking the subnormal with I.Q. below 50 has not in the past been considered capable of employment in the open community, a number of case studies is now available (Craft, 1962; Gunzburg, 1968) indicating that such persons are employable outside the institution. It will be important to screen out those with the best prospects if a choice has to be made. Qualities such as acceptance of directions, acceptable work habits, co-operation with other workers, relative speed in learning new work skills, will be appreciated by employers; test results are usually validated against such criteria.

Whilst it has now become widely accepted that imbeciles can be trained to a level which enables them to contribute financially to their support, it is less clear that skills acquired in relation to a particular task can be transferred to a new situation. This is important if a severely subnormal person is to work outside the protective sheltered workshop in ordinary conditions.

A number of studies (Clarke and Hermelin, 1955; Clarke and Blakemore, 1961) throw light on this question and have practical repercussions on classroom and workshop practice. 'Transfer of training' was shown to take place, as well as retention of learning over long periods of non-practice. It was even found (Clarke, 1966) that 'within limits the more complex the task the greater the transfer to another task with different content, though with similar demands. The practical corollary of these investigations is that transfer is maximal where there has been substantial learning preceding the acquisition of a task and that mere practice on a simple task will neither help in this situation nor will there be generalisation to others'.

There are now many studies of discrimination learning and transfer, but most of them refer to children (House and Zeaman 1958, 1960; Girardeau, 1959; Bryant, 1963). Nevertheless, enough work relating to adolescent and adult imbeciles has now been published (summarized by Clarke and Clarke, 1965) to suggest that a good deal can be done outside the artificial psychological laboratory situations. The unexpectedly rapid development of the sheltered workshop where highly complex operations are carried out by people who once vegetated in institutional wards testifies to the reality of these findings.

The influence of personality make-up on the work performance of imbeciles was investigated by Claridge (1956, 1959) and Claridge and O'Connor (1957), who differentiated two personality types on the basis of a behaviour rating scale. It was found that 'apathetic imbeciles' tended to improve steadily on their work performance irrespective of whether there were incentives or not. On the other hand, 'excitable imbeciles' who had a comparatively inferior ability for improvement could be encouraged by special incentives. However, they showed a tendency to decline when incentives were removed, whilst the 'apathetic imbeciles' still continued to improve. Such findings link up with general psychological theory as presented by Eysenck (1955) and Pavlov relating to inhibition and excitation.

These findings are, if corroborated by other research, of considerable relevance since they would not only explain differences in the training process but would enable the staff to make the necessary allowances in the training programme and in the type of supervision required (O'Connor and Tizard, 1956).

IV CONCLUDING REMARKS

The adult, particularly the adolescent mentally subnormal, no longer necessarily requires full and complete support. Vulnerable as he is, proper assessment of his abilities and encouragement and direction of his social education and training can be most successful as long as society can afford to have him as a wage-earning handicapped member in its midst. The psychological contribution in this field by now far exceeds mere diagnostic assessment and doubtful predictions based on them. Guided by detailed assessments relating to practical problems of living and working in the community, programmes of educational and social treatment of adolescents and adults have been developed by psychologists who deal directly with crucial issues (e.g. Neale and Campbell, 1963; Gunzburg, 1963, 1968). This work is in its beginnings, because the field has been for too long dominated by the psychometric approach of intelligence testing.

There is little doubt that neither the individual tests, mentioned in the foregoing paragraphs, nor large assortments of tests of varying character (O'Connor and Tizard, 1956; Clausen, 1966) provide ready made answers to questions which the psychologist is likely to be asked in individual cases. Nevertheless, they contribute in each particular case to the available evidence; the consistency or inconsistency of the observations made is of great value in arriving at decisions, all of which should be reviewed and revised from time to time.

REFERENCES

ABEL, T. M. and KINDER, E. F. (1942) *The Subnormal Adolescent Girl*. New York: Columbia.

ABEL, T. M., PIOTROWSKI, Z. and STONE, G. (1943-44) Responses of negro and white morons to the Rorschach Test. *Am. J. ment. Def.*, **48**, 253-257

ALPER, A. E. and HORNE, B. M. (1959) Changes in I.Q. of a group of institutionalized mental defectives over a period of two decades. *Am. J. ment. Def.*, **64**, 472-475.

AYLLON, T. and MICHAEL, J. (1959) The psychiatric nurse as behavioural engineer. *J. exp. Anal. Behav.*, **2**, 323-334.

BALLER, W. R. (1936) A study of the present social status of a group of adults, who, when they were in elementary schools, were classified as mentally deficient. *Genet. Psychol. Monogs.*, **18**, 165-244.

BARCLAY, A., GOULET, L. R. and SHARP, A. R. (1964) Short-term changes in intellectual and social maturity of young non-institutionalized retardates. *Proc. Copenhagen Congress*, 679-683.

BAROFF, G. S. (1959) W.I.S.C. patterning in endogenous mental deficiency. *Am. J. ment. Def.*, **64**, 482-485.

BAUMEISTER, A. A. (1967) A survey of the role of psychologists in public institutions for the mentally retarded. *Ment. Retard.*, **5**, 2-5.

BERG, J. M. (1965) The aetiological aspects of mental subnormality: pathological factors. *In* CLARKE and CLARKE (1965).

BERGMAN, M. and FISHER, L. A. (1953) The value of the thematic apperception test in mental deficiency. *Psych. Quarterly Suppl.*, **27**, 22-42.

BERNSTEIN, B. (1960) Language and social class. *Brit. J. Sociol.*, **2**, 271-276.

BERNSTEIN, B. (1962) Linguistic codes, hesitation phenomena and intelligence. *Language and Speech*, **5**, 31-46.

BRENNAN, W. K. (1963) Moral judgment and the child. *J. ment. Subnorm.*, **9**, 13-20.

BROWN, R. I. (1965) Distractibility and some scholastic skills. *J. child Psychol. and Psychiat.*, **6**, 55-62.

BROWN, R. I. and BOOKBINDER, C. E. (1965) *Audio Visual Programmed Reading Material.* Bristol: Educational Media and Technical Aids.

BRYANT, P. (1963) *The effects of language on the formation of concepts in imbecile children.* Unpublished Ph.D. Thesis, University of London.

CAIN, L. F., LEVINE, S. and ELZEY, F. (1963) *Manual for the Cain-Levine Social Competency Scale.* Palo Alto: Consulting Psychologists Press.

CASSEL, R. H. (1949) Notes on pseudo-feeblemindedness. *Train. Sch. Bull.*, **46**, 119-127.

CASTELL, J. H. F. and MITTLER, P. (1965) Intelligence of patients in subnormality hospitals: a survey of admissions in 1961. *Brit. J. Psychiat.*, **111**, 219-225.

CHARLES, D. C. (1953) Ability and accomplishment of persons earlier judged mentally deficient. *Genet. Psychol. Monogs.*, **47**, 3-71.

CHIPMAN, CATHERINE E. (1929) The constancy of the Intelligence Quotient of mental defectives. *Psychol. Clinic.*, **18**, 103-111.

CLARIDGE, G. S. (1956) *Factors affecting the motivation and performance of imbeciles.* Unpublished Ph.D. Thesis, University of London.

CLARIDGE, G. S. (1959) A re-analysis of 'excitability' and its relationship with improvement in performance. *J. ment. Def. Research*, **3**, 116-121.

CLARIDGE, G. S. and O'CONNOR, N. (1957) The relationship between incentive, personality type and improvement in performance of imbeciles. *J. ment. Def. Research*, **1**, 16-25.

CLARK, D. F. (1960) Visual feedback in the social learning of the subnormal. *J. ment. Subnorm.,* **10,** 30-39.

CLARK, D. F. (1968) A reassessment of the role of the clinical psychologist in the mental deficiency hospital. *J. Ment. Subnorm.,* **14,** 3-17.

CLARKE, A. D. B. (1966) *Recent Advances in the Study of Subnormality.* London: N.A.M.H.

CLARKE, A. D. B. and BLAKEMORE, C. B. (1961) Age and perceptual motor transfer in imbeciles. *Brit. J. Psychol.,* **52,** 125-131.

CLARKE, A. D. B. and CLARKE, A. M. (1953) How constant is the I.Q.? *Lancet,* **2,** 877-880.

CLARKE, A. D. B. and CLARKE, A. M. (1954) Cognitive changes in the feeble-minded. *Brit. J. Psychol.,* **45,** 173-179.

CLARKE, A. D. B. and CLARKE, A. M. (1955) Pseudo-feeblemindedness – some implications. *Am. J. ment. Defic.,* **59,** 507-509.

CLARKE, A. D. B. and CLARKE, A. M. (1965) The abilities and trainability of imbeciles. *In* CLARKE and CLARKE (1965).

CLARKE, A. D. B., CLARKE, A. M. and REIMAN, S. (1958) Cognitive and social changes in the feebleminded – three further studies. *Brit. J. Psychol.,* **49,** 144-157.

CLARKE, A. D. B. and HERMELIN, B. F. (1955) Adult imbeciles: their abilities and trainability. *Lancet,* **2,** 337-339.

CLARKE, A. M. and CLARKE, A. D. B. (1965) *Mental Deficiency; The Changing Outlook* (2nd Ed., 1st Ed. 1958). London: Methuen.

CLAUSEN, JOHS (1966) *Ability Structure of Subgroups in Mental Retardation.* Washington: Spartan Books.

CRAFT, M. (1962) The employment of the adult imbecile: a follow-up. *J. ment. Subnorm.,* **8,** 26-27.

DOCTER, R. F. and WINDER, C. L. (1954) Delinquent vs. non-delinquent performance on the Porteus Qualitative Maze Test. *J. consult. Psychol.* **18,** 71-73.

DOLL, E. A. (1941) The essentials of an inclusive concept of mental deficiency. *Am. J. ment. Def.* **46,** 214-219.

DOLL, E. A. (1953) *A Manual for the Vineland Social Maturity Scale.* The Measurement of Social Competence. Minneapolis: Educational Test Bureau.

EARL, C. J. C. (1933) The human figure drawings of adult defectives. *J. ment. Sci.,* **79,** 305-328.

EARL, C. J. C. (1940) A psychograph for morons. *J. abnorm. soc. Psychol.,* **35,** 428-448.

EARL, C. J. C. (1961) *Subnormal Personalities: Their Clinical Investigation and Assessment.* London: Baillière, Tindall & Cox.

EDGERTON, R. B. (1967) *The Cloak of Competence.* Berkeley: Univ. of California Press.

ELLIS, N. R. (1963) Toilet training the severely defective patient on S-R reinforcement analysis. *Am. J. ment. Def.,* **68,** 98-103.

EYSENCK, H. J. (1955) A dynamic theory of anxiety and hysteria. *J. ment. Sci.*, **101**, 28-51.

FERGUSON, R. G. (1958) *Evaluation of the Potential for Vocational Rehabilitation of Mentally Retarded Youths with Muscular, Orthopaedic and Emotional Impairment.* Second Annual Report. Sheltered Workshop of the MacDonald Training Center, Tampa, Fla.

FISHER, G. M. (1960) The altitude quotient as an index of intellectual potential: W.A.I.S. data for familial and undifferentiated mental retardates. *Am. J. ment. Def.*, **65**, 252-255.

FITZPATRICK, F. K. (1956) Training outside the walls. *Am. J. ment. Def.*, **60**, 827-837.

FOREMAN, M. E. (1962) Predicting behavioural problems among institutionalized mental retardates. *Am. J. ment. Def.*, **66**, 580-588.

GALLAGHER, J. J. (1947) A comparison of brain-injured and non-brain-injured mentally retarded children on several Psychological variables. *Monogr. Soc. Res. Child Dev.*, **22**, 329-333.

GIRARDEAU, F. L. (1959) The formation of discrimination learning sets in mongoloid and normal children. *J. comp. physiol. Psychol.*, **52**, 566-570.

GOLDSTEIN, K. (1943) Concerning rigidity. *Character and Personality*, **2**, 209-226.

GOULET, L. R. and BARCLAY, A. (1962) The Vineland Social Maturity Scale: utility in assessment of Binet M. A. *Am. J. ment. Def.*, **67**, 916-921.

GRAHAM, E. E. and KAMANO, D. (1958) Reading failure as a factor in the W.A.I.S. subtest patterns of youthful offenders. *J. clin. Psychol.*, **14**, 302-305.

GRAJALES, M. L. (1948) *Porteus Qualitative Maze Test as a Measure of Delinquency.* New York: Fordham Univ. Thesis.

GUNZBURG, H. C. (1955a) Scope and limitations of the Goodenough Drawing Test method in clinical work with mental defectives. *J. clin. Psychol.*, **11**, 8-15.

GUNZBURG, H. C. (1955b) Projection in drawings. *Brit. J. med. Psychol.*, **28**, 72-81.

GUNZBURG, H. C. (1956) The role of the psychologist in the mental deficiency hospital. *Int. J. Soc. Psychol.*, **1**, 31-36.

GUNZBURG, H. C. (1958) Psychotherapy with the feebleminded. *In* CLARKE and CLARKE (1958, 1965).

GUNZBURG, H. C. (1959) Earl's moron battery and social adjustment. *Am. J. ment. Def.*, **63**, 92-103.

GUNZBURG, H. C. (1960) *Social Rehabilitation of the Subnormal.* London: Baillière, Tindall & Cox.

GUNZBURG, H. C. (1963) *Senior Training Centres.* An outline of the principles and practice of social education and training for older mentally subnormal people. London: N.A.M.H.

GUNZBURG, H. C. (1964) The reliability of a test of psycholinguistic abilities (I.T.P.A.) in a population of young male subnormals. *J. ment. Subnorm.*, **19**, 101-112.

GUNZBURG, H. C. (1966) Teaching aids for the subnormal. In *The Application of Research to the Education and Training of the Severely Subnormal Child. J. ment. Subnorm. Monograph Supplemt.*

GUNZBURG, H. C. (1968) *Social Competence and Mental Handicap.* London: Baillière, Tindall and Cassell.

GUNZBURG, H. C. (1969) *The P-A-C Manual.* London: N.A.M.H.

HASKELL, S. H. (1966) Programmed instruction and the mentally retarded. In *The Application of Research to the Education and Training of the Severely Subnormal Child. J. ment. Subnorm. Monograph Supplemt.*

HEBER, R. (1959) *Manual on Terminology and Classification in Mental Retardation.* Am. Ass. on Ment. Def.

HILLIARD, L. T. and KIRMAN, B. H. (1965) *Mental Deficiency* (2nd Ed.) London: Churchill.

HOAKLEY, Z. PAULINE (1932) The variability of intelligence quotients. *Am. Assn. Stud. Feebleminded.*, **37**, 119-148.

HOUSE, B. J. and ZEAMAN, D. (1958) A comparison of discrimination learning in normal and mentally defective children. *Child Develop.*, **29**, 411-416.

HOUSE, B. J. and ZEAMAN, D. (1960) Transfer of a discrimination from objects to patterns. *J. exp. Psychol.*, **5**, 298-302.

HUNDZIAK, M. *et al.* (1965) Operant conditioning in toilet training of severely mentally retarded boys. *Am. J. ment. Def.*, **70**, 120-124.

HURTIG, M. C., MERLET, L., SANTUCCI, H. and ZAZZO, R. (1962) An experimental examination of the concept of mental deficiency. *Proc. London Conf. Scient. Stud. Ment. Def.*, **2**, 650-658.

JASTAK, J. (1949) A rigorous criterion of feeblemindedness. *J. abnorm. soc. Psychol.*, **44**, 367-378.

JOHNSON, ELIZABETH Z. (1953) Klopfer's Prognostic Scale used with Raven's Progressive matrices in play therapy prognosis. *J. proj. Tech.*, **17**, 320-326.

JOLLES, I. (1947) The diagnostic implications of Rorschach's Test in case studies of mental defectives. *Genetic Psychol. Monographs*, **36**.

JORDAN, T. E. (1964) Early developmental adversity and classroom learning – a prospective inquiry. *Am. J. ment. Def.*, **69**, 360-371.

JORDAN, T. E. and DE CHARMS, R. (1959) The achievement motive in normal and mentally retarded children. *Am. J. ment. Def.*, **64**, 457-466.

KALDECK, R. (1958) Group psychotherapy with mentally defective adolescents and adults. *Int. J. Group Psychotherapy*, **8**, 185-193.

KARPELES, L. M. (1932) A further investigation of the Porteus Maze Test as a discriminative measure in delinquency. *J. appl. Psychol.*, **16**, 427-437.

KENNEDY, R. J. R. (1948) *The Social Adjustment of Morons in a Connecticut City.* Hartford Coun: State Office Buildings.

KENNEDY, R. J. R. (1962) *A Connecticut Community Revisited.* A study of the social adjustment of a group of mentally deficient adults in 1948 and 1960. V.S. Office of Voc. Rehabilit.

KOHS, S. C. (1923) *Intelligence Measurement.* New York: Macmillan.

KRISHEF, C. H. (1959) The influence of rural urban environment upon the adjustment of discharges from the Owatonna State School. *Am. J. ment. Def.*, **63**, 860-865.

LECK, I., GORDON, W. L. and MCKEOWN, T. (1967) Medical and social needs of patients in hospitals for the mentally subnormal. *Brit. J. prev. and soc. Medic.*, **21**, 115-121.

LINDSLEY, O. R. (1960) Characterisation of the behaviour of chronic psychotics as revealed by free operant conditioning methods. *Diseases of the Nervous System.* Monograph Suppl., **21**, 66-78.

LOCKING, J. R. (1966) An arithmetic programme for the subnormal pupil. In *The Application of Research to the Education and Training of the Subnormal Child. J. Ment. Subnorm. Monograph.*

LOOS, F. M. and TIZARD, J. (1955) The employment of adult imbeciles in a hospital workshop. *Am. J. ment. Def.*, **59**, 395-403.

LUBIN, N. M. (1955) The effect of color in the TAT on productions of mentally retarded subjects. *Am. J. ment. Def.*, **60**, 366-370.

LURIA, A. R. (Ed.) (1963) *The Mentally Retarded Child.* London: Pergamon Press.

LURIE, LOUIS A., ROSENTHAL, FLORENCE M. and OUTCALT, LOUISA C. (1942) Diagnostic and prognostic significance of the difference between the intelligence quotient and the social quotient. *Am. J. Orthopsychiatry.*, **12**, 104-114.

LYLE, J. G. (1959) The effect of an institution environment upon the verbal development of imbecile children, Part I. *J. ment. Def. Res.*, **3**, 122-128.

LYLE, J. G. (1960) The effect of an institution environment upon the verbal development of imbecile children. Parts II and III. *J. ment. Def. Res.*, **4**, 1-23.

MANNE, S. H., KANDEL, A. and ROSENTHALL, D. (1962) Differences between performance I.Q. and verbal I.Q. in a severely sociopathic population. *J. clin Psychol.*, **18**, 73-77.

MARSHALL, A. (1967) *The Abilities and Attainments of Children Leaving Junior Training Centres.* London: N.A.M.H.

MASLAND, R. L., SARASON, S. B. and GLADWIN, T. (1958) *Mental Subnormality.* New York: Basic Books.

MATTHEW, G. C. (1964) The social competence of the subnormal school leaver. *J. ment. Subnorm.*, **10**, 83-88.

MEIN, R. and O'CONNOR, N. (1960) A study of the oral vocabularies of severely subnormal patients. *J. ment. Def. Res.*, **4**, 130-143.

MINOGUE, BLANCHE M. (1926) The constancy of the I.Q. of mental defectives. *Ment. Hyg.*, **10**, 751-758.

MUNDY, L. (1957) Therapy with physically and mentally handicapped children in a mental deficiency hospital. *J. clin. Psychol.*, **13**, 3-9.

NEALE, M. D. and CAMPBELL, W. J. (1963) *Education for the Intellectually Limited Child and Adolescent.* Sydney: Novak.

O'CONNOR, N. and HERMELIN, B. (1963) *Speech and Thought in Severe Subnormality*. London: Pergamon.

O'CONNOR, N. and TIZARD, J. (1951) Predicting the occupational adequacy of certified mental defectives. *Occup. Psychol.*, **25**, 205-211.

O'CONNOR, N. and TIZARD, J. (1956) *The social Problem of Mental Deficiency*: London: Pergamon.

P-A-C 2 (Progress Assessment Chart 2 of Social Development). London: N.A.M.H.

P-E-I 2 (Progress Evaluation Index 2 of Social Development). London: N.A.M.H.

PIAGET, J. (1952) *The Child's Conception of Number*. London: Routledge and Kegan Paul.

PORTEUS, S. D. (1941) *The Practice of Clinical Psychology*. New York: Am. Book Co.

PORTEUS, S. D. (1950) *The Porteus Maze Test and Intelligence*. Palo Alto: Pacific Books.

PORTEUS, S. D. (1959) *The Maze Test and Clinical Psychology*. Palo Alto: Pacific Books.

PFEIFFER, E. (1966) Remarques sur la pratique de la psychologie en milieu hospitalier. *Ann. Med. Psychol.*, **124**, (11) 3, 339.

The President's Panel on Mental Retardation (1962) *A Proposed Program for National Action to Combat Mental Retardation*. Superintendent of Documents, U.S. Government Printing Office, Washington, U.S.A.

PRINGLE, M. L. KELLMER (1966) *Social Learning and Its Measurement*. London: Longmans.

PROUTY, RUTH A. (1929). Psychological classification versus clinical diagnosis *Psychol. Clinic.*, **18**, 213-220.

ROBERTS, A. D. (1945) Intelligence and performance test patterns among older mental defectives. *Am. J. ment. Def.*, **49**, 300-303.

ROBINSON, H. B. and ROBINSON, N. M. (1965) *The Mentally Retarded Child*. New York: McGraw-Hill.

ROSWELL-HARRIS, D. (1958) *Some aspects of cognitive and personality test changes in a group of one hundred feebleminded young men*. Unpublished M.A. Thesis, Univ. of Reading.

SAENGER, G. (1957) *The Adjustment of Severely Retarded Adults in the Community*. Albany: New York State Interdepartmental Health Resources Board.

SARASON, S. (1953) *Psychological Problems in Mental Deficiency* (2nd Ed.). Harper & Row.

SARASON, S. B. and POTTER, E. H. (1947) Colours in the Rorschach and Kohs block designs. *J. consult. Psychol.*, **11**, 202-206.

SARASON, S. B. and SARASON, ESTHER KROOP (1946) The discriminatory value of a test pattern in the high grade familial defective. *J. clin. Psychol.*, **2**, 38-49.

SHAFTER, A. J. (1957) Criteria for selecting institutionalized mental defectives for vocational placement. *Am. J. ment. Def.*, **61**, 599-616.

SILBERMAN, H. F. (1962) Self-teaching devices and programmed materials. *Rev. ed. Res.*, **32**, 119-193.

SKEELS, H. M. and DYE, H. B. (1939) A study of the effects of differential stimulation on retarded children. *Proc. Am. Assoc. Ment. Def.*, **44**, 114-136.

SKEELS, H. M. and HARMS, I. (1948) Children with inferior social histories, their mental development in adoptive homes. *J. genet. Psychol.*, **72**, 283-294.

SKINNER, B. F. (1965) The technology of teaching. *Proc. Roy. Soc. (B.)*, **162**, 427-443.

SKODAK, M. and SKEELS, H. M. (1949) A final follow up study of one hundred adopted children. *J. genet. Psychol.*, **75**, 85-125.

SNYDER, R. and SECHREST, L. (1959) An experimental study of directive group therapy with defective delinquents. *Am. J. ment. Def.*, **64**, 117-123.

SOLOMON, P. (1955) Differential Rorschach scores of successfully and unsuccessfully placed mental defectives. *J. clin. Psychol.*, **11**, 294-297.

STACEY, C. L. and DE MARTINO, M. F. (Ed.) (1957) *Counseling and Psychotherapy with the Mentally Retarded*. Glencoe, Illinois: The Free Press.

STAHLECKER, L. V. (1967) *Occupational Information for the Mentally Retarded*. Springfield, Illinois: Thomas.

STEVENS, S. S. (1951) *Handbook of Experimental Psychology*. New York: Wiley.

STOLUROW, L. M. (1960) Teaching machines and special education. *Educ. Psych. Meas.*, **20**, 429-448.

STOLUROW, L. M. (1961) *Teaching by Machine*. U.S. Department of Health, Education and Welfare, Office of Education, Co-operative Research Monographs No. 6. Wasington, D.C.: Government Printing Office.

STOLUROW, C. M. (1963) Programmed instruction for the mentally retarded. *Rev. of ed. Res.*, **33**, 126-136.

TAYLOR, EDITH MEYER (1959) *Psychological Appraisal of Children with Cerebral Defects*. Cambridge, Massachusetts: Harvard Univ. Press.

TIZARD, J. (1964) *Community Services for the Mentally Handicapped*. London: Oxford Univ. Press.

TIZARD, J. and O'CONNOR, N. (1950) The employability of high grade mental defectives. *Am. J. ment. Def.*, **54**, 563-576; **55**, 144-157.

TIZARD, J. and O'CONNOR, N. (1952) The occupational adaptation of highgrade mental defectives. *Lancet*, **2**, 620-623.

TOBIAS, J. and GORELICK, J. (1962) The Porteus Maze test and the appraisal of retarded adults. *Am. J. ment. Def.*, **66**, 601-606.

TOWN, CLARA H. (1931) An investigation of the adjustment of the feebleminded in the community. *Psychol. Clinic.*, **20**, 42-54.

TREDGOLD, R. F. and SODDY, K. (1963) *Tredgold's Textbook of Mental Deficiency*. London: Baillière, Tindall and Cox.

VAIL, D. J. (1955) An unsuccessful experiment in group therapy. *Am. J. ment. Def.*, **60**, 144-151.

WAGNER, E. E. and HAWVER, D. A. (1965) Correlations between psychological tests and sheltered workshop performance for severely retarded adults. *Am. J. ment. Def.*, **69**, No. 5, 685-691.

WALTON, D. and BEGG, T. L. (1957) Cognitive changes in low grade defectives. *Am. J. ment. Def.*, **62**, 96-102.

WARREN, S. A. and KRAUS, M. J. (1961) W.A.I.S. verbal minus performance I.Q. comparisons in mental retardates. *J. clin. Psychol.*, **17**, 57-59.

WATSON, L. S. (1964) Programmed instruction with the retarded. *Mental Retardation Abstracts*, **1**, No. 28030.

WATSON, L. S. (1967) Application of operant conditioning techniques to institutionalized severely and profoundly retarded children. *Mental Retardation Abstracts*, **4**, No. 1, 1-18.

WATSON, L. S. and LAWSON, R. (1966) Instrumental learning in mental deficiency. *Mental Retardation Abstracts*, **3**, 1-20.

WECHSLER, D. (1958) *The Measurement and Appraisal of Adult Intelligence* (4th Ed.). Baltimore: Williams and Wilkins.

WILE, I. S. and DAVIS, R. (1930) A comparative study of the Kohs block design tests. *Amer. J. Orthopsychiat.*, **1**, 89-103.

WINDLE, C. (1962) Prognosis of mental subnormals. *Am. J. ment. Def.*, *Monograph*. **66**, 5.

WOLF, M., MEES, H. and RISLEY, T. (1964) Application of operant conditioning procedures to the behaviour problems in the autistic child. *Behav. Res. Therapy*, **1**, 305-312.

WOODWARD, M. (1959) The behaviour of idiots interpreted by Piaget's theory of sensori-motor development. *Brit. J. educ. Psychol.*, **29**, 60-71.

WOODWARD, M. (1961) Concepts of number in the mentally subnormal studies by Piaget's method. *J. child Psychol. Psychiat.*, **2**, 249-259.

WOODWARD, M. (1962a) Concepts of space in the mentally subnormal studies by Piaget's method. *Brit. J. soc. clin. Psychol.*, **1**, 25-37.

WOODWARD, M. (1962b) The application of Piaget's theory to the training of the subnormal. *J. ment. Subnorm.*, **8**, 14, 17-25.

WRIGHT, C. (1944) The qualitative performance of delinquent boys on the Porteus Maze tests. *J. consult. Psychol.*, **8**, 24-26.

ZAZZO, R. (1960a) Une recherche d'équipe sur la débilité mentale. *Enfance*, **4-5**, 335-364.

ZAZZO, (1960b) *Manuel Pour L'Examen Psychologique de L'enfant*. Paris: Delachaux et Niestle.

ZIGLER, E. (1962) *Readings on the Exceptional Child. New York:* Appleton-Century-Crofts.

II

Geriatric patients

Moyra Williams

The psychological study of geriatric patients has changed greatly in the past decade. Instead of remaining a categorizing science, it has become an experimental one. It is no longer interested in listing symptoms; it is trying to ascertain the factors relating to them and the mechanisms involved. Sometimes this necessitates the construction of models, and analogies with computers are becoming as common in interpretations of the ageing process as in other areas of psychological investigation.

In the case of geriatrics the picture is complicated by a tendency to equate the processes of normal ageing with the effects of disease. The common and misguided belief that old age is similar to dementia has led to some confusion, and one of the purposes of the present chapter will be to distinguish more clearly the differences between them. Thus a person may have difficulty remembering new names and faces due to his increasing age, but this does not render him incapable of leading a useful social existence. He may have rigid 'old-fashioned' attitudes towards pop music and politics but be quite capable of running a household or even a business. He may be slow in his response to changing signals but remain a safe car-driver. In general, the tendency is for psychologists to approach the subject of ageing either from the experimental or from the clinical point of view. The latter still concentrates on defining symptoms and measuring their changes, the former on estimating the alterations of mental performance associated with increasing age. In this paper recent work in the two fields will be considered independently, but an attempt will be made to see how they overlap or enlighten one another.

I THE EFFECT OF AGE

1 General ability

Current work mainly confirms the previous observations that speed, sensory efficiency, flexibility and the power to assimilate new skills decrease with age, as reflected in performance on a number of mental tests. Recent observations, however, have concentrated much more than in the past on ascertaining the *rate* of decline in individual skills and mental functions rather than in measuring overall fall-off. Skills specifically involving reorganization of perceptual data decline first and most quickly, whereas those involving the utilization of information acquired in the past (especially verbal skills) decline more slowly. Cattell has characterized these two types of performance as fluid and crystallized intelligence and in a study by Horn and Cattell (1966) it was noted that whereas fluid intelligence begins to decline in the early twenties, crystallized intelligence may show gradual improvement throughout life till the age of 60 or over. Trembley and O'Connor (1966) found moreover that it is not only the speed of decline which differs with different skills. In 33,283 men varying in age from 10 to 60 years, they found that four different primary abilities (tonal memory, designs from memory, number memory and inductive reasoning) varied in the time at which each reached its peak in development. These authors further put forward the hypothesis that the traits which develop earliest show the longest plateau and the slowest decline.

The manner in which these differences are reflected in mental tests and in the different subtests of the Wechsler battery has been demonstrated in many publications (e.g. Reed and Reitan, 1963). It has been illustrated graphically in Figs. 11.1 and 11.2, which are taken from Bromley (1966). Most of the observations are based on cross-sectional samples from different age groups.

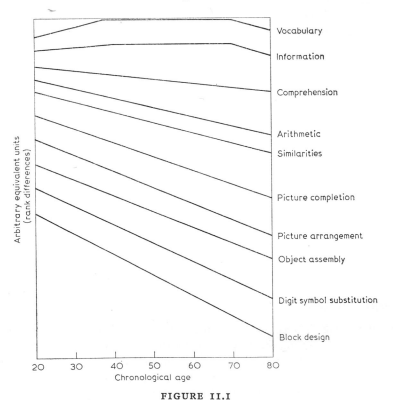

FIGURE 11.1

Showing the relative age-differences on the Wechsler-Bellevue subtests in arbitrary equivalent units (adapted from Bromley, 1966).

Only two longitudinal studies have been reported, and these only cover two to three years. Fisher and Piarce (1967) confirmed the picture of the W.A.I.S. subtest deteriorations in their survey, and suggest that two additional factors can be distinguished. These were ascertained from rating scales and are called by the authors Cognitive Accessibility (orientation, attention and consciousness) and Social Accessibility (rapport and affect). In the other investigation Eisdorfer

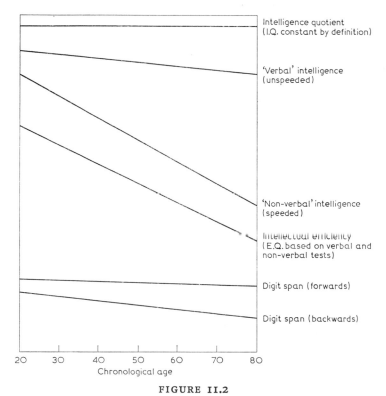

Intelligence quotient
(I.Q. constant by definition)

'Verbal' intelligence
(unspeeded)

'Non-verbal' intelligence
(speeded)

Intellectual efficiency
(E.Q. based on verbal and
non-verbal tests)

Digit span (forwards)

Digit span (backwards)

20   30   40   50   60   70   80
Chronological age

FIGURE II.2

Showing the age differences in Wechsler-Bellevue functions expressed in arbitrary equivalent units (adapted from Bromley, 1966).

(1963) re-tested 165 subjects from the Duke University Project after a three-year interval. He found little overall decline over this time-period and only minor changes in line with a general regression towards the mean.

This last paper raises the question of the effect of other factors (e.g. social and/or environmental) on both test performance and mental ability. Eisdorfer and Cohen (1961) found a number of differences between subjects in the Duke Project and those from Kansas which raise an additional question of cultural environment. The effect of life-long skills has also been raised. Williams (1960) compared the Vocabulary and Object Assembly performances of 100 people over the age of 60 and noticed that performance on the latter was often very much better than on the former (contrary to the general pattern) in subjects who had practised manual and perceptual skills throughout their working lives. Another important factor in the performance of older people is that of motivation. Granik and Friedman (1967) who gave 33 tests, including the W.A.I.S., to 77 subjects varying in age and education found motivation to effect performance. However, Ganzler (1964) found that although increased motivation effected the effort which older subjects put into mental tests (and did indeed improve their performance on a test of visual organization) it did not influence the performance of either older or younger people on the Shipley Abstraction test.

Conceptual thinking in the older age groups has not been studied in great detail. Sanders *et al.* (1966) asked a number of older subjects to solve Piaget-type spatial problems and found them less able to give causal explanations than younger subjects. It was not clear, however, why this should be so or what to infer from the observations. The findings may well be in line with Welford's (1958) observation that when asked to explain incompatible sentences older subjects tend to give inconsistent or associative responses rather than logically deductive ones. To presume that either of these findings indicate a tendency to child-like thinking in the elderly would, of course, be wrong although in both conditions subjects may be responding with the first available reaction instead of suppressing this and working through to a more acceptable one.

2 Speed and perception

One of the findings most generally agreed upon by all workers is that age slows up psycho-motor-responsiveness, but why and how it does so still remains a problem. Birren (1960) has reviewed a mass of experimental work on animals as well as men aimed at discovering the reasons for slowing up. Speed of conduction along nerves does not decrease with age after maturity, and although many reflex actions are reduced in older people, there are a variety of reasons why this might be so. Birren concludes 'at present it is unknown whether the slowing is a consequence of a single mechanism with a precise anatomical locus or whether it represents diffuse multi-faceted changes'.

Perceptual tasks and reaction time almost invariably show fall-off in speed with age. Rajalakshuri and Jeeves (1963) compared the time taken by subjects in each decade from 10 to 70 to identify an odd figure out of five shown to them tachistoscopically. Very young children and those over 70 both showed retardation. They argue that this could not be accounted for by the same mechanism in the young as in the old. Whereas in the young it can be regarded as being due to lack of experience, a different explanation is required for older subjects, and these authors tend towards the popular idea of reduced signal-noise ratio requiring more information before a response can be made. A similar explanation is assumed by Rabbitt (1964, 1965) to account for increased reaction time to multiple-choice tasks, and by Talland (1964) to account for the inability of older subjects to profit from warning signals on a simple reaction time task. In the last situation Talland goes so far as to suggest that the warning signal causes confusion by actually adding to the 'noise'. On the other hand, Botwinick and Thompson (1967) found that, with short, regular, preparatory signals, reaction time to auditory stimuli decreased quicker in older subjects than in younger ones. This difference was especially marked in females.

Reaction time is not only increased to simple perceptual tasks. On word association tests it is also longer than in younger subjects (Riegel and Birren, 1965). On perceptual tasks it is difficult to distinguish between time taken for subjects to appreciate signals and that taken by them to make a response, and Eisdorfer *et al.* (1963) argue that much of the apparent slowness may be due to response rather than perception time.

The tendency for older subjects to miss out sensory signals (an important factor in industrial employment) cannot be accounted for altogether by loss of sensory acuity. Set and expectancy are important factors in signal response, and if, as has already been suggested, the older person is less capable than the younger one of excluding irrelevant stimuli from his surrounding environment, it follows that he will have greater difficulty in retaining the necessary set towards signal detection. Birren (1964) has discussed the relationship between sensory acuity and behaviour at some length. He finds that the major conditions influencing response speed are (1) the complexity of the situation, (2) strength and familiarity of the stimulus, (3) the subject's response set and (4) the complexity of the response required. 'In other words, the quick response is made to a stimulus if the stimulus is expected, familiar, strong and unambiguous, and the response is simple' (p. 113).

3 Memory and learning

The fall-off in these spheres is one of the most marked features of ageing, and various hypotheses have been put forward to account for it. These are examined and classified by Crovitz (1966) as (1) cerebral alteration; (2) interference; (3) disuse; (4) motivation. Again, more can probably be learned about the mechanisms involved from studying the variables influencing performance than from listing the defects observed, and a good deal of work has been devoted to this end.

Pacing is a variable which has received some consideration. Canestreri (1963) allowed subjects to pace themselves on a paired-associate learning task, but although older subjects made less mistakes under these conditions than when pressed for speed, they still made more than younger ones. Thus even when the time factor is excluded the learning difficulty remains.

I.Q. is another variable which has received attention, and there is evidence that high I.Q. older subjects can learn lists of words just as well as low I.Q. younger ones (Eisdorfer and Service, 1967).

Context has long been recognized as important and the effect of retro-active inhibition has been studied by Hulicka (1967) and Talland (1967). That older people are more subject than younger ones to the effect of retro-active inhibition is a fairly constant finding; various models have been put forward to explain the memory difficulties of older people (Arenberg, 1967).

That the manner in which events are retained is different in the old from in the young has also been recognized (Gomulicki, 1953) and this has led to some interesting work on the study of *learning strategies* in the different age groups. The use of mediators on association learning tasks can be extremely helpful to older people who appear to employ them spontaneously rather less than the young (Hulicka and Grossman, 1967). The use of movement (Chown *et al.*, 1967) and verbalization (Crovitz, 1966) in the learning situation can both be helpful and may be on a par with the use of cross-modal association techniques in the teaching of subnormals. These findings point to the fact that cross-modal associations can still be built up in older people as in younger ones, and so detracts from the suggestion that the learning difficulties experienced by older people are based on the scarcity of available neural mechanisms. Why older people do not attempt to use these mediators spontaneously has not yet been considered.

Little systematic attention has been paid to the relative ease with which events in the different modalities can be remembered in the different age groups, or to the fact that different aspects of memory function are affected differently. It has long been recognized that the immediate memory span for digits repeated forwards shows little change with age, whereas that for digits repeated backwards does. It has also been demonstrated that the ability to repeat pairs of digits presented dichotically (Caird, 1966) falls off considerably with age. This is probably due to the interference of the primary perception caused by the tasks involved. It has also been shown that the performance of older subjects on tests involving the immediate reproduction of visual material or the learning of spatial relationships (Williams, 1968) is affected by age and shows much the same decrements as those due to brain damage. This latter point will be taken up more fully in the next section, but is in line with the observation that the manipulation of visual data begins to fall off sooner than that of verbal material.

4 Personality

Controlled studies by psychologists of the personality changes which occur with ageing in the individual are a rarity. The impression gained from words and biographies is that people stabilize rather than change. This is supported in an interesting study by Lowell-Kelly (1962), who was able to re-test 278 married couples 20 years after they had first been seen at college. The subjects, who had been volunteers in a large-scale survey and had been given a number of rating scales and personality inventories, showed remarkable consistency (45%-48%) on both values and vocational interests. Their consistency on self-ratings was lower (31%), but on attitudes was very low indeed (8%). A similar consistency of personality traits was found by Hardyk (1964) on the M.M.P.I. after a much shorter time-interval. Where changes of attitude occur, these may be due to general physical health (Ludwig and Eichhorn, 1967) and social involvement (Bell, 1967).

Changes in attitude to specific topics have been studied by Friedman and Granick (1963), who investigated the attitude towards the expression of anger by asking subjects in various age groups to rate themselves on the Clyde Mood Scale and then to rate the permissibility of various forms of aggressive behaviour. Their findings may have reflected the social and cultural backgrounds of the places and time in which the individuals were brought up rather than age changes,

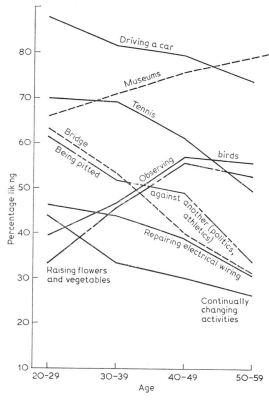

FIGURE 11.3

Changes with age in various interests as measured by the Strong Test (Pressey and Kuhlen, 1957).

and are, therefore, difficult to evaluate. Sex differences have, however, been noted in respect to authoritarianism by Neugarten and Gutman (1958). In youth and middle age the man is generally regarded as taking the dominant role, whereas in the older age groups they are regarded as being more submissive and less authoritarian than the woman.

Changes in interests have been reported by Pressey and Kuhlen (1957). As might be expected, the sedentary and intellectual interests show an increase with age in contrast to the active ones.

M

In summarizing this section, the main conclusions seem to be that whereas the tendency to take in new material or to respond quickly to external stimuli decreases with age, these tendencies are not due to loss of power or ability but rather to an increasing tendency on the part of the individual to utilize strategies that have been built up in the past, and a reluctance to replace these by new views or methods. The individual solidifies and stabilizes but in doing so may actually cut himself off from his environment. The hypothesis of altered signal/ noise ratio may be just another way of saying the same thing.

II CLINICAL PROBLEMS IN OLD AGE

The problems of ageing in the clinical field are very different from those in the general population. Geriatric patients are subject to illnesses rarely seen in younger people and respond to the same illnesses that affect younger people in a very different manner. The psychologist's main role in geriatric medicine is two-fold: (1) in helping to distinguish one illness from another (diagnosis) and (2) in helping to devise or discover means by which the older patients can overcome or compensate for their disabilities. In this chapter only the first of these roles will be discussed.

The most common illnesses of geriatric patients in which psychological assessment is required are as follows:

Organic
  Conditions of physical inadequacy (respiratory or cardiac failure, avitaminosis, anaemia)
  Senile psychosis
  Arteriosclerosis
  Brain damage due to strokes

Psychogenic (functional)
  Depression
  Paraphrenia

The psychological effects of all illness or malaise in older people often appear similar at first glance. Confusion and disorientation occur in severe depression just as in physical illnesses. A careful study of the qualitative aspects of performance, can however, often clarify the underlying cause.

1 Changes due to brain damage compared with those due to ageing

It is a common belief that the fall-off in mental performance due to brain damage and that due to ageing are similar. Thus generalized cerebral disorder in young subjects certainly often results in (1) psycho-motor slowing up; (2) defects of memory and learning, particularly retention; (3) poor performance on perceptual and constructive tasks. Even the difference between performance on the Hold-Don't Hold sub-tests of the W.A.I.S. battery shows the same discrepancy in brain-damaged subjects under 40 years as is shown by normal old people over 70 (Inglis, 1958; Reed and Reitan, 1963). Defects in visuo-motor performance and especially in the retention of perceptual material (Bender-Gestalt, Rey-Davis, Designs from Memory), are particularly evident in both young brain-damaged subjects and normal older people. Thus an estimation of brain damage (or organic deterioration) in younger people can often usefully be based on the degree to which their test performance simulates that shown by older subjects.

In older people, however, the situation is very different. In the first place, as has already been pointed out, older subjects can show all the signs of brain damage seen in younger ones without being abnormally incapacitated. In the second place, there is little connection, as has been frequently shown, between the degree of mental incapacity shown by older subjects and macroscopically verified cerebral lesions. *Hence the estimation of intellectual deterioration in geriatric patients is of little practical value in either diagnosis or prognosis and can on no account be used as an estimation of cerebral degeneration* (Post, 1965).

The effects of ageing may even be seen independently of brain damage in elderly people. Fitzhugh *et al.* (1964) showed that subjects with long-standing brain damage showed similar effects of ageing to normal people, but noted that the loss of abstraction was greatest in those who had suffered damage youngest. Hallenbech (1964) studied the performance of brain-damaged older subjects on the usual battery of mental tests and found that age changes were more consistent than those of brain damage. These changes extended even to performance on the Bender-Gestalt and to after-effects of Archimedes spiral.

III THE MEASUREMENT OF ABILITY IN OLDER SUBJECTS

Although the estimation of intellectual deterioration in geriatric patients is of doubtful value, the estimation of level of functioning is often of immense importance from the point of view of present management. Thus, if the general ability to perform mental and physical tasks falls below a critical level, life expectation in the elderly is extremely poor. Cosin *et al.* (1957) investigated with a variety of mental and physical tests 50 consecutive admissions to the Oxford Geriatric Unit. The patients were divided into three groups depending on their test performance: (1) good, (2) moderate, (3) poor. Six months later a far greater proportion of the patients in group 3 were dead than in either of the other two groups, even though at the same time of admission they had not appeared to be physically ill. Jarvik and Falek (1963) also found, on a five-year follow-up of old people, that there was a positive relationship between survival and stability of scores on the W.A.I.S. Vocabulary, Digit Symbol and Similarities tests, while Klonoff and Kennedy (1966) found a significant relationship between general health and test performance in hospitalized patients.

No less important than the assessment of functional level in the elderly is the measurement of slight degrees of intellectual change. This problem becomes particularly important in research aimed at estimating the effectiveness or dangers of specific methods of treatment – e.g. thalomolysis for Parkinsonism, ECT for depression.

The difficulties here are immense and stem principally from the wide range of base lines from which different individuals may start. The slight changes of ability shown by a person with an original I.Q. of 150 are very different from those shown by one of I.Q. 70, and no measuring scale which is sensitive enough to reflect the former would be certain to show up the latter. It is probably for this reason that rating scales are often more effective in this field than are cognitive tests. Two research projects have demonstrated this quite clearly.

In a survey into the possible intellectual fall-off in older people following anaesthesia Simpson *et al.* (1961) applied both mental tests and rating scales to all patients over 65 years old who entered the United Oxford Hospitals for surgical procedures during the year 1959. The rating scales covered daily activity, help required, outside activity, etc. Mental tests were also given to measure reasoning (Matrices) verbal learning (Wechsler Memory Scale) and manual dexterity. Whereas no changes were found in any spheres which could be related to anaesthesia, the rating scales showed marked differences related to symptom alleviation, but the mental tests showed little variation. A similar result was found by Paolino *et al.* (1966), who were also investigating post-operative changes in the elderly. Again no differences were found in the usual mental tests, but slight changes were found in tests of manual dexterity and speed (finger-tapping). Riklan and Levita (1966) used a number of standard psychometric tests to assess the effect of subcortical interference (thalomolysis) for the relief of Parkinsonism. The pre-operative test performances showed some abnormalities of personality and cognitive ability correlated with severity rather than duration of symptoms. However, there was little change seen in the six months post-operative follow-up of these patients although a number of typical 'organic signs' were sometimes seen in the early post-operative stages. It was noted that these signs were more intense and cleared up more slowly in the older subjects than in the younger ones.

A similar difference between rateable behaviour changes and psychometric stability was noted by Cosin *et al.* (1958) when assessing the variability of behaviour in a group of grossly confused geriatric patients who were subjected to a variety of different social and occupational stimuli. Performance on a group of mental tests showed little variation no matter how the patients were treated, but degrees of meaningful activity and conversation (measured on rating scales) closely paralleled the degree of stimulation the patients received.

Since measurements of overall ability and measurements of change are of importance in geriatric patients, and since the psychometric procedures currently used in younger subjects are unsuitable for this task, the question remains how are the measurements to be made? Are there any standardized tests or rating scales of value in this sphere? Are there any cut-off points below which an old person's mental ability can be regarded as definitely abnormal for his age? It will be clear from the foregoing that only tests standardized on geriatric people themselves will be of any real value, and of these the three most useful seem to be:

(1) *The Stockton Geriatric Rating Scale* (Meer and Baker, 1966). This consists of 33 items which factor analysis has shown to cover four factors – (1) physical disability, (2) apathy, (3) communication, and (4) social behaviour.

(2) *The Tooting Bec Questionnaire* (Doust *et al.*, 1953). This consists of 18 questions covering orientation for person, place and time, general information (past and present) and the ability to retain an address for a limited and controlled time period. Scores indicating mild, moderate and severe dementia are provided by Cosin *et al.* (1957).

(3) *The Measurement of Mental Performance in Older People* (Williams, 1961). This contains two parallel scales of tests using material from the Wechsler Bellevue, Wechsler Memory Scale, and Ravens Matrices, as well as tests of delayed recall and manual dexterity. Scores are based on the amount of assistance or the number of cues subjects have to be given in order to perform to a set criterion. Cut-off points indicating dementia have been calculated from the performance of over 200 subjects aged 65 and over.

The above scales and tests can profitably be used for assessing the level of mental functioning below which subjects should be regarded as 'at risk'. They can also be used for distinguishing the sick from the healthy, older person. They do not serve to distinguish one kind of illness from another or provide a differential diagnosis between organic and functional illnesses in the elderly.

IV DIFFERENTIAL DIAGNOSIS BETWEEN ORGANIC AND
FUNCTIONAL ILLNESSES IN THE ELDERLY

In his diagnostic work the psychologist is not so much concerned with establishing levels of function as described in the previous section, but is expected to elicit categories of behaviour that can be related to different illnesses. Thus, although a patient suffering from senile psychosis may be functioning at the same general level as one suffering from a depressive illness (Goldman and Plotnik, 1967), there will be characteristic differences in their behaviour which distinguish them. The psychologist usually hopes to be able to quantify these differences in order to measure them.

The tests in current psychometric use, however, have not proved very helpful, except in clearly distinct diagnostic groups. Thus, Roth found differences in the pattern of performance between elderly patients suffering from organic as opposed to psychotic illnesses (Roth and Hopkins, 1953; Roth, 1955). In the senile psychotics perception and retention of orientation and current events were very poor compared to word definition and digit repetition. The performance of a group of arteriosclerotic patients fell between the seniles and the psychotics (paraphrenics and depressives). Newcombe and Steinberg (1964) found that the most helpful test in differentiating organic from functional illnesses in old people was one of delayed recall. It is a consistent (but not fully appreciated) finding that, in the organic memory impairments, immediate memory, such as that tested on digit repetition, can be comparatively unimpaired, the main difficulty found being in recall after a time interval.

The findings quoted above have been made on groups of clear-cut cases on whom the clinical diagnosis was never in doubt. The psychologist in the course of his daily work would seldom be asked to assist in the diagnosis of such cases, those being referred to him usually showing far more equivocal signs of a not-so-easily quantifiable nature. Thus the diagnosis often has to be based on qualitative rather than quantitative aspects of behaviour and the test is used as a standard situation to elicit the signs rather than as a measuring device. The most consistent of these signs are summarized in Table 11.1 and are described in detail below.

Activity	Organic	Functional
Emotional expression	Labile, dependent on immediate stimulus.	Consistent with internal preoccupations; unchanging.
Psychomotor behaviour	R.T. brisk. Actions repetitive and stereotyped. Tend to be restless. Non-goal orientated.	R.T. slow. Little spontaneous activity. Goal orientated.
Verbalization	Vocabulary and sentence structure usually intact, but statements contradictory or meaningless.	Form intact, but content refers principally to pre-occupations.
Orientation	Poor for time and often also for place. Orientation for person best retained.	Usually intact, but may depend on pre-occupation.
Perception	Misperception evident in response to visual and verbal stimuli.	Respond to external stimuli appropriately, despite pseudo-hallucinations and delusions.

TABLE II.I

The main signs differentiating organic from functional disorders in various spheres of mental activity.

1 Emotional lability

The organic patient may be in floods of tears at one moment, e.g. when talking about a dead spouse, and yet can be roused to merry laughter a few seconds later if the subject of conversation is changed. It is also typical of an organic patient that in a test situation which is beyond his capacity he may appear severely disturbed and agitated (the catastrophic reaction) but if given one within his capacity will be full of smiles and optimism the next moment. The speed with which such changes of mood can be brought about and the degree to which they can be controlled by the manipulation of the environment are in great contrast to the state shown by the depressed older patients who remain sad, despondent and self-derogatory, however easy a task they are asked to perform.

2 Psycho-motor behaviour

The organic patient usually responds to all tests and questions with little delay in contrast to the depressed older patient who usually exhibits retardation. The organic patient does not, however, necessarily respond appropriately. He has difficulty in dressing himself, in finding his way around and in carrying out any truly purposeful task. This is not for lack of the necessary motor skills (as in apraxia) but appears to be based on poor goal-orientation. Thus the organic patient cannot remember whether he should be dressing or undressing himself and hence puts some clothes on at the same time as he is taking others off. His difficulty in finding his way around is due to the fact that he cannot remember where he is going, not to the fact that he cannot find the way there.

3 Verbalization

The organic patient's responses to questions are usually given quickly but are typically relevant only to the immediate question and to no other aspects of a conversation or situation. Thus they often demonstrate gross inconsistencies which the patient, if pushed, will rationalize in a glib manner. The following may serve as an illustration:

> How old are you? – Forty-eight.
> Are you married? – Yes, I'm a grandmother.
> How old are your grandchildren? – The oldest is fifty.
> How can you only be forty-eight if your oldest grandchild is fifty – Well, he is married too.

In contrast to this, the patient suffering from a depressive illness tends to answer questions slowly, but the content of his speech, even if abnormal, will centre unshakeably around his pre-occupations or delusions.

4 Orientation

The organic patient is distracted from a task by any external stimulus and is often more inclined to concentrate on minute details of the situation than on the whole. Thus, if asked to describe a picture, a senile patient will spend a long time describing minute details, apparently oblivious of its implications as a whole, and will frequently break off from an interview to wander around the room or building. If asked to explain his actions, inconsistency is again the keynote of the responses. Thus a female patient may walk out of the interview room and if asked where she is going will say it is to prepare dinner for her husband. If asked again on arrival at the end of the corridor, she may say it is to find her hat and coat, as she is going for a walk. If asked again when she reaches the front door, she may say that she has come to meet an expected visitor.

In contrast to the behaviour described above the depressed or paranoid patient is likely to be far more consistent in his behaviour and to rationalize actions by referring to his own constant preoccupations.

5 Perception

Whereas the depressed old lady usually knows very well what is going on around her, even if she is slow to respond to it, the senile patient often appears to mis-identify visual and verbal stimuli. If asked to name objects she will show no difficulty in word-finding but will name something perceptually similar. Thus a picture of a windmill might be called a pepper-pot, a drum is called a powder puff. This is in contrast to the patient with a focal lesion in the speech area (dysphasia) who can demonstrate clearly that she knows the nature and functions of an object even when she cannot find its name ('It's a thing that goes round and round').

The comprehension of words is often grossly defective in the senile patient, but in view of the patient's own fluent verbalization this sometimes goes un-noticed. If patients are asked to match one of four words with the picture it names, the senile patient will often be unable to comply with the instructions at all (Rochford and Williams, 1964). He may point to each word, read each word correctly, or attempt to put pictures and words into a single pile. The depressed patient, on the other hand, may be very slow and reluctant to perform such tasks, but will usually perform both naming and comprehension tasks correctly. The shorter a command, the better a senile patient understands it, but much depends on orientation at the moment. Lengthy instructions may simply allow the patient's attention to wander.

V DIFFERENCES BETWEEN FOCAL AND GENERALIZED CEREBRAL LESIONS IN THE ELDERLY

A problem often presented by older subjects is that of distinguishing between the mental effects of focal as opposed to generalized cerebral lesions. Since the former can sometimes be treated surgically and may carry a better prognosis than the latter, the distinction can be of great importance.

Since the effects of generalized cerebral lesions usually consist in a summation or mixture of focal signs the distinction is not easy, but again qualitative aspects of behaviour may be usefully differentiated (see Table 11.2). These can be seen in the following spheres:

1 Disorders of memory

Inability to remember or recognize stimuli which have been presented just a few seconds before is characteristic of patients with focal lesions affecting the limbic system, as also of those with generalized cerebral derangement or atrophy. All these patients may be able to name or describe pictures adequately, and yet, as soon as the picture is removed, will deny having been shown anything at all. If shown a selection from which to pick out that seen before, it is typical of such patients to claim to have seen everything which they can recognize easily (e.g. mis-recognize pictures of familiar objects).

Despite this lack of conscious recall, patients can often be taught simple motor habits, e.g. mazes (Williams, 1956a, b), and, as already mentioned immediate reproduction of digits or sentences may be intact.

In a patient with a focal as opposed to a generalized lesion, the retention disorder mentioned above usually appears as a fairly isolated symptom, or associated only with disorders of mood and insight. Speech, visual perception and motor skills remain intact. In the patient with generalized lesions there are usually a number of other recognizable disorders as well (see Table 11.2).

2 Disorders of language

Patients with focal cerebral lesions of the dominant hemisphere usually demonstrate some defects of language, typically inability to name objects (Nominal Dysphasia) or to find rare words as required. The difficulty may extend to the formation of sentences (Dysgrammaticality) and to reading and writing (Dyslexia and Dysgraphia). In these patients comprehension is usually better retained than expression, and there is a considerable reduction of output varying from slow, painstaking searching for words (or perseveration of single stock phrases) to complete mutism. The patients can usually remember what they were asked to do or say and a typical remark, when shown an object for a second or third time is 'That's the one I can never name'.

Patients with generalized lesions and especially those suffering from senile dementia, may also show many abnormalities of speech, but their expression is characterized by an over-abundance of output rather than a diminution of it; by incongruity of word sequences rather than ungrammaticality (jargon) and evidence of misperception of objects rather than difficulty in naming those they perceive correctly. Mistakes are unrelated to frequency of the word sought (as in dysphasics), and, indeed, if an object can be easily identified it can usually be named (Rochford and Williams, 1964). The ability to read and write single

M*

	Focal	*General*

Disorders of Memory (eliciting tests and situations: Benton's Designs from Memory Test, Wechsler's Memory Scale, Williams' Memory Scale).

	Focal	*General*
Abilities lost	Retention (especially of recent events) and learning in all sensory modalities.	Retention and learning, speech, perception, and reasoning.
Abilities retained	Immediate memory span, speech, logical reasoning and visual perception.	Immediate memory span.
Orientation	Poor for time and place.	Poor for time and place.
Insight	Often quite good.	Usually poor.
Mood	Usually euphoric.	Agitated, perplexed, confused.
Response to cues	Usually good, tendency to confabulate if very severe.	Confabulation and distraction.

Disorders of Language (eliciting tests and situations: Rochford and Williams' Scale for measurement of Dysphasia, Eisenson's Dysphasia Test).

	Focal	*General*
Abilities lost	Expression and naming worse than comprehension. Reading aloud worse than recognition of written words. Errors indicate correct recognition of objects.	Comprehension as bad or worse than expression. Recognition of written words worse than reading aloud. Errors indicate misrecognition of objects.
bilities retained	Memory, reasoning and visual perception.	None completely retained.
Orientation	Good.	Poor.
Insight	Good.	Usually poor.
Mood	Distressed by failure to find right words.	Appear perfectly satisfied by own performance.
Response to cues	Assisted by any semantic or mechanical lead-in.	Distracted by all cues.
Perseveration	Some words repeated in identical form despite S's awareness of their irrelevance. Ex. chair = 'Chair', Book = 'Chair – No! – Chair'.	Portions of words or phrases often carried over from one sentence to another with elaboration or correction. Ex. chair = 'A sitting on machine'. Book = 'A sitting on reading machine'.

	Focal	*General*

Disorders of Perception (eliciting tests and situations: Bender-Gestalt, Block Construction, Picture Naming, Picture-word Matching, Walking around Ward!).

	Focal	*General*
Abilities lost	Unable to appreciate whole or relationship between its parts although individual parts recognized.	Whole object misidentified. Parts regarded as adequate wholes.
Abilities retained	Speech, memory, logical reasoning.	All lost to some degree.
Orientation	Spatial orientation poor. Orientation for time and person usually retained.	All poor.
Insight	S often perplexed and worried; feels 'something is wrong', but may attribute his difficulties to 'madness' or 'poor memory'.	Little insight, S usually satisfied with poor performance.
Mood	Perplexed and distressed when disorder elicited.	Undisturbed by errors, but agitated if lost in ward.
Response to cues	May be helped by verbal directions, and can often learn to orientate themselves using verbal cues.	Distracted and confused by cues.

Disorders of Motor Skills (eliciting situations: dressing, tying a bow, lighting cigarette or candle, placing pegs in board).

	Focal	*General*
Abilities lost	Complicated sequencing of acts (apraxia).	Goal towards which act is directed.
Abilities retained	All others.	Individual finger skills usually good.
Orientation	Good.	Poor.
Insight	Good.	Poor.
Mood	Agitated by failure.	Agitated when really confused – i.e. if clothes are on back to front.
Response to cues	Little improvement unless complexity of situation is reduced. Verbal directions do not assist.	Improvement if continually reminded of goal.

TABLE II.2

The main signs differentiating focal from generalized cerebral lesions in various spheres of mental activity.

words is often better retained than the ability to give written words an accepted meaning, and there is little evidence that past stimuli or mistakes are remembered.

3 Disorders of perception

Patients with focal lesions in the parietal lobes exhibit many defects of visual perception, especially right-left disorientation, difficulty in seeing two or three objects presented simultaneously (simultanagnosia), difficulty in distinguishing figure from ground (Critchley, 1953). These troubles lead to difficulty in finding their way around in familiar surroundings, difficulty with constructional tasks and often to difficulties in recognizing familiar people or places.

Patients with more generalized lesions may also exhibit any or all of these defects, but in addition they usually show loss of goal-orientation – i.e. they forget what they are looking for. Recognition is influenced by sets and expectancies built up either by preoccupations or by other stimuli in the immediate present. Thus, these patients are grossly distractible. Disorders of verbal comprehension usually run parallel with the visual ones. Each single stimulus in a verbal sequence or part of the visual field is interpreted singly; there is no summation of sequences or rejection of irrelevant material.

4 Disorders of motor skill

Patients with focal lesions of the parietal lobe often exhibit loss of complex skills (apraxia). They cannot carry out familiar sequential acts like tying bows, lighting cigarettes, dressing, etc., although they know perfectly well what they want to do and can recognize the completed act as correct. Patients with generalized lesions often also fail to execute complex skills, but usually do so because they lose track of what they started doing rather than because they cannot do it. Thus, if reminded continually of the goal for which they are aiming, their performance may become adequate. Fine manual skills like tying bows and lighting cigarettes are seldom impaired although the cigarette once lit may well be used two minutes later as if it were a comb or a pencil.

VI CONCLUSION

In this chapter an attempt has been made to clarify some of the problems associated with the psychological assessment of older subjects and to distinguish the changes due to ageing from those due to diseases of various kinds. Because the differentiations are at present based primarily on qualitative aspects of behaviour and are, therefore, difficult to measure in quantitative terms, they might be criticized by some as unscientific. What is the psychologist doing during his examination that a medically trained clinician could not do just as well? The answer is that the psychologist is controlling the situations by which the signs are elicited. He is measuring the conditions in which they vary, and in this way he hopes one day to be able to throw some light on the mechanisms involved in particular mental skills and their disruption. The clinical psychologist is in fact doing very much the same thing as the experimental psychologist studying the effect of ageing on 'normal' people, but the clinical psychologist is working with different tools on different material. This does not mean to say that the two cannot work happily and profitably together: indeed, unless they do so they are both liable to miss much.

REFERENCES

ARENBERG, D. (1967) Age differences in retroaction. *J. Gerontol.*, **22**, 88-91.

BELL, T. (1967) Social involvement and feeling old. *J. Gerontol.*, **22**, 17-22.

BIRREN, J. E. (1960) Psychological aspects of ageing. *Am. Rev. Psychol.*, **2**, 161-198.

BIRREN, J. E. (1964) *The Psychology of Ageing*. New Jersey: Prentice Hall.

BOTWINICK, J. and THOMPSON, L. W. (1967) Practice of speeded responses. *J. Gerontol.*, **22**, 72-76.

BROMLEY, D. B. (1966) *The Psychology of Human Ageing*. Harmondsworth: Penguin Books Ltd.

CAIRD, W. K. (1966) Age and short-term memory. *J. Gerontol.*, **21**, 295-299.

CANASTRERI, R. E. (1963) Paced and self-paced learning and age. *J. Gerontol.*, **18**, 165-168.

CHOWN, S., BELBIN, E. and DOWNS, S. (1967) Paired associate learning. *J. Gerontol.*, **22**, 212-219.

COSIN, L. Z., MORT, M., POST, F., WESTROPP, C. and WILLIAMS, M. (1957) 50 cases of persistent senile confusion. *Int. J. Soc. Psychiat.*, **3**, 195-202.

COSIN, L. Z., MORT, M., POST, F., WESTROPP, C. and WILLIAMS, M. (1958) Experimental treatment of senile confusion. *Int. J. Soc. Psychiat.*, **4**, 24-42.

CRITCHLEY, MCD. (1953) *The Parietal Lobes*. London: Arnold.

CROVITZ, E. (1966) Ageing and visual discrimination learning. *J. Gerontol.*, **21**, 236-238.

DOUST, J. W. L., SCHNEIDER, R. A., TALLAND, G. A., WALSH, M. A. and. BARKER, G. B. (1953) Studies on the physiology of awareness. *J. nerv. ment. Dis.*, **117**, 383-398.

EISDORFER, C. (1963) W.A.I.S. performance of the aged: A retest evaluation. *J. Gerontol.*, **18**, 169-172.

EISDORFER, C., AXELROD, S. and WILKIE, F. L. (1963) Exposure time and serial learning in the aged. *J. Abn. Psychol.*, **67**, 594-600.

EISDORFER, C. and COHEN, L. D. (1961) W.A.I.S. Standardization for the aged. *J. Abn. Psychol.*, **62**, 520.

EISDORFER, C. and SERVICE, C. (1967) Intelligence and learning in the aged. *J. Gerontol.*, **22**, 158-161.

FISHER, J. and PIERCE, R. C. (1967) Assessment of intellectual functioning in the aged. *J. Gerontol.*, **22**, 166-173.

FITZHUGH, K. B., FITZHUGH, L. C. and REITAN, R. M. (1964) Changes of ability due to age in patients with cerebral dysfunction. *J. Gerontol.*, **19**, 132-134, 479-484.

FRIEDMAN, A. S. and GRANICK, S. (1963) Anger and aggression in old age. *J. Gerontol.*, **18**, 283-285.

GANZLER, H. (1964) Effects of motivation on age deficits. *J. Gerontol.*, **19**, 425-429.

GOLDMAN, J. and PLOTNIK, M. M. (1967) Diagnosis of brain dysfunction. *J. Gerontol.*, **22**, 14-16.

GOMULICKI, B. (1953) The development and present status of the trace theory of memory. *Brit. J. Psychol.*, Monog. Supp.

GRANICK, S. and FRIEDMAN, A. S. (1967) Age and psychometric test performance. *J. Gerontol.*, **22**, 191-195.

HALLENBECH, C. E. (1964) Evidence for a multiple process of mental deterioration. *J. Gerontol.*, **19**, 357-363.

HARDYK, C. D. (1964) Age differences in M.M.P.I. scores. *J. Gerontol.*, **19**, 78-82.

HORN, J. L. and CATTELL, R. B. (1966) Intellectual functioning in the elderly. *J. Gerontol.*, **21**, 210-220.

HULICKA, I. M. (1967) The effect of interference on recall. *J. Gerontol.*, **22**, 180-184.

HULICKA, I. M. and GROSSMAN, J. L. (1967) The effect of mediators in learning. *J. Gerontol.*, **22**, 46-51.

INGLIS, J. (1958) Cognitive deficit in elderly psychiatric patients. *Psychol. Bull.*, **55**, 197-214.

JARVIK, L. F. and FALEK, A. (1963) Intellectual stability and survival. *J. Gerontol.*, **18**, 173-176.

KLONOFF, H. and KENNEDY, M. (1966) The effect of hospitalization on performance. *J. Gerontol.*, **21**, 239-243.

LOWELL-KELLY, E. (1962) Consistency of the adult personality. *In* SARASON, E. G. (Ed.) *Contemporary Research in Personality*. New Jersey: Van Nostrand.

LUDWIG, E. G. and EICHHORN, R. L. (1967) Age and disillusionment. *J. Gerontol.*, **22**, 59-65.

MEER, B. and BAKER, J. A. (1966) The Stockton Geriatric Rating Scale. *J. Gerontol.*, **21**, 393-403.

NEUGARTEN, B. L. and GUTMANN, D. L. (1958) Age sex roles in middle age. *Psychol. Monog.*, **72**, No. 470.

NEWCOMBE, F. and STEINBERG, B. (1964) Learning and memory in older patients. *J. Gerontol.*, **19**, 490-493.

PAOLINO, A. F., WOLIN, L. R., SALERS, K. and SIMEONE, F. A. (1966) Surgery and the aged. *J. Gerontol.*, **21**, 271-277.

POST, F. (1965) *The Clinical Psychiatry of Later Life*. Oxford: Pergamon Press.

PRESSEY, S. L. and KUHLEN, R. G. (1957) Changes with age in various interests as measured by the Strong Test. *In Psychological Development Through The Life Span*. New York: Harper & Row.

RABBITT, P. (1964) Age and choice response. *J. Gerontol.*, **19**, 301-306, 307-312.

RABBITT, P. (1965) Age and irrelevent information. *J. Gerontol.*, **20**, 233-238.

RAJALAKSHURI, R. and JEEVES, M. A. (1963) Form perception and age. *J. Gerontol.*, **18**, 275-278.

REED, H. B. C. and REITAN, R. M. (1963) Normal ageing and brain damage. *J. Gerontol.*, **18**, 177-181, 271-274.

RIEGEL, K. F. and BIRREN, J. E. (1965) Age and differences in associative behaviour. *J. Gerontol.*, **20**, 125-130.

RIKLAN, M. and LEVITA, E. (1966) Effects of subcortical surgery on Parkinsonism. *J. Gerontol.*, **21**, 372-279.

ROCHFORD, G. and WILLIAMS, M. (1964) The Measurement of Language disorders. *Sp. Path. and Ther.*, **7**, 3-21.

ROTH, M. (1955) The natural history of mental disorder in the elderly. *J. ment. Sci.*, **101**, 281-301.

ROTH, M. and HOPKINS, B. (1953) Test performance of patients over 60. *J. ment. Sci.*, **99**, 439-450, 451-463.

SANDERS, S., LAUVENDEAU, M. and BERGERON, J. (1966) Ageing and the concept of space. *J. Gerontol.*, **21**, 281-286.

SIMPSON, B. R., WILLIAMS, M., SCOTT, J. F. and CRAMPTON-SMITH, A. (1961) Effects of Anaesthesia on old people. *Lancet*, *ii*, 887-893.

TALLAND, G. A. (1964) Age and warning effect on R.T. *J. Gerontol.*, **19**, 31-38.

TALLAND, G. A. (1967) Age and the immediate memory span. *The Gerontologist*, **7**, 4-9.

TREMBLEY, D. and O'CONNOR, J. (1966) Primary mental abilities in the elderly. *J. Gerontol.*, **21**, 9-12.

WELFORD, A. T. (1958) *Ageing and Human Skill.* London: Nuffield Foundation.

WILLIAMS, M. (1956a) Spatial Disorientation in senile dementia. *J. ment. Sci.*, **102**, 291-299.

WILLIAMS, M. (1956b) Studies of perception in senile dementia. *Brit. J. med. Psychol.*, **29**, 270-279.

WILLIAMS, M. (1960) The effect of past experience on mental test performance of the elderly. *Brit. J. med. Psychol.*, **33**, 215-219.

WILLIAMS, M. (1961) *The Measurement of Mental Performance in Older People.* London: Nuffield Foundation.

WILLIAMS, M. (1968) A scale for the measurement of memory. *Brit. J. soc. clin. Psychol.*, (in press).

PART THREE

Assessment of Children

12

Assessment of handicapped children:
some common factors

P. J. Mittler

The psychologist's concern is primarily with the individual child. There is no substitute for skilled observation and assessment; nothing easier than finding what one is looking for and missing the unexpected; nothing harder than keeping an open mind. Even where generalizations that are made about children suffering from one or other disability are valid, it cannot be too strongly emphasized that handicapped children have many problems in common. It is likely, moreover, that for every child who is typical in respect of a particular characteristic, there is another who is an exception to the rule.

Our limited knowledge of handicapped children is in some respects an advantage, since it helps us to assess each child as unique and to avoid stereotypes which are thought to be associated with one condition. While the professional psychologist's work will be on poor foundations if he is not aware of attempts to systematize knowledge about particular conditions, the aim of scientific precision may not be in harmony with his clinical experience. Systematization may easily be at the cost of flexibility; stereotypes may or may not be based on systematic observations, but at best they express no more than a probability, and may, indeed, be one illustration of the psychology of rumour.

I THE CONCEPT OF MULTIPLE HANDICAP

1 The dynamics of growth

Whatever the nature or extent of the handicap, it is bound to affect development to some extent. The psychologist has to try and assess how far a child's opportunities for growth and development have been affected by the main handicap and also by the secondary or associated handicaps, including environmental factors in the child's family, school and social experiences. This he can rarely do other than by a blend of clinical intuition and inspired guesswork. His knowledge of developmental psychology is the cornerstone of his work, because it helps him to understand something of the nature of psychological and physical growth, and the interrelationships between them. To describe the stages of growth is not necessarily to describe the process. We have to learn to think of growth as a dynamic process, but one which is by no means inevitable. Curiously enough, it is only comparatively recently that the notion of a 'developmental dynamic' has come to exert an influence in child psychology and in medicine. In the past, growth tended to be regarded as so inevitable, so strongly biologically programmed, that it was hardly a worthy object of scientific investigation. It was only necessary to collect norms on the amount of growth that could be expected at different ages, so that the individual child could be compared against the norm and appropriate measures taken to correct any deficiencies that came to light. A static view of growth lies at the back of many oversimplifications in the field of child development in general and of handicaps in particular (Hunt, 1961). While some element of generalization is both necessary and justifiable, the effect of a handicap is both complex and age-specific. Sensory defects, for example, begin to affect development from the first weeks of life, since they deprive the child of visual or auditory experiences at a time when the intact child is already able to make use of them, whereas the effect of a motor handicap such as a mild cerebral palsy may only become apparent relatively later. Similarly, a child who is mildly subnormal and also living in an unstimulating and socially adverse environment may only come to notice once he reaches school or is exposed to more formal learning situations; nevertheless, the development of his language and conceptual skills is likely to have been unduly retarded at a much earlier age as a result of poor environmental conditions, some of which might have been overcome or their effects modified by 'intervention' or compensatory education programmes (Jensen, 1967).

The assessment of a handicapped child is a complex process, because the psychologist has not only to interpret his test findings as such, but to relate them to what he can discover of the child's background and the opportunities available to him. The difficulty springs from the 'multifactorial' approach which is necessary. We are accustomed to think in terms of the single aetiology and are inclined to search for the single explanation of a handicap, even though we realize that such a search can only oversimplify. We salve our consciences by talking about 'primary' and 'secondary' factors, but the distinction between these is often arbitrary and difficult to draw in practice. There is a danger, moreover, in calling off the search when a plausible 'cause' appears to have been found. A case history may illustrate this danger.

Robert was referred to a child guidance clinic at the age of $10\frac{1}{2}$ as a virtual non-reader. He could barely read any words on standard reading tests, and had only a hazy notion of letters. He attended an excellent primary school, where every effort had been made to overcome his difficulties, both by the headmaster and by a teacher specially trained in remedial methods. His tested intelligence on both verbal and non-verbal tests was well within the average range, and extensive investigations revealed no evidence of perceptual, motor, drawing or visuo-spatial deficits or problems of auditory discrimination; there was no evidence of left-handedness in himself or in his family, and there was nothing in the history or in clinical examinations to suggest a neurological basis for his problem. It was therefore concluded by a child psychiatrist that his difficulties must be 'emotionally based' and stemmed partly from jealousy of an achieving sibling. Further remedial measures were begun, but little progress was noted, and his mother discontinued attendance. Her co-operation throughout had been lukewarm, and the psychiatric social worker felt that she was withholding information.

At the age of 12, Robert suddenly went into *status epilepticus*, after blowing up a balloon which induced a seizure as a result of hyperventilation. Emergency hospital treatment was successful, he made a good recovery and was able to resume his normal life, apparently none the worse for his almost fatal experience. As a result of this attack, he was given serial EEG and other investigations, which revealed that his left frontal lobe had virtually not grown since infancy. It was felt that the evidence of a cerebral agenesis was sufficient to account for his 'dyslexia', but the mother now told the neurologist that she herself was also virtually illiterate as a result of exactly the same kind of reading difficulty shown by Robert. The mother was of average intelligence and had tried, both during her childhood and since, to overcome her own 'dyslexia'.

In this case, three distinct aetiologies could be postulated: psychogenic, neurological and genetic. The last two are commonly recognized as causal factors in this condition (Vernon, 1957), though they are rarely found in combination, and there is room for argument about the first as a primary determinant of reading disorder on such a scale.

2 Classification and educational need

Classification is necessary but dangerous in clinical work. Its traditions stem from the biological sciences and more directly from medicine and constitute an invaluable source of historical reference. Its dangers lie in the overconfident applications of assumptions which derive from adult medicine. The emphasis on correct diagnosis is as important in the field of children's developmental disorders as in medicine, but the tradition can be constricting. Its influence can be seen most clearly in the administrative definitions of educational handicap which were first formulated in the 1944 Education Act, which distinguished between ten categories of handicap. Table 12.1 adapted from the Plowden Report (Central Advisory Council for Education, 1967), lists the officially recognized handicaps and the prevalence of each in the school population in 1966.

There is growing evidence of overlap between these categories, evidence which suggests that multiple handicap is the rule rather than the exception. We are accustomed to the notion of multiple handicap of the grosser disorders – the deaf-blind and the physically handicapped subnormal child are obvious examples – but most handicapped children, and many who do not fall within the present system of classification at all, can be regarded as suffering from more than one handicap. There is now a case for revising the official categories of handicap and replacing them by a wider category of 'learning disorder'. This would have the advantage of stressing the educational and developmental aspects of the problem, as distinct from primarily medical or administrative considerations, and would have the additional advantage of helping teachers to escape from what may be the excessive specialization which has resulted from training courses devoted primarily to one handicap. Handicapped children have educational needs which are not usually fundamentally different from those of other children – they need an environment in which their skills can be developed and in which their learning problems, from whatever cause, can be competently recognized and tackled.

	1966	
Categories	*No. of children*	*Prevalence per 10,000 of school population*
Blind	1,337	1·7
Partially sighted	2,326	3·0
Deaf	3,281	4·2
Partially hearing	3,296	4·2
Physically handicapped	11,616	14·8
Delicate	10,418	13·3
Maladjusted	8,548	10·9
Educationally sub-normal	55,514	70·9
Epileptic	877	1·1
With speech defect	224	0·3
Total	97,437	124·4

TABLE 12.1

Numbers of handicapped pupils receiving and awaiting special education (in special schools, classes, units, in hospitals and at home) and prevalence per 10,000 of the school population in England and Wales, 1966. (adapted from Table 17, *Children and their Primary Schools*, Plowden Report, 1967, 299).

Evidence for overlap between different classes of handicap comes from a variety of sources, but is probably best documented in the areas of slow-learning and maladjustment. Surveys by Chazan (1962, 1964; see also Chapter 18) suggest that more than a third of children classified as educationally subnormal in schools in South Wales have scores well within the maladjustment range on instruments such as the Bristol Social Adjustment Guides (Stott, 1966) – more than three times as many as in a normal control group. Similarly, a significant proportion of children deemed to be maladjusted show evidence of serious learning difficulties, in a setting of normal intelligence. More specifically, there is an extensive literature on the relationship between maladjustment and reading difficulties (Sampson, 1966). This is not, of course, to deny the importance of other factors in the aetiology of reading disabilities, nor is it suggested that maladjustment can be regarded as an established 'cause' of these difficulties. It is reasonably clear, however, that the two are frequently associated, and it follows from this that no clear administrative line can be drawn between them. The implications for the assessing psychologist in present circumstances are often difficult since he has to decide on an alleged entity called a 'primary disorder', and make appropriate recommendations.

More obvious cases of multiple handicap (or of frank misdiagnosis) can be seen in mentally subnormal children in whom sensory and perceptual deficits are still missed. Not all psychologists, for example, are trained to carry out audiological screening, though there are opportunities in London for them to receive instruction in this field; nevertheless, they can learn to be more vigilant in the course of observing children in test and play situations, and refer for specialist advice children who show suspicious signs of hearing impairment. Screening tests for this purpose are now widely available (see Chapter 14 of this volume). Surveys of subnormal children in hospitals (Kodman, 1963) have revealed a high percentage of children with significant degrees of previously undetected hearing impairment. Mistakes of this kind are rarer in cases of visual defect, though Williams (1966) has published a remarkable case history of a boy diagnosed as an imbecile and placed in a subnormality hospital, whose intellectual functioning rose to within normal limits once his blindness was recognized and he was placed in a school for blind children.

Multiple handicaps are extremely common in the cerebral palsies. Reynell (Chapter 15) discusses surveys of the distribution of intelligence and of educational attainments in C.P. populations, most of which agree that about half of all C.P. children have I.Q.s under 70, and that many of those with higher intellectual levels show learning problems of various degrees of severity. The problem of intellectual underfunctioning and educational retardation in these children has not been widely investigated, though there are a number of reports in the English literature giving an account of the problem and of some educational approaches that are being used in schools in Great Britain.

The concept of 'minimal brain damage' is being extensively explored at present, and is probably of considerable educational significance (Bax and McKeith, 1963; Gubbay *et al.*, 1965; Rutter *et al.*, 1969), though it is hard to define. There are children who, while not showing obvious or 'hard' neurological signs, appear to be poorly co-ordinated, have marked attentional deficits and other handicaps, and often a non-specific abnormal EEG. They merit much more interdisciplinary research.

II ASSESSMENT AIMS AND METHODS

Awareness of the complexity of children's handicaps should lead to the development of more precise and more penetrating methods of assessment. Our tools should match our understanding.

Few psychologists can be described as thoroughly satisfied with currently available tests and assessment techniques, or with the uses to which they have to be put. The traditional intelligence tests have certainly made an immeasurably significant contribution to assessment, and no doubt they will continue to play a central role in the psychologist's work with handicapped children. But there is increasing recognition that they should be only the first step in the assessment process, and that there is now a need to go beyond what the traditional test has to offer. This section will outline some tentative steps in this direction: profile analysis; study of cognitive processes; the assessment of personality and non-cognitive variables; observation of play and behaviour.

1 Profile analysis

Dissatisfaction with 'global' methods of assessment has led to attempts to develop tests which aim to give a reliable analysis of a child's cognitive assets and deficits. The aim is to break down 'intelligence' into at least some of its constituent processes and skills, so that remedial work can be based on a careful analysis of specific abilities and disabilities. The emphasis should be on the child's present level of functioning in the context of his immediate learning skills and difficulties.

Profile analysis is certainly attractive to psychologists who wish to use their assessment constructively to help in the planning and evaluation of a remedial programme. But great care is necessary if this approach is to be followed. In the first place, we are still far from confident that 'the constituent processes' of the construct labelled 'intelligence' can in fact be identified and isolated by present methods. Secondly, even if more penetrating profile analysis became possible, there still remains the formidable task of developing teaching methods which are closely linked with the processes that have been analysed.

Nevertheless, despite the difficulties inherent in these methods, there is undoubtedly an urgent need to develop assessment techniques which can be closely related to educational and other treatment. Intelligence tests have not, on the whole, yielded more than general statements about a child's educational needs. They were never intended as instruments which might provide specific guidance for the educator to help him plan a detailed teaching or remedial programme. Many psychologists have developed considerable skill in 'looking beyond the I.Q.', and in reporting on more detailed cognitive processes. The Wechsler scales, amongst others, lend themselves to this aim, but technical problems related to the low reliability of the subtests have in practice resulted in a tendency to confine further analysis of the 'global' I.Q. to statements about the significance of verbal-performance discrepancies (see Savage, Chapter 2).

Psychologists should not be the slaves of constructs inherited from the past. 'Intelligence', 'memory', 'perception' and the like may be convenient headings in our textbooks, but they need not necessarily be as relevant in applied work as they are in teaching students. It may be convenient to collect a group of studies under headings such as 'intelligence' or 'personality', but these terms should not be reified unduly. Many processes are involved, even though a general factor does explain a substantial proportion of the variance.

The 'profile' approach to assessment is the keynote of several chapters in the present volume, and is separately discussed by Tyson in Chapter 22. Its theoretical basis owes much to factorial studies, especially Thurstone's work on primary mental abilities (Thurstone, 1938; Meyers *et al.*, 1962), though it should be emphasized that the clinical use of more detailed assessment processes and profile analysis need not involve any theoretical assumptions about *g*. In other words, it is not necessary to adopt any particular theoretical position about the relationship between general and specific abilities. It is, however, necessary to demonstrate that the tests used are reliable and valid, and that they contribute significantly to assessment. The new British intelligence scale (see Chapter 24) is an example of a scale which is composed of a number of subtests, each of which measures a component of intelligence, even though most of the variance on this, as on most other tests available, is still accounted for by a general factor. There are examples of cognitive tests other than those primarily concerned with intelligence which have been developed in recent years. The Illinois Test of Psycholinguistic Abilities (McCarthy and Kirk, 1961; see Chapter 20) in the field of language, and the Frostig Tests (Frostig *et al.*, 1964) in the field of perception, both attempt to describe constituent processes. There are, however, serious problems of interpretation that arise from the reliability of the subtests and consequently from the even lower reliabilities of the differences between subtests (see Savage, Chapter 2). These problems are difficult to overcome, and care must always be taken to avoid attaching undue significance to subtest differences, since these are bound to be affected by the degree of reliability of the measures used (Phillips, 1961).

2 Cognitive processes

One of the disadvantages of standardized assessment procedures stems from the constraints imposed by scoring conventions. While it is obviously essential to adhere more or less rigidly to standardized procedures in administration and scoring, especially if the result is to be used as a basis of comparison between a particular child and a normative population, it is often instructive to inquire more closely into the underlying cognitive processes involved in both correct and incorrect solutions to a problem. Most standardized tests are not designed to afford such insight, and only allow for dichotomous right/wrong categories of scoring, or more rarely for a trichotomous system, as in the Wechsler scales, where scores of two, one or zero points may be awarded for the 'degree of correctness' of a response. Because of the need to classify responses in this way, the psychologist is debarred from inquiring more closely into the strategies of problem-solving that the child has used, since this kind of 'testing the limits' is not part of the orthodox testing procedure and might, in any case, provide practice or transfer effects that would affect later questions.

It is therefore relevant to ask whether use cannot be made of concepts and methods which originate in the psychological laboratory. A variety of approaches have already been used, and others may well suggest themselves. The most obvious example of techniques designed to throw light on the nature of the problem-solving strategies is Piaget's 'clinical' method; this is fully described by Woodward (Chapter 23), but it is relevant to refer to it here because Piaget's system can be modified even more widely than it already has been. Its advantage lies in allowing the psychologist to use any toys or activities in which the child is already showing some interest in order to investigate, say, to what extent a young handicapped child has acquired 'permanence of objects'. Knowledge of the developmental stages allows the psychologist to manipulate the situation in order to explore the child's concepts more freely by devising variations on the child's play as it develops. Much can be learned by simply watching the child's play, but such observations are better guided by some kind of theoretical framework. For example, a knowledge of Piaget's work on the development of play in relation to the growth of cognitive skills is highly relevant in assessing the degree of symbolic representation achieved by a non-verbal child. Such observations are not wholly unsystematic, though their limitations are obvious enough.

Other approaches to underlying cognitive processes can be seen in the work of more experimentally orientated psychologists, such as Bruner and his associates (Bruner *et al.*, 1966) at the Harvard Centre for Cognitive Studies, and O'Connor and Hermelin (1963) in Britain. Bruner has been responsible for a series of experimental variations on the Piagetian theme of conservation of quantity and has shown, at least by implication, that children's concepts of number can be examined by fairly precise means, which provide the experimenter with information on the hypotheses which the child appears to be using to reach a particular solution. O'Connor and Hermelin, although working along different lines, have devised numerous simple experiments, many involving little or no apparatus, which throw light on the way in which children form discriminations, and how these vary in different sensory modalities; they have also devised a series of 'visual analogues' to language operations, and demonstrated that even severely handicapped and withdrawn, unco-operative children are 'testable' under fairly formal experimental conditions (O'Connor and Hermelin, 1963, 1967).

A considerable amount of work along operant conditioning lines has also shown that severely disturbed children can respond to more complex equipment, provided appropriate controls and procedures are applied (Lovaas, 1966; Bijou and Baer, 1966). Operant techniques have until recently been employed for teaching rather than testing purposes, but it is likely that further work along these lines will include attempts to develop methods which will permit some degree of 'automated' testing to proceed without the presence of an examiner. This may be necessary for certain children who make little response to conventional testing or who may not tolerate an examiner at all; such methods may also be used to supplement more conventional assessments. It is possible to leave a child alone with a piece of 'learning apparatus' either in a clinic or even in his own home; his approaches to the machine, exploratory play, lever manipulations, etc., are automatically recorded, together with any reinforcements that he receives. The experimenter can return at the end of the day and, by examining the records, determine whether the child has exceeded chance criteria of learning (Baumeister, 1968; Malpass, 1968; see also Chapter 25 of this volume). Such methods also provide validational data for more orthodox assessment procedures: it is clearly useful to know what relationship exists between abilities and skills displayed in a formal test situation and those displayed by the child confronted only by a piece of apparatus. Needless to say, the final validity of both procedures can only be determined by relating them to learning processes as displayed in the classroom and in other more realistic settings.

3 Personality and non-cognitive variables

Concentration on cognitive skills and educational performance has led to an unfortunate neglect of personality assessment in handicapped children. No doubt theoretical and methodological problems related to the definition of and identification of personality variables are also partly responsible, as well as the obvious difficulty of assessing a developing system, while having only the most general notions either about levels of personality development that can be expected at any given age, or about the nature of the 'mature' personality (see Griffiths, Chapter 3).

It is difficult in practice to draw a clear distinction between cognitive and non-cognitive factors in a given child, and it is likely that the boundary between them is not as clear-cut as the textbooks sometimes suggest. The effective deployment of intellectual skills depends not only on genetic potential and appropriate environmental experiences, but on motivational forces both within the child and impinging on him in the form of parental encouragement and attitudes (see Section III 3). Moreover, experimental and physiological psychology now suggest that performance both on intelligence tests and on laboratory tests of learning is related to drive and arousal variables which can be linked to the introversion-extraversion dimension (Eysenck, 1967, 1968).

Wachs (1966) has reviewed some recent studies on personality assessment of handicapped populations, though these were more often on adults than on children. Both objective and projective methods have been applied to blind, deaf, speech-impaired and physically handicapped subjects. Some of the personality tests in current use can be applied to handicapped children, including fairly superficial check-list inventories which are filled in by teachers or parents. The Bristol Social Adjustment Guides (Stott, 1966) have been shown to be useful for severely subnormal children; Marshall (1967) in a study of 165 fourteen-year-old children in Junior Training centres found that children characterized as 'unforthcoming' or 'withdrawn' on the Bristol Guides made a poorer response to teaching than those receiving high ratings on other variables such as the 'hostile-aggressive' syndrome. Techniques designed to provide insight into the child's perception of the family – e.g. the Family Relations Test (Bene and Anthony,

1957) – can also be used for at least some groups of handicapped children; similarly, instruments such as the Junior Eysenck Personality Inventory (Eysenck, 1965) are relevant for some children, or for research purposes. Chazan (see Chapter 18 of this volume) reviews the main personality techniques used on emotionally disturbed and maladjusted children.

4 Observation of behaviour and play

Psychologists are now experimenting with methods designed to supplement information gained from standardized testing procedures and to use these in cases where severely handicapped or disturbed children cannot be assessed by conventional methods. It is now appreciated that 'observation' is not an excuse for inaction, and that much can be learned by systematic study of the child's behaviour. Psychologists have in the past been beset by the urge to 'do something' – to give children problems and puzzles to solve and generally to manipulate them into some form of activity. Wright (1960), reviewing observational studies over a 70-year period, reported that only 8% of the child-development literature came into the 'observation' category. Interference with the 'stream of behaviour' was regarded as controlled and scientific, whereas observation was thought by many to be inevitably 'soft'. He reviews some old and new techniques which lend themselves to objective recording and analysis, e.g. systematic diary recording, specimen descriptions, time sampling, event sampling, field unit analysis and trait rating.

The work of the animal ethologists has also given some impetus to child observation studies. Hutt and his associates (Hutt and Hutt, 1965) are reporting a series of studies in which both normal and different types of handicapped children are observed in rooms of different degrees of complexity. Their movements, gestures, exploratory behaviour and orientation to new objects and situations can be objectively recorded and analysed, and changes in behaviour consequent on increasing complexity of environment have been reported. Similarly, O'Connor and Hermelin (1967) have used basically simple measures of approach and avoidance behaviour to compare the response of autistic and subnormal children to different stimuli – visual, auditory and human. These and similar methods call for careful recording methods and may involve the development of some form of shorthand notation to describe different types of behaviour, but they have the advantage of leaving the child to his own devices and not requiring him to adjust to a relatively unfamiliar task or to orientate himself to apparatus. The psychologist can, of course, proceed from base-line observations of this kind towards making specific alterations in the environment, and then assess the relative changes which appear to follow each type of manipulation of the environment.

Another approach derives from informed observation of the play activities of young children. This can be done quite easily before, during or after the test situation itself; there is much to be said for a 'warm-up' session in which the child is allowed or encouraged to choose from a range of suitable toys. Most young children seem to play more naturally in the presence of their mothers rather than when left alone with a stranger, but this is not always the case. In the case of very young children, observations are usually guided by a Piagetian framework; 'permanence of objects' can be tested by observations on the child's behaviour in relation to toys which seem to have 'disappeared'; symbolic, representational play in which an object 'stands for' another object (e.g. a pencil for a moving train, etc.) is clearly a landmark of early intellectual development, since it provides the foundation for the more advanced symbolic skills of language and conceptualization. Imaginative and 'pretend' games are also relevant in this connection; similarly, constructional skills with bricks and building apparatus are sometimes more apparent in free play than in test situations; many psychologists have been embarrassed to note that a child who had 'failed' a brick building item such as the Binet 'bridge' or the Merrill-Palmer 'little pink tower' could later be observed incorporating these tasks into even more complex activities. Notions of seriation and order can also be observed by watching a child line up cars or dolls in order of size, and simple number concepts can be observed in operation when a child allots an equal number of pennies or sweets to two dolls. If the time is ripe, the psychologist can gently inveigle himself into the child's play to move a toy here, make a suggestion there, or adapt the child's play in order to try and elicit a modification of the free play for his own purposes.

III RELIABILITY AND VALIDITY

However skilful a psychologist may be in handling, understanding or testing a child, he needs to be aware of many possible factors that are likely to affect both the reliability and validity of the assessment process. This section will not be concerned with questions of reliability and validity in the more restricted sense of these terms but will discuss some features of psychological assessment in a clinical rather than a purely psychometric or research setting. The topics that will be briefly covered include: (1) lack of co-operation; (2) distractibility; (3) restricted experiences for development; and (4) prediction and I.Q. constancy.

1 Lack of co-operation

Lack of co-operation is sometimes all too obvious. A child may be quite unbiddable in a formal test situation: he may simply be uninterested in anything the psychologist has to offer, or rush wildly round the room, picking up a piece of test material only to hurl it across the room. More disconcertingly, he may during the course of such a stormy session come to rest just long enough to complete a performance test not requiring verbal instructions (such as a Form Board) and then resume his hyperkinetic activities. The significance of an isolated 'island of co-operation or skill' on a non-verbal test is difficult to estimate (Mittler, 1964).

Psychologists are thus understandably cautious in interpreting their findings on apparently unco-operative children, and are apt to emphasize such sources of reliability. On the other hand, it is sometimes surprising to find that a test administered under what appear to be appalling conditions may turn out to predict later performance under far better conditions with remarkable accuracy. Rutter *et al.* (1967) report a follow-up study of 63 psychotic children originally tested in a highly disturbed condition at the Maudsley Hospital and retested about seven years later in the adolescent period when they were much less disturbed; he found that the early I.Q. correlated around 0·6 with the final assessment. Similarly, Mittler *et al.* (1966) found that the early I.Q. predicted final outcome in another group of psychotic children rather more accurately than for a matched group of mentally subnormal children or for another group of disturbed children with only mild psychotic features.

Lack of co-operation is not always obvious, and the psychologist frequently suspects that a child is poorly motivated or just disinterested, though appearing superficially polite and attentive. Erratic performance often provides a clue, but it should not be assumed that this is in itself a sign of poor motivation or disturbance, since it may represent the child's characteristic approach strategy to an unfamiliar situation. Eysenck (1967) illustrated five different 'strategies' in five imaginary children on a five-item test. Although each child obtains a total of two correct responses, no two children achieve this total in the same way. Responses are symbolized as either right (R), wrong (W), not attempted (N) or abandoned (A); the following table illustrates the alternatives.

	1	*2*	*3*	*4*	*5*	*Total score*
Jones	R	R	N	N	N	2
Charles	W	R	W	R	N	2
Smith	R	A	A	R	A	2
Lucy	R	A	R	N	N	2
Mary	R	W	R	W	W	2

TABLE 12.2

Five-item intelligence test, administered to five children, all having a score of 2 (adapted from Eysenck, 1967).

R = Right answer.　　　W = Wrong answer.
A = abandoned item.　　N = Item not attempted.
(In most tests A and N cannot be distinguished.)

'Lack of co-operation' takes many forms, and is not always obvious. More than one assessment is usually desirable, if not always practicable; it is also useful to see the child in more than one setting, and to see him in the classroom if possible.

Some children react adversely to being seen in hospitals or clinics, though their confidence in the psychologist may improve on a second visit. Similarly, some children are at their best only if the mother is present, whereas in other cases a marked improvement in concentration seems to occur when psychologist and child are alone; here again, this may last for only a few minutes, and it is then helpful to bring the mother back. It will be obvious that there are no valid generalizations on the usefulness or otherwise of the mother in an assessment situation. Each child's functioning is different in different situations, and the application of general rules and principles is dangerous.

The skilful psychologist has somehow to steer a course between the Scylla of flexibility and the Charybdis of objectivity. He recognizes that it may take several visits to secure an adequate assessment, that observation of the child's behaviour and the quality and nature of his free play may be as valuable as a formal test result in some circumstances. It is often futile to hope to administer a full 'Binet' in the name of science, when the child lacks the motivation and the concentration to cope with the demands of a formal test. But there is much that can be achieved by observation, and by attempts to administer isolated items (e.g. the Merrill Palmer test (Stutsman, 1931) lends itself well to this purpose). Instruments such as the Vineland Social Maturity Scales (Doll, 1953) and the Progress Assessment Charts (Gunzburg, 1966) and, for the less handicapped, the Manchester Social Adaptation Scales (Lunzer, 1967) provide basic information on the child's skills and competence in specific areas and give a useful indication of his functioning in real life. It may be a counsel of perfection to argue that psychologists have much to gain by supplementing their observations of children in clinics and hospitals by reassessing them in school or in their own homes. But if repeated assessments over a short period are possible, the psychologist can try to validate his findings against the child's skills and functioning in other situations. It is also invaluable to share his findings with teachers and any other therapists who have frequent contact with the child, so that notes can be compared; observations of others including parents often provide the psychologist with leads for further investigations.

Although it is likely that pressure of time and absence of appropriate facilities may militate against a productive assessment process, it is apparent that a number of children present formidable problems because of their lack of interest and motivation in the test situation. This applies to a minority with severe autistic disturbances, and some other children who seem to lack even the simplest forms of exploratory drive and curiosity. These children appear to lack interest not only in the test apparatus, but in play with bricks and other materials. Some are destructive, but many appear to take no notice of anything that is put in front of them (Mittler, 1966). If this behaviour reflects a general lack of interest in exploratory and manipulative play and is not merely confined to the test situation, the outlook for general cognitive development may be poor, in view of the close relation between play and representational and symbolic skills (Piaget, 1951). Nevertheless, few children can be described as 'uninterested in everything' and a resourceful psychologist may be able to exploit such interests as the child does show, no matter how primitive, in order to explore or even manipulate the behaviour within the framework of the psychological examination (Woodward, 1963; Chapter 23 of this volume). To describe a child as untestable tells us more about the psychologist than the child.

2. Distractibility

Severely handicapped children are often described as untestable on account of distractibility: this is especially common in children with the hyperkinetic syndrome (Ounsted, 1955) who may show a characteristic pattern of 'perseveration with distractibility'. A child with this type of behaviour enters a room, fixes his attention on some object or fixture, 'plays' with it for a short while, then rushes from object to object, only to return again to the central object which has first captured his attention. This form of behaviour has been described as 'cyclical re-entrant play'. This is an extreme form of play abnormality, but milder varieties of stereotyped behaviour and perseveration are not uncommon. It has been suggested that stereotopies may be a function of the complexity of the environment. Hutt and his colleagues (Hutt and Hutt, 1965) have reported a series of experiments in which stereotopies found in autistic children increased as a direct function of the increasing complexity of the environment; children were placed in an empty room and their behaviour and movements objectively recorded; visual, auditory and, finally, human stimuli were gradually introduced and the effects on behaviour recorded. Similar experiments have been conducted on the effects of overcrowding and on drug effects. These and similar studies, so far applied in strictly controlled experimental situations, suggest that behavioural abnormalities may be a function of the nature of the environment in which the child is being seen; it is also apparent that the psychologist in a clinical situation can, within obvious limitations, try and introduce some modifications into the assessment setting, in order to test empirically whether a particular child appears to function better in some situations rather than others.

Similar implications are apparent in work by Brown (1966). In a series of studies, young subnormal children showed errors of attention and distractibility when placed in unfamiliar environments; these difficulties were less marked when they were assessed in more familiar surroundings. Experience with normal nursery-school children confirms that they may react unfavourably to being taken, not only by a comparative stranger but even by their own teacher, to less familiar surroundings. Brown described a tendency to gaze around the room, to stare fixedly at a person and to remain motionless for several minutes. In some respects this behaviour is comparable to the behaviour of normal infants under seven months removed to hospital for short periods, described by Schaffer (1958) as showing 'extreme preoccupation with their environment, characterized by constant scanning of surroundings, without apparently focusing on any particular feature, and letting eyes sweep over all objects without attending to any particular one'.

These considerations may be relevant in view of the experimental studies of Zeaman and House (1963) and Zeaman (1966), which emphasize the prominence of attention defects shown by subnormal children in discrimination learning experiments. The implications of these findings for the assessment of an individual child are that time may be needed to allow a child to become familiar with new materials or an unfamiliar environment. Very few attempts have been reported to overcome attention and motivation defects, though this is clearly an essential preliminary to psychological assessment, and to teaching or therapy of any kind.

3 Restricted experiences for development

A child may be highly motivated, co-operative and anxious to please but may still for reasons outside his control be at a disadvantage when being tested. In general terms, it might be appropriate to describe such disadvantages as related to restrictions in the child's experience before he enters the assessment situation. Tests standardized on normal children assume that a child has had adequate and appropriate stimulation and experiences to help him to develop mentally and physically. Such experiences may be lacking in the life of a handicapped child: his primary handicap may have restricted his opportunities for acquiring critical experiences, but associated or secondary handicaps are also relevant. Similarly, a handicapped child may have inadequate opportunities for social relationships, for normal play experiences and for appropriate language stimulation. Moreover, periods of hospitalization may not only have restricted his learning opportunities and perceptual experiences, but affected his social and emotional development to some degree. Finally, his home background may have been unfavourable, either due to severe material hardship, inadequate or inconsistent stimulation or because he himself has caused stress and anxiety in the home.

The psychologist cannot know about all the circumstances of a child's life, and can usually only make a guess about his opportunities for intellectual and psychological development. Even a well-documented dossier may not tell him very much about the quality of the child's day-to-day life. It is therefore dangerous to jump to hasty conclusions in trying to relate a child's behaviour in the test situation to one's knowledge of his past history. It is salutary to find a child who has suffered apparently appalling deprivations emerge resilient, inquiring and eager to learn, and, as far as one can tell, remarkably unscathed by experiences which would have distorted the development and personality of others in similar circumstances. The reactions of children subjected to severe physical and psychological hardships are too varied to be dismissed to the compartment labelled 'individual differences'. We are entirely ignorant why, for example, a subnormal child who has been abandoned by his parents, been in countless children's homes and rejected by foster home after foster home, who lacks many opportunities that most children take for granted, should nevertheless be able to leave school, find a job and remain a useful and healthy individual for the rest of his life.

N

These basic questions confronting the student of child development are no nearer solution now than they ever were. Such knowledge as we have enables us to make only the broadest generalizations about the likely effects of environment on behaviour, of parental practices on development. Even where firm causal connections have been established, as, say, in the general area of 'maternal deprivation', studies of large groups always reveal a substantial minority of individuals who behave exactly counter to expectations. Researchers have on the whole paid scant attention to them, and have rejoiced in the demonstration of significant relationships, secure in the knowledge that to demonstrate a 'trend' is sufficient, since no one expects all members of a group to behave in the same way. But a more firmly established 'science of individual differences' would enable us to look more closely and penetratingly at these deviant individuals. What, for example, are the characteristics of those lower working-class children who *are* school achievers (Jackson and Marsden, 1962); of 'deprived' children who are *not* psychologically damaged (Lewis, 1954); of severely subnormal children who show exceptional literary abilities (Hunt, 1968)? These cases are of interest not only in themselves but for what they teach us about the nature of the whole developmental process and the complexity of the variables influencing 'individual differences'.

There has for many years been a general awareness of the importance of 'environmental factors' and their effects on the development of both normal and handicapped children. But it is only comparatively recently that attempts have been made to specify with some degree of accuracy the precise nature of the forces at work. Both animal and human studies have described the effects on later behaviour of variations in the early experience of the young organism. The effects of handling, of exposure to controlled perceptual stimuli and also the effects of deprivation of certain experiences have been well documented (Hunt, 1961; Barnett, 1962; Stephenson *et al.*, 1967). In the case of children, the evidence is necessarily less experimental: the Iowa studies of the 1930s (Wellman and Pegram, 1944; Jones, 1954) were concerned with the effects on intellectual functioning of the provision of supplementary experiences, usually schooling, to children in institutions and orphanages. Despite serious methodological short-comings (McNemar, 1945), these studies have by no means been discredited. Larger groups have been studied in attempts to evaluate the relative contribution to development of home and school variables, and to specify the precise nature of the environmental variables involved. Recent studies are thus characterized by a more analytical approach in which concern for 'environment in general' is being replaced by an attempt to isolate specific factors, which can then, by factorial or other methods, be examined for broader patterns or clusters of factors.

The Manchester surveys reported by Wiseman (1964, 1966, 1967) may be considered as examples, though other large-scale studies have concerned themselves with similar problems and reached similar conclusions (e.g. Fraser, 1959; Douglas, 1964; Kellmer Pringle *et al.*, 1966). Wiseman studied a population of

10-year-olds from 44 primary schools in the Manchester area; intelligence and attainment tests were available on these children since the age of 7, together with a total of 52 environmental variables – 18 concerned with home and neighbourhood, 34 with the school buildings, equipment, teachers and 'atmosphere'. The findings indicated that younger children are relatively more affected by environmental variables than older ones; that the effects of adverse environmental factors are greatest on abler children, and that home and neighbourhood factors, particularly those concerned with the quality of care in the home, affect educational functioning even more than factors in the school itself. Despite the strong environmental emphasis of these findings, Wiseman draws attention to the strength of the genetic factor suggested by the close association between home and school variables, since 'home variables are affected by and affect the parents of the children, while school variables are those which affect children only' (Wiseman, 1966). The following variables were among those which showed the highest associations with school performance: cleanliness of the home, proportion of verminous children, inadequate material needs, provision of free meals, parental occupation. As far as the school variables were concerned there were strong associations between school performance and attendance, sociability and streaming.

Other studies have focused more sharply on the increasingly impressive evidence for the contribution of parental attitudes to educational progress. Douglas's longitudinal studies (1964, 1968) have suggested that children from middle-class homes where attitudes to the child's school are encouraging and positive, were more likely to be selected for 'A' streams at the age of 7, made better progress in their primary schools, and stood a better chance of selective education in 1957 than working-class children within the same ability range. Even more carefully documented evidence on parental attitudes comes from the National Survey conducted in connection with the Plowden Report, *Children and their Primary schools* (Central Advisory Council for Education, 1967). Table 12.3 adapted from the Plowden Report (see especially Peaker, appendix 4, volume 2) shows the percentage of the variation in performance on a test of reading comprehension which is attributable to parental attitudes, home circumstances, state of school and unexplained variables. Between school and within school calculations are reported separately. It will be seen that parental attitudes constitute the largest single source of variance.

There has also been a growing interest in the relationship between response to schooling and the nature of the child's linguistic environment in the home. This is not only a matter of how much language stimulation the child receives, but also of the effects on his cognitive skills of different types of linguistic code. Bernstein (1965) has postulated different linguistic codes ('restricted' and 'elaborated' in working- and middle-class homes and Lawton (1968) has provided some empirical confirmation of Bernstein's main thesis. (See also Ravenette, Chapter 19).

These studies are for the most part concerned with large populations of non-handicapped children and their findings cannot be extrapolated to populations of handicapped children without further study. Nevertheless, it is likely that a detailed examination of environmental factors will indicate at least an equally suggestive relationship. It is already clear, for example, that milder mental handicaps (corresponding to the category of mild subnormality, feeble-mindedness or educational subnormality) are concentrated in the lower socio-economic levels, and are particularly to be encountered in association with conditions of poverty, overcrowding, unemployment and chronic ill-health in a parent (Goldstein,

A. BETWEEN SCHOOLS						
	Top Juniors	*Lower Juniors*	*Infants*	*All boys*	*All girls*	*All pupils*
Parental attitudes	39	20	24	31	25	28
Home circumstances	17	25	16	14	25	20
School variables	12	22	20	17	17	17
Total	68	67	60	62	67	65

B. BETWEEN PUPILS WITHIN SCHOOLS						
	Top Juniors	*Lower Juniors*	*Infants*	*All boys*	*All girls*	*All pupils*
Parental attitudes	29	15	16	18	21	20
Home circumstances	7	9	9	7	11	9
School variables	22	15	14	19	15	17
Total	58	39	39	44	47	46

TABLE 12.3

Percentage variations in performance on a test of reading comprehension attributable to parental attitudes, home circumstances and state of school (adapted from Table 3, *Children and their Primary Schools*, 2, Plowden Report, 1967, Appendix 4, 208).

1964). Similarly, premature births, with which several handicaps are associated, but particularly cerebral palsy and some types of mental subnormality, occur more frequently in social classes IV and V (Drillien, 1964); it has been suggested that, as far as prematurity is concerned, the general health and physique of the mother are more important than the course of the pregnancy itself (Walker, 1966). Pasamanick and his associates have postulated the notion of a 'continuum of reproductive casualty' which is associated with later abnormalities ranging from the milder to the severer handicapping conditions (Pasamanick and Knobloch, 1961).

There is thus growing evidence from these and other studies of the strength of the environmental contribution to the already complex multiple handicaps discussed at the beginning of this chapter. Environmental factors have been discussed at some length, because it seems relevant to emphasize that they do not constitute an amorphous set of forces which are important but impossible to estimate in a single case. In assessing handicapped children, it is important to make some attempt to estimate the contribution of such factors as the nature of the opportunities to gain experiences, the kind of parental attitudes, not only to the child's handicaps, but to the provision of intellectual and social stimulation, and the type of linguistic environment in which he lives. In estimating the influence of these factors, there can be no necessary assumption of a causal connection between any one of these factors and any one aspect of the child's handicap. It is equally possible to attribute too much to an adverse environment or to assume that what appears on the surface to be 'a good home and loving parents' necessarily provides a favourable environment in all cases. Value judgements about what is a 'good' or a 'bad' home are obviously to be avoided, since it is not only difficult to arrive at a valid judgement of the home environment in which a handicapped child is living, but also difficult to justify the assumptions behind such judgements. A home can be overcrowded and poverty-stricken, but still emotionally warm: conversely, comfortably off parents may not necessarily provide an appropriate emotional atmosphere. These factors are extremely complex and difficult, if not impossible, to describe objectively and it is imperative to avoid hasty generalizations.

Mention should also be made of work by psychologists and sociologists who have attempted to relate the behaviour of the child to the organization and structure of the institution in which he lives. Tizard *et al.* (1966) have developed a rating scale to describe child-rearing practices in different types of institution – e.g. different types of children's home and hospital – and have shown how variations in child-care practices and organization between institutions exert a significant effect on children's independence and social skills. Psychologists have not, on the whole, concerned themselves professionally with the social psychology and organizational structure of the institutions in which they work, but recent interdisciplinary studies have shown that these play a significant role in the development and attitudes of children (Butterfield, 1968). Other studies report attempts to alter institutional practices; ward regimes have been modified with the aim of changing patients' behaviour patterns, and the notion of a 'prosthetic environment' has been canvassed by behavioural engineers. Ayllon and Azrin (1964) have reported a series of studies in which the behaviour of chronic schizophrenics has been modified by ward extinction and shaping procedures; nurses and therapists can be trained to work to consistent schedules of reinforcement in the alteration of traditional ward routines and practices. These approaches are likely to be more widely used in the future, and psychologists assessing a child for the first time can usefully consider the kind of rewards and punishment schedules to which he may have been exposed.

One task that awaits the psychologist, therefore, is to develop instruments that will help him to gather more systematic information about the environment in which the child lives. Relatively little work in this area is available, though there are some indications of the lines along which progress might be made. The surveys referred to above have pinpointed factors of special relevance and these, together with previously isolated variables, could form the basis of an instrument which could be used to gather systematic information – e.g. degree of over-crowding, whether parents read to the child, availability of play materials possibility of contact with other children, the extent to which the child is taken out of the house, etc. Tizard and Grad (1961) developed a questionnaire for assessing some of these factors in their comparison of homes which cared for a severely mentally handicapped child and those who sought institutional care, and a follow-up study of this sample (P.E.P., undated) provides further examples of questionnaires designed to elicit objective information. Parental attitudes to handicapped children have been investigated by Pitfield and Oppenheim (1964), who compared attitudes to child-rearing of mothers of mongol, psychotic and normal children, roughly matched for social class. Allowance for social class factors is essential, in the light of the substantial differences in child-rearing methods and attitudes demonstrated by the findings of the Nottingham surveys (Newson and Newson, 1963, 1968). These surveys provide useful background data against which handicapped populations may be compared.

4 Prediction and I.Q. constancy

Our discussion has so far concentrated on factors which may affect the reliability and validity of test findings both at the time of the test and as a result of lack of previous opportunity for the child to gain experiences necessary to his intellectual development. It remains to consider the more long-term problem of the predictive power of tests, which is now seen to be a very much more complex matter than was previously assumed. Although some element of prediction is both inevitable and necessary, the emphasis at present tends to be more on careful description of a child's present level of functioning than on prediction of his future performance.

Nevertheless, the evidence for the predictive accuracy of the better known, reliable and well-standardized tests is well known. A large group tested longitudinally will almost certainly show a considerable degree of 'I.Q. constancy'. For example, textbooks often state that in a test with a Standard Error of five points, only one child in twenty would obtain a retest score which differs by ten points or more either way from his original score. Similarly, constancy is often expressed in the form of correlations between two test administrations. But these are superficial approaches to a complex matter; much depends on the length of the interval between the tests (e.g. one week or one year), the type of test used and the nature and age of the population being tested. Figures based on group averages and correlations refer to the characteristics of populations as a whole and tend to mask as much as they reveal. More specifically, a number of longitudinal studies have focused on individual patterns of growth and shown that intellectual development does not proceed at a uniform rate in the individual, that many – especially those some distance from the mean – fluctuate considerably, sometimes in apparent association with considerable changes in their environment but often without obvious explanation (see Bloom, 1965, for a particularly useful discussion of I.Q. constancy).

The California longitudinal study by Honzik *et al.* (1948) shows how a correlation as high as 0·8 between tests over an interval of three years can leave room for much fluctuation. In their sample of 200 children tested repeatedly during their school years, 9% showed changes of 30 or more I.Q. points; 58% showed changes of more than 15 points, and only 10% fluctuated less than 10 points. Sontag *et al.* (1958) and Wiener (1963) reported that in the Fels study the 'I.Q. risers' were predominantly boys, premature children and those who were rated as independent, aggressive and showing initiative and competitiveness; while the 'I.Q. descenders' included a disproportionate number of girls. Similar sex differences are being reported by Douglas (1968) in his national sample of 5,000 children in Great Britain (see also Ravenette, Chapter 19). Changes as high as 50 points have been reported in several studies, for reasons that could not necessarily be easily inferred.

The implication of these and other longitudinal studies (summarized by Kagan, 1964) is that the psychologist cannot count on I.Q. constancy in the individual child, and that predictions based on tests alone are exceedingly hazardous. This applies to attempts to predict a future I.Q., but even more to the prediction of future levels of educational functioning. Correlations between intelligence and educational performance are not high enough for groups or for individuals either predictively or even concurrently (see Williams, Chapter 16). Woodrow's (1946) classical study on the relationship between tests of intelligence and of learning ability showed that one factor of 'learning ability' could not account for improvement on either motor or intellectual tasks, and that there was no significant relationship between I.Q. and gains on educational attainment tests. Tyler (1965) quotes studies which suggest that even on teaching machines there is no evidence that 'brighter' children learn faster or better than those of somewhat lower levels of ability. She stresses that the duller child is handicapped by being presented with problems above his developmental level and suggests in this context that 'slow developer' is a more appropriate term than 'slow-learner', since speed of learning is not the most important variable here.

IV COMMUNICATION OF FINDINGS

1 With colleagues

Even the best conducted test administered in ideal circumstances can be a waste of time and effort unless the findings are communicated in such a way that they can be understood and acted on by those who read the report. Much has been written on the 'psychological report', but it is doubtful whether its properties can be specified, since everything depends on the purposes of the report, to whom it is addressed and how much psychological knowledge they may be expected to possess. Moreover, the psychologist has to consider that his report will probably be read by others than those to whom it is addressed. Many psychologists therefore prefer to write a fairly brief report, giving an account of the child's level of co-operation and interest in the test situation, naming the tests used and any special factors likely to affect the reliability of the results, coming to some general conclusions or making specific recommendations and suggestions for his treatment or education. There is also a growing tendency to avoid quoting I.Q. figures, but to express the findings in terms of a range of scores within which the child's performance appears to lie.

Short reports have certain advantages and are obviously time saving to both writer and reader, but it may be felt that more detailed notes and information and possibly a more technical report should also be available to those that need it and for the psychologist's own records. Now that psychologists are using a wider range of tests and supplementing these with other techniques, including experimental methods, there is obviously a need for a clear record of what was done and with what result. Some psychologists therefore write two reports – one fairly long and technical, and the other written specifically in answer to the referral request. This practice is particularly prevalent when reports are requested by official bodies, such as courts or social agencies.

2 With parents

Communicating findings to parents is one of the most difficult of the psychologist's skills, and also one of the most important. Psychologists, like teachers and doctors, vary greatly in their attitude to the presence of parents during the assessment; it is true that some parents find it hard to relax while their child is being tested by a stranger; they may feel convinced that a question was unfair or irrelevant, or that another was misunderstood. Some of this anxiety can be modified if the psychologist talks to the parents before he sees the child, explains what he is going to do, that the child may be given some tasks that are too difficult for him, but that this is part of the normal process of testing. Parents need also to be helped to understand that an intelligence test by its very nature is designed to test a child's reactions to new tasks, and not to test knowledge and attainment as such. This is not always a very convincing explanation, since some popular types of item such as arithmetic and vocabulary seem to contradict this principle. Parents are apt to see many items as unfair if, when testing school knowledge, they are obviously beyond the child or outside his range of experience; they may feel that certain non-verbal tests are unfair if the child has not 'played with that kind of toy before'; non-verbal tests such as form boards are sometimes considered irrelevant to the child's main difficulties. It may be too much to expect even the most co-operative and relaxed parent to understand the nature and purposes of the psychologist's examination at a single explanation, but it is likely that at least some misunderstanding can be prevented by talking to the parent beforehand. It must be admitted that this often presents practical difficulties where there is limited space, and where the psychologist would not feel it appropriate to discuss test procedures in the presence of the child himself.

Whether or not the parents have been present during the test, they should still be told as much as possible about why the child is being tested and what it is hoped to learn from the examination. Only in this way will they be in a position to participate in a discussion on the psychologist's findings. Since the psychologist will usually be interested in more than a global intelligence test, it is useful to be able to discuss with parents any findings or tentative suggestions that have emerged from the tests concerning specific assets or difficulties which seem to show. Apparent difficulties with immediate memory, or more general problems of concentration or attention may be very marked in the test situation, but may have escaped the parent's attention, possibly because they have failed to notice them, but perhaps because they are only apparent in artificial or new and unfamiliar settings such as that provided by a psychological examination. It is as well to 'validate' psychological reports before they are written by checking whether other observers who see much more of the child than the psychologist have made similar observations or whether their own observations complement those of the psychologist. This is a matter of collaboration with colleagues, but parents can be the best observers. Some allowance has to be made for bias and selectivity in reporting, but it is a sound principle that parents' observations of the child's present behaviour are probably more reliable than their memory of his behaviour and development in the past (Wenar, 1963; Donoghue and Shakespeare, 1967).

The psychologist should adapt his assessment in order to learn as much as possible about the child from the parents, and should also consider in each case to what extent the parents can be involved in helping the child. In some cases, a treatment or training programme can be planned in conjunction with the parents; this would be based on the psychologist's findings of the child's relative strengths and weaknesses and would be designed with the aim of providing experiences to help him to acquire certain skills and abilities. Psychologists do not on the whole involve parents very closely with treatment, though there are grounds for considerable optimism about the possibilities. 'Parent guidance' has been practised in the field of deaf education for many years (Ewing and Ewing, 1957; Broomfield, 1967); because of the importance of treating deafness at the earliest possible moment, parents are taught not only the correct way to use a hearing-aid on a 12-month-old baby, but also how to encourage listening and early language development. Similar help could be given to parents of other handicapped children. Parents of spastic or physically handicapped children can be taught how to give certain simple exercises and work closely with physiotherapists, occupational therapists and speech therapists.

The involvement of parents in the treatment of the child is probably one of the most important developments of the future. Findings reported earlier confirm,

N*

if any confirmation were needed, that parental attitudes and home background generally play a critical part in the child's educational and cognitive development. This involves more than mere recognition of the importance of these factors in the child's development. The central theme of the Plowden Report (1967) is the need to forge closer links between home and school and to do so as early as possible. Parents of school-age children, especially those who are in special schools, need to be brought as closely as possible in touch with the child's teaching. This is not an easy task, and is one which presents many practical difficulties, but there are possibilities of forging such links by the appointment of specially trained staff; these may be educational social workers or school counsellors, and one of their tasks would be to bring the parents into closer touch with the school – not merely by encouraging them to attend open days and displays of work, but by week to week contact with the school – either by direct visiting, or by being involved in detailed practical tasks which are suggested by the school.

It may be objected that parents are 'not qualified' to help their children in this way, and that direct participation of this kind may be harmful. Parents may either use 'different methods and thus confuse the child', or may be too 'involved' and thus cause 'emotional damage'. These fears have not been shown to be justified, though no doubt many individual instances could be quoted to substantiate the traditional attitudes of most of the professions. On the other hand, few serious or systematic attempts have been made to involve parents closely and intensively in the child's educational treatment. Closer participation by parents can most usefully begin long before school age. Now that there is general recognition of the importance of early diagnosis and widespread emphasis on the provision of appropriate experiences for young handicapped children, it seems only logical to enlist the support of parents at a time when society makes very little provision for handicapped pre-school children. Psychologists have a key role to play in helping parents to plan appropriate activities in the home which are likely to help the child to utilize his experiences beneficially. The psychologist works at three levels in this respect. In the first place, his knowledge of child development provides him with a general framework of information which will be of use in planning the kind of activities which will help to foster development; at a second level, his professional skills in analysing a child's assets and deficits should enable him to discuss their child's intellectual and other skills in some detail and not merely in general terms; finally, the psychologist should learn how to collaborate with a teacher or therapist in designing a remedial programme which is based to some extent on his detailed findings.

3 With the child

Just as parents need to know the purposes of the assessment, and to have the findings discussed fully and frankly, so does the child. This is obviously a minor issue with younger children (unless they have been badly prepared for the psychologist), but skilled communication of aims and findings may be as important (if not more important) for the child as for the parents. Obviously this point can only be made in a general way, since children will have different needs and each situation has different demands. Nevertheless, more attention could profitably be given by psychologists to this aspect of their work. Children are often lured into a room by people who may say anything from 'a man wants to see you' to 'go and do the puzzles and answer all the questions like a good boy'. Whether or not the aims and findings of the tests are explained to the child, he is likely to form his own impressions of the reasons for the procedures, and these will be distorted to the extent that no explanation is given. It is axiomatic that the relationship between psychologist and child should be as informal and friendly as possible, yet it cannot be denied that for school children, especially those used to fairly formal methods, a test is a test, no matter how friendly the tester. For many children, it is as well to be quite straightforward and frank about the purposes of the test, nor is there always a need to use circumlocutions such as 'games' or 'puzzles'. Many children are perspicacious enough to see through and even be contemptuous of these euphemisms ('He called them toys, but I knew they were really I.Q. tests', one child was heard to say to his mother). Similarly, frankness in discussing results is usually desirable, though the explanation has obviously to be appropriate, and can touch on details of his performance on particular items. This may to some extent compensate for what may appear to be the rigidity of the test administration itself, when the psychologist may have been deliberately non-committal with 'neutral' remarks such as, 'You're doing fine', when the child knew perfectly well that he had failed an item.

V CONCLUSIONS

This chapter has tried to emphasize that handicapped children, whatever the nature of the handicap, have much in common and that improvements in diagnostic and treatment facilities should not lead to hard and fast distinctions between different disabilities or rigid assumptions about the distinct needs of each. Each child's development is differently affected by his handicaps, and the psychologist has not only to estimate the effect of these on the child's development but also to try and suggest ways in which his development may be helped so that restraints on his intellectual and personality growth can be modified or removed. Psychologists now appreciate the complexity of the many influences that affect the development of handicapped children; it is apparent, for example, that although one handicap may for classification purposes be considered 'primary', most children have additional handicaps, including environmental and socio-cultural forces which restrict their development. In practice it is extremely difficult to balance the many considerations which have to be weighed when assessing a handicapped child. No decision about educational placement, for example, can be simple. To recommend a more appropriate school on educational grounds alone may ignore the effects of a change of school on the child and on his parents. A recommendation for residential education will affect parent's attitudes and management to an extent which may not be foreseen at the time.

A recognition of the complexity of the factors involved in the assessment of handicapped children implies rather different concepts of the aims and methods of assessment. At the present time, decisions of vital importance for a child's future may have to be taken on the basis of a relatively short period of assessment. Reports bearing closely on the child's future are sometimes written and acted upon after only one or two visits. Sheer pressure of time and numbers, combined with the absence of appropriate facilities, has forced these conditions on those professionally concerned with handicapped children. With the present dearth of psychologists, it seems rational to plan facilities and procedures to minimize the disadvantages of staff shortage. One way of improving assessment facilities would be for more areas to set up special assessment and observation classes for children who were not making progress in ordinary schools. These should be staffed by specially trained and experienced teachers and visited by psychologists and other specialists, who would examine the child over an extended period and also be in a better position to relate their findings to the child's response to skilled teaching. In this way, assessment can become a continuous dynamic process and decisions about a child's educational needs can be made on the basis of information and observations gathered over an extended period, and not based, as they all too often are at present, on the results of a test administered under far from ideal conditions. Moreover, assessment units of the kind envisaged here would need to involve parents as closely as possible.

Diagnosis will also become more effective with improved facilities for early diagnosis. There can be little doubt that this would increase the early detection of handicap and enable remedial and nursery school measures to be made available to a far greater extent than they are at present. Each area needs an assessment centre or class where children whose development is causing concern could be assessed over a lengthy period, and their educational and social needs fully investigated. The psychologist must clearly play a crucial role in early diagnosis and in devising a remedial programme in collaboration with the class teacher.

In the last analysis, full assessment cannot be carried out by a single individual, no matter how competent. A team approach to assessment is bound to be of advantage, not only for the child himself and for his parents, but for the team themselves. Each member of the team has his own skills to contribute, but he has also to learn to understand those of his colleagues. This is often achieved by day-to-day collaboration, but much more could be done to make the various members of the team aware of each other's contribution at a very early stage in their training. For example, psychologists could be given at least part of their post-graduate and professional training alongside doctors, social workers and teachers in special education. In this way, some of the less useful side-effects of specialization might be avoided and the foundations of a genuine interdisciplinary assessment established.

Whether a truly multidisciplinary concept of assessment can be achieved depends on the ability of psychologists to experiment with new methods of assessment which will make for an organic link between assessment and treatment.

REFERENCES

AYLLON, T. and AZRIN, N. H. (1964) Reinforcement and instructions with mental patients. *J. exp. Anal. Beh.*, **7**, 327-331.

BARNETT, S. A. (Ed.) (1962) *Lessons in Animal Behaviour for the Clinician.* London: Heinemann and Spastics Society.

BAUMEISTER, A. (1968) Learning abilities of the mentally retarded. *In* BAUMEISTER, A. (Ed.) *Mental Retardation.* London: University of London Press.

BAX, M. and MCKEITH, R. M. (Eds.) (1963) *Minimal Cerebral Dysfunction.* London: Heinemann and Spastics Society.

BENE, E. and ANTHONY, A. J. (1957) *The Family Relations Test.* London: National Foundn. Educ. Research.

BERNSTEIN, B. (1965) A socio-linguistic approach to learning. *In* GOULD, J. (Ed.) *Penguin Survey of Social Science.* Harmondsworth: Penguin Books.

BIJOU, S. W. and BAER, D. M. (1966) Operant methods in child behavior and development. *In* HONIG, W. (Ed.) *Operant Behavior: Areas of Research and Application.* New York: Meredith. Reprinted in BIJOU, S. W. and BAER, D. M. (Eds.) (1967) *Child Development: Readings in Experimental Analysis.* New York: Appleton-Century-Crofts.

BLOOM, B. S. (1965) *Stability and Change in Human Characteristics.* New York: Wiley.

BROOMFIELD, A. (1967) Guidance to parents of deaf children. *Brit. J. Dis. Communic.*, **2**, 112-123.

BROWN, R. (1965) Distractibility and some scholastic skills. *J. child. Psychol. Psychiat.*, **6**, 55-62.

BROWN, R. I. (1966) Problems of attention in the education and training of the subnormal. *Monog. Suppl. J. ment. Subn.*

BRUNER, J. S., OLVER, R. R. and GREENFIELD, P. M. (1966) *Studies in Cognitive Growth.* New York: Wiley.

BUTTERFIELD, E. C. (1968) The role of environmental factors in the treatment of institutionalized mental retardates. *In* BAUMEISTER, A. A. (Ed.) *Mental Retardation.* London: University of London Press.

CENTRAL ADVISORY COUNCIL FOR EDUCATION (1967) *Children and their Primary Schools* (Plowden Report). London: H.M.S.O.

CHAZAN, M. (1962) The relationship between maladjustment and backwardness. *Educ. Rev.*, **15**, 54-62.

CHAZAN, M. (1964) The incidence and nature of maladjustment in schools for the educationally subnormal. *Brit. J. educ. Psychol.*, **34**, 292-304.

DOLL, A. E. (1953) *Measurement of Social Competence*. Minneapolis: Educ. Test Bureau.

DONOGHUE, E. L. and SHAKESPEARE, R. (1967) The reliability of paediatric case history milestones. *Developm. Med. Child Neurol.*, **9**, 64-69.

DOUGLAS, J. W. B. (1964) *The Home and the School*. London: McGibbon and Kee.

DOUGLAS, J. W. B. (1968) *All our Future*. London: Peter Davis.

DRILLIEN, C. (1964) *The Growth and Development of the Prematurely Born Infant*. London and Edinburgh: Livingstone.

EWING, C. A. and EWING, I. (1957) *Educational Guidance and the Deaf Child*. Manchester: Manchester Univ. Press.

EYSENCK, S. (1965) *The Junior Eysenck Personality Inventory*. London: University of London Press.

EYSENCK, H. J. (1967) Intelligence assessment: a theoretical and experimental approach. *Brit. J. educ. Psychol.*, **37**, 81-98.

EYSENCK, H. J. (1968) *The Biological Basis of Personality*. Springfield, Ill.: Thomas.

FRASER, E. D. (1959) *Home Environment and the School*. London: University of London Press.

FROSTIG, M., LEFEVER, D. W. and WHITTLESEY, J. R. B. (1964) *Marianne Frostig Developmental Test of Visual Perception*. Palo Alto, Calif.: Consulting Psychologists Press.

GOLDSTEIN, H. (1964) Social and occupational adjustment. *In* STEVENS, H. A. and HEBER, R. (Eds.) *Mental Retardation: A review of Research*. Chicago: Chicago Univ. Press.

GUBBAY, S. S., ELLIS, E., WALTON, J. N. and COURT, S. D. M. (1965) Clumsy children: a study of apraxic and agnosic defects in 21 children. *Brain*, **88**, 295-312.

GUNZBURG, H. (1966) *The Progress Assessment Charts* (3rd Ed.). London: National Assn. Mental Health.

HERMELIN, B. and O'CONNOR, N. (1965) Visual imperception in psychotic children. *Brit. J. Psychol.*, **56**, 455-460.

HONZIK, M. P., MCFARLANE, J. W. and ALLEN, L. (1948) The stability of mental test performance between two and eighteen years. *J. exp. Educ.*, **17**, 309-324.

HUNT, J. MCV. (1961) *Intelligence and Experience*. New York: Ronald.

HUNT, N. (1968) *The World of Nigel Hunt*. London: Darwin Finlayson.

HUTT, C. and HUTT, S. J. (1965) Effect of environmental complexity on stereotyped behaviours of children. *Anim. Beh.*, **13**, 1-4.

JACKSON, B. and MARSDEN, D. (1962) *Education and the Working Class*. London: Routledge. (Revised Ed. Pelican Books, 1966.)

JENSEN, A. R. (1967) The culturally disadvantaged: psychological and educational aspects. *Educ. Res.*, **10**, 4-20.

JONES, H. E. (1954) The environment and mental development. *In* CARMICHAEL, L. (Ed.) *Manual of Child Psychology*. New York: Wiley.

KAGAN, J. (1964) American longitudinal research in child development. *Child Dev.*, **35**, 1-32.

KODMAN, F. (1963) Sensory Processes and mental deficiency. *In* ELLIS, N. R. (Ed.) *Handbook of Mental Deficiency*. New York: McGraw Hill.

LAWTON, D. (1968) *Social Class, Language and Education*. London: Routledge and Kegan Paul.

LEWIS, H. (1954) *Deprived Children: the Mersham Experiment*. London: Oxford Univ. Press.

LOVAAS, I. (1966) A program for the establishment of speech in psychotic children. *In* WING, J. K. (Ed.) *Early Childhood Autism: Clinical, Educational and Social Aspects*. London: Pergamon.

LUNZER, E. (1967) *The Manchester Scales of Social Adaptation*. London: National Foundn. Educ. Research.

MCCARTHY, J. J. and KIRK, S. A. (1961) *The Illinois Test of Psycholinguistic Abilities* (Experimental Ed.). Urbana, Ill.: Inst. for Research in Exceptional Children.

MCNEMAR, Q. (1945) Note on Wellman's re-analysis of I.Q. changes of orphanage preschool children. *J. genet. Psych.*, **67**, 215-219.

MALPASS, L. F. (1968) Programmed instruction for retarded children. *In* BAUMEISTER, A. A. (Ed.) *Mental Retardation*. London: University of London Press.

MARSHALL, A. (1967) *The Abilities and Attainments of Children Leaving Junior Training Centres*. London: National Assn. Mental Health.

MEYERS, C. E., ORPET, R. E., ATTWELL, A. A. and DINGMAN, M. F. (1962) Primary mental abilities at mental age six. *Monog. Soc. Res. Child Dev.*, **27**.

MITTLER, P. (1964) The use of form boards in developmental assessment. *Developm. Med. Child Neurol.*, **6**, 510-516.

MITTLER, P. (1966) Psychological assessment of autistic children. *In* WING, J. K. (Ed.) *Early Childhood Autism: Clinical, Educational and Social Aspects*. London: Pergamon.

MITTLER, P., GILLIES, S. and JUKES, E. (1966) Prognosis in psychotic children: report of a follow-up study. *J. ment. Def. Res.*, **10**, 73-83.

NEWSON, J. and NEWSON, E. (1963) *Infant Care in an Urban Community*. London: Allen and Unwin. (Reprinted as *Patterns of Infant Care*. London: Penguin Books, 1965.)

NEWSON, J. and NEWSON, E. (1968) *Four Years Old in an Urban Community*. London: Allen and Unwin.

O'CONNOR, N. and HERMELIN, B. (1963) *Speech and Thought in Severe Subnormality*. London: Pergamon.

O'CONNOR, N. and HERMELIN, B. (1967) The experimental study of psychotic children. *Proc. Roy. Soc. Med.*, **60**, 560-563.

OUNSTED, C. (1955) The hyperkinetic syndrome in childhood. *Lancet*, **169**, 303-311.

PASAMANICK, B. and KNOBLOCH, H. (1961) Epidemiologic studies in the complications of pregnancy and the birth process. *In* CAPLAN, G. (Ed.) *Prevention of Mental Disorders in Children*. New York: Basic Books.

PHILLIPS, C. J. (1961) On comparing scores from tests of attainment with scores from tests of ability in order to obtain indices of retardation by differences of ratios. Unpublished thesis, Univ. of Birmingham (cited by P. WILLIAMS, Chapter 16 of this volume).

PIAGET, J. (1951) *Play, Dreams and Imitation in Childhood*. London: Heinemann. (Tr. C. Gattegno and F. M. Hodson.)

PITFIELD, M. and OPPENHEIM, A. N. (1964) Child rearing attitudes of mothers of psychotic children. *J. child. Psychol. Psychiat.*, **5**, 51-57.

POLITICAL AND ECONOMIC PLANNING (undated, 1965?) *Mental Subnormality in London*. London: P.E.P.

PRINGLE, M. L. KELLMER, BUTLER, N. R. and DAVIE, R. (1966) *11,000 Seven Year Olds*. London: Longmans Green.

RUTTER, M., GREENFIELD, D. and LOCKYER, L. (1967) A five to fifteen year follow-up study of infantile psychosis. *Brit. J. Psychiat.*, **113**, 1183-1199.

RUTTER, M., GRAHAM, P. and YULE, W. (1969) *Neurological Disorders in Childhood: A Study in a Small Community*. London: Heinemann (in press).

SAMPSON, O. C. (1966) Reading and Adjustment: a review of the literature. *Educ. Res.*, **8**, 184-190.

SCHAFFER, H. (1958) Objective observations of personality development in early infancy. *Brit. J. med. Psychol.*, **31**, 174-183.

SONTAG, L. W., BAKER, C. T. and NELSON, V. L. (1958) Mental growth and personality development. *Monogr. Soc. Res. Child Developm.*, **23**, 1-85.

STEPHENSON, H. W., HESS, E. H. and RHEINGOLD, H. (1967) *Early Behavior*. New York: Wiley.

STOTT, D. H. (1966) *The Social Adjustment of Children* (3rd Ed.). London: University of London Press.

STUTSMAN, R. (1931) *Mental Measurement of Preschool Children*. New York: World Books.

THURSTONE, L. L. (1938) *Primary Mental Abilities*. Chicago: Chicago Univ. Press.

TIZARD, J. and GRAD, J. (1961) *The Mentally Handicapped and their Families: A Social Survey*. London: Oxford Univ. Press.

TIZARD, J., KING, R. D., RAYNES, N. V. and YULE, W. (1966) The care and treatment of subnormal children in institutions. In *What is Special Education*. London: Assn Special Education.

TYLER, L. (1965) *The Psychology of Individual Differences* (3rd Ed.). New York: Appleton-Century-Crofts.

VERNON, M. D. (1957) *Backwardness in Reading*. London: Cambridge Univ. Press.

WALKER, J. (1966) Pregnancy and perinatal association with mental subnormality. *In* MEADE, J. S. and PARKES, A. S. (Eds.) *Genetic and Environmental Factors in Human Ability*. London and Edinburgh: Oliver and Boyd.

WACHS, T. D. (1966) Personality testing of the handicapped: a review. *J. proj. Techn.*, **30**, 339-355.

WELLMAN, B. and PEGRAM, E. L. (1944) Binet I.Q. changes of orphanage and preschool children. *J. genet. Psychol.*, **65**, 239-263.

WENAR, C. (1963) The reliability of developmental histories: summary and evaluation of evidence. *Psychosom. Med.*, **25**, 505-509.

WIENER, R. G., RIDER, R. V. and OPPEL, W. (1963) Some correlates of I.Q. changes in children. *Child Dev.*, **34**, 61-67.

WILLIAMS, C. E. (1966) A blind idiot who became a normal blind adolescent. *Developm. Med. Child Neurol.*, **8**, 166-169.

WISEMAN, S. (1964) *Education and Environment*. Manchester: Manchester Univ. Press.

WISEMAN, S. (1966) Environmental and innate factors and educational attainment. *In* MEADES, J. E. and PARKES, A. S. (Eds.) *Genetic and Environmental Factors in Human Ability*. London and Edinburgh: Oliver and Boyd.

WISEMAN, S. (1967) The Manchester Survey. *In* Central Advisory Council for Education (The Plowden Report) *Children and their Primary Schools*, **2**, Appendix 9. London: H.M.S.O.

WOODROW, H. (1946) The ability to learn. *Psychol. Rev.*, **53**, 147-158.

WOODWARD, W. M. (1963) The application of Piaget's Theory to research in mental deficiency. *In* ELLIS, N. R. (Ed.) *Handbook of Mental Deficiency*. New York: McGraw-Hill.

WRIGHT, H. F. (1960) Observational child study. *In* MUSSEN, P. H. (Ed.) *Handbook of Research Methods in Child Development*. New York: Wiley.

ZEAMAN, D. (1966) Learning processes of the mentally retarded. *In* OSLER, S. F. and COOKE, R. E. (Eds.) *Biosocial Basis of Mental Retardation*. Baltimore: Johns Hopkins Press.

ZEAMAN, D. and HOUSE, B. (1963) The role of attention in retardate discrimination learning. *In* ELLIS, N. R. (Ed.) *Handbook of Mental Deficiency*. New York: McGraw-Hill.

13

Visual perceptual difficulties

Winifred Langan

The Department of Education and Science recognizes two categories of children with visual perceptual difficulties, the blind and the partially sighted. There is, however, a third group of children who have grave difficulties of perception. These children need to be recognized during the ascertainment programme as they have sometimes been considered to be severely subnormal in the same way as a child with a slight or unusual hearing loss is often underestimated.

This chapter, therefore, will be divided into three parts, the first dealing with the blind, the second with the partially sighted, followed by a short comment concerning those children who can see but who do not perceive – a special category of the 'partially sighted'.

I BLIND CHILDREN

1 Definitions and incidence

'Blind pupils – those who have no sight or whose sight is or is likely to become so defective that they require education by methods not involving the use of sight.'

It is important to note that the definition of blindness is given in terms of the type of education the child will need. In fact, there are few totally blind children in schools for the blind, the vast majority having at least dark/light sense and many an ability to see fingers raised at a distance of one foot. Naturally such sight does not allow of conventional methods of teaching but will often help with the problems of mobility.

In *The Health of the School Child 1964 and 1965* (H.M.S.O.), the latest report of the Chief Medical Officer of the Department of Education and Science, the incidence of blindness is given as 1·9 per 10,000 of the school population with 1,387 children in schools for the blind. In December 1967 there were 1,392 places provided for blind children in England and Wales, plus 133 places for blind children with additional handicaps.

2 Schooling

The distribution of the schools is interesting. With the exception of one Roman Catholic School in Liverpool, the northern counties have followed the pattern of sighted schools and separated primary from secondary children. So Henshaw's Institute for the Blind in Manchester, a Modern School, is fed by the three

Junior Schools in Liverpool, Newcastle and Sheffield. The rest of the country has all-age schools, although, of course, the two Grammar and one Technical school take appropriate children from anywhere in England and Wales.

Type	Number	Places
Nursery	5	130
Junior	3	216
Secondary	1	109
Grammar	2	135
Technical	1	65
All age	6	737
Total	18	1,392

TABLE 13.1
Schools for blind children

Since the days of asylums for the care of blind children and adults, blind education has traditionally been in boarding schools. Arising from the early idea of blind people needing to be permanently protected from the seeing world, the early education of young blind children was mainly custodial although some handicrafts were taught. Very gradually an awareness grew of the much greater potential of many blind children and over the last 50 years a gradual change has taken place. In 1934 a Ministry Committee sat to consider the needs of partially sighted children. They advised the separation of partially sighted children from blind children and the implementation of their recommendations after the 1939-1945 war began a new era of education for both groups. Table 13.2 shows the changes which have occurred since 1946.

	Schools for blind	Schools for P/S	Schools for both
1945	16	30	14
1955	22	27	3
1965	18	30* (boarding)	2

TABLE 13.2

* Many of these schools take some physically handicapped, E.S.N. or delicate children. There are also a number of units for P/S children in ordinary schools and it is very difficult to discover from published tables the exact number of P/S children having special education.

Over the past few years, those concerned with the education of blind children have come to a better understanding of the need for these children to have a closer attachment to their homes. So, although all schools for blind children remain boarding schools, as many children as possible return home each week-end and a few children living near enough are allowed to sleep at home every night. There is no real shortage of places for blind children and, with the exception of the rise in the number of cases of retrolental fibroplasia (blindness caused by too much oxygen being given to prematurely born children) particularly between 1948 and 1952, the number of children requiring special education because of blindness has remained relatively stable for the past 20 years.

Because blind education is the earliest type of education to have been started in this country, it remained rather behind other types of special education for a long time. Within the schools recently, however, there has been much steady progress. The last relics of the 'institutionalized' asylum have been swept away and signs of progress abound. 'Symptoms of this change are to be found in the expansion of braille libraries in the schools, the development of athletics and in a freer, more natural routine with more contacts with the outside world.' Some schools send selected pupils to local grammar schools to prepare for G.C.E. subjects, but keep them based in the blind school so that they can be helped in the preparation of their work. There is much difference of opinion about this but those who have had experience of the arrangement over a period of time tend to think it is a step forward.

There has also been considerable change in the attitude to training and work potential. In 1956 a new type of training establishment was set up at Reigate for blind children over the age of 16. This gives them both further education and training aimed to equip them for making an appropriate choice of occupation. Blind adults can now be found in many different types of factory and office as well as in the more traditional occupations of craftwork, telephony, physiotherapy, etc.

In the schools themselves, although change has been rather slow, advantage has been taken of the results of research into new methods undertaken for use in schools for sighted children. As more knowledge in general education has become available, methods in schools for the blind have changed and as more teachers have taken advantage of research in related fields, more of them are coming to the conclusion that blind children should pursue the same curriculum as sighted children. Doubt is now being expressed as to whether there is such a thing as 'Geography for the Blind' or different arts and crafts for the blind (about which many articles used to be written in 'blind' journals), but rather that there should be a different approach.

Side by side with academic teaching (and often, too, as a part of it), there is much more social and general training than is normally found in general education. Jervis (1959) suggested that 'a major focus of a program for blind children may be on helping the child to a better understanding of himself as a person'. He is of the opinion that the learning of specific subjects is less important than helping a child to 'a realization of personal worth'. 'Such children may respond to learning experience directed at broadening their knowledge of people, of the community and of the world in which they are living'.

In 1957 the American Foundation for the Blind published the proceedings of a National Work Session held in New York at which the 'Plus Curriculum' necessary for blind children was discussed. The importance of self-concept was emphasized together with the need for the child to have insight into his own feelings about his blindness and its relationship to his personal problems. The members of this meeting also spent some time in discussing the problems of mobility for blind children. Orientation and mobility skills are certainly more important than was recognized a few years ago and many British schools and adult agencies are taking an increasing interest in research orientated towards such skills. However able, however learned, however 'well educated' a person may be, he can never fulfil his potential if he is dependent upon the services of another person to get about; nor does he feel as efficient or as socially well adjusted.

3 Intellectual abilities

(a) *Finger Sight*

So much has already been written on the creation, history and development of braille that it is not necessary to go into any detail here. It is sufficient to say that the six-dot cell on which braille is based does not exceed the field of tactility, so that the perception is rapid (Ritchie, 1930).

What must be stressed here, however, is the great variation of teaching methods in schools. Some schools teach the alphabet straight through; some teach first the three letters based on the same group of dots, A, K, U/B, L, V; etc.; some teach letters in the pairs which are most likely to be confused, D, F/ H, J/ etc. Yet other schools do not teach the alphabet at all, but start at once with Grade II. Again, in some schools, teachers feel very strongly that reading and writing should be learnt together, while others feel just as strongly that their pupils need to read proficiently before they can be allowed to attempt writing.

It will be appreciated that the various methods of teaching, which in some cases are not even continuous throughout a school, combined with the temperamental differences in the children which seem to affect braille reading ability, make for lack of uniformity in braille facility – not only from school to school, or even from class to class, but from child to child. Time of entry into school, number of years of schooling and age at loss of sight, all tend to affect braille reading results, but not in a uniform manner. A group of children may be gathered together in which these conditions are essentially the same, who will yet vary considerably in both rate and comprehension of reading.

Many reading disabilities may have similar causes as poorness of reading in sighted children, but there are many other difficulties to aggravate the condition, not the least of them being differences in tactile acuity, sense of space relationships and temperament.

(b) *Tactile Acuity*

For many years it has been a generalization that men and women deprived of one sense are automatically compensated by more acute development of reactions in the other senses. Work by Babcock (1915), Seashore (1918), Hayes (1933) and many other workers during the past 50 years does not bear out this 'vicariate of the senses', as Hayes names it. Experiments in touch, taste, smell and direction-finding have been widely used and no essential differences between the blind and the sighted could be demonstrated. Such experiments are made, however, under conditions which are not natural day-to-day experiences of either the blind or the seeing. What really appears to happen in daily life is that experience teaches the blind to *interpret* what they hear, smell or touch in a much more accurate manner, not necessarily to discriminate better. (A blind person needs to interpret whatever stimuli reach him, whereas a sighted person turns to such stimuli and leaves his eyes to interpret them. The question of interpretation in this sense rarely enters into laboratory experiments.) In fact, Griesbach found that among the blind the finger most often used for reading was less sensitive than the other fingers, and Kunz concluded from this that braille reading actually blunts the sense of touch and that it is not until the finger tip has become hard and leathery that good braille reading can be accomplished.

(c) *Space Relationships*

It is sometimes forgotten that once anything is offered to a blind person which is bigger than 'the field of tactility' he has to use a type of synthetic exploration in order to understand it. A good deal of movement is necessary before he can comprehend the parts; he must then combine them within this comprehension to make a whole. Where the object is very large there is likely to be a good deal of vagueness or even misunderstanding of the built-up composite, for he has to learn the parts well enough to hold them all in mind together.

Villey (1930) does not speak of synthetic and analytic touch, but of 'the two essential elements of touch', which he thinks are: (1) passive contact and (2) movement; or, as he prefers to describe them, the skin's sense of (1) place and (2) mobility, which is 'the faculty of recognizing as distinct two excitations very near together'. Fortunately, those parts of the body 'in which there are the most tactile nerves are also those which have the most motory nerves, an arrangement singularly propitious for the sense of touch'. The pulp of the fingers is one of these areas.

Obviously, large representations or models of objects are very difficult for the blind child to comprehend completely, but many writers have spoken of the ease with which an object not much larger than the hand can be explored and understood. It is of such objects that a man can most easily build up an exact representation and by 'extensive contact', then detailed exploration, experience great satisfaction in the completeness of the image he conjures up. In this image there may, of course, occur incorrect details, but we should be satisfied if a good general idea has been obtained and no sense of frustration experienced.

Experiments have shown that one of the few ways in which the abilities of the blind exceed those of the seeing is in their speed of touch. This, says Villey, 'is the effect of a habit contracted under the command of a psychological force. The speed of the movement helps, in a remarkable way, the action of memory and favourizes the blending of successive elements into a simultaneous spatial representation. It is, perhaps, necessary for this.' Within this theory may lie the answer to many of the questions that arise in our teaching, especially those concerned with the comprehension of maps and models and with the association between speed and comprehension in reading.

4 Personality and social adjustment

As long ago as 1930, Ritchie asked, 'To what extent and in what manner does blindness affect temperament?' Although the importance of this question has long been recognized, little systematic research has been reported on it, so that most of the information available has to be obtained from autobiographies or other books written by blind people. Pierre Villey's (1930) book, is probably as illuminating as any in this respect, although now out of print. More recent books have added to our knowledge, but few can approach the standard of insight shown by him.

From the available literature it would appear that the blind population covers a complete cross-section of society, but it seems probable that, whatever the temperament, individual differences tend to be exaggerated. There is more acute response to praise and blame, frustration is experienced more quickly, etc. This suggests that physical perspective has some influence on psychological perspective. Ritchie (1930) refers more than once to 'the consciousness of limitation' without, apparently, being able to pin-point the cause of the limitation. Although, therefore, every effort may be made to give blind children as normal a life as possible, it has to be accepted that there are severe limitations to what the majority of them can achieve so that it is not surprising that many of them throw up a 'subtle, egocentric buttress' and often come to feel that their 'output of effort, perseverance and concentration is out of all proportion to the results achieved.' (Ritchie). This often affects their output in the learning situation so that achievement levels in these children are generally lower than their learning potential.

In spite of the fact that very little work on the personality of the blind has been undertaken methodically by trained workers (Pringle, 1964), examination of available literature suggests that certain broad groups can be observed among these children.

One child is extremely active, enjoying the stimulation of movement and sound in the environment, another may be quite the opposite, finding his greatest satisfaction in just sitting and, perhaps, a tremendous pleasure in touching and examining in minute detail. Then there is the type of child who Villey (1930) so expressively calls 'the motory type'. With this child, movement is again the main characteristic; not, however, movement outside himself that brings peace through attention to auditory stimuli, but the movement of himself, or parts of himself, which excites and begets further movement – jumping, clapping stamping, skipping, even shouting, provided it is loud enough! To him the whole world is movement; this in spite of his paucity of experience of much of the movement of which he speaks, e.g., 'a running dog', 'a galloping horse'. Cutsforth (1933) says that it is impossible to give a blind child an image of a moving object. This is probably true in terms of a model depicting movement, yet there is certainly a group of blind children who, besides finding their greatest joy in what may be termed 'static movement' (i.e. movement of their bodies while remaining in one place), also tend to imagine everything in movement.

These differences are, of course, observable in sighted children, but not in nearly so exaggerated a form, mainly because the principal medium of casual experience in these children is the eye and, this being a sighted world, the stimulation, with all its implications, is understood and accepted by the majority of people. Little adjustment is needed where everyone is speaking in the same terms. From the point of view of the blind children, of course, we should speak of *our* adjustment to *them*, rather than of *their* adjustment to *us*, and only the fact that this is a sighted world gives us any right to make our own standards of behaviour the criterion in the matter.

It must be realized, of course, that many children do not fall sharply into any one of these groups, but have one or more qualities, in greater or less degree, and the less clearly defined any one characteristic may be the more general attention will need to be given to it. 'The role of the attention is perhaps increased in proportion as the sensorial organization is more imperfect; attention must then act as its substitute to a greater degree (Villey, 1930).

It is obvious that practically everything in life is going to be just that much harder for the blind child than for the sighted. According to their endowed temperament and their environmental training they may either fight life, tooth and nail, in order to make a place in it for themselves, become completely crushed and frustrated, retiring into a rather depressed and sour personality, or make spasmodic efforts to overcome their difficulties, altering with periods of depression and weakness. Few handicapped children have to make such persistent effort for such apparently small results. For every Helen Keller or Marie Heurtin there are scores of Joans and Marys, unknown and undistinguished, striving, hoping, longing, often with some success, but just as often with little but the result of being able to live from day to day.

All this presents a very gloomy picture, yet the blind world is by no means a gloomy one. This discussion has been concerned with some of the inner, more difficult adjustments that the blind need to make, but, on the whole, blind people are gregarious and socially inclined. After all, they can hear and speak and these are two of the main pillars of social life to which they can most certainly make a contribution. Where failure occurs in this sphere, it comes not so much from the fact that they are blind, but from the fact that they are selfish, greedy or bad-tempered, or have some other characteristic which is not acceptable to the general community. Their tendencies towards these characteristics may be exaggerated because of their blindness (as indeed may their good qualities), but they are not necessarily caused by the fact of blindness. It is extremely important that people working in this field should constantly remind themselves of this fact and guard against the danger of attaching labels which are only half correct.

Hector Chevigny (1947) puts the blame for lack of adjustment in the blind on the shoulders of the sighted. He maintains in principle that the maudlin pity, unreasoning prejudice and sheer ignorance of the sighted population creates dependence and self-pity in all but the strongest-willed blind person. This is possibly true of the person blinded after adolescence, but it is by no means true of the child who loses his sight in the early years. His temperament is likely to be at least as strong a factor in his social adjustment as the opinions of his sighted contemporaries or even of the adults in his environment. The object of his teachers and friends should be to help him (as they would help a sighted child) to adjust his particular temperament to the environment in which he has to live. In as far as he comes to terms with himself and his surroundings, just so far will the blind child find satisfaction and happiness in his life and, incidentally, just so far shall we of the sighted world consider he has 'adjusted himself to blindness'. What a blind child needs to do is precisely what a sighted child needs to do in order to get the best out of life (although he may have a harder task in achieving it) – that is, to make terms with it acceptable to himself and to his particular community.

All children are affected by the environmental influences of their developmental period but, because of their relatively greater dependence on adults, blind children are particularly susceptible to such experiences (Maxfield, 1950). Many parents of blind children are naturally anxious concerning their safety and tend to over-protect them, so that they sometimes appear to be either severely retarded or even subnormal. In some cases, the unconscious guilt of the mother in producing this 'defective' offspring can so affect the child that he is not only retarded socially and intellectually but is also, to a lesser or greater extent, maladjusted by the time he should be ready for nursery education. Yet Norris, Spaulding and Brodie (1957), in their interesting five-year study of all the pre-school blind children in Chicago (295 children), claimed that they were able to identify the conditions conducive to optimum development in blind children. So, if such young children could be assessed at an early age and they and their parents given the regular advice and support of a team, rather like young deaf children are given in Manchester University Department of Education of the Deaf, it would appear that retardation due to wrong handling could be largely eliminated. Norris, Spaulding and Brodie (1957) claim that, 'Under these conditions the blind child can develop into an independent, responsible, freely functioning child whose use of his potential compares favourably with that of most sighted children of his age'. They are convinced that 'favourable opportunities for learning ... are more important in determining the child's functioning level than such factors as his degree of blindness, his intelligence ... or the social, economic or educational background of his parents'. Stress is also laid on the child's security within the family environment and the consistent application of the principles of normal growth within the restrictions which blindness imposes in the total situation: 'Failure to provide the essentials for healthy personality development may result in grossly retarded functioning and extreme emotional problems'. The need to give early support to blind children and their families is obvious and the establishment of more parent/child units is urgent.

Sommers (1944) supports the work of Norris *et al.* Her work was concerned with the influence of parental attitudes and social environment on blind children and, although it was actually carried out with 143 blind adolescents and their parents, she concluded that the child's reaction to his handicap was largely dependent on his social experience, particularly within his family in early childhood. In her opinion, the effectiveness of the blind child's education was largely determined by 'the effective education of the parents'. These results are also supported by the work of Barry and Marshall (1953). They found that early maternal rejection often resulted in poor social adjustment in the school period, while early maternal training made good adjustment in school much more likely. Hallenbeck (1954), however, suggests that while a good positive relationship with an adult is essential, this need not necessarily be the mother.

5 Assessment

Problems concerned with the assessment of blind children have tantalized psychologists and educationists for very many years.

As long ago as 1914, Irwin and Goddard met together in Vineland, U.S.A., to discuss the possibility of adapting new tests, put forward by Binet as assessing the intelligence of sighted children, for use with a blind school population. In England a year later, in an article in *The Teacher of the Blind*, Drummond also suggested that such a scale might be devised for blind children. 1916 saw the first published results on 224 blind children in Ohio and by 1918 probably 1,000 American children in blind schools had been tested individually. From this time, testing of the blind took a hold in America and every few years saw the publication of test results of one sort or the other, for the blind, for partially sighted, group tests, individual tests, some new, some adaptations of sighted tests already in existence.

In England, meantime, Drummond's first article was never followed up until he began to consider a subject for his M.D. Thesis. In 1920 he published the results of trying out the Haines Test with 133 blind children in England and Scotland (Drummond, 1920). Work in Austria was proceeding at the same time and Burklen published results of Bobertag's version of the Binet both in 1918 and 1921.

Although fairly systematic testing in blind schools was started in America in 1916, it was not until 1923 that Hayes produced anything that could be said to compare closely with the Terman revision of the Binet. In that year, however, he produced his 'Scissors and Paste' guide which enabled typed slips of paper to be pasted into the Terman Instruction book where alternative tests had been added for use with the blind. The position of these was based partly on the statistical study of passes and failures at each age and partly on 'the judgement of the psychometrists'. A good deal of difference of opinion seems to have existed even at this time on the wisdom of making such judgements, for Irwin had realized very much earlier that, in spite of his wide experience with the blind, some of the tests he had considered most suitable had proved the opposite and many had been placed in the wrong years.

In the meantime, Haines and Drummond had become involved in the question of degree of vision and age at onset of blindness and work virtually ceased in England. These questions have dogged psychologists ever since. Hayes, however, held the opinion that too much stress has been laid on these matters. He was 'inclined to stress the practical need for a scale which would measure all of the children who came to schools for the blind, as well as the advantage of comparing them with seeing children of the same age' (1941).

In England, Dr Ritchie of the London Society for Teaching and Training the Blind, had interested F. M. Earle in the subject and in 1928 a week's course in mental testing was given to 25 teachers of the blind who were then to go back into their schools and use their skills in trying to discover the association between test results and ability in school work. This would have been valuable information indeed, but the results were never collated nor any findings published. The only indication we have in this connection lies in a thesis presented at Manchester University (J. M. Murray) but not published, where the correlation between achievement in English and the Williams verbal intelligence test was found to be 0·89 on the basis of mental age and 0·61 on the basis of I.Q. when raw scores only are considered. This English achievement test covers an age range of 9-16, so a fairly wide difference in the correlation co-efficients was to be expected. Where a mixed intelligence test was used (Langan adaption of the Binet), the correlation was 0·85 on a very small sample.

The 1930 Hayes revision in America was the beginning, in that country, of widespread testing of children in schools, clinics and mental defective institutions. Then in 1942 he published a blind version of the Wechsler-Bellevue Test and examinations were extended right through the adolescent years. In the same year, Pintner published a report on the results of using the Terman-Merrill Test on partially-sighted children by having the visual material photostatically treated. It was ten years later before this type of test became available in England.

In 1943 Hayes produced an adaptation of the Binet which was, virtually, a verbal test. With only two exceptions, the 96 items taken from the Terman-Merrill Test were placed in the same position in which they appear in the sighted version. This was necessary in view of Hayes' statement that he intended making a 'selection of tests from the "L" and "M" forms of the Terman-Merrill revision of 1937 which may be used with the blind without change'. Apparently, this was in the hope that a direct comparison might be made both between this and other tests and also between the sighted and the blind results on the Binet Test. Whether such a comparison can be really valid, in view of the completely verbal nature of the tests, is a matter of conjecture.

1945 brought the first English version of the adaptation of the Terman-Merrill test for use with the blind and here the balance between verbal and practical tests was kept almost the same as in the sighted version and the position of the verbal tests in each year left unchanged. This allowed some comparison to be made between sighted and blind children, giving a rough idea how a particular blind child will fit into a sighted, competitive world. This has been used all over Europe and the Commonwealth now and appears to be giving fairly satisfactory results.

In 1957 the Williams Test for Children with Defective Vision came on the market. Miss Williams had undertaken a survey in connection with the Blind adaptation of the Terman-Merrill Test under the auspices of the National Founda-tion for Educational Research and this stimulated her interest in the testing of both blind and partially sighted children. This test is composed almost entirely of items selected from material already standardized on large groups of seeing children. Practically all items are verbal but, 'in order to furnish variety in the nature of tasks to be required from the younger subjects it did seem essential to include a small number of items of the performance type in the lower part of the scale'. These are not scored. This test may be obtained from Miss M. Williams of the Department of Education of Birmingham University.

Psychologists using tests to assess blind children cannot be expected to have a complete understanding of the many types of visual defect found among school children. They should, however, have a general knowledge of what the various defects mean to the children: myopia (short sight), hypermetropia (morbidly long sight), cataract (opacity of lens of eye), corneal opacities (cornea = transparent horny part of anterior covering of eyeball), restricted field, severe astigmatism (structural defect in eye or lens preventing rays of light from being brought into common focus, arising from unequal refraction at different points), loss of peripheral vision, defective or detached retina: all create different difficulties for the children who suffer from them. One of the best books for making these problems clear is *The Science of Seeing* (Mann and Pirie, 1946). Plate VIII opposite page 99 shows vividly that the words 'blind' and 'partially sighted' are blanket terms, covering many different types of defects. If this book is not obtainable, a good though rather technical book is *The Eye and its Function* (R. A. Weale, 1960). *The Seeing Eye* (Asher, 1961) is another useful reference although written in a racy style (See also Gregory, 1966, for a clear exposition of visual and perceptual processes.)

(a) *Types of Test*

There are two types of test which can be used with blind children, mainly verbal tests or mixed tests of the Binet type, both of which have been specifically prepared for such children. Verbal sections of tests which have not been standardized on blind children should never be used.

The advantage of a verbal test, such as the Williams, is that it cuts out some of the problems associated with degree of vision and age at onset of blindness, although we must always be aware when we are testing children totally blind from birth that words do not, necessarily, have the same meaning for them. 'Big' and 'small', 'far' and 'near' and all words involving distance, size, height, etc., are likely to have different associations for them according to the degree of vision and the age at onset of blindness in the child being tested. This is a problem that has bedevilled research into blind tests for many years and there is a certain amount of evidence concerning the importance of these factors. Haines (1916) and Drummond (1920) were so sure of their significance that they decided to base their tests on results obtained only from children born blind. S. C. Swift (unpublished thesis) quoted by Hayes agreed in principle but made a distinction between those born blind and those who had vision long enough to gain and retain visual images.

Hayes' (1941) attitude was that these opinions raised rather than settled the question and he proceeded to do a number of experiments to discover whether age at onset of blindness was as important as these writers considered. He surveyed 600 children of different ages and degrees of vision and visual experience being educated in 9 different schools. They were all given 11 different tests involving English composition and grammar, geography, vocabulary, reading, etc. These included several tests in which children with visual imagery *ought* to have done better than those born blind. In every test the attainment of those born blind measured up well to the median of the attainment of the whole number tested, in most cases no upward trend was observed with increased years of visual experience and 'in all the tests a considerable percentage of the highest scores was made by pupils of the early blind group'. While there may be many fields in which those without visual imagery might suffer, Hayes found no evidence of this in his research. He ends this chapter of his book by saying, 'The *mental constitution* of those born blind may well be essentially different from that of the other group, but the *functioning* of their minds as measured by our tests shows no such difference'.

The second advantage of a purely verbal test is that it makes it easier to compare one child with another. At least this is an interesting theory, but the previous warning about the use of words must always be heeded. Perhaps it is fair to say that a verbal test standardized on the complete blind school population gives a better method of comparison of blind to blind than any other method yet devised.

Its third advantage is that it fits very well into the present system of blind education which has quite a strong verbal bias. A good deal of emphasis is laid on verbal explanation and there is not a great deal of experimentation, as yet, of more active forms of learning, except in a few schools.

Its one great disadvantage is that it might easily accentuate differences in environment. A good deal of sighted research has been published on this point and differences between school/school and home/home could easily bias the results of a purely verbal test unless it was most carefully constructed.

The advantages and disadvantages of mixed tests of the Binet type have now to be considered.

It is important to remember that if an adaptation of the Terman-Merrill Test is used it is almost bound to have the same strengths and weaknesses as the original. These we all judge for ourselves and those who like the informal structure of the sighted test will welcome the adaptation, others will not.

This adaptation has the advantage of offering some comparison with the sighted population. That is to say, where it is an advantage to know roughly where a blind person is likely to be on the general ability scale in comparison with his sighted brother (as distinct from how he does as a blind person among blind children – the 'forte' of the schools), an adaptation of a sighted test with about the same proportion of verbal to practical items can be very useful. In adapting this test all eyesight tests were removed and touch-sight tests were inserted. These new tests were standardized on the blind population but the verbal side was left undisturbed.

Its most important asset perhaps, lies in the use of touch, for blind children must, and do, learn much from tactile clues, adding them to auditory ones almost without knowing it; in order to succeed, their sense of space relationships must also be good. Interpretation of all these clues as one whole stimulus is important.

(b) *Administration and Recommendation*

There are very few problems associated with the administration of blind tests that an experienced tester would not foresee. The voice is important, of course for it takes the place of the smile given to the sighted child and is the means of establishing rapport. The voice must have much vitality and variety to guard against monotony and boredom and the use of the word 'look' should not be avoided, for blind children 'look' with their hands as we look with our eyes.

Care should be taken that any article to be used by the child lightly touches his hands as it is passed over so that no time is lost in searching. All practical work should be done on a large tray with raised sides which has been covered with some type of rough material to minimize unnecessary movement of small articles needed by the child.

When administering the Williams Test it must be remembered that it is particularly useful for comparing one blind child with another and has a high correlation with success in the school situation. However, since the test gives no indication of a child's practical ability, any psychologist using this alone will wish to make other assessments of his behaviour in situations involving objects where the child needs to use his hands. It is often difficult without this thorough investigation for anyone who is not well acquainted with the behaviour of blind children to disentangle the effects of blindness from those of mental retardation. This will also help to offset the problems raised by the effect of the verbal fluency of many blind children. They often have a wide vocabulary and are facile talkers as this has been their main means of participating in a sighted world, but it has sometimes led to serious errors in educational placement and expectation.

Manufacture of the adaptation of the Terman-Merrill Test for use with blind children has now been discontinued, but many clinics have the apparatus and are willing to lend it. If any difficulty is experienced the author always has a set available for loan.

As with any other type of handicap, the psychologist must know the main facts concerning the developmental period before a realistic recommendation can be made. He must be aware of any past or present circumstances which could affect the decision to be made. Where a social worker's case history is not available, such information should be obtained from the adult accompanying the child before the test is started. An ophthalmologist's report should also be requested (Asher, 1961, Chapter X, will help in understanding this) and when a child has to be seen without such a report, this should be stated at the time that the recommendations are made.

It is rarely wise to make a final assessment after one interview, and whenever possible there should be several periods of observation when the child's reaction to his environment, his responses to stimulation and his ability to integrate with other children can be observed. Gesell and Amatruda (1947) not only stress the need for long periods of observation in order to arrive at a proper diagnosis but also point out that 'vision is a social sense as well as an intellectual' one and the lack of sight may affect the development of personality more than intellectual development. The lack of active play may also affect the child's physical health and tend to make him apathetic or nervous of a new environment, and so affect his response to testing, however expertly done. It is often helpful to give the same simple task (such as a form board, Wallin A or some other simple, learning task) on successive days, not as a test but as a means of assessing the child's ability to learn.

Where expert advice to the parents has been available but disregarded, a period of parent consultations will be needed alongside the work with the child; a great deal can be done in the rehabilitation of a blind child when the parents virtually become an extension of the clinic team. After a period of parent/child/therapist experience, it is sometimes helpful to integrate the child into a small group of two or three sighted children. Such a play group can be beneficial to both blind and sighted and often makes the psychologist's eventual recommendation more realistic.

(c) *The Assessment of Young Blind Children*

When psychologists are asked to see pre-school blind children, it is generally because they have been to a Sunshine Home and failed. In cases where this is not so, a period at a Sunshine Home may be recommended as giving opportunity for extended observation, although the child must be stable emotionally and not obviously backward for the prognosis to be good in such an environment. Another possibility is to refer the family to the parent-child advice unit run by the R.N.I.B. (224-228 Great Portland Street, London, W.1) at 60 Hallowell Road, Northwood, Middlesex.

There are particular difficulties inherent in the testing of young blind children, partly due to the inadequacy of our testing techniques and partly to the wide differences in children's upbringing. In those cases where children have been so restricted in early experiences that they have had little opportunity of indirect learning, they have neither the desire nor the ability to respond to the testing situation. With these young children, therefore, a period of observation is not just desirable but essential. After a period of individual stimulation, these children will need the experience offered by a small pre-school play group under the experienced eye of the psychologist; where no such group is available, an extended period of observation and stimulation should be arranged individually. Only in this way can their response to stimulation, frustration, friendship, direct teaching, etc., be fairly estimated. Norris, Spaulding and Brodie (1957) found that 'qualitative descriptive observations of the child were often more significant than his response to the test items'.

II PARTIALLY SIGHTED CHILDREN

1 Definition and incidence

'Partially sighted pupils – pupils who by reason of defective vision cannot follow the normal regime of ordinary schools without detriment to their sight or to their educational development, but can be educated by special methods involving the use of sight'.

Once again the definition is given in terms of the schooling required and because of this partially sighted schools and units have a heterogeneous group of children living and learning within them. Many children see adequately for all normal activities but cannot use standard print at a normal rate. Others, however, are borderline 'blind' and it is sometimes difficult to know the best placement for them. The decision is generally made on whether or not the child can manage print of any kind (with every type of lens help possible). Where this is not possible, that child must learn braille and must, therefore, attend a school for the blind.

Latest statistics (1965) give the incidence of partially sighted children as 3·2 per 10,000 school population: 2,265 children, roughly nearly twice as many as the blind school population. It is virtually impossible to state accurately the

o

number of places provided for partially sighted children because so many schools are shown as taking partially sighted children plus other types of handicap; also, the number of places available in units attached to ordinary schools is not published separately. Some facts are known, however.

2 Schooling

There are six all-age boarding schools catering mainly for partially sighted children which have 718 places, plus two for blind plus partially sighted children, taking 236 overall. Nineteen day schools take 1,116 partially sighted children only and a further five for partially sighted plus physically handicapped or delicate children have 960 places. Three of the boarding schools have together 30 places for day pupils and added to this must be the number of children who attend units in ordinary schools. The overall number of places seems adequate.

Much of the work with these children is individual as their problems vary so much, but music, P.E. and other group work is done wherever possible. Learning is slower than that in a comparable group of fully sighted children largely because of the inability of most partially sighted children to scan a page of reading – each line must be carefully studied. Naturally, there is much oral work.

There is some difference of opinion as to what shape the future education of partially sighted should take. The content of the curriculum is very much like that of any other school, although it is obvious that it may not be able to be so broad because of the greater amount of time needed for learning. The place where it should be given, however, is still hotly debated.

In theory, the obvious place is in a unit in a primary school for the primary-age child and in a secondary school for the older child. This makes integration much easier and group lessons can be taken with sighted children. In practice, however, it seldom seems to work out in this way. If partially sighted are to mix for any lesson with seeing children, very careful preparation must be made. For example, if they are going to a mixed cookery lesson, they must be prepared before hand for the recipe they will be using as it takes too long to stop and read something entirely new. The same difficulty obtains for a music lesson: they cannot read off quickly enough the words and music of a new song and they hold back the rest of the class. Very close co-operation must be maintained between the teachers within the school and the unit if any real integration is to take place. The children themselves have also to be taught an accepting attitude for only rarely do partially sighted and fully sighted children play together in the playground or hall and even less frequently do real friendships spring up between the groups.

From the point of view of the staff it is claimed that units in ordinary schools are unsatisfactory. The 'partially sighted teacher' always seems a little different from the rest of the staff and is sometimes resented because his children need certain privileges. To some extent this type of teaching has little future for the staff as there are rarely more than two or three teachers in any one unit and graded posts are not often available.

There seems a good case, therefore, for schools for partially sighted children and, indeed, there are some very successful schools in existence in this country. Here, however, although the problems are different, they do exist. Perhaps the biggest difficulty for both staff and children is isolation. This, of course, is a hazard of all boarding schools, but there is a double hazard here, for the children themselves are already a little isolated from fully seeing children by their handicap and the staff somewhat isolated from their teacher contemporaries because of special teaching techniques. A further difficulty is that of making friends when the children return to their own area during the holidays. While this is a problem for all children attending boarding schools, it poses added problems for the partially sighted child. Except in large urban areas there are not enough partially sighted children living close enough together to form a day school.

3 Intellectual abilities

Although general surveys on handicapped children suggest that the general ability of partially sighted children covers the normal range, they appear to bunch rather heavily in the area of 'low average' and 'a little below average'. However, so little work has been done in this field that it is impossible to say whether this is a fact or whether testing techniques for this type of child are inadequate.

In 1954, the standing committee of the National Society for the Prevention of Blindness, New York, reported on 'Research Needs Related to Partially Seeing Children'. Because of insufficient data they suggested the following:

(*a*) Periodic surveys of both rural and urban areas to determine actual incidence.

(*b*) A survey to determine the causes of partial sight to be undertaken every 3-4 years (the last accurate data was gathered in 1951 (Kerby, 1952).

(*c*) Experiments to ascertain the size of type most appropriate for individual children.

(*d*) A follow up of the experimental study in Ohio, 1954, which appeared to show that the majority of children had near visual acuity good enough to enable them to read material of the standard size for their age group (an endeavour was made to follow up (*c*) and (*d*) in England in the early sixties, but no results were published).

(*e*) More knowledge is needed relating to the fitting and use of special optical devices (Exhall Grange, Coventry, the largest boarding school in England for partially sighted children, has numerous devices and lenses available to any child who needs them, but they are rarely used).

(*f*) A study is needed of eye defects by type and degree and their effect on visual functioning.

(*g*) The reasons for placement of partially sighted in special education need to be known with particular reference to –

    (i) socio-economic and emotional factors

    (ii) parental acceptance or rejection

    (iii) travel distance to a unit

    (iv) isolation from their own social group

    (v) the kind and amount of counselling by ophthalmologists, social workers, nurses, teachers.

(*h*) More must be known about the most effective procedures for ascertaining mental and vocational aptitudes.

(*i*) Personality studies are wanted.

(*j*) New testing methods should be tried.

(*k*) A comparative study is needed of the effectiveness of teaching in special classes, special units and help in the ordinary class. Such a study must be related to the total adjustment of the child, not just to academic achievement.

(*l*) The relative effects of the home and the school in total need to be investigated.

(*m*) Better integrated research is needed on the application of inter-professional teamwork – doctors, social workers, nurses, teachers, psychologists, etc.

(*n*) Much more must be known about the whole range of the educational programme.

It is obvious that more questions are being asked about partially sighted children than answered. There are several possible reasons for this; there is no university department specifically concerned with partial sight so that research planning is rather more difficult; there is no very strong organization such as the R.N.I.B. or the R.N.I.D. and perhaps the problem of partial sight does not evoke as much interest and sympathy as blindness.

While it is known that the intellectual ability of partially sighted children covers the whole range of intelligence, their achievement in school subjects tends to be lower than that of their fully sighted contemporaries. This may be partly due to the greater effort required in their studying and partly to an attitude of general rebellion or inefficiency which many of them hold. Just as some blind children are overprotected, so many partially sighted children are underprotected. Frequently far too much independence is demanded of them, particularly from parents who are not always aware of the nature and extent of their children's difficulties. Psychologists can often be helpful in explaining some of these problems to the parents and in helping them to understand why a child finds it so difficult to negotiate traffic or to manage alone on stairs, etc. Teachers of partially sighted children are generally more alive to these difficulties but cannot, alone, give them the confidence to face life that only comes by feeling at home in the environment and being able to deal adequately with day-to-day happenings.

Another group who sometimes need more understanding patience by both parents and teachers are children with a 'lazy' eye (this is an eye which, although physically competent, is not functioning properly so that the other eye is over-worked). When the good eye is first occluded some children react strongly by fear, aggression or depression. They find the experience very frustrating and if they are reprimanded for carelessness or untidy work, they find the situation almost unbearable. The resulting aggression or withdrawal can put them back several months in their school work.

4 Personality and social adjustment

If little has been written concerning the personality of blind children, virtually nothing has been written about partially sighted children. For many years blind and partially sighted children lived and worked together and certainly many of their problems are the same. Nevertheless, partially sighted children often have a much more difficult time than their blind peers.

A partially sighted child sometimes reaches school age before his handicap is realized. Before this time he is often punished for being 'careless' or for not looking where he is going and bumping into things. Even when a young child is known to be handicapped by poor sight, he tends to get less sympathy than a blind child because his problems are less obvious to people; outside the house they may not be known at all. Such children are also at much greater risk physically because no one rushes forward to help them down steps or across roads – they are just not recognized as having a need for help.

The report of the U.S.A. Children's Bureau (1952) points out that handicapped children, even more than others, need to feel loved and accepted. This, they suggest, is partly because, however physically real the handicap may be, the child is inclined to interpret it as punishment for his deeds and thoughts, or to think of it as the result of parental rejection or as a sign that he is an outcast. Wright (1960) does not believe this, but considers that in spite of very little research on the subject, there is no evidence that there is 'a positive relationship between adjustment and degree of disability'. The manner in which an individual accepts his handicap depends to a great extent on the attitude of those around him who are closely associated with him in his immediate environment. The facts that a partially sighted child is not diagnosed early, often peers intently with a forward bending head or wears thick, rather pebble-like glasses, seem to affect those around him who either neglect him or make fun of him. Both Wright and the personnel of the Children's Bureau may be correct and the attitude of other people may be the cause of some of the reactions seen in the child (compare Chevigny, 1947, concerning blind children).

Only one piece of research is known on this theme, that of Greenberg and Jorden (1957), which was concerned with high-school students in four residential schools for the blind. Whether their findings would be valid for younger children is doubtful. Their hypothesis was that the blind are (*a*) less neurotic, (*b*) more self-sufficient, (*c*) more dominant and (*d*) less authoritarian than partially sighted students. Two tests were given and an individual 'personal data form' administered. No significant differences were found except in the degree of authoritarianism – the partially sighted showed considerably more authoritarianism than the blind. The authors themselves stress the need for more research in this area and make several suggestions which they consider would improve the experiment.

Maxfield and Fjeld (1942) did an interesting study on what they term 'visually handicapped' children which showed that the mean quotient on the Vineland Social Maturity scale for these children was 83·5, well below the average for sighted children. The implication is, however, that these children were blind, not partially sighted, in spite of the title of the paper.

Morgan's (1944) research compared the emotional adjustment of visually handicapped boys, normal boys, and a group of boys in state reform schools. Those with visual handicaps showed social maladjustment considerably higher than that of the boys in the ordinary schools but lower than that of the boys in state reform schools. There was a tendency for the more intelligent handicapped to be less maladjusted.

If, however, Norris, Spaulding and Brodie found that under good conditions a blind child can develop quite normally, becoming independent and fully functioning, the same is likely to be true of the partially sighted child. Again, we return to the importance of the parent/child relationship and the developmental conditions of the early years. Plants' (1950) conclusions concerning blind children apply to the partially sighted also – 'It is imperative that they be given the opportunity for self understanding and that such understanding is not blocked off by so much physical and intellectual activity that they are left little time or energy for learning to know themselves'.

5 Assessment

Occasionally a partially sighted child can be given the standard version of the Terman-Merrill Test (1961 edition). Often, however, their sight is not sufficient for this and the special adaptation prepared in 1952 of the 1937 version of the Terman-Merrill Test for partially sighted children must be used. In this, the designs and pictures of the envelope material have been redrawn, photostatically treated and printed on very white paper. This makes the whole more black and white so that details are more easily seen. The printed material is in large lettering which is easier to see than in the standard version.

The Williams Test may also be used if a verbal test is required. The standardization of this test included a proportion of partially sighted children.

Any psychologist who can use the Terman-Merrill Test can administer either of these tests; no special technique is needed although the test takes longer to give. The child must be allowed to handle the material and place it in the position which allows of optimum advantage according to the type and degree of partial sight.

III CHILDREN WITH PERCEPTUAL IMPAIRMENT

1 The problem

The children who will be considered in this section are those who, having adequate vision for all their needs, yet fail to perceive.

If we accept Goins' (1958) definition that 'visual perception is that process by which phenomena are apprehended by the mind through the medium of the eye', it will be obvious why so many people consider children with perceptual impairment to be brain-damaged children. While this may eventually prove to be so, there is not yet enough evidence to state it as a fact. Much of the work on perceptual impairment has been done with cerebral palsied children (Strauss and Lehtinen, 1947; Abercrombie, 1964; Wedell, 1964) and these children are of course, brain injured. Nevertheless, there have been studies, many unpublished, in which various forms of perceptual impairment have been found in children with no observable signs of brain injury and in whom no unusual EEG results are obtained, nor anything unusual in a full neurological examination. This is particularly so in many cases observed in a large Child Guidance Service in the North of England where this problem has created a special interest.

It must be emphasized that these children have no difficulty in actually seeing a shape, a word or an object, only in interpreting whatever is 'eye-seen'. Goins (1958) makes a necessary distinction between the 'sensory aspects of *receiving* the visual stimuli – and the *transmission* of appropriate nervous impulses to the brain' (emphasis Goins). So what these children lack is the ability to interpret a seen stimulus into a meaningful concept or even, in some cases, to see the whole at all.

Thurstone (1938, 1941) suggested a factor of 'perceptual fluency and speed' and Renshaw's (1945) work with naval personnel in the recognition of aircraft supported this view as he discovered that it was not so much the spanning area of the eye which was important but the fluency and speed of perceptual field structuring. Some experimenters (e.g. Gates, 1922) have found little correlation between various forms of visual perception and have concluded that there is no general factor of visual perception but specific factors, such as the ability to interpret and remember words, geometrical figures, digits, etc.; yet experience shows that many of these children fail in all forms of visual perception. Fendrick's (1935) work on reading ability certainly suggests a specific factor for visual perception. Nine tests involving perception were used and mean scores of all were significantly higher for the good readers.

Among children it may be a general weakness which gradually differentiates the various fields as maturity develops. For where children are concerned, not only must they *see* through unimpaired visual acuity, then *perceive* the object as a whole but they must already have known and formed a *concept* of that object so that it can be interpreted. Wedell (1967) makes this point clear when he described seven different functions involved in the drawing of a square.

Thurstone's 'P' factor seems the nearest we can get to this general ability of being able to perceive 'detail that is embedded in irrelevant material'. Tests of reading readiness often contain this type of task and the children we are considering not only tend to be slow at reading but sometimes fail at mathematical tasks also. Wedell (1967) points out that 'number, usually taught in terms of the spatial arrangement of materials, is also likely to be affected by perceptual impairment'. Schonell and Schonell (1957) suggest that inadequate development of visual imagery may constitute a handicap in calculation.

2 Recognition and assessment

Recognition of these problems can often be discovered during a routine Terman-Merrill or W.I.S.C. Test. In the Terman-Merrill Test the child will do badly at designs, paper cutting, paper folding, complete a man and possibly reading and number items. Designs may be correct but drawn upside down or on their side, in completing a man, the child may draw the necessary additions correctly but not attached. On the other hand, the subject sometimes cannot do these tests at all. Young children may not be able to name the picture vocabulary although they know the objects – they often name one part of the picture. The Performance Scale of the W.I.S.C. is generally low.

If no testing is being done, much evidence can be found in their response in the playroom or classroom for they find it very difficult (1) to recall and reproduce visual patterns, (2) to discriminate between figure and ground in a picture and (3) to appreciate the significance of separate items on a page.

Such children often have defective body image, drawing the human figure badly, omitting parts or drawing it sideways or upside down. This is probably Robinson's (1946) meaning when she mentions 'bodily well-being' as one of the elements involved in visual perception. Such children seem to remain at Piaget's sensori-motor stage: they still need to use every type of exploration and only the evidence of their hands, their feet, often their tongues, can be believed or understood (a young boy of $5\frac{1}{2}$ still puts everything to his mouth and he paints a man by a heavy blob rather like a near-blind child does). Possibly the most important factor for these children with visual impairment but no obvious brain lession is their lack of body image. When we are sure of ourselves in space we have a point of reference to judge position and distance. Without this we tend to confuse 'up' and 'down', 'above' and 'below', 'in front' and 'behind'. Indeed there are some children who need to be taught the meaning of such words by direct demonstration as though they were words in a foreign language. Even when objects are clearly seen, the children find it difficult to judge the relative positions of objects, their distance from one another. Picture mass confuses them, they tend to notice small details rather than the whole picture and so lose the clue and cannot interpret.

Reading and writing are vitally affected and sometimes mathematics. Worse than this, however, is the effect on their general living as all orientation is so difficult and so much energy is given to trying to sort out things. It is not surprising that such children lose confidence and virtually stop learning. So often they are told 'Oh, don't talk nonsense' or 'Don't be silly' that in the end they become silent and withdrawn or become aggressive exhibitionists.

Psychologists and medical officers testing for possible E.S.N. placement need to be aware of these childrens' difficulties as they are so often considered very retarded. In severe cases verbal responses also become affected, partly because of lack of interpretation, partly because of lack of confidence in speech – so many times they have been wrong that they now presume they will be wrong and refuse to answer questions.

3 Teaching suggestions

Therapeutic work with these children must take place in three ways: (1) their confidence must be built up by giving them activities in which they can succeed, (2) they must be given a clear body image and (3) some concentrated work on perception must be undertaken. These activities should take place outside the classroom for the child has already suffered considerably from being thought slow or odd or unco-operative and he will only do good work if he is alone with the therapist. As a rule, however, such children can remain in an ordinary school, especially if the class teacher takes an interest in their experimental work and encourages effort rather than result.

Better understanding of body image will gradually develop if the child stands opposite the therapist to see and touch parts of the body. When he is sure of this he can translate it to his own, seen body and, much later, to his unseen body (eyes closed). At the same time, moving over, under, round objects or between them will help him to know himself in space. According to age, various moving objects may also be used such as swing boats, scooters, cycles, etc.; only after considerable experimentation are such children happy standing on one leg, hopping, climbing, etc., but this must come before the work is finished.

Concentrated work on perception can go on all the time but most of the apparatus must be home made because there is so little on the market. Things like the Bates 'Tests' can be used as exercises; some of the 'shape' material of the various infant school suppliers – blocks, cones, etc. – and other mathematical tools are all useful. Clear, simple pictures are important; paints, crayons, clay, Lego and other constructional toys can be used for shapes. There is really no end to the ordinary play material that can prove effective in educating the visual perceptual abilities of these children. Reading and mathematical text books will come into their own as the children progress.

Frostig (1961), Kephart (1961), Frostig and Horne (1964) and Tansley (1967) have all produced programmes helpful to these children, but all need supplementing to meet the needs of the individual child. The younger the child the better the prognosis – in fact, with many older children therapy must be directed towards helping the child to find a way round his problem as it is often too anxiety provoking to take him right back to basic principles. Children vary a

o*

great deal in the amount of help they can use and there is a need for much more research to find out which children are likely to improve and why. There is no doubt, however, that the younger the child, the more hope there is.

REFERENCES

ABEL, G. L. (1959) Problems and trends in the education of blind children and youth. *In Concerning the Education of Blind Children*. New York: American Foundation for the Blind.

ABERCROMBIE, M. L. J. (1964) *Perceptual and Visuomotor Disorders in Cerebral Palsy*. London: Heinemann. Little Club Clinics in Developmental Medicine.

ALLEN, F. H. and PEARSON, G. H. J. (1928) The emotional problems of the physically handicapped child. *Brit. J. med. Psychol.*, 8, 212-235.

AMERICAN FOUNDATION FOR THE BLIND (1957) Group Report V. Itinerant Teaching Service for Blind Children.

ASHER, H. (1961) *The Seeing Eye*. London: Duckworth.

BABCOCK, R. H. (1915) The blind and their sense perception. *The Outlook*, III, 871-872.

BARRY, H. and MARSHALL, F. E. (1953) Maladjustment and maternal rejection in retrolental fibroplasia. *Mental Hygiene*, 37, 570-580.

BERTIN, M. A. (1959) A comparison of attitudes towards blindness. *Int. J. Educ. Blind*, 9, 1-4.

BUELL, C. (1946) Guidance of visually handicapped youth. *J. Except. Children*, 13, 78-82, 92.

CHEVIGNY, HECTOR (1947) *My Eyes have a Cold Nose*. London: Michael Joseph.

CHEVIGNY, HECTOR and BRAVERMAN, S. (1950) *The Adjustment of the Blind*. New Haven: Yale U.P.

COWEN, E. L., UNDERBERG, R. P., VERRILLO, R. T. and BENHAM, F. G. (1961) *Adjustment to Visual Disability in Adolescence*. New York: American Foundation for the Blind.

CUTSFORTH, T. D. (1933) *The Blind in School and Society* (reprinted 1951). New York: Appleton.

CUTSFORTH, T. D. (1950) Personality and Social Adjustment among the Blind. *In* ZAHL, P. A. (Ed.).

DEPARTMENT OF EDUCATION AND SCIENCE. *The Health of the School Child, 1964 and 1965*. London: H.M.S.O.

DRUMMOND, W. B. (1920) A Binet scale for the blind. *Edinburgh Journal*, 24, 16-31, 91-99.

FENDRICK, PAUL (1935) Visual characteristics of poor readers. *Teachers College Contributions to Education*, No. 659. New York: Columbia University, Teachers College.

FROSTIG, M. *et al.* (1961) A development test of visual perception. *Percept. Mot. Skills*, **12**, 383-394.

FROSTIG, M. and HORNE, D. (1964) *The Frostig Program for the Development of Visual Perception.* Chicago: Follett Publishing Co.

GALLAGHER, J. J. (1966) Children with developmental imbalance. *In* CRUICK-SHANK, W. M. (Ed.) *The Teacher of Brain-Injured Children.* New York: Syracuse U.P.

GATES, A. I. (1922) The psychology of reading and spelling. *Teachers College Contributions to Education*, **129**, N.Y.: Columbia Univ.

GESELL, A. and AMATRUDA, C. S. (1947) *Developmental Diagnosis* (2nd Ed.). New York: Hoeber.

GESELL, A., ILG, F. L. and BULLIS, G. E. (1949) *Vision: its Development in Infant and Child.* New York: Hoeber.

GOINS, J. T. (1958) *Visual Perceptual Abilities and Early Reading Progress.* Supplementary Educational Monographs, No. 87. Univ. Chicago Press.

GREENBERG, H. and JORDEN, S. (1957) Differential effects of total blindness and partial sight on several personality traits. *Except. Children*, **24**, 123-124.

GREGORY, R. (1966) *Eye and Brain.* London: Weidenfeld and Nicolson.

GRIFFIS, G. (1958) *Adjustment Problems of Adolescents with Defective Vision.* M.A. Thesis, University of Chicago.

HAINES, T. H. (1916) *Mental Measurement of the Blind.* Princeton: Psychological Review Co.

HALLENBECK, J. (1954) Two essential factors in the development of young blind children. *New Outlook for the Blind*, **47**, 308-315.

HAYES, S. P. (1933) New experimental data on the old problem of sensory compensation. *The Teachers Forum*, **6**, 22-24.

HAYES, S. P. (1935) Where did that sound come from? *The Teachers Forum*, **7**, 47-51.

HAYES, S. P. (1941) *Contributions to a Psychology of Blindness.* New York: American Foundation for the Blind.

JERVIS, F. (1959) A comparison of self-concepts of blind and sighted children. In *Guidance Programmes for Blind Children.* Perkins School for the Blind, Watertown, Mass.

KAISE, E. MORLEY (1949) Reversals in reading: a problem in space perception. *El. School J.*, **69**, 278-284.

KEPHART, N. C. (1961) *The Slow Learner in the Classroom.* Columbus, Ohio: C. E. Merrill Books Inc.

KERBY, C. E. (1952) A report on visual handicaps of partially seeing children. *Except. Children*, **18**, No. 5.

LANGAN, W. (1948) The education of the blind mental defective. *Am. J. Ment. Def.*, **52**, 272-277.

LOWENFELD, B. (1959) The blind adolescent in a sighted world. *Except. Children*, **25**, 210-235.

MANN, H. and PIRIE, H. (1946) *The Science of Seeing.* Pelican Books.

MAXFIELD, K. E. (1950) The pre-school blind child. *In* ZAHL, P. A. (Ed.).

MAXFIELD, K. E. and BUCHHOLZ, S. (1957) *A Social Maturity Scale for Blind Pre-School Children*. New York: American Foundation for the Blind.

MAXFIELD, K. E. and FJELD, H. A. (1942) The social maturity of the visually handicapped pre-school child. *Child Devel.*, **13**, 1-27.

MINISTRY OF EDUCATION. *Education of the Handicapped Pupil 1945-1955*. Pamphlet No. 30 (out of print).

MOOR, PAULINE M. (1961) Blind children with developmental problems. *Children*, **8**, 1.

MORGAN, D. H. (1944) Emotional adjustment of visually handicapped adolescents. *J. educ. Psychol.*, **35**, 65-81.

NATIONAL SOCIETY FOR THE PREVENTION OF BLINDNESS, NEW YORK (1954) Research needs related to partially seeing children. *Sight Saving Review*, **24**, No. 2, 1954.

NORRIS, M., SPAULDING, P. J. and BRODIE, F. H. (1957) *Blindness in Children*. Chicago: University of Chicago Press.

PETRUCCI, D. (1953) The blind child and his adjustment. *Outlook for the Blind*, **47**, 240-246.

PIRRENE, H. (1967) *Vision and the Eye* (2nd Ed.). London: Chapman and Hall.

PLANTS, S. E. (1950) Home teaching and casework with the blind. *In* ZAHL, P. A. (Ed.).

PRINGLE, M. L. KELLMER (1964) *The Emotional and Social Adjustment of Blind Children*. London: N.F.E.R.

RENSHAW, SAMUEL (1945) The visual perception and reproduction of forms by tachistoscope methods. *J. Psychol.*, **20**, 218.

RITCHIE, J. M. (1930) *Concerning the Blind*. London and Edinburgh: Oliver and Boyd.

ROBINSON, HELEN M. (1946) *Why Pupils Fail in Reading*. Chicago: University of Chicago Press.

SCHONELL, F. J. and F. E. (1957) *Diagnosis and Remedial Teaching in Arithmetic*. Edinburgh and London: Oliver and Boyd.

SEASHORE, C. F. and LING, T. L. (1918) The comparative sensitiveness of blind and seeing persons. *Psychol. Rev. Monog.*, **25**, 148-158.

SMITH, I. M. (1964) *Spatial Ability*. London: University of London Press.

SOMMERS, V. S. (1944) *Influence of Parental Attitudes & Social Environment*. New York: American Foundation for the Blind.

SPENCER, M. B. (1960) *Blind Children in Family and Community*. Minneapolis: University of Minnesota Press.

STRAUSS, A. A. and LEHTINEN (1947) *Psychopathology and Education of the Brain Injured Child*. New York: Grune and Stratton.

SYMPOSIUM (1961) Self-image: a guide to adjustment. *New Outlook for the Blind*, **55**, 71-103.

TANSLEY, A. E. (1967) *Reading and Remedial Reading*. London: Routledge and Kegan Paul.

THURSTONE, L. L. (1938) The perceptual factor. *Psychometrika*, **3**, 9.

THURSTONE, L. L. and T. G. (1941) Factorial studies of intelligence. *Psychometric Monographs*, No. 2.

THURSTONE, L. L. (1944) A factorial study of perception. *Psychometric Monograph*, No. 4.

VERNON, M. D. (1937) *Visual Perception.* London: University of Cambridge Press.

VILLEY, PIERRE (1930) *The World of the Blind.* London: Duckworth.

WEALE, R. A. (1960) *The Eye and Its Function.* The Hatton Press.

WEDELL, K. (1964) Some aspects of perceptual-motor development in young children. *In* LORING, J. (Ed.) *Learning Problems of the Cerebral Palsied.* London: Spastics Society.

WEDELL, K. (1967) Some implications of perceptual-motor impairment in children. *Rem. Educ.*, **2**, 5-9.

WEINER, L. H. (1962) Educating the emotionally disturbed blind child. *Int. J. Educ. Blind*, 77-79.

WRIGHT, B. A. (1960) *Physical Disability: a Psychological Approach.* New York: Harper.

ZAHL, P. A. (Ed.) (1950) *Blindness: Modern Approaches to an Unseen Environment.* Princeton: Princeton University Press.

14

Deaf and partially hearing children

Michael Reed

I THE PROBLEMS INVOLVED

The first problem to be met in work with children with hearing defects is that of definition. However well 'deaf' and 'partial hearing' are defined, these terms have different values for different people. The American Academy of Ophthalmology and Otolaryngology (1960) offers a definition of hearing impairment as the most general term for malfunction of the auditory mechanism. It does not distinguish either the anatomical area primarily involved or the functional nature of the impairment. It further defines 'deafness' as a term describing severe or complete impairment of hearing and should be used only if the hearing level for speech is 82 db (I.S.O.)* or worse.

Impairment of hearing can, of course, be shown graphically, as in pure tone audiometry and in speech audiometry (Hirsh, 1952).

The Ministry of Education (1962) defines 'deaf' and 'partial hearing' in terms of educational need.

(a) deaf pupils, that is to say, pupils with impaired hearing who require education by methods suitable for pupils with little or no naturally acquired speech or language;

(b) partially hearing pupils, that is to say, pupils with impaired hearing whose development of speech and language, even if retarded, is following a normal pattern, and who require for their education special arrangements or facilities, though not necessarily all the educational methods used for deaf pupils.

These definitions are controversial and mean different things to different people. It is difficult, however, to provide a precise definition which will suit all conditions.

Hearing impaired children present problems not always readily understood by less experienced workers in this field. Some of the problems are:

1. recognition of impaired hearing in a child to be examined;
2. knowing the nature and effect of impaired hearing, particularly when associated with other defects;
3. the possible role of impaired hearing in a child who pays little or no attention to sound;
4. the assessment of children known to have impaired hearing.

* I.S.O. International Standards Organisation: decided to adopt an international standard for Odb, British, American and French standards being different.

Recognition of profound deafness is relatively simple, but some forms of partial hearing present considerable difficulties. Even the nomenclature is often ambiguous. A child may be described as 'deaf' in a school for normally hearing children, yet be more properly described as 'partially hearing' in a clinic or special school for such children.

Problems 2 and 3 above require workers specially trained and experienced in this field. All too frequently it is thought to be simple, and assessments are made by doctors, teachers, psychologists and others without sufficient additional training for the more obscure cases. However, much basic screening can be effective with a minimum training provided the nature of hearing impairment is understood. Intellectual assessment requires knowledge of those tests valid for children with impaired hearing, the ability to make contact with children with little or no normal communication and the ability to present instructions in a non-verbal form without invalidating the test procedure.

A clear distinction must be drawn between awareness of sound and complete comprehension of sound. A child may be fully aware that a person has spoken without any understanding of what has been said because his hearing is distorted and not because his intellect is inferior. For example, a child with a severe high-frequency loss of hearing may be aware of a pattern of speech because he hears most of the vowel sounds at normal level of loudness, yet may understand little of what he hears because he fails to hear many consonants.

A child who has a moderate degree of impaired hearing may or may not understand, depending upon the kind of speech pattern used or the listening conditions of the moment. Simple question forms such as 'What is your name?' 'How old are you?' are so familiar that the rhythm and vowel patterns are enough to provide understanding, but other less familiar expressions may not be understood. If the child's attention is directed elsewhere speech patterns which are understood may not be heard as they are subliminal at that moment. These differences in hearing and understanding give rise to misinformed expressions about the child such as, 'He hears when he wants to', or 'He is lazy and doesn't listen'.

For most co-operative children over a mental age of 3 years, it is relatively simple to establish the degree of hearing impairment if the examiner understands the real meaning of hearing and deafness. Less mature children and those who, for various reasons, are not readily co-operative are more difficult to assess and may take skilled and long-term observation and testing.

An effort is made by most local authorities to discover deafness in children as early as possible (Ewing, I. R., 1957; Humphries, 1957). It is now usual for the Medical Officer of Health to keep a register of babies 'at risk' (Sheridan, 1962). If there is a family history of deafness (or other defects), a history of rubella or other virus infections during the first three months of pregnancy, adverse birth conditions or severe neonatal illness, the baby's name is placed on the risk register and particular attention is paid to the development of the child by the Medical Officer and health visitor. In the case of investigation of hearing, the baby is given a screening test of hearing by a health visitor or Medical Officer some time after the sixth month, to ascertain whether there is normal hearing or not. Some authorities have tried to screen all babies for normal hearing, but usually only those 'at risk' are so screened. Many children with impaired hearing are found in this way but, unfortunately, many children with impaired hearing are missed and not found for many years. Meanwhile social, emotional and educational problems are developing in these children.

II INCIDENCE

Difficulties in definition and sampling have caused surveys of incidence to vary quite considerably. At borderline zones examiners may differ widely between 'deaf' and 'partially hearing' and between 'partially hearing' and those remaining in normal schools and not considered 'partially hearing'.

The Fifeshire survey (the Scottish Council for Research in Education, 1956) used levels of hearing loss as shown by pure tone audiometry. The approximate decibel equivalent for dividing lines for hearing (A)/partial hearing (B) and partial hearing (B)/deaf (C) were taken as 35 db and 60 db. In the Board of Education Report (1938) the terms used were Grade I, Grade II and Grade III which depended upon other factors as well as loss of hearing but were roughly equated to A, B and C above. The Advisory Council on Education in Scotland (1950) also reported an incidence.

	Board of Education	Advisory Council	Fifeshire Survey
Grade I		50-80	73 per 1000
Grade II	1·0-2·5	2·5-10	3·4 per 1000
Grade III	0·7	0·7	1·9 per 1000

Johnson (1962) tables returns from local authorities which show a variation in incidence from 0·38 to 1·34 per thousand of the total school population.

The Department of Education and Science publishes figures of children in special schools and units of all kinds and it is interesting to note the change over the years 1938 to 1967, excluding the war years during which time statistics were not collected (see Table 14·1).

As education became re-established after the war, the number of children in schools for the deaf increased until 1954 and then steadily decreased. The number of children in partially hearing schools and units has steadily increased throughout the whole period. There are several reasons for these changes. From 1949 there has been a steady growth of assessment centres in hospitals and in local authorities and a greater awareness of the need for early discovery and pre-school guidance and the early and continuous use of hearing aids. The result of this is that more children can make more effective use of what hearing they have, and therefore there has been a shift from 'deaf' to 'partially hearing' to being able to receive education in normal classes. That is, some

(1) Year	(2) School population	(3) Deaf pupils in special schools	(4) Rate per 10,000	(5) Partially hearing pupils in special schools and special classes of ordinary schools	(6) Rate per 10,000	(7) Other school children also provided with hearing aids	(8) Rate per 10,000	(9) Total rate per 10,000
1938	5,053,644	3,585	7·09					
1939 to 1946	NATIONAL STATISTICS WERE NOT COLLECTED DURING THESE YEARS							
1947	5,174,674	2,644	5·10	895	1·73			6·83
1948	5,503,668	3,065	5·56	751	1·36			6·92
1949	5,680,243	3,130	5·51	854	1·50			7·01
1950	5,805,102	3,252	5·60	964	1·66			7·26
1951	5,895,422	3,439	5·83	1,030	1·75			7·58
1952	6,132,334	3,632	5·92	1,093	1·78			7·70
1953	6,373,096	3,816	5·99	1,089	1·71			7·70
1954	6,545,815	3,979	6·00	1,218	1·86			7·86
1955	6,688,840	3,915	5·85	1,295	1·94			7·79
1956	6,824,870	3,894	4·71	1,299	1·90			6·61
1957	6,954,934	3,692	5·31	1,337	1·92	714	1·03	8·26
1958	7,027,156	3,548	5·04	1,357	1·93	1,562	2·22	9·19
1959	7,093,734	3,477	4·90	1,456	2·05	2,127	2·99	9·94
1960	7,123,007	3,463	4·86	1,453	2·04	3,079	4·32	11·22
1961	7,162,125	3,371	4·70	1,480	2·07	3,865	5·40	12·17
1962	7,168,287	3,255	4·54	2,066	2·88	3,925	5·48	12·90
1963	7,133,057	3,016	4·23	2,469	3·46	4,703	6·59	14·28
1964	7,245,501	3,155	4·35	2,567	3·54	4,555	6·29	14·18
1965	7,306,618	3,110	4·25	2,739	3·75	5,243	7·18	15·18
1966	7,400,486	3,048	4·12	2,980	4·03	5,467	7·39	15·54
1967	7,441,600*	2,923	3·93	3,479	4·68	6,006	8·07	16·68

* Approximate.

Notes

(a) Column 2 does not include pupils in independent schools.
(b) Column 3: the figure for January, 1938, includes pupils who would now be classified educationally as partially hearing.
(c) Column 5 does not include pupils in special classes before 1962. The first special class for partially hearing pupils at an ordinary school was opened in 1947. Information about the number of such classes in England and Wales was collected for the first time in 1960, followed in 1962 by the first annual return of numbers of pupils in attendance.
(d) Column 7: the figures are calculated from annual returns made for the first time in 1957 of school children provided with hearing aids. The provision of hearing aids under the National Health Service for adults and children began in July, 1948.
(e) Column 9: the first 10 sets of figures represent rate per 10,000 in special schools only.

TABLE 14.IA

Pupils with impaired hearing in England and Wales, classified by educational category and type of school attended, 1938-1966

Department of Education and Science, 1968).

children who would have been taught as 'deaf' children can be taught as 'partially hearing' children and some children who would have been taught as 'partially hearing' children became able to be taught in normal classes. As

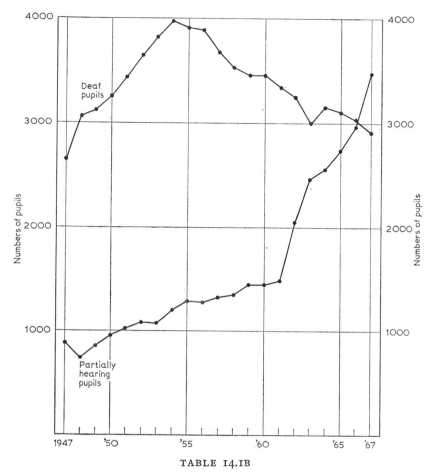

TABLE 14.1B

Pupils with impaired hearing in England and Wales. Graph to illustrate the figures in columns 3 and 5 of Table 14.1A (Department of Education and Science, 1968)

units for hearing impaired children were developed in normal schools some children who would have remained in normal classes were placed in such units. Hence the rise and fall in numbers in schools for the deaf and the steady rise in numbers in schools and units for partially hearing children.

III   CAUSES OF DEAFNESS

Various surveys of causes of deafness differ from area to area, probably because it is very difficult for parents to remember events which have taken place many years earlier and because it is almost impossible to know the details of one's family history beyond one or two previous generations.

In *The Deaf Child* (Whetnall and Fry, 1964) the following comprehensive classification of causes of deafness, both sensori-neural (perceptive) and conductive, is given.

Classification of causes of deafness

I. Prenatal
    A. 1. Hereditary:
          Dominant
          Recessive
      2. Familial
    B. Non-hereditary:
      1. Maternal infection, especially virus diseases:
        rubella   glandular fever
        influenza   Asian influenza
      2. Maternal nutritional deficiencies:
        the malabsorption syndrome
        beri-beri   diabetes
      3. Drugs and chemicals:
        streptomycin   quinine
        salicylates   thalidomide
      4. Toxaemia of pregnancy
        Endocrine – cretinism

II. Perinatal
    1. Birth injuries
    2. Haemolytic disease, due usually to Rh incompatibility – kernicterus
    3. Prematurity

III. Postnatal
    1. General infections, virus and bacterial:
      mumps   measles   other specific fevers
      tuberculous meningitis
      meningococcal and pneumococcal meningitis
      encephalitis
    2. Otitis media
    3. Trauma
    4. Ototoxic antibiotics:
      streptomycin   neomycin   kanamycin

Statistics relating to causes will vary depending upon variability of hospital populations, incidence of epidemics such as rubella and improvements in medical treatment and hygiene.

IV   THE NATURE OF HEARING AND DEAFNESS

The range of hearing in normal ears extends from about 20 Hz.* to about 20,000 Hz., but both frequency and intensity determine whether sound is heard or not (Davis and Silverman, 1960). For speech interpretation the important frequencies are from 250 Hz. to 4,000 Hz. If hearing is normal within this range a child is likely to learn to understand and to develop normal speech provided there are no other complicating conditions. In this context, frequencies below 1,000 Hz. are referred to as low frequencies and those above as high frequencies.

One form of measurement of hearing is that of pure tone audiometry. A pure tone audiometer is an instrument which produces pure tones, usually at octave or half-octave intervals, the intensities of which can be altered by 5 db steps. Some pure tone audiometers are continuously variable through frequency and intensity (Bekesy, 1947). The decibel (db) is the unit of measurement of intensity, the decibel scale being logarithmic. The lower threshold of hearing is the least intensity which can be heard at frequencies between 125 Hz. and 8,000 Hz. That is a range just wider than that necessary for good speech interpretation. This graph is the pure tone audiogram. The normal threshold of hearing for pure tones was found empirically and is referred to as O db.

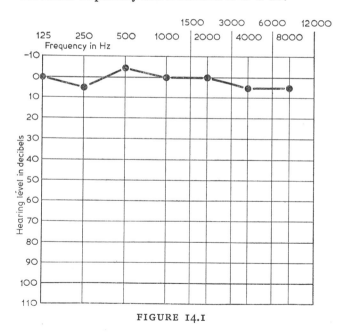

FIGURE 14.1

Figure 14·1 is a representation of normal hearing. Losses up to 20-25 db are assumed not to be significant although minor losses of this order have not been

* Since the U.K. Government decided to adopt the metric system, c.p.s. has been changed to Hz. (Herz).

studied sufficiently under varying conditions and, in some learning situations, might prove to be significant.

The following table gives an approximate indication of the relation of some everyday complex sounds to the decibel scale:

	Intensity at the ear
A whispered voice at 3 feet from the ear	35 db
A conversational voice at 3 feet from the ear	65 db
A loud voice at 3 feet from the ear	80 db
A pneumatic drill at 3 feet from the ear	100 db

Vowels and consonants in speech are complex sounds made up of many different frequency components. Vowels can usually be discriminated by their frequency components below 1,000 Hz. and consonants by their frequency components above 1,000 Hz. Vowels produce power in speech whereas consonants afford intelligibility. With this knowledge a very rough assessment may be made of a child's ability to perceive speech, without the use of amplification, from his pure tone audiogram. It must be stressed, however, that this can only be a very rough guide as many other factors, such as age of onset of deafness, age of discovery, use of a hearing aid, training, intelligence, personality, etc., will affect the judgement. The relationship between pure tone thresholds and speech perception is not a simple one and there is much controversy over this relationship except as a rough approximation.

In some cases of hearing impairment very little amplification is required to reach the threshold of pain. This phenomenon is known as loudness recruitment and although more common in elderly people nevertheless is present in some children (Davis and Silverman, 1960). It is a reason for some children disliking and rejecting the use of hearing aids. Very great care has to be taken with the use of hearing aids in such cases.

It would seem that the earlier experience in listening to sound is provided, the better the interpretation thereof. It is therefore important to discover children handicapped by hearing impairment as early as possible, to provide hearing aids as soon as possible and ensure the careful and continuous use of amplification of sound.

V THE EFFECT OF IMPAIRED HEARING ON ORAL COMMUNICATION

The most handicapping effect of impaired hearing is on speech reception – and therefore on learning, and on speech production – and therefore on easy communication. This, in turn, will also affect personal relationships and emotional stability. Although a hearing impaired child is able to gain much from experiences of seeing, touching, moving, etc., and should therefore be given the maximum experience through his normal senses, nevertheless the development of complete concepts cannot take place. The modification of experience by speech and other sounds, which normally take place alongside most experiences for hearing children, is often absent for deaf children. Many concepts which, at first sight, appear to depend entirely on visual information, frequently depend upon the relationship between the experience and a 'sound' factor in juxtaposition.

1 Speech reception

Speech reception will depend upon many factors such as past experience, the intensity of speech, use of amplification and so on. Therefore, for purposes of

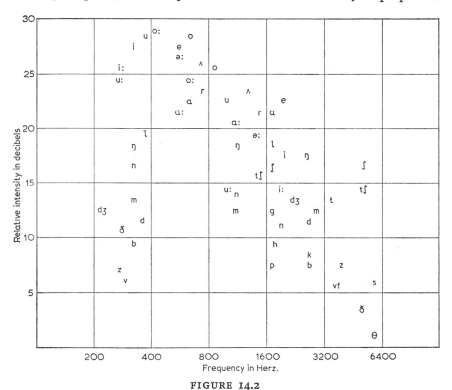

FIGURE 14.2

The principal frequency components of English sounds
(Whetnall and Fry, 1964)

this discussion, a standard set of conditions is envisaged such as a normal conversational voice at 3 feet from a child who has been exposed to a normal speech environment for many years and who is listening attentively without the use of a hearing aid and not lip-reading.

Figure 14·2 shows the frequency bands which are most important for each of the English speech sounds and also gives the relative intensities of the components in their complex structure. The position of any phonetic symbol is the mid-point of a narrow frequency band. For all voiced sounds there is an additional low-frequency fundamental component in the band covered by the vocal cord vibrations (Whetnall and Fry, 1964).

Figure 14·3 shows the relative intensities of English speech sounds expressed in decibels above the level of the weakest sound 'th' as in 'thin'. The speech sounds will vary depending upon the power of the speaker's voice, but the relationships will remain the same.

An examination of the distribution of speech sounds of the pure audiogram can give a rough approximation of the difficulties a hearing impaired child, or adult, will have in recognition of speech sounds. It can only be an initial rough approximation to actual speech reception as many other factors are involved.

o:	29	i	22	tʃ	16	k	11
o	28	u:	22	n	15·5	v	10·5
a:	26	i:	21	dʒ	13·5	ð	10·5
ʌ	26	r	20	ʒ	13	b	8·5
ə:	25	l	20	z	12	d	8·5
a	24	ʃ	19	s	12	p	7·5
u	24	ŋ	18·5	t	11·5	f	7
e	23	m	17	g	11·5	θ	—

FIGURE 14.3

The relative intensity of English sounds (in decibels)
(Whetnall and Fry, 1964)

With a hearing loss represented by Figure 14·4, listening carefully, a child would be expected to hear and understand everything that is said to him. If, however, his attention is directed elsewhere, he may not be attracted to speech as quickly as a child with completely normal hearing. It is possible, therefore, that such a child could be said to hear when he wants to hear. A hearing aid would not help in such cases, as this would probably introduce too much noise and distortions and make most sounds too loud for comfort. The problem is really one of attention or raising the speaker's voice slightly. If this loss of hearing were present from birth, speech comprehension might be delayed – but not significantly and not in the early years as speech is usually directed to the child and close to him.

With a hearing loss represented by Figure 14·5, without the use of a hearing aid or lip-reading and at 3 feet from the speaker, a child would be aware of speech sounds but it is unlikely that they would be loud enough to interpret.

If, however, the speech is made loud enough by speaking close to the ear, or by the use of a hearing aid, then, provided the language is within the knowledge of the child, it will be understood.

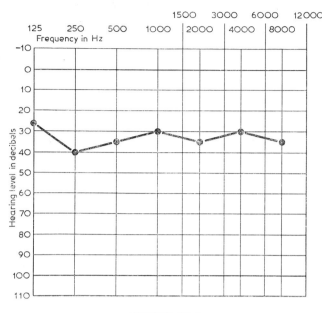

FIGURE 14.4

If the condition has been present since birth, or soon afterwards, then there is the additional problem of developing an understanding of language. Speech must be loud enough for language development to take place. It would seem

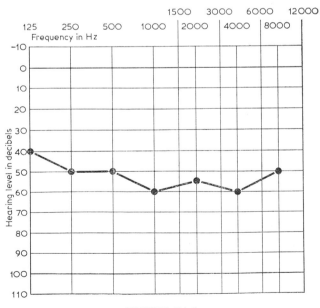

FIGURE 14.5

that the earlier speech patterns are received the greater the development of language (Whetnall and Fry, 1964). Therefore, it becomes important to have the careful use of a hearing aid from as early an age as possible and the maximum use of speech in meaningful situations on all possible occasions so that the handicap caused by the defect can be minimized.

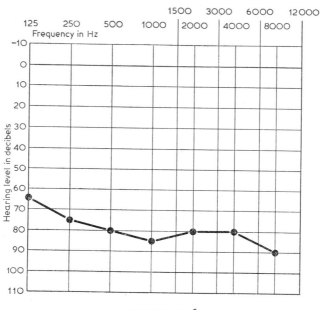

FIGURE 14.6

With a hearing loss as represented by Figure 14·6, speech at 3 feet and without a hearing aid or lip-reading is unlikely to be heard at all. If such a hearing loss occurs after language has developed, then the use of a hearing aid would probably be of great advantage and speech almost normally understood, provided there are no other problems. If the condition were congenital then the task of developing language, and therefore comprehension, is a severe one. With this degree of loss of hearing, the age of discovery is a critical factor. If the threshold of hearing is below that of speech awareness, so that there is no experience of any part of this form of communication, the greater the delay in the use of hearing aids the greater seems to be the difficulty in learning to understand through hearing. It is not impossible, however, at almost any age to develop some understanding, provided there is some useful hearing, and even at the age of 19 years it has been possible to develop an understanding of speech, within the limits of a developing language pattern, through the use of a hearing aid and other means, although a severe impairment of hearing was present. The prognosis for a child with this degree of impaired hearing is good, other things being equal, if found in the first two or three years, given a hearing aid and the parents trained to help.

Deafness of a greater order than this presents proportionally greater difficulty until a point is reached at which lip-reading provides more information than hearing. The earlier even limited hearing is trained the less difficult speech recognition becomes.

Hearing impairment such as in Figures 14·7 and 14·8 presents different problems, as this kind of impairment produces gross distortions in speech recognition, due to an imbalance of speech sounds. This kind of impairment is

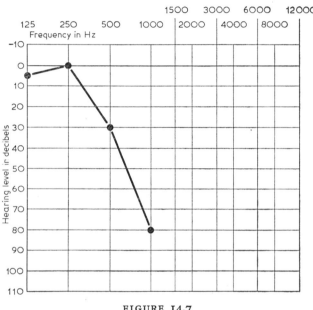

FIGURE 14.7

referred to as high-frequency deafness. That is, there is a considerable difference between hearing for low frequencies and hearing for high frequencies, whether the hearing for low frequencies is normal or not.

With a loss such as Figure 14·7, a child would be as aware of speech sounds as anyone with normal hearing, because he would hear the low-frequency components of speech at normal levels, yet be unable to interpret what is heard because vowel sounds but almost no consonants would be heard. This child would hear a good rhythmic and tuneful pattern of speech composed almost entirely of vowels and may learn to understand a few very familiar phrases in his early years. As speech becomes more complex, as he grows older, he will understand virtually nothing unless special help is given. A large number of children are born with such losses, particularly those with severe anoxic conditions at birth (Fisch, 1955). These children are not easily recognized as having an impairment of hearing and are frequently thought to have various defects other than deafness, such as receptive asphasia, psychogenic deafness, educational subnormality, autism, etc. The use of a hearing aid does not generally help unless there is some deafness at low frequencies as well. In this case the hearing aid has the limited use of bringing the speech up to optimal listening levels so that speech recognition will be maximal, but it can never give 100% recognition through hearing alone.

With a hearing loss such as Figure 14·8 the distortions will not be so severe as in Figure 14·7 and speech will be partially heard and understood. The use of a

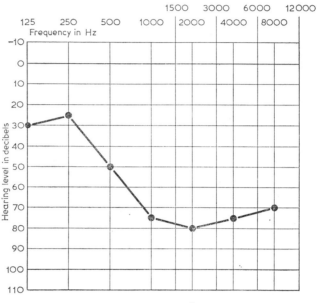

FIGURE 14.8

hearing aid will undoubtedly be of help and with specially selected hearing aids which might reduce the amplification of the lower frequencies they could be of even greater use. As far as is known at present, the variation of the hearing aid characteristic has only a marginal effect on speech recognition, but there is limited experience of this with children and no conclusive experimental evidence so far with children using hearing aids with differing characteristics (Johannson, 1966; Ling, 1968).

A loss represented by Figure 14·9 can only be described as profound deafness. Use of a hearing aid from a very early age may offer rhythmic and possibly voice tonal differences which could be of some minimal use in speech perception. There is much information to be had from low frequencies which should be used; therefore, however deaf a young child may appear to be, and usually a very deaf child is thought to be deafer than he is, a hearing aid should always be used for a considerable time so that he may be trained, if at all possible, to learn to extract as much information as possible through residual hearing.

2 Speech production

If a child is congenitally hearing-impaired, then speech production can be said to be highly correlated with speech perception, although this can be altered somewhat by measures taken by parents, teachers and speech therapists.

With a loss shown by Figure 14·4 there may be no noticeable effect on speech production. A mother talks to her baby in simple phrases when she is usually very close to him, so it is likely that he will hear well and reproduce these in

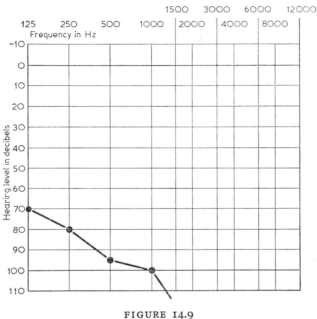

FIGURE 14.9

time. When walking he will be further away and hear less well, but the effect would be so slight that it would not be noticed in the considerable variation of speech in a normal group of children.

With a hearing loss such as Figure 14·5 there will be a marked delay and speech defect. The degree of this will depend upon the exact degree of impairment, the age of discovery, the provision and use of a hearing aid and the amount of training given. If discovered early enough and sound advice given, there need be only a minimal delay and almost no speech defect.

With a hearing loss as in Figure 14·6 speech will not develop at all or, at the best, very rudimentary speech, unless a hearing aid and training is provided. As with speech reception, the age of discovery now becomes critical and more so as the degree of loss of hearing exceeds this level. Amplification and regular training by parents and, later, by teachers of the deaf are essential. Under the best conditions eventual achievement in speech production could be almost normal, whereas without an aid and special help the child could remain dumb.

With high-frequency losses such as Figure 14·7, fluency of speech as shown by rhythm and voice modulation would be hardly affected, but probably the speech would not be understood by many. With a loss such as that in Figure 14·8, the rhythm and tone might be somewhat affected and speech generally more delayed than Figure 14·7, but there would be a reasonable tone and rhythm because much of the low-frequency element would be heard.

In both cases there would be a jargon developing with which the immediate families might be familiar and understand to a limited extent, but rarely understood by strangers.

With a loss as shown by Figure 14·9, profound deafness, without the use of a hearing aid, no speech will develop through hearing alone. With early help and pre-school guidance some children will be able to develop speech which their intimates may understand.

In *all* cases the early provision of hearing aids and parent guidance must be provided. Not only must a child hear other people speaking but also be able to monitor his own, sometimes rudimentary, speech, if the latter is to develop.

VI   SCREENING AND MEASUREMENT

Screening tests are quite distinct from tests which set out to measure an exact level, whether this is related to speech tests or tests of responses at threshold levels through a range of frequencies. Screening tests should discriminate between those who have normal hearing and all others who might have some significant impairment of hearing. They are devised so that observations can be made of reactions to minimal sounds. Mistakes can be made by presenting sounds well above threshold levels, or sounds which are complex, and to which children with slight hearing losses make responses and therefore are thought to have normal hearing.

1 Babies

Local Authorities keep a register of babies 'at risk' of being handicapped (Sheridan, 1962), deafness being one of the handicaps. During the latter part of the first year of life such babies should be screened for loss of hearing. That is, the baby is observed by a competent examiner in the first instance only to find out whether or not the baby appears to react normally to sound. In some areas Health Visitors are used and in other areas this work is done by a Medical Officer of Health. If a baby has not responded normally the second stage should be carried out by an experienced medical officer to confirm the absence of normal responses and to conduct the first stage of differential diagnosis, as lack of response to sound may not necessarily indicate hearing impairment. Some babies may not be able, physically, to make responses expected. If the absence of response is thought to be due to possible hearing impairment, the baby should then be referred to a specialized audiology unit for special tests and prolonged observation and advice (Ewing and Ewing, 1961).

Sound stimuli used in screening tests for babies are speech sounds such as 's' or very gently shaken rattles. These sounds must be at minimal levels if they are to be truly screening sounds and therefore the test must be given in quiet conditions. If the sound is produced from each side while the baby's attention is to the front, the usual reaction to a sound stimulus is a turn of the head towards the sound. At six to seven months, the average baby will be able to do this. Lack of ability to localize could be a sign of hearing impairment, but it could also be due to lack of attention or a physical condition preventing movement of the head. If there is any doubt a more careful observation must be made at the Maternal and Child Welfare Clinic. Similar screening procedures should be carried out and full history taken. If a baby is generally immature he may not be able to make the expected reactions even if he has normal hearing and therefore a full examination of the child and knowledge of his environmental conditions must be taken into account before assuming hearing impairment.

The next stage is to attempt to measure the level of hearing if there is good reason to suspect that this is not normal. Sound stimuli of varying kinds may be made but the frequency spectrum and the intensity levels must be known if correct judgements are to be made of the meaning of responses obtained to complex stimuli. A loudness level meter is used, at the same distance as that between the child and the sound source, to determine the intensity levels used when the child responds.

The child should sit squarely on his mother's lap, not leaning against her, facing an observer who attracts the child's attention and indicates to his assistant when to present a sound stimulus. There should always be two people to conduct this kind of test. The assistant must be out of the field of vision of the child and vary the position from which the sound is produced. This would be from either side or above the child's head. Only the observer in front of the child is in a position to know the right moment to produce the sound stimulus. The baby's attention should not be too fixed on the observer or his actions, nor should he be restless and impatient. An important part of this technique is to know the right moment for presenting the stimulus and only experience of babies and this kind of test situation will provide such knowledge.

The sounds must be produced without giving the baby any other clue, by shadow or tactile sensation such as the movement of his mother, that some event has taken place behind him. Not all babies respond in exactly the same way and therefore any change in state of the baby which is consistent with the sound stimulus offered may be accepted, with caution, as a response.

Pure tones may be offered as the stimuli but not all babies respond to them. However, they should be used over a period of time, as a better picture can then be built up of the child's level of hearing. Earphones cannot be used for this purpose, but an audiometer using a loudspeaker at a fixed distance may produce reliable data. If such tests can be used during light sleep very clear responses may be observed, such as a movement of a baby's eyelid, hand or foot.

2 Infants

The period between $1\frac{1}{2}$ and 3 years is probably the most difficult in which to obtain clear results to tests of hearing. It is beyond the stage of routine screening procedures and usually such children are brought forward because of delayed speech or obvious lack of response to sound. It is also a period when parents are diverted from having their children examined by audiologists because many are told not to worry. 'Speech will come', 'The child is a late developer' or 'is lazy' or 'you are over-anxious'. It is a difficult period because the child is shy of strangers, is more eager to play than to co-operate, or wants to explore and not remain quietly sitting and listening. If the child will sit quietly and play with an observer, either on his mother's lap or at a small table, the procedure is as with babies, i.e. two examiners, one to engage the child and observe responses and the other to make the sounds as directed by the observer. The two examiners must work as a team and know each other's procedure.

At this stage an infant may know the names of some toys such as animals and by asking the child to pick up an animal by name, knowledge of his ability to discriminate certain names will suggest certain kinds of hearing impairment. For example, if he can pick up toys to order only if the speaker uses a very loud voice it suggests a moderate or severe loss of hearing. If he makes mistakes with names with similar vowels but not if the vowels are dissimilar it might suggest a high frequency loss of hearing. The names of the toys must, of course, be known to the child.

3 Young children

With children over a mental age of 3 years the test procedure becomes much easier to undertake. Most children are co-operative at this stage provided the examiner is used to establishing rapport with a young child, probably without fluent communication. Without such rapport no valid results can be obtained.

There is little opportunity to screen children of this age unless they are in nursery schools or classes. In this kind of organized situation simple screening tests can be used, such as asking the child to point out certain pictures from selected rows of pictures, using minimal speech intensity. The names of the pictures in each row should contain a common vowel so that the ability to select the picture must depend upon the child's ability to discriminate consonants. If there is any significant impairment of hearing the child will fail this test (Reed, 1960).

Using play audiometry co-operative children (and with skilled audiometry most children are co-operative) a pure tone audiogram can be obtained provided a careful approach is made through several stages. The most difficult cases are those in which there is no normal communication. These procedures will therefore be discussed in detail. If there is some normal communication the task is easier, but generally with young children all the steps should be taken in turn to be certain of a valid result.

The instruction which the child has to understand is that he should make a response when, and only when, a stimulus is given. This is finally a sound stimulus.

A drum is used in the first stage because this, when beaten, produces a loud complex sound which, except in rare cases, will always be heard, even by profoundly deaf children. Those children who may not hear any part of the sound spectrum may perceive the stimulus through tactile sensation. It is unlikely, therefore, that this stimulus may not be perceived so that all children who are at this mental level and who are physically capable of responding are likely to learn the condition. With severely physically handicapped children it is usually possible to find some movement of a foot or leg or head to produce a consistent response.

An assistant may be needed to demonstrate what is required for a child without normal communication. The assistant watches the examiner and moves a toy when the drum is beaten. This may be taking a ring off a peg, one beaker out of another, or the use of any toy which interests the child and which produces a deliberate movement. If this is repeated several times so that the child may observe that the movement is made when, and only when, the drum is beaten, most children will learn such a sequence and be ready to take part in the game. Thus the first stage of offering a response to a visual, and possibly an auditory, stimulus is complete. The second stage cannot be undertaken unless this first stage is learned.

The second step is to repeat this procedure behind the assistant so that the response is now to an auditory (or tactile) stimulus. This is to teach the child that a response is expected although the stimulus is unseen. Most children learn and respond to this procedure. Thus the stage has been reached when the child responds to an auditory, though complex, stimulus.

The third step is to use pitch bars (or pitch pipes). These produce tones which, although not pure tones, are relatively so. Whether you continue to use the assistant or not depends upon a judgement of the speed with which the child reacts to the changed conditions. A procedure similar to that with the drum is used – first a visual and auditory stimulus, and then unseen from behind the child. A profoundly deaf child may fail at this stage, but if the responses have been consistent it may be reasonably deduced that the child responds to a loud complex sound and not to pitch bars (e.g. 250 Hz., 500 Hz., 1,000 Hz.) and therefore has very little useful hearing. If there are responses, then the way in which the responses are given to sounds of high or low intensity will suggest the hearing level of the child. Use of a loudness level meter will give a more accurate assessment of intensities.

P

From this it is a relatively simple step to use pure tones from an audiometer, using a loudspeaker system or telephone receivers. The latter is the more standard procedure, but sometimes very young children will not tolerate telephone receivers on their heads but will respond to tones from a loudspeaker. If a loudspeaker is used then a fixed distance must always be observed so that the value of the resulting pure tone audiogram can be assessed. The first pure tone audiograms of very young children may not be their true threshold, but if the tests are carefully carried out they should offer a very good approximation of the hearing level of the child. As in all assessments of young children, tests are repeated from time to time to test validity.

In many cases some of the steps may be omitted but if in doubt all should be gone through. *Very great care must be taken to ensure that the only real stimulus is the one the examiner intends to provide.* Some children are very quick to observe any extraneous clue such as shadows, mirror images or eye indications when stimuli are made and respond to these and not to the stimulus the examiner thinks he is providing.

The response to stimuli as described above is usually the movement of a toy and is generally called play audiometry. Some children require greater motivation to induce them to respond or continue to respond. Ewing (1930) used a toy train in a tunnel to provide the interest and reinforcement but did not continue with this, preferring generally to use a variety of simple toys. Hallpike and Dix (1947) used a peep-show apparatus. With this apparatus the child's response was to press a button which illuminated a picture, this being his reward for responding. The illumination could take place only if the stimulus had been presented, thus the child had to learn that the reward came only under certain conditions. However, looking at static pictures is not a very rewarding situation and Denmark (1950) used a roundabout as a moving toy reward. These improvements were suggested for general play audiometry, but skilled audiologists usually find that with most children simple toys which can be manipulated by hand produce quick and reliable results.

For subnormal children and those who are markedly withdrawn more elaborate equipment has been used with favourable results. Lloyd, Spradlin and Reid (1968) describe their apparatus from which, if the response is correct, different kinds of sweets are produced. Fulton and Spradlin (1967) used this apparatus with severely retarded children and concluded that 'operant audiometry' did provide reliable thresholds for the children with whom they experimented.

All these devices need a switching arrangement so that the reward is given only when the stimulus is presented. The reward must be highly desirable and changed frequently enough to maintain interest. Apparatus such as described by Lloyd is technically sophisticated and expensive to produce so that very few centres could obtain this. However, simpler versions can be built depending upon the technical knowledge and ingenuity of those working with such children.

4 School age children

At school age, screening tests in schools are generally undertaken and usually these are in the form of pure tones. Pure tones at a standard intensity, but which may vary from authority to authority, are used. The most usual intensity level is 20 db and the frequencies used are 250 Hz., 500 Hz., 1,000 Hz., 2,000 Hz. and 4,000 Hz. These frequencies are presented to the child, each ear in turn, and responses observed. All the children in a school may be quickly tested in this way and doubtful cases referred to a specialist clinic (Scottish Council for Research in Education, 1956).

At the specialist clinic (audiology unit) standard pure tone audiometry (using a hand signal or pressing a light switch as a response) or play audiometry is used to establish a hearing threshold (pure tone audiogram).

5 Unco-operative children

These frequently present great difficulties. Unless a child is ready to respond willingly and consistently, an exact and reliable test cannot be carried out. However, some evaluation is possible by skilled and careful observation of a child's responses to a variety of sounds. Over a period of time such observations can eliminate various degrees of deafness, so that a reasonable assessment of the problem can be made. For example, if a child has made many responses to fairly loud complex sounds by stopping his play or turning to try to locate the sound, it can be assumed that he is not profoundly deaf but is aware of some sound. The sound stimuli have to be well separated in time because many children will respond only once. If such responses are to quiet but complex sounds, it could be deduced that he has considerable hearing for some frequencies, but the extent through the frequency range would be unknown. The child could have normal hearing but there could also be a severe loss for some frequencies (e.g. high-frequency deafness). If the sound spectrum of various sounds presented were known, reasonable deductions could be made by judicious selection of such sounds.

It is not, however, until consistent responses are being made to pure tones at threshold levels, or there is consistent ability to discriminate rhyming words spoken at minimal intensity levels, that hearing loss can be eliminated as a significant defect.

Some reaction to complex sounds or to speech does not necessarily exclude loss of hearing although it may exclude profound deafness. It is usually possible in many cases to arrive at an estimate in terms of broad zones, e.g. profound deafness, moderate deafness, slight deafness or not very significant deafness.

6 Objective tests of hearing

Tests of hearing usually demand attention, judgement and willingness to partake in the test situation. With malingerers or children who will not or cannot participate, objective tests of hearing would overcome these difficulties.

Highly specialized electrophysiological tests have been designed to eliminate any subjectivity on the part of the child being examined. They are not, however, routine at the present time and demand great skill and interpretation on the part of the examiner and therefore may not be quite as objective as at first the procedure would appear to be. They are used in only a few very specialized centres, but if these centres were regionalized, methods of this kind could be used in those cases in which the diagnosis was obscure.

(a) Psychogalvanic Skin Resistance Test (P.G.S.R.)
This is sometimes referred to as electrodermal audiometry (EDA). It is based on the well-known change in electrical resistance in the skin under certain conditions and which can be measured and recorded. Pavlovian techniques used in conjunction with the galvanic skin response offer an objective hearing test when used in audiometry. The conditioned stimulus is a pure tone. This precedes a mild electric shock (which is the unconditioned stimulus). After several presentations, sweating occurs which alters the skin resistance to an electric current. When this situation arises there will be a change in electrical resistance on simple presentation of a pure tone *if it is heard* (Hardy and Bordley, 1951; Hardy and Pauls, 1952).

The use of this method spread widely through the U.S.A. and into other countries. Hardy implied that this method was the equivalent of subjective pure tone audiometry. However, there have been criticisms of this. Bordley (1956) believes that the auditory-sympathetic reflex lies below cortical level.

Many children refuse to participate in this kind of test. Others accept the apparatus but cry on being given the slight electric shock necessary, and others are very active and restless, both of which conditions affect the results. It has frequently been found that the very children for whom such a test is required are those with whom this procedure proves to be unreliable.

Cerebral palsied children, who frequently have a loss of hearing (Fisch, 1955) are said to be difficult to test by conventional means. By understanding the individual C.P. child's muscular difficulties and by finding one voluntary movement it is often easier to provide valid pure tone audiograms in the conventional way than by using P.G.S.R. which may be unreliable because of the artefact produced by involuntary movement.

Most studies (Goldstein *et al.*, 1954; Barr, 1955; Statten and Wishart, 1956; O'Neil *et al.*, 1961; Moss *et al.*, 1961) discuss the difficulties of this method and reach the conclusion that generally most cases in which there is lack of success in measuring hearing with standard methods also fail with this method.

There is now greater understanding of the limitations, advantages and disadvantages of this procedure, and in the hands of skilled and experienced technicians it may still have a place in a battery of tests.

(b) Electroencephalographic Audiometry (EEG)
This is sometimes called Evoked Responses Audiometry and has been studied for some years (Withrow and Goldstein, 1958; Derbyshire *et al.*, 1956; Derby-

shire and Farley, 1959; Taylor, 1964). This method would appear to achieve better results than P.G.S.R. as children can be sedated and therefore some of the problems involved, such as fear and movement, can be eliminated. However there is still the problem of validation to be considered. Goldstein considers that EEG audiometry is more successful than P.G.S.R. audiometry but nevertheless there is still a need to consider the use of both, together with standard procedures, in order to achieve more answers to many of the difficult questions.

The apparatus is costly and the technicians require great skill and experience in the procedure, particularly in interpretation of the recordings. Beagley and Knight (1956-66, 1967), using a digital computer in conjunction with their EEG apparatus for averaging out the recordings, are showing some useful results which suggest the possibility of a bright future for this method with different children and as a tool to be used in differential diagnosis.

7 Differential diagnosis

The varying reasons for lack of response or lack of discrimination to sound are hearing impairment, mental retardation, receptive aphasia, autism, severe social deprivation or some combination of these conditions. In doubtful cases it is often wise to put the child into a mental test situation first as many indications may come out of this situation provided a non-verbal test is given. Tests of hearing related to the mental test can then be given. Children with uncomplicated loss of hearing have in the past been thought to be duller than they were because verbal tests of ability had been given. If skilled assessment is made and non-verbal as well as verbal tests are given, a clear differential may be observed which would eliminate the simpler mistakes.

In conditions of simple developmental receptive aphasia there should be no great difficulty in differentiation as the child should respond to pure tones at a normal level but have little or no understanding for speech commensurate with his mental maturity. With cases of mixed conditions of hearing impairment and receptive aphasia there is more difficulty in differentiation and assessing the relative effects, as there seems to be no direct method of testing for receptive aphasia. The history of birth conditions or subsequent severe illness may suggest the possibility of this condition being present. A working definition of receptive aphasia is that understanding of speech is not commensurate with the level of hearing and the mental maturity of the child, providing the speech environment has been normal. Therefore, the condition can only be established by elimination of those factors which can be measured, even if only approximately, or reasonably observed.

If hearing impairment and receptive aphasia are both present, the latter can only be deduced if, after a long period in learning situations for a child with a hearing impairment, the child has not learned to understand speech within the limits imposed by his hearing impairment, mental maturity, emotional stability and home environment.

Autism presents a major problem in differential diagnosis as lack of relationship with people is a foremost symptom of the condition. Unless the child does, at some stage, respond willingly to test sounds, it is unwise to eliminate a possible hearing impairment. Tests have to be given as for unco-operative children and deductions made over a long period. For treatment it would be necessary to treat the child as if he hears and also as if he is deaf, but essentially one must try to establish relationships as, without this, very little learning can take place, whatever the other conditions (see Chapter 20).

Treatment, in a social and educational sense, should not be delayed because of uncertainty of diagnosis. A child who appears not to be aware of sound or appears not to understand the meaning of sound can be placed in a teaching/diagnostic situation until a complete diagnosis is made.

VII   TESTS OF INTELLIGENCE

Since Pintner and Patterson (1923) devised a battery of non-verbal tests for use with deaf children there have been many surveys on deaf populations, with following controversial discussions on the relationship between deafness and intelligence. Pintner concluded that the deaf were inferior, probably due to the existence of brain injury. Blair Hood (1949), using the Alexander Performance Scale with 401 hearing-impaired children, found a mean I.Q. of 99·3 but with a standard deviation of 24·9. He reported a bi-modal distribution having a secondary peak towards the low end of the scale. Ewing and Stanton (1943), using Raven's Progressive Matrices (1938), reported results much inferior to those of Blair Hood. Gaskill (1957), using the Coloured Matrices (1947) on 289 deaf pupils, found a mean I.Q. of 97·9 with a standard deviation of 20·8, and considered this to be an adequate test for children in schools for the deaf. Using the W.I.S.C. with deaf children aged 10-15 years he found no statistically significant difference between congenitally and adventitiously deaf children, but the partially hearing children of his sample tended to be below average. He suggests that this could be due to selective influences in school placement. This is likely to be true.

Kendall (1957) found no significant difference at any age level when performance tests (Merrill Palmer) were administered to representative groups of deaf and hearing children. This clearly supported the hypothesis that deaf children of pre-school age are not handicapped in solving sensori-motor problems.

Murphy, L. J. (1957) reported the use of W.I.S.C. (P) with hearing impaired children in schools for the deaf aged 6-10 years. He found in his investigation a reasonably normal distribution of I.Q.s.

Murphy, K. P. (1957) conducted a survey of all schools for the deaf in England, Wales and Eire in which the single age year 12-13 could be found. As part of the survey he used the Wechsler-Bellevue I Scale of Intelligence and found that the mean I.Q. of the group was not significantly different from the standardizing population of Wechsler or L. J. Murphy's groups of children aged 6-10 years.

It is evident from all the reports, and from the writer's experience, that the administration of any test to hearing impaired children requires a high degree of skill in manipulation and wide experience of deaf children.

In more recent years much thought has been given to other forms of investigating mental processes of deaf children. Following the developing interest in the work of Piaget, Oléron and Herren (1961), Darbyshire (1965) and Furth (1966) have investigated the ability of hearing impaired children to solve Piagetian problems. Oléron (1953) in a card-sorting operation found that deaf children were inferior to a control group of hearing children.

Rosenstein (1960) gave non-verbal visually presented tests of perceptual discrimination, multiple classification and concept attainment and usage to 60 orally trained deaf children and 60 hearing children and found no significant difference between the two groups. He suggested that deaf children are capable of cognitive behaviour and that they must be exposed to more linguistic experience. This might be interpreted that mere exposure is enough. It is probably true that if deaf children could attain normal linguistic attainments they would show similar mental functioning to that of hearing children. However, this is one of the most difficult of all learning tasks and, therefore, because profoundly deaf children find it difficult to attain reasonable linguistic attainments, it follows that in any task having a linguistic component they will be inferior to hearing children.

It is generally agreed that children must have varied experiences to develop their intelligence to the full and deaf children are no exception to this. However, many apparently non-verbal experiences are influenced by speech of others in the vicinity to enrich that experience. Thus environmental influences for deaf and hearing children are rarely similar. Luria (1961) suggests that verbal control helps in the execution of certain motor tasks and regards speech as a regulator.

Furth (1966) is convinced that intellectual functioning cannot depend basically upon language. This may be true for the formation of many concepts, but those of a higher order may depend somewhat on linguistic ability. There are concepts which depend upon concrete experiences, the complete development of which can be hastened by linguistic description which may not be available to deaf children. Furth designed several experiments to prove his hypothesis and which would show different characteristics of intelligent behaviour. He points out that 'the deaf' are not a homogeneous group, a fact frequently unrecognized. Not only are there all the variables found in a hearing population, but there are also different degrees of hearing loss, hearing distortions, different C.N.S. disorders due to the varying causes of deafness, different ages of onset of deafness, etc. He suggests there is no psychology of the deaf. However, there is a psychology of deafness in which, knowing all the variables, trends can be discussed.

Furth (1961) conducted tests on 'Sameness' and 'Opposition' on deaf and hearing subjects. On the first two tests there was no significant difference but on the third test the hearing subjects had better scores than the deaf subjects. He attributes this to the assumption that verbal language gives hearing children a specific advantage. In a later experiment (Milgram and Furth, 1963) with retarded children it was postulated that the results would be similarly different in relation to normally hearing children. This was found to be so.

Furth found that deaf children were behind hearing children in their ability to perform Piagetian tasks successfully, but they succeeded eventually. He also describes experiments in logical thinking with deaf children, but did not relate this to any study with hearing children (Furth, 1966).

Darbyshire (1965), having noted that others had found that hearing impaired children performed less well than hearing children in Piaget-type tests, and, thinking that part of their failure could be due to incomplete understanding of the test instructions, decided to include only those tests for which he considered comprehension of instruction would be within the scope of his hearing impaired subjects. From his results he concluded that the performance of hearing impaired children was not inferior.

Ives (1967) discussed the Piaget approach in relation to the development of intelligence in deaf children and points out that in the task, 'conserving quantities of liquid', Furth's sample of deaf subjects was more successful than Oléron's group and infers that this might be because Furth took very great care to ensure that his subjects learned the nature of the task. Both groups were less successful than hearing subjects. Ives suggests that this may be due to the lack of linguistic skills and suggests further use of the Illinois Test of Psycholinguistic abilities as a possible tool for further study in this field (McCarthy and Kirk, 1961; see Mittler, Chapter 20).

It is clear, as Furth and others have pointed out, that verbal tests are invalid for testing hearing impaired children unless the intention is to measure verbal ability. It is also important, but perhaps not so clear, that deaf children should be tested by examiners who can make the instructions understood without indicating the answer. Mime does not always clearly convey to the subject exactly what is in the mind of the examiner. The part played by verbal experience in developing those concepts which superficially appear to have no verbal component is not fully understood and could be studied with some benefit. It has been observed by the writer that scores on W.I.S.C. (P) subtests picture completion and picture arrangements by deaf children who have been discovered very late have improved after their linguistic development has improved.

Knowing the way in which a child performs at the kind of tasks presented by tests of intelligence is an important part of the assessment of handicapped children and particularly so with hearing impaired children, and in attempting to investigate those children who present obscure conditions. If there is an apparent, or real, hearing impairment it is evident that a verbal test is not valid, although the presentation of both verbal and non-verbal tests may reveal, by the different results, the effect of the impairment on the development of verbal ability. Even if a child using a hearing aid can understand the instructions, a verbal test may not be valid as the child may have been given the hearing aid many years after an early onset of deafness. Such a child would not have had the normal exposure to a speech environment. A non-verbal test with verbal instructions becomes a verbal test with very deaf children.

1 The tests

(a) The Ruth Griffiths Scale (Griffiths, 1954)

Age range: up to 2 years (now being developed beyond 2 years). This presents a standardized situation; the resulting profile may give a good indication of loss of hearing. In the case of a hearing impaired child the D.Q. (developmental quotient) as a combination of all the five scales may not have much meaning, but the profile is useful.

(b) The Merrill Palmer Scale (Stutsman, 1931)

Age range: $1\frac{1}{2}$ years to 5 years. This is a very useful test as there are very few verbal items and the instructions can be interpreted by demonstration. Verbal items can be omitted as omissions, together with refusals, are accepted within the framework of the scoring procedure. The test requires very little normal communication and is therefore useful even with children with whom it is difficult to establish any real relationship (Kendall, 1957).

(c) The Nebraska Test of Learning Aptitude (Hiskey, 1955)

Age range: 3 years to $11\frac{1}{2}$ years. This test was standardized on deaf and partially, hearing children, for whom there are different norms. This difference tends to show, as other work has shown (Maxwell, 1959), that even with so-called non-verbal tests there could be verbal influences. The instructions may be given in mime form so that the test is entirely non-verbal in presentation. Some of the pictures reflect an American culture and one of the subtests, puzzle blocks, contains a factor of colour which influences the child in solving the puzzle and yet does not influence the scoring. It may even be a negative influence. There are items such as analogies and classification which are similar to those of the usual verbal tests.

The test is time consuming and the material rather drab, but for severely deaf children may give a good indication of learning ability, as this is understood in a school situation. It is more useful for very deaf children than partially hearing children, for whom the W.I.S.C. is usually more suitable. It is not very useful for disturbed children as the material is not sufficiently attractive and demands more co-operation and contact with the examiner than such children may give.

It is useful for children with communication difficulties for reasons other than hearing impairment.

(d) The Drever Collins Scale

Age range: 5 years to 16 years. This is a test which was standardized on deaf children. Almost all the items are of the 'form board' or 'construction' type of

p*

material, and therefore samples only a narrow range of abilities. It does not provide a good indication of future progress in an educational environment, but has a value for use with those children who do not readily co-operate, as presentation requires very little contact between a child and his examiner. With such children it could indicate some kind of ability and will provide some information not otherwise obtainable.

(e) Wechsler Intelligence Scale for Children (W.I.S.C.) (Wechsler, 1949)
Age range: 5 years to 16 years. This is a most useful test for both deaf and partially hearing children. It has a verbal and non-verbal scale and therefore can be a useful guide, by comparison of the two results, to the effect of hearing impairment on verbal ability. However, very deaf children may not be able to provide any useful results on the verbal scale.

The instructions are generally verbal, but these can be given in a non-verbal form for those children without normal communication (Murphy, L. J., 1957). The items 'block design', 'object assembly' and 'coding' can be understood easily by deaf children. Alternative methods of instructing deaf children for the two items 'picture completion' and 'picture arrangement' may have to be given. Using pencil drawings of a face with a different part missing in each presentation, first drawing in the missing part for him and subsequently letting the child draw in the missing part, will soon teach him that every time he is presented with a picture he will have to indicate a missing part. With the test pictures he can draw in the missing part using a dry paint brush. In this way there can be no ambiguity in his responses. Picture arrangement can be more difficult to present. One method is to give the child a series of numbers to put in order, then a series of letters and finally a series of pictures, demonstrating each time what he has to do. Once he understands the procedure the test pictures are presented.

The items 'picture completion' and 'picture arrangements' appear to be verbally loaded and therefore lower weighted scores are often obtained on these than on the other three items of the performance scale. With greater language development these differences tend to disappear.

This test was standardized on hearing children and later the scale was re-standardized on British deaf and partially hearing children (Murphy, L. J., 1957).

(f) The Snijders-Oomen Test (S.O.N.) (Snijders and Snijders-Oomen, 1959)
Age range: 5 years to 16 years. This is a non-verbal test originating in Holland and standardized on Dutch deaf children. Since then it has been used in many European countries and is now being used in England. It appears to be a useful test for deaf and partially hearing children. It is time-consuming. The instructions are in mime. No large-scale use has yet been reported in England and therefore its validity is not yet known for use with English children.

(g) *Raven's Progressive Matrices* (Raven, 1938, 1947)

Both forms of this test are easy to use with hearing-impaired children. It does not seem to sample a wide range of mental activity and though not very useful with handicapped pupils, is a useful supporting test.

There are other tests, such as the Chicago, the Leiter, the Ontario tests which have been used in the U.S.A., Canada and this country on hearing impaired children but on which there has so far been little reported.

2 Practical problems

In establishing rapport with a deaf child the situation should never be allowed to depend upon speech until it is certain how the child is able to communicate. Deaf children have so often been placed in situations which they have not understood, that they tend to withdraw if they are spoken to by strangers. Good rapport can be established by offering toys with a smile and co-operating in simple play without speech. Through such play, by using speech incidentally but not making the situation depend upon it, the ability of the child to communicate normally, or in any other way, can be established. For example, the child can be asked during play to pick up a car or a doll or be asked to put a ball in a box. By the response to these orders a judgement on the child's ability to hear and understand can be made. Few incidents can cause a relationship to break down more quickly than trying to communicate with a child in a way he doesn't understand.

Children with impaired hearing are usually quick in responding to any visual clue and watch for facial expression to indicate success or failure. Although smiles are necessary for rapport and encouragement, it is important to remember that they may also give an indication, at the wrong moment, of success and thereby encourage him in making a wrong response as well as helping him to make a correct response when he doesn't really know the answer.

An instruction which is normally verbal has to be changed into a non-verbal form so that the child will understand what is required of him but will not indicate what the answer should be. A simple demonstration will sometimes suffice, but this may sometimes indicate the response. Simple learning situations will frequently teach the instruction, as with the W.I.S.C. It is preferable if the instruction is built into the presentation of material, as in the Nebraska and S.O.N. tests.

VIII EDUCATIONAL ASSESSMENT

As deafness is a barrier to communication it is reasonable to presume that a secondary effect is educational retardation. There are two different levels on which educational assessment may be carried out. One is to use normal procedures and the other is to use special tests for hearing impaired children.

It is often important to know how the hearing-impaired child's achievement compares with that of normally hearing children, particularly if placement into normal schools or employment is to be considered. Sometimes, however, the rate of learning for severely deaf children is so slow that special tests have to be devised for a child to get on to the scale and also for a spread of scores within a deaf population. If deaf children can achieve results which can be scored on existing tests for normal children, it would appear to be preferable to use such tests as this would provide information within the deaf group and also relative to the normal population. Severely deaf children usually have to spend a very long period within education to reach the lowest level of most linguistic tests.

Murphy, K. P. (1957) in his survey of 12-year-old deaf children found a normal distribution of intelligence, using the Wechsler-Bellevue I Scale. The reading vocabulary score, using Gates Reading Vocabulary Scale:

Hearing Loss	Boys	Girls
Below 60 db	Mean 12·3 yrs S.D. 10·25	Mean 13·3 yrs S.D. 12·17
60 – 80 db	Mean 8·66 S.D. 6·8	Mean 8·11 S.D. 7·7
80+ db	Mean 7·48 S.D. 6·4	Mean 7·7 S.D. 4·7

TABLE 14.2

Johnson (1962) surveyed those children educated in normal schools in Cheshire although suffering a hearing loss. The distribution of Reading Ages for the 65 children were as follows:

No. Tested	Ahead of age	Average	Retarded by						
			1	2	3	4	5	6	7
			years or more						
65	9	13	17	11	3	7	3	1	1

TABLE 14.3

A recent survey by Simpson (1963) investigated the abilities of those children born in 1947 and attending schools for the deaf in 1962-63. These would be children about to leave school unless they were remaining on at school for special reasons, e.g. at the Mary Hare Grammar School. Three hundred and fifty-nine pupils were interviewed, and 13 children failed to be seen. Simpson found it surprising that of 44 children with an I.Q. of over 120 (W.I.S.C.P.), only 14 were in the two selective schools, the Mary Hare Grammar School and the Burwood Park Technical School for Boys. Profound deafness is such a tremendous barrier to communication that perhaps it is not so surprising, as so many factors other than intelligence play such an important part in achieving oral communication (D.E.S., 1968) and both the two schools concerned are exclusively oral. Bates (1956) has reported that the results from tests using W.I.S.C. (P) are poor predictors of academic achievement. This is probably true if oral communication is essential, but it is possible that there could be other means of communication, such as manual communication, by which means more deaf children could achieve higher attainment levels. This is discussed in the report from the Department of Education and Science, *The Education of Deaf Children* (1968).

1 Reading

It must be remembered that a test of mechanical reading may be impossible for many profoundly deaf children and, in any case, is more a test of their ability to speak than to read. However, tests of reading comprehension are valid, particularly if the test of comprehension is to perform an action after reading. Most tests of comprehension for normal children can be used with hearing-impaired children provided they can reach the base level.

2 Arithmetic

Tests used for normal children can be used provided any language used in problems and any instructions used are understood by the deaf child.

The examination for the selection of children for the Mary Hare Grammar School and Burwood Park Technical School show that deaf children are retarded in arithmetic. It is not clear why this should be, although it is possible that so much time is spent on developing language and communication in schools for deaf children that too little time is available for arithmetic, and also that there is far more language involved in the development of complete mathematical concepts rather than simple computation.

Murphy, K. P. (1957) also found that severely deaf children were retarded in arithmetic and suggests several reasons for this.

3 Tests peculiar to education of hearing impaired children

In educating severely hearing impaired children, the greatest task is that of developing communication. This implies the development of linguistic concepts through the medium of hearing, lipreading, writing and perhaps a manual mode of communication. The latter aspect is, in most countries, an emotional and controversial issue. In Great Britain it is probable that the majority opinion is to attempt to teach children to communicate orally until it is proven that the child cannot learn in this way.

Opportunities are provided, in pre-school guidance and in school, so that a child may develop what hearing he has and to learn to lipread and, at the same time, form linguistic concepts. At a later stage writing is added. The degree of dependence on hearing or lipreading will depend on the level of hearing of the child. *Ad hoc* tests of comprehension through hearing and/or lipreading have to be devised by teachers and psychologists to assess progress. These have to be different from school to school, initially, as the tests will have to depend on the words which have been actively presented to the child. In the initial stages of learning a very deaf child has no background of words, each word or phrase having to be taught actively. There is virtually no passive learning linguistically. Tests need to be recorded on tape for hearing assessment or on film for lipreading assessment. Sporadic attempts are made for the former, but rarely, except for research, is the latter kind of test developed.

It is more difficult to assess linguistic ability particularly of young deaf children. The lack of homogeneity in any deaf population makes it particularly difficult to establish a norm. Owrid (1958) has endeavoured to measure this.

IX PERSONALITY

There have been fewer studies of emotional aspects of personality of deaf children than of intellectual abilities. Lyon (1934), using the Thurstone Personality Schedule, found that the percentage of deaf pupils classified as emotionally maladjusted or needing psychiatric advice were twice as many as hearing college freshmen of approximately the same age. Brunswig (1936) found similar results using a test she had standardized on deaf students. Other studies have shown that deaf children have social and behavioural problems, which is only to be expected if the normal channel of communication is defective. Many personality deviations which are secondary to hearing impairment are likely to be alleviated if guidance is given to the parents of such children and the problems of deafness explained to them. If this is begun when the child is very young and they are able to establish some sort of communication with their developing babies, many personality difficulties need never arise. There will be some, particularly the profoundly deaf children, with whom it will be difficult to establish any reasonable oral communication and emotional difficulties will develop which could be resolved later on within a special school situation. There is a point of view which suggests that in such cases a non-oral communication system might help, but this is very controversial (D.E.S., 1968).

Levine (1956) used the Rorschach technique in a study using an experimental group of 31 deaf subjects from an oral residential school for the deaf and a control group of 100 hearing subjects of comparable age. She found that the deaf subjects were characterized by:

(i) pronounced underdevelopment of conceptual forms of mental activity;
(ii) emotional underdevelopment;
(iii) a substantial lag in understanding the dynamics of interpersonal relationships as well as the world about;

(iv) a highly egocentric life perspective;

(v) a markedly contracted life area;

(vi) a rigid adherence to the book of etiquette code rather than inner sensibility, as standards for behaving and even for feeling.

However, Levine pointed out that this may not be maladjustment in the true sense of the word.

This group was, however, a selected population from a particular kind of segregated community. The total population of deaf school children is very heterogeneous and so much depends upon what action is taken by parents and teachers. In addition, a technique such as the Rorschach can only be used with those deaf subjects who have reasonable verbal ability.

Levine (1960) concludes from her experience that personality evaluation of deaf school-age children is better accomplished through clinical observation and case history than through formal testing. The writer would agree completely with this, but it needs an examiner with long experience of hearing impaired children of all ages and different environmental conditions.

X USE OF HEARING AIDS

Aids to hearing have been used for many years. Before the use of electrical aids, hard of hearing people used horns of various shapes but not many were used as they tended to become figures of ridicule, and certainly no child in school would use one. Some elderly people do make use of them as, in many cases, the reproduction is clear and of more use to them. Since the advent of the small wearable hearing aid more people have used them, particularly since they were obtainable free through the National Health system and very few people, adults or children, are now embarrassed by wearing them, particularly in those cases where the benefit is marked.

If children are given hearing aids at an early age, there is usually no difficulty in getting them to wear the aid continuously. If they are offered late in a child's development then it becomes relatively more difficult to induce him to wear an aid, particularly out of school. In adolescence it becomes quite difficult to induce a child to begin to wear an aid and sometimes those who have worn hearing aids for many years now refuse them. However, aids are becoming smaller yet still efficient and sometimes a boy or girl who has begun to discard a hearing aid will accept a small aid which can be worn behind the ear and be inconspicuous. The greater the benefit, the more likely the child will be to wear the aid.

Not all children with impaired hearing reap the same benefit. Those children with distorted hearing as shown by Figures 14·7 and 14·8 benefit less than those with relatively undistorted hearing losses. Other children, although quite seriously deaf, cannot tolerate loud sounds, and therefore have to wear hearing aids which incorporate automatic volume control or some equivalent technical restriction of output of the aid. Great care, therefore, has to be exercised in advising children how to use their hearing aids and it is essential to have advice from an audiologist.

Most hearing aid users have a single aid which is worn in one ear. This may or may not be the better ear although in cases of severe deafness almost always it is used on the better ear unless there is a medical reason for not so doing. Sometimes a single aid has a Y-lead and a receiver in each ear. This is particularly so with very young children before it is known which is the better ear. This is not true binaural hearing, of course, and there is some experimentation going on with the use of two hearing aids but generally in a haphazard fashion with anecdotal reporting.

Jerger, Carhart and Dirks (1961) used tests of speech intelligibility on subjects with sensori-neural deafness and found that results failed to reveal any appreciable advantage for using two hearing aids over one.

Dirks and Carhart (1962) used a questionnaire method to discover the various aspects of efficiency in everyday listening using binaural and monaural hearing aids. There were 26 different environmental conditions. In quiet conditions the subjects preferred the use of binaural hearing aids; in noisy conditions both binaural and monaural aids were poor.

At the present time binaural or monaural aids are issued, depending upon the beliefs of the examiner, which seem to be largely an emotional conviction. There should be more research in this field under different conditions.

XI SCHOOL PLACEMENT

There is a great deal of controversy over placement of hearing impaired children into the educational system, much of which is extremely emotionally toned. There are boarding and day schools for deaf children, schools and units for partially hearing children and some schools which still accept both deaf and partially hearing children.

Before schooling, in most areas, there is some pre-school guidance for the family. It is understandable that many parents do not like their children leaving home to go to a boarding school. It is also reasonable to believe that the child needs the family situation especially when very young. The Education Act (1944) requires a local authority to provide education (not necessarily within its own boundaries) for hearing impaired children from the age of 2 years if the parents wish it.

There is no doubt that early assessment and pre-school guidance is necessary and a balance has to be struck between a young child's need for its mother and its need for expert help, a balance which is not easy to determine. It depends so much on the degree of hearing impairment, the amount of help which can be given locally, the ability of the family to help the child and the social and emotional conditions within the home. Day provision can be accepted more easily and earlier than boarding provision as a general rule.

At the age of 5 years, education is mandatory – the controversy then becomes one of the type of school to which a child should go. In many areas there is a determined avoidance of 'deaf' school placement as it is considered that here a child will learn to 'sign' to the detriment of language development and oral communication. There is no doubt that the 'deafer' the child, the more likely he is to use 'gesture' to communicate his desires and emotions. It has never been proven that this is necessarily bad, and emotionally is probably good. It is unlikely that anyone would argue that no attempt should be made to endeavour to teach the child to be 'oral', but there is no real evidence that if a child uses gesture and if a deaf child is placed in such an environment that he will not develop 'orally' if the school, and in particular the home, endeavours to develop oralism.

The issue of placement must depend upon a forecast, for the immediate future, of the rate at which the child is going to develop linguistically and the rate at which he will be able to receive oral communication, for the essential difference between 'deaf', 'partially hearing' and normal education is that of the rate of receiving oral communication – either through hearing, lipreading or some combination of both. This initial placement is not irrevocable and transfers in either direction should always be possible.

It is likely that nursery and even infant special education could be organized more often locally for deaf and partially hearing children in units in normal schools, if the two categories were taken together, and it is not likely at this stage to affect either adversely. By the infant stage a better, more complete and reliable assessment could be reached and a more realistic placement into one or other of the educational establishments for hearing-impaired children could be made. There are so many factors involved that it takes time to reach a reliable assessment, yet the child may need daily and more expert help than can be provided by pre-school guidance alone (D.E.S., 1968).

To carry out continuous assessment requires a team approach. The essential members are an otologist, a psychologist, a teacher of the deaf, a social worker, an audiology technician and the services frequently of a neurologist, paediatrician and psychiatrist.

REFERENCES

ADVISORY COUNCIL ON EDUCATION IN SCOTLAND (1950) *Pupils who are Defective in Hearing*. Edinburgh: H.M.S.O. (Cmd 866).

AMERICAN ACADEMY OF OPHTHALMOLOGY AND OTOLARYNGOLOGY (1960) *A Guide to the Care of Adults with Hearing Loss*.

BARR, B. (1955) Pure tone audiometry for pre-school children. *Acta Otolaryng.* Supplement *121*.

BATES, A. (1956) Selection of pupils for the Mary Hare Grammar School. *Teacher of the Deaf*, **54**, 172-182.

BEAGLEY, H. and KNIGHT, J. J. (1966) Methods of objective audiometry. *J. Laryng. and Otol.*, **80**, 1127-1134.

BEAGLEY, H. and KNIGHT, J. J. (1967) Changes in auditory evoked response with intensity. *J. Laryng. and Otol.*, **81**, 861-873.

BEKESY, G. VON (1947) a new audiometer. *Acta Laryngologica*, **35**, 411-422.

BOARD OF EDUCATION (1938) *Report of the Committee of Inquiry into Problems relating to Children with Defective Hearing*. London: H.M.S.O.

BORDLEY, J. E. (1956) An evaluation of the psychogalvanic skin resistance technique in audiometry. *Laryngoscope*, **66**, 1162-1185.

BRUNSHWIG, L. (1936) *A Study of some Personality Aspects of Deaf Children*. New York: Colombia University Teachers College Contributions to Education.

DARBYSHIRE, J. (1965) *The development of reasoning in the deaf, along with an experimental study in the use of adaptations of some of Piaget's tests with groups of deaf and hearing children*. Unpublished thesis for Ph.D. at Queens University, Belfast, N. Ireland.

DAVIS, H. and SILVERMAN, RICHARD S. (1960) *Hearing and Deafness*. New York: Holt, Rinehart and Winston.

DENMARK, F. G. W. (1950) A development of the peep-show audiometer. *J. Laryng. and Otol.*, **64**, 357-360.

DEPARTMENT OF EDUCATION AND SCIENCE (1968) *The Education of Deaf Children*. London: H.M.S.O.

DERBYSHIRE, A. J., FRASER, A. A., MCDERMOTT, M. and BRIDGE, A. (1956) Audiometric measurements by electroencephalography. *Electroencephalog. & clin. Neurophysiol. J.*, 8, No. 3.

DERBYSHIRE, A. J. and FARLEY, J. C. (1959) Sampling audiometry responses at the cortical level: a routine for e.e.g. audiometry testing. *Ann. Otol. Rhin. & Laryng.*, **68**, 675-697.

DIRKS, D. and CARHART, R. (1962) A survey of reactions from users of binaural and monaural hearing aids. *J. Speech and Hearing Disorders*, **27**, 311-322.

DREVER, J. and COLLINS, M. (1946) *Performance Test of Intelligence*. London and Edinburgh: Oliver and Boyd.

EWING, A. W. G. (1930) *Aphasia in Children*. London: Oxford Medical Publications.

EWING, I. R. and EWING, A. W. G. (1961) *New Opportunities for Deaf Children*. London: University of London Press.

EWING, A. W. G. and STANTON, D. A. G. (1943) A study of children with defective hearing. *Teacher of the Deaf*, **41**.

EWING, I. R. (1957) *In* EWING, A. W. G. (Ed.). *Educational Guidance and the Deaf Child*. Manchester University Press.

FISCH, L. (1955) The aetiology of congenital deafness and audiometric patterns. *J. Laryngol. & Otol.*, **69**, No. 7.

FISCH, L. (1955) Deafness in cerebral palsied school children. *Lancet*, **2**, 370-371 (Aug. 20).

FULTON, R. T. and SPRADLIN, J. E. (1967) *Reliability of Operant Audiometric techniques in Severely Retarded Children*. Parsons Demonstration Project Report No. 79. Parsons State Hospital and Bureau of Child Research, Kansas City.

FURTH, H. (1961) Visual paired associate tasks with deaf and hearing children. *J. Speech and Hearing Research*, **4**.

FURTH, H. (1966) *Thinking Without Language*. New York: The Free Press.

GASKILL, P. (1957) *In* EWING, A. W. G. (Ed.) *Educational Guidance and the Deaf Child*. Manchester University Press.

GOLDSTEIN, R., LUDWIG, H. and NAUNTON, R. F. (1954) Difficulty in conditioning galvanic skin responses: its possible significance in clinical audiometry. *Acta Oto-Laryng.*, **44**, 67-77.

GRIFFITHS, R. (1954) *The Abilities of Babies*. London: University of London Press.

HALLPIKE, C. and DIX, M. (1947) Peepshow: a technique for pure tone audiometry. *Brit. med. J.*, **2**, 719 (Nov. 8).

HARDY, W. G. and BORDLEY, J. E. (1951) Special techniques in testing the hearing of children. *J. Speech and Hearing Disorders*, **16**, 122.

HARDY, W. G. and PAULS, M. D. (1952) The test situation in P.G.S.R. audiometry. *J. Speech and Hearing Disorders*, **17**, 15 (March).

HIRSH, I. (1952) *The Measurement of Hearing*. New York: McGraw-Hill.

HISKEY, M. S. (1955) *Nebraska Test of Learning Aptitude* (revised). University of Nebraska.

HOOD, H. B. (1949) A preliminary survey of some mental abilities of deaf children. *Brit. J. Educ. Psych.*, **19**, 210-219.

HUMPHRIES, B. (1957) The ascertainment and management of defective hearing in the very young. *Public Health*, **71**, 221-228.

IVES, L. (1967) Some possible effects of congenital deafness on the development of intelligence and psycho-linguistic skills. *Teacher of the Deaf*, **65**.

JERGER, J., CARHART, R. and DIRKS, D. (1961) Binaural hearing aids and speech intelligibility. *J. Speech and Hearing Research*, **4**, 137-148.

JOHANNSON, B. (1966) The use of the transposer for the management of the deaf child. *J. Internat. Audiol.*, **5** (3).

JOHNSON, J. C. (1962) *Educating Hearing Impaired Children in Ordinary Schools*. London: Manchester Univ. Press.

KENDALL, D. (1957) *In* EWING, A. W. G. (Ed.) *Educational Guidance and the Deaf Child*. London: Manchester University Press.

LEVINE, E. G. (1956) *Youth in a Soundless World*. New York: New York University Press.

LEVINE, E. S. (1960) *The Psychology of Deafness*. New York: Columbia University Press.

LING, D. (1968) Three experiments in frequency transposition. *Amer. Annuals of the Deaf*, **113** (March).

LLOYD, L., SPRADLIN, E. and REID, M. (1968) An operant audiometric procedure for difficult to test patients. *J. Speech and Hearing Disorders*, **33**, 236-245.

LURIA, A. R. (1961) *The Role of Speech in the Regulation of Normal and Abnormal Behaviour Patterns*. London: Pergamon Press.

LYON, V. (1934) The use of vocational and personality tests with the deaf. *J. Applied Psychology*, **18,** 224.

MCCARTHY, J. J. and KIRK, S. A. (1961) *The Illinois Test of Psycholinguistic Abilities* (Experimental edition). Urbana, Ill.: The Institute for Research on Exceptional Children.

MAXWELL, A. E. (1959) A factor analysis on the W.I.S.C. *Brit. J. Educational Psychology*, **29.**

MILGRAM, N. A. and FURTH, H. (1963) *Amer. J. Ment. Def.*, **67,** 733-739.

MINISTRY OF EDUCATION (1944) *Education Act.* London: H.M.S.O.

MINISTRY OF EDUCATION (1962) Children with impaired hearing. Circular 10/62. London: H.M.S.O.

MINISTRY OF HEALTH (1961) Services for young children handicapped by impaired hearing. Circular 23/61. London: H.M.S.O.

MOSS, J. W., MOSS, M. and TIZARD, J. (1961) Electrodermal response audiometry with mentally defective children. *J. Speech and Hearing Research*, **4** (March).

MURPHY, K. P. (1957) *In* EWING, A. W. G. (Ed.) *Educational Guidance and the Deaf Child.* London: Manchester University Press.

MURPHY, L. J. (1957) *In* EWING, A. W. G. (Ed.) *Educational Guidance and the Deaf Child.* London: Manchester University Press.

OLÉRON, P. (1953) Conceptual thinking of the deaf. *Amer. Annals of the Deaf,* **98,** 304-310.

OLÉRON, P. and HERREN, H. (1961) L'acquisition des conservations. *Enfance,* June-October.

O'NEIL, J. T., OYER, HERBERT J. and HILLIS, JAMES W. (1961) Audiometric procedures used with children. *J. Speech and Hearing Disorders*, **26,** 61-68.

OWRID, L. (1958) *Tests and developmental schedules for the evaluation of linguistic development in deaf children.* Unpublished thesis for Ph.D. in Manchester University.

PINTNER, R. and PATTERSON, D. G. (1923) *A Scale of Performance Tests.* New York: Appleton-Century-Crofts.

RAVEN, J. D. (1938) *Guide to using the Progressive Matrices.* London: H. K. Lewis.

RAVEN, J. D. (1947) *Coloured Progressive Matrices* London: H. K. Lewis.

REED, M. (1960) *Hearing Test Cards.* London: Royal National Institute for the Deaf.

ROSENSTEIN, J. J. (1960) Cognitive abilities of deaf children. *J. Speech and Hearing Research*, **3,** 108-119.

SCOTTISH COUNCIL FOR RESEARCH IN EDUCATION (1956) *Hearing Defects of School Children.* London: London University Press.

SHERIDAN, M. D. (1962) Infants at risk of handicapping conditions. *Monthly Bulletin, Ministry of Health Laboratory Service*, **21,** 238.

SIMPSON, E. (1963) *Survey of Children born in 1947 who were in Schools for the Deaf in 1962-63.* The Health of the School Child 1962 & 63. London: H.M.S.O.

SNIJDERS, J. TH. and SNIJDERS-OOMEN, N. (1959) *Non-verbal Intelligence Test.* Groningen: J. B. Wolters.

STATTEN, P. and WISHART, D. E. S. (1956) Pure tone audiometry in young children; psycho-galvanic skin resistance & peepshow. *Ann. Otol. Rhin. & Laryng.*, 65, 511.

STUTSMAN, R. (1931) *Mental Measurement of Pre-School Children*. New York: World Book Co.

TAYLOR, I. G. (1964) *Neurological Mechanisms of Hearing and Speech in Children*. London: Manchester University Press.

WECHSLER, D. (1949) *Intelligence Scale for Children* New York: Psychological Corporation.

WHETNALL, E. and FRY, D. B. (1964) *The Deaf Child*. London: William Heinemann Medical Books.

WITHROW, F. B. JR. and GOLDSTEIN, R. (1958) An electrophysiological procedure for determination of audiological threshold in children. *Laryngoscope*, 68, 1674.

15

Children with physical handicaps

Joan Reynell

I CLINICAL FEATURES

The two main groups of physical handicap are: (1) those which are associated with or result from abnormal brain function and (2) those in which there is no brain involvement. In the first category are children with cerebral palsy, and children who have spina bifida with associated hydrocephalus. In the second category are children with muscular dystrophy, limb deficiency, and handicaps following poliomyelitis.

This distinction is an important one, as the implications for testing procedures and the significance of the test findings are different in each category. Table 15.1 shows a comparison between these different types of physical handicap in respect of a number of relevant factors.

Children who have abnormal brain function must be considered to have complex handicaps. In addition to the physical handicaps there is often some general or specific intellectual impairment; there may be perceptual disorders; there may be sensory handicaps and there may be speech and language disorders.

Children without brain involvement have a primary physical handicap which may involve secondary handicaps such as emotional disturbance, but the primary interference with learning and development is confined to the physical handicap.

In this chapter the main consideration will be given to those with brain involvement, because from the point of view of a psychological assessment they are the most complex, but this in no way minimizes the importance of those handicaps which, although more circumscribed, may by secondary involvement cause serious interference with the child's total development.

Figure 15.1 shows the effect of both categories of physical handicap on the total learning process. For full learning to take place there must be: (1) a learning situation appropriate to the child's level and range of function; (2) intact sensory channels, so that the information can be received; (3) adequate perceptual processes, so that sensory input can be assimilated and categorized; (4) adequate brain function so that the processed learning may be recoded in order that some expressive (e.g. language) or motor function may result; (5) adequate expressive (e.g. speech) or motor ability to allow some output as a result of the learning input, and as a basis for further learning.

Children with abnormal brains may be handicapped at any or all of these stages, whereas most children with physical handicaps not involving brain function will

Handicap	Brain involvement	Type	Unimpaired learning experience	Intellectual learning disorder	Extent of handicap	Remedial measures
Cerebral Palsies	yes	congenital	usually none	primary	multiple	aids and special teaching
Spina bifida with associated hydrocephalus	yes	congenital	usually none	primary	multiple	aids and special teaching
limb deficiency	no	congenital	usually none	none or secondary	usually confined to physical disability	aids and special teaching
poliomyelitis	no	acquired	usually some, often much	none or secondary	usually confined to physical disability	aids
Muscular dystrophy	no	acquired	usually some, often much	none or secondary	usually confined to physical disability	aids

TABLE 15.1

Factors involved in different types of physical handicap

have primary handicaps confined to the more peripheral learning areas, as shown in Figure 15.1.

Manipulation of the environment, such as the provision of mechanical aids, may be enough to allow children without brain involvement to learn normally, but children with cerebral palsy and hydrocephalus will probably need more help, such as special teaching methods geared to their particular level and range of handicap.

Table 15.1 also shows the distinction between handicaps which are congenital and those which are acquired. Children with acquired handicaps have had some unimpaired learning in the early years, which gives them an enormous advantage over those with congenital abnormalities who have never known normal learning experience. Conditions involving abnormal brain function are usually congenital, such as the cerebral palsies, and spina bifida with associated hydrocephalus; but physical handicaps may be acquired after a head injury or disease such as meningitis. In most conditions which do not involve the brain, the physical handicaps are acquired after a period of normal learning experience. This is the case with the muscular dystrophies and handicaps following poliomyelitis, but limb deficient children are usually handicapped from birth.

The most common conditions in which physical handicaps are associated with brain abnormality are: (1) the cerebral palsies and (2) spina bifida associated with hydrocephalus. These conditions are congenital and usually involve complex multiple handicaps. These two handicapping conditions will form the main basis of this chapter.

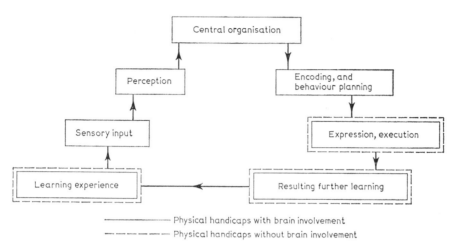

FIGURE 15.1
Stages in the learning process which are affected by different categories of physical handicap.

1 Cerebral palsy

In the cerebral palsies the physical handicap results directly from brain abnormality. There are a number of different ways of classifying the cerebral palsies; different authors may use different nomenclature and different subdivisions. The classification is discussed at length by Ingram (1964), and a detailed description of the different types can be found in this work and in Mitchell (1961).

The main categories are:

(1) The spastic conditions, classified according to the number of limbs involved, such as 'hemiplegia', 'diplegia', and 'quadriplegia'. Spastic muscles are described by Mitchell (1961) as having an 'exaggerated stretch reflex'.
(2) Ataxic conditions, in which there is inco-ordination of movement.
(3) Dyskinesia (Ingram, 1964), including athetosis, in which the predominant handicap is that of involuntary movement. These conditions are usually

generalized, but when there is only partial involvement they may be classified according to the number of limbs involved, as in the spastic conditions.

Estimates of the incidence of cerebral palsy in Great Britain range between 1·5 and 2·5 per thousand. Details of the figures for Great Britain and other countries may be found in Henderson (1961) and Ingram (1964). Spastic hemiplegia and spastic diplegia account for more than two-thirds of the total, and athetosis is usually estimated at not more than 10% of the total cerebral palsied population.

In the Dundee survey of 133 school-age children with cerebral palsy, Cockburn (1961) gives a table showing how the children were placed educationally. She found that approximately 50% were in ordinary school, approximately 25% in some sort of special school, including Training Centres, and approximately 25% at home or in institutions. Of the 133 school-age children, 19·5% were considered by the author to be unsatisfactorily placed.

Bowley (1967) reports in detail on the preliminary findings of a follow-up study of 64 cerebral palsied children of I.Q. above 50, who had attended the Cheyne (Nursery) Centre and who had been followed up into the first two years of school. Of these 64 children, 11 attended ordinary schools, 36 attended day schools for the physically handicapped, and 17 were placed in residential or hospital schools. Bowley found that 28 of the children made average or good progress at school, 13 were not making good progress despite good intelligence, and 23 failed at school because of poor intelligence, epilepsy, sensory or speech defects.

The selection of a suitable school for a child with cerebral palsy, if he is not able to go to the ordinary school, will depend on the nature and severity of the handicaps. If the physical handicap is severe and necessitates regular physiotherapy, a school for the physically handicapped may be most suitable, but if the intellectual or sensory handicaps predominate, this may influence the choice of school towards one which can provide the best help for that type of handicap. There are a few schools in England specially for cerebral palsied children, including one school which also caters for children in whom the only real handicap is a specific learning disorder. School provision varies considerably with each area, and in some rural areas the only possibilities of special schooling are residential. This is usually a major step for parents and children and some of the difficulties and ways in which these may be helped are discussed in a symposium edited by Loring and Mason (1966).

Some degree of intellectual handicap, general or specific or both, is usually associated with cerebral palsy. There have been many surveys and studies of the intellectual abilities of cerebral palsied children and most of the published work gives at least some space to this aspect. Surveys which are specially concerned with intellectual and other psychological aspects include those of Dunsdon (1952), Floyer (1955), Cruikshank and Raus (1955) and Schonell (1956). The distribution of intelligence found in some of the surveys is shown in Table 15.2.

Some works, such as that of Meyer Taylor (1959), are concerned more with qualitative aspects of intellectual function, and a review of the work on some of the specific intellectual disabilities has been presented by Abercrombie (1964). Estimates of the incidence of specific learning handicaps vary widely according to the particular criteria used, and according to sampling. Abercrombie discusses this at some length.

Various attributes have been linked with the so-called 'brain-damage' syndrome, such as distractability, hyperactivity, emotional lability, and perseveration. These attributes are discussed by many authors, including Strauss and Lehtinen (1947), Cruikshank and Raus (1955), and Schonell (1956). Cruikshank *et al.* (1961) report a pilot study of a special educational programme

	Birmingham Total no. 354	*Liverpool* Total no. 166	*New Jersey* Total no. 1,000	*Dundee* Total no. 223	*Sheffield* Total no. 356
I.Q.					
130+	0·6	0	1·6	2·2	0·4
110–129	3·4	3·6	5·3	8·1	5·9
90–109	20·1	17·5	21·6	16·1	21·6
70–89	26·8	30·7	22·7	25·1	31·4
50–69	22·9	21·7	20·4	21·1	17·6
0–49	22·3	25·3	28·4	27·4	23·1
Not yet assessable	3·9	1·2	—	—	—

TABLE 15.2

I.Q. distribution in published studies

Figures refer to a percentage of the sample in each case.
Reproduced by kind permission from *Assessment of Cerebral Palsy*, Vol. II (1967), by K. S. Holt and J. K. Reynell. London: Lloyd-Luke (Medical Books).

for what they term 'brain-injured and hyperactive children'. A summary, including many abstracts from some of the major works on personality and learning difficulties of cerebral palsied children, is included in a symposium edited by Birch (1964). Schulman *et al.* (1965) reported a study of behaviour constellations in 'brain-damaged' children, in which an attempt was made to discover significant patterns. They found that the only behaviour attribute which significantly characterized 'brain-damaged' children was distractibility. They did not find a significantly high activity level, as measured by actometers attached to the children's wrists and ankles. This evidence argues against the assumption by many authors that such children are 'hyperactive', although they appear to be hyperactive in many cases because the mobility is not effectively canalized. There seems to be a general agreement that attention difficulties may be among the very real learning handicaps suffered by children with cerebral palsy (Holt and Reynell, 1967), and this is an important consideration in assessment.

2 Spina Bifida

In spina bifida with associated hydrocephalus, the physical handicaps may arise either from the spinal lesion or from the cerebral abnormality, or both.

A simple and very clear explanation of the handicaps involved, written for parents, is given by Swinyard (1964), and a fuller description can be found in the proceedings of a symposium published as an 'Action for the Crippled Child' monograph (1965). Some of the research aspects are reported in a symposium published by the Spastics Society (1967).

The main handicaps are likely to be paraplegia and failure of bladder function, resulting from the spinal lesion, and possibly intellectual and other handicaps resulting from brain abnormality if there is associated hydrocephalus. The extent and range of handicaps will depend on the severity and position of the spinal lesion and the extent of the brain abnormality resulting from hydrocephalus.

The incidence is most usually reported as in the region of three per thousand births (Smithells, 1965) in the British Isles, and about 2·5 per thousand now survive. The incidence in the school-age population can therefore be expected to be at least as great, if not greater than that of cerebral palsy.

There is still a great deal of work to be done on the intellectual and other psychological aspects of this handicap, and little has yet been published. Ingram and Naughten (1962) discussed some of the psychological aspects of cerebral palsy associated with hydrocephalus. They report a high incidence of a superficial, facile verbosity, which gives a superficial impression of higher intelligence than can be used. The authors found that 'in all except two cases (out of 20) the vocabulary level was above the general psychometric level', and that 'progress is often disappointing, and educational abilities slow to mature, compared with conversational ones'. These authors were only concerned with the association of cerebral palsy with hydrocephalus, however, so their findings will not necessarily apply to children with spina bifida. The particular psychological syndrome they describe seems to occur in some, but by no means all of the children who have hydrocephalus associated with spina bifida, and work is now in progress to relate different types of intellectual abilities and handicaps to different clinical aspects.

Stephen (1963) reports on the educational status and intellectual level of children with meningomyelocele (spina bifida involving external protrusion of the spinal cord). She reports that the majority of the children of school age were 'educable' in terms of I.Q., and have responded to education. She found that the children with meningomyelocele and associated hydrocephalus tend to be of lower intelligence than those without hydrocephalus.

II ASSESSMENT

1 Purpose of assessment

The purpose of the psychological assessment of a child with multiple handicaps is usually to elucidate learning assets and learning handicaps, so that the environment and teaching may be suitably modified to allow maximum function and development. 'Learning' is here regarded in the very widest sense and from the earliest age, in line with Piaget's view of the way in which intelligence evolves as the outcome of the interaction between the child and his environment (Piaget, 1953).

Children with multiple handicaps may have both a depressed level of intellectual function and an unusual and uneven balance of intellectual abilities (Holt and Reynell 1967). There may be difficulties at any stage in the sequence shown in Figure 15.1, and these difficulties could occur in any sensory or expressive modality.

The investigation of such complex handicaps as these must be broadly based and qualitative. Every stage, every modality, and all combinations must be assessed, although of course they do not all have to be assessed separately. The procedure is not as complicated as this may suggest, as it depends more on the examiner's understanding of what he is assessing than on the actual testing.

The broad and qualitative approach must be maintained, however limiting the handicaps. It is tempting to use only the most easily accessible channels of communication, such as a verbal test for children who have severe visual difficulties and restricted hand function, but this is inadequate for a full assessment. We also need to know what use a child is able to make of such vision as he has, his ability for spatial orientation and how to help him understand the properties of material objects in spite of his manipulative handicaps.

The value of such assessment lies in the leads given for remedial measures, and appropriate adaptations in daily living. Help with some form of communication is very important, using whatever means, and at whatever level the child can manage.

Severely handicapped children sometimes are unable to use the common learning experiences of everyday living which form the basis for intellectual development in non-handicapped children, so the environment must be adapted to meet their developmental needs. Without an understanding of the particular needs of each child, and suitable adaptations, their development may become unnecessarily skewed or delayed. An immobile child who spends all his time lying on his back may be considered by his parents to be 'intelligent' because he can repeat nursery rhymes and count up to ten, so this detached verbal skill is fed at the expense of all sensori-motor learning, and he has little chance of linking verbal learning to an understanding of the material world. The balance can usually be redressed to some extent by propping him up so that he can use such hand-eye co-ordination as he has, and by deliberately teaching him to link linguistic and sensori-motor experiences.

Parents, teachers and therapists can devise ways of helping handicapped children, but psychologists and paediatricians have an essential role to play in assessing the developmental needs and suggesting directions for help.

The purpose of the assessment has been discussed at some length in order to see the assessment procedures in perspective and to stress the developmental orientation. Test procedures with children who have multiple handicaps should always have this developmental orientation. The orientation may be different when the handicaps are acquired late in childhood, but when the handicaps are congenital or acquired very early in childhood, they become part of the total development.

The use of assessment for prediction is subordinate to that of meeting present needs in this group of children. The procedure should be regarded as *assessment* rather than diagnosis, and for *present help* rather than for prediction. Subsequent progress, particularly in children under four years, will depend to a large extent on how far it is possible to help the development at each stage.

2 When to assess

Children with multiple congenital handicaps should be assessed as early as possible, and followed up regularly until school age and at critical periods after this. These children have learning handicaps from birth and early sensori-motor learning is likely to be interfered with unless the environment can be suitably adapted to allow the learning to take place despite the handicaps. A great deal can be done to help children at this early stage if the full extent of the present handicaps are known and the parents are given guidance on how to help. It is not within the scope of this chapter to go into remedial measures, but the interested reader is referred to the following works: Barrett and Jones (1967), Bobath (1967) and König (quoted by Ellis, 1966).

From a mental age of 18 months the investigation of linguistic processes becomes important, as this is a major developmental aspect of this age. This involves the reception of communication of all types (not only speech), the use of 'inner language' (Sheridan, 1964) for self direction and thinking and communication directed to others by whatever means the handicaps allow. The early stages of difficulties may be revealed, and suitable help be provided.

By 4 to 5 years assessment will be geared towards school placement, bearing in mind all aspects of school life. For example, attention difficulties, ability to conform, emotional maturity and ability to cope with a new environment without the support of the mother, are all important considerations for school readiness. School entry is usually a more formidable step for most handicapped children who are necessarily more dependent than the non-handicapped.

It is often wise to reassess at 7 years, when education becomes more formal and the more subtle learning difficulties may appear, such as some of the visuo-motor and language disorders which may only become evident when more specific and higher level demands are made. The more severe learning difficulties will have become evident earlier. Assessments at this stage, with children who have been previously assessed, may usefully take a more specific form, geared towards the elucidation of any particular learning difficulties which may be suspected by the teacher, with a view to advising on remedial measures.

After this age it is not usually necessary to continue regular assessments unless special difficulties occur, and reassessment is specially requested by teachers, doctors or therapists. Such requests occur sometimes in adolescence when the children become most acutely aware of their handicaps, and emotional disturbance or discouragement may lead to a lowering of functional level.

Assessments at school leaving age do not necessarily involve any form of testing, but can usefully take the form of a conference between psychologist, doctor, teacher and Youth Employment Officer. Intellect, personality, social behaviour and competence, physical ability, physical appearance, and speech difficulties all play a part in suitability for employment. Intelligence, even if this is average or above, is unfortunately not enough, and a realistic approach is necessary to the problem as a whole (Ingram *et al.*, 1964).

3 How to assess

The method of assessment will depend on the child's age and handicaps, and on the purpose of the assessment. Each child has a different combination of assets and handicaps, so there can be no general rule covering all children in the choice of methods.

With children who are severely handicapped, there is a temptation to circumvent the handicap as far as possible in testing the children, and to search for a hypothetical 'intelligence' which is able to function in isolation; for example, the use of only a picture vocabulary test with a child who has impaired speech and hand function, because his handicaps do not interfere with this particular test procedure; or the use of only a performance test with a child who has no speech. If the children are handicapped from birth or from a very young age there can be no such separable 'intelligence' untouched by and independent of all handicaps. The children have developed as a whole. Reference back to Figure 15.1 will illustrate how the handicaps, as part of that whole, are also part of the total development, including intellectual development. Obviously we want to find the highest level at which each child can possibly function, and search for this should be diligent, but is not enough. We must also assess the total handicaps and their effects in order to help the children make the best of their assets. In order to prevent a skewed intellectual development we need to find ways in which his learning assets can be used to help him in the areas in which he is most handicapped. The choice of method must allow for the assessment of the child as a whole and must include a broad qualitative approach.

The two main methods of assessment to be discussed are: (1) the use of standardized tests and (2) observation methods. In most cases it is wise to use both approaches. Standardized testing alone is not usually enough, particularly with very young children, with school-age children who have specific learning difficulties, with the very severely handicapped or when assessing for employment.

With very heavily handicapped children, standardized testing may even be inappropriate. This does not mean that no *standards* must be used, but that a sound knowledge of developmental processes is sometimes a more useful guide than a standardized test, which can only be used with many unstandardized modifications. Such procedures are dependent on the knowledge and experience of the examiner and conclusions should be drawn with caution.

4 Standardized testing

(a) *Establishment of Two-way Communication*

The establishment of two-way communication is the first consideration. This is not the same as the usual 'rapport' referred to in most test manuals. Referring again to Figure 15.1, unless there is some way in which the child can receive communications from the examiner and some way in which he can communicate his answer, there can be no testing. Nearly all children who are intellectually capable of this have some form of communication which can be used, however limited. Parents, teachers and therapists who have regular contact with the child may be able to help, and in some cases may be used as intermediaries. If communication is severely limited, the parents and child may have evolved some sort of signal system which the child does not readily transfer to a stranger. This may be crude gestures, vocalization, facial expression or eye movements, according to what the handicap allows.

Communications from the child, such as facial expression and eye movements, may be 'read' by the examiner even if they are not deliberately communicated by the child. This can be useful with very young children, with the severely mentally handicapped, or with children who are withdrawn and unco-operative. The use of eyes for communication in testing is discussed below.

Communication from examiner to child is equally important. The examiner must be quick to establish a suitable level, range and modality before co-operation is lost. Some severely handicapped children have become so used to receiving incomprehensible signals from others that they quickly cease to try unless communications come within their range at an early stage in the relationship. A suitable level and modality can often be established with the help of the case notes, conversation with parents, and seeing the child in the waiting-room first, so that the test interview can start off on the right footing.

Many very severely handicapped children, with a mental age of not less than 18 months, have some way of indicating 'yes' and 'no'. At first this is not a deliberately worked out code, but perhaps just an incidental smile for 'yes' and frown or turning of the head for 'no', but provided this initial stage is there, this can be built on and used for testing.

The use of the eyes is the greatest asset in the assessment of severely handicapped children. With children under 5 years, particularly, or with very shy children, a great deal can be done by watching the eye movements before any further co-operation is needed.

The use of the eyes in testing is referred to as 'eye-pointing', and it is always wise to use this as well, even if there is some hand function. Children should be positioned so that their eyes can be carefully watched all the time. Some eye control is usually possible even in the most severely handicapped children, although this may not be easy and needs careful observation on the part of the examiner.

Eye-pointing is simply a communication from the child, which may not even be deliberate, indicating his response to a question or situation. The question must be such that a single selective response is possible. The question may be spoken, or the task may be visual if the child is deaf, or may be framed in any modality he is able to receive. The test objects or pictures are so spaced out in front of the child that visual selection can be observed, and yet so that they are within the child's span of visual attention. As the question is asked, the examiner watches the child's eyes (preferable from right angles so that the child does not feel too much under scrutiny) and notes the object or picture at which the child's eyes become focused.

With children who have good eye control there is usually a brief scanning of all objects, followed by a fixation of the one selected. The examiner should be quick to reinforce the response with praise so that the child knows there is communication. On the other hand, care must be taken not to arrest the scanning at the appropriate object by a too early reinforcement or the child may learn to scan until the selection is made for him by the examiner. Some children will just fixate the object, others may fixate and smile, or fixate and attempt to point with the arm. If eye control is not good it is wise to have a practice period with a few easy objects first so that the examiner may learn what constitutes a true response for that particular child.

The greatest difficulty is likely to be encountered with children who have athetosis, with persisting primitive reflexes, and who cannot co-ordinate hand and eye. Such a child may try to reach out for an object, and his eyes will then lose it, and the resulting arm movement go astray. In such cases an initial brief selective glance may be all the indication the examiner will get, and must be carefully watched for. It is usually advisable to train such a child to respond with his eyes only. If the arms are very gently restrained by a familiar adult (preferably the mother) and if he understands that his eye communication is received, he may be able to learn to respond with eyes alone and so allow a more prolonged visual fixation. Figure 15.2 shows a child being tested in this way.

Tests which can be used for eye-pointing are necessarily selection tests, such as the Columbia Mental Maturity Scale (Burgemeister *et al.*, 1959), Raven's Matrices, the Peabody Picture Vocabulary and others of this type. There is now a fairly wide range of such tests, including a test of verbal comprehension for children aged 1 to 5 years which is specially designed for eye-pointing (Reynell, 1969).

The range of communication methods which can be selected according to the child's handicap, can be summarized as follows:

Examiner to child: Speech, gesture, touch, movement (kinaesthetic), or any combination of these in direct or coded form; special signalling systems, usually via the parents.

Q

Child to examiner: Speech, hand function, gestures, 'yes-no' indications, eye-pointing, vocalization other than speech, or any specific learnt signalling system.

Many children handicapped by cerebral palsy or hydrocephalus will be able to communicate in a normal way, in which case the ordinary test procedures may be used. This discussion refers to children with whom the usual methods of communication are not possible.

(b) *The setting*

The general setting and seating arrangements will be discussed only briefly, because most of the points will apply also to non-handicapped children and are discussed in other chapters. For a more detailed discussion of the points which apply specially to cerebral palsied children the reader is referred to Holt and Reynell (1967).

The main considerations which particularly concern children with cerebral palsy and hydrocephalus are as follows:

The room, and particularly the testing table, should be clear of all distractions. These children often have difficulty in selective attention and more than usual care should be taken to keep possible distractors out of the way.

Positioning is extremely important and can make a good deal of difference to the child's functional ability. Physiotherapists and parents can often advise as to the most suitable position for full function of arms, eyes, or whatever means is to be used. Figure 15.3 shows a child suitably placed so that he is well supported, yet not restricted in movement. He has his feet firmly on the ground, which is important for sitting balance, and the chair and table are of the right height to allow the best use of hand-eye co-ordination.

Some children who have spent a great deal of time lying on their backs have difficulty in focusing and manipulating objects on the table, although they may be able to do this at eye level. Tests which can be carried out at eye level include items from the developmental scales for the younger children, or the Columbia Mental Maturity Scale, Picture Vocabularies, Raven's Matrices and parts of other scales for the older children. This difficulty usually only applies to very young children, however, as most older children spend a good deal of time propped up in a sitting position.

Children with multiple handicaps often have a very short span of interest and may tire easily, because in general everything is more effort to them than to the non-handicapped. A rapid change of test material may be necessary to hold their interest, or a change to a different method of assessment such as observation. The interview may have to be shorter than usual and further testing deferred for a second interview, rather than continuing beyond the point of the child's optimum function. Other children may be very slow to respond, and may find difficulty in transferring from one mental set to another. These children may need a much longer assessment time than is usual. Again there can be no generalizations. The child sets the pace and length of the interview, and the examiner must adjust accordingly.

(c) *Choice of test procedures*

The choice of tests will depend on the age and handicaps of the child, on the purpose of the investigation, and on possible channels of communication.

As a minimum, the areas which should be investigated are sensori-motor and linguistic. The term 'sensori-motor' is here used to include all non-linguistic processes, however complex, in which there is a motor response to a sensory input. The term 'linguistic' refers to all coded and symbolic processes, not necessarily verbal.

It is usually advisable to use more than one test scale, particularly if the physical handicaps are very limiting or if the child is under school age. There is a wide choice of test material for school age children, and a reasonably good range of profile-type developmental scales for children under 2 years. The age range 2 to 5 years is less well served at present, although it is hoped that this gap will be filled in the next few years by test scales which are now in process of construction.

Multiple-handicapped children are not a homogeneous group, as all have different combinations of handicaps. It makes no sense to standardize tests on a cerebral palsy population, as has been done for deaf and blind children. The test scales used are those which have been standardized on the normal population, although many of them are designed to be used with the handicapped, and their construction is the outcome of this clinical need (Burgemeister *et al.*, 1959; Reynell, 1969).

Questions to be answered in selecting tests to be used are:

(1) Which test scales cover the relevant mental age range?
(2) Which will allow enough two-way communication for interference with scoring to be minimal?
(3) Which will elucidate the particular intellectual processes relevant to the assessment?

As far as possible it is wise to select test scales which can be administered without modification and without omissions, rather than to use parts of test scales which are not applicable as a whole. For example, to test a child on the Terman Merrill Scale when he has impaired language and impaired hand function will necessitate so many omissions and modifications that it is no longer a standardized test and any score obtained by this procedure could be very misleading. Profile-type tests may be used in this way for special investigations, provided the whole of one subscale is used and scored as a subscale only.

5 Procedure: analysis and synthesis

The procedure is, first of all to find the optimum level at which the child can function, to follow this by an analysis of his assets and difficulties and finally to synthesize all the findings so that the child is seen as a whole, and advice given as to how his assets may be used to help the areas in which he is most handicapped.

To find the optimum level, a standardized test battery is chosen such that two-way communication may be as free as possible, and where the handicaps will interfere least. If only the lower limbs are involved, any of the usual test batteries may be used. If the upper limbs are severely involved but the child has speech and hearing any verbal test may be used, together with any performance test in which the response is by selection (such as Raven's Matrices and the Columbia Mental Maturity scale). If the child has neither hand function nor speech, but good hearing, many of the verbal tests will not be applicable, but both verbal and performance tests must be chosen so that response may be by selection. Suitable verbal tests are any of the picture vocabularies, the Reynell Verbal Comprehension Scale 'B' and some of the subscales from the Illinois Test of Psycholinguistic Abilities (McCarthy and Kirk, 1961). If the child has neither hearing, speech nor hand function, testing must depend on the ingenuity of the examiner in finding ways of presenting the tasks and receiving the response in a visual modality. There are so far no test scales specifically for this combination of handicaps, but some test batteries contain a few suitable items which could be adapted without much distortion, such as the shape-matching item from the Terman Merrill scale. Children with upper limb involvement and severe visual difficulties may be assessed on the Williams Scale for the Blind and Partially Sighted, as this is a purely verbal scale.

Having found the optimum level at which the child can function by using the test scale least interfered with by his handicaps, further investigation must be carried out to find out which are the particular areas in which he can function best, in terms of intellectual processes, and which are the areas in which he is most handicapped. The exact procedure must depend on the age, intelligence and range of handicaps of each child, and it is not possible to cite every combination in detail here. The reader has only to refer back to Figure 15.1 to see that the possible combinations in children with cerebral palsy are almost limitless. A pattern which commonly presents difficulties with physically handicapped children is that of poor hand function combined with little or no speech, a combination of handicaps which is found in many athetoid children. This pattern of handicaps will be cited as an example of the procedure in 'analysis' of learning assets and handicaps.

For a general assessment, the test scales are chosen so that auditory and visual input can be used, with an eye-pointing or 'yes-no' response. Within these limits the child's linguistic and sensori-motor intelligence must be investigated. The test scales will be limited to multiple or dual choice type of response, because the mode of possible response is severely limited by the handicaps. Suitable tests, sensori-motor and linguistic, which come within this category are mentioned above. Having achieved a basic score for verbal and performance tests, it is wise to use such hand function and such vocalization as he has to amplify the quantitative tests with a full qualitative assessment. There may be enough hand function to use some performance test items from the W.I.S.C., Merrill Palmer, Nebraska or other scales, so that from the way he tries to do them, an idea of his sensori-motor intelligence may be inferred. For example, has he been able to see the gestalt in the W.I.S.C. Object Assembly tests, even though he cannot move the pieces with enough control to construct this without help?

Linguistic processes can be further investigated by getting him to attempt, by gesture and/or vocalization, some verbal test questions such as the W.I.S.C. or Terman Merrill. Experienced psychologists will have a good idea of the common answers to these familiar tests, so that it is often possible to get some idea of what a child is trying to communicate. This is another advantage of using familiar standardized tests for a qualitative amplification of the assessment. Such qualitative information will widen the rather narrow vocabulary information from the scorable tests. The reception of verbal information, its processing and recoding, as in the 'similarities' tests, is a more advanced and complex process than selecting a picture in response to a word or phrase.

If the child has no hand function, but has comprehensible speech, the range of linguistic processes which can be investigated can be vastly increased, and most untimed verbal tests can be used. It is important to stress the 'untimed', because many children with multiple handicaps have a slow or delayed response, even though this may be at a reasonably high level. The timing aspect is, of course, even more important in performance tests.

Some physically handicapped children, particularly those with certain types of hydrocephalus, have a superficially easy verbal flow, which can be misleading unless all intellectual processes are carefully investigated. Such children may develop speech early and use it freely in conversation, giving a superficial impression of good intelligence. In such cases, the overall score on a verbal test such as the Terman Merrill scale, which includes many memory items and relatively automatic verbal responses such as 'a father is a man, a mother is a . . .', may be a poor guide to their total learning ability. There may be advanced speech development, with a rather automatic pattern of repetitive phrases which are not necessarily used appropriately. It is important to find out how far this linguistic development is linked to reality and how far it can be used for reasoning. In testing such children it is often necessary to break through their verbal flow, bring them back to the problem, and hold their attention firmly. This verbal flow can act as a distractor, and actually become a barrier to further learning unless it can be harnessed to the material world and so form a basis for thinking. In such children it is very important to find out how to help them to use this particular skill to enhance thought, rather than to distract.

6 Investigation of specific learning processes

It is well known that children with cerebral palsy often have specific intellectual difficulties over and above a more general retardation or in the absence of any general retardation. Children with spina bifida and associated hydrocephalus may also have an imbalance of intellectual processes, often taking the form described above. It is an important part of the assessment to investigate all such difficulties, so that remedial measures may be instigated where appropriate.

Among the most commonly encountered learning difficulties of cerebral palsied children are the perceptual, visuo-motor and allied handicaps involving the sequence shown in Figure 15.4.

FIGURE 15.4

The visuo-motor input-output sequence.

Interest was aroused in this type of difficulty by Strauss and Lehtinen (1947) and since then there has been a great deal of work on the subject. The work up to 1964 is summarized by Abercrombie (1964). Difficulties may occur in any perceptual modality, but the most fully investigated, and possibly the commonest in cerebral palsy are those involving visual perception and motor function. Children with visuo-perceptual handicaps may have difficulties in distinguishing figure from ground, in recognizing a picture and in matching shapes. Colours are often a help, and both investigation and training may be aided by using coloured material rather than line drawings. Children with visuo-motor handicaps may have normal perception but have difficulty in translating a visual input into a motor response. Such children may have difficulty in copying two dimensional patterns or in copying a three dimensional model. At a still later stage in the sequence (Fig. 15.4) children may have difficulty in formulating their own assimilated ideas in terms of an executive or expressive function. They may perceive correctly and be correctly orientated within themselves, so that they know what they want to express and yet fail to act in line with their own ideas. For example, they may copy a model correctly but fail to create a model where there is none to copy, or fail to order their response correctly although the content is correct. Other children may suffer from such global spatial disorientation that adaptation to ordinary living is severely impaired. Such a child may be unable to orientate himself in a strange room, so that although he can see the door, he cannot find his way to it. He may not be able to dress himself because he cannot get his clothes the right way round and the right way up, and relate them to the relevant parts of his own body.

There is need for a great deal more study of this type of handicap, so that the different forms may be investigated independently at an early stage and suitable remedial help given. Most of the work so far has been on school-age children, in whom the difficulties are well established.

Of the tests designed to reveal this type of difficulty, the most commonly used are paper and pencil tests such as the Frostig tests (Frostig *et al.*, 1961), and the Bender Gestalt Test to which a developmental scoring system has been worked out by Koppitz (1964). It is important, particularly with younger children who may not have reached the stage of paper-and-pencil skills, to recognize the difficulty early by means of three-dimensional tests such as block building. Many of the Merrill Palmer tests will reveal such difficulties. This scale includes tests which depend on different aspects of perceptual and visuo-motor function. The Seguin Form Board, for example, is mainly a perceptual task; the block bridge is a constructional matching task; the nest of cubes involves size ordering; and copying a circle, cross and star are two-dimensional visuo-motor tasks. Some children show differential difficulty on some of the tests and not others. It is well worth considering the particular type of ability involved in a particular pattern of failure on this test battery. There may also be an early indication of such difficulties in the Terman Merrill scale, in a failure on the reversed form board and the block bridge out of step with other successes. Typically, an attempt is made to construct the block bridge upside down. Gibbs (1959) pointed out that a specific pattern of refusals of spatial tasks in 2- or 3-year-old children may occur with children who have disorders of this type.

Many useful methods have been described for studying different aspects of spatial disorders in young handicapped children.

Graham (1962) compared children who had experienced perinatal anoxia with a group of controls. She used separate batteries of 'conceptual' and 'perceptual motor' tasks. The 'conceptual' task, using form boards with blocks of different form, colour and size, required the building up of concepts at four different levels of difficulty. The 'perceptual motor' battery included figure-ground and tactile tests. She found that the children who had experienced perinatal anoxia were poorer than the controls on the 'conceptual' tasks but not in perceptual-motor function.

Albitreccia (1958) used a battery of tests with the main emphasis on the relationships of body parts, and orientation in space.

Holzel (1965) used a sensory approach to investigate sensory and perceptual disorders in cerebral palsied children of nursery school age.

Monfraix *et al.* (1961) have worked out a test of manual perception and compared cerebral palsied children with normal controls. By means of this test they compared 'gnostic age' with mental age in each child, for each hand separately.

A test scale with rather similar orientation to that of Albitreccia has been devised and standardized for ages 2 to 5 years (Reynell, 1963). The material for this test is shown in Figure 15.5. The tasks are: (1) recognition of parts of a doll, (2) putting the parts on a coloured picture of a house, (3) putting the features on a face, with naming of each part by the examiner (e.g. 'here are the eyes', 'this is his nose'), (4) putting the features on a face without the help of naming, (5) putting together a manikin, complete with coat, trousers and hat. Each part is scored for position and angle. In these tests the plywood pieces are laid on to the picture, without specific holes into which they must fit, so only minimal hand function is needed. It is a spatial construction task, in so far as there is no guide as to where the pieces are to be put and no model to copy (the first face being removed before the second one is produced). It is not a pure spatial test battery, as it has a linguistic component, but it is useful for elucidating the stage that the child has reached in linking language and performance. For example, the normative study showed that children aged less than $3\frac{1}{2}$ years had much more difficulty with the second face where the parts were not named by the examiner, than with the first face where they were named. Some children showed a transitional stage at which they themselves named the pieces correctly, but they still could not put them in the right place. From the age of about $3\frac{1}{2}$ years, this naming process seemed to be internalized so that the second face was as easy or easier than the first. The development and significance of this linkage stage is discussed by Luria (1961). This stage of development may be delayed or its effectiveness impaired by a discrepancy between linguistic and sensori-motor development. This can occur as a result of a visuo-motor lag, as in many cerebral palsied children, or a pseudo-linguistic advance, as in some children with hydrocephalus.

FIGURE 15.6

Visuo-motor and linguistic input-output sequences combined.

When difficulties in visuo-motor function are suggested by any of the usual intelligence test batteries, they need further analysis based on the sequence shown in Figure 15.4. Vision and hand function are peripheral and should be investigated by appropriate means beyond the scope of this chapter (Holt, 1965; Holt and Reynell, 1967). It is difficult to separate the remaining three stages, but it should be possible, by means of matching techniques and other mainly perceptual tests, to find out whether visual perception is normal. If perception is normal, the difficulty must lie in either or both of the remaining two stages. The distinction between perception and visuo-motor function is discussed fully by Abercrombie (1964).

Any tests which involve matching rather than copying are more perceptual than visuo-motor, as the motor component is reduced to a minimum. The shape matching test in the Terman Merrill scale is a familiar perceptual task. Frostig *et al.* (1961) includes perceptual tests in her battery, in addition to some visuo-motor tests. Birch and Lefford (1964) have worked out tests of perceptual recognition, perceptual analysis and perceptual synthesis and have compared cerebral palsied and normal children. This approach could be very helpful for analysing perceptual difficulties in school-age children.

There is no easy recipe for such investigations. The important thing is for the examiner to know exactly what he is trying to do in terms of the sequence shown in Figure 15.4 and its co-ordination with the linguistic sequence (Fig. 15.6).

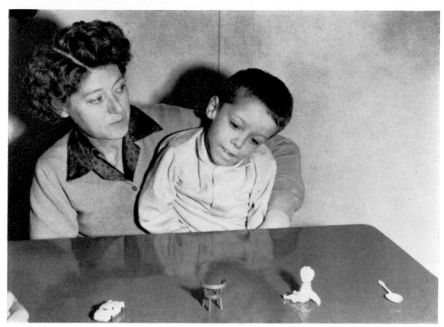

FIGURE 15.2

A child responding to a test question by means of eye-pointing (Holt and Reynell, 1967)

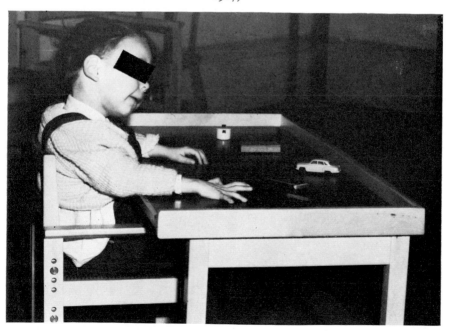

FIGURE 15.3

Seating arrangements for testing a child with physical handicaps.

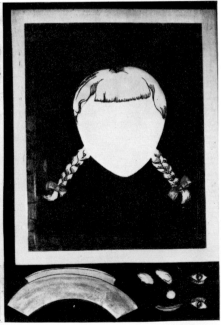

FIGURE 15.5

A 'spatial' test which depends on the ability to link language
with sensori-motor processes.

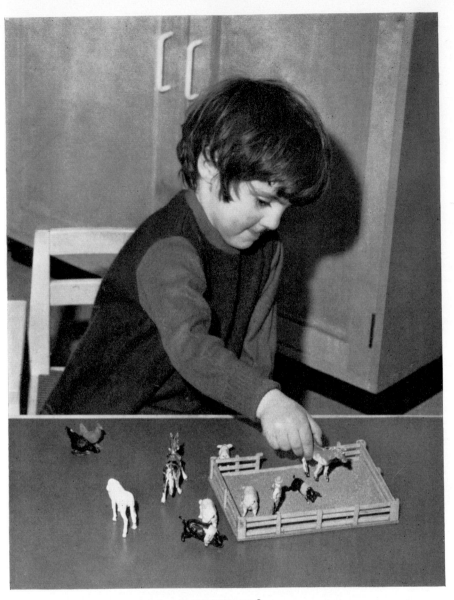

FIGURE 15.8

Verbal comprehension test. Child responding to the request, 'Make one of the horses walk through the gateway'.

Before discussing the linguistic sequence it should again be stressed that 'language' may cover any sort of coded communication, not necessarily verbal (Fig. 15.6). Verbal language is clearly the most valuable asset, but for children who have no hearing and no speech language may assume some other form such as sign language. Non-verbal communication has already been discussed in relation to severely handicapped children, so the following discussion will apply only to verbal communication.

7 Language and tests

For a detailed investigation of verbal language, the sequence shown in Figure 15.7 must be broken down, and each stage separately assessed.

FIGURE 15.7

Verbal language input-output sequence.

Hearing-for-speech and speech mechanisms are usually investigated by audiologists and speech therapists, but the other three stages also come within the psychologist's field.

These processes can be analysed by means of the Illinois Test of Psycholinguistic Abilities (McCarthy and Kirk, 1961). This battery of tests is so constructed that receptive and expressive communication may be assessed at different stages and in different modalities on two levels: automatic and associative. The test battery has certain disadvantages for use with the younger handicapped children in this country, because (1) there are no British norms as yet and some of the items have a considerable cultural bias and (2) it is not designed to cover the very early stages of language development from 1½ years. It is valuable for elucidating learning difficulties in school-age children, however, and Frostig (1966) includes it in her diagnostic battery in assessment for remedial education.

It is important to investigate language problems as early as possible in handicapped children, so that suitable help may be given in the early stages. The language and verbal comprehension scales described below were devised specifically for this purpose, as the outcome of work with handicapped children (Reynell, 1969).

These scales allow for the separate assessment of verbal comprehension and expressive language over the age range 1 to 5 years. There are two parallel comprehension scales: (*a*) one is dependent on some hand function but does not need speech, (*b*) the other is designed for use with eye-pointing throughout and requires neither hand function nor speech. The test material consists of everyday objects, such as a cup, spoon, brush, sock and toys which have been found to be familiar to most handicapped children, such as cars, dolls and farm animals. It

Q*

was found that toys held the attention of distractable children much better than pictures, and the play atmosphere enables even the shyest children to co-operate. Figure 15.8 shows a child carrying out one of the test items, following the instruction 'make one of the horses walk through the gateway'. The vocabulary is kept simple throughout, increasing difficulty being related to sentence length and ideational content.

The aim of these tests is to give a quantitative estimate of a child's level of comprehension relative to norms for his age, and to elucidate, in a qualitative way, any aspect which may be particularly difficult for the child. For example a child may have more difficulty with increasing sentence length than with increasing difficulty of content.

The expressive language scale covers three aspects: (1) the developmental aspects of language structure from the earliest vocalizations to the use of subordinate clauses, (2) vocabulary, using objects, coloured pictures and spoken words, increasing in difficulty but within the experience of even the most house-bound handicapped child, and (3) language content, ability to use language for creative expression, in talking about coloured pictures. This last section is particularly revealing with children who have a deceptively easy flow of speech but with a limited and stereotyped content. This scale is also designed to give a quantitative estimate of expressive language as compared to age norms, and a qualitative assessment of particular areas of difficulty.

There are a number of other methods of investigation of language disorders, such as the sentence length method used by McCarthy (1943) and a similar scheme at present being used by Mason (1967). It is not possible to go into all these different methods in the space available, but a good coverage of the work up to 1957 can be found in Templin's book (Templin, 1957) (See also Chapter 20 of this volume).

The aim of describing one or two tests fully, rather than attempting a more superficial coverage of all tests, is to illustrate the *method* of assessment, and points governing the selection of tests, rather than to try to specify which particular tests should be used in different cases. Any test is at best only a tool, and it is perhaps not out of place to stress once again that however many tests are devised, their value depends ultimately on the insight of the examiner. There are so many possible influences and, in the case of the multiple handicapped, so many possible areas of interference, that the results of analytical investigations of specific learning processes and difficulties must constantly be related to the overall developmental picture of the child with his own particular handicaps and his own particular environment. Investigations should always be relevant to their purpose, which is that of advising on the provision of remedial measures. Detailed and extensive investigations should only be carried out when their significance and purpose is fully understood. Handicapped children are sometimes overtested, perhaps for demonstration or research purposes, and as a result they may become over aware of their disabilities. The child's total welfare must come first.

8 Observational methods of assessment

Observation is a much neglected method of assessment, although its value for research in child development has long been recognized (Wright, 1960). If it is to have value for assessment, such a method must be carefully designed and controlled, and the observations evaluated against established standards of child development and behaviour.

Situations in which the need for such procedures may arise with multiple handicapped children are:

(1) When the child is too withdrawn or too out of touch with reality to respond to standardized tests;

(2) when the handicaps are too severe and communication too limited for formal testing;

(3) for the assessment of factors which are important for learning and development, but which are not scorable in the ordinary way, e.g. attention, drive, fatigue tolerance, dependence and perseverance;

(4) to assess adjustment and application in different types of learning situations;

(5) to assess response to other children;

(6) when attempts at standardized testing are considered inadequate;

(7) as an extension of the test interview when the child has not enough attention or interest to complete the testing.

Many of these situations are equally applicable to children without physical handicaps, but they arise more frequently with the handicapped.

The observation may be carried out in an unstructured play situation, or in a carefully structured setting such as that used by Hutt *et al.* (1963). It may be short term, covering one observation period, or long-term, with repeated or continuous observation over a period of time. A one-way screen is, of course, an asset, but it is not essential, provided the room is large enough to allow free play and for the observer not to loom too large.

Examples

(1) In a free-play situation, with or without other children, the standards used may be the normal developmental stages of play; the repetitive banging or throwing; exploratory play often involving pulling things apart; constructive play such as building; and creative, imaginative or symbolic play.

Guanella (1934) studied block building with a group of children from 1 to 7 years. She cited the following stages: (i) non-structured play (banging and throwing), occurring most frequently under 1 year; (ii) the linear stage (arranging blocks in rows or piles), occurring most frequently at 97 weeks; (iii) the areal stage (walls or floors in two dimensions), observed most frequently at 133 weeks; (iv) the three-dimensional stage, at 190 weeks; and (v) more complex structures, often with imaginative accompaniment, from 4 to 7 years. This is an example of an attempt at developmental standards for a partially structured play situation.

Symbolic play with small toys, such as dolls, beds and cups, normally begins at a mental age of about 18 months and becomes increasingly complex. It is hoped that the findings of current research will eventually enable this type of play to be used as an additional standard assessment procedure in certain cases. The ability to use symbolic play material is usually considered to be an indication of the development of 'inner language' (Sheridan, 1964). Since language is essentially dependent on symbols, the ability to use symbols in play is considered to be a prerequisite of language development. Myklebust (1961) believed this ability to be deficient in children with aphasia, and he used symbolic play material in his training programme for aphasic children.

Even very severely handicapped children can sometimes indicate, by their attempts at play, in a structured or free situation, which basic level has been reached.

(2) In a play situation with other children, some idea can be gained of the level of social play. Children rarely play together in a truly co-operative way until a mental age of 3 to $3\frac{1}{2}$ years, although parallel play is common before this.

Parten and Newhall (1943) studied the social behaviour of pre-school children. They found that children under 3 years rarely played co-operatively, and that there is a marked increase in the proportion of co-operative play between 3 and 4 years.

These two examples illustrate some of the ways in which observation may amplify a test interview, and some of the controls which are needed in the use of such methods.

Observation over a period of time, in learning situations such as those likely to be encountered at school, is now used increasingly. This means admitting the child to a small observation unit where there is constant expert supervision and keeping daily records of his progress in the particular areas to be assessed, such as attention, conformity to simple routines and progress on simple learning tasks.

This sort of observation is carried out at the Katharine Elliot School in Shropshire (Rabinowitz 1966). This is a nursery school for multiple-handicapped children, originally under the direction of a psychologist who carried out the assessment over a period of time.

9 Procedures when formal testing is impossible

A special form of structured observation applies to children who are so severely handicapped that no formal testing is possible, and when the extent of the handicap precludes any of the usual sort of play. It will be clear from previous sections of this chapter, that there are very few children in this category, because the range of testing methods is now so wide. Unless there is also severe mental retardation, some form of standardized testing can usually be carried out.

For this small group of children, who are handicapped in all four limbs, speech, head control and probably eye control as well, the approach must be based on a knowledge of the stages of intellectual development, as, for example, those described by Piaget (1953, 1955), and as used by Woodward (1959) for severely retarded children.

Two examples of this type of assessment follow:

(1) Elizabeth is 10 years old. She has severe athetosis involving all four limbs. She has no head control, very limited eye control, no speech, and continual spasms so that she cannot sit.

The aim in assessing Elizabeth at this age was to suggest ways in which her parents, teachers and therapists could use whatever she has to build on for communication, and greater ease of management.

Her hearing and vision are adequate to use as channels of communication in an input direction, but communication in an outward direction is more difficult.

The best testing position was found to be supporting her in a half-standing position leaning against her mother, so that her head could be controlled against her mother's shoulder and such eye control as she has could be used. She became wildly excited by the new situation, which increased her spasms, so that quiet and time were essential to allow her to become used to the situation and to the examiner's voice.

A few familiar objects such as a cup, spoon, doll and brush, from the Reynell Verbal Comprehension Scale were put on the table and she was allowed plenty of time to look at them. Then her eyes were carefully watched as the objects were named. Each object had to be named several times in a different order, to be sure of her response, because this consisted only of a brief selective glance, before her eyes slid away. A measure of her verbal comprehension was obtained in this way and, although it proved to be very low, there was something to build on.

In response to 'shall we get out some more toys?', she smiled, showing an indication of 'yes', which, although not a deliberately coded message, was at least some communication which could be used to build up a simple 'yes-no' code system.

The value of this assessment, limited though it was, lay in the bases found for building on future learning of a level, pace and kind that she could manage. She has the beginnings of 'yes-no' communication, she has some partially controlled eye movements which she can be taught to use more effectively, and she has an intellectual level well within the range of ability for learning simple daily routines to help her management, if suitable means can be devised by her therapists. The next stage is for her therapists and parents to carry this further by regular teaching.

(2) Diana is $4\frac{1}{2}$ years old. She has spastic quadriplegia with no leg control, and only minimal arm control. She has no speech, but has reasonably good vision and hearing.

The questions to be answered were: (*a*) what sort of education would be suitable in terms of school placement? and (*b*) what type and level of learning could help her present development?

She could only sit if supported on an adult's lap, and the procedure was constantly interrupted by minor fits, during which she had to be prevented from banging her head on the table.

She showed a good personal response by her facial expression, and an interest in the test material, watching and becoming excited as each new item was produced. She was selective in her choice of test material and had no difficulty in communicating acceptance or the reverse by means of gross arm or body movements. She was already demonstrating a clear basis for communication. She could indicate her selection of appropriate holes in the Griffith's form board tests, although she could not put the pieces in. She succeeded in all but the reversals, all of which she failed. She was able to select objects correctly on the Reynell Verbal Comprehension Scale up to a 20-month level, but she could not attempt any naming. When given symbolic play material, a small doll, bed and blanket, she managed by means of her own arm movements with some practical assistance from the examiner, to put the doll on the bed and cover it with a blanket, indicating a play level of at least 18 months.

It was now possible to answer the questions posed at the beginning of the test interview: (a) she reached a ceiling in the tests she could attempt, such as the form boards and verbal comprehension, at a level well below suitability for education beyond Training Centre level; (b) she had demonstrated a level and type of communication which could be built on and used for teaching. She had demonstrated an interest in symbolic play, which could be used as a medium for teaching.

The type of assessment illustrated by these two examples is really a combination of standardized tests and structured observation, with a basis of a sound knowledge of developmental processes against which to evaluate the findings.

III CONCLUSION

It has proved difficult to describe, in any practical detail, the methods used in the assessment of children who have handicaps as complex and varied as those discussed in this chapter. Clearly the actual procedure, the tests selected and the method of communication must vary with each child, and always it is the examiner who must adapt to the child. A developmental orientation is adopted, so that each child with his own particular complex of assets and handicaps, is seen as a dynamic and developing whole. The complexity must be unravelled and analysed so that the details of all learning processes may be assessed, and then the whole must be resynthesized so that helpful remedial measures may be initiated using the child's assets to help the areas in which he is most handicapped. In this way it is hoped that he may be able to make the most of such potential as he has, and any disbalance of ability may be minimized. Although he still has to live with his handicaps, he may be helped to find ways of circumventing them.

REFERENCES

ABERCROMBIE, M. L. J. (1964) *Perceptual and Visuo-motor Disorders in Cerebral Palsy*. Little Club Clinics in Developmental Medicine No. 11. London: Spastics Society and Heinemann.

ALBITRECCIA, S. I. (1958) Recognition and Treatment of Disturbances of the Body Image. *Cerebral Palsy Bull.*, 4, 12-17.

BARRETT, M. L. and JONES, M. H. (1967) The sensory story. A multisensory training procedure for toddlers. *Dev. Med. Child Neurol.*, 9, 448-456.

BIRCH, H. G. (Ed.) (1964) *Brain Damage in Children. The Biological and Social Aspects*. New York: Williams and Wilkins.

BIRCH, H. G. and LEFFORD, A. (1964) Two strategies for studying perception in brain-damaged children. *In* BIRCH, H. G. (Ed.) *Brain Damage in Children.* New York: Williams and Wilkins.

BOBATH, BERTA (1967) The very early Treatment of cerebral palsy. *Dev. Med. Child Neurol.*, 9, 373-390.

BOWLEY, A. (1967) A follow-up study of 64 children with cerebral palsy. *Dev. Med. Child Neurol.*, 9, 172-182.

BURGEMEISTER, B. B., BLUM, L. M. and LORGE, I. (1959) *Columbia Mental Maturity Scale*. New York: World Book Company.

COCKBURN, J. M. (1961) Psychological and educational aspects. *In* HENDERSON, J. L. (Ed.) *Cerebral Palsy in Childhood and Adolescence*. Edinburgh and London: E. and S. Livingstone.

CRUIKSHANK, W. M., BONTZEN, F. A., RATZBURY, F. H. and TANHAUSER, M. T. (1961) *A Teaching Method for Brain Injured and Hyperactive Children*. New York: Syracuse University Press.

CRUIKSHANK, W. M. and RAUS, G. M. (1955) *Cerebral Palsy: Its Individual and Community Problems*. New York: Syracuse University Press.

DUNSDON, M. I. (1952) *The Educability of Cerebral Palsied Children*. London: Newns.

ELLIS, E. (1966) The very early treatment of cerebral palsy. *Dev. Med. Child Neurol.*, 8, 206-207.

FLOYER, E. B. (1955) *A Psychological Study of a City's Cerebral Palsied Children.* London: British Council for the Welfare of Spastics.

FROSTIG, M. (1966) The relationship of diagnosis to remediation in learning problems. *In International Approach to Learning Disabilities of Children and Youth*. New York: The Association for Children with Learning Disabilities.

FROSTIG, M., LEFEVER, D. W. and WHITTLESEY, J. R. B. (1961) A developmental test of visual perception for evaluating normal and neurologically handicapped children. *Percept. and Mot. Skills*, 12, 383-394.

GIBBS, N. (1959) Some learning difficulties of cerebral palsied children. *Spastics Quart.*, **8**, 21-23.

GRAHAM, FRANCES (1962) Development three years after perinatal anoxia and other potentially damaging new born experiences. *Psychological Monograph*, **76**, 3.

GUANELLA, FRANCES (1934) Block building activities in young children. *In* WOODWORTH, R. S. (Ed.) *Archives of Psychology*, No. 174. New York.

HENDERSON, J. L. (1961) *Cerebral Palsy in Childhood and Adolescence*. Edinburgh and London: E. and S. Livingstone.

HOLT, K. S. (1965) *Assessment of Cerebral Palsy* (Vol. 1). London: Lloyd Luke.

HOLT, K. S. and REYNELL, J. K. (1967) *Assessment of Cerebral Palsy* (Vol. 2). London: Lloyd Luke.

HOLZEL, F. (1965) Sensory and perceptual difficulties in brain-injured children. *Spastics Quart.*, **14**, 23-27.

HUTT, C., HUTT, S. J. and OUNSTED, C. (1963) A method for the study of children's behaviour. *Dev. Med. Child Neurol.*, **5**, 233-245.

INGRAM, T. T. S. (1964) *Paediatric Aspects of Cerebral Palsy*. Edinburgh and London: E. and S. Livingstone.

INGRAM, T. T. S., JAMESON, S., ERRINGTON, J. and MITCHELL, R. G. (1964) *Living with Cerebral Palsy*. Clinics in Developmental Medicine No. 14. London: Spastics Society and Heinemann.

INGRAM, T. T. S. and NAUGHTEN, J. A. (1962) Paediatric and Psychological Aspects of Cerebral Palsy Associated with Hydrocephalus. *Dev. Med. Child Neurol.*, **4**, 287-292.

KOPPITZ, E. M. (1964) *The Bender Gestalt Test for Young Children*. New York: Grune and Stratton.

LORING, J. and MASON, A. (Eds.) (1966) *The Spastic School Child and the Outside World*. London: Heinemann.

LURIA, A. (1961) *The Role of Speech in the Regulation of Normal and Abnormal Behaviour*. London: Pergamon Press.

MCCARTHY, D. (1943) Language development of the preschool child. *In* BARKER, R. G., KOUNIN, J. S. and WRIGHT, H. F. (Eds.) *Child Behaviour and Development*. New York: McGraw-Hill.

MCCARTHY, J. J. and KIRK, S. A. (1961) *Illinois Test of Psycholinguistic Abilities* (Experimental Edition). Urbana, Ill.: Institute for Research on Exceptional Children.

MASON, A. (1967) Specific (developmental) dyslexia. *Dev. Med. Child Neurol.*, **9**, 183-190.

MITCHELL, R. G. (1961) Analysis of each type of cerebral palsy. *In* HENDERSON J. L. (Ed.) *Cerebral Palsy in Childhood and Adolescence*. Edinburgh and London: E. and S. Livingstone.

MONFRAIX, C., TARDIEU, G. and TARDIEU, C. (1961) Development of manual perception in children with cerebral palsy. *Cerebral Palsy Bull.*, **3**, 544-552.

MYKLEBUST, H. R. (1961) Aphasia in children. Suggestions for management and training. *J. South African Logopedic Soc. June*, 6-13.

NATIONAL FUND FOR RESEARCH INTO POLIOMYELITIS AND OTHER CRIPPLING DISEASES (1965) *Proceedings of a Symposium on Spina Bifida*. London: Action for the Crippled Child Monograph.

PARTEN, M. and NEWHALL, S. M. (1943) Social behaviour of the preschool child. *In* BARKER, R. G., KOUNIN, J. S. and WRIGHT, H. F. (Eds.) *Child Behaviour and Development*. New York: McGraw-Hill.

PIAGET, J. (1953) *The Origin of Intelligence in the Child*. London: Routledge and Kegan Paul.

PIAGET, J. (1955) *The Child's Construction of Reality*. London: Routledge and Kegan Paul.

RABINOWITZ, A. (1966) A nursery school in Shropshire. *Spec. Educ.*, **55**, 30-32.

REYNELL, J. K. (1963) A spatial test for preschool children. *In Factors affecting Response to Treatment in Cerebral Palsy*. Ph.D. Thesis, University of Sheffield.

REYNELL, J. K. (1969) *Test Manual. Reynell Developmental Language Scales. Experimental Edition*. London: National Foundation for Educational Research.

SCHONELL, F. E. (1956) *Educating Spastic Children*. Edinburgh and London: Oliver and Boyd.

SCHULMAN, J. L., CASPAR, J. C. and THORNE, F. M. (1965) *Brain Damage and Behaviour*. Springfield, Ill.: Thomas.

SHERIDAN, M. O. (1964) Development of auditory attention and language symbols in young children. *In* RENFREW, C. and MURPHY, K. (Eds.) *The Child who does not Talk*. London: Spastics Society and Heinemann.

SMITHELLS, R. W. (1965) The epidemiology of spina bifida. *In Proceedings of a Symposium on Spina Bifida*. London: National Fund for Research into Poliomyelitis and other Crippling Diseases.

SPASTICS SOCIETY (1967) Research into hydrocephalus and spina bifida. *Dev. Med. Child Neurol. Supplement No.* 13. London: Heinemann.

STEPHEN, ELSPETH (1963) Intelligence levels and educational status of children with meningomyelocoele. *Dev. Med. Child Neurol.*, **5**, 572-576.

STRAUSS, A. A. and LEHTINEN, L. E. (1947) *Psychopathology and Education of the Brain-injured Child*. New York: Grune and Stratton.

SWINYARD, C. A. (1964) *The Child with Spina Bifida*. New York: Association for the Aid of Crippled Children.

TAYLOR, E. M. (1959) *Psychological Appraisal of Children with Cerebral Defects*. Cambridge, Mass.: Harvard University Press.

TEMPLIN, M. C. (1957) *Certain Language Skills in Children*. Minneapolis: Univ. Minnesota Press.

WOODWARD, M. (1959) The behaviour of idiots interpreted by Piaget's theory of sensori-motor development. *Brit. J. educ. Psych.*, **39**, 60-71.

WRIGHT, H. F. (1960) Observational child study. *In* MUSSEN, P. H. (Ed.) *Handbook of Research Methods in Child Development*. New York: Wiley.

16

Slow-learning children
and educational problems

Phillip Williams

I INTRODUCTION

During the latter half of the nineteenth century one of the most controversial issues was the question of compulsory education for all children. On the one side were ranged the reformers, including J. S. Mill, who argued for the 'unlimited possibility of improving the moral and intellectual condition of mankind through education'. On the other side lay the traditionalists, including the Member for Newark, who argued that 'You may train your hounds and your pointers, but never the hare or the fox'. The reformers prevailed and the way was opened for the establishment in this country of an educational system for all children. Today, when the value of education is appreciated more than ever before, it is hard to believe that the issue might have been resolved in any other way: indeed it is almost inconceivable that the reformers should have been opposed at all. What is of more immediate interest to this chapter is the effect which was produced when large numbers of children, many of whom had hitherto spent their childhood literally roaming the streets of the large conurbations in bands, were compelled to attend school (Burt, 1957).

In its 1861 Revised Code of Elementary Instruction, the Board of Education laid down a scheme of educational standards which suggested appropriate levels of attainment for different age-groups. This can be regarded as the germ of the idea of an age-scale type of measurement, antedating Binet by more than 40 years. Salaries of teachers were linked to the performance of their pupils in relation to the Board's standards. After the 1870 Education Act this education system had to cope with, in words quoted by Burt, 'an aggregation of difficult children, urchins who could not be taught, ruffians who could not be controlled'. It soon became clear that there were numbers of children for whom these standards were quite unattainable, in spite of the most devoted teaching, and for whom new arrangements were necessary. In some areas classes called 'standard O' were established for this group of children: in others (e.g. Bradford) schools catering specifically for them were established. By the last decade of the nineteenth century special provision of some kind for those children who could not respond to the challenge of the new educational system had begun (Pritchard, 1963).

II DEFINITION

Since that time this group of children (the slow responders) has been defined and named in a variety of ways. During the years between the wars the intelligence quotient was the criterion used; the group of children with I.Q.s below 70 were known as mentally defective children. The legislation following the 1944 Education Act used the criterion of educational competence; the Ministry of Education in its pamphlet *Special Education* (1946) suggested that children whose standard of school work fell below that of children 20% younger should form the educationally subnormal group. The change in name is interesting, the change in criterion more so. With adults the criteria of subnormality have changed from emphasizing social competence to emphasizing measured intelligence; with children the reverse has taken place and educational competence has replaced measured intelligence.

Today there is increasing dissatisfaction with the use of the term 'educationally subnormal'. The Department of Education and Science in its booklet *Slow-learners at School* (1964) suggests using the name 'slow-learning' for children of any degree of ability who are unable to do work commonly done by children of their age; the Plowden report (1967) recommends substituting 'slow-learning' for 'educationally subnormal'. Regrettably any term used to describe our slow responders seems in time to acquire its own odium, and a quarter of a century seems to represent the limit of its useful life.

The term 'slow-learning' today is generally interpreted as referring to all children whose educational standards fall below those of children at least 20% younger (note that this is an educational criterion, quite independent of measured intelligence). This is not a very precise definition for reasons which will be discussed later. But before looking at the problems of the criterion, it is important to emphasize that within the group encompassed by this definition lie a number of children with very special needs, who are the subjects of separate treatment in other chapters. These are the children whose learning problems are such that they need provision outside the education system – even outside the special school framework. These extreme cases of slow-learners are found in training centres and hospitals for the subnormal. In general they are of much lower intelligence than the children with whom we are mostly concerned in this chapter, although marked overlaps between the intelligence levels of the groups occur, and these overlaps are of great theoretical interest. Thus there are some children in subnormality hospitals who are of average or above average intelligence (British Psychological Society, 1966). Probably all these children can be described as 'slow-learning' following the interpretation given at the start of this paragraph, but the problems of the children in subnormality hospitals are so much more acute that they are described and treated as a separate group. The same point applies to children in training centres.

This chapter deals with the rest of the slow-learners, those whose difficulties are less acute than the training centre and hospital children, whose intelligence levels are mainly higher (Williams and Gruber, 1967) and who are found in special schools, special classes and in the ordinary schools.

III INCIDENCE

Estimates of the incidence of slow-learning children vary considerably, and are bound to do so while our criteria are imprecise. The meaning of 'educational standards' is open to different interpretations. Should a child whose standards in the key areas of reading and language skills fall into the slow-learning zone, but whose number work and practical skills are only mildly below average, be described as a 'slow-learner'? Questions of this nature do not seem to have been answered. From a practical point of view the sort of label that is attached to a child should make little difference to the education which he needs – in this case special help with his reading and language – but it is because of reasons such as this that incidence figures of slow-learners must be treated with care.

Different countries have adopted different systems of classifying the children we describe as 'slow-learners'. Later in this chapter reference is often made to American studies, usually concerned with mentally retarded children. In interpreting the findings of these studies it must be remembered that in this country these children might often be found in training centres or hospitals.

Shortly after the 1944 Act the Ministry of Education (1945) suggested that 5-10% of the school population could fall into this category of children whose educational standards were below those of children 20% younger than themselves. In a later publication the Ministry of Education (1946) suggested that as a rough guide education authorities should plan on the assumption of about 10% of the school population falling into this category. This latter estimate is similar to the estimated incidence of backwardness in the school population, using a somewhat different criterion, made in 1917 by Burt and quoted in Burt (1937).

During the 1940s and 1950s in particular a large number of estimates were made of the incidence of children needing special help because of low attainment. In the main, two sorts of criteria have been used: (a) *'Difference' scores*: there were many inquiries in which a set difference between chronological age and attainment age was used as a criterion. Thus a difference of two years between chronological age and attainment age might be regarded as an appropriate criterion. (b) *Quotients*: some inquiries preferred to take a quotient on a standardized test of attainment as a criterion, for example a quotient of 85 or below. The standardization characteristics of the test used are crucial to the incidence figures. (c) *'Percentage-based' differences*: there is a third sort of criterion, viz. that suggested by the Ministry of Education itself. Few inquiries used this criterion, i.e an attainment age lower than a chronological age 20% below the child's own chronological age. This can be expressed as an attainment age which is less than 80% of the child's chronological age. A moment's reflection indicates that the use of this criterion increases the labour of calculation in comparison with criterion (*a*), although perhaps providing greater comparability of incidence at different age levels.

Schonell (1949) has summarized the results of surveys into the incidence of slow-learning children up to the late 1940s. One of his conclusions is that 'it is not at all unlikely that the figure for general backwardness throughout the country is nearly 20%.'

Recently the approach to this problem has been through questionnaire inquiries as well as surveys using standardized tests. Two recent surveys show an interesting unanimity of estimate of children in need of special education. In the first report of the National Child Development Study, Kellmer Pringle, Butler and Davie (1966) reported head teachers' views that 13% of their sample of 11,000 7-year-olds could with advantage have been given special educational help (not merely with reading). Morris (1966), reporting the second N.F.E.R. reading inquiry in Kent, stated that 14% of her sample of 711 children in ten specially selected Kent schools were either non-readers or extremely poor readers. Thus, in spite of the great improvement of educational standards, the incidence of slow-learners needing some form of special help still seems to lie between 10% and 20%. This underlines the fact that backwardness, slowness to learn and educational subnormality are all relative concepts. No matter how much we improve the speed of the group, there will always be those who will be its slower members.

IV IDENTIFICATION

Identification of slow-learning children is in essence a question of locating children with low attainments. Standardized tests are used, but are only part of a procedure which involves close consultation with school staffs and possibly other colleagues as well. Test scores are needed, but not test scores alone. While there is no logical reason why individual tests should not be used, in practice educational psychologists tend to use group tests for surveying large populations, for reasons of convenience and economy of time. Whether the criterion used is a 'difference', a 'percentage' or a 'quotient', it is vital that the tests used match up to acceptable standards of construction. As with all standardized tests, attainment tests should provide the data on reliability and validity discussed in standard texts on psychological tests, e.g. Anastasi (1961) or Cronbach (1961). It is dangerous to suggest that reliability coefficients should not fall below certain minimum values. Reliability values depend on so many factors, such as type of reliability, homogeneity of the population on which the reliability was calculated, etc., that it is better for the psychologist to evaluate each quoted reliability in the light of these factors. Fortunately there are at present numbers of group attainment tests available with acceptable reliability and validity data.

The other main factor to be considered in choosing suitable tests for identifying slow-learning children is the nature of the standardization sample. It cannot be emphasized too strongly that a test score has relevance only in relation to the sample of children on which the test was standardized. If we decide to identify as slow-learners all 9-year old children with a reading age of 7 years or less on a Southgate Reading Test (Southgate, 1958) then we are identifying all 9-year-old children whose reading standard today is not higher than that of those 7-year-olds in the City of Worcester on whom the test was standardized in June 1957.

It is essential to know the characteristics of the standardization population, for in this way we gain a better understanding of the meaning of the scores that the children obtain. A well-standardized test may provide information on the social class composition, on the urban-rural breakdown and the intelligence distribution of the standardization population. The Illinois Test of Psycho-linguistic Abilities (McCarthy and Kirk, 1961) is a good example of a test which does just this. It is regrettable that few of the British group attainment tests, which might be used by an educational psychologist to identify slow-learning

	Approximate reading age			
Raw score of 15 on	1948	1952	1956	1964
Watts/Vernon test	12 y. 5 m.	12 y. 1 m.	11 y. 8 m.	11 y. 0 m.

TABLE 16.1
Equivalent reading standards at different dates

children, provide adequate standardization data. Where it does appear that good data have been provided, there are three points to which attention might still need to be paid in this country.

One is the extent to which private schools were included in the standardization sample. About 6% of the school population are educated in the private school sector (Department of Education and Science, 1967), but in some areas social pressures lead to private education being used for a much higher percentage of the child population – in the South Eastern Region, for example, over 10% of the child population are educated in independent schools (Table 2, Department of Education and Science, 1967) – with the result that a markedly truncated population attends the state schools. If tests are standardized in the state schools in such areas then a strange distribution of scores will be obtained if the test is used in an area where private education caters for a low percentage of the child population (the converse is, of course, also true).

The second point to which attention should be paid is the date at which the test was standardized. Attainment levels in England and Wales have been rising steadily for the last 20 years or so. Examples of the way reading standards of school children have improved are given in reports of the Ministry of Education and the Department of Education and Science published in 1950, 1957 and 1966, also in the reports of the Central Advisory Council for Education published in 1963 and 1967 (the Newsom and Plowden reports). The findings for 11-year-olds in 1964 are summarized in Table 16.1, based on Peaker (1967).

Clearly reading tests which were standardized before the last year or so are likely to give highly misleading information if used to identify slow-learning children. This change in levels of attainment across time is known as zero-error. While it is very important in the interpretation of results of attainment tests it is less important though still observable in tests of intellectual development (see Pilliner, Sutherland and Taylor, 1960, for a discussion of this point).

The third point is the locality in which the test was standardized. There are wide local differences in attainment standards, e.g. Vernon, O'Gorman and McLellan (1955).

It is for reasons such as these (and others) that Vernon (1956, 1960) advocates that psychologists should construct their own norms for the areas in which they work and should revise these norms periodically. Local standardizations of this sort provide information which is essential for psychologists concerned with the accurate identification of slow-learning children in parts of the country which may differ widely in their standards of attainment. The process of restandardizing is not difficult: a standard technique is described by Lawley (1950).

1 Surveys for identifying slow-learning children

Survey work is often the first stage in the educational psychologist's identification task. Conducting educational surveys involves a sequence of operations.

First the survey has to be planned, starting with a clear definition of its aim. Perhaps the next point, the need to establish a good relationship with the schools and the staff who are likely to be asked to participate in the survey, is the most important of all. No survey can proceed without goodwill, particularly from the administrators and headteachers involved. It is often valuable to establish a small survey steering committee, especially if a survey is being conducted for the first time.

At the planning stage decisions have to be made about the method of the survey. No survey should be purely a psychometric affair, if only because of the standard errors of the tests used; the way in which teachers can draw attention to apparent anomalies should be discussed at an early stage. This may involve no more than a space on a form in which personal comments on the children can be entered; it may also involve an agreed arrangement to visit each school for personal discussions on the survey's findings.

It is at the planning stage that marking and scoring procedures can be agreed. The design of return forms is another point which needs tackling – well-designed forms can repay many times over the time spent on their design. Fieldhouse (1957) gives simple examples of forms which have been found useful and also provides an elementary guide to practical procedures involved in conducting a survey of reading. If it is intended to carry out more than a very simple analysis of the results, then it can be advantageous to use computer procedures, and in this case the return forms should be designed with ease of transference of data from form to card (or whatever form of in-put is used) uppermost.

It is at the planning stage too that clear cut instructions for the participating schools must be formulated. It is important to decide beforehand which age group will be surveyed. Usually, but not necessarily, a year-group of children is chosen and the age limits set to coincide with the limits of a school-year group. This is administratively convenient for the schools since it avoids disrupting two year-groups in order to assemble the children taking part in the survey. But in any school system there are almost always a few children who, for various reasons, are placed out of their chronological age-group. These are often the very children on whom the survey's accurate information is most necessary, and the need to include them in the arrangements for the survey must be made clear. The question of children in special schools and units also needs deciding. Unless the survey is being conducted for research purposes there is usually little point in including children who are already receiving special education in a school for the physically handicapped, for example; but there may be occasions when it is highly appropriate to include children who are already attending special schools and classes for the slow-learning in surveys designed to identify other slow-learning children in need of special provision.

Questions such as these lead to a careful consideration of the population to be included in the survey. If slow-learners are to be identified so that they can be given special help, then it is appropriate for all children of the age-group to participate in the survey. This is the situation which has been assumed so far, but if provision for slow-learners is insufficient and the survey is intended to shed light on the needs of the area, i.e. if it is an 'incidence' survey and not a pure 'identification' survey, then there is no need to cover all the population; a sample will provide the information much more economically. Thus if a survey is designed to estimate the incidence of slow-learning children among an age-group of four thousand second-year juniors in a large authority, there is no need to assess all four thousand. The psychologist could draw a random sample of 960 children, i.e. 24% of the population, and find the incidence of slow-learners in this sample.

The penalty which has to be paid for the lighter work of a smaller survey is the loss of precision that sampling entails. Let us suppose that in relation to the particular criteria for 'slow-learning' employed in this survey 20% of the sample are slow-learners. We now need to know the reliability of this estimate of 20% as far as the population of 4,000 children is concerned.

The standard error of a percentage is given by the formula (adapted from Garrett, 1953, p.196):

$$\text{S.E.\%} = \sqrt{\frac{P.Q}{S}} \times \text{f.p.c.}$$

where $\quad P$ = percentage incidence

$Q = 100 - P$

S = number of individuals in the sample

f.p.c. = finite population correction

$$= \sqrt{\frac{N-S}{N-1}} \text{ where}$$

N = number of individuals in the population.

So for our example:

$$\text{S.E.}\% = \sqrt{\frac{20 \times 80}{960}} \times \sqrt{\frac{4{,}000-960}{3{,}999}} = 1{\cdot}13$$

This suggests that if they were to repeat our survey a number of times the estimate we would obtain would probably fall within the range of $20{\pm}1{\cdot}13\%$ on two occasions out of three. The standard error is of course the standard deviation of this distribution of estimates, and since it is not unreasonable to expect this distribution to be a normal one, then 68%, or approximately two-thirds of the estimates, will fall within one standard deviation on either side of the estimate obtained, i.e. $20{\pm}1{\cdot}13\%$. But psychologists often prefer to work with a range within which the estimates obtained on replication would fall on 19 occasions out of 20, i.e. the $0{\cdot}95$ confidence band. Nineteen out of 20 of the estimates will fall within $1{\cdot}96$ standard errors on either side of the estimate obtained. So we find the $0{\cdot}95$ confidence band for the percentage of slow-learners in the population of 4,000 children is $20{\pm}1{\cdot}96 \times 1{\cdot}13 = 20{\pm}2{\cdot}21$.

So we can be reasonably sure that the whole age group contains between $17{\cdot}8\%$ and $22{\cdot}2\%$ of slow-learners.

This amount of inaccuracy may be quite tolerable for an education authority which requires an approximate estimate only of the provision which it ought to make for slow-learning children, but if more exact estimates are required then larger samples must be drawn.

In educational psychology, however, random samples are rarely drawn for survey work of this nature. In the example given above each one of the 4,000 children would have to be listed and numbered before a truly random sample could be drawn. Not only is this a laborious procedure in itself but also it is not always easy for schools to withdraw sample members from classes to give them special assessments. Both difficulties can be eased if 'cluster sampling' is adopted. Cluster sampling involves sampling by groups, or clusters, and not by individuals. The clusters used in educational work are usually schools or classes. In the foregoing example the 4,000 children might have been taught in, let us say, 125 classes. It is a much easier process to list the 125 classes, or clusters, and draw a random sample of perhaps 30 classes. The 960 children who might be found in this group of 30 complete classes can be surveyed much more easily than the 960 children scattered through all the schools who constituted the random sample in the foregoing example.

But once again we have to pay for convenience with precision. Since the clusters themselves are not homogeneous with respect to the incidence of slow-learners, our sampling will be somewhat 'lumpy'. We must therefore expect a greater standard error of our estimate of slow-learners in the population when we base the estimate on a sample of clusters than when we base it on a random sample of individuals.

Let us assume that the numbers of slow-learners identified in each of the 30 classes is as follows:

$$4, 6, 10, 5, 3, 8, 7, 0, 12, 17, 3, 0, 4, 5, 10,$$
$$7, 3, 6, 0, 7, 9, 5, 6, 11, 3, 5, 9, 12, 8, 7.$$

(Note that the incidence of slow-learners can be calculated as 192/960 = 20% again.) The incidence has been deliberately made the same so as to facilitate comparisons between the precision of this and the previous estimate.

Let N = the number of children in the population   (4,000)
    A = the number of clusters   (125)
    a = the number of clusters in the sample.   (30)
    B = the number of children in each cluster.   (32)
    x = the number of slow learners in the sample
            $(4+6+10+5+3+8 \ldots +8+7 =$ 192)
    y = the sum of the squares of the numbers of
        slow-learners in each cluster
            $(4^2+6^2+10^2+5^2 \ldots +8^2+7^2 =$ 1,660)

Then S.E.% $= 100 \sqrt{\left[\frac{1}{a} - \frac{B}{N}\right]\left[\frac{1}{(a-1)B^2}\left(y - \frac{x^2}{a}\right)\right]}$

(adapted from Kish (1965), p. 154)

$$= 100 \sqrt{\left[\frac{1}{30} - \frac{32}{4000}\right]\left[\frac{1}{29 \times 32^2}\left(1{,}660 - \frac{192^2}{30}\right)\right]}$$

$$= 100 \sqrt{\frac{304}{12{,}000} \times \frac{1}{29 \times 32^2}\left(\frac{12{,}936}{30}\right)}$$

$$= 100 \sqrt{\frac{304 \times 12{,}936}{12{,}000 \times 29 \times 32^2 \times 30}}$$

$$= \sqrt{\frac{304 \times 12{,}936}{1 \cdot 2 \times 29 \times 32^2 \times 30}}$$

$$= 1 \cdot 92.$$

So our 0·95 confidence band for the percentage of slow-learners in our population of 4,000 children is now $20 \pm 1 \cdot 96 \times 1 \cdot 92 = 20 \pm 3 \cdot 76$.

So we could be reasonably sure that the whole age-group contains between 16·2% and 23·8% of slow-learners.

Note that the use of cluster sampling has appreciably diminished the precision of our estimate in comparison with that obtained in our previous survey, based on a random sample.

The formula given above can be used for most educational surveys, even though the classes or clusters are not of equal size, but only approximately so. In this case the mean number of children per cluster will be used for B in the formula, but the formula cannot be used where the clusters differ markedly in size, as would be the case if a sample of schools were drawn. If it is necessary to sample this way, then Kish (1965), Butcher (1966) or Yamane (1967) should be consulted.

Occasionally it may be necessary to provide information about the incidence of slow-learning children in each of several subgroups of the population, e.g. the subgroup of boys and the subgroup of girls, or the subgroup of summer-born children and the subgroup of winter-born children. Let us consider the case of the boys' subgroup. In this case the data might be handled by treating each of the classes as a cluster of boys drawn from the total population of boys. The problem now is to estimate the error associated with our estimate of the incidence of slow-learning boys which is based on that obtained from our sample of 30 clusters out of the total population of, let us say, 2,000 boys arranged in 125 clusters.

If all the authority's schools are mixed, then we can proceed as previously, remembering that in this case

$$N = 2,000$$
$$B = 16$$

But if the authority runs some single-sex schools, then the size of our clusters will differ markedly from their mean of 16; in fact, some will be 32 (all boys) while some will be zero (all girls). In this situation the psychologist should use one of the approaches for clusters of unequal size, described in Kish (1965) or Butcher (1966).

After decisions about the survey sample have been taken, the planning stage gives way to the administration. Fieldhouse (1957) gives useful suggestions about the practical details which need watching if the administration is to be successful. It is of course particularly important to ensure that the information which will have been drafted about the procedures to be followed by teachers responsible for administering and scoring the tests is both understood and followed. The pre-survey briefing meetings which Fieldhouse recommends are especially important here. Fieldhouse's points can be summarized as follows:

1. calculation of test materials needed by each school;
2. early and generous ordering of materials;

3. making a survey schedule specifying days and times of testing;
4. drafting a memorandum about test administration in schools;
5. early despatch of test materials;
6. drafting a memorandum about the scoring procedures;
7. preparing scoring schedules to be completed by the schools;
8. preparing a special memorandum about the survey organization for headteachers.

It is not suggested that all these steps need to be taken in every survey, but it is suggested that they illustrate the need to programme every survey carefully. Practical experience serves only to emphasize the importance that these steps attach to communication.

The last stage of the survey is the presentation of the results. It is at this point that the design of the return forms is important. If the survey is designed to determine the incidence of slow-learning children, or to identify them, there is little point in preparing the data for analysis by computer, but if the survey covers a range of data and it is intended to present tables of information of incidence of slow-learners by sex, by social class, by area, etc., then it is worth while preparing the data for analysis by one of the survey analysis package programmes that are usually available for computer systems.

2 Surveys for identifying 'remedial' children

Many educational psychologists are required to run surveys to identify children needing remedial education. Although there is a difference between the 'remedial' children and the slow-learners, nevertheless the survey problems are very similar – in fact the same survey is often used as a vehicle to identify both groups of children. It is for this reason that it seems appropriate to place this section here.

Consider an intelligent child who has had an extended illness. His educational standards may be such that he could be correctly identified as a slow-learner, but it would not be appropriate to place him in a school or class for slow-learning children, where the gradual approach to learning would not suit his ability. Equally a busy teacher in a large class might not be able to give him the extra attention that he needs. The special attention, usually part-time, which is provided for children like this is commonly called 'remedial education'. There are many reasons, other than the absence from school mentioned in the example, why children might need help of this sort. Emotional problems are frequently found to lie behind the educational difficulties exhibited. Notwithstanding the variety of causes, these children share the characteristic of a retarded educational development. In the words of the Department of Education and Science (1964) they are 'children whose attainments are falling markedly behind their apparent level of ability'.

Note that both 'ability' and 'attainment' are involved. Putting on one side the arguments about the meaning that can be attached to comparisons between

scores on tests of ability and tests of attainment – for discussions of this controversial question see Levy (1962, 1963), correspondence in Vol. 16 of the *British
Journal of Statistical Psychology* (Brimer, Burt and Peaker, 1963) and Curr and
Hallworth (1965) – the fact remains that many educational psychologists are
required to conduct surveys based on this comparison. Whereas slow-learning
children are identified from their scores on an attainment test or tests, remedial
children are usually identified on the basis of the difference between their scores
on an attainment test or tests and intelligence test or tests. The interpretation of
a difference score of this sort is discussed in detail by Phillips (1961). He shows
clearly how test regression affects the interpretation of difference scores. To give
a qualitative example, let us consider a survey designed to identify remedial
children, in which all children took an intelligence test 'I' and an attainment test
'A'. Since the two tests are not perfectly correlated, there will be a regression
effect between scores that children obtain on the two tests. Children with high
'I' scores will be likely to have 'A' scores which are lower; children with low 'I'
scores are likely to have 'A' scores which are higher. Many of the children with
'I' scores of 120 will have 'A' scores of 110; few of the children with 'I' scores of
80 will have 'A' scores of 70. Yet the 'I-A' difference of 10 points is the same in
both cases. It may therefore be wise for psychologists to vary the criterion for
admission into remedial education in accordance with the child's intelligence. At
higher 'I' levels it would be more appropriate to require higher 'I-A' scores
before children are admitted, lest the remedial groups contain an unduly high
proportion of the highly intelligent section of the child population (see Phillips,
1961, for a table of difference scores of equivalent probability of occurrence).

A purely psychometric approach to surveys is insufficient. Not only should
there be flexibility in the light of the views of teachers and others about the
suitability of individuals for remedial work: recently there have been interesting
findings about the ways in which psychometric criteria operate. Although Lytton
(1967) suggests that the I.Q. is a good pointer to relative progress in remedial
work, Dunham (1960) finds that reading gains are 'associated at least as closely
with improvements in attitude as I.Q.'.

Lytton (1961, 1967) suggests that in reading there is no significant difference
in effectiveness between selection by tests and selection by teachers' judgements.
In appraising this interesting finding Lytton's very carefully worded guide for
class teachers must be borne in mind. Educational psychologists using teachers'
judgements as the basis of procedures for identifying 'remedial' children should
find it valuable to prepare a similar schedule before relying on judgements which
may otherwise be less accurate.

Lytton found in relation to arithmetic that higher gains following remedial
work 'are definitely associated with selection by tests, and this may therefore be
preferred'. This is an interesting difference between remedial arithmetic and
remedial reading, but in any discussion of the relative advantages of selection by
test and selection by judgement, the background of information against which
teachers' judgements are made must not be forgotten. With the wider availa-

bility of standardized tests in schools, teachers' judgements are themselves influenced by the previous performances of their pupils on tests. Often the educational psychologists of the School Psychological Service are instrumental in making standardized tests more widely available to the schools (Association of Educational Psychologists, 1965, p. 8), and the problems involved in the measurement of educational standards are relevant to our discussion.

V MEASUREMENT OF READING AND LANGUAGE DEVELOPMENT

Although Smith, Cambria and Steffan (1964) have given an interesting analysis of the reading process from the physiological standpoint, a comprehensive and definitive psychological analysis of reading remains to be made. Factor analytic studies of reading derive factors which vary according to the type of analysis carried out. See, for example, Thurstone's (1946) re-analysis of Davis's (1944) data. In this country reading specialists usually accept that there are three reasonably separate aspects of reading, word recognition, comprehension and rate (Vernon, 1960). There are tests available for each of these aspects of reading, and some tests use the same material to provide measures of all three. *The Neale Analysis of Reading* is a British test which is designed to do this (Neale, 1966), but before looking at other examples of tests for the assessment of reading it is important to remember the need to interpret test findings in the light of the points discussed on p. 474. In addition there are other points which are relevant to reading tests in particular.

Although some reading tests give results as deviation quotients – the *Sentence Reading Test* (National Foundation for Educational Research, 1958) is an example of a group test involving comprehension which does this – the majority of reading tests express their findings as reading ages. This is convenient educationally, but can be misleading, since educational age units are not equivalent. A gain of one year of reading age from reading age 13 years to reading age 14 years is entirely different from a gain of one year of reading age from reading age six years to reading age seven years. Williams (1961) has shown, for word recognition, the relation between reading age on the Schonell R.1 test and size of reading vocabulary. Figure 16.1 demonstrates this.

It is worth connecting this point to the discussion on incidence of slow-learners on p. 473. A 15-year-old with a reading age (word recognition) of 12 years will have a reading standard of children 20% younger. He can also fall into the group of children with attainments below those of children two years younger than himself. It is possible (although we could not be sure without knowing the standard deviation of the reading ages obtained on this test with this age-group) that a reading quotient derived from this score would fall below 80. So on a percentage criterion, a difference criterion and possibly on a quotient criterion as well, our 15-year-old is a slow-learner as far as word recognition is concerned. But a word recognition age of 12 years is so little different from that of 15 years that to describe the child as a slow-learner, even in this one respect, seems very artificial. Again, we have to be wary of attaching too much significance to incidence figures for slow-learners without knowing something of the educational conditions represented.

1 Group tests of reading

Few group tests of reading are designed with the intention of being useful in the identification of slow-learners. Most are intended as instruments for general educational guidance, giving information about the whole range of reading ability. An example of a widely used group test for survey purposes is the

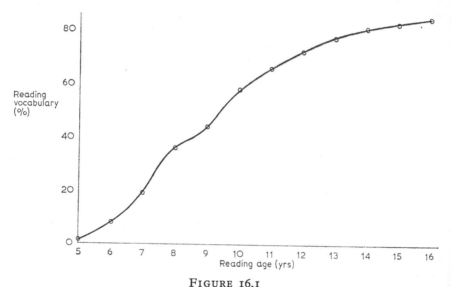

FIGURE 16.1

The relationship between Schonell R.1 Reading Age and size of reading vocabulary, expressed as % of dictionary sample.

N.F.E.R. (1958) *Sentence Reading Test*, suitable for children of primary school age. It has advantages of ease of administration and cheapness, but as the manual states, errors at the extremes are 'not inconsiderable'. The *Manchester Reading Comprehension Test, Senior* 1 (Manchester School of Education, 1959), is another group test suitable for the upper secondary school, giving separate norms for boys and girls. Both these scales convert raw scores to deviation quotients, whereas the older Schonell (1942) *Silent Reading Tests* A and B, his tests R.3 and R.4, are group tests of comprehension which express results as reading ages. Although these two latter tests provide norms for reading ages from 6 years 8 months to 13 years 9 months (the range for R.3 is 6 years 9 months to 12 years 4 months) their survey usefulness is at its best in the middle primary school range. Both tests need restandardizing.

The *Southgate Test* (Southgate, 1958) is an interesting attempt to provide a group test of word recognition. Although the skill measured is in fact different from word recognition as this is usually understood – instead of pronouncing a single word the child is required to identify from a set of five printed words the one which the tester pronounces – nevertheless the test is of considerable value. While the norms provide reading ages from 5 years 9 months to 7 years 9 months, the test gives particularly good discrimination in the early stages of reading, between reading ages of about 6 years to 7 years, and can be used for accurate identification of poor readers or for surveying slow-learning classes, particularly at primary school level. The parallel forms are useful, and the test deserves a better standardization sample.

2 Individual tests of reading

For many years individual tests of word recognition have been very popular instruments in reading assessment. Word recognition has usually been tested by the child's ability to pronounce correctly a set of separate words of gradually increasing difficulty, a test procedure which is both easy and speedy. The Burt (1921), Vernon (1938) and Schonell (1942) graded vocabulary tests all give reading ages which cover the range that the educational psychologist is likely to need, and are tests which are not too difficult to renorm locally. The *Holborn Reading Scale* (Watts, 1948) uses a set of sentences of gradually increasing difficulty to measure word recognition. In fact this method introduces other skills such as the ability to use contextual clues, but is a less artificial method of testing word recognition than a graded vocabulary test. The *Holborn Scale* does not give very good discrimination, which would suggest that it is not likely to be of value where accurate assessment is needed. It provides reading ages over the range 6 years 9 months to 13 years. Although it purports to measure comprehension, no norms are provided and the whole test could well be restandardized.

The *Standard Test of Reading Skill* (Daniels and Diack, 1958) also uses graded sentences as a means of measuring reading accuracy. The most interesting feature of this scale, however, is the deliberate attempt on the part of the authors to break away from the orthodox methods of expressing a child's reading attainment as a reading age or a deviation quotient. The authors discuss the dangers of applying the normative measuring scales of psychometrics to education, and try to devise a scale of reading growth which is independent of the average perform- ance of a standardization population. To do this they analyse reading development into stages, a technique which has similarities with the Piagetian analysis of intellectual development into stages. They characterize each stage qualitatively and provide a number of useful diagnostic tests for investigating the difficulties of children whose progress up the reading ladder is slow. A reading age table for reading accuracy is also provided if a more conventional measure is needed. This set of tests is an original contribution which deserves developing.

The *Neale Analysis of Reading Ability* (Neale, 1966) is a scale which uses a

R

set of graded paragraphs as its measuring instrument. It provides reading age norms for the ages 6 to 13 years.

The test has two particularly useful features. As stated above, it measures accuracy, comprehension and rate from a child's performance in reading one set of paragraphs. It also provides three parallel forms, which greatly increases its clinical usefulness. It is attractive, quite well standardized – the second edition giving revised norms – and provides a scheme of error analysis and diagnostic tests which are a useful introduction to the analysis of reading difficulties. It can be criticized in that it exposes a child to failure by requiring him to read a passage in which he makes 16 errors. It also has rather a high 'floor', making it inappropriate for children at the very early reading stages. Nevertheless, as an individual test of reading abilities over the junior school range, the writer can endorse Vernon's (1960) description of it as much the best test of its type.

3 Tests of reading readiness

As the importance of the early identification of slow-learning children becomes increasingly appreciated, techniques for use with children of infant school age become more relevant. Tests of reading readiness are used to evaluate whether children can profitably be introduced to formal reading material, and are at present some of the few widely available techniques which attempt to assess cognitive and perceptual development in children in the infant school. Most of the reading readiness tests which are currently available are not based on any well-established framework of theory and usually consist of subtests probing those skills and abilities, such as visual discrimination, which the test author considers relevant in the light of personal clinical experience. For this reason different tests often measure quite different aspects of development.

A useful discussion of the topic can be found in the papers by Standish (1959) and Sanderson (1963). Standish (1960) also provides a résumé of available reading readiness tests. There do not seem to be any British readiness tests, which obviously limits severely the usefulness of material in which the norms do not apply. Nevertheless, the tests are of use in clinical work with non-readers, irrespective of age, and for providing information about the comparative development of infant school children in the qualities measured by the tests.

One of the tests quite frequently used in this country is the *Harrison Stroud Scale* (Harrison and Stroud, 1956). This consists of six subtests which between them measure the eight skills which the authors consider essential to beginning reading. Although the standardization needs re-working to make it appropriate for this country, and although some technical weaknesses are highlighted in Buros (1954), the scale is an attractive device which can be used in its present form with groups of infant school children to provide information of clinical value.

4 Language development

Techniques for the assessment of language stem from the theory of language. The older tests of language measure qualities such as comprehension vocabulary spoken vocabulary, knowledge of grammar, spelling, etc. (Reading can clearly be included as an aspect of language, but is omitted here since it has already been discussed.) Examples of these older assessment instruments can be found in Burt's Mental and Scholastic Tests, published in 1921. F. J. Schonell (1942, 1950) published tests in the same tradition, and his *Diagnostic English Test* covers five separate areas of English language skills.

Both the Burt and Schonell scales are characterized by an emphasis on the measurement of language skills taught in the school situation; they also present their results in terms of attainment ages. During recent years the presentation of test findings as ages has diminished, and one line of development has been the production of tests of language skills which cover similar attainment areas to those of the Burt and Schonell scales, but which convert raw scores to deviation quotients. The National Foundation for Educational Research, for example, has produced a number of tests which cover the range of English skills from middle primary to school-leaving age in this way.

The other line of development has been the development of tests which measure aspects of language other than those formally taught in the school situation. Watts (1944) produced a range of interesting and imaginative scales for testing the growth of language skills, such as following a train of thought, understanding relationships in time and acquiring specialized vocabularies. Since Watts gives average performances for children of preschool age in some of his scales, the material is often appropriate for younger slow-learning children and might well have enjoyed a wider use than has been the case.

But the greatest step forward in the assessment of language development has been the production of tests which follow psycholinguistic theories, in particular the theory outlined by Osgood (1957). The classical assessment instrument in this category is the *Illinois Test of Psycholinguistic Abilities* (McCarthy and Kirk, 1961). The I.T.P.A. is an individual test which provides a measure of language development in each of nine different areas for children between the ages of 2 years 6 months and 9 years. The test is discussed in detail elsewhere (Chapter 12). In the context of this chapter it is relevant to stress its value in work with slow-learning children, particularly in the assessment of the linguistic assets and deficits of children, upon which a programme of remediation can be suggested. For example, Harborth (1968) feels that the I.T.P.A. can be of considerable diagnostic value in cases of children with reading problems.

The psycholinguistic approach to the assessment of slow-learning children is being considerably developed at present. Techniques similar to those pioneered by Berko (1958) have been applied to slow-learning children in this country by Preston (1968) with results which show the great syntactic handicaps in the language of slow-learning children.

Of less interest theoretically but of great value practically has been the development of picture vocabulary tests. Where conventional vocabulary scales (e.g. the Terman-Merrill or W.I.S.C. scales) require the child to give an oral definition of a word spoken by the examiner, a picture vocabulary test requires the child to identify, from a set of several pictures, the one which most nearly represents the word which the examiner has spoken. The advantages of this approach for the assessment of vocabulary in children with severe speech defects, such as some cerebral palsied children, is obvious. As long as the child can point to a picture, or indicate a choice in another way, a measure of vocabulary can be made. Many slow-learners have speech defects (Williams, 1966) and many have emotional problems which hinder their free response to the oral situation of the conventional vocabulary test. For reasons such as these picture vocabulary scales, though measuring abilities somewhat different from those measured by the conventional vocabulary tests, are very useful instruments in the assessment of slow-learning children.

One of the earlier scales is the Ammons and Ammons (1948) Full-Range Picture Vocabulary Test. This is an American test, providing two parallel forms, which covers a span from 2 years to superior adult level. It is not as well standardized as the Peabody Picture Vocabulary Test, or P.P.V.T. (Dunn, 1959) which is especially relevant for our purposes since it was constructed with the intention of using it for mentally retarded children. The P.P.V.T. is essentially a booklet of 150 pages, each of which contains four pictures, one of which is a reasonable representation of a stimulus word spoken by the examiner. Norms provide vocabulary ages and vocabulary quotients for the age range from 21 months to 18 years. Parallel forms are available and there are a number of studies which report the use of the P.P.V.T. with slow-learning children (e.g. Dunn and Brooks, 1960).

Moss and Edmonds (1960) used the P.P.V.T. with English children and reported, 'Although it can evidently be used in its present form with the American norms, it should be restandardized for English usage'. Brimer revised the P.P.V.T. material to remove the more obvious Americanisms before restandardizing on English children in Wiltshire. The final products of this work are sufficiently distinct to be renamed the English Picture Vocabulary Tests, or E.P.V.T.s (Brimer and Dunn, 1966).

The E.P.V.T.s have one major disadvantage – they do not provide norms for preschool children – so for assessing the response of under-fives to a picture vocabulary test it is necessary to rely on an American scale such as the P.P.V.T. However, as well as being standardized on English children, the E.P.V.T.s have the additional advantage that one form can be given as a group test. Test 1 covers the age range 5·0-8·11 years and is intended for individual administration. Test 2 covers the age range 7·0-11·11 years and can be used with groups or individuals. Each test contains 40 items, preceded by practice items. The test has been carefully standardized and the manual reviews a research study which demonstrates the applicability of the E.P.V.T. to slow-learning children whose ages are above the age-ceiling of the test.

An ingenious variant of the picture vocabulary test idea is the Quick Test, or Q.T., produced by Ammons and Ammons (1962). Instead of using a new set of pictures for testing the child's knowledge of each word, the Q.T. uses one set of pictures throughout the test. The set of four pictures is available on a cardboard sheet, and this and an answer form is all the equipment the examiner needs. The scale which gives mental age norms between 1·5 and 19·0 years, by steps of 0·5 or 1·0 year, is short but quite good reliability figures are quoted in Ammons and Ammons (1962). There are in all three parallel forms of the test, which has potential as a rapid screening device or as a research instrument when a short individual examination of a number of children is needed. A British restandardization would be valuable.

VI MEASUREMENT OF NUMBER AND MATHEMATICAL SKILLS

Perhaps the most striking feature of backwardness in the area of number and mathematics is the relative lack of interest that it has aroused among researchers. While the journals contain many articles on remedial reading (e.g. Chazan, 1967) there are very few to be found on remedial arithmetic. Schonell and Schonell's (1957) *Diagnosis and Remedial Teaching in Arithmetic* stands virtually alone in this field. One exception is Biggs (1967) who discusses (pp.153-154) the effectiveness of structural methods for remedial treatment in arithmetic.

At the same time, however, there has been great interest in the difficulties inherent in developing number and mathematical skills, difficulties which are faced in varying degrees by all children. As routine computation in our society is increasingly being taken over by mechanical and electronic aids, so the necessity for our schools to produce children who are proficient calculators has diminished. It has been replaced by the need to give children an appreciation and understanding of mathematical ideas. This situation may be one of the reasons why the contribution of Jean Piaget has been so timely. Isaacs (1961) provides a useful brief introduction to Piaget's work in general, while Flavell (1963) provides a more detailed discussion; for material which is more directly concerned with the growth of children's understanding of number, Churchill (1961) or Lovell (1961) should be consulted. Piaget's (1952) original material on this topic is contained in *The Child's Conception of Number*. Piaget emphasized that the key to facilitating the acquisition of number skills lay in understanding the sequence of stages of cognitive development through which all children pass. Although Piaget's original work was carried out with normal children, Woodward (1963) has discussed its relevance to subnormal children; various studies – e.g. Griffiths, 1964 – have demonstrated its applicability to slow-learning children.

Parallel with the arousal of interest among educators in Piaget's child-centred approach to number work have been developed a variety of 'structural methods' of teaching the subject. Williams (1962) gives an interesting survey of these methods, designed to increase the child's understanding of mathematical ideas. The effect of these twin forces – Piaget and structural methods – on the traditional arithmetic curriculum of the primary school, has been immense. The traditional emphasis on content has been replaced by an emphasis on understanding and functioning.

1 Testing number readiness

Number readiness has always been a neglected field. The new approach to number work has illustrated the pointlessness of asking children to manipulate abstract symbols before the Piagetian stage of conservation of number has been reached, but the new approach has not as yet been followed by appropriate assessment devices. It may be, at these early stages, that no formal assessment devices are necessary at all. In this case the teacher or psychologist would observe the child's response to a series of Piaget-type situations over a period of time which might be a few days or might be a few weeks (see Jackson (1968),pp.116-24, for some useful suggestions). This intensive individual study, relying on careful observation and skilled interpretation, is probably the best method of estimating a child's readiness for formal number. Indeed, with this careful approach the introduction of a planned sequence of number work becomes so smooth that the concept of number readiness loses much of its meaning. Nevertheless, there are occasions when a busy educational psychologist needs to have a quick estimate of a child's readiness for work with number symbols. Churchill (1961) suggests some short investigations that can yield useful information.

The first two year-groups of the Burt (1921) *Mental Arithmetic Test* provide a number of items which bear directly on the question of a child's stage of readiness for number work. The age norms provided are of course nearly half a century out of date, but the ideas behind the items are still fresh and relevant to the development of a child's early number sense. The use of these items provides helpful qualitative information on the early stages of number readiness.

2 Measurement of attainment in number

Traditionally tests of 'number' fell into three main categories: tests of mechanical arithmetic, problem arithmetic and mental arithmetic. During the 1930s and 1940s attainment in these areas was measured through using scales such as those devised by Burt (1921) and Schonell (1942). Both these authors produced tests which transformed raw scores into arithmetic ages and which were of use for children with arithmetic ages up to 14 years. The norms are today inappropriate, and indeed, in line with the comments on the changing approach to the teaching of a number, so is the content.

The Burt and Schonell scales were not very suitable for 6- and 7-year-olds. A scale which provides reasonably good discrimination at these ages is the *Staffordshire Arithmetic Test,* by Hebron (1958). This is a test which is traditional in content, fairly widely used and covers the full spread of arithmetic ages needed to identify the slow-learner. It is an easily administered group test, giving standard scores, percentiles and arithmetic quotients as well as ages, but, as with so many attainment tests, it needs an up-to-date restandardization.

The National Foundation in Educational Research (N.F.E.R.) have produced a series of *Arithmetic Progress Tests* which measure attainment in mechanical and problem arithmetic combined, to give an arithmetic quotient. For example, A.1 and A.2 are parallel tests appropriate to children in the second year of the junior school (Land, 1963). Details of the range of N.F.E.R. group tests for the assessment of arithmetic attainment are given in a catalogue '*Educational Guidance in Schools*' (National Foundation for Educational Research, various dates). Like nearly all N.F.E.R. tests these are valid, with high K.R.20 consistencies and convenient to administer in the classroom situation, but they do not discriminate finely between slow-learning children.

In the clinic situation there is a need for an assessment instrument which covers a wide age range, and which provides a speedy estimate of the attainment of an individual child. For many years the most suitable instrument has been devised by Vernon (1949). His graded Arithmetic-Mathematics test provides a quick estimate of A-M ages from 6 years to 21 years. The test is an age-scale, with five items per year-group. Although the higher age levels are of no use in the assessment of slow-learning children (the test was not designed for this purpose), the lower levels provide a quick rough guide to their formal arithmetic standards. One of the difficulties in using arithmetic tests involving problems is the presence of material requiring high reading ability. In the Vernon test the reading difficulty has been kept low, but children probably need a reading age of at least 7 years before they can do justice to the written problems that the test contains. A modern version of the test would be a most useful addition to the educational psychologist's armoury.

Recently Piagetian ideas have been incorporated into the teaching of number to slow-learning children (e.g. Tansley and Gulliford, 1960). The revolution in the approach to the teaching of number in ordinary and special school alike is rendering many of the traditional assessment devices for measuring attainment in number, including those mentioned above, obsolescent or obsolete in many areas. Unfortunately there is a time-lag between the introduction of a new teaching programme and the availability of assessment instruments to measure learning. Replacement tests have only become available in the last few years (thus, at the time of writing the assessment guides to the Nuffield mathematics scheme are still being developed).

One of these scales is the N.F.E.R. *Number Test* 1 (Barnard, 1966) designed to measure a child's *understanding* of the four number processes (addition, subtraction, multiplication and division) rather than his *attainment* in them. The test has been standardized on children in an urban and a county authority and provides norms for the age range 10·6 to 12·6 years.

Arithmetic Concept Tests A and B were designed for the study reported by Biggs (1967). They attempt, according to Biggs, to measure the child's conceptual understanding of arithmetic and are appropriate to the third year of the junior school. Test A, which is a short 15-item test, attempts to assess the child's ability to apply his knowledge of already learned concepts to problem situations without involving him in computation. For example: 'Looking under a fence I counted 56 legs belonging to sheep. Tick what I would have to do to find out how many sheep there were: ADD, MULTIPLY, SUBTRACT, DIVIDE, NONE OF THESE.'

Test B, according to Biggs, emphasizes 'the child's ability to recognize certain basic arithmetical concepts when they are presented to him in an unusual or unfamiliar way, and to see if he can relate this unconventional presentation of the structure to the familiar symbolic representation of it. Thus the child whose concept of addition is broadly coded should see that

embodies the same structure as $3+2 = 5$, whereas the child whose coding is narrowed to the specifics of a certain layout, or the symbol "+", or the instructions "add" or "collect", would probably not recognize the similarity between the test item and the symbolic example.'

VII ATTAINMENT TESTING – PROSPECTS FOR CHANGE

For many decades educational attainment has been measured by standardized tests. The scores obtained on these tests have meaning through the comparisons made with average performances on the tests. In some attainment tests the score of an individual child is related to the average performance of his own age group (e.g. deviation quotient). In other attainment tests the score of an individual child is interpreted as an average performance of an age-group other than his own (e.g. attainment age).

This approach to the testing of attainment, the normative approach, has proved very useful. Attempts have usually been made to provide standardization samples which are representative of the national population, so that the yardstick against which a child's performance is assessed is in effect the performance of the nation's children. But a moment's reflection will indicate that the usefulness of this approach depends in no small measure on the consistency with which a particular subject is taught throughout the nation's schools. To take an extreme example, it would be of little value using a Neale reading test in a class of 7-year-old immigrants where the teacher had decided to emphasize the development of oral language facility, and then to introduce reading via i.t.a. Equally, a Staffordshire arithmetic test, with a content which emphasizes the acquisition of the four rules of number and money, would be quite inappropriate for giving information about the number development of children in a school which had adopted the new mathematics.

These two examples illustrate the relationship between school curriculum and the assessment of attainment. But these two examples of curriculum change are but the fore-runners of many such changes that are likely to occur in the next few years. Curriculum development is one of the future growth areas of education. The Schools Council is itself now supporting over 20 major national curriculum development projects, most of which will be making a considerable impact on the work of the schools during the next decade.

There are many consequences for attainment testing which will follow from these developments, two of which deserve further brief discussion.

The first consequence is the decrease in usefulness of nationally normed tests. Indeed, it may be that in any subject there will arise a series of separate attainment tests, each dealing with the subject as approached by a particular curriculum project and normed on the schools which are participating in that project.

The second consequence relates to the procedures through which tests are standardized. One of the by-products of curriculum development is a detailed analysis of the objectives of a subject area. Often the best sequence in which the objectives may be tackled is suggested by an analysis of this sort. (Bloom's (1965) *Taxonomy of Educational Objectives* has been a classic text in this field.) In the light of an analysis of this nature it may be more relevant to determine how many objectives an individual child has attained rather than to determine how many standard deviations he falls below the average of his peer group in the subject as a whole. If we regard attainment as a ladder up which a child is encouraged to climb it may be more relevant to specify the rung he has reached rather than to describe the distance between him and the average climber. The analogy is of course a simple one and needs to be extended in various ways.

Both of these consequences have implications for slow-learners. One of the gaps in assessment work with slow-learners is the absence of appropriate attainment tests. Most tests are designed with the normal school population in mind and discriminate poorly between children whose attainment is weak. A carefully designed check-list of objectives, finding out which steps a child has grasped and where his understanding stops would be equally useful throughout the whole range of attainment. It would be much more valuable for the teacher since its findings would be related directly to the teaching situation. Finally, such an instrument would not necessarily reject the traditional normative approach, since it would not be difficult to convert overall score into a standardized score for those who find this information helpful.

VIII DIAGNOSTIC ASSESSMENT

So far we have been concerned with the identification of slow-learning children. This is merely the first step in a sequence of procedures aimed at helping the development of the slow-learners. These procedures will involve clinical work with the children's families, discussions with their teachers, co-operation with other interested professions and various other activities. The procedures will

R*

lead in many cases to placement in special classes and units and to regular consultations and follow-up. These activities are all important. They are not dealt with in this chapter, not because their significance is underestimated, but because their significance is so great that it is not possible to do other than acknowledge it within this chapter.

Between the initial step of identification and the final step of follow-up there does lie one activity which is of direct relevance to our theme of assessment. This is the diagnostic work which the psychologist carries out with the slow-learners who have been identified by the methods which have already been described, and this diagnostic assessment is the theme of the rest of this chapter.

1 The importance of diagnosis

Medically, diagnosis has involved the recognition of symptom groupings or syndromes and their reference to demonstrable causes. The advantages of proceeding in this way lie in the provision of experimentally tested treatment procedures and a knowledge of the prognoses associated with the treatments. This approach has been tried in the attempts of the teacher and the psychologist to understand and help the slow-learner. Both Burt (1937) and Schonell (1942) described the factors which can be held to cause poor response to the school situation, but, although this has provided a useful 'check list' of possible causes which the psychologist must explore when he is working with the slow-learner, nevertheless the approach has not as yet been as fruitful as the analogous approach in medicine. This may be because our study of slow-learning is much younger than our study of ill-health; it may be that the web of cause and effect is much more difficult to disentangle – Lovell (1967) in fact considers some of the possible causes of backwardness as 'conditions associated with' rather than 'causes of' – or both youth and difficulty may be involved. Whatever the reasons, there is no doubt that the diagnostic approach has its limitations, and these are the limitations which have led Robinson and Robinson (1965) to point out that a great deal of effort has been wasted in debating and redefining such classificatory labels as 'autistic', 'schizophrenic', 'defective', 'pseudofeebleminded', 'oligophrenic' and the like. They suggest that the classificatory approach of traditional diagnosis might be replaced by a descriptive approach, concerned to evaluate each child along agreed dimensions of behaviour. A similar view is held by Gallagher (1957, quoted in Robinson and Robinson, p. 266), who asks, 'Does the educator not gain more information from the fact that a child is perceptually disturbed than from the fact that he is brain injured?'

This approach has the great advantage of focusing attention on the individual, on his assets and his deficits, and permitting the 'prescriptive education' that is sometimes advocated, but at the same time our little knowledge of the future development of slow-learners seems as yet to be mainly related to the diagnostic categories that have so far been established. We know, for example, that the retardation associated with phenylketonuria is likely to be severe (Partington,

1962), although the effects of early diagnosis and dietary control have been disputed (Berman *et al.*, 1961, 1966; Birch and Tizard, 1967) (see also Woolf's (1967) comment on Birch and Tizard). We know that the children who respond best to the special education provided at schools for the educationally subnormal are largely the 'sociocultural' slow-learners, whereas those who show the least response are largely the 'organically damaged' slow-learners (Williams and Gruber, 1967). For these reasons the knowledge that has so far been painfully gained by the traditional approach should not be discarded and an outline of a diagnostic framework is necessary. It is essential however, to stress that, whatever the diagnostic framework used, it is always possible that a slow-learning child may fall into more than one category – he may in fact be 'multiply handicapped'. An organically damaged slow-learner may also grow up in a limited environment; he may also come from a broken family and exhibit marked maladjustment. In short, all possible categories need to be explored.

2 Diagnostic framework

One of the problems confronting the diagnostician in this field is the established category of 'educationally subnormal pupil'. When the legislation which followed the 1944 Education Act included these pupils in the categories of handicapped pupils, it placed them alongside the children suffering from physical handicap, the deaf and the partially sighted, for example. The intention was admirable – the attitude of the community to the children with psychological handicap was changed for the better – but one effect has not been fully appreciated. There is an important difference between the child with a physical handicap and the child who is educationally subnormal. The former explains a child's need of special educational help; the latter merely describes it. The former is a diagnosis, the latter is not (Williams, 1965). It has been too easy in clinical work with slow-learners to regard a label of 'educationally sub-normal' as the end of a diagnostic process, whereas it is in fact merely the beginning. There is considerable substance in Stott's (1963a) contention that the term 'educationally subnormal' is an aetiological dustbin.

Many attempts have been made to provide a scheme of classification. The work of Burt (1937) and Schonell (1942) collated the results of their own and other researches, and suggested methods of grouping or describing the different cases studied. Burt, for example, listed four main groups of conditions shown by backward children (equivalent to our slow-learners). These were:

I Inherited conditions.
II Environmental conditions:
    A. School conditions
    B. Social conditions.
III Physical conditions:
    A. Developmental
    B. Pathological.

IV Psychological conditions:
  A. Intellectual
  B. Temperamental.

These categories were broken down into 16 subgroups. Burt was also very careful to point out that 'in most cases not one cause, but several, are at work'.

It is interesting to compare a classification system such as Burt's, which is based on British research with slow-learners in school, with the American systems of classification which are based largely on experience with more seriously mentally retarded children. Most American writers distinguish between two broad causal categories, the exogenous or brain-injured group, and the endogenous or familial group. Masland, Sarason and Gladwin (1958) write, ' . . . within certain broad limits one can distinguish those mentally subnormal individuals whose disability is attributable primarily to a demonstrable defect of brain structure or chemistry from those whose malfunction is the result of learning difficulties resulting from unfavourable environmental influences'. The main point of interest in this comparison is the apparent lack of emphasis on inheritance, which Burt places first among his groups of conditions shown by backward children, suggesting that intellectual potential is genetically determined.

Heber (1959) reports the classification adopted by the American Association on Mental Deficiency. This is a medical classification describing eight categories, seven of which are different groups of diseases and conditions. The eighth category is the only one which refers to non-medical causation, and in this case the category title 'Due to uncertain (or presumed psychologic) cause with functional reaction alone manifest' is clearly far from certain of the advisability of admitting psychologically determined examples of causation. Note also the absence of emphasis on inheritance of intelligence. An interesting short discussion on different approaches to the classification problem, though again geared largely to the more severely retarded, is to be found in Benton's chapter in Stevens and Heber (1965).

The diagnostic framework which is used as a background for the rest of this chapter is adapted from Robinson and Robinson (1965).

(*a*) Genetic causation:
  1. chromosomal aberration, e.g. mongolism
  2. specific defective genes, e.g. phenylketonuria (p.k.u.)
  3. genetically determined tendencies, e.g. epilepsy.
(*b*) Physical damage:
  1. cretinism
  2. skull and brain anomalies, e.g. microcephaly
  3. cerebral palsy
  4. brain infections, e.g. encephalitis.
(*c*) Psychological damage.

Here Robinson and Robinson do not attempt to list recognizable diagnostic categories, but provide a set of psychological factors which can lead to intellectual damage.

(1) inadequate early care, e.g. through institutionalization, sensory deprivation, rejection, indifferent maternal care;
(2) subnormal parents;
(3) family size;
(4) education;
(5) socio-economic class;
(6) ethnic and racial groups;
(7) intrapsychic variables, e.g. achievement motivation or anxiety.

Group (*a*) represents a set of conditions which are unlikely to come the way of the psychologist working in the ordinary school system very frequently. Nevertheless, he will meet slow-learners who fall into one of the many different sorts of genetically determined conditions of group (*a*), and one of the obvious implications is the need for the psychologist to be aware of the medical contribution to diagnostic work with slow-learners.

Another point about the conditions of group (*a*) is the allowance that this group can make for inherited qualities in the causation of slow-learning. Although recent work in this field has tended to emphasize the importance of environmental conditions, e.g. Fraser (1959), Wiseman (1964), Douglas (1964), nevertheless, as Jensen (1967) points out, the polygenic inheritance of intelligence is still a powerful explanatory weapon.

Children of group (*b*), like those of group (*a*), are also very much of a minority among the slow-learners with whom the educational psychologist works. Like those of group (*a*) they serve to emphasize the need for close and frequent co-operation between doctor and psychologist. With increases in medical knowledge it may well be that the number of identifiable syndromes in groups (*a*) and (*b*) will increase considerably in the future.

The conditions listed in group (*c*) are much more frequently encountered by the educational psychologist. Perhaps the most needed change, in order to bring the classification in line with British work with slow-learners, is to increase the emphasis on (*c*) (4), education. Factors such as absence from school, several changes of school, inappropriate teaching, school-home disharmony, figure fairly prominently in the work of British investigators. Thus Burt (1937) named 'school conditions' [as the major condition existing in nearly 9% of the cases of backwardness that he described. More recently the 'summer birthday effect' (e.g. Williams, 1964; Pidgeon, 1965) which appears at present to be largely, though possibly not entirely, determined by the organization of the educational system, has been shown to be another factor in this group.

Sensory deprivation, one of the illustrations of (*c*) (1) – inadequate early care – refers to the critical importance of early sensory stimulation in preventing later mental retardation. But there is another sort of sensory deprivation, loss of stimulus through hearing damage or visual defect, which is frequently found among slow-learners, and to which psychologists need to be alert. Although figures of the incidence of hearing loss among retarded children vary, Kodman (1963) has suggested that where the same criterion of impaired hearing is used for populations of normal and retarded children, the incidence of hearing loss in the latter is usually four times that in the former. Points such as this warn the psychologist to be on guard lest undetected hearing losses occur among slow-learners referred to him.

The writer would also like to see a more detailed treatment of the emotional conditions associated with slow-learning. (*c*) (1) quotes rejection as an important condition, but most British work emphasizes the close and intimate relationship between school progress and the emotional stability of the home. Fraser's (1959) comment 'a normal home background, emotional stability, freedom from tension and from economic insecurity, and consistent encouragement from the parents, are necessary for a child if his school work is to reach the level allowed by his intelligence'. is a précis of her research findings.

The extra emphasis suggested on educational conditions, sensory loss and emotional problems once again underlines the multidisciplinary nature of diagnostic work with slow-learners. Teachers, doctors, social workers, as well as psychologists, all have contributions to make; ignoring these contributions by working in isolation impoverishes the quality and effectiveness of any one individual's effort.

IX DIAGNOSTIC METHODS

Diagnostic work with slow-learners resolves itself into two main areas:

(*a*) collaboration with colleagues in trying to decide if the child should be treated as belonging to one or more of the three major symptom groupings;

(*b*) at the same time providing an evaluation of the slow-learner's psychological assets and deficits so that the educator can design appropriate teaching and treatment methods.

The psychological assessment that these tasks demand requires the observance of the same principles that have been discussed in other chapters of this text, but there are some special problems relating to slow-learners, and in the rest of this chapter an attempt will be made to keep these in mind in presenting some of the methods which can be used in diagnostic work with slow-learners.

1 Intellectual development

It is interesting to observe that more than 60 years after the appearance of the prototype test of intelligence, the Binet-Simon scale, its direct descendant, the 1960 Terman-Merrill Form L-M is still in wide use. The survival properties of the Binet family of intelligence tests are particularly strong where the assessment of slow-learners is concerned – the purpose for which the first test was constructed in 1905.

The Binet scales have been well described and evaluated by Anastasi (1961) and Cronbach (1961). Factor analyses show, however, that the factorial structure of Binet I.Q.s differs at different age levels. The test is fairly heavily weighted with verbal abilities (e.g. Jones, 1949), and the verbal loading is greater at older age levels than younger ones (McNemar, 1942). Now the majority of slow-learners are children from homes which are culturally limited – the 'cultural-familial' group of our classification. Williams (1966) describes 55% of his population of children attending special schools for the educationally sub-normal as coming from homes of social class IV or V. We know that perhaps the greatest effect of growing up in a deprived home is damaged language development (Deutsch, 1963). It might therefore be argued that using an intelligence test like the Binet scale will give a misleading impression of intellectual development in slow-learners, particularly at older age levels where the verbal content of the test is high (see the discussion on test content in Brown, 1967). By these older age levels, too, the 'cumulative deficit' in language, which Deutsch has argued, will have become marked. Rushton and Stockwin (1963) show that changes in Binet scores obtained by boys attending a school for educationally subnormal pupils are in accord with expectations based on a knowledge of the boys' homes and the structure of the Binet test.

Anastasi (1961) summarizes some of the vast body of literature on the reliability of the Binet scales by commenting that the Binet tends to be 'more reliable for the older than for the younger ages, and for the lower than for the higher I.Q.s'. While Rushton and Stockwin's work does not cut across this general conclusion, it does warn of the danger of an uncritical acceptance of the Binet I.Q., and of the need to interpret it in relation to the nature of the environment in which a slow-learner has been nourished. Stott (1960) also reports work which casts doubt on the reported stability of low Binet I.Q.s as far as children attending schools for the educationally subnormal are concerned. In his examination of 1,358 test-retest comparisons he found that 28% gave discrepancies of 10 I.Q. points or more, an appreciably higher proportion than would be expected from the stability characteristics quoted for the test at the ability levels concerned. He argues that part of the variation in scores that he reported is due to faulty standardization of the Binet, but that the variation is due in large part to real changes in the rate of mental development of subnormal children of school age.

While it is right to draw attention to reported drawbacks of the Binet scale, it is also important to underline its usefulness for the assessment of slow-learners. It is a scale which is attractive to the subject, can measure low intelligence levels, can be used over a wide age-range and which correlates well with educational success. The verbal loading which is in one sense a disadvantage (*v. supra*) is in another sense an advantage, especially when the psychologist is concerned with the prediction of educational performance.

The problem of the verbal content of the Binet scales has been dealt with in the Wechsler group of intelligence scales by providing two subscales, one of which measures the subject's verbal ability, while the other measures his ability on performance tests. Scores on the two subtests can be combined if a measure of global intelligence is required. So the Wechsler scales each yield three measures, expressed as deviation quotients, a verbal quotient, a performance quotient and a full-scale quotient. The Wechsler-Bellevue Intelligence Scale (Wechsler, 1939), and the Wechsler Adult Intelligence Scale or W.A.I.S. (Wechsler, 1955) are rarely relevant to slow learners; the two Wechsler scales which are frequently used are the Wechsler Intelligence Scale for Children, or W.I.S.C. (Wechsler, 1949), and the Wechsler Pre-School and Primary Scale of Intelligence, or W.P.P.S.I. (Wechsler, 1967). Apart from the encouraging preliminary findings of Yule *et al.* (1969) and Brittain (1969) too little is yet known about the use of the W.P.P.S.I. to justify informed discussion. Yule's warning that in his sample of $5\frac{1}{2}$-year-old children (a) the mean Full Scale I.Q. was 105 and (b) Verbal-Performance discrepancies were larger than expected should be noted, however.

One of the practical drawbacks to the theory underlying the construction of the W.I.S.C. is the factorial validity of the scales. Jones (1962) and Maxwell (1959) show that the two subscales are not as clearly differentiated as their titles would suggest. Thus two of the six subtests on the performance scale, picture completion and picture arrangement, are quite heavily verbally loaded. Although it is doubtless possible to construct scales which differentiate verbal and performance skills more clearly than does the W.I.S.C., nevertheless the difference between the W.I.S.C. verbal and performance quotients can provide useful diagnostic information. Cronbach (1961) suggests that a difference of 15 points between the verbal and performance quotients on the Wechsler scales is enough to justify drawing conclusions based on the existence of a real difference between verbal ability and performance ability. Robinson and Robinson (1965), referring specifically to the W.I.S.C., suggest that differences between the verbal and performance I.Q.s are not unusual until they reach a magnitude of 25 points or more, and thus should be interpreted cautiously.

While observations such as these are of general value in that they call attention to the dangers of readily attaching significance to small differences between subscales, nevertheless it is also too easy to apply rule-of-thumb procedures in situations to which they are not appropriate. The meaning which can be attached to difference scores depends in no small measure on the scores themselves, a situation which is very important for work with slow-learning children. For example, it is not at all unusual for children with W.I.S.C. performance quotients of 100 to have verbal quotients of 90, but it is very unusual for children with W.I.S.C. performance quotients of 60 to have verbal quotients of 50. Although the difference between the subscales is the same in both cases the interpretation for the slow-learner is different from that for the child of average ability. For a discussion of the theoretical issues behind this point the reader is referred to Payne and Jones (1957), while Phillips (1961) provides tables which give the probability of occurrence of difference scores for tests of varying characteristics.

The interpretation of differences between the subtests of the W.I.S.C. verbal and performance scales is an even more hazardous operation. The data which Wechsler provides in the test manual enable the probability of occurrence of difference scores to be determined, but the reliability of the subtests is so low, mainly less than 0·80, that the lower reliabilities of difference scores make their interpretation usually unjustifiable. Profile analysis on the W.I.S.C. has not received the same attention as it has on the W.A.I.S. (Wechsler, 1955), but for these reasons of unreliability of differences, among others, it is unlikely that it would yield any less unsatisfactory results.

Littel (1960) gives a reasonable appraisal of the W.I.S.C. Although he criticizes in his review the rationale and absence of predictive validity data, he also comments that 'the W.I.S.C. appears to be a relatively well standardized test with many virtues. It correlates consistently well with other measures of intelligence, appears to be widely accepted and used, and in general seems to merit further research and development.' Some of this development has been discussed by Glasser and Zimmerman (1967), who provide a useful review of short forms of the W.I.S.C. as well as a detailed commentary on subtest analysis: they should be consulted when questions of subtest differences are important.

One of the major disadvantages of the W.I.S.C., i.e. its age floor of 5 years, has been dealt with by the introduction of the W.P.P.S.I., which makes the Wechsler approach to the measurement of intelligence available to a lower age-limit of 4 years. However, the other chief drawback of the W.I.S.C. scales, their inability to measure very low (or very high) intelligence levels (the full scale estimates I.Q.s between the limits of 45 and 155) remains a potential weakness for work with some slow-learners.

The measurement of the intellectual development of the very young child who is suspected of being a slow-learner is a fascinating but specialized field, too complicated to be adequately covered in this chapter. While it seems possible to make reasonably accurate predictions of very limited intellectual development as early as the first year of life (Illingworth, 1966), the test-retest stability figures of assessments made at this period are in general very low (Bayley, 1949). Usually the investigator uses techniques containing – inevitably – a weighting of sensori-motor items which would not be expected to relate highly with later intellectual functions. The *Gesell Developmental Schedules* (Gesell and Amatruda, 1947) are among the oldest and most widely used schedules, whereas the Merrill-Palmer Scale (Stutsman, 1931) is one of the most widely used scales of intelligence for young children over the age of two years. The *Griffiths Mental Development Scale* (Griffiths, 1954) covers the age range from birth to 2 years. Psychologists working with young children should read Illingworth (1966) and Sheridan (1960a) as useful introductory material to the problems of identification of young handicapped children, which are dealt with in greater detail in Chapter 15.

The use of a standardized test of intelligence with slow-learners can, in the hands of a skilled clinician, provide a wealth of information about a child's special aptitudes and personality characteristics, quite apart from the information about intellectual development that the test affords. Developments in assessment procedures have now enabled the psychologist to obtain more objective measurements of attributes which might previously have been largely assessed through the 'standardized interview' situation of the intelligence test. The rest of this section on diagnostic assessment will discuss the evaluation of the slow-learner's non-verbal skills, his perceptual development, his emotional condition, his social maturity and his sensory processes. It is not suggested that these are the only areas in which assessment should be made: language development is not included simply because it has already merited a brief discussion. Nor is the order of presentation intended to reflect importance, but it is suggested that these areas illustrate some of the more important fields in which assessments of slow-learners can usefully be made.

2 Non-verbal skills

The W.I.S.C. performance scale is a most useful battery of short performance subtests, but there is often a need to obtain a more detailed picture of a slow-learner's non-verbal skills than is provided by the W.I.S.C. performance scale alone. The psychologist has a wide variety of techniques from which to choose. One of the simplest to administer, the Goodenough *Draw-a-man Test* has been revised by Harris to produce the *Harris-Goodenough Test of Psychological Maturity* (Harris, 1963). The child is asked to make a drawing of a man and of a woman. The drawings are scored on a points system, the child's score being converted into a deviation quotient with a mean of 100 and a standard deviation of 15 points. There is also a quick scoring method, using a set of drawings typical of different levels of development, but once again the gain in time is paid for by a loss of reliability. Norms are provided for the age-range 3 to 15.

The reliability of such a short test could not be expected to be high. Harris himself quoted stability coefficients of the order of 0·90 over a time interval of a few weeks. On the other hand Kellmer Pringle and Pickup (1963), working with an admittedly small sample of children, found stability coefficients for the original Goodenough of less than 0·50 for time intervals of one to three years. Strümpfer and Mienie (1968), again with a small sample, found a stability coefficient across a four-month time interval of 0·80 for the combined man and woman drawings of the *Harris-Goodenough*.

Validity findings also vary. Correlations between the *Goodenough Scale* and the 1937 Binet have ranged up to 0·70, including a study by Birch (1949) with mentally retarded children, in which a correlation of 0·62 was found, but Kellmer Pringle and Pickup found correlations between 0·12 and 0·37. With the W.I.S.C. quotients, Kellmer Pringle and Pickup found correlations between 0·01 and 0·40. Strümpfer and Mienie found correlations of the order of 0·50 between the *Harris-Goodenough* and South African group and individual tests of verbal and non-verbal intelligence. The interpretation of these and other findings reported in Harris and in Vane (1967), who suggests that the Harris version may not be as adequate as the original Goodenough, depends upon fuller details of population characteristics, time intervals, etc., than it is possible to give in this brief comment; but, in spite of its great popularity as a non-verbal clinical test in the United States (Sundberg, 1961), it would seem reasonable to regard the *Draw-a-man Test*, even in the Harris-Goodenough version, as a most useful shock-absorber, providing interesting supplementary information, but in no circumstances a substitute for more valid measures of intellectual development. Yule *et al.* (1967), referring to children aged 9-11 years, regarded their validity findings as '. . . far too low to warrant the acceptance of the Goodenough-Harris Drawing test as a test of general intelligence with children aged 9 to 11 years'. There is little evidence that this conclusion should be varied for slow-learners generally.

The *Progressive Matrices* family of tests contains two scales, the *Standard Progressive Matrices* and the *Coloured Progressive Matrices*, which are often used as non-verbal tests with slow-learners. A bibliography of references to the literature on the tests is given at the back of each of the manuals (Raven, 1962, 1964).

The tests were developed as measures of Spearman's *g*, and there is evidence that the *Progressive Matrices* is heavily loaded with this factor. Perhaps the most relevant application of the matrices scales to slow-learners has been the suggestion that performances on these scales are less affected by deprived cultural and educational backgrounds than is the case with other scales of intelligence (MacArthur and Elley, 1963). This clearly has considerable application for the psychologist concerned to evaluate the intellectual development of the cultural-familial slow-learners. Findings on this point have not, however, been entirely clear cut, and Vernon (1965) does not feel that the *Progressive Matrices* is as suitable as the W.I.S.C. verbal scale for measuring the educational potential of West Indian immigrants. A review of earlier findings on the Progressive Matrices is given by Burke (1958).

The *Progressive Matrices* ceiling is much too high for slow-learners, and when the test is given in the untimed version it can be a discouraging experience for this reason. The *Coloured Matrices*, covering an age-range of 5 to 11 years, is a more suitable test, and Freyberg (1966) discusses its use as a group test, concluding that it has useful potential, although it is still not entirely clear what the test is measuring.

The *Columbia Mental Maturity Scale* (Burgemeister *et al.*, 1959) is a useful non-verbal instrument for slow-learners who have gross motor handicaps. It consists of 100 cards, on each of which the child has to select the inappropriate drawing from a set, and is best used to give mental ages between the ranges of 3 and 11 years. It can be used with children whose responses may be limited to pointing or gesturing, and is particularly useful for the assessment of cerebral palsied children (British Psychological Society, undated), but is of general interest for slow-learners. It does not, of course, measure the same qualities as the W.I.S.C. or Binet, and the correlation with the Binet varies appreciably with age.

Among the large number of other tests of non-verbal skills the *Porteus Maze Test* (Porteus, 1952) is an old but often-used scale. This consists of a set of paper-and-pencil mazes, giving mental age norms from 3 years to adult level. Porteus has claimed that the scale is particularly valuable in predicting success in meeting the practical and social demands of life. The scale can also be used to provide a 'Qualitative' or Q-score, which is said to differentiate delinquents from non-delinquents. Gibbens (1958) has discussed this claim in relation to Borstal lads, and has also shown that a high Q-score is related to intellectual dullness and to other intellectual and social characteristics.

3 Perceptual development

The classic test in this field is the *Bender-Gestalt* (Bender, 1938) which requires the child to reproduce designs on each of nine cards, presented separately. Billingslea (1963) has surveyed research findings on the test. The use of this scale with children, including the provision of norms, has been discussed by Koppitz (1960, 1964). Poor performance on this scale is characteristic of a variety of conditions, but it seems clear that mentally retarded children perform poorly (Goldberg, 1957; Koppitz, 1958). The use of the test to identify those slow-learners who are brain-damaged is of doubtful value, and Feldman's study although relating to individuals of very limited ability, supports this point of view (Feldman, 1953).

The *Benton Visual Retention Test* (Benton, 1955) requires the subject to reproduce from memory a set of ten designs, presented individually. The method of presentation can vary, and there are equivalent series of drawings for use with the alternative presentations. The raw scores obtained are interpreted in relation to intelligence level, and not only is this information of intrinsic interest, but Benton also suggests the likelihood of a given raw score indicating organic damage at the subject's intelligence level. The idea is an interesting one, but with slow-learning children the average performance is so near the floor of the test that differential diagnosis of this sort becomes extremely difficult. Birch (1964) and Horne and Justiss (1967) should be read on this general problem of identifying the brain-damaged group of slow-learners. Horne and Justiss suggest that their findings point to the conclusion that we cannot at present outline any sharply defined set of characteristics which are common to all brain-injured mentally retarded individuals, a conclusion which they suggest is shared by other writers. Birch *et al.* (1967), in an interesting article, compared the relationship between neurological evidence of brain damage in E.S.N. children attending a special school, and pattern of W.I.S.C. scores. No systematic association was found.

The *Frostig Developmental Test of Visual Perception* (Frostig, 1964) is designed to measure perceptual development in children aged 3 to 8 years. Like the other tests of perception mentioned above, the standardization is American. There are five subtests; eye-motor co-ordination, figure-ground discrimination, form constancy, position in space and spatial relations. The test measures development in 'perceptual ages'. Associated with the theory of the scale is a set of perceptual exercises (Frostig and Horne, 1964), which can be used to provide special training in those areas of visual perception which the test shows to be poorly developed.

4 Emotional development

Slow-learners may be intellectually limited, but it does not follow that their emotional life is similarly limited (e.g. Tansley and Gulliford, 1960). There are nevertheless restrictions which intellectual limitation can place on the measurement of emotional development. Slow-learners usually respond in a less rich and detailed way to the stimuli of projective tests than do other children, and this makes the use of projective tests less rewarding. Their lower standards of reading and writing make the use of personality schedules requiring these abilities difficult. These two considerations are examples of points to be borne in mind in attempting to evaluate the emotional development of slow-learners.

In this short section no attempt will be made to discuss the theory of emotional development and methods of assessment. Five approaches to the assessment of emotional development (interpreted widely) will be briefly mentioned in relation to slow-learners.

(a) *Assessment by Teachers*
Workers with slow-learning children have found the Bristol Social Adjustment Guides (Stott, 1963b) a useful technique (e.g. Chazan, 1964; Chapter 18 of this volume). Teachers can complete the 'Child in School' Guide by underlining the statements which best describe a child's behaviour in given situations. These views are then transformed into measures of the nature and extent of any maladjustment present.

Vernon (1964) comments on the strengths and weaknesses of the Guides. It is also worth noting Tizard's (1968) views that 'teacher questionnaires alone cannot be regarded as valid indices of maladjustment'. For work with slow-learning children the Guides can be regarded as useful examples of techniques for structuring teacher's views on children's behaviour into quantifiable form. Rutter (1967) has recently published a 26 item *Children's Behaviour Questionaire* which appears to be reliable in the screening of children with behavioural and emotional disorders.

(b) *Assessment by Parents*
There are a number of questionnaires available for assessing the emotional development of children. The Bristol Guides (*v. supra*) contain an example and Rutter and Graham (1966) devised one for their research. There seems little work specifically directed towards the use of this approach with slow-learners, although in the clinical situation the use of parent-supplied information is of course of vital importance.

(c) *Assessment by Peers*

The various sociometric techniques outlined in Evans (1962) can be used to establish the social structure of the classroom, and hence to identify the isolates and the neglectees. This approach has had some use with slow-learners and Johnson's (1950) study has been of importance in determining attitudes to the issue of 'segregating' slow-learners in special classes. Laing and Chazan (1966) discuss findings based on the use of this approach with slow-learners in this country.

With younger slow-learners who find writing difficult the normal sociometric technique is unsuitable. A modified method which is sometimes used with small groups requires each child to be labelled with a large, clearly visible number. The children respond to the question by writing down the number appropriate to their choice.

(d) Self-assessment

Self-assessment schedules designed for the use of children are fairly widely available. There are examples of schedules with a psychometric, factorial rationale (e.g. Eysenck, 1965), and schedules which reflect a more clinical approach (e.g. Mooney and Gordon, 1950). If valid instruments of this nature could be developed for use with children of poor reading standards, their use with slow-learners would be much more widespread. This development has already occurred with group tests of intelligence (e.g. Young, 1966; Cornwell, 1952), but there are fewer problems to be overcome in the cognitive field.

(e) *Global Assessment*

Each of the approaches discussed so far is but one way of attempting to obtain a picture of emotional development. Each way has something different to contribute. Observation of a child's behaviour in different situations, at home, at school and at play for example, helps to round out the picture. Longitudinal studies, involving repeated observations over periods of time, give the picture depth and perspective. Notes made in the course of activities such as individual intelligence testing add detail. In short, the many assessment techniques with which the psychologist is acquainted should all be brought into play to provide the comprehensive evaluation of the slow-learner's emotional development which is sometimes required.

5 Social competence

Social competence has long been a crucial concept in work with slow-learners. Stott (1963a) has argued that an assessment of 'real life ability' is of more relevance to the slow-learner than is an assessment of intelligence. Kellmer Pringle (1960) has presented a general review of work on social competence.

For many years the standard instrument in the field has been the *Vineland Scale of Social Maturity* (Doll, 1947). Although this scale was produced for work with slow-learners, its standardization renders the norms inapplicable to present-day English children for a variety of reasons. In addition, the small number of items per year-group renders effective discrimination difficult.

Lunzer (1966) has developed Doll's ideas and has produced the *Manchester Scales of Social Adaptation*. The scales are individually administered, and most items require a child to answer the tester's questions orally. There are ten sub-scales arranged in two groups, 'social perspective' and 'self-direction'. Percentile norms are provided for children between the ages of 6 and 15 for each subscale, group of subscales, and for the full test. The present scales are provisional, but promise to be a very useful instrument for work with slow-learners.

There are a number of unstandardized schedules used in research studies on slow-learning children, which incorporate items of interest to psychologists working in this field (Matthew, 1963; Haigh, 1966). Leland *et al.* (1967) have presented a report of their efforts to develop a scale of adaptive behaviour in relation to mental retardation. In this scale adaptive behaviour is defined in terms of the individual's ability to (1) function independently, (2) assume personal responsibility and (3) show social and civic responsibility. Although for many years the *Vineland Scale* has stood virtually alone, there are signs that the psychologist working in this field will be able soon to select from a variety of instruments the one which best suits his purpose.

6 Sensory deficits

The identification of sensory deficits is not the psychologist's task, although psychologists who have specialized in this field can make valuable contributions to assessment teams, but all psychologists working with children must be alert to the possibility of damaged vision or hearing as aetiological factors in the problems with which they deal. This possibility becomes stronger with slow-learners and the increased incidence of damaged vision and hearing in this group has already been mentioned. Ideally, all children should be medically examined at referral to the psychologist, but this is not always practicable, for a variety of reasons. Consequently short screening tests, which can suggest the need for more specialized medical examinations, should be used almost as a matter of routine in the psychologist's work with slow-learners.

The *Stycar Vision Test* (Sheridan, 1960b) aims to test short-sightedness in children who do not know the names of the letters and hence cannot be tested with the normal Snellen chart. It is intended to fill a need in work with young children and retardates. The principle of the test is to require children to match letters rather than name them as in the Snellen test, and it can be used down to a floor mental age of about 3 years. Testing is individual and, once rapport has been established, only takes a few minutes.

Hearing loss has attracted more attention than visual problems, and there are a number of short screening techniques. Sheridan (1958) has produced the *Stycar Hearing Test* for children with mental ages between 6 months and 7 years.

This is an attempt to solve the very difficult problem of identifying hearing loss in very young children, and Sheridan has perhaps not been quite as successful with hearing as she has with vision. Nevertheless, in spite of the lack of validation data the test has a definite place in work with the very young.

With children above the mental age of about 3 years the *Picture Screening Test* of hearing (Reed, 1960) is very useful. The purpose of the test is to screen for 'social' or 'educational' hearing loss. Like all the tests in this section it is individual and, given satisfactory rapport, it takes a few minutes to administer. The test consists of a series of cards. A card bears four pictures representing monosyllabic words with similar vowel sounds but different consonants. The child has to indicate the appropriate picture in response to the word spoken by the examiner.

Other approaches to screening for hearing loss are provided by the 'word-list' method in which pairs of phonetically balanced words are presented to the child, who has to indicate whether the words in each pair are similar or different. Details of this approach and of appropriate word lists can be found in Dale (1962). However, it must be emphasized that it is not the educational psychologist's task to decide the presence or absence of hearing loss in a child referred because of a learning problem. His task is to be on the alert for any sign of hearing loss and 'when in doubt, refer'.

It is convenient, though not entirely logical, to attach to this section a note on the measurement of motor impairment in slow-learners. The *Lincoln-Oseretsky Motor Development Scale* (Sloan, 1955) is a revision of an earlier version, and gives a measure of the motor development of children between the ages of 6 and 14. More recently, Stott, Moyes and Headridge (1966) have produced a new scale, called *Test of Motor Impairment*, which measures to an age floor of 5 years. The manual contains a section on the assessment of educationally subnormal children, and the scale is therefore of special interest. The growth of medical and educational interest in the 'clumsy child' (e.g. Walton *et al.*, 1962) and the high incidence of motor defect in children attending special schools for the educationally subnormal (Williams and Gruber, 1967) suggests that this is an area of assessment in which the psychologist working with slow-learners should be competent.

X CONCLUSIONS

This chapter has attempted to provide a brief sketch of the problems and procedures associated with the assessment of slow-learning children.

Complex though these procedures may be, they are only part of the professional activity of the psychologist working in this field. He must carry out his assessment with due regard to the legal aspect of work with slow-learners – for example the way in which legislation has laid on local authorities obligations towards slow-learners, while at the same time safeguarded parental rights.

He must also be able to communicate his findings to colleagues and to parents. This is an essential part of the psychologist's expertise, involving close and co-operative teamwork with teachers, medical officers, psychiatrists and many others.

Finally, the psychologist must be aware of the purpose of assessment procedures, in short, the action which needs to be taken when assessment is complete. This is outside the scope of this chapter, but just as important. Assessment without action is as ineffective as action without assessment.

ACKNOWLEDGEMENTS

The author is grateful to Mr C. J. Thomas, Head of the Department of Economic and Social Statistics of the University of Southampton, for kindly reading part of the section on surveys for identifying slow-learning children and making helpful suggestions. He is also grateful to Miss P. Jones and Mrs S. Williams, who undertook the typing.

REFERENCES

AMMONS, R. B. and AMMONS, C. H. (1948) *Full-range Picture Vocabulary Test*. Missoula, Montana Psychological Test Specialists.

AMMONS, R. B. and AMMONS, C. H. (1962) *The Quick Test (Q.T.) Provisional Manual*. Missoula, Montana: Psychological Test Specialists.

ANASTASI, A. (1961) *Psychological Testing* (2nd Ed.). New York: Macmillan.

ASSOCIATION OF EDUCATIONAL PSYCHOLOGISTS (1965) *Evidence Prepared for the Department of Education and Science, Working Party on Educational Psychologists*. London: Association of Educational Psychologists.

BARNARD, E. L. (1966) *Number Test 1*. London: National Foundation for Educational Research.

BAYLEY, N. (1949) Consistency and variability in the growth of intelligence from birth to eighteen. *J. Genet. Psychol.*, **75**, 165-196.

BENDER, L. (1938) *A Visual Motor Gestalt Test and its Clinical Uses*. New York: American Orthopsychiatric Association, Research Monog. No. 3.

BENTON, A. L. (1955) *Benton Visual Retention Test* (Revised Ed.). New York: Psychological Corporation.

BERKO, J. (1958) The child's learning of English morphology. *Word*, **14**, 150-177.

BERMAN, P. W., GRAHAM, F. K., EICHMAN, P. L. and WAISMAN, H. A. (1961) Psychologic and neurologic status of diet-treated phenylketonuric children and their siblings. *Pediatrics*, **28**, 924.

BERMAN, P. W., WAISMAN, H. A. and GRAHAM, F. K. (1966) Intelligence in treated phenylketonuric children: a developmental study. *Child Develop.*, **37**, 731.

BIGGS, J. B. (1967) *Mathematics and the Conditions of Learning*. London: National Foundation for Educational Research.

BILLINGSLEA, F. Y. (1963) The Bender-Gestalt: a preview and perspective. *Psychol. Bull.*, **60**, 233-251.

BIRCH, J. W. (1949) The Goodenough Drawing Test and older mentally retarded children. *Amer. J. Ment. Defic.*, **54**, 218-224.

BIRCH, H. G. (1964) (Ed.) *Brain Damage in Children*. New York: Williams and Wilkins.

BIRCH, H. G., BELMONT, L., BELMONT, I. and TAFT, L. T. (1967) Brain damage and intelligence in educable mentally subnormal children. *J. Nerv. Ment. Dis.*, **144**, 246-257.

BIRCH, H. G. and TIZARD, J. (1967) The dietary treatment of phenylketonuria: not proven? *Develop. Med. Child Neurol.*, **9**, 13-21.

BLOOM, B. S. (1965) (Ed.) *Taxonomy of Educational Objectives*, Vol. I. London: Longmans.

BRIMER, M. A. B. (1963) Ability and attainment. III: Note on Levy (1962). *Brit. J. Statist. Psychol.*, **16**, 112-115.

BRIMER, M. A. and DUNN, LL. M. (1966) *English Picture Vocabulary Test* (2nd Ed.). London: National Foundation for Educational Research.

BRITISH PSYCHOLOGICAL SOCIETY (undated – 1966?) *Notes on the Assessment of Children with Physical Handicaps*. Unpubl. Manual.

BRITISH PSYCHOLOGICAL SOCIETY (1966) *Children in Hospitals for the Subnormal*. London: British Psychological Society.

BRITTAIN, M. (1969) The WPPSI: A Midlands Study. *Brit. J. Educ. Psychol.*, **39**, 14-17.

BROWN, R. I. (1967) (Ed.) *The Assessment and Education of Slow-learning Children*. London: U.L.P. for University of Bristol Institute of Education.

BURGEMEISTER, B., BLUM, L. H. and LORGE, I. (1959) *Columbia Mental Maturity Scale, Revised Edition*. New York: Harcourt Brace and World.

BURKE, H. R. (1958) Raven's Progressive Matrices: a review and critical evaluation. *J. genet. Psychol.*, **93**, 199-228.

BUROS, O. K. (1954) *The Fifth Mental Measurements Year Book*. Gryphon Press.

BURT, C. (1921) *Mental and Scholastic Tests*. London: King.

BURT, C. (1937) *The Backward Child*. London: University of London Press. (3rd Ed., 1950).

BURT, C. (1957) *The Causes and Treatment of Backwardness* (4th Ed.). London: University of London Press.

BURT, C. (1963) Ability and attainment. II: Note on Peaker (1963). *Brit. J. Statist. Psychol.*, **16**, 106-112.

BUTCHER, H. J. (1966) *Sampling in Educational Research*. Statistical Guides in Educational Research No. 3. Manchester: Manchester University Press.

CENTRAL ADVISORY COUNCIL FOR EDUCATION (1967) *Children and Their Primary Schools* (the Plowden Report). London: H.M.S.O.

CENTRAL ADVISORY COUNCIL FOR EDUCATION (1963) *Half our Future* (the Newsom Report). London: H.M.S.O.

CHAZAN, M. (1964) The incidence and nature of maladjustment among children in schools for the educationally subnormal. *Brit. J. educ. Psychol.*, **34,** 292-304.

CHAZAN, M. (1967) The effects of remedial teaching in reading: a review of research. *Remedial Education*, **2,** 4-12.

CHURCHILL, E. M. (1961) *Counting and Measuring*. London: Routledge.

CORNWELL, J. (1952) *An Orally Presented Group Test of Intelligence for Juniors*. London: Methuen.

CRONBACH, L. J. (1961) *Essentials of Psychological Testing* (2nd Ed.). New York: Harper and Row.

CURR, W. and HALLWORTH, H. J. (1965) An empirical study of the concept of retardation. *Educational Review*, **18,** 5-15.

DALE, D. M. C. (1962) *Applied Audiology*. Springfield, Ill.: C. C. Thomas.

DANIELS, J. C. and DIACK, H. (1958) *The Standard Reading Tests*. London: Chatto and Windus.

DAVIS, F. B. (1944) Fundamental factors of comprehension in reading. *Psychometrika*, **9,** 185-197.

DEPARTMENT OF EDUCATION AND SCIENCE (1964) *Slow Learners at School*. London: H.M.S.O.

DEPARTMENT OF EDUCATION AND SCIENCE (1966). *Progress in Reading*, 1948-1964. London: H.M.S.O.

DEPARTMENT OF EDUCATION AND SCIENCE (1967) *Statistics of Education*, 1966, Vol. I. London: H.M.S.O.

DEUTSCH, M. (1963) The disadvantaged child and the learning process. *In* PASSOW, A. H. (Ed.) *Education in Depressed Areas*. New York: Teachers College, Columbia University.

DOLL, E. A. (1947) *Vineland Social Maturity Scale*. Minneapolis: Educational Test Bureau.

DOUGLAS, J. W. B. (1964) *The Home and the School*. London: MacGibbon and Kee.

DUNHAM, J. (1960) The effects of remedial education on young children's reading ability and attitude to reading. *Brit. J. educ. Psychol.*, **30,** 173-175.

DUNN, LL, M. (1959) *Peabody Picture Vocabulary Test*. Minneapolis: American Guidance Services.

DUNN, LL. M. and BROOKS, S. T. (1960) Peabody picture vocabulary test performance of educable mentally retarded children. *Train. Sch. Bull.*, **57,** 35-40.

EVANS, K. M. (1962) *Sociometry and Education*. London: Routledge.

EYSENCK, S. B. G. (1965) A new scale for personality measurement in children. *Brit. J. Educ. Psychol.*, **35,** 362-367.

FELDMAN, I. S. (1953) Psychological differences among moron and borderline mental defectives as a function of aetiology. *Amer. J. Ment. Defic.*, **57,** 484-494.

FIELDHOUSE, A. E. (1957) *How to Conduct a Reading Survey*. Studies in Education No. 15. Wellington: New Zealand Council for Educational Research.

FLAVELL, J. H. (1963) *The Developmental Psychology of Jean Piaget.* Princeton New Jersey: Van Nostrand.

FRASER, E. (1959) *Home Environment and the School.* London: U.L.P. for Scottish Council for Research in Education.

FREYBERG, P. S. (1966) The efficacy of the coloured progressive matrices as a group test with young children. *Brit. J. Educ. Psychol.,* **36,** 171-177.

FROSTIG, M. (1964) *The Marianne Frostig Developmental Test of Visual Perception* (3rd Ed.). Palo Alto, California: Consulting Psychologists Press.

FROSTIG, M. and HORNE, D. (1964) *The Frostig Program for the Development of Visual Perception: Teachers' Guide.* Chicago: Follett.

GALLAGHER, J. J. (1957) A comparison of brain-injured and non-brain-injured mentally retarded children on several psychological variables. *Monogr. Soc. Res. Child Developm.,* **22,** No. 2. Quoted in Robinson and Robinson (1965).

GARRETT, H. E. (1926) *Statistics in Psychology and Education.* New York: Longmans (4th Ed. 1953).

GESELL, A. and AMATRUDA, C. S. (1947) *Developmental Diagnosis* (2nd Ed.). New York: Hoeber.

GIBBENS, J. C. N. (1958) The Porteus Maze Test and delinquency. *Brit. J. educ. Psychol.,* **28,** 209-216.

GLASSER, A. J. and ZIMMERMAN, I. L. (1967) *Clinical Interpretation of the Wechsler Intelligence Scale for Children* (W.I.S.C.). New York: Grune and Stratton.

GOLDBERG, F. H. (1957) The performance of schizophrenic, retarded and normal children on the Bender-Gestalt Test. *Amer. J. Ment. Defic.,* **61,** 548-555.

GRIFFITHS, R. (1954) *The Abilities of Babies.* London: University of London Press.

GRIFFITHS, E. J. (1964) *A Study of Natural Number Concepts of Educationally Subnormal Children.* Unpublished dissertation for the Diploma in the Education of Backward Children, University College of Swansea.

HAIGH, C. R. (1966) *A Comparison of the Social Competence of Special School and Secondary Modern School Pupils.* Unpublished dissertation for the Diploma in Educational Psychology, University College of Swansea.

HARBORTH, M. (1968) Psycholinguistics and Reading Failure. Contribution to *3rd International Reading Symposium,* Eds. DOWNING, J. and BROWN, A. C. London: Cassell.

HARRIS, D. B. (1963) *Children's Drawings as Measures of Intellectual Maturity.* New York: Harcourt Brace.

HARRISON, M. L. and STROUD, J. B. (1956) *The Harrison-Stroud Reading Readiness Profiles.* Boston: Houghton Mifflin.

HEBER, R. F. (1959) A manual on terminology and classification in mental retardation. *Amer. J. ment. Defic.,* **64,** Monogr. Suppl.

HEBRON, M. (1958) *Staffordshire Arithmetic Test.* London: Harrap.

HORNE, B. M. and JUSTISS, W. A. (1967) Clinical indicators of brain damage in mentally retarded children. *J. clin. Psychol.,* **23,** 464-465.

ILLINGWORTH, R. S. (1966) *The Development of the Infant and Young Child, Normal and Abnormal*, (3rd Ed.). London: Livingstone.

ISAACS, N. (1961) *The Growth of Understanding in the Young Child*. London: Ward Lock.

JACKSON, S. (1968) *A Teacher's Guide to Tests*. London: Longmans.

JENSEN, A. R. (1967) The culturally disadvantaged: psychological and educational aspects. *Educ. Res.*, **10**, 4-20.

JOHNSON, G. O. (1950) A study of the social position of mentally handicapped children in the regular grades. *Amer. J. ment. Defic.*, **55**, 60-89.

JONES, L. V. (1949) A factor analysis of the Stanford Binet at four age-levels. *Psychometrika*, **14**, 299-331.

JONES, S. (1962) The Wechsler Intelligence Scale for Children applied to a sample of London primary school children. *Brit. J. educ. Psychol.*, **33**, 119-132.

KISH, L. (1965) *Survey Sampling*. New York: Wiley.

KODMAN, F. (1963) *In* ELLIS, N. R. (Ed.) *Handbook of Mental Deficiency*. New York: McGraw-Hill.

KOPPITZ, E. M. (1958) The Bender-Gestalt Test and learning disturbance in young children. *J. clin. Psychol.*, **14**, 292-295.

KOPPITZ, E. M. (1960) The Bender-Gestalt Test for Children: a normative study. *J. clin. Psychol.*, **16**, 432-435.

KOPPITZ, E. M. (1964) *The Bender-Gestalt Test for Young Children*. New York: Grune and Stratton.

LAING, A. F. and CHAZAN, M. (1966) Sociometric groupings among education-ally subnormal children. *Amer. J. ment. Defic.*, **71**, 73-77.

LAND, V. (1963) *Arithmetic Progress Tests A_1 and A_2*. London: National Foundation for Educational Research.

LAWLEY, D. N. (1950) A method of standardizing group tests. *Brit. J. statist. Psychol.*, **3**, 86-89.

LELAND, H., HIHINA, K., FOSTER, R. and SHELLHAAS, M. (1967) The demonstration and measurement of adaptive behaviour. *Excerpta Medica* 153. Amsterdam: Excerpta Medica Foundation.

LEVY, P. M. (1962) Ability and attainment: a new psychometric formulation of the concept of educational retardation. *Brit. J. statist. Psychol.*, **15**, 137-147.

LEVY, P. M. (1963) Ability and attainment. IV: Note on Brimer (1963). *Brit. J. Statist. Psychol.*, **16**, 116-117.

LITTEL, W. M. (1960) The Wechsler Intelligence Scale for Children: review of a decade of research. *Psychol. Bull.*, **57**, 132-156.

LOVELL, K. (1961) *The Growth of Basic Mathematical and Scientific Concepts in Children*. London: University of London Press.

LOVELL, K. (1967) *Educational Psychology and Children* (9th Ed.). London University of London Press.

LUNZER, E. A. (1966) *The Manchester Scales of Social Adaptation*. London: National Foundation for Educational Research.

LYTTON, H. (1961) An experiment in selection for remedial education. *Brit. J. educ. Psychol.*, **31**, 79-94.

LYTTON, H. (1967) Follow-up of an experiment in selection for remedial education. *Brit. J. educ. Psychol.*, **37**, 1-9.

MACARTHUR, R. S. and ELLEY, W. B. (1963) The reduction of socio-economic bias in intelligence testing. *Brit. J. Educ. Psychol.*, **33**, 107-108.

MCCARTHY, J. J. and KIRK, S. A. (1961) *The Illinois Test of Psycho-linguistic Abilities*, (Experimental Ed.). Urbana, Ill.: University of Illinois Press.

MCNEMAR, Q. (1942) *The Revision of the Stanford Binet Scale: an Analysis of the Standardisation Data*. Boston: Houghton Mifflin.

MANCHESTER SCHOOL OF EDUCATION (1959) *Manchester Reading Comprehension Test*. London: University of London Press.

MASLAND, R. L., SARASON, S. B. and GLADWIN, T. (1958) *Mental Subnormality*. New York: Basic Books.

MATTHEW, G. C. (1963) *The Post-School Social Adaptation of Educationally Subnormal Boys*. M.Ed. Thesis University of Manchester.

MAXWELL, A. E. (1959) A factor analysis of the Wechsler Intelligence Scale for Children. *Brit. J. educ. Psychol.*, **29**, 237-241.

MINISTRY OF EDUCATION (1945) *Training and Supply of Teachers of Handicapped Pupils*. London: H.M.S.O.

MINISTRY OF EDUCATION (1946) *Special Educational Treatment*. London: H.M.S.O.

MINISTRY OF EDUCATION (1950) *Reading Ability*. London: H.M.S.O.

MINISTRY OF EDUCATION (1957) *Standards of Reading*, 1948-1956. London: H.M.S.O.

MOONEY, R. L. and GORDON, L. V. (1950) *The Mooney Problem Check Lists*. New York: Psychological Corporation.

MORRIS, J. M. (1966) *Standards and Progress in Reading*. London: National Foundation for Educational Research.

MOSS, J. W. and EDMONDS, P. (1960) The Peabody Picture Vocabulary Test with English Children. *Brit. J. educ. Psychol.* **30**, 82-83.

NATIONAL FOUNDATION FOR EDUCATIONAL RESEARCH (1958) *Sentence Reading Test*. London: National Foundation for Educational Research.

NATIONAL FOUNDATION FOR EDUCATIONAL RESEARCH (various dates). *Educational Guidance in Schools*. London: Newnes Educational Publishing Co. Ltd.

NEALE, M. D. (1966) *The Neale Analysis of Reading Ability* (2nd Ed.). London: Macmillan.

OSGOOD, C. E. *et al.* (1957) *The Measurement of Meaning*. Urbana, Ill.: Univ. of Illinois Press.

PARTINGTON, M. W. (1962) Variations in intelligence in P.K.U. *Canad. Med. Ass. J.*, **86**, 736-743.

PAYNE, R. W. and JONES, H. G. (1957) Statistics for the investigation of individual cases. *J. clin. Psychol.*, **13**, 115-121.

PEAKER, G. F. (1963) Abilities and attainment. I: Letter to Editor. *Brit. J. Statist. Psychol.*, **16**, 105-106.

PEAKER, G. F. (1967) Standards of reading of Eleven-Year-Olds, 1948-64. *In* CENTRAL ⌐ADVISORY ⌐COUNCIL FOR EDUCATION, *Children and Their Primary Schools.* London: H.M.S.O.

PHILLIPS, C. J. (1961) *On Comparing Scores from Tests of Attainment with Scores from Tests of Ability in order to obtain Indices of Retardation by Differences or Ratios.* Unpublished thesis, University of Birmingham Institute of Education.

PIAGET, J. (1952) *The Child's Conception of Number.* London: Routledge.

PIDGEON, D. G. (1965) Date of birth and scholastic performance. *Educ. Res.*, **8**, 3-7.

PILLINER, A. E. G., SUTHERLAND, J. and TAYLOR, E. G. (1960) Zero error in Moray House Reasoning Tests. *Brit. J. educ. Psychol.*, **30**, 53-59.

PORTEUS, S. D. (1952) *The Porteus Maze Test Manual.* London: Harrap.

PRESTON, B. M. A. (1968) *The Use of Ten Parts of Speech by Normal and E.S.N. Special School Children.* Unpublished Dissertation for the Diploma in the Education of Backward Children, University of Leeds.

PRINGLE, M. L. KELLMER (1960) Social learning and its measurement. *Educ. Res.*, **2**, 194-206.

PRINGLE, M. L. KELLMER, BUTLER, N. R. and DAVIE, R. (1966) 11,000 *Seven-Year-Olds.* London: Longmans.

PRINGLE, M. L. KELLMER and PICKUP, K. T. (1963) The validity and reliability of the Goodenough Draw-a-Man Test. *Brit. J. educ. Psychol.*, **33**, 297-306.

PRITCHARD, D. G. (1963) *Education and the Handicapped, 1760-1960.* London: Routledge.

RAVEN, J. C. (1962) *Coloured Progressive Matrices (Revised Order 1956).* London: H. K. Lewis.

RAVEN, J. C. (1964) *Standard Progressive Matrices (Revised Order 1956).* London: H. K. Lewis.

REED, M. (1960) *Picture Screening Test of Hearing.* London: Royal National Institute for the Deaf.

ROBINSON, H. B. and ROBINSON, N. M. (1965) *The Mentally Retarded Child* (2nd Ed.). New York: McGraw-Hill.

RUSHTON, C. S. and STOCKWIN, A. E. (1963) Changes in Terman Merrill I.Q.s of educationally subnormal boys. *Brit. J. educ. Psychol.*, **33**, 132-142.

RUTTER, M. and GRAHAM, P. (1966) Psychiatric disorders in 10 and 11-year-old children. *Proc. Roy. Soc. Med.*, **59**, 382-387.

RUTTER, M. (1967) A children's behaviour questionnaire for completion by teachers: preliminary findings. *J. child Psychol. Psychiat.*, **8**, 1-11.

SANDERSON, A. E. (1963) The idea of reading readiness: a re-examination. *Educ. Res.*, **6**, 3-9.

SCHONELL, F. J. (1942) *Backwardness in the Basic Subjects.* Edinburgh: Oliver and Boyd.

SCHONELL, F. J. (1949) The development of educational research in Great Britain. Pt. V: Handicapped children. *Brit. J. educ. Psychol.*, **19**, 82-99.

SCHONELL, F. J. (1950) *Diagnostic and Attainment Testing.* Edinburgh: Oliver and Boyd.

SCHONELL, F. J. and SCHONELL, F. E. (1957) *Diagnosis and Remedial Teaching in Arithmetic.* Edinburgh: Oliver and Boyd.

SHERIDAN, M. D. (1958) *The Stycar Hearing Test.* London: National Foundation for Educational Research.

SHERIDAN, M. D. (1960a) *The Developmental Progress of Infants and Young Children.* London: H.M.S.O.

SHERIDAN, M. D. (1960b) *The Stycar Vision Test.* London: National Foundation for Educational Research.

SLOAN, W. (1955) The Lincoln Oeseretsky Motor Development Scale. *Genet. Psychol. Monogr.*, **51**, 183-252.

SMITH, K. W., CAMBRIA, R. and STEFFAN, J. (1964) Sensory feedback analysis of reading. *J. appl. Psychol.*, **48**, 275-286.

SOUTHGATE, V. (1958) *Southgate Group Reading Tests.* London: University of London Press.

STANDISH, E. J. (1959) Readiness to read. *Educ. Res.*, **2**, 29-38.

STANDISH, E. J. (1960) Group tests of reading readiness. *Educ. Res.*, **2**, 155-160.

STEVENS, H. A. and HEBER, R. F. (1965) *Mental Retardation.* Chicago: University of Chicago Press.

STOTT, D. H. (1960) Observations on retest discrepancy in mentally subnormal children. *Brit. J. educ. Psychol.*, **30**, 211-219.

STOTT, D. H. (1963a) The assessment of mentally handicapped children. *Medical Officer*, **110**, 235-239.

STOTT, D. H. (1963b) *The Social Adjustment of Children* (2nd Ed.). London: University of London Press.

STOTT, D. H., MOYES, F. A. and HEADRIDGE, S. E. (1966) *Test of Motor Impairment.* Glasgow: Department of Psychology, the University of Glasgow.

STRÜMPFER, D. J. W. and MIENIE, J. P. (1968). A validation of the Harris-Goodenough Test. *Brit. J. educ. Psychol.*, **38**, 96-100.

STUTSMAN, R. (1931) *Mental Measurement of Preschool Children.* Tarrytown on Hudson: World Book Co.

SUNDBERG, N. D. (1961) The practice of psychological testing in clinical services in the United States. *Bull. Brit. Psych. Soc.*, **44**, 1-9.

TANSLEY, A. E. and GULLIFORD, R. (1960) *The Education of Slow-learning Children* (3rd Ed.). London: Routledge.

THURSTONE, L. L. (1946) Note on a reanalysis of Davis's Reading Tests. *Psychometrika*, **11**, 185-188.

TIZARD, J. (1968) Questionnaire measures of maladjustment: a postcript to the symposium. *Brit. J. educ. Psychol.*, **38**, 9-13.

VANE, J. R. (1967) An evaluation of the Harris revision of the Goodenough Draw-a-Man Test. *J. clin. Psychol.*, **23**, 375-377.

VERNON, M. D. (1957) *Backwardness in Reading*. Cambridge: Cambridge University Press.

VERNON, P. E. (1938) *A standardisation of a Graded Word Reading Test*. London: University of London Press.

VERNON, P. E. (1949) *Graded Arithmetic Mathematics Test*. London: University of London Press.

VERNON, P. E. (1956) *The Measurement of Abilities*. London: University of London Press.

VERNON, P. E. (1964) *Personality Assessment: a critical Survey*. London: Methuen.

VERNON, P. E. (1965) Environmental handicaps and mental development, Part II. *Brit. J. educ. Psychol.*, **35**, 117-126.

VERNON, P. E. (1960) *Intelligence and Attainment Tests*. London: University of London Press.

VERNON, P. E., O'GORMAN, M. B. and MCLELLAN, A. (1955) A comparative study of educational attainments in England and Scotland. *Brit. J. educ. Psychol.*, **25**, 195-203.

WALTON, J. N., ELLIS, E. and COURT, S. D. M. (1962) Clumsy children: developmental apraxia and agnosia. *Brain*, **85**, 603-612.

WATTS, A. F. (1944) *The Language and Mental Development of Children*. London: Harrap.

WATTS, A. F. (1948) *The Holborn Reading Scale*. London: Harrap.

WECHSLER, D. (1939) *The Measurement of Adult Intelligence*. Baltimore: Williams and Wilkins (4th Ed., 1958).

WECHSLER, D. (1949) *Wechsler Intelligence Scale for Children*. New York: Psychological Corporation.

WECHSLER, D. (1955) *Wechsler Adult Intelligence Scale*. New York: Psychological Corporation.

WECHSLER, D. (1967) *Wechsler Preschool and Primary Scale of Intelligence*. New York: Psychological Corporation.

WILLIAMS, J. D. (1962) Teaching arithmetic by concrete analogy. II: Structural systems. *Educ. Res.*, **4**, 163-192.

WILLIAMS, P. (1961) The growth of reading vocabulary and some of its implications. *Brit. J. Educ. Psychol.*, **31**, 104-105.

WILLIAMS, P. (1964) Date of birth, backwardness and educational organisation. *Brit. J. educ. Psychol.*, **34**, 247-255.

WILLIAMS, P. (1965) The ascertainment of educationally subnormal children. *Educ. Res.*, **7**, 136-146.

WILLIAMS, P. (1966) Some characteristics of children entering special schools for the educationally subnormal in South Wales. *Brit. J. Psychiat.*, **112**, 79-90.

WILLIAMS, P. and GRUBER, E. (1967) *Response to Special Schooling*. London: Longmans.

WISEMAN, S. (1964) *Education and Environment*. Manchester: Manchester University Press.

WOODWARD, W. M. (1963) The application of Piaget's Theory to research in

s

mental deficiency. Chapter in ELLIS, N. R. (Ed.) *Handbook of Mental Deficiency.* New York: McGraw-Hill.

WOOLF, L. I. (1967) Letter to Editor. *Develop. Med. Child Neurol.,* 7, 244-250.

YAMANE, T. W. (1967) *Elementary Sampling Theory.* Englewood Cliffs, New Jersey: Prentice Hall.

YOUNG, D. (1966) *Intelligence Test for Non-Readers* (2nd Ed.). London: University of London Press.

YULE, W., LOCKYER, L. and NOONE, A. (1967) The reliability and validity of the Goodenough-Harris Drawing Test. *Brit. J. educ. Psychol.,* 37, 110-112.

YULE, W., BERGER, M., BUTLER, S., NEWHAM, V. and TIZARD, J. (1969) The WPPSI: an empirical evaluation with a British sample. *Brit. J. Educ. Psychol.,* 39, 1-13.

17

Severely subnormal children

Rosemary Shakespeare

I INTRODUCTION

Severe subnormality is defined by the Mental Health Act (1959) as 'A state of arrested or incomplete development of mind which includes subnormality of intelligence and is of such a nature or degree that the patient is incapable of living an independent life or of guarding himself against serious exploitation, or will be so incapable when of an age to do so'.

Most psychologists accept an I.Q. of 55 as the maximum level of intelligence of the severely subnormal child (British Psychological Society, 1963), the minimum, of course, being theoretically nil. In terms of mental age this will mean that his level of mental development, as measured by a standard cognitive test, will be half or below half his actual age, though he may be more mature in other aspects of development.

II THE PURPOSES OF ASSESSMENT

There are usually four aims involved in any assessment of a severely subnormal child:

1. *General Diagnosis*
   To discover if he is mentally retarded: this is usually not a difficult question, though in some cases general impressions can be misleading.
2. *Degree of Handicap*
   If so, to what degree is he handicapped by low intelligence?
   Usually the important question to ask is whether he is able to benefit from training.
3. *Plan for Training*
   How can he best be trained? This involves considering his strengths and weaknesses so the gaps can be filled, and deciding what the next stage in his development can be expected to be.
4. *Prediction*
   What is the eventual outcome of training likely to be? What can we predict for his adult life?

III THE LIMITATIONS OF STANDARD COGNITIVE TESTS

Psychologists have tended to concentrate mainly on the application of standard tests in assessing the cognitive levels of the severely subnormal (Sarason, 1949;

Gunzburg, 1958; Benton, 1964). However, many severely subnormal children are too handicapped to score on even the earliest items of these tests. In a survey of 403 children admitted to hospitals for the subnormal, it was found that 155 had been given a standard intelligence test, 120 were assessed by other means, such as development scales and 87 could not be tested (10% were not referred to the psychologist) (British Psychological Society, 1966).

It is usually possible to use a formal intelligence test with children whose mental age is above 18 months, unless the child is too emotionally disturbed to co-operate. Tests which were originally standardized on pre-school children are usually used, e.g. the Stanford-Binet Intelligence Scale (Terman and Merrill, 1960) the Minnesota Pre-School Scale (Goodenough, Maurer and Van Wagenen, 1940) the Merrill Palmer Test (Stutsman, 1931) the Peabody Picture Vocabulary Test (Dunn, 1959).

When using these tests it is important to remember that they were mainly standardized on normal children below 5 years of age and that reliability coefficients tend to be lowest for this age-range. This may be because the very young child has not yet learnt that he is expected to work as quickly and as well as he can when being tested; this attitude probably only develops when the child goes to school. A similar argument may well apply to the severely subnormal child whose mental age is below 5 years, for there tends to be less emphasis on competition and high achievement either in the home or the school life of the mentally handicapped than in the general community.

IV ASSESSMENT BELOW THE M.A. 18 MONTHS LEVEL

A child whose mental age is below 18 months will need a different approach in testing from the more intelligent child. Whereas some speech can be used in administering preschool tests, testing has to be based mainly on sensory and motor abilities below this level. At the preschool level, the examiner can ask the child to perform specific activities in the way that the examiner wants, but below the 18-month level, testing will be in a less directed situation, relying more on observation of the child's spontaneous behaviour.

Whereas preschool testing tends to consist of a number of items which are probably not of great interest in themselves, but correlate well with general mental ability (e.g. naming objects, copying drawings), testing at the baby level is much more likely to consist of items which are in themselves important stages of development, e.g. ability to grasp, using a spoon, sitting without support.

Similarly, much of the assessment of the severely subnormal child tends to be based on what the child does in his normal daily life, particularly his locomotor behaviour, feeding attainments, dressing abilities, toilet training and speech development. Progress in all these areas is important in itself as the more advanced a child is in these areas, the more independent he will become.

For this reason reliability tends to be a more important consideration than validity in such assessments. It is important to ask if two different investigators will reach the same conclusion about an item or if two people who know the child well are likely to give the same information. Once the method of assessment is found to produce consistent results, the question of whether the test is measuring what it aims to measure is less of a problem as it can usually be seen to do so directly; the main problem of validity is usually in discovering if items are placed at the correct age level. Normal children vary a great deal in the age at which they reach the various stages, but an average age is usually used.

1 Sources of information

There are two sources of information that the psychologist can use in assessing the mental level of the severely subnormal child; observation of the child's behaviour either in the test situation or in a free situation and, secondly, information from the parents, foster parents, nursing staff or whoever has charge of the child. It is advisable to make use of both these whenever possible, as in many cases this will provide a built-in reliability check; if the child is seen in a clinic or out-patient department, he may be upset by strange surroundings, or unpleasant associations from former visits, and may not show typical behaviour; moreover, it is often not possible to convey to a severely subnormal child that you want him to do his best. On the other hand, parents are not always completely objective and it is useful to check parents' or nurses' impressions by watching the child. It is advisable to put questions to informants in such a way as to try to elicit facts about what he usually does, rather than what he can do, e.g. '*Does* he feed himself with a knife and fork?' is preferable to '*Can* he feed himself with a knife and fork?' as informants are sometimes convinced that a child 'could if he wanted to' but this cannot be used in an assessment.

Birch *et al.* (1962) made use of parents' observations of their (normal) children to study individual patterns in development. They restricted their information to factual accounts rather than asking the parents to evaluate, and found that the nearer in time to the interview, the more valid the observation. At the closest time to the interview, data agreed at between 0·05 and 0·01 level of confidence.

If the information required is retrospective, it may be a little less reliable, though more factual information seems to be recalled best; Donoghue and Shakespeare (1967) found that the mother's recollection of birth-weights correlated 0·96 with the child's actual birth-weight but their estimates of the age when a child first talked only correlated 0·21 with evidence gathered at the time. One reason was felt to be that the milestone is much harder to define.

Studies on the recall of normal children's early milestones (e.g. Pyles *et al.*, 1935; McGraw and Molloy, 1941; Haggard *et al.*, 1960; Mednick and Schaffer, 1963; Robbins, 1963) are difficult to summarize as the studies used different methods. However, the overall impression of them is that the majority of mothers recall a large number of their children's milestones and their memories are likely to be roughly correct, but only large differences – usually more than two or three months – between two age estimates or average ages can be considered as due to anything other than inaccuracies of memory.

This work, of course, was concerned with normal children. Whether the parents of severely subnormal children remember better because development was slower or they were anxious at delays or alternatively have distorted memories for similar reasons is unknown. It is probably safer to disregard any differences smaller than about three months between a recalled age and average development scale estimates.

An important point is made by the Paediatric Society Working Party, S.E. Met. Region (1962) on the subject of testing. They comment that parents are apt to be suspicious of intelligence tests, especially as they often form part of a very critical examination to decide if the child is educable, and 'justice must be seen to be done'. They feel that whenever possible the child should be seen in his own home after the examiner has become known to the family. Tests in unfamiliar surroundings after perhaps a long journey and time spent waiting may be thought by the examiner to give satisfactory results but the parents may disagree.

If testing in the child's home is not possible it must still be remembered that, as with cognitive testing at higher levels, the examiner should aim at eliciting the child's best response and should make sure that the child is comfortable, warm enough, not hungry or sleepy and not too frightened, e.g. by a white coat, too much noise, too many people, etc., to give his best performance.

2 Criteria of assessments

Most psychological tests in use today involve assessing the patient's characteristics with reference to a criterion group. Two criterion groups have been used with the severely subnormal; by far the most common approach is to assess the child with reference to the abilities of normal babies and children, but an alternative approach is to assess the child comparing him with other severely subnormal children. The latter approach, however, usually makes use of knowledge of normal children's development in order to rank items in order of difficulty.

Using the 'normal' as a criterion has the advantage that it is a familiar standard to most people, even without special training. It also provides a criterion for progress and gives an order in which a series of items of behaviour can be expected to appear; it is usually found that the subnormal child goes through the same stages of development as does the normal child, but much more slowly (Woodward 1959).

The disadvantage of using the normal as a standard is that the subnormal child can never hope to attain the later levels to which these scales are leading, and in the case of a scale which yields a global mental age score, the child's own pattern of abilities, which is likely to vary from the more even pattern of the normal child, will be lost.

The developmental approach to assessing handicapped children is fully described by Stephen and Robertson (1965). They describe the approach as the application of the facts of child development to the guidance of handicapped children. They consider how the environment of the subnormal child may differ from that of the normal child in that he is more likely to have periods in hospital, and how he may himself cause his surroundings to be limiting because of his handicaps. He will then be likely to have particular difficulties in verbal communication, co-operation and in emotional development, in addition to his intellectual limitations. They also discuss how, if perception cannot develop normally, the child's experiences need to be arranged to attempt to compensate for the loss. The developmental approach, once the facts about normal children are known, should indicate not only what to teach the child, but when is the important stage to do this; otherwise concepts which are built up from information from various modalities, e.g. body image, may become distorted by motor and sensory limitations.

Then they show how developmental stages, besides being used for diagnosis of general mental handicap and special handicaps, can also be used to plan treatment and assess results.

V SCALES DEVELOPED WITH NORMAL YOUNG CHILDREN

Various scales have been developed whose main intention is to assess the development of babies; the most common ones will be described here.

1 Gesell's Developmental Schedules

Gesell and his associates began a longitudinal study in 1927 of 107 infants who had no known defects and came from families of middle socio-economic status, and were close to the average in education and occupational level.

These children were observed at frequent intervals and the study supplemented by observations of clinical cases. The data from these combined observations formed the basis of the Gesell Developmental Schedules (Gesell and Amatruda, 1947).

Gesell views the child as a 'growing action system' and sees growth as a patterning process. Behaviour patterns are 'the authentic end-products of a total developmental process which works with orderly sequence'. He emphasizes that the development of behaviour and mind is closely related to the underlying physical structures and that developmental diagnosis is possible because behaviour patterns are objective items which conform to general laws of development.

He assesses four areas of behaviour: motor behaviour, which covers both gross bodily control and finer motor co-ordinations; adaptive behaviour, which entails observing the child's reactions to objects and situations around him; language behaviour, which, besides articulate speech and pre-verbal vocalizations also includes facial expression and gesture; and personal-social behaviour, which comprises the child's personal reactions to the social culture in which he lives, as in toilet training, feeding, learning co-operation. Information is gathered both from observation of the child's reaction to various standard test objects and from interview with the parent or parent substitute.

The schedules are not scored as a composite measure, but an approximate developmental level, in months, can be found for each of the four areas by comparing each record with descriptions given of various 'key ages' – 4, 16, 28 and 48 weeks; and 12, 18, 24 and 36 months. Neither Gesell nor most authors of developmental schedules give estimates of the range of variation about the mean age of achieving each behaviour pattern. Gesell says that they have noted variations but that 'these variations cling closely to a central average'. He says that most children are at a similar level in each of the four areas, but in 'atypical, deviated or defective development they often show discrepancies'. No reliability or validity studies are reported and the schedules are not so much a test as a means of organizing the usual qualitative information obtained clinically by paediatricians. This is in contrast to most development scales, and makes it difficult to use for research purposes, although standard mental ages have been applied (Richards and Nelson, 1939).

It should be mentioned, however, that as Illingworth (1966) points out, there is a difference between using Gesell's tests and using Gesell's methods; the latter includes a very full social and developmental history and consideration of the 'whole' child, besides developmental testing.

2 Cattell Infant Intelligence Scale (Cattell, 1947)

This scale was developed as a downward extension of the 1937 Stanford-Binet (Form L) and includes items from the Stanford-Binet, and the Gesell Schedules as well as some original ones, so that continuity between this scale and the Stanford-Binet can be attained. The items are grouped into age levels from 2 to 30 months at intervals of one month during the first year, at two-month intervals during the second year and at three-month intervals from 24 to 30 months; a mental age and ratio I.Q. are computed, as in the 1937 Binet.

The scale was standardized using a longitudinal study of 274 children, a majority of whom were tested at each of eight ages.

At the youngest ages the items are largely perceptual – watching moving objects, etc. – with increasing use of motor items with increasing age. Verbal items are brought in at the higher ages.

Split-half reliabilities were between 0·71 and 0·90 except for the three-month level where the correlation was only 0·56. The validity of the test was assessed by correlating I.Q.s on the Cattell Scale with I.Q.s on the Stanford-Binet at 36 months. Correlations between I.Q. at 3 years and tests given at 3, 6 and 9 months were 0·10, 0·34 and 0·18 respectively. After 9 months they were, however, much higher and correlations between I.Q.s at 36 months and those at 12, 18, 24 and 30 months were 0·56, 0·67, 0·71 and 0·83 respectively.

Although prediction from I.Q. during the first few months was poor, Cattell found that extreme deviants tended to retain their relative positions, and that this was particularly marked in the case of children who scored well above the mean.

3 The Bayley Infant Scales of Mental and Motor Development

These scales were developed from the California Infant Scale of Motor Development (Bayley, 1935) and the revised scale is now being used extensively for research purposes in America and in many other countries (e.g. Bayley, 1965).

The applicability of the norms to an English sample has been investigated (Francis-Williams and Yule, 1967). No significant differences in abilities were found to be due to sex or social class, but absence of a sibling in the early months produced an increase in the Mental Scale score. Some differences were found between the scores of the English and American samples and the authors recommended that the scale is used only for 'cautious research work'.

4 The Griffiths Mental Development Scale (Griffiths, 1954)

The scale has five sub-scales: Locomotor, Personal/Social, Hearing and Speech, Hand and Eye Development, and Performance. The original scale was designed for the assessment of children from ages 0 to 2 years and had one item at each month of age between these points on each scale. An extension of the test from age 2 upwards is now being produced. It is necessary to attend a course of instruction before using this test.

The Griffiths test is the only one in general use which was developed and standardized on English babies.

The test is designed to yield quotients from each subscale and a general quotient from the whole test.

Hindley (1960) has investigated the stability of means and standard deviations from age to age and the effects of tester, sex and social class. He found that group mean scores on the test were fairly stable between 3, 6 and 12 months though they tended to be above 100. The test appeared to become more difficult at 18 months as the mean score decreased, almost down to 100. However, he points out that this tendency may have been due to the sample being unrepresentative of the general population. Standard deviations were stable with large numbers.

5 Other scales available

A developmental schedule by Sheridan (1960) is also available and is aimed not at producing a quotient but at providing a list of items which need a minimum of special material and which it is hoped will help medical practitioners assess progress in normal children, and detect and assist handicapped and maladjusted children as early as possible. Items are divided into four areas: Posture and Large

s*

Movements, Vision and Fine Movement, Hearing and Speech, Social Behaviour and Play; the chart covers age-levels from 1 month to 5 years.

Scales for assessing the development of babies have also been designed by Stutsman (1931), Shirley (1933), Buhler (1935), Buhler and Hetzer (1935) and Brunet and Lezine (1951).

VI   THE RELIABILITY OF DEVELOPMENT SCALES

Studies have usually been done with normal babies and little is known about the reliability of these scales with subnormal children.

With a normal group, tests seem least reliable at the earliest stages. Herring (1937) found test-retest reliabilities of 0·67 at 1 month, 0·40 at 2 months and 0·83 at 3 months, and split-half reliabilities of 0·75 to 0·92, but used only small numbers of children. Conger (1930), using the Linfert-Hierhalzer Scale, found test-retest correlation of 0·24 at 1 month, 0·44 at 2 months and 0·69 at 3 months.

Bayley (1933), using the scale mentioned earlier, found split-half reliabilities of 0·51 to 0·74 up to 3 months, and from 6 months upwards, correlations of 0·75 to 0·95.

Richards and Nelson (1939) used the Gesell scales but with a standard mental age scoring and found split-half correlations of 0·79 to 0·89 from 6 to 18 months.

Hindley (1960), summarizing this work, shows that most of the findings indicate that in no case does the proportion of the variance of the second test which is predictable from the first test exceed 50%. Using the Griffiths test, he found that predictions from one age to another produced correlation coefficients of 0·46 to 0·58, though Griffiths has previously reported a retest reliability of 0·87 for 60 cases over various intervals.

It has been suggested that the reason for these fairly low reliabilities at this level, as compared with the higher reliabilities usually achieved with cognitive tests at the higher ages, is that different abilities are measured at different levels. Hofstaetter (1954), using data from Bayley's (1949) longitudinal study analysed common factors in the items of infant, preschool and school-age intelligence tests and found that up to about 20 months – the phase before speech develops – items seemed to involve a factor which he called 'sensori-motor alertness' whereas from 20 to 40 months, after speech has begun, items involved a factor of 'persistence' or 'a tendency to act in accordance with an established set rather than upon interfering stimulation'.

After 40 months a third factor which he felt measured 'abstract behaviour', 'planning' or 'general intelligence' became most important.

Smart (1965) analysed some of Bayley's data and also analysed data from tests given to 50 children in the course of the Sontag *et al.* (1958) study. His subjects were too old to allow him to confirm Hofstaetter's first factor, but he found two factors similar to Hofstaetter's second and third factor; Smart felt, however, that the second was in fact a non-verbal factor and he preferred to re-name the third 'manipulation of verbal symbols' or possibly 'symbolic reasoning' or 'verbal reasoning'.

However, Cronbach (1967) has shown that the emergence of these factors at these ages is not due to actual differences in abilities shown by the children at different ages, but can be explained by the ages chosen for testing and the particular age-range covered. By analysis of several sections of the test data, he shows that the factorial separations would have appeared at other ages if the tests had been spaced differently along the age continuum.

An additional factor may be that the amount of change which actually occurs in children between birth and 18 months may be much greater than the amount of change found later. It is generally accepted that children do have varying rates of development and plateaux may occur at different ages for each child.

VII SCALES DESIGNED FOR ASSESSING THE SUBNORMAL BASED ON NORMAL DEVELOPMENT

The following two development scales are based on studies of normal children but designed for the purpose of assessing the mentally handicapped.

1 The Vineland Social Maturity Scale

This scale was designed by E. A. Doll in 1935 to assess levels of social competence, and consists of 117 items arranged in average order of difficulty and covering eight categories of behaviour: General Self-Help, Self-Help in Eating, Self-Help in Dressing. Self-Direction, Occupation, Communication, Locomotion and Socialization. It assesses development over the age-levels of 0-25 + years. A Social Age and a Social Quotient can be derived from the total score.

The present norms, derived in 1947, are based on a tentative standardization sample of 620 subjects, 10 of each sex for each year from birth to 30 years.

The reliability of a score from a test of this kind may be affected by the particular examiner, by the informant or by features of the scale itself. Doll (1953) reported 123 retests after various intervals between 1 day and 9 months with various combinations of same/different examiner and same/different informant: the overall reliability coefficient was 0·92. Hurst (1962), in a study of the meaning of differences between scores on the Vineland Scale and the Stanford-Binet, felt it advisable to allow for variation in reliability estimates and produced two series of significant difference scores, using an upper (0·92) and a lower (0·80) estimate of reliability.

One of the uses for this scale suggested in the manual is to distinguish between mental retardation with and mental retardation without social competence; there is evidence, however, that social competence as measured by the scale and mental ability are not entirely unrelated. Hurst (*op. cit.*) reports results from five studies where Stanford-Binet Mental Ages and I.Q.s were compared with Social Ages and Social Quotients from the Vineland Scale. The M.A./S.A. correlations ranged from 0·66 to 0·96, and the I.Q./S.Q. correlations from 0·41 to 0·82. Coefficients of this size do, in fact, justify use of the Vineland Scale as a substitute for cases where the child is too unco-operative to be given a standard test, and justify its use as supporting evidence in cases where there is doubt about the reliability of one test result.

It seems important to note, though, that most work has been done with scores at the lower social age levels either with primary school children or with mentally retarded subjects, and inspection of the items at these age levels suggests that many of them assess functions similar to those assessed by intelligence tests, e.g. 'follows simple instructions', 'uses names of familiar objects', 'cuts with scissors', 'uses pencil or crayon for drawing', etc. Even when items are less closely related to intelligence test items, they tend to be concerned with activities normally learnt by all children regardless of culture, class or social environment, e.g. 'stands alone', 'goes about house or yard', 'avoids simple hazards', 'cares for self at toilet', etc. But when one looks at the items for the higher age-groups it seems likely that many of them would be likely to depend on the cultural environment of the child and the attitude of his parents, e.g. 'answers ads'; 'purchases by mail' at the 10-11 year level is probably more common amongst American children and would presumably depend as much on the parents' attitude as on the child's ability. At the highest level, 25 +, the items, besides being rather difficult to score (e.g. 'inspires confidence') seem to be too dependent on individual interest and opportunity to be a good measure of individual social development, e.g. 'advances general welfare', 'performs expert or professional work', 'directs or manages affairs of others'.

2 The application of Piaget's theory of development

Woodward (1959) has described the application of Piaget's theory of the process of intellectual development to research in assessment of the very severely subnormal; Piaget calls the first phase of intellectual development the Sensori-Motor Stage, which in normal children extends from birth to around 18 months to 2 years. This approach must at present be used cautiously in individual assessment as little is yet known about the reliability of assessments from different examiners or on different occasions, and the technique has so far been used mainly for research purposes. However, it is potentially one of the most useful techniques available; it has the advantage that it does not involve the administration of prescribed test items but relies on the evaluation of the child's responses in a play situation. Sensori-Motor behaviour can be observed at a distance if the child is too shy or disturbed in a person to person situation, and children who are physically handicapped by deafness, blindness or cerebral palsy, can also be a assessed.

For example, any convenient toy which the child seems interested in can be used and the child's spontaneous reactions, such as whether he grasps it, watches it moving, bangs or rattles it are observed. Simple problem situations can be arranged using a toy the child likes or a sweet or biscuit to see if the child can retrieve it when it is hidden or placed out of reach on a cloth or string which he can grasp. Deaf children will often show interest in bright, interesting looking toys, blind children may enjoy playing with a bell or rattle and large, simple, easy to handle toys may be easier for a child with a motor handicap.

VIII   COMPARING THE CHILD WITH OTHER HANDICAPPED CHILDREN

1 Progress Assessment Charts: Gunzburg

Gunzburg (1964) has pointed out that most scales of measurement suitable for use with mentally handicapped individuals have been related to a standard of normality, which can never be attained. The Progress Assessment Charts (Gunzburg, 1963b) describe how much better or worse the handicapped person is in relation to other handicapped people.

The chart is an inventory of 120 skills graded according to difficulty and divided into four areas of social competence: Self-help, Communication, Socialization and Occupation and the items are scored Pass or Fail by someone who knows the child well. It was not originally designed to give scores or quotients though percentage scores for each area have been used (e.g. Marshall, 1967). General norms, in fact, would not be appropriate as social training is so dependent on varying local conditions, e.g. volume of traffic will affect how much the child goes out independently. Hence local norms should be much more useful in providing aims for teaching.

Whether a child passes or fails an item is recorded on charts which have a figure consisting of concentric circles and divided into quadrants. The easiest items appear in the centre of the circle, the hardest on the outside, and each quadrant represents one area of social competence (as above, and see Figure 17.1).

IX   EXPRESSING THE RESULTS OF ASSESSMENTS

The Intelligence Quotient has long been used to express results of tests of mental level as it provides a convenient description of the relationship between a child's mental age and his actual or chronological age. The concept is based on the assumption that intelligence is normally distributed in the general population and the I.Q. figure (when the mean and standard deviation of the test is known) describes a particular child's level in relation to the rest of the population. Assuming that intelligence is normally distributed, 99% of the population will have I.Q.s between $\pm 2 \cdot 58$ standard deviations from the mean, i.e. if the standard deviation is 15 points, between I.Q. 61 and 139: only $\frac{1}{2}$% should have I.Q.s below $2 \cdot 58$ standard deviations.

Penrose (1949) has pointed out that there are far more people whose abilities are below three standard deviations from the mean than would be expected on statistical grounds. Most severely subnormal children cannot properly be considered, then, as being assessable in terms of the normal distribution. If a child has an I.Q. of 117 on the Wechsler Intelligence Scale for Children (which has a standard deviation of 15 points) this can be easily interpreted as meaning that he has scored as high as roughly 87% of his age-group.

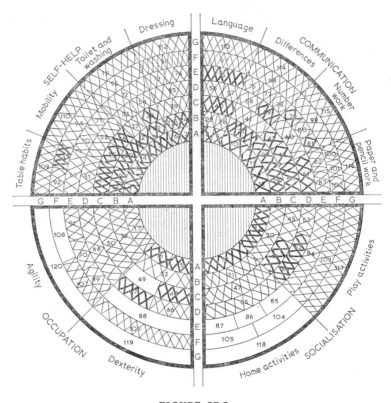

FIGURE 17.1
Diagram from Progress Assessment Chart 1
(Gunzburg, 1963b).

If, however, a 14-year-old has a mental age of 1 year, his I.Q. could be computed as 7; this, however, cannot meaningfully be interpreted as a percentile. The only advantage in using an I.Q. at this level might be either to rank children in terms of ability or to assess relative increase or decrease in mental ability in the same child retested some time later.

When using tests standardized on a normal population, it would seem best to express the results in terms of mental age; it will usually be necessary to quote several mental ages if a standard test is used together with development scales.

X INTERRELATIONSHIPS BETWEEN ABILITIES

1 Mental age and social maturity

The four sections of the Progress Assessment Charts have been found to have positive correlations with mental tests within the severely subnormal group; Marshall (1967) compares total percentage of items passed on the whole P-A-C 1 Scale and found a correlation of 0·57 with the English Picture Vocabulary Test, 0·56 with Stanford-Binet Vocabulary score, 0·59 with the Goddard Seguin Form Board Test, 0·62 with the Goodenough Draw-a-Man Test, and 0·64 with a Design Drawing Test.

The comparatively high correlations between Stanford-Binet Intelligence Scale scores and Vineland Social Maturity Scale scores has already been mentioned. Vineland scores do, however, tend to be higher than M.A. scores with subnormal groups, presumably because they have had more experience than normal children of the same mental age. Gunzburg (1964) illustrates this with diagrams of scores of two groups of subjects.

2 Mental level and daily living attainments

Within a group of 34 children aged between 1 year 1 month and 13 years 8 months whose mental ages were between 1 or 2 months and 3 years 3 months, Whitehead found that assessments of mental age using Woodward's application of Piaget's theory, correlated 0·40 with locomotor abilities, 0·52 with feeding abilities, 0·43 with dressing abilities, 0·45 with toilet training level and 0·55 with speech development. The children tended to be more advanced in Locomotor, Feeding and Dressing Attainments and less advanced in speech as compared with the mental age estimates (unpublished study).

Woodward and Stern (1963), investigating a group of 83 severely subnormal children below 9 years of age, found that locomotor development appeared to be in advance of sensori-motor development, which in turn was in advance of speech level.

Garfield and Shakespeare (1964) found that, in a group of 92 mentally retarded children with cerebral palsy, there were high positive relationships between development according to Piaget's theory and locomotor behaviour, oculomotor co-ordination, feeding and speech: correlations were 0·61, 0·76, 0·64, 0·54 respectively; moreover the daily living skills were closely interrelated, which seemed to suggest that development in the various areas was affected by the same limiting factors, which might be lack of experience, low intelligence or a combination of these.

3 Speech and other abilities

Speech is generally found to be delayed in subnormal children, particularly in those who grow up in hospital or some other institution. A number of studies have shown that normal children, too, tend to develop speech more slowly if they are brought up in an institution than if they are brought up in a normal home environment (McCarthy, 1954).

Lyle (1959, 1960, 1961) found that 77 imbecile children, aged $6\frac{1}{2}$ years to $13\frac{1}{2}$ years, whose non-verbal I.Q.s were between 20 and 50 and who were living in a hospital were significantly retarded in verbal ability compared with a sample of 117 imbeciles of the same age and non-verbal intelligence who lived at home with their parents. He found that disturbances in mother/child relationships before coming into hospital and inability of the child to speak before coming into hospital were associated with poor verbal ability at the time of investigation; children who could speak on admission were more retarded in verbal ability compared with non-institutionalized children; age of admission was unrelated to verbal ability. However, Woodward and Stern (1963) found that new admissions to hospital were not significantly advanced in speech compared with those who had been in hospital longer: they point out, however, that their study was mainly of pre-verbal utterances; their children were younger than Lyle's, and most of the children were not developed enough to get a basal score on the Binet test, i.e. $1\frac{1}{2}$ – 2 year level.

XI SUGGESTIONS FOR TRAINING

Whenever possible, assessment should be aimed at providing a basis for a training programme. If child development scales of the type based on walking, feeding, dressing, etc., are used then the next stage beyond the one at which the child 'passes' can be suggested as an immediate aim. These stages are generally known as 'milestones'. Sheridan (1962) prefers to call them 'stepping-stones' because, though they appear in constant sequence, they do not occur with predictable regularity and are most usefully regarded not as the end of a stage but as an achievement which prepares the child to progress to the next stage.

Gunzburg's Progress Assessment Charts were designed specifically for the purpose of planning training programmes and Woodward's application of Piaget's theories can also be used as a basis for recommendation of play materials or of the kind of play that should be encouraged next.

1 Suitability for Training Centre

Most severely subnormal children living at home will be ascertained and deemed 'unsuitable for education at school'. Then, in most areas, they cease to become the responsibility of education authorities and are looked after by the health authorities who provide Training Centres for them. Gunzburg (1963a) says there are probably about 20,000 such children of school age, though numbers are difficult to estimate accurately.

There are some children, however, who are not suitable for training in Training Centres. These may be children who have the mental level necessary to benefit but are too physically handicapped or have severe behaviour problems, children whose I.Q. is too low for them to benefit or those who need to be carefully observed to decide if they are trainable. For these children, many local authorities are now providing Special Care Units which are usually associated with Training Centres (Rose, undated).

Woodward's application of Piaget's theory has been used to recommend when a child should attend a Training Centre. Woodward and Stern (1963) suggest that a child is ready to benefit from attending a Training Centre when he has reached the end of the sensori-motor stage of development; at this level, the child has a good concept of the permanence of objects, which Piaget believes is necessary for the child to acquire meaningful speech. The children of this level in Woodward and Stern's study had some verbal comprehension – enough to understand the earliest verbal comprehension items of the Binet — and were able to draw in a more advanced way than the vigorous scribbling of preceding stages; it was only children at this stage who would indicate that they wanted assistance or adult attention.

It is generally agreed that a child needs a mental age of about 18 months to 2 years to benefit from attending a Training Centre, though below this level a Special Care Unit can be used. In any particular case, however, whether he is suitable for his local Training Centre may also depend not only on mental age but also on whether he can walk and is continent. These attainments are not usually necessary if the Training Centre is in a new purpose-built building with easy access to doors, no stairs and good washing facilities, but some Training Centres which still use a local hall not designed for the purpose find it impossible to cope with non-ambulant or incontinent patients. Training Centres do not always take children below 5 years of age, though they are doing so in increasing numbers; subnormal children will often derive enormous benefit from attending an ordinary nursery school. Sheridan (1962) feels that the ordinary nursery school can carry 10% – 15% of handicapped children without undue strain.

Kirk (1958) has shown that adequate pre-school experience can produce gains in the mental growth of the retarded child in the case of children from inadequate home backgrounds. In his studies, children who went from their inadequate homes to foster homes and also received pre-school training showed most improvement, whilst children who remained in inadequate homes but underwent the pre-school programme showed less progress. Kirk also showed that children living in hospital benefited from undergoing pre-school training when compared with children who stayed on the wards until they went to school. Children whose retardation was due to non-organic factors seemed most likely to benefit. However, children from relatively adequate homes tended to increase in rate of development without pre-school education.

Another question which may arise is that of how long training should continue: there has been a tendency in the past to emphasise 'training' till 16 years, then to assume that only industrial work is needed after that age.

Gunzburg (1964) analysed Progress Assessment Charts of 286 children attending 8 Training Centres in a large industrial town and found that there was a gradual learning of social skills in all four P-A-C areas up to 12 years, but little progress was evident after that; this could be due to a latent period in development of a faulty attitude to teaching at this level but it probably does not mean that the children have finished learning. Gunzburg found that trainees at the National Society for Mentally Handicapped Children's National Hostels and Workshops at Slough, who were aged 16-25 years, were able to benefit from intensive social training in areas where they had been relatively backward before, though they improved much less in areas where they were already fairly competent or which were difficult to teach, like reading and writing.

XII PREDICTION OF FUTURE INTELLECTUAL LEVEL

Most evidence seems to suggest that within a normal group the results of baby tests have no value in predicting future intellectual levels; attempts have often been made to make early assessments particularly so as to know if a child should be recommended for adoption or not, but the general conclusion has been that tests have not been able to predict successfully the child's future intellectual capacity. Clarke and Clarke (1965) summarize previous studies and reviews; Honzik *et al.* (1948), Bayley (1949), MacFarlane (1953) and Wittenborn (1956) all agreed on the poor predictive validity of scales for young children.

Illingworth (1966), in a critical review of these studies, suggests that the failure of some workers to find higher correlations between early and later tests is due to too much reliance on objective tests, to the exclusion of consideration of the whole child – scoring items 'pass' or 'fail' without considering the 'maturity' with which he performs the test, assessing sensori-motor development but not the child's alertness, responsiveness, etc., using only a single examination, erroneous interpretation of previous studies, absence of full physical and neurological examination and selection of samples to exclude mentally retarded children. He does conclude, however, that mental retardation and neurological defects can be detected in early infancy, but that there is little evidence that mental superiority can be identified then.

Most writers agree that severely subnormal children can often be identified at an early age and identification may be possible at birth or in the first few months if the child has physical stigmata associated with mental defect, e.g. Down's Syndrome, anencephaly, etc.

Illingworth and Birch (1959) followed up 135 children who were considered to be mentally retarded at the first examination before 2 years of age. The diagnosis was made from a developmental history and physical and developmental examinations including the Gesell Schedules. Children with mongolism, cretinism, hydrocephalus and anencephalus were excluded. The children were later tested (when the oldest was 10 years), on the Stanford-Binet Intelligence Test, except for 32 who had died and 2 who could not be traced. At follow-up 59 were ineducable, 24 had I.Q.s between 50 and 75, 13 had I.Q.s between 76 and 94 and 5 had I.Q.s above 100. The initial rough diagnosis was divided into severe, moderate and slight retardation. Where this initial diagnosis was severe, 82% were later found to be ineducable with I.Q.s below 50, where the initial diagnosis was moderate or slight, 28% and 10% respectively were found to be ineducable. In the whole sample, 16 fared better than expected, 4 fared worse. They conclude that mental retardation can be diagnosed before 2 years in a high proportion of cases.

In another paper, Illingworth (1961) relates later I.Q. assessments to diagnosis made during the first year, again excluding mongolism, hydrocephalus and cretinism. Of the 87 children available for later testing, 6 had an I.Q. of 100 or more, 20 scored between 70 and 99, 10 scored between 50 and 69 and 51 had I.Q.s of less than 50. Of the 39 diagnosed in the first six months, figures were 3, 9, 8 and 19 for the same groups. Hence on these figures, the early diagnosis of mental defect (I.Q. below 70) was correct in 75% of the children. Prediction for the individual child, however, must be cautious for there were, of course, 25% in this study who had I.Q.s above 70 in later life.

Adverse environment and lack of stimulation are among the factors which may give the impression that the child is mentally retarded when he later proves to be of normal intelligence. A striking example of this was reported by Williams (1966); a boy admitted to hospital, aged 5 years, with infantile hydrocephalus appeared to be an idiot, as he was unable to feed himself, walk, speak, or see and he had a Social Age of $9\frac{1}{2}$ months on the Vineland Social Maturity Scale. Little is known of his very early history, but he appears to have been totally rejected by his mother and to have lived in various foster homes and institutions. The child gradually progressed until, when he was 18, Williams visited him at the Royal Normal College for the Blind; he then had an I.Q. of 102 (Williams Intelligence Test) and created an impression of higher intelligence than this by his variety of interests and fund of knowledge.

Craib and Woodward (1958) report a follow-up survey of 42 children who were admitted to a mental deficiency hospital but who were subsequently accepted as educable; three of these children proved later to be of normal intelligence and they had all suffered parental rejection or separation before admission.

Cases such as these are not by any means common, but should serve to remind us that environmental effects can make prediction very difficult. Dennis and Najarian (1957) have shown that lack of experience and stimulation can retard development at some stages in infancy.

Clarke and Clarke (1959) in a six-year study showed that I.Q. increases in 200 feeble-minded adolescent hospital patients were greater in those who had suffered most environmental deprivation. The group with a history of the greatest deprivation (which was assessed independently) showed an initial rapid improvement, followed by a deceleration in the rate of improvement when they lived in a more stimulating situation; they showed an average increase in I.Q. of 16 points over the six years. In a group with a history of comparatively less deprivation, the increase was roughly linear with time and the average increase was 10 points.

They had formed the impression that the increments seemed to be due to withdrawal from the adverse situation rather than to entry into the new one. To test this impression, they studied a group, over four years, who were working outside the hospital in the community. Though the social changes were for them much greater, the I.Q. increase – an average of 12 points – was the same as for those who remained in the institution. A further increase seems likely if the patient is rehabilitated to a fairly normal life. Mundy (1957) followed the progress of 75 female patients aged 18-60 years who were initially mostly of imbecile intelligence level. Over three years, 25 who remained in an institution showed a mean increase of 3·76 I.Q. points, 25 who lived in a hostel and worked in open employment showed a mean increase of 7·88 points and 25 who had been rehabilitated to both living and working in the community showed a 16·08 increase on average.

Stott (1962a, 1962b) has pointed out that maternal deprivation may not be the only factor involved in cases where mental subnormality has been thought to be due to maternal deprivation; he argues for the possibility of a hitherto neglected congenital factor which may be more likely to be present in children who are also deprived of normal maternal attention and stimulation. In the second paper he describes the histories of 14 children who had suffered abnormal mothering and demonstrates that in no case was there an absence of another feasible cause; the adverse family environment seemed to be one of several contributing factors.

XIII SUMMARY

Four aims are usually involved in any assessment of the severely subnormal child:

1. To discover if he is mentally retarded. For this purpose a scale based on normal child development is most appropriate. It must, however, be remembered that such scales were standardized on normal children living at home; children who have been reared in institutions may not have had comparable experiences. It is usually best, in administering the scale, to make use, wherever possible, of information from observing the child and of information from discussion with the parents, nursing staff or whoever looks after the child.

If the child's I.Q. score is below 55 or his mental age on the test is less than half his actual age, he is said to be functioning at severely subnormal level assuming that the test is reliable and that the child has co-operated.

2. To decide into which category of severe subnormality he falls. One possible division is into trainable and non-trainable groups, i.e. suitable for Training Centre.

Before the present Mental Health Act, the group that is now called severely subnormal was divided into imbecile and idiot categories, usually taken to be divided at about I.Q. 20. These categories tended to correspond fairly well to the trainable/untrainable categories and are still sometimes used as descriptive terms.

3. How can he best be trained? A scale which has items which are themselves relevant to daily living is obviously most useful for this purpose. Here knowledge of other handicapped people and the interrelationships between skills and their developmental patterns is useful to give detailed guidance as to what to expect from the child, and what not to expect if he is already typical of this group. Local norms are often more useful than general norms.

4. What is the eventual outcome of training likely to be? We have seen that prediction of future level from a young age is not too difficult with very severely subnormal children; a very deprived environment from an early age may have a marked effect on development.

The best way to attempt prediction is from a series of tests at regular intervals, which make it possible to assess the rate and quality of development. Assessment of the severely subnormal has been a comparatively neglected field but there are signs that more interest is being taken now, and more research reports are appearing concerned with patients whose responses to their environment are like those of young children in their first two or three years.

It is to be hoped that more techniques will be developed for assessing the severely subnormal child and planning his training programme.

REFERENCES

BAYLEY, N. (1933) Mental growth during the first 3 years: a developmental study of 61 children by repeated tests. *Genet. Psychol. Monog,* **14**, 1-92.

BAYLEY, N. (1935) The development of motor abilities during the first three years. *Monogr. Soc. Res. Child Develop.,* **1**.

BAYLEY, N. (1949) Consistency and variability in the growth of intelligence from birth to 18 years. *J. genet. Psychol.,* **75**, 165-196.

BAYLEY, N. (1965) Comparisons of mental and motor test scores for ages 1 through 15 months by sex, birth order and race, geographical location and education of parents. *Child Develop.,* **36**, 379-411.

BENTON, A. L. (1964) Psychological evaluation and differential diagnosis. *In* STEVENS, H. A. and HEBER, R. (Eds.) *Mental Retardation.* Chicago and London: University of London Press.

BIRCH, H. G., THOMAS, A., CHESS, S. and HERTZIG, M. E. (1962) Individuality in the development of children. *Devel. Med. Child Neurol.,* **4**, 370-379.

BRITISH PSYCHOLOGICAL SOCIETY (1963) Report of the working party on subnormality. *Bulletin of the Psychological Society,* **16**, 53-67.

BRITISH PSYCHOLOGICAL SOCIETY (1966) *Children in Hospitals for the Subnormal: A Survey of Admissions and Educational Facilities.* London: British Psychological Society.

BRUNET, O. and LEZINE, I. (1951) *Le Dévelopment Psychologique de la Première Enfance*. Paris: Presses Universitaires de France.

BUHLER, C. (1935) *From Birth to Maturity*. London: Kegan Paul.

BUHLER, C. and HETZER, H. (1935) *Testing Children's Development from Birth to School Age*. London: Allen and Unwin.

CATTELL, P. (1947) *The Measurement of Intelligence of Infants and Young Children*. New York: Psychological Corporation.

CLARKE, A. D. B. and CLARKE, A. M. (1959) Recovery from the effects of deprivation. *Acta Psychologica*, **16**, 137-144.

CLARKE, A. M. and CLARKE, A. D. B. (1965) *Mental Deficiency; the Changing Outlook* (2nd Ed.). London: Methuen.

CONGER, J. A. (1930) An evaluation of the Linfert Scale for measuring the development of infants. Unpublished Master's Thesis, Univ. of Minnesota (see MAURER, K. M. (1946) *Intellectual Status at Maturity as a Criterion for Selecting Items in Pre-School Tests*. Univ. Minn. Inst. Child Welf. Monog: Series 21. Minneapolis: Univ. of Minnesota Press).

CRAIB, M. F. and WOODWARD, M. (1958) A survey of 44 children admitted to the Fountain Group Hospital under the Mental Deficiency Act and subsequently accepted as educable. *J. ment. Sci.*, **104**, 115-122.

CRONBACH, L. J. (1967) Year to Year Correlations of Mental Tests: A Review of the Hofstaetter Analysis. *Child Development*, Vol. 38, No. 2, 283-289.

DENNIS, W. and NAJARIAN, P. (1957) Infant development under environmental handicap. *Psychol. Monog.*, **71**, 1-13.

DOLL, E. A. (1953) *The Measurement of Social Competence*. Minneapolis: Educational Publishers.

DONOGHUE, E. C. and SHAKESPEARE, R. A. (1967) The reliability of paediatric case history milestones. *Devel. Med. Child Neurol.*, **9**, 64-69.

DUNN, L. M. (1959) *Peabody Picture Vocabulary Test*. Nashville, Tenn.: American Guidance Service.

FRANCIS-WILLIAMS, J. and YULE, W. (1967) The Bayley Infant Scales of Mental and Motor Development: an exploratory study with an English sample. *Devel. Med. Child Neurol.*, **9**, 391-401.

GARFIELD, A. and SHAKESPEARE, R. A. (1964) A psychological and developmental study of mentally retarded children with cerebral palsy. *Devel. Med. Child Neurol.*, **6**, 485-494.

GESELL, A. and AMATRUDA, C. S. (1947) *Developmental Diagnosis*. New York: Hoeber.

GESELL, A., THOMPSON, H. and AMATRUDA, C. S. (1938) *The Psychology of Early Growth*. New York: Macmillan.

GOODENOUGH, F. L., MAURER, K. M. and VAN WAGENEN, M. J. (1940) *Minnesota Pre-School Scale: Manual*. Minnesota: Educational Test Bureau.

GRIFFITHS, R. (1954) *The Abilities of Babies*. London: University of London Press.

GUNZBURG, H. C. (1958) Psychological assessment in mental deficiency. *In* CLARKE, A. M. and CLARKE, A. D. B. (Eds.) *Mental Deficiency: The Changing Outlook* (2nd Ed.). London: Methuen.

GUNZBURG, H. C. (1963a) *Junior Training Centres*. London: N.A.M.H.

GUNZBURG, H. C. (1963b) *Progress Assessment Charts*. London: N.A.M.H.

GUNZBURG, H. C. (1964) Social competence of the imbecile child: landmarks and directed training. *Proc. of the Int. Copenhagen Congress on the Scient. Study Ment. Retard.*, **2**, 703-706.

HAGGARD, E. A., BREKSTAD, A. and SKARD, A. G. (1960) On the reliability of an amnestic interview. *J. Abnorm. soc. Psychol.*, **61**, 311-318.

HERRING, A. (1937) An experimental study of the reliability of the Buhler Baby Test. *J. exp. Educ.*, **6**, 147-159.

HINDLEY, C. B. (1960) The Griffiths Scale of Infant Development: scores and predictions from 3-18 months. *J. Child Psychol. Psychiat.*, **I**, 99-112.

HOFSTAETTER, P. R. (1954) The changing composition of intelligence: a study in T-technique. *J. genet. Psychol.*, **6**, 159-164.

HONZIK, M. P., MCFARLANE, J. W. and ALLEN, L. (1948) Stability of mental test performance between 2 and 18 years. *J. exp. Educ.*, **17**, 309-324.

HURST, J. G. (1962) The meaning and use of difference scores obtained between performance on the Stanford Binet Intelligence Scale and the Vineland Social Maturity Scale. *J. clin. Psychol.*, **18**, 153-160.

ILLINGWORTH, R. S. and BIRCH, L. B. (1959) The diagnosis of mental retardation in infancy. *Arch. Dis. Child.*, **34**, 269-273.

ILLINGWORTH, R. S. (1961) The predictive value of developmental tests in the first year with special reference to the diagnosis of mental subnormality. *J. Child Psychol. Psychiat.*, **2**, 210-215.

ILLINGWORTH, R. S. (1966) *The Development of the Infant and Young Child* (3rd Ed.). Edinburgh and London: Livingstone.

KIRK, S. A. (1958) *Early Education of the Mentally Retarded*. Urbana, Illinois: Univ. of Illinois Press.

LYLE, J. G. (1959) The effect of an institution environment upon the verbal development of imbecile children: (1) verbal intelligence. *J. ment. Def. Res.*, **3**, 122-128.

LYLE, J. G. (1960) The effect of an institution environment upon the verbal development of imbecile children: (2) speech and language. *J. ment. Def. Res.*, **4**, 1-13.

LYLE, J. G. (1961) Some factors affecting speech development of imbecile children in an institution. *J. child Psychol. Psychiat.*, **I**, 121-129.

MCCARTHY, D. (1954) Language development in children. *In* CARMICHAEL, L. (Ed.) *Manual of Child Psychology*. New York: Wiley.

MACFARLANE, J. W. (1953) The uses and predictive limitations of intelligence tests in infants and young children. *Bull. World Health Org.*, **9**, 409-415.

MCGRAW, M. B. and MOLLOY, L. B. (1941) The paediatric anamnesis: inaccuracies in eliciting developmental data. *Child Devel.*, **12**, 255-265.

MARSHALL, A. (1967) *The Abilities and Attainments of Children leaving Junior Training Centres*. London: N.A.M.H.

MEDNICK, S. A. and SCHAFFER, J. B. P. (1963) Mother's retrospective reports in child-rearing research. *Amer. J. Orthopsychiat.*, **33**, 457-461.

MUNDY, L. (1957) Environmental influence on intellectual function as measured by intelligence tests. *Brit. J. Med. Psychol.*, **30**, 194-201.

PAEDIATRIC SOCIETY WORKING PARTY OF THE S.E. MET. REGION (1962) *The Needs of Mentally Handicapped Children*. London: N.A.M.H.

PENROSE, L. S. (1949) *The Biology of Mental Defect*. London: Sidgwick and Jackson.

PYLES, M. K., STOLTZ, H. R. and MCFARLANE, J. W. (1935) The accuracy of mother's reports on birth and developmental data. *Child Devel.*, **6**, 165-176.

RICHARDS, R. W. and NELSON, V. L. (1939) Abilities of infants during the first eighteen months. *J. genet. Psychol.*, **55**, 299-318.

ROBBINS, L. C. (1963) The accuracy of parental recall of aspects of child development and of child rearing practices. *J. abnorm. soc. Psychol.*, **66**, 261-270.

ROSE, G. (Undated) *Special Care Units*. London: N.A.M.H.

SARASON, S. B. (1949) *Psychological Problems in Mental Deficiency*. New York: Harper.

SHERIDAN, M. (1960) *The Developmental Progress of Infants and Young Children*. H.M.S.O. (Reports on Public Health and Medical Subjects No. 102).

SHERIDAN, M. D. (1962) Mentally handicapped children. *Devel. Med. Child Neurol.*, **4**, 71-76.

SHIRLEY, M. M. (1933) *The First Two Years: A Study of Twenty Five Babies*, Vols. I-III. Minneapolis: Univ. Minnesota Inst. Child Welfare.

SMART, R. C. (1965) The changing composition of 'intelligence': a replication of a factor analysis. *J. genet. Psychol.*, **107**, 111-116.

SONTAG, L. W., BAKER, C. T. and NELSON, V. L. (1958) *Mental Growth and Personality Development: A Longitudinal Study*. Monographs of the Society for Research in Child Development, **23**, No. 2.

STEPHEN, E. and ROBERTSON, J. (1965) Normal child development and handicapped children. *In* HOWELLS, J. G. (Ed.) *Modern Perspectives in Child Psychiatry*. Edinburgh and London: Oliver and Boyd.

STOTT, D. H. (1962a) Abnormal mothering as a cause of mental subnormality. I: A critique of some classic studies of maternal deprivation in the light of possible congenital factors. *J. child Psychol. Psychiat.*, **3**, 79-91.

STOTT, D. H. (1962b) Abnormal mothering as a cause of mental subnormality. II: Case studies and conclusions. *J. child Psychol. Psychiat.*, **3**, 133-148.

STUTSMAN, R. (1931) *Mental Measurement of Pre-School Children*. Yonkers: World Book Co.

TERMAN, L. M. and MERRILL, M. A. (1960) *Stanford-Binet Intelligence Scale: Manual for the Third Revision, Form LM*. Boston: Houghton-Miffin.

WHITEHEAD, K. Unpublished study. Queen Mary's Hospital, Carshalton, Surrey.

WILLIAMS, C. E. (1966) A blind idiot who became a normal blind adolescent. *Develop. Med. Child Neurol.*, **8**, 166-169.

WITTENBORN, J. R. (1956) A study of adoptive children. II: The predictive validity of the Yale Developmental Examination of Infant Behaviour. *Psychol. Monog.*, **70**, 59-92.

WOODWARD, M. (1959) The behaviour of idiots interpreted by Piaget's theory of sensori-motor development. *Brit. J. educ. Psychol.*, **29**, 60-71.

WOODWARD, M. and STERN, D. (1963) Developmental patterns of severely subnormal children. *Brit. J. educ. Psychol.*, **33**, 10-21.

18

Maladjusted children

Maurice Chazan

I INTRODUCTION

Since the end of the nineteenth century there has been a growing interest in this country in the investigation and treatment of emotional and behaviour difficulties in children. In spite of a shortage of skilled personnel which still exists, there has been a gradual extension of child guidance facilities provided by local authorities as well as hospitals. The child guidance team, which, following the American pattern, originally consisted of personnel qualified in psychiatry, psychology and psychiatric social work, now includes, in a number of instances, specially trained psychotherapists, speech therapists and remedial teachers. Furthermore, the child guidance service has been greatly aided by the development of special educational treatment for children with emotional difficulties which followed the official recognition, as a result of the Education Act (1944), of a category of 'maladjusted pupils'. Such educational treatment is now provided in a variety of day and boarding schools as well as in special full-time or part-time classes, and while there are still big gaps in provision of this kind in several parts of the country, most child guidance clinics are able to work in conjunction with some special educational facilities for maladjusted children within their own area or with residential schools further afield.

The National Health Service Act (1946) made it a duty for regional hospital boards to provide specialist mental health services and, although in-patient accommodation for disturbed children and adolescents is still very scarce, there have been some recent developments in facilities for children with emotional or behaviour disorders who require to be treated within a hospital setting. The Children Act of 1948 and the Children and Young Persons Act of 1963 have resulted in an extension of local authority welfare provision for children who are neglected or deprived, and Children's Departments have undertaken increasing responsibility for rehabilitating families in difficulties, a considerable proportion of whose children tend to be maladjusted to some extent.

Developments such as these have meant that the assessment of maladjustment in children with a view to appropriate treatment has become considerably more complex in recent years. The child guidance team has to decide which out of a variety of possible measures will be the most suitable for a particular child and, in present-day conditions, this decision has usually to be made without unduly prolonged investigation. The majority of child guidance clinics have long waiting-lists, so that it is not possible for all cases to be subjected to lengthy diagnostic procedures, even if this were desirable. Furthermore, clinics are often called upon to make recommendations about individual children to juvenile court magistrates while being given only a short period of time to conduct the necessary investigations.

It may in fact be said that, as other agencies increasingly contribute to the treatment and rehabilitation of maladjusted children, the child guidance clinic tends to emphasize its diagnostic and advisory functions and to undertake the direct treatment of only a small and selected proportion of children. Since recent surveys (Douglas, 1964; Rutter and Graham, 1966; Pringle, Butler and Davie, 1966) have suggested that a not inconsiderable proportion of school children need help or advice on account of some degree of maladjustment, it would seem that the only realistic way of tackling this problem is to increase the participation of teachers, parents, social workers and youth leaders in the treatment programme. If this is done, however, it still remains important that the initial diagnostic investigation should be skilfully and thoroughly carried out.

It has long been recognized that maladjustment is much easier to treat when dealt with at an early stage and that many children are referred far too late. It has been the policy of the School Health Service and, more recently, of the School Psychological Service to encourage parents and teachers to make known to them those children who appear to be in any way emotionally maladjusted. Some School Psychological Services make surveys of the school population at particular ages in order to ascertain which children may need special help, and the need has been felt for developing procedures which will pick out children 'at risk' on account of maladjustment.

This chapter will consider what methods of assessing maladjustment are in current use and to what extent they are adequate. Much less interest has been shown by psychometricians in the personality assessment of children than that of adults and, indeed, it is much more difficult to devise reliable and valid techniques for measuring social and emotional development than it is to construct tests of cognitive ability and scholastic attainment. The particular difficulties of assessing maladjustment will now be discussed.

II PROBLEMS IN THE ASSESSMENT OF MALADJUSTMENT

There is little need to emphasize that measurement is rendered much easier if there is general agreement about what is to be measured. No such agreement exists about the definition of 'maladjustment'. Furthermore, as Schonell (1952) points out, difficulties of definition reflect difficulties of classification. The nature of these difficulties will be discussed below. It will also be necessary to comment on our lack of norms of children's emotional and social development, the inconsistency of children's behaviour, and the low correlations usually found between various measures of maladjustment.

1 Difficulties of definition

The term 'maladjustment' was first used in the 1920s but was not in general use until after the second World War (Ministry of Education, 1955). 'Maladjusted pupils' were defined in the Handicapped Pupils and School Health Service Regulations, 1945, as 'pupils who show evidence of emotional instability or psychological disturbance and require special educational treatment in order to effect their personal, social or educational re-adjustment'. The Underwood Committee (Ministry of Education, 1955) did not recommend any change in the legal definition of maladjustment, as this definition achieved its purpose in making it possible for special educational treatment to be provided for a wide range of children with emotional problems or behaviour difficulties, but they considered that the definition was unsatisfactory for a number of reasons, including the failure to offer any help in the identification of maladjustment in particular children. Indeed, 'emotional instability' and 'psychological disturbance' are terms which themselves require clarification. The Underwood Report in attempting its own definition, emphasized that maladjustment described a relationship between the individual and his environment and that the maladjusted child was 'developing in ways that have a bad effect on himself or his fellows and cannot without help be remedied by his parents, teachers and the other adults in ordinary contact with him'. This definition has itself been subject to criticism, for example by Lovell (1958), who stresses that there are degrees of maladjustment and that we should also be concerned to help those children whose maladjustment is slight. A Report of the Scottish Education Department (1964) also finds difficulty in arriving at a satisfactory definition of maladjustment, but concludes that the term serves the legal and administrative purpose of describing in general terms a group of children for whom special educational treatment needs to be provided.

From the legal and administrative point of view, therefore, the term maladjustment seems no less satisfactory than any other which might replace it. It has certain advantages in that it avoids giving the impression that the child presenting difficulties in his emotional and social development is necessarily behaving 'abnormally' or is 'ill' in any way. Nevertheless, it should be clearly understood that the use of the term does not imply a precise diagnosis, and in fact to call a child 'maladjusted' does no more than to indicate that he needs some kind of help because of emotional or behavioural difficulties or because of an unsatisfactory school or home situation. It should not become a fixed label, and it should refer only to difficulties at a particular time and in a specific situation. Behaviour which is considered pathological or maladjusted in one culture may be quite acceptable and customary in another (Slotkin, 1959); and within cultures, too, there is considerable divergence of opinion among various sections of the public regarding what constitutes good and poor adjustment (Scott, 1959).

The clinician, therefore, will not be content with a diagnosis of 'maladjustment' but will seek to ascertain precisely what is wrong with the child or his situation and, as far as possible, to discover the causes of the maladjustment. This assessment will be greatly aided if the clinician makes use of a satisfactory scheme of classification. However, the classification of symptoms and types of maladjustment has presented a great deal of difficulty.

2 Problems of classification

As Schonell (1952) stated, the complexity of the factors involved makes it difficult to classify forms of maladjustment into clear-cut categories, and even a straightforward classification according to symptoms is not very helpful, as it is common for maladjusted children to present symptoms characterizing a number of disorders. Rutter (1965) points out that a generally acceptable classification of psychiatric disorders which occur in childhood is urgently needed and that the lack of such a classification has been a serious obstacle to progress in child psychiatry. He stresses that until a disorder can be identified and characterized it cannot be adequately studied. Among the difficulties encountered in attempting to draw up an acceptable scheme of classification, Rutter mentions that: (i) the same children may show different kinds of disorder at different ages; (ii) what is considered a problem at one age may be normal or acceptable behaviour at another (e.g. enuresis); (iii) severity and duration of disorder are important variables but are difficult to measure; and (iv) no theory has gained sufficient general support for it to be used as a basis for classification. There is the further problem of trying to take into account, in any classificatory scheme, work relating to symptom clusters, aetiology, response to treatment and long-term prognosis.

Rutter's own tentative classification of emotional and behaviour disorders in childhood is worthy of consideration as a basis for further work leading to a more refined scheme. He suggests that the following types of disorder can be differentiated to a greater or lesser extent:

(1) 'neurotic', 'personality' or 'emotional' disorders;
(2) 'anti-social' or 'conduct' disorders;
(3) a mixed group in which neither neurotic nor anti-social symptoms predominate;
(4) 'developmental' or 'habit' disorders, e.g. enuresis, speech abnormalities;
(5) the 'hyperkinetic' syndrome;
(6) child psychosis, with onset before pubescence;
(7) psychosis developing at or after puberty;
(8) mental subnormality;
(9) educational retardation as a primary problem.

Rutter recognizes that these categories may overlap to some extent and remains uncertain to what extent it is justifiable to separate depression and adult-type neurotic illnesses from the neurotic behaviour disorders which form the first category above.

Various other types of classification have been proposed, some of which will be discussed later in connection with the consideration of the various techniques of assessing maladjustment. Most classification schemes, however, agree in recognizing a distinction between 'neurotic' or 'emotional' disorders of an introverted type, characterized by inhibition and unhappiness, and 'conduct' disorders, characterized by anti-social or aggressive behaviour. Schemes of classification worthy of study include those put forward by Hewitt and Jenkins (1946), Cameron (1955, 1958), Anna Freud (1962), Stott (1963), and Eysenck and Rachman (1965a). Appendix B of the Underwood Report (1955) lists a classification which is used in many child guidance clinics in this country, but there are still great variations in the classificatory schemes used and in the ways in which basic information about children are recorded.

3 Paucity of normative data on children's emotional and social development

The significance of particular types of behaviour can be reliably assessed only if we know how common such behaviour is at different ages. The fact that a particular kind of behaviour pattern is common in an age-group does not necessarily mean that the behaviour manifested is *desirable* from the adult point of view, but we still need to know what is normal (in the sense of being usual or frequently found) at any stage of emotional or social development before we can call a personality trait or form of behaviour 'deviant' or 'abnormal'. Such norms can be reliably obtained only through the longitudinal study of large groups of unselected children. There has been a paucity of such studies in this country and we have tended to rely heavily on normative data derived from American research work. Recently, however, the gap is being filled by the results emerging from longitudinal investigations of representative samples of the child population in Great Britain, notably those by Douglas (1964), Moore (1966) and Pringle, Butler and Davie (1966).

There is little need to stress the point that the training of those engaged in the assessment of maladjustment should include a thorough study of the emotional and social development of normal children.

4 Lack of constancy in children's behaviour

As stated above, a diagnosis of 'maladjustment' should never be regarded as necessarily applicable to a child for a fixed period of time. Changes of behaviour and attitude often occur, particularly in the case of young children and adolescents, and the maladjusted child's behaviour may be modified as a result of maturation as well as through treatment or alteration in his environment. A new teacher or a new friend may cause a gradual, or even sudden, transformation in a child's behaviour. Maladjustment, therefore, is to be regarded as a handicap which in many cases will not be a permanent one. Long-term follow-up studies of maladjusted children have been sparse, but there is evidence to suggest, for example, that children with 'neurotic' disorders are more likely to respond to treatment than children with aggressive-type disorders (Morris, H. M., Escoll and Wexler, 1956; Morris, D. P., Soroker and Burrus, 1957; O'Neal and Robins, 1958; Rutter, 1965). Except when dealing with psychotic children, where some improvement is reported to occur in only about one-quarter to one-third of cases (Rutter, 1966), it is usually possible, with good treatment facilities, to effect some change in a maladjusted child's emotional state and behaviour.

Recent surveys have highlighted to what an extent children may behave differently in different situations. Rutter and Graham (1966) investigated the incidence of psychiatric disorder in children aged 10 and 11 years on the Isle of Wight. Screening procedures involving questionnaires to parents and teachers showed that about 13% of 2,193 children needed more intensive study, as they showed some evidence of possible disturbance. The proportions of the sample selected by parents and teachers were much the same (6% were selected by means of the parents' responses and 7·1% through the teachers' replies), but there was very little overlap between the children chosen through the parents and those selected through the teachers. Only 19 out of the 284 children picked out were selected by *both* teachers *and* parents. There are several possible explanations for this discrepancy (Graham, 1967), but there is little doubt that a considerable number of the children genuinely showed disturbance only, or mainly, at home or only, or mainly, at school. Furthermore, the symptoms of disturbance shown at home by maladjusted children may differ from those shown in school. These findings are supported by the results of the survey carried out by Mitchell and Shepherd (1966) who investigated, through questionnaires completed by parents and teachers, the behaviour of a one-in-ten random sample of children aged 5 to 15 years attending local authority schools in Buckinghamshire. Completed questionnaires from both teachers and parents were available for 6,077 children. Although the children whose parents reported that they were free of deviant behaviour were also the most problem-free group at school and, similarly, children who presented problems to their parents were more likely to have problems at school than those who were not deviant at home, a substantial number of children whose behaviour was deviant presented difficulties only at home or only at school. Mitchell and Shepherd found it impossible to assess how far the difference between the reports lay in the children's actual behaviour and how far it was due to the skill in observing and the frames of reference of the persons making the report. These studies, however, emphasize that any comprehensive procedure for assessing maladjustment, whether in screening large numbers of children or in the investigation of a single case, must include a study of the child in both the home and the school situation.

5 Low correlation between various measures of maladjustment

In view of the lack of agreement about the nature, classification and aetiology of maladjustment and the evidence that children can behave very differently in different situations, it is not surprising that comparisons of the relationships among measures of adjustment show mainly low correlations. Tindall (1959), for example, compared the results obtained from using techniques representative of the five major types of measuring devices currently employed to assess adjustment:

(1) questionnaires and inventories;
(2) ratings by adult judges;
(3) ratings by peers using sociometric techniques;
(4) projective techniques;
(5) systematized direct observation (through time samples of behaviour).

The sample consisted of 66 adolescent boys known to be varying in their adjustment status in a residential institution in Ohio. While the boys, having lived in the institution for an average of six years, constituted an atypical group in some respects, they were all from a similar immediate environment and were well known to the adult judges. The analysis of the intercorrelations among the various indices of adjustment showed, in general, a positive but low correlation among the different arrays, the median intercorrelation coefficient being 0·228. Tindall concluded that this indicates a slight relationship among these common approaches to measurement of adjustment, but stated that the results do not strongly support a global concept of adjustment; assessment of adjustment by one technique has little predictive value in terms of results which might be obtained by using another technique. He recommends that several indices should be used rather than a single method before any general conclusions in regard to adjustment status are drawn. Petrie (1962), who used a number of different approaches to assess the progress in adjustment of a group of 23 maladjusted children in a special boarding-school, also found very little relationship between the various techniques he employed.

Such investigations point to the need for caution in using tests which claim to measure adjustment globally and in making inferences about behaviour or personality which go beyond the scope of the data provided by a particular test. Indeed, current techniques of measuring adjustment and personality are frequently criticized as being low in validity (Vernon, 1964), that is, we are not sure exactly what they measure and how well they fulfil their purpose. As will be seen from observations on the validity of the tests and techniques to be described later, few of these report validation studies of a high standard. The question of the validity of tests of adjustment or personality is too complex to be dealt with adequately here; comprehensive discussions of the problems involved will be found in Cronbach (1960), Rabin and Haworth (1960), Anastasi (1961) and Vernon (1964).

6 Need for new techniques of assessment

As previously stated, relatively little attention has been given to the development of techniques for the assessment of maladjustment. Most of the techniques

T

which are available have been standardized on small samples and have not been modified in the light of new knowledge about maladjustment. Most, too, particularly questionnaires and inventories, have been devised and standardized in the United States and are not suitable without modification for use in this country. There is an urgent need, therefore, for the revision of the best of our existing techniques in the light of experience and recent knowledge, and for the development of new instruments.

However, in the assessment of maladjustment, the quality of the assessor is as important as the quality of any techniques used, and it is essential that too much reliance should not be placed on the results of tests. Much depends on the assessors' practical and theoretical knowledge of a wide range of children as well as on their training in and experience of those techniques which they adopt. It has been shown, too, that much maladjustment is situation-specific and so a full picture of the child in a variety of situations needs to be built up. Furthermore, although a decision about treatment for a maladjusted child usually needs to be made at an early stage after referral for examination, the assessment of his condition and needs should constantly be reviewed in the light of accumulating knowledge of his behaviour and his response to the treatment measures recommended.

III   SCREENING AND SURVEY PROCEDURES

1 School surveys

It is now customary for local education authorities, usually through their school psychological service, to carry out surveys of their school population in order to ascertain which children may be in need of special educational treatment. Such surveys have tended to be made in the early years of the junior school, and to be aimed mainly at discovering children who are educationally subnormal or slow learning. Although few authorities have, as yet, the resources to deal adequately with the problems of maladjustment, there has been an increasing interest in discovering children who may be maladjusted. As a number of studies (Chazan, 1962a; Sampson, 1966; Morris, 1966) have shown, there is a considerable overlap between maladjustment and learning difficulties in school, and there is likely to be a high incidence of maladjustment among children who are handicapped either physically or mentally, but school psychological services wishing to make comprehensive surveys to discover maladjusted children need to adopt techniques additional to those normally used to ascertain slow-learning children. Approaches which seem particularly suitable for screening and survey procedures will now be considered.

(a) *Discussions with Teachers and Social Work Agencies*
There are good reasons for not carrying out formal screening procedures in the case of children in the infant school. For instance, each child needs to be given

ample opportunity for settling down in school and for showing his capabilities; the giving of tests at the infant stage should be avoided as far as possible; and teachers are justifiably reluctant to make formal judgements concerning young children whose progress and behaviour fluctuate rapidly. Nevertheless, it is undesirable that help should be delayed in the case of children who show signs of emotional disorder in the infant school, or, indeed, before starting school. Many parents have anxieties about their children's emotional development from an early age (Brandon, 1960) and, while not all such anxieties are well-founded, worried parents should be given advice before their anxiety has an adverse effect on the child, perhaps producing disturbance where there was none previously. A number of children, too, spend the early years of their life in grossly adverse home circumstances, and these children are 'at risk' with respect to maladjustment.

The school psychological service, therefore, should encourage nursery and infant schools to make known to them those children whose development is in any way giving cause for concern. Discussions between the educational psychologist and the staffs of nursery and infant schools should be held at intervals to consider which children might be in need of a psychological investigation and which should be closely observed in the school situation. Such discussions help to put problems in perspective and encourage a greater awareness of the significance of difficulties in emotional and social development. There should also be good liaison between the school psychological service, the school health service and the social work agencies of the area to ensure that co-ordinated efforts are made to help children and families at risk.

(b) *Rating Scales*
Rating scales, completed by adult judges, are very useful for obtaining a fairly rapid personality assessment of children well known to the judges and are commonly used as part of record forms kept in the case of each child by many schools; a great variety of rating scales are employed in this way (Walker, 1955). A number of scales have been specifically designed for the detection of maladjustment, an example being the Haggerty-Olson-Wickman Behaviour Rating Schedules (Olson, 1930). These schedules (A and B) were validated against an external criterion, i.e. a particular item contributes to a score for maladjustment, not because it appears to imply socially undesirable behaviour, but on the basis of the extent to which the behaviour described has actually been found to be applied to problem children.

Examples of the type of items used in Schedule B are as follows:
25. Is he even-tempered or moody?

Stolid; rare changes of mood (3)	Generally very even-tempered (1)	Is happy or depressed as conditions warrant (2)	Strong and frequent changes of mood (4)	Has periods of extreme elations or depressions (5)

26. Is he easily discouraged or is he persistent?

Melts before slight obstacles or objections (5)	Gives up before adequate trial (3)	Gives everything a fair trial (1)	Persists until convinced of mistake (2)	Never gives in; obstinate (4)

The scores are weighted, a score of 1 being given for descriptions rarely applied to problem children, and a score of 5 for responses characteristic of this group. The scale seems to have been little used in this country, although studies in the U.S.A. have found it valuable (Horrocks, 1964).

Rutter (Rutter and Graham, 1966; Rutter, 1967) has developed two Behaviour Rating Scales, one for completion by parents and the other to be answered by teachers. These scales are essentially symptom counts, each item being selected as discriminating 'normal' children from maladjusted children attending child guidance clinics. Examples of the items in the teachers' scale are:

(1) Very restless. Often running about or jumping up and down. Hardly ever still.
(2) Truants from school.

24. Has a stutter or stammer.

Mostly, each item is weighed 2, 1 or 0 according to whether it is marked 'Certainly Applies', 'Applies Somewhat' or 'Doesn't Apply' by the respondent. The sum of the weights is the child's score, and a particular score (e.g. 9 or over on the teachers' scale) can be taken as the point at which it is worth following-up a child as possibly maladjusted. Both the teachers' and parents' scales incorporate subscales which indicate whether the child's maladjustment takes the form of the 'neurotic' or 'anti-social' type. The development of the questionnaire for completion by teachers is discussed by Rutter (1967). Satisfactory re-test and inter-rater reliability is claimed, and the scale is said to be reasonably efficient in differentiating children with neurotic or anti-social disorders. The scale is, as Rutter states, simple to complete and to score, and should prove extremely useful in screening children for maladjustment through school surveys. The author, however, is careful to mention its limitations. Its simplicity means that further information about a child is required; it cannot be used in the way suggested for picking out children with only one symptom of disorder; and the scale will not select children with symptoms which are manifested only outside the school situation.

Mitchell and Shepherd (Mitchell, 1965; Mitchell and Shepherd, 1966) also used specially devised questionnaires, to be completed by parents and teachers, in their survey. The questionnaire to parents included:

(i) A series of 22 triple-choice questions on behaviour traits asking for the parent's estimate of *intensity* of behaviour, e.g.

52. Very irritable, easily becomes cross or annoyed.

Occasionally becomes cross (for instance, if tired or provoked by other children).

Very placid nature, practically never gets cross or annoyed.

(ii) A series of 15 items in which the parent had to record an estimate of the *frequency* of certain kinds of behaviour on an eight-point scale, e.g.

72. *Wets the bed*

(a) Every day or almost every day	(b) Two or three times a week	(c) About once a week	(d) About once every two weeks
(e) About once a month	(f) About once in two or three months	(g) Two or three times a year	(h) Never, or less than once a year

The teachers' questionnaire (Mitchell and Shepherd, 1966) included items on attendance, attainment and physical disabilities as well as a list of 21 behaviour problems, to be underlined if applicable, e.g.

(a) very restless, can't sit still for a moment;
(b) cries more than most children;
(c) has a stammer.

In using the data provided by the completed questionnaires the investigators decided to adopt a concept of 'deviant behaviour' framed in terms of a 10% limit, i.e., if any behaviour was reported to have occurred at an intensity or frequency found in 10% or less of any age (yearly) or sex group, then it was considered as deviant for that age and that sex. This method of scoring has the merit of taking into account age and sex trends, but it is doubtful whether it can be justifiably assumed that disturbed behaviour occurs in 10% or less of any age-group. The parents' questionnaire, although suitable for research purposes, is overlengthy for use in screening surveys, but the teachers' form is straightforward and takes little time to complete.

Other useful scales of a fairly similar type have been used in studies by Douglas and Mulligan (1961) and Mulligan *et al.* (1963). A number of research workers (Brandon, 1960; Ryle *et al.*, 1965) have employed the MacFarlane Scales, or a modification of these, which consist essentially of a series of five-point scales requiring ratings of various symptoms and characteristics indicating behaviour or emotional disturbance (MacFarlane *et al.*, 1954). Ross *et al.* (1965), using an extreme-group procedure and factor analysis, have developed a behaviour checklist for boys aged 6-12 years (the Pittsburgh Adjustment Survey Scales). An initial pool of statements related to the dimensions of aggressive, withdrawn and prosocial (well-adjusted) behaviour was reduced after analysing the results of applying the statements to children nominated by teachers as aggressive, withdrawn, or well-adjusted – and by factor analysis of data subsequently obtained four scales were produced: Aggressive-Behaviour Scale (25 items); Withdrawn Behaviour Scale (19 items); Pro-Social Behaviour Scale (20 items); and Passive-Aggressive Behaviour Scale (13 items).

All the scales described above merit further validation studies. It is important that in making ratings of any kind, judges should be fully aware of the distortions that can easily creep into assessments of personality and behaviour (Warburton, 1961; Vernon, 1964). They should be encouraged to make use of the whole scale, including the extreme categories where applicable, and to observe the subjects in a variety of situations for a substantial period of time before making a rating. This will help to avoid the 'halo' effect – e.g. the tendency to look more kindly on a pupil's misbehaviour because he is good at his school work.

(c) *Bristol Social Adjustment Guides*

The Bristol Social Adjustment Guides (Stott, 1963) are described by Vernon (1964) as a compromise between ratings and more detailed short-term behaviour observations. There are separate Guides for the Child in School, the Child in Residential Care and the Child in the Family, to be completed by teachers, houseparents or social workers as the case may be. The 'Child in School' Guide, for example, has 166 items possibly indicative of maladjustment and many more items describing normal behaviour, e.g.

Ways with other children

Gets on well with others; generally kind, helpful / sometimes nasty to those outside own set / squabbles, makes insulting remarks / selfish, scheming, a spoil sport / hurts by pushing about, hitting / spiteful to weaker children / tells tales, underhand (tries to get others into trouble) / nothing noticeable.

Plays only or mainly with older / younger children / those of own age.

The teacher underlines those descriptions of behaviour which best fit the child. The items indicative of deviant behaviour are coded on a special diagnostic form, on which these items are grouped according to the nine syndromes which are recognized by Stott, i.e.:

Unforthcomingness (U)
Withdrawal (W)
Depression (D)
Anxiety or uncertainty about adult interest and affection (XA)
Hostility to adults (HA)
Anxiety for approval of and acceptance by other children (XC)
An attitude of unconcern for adult approval and a 'writing-off' of adults (K)
Hostility to other children (HC)
Restlessness (R)

There are, in addition, two groupings of miscellaneous symptoms of emotional tension and nervousness. Details of environmental disadvantages, degree of backwardness, sexual maturity and physical condition are also recorded on the diagnostic form. Recently, Stott (1966) has suggested the addition of an 'inconsequential' syndrome, applicable to children showing very restless and purposeless behaviour; this seems to be a useful concept (Chazan, 1968).

In the Manual to the Guides, Stott emphasizes that they are intended for use in schools or residential centres and by the psychological services and that, where the assessment of an individual child for the practical purposes of treatment or special placement is at stake, the actual information given through the Guides should be used rather than any summation of symptoms in the form of numerical scores. In research, however, such scores may be used, and in a number of studies (Chazan, 1964; Pringle *et al.*, 1966) the following scoring system has been used:

Number of 'adverse' items underlined	*Category*
0-9	'stable'
10-19	'unsettled'
20 or more	'maladjusted'

The diagnostic form, in fact, grades the items in order of severity and draws a dividing line between milder symptoms indicating 'unsettledness' and more severe ones suggesting 'maladjustment'. In earlier editions of the manual Stott recommended that the 'maladjusted' items should be given double the weight of the 'unsettled' ones, but in the 1966 edition, he no longer advocates this as a general principle.

The Bristol Social Adjustment Guides have a number of merits. They are meaningful and simple to use; they are comprehensive, giving an all-round picture of the child, and they help the observer to be more perceptive. A retest reliability coefficient of about 0·80 is claimed. They need, however, a more thorough statistical analysis (Vernon, 1964) and the classification might be altered in the light of general research findings on maladjusted children. Stott's original idea of weighting by severity of symptoms is a sound one, but more research is needed before this can be reliably implemented. It should be borne in mind, too, that the behaviour items have a different significance at different ages, and that, in the case of the 'Child in School' Guide, secondary school teachers, who see their pupils only in a limited number of situations, tend to have more difficulty in completing the form than primary school teachers. However, the Guides certainly merit a comprehensive standardization on representative samples of 'normal' and 'maladjusted' children.

Adjustment pointers. For screening purposes, the Bristol Social Adjustment Guides may require too much time from class teachers and, instead, the teachers could be asked to fill in the six adjustment pointers, which take very little time.

All the teacher does is to answer Yes or No to the following questions (Stott, 1963):

(1) In his general manner such as you would expect of a normal, alert child of his age?
(2) Is he exceptionally quiet, lethargic, depressed or very variable in energy?
(3) Does he lack concentration or is he restless in a way that seriously hinders his learning?
(4) Is he a nuisance or untrustworthy?
(5) Does he get on well with other children generally?
(6) Is there anything in his behaviour or appearance to make you think he might be emotionally unstable or suffer from nervous trouble?

When any of the six questions is adversely answered in the case of an individual, the child should be further investigated, for example through the completion of the full Guide.

Delinquency prediction instrument (Stott, 1961). By the use of a special template, a delinquency prediction score can be obtained from the completed Bristol Social Adjustment Guide. In constructing the prediction instrument, a selection was made of the behavioural indications most typical of delinquents and the 54 items occuring at least four times more frequently among delinquents compared with non-delinquent schoolmates were included. These items have been given weights according to the number of times they occurred more frequently among the delinquents than the non-delinquents.

A preliminary sorting procedure is suggested by Stott for the detection of potential delinquents, in which six questions are given to the teacher, who underlines Yes or No in response. Examples of the questions are:

(1) Is he a nuisance, or does he take correction badly?
(2) Has he been involved in wanton damage to property, truancy, or dishonesty or other undesirable behaviour?

These instruments are likely to prove very useful, although they are still in the early stages of validation.

(d) *Sociometric Techniques*

Sociometric techniques can be of great value in supplementing information obtained on a child from himself and from adults who know him. The status of a child in the classroom group is usually a good indicator of his degree of social adjustment. There may, of course, be some maladjusted children who are very popular in class, despite their maladjustment, because of prowess at games; and there may be cliques of maladjusted children who support one another socially. But, in general, maladjusted children tend to be low in sociometric status (Belfield, 1963) and children who are ignored or rejected by their peers are likely to be in need of help on account of maladjustment (Evans, 1962).

A variety of sociometric approaches can be used, and these are described in detail by Gronlund (1959) and Evans (1962). A simple method for the detection of 'isolates' is the 'Companionship Choice' approach, in which, for example, the pupil is asked to name three children, out of the classroom group or other specified group, with whom he would like to associate on each of a number of criteria (usually three), e.g. 'Which child in the class would you like to sit next to?' Those children who receive either no choices or just one or two – the 'isolates' or 'neglectees' – should be considered worthy of further investigation.

Other methods include (i) the 'Guess Who?' approach, e.g. asking pupils 'Which three children work hardest at their lessons?' 'Which children are always miserable?' and other questions of a similar type. A pupil's rating for various characteristics is obtained by counting the number of times a trait is assigned to him; (ii) 'Social Distance' Measurement (Bogardus, 1925; Cunningham *et al.*, 1951), where each member of a group rates each of his peers on desirability as an associate, usually on a five-point scale such as the following (Shaw, 1954):

(1) I would like to have him/her as one of my best friends.
(2) I would like to have him/her in my group but not as a close friend.
(3) I would like to be with him/her once in a while but not often or for a long time.
(4) I don't mind his/her being in the room but I don't want to have anything to do with him/her.
(5) I wish he/she were not in the classroom.

A combination of 'Companionship Choice', 'Guess Who?' and 'Social Distance' approaches can provide a sensitive index of sociometric status, though it must be remembered that groupings among children may change rapidly and that the information obtained from the techniques described above is fairly superficial. Probing for the reasons for choice and rejection gives a less superficial picture, but this is not to be recommended as part of normal screening procedures, as such probing ought to be carried out only on an individual basis.

(e) *Questionnaires and Inventories (self-rating)*
Self-reports of personality and attitudes have obvious weaknesses particularly in that they tend to be superficial and subject to distortion. The respondent naturally wants to present himself in the best light and he will also be anxious to give socially desirable responses (Edwards, 1957); in many cases it is genuinely difficult for a subject to give a clear-cut response to a question. However, as Vernon (1964) observes, self-reports have a number of advantages, as they are easily scored and readily standardized, and they offer an impersonal situation which is to the liking of some subjects.

It is doubtful whether self-report tests should be included in regular screening procedures, particularly in the case of young children, though they can be useful in many research surveys. Where such tests are given to samples of children, care must be taken to find out whether all the children who are asked to complete them can read and write adequately; otherwise the test should be given

T*

orally and individually. As there is usually a far greater incidence of maladjustment in the backward classes of a school than in the other classes (Chazan, 1963), this is a very important point to bear in mind if the results of a survey are to be meaningful.

(i) *British questionnaires and inventories.* There are surprisingly few standardized British self-report questionnaires and inventories. The most recent self-report test is the Junior Eysenck Personality Inventory (Eysenck, S., 1965a), which has supplemented the well-known Maudsley Personality Inventory (Eysenck, H. J., 1959) and the Eysenck Personality Inventory (Eysenck and Eysenck, 1964), both inventories much used with adults. The J.E.P.I. is designed to measure the two major personality variables of neuroticism/stability and extraversion/introversion which Eysenck and his colleagues have discussed in numerous publications (Eysenck, H. J., 1947, 1957, 1960; Eysenck and Rachman, 1965a, b). It has been constructed for the age-range 7-16, and contains 60 items, of which 24 measure extraversion, 24 assess neuroticism and 12 constitute the Lie scale for the detection of faking. The subject merely has to answer 'Yes' or 'No' to the 60 questions, examples of which are as follows:

> Do you like plenty of excitement going on around you?
> Are you moody?
> Can you get a party going?
> Have you ever told a lie?

Test/retest reliabilities for the scales average between 0·7 and 0·8. No extravagant claims are made for the validity of the inventory, though preliminary testing of child guidance clinic subjects has suggested that the scale may be valid for clinical investigations. The scale does not go deeply into a child's personality make-up, but item analyses and factor analyses for all the questions used and for the various age-groups separately have been carried out (Eysenck, S., 1965b). It is claimed, therefore, that the J.E.P.I. is an improvement on the Junior Maudsley Personality Inventory constructed by Furneaux and Gibson (1961), which is based on the American inventory devised by Pintner *et al.* (1938) and has not been standardized to the same extent as the new Eysenck scale. Gibson (1967) suggests that the discriminative power of standard personality inventories could be improved by item analysis carried out on the data obtained from a specific population. While the new scales thus derived would not be relevant in other contexts, they would be more meangingful than the standard ones for the particular population being studied.

(ii) *American inventories.* Questionnaires and inventories standardized in the U.S.A. need to be used with caution because of the wording of many items which may not, without emendation, be appropriate for British children. However, a number of American tests of personality and adjustment have been used in a variety of surveys and studies in this country. Examples of these tests are (*a*) personality questionnaires devised by Cattell and his colleagues at the

Institute for Personality and Ability Testing in Illinois (the I.P.A.T. scales), (*b*) the Mooney Problem Check Lists, (*c*) the Bell Adjustment Inventory, (*d*) the California Test of Personality, (*e*) the Minnesota Counselling Inventory and (*f*) Cassell's Test of Social Insight. These approaches will be discussed briefly below.

(a) *The I.P.A.T. Scales.* Cattell and his colleagues have now provided a range of personality questionnaires covering the age ranges 4 years to adult levels. The Pre-School Personality Questionnaire is designed for 4- to 6-year-olds; the Early School Personality Questionnaire (E.S.P.Q.) caters for the ages 6 to 8 years (Coan and Cattell, 1966); and the Children's Personality Questionnaire (C.P.Q.) is intended mainly for 8- to 12-year-olds (Porter and Cattell, 1963). At the secondary stage, there is the High School Personality Questionnaire (H.S.P.Q.), with norms for 12- to 18-year-olds (Cattell and Beloff, 1963); and the 16 Personality Factor Questionnaire (16 P.F.), suitable for older adolescents and adults (Cattell and Stice, 1964). These questionnaires give a picture of personality development in terms of a number of distinct dimensions or traits of personality, e.g. cyclothymia (warm, sociable) versus schizothymia (aloof, stiff). The C.P.Q., for example, assesses personality in terms of 14 such dimensions. The children are asked to answer 70 questions in each of four parts, being required to read a question and mark an ' × ' on the side that 'fits you better', e.g

Would you like to play with mechanical toys ☐ or ☐ with friends?

Does almost everyone like you ☐ or ☐ only some people?

Savage (1966) considers this test to be the best personality questionnaire available for children of this age-group.

The Junior-Senior H.S.P.Q. contains 142 triple-choice questions, e.g.

Do you sometimes feel that you are not much good and that you never do anything worthwhile?

a. yes   *b.* perhaps   *c.* no

The wide age-range covered by the I.P.A.T. questionnaires make them very useful, though it is doubtful whether the E.S.P.Q. should be, as suggested by the authors, given to school classes of 20-30 children. Individual testing is more appropriate at the age-range for which this scale is intended.

(b) *The Mooney Problem Check Lists* (Mooney and Gordon, 1950). This check list is extremely simple to complete and yet is quite comprehensive. There are forms for different age-ranges at the secondary school stage and beyond, consisting of a long list of problems to be underlined if applicable to the subject. Any problem causing particular concern to the respondent is circled and there are also some open-ended questions. The problems are classified in a number of categories, e.g. Health and Physical Development, Courtship, Sex and Marriage and Home and Family.

The authors emphasize that the Problem Check List is not a test; it does not give scores relating to personality traits or permit any direct statements about the adjustment status of the respondent. The list is, rather, a preliminary basis for understanding a pupil's problems and for counselling. It is refreshing to find a technique for which such modest claims are made and it can usefully be employed as a screening device and in surveys.

(c) *The Bell Adjustment Inventory* (Bell, 1961). This inventory, designed for American high school and college students, contains 140 questions requiring a choice of answers from Yes/No/?, for example:

Do you day-dream frequently?
Do you enjoy social gatherings just to be with people?
Are you troubled with feelings of inferiority?

The test measures four aspects of personal and social adjustment: (*a*) home, (*b*) health, (*c*) social and (*d*) emotional adjustment. Coefficients of reliability between 0·80 and 0·89 are claimed for the subscales, and of 0·93 for the total score. Items for each section were included only when they clearly differentiated between the upper and lower 15 % of the individuals in a distribution of scores, and results were checked with interviews with 400 subjects over a period of two years. This inventory, being free for the most part of linguistic usage appropriate only in the American context, is suitable for use with British adolescents, although, as with most inventories of this kind, answering some of the questions will cause the majority of respondents considerable difficulty.

(d) *The California Test of Personality* (Thorpe, Clark and Tiegs, 1953). This test has five levels, ranging from kindergarten to maturity. Yes or No answers are required to questions such as (in the case of the youngest level):

Is it easy for you to play by yourself when you have to?
Do the children think you can do things well?

Percentile scores can be calculated for Personal Adjustment, Social Adjustment and Total Adjustment, as well as for 12 aspects of personal and social adjustment. A personality profile is thus provided as a helpful first step in the interpretation and use of the test results. Cronbach (1960) finds the evidence on validity given in the manual to be incomplete, and questions the worth of some of the subscores; Anastasi (1961) quotes this test as an example of one which relies primarily on content validation, and Horrocks (1964) considers that it provides useful measures, but stresses its limitations as a test of 'personality'.

(e) *The Minnesota Counselling Inventory* (Berdie and Layton, 1957). This inventory is designed to help counsellors of high school students, mainly in the age-range 15 to 18 years. Based on the Minnesota Personality Scale, it yields nine scores. Three of these scores relate to adjustment in the areas of family relationships, social relationships and emotional stability. Four scores indicate characteristic ways of meeting problems and behaviour in social groups, under the headings of conformity, adjustment to reality, mood and leadership. The remaining two scores ('Question' and 'Validity' scores) are meant to check on the test-taking attitude of the respondents and to assess the degree of defensiveness and over-anxiety to display socially acceptable characteristics which they may show.

The inventory consists of 355 items to which the respondent answers in terms of 'true' or 'false', e.g.:

During the past few years I have been well most of the time.

My parents treat me more like a child than a grown-up.

I get discouraged easily.

Wider experience of this instrument should enable users to make a more valid interpretation of it (Cronbach, 1960); it is recommended by Anastasi (1961) that the inventory should be employed only by those well-trained in its use.

(f) *The Test of Social Insight, Youth Edition* (Cassell, 1959). This is a 60-item untimed test which claims to assess adolescent social problems. The items are of the multiple-choice type, each item having five alternatives; the respondent can choose to resolve a problem by means of withdrawal, passivity, co-operativeness, competitiveness or aggressiveness, e.g.:

A teacher has given you a much lower grade than you think you deserve, What do you do?

(i) Insist that you receive a fair grade.

(ii) Ask the teacher for an explanation.

(iii) Do nothing, and act natural.

(iv) Transfer to another class.

(v) Ask to take an examination to show that you know the class materials.

This is an interesting approach, but it is likely that the subject's choices are as much determined by his level of intelligence as by his social adjustment.

(f) *A Comprehensive Approach to identifying Maladjustment in School*

Bower (1960) suggests a comprehensive approach to the early identification of emotionally handicapped children in school. He advocates the adoption of three main types of procedure: (1) a pupil behaviour rating scale; (2) a class play; (3) 'Thinking about yourself'.

(i) *The pupil behaviour rating scale* asks the teacher to rate each pupil's behaviour on a five-point scale, e.g.:

This pupil gets into fights or quarrels with other pupils – (1) Seldom or never, (2) Not very often, (3) Not observed, (4) Quite often, (5) Most of the time.

After rating, the teacher ranks the class from highest score to lowest, i.e. from 'most' to 'least' maladjusted.

(ii) *The class play* is a form of sociometric technique, which has two parts. In Section I (Peer Perception), each child is asked to act as a director of a play and to choose fellow-pupils for 15 specific parts e.g.:

Choose . . . . someone who could play the part of a true friend

. . . . some girl who could play the part of a mean, bossy sister.

In Section II (Self Perception), each child answers a number of questions relating to the 15 roles listed in Section I, for example:

Which *two* parts would you like to play best of all?

Which *two* parts would you think the children in the class would pick for you?

Scores for 'peer-perception' and for 'self-perception' are calculated on a specified formula, and the class is ranked highest to lowest on the basis of the 'peer-perception' scores.

(iii) *'Thinking about yourself'* is a self-rating questionnaire which has 53 items, consisting of descriptions of personal characteristics or behaviour, e.g.

This boy/girl . . . . has bad dreams
. . . . hates school
. . . . is happy.

For each item, the subject records whether, firstly, he is like the boy described and, secondly, he wants to be like him, in terms of always/frequently/seldom/never. The score is the sum of the differences in the rating of the two questions for each item, and again the class is ranked from highest to lowest.

After ranking the pupils in his class, the teacher draws a line under the pupils receiving the five highest scores on the 'Pupil Behaviour Rating Scale' and another line under the pupils receiving the five highest scores on 'A Class Play' (Section I). In the rankings on 'Thinking about Yourself', a line is drawn under the third highest boy and the third highest girl. Those pupils who are above the line in two out of the three rankings or on all three of the rankings are selected for screening purposes.

This screening method was tested for validity by asking clinical psychologists to examine individually an unselected random group of 225 screened children, 169 boys and 56 girls in grades 3 to 7. Ninety per cent of the screened group were found to have moderate to severe emotional problems on the basis of a clinical examination. Bower's method has the advantage of combining teacher assessment, peer ratings and self-report, and would seem to merit use in junior schools with some modification in the phraseology in 'A Class Play' and 'Thinking About Yourself'. The items are interesting to children, and the slightly indirect way in which they are expressed is likely to make them more acceptable.

(g) *Selection of Techniques*

As the selection of techniques for screening purposes will depend on a variety of factors, such as the particular scope of the survey, the age-range and number of children involved, and the personal choice of the psychologists concerned, it is difficult to make recommendations about this which might serve as a guide-line to School Psychological Services. Nevertheless, it might be suggested that, as a first step in junior school surveys, teachers might be invited to complete Stott's Adjustment Pointers or Rutter's Child Scale B. In the case of children picked out by this method as possibly maladjusted, teachers could then be asked to provide more detailed information by, for example, completing the full Bristol Social Adjustment Guide. On this basis, those cases could be selected where contact with the parents and possible clinical investigation would seem desirable. With older children, particularly in schools where there is a counselling service, such techniques as the I.P.A.T. questionnaires and the Mooney Problem Check List could be used in the second stage, but generally it is desirable to avoid involving the child directly until the parents have been consulted.

IV CLINICAL PROCEDURES

1 Obtaining reports on the child

The child guidance team has always spent a great deal of time in compiling a full case-study of each child referred on account of maladjustment, and it has been the usual practice for the psychiatrist, the psychologist and the psychiatric social worker to contribute to the information which is amassed as a basis for diagnosis. Because of staff shortages or through deliberate policy, this practice, which is costly and time-consuming, is not always maintained, but it should be emphasized that a sound diagnosis in the case of a maladjusted child can rarely be made without comprehensive information on his physical history and condition, his home background and his school situation. Over-emphasis on one aspect of the child's life may lead to ignoring important factors contributing to his maladjustment, and it is usually the case that a number of factors combine to produce emotional or behaviour disturbance.

The time spent on each child and his family by members of the clinic team will be used more profitably if full reports are obtained from those who already know the child. These reports, in the main, will be concerned with the child's physical history and condition, his home background, and his progress at, and behaviour in, school.

(a) *Physical History and Condition*

The School Health Service normally keeps full records of the physical history and condition of children at school, and these should be made available when necessary to the child guidance clinic. In addition to the information provided by the parents, the family doctor may be able to add to the picture, and the class teacher should not be overlooked as a possible source of information about defects of vision or hearing and about physical disabilities which may have been revealed in the school situation. It may be thought desirable for a physical examination to be carried out at, or through, the child guidance clinic. In a number of cases, especially when children show a hyperkinetic type of disorder or when periodic outbursts of violence or temper are reported, EEG readings prove valuable (Rutter, 1965), and neurological investigations may throw some light on cases of severe reading disability. Stott's Systematic Interview Guides (Stott, 1967) will be found particularly useful for recording the mother's report on a child's early physical development.

(b) *Home Background*

The role of the parents in the causation of maladjustment has long been recognized by child guidance workers, and it is the custom for the psychiatric social worker to obtain a detailed and systematic report on the home background, both from the material and the psychological points of view, usually through visiting the home. However, both in the U.S.A. and Great Britain, there has been a tendency for case work agencies to concentrate on the mother and to overlook the role played by the father in the family (Pollack, 1956; Andry, 1960, 1962).

It is now being increasingly recognized that, as far as is practicable, the father as well as the mother should be seen in the early stages of investigating a case. In some instances, the child and the family will already be known to the Children's Department, the Probation Department or other agencies and it is essential that in these cases reports should be obtained from the department concerned.

(c) *School Situation*

Sometimes the part played by the school in the emotional and social life of the child is underestimated by child guidance clinics which concentrate on dynamics within the family. There is a good deal of evidence, however, to confirm that school factors may contribute to a child's maladjustment (Chazan, 1962b; Moore, 1966; Mitchell and Shepherd, 1966); it is thus essential that a school report should be available on every child referred to a child guidance clinic. Such a report may be obtained by means of the Bristol Social Adjustment Guide (Child in School) or through a specially devised report form, which should include specific questions on the child's scholastic progress, intellectual ability, attitudes towards teachers and children and behaviour in school. It is valuable if written reports can be supplemented by personal discussions between the psychologist and the head or class teacher.

On the basis of the information available about a child and after an initial interview with the child and his parents at the clinic, the team will decide whether further diagnostic procedures are warranted and, if so, what form these should take. Intensive personality testing on the child's first visit to the clinic is not usual, nor is it desirable to attempt to probe too deeply on this occasion, at least as far as the child himself is directly concerned. Most psychologists prefer to administer individual tests of intelligence as a first step, not merely because of the information they give about the child's intellectual functioning but because the intelligence test situation provides a good means of gaining rapport with the child and of observing his reactions in a standard situation. A variety of techniques for clinical use by the psychologist are now available and the selection of particular approaches will depend largely on training and experience as well as on personal preference. However, thought needs to be given to choosing techniques which are particularly appropriate for an individual child and to formulating hypotheses which personality testing might help to confirm or reject. For example, time can be wasted in attempting to use tests which require imaginative or high-level verbal responses with dull children, in whose case different techniques might be more appropriate.

The clinical procedures used by the psychologist to assess maladjustment will be considered below. Many of these are well-known and have been fully discussed elsewhere, so that only the more recently devised techniques will be described in detail.

2 Interviewing

Interviewing in the clinical context, whether carried out by a psychiatrist, psychologist or psychiatric social worker, is particularly difficult in that the interviewer seeks to obtain data and to make judgements on many aspects of the child's background, attitudes and relationships in a fairly structured form, and yet the structured type of interviewing is hardly appropriate to the situation. Without the establishment of good rapport between the interviewer and the child or his parents in the early stages of contact, little progress can be made, and this consideration has to be kept in mind as well as the desirability of obtaining complete and accurate information on a case. A single interview session, therefore, is rarely sufficient for diagnostic purposes, as freer communication is more likely on a second occasion.

The problems of gaining rapport with children and parents are discussed by Kanner (1948) and questions which may produce interesting responses and provide leads for discussion are suggested by Kahn and Giffen (1960). It may be said that psychologists have tended to neglect direct discussion with children in favour of using tests of some kind, but test findings can be more reliably interpreted if supplemented by free and open discussion, and it is important that the child's own view of his home and school situation should be taken into account. More emphasis, therefore, might be given in the training of psychologists to techniques of interviewing both children and parents.

3 Observation of behaviour

The members of the clinic team can often learn much about a child from direct observation, but it is unwise to draw too many inferences from the behaviour of a child in the artificial setting of the clinic. Many children who are highly aggressive in school or at home may not exhibit any signs of aggressiveness at the clinic, and some otherwise uninhibited children may display a lack of emotional response in this situation. However, children who are perpetually restless, highly inhibited or psychotic are likely to show direct evidence of their characteristic behaviour to the clinician. As previously mentioned, the individual test situation gives an opportunity for the psychologist to note such reactions as lack of co-operation, sullenness, sensitivity to failure, lack of persistence or disinhibition, and to record any impairment of speech, hearing or motor co-ordination which seems to handicap the child.

Many psychiatrists and psychologists like to give the child opportunities for free individual play with a variety of toys, or else they may have a standard set of toys or figures with which the child is encouraged to play, while a conversation is carried on with him. It is also useful to have a number of activity play groups conducted in the clinic, where the child may play freely with other children of his age and can be observed in a more natural setting than that afforded by the consulting-room (Slavson, 1952).

4 Questionnaires and inventories

In addition to the questionnaires and inventories described earlier, there are several scales which may be found useful in the clinic. Although questionnaires and inventories are used mostly for survey purposes, they can be valuable in providing starting-points for discussion in the case of children referred for clinical investigation, especially with adolescents. Among inventories suitable for use in clinical work is the Rogers Personal Adjustment Inventory (Rogers, 1961), which is described as a series of character and personality tests for 9- to 13-year-old children. This inventory aims to assess the extent to which a child is satisfactorily adjusted to his fellows, his family and to himself, and also to provide information about the ways in which he meets his difficulties. The type of question asked is rather more imaginative than usual and four diagnostic scores are obtained from the responses: (1) personal inferiority; (2) social maladjustment; (3) family maladjustment; (4) daydreaming score (fantasy life). The norms, as Rogers himself states, are not up to date, nor are they based on adequate numbers of children. The test-retest reliability coefficient is 0·72, but the validity (correlation between the test and the ratings of clinicians) ranges between 0·38 and 0·43, low enough to indicate that only cautious predictions should be made on the basis of this inventory. The Personal Adjustment Inventory has proved of value to clinical workers, and merits an up-to-date standardization.

Several anxiety scales have been used in clinical work, notably the Taylor Manifest Anxiety Scale (Taylor, 1953) and the Sarason General Anxiety Scale for Children (Sarason *et al.*, 1960). The Taylor Scale consists of 50 questions to which the subject responds 'true' or 'false' e.g.

I do not tire quickly
I have very few headaches
I feel anxious about something or someone almost all the time.

There is also a children's form of the Manifest Anxiety Scale (Castaneda, McCandless and Palermo, 1956), containing 42 items, which has been found useful with children from about 8 to 12 years.

The Sarason Inventory has 34 items, plus 11 items constituting a Lie Scale, to which the respondent answers 'Yes' or 'No', e.g.

When you are away from home, do you worry about what might be happening at home?
Are you afraid of things like snakes?

Such scales are useful when employed with individuals, not so much because of the scores which may be derived from them but rather because they may indicate possible areas for deeper investigation which might otherwise have been missed. Anastasi (1961) considers that, until more is known about its reliability and validity, the Manifest Anxiety Scale should be regarded as a research instrument rather than a tool for clinical investigation.

5 Objective tests

Relatively little work has been done to develop tests of personality other than questionnaires and inventories which can be scored objectively. Himmelweit and Petrie (1951) describe an experimental investigation of neuroticism in children in which a number of objective tests were tried out. The tests which discriminated between samples of 50 'neurotic' children and 50 'normal' children (aged 9-14 years) included:

(i) *Persistence at a Task in face of Impossibility of Completion*
Here the child was given two jig-saw puzzles with pieces missing from each, and was asked to complete one of them; the score was the time in minutes spent on the task before giving up. Neurotic children gave up more readily than the normals.

(ii) *Myokinetic Test (9th Circle)*
This is a test of expressive movement designed by H. J. Eysenck. A prepared circle of four inches in diameter was placed before the child, who was asked to trace this once with his eyes open and then 10 times with his eyes shut. Without interrupting, the examiner, who sat next to the subject, marked the ninth circle which was used for the purpose of measurement. Neurotic children tended to place their circles further away from the centre of the original one compared with the normal children.

It would seem well worth while to continue to develop objective tests of this type, although scores derived from such tests, even when they discriminate between *groups* of maladjusted and well-adjusted subjects, have to be interpreted carefully in the case of any *individual*, in view of the possible overlap between the scores of groups.

The Porteus Maze test has been used qualitatively to study the characteristics of delinquents and neurotics (Porteus, 1942, 1959; Foulds, 1951), and more recently Gibson (1961, 1964) has devised a Spiral Maze test derived from the idea of the Porteus Maze technique. Gibson claims that psychomotor tests have advantages in personality investigation, in that they are simple to administer and scorable by objective means and they have little obvious connection with neuroticism or behaviour disorder.

The 'maze' is a spiral design printed on a large card and presenting a pathway bordered by heavy black lines. Obstacles, in the form of the letter O in heavy type, are scattered along the whole length of the pathway. The test is scored in terms of the *time* in seconds taken by the testee to complete the maze and the *number of errors* made through touching or penetrating the obstacles or lines at the side. Norms are limited at present, but the manual claims that, at age 9, the Error score clearly discriminates 'good' boys from 'naughty' boys as assessed by their teachers and that delinquents tend to sacrifice accuracy to speed. The value of making broad generalizations on the basis of a test which takes less than two minutes is questionable, but there is no doubt that psychomotor tests merit a place in any battery of objective tests which may be constructed to help in the assessment of personality.

6 Projective techniques

Projective techniques are widely used in child guidance clinics. Essentially, they are ways of stimulating the imagination in a situation of 'make-believe'; the subject speaks out or acts out responses which he invents as he proceeds (Anderson and Anderson, 1951). The clinician wishes to discover the conscious and unconscious drives, feelings, complexes and conflicts of the subject, and provides stimuli, verbal or pictorial, which will help to uncover these. In the case of the more complicated techniques, the skill and experience of the user of the test is as important as the quality of the test itself. Although projective techniques are usually administered according to the recommended standard procedure, they tend to be interpreted in different ways by different psychologists. In addition to the highly subjective nature of the interpretation, there is the added difficulty of disentangling the respondent's own projected feelings from material of no personal significance. For example, a child may repeat, in response to a presented picture, a story he has just heard at school or seen on television. In spite of these difficulties, however, projective techniques can provide the clinician with clues to the inner thoughts, worries and fears of the subject, and encourage a less superficial approach to the diagnosis of maladjustment. Projective techniques can be used with objective scoring methods (Himmelweit and Petrie, 1951), but this limits their flexibility.

Projective techniques have been discussed very fully in a number of works (Bell, 1948; Anderson and Anderson, 1951; Cronbach, 1960; Rabin and Haworth, 1960; Anastasi, 1961; Lindzey, 1961; Vernon, 1964), so that it will suffice here to comment briefly on the main approaches and to refer to recent publications of relevance.

(a) *Rorschach Technique*
The famous Rorschach Ink-Blot Technique (Klopfer and Kelley, 1946; Klopfer *et al.*, 1954, 1956; Alcock, 1963) can yield a rich personality picture in the hands of an expert in the technique, but it is extremely time-consuming to score and interpret. For this reason, as well as on the grounds of dubious validity (Benton, 1950; Sarason, 1954), it is not widely used in this country. It would seem to be

of more use in the case of older children suspected of being psychotic or near-psychotic, or showing other extreme forms of disturbance, than in the case of children with milder types of maladjustment. Objective scoring can be obtained by the use of the Harrower Rorschach Multiple Choice Blank (Harrower and Steiner, 1951).

(b) *Apperception and other Pictorial Tests*
Apperception tests involve the presentation of a series of pictures to the subject, who is encouraged to invent stories about them. Murray's Thematic Appercep-tion Test (T.A.T.) has been widely used with older children and adolescents (Murray, 1938, 1943), and the Bellak Children's Apperception Test (C.A.T.), which uses pictures of animals rather than human beings in different situations, is a version of the T.A.T. for younger children (Bellak and Bellak, 1950; Bellak, 1954). Tests of a similar nature are the Michigan Picture Test, for the age-range 8–14 years (Hartwell *et al.*, 1951), and the Symonds Picture-Story Test, for adolescents (Symonds, 1948, 1949). The Object Relations Technique has been developed in Great Britain by Phillipson (1955), who bases it on object relations theory (Fairbairn, 1952) and has designed pictures to elicit responses to one-person relationship, two-person relationship, three-person relationship, and group relationship situations. Westby (1959) commends the specificity of the theoretical framework and the novelty of construction of this test, into which much careful preparatory work has gone. Other pictorial tests include the Blacky Pictures (Blum, 1950), consisting of a set of 12 black-and-white cartoons which depict the story of a dog called Blacky and his family. Blum's approach is based on psychoanalytic theory, but neither Cronbach (1960) nor Horrocks (1964) consider that the validity of the test is established.

The Rosenzweig Picture-Frustration Study (1948) examines the reaction to frustrating situations depicted in 24 pictures; it claims to measure such tendencies as consideration for others, dependency, penitence over wrong-doing, and aggressiveness. Schneidman's (1947) Make a Picture Story ('MAPS') technique provides structured and ambiguous pictorial backgrounds, together with cut-out figures of persons and animals; a miniature theatre can be used with these. The subject chooses one of the backgrounds and uses the figures to enact a drama or tell a story, which the psychologist interprets. This is an attractive technique, but, as Williams (1965) states, its validity has yet to be proved.

While pictorial projective techniques can sometimes provide psychologists with insight into a subject's deep-seated problems, they are open to the criticism of them made by Vernon (1964) to the effect that they tend to cover too much ground too thinly to provide precise answers to any definite problem.

(c) *Mosaic Test* (Lowenfeld, 1929)
The Mosaic Test was first devised in 1929 by Margaret Lowenfeld, who used a set of 465 small wooden pieces of different colours and shapes, with which the

subject makes whatever he likes. It is claimed that particular types of mosaic arrangements are typical of different diagnostic categories such as schizophrenia, organic disorder, or psychopathic personality. Little systematic work with this test has been carried out on children, and, as Rabin and Haworth (1960) comment, the test lacks both a sound theoretical basis and a well-defined objective method of scoring. Nevertheless, the test is attractive enough to merit further research work on representative samples of children.

(d) *Raven's Controlled Projection Test*
Raven (1951) has worked out a technique which aims at recording, for comparative study, what meaning a child attaches to everyday situations. The method consists of inviting a child to draw, and while he is doing so, to respond imaginatively to a series of questions, e.g.

Once there was a boy (girl).
   (*a*) What did he like doing?
   (*b*) When he was playing, who did he like being with?
   (*c*) Who did he not like being with?

The manual gives records of the test responses of normal children as well as those of a number of groups of children showing various kinds of emotional or social disturbance. Child guidance clinics find this test useful, though of limited value with children who do not talk very easily.

(e) *Sentence Completion*
Vernon (1964) describes the sentence completion technique as very flexible and easily administered, a fruitful source of material for clinical exploration. The technique consists of giving the subject a number of incomplete sentences which he is asked to finish in any way he chooses. An existing test may be used (e.g. Rohde and Hildreth, 1940; Rotter and Rafferty, 1950), or a specific list of incomplete sentences may be drawn up to elicit responses which are relevant to a particular inquiry. Bene (1957) discusses a method for coding responses to the sentence completion test which enables a more objective score to be obtained. She considers that the test is a useful tool for clinical psychologists, and that it can furnish valuable information about some aspects of an individual's personality. Sentence completion techniques in their various forms are discussed, too, by Anderson and Anderson (1951) and Brower and Abt (1952).

(f) *Other Projective Techniques*
A variety of other methods can be used to encourage the child to express his feelings. Child guidance clinics make much use of painting and drawing for this purpose, and Woltmann (1951) has described the use of puppetry as a projective method; Haas and Moreno (1951) have discussed the value of psychodrama. Such approaches which usually have a therapeutic as well as a diagnostic aim, are attractive to children. Cassell and Kahn (1961) have devised a Group Personality Projective Test, employing 90 stick-figure drawings portraying a variety of

everyday activities, each with little situational structuring; the subjects are required to choose one of five answers to a question about the picture. The test aims to assess 15 personality needs in three areas: (i) personal needs; (ii) social needs; and (iii) emotional needs.

7 Tests of Family Relations

Research into the aetiology of maladjustment in childhood has stressed the importance of interpersonal relationships in the family setting (O'Connor and Franks, 1960), and it has long been the practice for the child guidance team to obtain detailed information about these. However, family relationships are usually seen through the eyes of the parents – often only the mother – and too little attention may be paid to the child's own view of his relationships with other members of the family. Structured tests of family relations can be helpful in obtaining the child's point of view without causing him embarrassment, and British tests of this type which have been devised in recent years include the Bene-Anthony Family Relations Test (1957), the Family Relations Indicator (Howells and Lickorish, 1962) and the London Doll-Play Technique (Ucko and Moore, 1963).

(a) *Bene-Anthony Family Relations Test* (1957)

This test consists of 20 figures representing different members of a family, sufficiently stereotyped to represent any child's family, yet ambiguous enough to become a specific family unit; there is also a figure called 'Nobody'. Each figure is attached to a small box which has a slit in the top, and there are a number of small cards, on each of which a statement is printed. The form for younger children has 40 test items. These items indicate positive or negative feelings coming from the children or going towards the child, e.g.

> This person in the family is very nice (mild positive feelings coming from the child).
> Sometimes I wish this person in the family would go away (strong negative feelings coming from the child).
> This person in the family likes to kiss me (strong positive feelings towards child).
> This person in the family hits me a lot (strong negative feelings towards child).

The child chooses his own family from the 21 figures and is then told that the cards contain messages and that his task is to put each card 'into the person' whom the message it conveys fits best. 'Nobody' is used for those items that are not felt to apply to anyone in the family. The scoring consists of placing check marks on the scoring sheet, which is arranged in rows and columns, the rows standing for Nobody, the Self, Father, Mother, Siblings and Others in the Family. The number of items going to each person within each area is totalled, the totals showing how much of each kind of feelings the child has assigned to each member of the family. The data are summarized in the form of tables, and conclusions are reached on the basis of both the quantitative and qualitative results.

The test is simple to use, and attractive to children. Its validity and reliability need further investigation, though the manual claims that reasonable confidence in the test may be justified. It has the advantage of requiring no verbalization on the part of the child, so that it is particularly useful with younger children and can even be given to E.S.N. pupils (Chazan, 1964, 1965); it is perhaps less suitable for adolescents.

(b) *Family Relations Indicator* (Howells and Lickorish)

This is a type of projective technique which is similar in some respects to Jackson's Test of Family Attitudes (1952) and makes use of a series of 33 pictures on cards, some designed for boys, others for girls. On each card a simple scene is depicted involving one, two or more members of a family. The pictures show six face-to-face situations in domestic settings, each basic relationship being repeated twice or three times in different material environments.

The child is not asked to tell a story about the pictures, but is encouraged to make 'factual' statements about the people depicted. In the analysis of the child's responses emphasis is focused on those units (called 'behavioural units') which reveal family attitudes and relationships. Each behavioural unit is recorded on a Behaviour Item Sheet under the following headings: Attitudes, Verbalizations, Actions, Deprivations, Delinquency and Guilt Feelings. This sheet is in effect a summary of the analysis, showing the person who produces a particular action or attitude and also the object of the attitude or action.

The Family Relations Indicator makes only modest claims: it does not attempt to evaluate unconscious motives, but merely takes the replies to the pictures at their face value. In fact, the authors stress that too much information should not be extracted from the responses. The analysis and scoring are somewhat time-consuming and the sample used in the validation study was limited, but the Indicator is worthy of being tried out with children below secondary school age.

(c) *The London Doll-Play Technique*

Moore and Ucko (1961, 1963) describe the use of a doll-play technique with boys and girls aged 4 to 6, and stress the value of this approach for studying children's perceptions and fantasies about the roles of people who are important to them. The technique, although structured, gives the child opportunities for free play. There is a fixed sequence of situations, but the child can introduce any member of the doll family as often as he wishes in roles chosen by himself.

This is an attractive test for very young children, and although lengthy and designed for research purposes, promises to be of clinical value in selected cases.

8 Selection of techniques

It has been shown that the psychologist has a large variety of techniques at his disposal for use in clinical work, and, although the selection of particular techniques will inevitably depend on the personal bias and training of the psychologist and the context within which he is working, it is very useful to have available a wide range of approaches to the study of personality. In this way the technique most suitable for a particular case can readily be used. Yet, especially in the case of projective techniques, it is desirable that the psychologist should gain a good deal of experience with a limited number of tests. A possible battery to be used more frequently than other techniques might consist of the following: Murray's Thematic Apperception Test, the Rosenzweig Picture-Frustration Study, Raven's Controlled Projection Test, Sentence Completion tests and the Bene-Anthony Family Relations Test. In addition, it will usually be of value to administer an appropriate inventory, as such tests take little time and cover much ground. In view of the current pressures on clinical staff, psychologists are likely to make most use of the less time-consuming procedures, but the lengthier approaches may have something to offer where there is an opportunity for studying children in depth.

V RELATING DIAGNOSIS TO TREATMENT

1 Roles of different members of the clinic team

As the facilities for helping maladjusted children develop, there is an increasing need for the roles of the different members of the clinic team to be interpreted with some degree of flexibility. The psychologist, for example, should not be seen solely as an administrator of tests for diagnostic purposes, but as a member of the team who can contribute much to certain forms of treatment, e.g. activity group play therapy, behaviour therapy, or remedial education. Nor is it entirely satisfactory for the social worker in the clinic to confine herself to seeing parents, without some direct knowledge of the children who are the subjects of investigation. Such changes in the roles of child guidance personnel have implications for training which should be carefully considered.

Diagnosis should be thought of as a continuing process in many cases, with a regular feed-back from all who are involved in the treatment of the child. The psychotherapist or remedial teacher, for example, may discover new facts about the child in the process of treatment which may confirm the original diagnosis or lead the team to modify this. Similarly, if a child goes to a special unit for maladjusted children, there should be a continuous reappraisal of the child's condition and needs in the light of new information about him gained by the staff of the unit. In such cases, the teacher has a particularly valuable part to play in that he may see a good deal of the child in a variety of situations, and the teacher of maladjusted pupils needs to be well trained and to have suitable personal qualities (Chazan, 1966); but it is essential that everyone concerned with the child should feel free to contribute to the picture of the child which is gradually being built up.

2 Communication of findings within the clinic and to outside agencies

When several members of staff are concerned with a case, there is always the danger, even in a close-knit unit, that communication between them may not be entirely satisfactory. It will help if each member of staff makes records of his contacts with a child, or members of his family or outside professional workers, in such a form that they are easily comprehensible to colleagues. Furthermore, regular internal case-conferences, time-consuming as these may be, are worth while to ensure that all working are in the same direction and that those members of staff with the most appropriate skills and interest have undertaken the treatment or supervision of the case. It is a useful practice to invite external professional workers (e.g. child care officers, probation officers) involved with the child or his family to participate in such case-conferences. These may not only provide the clinic team with valuable information but serve to give outside workers some insight into the methods of the child guidance service.

It is important, too, for the clinic team not only to ask for information about a child from outside agencies but to feed information gained about a child back to these agencies. It is obvious that it will greatly help the school, the child, and the clinic if the teachers interested in the child are informed of the clinical findings and of the treatment or disposal recommended by the clinic. The document on the school psychological service published by the British Psychological Society (1962) stresses that the psychologist should be careful to communicate information from the clinic which might be helpful to teachers, particularly while a child is receiving treatment, so that teachers may understand variations in behaviour which may result. Through personal discussion between the psychologist and teachers, further insight is gained into the educational and psychological needs of children.

The clinic team will, of course, not wish to disclose highly confidential details of the family history to some outside agencies, but valuable inter-communication can always take place even in such circumstances, provided that the reports transmitted from the clinic are worded in language appropriate to the recipient.

3 Selection of appropriate methods of treatment or disposal

The methods of treatment or disposal employed in the case of maladjusted children will naturally vary according to the school of thought to which the individual members of the clinic team adhere. Most child guidance clinics today, however, look at this problem from a broad frame of reference and consider a wide range of measures which may help the child's adjustment. These may include modifying the attitudes of parents or teachers to the child, direct psychotherapy (individual or group), the use of medication or bringing about a temporary or permanent change of home or school. Most maladjusted children will remain at their usual school and a recommendation that a child should be removed to a special unit for maladjusted pupils will be made only if less drastic measures are thought unlikely to succeed. Similarly, removal from home will be recommended only in extreme circumstances. Where the child is taken away from his normal environment, such a step should not be regarded as a final one, nor a sufficient one without further work with the child's family. As the Underwood Report (1955) pointed out, residential treatment is not likely to be successful unless it is based on a plan which includes the parents as well as the child, and unless consultation is maintained throughout the period that the child is away from home between the authority, the recommending clinic, the parents and the establishment providing the treatment.

In considering long-term psychotherapy for a child, the clinic will usually take into account, as well as its own treatment resources, the child's emotional condition and intellectual level, the circumstances at home and the school situation. Subnormal children may not always be unsuitable for psychotherapy (Neham, 1955; Evans, 1956; Mundy, 1957; Gunzburg, 1965), but most clinics are forced to adopt some kind of system of priorities.

Whatever measures may be instituted, it is important that the parents, and if possible the child himself, should be fully aware of the nature and aims of the recommended treatment.

4 Evaluation of assessment procedures

As Vernon (1964) states, personality diagnosis and assessment is carried out in such varied circumstances and with such varied purposes that there is bound to be considerable subjectivity in interpreting and weighing up the relevance of data obtained from tests, interviews or other methods. It is important, therefore, that a clinic should attempt to evaluate its own assessment procedures by a careful long-term follow-up of at least a sample of cases seen. We need to know far more about the response of particular types of disturbance to particular kinds of treatment, and although practice will vary greatly from place to place, reports from clinics on the validity of diagnostic procedures will help us to arrive at a better evaluation of methods of assessing maladjustment. Although, as previously mentioned, we have had some valuable studies of the effects of treatment, we still know surprisingly little about how children deemed maladjusted adjust to life as older adolescents and adults. Only by well-planned follow-up studies can we begin to assess the efficacy of our diagnostic and treatment procedures.

REFERENCES

ALCOCK, T. (1963) *The Rorschach in Practice*. London: Tavistock Publications.

ANASTASI, A. (1961) *Psychological Testing* (2nd Ed.). New York: Macmillan.

ANDERSON, H. H. and ANDERSON, G. L. (1951) *An Introduction to Projective Techniques*. New Jersey: Prentice Hall, Inc.

ANDRY, R. G. (1960) *Delinquency and Parental Pathology*. London: Methuen.

ANDRY, R. G. (1962) *Paternal and Maternal Roles and Delinquency*. Geneva: W.H.O. Public Health Papers, **14**.

BELFIELD, D. J. (1963) *The social adjustment of most accepted and least accepted children in junior schools*. M.Ed. Thesis, University of Manchester.

BELL, H. M. (1961) *The Adjustment Inventory*. Palo Alto, California: Consulting Psychologists Press, Inc.

BELL, J. E. (1948) *Projective Techniques*. New York: Longmans, Green.

BELLAK, L. and BELLAK, S. S. (1950) *Children's Apperception Test*. New York: C.P.S. Co.

BELLAK, L. (1954) *The Thematic Apperception Test and the Children's Apperception Test in Clinical Use*. New York: Grune and Stratton.

BENE, E. (1957) The objective use of a projective technique, illustrated by a study of the differences in attitudes between pupils of grammar schools and of secondary modern schools. *Brit. J. educ. Psychol.*, **27**, 89-100.

BENE, E. and ANTHONY, J. (1957) *Family Relations Test*. London: N.F.E.R.

BENTON, A. L. (1950) The experimental validation of the Rorschach test. *Brit. J. med. Psychol.*, **23**, 45-58.

BERDIE, R. F. and LAYTON, W. L. (1957) *Minnesota Counseling Inventory*. New York: The Psychological Corporation.

BLUM, G. S. (1950) *The Blacky Pictures*. New York: The Psychological Corporation.

BOGARDUS, E. S. (1925) Measuring social distance. *J. applied Sociol.*, *IX*, **5**, 299-308.

BOWER, E. (1960) *Early Identifications of Emotionally Handicapped Children in School*. Springfield, Illinois: Charles C. Thomas Co.

BRANDON, S. (1960) *An epidemiological study of maladjustment in childhood*. M.D. Thesis, University of Durham.

BRITISH PSYCHOLOGICAL SOCIETY (1962) Document on the School Psychological Service. London: British Psychological Society.

BROWER, D. and ABT, L. E. (1952) *Progress in Clinical Psychology*. New York: Grune and Stratton.

CAMERON, K. (1955) Diagnostic categories in child psychiatry. *Brit. J. med. Psychol.*, **28**, 67-71.

CAMERON, K. (1958) Symptom classification in child psychiatry. *Revue Psychiat. Infantile*, **25**, 241-245.

CASSELL, R. N. (1959) *Test of Social Insight*. New York: Martin M. Bruce.

CASSELL, R. N. and KAHN, T. C. (1961) *Group Personality Projective Test (GPPT)*. *Psychol. Reports*. Monograph Supplement, I-V8.

CASTANEDA, A., MCCANDLESS, B. R. and PALERMO, D. S. (1956) The Children's Form of the Manifest Anxiety Scale. *Child Dev.*, **27**, 317-326.

CATTELL, R. B. and BELOFF, H. (1963) *Junior-Senior High School Personality Questionnaire (HSPQ)*. Illinois: Institute for Personality and Ability Testing.

CATTELL, R. B. and STICE, G. F. (1964) *The Sixteen Personality Factor Question-naire*. Illinois: Institute for Personality and Ability Testing.

CHAZAN, M. (1962a) The relationship between maladjustment and backward-ness. *Educ. Rev.*, **15**, 1, 54-62.

CHAZAN, M. (1962b) School Phobia. *Brit. J. educ. Psychol.*, **32**, 209-217.

CHAZAN, M. (1963) Maladjustment, attainment and sociometric status. *Univ. Coll. of Swansea Faculty of Education Journal*, 4-7.

CHAZAN, M. (1964) The incidence and nature of maladjustment among child-ren in schools for the educationally subnormal. *Brit. J. educ. Psychol.*, **34**, 292-304.

CHAZAN, M. (1965) Factors associated with maladjustment in E.S.N. children. *Brit. J. educ. Psychol.*, **35**, 277-285.

CHAZAN, M. (1966) Teaching maladjusted children. *Univ. Coll. of Swansea Faculty of Ed. J.*, 23-25.

CHAZAN, M. (1968) Inconsequential behaviour in school children. *Brit. J. educ. Psychol.*, **38**, 5-7.

COAN, R. W. and CATTELL, R. B. (1966) *Early School Personality Questionnaire (ESPQ)*. Illinois: Institute for Personality and Ability Testing.

CRONBACH, L. J. (1960) *Essentials of Psychological Testing* (2nd Ed.). New York: Harper and Bros.

CUNNINGHAM, R. *et al* (1951) *Understanding Group Behaviour of Boys and Girls*. New York: Bureau of Publications, Teachers College, Columbia University.

DOUGLAS, J. W. B. (1964) *The Home and the School*. London: MacGibbon and Kee.

DOUGLAS, J. W. B. and MULLIGAN, G. (1961) Emotional adjustment and educa-tional achievement – the preliminary results of a longitudinal study of a national sample of children. *Proc. roy. Soc. Med.*, **54**, 885-891.

EDWARDS, A. L. (1957) *The Social Desirability Variable in Personality Research*. New York: Dryden Press.

EVANS, D. (1956) *An experimental study of a group of seriously-maladjusted E.S.N. children*. M.A. (Education) Thesis, University of Birmingham.

EVANS, K. M. (1962) *Sociometry and Education*. London: Routledge and Kegan Paul.

EYSENCK, H. J. (1947) *Dimensions of Personality*. London: Routledge & Kegan Paul.

EYSENCK, H. J. (1957) *The Dynamics of Hysteria and Anxiety*. London: Routledge and Kegan Paul.

EYSENCK, H. J. (1959) *Maudsley Personality Inventory*. London: University of London Press.

EYSENCK, H. J. (1960) *The Structure of Human Personality*. London: Methuen.

EYSENCK, H. J. and EYSENCK, SYBIL B. G. (1964) *Eysenck Personality Inventory*. London: University of London Press.

EYSENCK, H. J. and RACHMAN, S. J. (1965a) The application of learning theory to child psychiatry. *In* HOWELLS, J. G. (Ed.) *Modern Perspectives in Child Psychiatry*. London: Oliver and Boyd.

EYSENCK, H. J. and RACHMAN, S. J. (1965b) *The Causes and Cures of Neurosis*. London: Routledge and Kegan Paul.

EYSENCK, S. (1965a) *Junior Eysenck Personality Inventory*. London: University of London Press.

EYSENCK, S. (1965b) A new scale for personality measurement in children. *Brit. J. educ. Psychol.*, **35**, 362-367.

FAIRBAIRN, W. R. D. (1952) *Psycho-Analytic Studies of the Personality*. London: Tavistock Publications.

FOULDS, G. A. (1951) Temperamental differences in maze performance. *Brit. J. Psychol.*, **42**, 209-217.

FREUD, A. (1962) Assessment of child disturbances. *Psychoanal. Study Child*, **17**, 149-158.

FURNEAUX, W. D. and GIBSON, H. B. (1961) A children's personality inventory designed to measure neuroticism and extraversion. *Brit. J. educ. Psychol.*, **31**, 204-207.

GIBSON, H. B. (1961) *Gibson Spiral Maze*. London: University of London Press.

GIBSON, H. B. (1964) The Spiral Maze: a psychomotor test with implications for the study of delinquency. *Brit. J. Psychol.*, **54**, 219-255.

GIBSON, H. B. (1967) Teachers' ratings of schoolboys' behaviour related to patterns of scores on the new Junior Maudsley Inventory. *Brit. J. educ. Psychol.*, **37**, 347-355.

GRAHAM, P. (1967) Perceiving disturbed children. *Spec. Educ.*, **56**, 29-33.

GRONLUND, N. E. (1959) *Sociometry in the Classroom*. New York: Harper and Bros.

GUNZBURG, H. C. (1965) Psychotherapy with the feeble-minded. *In* CLARKE, A. M. and CLARKE, A. D. B. (Eds.) *Mental Deficiency: the Changing Outlook* (2nd Ed.). London: Methuen.

HAAS, R. B. and MORENO, J. L. (1951) Psychodrama as a projective technique. *In* ANDERSON and ANDERSON (1951).

HARROWER, M. R. and STEINER, M. A. (1951) *Large Scale Rorschach Techniques*. Springfield, Illinois.

HARTWELL, S. W., HUTT, M. L., GWEN, A. and WALTON, R. E. (1951) The Michigan Picture Test: diagnostic and therapeutic possibilities of a new projective test for children. *Amer. J. Orthopsychiat.*, **21**, 124-137.

HEWITT, L. E. and JENKINS, R. L. (1946) *Fundamental Patterns of Maladjustment: the Dynamics of their Origin*. Illinois: Green.

HIMMELWEIT, H. T. and PETRIE, A. (1951) The measurement of personality in children. *Brit. J. educ. Psychol.*, **21**, 9-29.

HORROCKS, J. E. (1964) *Assessment of Behavior*. Columbus, Ohio: Charles E. Merrill Books, Inc.

HOWELLS, J. G. and LICKORISH, J. R. (1962) *Family Relations Indicator*. London: N.F.E.R.

JACKSON, L. (1952) *Test of Family Attitudes*. London: Methuen.

KAHN, T. C. and GIFFEN, M. B. (1960) *Psychological Techniques in Diagnosis and Evaluation*. Oxford: Pergamon Press.

KANNER, L. (1948) *Child Psychiatry* (2nd Ed.). Oxford: Blackwell Scientific Publications.

KLOPFER, B. *et al.* (1954) *Developments in the Rorschach Technique*, Vol. I. New York: World Books.

KLOPFER, B. *et al.* (1956) *Developments in the Rorschach Technique*, Vol. II. New York: World Books.

KLOPFER, B. and KELLEY, D. M. (1946) *The Rorschach Technique*. New York: World Books.

LINDZEY, G. (1961) *Projective Techniques and Cross-Cultural Research*. New York: Appleton-Century-Crofts.

LOVELL, K. (1958) *Educational Psychology and Children*. London: University of London Press.

LOWENFELD, M. (1929) *Mosaic Test*. London: Badger Tests Co. Ltd.

MACFARLANE, J. W., ALLEN, L. and HONZIK, M. P. (1954) *A Developmental Study of the Behaviour Problems of Normal Children between Twenty-one Months and Fourteen Years*. University of California Publications on Child Development, 2. Berkeley: University of California Press.

MINISTRY OF EDUCATION (1955) *Committee on Maladjusted Children* (*The Underwood Report*). London: H.M.S.O.

MITCHELL, S. (1965) *A study of the mental health of school children in an English county*. Unpublished Ph.D. Thesis, University of London.

MITCHELL, S. and SHEPHERD, M. (1966) A comparative study of children's behaviour at home and at school. *Brit. J. educ. Psychol.*, **36**, 248-254.

MOONEY, R. L. and GORDON, L. V. (1950) *The Mooney Problem Check Lists*. New York: The Psychological Corporation.

MOORE, T. (1966) Difficulties of the ordinary child in adjusting to primary school. *J. child Psychol. Psychiat.*, **7**, 17-38.

MOORE, T. and UCKO, L. E. (1961) Four to six: constructiveness and conflict in meeting doll-play problems. *J. child Psychol. Psychiat.*, **2**, 21-47.

MORRIS, D. P., SOROKER, E. and BURRUS, J. (1957) Follow-up studies of shy, withdrawn children: evaluation of later adjustment. *Amer. J. Psychiat.*, **24**, 743-754.

MORRIS, H. M., ESCOLL, P. J. and WEXLER, R. (1956) Aggressive behaviour-disorders of childhood: a follow-up study. *Amer. J. Psychiat.*, **112**, 991-997.

MORRIS, J. (1966) *Standards and Progress in Reading*. London: N.F.E.R.

MULLIGAN, G., DOUGLAS, J. W. B., HAMMOND, W. A. and TIZARD, J. (1963) Delinquency and symptoms of maladjustment: the findings of a longitudinal study. *Proc. roy. Soc. Med.*, **56**, 1083-1086.

MUNDY, L. (1957) Therapy with physically and mentally handicapped children in a mental deficiency hospital. *J. clin. Psychol.*, **13**, 3-9.

MURRAY, H. A. (1943) *Thematic Apperception Test*. Harvard Univ. Press.

MURRAY, H. A. (1938) *Explorations in Personality*. New York: Oxford University Press.

NEHAM, S. (1955) Psychotherapy in relation to mental deficiency. *Amer. J. ment. Defic.*, **60**, 557-572.

O'CONNOR, N. and FRANKS, C. (1960) Childhood upbringing and other environmental factors. *In* EYSENCK, H. J. (Ed.) *Handbook of Abnormal Psychology*. London: Pitman.

OLSON, W. C. (1930) *Problem Tendencies in Children: A Method for Measurement and Description*. Minneapolis: University of Minnesota Press.

O'NEAL, P. and ROBINS, L. N. (1958) The relation of childhood behaviour problems to adult psychiatric status: a 30 year follow-up study of 150 subjects. *Amer. J. Psychiat.*, **114**, 961-969.

PETRIE, I. R. J. (1962) Residential treatment of maladjusted children: a study of some factors related to progress in adjustment. *Brit. J. educ. Psychol.*, **32**, 29-37.

PHILLIPSON, H. (1955) *Object Relations Technique*. London: Tavistock Publications.

PINTNER, R., LOFTUS, J., FORLANO, G. and ALSTER, B. (1938) *Aspects of Personality*. New York: World Books.

POLLACK, O. (1956) *Integrating Sociological and Psychological Concepts*. New York: Russell Sage Foundation.

PORTER, R. B. and CATTELL, R. B. (1963) *Children's Personality Questionnaire (CPQ)*. Illinois: Institute for Personality and Ability Testing.

PORTEUS, S. D. (1942) *Qualitative Performance in the Maze Test*. Vineland, N.J.: Smith Printing House.

PORTEUS, S. D. (1959) *The Maze Test and Clinical Psychology*. Palo Alto, California: Pacific Books.

PRINGLE, M. L. KELLMER, BUTLER, N. R. and DAVIE, R. (1966) *11,000 Seven-Year-Olds*. London: Longmans.

RABIN, A. I. and HAWORTH, M. R. (1960) *Projective Techniques with Children*. New York: Grune and Stratton.

RAVEN, J. C. (1951) *Controlled Projection for Children* (2nd Ed.). London: H. K. Lewis.

ROGERS, C. R. (1961) *Personal Adjustment Inventory*. New York: Association Press.

ROHDE, A. R. and HILDRETH, C. (1940) *Sentence Completions*. New York: The Psychological Corporation.

ROSENZWEIG, S. (1948) *The Children's Form of the Rosenzweig Picture-Frustration Study*. Psychology Laboratory, Western State Psychiatric Institute and Clinic.

ROSS, A. O., LACEY, H. M. and PARTON, D. A. (1965). The development of a behaviour checklist for boys. *Child Dev.*, **36**, 1013-1027.

ROTTER, J. B. and RAFFERTY, J. E. (1950) *Manual for the Rotter Incomplete Sentences Blank, College Form*. New York: The Psychological Corporation.

RUTTER, M. (1965) Classification and categorization in child psychiatry. *J. child Psychol. Psychiat.*, **6**, 71-83.

RUTTER, M. (1966) Prognosis: psychotic children in adolescence and early adult life. *In* WING, J. K. (Ed.) *Early Childhood Autism: Clinical, Educational and Social Aspects*. Oxford: Pergamon Press.

RUTTER, M. (1967) A children's behaviour questionnaire for completion by teachers: preliminary findings. *J. child Psychol. Psychiat.*, **8**, 1-11.

RUTTER, M. and GRAHAM, P. (1966) Psychiatric disorder in 10- and 11-year-old children. *Proc. roy. Soc. Med.*, **59**, 382-387.

RYLE, A., POND, D. A. and HAMILTON, M. (1965) The prevalence and patterns of psychological disturbance in children of primary age. *J. child Psychol. Psychiat.*, **6**, 101-113.

SAMPSON, O. (1966) Reading and adjustment: a review of the literature. *Educ. Res.*, **8**, 184-190.

SARASON, S. B. (1954) *The Clinical Interaction with Special Reference to the Rorschach*. New York: Harper and Bros.

SARASON, S. B. *et al.* (1960) *Anxiety in Elementary School Children: A Report of Research*. New York: Wiley.

SAVAGE, R. D. (1966) Measuring Children's Abilities. *Spec. Educ.*, **55**, 27-30.

SCHNEIDMAN, E. S. (1947) *Make a Picture Story (MAPS)*. New York: Psychological Corporation.

SCHONELL, F. J. (1952) The development of educational research in Great Britain. Pt. VII: Maladjusted pupils. *Brit. J. educ. Psychol.*, **22**, 30-44.

SCOTT, W. S. (1959) Definitions of mental health and illness. *In* GORLOW, L. and KATKOVSKY, W. (Eds.) *Readings in the Psychology of Adjustment*. New York: McGraw-Hill.

SCOTTISH EDUCATION DEPARTMENT (1964) *Ascertainment of Maladjusted Children*. Edinburgh: H.M.S.O.

SHAW, H. (1954) A study of popular and unpopular children. *Educ. Rev.*, **6**, 208-220.

SLAVSON, S. R. (1952) *Child Psychotherapy*. New York: Columbia University Press.

SLOTKIN, J. S. (1959) Culture and psychopathology. *In* GORLOW, L. and KATKOVSKY, W. (Eds.) *Readings in the Psychology of Adjustment*. New York: McGraw-Hill.

STOTT, D. H. (1961) *Delinquency Prediction Instrument*. London: University of London Press.

STOTT, D. H. (1963; 3rd ed. 1966) *The Social Adjustment of Children (Manual to the Bristol Social Adjustment Guides)*. London: University of London Press.

STOTT, D. H. (1966) *Studies of Troublesome Children*. London: Tavistock Publications.

U

STOTT, D. H. (1967) *Manual to the Systematic Interview Guides* (*No. 1. Birth to Five Years; No. 2. Prenatal Period*). London: University of London Press.

SYMONDS, P. M. (1948) *Symonds Picture Story Test*. New York: Teachers College, Columbia University.

SYMONDS, P. M. (1949) *Adolescent Fantasy*. New York: Columbia University Press.

TAYLOR, J. A. (1953) A personality scale of manifest anxiety. *J. abnorm. soc. Psychol.*, **48**, 285-290.

THORPE, L. P., CLARK, W. W. and TIEGS, E. W. (1953) *California Test of Personality*. California Test Bureau.

TINDALL, R. H. (1959) Relationships among measures of adjustment. *In* GORLOW, L. and KATKOVSKY, W. (Eds) *Readings in the Psychology of Adjustment*. New York: McGraw-Hill.

UCKO, L. E. and MOORE, T. (1963) Parental roles as seen by young children in doll play. *Vita Humana*, **6**, 213-242.

VERNON, P. E. (1964) *Personality Assessment*. London: Methuen and Co.

WALKER, A. (1955) *Pupils' School Records: A Survey of the Nature and Use of Cumulative School Records in England and Wales*. N.F.E.R. Publications No. 8. London: Newnes.

WARBURTON, F. W. (1961) The Measurement of Personality, I. *Educ. Res.*, **4**, 2-17.

WESTBY, G. (1959) Review of Object Relations Technique (Phillipson, H., 1955). *In* BUROS, O. K. (Ed.) *The Fifth Mental Measurements Yearbook*. New Jersey: The Gryphon Press.

WILLIAMS, MOYRA (1965) *Mental Testing in Clinical Practice*. Oxford: Pergamon Press.

WOLTMANN, A. G. (1951) The use of puppetry as a projective method in therapy. *In* ANDERSON, H. H. and ANDERSON, G. L. (1951).

19

Culturally handicapped children

A. T. Ravenette

I INTRODUCTION

The implications of social class membership for the development of intelligence have only recently, i.e. within the last decade, become a serious research issue. In America the rise of new technologies and, in this country, the development of political ideas of equal opportunity, seem to have been the major influences behind this interest. There seems to have been less impetus from within the fields of education or of academic psychology. It is difficult to define the reasons for the educationists' lack of concern except, perhaps, to suggest that education has tended to be traditionally minded and that the 1944 Education Act, which stated the aim of 'education according to age, aptitude and ability' provided the basis for another set of traditions. It was, of course, true that educationists saw 'ability' as the intelligence which was measured from performance on paper and pencil tests. After all, psychologists had guaranteed the reliability and validity of such tests and, pragmatically, these tests seemed to serve the purpose for which they had been designed.

The lack of interest shown by academic psychologists seems largely to have stemmed from the great concern with 'factor analytic' models of the structure of intelligence (Vernon, 1950). The controversies which arose from the use of different factor analytic approaches obscured the central issue of what exactly is meant by cognitive growth and what is the nature of the forces which hinder or accelerate growth. Underlying this controversy there seemed to be an apparent satisfaction with the notion that intelligence was primarily determined by heredity factors and, that being the case, little could be done about it except measure and analyse the structure in which intelligence was manifest across large populations of individuals.

It is not, perhaps, surprising that the work of Piaget (Flavell, 1963) made little impact on psychologists or educationists until the 1950s, despite the fact that he was concerned with the nature and development of cognitive processes. His methods were neither easily quantifiable nor standardizable. He worked extensively with small numbers of children, each seen individually, so that such research was bound to be expensive and time consuming. His experimental techniques could not easily be transformed into pencil and paper tests and thus were not practical for the group testing of large numbers of children. Even as late as Flavell's (1963) extensive review of Piaget's work, however, there seems to have been little or no research on Piagetian lines into the effect of social class membership on the development of intelligence. Neither the terms 'social class' nor 'socio-economic status' even appear in the index of Flavell's book.

The theoretical ideas underlying the most recent work on social class and intelligence stem from a re-appraisal of the role of experience in setting either limits or opportunities for intellectual growth. Hunt (1961) provides a stimulating biographical history of cognitive studies and cognitive theories, but even he seems little concerned with social class issues. The major influence, however, has come from new thinking about the role of language in cognitive development. Luria and Yudovich (1959) and Luria (1961) clearly see language as the most important skill both for the regulation of behaviour and for the ability to understand and cope with the environment. Language in fact becomes a mediator between the individual and his world of objects and of people. Vygotsky (1962) spells out very effectively the relationship between thought and language and suggests some developmental lines which are essential if the child is to acquire adequate mental ability to master the many problems with which he will be confronted. The linguists Sapir (1933) and Whorf (1956) had already suggested that the language which an individual uses will, in part, determine what he sees and understands. Carroll (1958) argued that language provides a lattice through which the world is perceived and, like all lattices, reveals some aspects but hides others. An understanding of the role and importance of language must now be considered essential if we are to understand cognitive growth and cognitive performance.

In this country a watershed was reached when Bernstein (1959), a sociologist interested in social class and language, put forward the idea that the two major social classes, middle and working, could be characterized by distinctive linguistic styles or linguistic codes. More important than the recognition of this difference was an awareness that the linguistic code might itself be a means of helping or hindering cognitive development. In fact, Bernstein was responsible for bringing together the ideas of the linguists, the psycho-linguists and the Russian psychologists. He applied this synthesis to problems of sociology and subsequently to problems which involved psychology and education. The work which has stemmed from this way of thinking is as yet only small in quantity, partly because it is expensive to carry out and also because it is very time consuming. The potential, however, for educationists and for psychologists is very great.

It is the aim of this chapter to report some of the earlier cognitive studies related to social class, but not related to language, then to present Bernstein's formal statement of linguistic codes, together with some of its implications. The next section will deal with studies which, following Bernstein, are concerned with the pattern, as opposed to the level, of ability of working-class children, and the following section will be concerned with changes in cognitive status. The subsequent section will present evidence directly related to linguistic differences and the final section will attempt a broader look at the topic.

Some comment needs to be made about the expression 'culturally handicapped'.

The label has many variants – 'disadvantaged', 'culturally disadvantaged' and so on – but whatever the label it contains a number of value judgements, the most important being that, in some ways, children who are culturally handicapped are inferior to those who are not. It is, of course, true that most of the evidence shows that children from working-class backgrounds do not develop educationally and cognitively in the same way as middle-class children, but this could equally well arise from failures in the educational system rather than from inherent defects in a working-class child. This alternative interpretation of the evidence is now becoming increasingly recognized as having some validity (c.f. the Newsom Report, 1963, and the Plowden Report, 1967) but it is unfortunately true that the question has not been asked whether or not there are ways in which working-class children may be better adjusted and more effective members of society than middle-class children. The criteria which are used seem to be those of the middle class and there is no absolute reason why these should always be the best. That aside, for the purpose of this chapter, 'culturally handicapped' children are deemed to be children of lower working-class parents. It must be remembered, however, that not all such children fail to measure up to middle-class standards when they grow into adulthood. What is reported represents consistent trends within populations, not hard facts about individual children.

II STUDIES OF SOCIAL CLASS AND ABILITY WHICH ARE UNRELATED TO CONSIDERATIONS OF LANGUAGE

Sarason and Gladwin (1958), writing about mental subnormality, give a fairly considerable review of intelligence and cultural background. Some of the studies they quote have now become textbook classics, e.g. Sherman and Key (1932), Wheeler (1932) and Asher (1935). The general finding in these studies is that children in isolated parts of the U.S.A. show low I.Q.s on standardized tests of intelligence. Retesting of the same population at a later date also showed a relative decline in test scores. The most interesting comparative study is Wheeler's (1942) repeated investigation of his population (East Tennessee mountain children) 10 years later. He then found that the test scores at all grades were higher than were test scores for comparable grades 10 years previously. More important, however, he found that on each occasion of testing the I.Q. declined progressively with age. In other words, these children failed to develop at the same pace as children in more favoured areas.

Even earlier in this country Gordon (1923) found that canal children were inferior in ability to children brought up in more normal surroundings. Re-testing by Gaw (1925), however, using performance tests, showed that these children were impaired by some 12 points on the Binet Simon Test with which they had first been tested. In other words, these children were impaired when tested with a more verbal type of test.

These studies are concerned with extreme groups with well-defined social and geographical features and not with subcultures in apparently homogeneous areas. The largest single study of *social* class differences in cognitive ability is by Eells *et al.* (1951).

They tested some 5,000 children in one township in the U.S.A. using two verbal and two or three non-verbal tests at the ages of 9-10 years and 13-14 years. They were concerned to investigate the relationship between socio-economic status and various aspects of cognitive ability. They found intercorrelations varying from 0·02 to 0·43 depending on the tests, and mean differences in I.Q. from 8 to 23 points. The overlap between different socio-economic divisions, however, was considerable. The main status differentials were largest for verbal items and least for pictorial, geometric and stylized drawing items. Their major conclusion was that 'variations in opportunity for familiarity with cultural words, objects or processes required for answering test items seem to the writer to appear as the most adequate general explanation of the findings'.

Despite this extensive research operation, the next step was to attempt the development of 'culture-free' tests as though it was the test instruments which had been investigated, not the children who comprised the population (cf. also Stodoltsky and Lesser, 1967).

Fraser (1959) in Scotland was interested in the relationship between home background, school attainment and intelligence. She found that various features in the family background showed positive correlations of 0·752 and 0·659 with both school attainment and verbal intelligence. She makes the point, however, that had non-verbal tests been used the correlation with intelligence would probably have been far less.

A study which requires rather full comment is by Crawford (reported in Mays, 1962). The main aim of her work was to investigate the relationship between reading attainment and intelligence for children aged 6 years 10 months to 8 years 9 months who attended schools in Liverpool. Seven hundred and ninety children comprised the sample (3·29% of the total population) which was subdivided according to the postal district, which in turn was related to the social class of the inhabitants. The key area with respect to the lower working class was the Crown Street area (postal districts 7 and 8). The measure of intelligence used was the Terman Merrill Scale Form L (Terman and Merrill, 1937) administered by a team of specially trained teachers aided by two specialist remedial teachers.

The mean overall I.Q. was 104·39. The mean I.Q.s within the various postal districts ranged from 95·21 to 132·25, but the sample sizes for these areas also varied from 4 to 93. Children within the Crown Street area (36 children) had a mean I.Q. of 100·05. Crawford draws the following conclusion:

> If they are handicapped in education by their poor cultural environment, which is to some extent taken for granted rather than established, they should have been handicapped in their performance on the Terman Merrill Intelligence Tests. The average I.Q. of 100 suggests that they have not been so handicapped and the wide range of I.Q. found within the group of thirty-six

children would confirm this suggestion. It seems to the writer that there is no real evidence of cultural handicapping for the majority of children to justify the generally low proportion of children selected for selective secondary education at the age of 11 years.

Whilst the facts are not in dispute, they are only understandable within a framework of questions. If the initial hypothesis has been that these children were not handicapped, the answer which was found might be considered satisfactory. If, however, the hypothesis had been that these children were handicapped, the answer would be the starting-point for a series of new questions. Some of these can be stated.

Is the Terman Merrill Scale adequately standardized? One answer to this question has been provided by Jones (1962), who compared W.I.S.C. (Wechsler, 1949) and Terman Merrill I.Q.s for a North London population. Her sample may have been slightly under-representative of lower-class children (Maxwell, 1960), but the mean Terman Merrill I.Q. was not 100 but 114·9. By contrast, the W.I.S.C. mean I.Q. was 106·4. Perhaps the Terman Merrill standardization was unsatisfactory. A second question concerns the content of the Terman Merrill Scale. The items are a mixed bag of pictorial, memory, performance and verbal tests. The verbal items become more and more important with increasing age, especially after the age of 7 years. Was there any pattern of differential success and failure with the Crown Street sample such that differential handicapping could be assessed? No such analysis was made.

Is a scale such as the Terman Merrill subtle enough, or discriminating enough, to be sensitive to differential handicap? Six questions to represent one year of mental age is a very small sample of potential ability for drawing conclusions about cultural handicap.

Since Crawford's primary concern was with reading and intelligence, for which her sample may have been adequate, her findings about social class were, to a great extent, incidental. She had not set out to investigate this particular problem and consequently it might have been wiser to have drawn more cautious conclusions from the limited data at her disposal. On the other hand, her results could provide a good basis for repeated assessment on more detailed measures of cognitive ability at a later stage in order to see if her predictions for children aged 7 to 9 years were justified.

The final study to be reported in this section is that by Wiseman (1964), as published in the Plowden Report (1967). Wiseman was not primarily concerned with cognitive ability but with the relationship between a wide variety of variables concerned with home, school and children's ability as measured on a variety of tests of intelligence and attainment. He isolated two groups of children: those characterized by brightness (I.Q. >115) and those characterized by dullness (I.Q. <85), and factor analysed his data for these groups separately. It is not a wise procedure to separate the intelligence measures from the complex of data which Wiseman presents. His conclusions, however, are interesting. Both for backwardness and brightness, factors associated with the home and the neighbourhood are more important (as determined by size of correlation) than factors associated with schools. Of these factors, paternal interest was associated with brightness and lack of maternal care with backwardness.

This study was a major undertaking, involving the study of 87 variables. It is, however, primarily of educational rather than psychological interest and seems to have been planned as a survey rather than as a test of hypotheses.

In summary, it is worth quoting Sarason and Gladwin (1958), who make the following criticism of most studies to the time of their writing:

> With a few notable exceptions more effort has been expended on establishing that I.Q. varies with, for example, social class, than has been devoted to finding out why lower class children test lower. Even where reasons have been sought, the focus has commonly been on the test situation – motivation, speed, competitiveness, comprehension and the like – rather than upon the kinds of thinking which on the one hand are necessary to solve test problems, and on the other are likely to be learned in various environmental contexts. We thus find available for both retarded and standard populations a wide array of correlations between the I.Q. and almost any other factor imaginable, but in these studies one finds few hints as to specific causal relations.

III THE LINGUISTIC APPROACH – BERNSTEIN'S ARGUMENT

The great merit of Bernstein's approach is that it suggests a link between environmental factors and the ability to solve some of those problems which comprise tests of intelligence. He recognizes two major speech codes, the 'restricted' and the 'elaborated'. The former is held to characterize the verbal communications in close-knit communities, e.g. the family, clubs and the armed forces. The essence of these situations is that in each there exist strong feelings of common identity, common purpose and common aspirations. Under these circumstances a single word will carry a wealth of unspoken meaning which does not need to be verbally explicated. The meaning, in fact, is often carried by the gesture or intonation, not by the semantic meaning of the word. The linguistic code which is generated in such circumstances is called 'restricted' and has the following characteristics (quoted from Bernstein, 1960):

(1) Short, grammatically simple sentences with poor syntactic form.
(2) Simple and repetitive use of conjunctions ('so', 'then' and 'because').
(3) Little use of subordinate clauses to break down the initial categories of the dominant subject.
(4) Inability to hold a subject through a speech sequence, so that a dislocated informational content is facilitated.
(5) Rigid and limited use of adjectives and adverbs.
(6) Infrequent use of impersonal pronouns as subjects of conditional clauses or sentences.
(7) Frequent use of statements where reason and conclusion are confounded to produce a categoric statement.

(8) A large number of statement/phrases which signal a requirement for the previous speech sequence to be reinforced: 'Wouldn't it?', 'You see?', 'You know', etc. This process is called sympathetic circularity.

(9) Individual selection from a group of idiomatic phrases or sequences will frequently occur.

(10) The individual qualification is implicit in the sentence organization: it is a language of implicit meaning.

An elaborated code will be generated in circumstances where common aspiration, common identity and common purpose are not taken for granted. In such situations the speaker has to make clear his point of view as he cannot know if the listener will share it. He must attempt to clarify his meaning by the use of verbal modifiers (adverbs, adjectives, clauses, etc.) in order to communicate with some precision just what his meaning is. The characteristics of an 'elaborated code' are:

(1) Accurate grammatical order and syntax regulate what is said.

(2) Logical modifications and stress are mediated through a grammatically complex sentence construction, especially through the use of a range of conjunctions and subordinate clauses.

(3) Frequent use of prepositions which indicate logical relationships as well as propositions which indicate spacial and temporal continuity.

(4) Frequent use of impersonal pronouns 'it' and 'one'.

(5) A discriminative selection of adjectives and adverbs.

(6) Individual qualification is verbally mediated through the structure and relationships within and between sentences.

(7) Expressive symbolism discriminates between meanings within speech sequences rather than reinforcing dominant words or phrases, or accompanying the sequence in a diffuse generalized manner.

(8) It is a language which points to the possibilities inherent in a complex conceptual hierarchy for the organizing of experience.

It is Bernstein's contention that the nature of working-class family life and working-class culture is of the sort that will tend to generate a 'restricted' and not an 'elaborated' code. Life in middle-class families, on the other hand, will make it possible for both codes to be generated, and therefore available to the children. In fact, observation of middle-class mothers talking to their children will demonstrate that the teaching of the 'elaborated' code is part of the normal communication process. Observation of working-class mothers demonstrates that, if anything, they frequently inhibit the development of an 'elaborated' code by using categorical rather than logical reasons, and appeals to accepted authorities rather than appeals to the person. Further evidence on this will be presented in a later section.

An important implication of these codes is that the 'elaborated' code is quite clearly related to verbal ability and verbal intelligence. Bernstein argues that

U*

the 'restricted' language user will tend to be relatively impaired on verbal tests rather than on non-verbal tests of intelligence. More specifically, if working-class children tend to be limited to a 'restricted' code, then they will tend to be impaired on verbal tests as opposed to non-verbal. Moreover, since verbal tests involve the progressive development of verbal ability, i.e. the progressive elaboration of verbal codes, working-class children will appear, in comparison with middle-class children, to show a cumulative deficit in verbal ability, but not necessarily in non-verbal ability. This is a very important argument since the issue is not one of general intelligence but rather of a pattern of ability and the differential growth of ability.

If there is any validity in Bernstein's argument, it is necessary to show that there are differences in the linguistic usage of different social classes and also that the apparent intellectual impairment of working-class children is not total but differential.

IV   THE PATTERN OF ABILITY OF WORKING-CLASS CHILDREN

1 Late adolescent boys

Bernstein (1960) examined the problem of differential ability by testing a sample of 45 middle-class boys attending a Public School and 61 working-class boys attending day-release classes. The age-range was from 15 to 18 years. Verbal ability was measured by the Mill Hill Vocabulary Test and non-verbal ability by the Progressive Matrices Test.

Extrapolating raw scores to I.Q. equivalents for an age of 16 years it was found that the mean non-verbal P.M. I.Q. for middle-class boys was 8-10 points higher than the mean for the working-class boys, but the mean for the Mill Hill I.Q.s was 23-24 points higher for the middle-class boys, i.e. a difference three times as large. Moreover, as many as 60% of the working-class boys had non-verbal I.Q.s over 110, but not one of them had a verbal I.Q. over 109. In the middle-class sample, the proportion of boys at each level of ability on both tests was substantially the same.

The results justify the conclusion that, for this particular sample, a different relationship between verbal and non-verbal ability obtains – a difference characterized by relatively impaired verbal ability in the working-class sample.

2 Secondary school boys and girls

Ravenette (1963), following Bernstein's lead, set out to test the hypothesis that, in a working-class population, secondary school children would show relatively impaired verbal ability in comparison with non-verbal ability. A subsidiary hypothesis was that the impairment would increase with age, but the evidence in connection with this hypothesis will be presented in the next section.

The sample comprised West Ham children born in October 1947, 1948 and 1949. At the time of testing they were aged $12\frac{1}{2}$, $13\frac{1}{2}$, and $14\frac{1}{2}$ years. This

Borough is populated almost completely by working-class families – the most optimistic estimate for middle-class residents would be no more than 10%.

The tests used were the Verbal and Perceptual Tests from the Morrisby Differential Test Battery (1955) and the control population was provided by the population on which the tests were standardized. It is a most important characteristic of these two tests that the cognitive operations which are being tested are strictly comparable between the two tests, the difference being that, in the verbal tests, words provide the elements for the problems, and in the perceptual tests, non-symbolic drawings. Moreover, the tests have standardization data for each year group of the test population.

The overall results are given in Table 19·1, from which it can be seen that verbal scores are significantly lower than perceptual scores at each age range

| | | BOYS | | | | |
Age	*N*	*Mean V*	*Mean P*	*Mean Diff.*	*t*	*p*
12½	82	89·4	94·6	5·2	2·94	<0·01
13½	77	93·0	97·6	4·6	4·01	<0·001
14½	126	94·4	99·2	4·8	4·65	<0·001
		GIRLS				
12½	97	92·8	101·2	8·4	7·32	<0·001
13½	118	90·3	98·0	7·7	7·73	<0·001
14½	102	91·2	97·3	6·1	5·95	<0·001

V = Verbal test.
P = Perceptual test.

TABLE 19.1
Verbal and perceptual I.Q.s of working-class
children by age and sex.

and for both sexes. The inclusion of non-readers and poor readers can be an embarrassment since it is not known whether their scores reflect low reading ability or low test ability. Using Head Teachers' assessments of reading ability, poor readers were omitted for one analysis but the only effect of this was at the 12½-year level for boys, when the differences between verbal and perceptual scores were no longer significantly different, although the discrepancy was in the predicted direction.

A comparison of boys' scores with girls' scores showed that at the 12½-year level the girls' perceptual scores were higher than the boys' (p <0·01), but at the 14½-year level boys' verbal scores were higher than the girls' (p <0·05). Overall, the girls showed a greater verbal deficit than the boys (p <0·05).

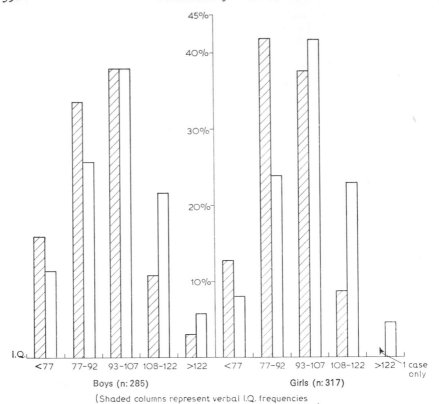

(Shaded columns represent verbal I.Q. frequencies
Open columns represent perceptual I.Q. frequencies)

FIGURE 19.1

Distribution of verbal and perceptual I.Q.s.

A mean difference is useful, but it is an inadequate statistic for showing the complexity of the results. This can best be shown by three other analyses.

One such analysis involves the distribution of scores and this is presented in Figure 19·1. The most noteworthy feature is the dearth of high scores on the verbal test. This is far more marked for girls than for boys.

Verbal score	Higher by 7 or more	Higher by 3-6	Within 2 points	Lower by 3-6	7-10	11 or more
Boys	0·68	10·9	51·5	29·8	7·1	—
Girls	0·63	5·0	51·7	36·3	5·7	0·63

4 points of Scaled score = 15 points of I.Q. score.

TABLE 19.2

Summary of the distribution of discrepancy scores (percentages).

A different measure is given by an examination of the distribution of difference or discrepancy scores (i.e. verbal score – perceptual score). This is shown in Table 19·2.

It would be the normal expectation for these discrepancy scores to be distributed symmetrically about the mean, but this table shows the heavy balance

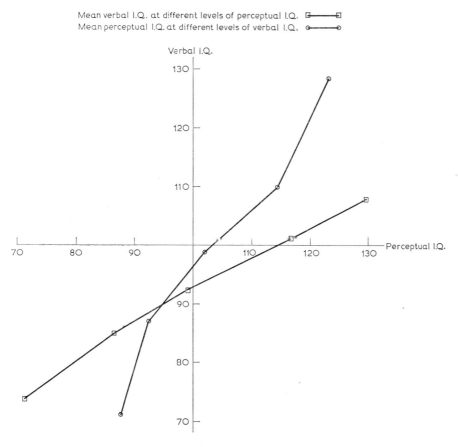

Mean verbal I.Q. at different levels of perceptual I.Q. ▭——▭
Mean perceptual I.Q. at different levels of verbal I.Q. ◦——◦

FIGURE 19.2

Calculated regression lines for verbal/perceptual data.

in the direction of discrepancies where the perceptual score is higher. Once again, the girls show up as being more seriously impaired than the boys.

A third analysis involves determining the average verbal score for different levels of perceptual ability and average perceptual scores for different levels of verbal ability. This analysis is presented graphically in Figure 19·2.

The most striking features which this graph demonstrates are, first, the regular increase in the decline of verbal score at successive levels of perceptual ability and, secondly, the fact that, at the highest level of verbal ability (I.Q.

124 and above), the mean perceptual I.Q. is 22 points lower. This is a surprising replication, at a lower age level, of Bernstein's finding previously reported.

Summing up these results, it can be said that this sample of secondary school children consistently shows non-verbal ability which is superior to verbal ability, that girls show a relatively greater deficit of verbal ability than do boys, and finally that the verbal ability deficit increases steadily with increasing non-verbal ability.

3 Primary and preschool children

There is, as yet, little evidence concerning the pattern of cognitive ability of working-class primary school children. Douglas (1964) suggests that between the ages of 8 years and 11 years there is a slight differential deterioration in the verbal as opposed to the non-verbal ability of these children, but his researches were not designed to investigate this particular question and his test instruments at the ages of 8 years and 11 years were not comparable.

At the preschool level, Hindley (1965) studied the cognitive development of infants at the age of 6 months, 18 months, 3 years and 5 years. At the two earliest ages the Ruth Griffiths Scale was used and at the later ages the Terman Merrill Form L Intelligence Scale. For the purposes of this chapter the·important findings were that measured ability and social class were positively and significantly correlated at ages 3 and 5 years, more markedly for girls than for boys. In other words, the social class differences in ability which have already been reported at higher age levels appear quite strongly in the preschool age-group. Unfortunately, however, it is methodologically difficult to demonstrate a differential pattern of ability at this age.

The Sociological Research Unit of the London Institute of Education (under the direction of Professor Bernstein) has been carrying out investigations of middle- and working-class infant school children, but the results of these researches are not yet available. Informal communication with Gahagan, who was involved with the work, suggests that there is evidence of patterns of ability which differentiate between middle- and working-class children even at the ages of 5 years and 6 years. The test instrument has been the W.I.S.C., but since the floor of this test is 5 years, the scale is of rather doubtful value as a discriminator between children with below average ability. The evidence, therefore, will need to be interpreted with some caution.

The fullest study of social class, language and cognition at the primary stage is by Deutsch (1965), and is concerned with an American population of children aged 6 years to 11 years from a wide range of social class and race. The development of language is central to his research and he devised various complex techniques for its measurement. Altogether he used 'over 100 variables concerned with home background, language functioning, conceptual behaviour, intelligence test performance, reading, general orientation, self-systems, various sub-components of language and assorted related factors'. The report deals with some of the findings, devised from a correlational analysis of 52 of these variables. He found that all verbal intelligence scores, and most of the other verbal measures, correlated significantly with socio-economic status at the 6-year level. At the 11-year level the relationships were generally even more marked.

He generalizes the results in the following manner: 'What is found is a deficiency, based on class and race, in the measures which reflect abstract and categorical use of language as opposed to denotative and labelling usage.' He further says:

> It is found that, as the complexity of the levels increases, from labelling, through relating to categorizing, the negative effects of social disadvantage are enhanced. It is also true, in looking at the enumeration scores, that, as labelling requirements become more complex and related to more diverse and variegated experience, lower class people with more restricted experience are going to have more difficulty in supplying the correct labels.

The research of Templin (1957), also in America, fits naturally into this section, although logically into a later section. She systematically observed the speech of some 480 children aged from 3 years to 8 years. She was especially concerned with the length of utterance, complexity of sentence structure, grammatical correctness and the development of syntactic form generally. Her primary concern was developmental, but within that context she found statistically significant differences between upper and lower socio-economic levels on most of her language measures. She is careful to point out that these differences might be partially accounted for by differences of intelligence. Her work effectively extends the findings of Deutsch to a younger age range in the same way that Hindley's work extends Douglas's findings on cognitive ability.

The evidence throughout the age range is consistent with the hypothesis that language development and verbal intelligence are closely related to social class status.

V CHANGE OF COGNITIVE STATUS OF WORKING-CLASS CHILDREN

1 Late adolescence

Venables (1961, 1963) studied working-class boys who, after leaving school, were studying as engineering apprentices. At the outset of their training they showed relatively impaired verbal ability and high non-verbal ability, but at the end of their training their verbal scores had greatly improved. Venables relates her findings to the fact that the students had to become acquainted with, and master, a language which was new to them (i.e. a different linguistic code). At the same time the students who stayed the course were concerned to pass their apprenticeships so that the mastery of some verbal ability was vitally important for them. Had this not been the case, it is open to question as to whether or not they would have improved their verbal scores.

2 Secondary school children

P. E. Vernon (1957) investigated the quality of schooling and its influence on measured intelligence and attainment of secondary school children in grammar, technical and secondary modern school children. The overall finding was that the I.Q.s of grammar school children tended to rise and those of the secondary modern school children to fall over a three-year period. The change in mean scores was positively related to a rating on 'stimulatingness' given by the Education Officers of the area in which the schools were situated. Vernon is careful to point out that a number of factors were probably responsible for the change on

				BOYS				
Age	N	MH	V	MH-V	p	P	MH-P	p
12½	62	97·8	95·1	+2·7	<0·02	98·2	−0·4	NS
13½	69	97·6	95·2	+2·4	<0·02	100·8	−3·2	<0·05
14½	100	104·6	97·4	+7·2	<0·001	102·7	+1·9	NS
				GIRLS				
12½	72	100·0	96·3	+3·7	<0·001	103·8	−3·8	<0·01
13½	78	99·0	93·1	+5·9	<0·001	100·5	−1·5	NS
14½	77	100·7	92·7	+8·0	<0·001	100·0	+0·7	NS

MH = Moray House test.
V = Verbal test.
P = Perceptual test.

TABLE 19.3

Comparison of Moray House Test scores at age 11 with verbal and perceptual scores at age 12½, 13½ and 14½.

cognitive status and he includes the fact that many of the secondary modern school children would have come from working-class backgrounds where the impetus to profit from schooling might be minimal. He also points out that the tests which were used gave no indication as to what aspects of intelligence were being measured over and above the verbal content of the tests which were used.

Ravenette (*op. cit.*) was also concerned to investigate whether or not there was a change in measured cognitive ability from age 11 years to age 14 years. He compared their Morrisby Verbal and Perceptual I.Q.s at 12½, 13½ and 14½ years with their Moray House Verbal Reasoning I.Q.s at 11 years. At each age-level the Morrisby Verbal I.Q. was significantly lower (more so for the girls than the boys) than the Moray House I.Q., but the perceptual I.Q. showed little difference. The results are given in Table 19.3.

The differences, however, might have arisen from differences in the standardization of the tests so that it was necessary to use an analysis of variance to examine the trend in the magnitude of those differences. In the outcome it was found that they increased from 11 to $13\frac{1}{2}$ and 11 to $14\frac{1}{2}$ for boys (p <0·001) and at all ages for girls (p <0·001). It was also found that there was a small decline in the perceptual scores from 11 to 14 for both boys and girls (p <0·05).

These results need to be treated with some caution since each age-group of children were tested on different forms of the Moray House Verbal Reasoning Tests. Since no evidence was available as a basis for equalizing the tests, the results could have arisen from inequalities in the Moray House Tests rather than because of change of cognitive status in the children themselves. Moreover, it is an assumption that there should be no difference between the three age-groups which were tested. In consequence, as many children as possible from the two younger age-groups of the original sample were retested two years later on the same verbal and perceptual tests as had been first administered. This work has not previously been reported.

Children who had been rated as poor readers or non-readers were omitted and a number of children had either left the area or were absent at the time of testing. The numbers for each year-group therefore were somewhat reduced. Table 19.4 gives the means, sample size and probability levels for verbal, perceptual and discrepancy scores. All tests of significance were correlated 't' tests. The shifts in scores over time are presented graphically in Figure 19.3.

It is difficult to determine changes in absolute level of ability, since it is frequently the case that children score better when retested on the same tests. If this is true for this particular sample, a relative drop in verbal ability may have been masked by a considerable practice effect. The important statistic, however, is the change in the verbal/non-verbal discrepancy score. When all the data are pooled, this discrepancy increases by about 2 I.Q. points (p <0·01). For the $12\frac{1}{2}$-year-old children retested at $14\frac{1}{2}$ the increase is not significantly different, but for the $13\frac{1}{2}$-year-olds retested at $15\frac{1}{2}$ the increase is about 3 I.Q. points (p<0·001). Boys and girls separately show an increase of discrepancy of about 2 I.Q. points (p <0·05). No single sex/age group, however, shows a difference large enough to achieve a satisfactory level of statistical significance.

In general, therefore, this evidence suggests that, on retest, these children tend to show a very slight but significant intensification of their pattern of ability. On the other hand it must be stressed that there was considerable variability between children both in the magnitude and the direction of change.

3 Primary school children

Douglas' (*op. cit.*) study of the interaction between family factors and changes in the ability of 8- to 11-year-old children has been seriously criticized by Burt (1965) for its lack of methodological sophistication and for the fact that the ability measures which were used were not detailed enough to answer the

BOYS

n = 55

Age	Test	Mean	Test	Mean	d(V-P)
12½	V₁	9·14	P₁	9·62	NS
14½	V₂	9·14	P₂	10·16	<0·01
p (test-retest)		NS		NS	

n = 70

Age	Test	Mean	Test	Mean	d(V-P)
13½	V₁	8·90	P₁	10·18	<0·05
15½	V₂	9·66	P₂	11·49	<0·001
p (test-retest)		<0·05		<0·001	

GIRLS

n = 74

Age	Test	Mean	Test	Mean	d(V-P)
12½	V₁	9·27	P₁	11·53	<0·001
14½	V₂	9·24	P₂	11·42	<0·001
p (test-retest)		NS		NS	

n = 75

Age	Test	Mean	Test	Mean	d(V-P)
13½	V₁	8·72	P₁	10·51	<0·001
15½	V₂	8·35	P₂	11·37	<0·001
p (test-retest)		NS		0·001	

Scores are standardized to—

$$M = 10·5$$
$$SD = 4$$

TABLE 19.4

Means, mean differences and probability levels for boys and girls aged 12½ and 13½ retested at 14½ and 15½ on the Morrisby Verbal (V) and Perceptual (P) tests.

questions which were being investigated. None the less Douglas' broad findings should not be summarily dismissed. The tenor of the evidence strongly suggests that children whose parents belong to the manual working class tend to deteriorate in their performance on tests of ability. It is unfortunate that, on each occasion of testing, only one test of intelligence was used and that the two tests for the different occasions were not comparable. Moreover, he pooled measures of intelligence with measures of attainment so that any selective change in

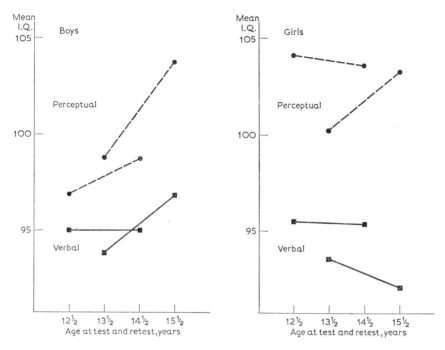

FIGURE 19.3

Mean verbal and perceptual I.Q.s at test and retest.

ability was masked. It was clear, however, that poor maternal care was associated with a deterioration in performance, whereas parental interest lead to an improvement. Poor attitudes to school work were associated with membership of the lower working class, favourable attitudes with membership of the middle class. These findings are supported by Wiseman's (*op. cit.*) much more elaborate inquiries, thereby providing some validation for Douglas' study.

At the infant school level no studies have as yet been published, but the Sociological Research Unit has been carrying out investigations which are likely to be published in 1968. Gahagan, who has been closely connected with work at the Unit, has indicated in a personal communication that working-class infant school children may well show a relative fall-off in verbal ability unless their teachers were able to provide an educational environment in which the intensive and extensive use of language was stressed.

In summary, the evidence on change in cognitive status supports the idea that working-class children show a differential pattern of cognitive growth in which non-verbal ability develops in comparable fashion to that of middle-class children, but verbal ability becomes relatively stunted. It is not known, however, at what age the differences arise, at what ages the differences are maximal or under what circumstances the pattern of ability of working-class children can be modified. Part of the research of the Sociological Research Unit has been to develop a language intervention programme for such children but it is too early as yet to present much by way of validatory studies. Some evidence, however, will be given at the end of the next section.

VI EVIDENCE IN SUPPORT OF THE 'RESTRICTED'/'ELABORATED' CODE DICHOTOMY

The analysis of language is a complex and time consuming activity, especially when the language is spoken. Unscripted free running speech, of course, could not even be collected before the advent of the tape-recorder. Because of the many difficulties, the samples which are used for analysis tend to be taken from small numbers of subjects, and the statistical techniques of necessity tend to be non-parametric. This type of methodology is still unfortunately comparatively rarely used in cognitive studies. Most of the evidence in this section is of this nature.

1 Late adolescence

Bernstein (1962a, b) investigated the spoken language of working-class and middle-class boys aged 15 to 18 years. The language was obtained by recording informal discussions held between three to five subjects. Five groups were constituted in order that comparisons could be made holding social class, pattern of ability and level of ability constant. Bernstein was concerned with two different aspects of linguistic practice: hesitations, length of utterance and rate of speech on the one hand, and the presence or absence of various grammatical features on the other. These features are associated with differences between codes. The general findings indicated that there were overall social class differences. Working-class subjects used a longer mean phrase length, spent less time pausing and used a shorter word length. This was still true when non-verbal intelligence was held constant, but within different subgroups of both middle- and working-class boys there were other minor differences. From the analysis of grammatical components of speech, the following differences appeared: middle-class groups used a high proportion of subordinations, complex verbal stems, passive voice (as opposed to active voice), total adjectives, uncommon adjectives, adverbs and conjunctions and egocentric sequences (i.e.

emphasizing the individuality of the speaker). The working-class groups used a higher proportion of total personal pronouns, more frequent use of 'you' and 'they' in various proportions, and sociocentric sequences (i.e. appealing to the collective assumptions and feelings of the group).

2 Secondary school boys

Lawton (1968) has reported a very detailed investigation into the use of language by middle- and working-class boys at the ages of 12 years and 15 years. He makes a clear distinction between different situations in which language may be elicited, e.g. through writing, through discussion and in a structured interview, and his three papers deal with each in turn. The subjects were matched both for verbal and non-verbal ability in order to hold level and pattern of ability constant. There were five subjects for each age and social class category, making a total of 20.

The general findings from all three studies confirmed the social class differences which had been postulated by Bernstein, but not all measures discriminated equally. The two major discriminants were the more extensive use of the passive voice by middle-class children, and the greater ability of these children to switch from a restricted to a more elaborate code when the occasion demanded. The former attribute probably represents a greater ability to plan speech in advance of what the individual is actually saying and the latter may reflect either that the working class do not have the elaborate code available or have too little confidence to use it if they have. Lawton warns against the use of single measures for discriminating purposes as the context in which language is elicited is likely to affect the form and structure of the language which is appropriate for the occasion.

Robinson (1965a, b) was concerned with boys only in one study, and boys and girls in the second. In the first study Robinson used a novel procedure. He selected sentences from middle-class and working-class boys elicited in free discussion and also from formal and informal letters that they had written. The sentences that were used in the test procedure included equal numbers from middle- and working-class language samples and were chosen to include formal and informal letter-writing and the spoken word as sources. The task was to fill in a word that had been omitted from the sentence. The analysis of responses showed that the working-class children's responses were much more alike than middle class responses and that the most frequent responses of the working-class children were not the same as the most frequent responses of the middle-class children. In other words, linguistic expectancy as typified by the sentence completion test was different for the two groups.

In the second study Robinson analysed the language which middle-class and working-class boys and girls used in a letter-writing situation. One letter was designed to elicit elaborate language, the other was such that restricted language could be used satisfactorily. This analysis was much less conclusive in its results than the previous studies which have been reported. The major differences appeared in the informal letter, not in the formal letter. The differences were, however, in line with those which were predicted on the basis of 'restricted' and 'elaborate' codes. The point might have been made that skill in writing lags behind skill in speaking (Vygotsky, 1962) and this might have affected the middle-class children more than the working-class children at this age, thereby tending to mask any differences between the two groups.

The general implications of these researches strongly support the idea that there are considerable differences in the linguistic usage of middle-class and working-class boys, and that the differences are fully consistent with Bernstein's formulation of the 'restricted' and 'elaborated' codes. It is perhaps surprising that most of the work has been done with boys. Future work should include the linguistic usage of girls as well.

3 Primary school children

The investigation of the language of primary school children has recently been undertaken by the Sociological Research Unit of the London Institute of Education under the direction of Professor Bernstein. As yet little of the material has appeared in print and much of the data is still being processed. Some reports, however, have been published and some are available from the Research Unit.

The sample populations which are involved are made up of 350 families from a predominantly working-class borough, each having a child who started school in September 1964. A further 150 subjects from a predominantly middle-class borough were added a year later. The mothers have been interviewed extensively and both the content of the answers and linguistic style of the mothers are available for analysis. The children have also been subjected to a wide number of cognitive tests, their speech is available for analysis, and some have been in classes where an attempt was made to build into the curriculum a language programme designed to develop the use of an elaborated code by the children. The investigations are being published, but some of the findings are presented here.

An experiment by Robinson and Creed (1968) involving 6-year-old working-class girls demonstrated that those who used a more elaborated code made fewer pointing errors and were more accurate in their descriptions in a task which involved spotting the differences between two similar pictures. This is an important finding since it relates linguistic code to operations which are clearly related to cognitive test performance.

Henderson (1968) in an unpublished report is able to show that at the age of 5-6 years middle-class children use more types of nouns, adjectives and verbs than their working-class peers. This difference discriminates more clearly than either sex, I.Q. or the nature of maternal communication with the child. This finding is completely in line with the differences already reported for secondary school children.

Rackstraw and Robinson (1967) report differences between middle- and working-class children in their use of language when they had to carry out certain naming or explanatory tasks. The middle-class children were characterized as being able to use 'language which reflected a more objective frame of reference and they chose more abstract and comprehensive words and structures'. The working-class child expressed things from his own point of view, giving concrete and particular details. The authors make the very interesting point that the working-class child's speech (and 'restricted' speech in general) seems closely related to 'ego-centric' speech as described by Piaget (1959)*. Using the same parallel, 'elaborate' speech is comparable to 'socio-centric' speech which, developmentally, comes next. Whereas, however, middle-class children progress to 'socio-centric' speech as a result of their verbal interactions with their parents, working-class children lack this experiential model within the home and develop, perhaps, to the more sophisticated 'restricted' speech of their parents.

From a different point of view, having postulated linguistic differences as in part determinants of cognitive growth, it is necessary to examine the communicational interactions between the parents and the child in order to see what models the child has available for learning. Very little has yet been done in this field but Hess and Shipman (1965) have produced one important contribution. They taught mothers from four different socio-economic groups how to carry out three simple tasks, and in their turn they had to teach these tasks to their children. Mother teaching her child provided a parent/child interaction session which could be studied. They report that there was little difference in maternal warmth between the different groups but there were considerable differences in the verbal and cognitive environments which they offered their children. Working-class mothers seemed to encourage passive learning styles, middle-class mothers were able to encourage active initiating behaviour from their children. Moreover, middle-class mothers were better able to verbalize both the task and the way to master the task and, at the same time, to regulate their own behaviour and the child's in tasks that required planning or care rather than verbal skill.

Differences in interaction such as these are likely to lead to differences at the infant school level when the children start school. If the school expects behaviour which is geared to the middle-class style of interaction then the working-class child will already be at a disadvantage.

Robinson and Rackstraw (1967) report differences between the middle- and working-class mothers of 5-year-old children on the basis of their answers to questions concerned with a child's 'Why?' questions. Although this is not observation of mother/child interaction, it must be assumed that what the parents said was relevant to what they actually did. The major differentiating variable in the responses was social class. The authors say:

> The middle-class mothers were more likely to answer the questions. The information was more accurate and there was more of it. The information was

* N.B. Piaget's terminology carries opposite meanings from that of Bernstein.

embedded in a less noisy context, and when the modes of answers to 'Why?' questions were categorized, the middle-class mothers were more likely to use arguments by analogy and a greater variety of purposive answers, and were less likely to repeat the question as an answer or use simple appeals to the regularity of events.

If the mothers actually do what they say they do, children from differing social classes are again exposed to differing verbal, cognitive and experiential situations, which in turn may help or hinder the child's own cognitive growth. Moreover, whereas the earlier evidence showed that the *children* differed linguistically, the speech sample of the *mothers* in this study extends the distinction up the age scale to the age of the mothers.

Another example of parental influence is reported by Bernstein and Young (1967). They investigated the attitudes of middle- and working-class mothers to toys. The data was obtained from interviewing the mothers and they were asked to indicate from a number of choices their attitudes towards toys for their children. The authors found that these attitudes were related both to social class and to the nature of the verbal communication between mother and child. More important, taking the statements 'So that they can find out about things' and 'To free the mothers so that they can do other things' as two ends of a scale and ranking parents on that scale, a correlation was found of $0 \cdot 17$ ($p < 0 \cdot 05$) with W.I.S.C. Verbal Scale I.Q., $0 \cdot 28$ ($p < 0 \cdot 001$) with Performance Scale I.Q., and $0 \cdot 25$ ($p < 0 \cdot 001$) with Full Scale I.Q. This would suggest that parents' stated beliefs are related to parental practice in the management of their children, which in turn leads to modification of cognitive development.

The final study to be reported in this section is by Gahagan and Gahagan (1967) and represents one piece of validation of the language intervention programme previously mentioned. The experimental task was to learn paired associate words and the children were encouraged to link these unconnected words by means of a verb in order to make some sense of the situation. Fifty-four children matched for verbal intelligence on the E.P.V.T. (Brimer, 1963) and drawn from three experimental classes and three each of two control classes were used. The measures which were important were the number of different linking verbs and the number of trials necessary for learning the paired associates. The outcome was that children who had been involved in the language programme produced a greater number of linking verbs and learned more efficiently than children from the control classes. The effect was greatest for the average and below average children. This evidence is certainly suggestive of the possibility of introducing educational techniques which will open up the chance for working-class children to acquire more adequate verbal skills and verbal ability.

This accumulating evidence provides most encouraging support for the idea that language is one of the major factors influencing cognitive ability, and that the cognitive differences which are found between middle- and working-class children reflect differences in the linguistic codes which these children acquire from their parents. The full implications of this finding have yet to be investigated.

It might be asked if the findings reported here are isolated to English-speaking cultures, or can they be paralleled elsewhere. Bruner (1966) gives one answer to this. Using Piaget techniques, and studying the cognitive development of children in what was formerly French West Africa, he found that even within those cultures developmental differences in cognitive growth could be distinguished between city and rural children and children who had schooling and those who did not. He states, 'The difference between the city child and the rural child derives from the differential exposure to problem solving and communication in situations that are not supported by context.' This exposure is achieved, of course, through the use of language. As he says elsewhere (Bruner, 1966), 'It is this concern (for the consequences that stem from the general properties . . . of language) that leads me to put language at the centre of the stage in considering the nature of intellectual development.' Language leads to a modification of the child's perception of the world, and this in turn leads to conceptual regrouping and, therefore, to abstraction.

VII IMPLICATIONS FOR THE PROFESSIONAL PSYCHOLOGIST

The findings reported in this chapter which relate social class, language and pattern of cognitive ability (as opposed to level of ability) are of considerable importance for the professional psychologist who is concerned with the cognitive assessment of working-class children. It is probably true to say that the intelligence test which is most widely used is the W.I.S.C., which is designed to measure separately verbal and performance ability. It would be predicted, therefore, that working-class children would tend to show a pattern of ability in which the verbal I.Q. was lower than performance I.Q. So far there are no extensive studies which are concerned with this problem, but Ravenette and Kahn (1962) demonstrated the prediction to be true for secondary school boys referred to a child guidance clinic in a predominantly working-class area. In detail, the discrepancy was about 13 I.Q. points ($p < 0.0001$). For secondary school girls the discrepancy was in the predicted direction but not sufficiently large to be statistically significant ($0.10 > p > 0.05$). For younger children mean verbal and mean performance I.Q.s did not differ significantly.

A word of caution needs to be added. The argument derived from consideration of language has been shown to have validity for children in working-class areas, but such areas are characterized by being highly urbanized and densely populated. No evidence has been adduced for rural populations. On the other hand, evidence is being accumulated for rural and 'tinker' children in Ireland (McKenna, personal communication) that for such children it is the performance I.Q.s on the W.I.S.C. which show a deficit, whereas lower verbal I.Q.s are a rarity. It is also reported, however, that Irish parents tend to have a negative attitude towards the provision of toys and educational materials to their children. This situation is comparable to that found by Bernstein (*op. cit.*) in which a negative attitude to toys is associated with poor performance I.Q.s even in families in industrialized working-class areas.

A further caution must be added in connection with immigrant children, for whom, except for West Indian children, little is known. P. E. Vernon (1965a, b) has studied West Indian children against a control sample of English children on a variety of cognitive measures and related these also to family factors. His general conclusions suggest that these children compare most favourably with English children on the W.I.S.C. Verbal Scale and that they are at a disadvantage on performance type items. Routine examination of West Indian immigrant children certainly is in agreement with his findings.

When, therefore, psychologists are concerned with understanding the pattern of ability of children whom they assess, all of these factors need to be borne in mind and this is a tacit admission that cognitive performance may be very much influenced by familial, cultural and environmental factors. Moreover, it becomes increasingly important to know what is 'normal' for the sample of the population from which an individual member comes in order to understand the most likely causes for the pattern of ability which he may demonstrate and, where necessary, to plan remedial programmes. In terms of absolute numbers, however, the largest group of the culturally handicapped will be that which is made up of children from industrialized working-class areas. The other groups need to be studied in as great detail as the working-class group.

One implication needs to be spelled out in some clarity. In working-class areas the number of children with I.Q.s of 70 and below must inevitably be inflated by virtue of impaired verbal ability. Such children are usually designated as educationally subnormal, especially if they present problems of behaviour in the ordinary school. It is not true to say, however, that this inflation has been recognized by administrators and planners of special school provision. Since the subnormality is to a great extent culturally determined, the question arises as to what provision they need in order to improve their learning potential. This particular problem, however, cannot be treated separately from the general problem of special help for the culturally handicapped. In this country, the Schools Council has recently launched a research project in compensatory education based on the Education Department of the University College of Swansea. Clearly it will be some time before any results become available. At the present moment methods and techniques of teaching have yet to be devised and, perhaps more important, the attitudes of the teachers of these children still need considerable modification. It may be that, in this double task, psychologists should play a major role.

The problem has been recognized in the U.S.A. for a number of years and special programmes for culturally handicapped children have been initiated in a number of places. Jensen (1967) offers an interesting review of some of the latest developments but suggests that evaluative studies to date are not very impressive. He seems to imply, moreover, that the problem is far more complex than had originally been thought.

VIII CONCLUSION

This evidence points very clearly to some aspects of the cognitive handicaps which are related to membership of the working class. The handicap is verbal rather than non-verbal, and the handicap would seem to increase with age. Linguistic differences run parallel to the cognitive differences. As yet, however, research has barely been started on tracing the specific effects of linguistic differences on measured cognitive ability. More important, it must be asked to what extent measures which are effective in improving language skills will lead also to cognitive improvement.

Despite the sophisticated methods of test construction which underlie most of our cognitive tests, these tests still provide comparatively crude measures of intelligence. There is a considerable need for much more subtle measures, both of verbal and non-verbal ability. Within each of these broad areas cultural handicap may be differently effective and the extent of this needs to be known.

From a developmental point of view, the acquisition of language and its relationship with parent/child interaction calls for much more intense investigation, and this cannot be divorced from the growth and shaping of personality. Studies of the role of cognition in the development of behaviour, and the role of behaviour in the development of cognition, each within a framework provided by linguistic usage, would seem to be long-term aims for research. Moreover, such work needs to be carried out on the basis of investigating how individual children behave rather than how large numbers respond to paper-and-pencil tests.

None of this will be of value, however, unless the results provide the basis for changes in the strategies, tactics and techniques used within the school setting. If culturally handicapped children are to receive special help, this is most likely to be given in the school and the givers will be teachers. Changes are taking place, but slowly, and part of the slowness is related to the lack of adequate knowledge and understanding of the implications of social class membership.

Finally, children are more than information processing and language using machines. Their behaviour is purposive, their aspirations are related to life as they see it. Life is lived within a matrix of communication and out of this matrix are developed beliefs, attitudes, hopes, expectations and identities. What is this matrix for a working-class child and how does it differ from that of his middle-class peer? How far are these children's choices determined by the cultural milieu, especially as enshrined in language, and what meanings to life can these children see? These are questions for psychologists to be concerned about, and the answers will be of more than theoretical importance if we are concerned with helping the culturally deprived.

REFERENCES

ASHER, E. J. (1935) The inadequacy of current intelligence tests for testing Kentucky mountain children. *J. genet. Psychol.*, **46**, 480-486.

BERNSTEIN, B. (1958) Some sociological determinants of perception. *Brit. J. Sociol.*, **9**, 159-174.

BERNSTEIN, B. (1959) A public language: Some sociological implications of a linguistic form. *Brit. J. Sociol.*, **10**, 311-326.

BERNSTEIN, B. (1960) Language and social class. *Brit. J. Sociol.*, **11**, 311-326.

BERNSTEIN, B. (1961) Aspects of language and learning in the genesis of the social process. *J. Child Psychol. Psychiat.*, **1**, 313-323.

BERNSTEIN, B. (1962a) Linguistic codes, hesitation phenomena and intelligence. *Language and Speech*, **5**, 31-46.

BERNSTEIN, B. (1962b) Social class, linguistic codes and grammatical elements. *Language and Speech*, **5**, 221-240.

BERNSTEIN, B. and YOUNG, D. (1967) Social class differences in conceptions of the uses of toys. *Sociol.*, **1**, 138-140.

BRIMER, M. A. and DUNN, L. M. (1963) *English Picture Vocabulary Tests*. London: National Foundation for Educational Research.

BRUNER, J. S. (1966) *Toward a Theory of Instruction*. Cambridge, Mass.: Harvard Univ. Press.

BRUNER, J. S., OLVER, R. R. and GREENFIELD, P. M. (1966) *Studies in Cognitive Growth*. New York: Wiley.

BURT, C. (1965) Critical notice: The home and the school. *Brit. J. Educ. Psychol.*, **35**, 259-264.

CARROLL, J. S. (1958) Some psychological effects of language structure. *In* HOCH, P. J. and ZUBIN, J. (Eds.) *Psychopathology of Communication*. New York: Grune and Stratton.

DEUTSCH, M. (1965) The role of social class in language development and cognition. *Am. J. Orthopsychiat.*, **35**, 78-88.

DOUGLAS, J. W. B. (1964) *The Home and the School*. London: MacGibbon and Kee.

EELLS, K., DAVIS, A. *et al.* (1951) *Intelligence and Cultural Differences*. Chicago: University of Chicago Press.

FLAVELL, J. H. (1963) *The Developmental Psychology of Jean Piaget*. Princeton: Van Nostrand.

FRASER, E. (1959) *Home Environment and the School*. London: University of London Press.

GAHAGAN, G. A. and GAHAGAN, D. M. (1967) The effect of a language development programme on a paired associate learning task. (Unpublished report.) Univ. of London Sociological Research Unit.

GAW, F. (1925) A study of performance tests. *Brit. J. Psychol.*, **15**, 374-392.

GORDON, H. (1923) *Mental and Scholastic tests among retarded children: An enquiry into the effects of schooling on various tests*. London: Board of Education Pamphlets No. 44.

HENDERSON, D. (1968) Social class differences in form-class usage among five-year-old children. *In Social Class, Language and Socialization.* Sociological Research Unit Monograph No. 1. London: Routledge and Kegan Paul (in press).

H.M.S.O. (1963) *Half Our Future (Newsom Report).* A report of the Central Advisory Council for Education (England).

H.M.S.O. (1967) *Children and their Primary Schools (Plowden Report).* A report of the Central Advisory Council for Education (England).

HESS, R. D. and SHIPMAN, V. (1965) Early blocks to children's learning. *Children,* **12,** 189-194.

HINDLEY, C. B. (1965) Stability and change in abilities up to five years: Group trends. *J. Child Psychol. Psychiat.,* **6,** 85-99.

HUNT, J. MCV. (1961) *Intelligence and Experience.* New York: Ronald.

JENSEN, A. R. (1967) The culturally disadvantaged: Psychological and educational aspects. *Educational Research,* **10,** 4-20.

JONES, S. (1962) The Wechsler Intelligence Scale for Children applied to a sample of North London primary school children. *Brit. J. educ. Psychol.,* **32,** 119-132.

LAWTON, D. (1968) *Social Class, Language and Education.* London: Routledge.

LURIA, A. R. (1961) *The Role of Speech in the Formation of Mental Processes.* London: Pergamon Press.

LURIA, A. R. and YUDOVITCH, F. A. (1959) *Speech and the Development of Mental Processes.* London: Staples.

MAXWELL, A. E. (1960) Discrepancies in the variances of test results for normal and neurotic children. *Brit. J. statist. Psychol.,* **13,** 165-172.

MAYS, J. B. (1962) *Education and the Urban Child.* Liverpool: University of Liverpool Press.

MORRISBY, J. R. (1955) *Differential Test Battery.* Slough: National Foundation for Educational Research.

PIAGET, J. (1959) *Language and Thought of the Child.* London: Routledge and Kegan Paul.

RACKSTRAW, S. J. and ROBINSON, W. P. (1967) Social and psychological factors related to variability of answering behaviour in five-year-old children. *Language and Speech,* **10,** 88-106.

RAVENETTE, A. T. (1963) *Intelligence, Personality and Social Class: an investigation into the pattern of intelligence and personality in working class secondary school children.* Unpublished thesis, University of London Library.

RAVENETTE, A. T. and KAHN, J. H. (1962) Intellectual ability of disturbed children in a working-class area. *Brit. J. Soc. clin. Psychol.,* **1,** 208-212.

ROBINSON, W. P. (1965a) Close procedure as a technique for the investigation of social class differences in language usage. *Language and Speech,* **8,** 42-55.

ROBINSON, W. P. (1965b) The elaborated code in working-class language. *Language and Speech,* **8,** 243-252.

ROBINSON, W. P. and CREED, C. D. (1968) Perceptual and verbal discriminations of 'elaborated' and 'restricted' code users. *Language and Speech*, 11, 182-193.

ROBINSON, W. P. and RACKSTRAW, S. J. (1967) Variations in mothers' answers to children's questions as a function of social class, verbal intelligence test scores and sex. *Sociol.*, 1, 259-276.

SAPIR, E. (1933) Language. *In* MANDELBAUM (Ed.) *Culture, Language and Personality*. Los Angeles: University of California Press.

SARASON, S. R. and GLADWIN, T. (1958) *Mental Subnormality*. New York: Basic Books.

SHERMAN, E. and KEY, C. B. (1932) The intelligence of isolated mountain children. *Child Development*, 3, 279-290.

STODOLTSKY, S. S. and LESSER, G. (1967) Learning patterns in the disadvantaged. *Harvard Educ. Rev.*, 37, 546-593.

TEMPLIN, M. C. (1957) *Certain Language Skills in Children: Their Development and Inter-Relationships*. Minneapolis: University of Minnesota Press.

TERMAN, L. and MERRILL, M. (1937) *Measuring Intelligence*. Boston: Houghton Mifflin.

VENABLES, E. C. (1961) Changes in intelligence test scores of engineering apprentices between the first and third years of attendance at college. *Brit. J. educ. Psychol.*, 31, 259-264.

VENABLES, E. C. (1963) Social differences among day release students in their recruitment and examination success. *Brit. J. Soc. clin. Psychol.*, 2, 138-152.

VERNON, P. E. (1950) *The Structure of Human Abilities*. London: Methuen.

VERNON, P. E. (1957) Intelligence and intellectual stimulation during adolescence. *Indian Psychol. Bull.*, 2, 1-6.

VERNON, P. E. (1965a) Environmental handicap and intellectual development, Part I. *Brit. J. educ. Psychol.*, 35, 9-20.

VERNON, P. E. (1965b) Environmental handicap and intellectual development, Part II. *Brit. J. educ. Psychol.*, 35, 117-126.

VYGOTSKY, L. S. (1962) *Thought and Language*. Massachusetts: M.I.T.

WECHSLER, D. (1949) *Wechsler Intelligence Scale for Children*. New York: The Psychological Corporation.

WHEELER, L. B. (1932) The intelligence of East Tennessee mountain children *J. educ. Psychol.*, 23, 351-370.

WHEELER, L. B. (1942) A comparative study of the intelligence of East Tennessee mountain children. *J. educ. Psychol.*, 33, 321-334.

WHORF, B. L. (1956) *Language, Thought and Reality*. Selected writings. CARROLL, J. B. (Ed.). New York: Wiley.

WISEMAN, S. (1964) *Education and Environment*. Manchester: Manchester University Press.

20

Language disorders

P. J. Mittler

Psychologists are increasingly aware of the urgent need for more detailed study of language behaviour, with an emphasis on underlying processes as well as on mere 'output', but are handicapped on the one hand by the absence of any generally accepted theory of language, and on the other by a shortage of adequate tests of language development and language skills. Fortunately, there are signs that both these deficiencies are being energetically tackled. It is possible to detect some convergence here: both at the level of theory and at a practical assessment level, there are signs of dissatisfaction with the global construct 'language' paralleled in some respects by dissatisfaction with other global constructs such as 'intelligence', 'memory' and the like. Instead, one may detect stronger emphasis on isolating constituent processes. 'Language' comprises many skills and processes. A model such as Osgood's (1957) distinguishing between decoding, encoding and association processes and between different channels of communication has been incorporated in the Illinois Test of Psycholinguistic Abilities (McCarthy and Kirk, 1961). A more detailed approach of this kind has obvious relevance to any attempt to use psychological tests as a basis for a more thorough analysis of an individual's cognitive processes, and is likely to provide a sound foundation to any attempt at planning a remedial programme or providing an appropriate learning situation.

I THE DEVELOPMENT OF LANGUAGE

A detailed knowledge of language development is obviously an essential part of the professional psychologist's knowledge. It is relevant not only for those working with children, or with mentally handicapped adults, but also for clinical psychologists who are likely to encounter linguistic disorders in schizophrenics and in neurologically and organically impaired patients. Since language is the cornerstone of most intellectual operations, an understanding of language processes and language disturbances is of the utmost importance. For an exhaustive review of earlier work on development, the reader is referred to McCarthy's now classical review (McCarthy, 1954). A more detailed normative study of selected aspects of development between three and eight years was carried out in Minnesota by Templin (1957); this study concentrates on articulation, speech sound discrimination, verbalizations (e.g. length of response, complexity, grammatical inaccuracies and sentence structure) and vocabulary, and with the interrelationships within these measures and between all of them and estimates of intelligence. The work of McCarthy and Templin is in the normative tradition, but the more recent interest in language acquisition has been from a psycholinguistic point of view. Perhaps the clearest and most readable introduction to these studies is provided by Roger Brown (1965) in a textbook on social psychology; among the most notable of the more recent research monographs concerned with language acquisition are Bellugi and Brown (1964), Smith and Miller (1966) and Lyons and Wales (1966). A good review of the psycholinguistic field as a whole is provided by Ervin-Tripp and Slobin (1966).

1 Theories of language development

A variety of models have been proposed to account for the language learning process, but space permits a brief account of only two contrasting theories: those based on learning theories, exemplified by Skinner (1957) and Lashley (1951), and more biologically orientated theories which lay emphasis on the construct of innate processes and on a 'language acquisition device'. These owe their origin chiefly to the work of Chomsky (1957, 1965) and have recently been placed in a broader biological framework by Lenneberg (1967).

(a) *Skinner's theory* is not only an attempt to explain the development of language on a selective reinforcement model, but is also significant for a classification of speech behaviour which can be used on both normal and abnormal populations. He maintains that his model is 'self-evident, since the basic facts to be analysed are well known to every educated person' (1957, p. 11). A baby exposed to a wide range of human speech sounds learns to associate certain regularly recurring patterns with perceptual or other situations. Thus, a conditioned stimulus (e.g. 'dog') is associated with the unconditioned stimulus (a real dog or picture of a dog) and comes to evoke the same conditioned response in the child. This has been likened to a classical conditioning paradigm, whereas the child's own speech is explained in terms of operant conditioning, the strength of the operant responses being a function of the strength of the positive reinforcements.

Skinner's classification of verbal behaviour is based on an attempt to describe the antecedent conditions which affect the probability of verbal responses. The following terms were coined to describe categories of verbal response:

- (i) *echoic:* immediate imitation of a heard stimulus;
- (ii) *mand:* an utterance which functions as a 'demand' and which is part of a drive state ('come!');
- (iii) *tact:* a response which is uttered when the child is in physical contact with an object ('stroke doggie');
- (iv) *intraverbal:* a broad category in which the response is at a different grammatical level from the stimulus, as when the child answers a question.

Other categories are *textual* (verbal responses to printed texts) and *audience* variables (modifications depending on the nature and expectations of listeners).

Skinner's classification forms the basis of an assessment technique, the Parsons Language Sample (Spradlin, 1963b), which will be summarized later (p. 632).

Skinner's model has been heavily criticized both by linguists and psychologists. Chomsky (1959) in a celebrated review of Skinner's *Verbal Behavior* (1957) which is at the same time a thoughtful critique of learning theories in general, accuses Skinner of 'complete naïvete with respect to grammatical mechanisms', for ignoring the whole problem of 'meaning' and for circularities in defining the terms 'stimulus', 'response' and 'reinforcement'. From a psychological point of view, Osgood (1963) concludes that Skinner was 'not false but insufficient'. He agrees with linguistic criticisms that there is nothing in Skinner's model about the meaning of signs or about semantic generalization, and adds that decoding processes are not adequately catered for.

(b) *Chomsky* (1957, 1965) is regarded as the source of an alternative, more biological theory of language acquisition, though his followers have provided more detailed accounts of the processes underlying language development than Chomsky himself.

Chomsky rejects the finite-state Markov model in which sentences are generated word by word in terms of their transitional dependencies. He argues for the existence of some inherent language acquisition device. The need for this is postulated because of the astonishing speed with which the child learns his own language, particularly the grammar. Reinforcement theories and imitation could not possibly, on this view, account for the rapid rate of growth. In an amusing calculation, Miller *et al.* (1960) demonstrate that the rules of left-right grammar – that is a system in which each word depends only on the preceding word – could not possibly be learned in a lifetime. They conclude that 'the child would have to hear about 3×10^{20} sentences per second in order to be exposed to all the information necessary for the planner to produce sentences according to these left-right rules of grammar' (p. 147).

Chomsky's theory and that of his followers rests on the distinction between 'competence' and 'performance'. Competence relates to the child's knowledge of a language which will enable him to understand and generate an infinite number of grammatical sentences of a language, and no non-sentences of that language. Performance refers to the actual use made of that knowledge. This fundamental distinction cannot be examined here, but its implications are developed in Smith and Miller (1966, especially the chapter by McNeill), and in Lyons and Wales (1966). The psycholinguistic studies which have appeared in the last few years postulate that from a very early stage of language development the child is already aware of and using, however inappropriately, a set of *rules* of grammar, especially syntax, but also of plurals, tenses, etc. The child who says 'I digged in the garden' is presumably merely misapplying a rule for forming the past tense; he is unlikely to be imitating. The task of the linguist, is to 'determine from the data of performance the underlying system of rules that has been mastered by the speaker-hearer, and that he puts to use in actual

x

performance' (Chomsky, 1965). Some examples of such performance are provided in the next section.

2 Prelinguistic utterances

Psychologists have not, on the whole, concerned themselves with direct observations on speech and language development before the end of the first year, although knowledge of this period is essential to the assessment of children with severely limited speech. This is partly because systematic observation and recording of early vocalization and babbling require a training in the use of the International Phonetic Alphabet, but is also partly attributable to the view held by many psychologists that these vocalizations occur on a maturational basis; for example, severely deaf babies babble up to about six months (Lenneberg, 1964). On the other hand, Irwin (1960) demonstrated that even in the first six months social class factors appeared to be associated with the wide range of individual differences demonstrated by detailed phonetic analysis of vocalizations. The vowel-dominated cooing of the first few months gradually gives way to a much more diversified type of babbling in which consonants play a greater part, especially with the development of teeth and the increasing mobility of the tongue. The function of the earlier babbling stages presumably includes that of providing practice for the maturing speech organs as well as opportunities for selective reinforcement of specific speech sounds, both by direct imitation from the mother and from associating certain vocalizations with subsequent relief of discomfort.

3 The first word

The process by which 'the first word' is differentiated from the 'noisy' background of babble is difficult to investigate and open to obvious subjectivity. For this reason it may be unreliable to place too much emphasis on the answer given by mothers to the question 'When did he start to talk?' or even 'When did he say his first word, other than Mummy or Daddy?' The answer is open to distortion not only because mothers remember discrete physical milestones much better than more psychological skills (Donoghue and Shakespeare, 1967) but mainly because the question is open to a variety of interpretations, and depends partly on the almost unanswerable question, 'What is a word?' Many studies have been reported on the first use of single words (Darley and Winitz, 1961), and there is wide agreement that it occurs around 12 months. The median age of many studies based on maternal report is around 11 months, but Shirley (1933), who conducted an exhaustively detailed study of 25 children in the first two years, did not herself hear the first word until an average age of 14 months. But the difficulties of definition are still formidable. Is the investigator to accept the mother's report that a particular phonemic combination always denotes a particular object or referent?

Be that as it may, the evidence from phonetic and spectrographic analyses indicates that the months immediately preceding word utterance are characterized by increasing control over pitch, volume and articulation. Tischler (quoted by Ervin-Tripp and Slobin, 1966) noted that almost all possible sounds could be recorded between 8 and 12 months, including a number not in the adult language, but that the maximum quantity and variety of vocalizations occurred between 8 and 10 months, and then showed a slight decline.

One of the most puzzling phenomena in language concerns the long plateau which follows the appearance of the first few words. Children learn to use about ten single words appropriately, but the rate of vocabulary growth is on average very slow until around 18 months. M. K. Smith (1926) found that the number of single words spoken in her group rose from 3 at 12 months to 22 at 18 months, but that the rise between 18 and 21 months was a further 96 words, followed by a further rise of 154 words between 21 and 24 months. Although Smith's data on the size of vocabulary have been disputed, partly on methodological grounds and partly because more recent studies such as Templin's (1957) suggest that children now speak a little earlier than they did, most investigators agree on the existence of this relatively long plateau, which is then followed by a rapidly accelerating curve.

4 Two-word utterances

The appearance of two-word utterances signals the beginning of a faster rate of language development, and allows the psychologist and linguist to collect data which will form the basis of generalizations about the nature of the underlying processes. This applies particularly to the development of grammar. The studies by Roger Brown and his associates (Brown and Fraser, 1964) analysed a sample of two word utterances and listed many examples in which the initial word acts as a 'pivot' on which the second word hangs as an 'open' class. (*No* dinner, *no* bed, *no* crying, etc.) Thus the pivot has relatively few members, but each pivot is used more frequently than the individual open class words. Quite apart from the pivot-open distinction, the interest of two-word utterances to the student of child language lies in regularities of the syntactic rules which seem to be followed from the very beginning of two-word combinations. The combinations which have been recorded by Menyuk (1963), Brown (1965) and McNeill (1966) cannot be explained directly as imitations or even as reductions of adult speech, but have their own logic. Here are some examples: '*Two boot; a gas here; hear tractor; see truck Mummy; there go one; put truck window; Adam make tower*'. Moreover, several studies have demonstrated that the child's early grammar is relatively impermeable to adult models; Brown (1965) instances a child saying '*Eve lunch*', to which only the context could give meaning – i.e. 'Eve (has had, will have, wants, is having, etc.) lunch'. Although the mother regularly expands the child's utterance, it seems that the original 'telegraphese' is preserved, and that the child does not expand the length of his sentences beyond a critical number of morphemes at any given time. Thus, the child's imitations do not increase as a function of the length of the adult's sentence, but there appears to be some regularity in the pattern of what is imitated. Nouns, main verbs and adjectives tend to be retained, while omissions include auxiliary verbs, articles, prepositions, the final -ing, etc. Brown has noted that the omitted words are mostly those which receive less stress.

Moreover, children cling stubbornly to their own grammatical idiosyncrasies, which constitute their interpretation of the rules of grammar. Further examples from Brown (1965) include: '*Cowboy did fighting me; put on it; why it can't turn off*'. Berko (1958) in an ingenious experiment first demonstrated the strength with which these rules were perceived; she presented children with drawings purporting to illustrate nonsense syllables, and then asked questions designed to elicit specific grammatical constructions. For example, a drawing named as a 'wug' was shown to 56 children at each age from 4 to 7 years; two further examples were shown to elicit the plural, always given correctly as wug/z. Similarly, the past tense was elicited from nonsense syllables such as spow, rick, gling; Berko found few differences between pre-schoolers and first grade children. Her groups were able to form plurals in / s / or / z /, but seemed to follow a regular rule that a final sibilant makes the word plural. Nouns forming irregular plurals (such as mouse, man, goose) are wrongly pluralized until four years or later. 'Mans' was elicited in 88% of a linguistically normal group of four year olds tested on the Illinois Test of Psycholinguistic Abilities (Mittler, 1969). The persistence of these misperceptions of rules is interesting in the light of Brown's and Fraser's (1964) comment that 'by the age of three children had about as complex a grammar as we could describe'.

5 Comprehension

Although language development is conventionally assessed by the yardstick of spoken utterances, it is equally important to know how far spoken language is understood by the child. Until very recently, almost nothing had been written, either descriptively or from a normative point of view, about the growth of language comprehension. It has always been known that comprehension precedes production, and that children appeared to react appropriately to single words and to increasingly complex commands from the age of about 9 months. At this time, for example, the baby is supposed to understand 'no', even if the appropriate stress, inflection and a general minatory manner are carefully excluded. It can be assumed that the developmental sequence certainly allows children to understand not only single words but simple sentences many months before they have reached the stage where they themselves can use these or similar words and constructions.

The fact that normative data on comprehension development are not available has forced itself on all psychologists who have dealt with mentally and linguistically handicapped children. Mothers frequently insist that even though their child is not speaking, 'he understands everything you say'. This statement should never be accepted without careful testing. It is all too easy for an alert child to guess the meaning of a mother's utterances either from the general context, or from her own (probably quite unconscious) gestures and eye-pointing. Children with impaired hearing and language development sometimes develop considerable facility in guessing from the slightest cues. But even if all situational cues are rigidly excluded and the message is entirely verbal, we cannot conclude from the fact that because a child behaves 'appropriately' to an adult's command, he has therefore fully understood the linguistic structure of the adult's sentence. If, for example, a child goes to sit at the table in response to the sentence 'Are you ready for your dinner?', he might have understood no more than the word 'dinner'; we cannot infer anything about his ability to understand the grammatical structure of the sentence. The child might still behave appropriately if the word order of the sentence was randomized.

Models of language comprehension derived from communication engineering are relevant in this connection. In listening to a noisy telephone link, or one in which segments of speech are artificially 'clipped off', decoding occurs in relation to sequential probabilities of the incoming message. Similarly, a child with a partial hearing loss at the higher frequencies learns in listening to speech to compensate for the 'missing consonants' or consonantal forms. There are limits to which such compensations can go, however, and the fact that a child can respond appropriately to an instruction does not allow us to assume that he can understand. The first obvious check is to ask him in simple terms to carry out a relatively unfamiliar or unexpected request, since it is possible that a comprehension difficulty may be masked by the ability to carry out a small number of commands in limited and restricted contexts.

Recent studies of children with language disorders have highlighted the difficulties which some of them experience in dealing with incoming messages. Children with 'receptive dysphasia' (now thought to be commoner than was at one time suspected) show primary decoding difficulties. Although they may have adequate hearing within the speech range, language seems meaningless to them; they have to be helped to make sense first of single words and then of phrases and sentences of gradually increasing length and complexity. Similarly, many autistic children have quite specific linguistic handicaps which makes it difficult for them to understand spoken language. In one recent experiment, Hermelin and O'Connor showed that autistic children could recall more words than a group of matched subnormal controls, but performed just as well whether the material to be recalled consisted of sentences or non-sentences, or whether the words used were of high or low frequency (Hermelin, 1968). These and similar experiments suggest that this group of autistic children shows rather characteristic difficulties of semantic and syntactic structuring which makes much of the language with which they are surrounded meaningless. Some authorities on autism (e.g. Rutter, 1968) go so far as to state that the language difficulty constitutes the primary handicap.

6 Further syntactic and semantic development

As this chapter is primarily concerned with disorders of development and their assessment, it would not be appropriate to enter in any detail into the growing complexity of language development which begins with the use of two-word utterances and simple sentences. Our methods of assessing both qualitative and quantitative aspects of language development are on the whole inadequate to deal with the richness and variety of language development after the age of about 3. Thereafter, all that the psycholinguist can hope to do is to examine very specific items of language behaviour, or carry out rather superficial surveys of populations. For all practical purposes the professional psychologist needs to be familiar with the earliest stages of speech and language development, so that he can relate what he knows of normal development to the assessment of any individual child who is not progressing normally. These considerations are relevant not only for children with obvious disorders of language and communication, but for a wide variety of handicaps. It is clearly of the utmost importance to be able to offer more than a 'global guess' about the degree and quality of language development in, for example, a child with sensory or motor defects, and to distinguish expressive from receptive disorders. But it is necessary to be aware of the importance of language skills when dealing with slow-learning and maladjusted children, and even more important to be aware of the more subtle linguistic handicaps which are found in working-class or in culturally impoverished populations (Bernstein, 1965; Lawton, 1968, see also Chapter 19 of this volume). Two of the more frequently used indices of language development will be briefly mentioned; McCarthy's (1954) review of earlier work is still among the most useful reference sources, and some of the methods which she describes are currently being revised and improved.

(a) *Length of sentence* is one of the widely used indices used. The standard technique is to engage the child in a semi-standard play situation with a set of toys and play materials and to record 50 consecutive remarks on magnetic tape. These can then be analysed for mean or maximum length of response. McCarthy (1954, p. 544) summarizes 14 such studies on mean length of response, but these figures are now thought to be too conservative an estimate; Templin (1957) who used the same criteria for defining a word as McCarthy and kept to the same testing conditions, reported a significantly higher mean number of words per remark. These differences may be due to sampling artefacts, or to a real difference in linguistic skills occurring, perhaps as a result of greater environmental stimulation in the period between the two studies. Templin's study goes some way towards throwing doubt on the widely held assumption that girls use longer sentences than boys. The sex differences were slight and largely insignificant on length of remark (except at age 5); in fact, in 230 comparisons of all her speech and language measures, covering eight age-groups, no 0·01 significance levels were recorded, only 15 reached even the 0·05 level and in four of these the boys' score exceeded that of the girls.

Tables 20.1a and 20.1b summarize Templin's (1957) results in greater detail in respect of mean number of words per remark (Table 20.1a) and Mean number of words in five longest remarks (Table 20.1b).

	Boys (N=30)		Girls (N=30)		USES (N=18)		LSES (N=42)		Total Subsamples (N=60)	
CA	Mean	SD	Mean	SD	Mean	SD	Mean	SD	Mean	SD
3	4·3	1·4	3·9	1·0	4·5	1·4	3·9	1·1	4·1	1·3
3·5	4·5	1·0	4·9	1·0	5·3	1·0	4·4	0·9	4·7	1·0
4	5·2	1·5	5·6	1·3	5·5	0·5	5·4	1·6	5·4	1·5
4·5	5·4	1·6	5·4	0·9	6·1	0·9	5·1	1·4	5·4	1·3
5	5·3	1·4	6·1	1·5	6·1	1·5	5·6	1·5	5·7	1·5
6	6·7	1·4	6·4	1·2	6·9	1·1	6·4	1·4	6·6	1·3
7	7·3	0·8	7·3	1·3	7·3	0·8	7·3	1·1	7·3	1·0
8	7·3	1·4	7·9	1·8	7·7	1·6	7·5	1·6	7·6	1·6

TABLE 20.1a.

Mean number of words per remark of boys and girls, upper and lower socio-economic status groups, and total subsamples, by age (Templin, 1957)

	Boys (N=30)		Girls (N=30)		USES (N=18)		LSES (N=42)		Total Subsamples (N=60)	
CA	Mean	SD	Mean	SD	Mean	SD	Mean	SD	Mean	SD
3	7·95	2·63	7·82	1·83	8·75	2·72	7·52	1·93	7·89	2·27
3·5	8·66	2·08	9·46	3·05	9·99	2·19	8·67	2·00	9·06	2·14
4	10·35	3·05	10·66	3·43	10·64	2·34	10·45	2·89	10·51	2·74
4·5	10·73	3·03	10·78	2·23	11·84	2·26	10·28	2·68	10·76	2·66
5	10·82	2·98	12·63	3·61	12·57	3·73	11·36	3·23	11·73	3·43
6	12·42	2·78	12·11	1·90	13·09	2·23	11·91	2·37	12·27	2·39
7	13·76	1·81	13·37	2·45	13·80	1·71	13·47	2·32	13·57	2·16
8	13·55	2·87	14·75	2·69	14·30	2·70	14·09	2·90	14·15	2·85

TABLE 20.1b.

Mean number of words in five longest remarks of boys and girls, upper and lower socio-economic status groups, and total subsamples by age (Templin, 1957)

It will be seen that these tables reflect a clear and significant superiority of the children from the upper socio-economic groups – a superiority which is consistently present in all the language and most of the speech assessments.

(b) *Complexity of verbalization* has been used by several investigators, including McCarthy (1930), Day (1932), Davis (1937) and again Templin (1957), who in this respect also confirmed the relatively more advanced complexity of present-day language samples of children compared to those studied by earlier writers. Following McCarthy and Davis, she isolated six major categories of complex sentence construction.

(1) Functionally complete, but structurally incomplete;
(2) simple sentences without phrase;
(3) simple sentence containing phrases used as adjective or adverb in apposition, compound subject or predicate or compound predicate;
(4) complex sentences with one main and one subordinate clause;
(5) compound sentence, with two independent clauses;
(6) elaborate sentences.

For further details of this classification, and also of her classification of incomplete sentences, the reader is referred to Appendix III of Templin's (1957) monograph, which includes a large amount of normative data on the age groups 3 to 8.

Shriner and Sherman (1967) in a series of studies have revived interest in length and complexity measures. They found that mean length of response was the best predictor of degree of language development, using multiple regression equations involving mean of five longest responses, the number of one-word responses, the number of different words and a structural complexity score.

II   DISORDERS OF LANGUAGE DEVELOPMENT

The programme of language development outlined in the preceding section is not intended to be a definite sequence through which all children pass. In discussing 'normal' language development, the wide range of individual differences must be emphasized. Some children are 'late talkers' for no apparent reason, but in others the delay in starting to speak may well be attributable to a complex of factors, no single one of which would be sufficient in itself to explain the delay. The problem for the parent and for those giving advice in the earliest stages when parents are asking for help is to distinguish the child who is merely a late but normal developer, from the one whose failure to speak may be due to a specific language disorder which requires careful investigation and early treatment. In cases where there is an absence of anything remotely resembling an aetiology, such a distinction is difficult to make and, for this reason, it can be argued that careful investigation of all late talking children is a justifiable preventive measure, even though many of the children investigated will turn out to be merely 'late developers'. Some authorities, in fact, have instituted such a screening procedure by instructing their health visitors to report any children who are 'not talking in sentences by three'. However crude such a classification may be, it seems to be a step in the right direction.

1 Types of speech and language defect

Although this chapter is mainly concerned with language rather than speech disorders, it may be appropriate to reproduce one suggested classification of the whole range of defects (Ingram, 1965).

---

1. Disorders of voicing (Dysphonia.)
2. Disorders of respiratory co-ordination. Hesitation. Stammer. (Dysrhythmia.)
3. Disorders of speech sound production with demonstrable dysfunction or structural abnormalities of tongue, lips, teeth or palate. (Dysarthria.)
    (a) Due to neurological abnormalities
        Upper motor neurone lesions
        Nuclear agenesis
        Lower motor neurone lesions
    (b) Due to local abnormalities

Jaws and teeth	Hypomandibulosis
	Other malocclusions
Tongue	Tie
	Thrust
Lips	Cleft
	Other
	Cleft ($\pm$ cleft lip)
Palate	The palatal dysproportion syndrome
	Other
Pharynx	Large pharynx
	Acquired disease
Mixed	

4. Disorders of speech sound production not attributable to dysfunction or structural abnormality of tongue, lips, teeth or palate, but associated with other disease or adverse environmental factors. (Secondary speech disorders.)
    (a) Associated with mental defect.
    (b) Associated with hearing defect.
    (c) Associated with true dysphasia.
    (d) Associated with psychiatric disorders.
    (e) Associated with adverse environmental factors.
    (f) Combinations of the above (the commonest).
5. The developmental speech disorder syndrome. (Specific developmental speech disorders.)
6. Mixed speech disorders comprising two or more of the above categories.

TABLE 20.2

Suggested classification of speech defects in childhood (Ingram, 1965).

Ingram distinguishes between the more 'physical' disorders, such as the dysphonias, dysrhythmias, dysarthrias and those secondary disorders of speech production which seems to be related to other primary defects such as mental

x*

subnormality, hearing loss, psychiatric disorders and, as he rightly points out, the all too frequent combinations of these. These in turn must be distinguished from the specific developmental speech disorders, 'in which the speech abnormality is not attributable to apparent associated disease or adverse environmental factors'. This disorder includes such diagnoses as receptive and expressive aphasia (or dysphasia), congenital auditory imperception (Worster-Drought, 1968), word deafness and central deafness (Renfrew and Murphy, 1964). Ingram's terminology has the advantage of not implying, as does 'aphasia' any fundamental similarity with aphasic disorders as seen in the adult whose fully developed language functions are impaired by a neurological lesion, such as a stroke or head injury. However, it is not intended to be more than a generic term and still requires more detailed study of the nature of the disability and of its underlying processes, particularly when individual programmes of therapy are being planned.

Moreover, developmental speech disorders must be distinguished from cases of 'true' or acquired dysphasia, in which some speech and language functions have been acquired but are then lost or impaired by a neurological lesion. Ingram (1965) notes that 'even up to the age of three years relatively few children show permanent loss of language ability as a result of brain damage which does not affect intelligence seriously. The majority of children eventually have quite normal speech though its development may be slow.' After the age of 3, however, speech and language impairment become more likely, especially if the damage occurs in the dominant hemisphere; in these cases the types of dysphasia seen are more similar to those shown by adult patients.

2 'Children who talk late'

Many children are now being referred to clinics as 'late talkers', and psychologists are becoming increasingly involved in their assessment. The way in which these referrals are handled varies greatly in different parts of the country, depending on local interest and local facilities. A fairly typical situation is one in which a mother who becomes worried because her child is 'not talking' first discusses the matter with the general practitioner. His advice is frequently along the lines of 'Don't worry, he'll talk when he's ready'. Although this advice is likely to be correct in the majority of cases there is a substantial minority who will need special investigation and help and who may not acquire useful language until four or five, or even later. It is obviously important to be able to identify those in need of special help and to increase the amount of provision for them, which is quite inadequate at the present time. Recent evidence from the Edinburgh Language and Reading Project (Mason, 1967) indicates that children who talk late are at risk for the development of severe difficulties of reading when they reach school, even though they may by then have made reasonable progress in speech and language development. It is likely that a proportion of children now regarded as 'dyslexic' have poorly developed language skills, and that these need specialized investigations, with instruments such as the Illinois Test of Psycholinguistic Abilities, which will enable a skilled remedial teacher to tackle their language difficulties alongside or as a preliminary to any remedial reading work that is done.

There are few detailed studies of the characteristics of late talkers and little agreement on the difference between the mere *late development* of language and some kind of specific *developmental disorders* of the dysphasic type. A child who is late in talking for whatever reason may possibly be referred to one of the rare paediatricians who have a special interest in the condition. In the more fortunate areas there is a hospital or local authority audiology unit or speech and hearing centre, the staff of which should be assisted by the inclusion of a psychologist who will, of course, need experience of language disorders and the appropriate assessment methods if he is to contribute adequately.

It is obviously important to exclude hearing loss and this involves careful and repeated assessment. The notion that a child is 'either deaf or not deaf' has not died altogether, and methods of testing for hearing loss vary greatly. Children with language disorders sometimes give odd and inconsistent responses to audiological tests. They may, for example, respond to pure tones at about 30 db, but not respond to complex tones or voice at much higher intensities (Murphy, 1964). They may also give inconsistent responses over several sessions. It is generally thought that pure tone audiometry, even where it is possible, should be only one of a number of assessment techniques. The psychologist should certainly be familiar with methods of assessing hearing functions (see Chapter 14), and should if possible attend a specialist course for this purpose.

If a significant degree of hearing loss has been confidently excluded, a number of other investigations can be undertaken. In addition to a full paediatric and (if possible) neurological examination, the psychologist may be asked to see the child 'to exclude subnormality'. It may be worth while to examine possible underlying assumptions behind this request. In the first place, there is no necessary association between subnormality of intelligence and retarded language development. If a child is suspected of a mild degree of mental retardation, this should not be regarded as sufficient explanation for the late development of speech and language. Both intelligence and language may be affected by a common factor; since the more reliable assessment techniques include a heavy verbal loading, it is difficult to disentangle the language assessment from the estimate of the child's intelligence. Indeed, since most tests require language comprehension, serious degrees of language disorder commonly lead to diagnoses of mental subnormality or even psychosis. Even if the child is quite obviously of subnormal intelligence, it is not at all uncommon for him to show language deficits far above those that would be expected on the grounds of low intelligence alone. If we consider a population of severely subnormal patients in hospitals (Lyle, 1960) we find that it is quite common for language to be extremely rudimentary even in patients who test at a mental age 5 on the Binet test. Strictly speaking, on a literal interpretation of 'mental age', we would expect a child (or adult) with a mental age as low as 2 years to be talking in sentences. This is manifestly not the case, and indicates that subnormal individuals have speech and language handicaps far above the level that might be predicted on the basis of their intelligence test scores. These defects have been demonstrated by Lyle (1960) and Mein (1960) and reviewed by Schiefelbusch et al. (1967). A series of experimental studies are also reported in O'Connor and Hermelin's (1963) monograph.

Where both subnormality of intelligence and a hearing loss can with some confidence be ruled out as at least a partial 'explanation' of failure to speak and/or comprehend, psychiatric investigation is usually considered necessary. This is partly to exclude autism in which a language disorder is certainly one of the most prominent symptoms, and partly with a view to obtaining an expert evaluation of the child's home background and the quality of the relationship there. The difficulty with this approach is that of distinguishing between cause and effect. A child who does not talk causes a complex pattern of reactions within a family and usually conflicting advice on management from well-meaning relatives and neighbours. Some mothers may react in terms of anxiety or they may institute on their own accord a language training programme, which may, for example, include withholding of food until 'please' has been extracted from the child; again, some mothers may over-react to the advice 'keep talking to him, even though he doesn't seem to understand', by bombarding the child with an incessant stream of commentary about the daily household activities to the point where such comprehension skills as he happens to have become severely stretched. Overstimulation may be as much a source of difficulty as understimulation, and the art of keeping a balance between them is difficult even for the most perceptive parent.

A child who is, as far as can be ascertained, free of any obvious psychiatric disability, and who does not appear to be unduly disturbed or immature emotionally may be living in an environment which is not conducive to language development for that child. Children living under adverse environmental conditions characterized by poverty, neglect or lack of contact between parents and child may show marked delays of language development as part of a wider syndrome of poor cognitive development and subsequent educational retardation or gross underfunctioning. Although delays of language development can sometimes be attributed to a poor environment, this should not be used as an argument against instituting a language enrichment or training programme, since there is evidence that subnormal children from culturally impoverished backgrounds stand to gain more from pre-school education than subnormal children from more stimulating backgrounds (Kirk, 1958). Similarly, Clarke (1968) summarizes a number of studies, including those conducted by him in the Manor Hospital, Epsom, which demonstrated significantly larger I.Q. increments in a sample of subnormal adolescents from particularly poor homes. These studies by Kirk, Clarke and also the well-known Brooklands experiment by Tizard (1964) demonstrated that the provision of a more stimulating environment even in the setting of a hospital could result in substantial improvements in intellectual functioning and educational attainment. It is likely, though not established, that the improvements could be partly attributed to a better use of language; certainly, the Brooklands study suggested that the rises were much greater on verbal than on non-verbal tests (Lyle, 1960).

There have been few detailed reports on the medical and psychological characteristics of children with specific developmental speech disorders. Ingram (1965) and Eisenson (1966) summarize the main clinical findings. The children are slower in standing and walking than their siblings or the general population. One of the most commonly reported findings is that they show late establishment of laterality, weak hand preferences, left-right confusion and difficulties with spatial orientation. Awkwardness for gross movements and deficits in finer motor co-ordination are stressed by Eisenson who distinguishes between 'hard' and 'soft' neurological signs. Out of 100 'aphasic' children studied at Stanford University, 20% had hard signs, 50% had soft signs and 60% had abnormal EEGs. He also reports a large number showing hyperkinetic features in infancy and continuing to be hyperdistractible and showing deficiencies in attention span. Ingram (1965) stresses positive findings in the family history, many of whom show late speech development, late acquisition of reading and writing, left-handedness or ambidexterity. The family history also reveals an excess of multiple births. It is likely, on the basis of these findings, that left handedness, late establishment of laterality or a family history of these, as well as of late acquisition of speech or reading, are found particularly frequently in children with language handicaps. In this connection, it should be remarked that handedness cannot be inferred merely by noting whether a pencil is held in the right or left hand. Hand preferences are not dichotomous, but may be regarded as graded characteristics. Humphrey (1951), working with adults, devised '20 questions on handedness', in which he asked his subjects which hand they used to cut, comb, throw, bat with, etc.

3 Developmental expressive dysphasia

In the primarily expressive disorders, we assume, after careful testing, that the main defect is one involving spoken language. The child uses only a very small number of single words or phrases or, in the more serious conditions, no intelligible words at all, though he may vocalize a good deal. When speech is finally acquired, Ingram (1965) reports that the grammatical structures which they produce are immature by about two years, that they omit articles, conjunctions, prepositions, auxiliary verbs, and are late in learning the correct use of the person and tense.

4 Developmental receptive dysphasia

It is often difficult to believe these children are not deaf, even though audiometric assessment consistently rules out a significant degree of hearing loss

Nevertheless, it has been pointed out that a child can have both a hearing loss and a receptive dysphasia (Taylor, 1964); moreover, Murphy (1967) stresses that repeated audiological assessment is essential, as a minority of these children do function as partially hearing on follow-up. The reasons for this are not clear, but the educational consequences may be critical.

5 Autism

Autism must be mentioned in any discussion on communication disorders, since a severe speech and language handicap is one of its most prominent features. A detailed discussion of autism, involving as it must a full clinical description, an attempt to differentiate autism from childhood schizophrenia and comments on aetiology and treatment is outside the scope of this chapter, but the condition is mentioned here because the assessment of autistic children presents the psychologist with problems very similar to those that he encounters in assessing children with language disorders and because a differential diagnosis between the two conditions is often a clinical and administrative necessity.

About half of the autistic children examined in recent surveys are almost competely mute, but those who do speak seem to display fairly character-istic linguistic idiosyncracies. Kanner (1957) has described these in general terms, while Cunningham and Dixon (1961) and Pronovost *et al.* (1966) have given more detailed case studies. In general, echolalia or delayed echolalia is very common; in addition, they frequently show the 'closed loop' pheno-menon (Rimland, 1965) in which the child will say 'Do you want some milk' when he means 'I want some milk'. Rimland argues that this inability to process and 'transform' linguistic input is due to a dysfunction at the level of the reticular system, though Rutter (1968) prefers the more parsimonious ex-planation that the phenomenon is merely another variant of echolalia. Wing (1966) also records a metaphorical use of language, in which for example, 'don't throw me off the balcony' means an emphatic 'no', and 'he knocked me down' is the equivalent for any accident or bump. A kettle is called 'a make a cup of tea' and a hammer 'a tap it'. Reference has already been made to recent experiments by Hermelin, (1968) who demonstrated a severe difficulty of structuring verbal material; these difficulties were more apparent for verbal than for visual material. Goldfarb (1961) reported that schizophrenic children fail to show voice disturbance under conditions of delayed auditory feedback which also suggests a serious disturbance of input and decoding mechanisms. These need not only full investigation but also an attempt by psychologist and teacher to devise remedial methods designed to overcome or at least compensate for the comprehension difficulties experienced by many autistic and dysphasic children.

The types of language disorders described above do not fall into watertight categories, and it may be inappropriate for the psychologist to be too concerned with the aetiology of the condition. In practice, much overlap between conditions will be found, and disorders of language development seem often to be related to a series of overlapping factors. A child may at one and the same time be suffering from multiple handicaps in which language impairment is considered the most significant at one particular time. With maturation, and with the provision of suitable remedial help, other handicaps may appear to become more prominent. It is therefore difficult to arrive at hard and fast decisions on the reasons for a child's language deficits. Even the most skilled investigations may fail to identify these with any real certainty. The psychologist must of course interest himself in aetiology, and be concerned with the total environment in which the child is acquiring experiences and skills, but his particular contribution lies in the full assessment of the child's level of development and in relating the results of his findings to soundly based ways of helping the child to realize his skills and, as far as is practicable, to overcome his handicaps.

III ASSESSMENT TECHNIQUES

The assessment of children with language disorders, whether these constitute a primary or secondary handicap, presents formidable problems. These stem partly from the difficulty of distinguishing between language and general cognitive processes, and partly from the absence of adequate measures of language functioning. A further difficulty arises from the problems of interpreting the significance of non-verbal tests.

Most of the children who come to psychologists for early assessment of a suspected language disorder are likely to be very young. With an increase in diagnostic and remedial facilities, psychologists are seeing many children as young as 2 or 3. This alone constitutes a further problem, since the validity of intellectual assessment in a pre-school population has been repeatedly brought into question by a series of longitudinal studies which have demonstrated a very small or even negative correlation between such early assessments and the results of tests administered when the child is 5 or older

A particular problem centres around the use of the 'baby' tests and infant developmental schedules, such as those developed by Cattell (1940), Gesell (1954), Griffiths (1954), and Bayley (1965). These tests have been heavily criticized on the grounds of inadequate standardization as well as poor predictive power, and even the validity of the different subscales – locomotor, speech and hearing, personal-social development, etc., has been questioned; a comprehensive critical review (Stott and Ball, 1965), after a factor analysis of the most widely used infant tests, questioned whether the main areas of development were appropriately named. A further problem in the application of such schedules to more severely handicapped older children arises from the fact that older children have had much more opportunity for gaining learning experiences than the very young children on whom the tests were standardized. These problems are not confined to children with language disorders and have been discussed in the more general context of assessing of all types of handicaps in an earlier chapter, but they are relevant here because some assessment of developmental level is essential in the assessment of very young children presenting with language disorders, since the question of their overall level of intellectual and social development is bound to arise at an early stage of the investigation. The view is taken here that some expression of opinion, based on careful assessment and observation, is part of the psychologist's responsibility. The obvious limitations of the currently used developmental schedules do not inevitably place them on a list of proscribed instruments which should not in any circumstances be used. Much depends on the use that is made of the information gained by these means, but there is no reason why they should not be used by an experienced psychologist who is aware of their poor predictive power. As has been argued earlier, psychologists now are somewhat less concerned with accurate prediction of future levels than with attempts to describe present levels of functioning in as accurate and objective a manner as possible. Seen in this light, developmental schedules, properly used and cautiously interpreted, have much to offer in the assessment of young children with delays and abnormalities.

1 Language assessment

The assessment of linguistic maturity in an individual child must rest on a good knowledge of the stages of language development as well as on the use of appropriate tests. The main landmarks of the language acquisition process have been outlined in an earlier section of this chapter, and it now remains to discuss some currently available tests and schedules of language development. It must be stressed at the outset that these are mostly in an early and experimental stage at present and most of them leave much to be desired by way of adequate standardization, freedom from social and cultural bias and ease of administration. Nevertheless, this is an active area of research and development reflecting current concerns with focusing on cognitive processes and on analysing and describing the various constituents of language.

(a) *Illinois Test of Psycholinguistic Abilities*
The clearest example of such an approach is provided by the *Illinois Test of Psycholinguistic Abilities* (McCarthy and Kirk, 1961). This test is based on Osgood's (1957, 1963) theoretical communication model, which in turn derives from some of the models developed by communication engineers. The purpose of such models is to 'provide the specifications for all the processes and all the levels that appear to be involved in understanding and speaking a language'. Osgood's model was quickly seen as a useful starting-point for the construction of a diagnostic test. It must be emphasized that by no means all the features of the theoretical model can be incorporated in a test, for reasons of length, practicability and relevance. Figure 20.1 represents the model as reflected in the subtests of the I.T.P.A. Further details can be found in the test manual

(McCarthy and Kirk, 1961) and in summaries of later work with the test (Bateman, 1965). A revised version of the test is available in which further subtests have been added, and essential improvements made.

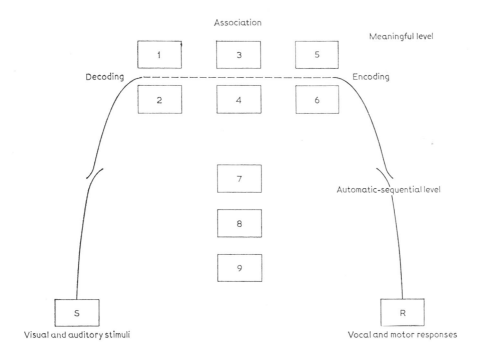

FIGURE 20.1

The clinical model for the Illinois Test of Psycholinguistic Abilities (McCarthy and Kirk, 1961).

Osgood distinguishes between levels of organization, psycholinguistic processes and channels of communication. *Levels of organization* can be subdivided into the representational level, which is broadly concerned with the subject's ability to deal with meaningful symbols, and the automatic sequential level which deals with the 'non-meaningful use of symbols, principally their long-term retention and the short-term memory of symbol sequences' (McCarthy and Olson, 1964).

Psycholinguistic processes are concerned with the development and use of the habits necessary for normal language functioning. The distinction here is between decoding processes, by which we obtain meaning from either visual or auditory linguistic stimuli; encoding processes, which make possible the expression of meaning in words or gestures; and association, which is the intermediate stage of internal manipulation of linguistic symbols.

Channels of communication describes the 'sensory-motor path over which linguistic symbols are received and responded to'. It is divided into the channels concerned with reception of stimuli and those concerned with response, of which only two combinations have been included in the present battery – the auditory-vocal and the visual-motor.

Thus, the test consists of the following nine subtests:

A. Six tests at the representational level –
  1. Auditory decoding: ability to understand simple questions.
  2. Visual decoding: the ability to comprehend and recognize pictures from a display.
  3. Auditory-vocal association: this is tested by a conventional analogies test in which the subject verbally completes an analogy.
  4. Visual-motor association: the ability to relate meaningful symbols is tested by a visual analogies method.
  5. Vocal encoding: the ability to express ideas in words is tested by asking the subject to describe a series of objects.
  6. Motor encoding: the subject has to supply an appropriate gesture for a series of objects which he is shown.

B. Three tests at the automatic sequential level –
  7. Auditory-vocal automatic: basically, a psycholinguistic test of performance in certain grammatical structures – e.g. plurals, tenses, comparatives and superlatives.
  8. Auditory-vocal sequencing: a modified forward digit repetition test.
  9. Visual-motor sequencing: the subject has to duplicate a sequence of pictures or symbols.

Each of these nine tests can be expressed in terms of a raw score, language age or standard score, together with a total score for the test. A profile analysis of an individual child or a mean profile of a group of children can be drawn up. Figure 20.2 is an example of such a profile taken from a study by Tubbs (1966) in which a comparison is made between groups of normal, subnormal and psychotic children, roughly matched on non-verbal tests.

This study demonstrated that psychotic children were significantly worse than younger matched normals on auditory decoding, auditory-vocal association, vocal encoding, motor encoding, auditory-vocal automatic and visual-motor sequential. It will be apparent that there was no difference on the auditory-vocal sequential task, confirming the clinical and experimental evidence that psychotic children are unimpaired at reading back from an immediate memory store. The remaining two tests reflected lower scores for the psychotic group, but not to a significant degree.

Olson (1961) reports a comparative study of deaf, receptive and expressive aphasic children with the I.T.P.A. and showed that the three groups could be

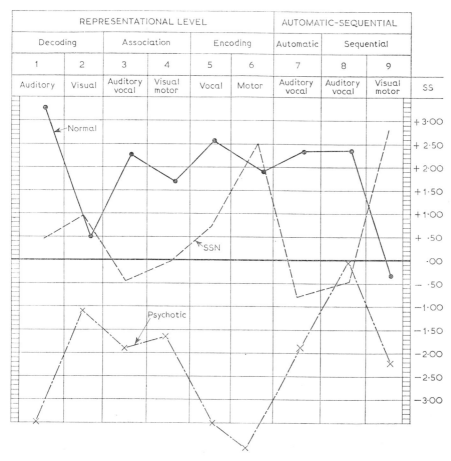

REPRESENTATIONAL LEVEL						AUTOMATIC-SEQUENTIAL			
Decoding		Association		Encoding		Automatic	Sequential		
1	2	3	4	5	6	7	8	9	
Auditory	Visual	Auditory vocal	Visual motor	Vocal	Motor	Auditory vocal	Auditory vocal	Visual motor	SS

FIGURE 20.2

Mean standard scores of normal, S.S.N. and psychotic children on I.T.P.A. (adapted from Tubbs, 1966).

differentiated on all except one of the subtests and that children diagnosed as 'expressive aphasics' were not a homogeneous group from the psycholinguistic point of view, which confirms clinical evidence relating to the variety of handicaps found in this group.

These studies are examples of research studies in which group differences have been compared, but the most promising application of the I.T.P.A. lies in its use for diagnostic purposes, and as a basis for the design of an appropriate remedial programme and the selection of an appropriate learning situation. Bateman (1965) reports a number of studies in which diagnostic use of the I.T.P.A. resulted in measurable improvements in those areas of psycholinguistic function which were significantly depressed. The main advantage of this instrument for assessment purposes is that it allows the composite and global term 'language' to be broken down into more detailed linguistic processes. The present experimental version of the test is standardized on 700 children between $2\frac{1}{2}$ and 9, but its use below four years presents difficulties.

(b) *The Parsons Language Sample*

The Parsons Language Sample (P.L.S.) (Spradlin, 1963a, 1963b) is closely modelled on Skinner's classification of verbal behaviour (see p. 612). It has two sub-sections, vocal and non-vocal:

Vocal subtests
Tact: samples object naming and pictures.
Echoic: sentences of varying degrees of complexity have to be repeated.
Intraverbal: answers to questions.

Non-vocal sub-tests
Echoic gesture: tests child's ability to imitate a motor act.
Comprehension: child has to complete motor tasks after both vocal and gestural instruction.
Intraverbal gesture: questions which can be answered by vocal and gestural responses.

The scale has good reliability, and a factor analytic study by Horner (1967) showed high correlations with I.T.P.A. total, and also indicated that the two scales were loading on similar factors – particularly immediate recall of auditory symbols, general linguistic ability and comprehension and/or expression. The test has so far been used mainly with mentally subnormal children, but has wider implications for assessment.

(c) *The Peabody Picture Vocabulary Test*

This test is now used almost routinely and needs little description. The original American standardization (Dunn, 1959) could be used on children from the age of about 21 months upwards, while Brimer and Dunn (1962) produced English revisions for children from 3 to 5, 5 to 7 years, and another for older children. In the basic form of the test the child is asked to point to one of four pictures corresponding to a word spoken by the examiner; the number of pictures correctly identified can be converted to a percentile or mental age score. This test has the advantage of not requiring more than a pointing response from the child, but it measures only vocabulary – obviously only a small segment of the comprehension complex. In a recent study, Carr *et al.* (1967) warn against the use of the P.P.V.T. as a 'quick' intelligence scale, even for screening purposes.

Shaw *et al.* (1966) had previously found only small correlations between P.P.V.T. and the W.I.S.C., and the Carr study indicated that the P.P.V.T. correlated moderately with only two of the I.T.P.A. subtests (Auditory-Vocal Association and Auditory-Vocal Automatic), though the variance accounted for by these two tests was only 38%. Hence, it cannot be concluded that the P.P.V.T. measures either general intelligence or even language comprehension, though it probably is a better reflection of the latter than the former.

(d) *Other Language Scales*

A variety of techniques of language assessment have been developed in recent years, but these have been mostly used in the context of specific research studies, rather than as attempts to provide tests for use on children with language disorders. The most extensive series of tests by Templin (1957) and her associates at the University of Minnesota has already been mentioned. Templin provides enough details of administration, scoring and norms to allow one or more of her tests to be applied to clinical populations. Reynell's tests (1969) are particularly useful with handicapped children and are fully described in Chapter 15 of this volume. In recent years, a number of investigators have concerned themselves with assessment of language functions in 'culturally disadvantaged' children, especially in the context of a language enrichment programme (see Chapter 19 of this volume). Details of language assessment techniques are also provided by Deutsch (1965) and Bereiter and Engelmann (1966), while Métraux (1950) describes 'typical profiles' from 18 to 54 months.

Finally, mention should be made of Lees' (1966) attempt to apply transformational grammar to evolve a 'developmental sentence type' in which a child's spoken language can be categorized according to the degree of maturity which would be predicted by Chomsky's model of language development (Chomsky, 1957, 1965).

IV TREATMENT

The treatment of children with language disorders is still at an early stage in Britain. This arises partly from a very real neglect of the problem and partly from the absence of a homogeneous and clearly definable handicap. Language disorders are found in association with other handicaps, and it is only rarely that a diagnosis of a primary language disorder can be confidently made, except in acquired cases where the defects follow a cerebral lesion or infection such as meningitis. For the most part, the problems presented are those of differential diagnosis, involving hearing loss, autism and mental subnormality. It is only when these can be excluded, or when the extent of these difficulties is not thought to be sufficient to account for the language delay, that appropriate treatment is begun. But there is no convincing reason why treatment should not be begun before the diagnosis is complete; indeed the term 'diagnostic therapy' is not inappropriate in this context, since it is only by beginning treatment that the problem becomes more sharply defined. Nevertheless rationally based, as opposed to exploratory treatment, must await a full diagnosis.

1 Speech therapy

There is a widespread assumption that speech therapy is not appropriate before the age of 5, but this rests on an outmoded concept of the methods and aims of speech therapy. Modern speech therapists are trained to do far more than correct articulation defects, though it is true that many of them spend much of their time on this kind of work, especially in school clinics and hospitals. A number of speech therapists are particularly involved in the treatment of language delays and language disorders (Renfrew and Murphy, 1964, Greene, 1967): their work is based on an attempt to stimulate first an 'inner' language, and on the development of comprehension as a series of carefully graded steps. It is also relevant to point out that many children referred for articulation disorders have a poorly developed language system; similarly, children with mild degrees of mental subnormality, including those in special schools and especially those from culturally and linguistically impoverished environments, may benefit from forms of speech therapy which are designed to facilitate linguistic development and the use of language in problem solving, in classifying experiences and forming concepts. Speech therapy of this type is increasingly applied for schoolchildren, but certain hospitals and local authority units now try to provide for speech therapy, possibly in a nursery school setting, for young children with poor or late development of language.

2 Educational treatment

A number of local authorities are now considering ways of providing units or classes in ordinary schools for children with special speech and language problems. The children in these classes tend to be very heterogeneous and to have a wide variety of language and learning problems, ranging from severe articulation disorders to almost complete absence of speech. It is only in the larger authorities that enough children are likely to be found who can constitute a more homogeneous group. In London, for example, there are a number of tutorial classes for 'aphasic' children, who spend half the day receiving special help suited to their individual needs and the rest of the day in a normal school. The educational needs of these children become increasingly complex as they grow older, because of the difficulties of reading and writing and of more advanced thought processes in which language is normally prominent.

For this reason there is an urgent need to increase the range of educational provision available. At the present time, there are only two residential schools in Great Britain which cater specifically for children with speech and language disorders – the John Horniman School at Worthing, Sussex, for children up to the age of about 9, and the Moor House School at Oxted, Surrey, for older children. Both of these schools are overwhelmed with applications, and the policy is to restrict selection to those of at least average intelligence.

Lea (1968) describes a language scheme designed to help children with receptive aphasia. Most of the children have acquired the ability to read and understand the printed word much better than the spoken word, but the structure of their written language is chaotic, as the following examples, all from children of average or higher intelligence between the ages of 11 and 15, will indicate (Lea, 1967):

> Very boy happy birthday; red a ball, garden pretty go to; today all is visiting day the finished in went going; a singing, a some, a slow, etc.

A linguist comments on these samples that although the clause structure here conforms readily to a Subject-Predicator-Complement type, the aphasia appears to be concentrating its effect on the 'lower' levels of grammar – noun and adverbial phrases and related propositional constructions (Crystal, 1967). Lea's scheme is based on the observation that the receptive aphasic has a difficulty of syntactic ordering and structuring: 'He does not appreciate that there are different types of words, each with a different function; all words are names, labels of equal value to be attached to a particular object or event' (Lea, 1968). He there- fore devised a scheme in which the different parts of speech are represented by different colours – e.g. nouns in red, verbs in yellow, adjectives in green, etc. In answering a written question, or in describing a picture, the answer is 'pre- structured' by drawing lines of the appropriate colour. For example, the answer to a written question 'What is the boy doing?' might be 'The boy is running'; the teacher draws a red (noun) line followed by a yellow (verb) line. These 'props' can be gradually faded as the child becomes increasingly skilled at structuring his own sentences.

Another, more elaborate, scheme for the treatment of aphasic children has been given by the late Mildred McGinnis (1963). The McGinnis method of teaching, which has been used on preschool as well as school-age children and which both speech therapists and teachers can learn, is based on 'association' techniques. A first attempt is made to teach 50 nouns by gradually building up individual sounds and then synthesizing them into words; the emphasis in this process is also on constant association between attention, retention and recall. Special attention is paid to sound sequences. Later stages (teaching units) increase the material to be learned by small steps and gradually increase the complexity of the language tasks. This method sounds rather formal, but it does seem to provide a carefully thought out means of structuring experience into small units, and avoids the danger of bombarding children with language.

3 Parent guidance

Parents have an essential role to play in the treatment of the child with a language disorder. Since early diagnosis and treatment are essential if a defect is not to become a handicap, parents should be involved in treatment to the maximum extent and not merely be given reassuring or anxiety-provoking comments. Work in the treatment of very young deaf children in this country (Ewing, 1957; Broomfield, 1967) has shown that parents can be helped to participate actively in a detailed treatment programme, first by being shown how to manage amplification and hearing aids and, almost from the start, being provided with a detailed scheme of language development. The psychologist who is familiar with the developmental aspects of the language acquisition process can help to design such a programme in collaboration with a teacher or speech therapist. By regular assessments, he can try to evaluate the progress the child is making, over and above the progress that would be expected merely on a maturational basis – not an easy distinction to make to parents who eagerly attribute any sign of progress to the effect of a treatment, rather than to the passage of time. Similarly, the psychologist should be able to plan for the next stage of the treatment and be on the alert for signs that the child is moving towards the next stage of development. His knowledge of play, particularly in its symbolization and imaginative aspects, should also enable him to advise parents on the kind of play that they might encourage, and which might act as a foundation for the advanced symbolic skills which are represented by language.

V CONCLUSIONS

Disorders of language and communication occur in a variety of handicaps and do not constitute a unitary syndrome. Children with mental subnormality and with hearing impairments commonly show poorer levels of language development than would be expected from the severity of their cognitive or perceptual handicaps and there are good reasons for suspecting that the learning difficulties which they show are to some degree attributable to their poor level of language ability and to their inability to harness language to problem solving processes. Even where there is reason to suspect a relatively 'pure' language disorder, and where disorders such as deafness, subnormality and autism can be fairly confidently excluded, the purity of the syndrome may be only temporary, since absence of language, both in its receptive and its expressive aspects, is likely to bring secondary handicaps in its train; in particular, behaviour and adjustment problems are to be expected, stemming partly from effects on family and teachers. At a cognitive level, absence of language as a tool for comprehension and communication is likely to make it more difficult for the child to progress to more complex forms of thinking, especially those involving abstraction, classification and concept formation. There is also evidence to show that children who talk late have particular problems in learning to read, even though they may by that time have acquired normal or near normal linguistic maturity.

Psychologists are seeing an increasing number of children, many of them very young, whose language development is giving cause for concern. Whether or not the language disorder is primary or secondary is less important than a full evaluation of the extent and nature of the child's language functions and some attempt to relate these to other aspects of his cognitive and personality development and to knowledge of the experiences available to him. By full evaluation is meant an attempt to break down the global, composite construct we call 'language' into its constituent processes. In this way some progress can be made towards relating diagnosis to treatment.

REFERENCES

BATEMAN, B. (1965) *The Illinois Test of Psycholinguistic Abilities. Summaries of Studies.* Urbana, Ill.: Institute for Research in Exceptional Children.

BAYLEY, N. (1965) Comparison of mental and motor test scores for ages 1-15 months by sex, birth order and race, geographical location and education of parents. *Child Develop.*, **36**, 379-411.

BELLUGI, U. and BROWN, R. W. (Eds.) (1964). The Acquisition of Language. *Monogr. Soc. Res. Child Dev.*, **29**, 1.

BEREITER, C. and ENGELMANN, S. (1966) *Teaching Disadvantaged Children in the Pre-School.* New Jersey: Prentice Hall.

BERKO, J. (1958) The child's learning of English morphology. *Word*, **14**, 150-177. Reprinted in SAPORTA, S. (1961) *loc. cit.*

BERNSTEIN, B. (1965) A socio-linguistic approach to learning. *In* GOULD, J. (Ed.) *Penguin Survey of Social Sciences.* Harmondsworth: Penguin Books.

BRIMER, R. and DUNN, L. (1962) *The English Picture Vocabulary Scale.* Bristol: Educ. Evaluation Enterprises.

BROOMFIELD, A. (1967) Guidance to parents of deaf children: a perspective. *Brit. J. Dis. Communic.*, **2**, 112-123.

BROWN, R. W. (1965) *Social Psychology.* New York: Free Press.

BROWN, R. W. and FRASER, C. (1964) The Acquisition of Syntax. *In* BELLUGI, U. and BROWN, R. W., *loc. cit.*

CARR, D. L., BROWN, L. F. and RICE, J. A. (1967) The PPVT in the assessment of language deficits. *Amer. J. ment. Def.*, **71**, 937-939.

CARROLL, J. B. (1964) *Language and Thought.* Englewood Cliffs, New Jersey: Prentice Hall.

CATTELL, P. (1940) *The Cattell Infant Intelligence Scale.* New York: Psychol. Corpn.

CHOMSKY, N. (1957) *Syntactic Structure.* The Hague: Mouton.

CHOMSKY, N. (1959) Review of Skinner's *Verbal Behavior. Language*, **35**, 26-58. Reprinted in JAKOBOVITS, L. A. and MIRON, M. S. (1967) *Readings in the Psychology of Language.* Englewood Cliffs, New Jersey: Prentice Hall.

CHOMSKY, N. (1965) *Aspects of the Theory of Syntax.* Cambridge, Mass.: M.I.T. Press.

CLARKE, A. D. B. (1968) Learning and human development. *Brit. J. Psychiat.*, **114**, 1061-1077.

CLARKE, A. D. B. and CLARKE, A. M. (1959) Recovery from the effects of deprivation. *Acta Psychol.*, **16**, 137-144.

CRYSTAL, D. (1967) Personal communication.

CUNNINGHAM, M. A. and DIXON, M. (1961) A study of the language of an autistic child. *J. Child Psychol. Psychiat.*, **2**, 193-202.

DARLEY, F. L. and WINITZ, H. (1961) Age of first word: review of research. *J. Speech hear. Dis.* **26**, 272-290.

DAVIS, E. A. (1937) *The Development of Linguistic Skill in Twins, Singletons with Siblings and Only Children from Age Five to Ten Years*. Minneapolis: Univ. Minnesota Press.

DAY, E. (1932) The development of language in twins. *Child Dev.*, **3**, 179-199; 298-316.

DEUTSCH, M. (1965) The role of social class in language development and cognition. *Amer. J. Orthopsychiat.*, **35**, 78-88.

DONOGHUE, E. L. and SHAKESPEARE, R. (1967) The reliability of paediatric case history milestones. *Developm. Med. Child Neurol.*, **9**, 64-69.

DUNN, L. (1959) *The Peabody Picture Vocabulary Scale*. Minneapolis: American Guidance Service.

EISENSON, J. (1966) Perceptual disturbances in children with central nervous system disfunctions and implications for language development. *Brit. J. Dis. Communic.*, **1**, 21-32.

ERVIN-TRIPP, S. and SLOBIN, D. (1966) Psycholinguistics. *Annual Review of Psychology*. Palo Alto.

EWING, C. A. and EWING, L. (1957) *Educational Guidance and the Deaf Child*. Manchester: Manchester Univ. Press.

GESELL, A. (1954) *The First Five Years of Life*. London: Methuen.

GOLDFARB, W. (1961) *Childhood Schizophrenia*. Cambridge, Mass.: Harvard Univ. Press.

GREENE, M. (1967) Speechless and backward at three. *Brit. J. Dis. Communic.*, **2**, 134-145.

GRIFFITHS, R. (1954) *The Abilities of Babies*. London: University of London Press.

HERMELIN, B. (1968) The experimental study of psychotic children. *In* MITTLER, P. (Ed.) *Aspects of Autism*. London: Brit. Psychol. Soc.

HORNER, R. D. (1967) A factor analysis comparison of the ITPA and PLS with mentally retarded children. *Except. Child.*, **34**, 183-189.

HUMPHREY, M. E. (1951) Consistency of hand usage. *Brit. J. educ. Psychol.*, **21**, 214.

INGRAM, T. T. S. (1965) Specific retardation of speech development. *Speech Path. Therapy*, **8**, 3-11.

IRWIN, O. C. (1960) Language and communication. *In* MUSSEN, P. H. (Ed.) *Handbook of Research Methods in Child Development*. New York: Wiley.

KANNER, L. (1957) *Child Psychiatry* (3rd Ed.). Springfield, Ill.: Springer.

KIRK, S. A. (1958) *Early Education of the Mentally Retarded*. Urbana, Ill.: Univ. Urbana Press.

LASHLEY, K. S. (1951) The problem of serial order in behavior. *In* JEFFRESS, L. A. (Ed.) *Central Mechanisms in Behavior*. New York: Wiley. Reprinted in SAPORTA, S. (Ed.) *loc. cit.*

LAWTON, D. (1968) *Social Class, Language and Education*. London: Routledge and Kegan Paul.

LEA, J. (1967) Personal communication.

LEA, J. (1968) Language and receptive aphasia. *Spec. Educ.*, **57**, 21-25.

LEES, L. (1966) Developmental sentence types: a method for comparing normal and deviant syntactic development. *J. Speech Hear. Dis.*, **31.**, 311-330.

LENNEBERG, E. H. (1964) Speech as a motor skill with special reference to nonaphasic disorders. *In* BELLUGI, U. and BROWN, R. W. (Eds.) *loc. cit.*

LENNEBERG, E. H. (1967) *Biological Foundations of Language*. New York: Wiley.

LYLE, J. G. (1960) The effect of an institution environment upon the verbal development of institutionalised children. (II) speech and language, (III) the Brooklands Residential Family Unit. *J. ment. Def. Res.*, **4**, 1-13; 14-23.

LYONS, J. and WALES, R. (Eds.) (1966) *Psycholinguistic Papers*. Edinburgh: Edinburgh University Press.

MCCARTHY, D. (1930) *The Language Development of the Pre-School Child*. Minneapolis: Univ. Minnesota Press.

MCCARTHY, D. (1954) Language development in children. *In* CARMICHAEL, L. (Ed.) *Manual of Child Psychology*. New York: Wiley.

MCCARTHY, J. J. and KIRK, S. A. (1961) *The Illinois Test of Psycholinguistic Abilities*. (Experimental Edition.) Urbana, Ill.: Institute for Research in Exceptional Children.

MCCARTHY, J. J. and OLSON, J. L. (1964) *Validity Studies on the Illinois Test of Psycholinguistic Abilities*. Milwaukee: University of Wisconsin.

MCGINNIS, M. (1963) *Aphasic Children*. Washington: Alexander Bell Assn.

MCNEILL, D. (1966) Developmental Psycholinguistics. *In* SMITH, F. A. and MILLER, G. A. (Eds.) *The Genesis of Language*. Cambridge, Mass.: M.I.T. Press.

MASON, A. (1967) Specific (developmental) dyslexia. *Develop. Med. Child Neurol.*, **9**, 183-190.

MEIN, R. (1960) A study of the oral vocabularies of severely subnormal patients. *J. ment. Def. Res.*, **4**, 130-143.

MENYUK, P. (1963) Syntactic structures in the language of children. *Child Dev.*, **34**, 407-422.

METRAUX, R. W. (1950) Speech profiles of the pre-school child 18-54 months. *J. Speech Hear. Dis.*, **15**, 37-53.

MILLER, G. A., GALANTER, E. and PRIBRAM, K. H. (1960) *Plans and the Structure of Behavior*. New York: Holt, Rinehart and Winston.

MITTLER, P. (1969) Psycholinguistic skills in four-year-old twins and singletons. Unpublished Ph.D. Thesis, University of London.

MURPHY, K. (1964) Development of normal vocalisation and speech. *In* RENFREW, C. and MURPHY, K. (Eds.), *The Child Who Does Not Talk*. London: Spastics Society and Heinemann.

MURPHY, K. (1967) Personal communication.

O'CONNOR, N. and HERMELIN, B. (1963) *Speech and Thought in Severe Sub-normality.* London: Pergamon.

OLSON, J. L. (1961) Deaf and sensory aphasic children. *Except. Child.,* 27, 422-424.

OSGOOD, C. E. (1957) A behavioristic analysis. *In Contemporary Approaches to Cognition.* Cambridge, Mass.: Harvard Univ. Press.

OSGOOD, C. E. (1963) Psycholinguistics. *In* KOCH, S. (Ed.) *Psychology: A Study of a Science.* New York: McGraw-Hill.

PRONOVOST, B. W., WAKSTEIN, M. P. and WAKSTEIN, D. J. (1966). A longitudinal study of speech behavior and language comprehension of fourteen children diagnosed atypical or autistic. *Except. Child.,* 33, 19-26.

RENFREW, C. and MURPHY, K. P. (1964) *The Child Who Does Not Talk.* London: Spastics Society and Heinemann.

REYNELL, J. (1969) *Reynell Developmental Language Scales.* London: NFER (In press.)

RIMLAND, B. (1965) *Infantile Autism.* London: Methuen.

RUTTER, M. (1966) Behavioural and cognitive abnormalities. *In* WING, J. K. (Ed.) *loc. cit.*

RUTTER, M. (1968) Concepts of autism. *In* MITTLER, P. (Ed.) *Aspects of Autism.* London: British Psychol. Soc.

SAPORTA, S. (Ed.) *Psycholinguistics. A Book of Readings.* New York: Holt, Rinehart and Winston.

SCHIEFELBUSCH, R. L., COPELAND, R. H. and SMITH, J. O. (1967). *Language and Mental Retardation.* New York: Holt, Rinehart and Wiston.

SHAW, H. J., MATHEWS, C. G. and KLOVE, H. (1966) The equivalence of WISC and PPVT I.Q.s. *Amer. J. ment. Defic.,* 70, 601-606.

SHIRLEY, M. (1933) *The First Two Years of Life: A Study of 25 Babies,* Vol. II. Minneapolis: University of Minnesota Press.

SHRINER, T. H. and SHERMAN, D. (1967) An equation for assessing language development. *J. Speech Hear. Res.,* 10, 41-48.

SKINNER, B. F. (1957) *Verbal Behavior.* New York: Appleton-Century-Crofts.

SMITH, F. A. and MILLER, G. A. (1966) *The Genesis of Language.* Cambridge, Mass.: M.I.T. Press.

SMITH, M. K. (1926) Measurements of the size of general English vocabulary through the elementary grades and high school. *Genet. Psychol. Monogr.* 24, 311-345.

SPRADLIN, J. E. (1963a) Language and Communication in Mental Defectives. *In* ELLIS, N. R. (Ed.) *Handbook of Mental Deficiency.* New York: McGraw-Hill.

SPRADLIN, J. E. (1963b) Assessment of speech and language in retarded children. *J. Speech hear. Dis., Monogr. Suppl.,* No. 10.

STOTT, L. H. and BALL, R. S. (1965) Infant and preschool mental tests: a review and evaluation. *Monogr. Soc. Res. Child Developm.,* 30, 101.

TAYLOR, I. G. (1964) *Neurological Mechanisms of Hearing and Speech in Children.* Manchester: Manchester University Press.

TEMPLIN, M. C. (1957) *Certain Language Skills in Children.* Minneapolis: Univ. Minnesota Press.

TIZARD, J. (1964) *Community Services for the Mentally Handicapped.* London: Oxford University Press.

TUBBS, V. K. (1966) Types of linguistic disability in psychotic children. *J. ment. Def. Res.,* **10,** 230-240.

WING, J. K. (Ed.) (1966) *Early Childhood Autism: Clinical, Educational and Social Aspects.* London: Pergamon.

WORSTER-DROUGHT, C. (1968) Speech disorders in children. *Developm. Med. Child Neurol.,* **10,** 427-440.

PART FOUR

Experimental Advances

21

Intensive assessment of the single case: an inductive-deductive approach

M. B. Shapiro

I   INTRODUCTION

The basic function of the applied scientist must be to develop, on the basis of a consideration of the current methods and findings of his science, principles which will provide a guide to the way in which he should carry out his practical work. The attempt to apply these principles may show that they have limitations or that they are incorrect. The applied scientist must then return to the study of his basic science in order to find ways of overcoming such difficulties. If the search is unsuccessful, he then has to develop his own methods and try to make his own discoveries. There needs, in effect, to be a kind of dialogue between applied and basic science. The effectiveness of the dialogue depends upon how well the applied scientist knows his science and how experienced he is in its application. This process, if ethical and scientific standards are to be maintained, does not work easily. Psychological research is developing very rapidly, and the applied problems are difficult. The busy practitioner has little time available for the study and thought which are necessary. An effective dialogue is therefore likely to remain more of an aspiration than an achievement. In such a situation one tends to avoid making public statements of one's present opinions, especially in writing. However, public discussion between applied scientists might lay the basis for a co-operative exercise which should speed up the solution of our problems. The need for such discussion is made greater by the fact that the applied scientist is, in general, the only person who can usefully conduct it. He is the only person who can be expected to know what questions should be asked of his basic science, and to extract from the answers the relevant generalizations and working hypotheses.

It seems necessary, if we are to carry out these tasks effectively, to keep two points in mind. First, we should always be ready to change our views in the light of new findings and considerations. Secondly, we should accept the possibility that quite serious mistakes may be made, and therefore adopt a detached attitude to the discussion of these mistakes – one's own as well as other people's.

It is the contention of this chapter that our present state of knowledge in the field of the psychological assessment of the individual gives rise to three important generalizations. The first of these is that there are sources of a substantial amount of error due to the imperfect reliability and the imperfect standardization of our techniques. This applies both to conventional psychological tests and to uncontrolled clinical observations. Secondly, a very large part of the organization of human traits, including those of ability and personality, may be accounted for by specific factors. Thirdly, while the organization of psychological traits is specific to a considerable degree, there does appear to be a considerable amount of generality in the mode of operation of the processes underlying these traits. This chapter will be concerned with a discussion of the nature and implications for the assessment of the individual, of these three ideas.

II ERROR

1 Unsystematic error

By unsystematic error we mean error of measurement in the classical sense of the term, i.e. fluctuations in scores which cannot be related to any identifiable factors and which have a mean of zero and a normal distribution about that mean. To the clinical psychologist, the validity of a test is much more important than its reliability. There would be no point in using a test which had perfect reliability and little, if any, validity. However, in our society, some tests are accepted as relatively independent criteria on the basis of which important decisions about patients are made. This applies particularly to intelligence tests like the various modifications of the Binet-Simon, presumably because there is some evidence available concerning the external validity of these tests. It is important, therefore, to be aware of the exact implications of unreliability and the way in which the unreliability can vary. For example, McNemar (1942) reports that the 1937 Terman Merrill has form-versus-form reliabilities which range from 0·83 for bright preschool children to 0·97 for dull schoolchildren. We can obtain an idea of what such reliability coefficients may mean in practice by using the usual formula s.e.m. $= $ s.d.$\sqrt{1-r}$ (s.e.m. $=$ standard error of measurement and s.d. $=$ standard deviation). One could define the s.e.m. of a test as the s.d. of the scores one would obtain if one were to give the same test an infinite number of times to the same person, without the psychological effects of such a procedure having any influence upon the results. The s.e.m. for a reliability of 0.83 would therefore be $\pm$ 0·4 s.d. and for a reliability of 0·97 about $\pm$ 0·17 s.d. We can assume that where the reliabilities are in the region of 0·8, the most likely true score will be very near to the observed score. Let us imagine that we have a preschool child who has an I.Q. of 120 and that the s.d. of the test norms is 16. An s.e.m. of $\pm$ 0·4 s.d. means that about 67% of the patient's scores will be between +0·4 s.d. and $-$ 0·4 s.d. around the true score, i.e. between an I.Q. of 113·6 (120$-$6·4) and an I.Q. of 126·4 (120+6·4), i.e. between 114 and 126. We may not be satisfied with the 67% level of confidence and want, because of the importance of a decision we have to make on the basis of the test result, to have a much higher level of confidence. We can obtain an estimate of all possible fiducial limits by using a table for the normal curve. We will find, for example, that for the 95% level we need limits which are about twice the s.e.m. In the case of our patient with an I.Q. of 120 we would conclude that 95% of his scores are likely to be between an I.Q. of 107·2 (120−12·8) and an I.Q. of 132·8 (120+12·8), i.e. between 108 and 133.

For a school-age subject with an I.Q. of 70 the fiducial limits would be a good deal narrower. At the 67% level they would be between 67·23 and 72·77, i.e. between 67 and 73. At the 95% level they would be between 64·46 and 75·54, i.e. between 65 and 76.

It can be seen that where the reliability is as low as 0·83, the impression given by a test result when taken by itself (i.e. a point estimate) is very different from the impression given by an examination of the fiducial limits (i.e. an interval estimate) at a reasonably high level of confidence. That is why it seems to be desirable for psychologists to include routinely a statement of the s.e.m. whenever they report a subject's test score. For example, in the case of a preschool child with an observed I.Q. of 120 on the Terman Merrill, one could report it thus: 120±6. One could gradually inculcate in one's non-psychological colleagues the idea that the number after the '±' means the range above and below the reported score in which two-thirds of the patient's scores are likely to be. If they want to be more confident about the result they could be advised to double the limits to obtain an estimate of the range within which 95% of the scores are likely to fall.

Some experienced and well-known psychologists resist this proposal to substitute interval for point-estimates very strongly, though not denying the fact that interval estimates are more accurate and less misleading than point estimates. The reasons given are usually that the use of interval estimates will confuse non-psychologists and make them have less confidence in our work. The counter-arguments are that the notion of error is not a strange one to intelligent people, that it is better for people to be confused temporarily about an accurate idea than to be clear permanently about an inaccurate one, that the admission of error will increase the confidence our colleagues have in us and, finally, that the popularization of the notion of interval estimates will lead to the more cautious and careful application of test results.

Not only do we find that well-known tests can have low reliabilities, but the reliabilities which are published are often of limited value. They are often presented, as they are in the case of the Wechsler tests, in terms of some form of internal homogeneity, such as the corrected split-half correlation. At best, this kind of estimate will only give us an idea of the reliability of the test when it is administered on a *single* occasion by the *same* testers. It does not give us the reliability of the test when it is administered on *different* occasions by *different* testers. This can only be done by some kind of 'equivalent-form' approach. There appears to be only one well-known test which provides a form-versus-form reliability: this is the 1937 version of the Terman Merrill (McNemar, 1942). Our difficulties are increased by the fact that there are indications that any single test may have a number of different reliabilities. For example, McNemar (1942) reports that in the case of the 1937 Terman Merrill, the reliabilities vary with both age and I.Q. level. He found that, on the whole, the higher the I.Q. the lower were the reliabilities, and the older the child the higher were the reliabilities. As we noted above, these reliabilities vary from 0·83 to 0·97, with strikingly different outcomes in terms of fiducial limits. The Terman Merrill (1937) is the only marketed test which presented these kinds of data, and now, alas, it has been replaced by a new version, the standardization of which is open to question. This matter will be discussed later.

2 Systematic error

By systematic error we mean that the score obtained on a test is different from the supposed 'true' score because of the operation of identifiable factors. One of the outstanding sources of such error lies in the method of calibration which is used for most tests. We are restricted, in our calibration of tests, to a form of ordinal scaling. This takes the form of ranking a subject's responses in relation to the ranked responses of a large sample which is representative of the population which interests us. It seems almost impossible to collect such a sample without some degree of bias. This is illustrated by Dearborn and Rothney's (1941) finding that the median score for nine different intelligence tests, when administered at different times over a period of years to 320 children, ranged from 94 to 110; '100' should have been the median score for every one of the tests.

Not only may similar tests differ from each other in their calibration, but some widely used tests have not been even standardized in the obvious way. The published norms consist essentially of extrapolations from other data which are thought to be relevant.

Two well-known intelligence tests belong to this class. One of them is the Standard Progressive Matrices (Raven, 1958) in its adult standardization (Foulds and Raven, 1948; Raven, 1948). In the first place, test results were gathered for what was said, but not proved, to be a representative sample of males with mean ages of 20 and 25 years. The test was then administered to a large sample of male subjects of all ages up to about 65, working in two large industrial concerns. The mean score for each of four percentile ranks (95th, 75th, 50th and 25th) was calculated for each five-year age group. The results showed, for each of the four percentiles, a fall in score with increasing age; the results for the two industrial firms were very similar to each other.

The means for the percentiles for the 20- and 25-year-old groups were found to be substantially higher than the means for the previously gathered 'representative' sample. It was thought that this reflected the fact that samples from the two industrial enterprises included very few unskilled labourers and no casual workers (Raven, 1948). To meet this difficulty the means for the previous percentiles of the older age groups in the industrial samples were lowered in accordance with the discrepancies found in the 20- and 25-year-old groups. The norms for adults over the age of 25 have not therefore been directly observed;

they are only estimates. The Mill Hill Vocabulary Test has been standardized in essentially a similar manner (Raven, 1958).

The second test whose norms appear to be largely an extrapolation is the third revision of the Stanford-Binet Intelligence Scale (Terman and Merrill, 1960). To achieve the re-standardization, a number of steps were taken. The two forms of the 1937 revision of the test were administered to nearly 5,000 subjects between $2\frac{1}{2}$ and 18 years of age. These subjects were not selected to represent any particular population, though we are assured, without any proof being offered, that 'great care was taken to make sure that special selective factors were avoided' (p.38). The second step consisted of comparing, for each item, the percentage passing at each mental age level with the percents obtained for the 1937 standardization. On the basis of this comparison, decisions were made about the retention, exclusion or re-allocation of items.

The third step consisted of further adjustments of the allocation of items in order to make mean mental ages more nearly equal to the mean chronological ages. For this purpose the findings for the 1937 standardization were used. Finally, the tables were so arranged that an s.d. of 16 could be achieved for each group. Again, for this purpose, the data gathered for the 1937 sample were used.

No work was carried out to investigate the results of these re-adjustments, nor are we given enough 'hard' data which enable us to judge the outcome for ourselves. In fact, the only 'hard' study consisted of the testing, with both Form L and M of the 1937 revision, of two stratified samples: one of 100 6-year-olds and another of 100 15-year-olds, drawn from two Californian communities. The percentage passing at each mental age level was compared with the percentages found for the 1937 revision. Very little difference appeared. This result indicated that it might be safer to use the 1937 than to use the 1960 version. We would at least continue to have the advantage of a pair of equivalent forms whose intercorrelations had been thoroughly investigated.

We have to conclude that not only can the fiducial limits of a test score be considerable but that there is a blur of uncertainty about the measures of central tendency and the measures of distributions of all tests.

III THE SPECIFICITY OF PSYCHOLOGICAL TRAITS

One of the outstanding findings which seems to emerge from the past 50 years of investigation of correlations between psychological traits is that specific factors account for a large part of the reliable variance between individuals. In the field of human ability most of the common variance, especially that part of it involved in attainment outside the testing-room, could be accounted for in terms of a general factor, a verbal education factor (*v:ed*) and a spatial motor factor (*k:m*). The remaining reliable variance could be accounted for in terms of relatively specific factors or group factors of narrow range, e.g. speed of wrist movement, rate of aim movements, auditory and visual reaction time (Vernon,

1964a). To talk of group factors of narrow range does not seem to be very different from talking about specific factors.

Vernon concluded (p.128, 1964a) 'it appears unlikely that vocational guidance can ever be reduced to the application of a battery of tests for measuring all the main ability factors, and expecting an individual's pattern of factor scores to tell us what jobs he is suited to. In order to tap minor job group factors, we should almost certainly have to resort to more elaborate, expensive and time consuming work-sample tests.' In other words, the only way in which we are likely to improve the validity of our methods of assessment is by developing methods of assessing specific factors. This conclusion was first arrived at in 1950; but in 1958 Vernon thought this conclusion still held. We seem, for practical purposes, to be very much closer to the original Spearman two-factor theory, or Thomson's sampling theory, than was recently thought possible.

In the field of personality the situation seems to be very similar. Vernon (1964a) quotes Cattell, whom he regards as having carried out the most exhaustive investigation yet of the organization of personality, as envisaging the clinical psychologist of the future measuring between 50 and 60 personality, motivational and interest factors in each of his patients. This seems to be another way of saying that there is, relatively speaking, a considerable amount of specificity in the organization of personality, even if we did not end up by discovering the existence of a still larger number of very narrowly specific factors as well

Another way of looking at specificity is in terms of the complexity of psychological phenomena. For example, one might have at one's disposal a perfectly valid test of hysteria; but this test would not give one unequivocal answers to such questions as to whether or not a given patient's defects were due to hysteria. For example, a patient might complain of deafness and produce very high scores on a hysteria test. The deafness could still be organic in origin.

One of the main conclusions from the finding of specificity is not only that current formal procedures of assessment have a limited degree of validity but that we are unlikely, in the foreseeable future, to develop sufficiently valid procedures for the exhaustive assessment of the individual.

IV THE GENERALITY OF PSYCHOLOGICAL PROCESSES

As has been pointed out previously (Shapiro, 1966a), the specificity of the outcome of psychological processes seems to co-exist with a generality of the character of these processes. For example, we appear to know something about the factors which can have predictable effects on the rate of conditioning, e.g. the time and strength relations of conditioned and unconditioned responses, physiological drive strength, frequency of reinforcement and so on. We can use this knowledge to develop conditioning programmes for individual subjects. However, as Inglis (1965) has pointed out, we cannot predict the rate of acquisition of any given response from the known rate of acquisition of another response. This is what is meant by specificity.

By the generality of processes, we mean that once we have established experimental control over a process in one individual, the general method of doing so would be applicable to other individuals and to various aspects of that particular individual's functions. This is another aspect of methodology of the single case which has been discussed in greater detail elsewhere (Shapiro, 1966b).

One of the most striking examples of the generality of processes and the specificity of outcome is provided by the findings of Hartshorne and May (1930) in their investigations of honesty. They found that the correlations between various tests of honesty were much lower than their estimated reliabilities. They also found that the size of these correlations was related to the degree of similarity in the content of tasks. They therefore doubted the existence of a general trait of honesty. Recent reanalyses of Hartshorne and May's data such as Burton's (1963) do not seem to add anything to this basic finding.

V CLINICAL APPLICATIONS OF THE IDEA OF ERROR

The awareness of error makes us look upon any psychological observation not as something conclusive but as the basis of one or more hypotheses about the patient. One's degree of confidence in any hypothesis suggested by an observation would depend upon the established degree of validity of that observation and upon other information about the patient concerned.

If one or more hypotheses are suggested by an observation, then steps must be taken to test them. In this way further observations are accumulated in a systematic manner. It should then become possible to arrive at a psychological description in which we can have greater confidence. The additional observations may in turn suggest new hypotheses which have in turn to be tested. We are thus led to the method of the systematic investigation as a means of improving the validity of our conclusions about an individual patient.

For example, let us suppose that we are concerned with a 25-year-old male patient whose medical and personal history suggests that there might be some impairment of his cognitive functions. The Mill Hill Vocabulary and Raven's Standard Progressive Matrices may have been given routinely. The results from these two tests are examined with this problem in view. Let us suppose that it is found that the Matrices score appears to be reliably, but not abnormally, lower than that of Mill Hill Vocabulary, these conclusions having been based upon an application of the formulae, supplied by Payne and Jones (1957), to the published means, reliabilities and inter-correlation of the two tests.

A re-examination of the patient's personal and medical history may then suggest that the cognitive deficit may be in the area of $k:m$. This suggests that tests with stronger $k:m$ components than the Matrices would show up an abnormal deficit. The Wechsler Adult Intelligence Scale is therefore administered, serving the purposes both of testing the hypothesis and providing checks against systematic and unsystematic errors in the first observations. It is found that not only is the Performance Scale score abnormally lower than that of the Verbal

Scale; but that the most abnormal difference is found between the vocabulary and block-design subtests. The Wechsler Vocabulary score is, however, within 0·5 s.d. of the Mill Hill Vocabulary, i.e. the two vocabulary scores are very similar to each other.

The results then are consistent with the hypothesis of an impairment of *k:m* abilities. However, speed plays an important part in the Performance Scale, and so the patient's relatively low score on these tests might have been due to a general slowness of cognitive function. This hypothesis can be checked by administering the Nufferno Speed and Level Tests (Furneaux, undated). One's conclusions and further investigation would depend upon the kind of results obtained.

The course of an investigation is dependent upon the kind of tests and upon the amount of time at one's disposal; these are the two limitations upon the conclusiveness of any investigation we might pursue. It is likely therefore that all we will have at the end of an investigation is a number of hypotheses of varying degrees of likelihood. These then become communicated to our clinical colleagues in the form of an opinion. *In fact, the definition of an opinion might well be that it consists of the hypotheses which the applied scientist thinks best account for the data at his disposal, and which he would choose to test next if he had sufficient time and suitable means.* One's clinical colleagues, who should understand the nature of an opinion, can then evaluate that opinion in terms of their own data and in terms of the psychologist's own estimation of the likelihood of his own opinion being correct.

The way in which an investigation is conducted depends presumably upon the particular skills and knowledge of the individual psychologist, and upon the kind of problem to be investigated. On the whole, certain rules do seem to promote economy of activity and clarity of findings. The first of these rules is that one should only make an observation if it can be seen as being capable of throwing light on a definite hypothesis. Secondly, the application of the principle of parsimony does seem to be useful at least in limiting the number of hypotheses which are tested. In the example we gave above, we ended up with a hypothesis of generalized slowness of cognitive function. If, for example, the W.A.I.S. picture arrangement subtest had produced one of the patient's best scores, then the hypothesis of general cognitive slowness would be ruled out, and we would not, at this stage, collect any more data concerning that hypothesis. This rule means that any general hypothesis must be taken literally and must account for every single observation made. One then goes on to test that hypothesis. If further testing is impossible, because of lack of time or opportunity, one bases one's opinions upon those hypotheses which account for the greatest part of the data.

The writer finds it useful, in the course of an investigation, to rank-order the available data from time to time, regardless of the initial framework in which it has been gathered. Even with a test like the W.A.I.S., there is no scientific reason why the subtests should only be grouped in terms of the verbal and performance scales. The rank-ordering of them, in such a way that they are easily available to the eye, can facilitate hypothesis making and testing.

Here is an example. The patient was referred to the psychologist because there was a discrepancy between the impression given by the patient during interview and the report given by the husband. The husband complained that the patient was silly and incompetent as a housewife, while the psychiatrist thought that she spoke quite sensibly. The Mill Hill and Matrices scores confirmed the husband's opinion. The W.A.I.S. was then administered in order to confirm the initial test results. The verbal and performance I.Q.s in fact did so. However, when all the results were rank ordered, in terms of their percentiles, the following set of results appeared:

Test	Percentile
Similarities	62
Picture completion	50
Objcct assembly	50
Comprehension	38
Digit span	24
Vocabulary	24
Digit substitution	24
Picture arrangement	18
Mill Hill Vocabulary	10
Block design	2
Raven's Progressive Matrices	Unscorable

These results suggest an initial reply to the psychiatrist's question to the effect that there might be disparities in the organization of the patient's abilities making possible an impression of about average verbal ability in the interview, of a below average performance in a vocabulary test and a very bad performance on the Matrices and certain kinds of practical work.

In applied science, no method of work can be adhered to too rigidly. It is conceivable that the psychologist might be completely puzzled by a case and decide merely to make a number of exploratory observations to 'see what comes out of it'. It is also conceivable that he would decide to test a given hypothesis, not because it is the most likely one but because he happens to have a short and appropriate test for it.

The way a psychologist's mind works may have little relation to the ultimate appearance of the investigation he carries out. Most of us are probably incapable of proceeding smoothly from problem to hypothesis and then to methods of testing them. One often thinks of a possible test before one thinks clearly of the relevant hypothesis or its clinical implications. The point, however, is that whatever the peculiarities of a particular psychologist's thought processes, it appears to be useful to force one's descriptive work into the framework of the systematic investigation. In this way one does not waste time answering irrelevant or clinically useless questions, and the answers obtained tend to be less equivocal.

Y*

It is important to be willing and able to admit to one's colleagues that one is not in a position to answer certain questions, so that one can spend time either carrying out those investigations that are within one's competence, or working in the library in order to improve one's competence.

VI THE IDEA OF SPECIFICITY AND THE DIRECT OBSERVATION OF CRITERION VARIABLES

The essential idea here is that a large part of the reliable variation between individuals, in personality and abilities, is an expression of specific factors. Content validity then becomes, for the clinical psychologist, one of the main forms of validity. A variable is said to have content validity if it is made up of items which can be regarded as a representative sample of the criterion variable. For example, in constructing a test of reading comprehension one has to find printed material which can be regarded as a representative sample of the kind of material which the subjects will be called upon to read. Similarly, in constructing an attitude test one has to select a number of items which constitute a representative sample of the kind of attitudes which are being investigated. The question does not arise of having to correlate the results on the test with some other criterion, as one would have to do in the case of a projective test being used to assess personality variables.

We will refer to methods of assessment which have content validity as 'direct' measures, because they are directly applied to the criterion variables. We will refer to methods which are not directly applied to the criterion, but which have in fact to be correlated with it before they can be accepted for use, as 'indirect' methods. Whether or not a method is direct or indirect depends upon the purpose for which it is used. Questionnaires obtaining verbal expressions of attitude might serve as direct measures of such verbal expressions; but they would become indirect measures if they were used to predict, say, the outcome of psychotherapy. In such a case we would have to determine the predictive validity of the test.

There are two aspects of a psychological dysfunction: (i) the direct behavioural manifestations, such as tics and compulsive behaviour, and (ii) actual experiences, such as feelings and perceptual experiences. These two aspects can be observed in three main ways:

(i) *Direct observation of the behaviour* in question, e.g. the frequency and intensity of aggressive or withdrawn behaviour, the degree of neglect of personal appearance, the slowness of gait, and so on. The actual technique used for recording and qualifying such observations will vary with the kind of observation, and the technical inventiveness and purpose of the observers.

(ii) *Self-report by the patient.* This is the only way in which some dysfunctions can be observed. Examples are all the various aspects of affective disorder such as feelings of guilt and hopelessness. Self-report can, of course, be applied to behaviour as well. The two main techniques for getting at this aspect consist of the interview and the questionnaire. The interview can be tape-recorded and the relevant aspects counted or rated in the manner of the client-centred therapists (Truax, 1966). The interview itself can vary in the degree of control and specificity of questioning.

(iii) *Reports by the patient's associates.* These usually take the form of ratings which are in effect questionnaires directed at the patient's associates. Such ratings can of course report both the patient's experiences and behaviour.

Techniques of direct observation are not yet well advanced in their development. We cannot yet list all the important artefacts and the ways in which they can be taken into account. We do not yet know exactly what skills have to be acquired by the clinical psychologist to ensure that this knowledge is applied effectively. A certain degree of sophistication has, however, been achieved, as consultation of Vernon's *Personality Assessment* (1964a) will show. In the case of the interview there seem to be two ways in which the validity of the interview can be increased. The first consists of the employment of 'surface' methods 'which make straight-forward inferences from the previous career, abilities and consciously expressed attitudes' (p. 148). The second consists of carefully defining the aims of the interview and acting closely in accordance with those aims. One might add a third condition: awareness of the ways in which artefacts may distort the outcomes of interviews. Examples of such artefacts are preconceptions of the subject's responses and the tendency for the interviewer actively to shape and to ignore the interviewee's responses in accordance with those pre-conceptions.

In the case of questionnaires a considerable literature has developed concerning the artefacts which can affect questionnaire responses. Outstanding among these is the finding that the form of a questionnaire may affect the content of the responses (Vernon, 1964b). However, the development of clinically appropriate questionnaire techniques which take into account the specificity of responses is as yet not far advanced. The first development along these lines was Stephenson's Q Sort Techniques (1956), which can be used to enable the subject to give an indication of the organization, in his own words, of his attitudes, feelings and beliefs about any subject at any particular time.

A more recent development of a specific individual-centred approach, which at the same time tries to minimize the influence of the usual questionnaire artefacts, is Shapiro's Personal Questionnaire technique (Shapiro, 1957). In this he aims at providing the patient with a means of expressing, at any given time, the severity of his own symptoms in his own words and on the basis of his own standards of distress. Neither the Q sort nor the Personal Questionnaire are sufficiently developed for the results from an individual patient to be taken at face value, without checking carefully on all other information.

In the case of behaviour sampling techniques their use has so far only been with children. Vernon (1964a) suggests that there might be difficulties in applying them to adults. A possible development for adults might consist of creating special situations which were designed to evoke the kind of behaviour under investigation. Vernon (1964a) reports that impressions of a subject's responses in such situations do have predictive validity.

Despite their lack of development, it does seem to be necessary and justifiable to use all available techniques of direct observation of criterion variables. It is necessary to bear in mind what is known of experimentally demonstrated artefacts and the steps that should be taken to counteract their influence.

Certain difficulties arise which need to be discussed. One of them is the definition of units of measurement. For example, in counting the frequency of tics per unit, one may find that it is difficult to arrive at a definition of a unit tic, as the movements involved will vary considerably in their amplitude and in the number of muscles involved. In the measurement of judgements of the intensity, say, of feelings or the severity of symptoms, it may be found impossible to utilize equal units without making the responses for the patient more difficult, e.g. graphic rating scale. Very disturbed patients might be unable to deal with such complications. This is why the Personal Questionnaire (Shapiro, 1957) makes use of paired comparisons.

In addition to problems of scaling there are questions of normative data. Shapiro and Nelson (1955) described an example of this. The patient, who was of well above average intelligence on the W.A.I.S. and who had a breakdown while studying for a degree, had been asked, during a psychiatric interview, to read aloud an extract from a daily newspaper. Subsequent questioning indicated that he could remember very little of what he had read. So far, we have a direct observation of a criterion variable which consisted of the fact that the patient was not able to remember material he had read aloud. This observation was confirmed by the administration of standard reading-aloud-comprehension test – a test which had been standardized on young children. However, when the test was given to a group of graduate psychologists, they, like the patient, produced poor scores and showed difficulty in remembering material they had read aloud, though not quite to the same extent as the patient. This example exemplifies the general proposition that, while the extremes of dysfunction can be reliably observed directly, one cannot draw reliable conclusions from such observations about the distribution of that dysfunction in the relevant normal population.

There are clinical problems, of course, in which this point is not of great importance. An example is that of the investigation of a 7-year-old boy with an obsessional disorder. The mother was interviewed at the clinic, where she appeared to be a very carefully dressed, meticulous woman who gave the impression of being a very fussy and meticulous mother. The social worker unexpectedly visited the home. She found the mother on her way to a night out with a man who was not her husband; the house was in a state of disarray, and the child apparently was about to be left on his own. Now, for the purpose of this investigation, the distribution of such behaviour amongst normal mothers is of great but not of crucial importance. What matters is that a theory about one possible factor in the child's disorder has been strongly contra-indicated. Further investigation might finally disprove it.

A similar example is given by a 10-year-old child who had a high score on all parts of a verbal test except the vocabulary subtest on which she did badly. One possible hypothesis was that the patient was an intelligent person who had been brought up in a home which was culturally deprived. This hypothesis was suggested by the income level of the family. In fact, independent inquiry showed the home to be sufficiently literate and cultured, to contra-indicate the deprivation hypothesis. Here again it is unnecessary to establish the frequency of literate and cultural activities in relation to income level, in order to obtain useful information by the direct observation of a criterion variable.

One can go further and say that not only are direct observations possible but that they must constitute a necessary part of the investigation. In fact, when formulating explanations and hypotheses to account for a set of results, the first step must be to check the hypotheses against the relevant uncontrolled observations. Once having done so, it may be decided that the best way of continuing the investigation is by gathering more information of this kind, rather than by tests of doubtful or assumed validity.

An example will illustrate. The patient had been initially referred to the psychologist to try to determine to what degree his silences in interviews and his low scores on intelligence tests were due to intellectual limitations or to his illness. He was reported by informants to have a very good and stable record as a factory worker before the onset of the illness. The psychologist decided to visit the factory and talk with the personnel officer as a check on the reality of the apparent discrepancy, and if possible in order to arrive at explanations of the findings. The psychologist was told by the personnel officer that the work done by the patient was of a very simple kind and could easily be carried out by a persistent person of very low intelligence. An inspection of the work being carried out by other workers confirmed the personnel officer's statements.

Another example is that of a young man of above average intelligence who had had about 60 different jobs before being admitted to hospital. In interview, the patient said he was liable to frequent very severe panic attacks, that he disliked very much being seen having these attacks and that after each attack he felt very exhausted for some time. These two factors combined to make him leave his jobs. If these claims were true, then further tests of the patient's vocational interests and abilities might be of little use. The main aim would be to check on the validity of the patient's statements both by direct observation and gathering evidence from the patient's associates.

It might be argued that this approach is no different from that of the social worker and psychiatrist. In fact, in a good team the psychologist would largely depend upon the information provided by the other members. However, should the circumstances demand it, he should not hesitate to seek the information himself. The frameworks for the psychiatrist and social worker are, however, different in that they work within the framework of making diagnostic and management decisions on the basis of *a priori* conceptions of the nature of mental disorder. The psychologist is concerned with the description of psychological dysfunctions as he finds them, and aims at placing his observations on an objective and reproducible basis; hence, the development of such techniques as the Q sort and the personal questionnaire. Secondly, he aims at relating to this kind of observation the results of all relevant research, especially about the mechanisms affecting the psychology of evidence and the psychology of personal interaction.

It might be argued that this approach is not different from using unvalidated methods like projective tests or the observation of behaviour during tests. The applied scientist must make a distinction between the relatively uncontrolled observation of criterion variables and the controlled observation of variables which only have a putative or attenuated relationship with criterion variables. For example, a subject might appear to be very systematic and careful when doing the W.A.I.S. block design test. One would not be able to infer from that observation that he will be systematic and careful in his work outside the testing room, i.e. one could not assume that the observation has external validity. The only sources of information concerning his carefulness at work would be interviews of his associates at work, and/or actual examples of the results of his work. This is what is meant by specificity.

This does not mean that the observation of behaviour in the test situation might not be of great importance. For example, a patient's carefulness in the test situation might have important implications for an investigation. One of the patient's main difficulties might be his reported carelessness at work and one might be seeking an explanation of this behaviour. His apparent carefulness in the test situation might lead to the formulation of a useful explanation of his behaviour at work.

This approach reflects the simultaneous application of the two generalizations: the generality of processes and the specificity of their outcomes.

VII   THE IDEA OF SPECIFICITY AND THE FULL CLINICAL
      INVOLVEMENT OF THE PSYCHOLOGIST

The idea of specificity not only leads to the concentration upon the direct observation of criterion variables but it influences the general style of the systematic investigation. It does so in two ways: (i) by directing the work at answering specific and concrete questions and (ii) by making the psychologist closely integrate his work with that of other members of the clinical team.

The failure to realize the precise implications of the idea of specificity is shown in the way in which many psychologists use relatively well validated tests such as intelligence tests. They often seem to be quite happy to administer such tests in response to very general or non-specific requests such as 'assessment of intelligence' or even 'I.Q. please'. The psychologist carries out the test, and then reports the results in terms of some simplified and arbitrary concepts such as Wechsler's categories of intelligence. The psychiatrist is then left to work out for himself the practical and clinical implications of the results. Actually the psychiatrist may have concrete problems in view; such as why does the patient have a bad work record? Why does she give an impression of intelligence in the interview while her husband says she is incompetent and stupid? Why does the patient have a reputation for being good at her work when she appears to be very stupid on the interview?

Which test one gives, if any, depends upon one's assessment of the validity of one's tools for answering a particular question, and then upon the initial hypotheses suggested by the patient's state and history. One might, for a given question, decide to conduct a series of interviews to establish the facts about a patient's work record rather than give any tests at all.

The advantage of clearly formulating the question is that when one has obtained one's results, one can ask oneself whether or not one has obtained an answer to the question, and communicate the result accordingly to one's colleagues. Sometimes the nature of the result leaves one with the conclusion that one does not have an answer to the question. For example, let us say we have a West Indian patient who has done very badly on a verbal intelligence test which was administered in answer to a question about the degree to which the patient's lack of response in an interview was due to lack of intelligence, cultural difficulties or to illness. An average score from the patient would indicate that the impression given in the interview was due to illness, though there could still be other explanations which required to be tested. If, however, the patient obtained a low score on the test we still would not know to what extent the patient's bad showing was due to his illness or a lack of intelligence, or cultural factors. In such a case one would make clear to one's colleagues that the question had not been answered by the test.

A second and related result of the emphasis upon specificity is that the psychologist does not leave the formulation of questions to his colleagues; nor does he evaluate the answers in isolation from them. As far as possible the psychologist should participate in the initial and interim clinical evaluations of the patient. He should, in terms of his knowledge of psychological processes, and in terms of the available techniques of assessment, be able to suggest relevant questions and help to exclude irrelevant ones. Likewise, when it comes to discussing the implications of a psychological observation, the other members of the clinical team should be able to give immediate assistance in checking the psychologist's hypotheses and suggesting more relevant and likely ones. A ten-minute discussion with the psychiatrist may sometimes save hours of work. This general approach means that the psychologist has to become a closely integrated member of a clinical team.

Communication by writing, in the form of a standardized request form and the written psychologist's report, should not be the standard and only methods of conveying problems and results. Ideally, the psychologist should be involved in all clinical discussions of the patient. The standardized request form and the written psychologist's report should only be used as a record of problems, findings and opinions which have already been discussed by everyone concerned.

In the minds of many psychiatrists and social workers, the psychologist often appears to be rather like the man who comes in to read the gas meter; he does not appear to be an applied scientist helping the clinic to do a day's work. The realization of the full implications of specificity should put an end to such a role. The idea of specificity leads to a realization of the need to formulate clearly the questions which have to be answered, of using direct methods of observation, and of checking carefully against all relevant clinical information the implications of the results which have been obtained. It also leads to the need to work closely with all members of the clinical team at all stages of the patient's career in the clinic. In this way, the psychologist's colleagues are not left to flounder with written communications which are often obscure and loaded with the psychologist's technical jargon. They can, instead, come to look upon the psychologist as a fully responsible colleague.

VIII THE CLINICAL APPLICATION OF THE GENERALITY OF
     PROCESSES

The idea of the generality of findings about psychological processes leads to the proposition that any method of experimental control of a criterion variable in a given patient will be found to be effective for that patient in all situations in which that process is involved. An example may make this proposition more meaningful. Let us suppose that we have been asked to give vocational advice about a patient who is said to be very intelligent but very 'withdrawn' and slow. Let us also suppose that we have checked these two observations: the first by interviewing a number of the patient's associates; the second by administering the Nufferno Speed and Level Test (Furneaux, undated) in which the patient was found to be at the top 1% in terms of the level of difficulty at which he could operate and at the bottom 1% in terms of speed. In order to investigate the slowness the psychologist then seeks a likely explanation of it. His fellow-clinicians may believe that the patient's slowness is a part of his 'withdrawnness'. It may be felt that the patient finds the presence of other people disturbing and that the psychologist's presence during the test is responsible for the patient's slowness. This formulation leads immediately to an experiment in which the patient is to be tested under two conditions: with the psychologist present and the psychologist absent. Of course, a number of technical difficulties would have to be overcome. A test with a number of equivalent forms would have to be found. Moran and Kimble's (1964) set of equivalent forms might be useful for this purpose. We would then have to test the patient under each of the two conditions. The two kinds of conditions would have to be appropriately balanced or randomized and there would have to be a sufficient number of occasions of each kind of measurement.

Let us assume that, as was in fact found in a similar experiment, the patient, contrary to expectation, could hardly perform at all when the psychologist was absent and that he maintained his usual poor rate in the psychologist's presence.

This finding would lead to the generalization that despite the apparent 'withdrawnness' of the patient, he was still dependent on the presence of other people for maintaining his responsiveness. This idea would have important implications for the patient's vocational adjustment. It would mean that he should not be given jobs in which he was left to himself; but rather that his work should involve interaction with other people, and that these people should be warned that, despite any appearances to the contrary, the patient was dependent upon this interaction for his admittedly poor rate of work.

The generalization would of course have to be checked by further observations. The patient's behaviour in the ward might then be observed to test the hypothesis that the patient was in fact interested in other people. It might then be found, in a relatively short behaviour sample of about 60 minutes, that the patient spent all his time in groups apparently listening, to judge by his posture and eye movements, to what was being said; but that he, himself, never initiated verbal interchange.

There are four important points to be borne in mind when considering the clinical implications of the results of an experiment. The first is that it might be necessary to have an indication of the amount of unsystematic error. Such an estimate becomes important when one fails to find a difference between the experimental conditions. Such a failure might be due to the fact that the method of observation was so unreliable that a 'real' psychological difference between the conditions might not have been able to show itself in the experiment. 'Unreliability' is therefore always a possible explanation of a finding of 'no difference'. There are various ways of trying to overcome this difficulty. One way is to build into one's method of measuring some kind of reliability assessment. In the case of the personal questionnaire (Shapiro, 1957) this is achieved by the use of paired comparisons. Other forms of testing might produce special problems. In the case of speed, perhaps it is best to use tests with a known reliability, or to use tests consisting of items with known and differing degrees of difficulty. In the latter case, one could calculate the correlation between speed and difficulty level over the items on each occasion of testing, and this has a minimum estimate of the reliability on each occasion.

A second point is concerned with the question of specificity. It is conceivable, for example, that a thorough investigation might show that an apparently very slow person was relatively fast in a very few activities. It would then be necessary to take advantage of the patient's specific abilities in arranging his vocational adjustment.

An appropriate example is found in a case reported by Bartlett and Shapiro (1956). Their patient had a reading disability. He appeared to be able to form the necessary associations quite efficiently within the visual modality, but not across the visual and motor modalities, i.e. linking the utterance of certain sounds with abstract shapes. In addition, the main difficulty of this patient seemed to lie in the *acquisition* of the relevant connections but not to their *retention*. There were, then, at least two kinds of specificities involved in the patient's inability to learn to read.

The experimental control over the patient's processes in learning to read might have been established along the lines suggested by Strauss and Lehtinen (1953) – the patient might have been found to learn most efficiently under conditions of minimal distraction, i.e. facing a grey wall and being taught by a teacher who wore very undistracting clothes. This might have led to greater speed in the making of connections across the visual and motor modalities.

The third point consists of the fact that the degree of experimental control established over a function would, if it is to be completely evaluated, itself need to be calibrated. For example, in the case of the very slow subject, the proportionate increase in slowness he showed when on his own might not have been very different from the increase that many normal people would have shown. In many cases, however, this question is not of central importance. What matters is that the patient, who is already very slow, is slower still when on his own. His adjustment would therefore be facilitated by making sure that he did not have to work on his own.

Finally, it should be remembered that, in all single-case experiments, a distinction has to be made between a reliable *difference* between sets of observations and a significant *association* between certain conditions and certain results. Let us assume that, in the case of the experiment on slowness, we had used 20 items, of the same difficulty level, on each occasion of testing. Let us also assume that we had used 30 occasions of testing, 15 with the psychologist present and 15 with the psychologist absent, in accordance with some kind of balanced design. Finally, let us assume that on each occasion of testing we timed each of the 20 items. We can obtain two kinds of results from these data.

The first tells us whether there is a reliable difference between the two kinds of conditions. For this purpose we would make use of all the 600 scores, i.e. 300 (15×20) with the psychologist absent and 300 with the psychologist present. The second kind of result indicates whether there is a significant association between the experimental conditions and speed. For this purpose, we only have a total of 30 scores at our disposal, each consisting of the total time for each of the 30 occasions of testing, 15 occasions on which the psychologist was present and 15 on which the psychologist was absent. The logic of a significant association is quite different from the logic of a reliable difference. It is clearly much easier to establish a reliable difference between conditions than it is to establish a reliable association with conditions.

This may seem an elaboration of the obvious, but this kind of confusion arises very easily in single case experimentation. An outstanding example is an experiment reported by Shapiro, Marks and Fox (1963). They report a significant association between their experimental conditions and personal questionnaire scores. Actually, the degrees of freedom and the estimate of error which they used took full advantage of the scores from the 20 items which were assessed on each occasion of testing. They did not establish that these items were independent in their responses. They were therefore only entitled to report a reliable difference between the experimental conditions. They were not, for example, entitled to report, as they did, a significant association between symptom scores and the immediate and delayed effects of treatment.

Finally it must be remembered that the best guarantee of the generality of the findings of an experiment must be to try to achieve the greatest degree of specificity of the variables which are brought under experimental control. For example, let us assume that we want to test a hypothesis that a person's asthmatic attacks are due to an unresolved conflict about his mother. One would then aim at doing an experiment in which the frequency and duration of asthmatic attacks could be related to the absence and presence of the mother. Metcalfe (1956) reports such an investigation; she found a significant association was found between visits from the mother and the frequency of severe attacks. One would not carry out an experiment in which the dependent variable consisted of responses to an inkblot or speed of word association. The notion of the generality of processes can only be applied with some confidence as long as one keeps as close as possible to the criterion variables.

IX   GENERAL EVALUATION AND CONCLUSIONS

The kind of approach which has been presented in this chapter has, in one form or another, been discussed by clinical psychologists for some time (Shapiro, 1951, 1957, 1966b; Payne, 1953; Jones, 1960). As far as one can see from the literature and from one's own practice, it has not developed very far. There have appeared in the literature a few studies which could be regarded as investigations in the sense described here, i.e. which consisted of the systematic testing of explanations about certain aspects of a patient's psychological disorder (Payne, 1953; Shapiro and Nelson, 1955; Bartlett and Shapiro, 1956; Beech and Parboosingh, 1962; Ravenette and Hersov, 1963).

At present, the intensive assessment of the individual demands a lot of thought and originality and is very laborious and time consuming. For example, the investigation by Shapiro and Nelson (1955) involved the following actions: (i) the application of a pair of reading attainment tests to the patient, (ii) the administration of one of the tests to a control group of normal subjects, (iii) the administration of one of the Nufferno Speed and Level Tests (Furneaux) to the patient and (iv) the administration of the Nufferno Speed and Level Tests to a control group of matched patients. Anyone who has tried to find and test small matched control groups will know how long this work actually took to complete. One can hardly see the hard-pressed clinical psychologist going over wholly, or even substantially, to work of this kind. Two developments are necessary to deal with this situation. The first lies in the routinization of the intensive assessment of the individual. This would be achieved by the production of manuals which would list under appropriate headings all the problems which can be encountered in clinical work, the hypotheses which could be advanced to account for them, and the methods which could be applied for testing these hypotheses.

It is possible to imagine such a manual written for the investigation of cognitive dysfunctions. A preliminary list of hypotheses could be written out on the basis of the present state of knowledge of the organization of human ability. Beside each item in this list could be written the various appropriate tests. In addition to tests, there could be listed different kinds of experiments for testing hypotheses. These could be described and appropriately indexed. Examples would be the experiments which have been discussed in this chapter. It is only when we reach this point that the intensive investigation of the individual case is likely to become a routine.

The second development which is necessary is a large increase in the number of clinical psychologists. It would then become possible for each psychologist to specialize in certain types of investigation. A realistic basis for the development of effective psychological work would be provided if there were at least as many psychologists as there were psychiatrists working in the mental health services. The effective channelling of the findings and methods of psychology into the day-to-day work of the Health Service can only be carried out by clinical psychologists. As staffing arrangements now stand, the clinical psychologists working in the Health Service cannot cope effectively with the wide range of problems which face them.

An understandable tendency develops to apply routine approaches of a superficial character, in order to deal with a sufficient number of patients. This further reduces the possibility of an effective contribution. Only when there has been a very large increase in the number of clinical psychologists will the intensive assessment of the individual patient cease to be an occasional feature of the clinical psychologist's work and become a basic part of his daily practice.

General attitudes are, however, more important than technical developments and facilities, if clinical psychology is to develop as an applied science. An essentially inductive approach seems to be necessary. The applied scientist must be concerned primarily with findings. For him, theory consists essentially of the generalizations which these findings imply, and the deductions which can be made from these generalizations. Hence, the notion of an inductive-deductive approach. This approach has been demonstrated in this chapter in a number of ways. First of all it is shown in the approach to the formulation of problems. The problems are those which are provided for the clinical psychologist by nature, as it were. The disorders of thinking, feeling, perception, behaviour and physiological function which he encounters in the clinic are not deduced from any theory. Their appearance at the clinic often amazes and surprises the psychologist. In fact, there seems to be no aspect of human experience and behaviour which will not, in some exaggerated, diminished or repetitive form, present itself sometime or another as a dysfunction.

Secondly, in seeking ways of dealing with these problems, the psychologist must give priority to those generalizations which are based on observations. The clinical psychologist has, therefore, continually to search his research literature for relevant findings, and try to develop from them generalizations which will at least provide him with working hypotheses.

Thirdly, in the processes of carrying out an investigation of an individual patient, the clinical psychologist, aware as he is of the traps of pre-conception, must constantly try to free himself from *a priori* considerations, and be ready to generalize afresh from his observations as he finds them. This applies to all three aspects of his work: casework, his research work and development of generalizations from the current state of knowledge.

We are in fact involved here with the application of Claude Bernard's (1865) principle of philosophical doubt. This principle is derived from the fact that the scientist is investigating phenomena which are independent of him and largely unknown to him. 'Even when an experiment apparently fully proves his pre-conceived ideas the experimenter must still doubt' (p. 52) and try to carry out experiments which will disprove these ideas. In this way, the scientist maintains absolute freedom of mind and creates the possibility of important discoveries.

ACKNOWLEDGEMENT

Acknowledgements are made to Dr S. Rachman for useful criticisms of this chapter.

REFERENCES

BARTLETT, D. S. and SHAPIRO, M. B. (1956) Investigation and treatment of a reading disability in a dull child with severe psychiatric disturbance. *Brit. J. educ. Psychol.*, **26**, 180-190.

BEECH, H. R. and PARBOOSINGH, R-C. (1962) An experimental investigation of disordered mental expression in a catatonic schizophrenic patient. *Brit. J. soc. clin. Psychol.*, **1**, 222-227.

BERNARD, C. (1865) *An Introduction to the Study of Experimental Medicine.* N.Y.: Dover, 1957.

BURTON, R. V. (1963) The generality of honesty reconsidered. *Psychol. Rev.*, **70**, 481-499.

DEARBORN, W. F. and ROTHNEY, J. W. (1941) *Predicting the Child's Development.* Cambridge, Mass.: Sci. Art.

FOULDS, G. A. and RAVEN, J. C. (1948) Normal change in the mental abilities of adults as age advances. *J. ment. Sci.*, **94**, 133-142.

FURNEAUX, D. (Undated) *Nufferno Speed and Level Test.* London: Nat. Found. Ed. Res.

HARTSHORNE, H. and MAY, M. A. (1930) *Studies in Deceit.* New York: Macmillan.

INGLIS, J. (1965) Problems in the retention of memory disorder. *Ontario Psychol. Assn. Quart.*, **18**, 85-89.

JONES, H. G. (1960) Applied abnormal psychology: the experimental approach. *In* EYSENCK, H. J. (Ed.) *Handbook of Abnormal Psychology. An Experimental Approach.* London: Pitman.

MCNEMAR, Q. (1942) *The Revision of the Stanford Binet Scale*. Houghton Mifflin.

METCALFE, M. (1956) Demonstration of a psychosomatic relationship. *Brit. J. med. Psychol.*, **29**, 63-66.

MORAN, L. J. and KIMBLE, J. P. JNR. (1964) Repetitive psychometric measures: equating alternate forms. *Psychol. Reports*, **14**, 335-338.

PAYNE, R. W. (1953) The role of the clinical psychologist at the Institute of Psychiatry. *Rev. Psychol. Appl.*, **3**, 150-160.

PAYNE, R. W. and JONES, H. G. (1957) Statistics for the investigation of individual cases. *J. clin. Psychol.*, **13**, 115-121.

RAVEN, J. C. (1948) The comparative assessment of intellectual ability. *Brit. J. Psychol.*, **39**, 12-20.

RAVEN, J. C. (1958) *Guide to the Standard Progressive Matrices*. London: H. K. Lewis.

RAVENETTE, A. T. and HERSOV, L. A. (1963) Speed of function and educational retardation: the psychological and psychiatric investigation of the individual case. *J. child. Psychol. Psychiat.*, **4**, 17-28.

SHAPIRO, M. B. (1951) An experimental approach to diagnostic testing. *J. ment. Sci.*, **97**, 748-764.

SHAPIRO, M. B. (1957) Experimental method in the psychological description of the individual psychiatric patient. *Internat. J. Soc. Psychiat.*, **3**, 89-103.

SHAPIRO, M. B. (1961) A method of measuring psychological changes specific to the individual psychiatric patient. *Brit. J. med. Psychol.*, **34**, 151-155.

SHAPIRO, M. B. (1966a) Generality of psychological processes and specificity of outcomes. *Percept. and Motor Skills*, **23**, 16.

SHAPIRO, M. B. (1966b) The single case in clinical-psychological research. *J. gen. Psychol.*, **74**, 3-23.

SHAPIRO, M. B., MARKS, I. and FOX, B. (1963) A therapeutic experiment on phobic and affective symptoms in an individual psychiatric patient. *Brit. J. soc. clin. Psychol.*, **2**, 81-93.

SHAPIRO, M. B. and NELSON, E. H. (1955) An investigation of an abnormality of cognitive function in a cooperative young psychotic: an example of the application of experimental method in a single case. *J. clin. Psychol.*, **2**, 344-351.

STEPHENSON, W. (1956) *The Study of Behaviour*. Cambridge University Press.

STRAUSS, A. and LEHTINEN, L. (1953) *Psychopathology and Education of the brain-injured child*. N.Y.: Grune and Stratton.

TERMAN, L. M. and MERRILL, M. A. (1960) *Stanford Binet Intelligence Scale. Manual for the Third Revision*. London: Harrap.

TRUAX, C. B. (1966) Therapist, empathy, warmth and genuineness and patient personality change in group psychotherapy: a comparison between interaction unit measures, time sample measures, patient perception measures. *J. clin. Psychol.*, **22**, 225-229.

VERNON, P. E. (1964a) *Personality Assessment: A Critical Survey*. London: Methuen.

VERNON, P. E. (1964b) *The Structure of Human Abilities*. London: Methuen.

22

The design of remedial programmes

Moya Tyson

REMEDIAL: *adj;* of or as a remedy; intended or helping to cure.
REMEDY: *n;*   that which cures disease, trouble or evil . . .
(*The Penguin English Dictionary*)

I INTRODUCTION

Although the purpose of this chapter is to consider the design of remedial programmes, it is perhaps not out of place to question first the necessity for such programmes. To remedy – or help to cure – what? In the sense in which the term 'remedial' frequently applies at present, it would seem that some classes are being instituted to remedy previous educational treatment, which might suggest that current educational methods for substantial numbers of children are incorrect, and failing in their purpose. The 1944 Education Act aspired to an education for each child according to his age, ability and aptitude. If this ideal state obtained, what need would there be for *remedial* education, as all education would be geared to the child's needs and capabilities, thereby eliminating the need for remediation (except possibly in a few special cases, as after severe illness or an accident). However, it may be a long time – if ever – before this perfection is attained and in the meanwhile it is as well to consider a more realistic approach to the question of remedial provision.

To begin with, a remedial programme implies that something is to be remedied. In this sense, is it valid to term classes for slow learners remedial (as is the case in many comprehensive schools) unless there is an intention to return the child to the educational mainstream? This, presumably, is where remedial education differs from special education, although in certain special education categories the intention is explicitly to help children to return or enter the general educational environment, as in the case of emotionally disturbed, dysphasic, or partially hearing children. The great difficulty when trying to elucidate terms such as 'remedial education' and 'special education' is that while these terms imply discontinuous groups, the child population does not divide naturally in this way, but is distributed across many continua: learning ability, sensory and motor handicaps, emotional stability, etc. On the whole, however, it could perhaps be accepted as a very rough division that special education implies a longer term provision than remedial education, where the aim is – or should be

– to make it possible for the child to return to his appropriate educational mainstream.

Another point of view on this subject of definition is that of Barsch (1967), who dwells at some length on his distinction between three types of children for whom educational provision is necessary: the curriculum model group, the special education group and the remedial group. The curriculum model group – also referred to as the integrating learner group – 'enters school at the appropriate age and systematically achieves expanded mastery of school subjects year after year'. This is the group of children (the majority group in the school population – Barsch suggests an arbitrary figure of about 50%) for whom, in a sense, the curriculum has evolved. Some infant teachers might suggest that these are the children who learn to read and write and to deal with numbers almost regardless of the method used and the classroom atmosphere, formal or informal. The special education group of children who 'are unable to survive on a day-by-day basis in the mainstream of education and require a special curriculum to suit their needs' comprises 'the deaf, blind, physically handicapped, mentally retarded, aphasic, emotionally disturbed and culturally disadvantaged' (this last category is not one that is usually considered as being in need of special education in the U.K.). Barsch quotes the size of this special education group in the U.S.A. as being estimated as between 3% and 20% depending on geographical area and educational provision generally, but takes a maximum figure of 20% in 'consideration of the improvement in diagnostic sensitivity leading to more discrete identifications'. The remaining 30% Barsch suggests are the remedial group. These are the children who, while appearing to have an adequate intelligence level, no obvious sensory or motor impairment or emotional disturbance, yet do not manage to keep pace with the educational lockstep. These are the children who gradually fall behind the curriculum model group and require 'emergency educational first-aid' for their educational problems. Among the people who will render this first-aid will be the remedial tutor and the successful results of such help will be that the child will be able to keep pace once more with his peers (whereas presumably the unsuccessful result will be that the child will continue to remain behind, perennially in a 'remedial' situation).

It could be speculated that if it were possible to predict beforehand which children would be unable to keep pace with the curriculum as designed for the majority of the ordinary school population and if there were enough teachers – particularly highly skilled teachers – to make really small classes the general rule at the Infant/Primary stage of education, the remedial group of Barsch's definition should either not exist or be a very small one indeed. As it is, although Barsch's figure of 30% seems startlingly high and may be queried on the basis of insufficient evidence, it is possible – taking into account evidence from surveys of reading disability, for example – that it is not too gross an exaggeration. For the present, in the U.K. at least, remedial classes continue to grow, more particularly for backward readers, and an expanding new professional association of remedial teachers with its own journal *Remedial Education* (Pergamon Press) has emerged from the need for specialized help for the child having difficulties in the educational milieu.

II THE DIAGNOSIS OF DIFFICULTIES

Given that there is a need for remedial help for children, the next point for consideration is the kinds of help – or remedial programmes – that are necessary. It seems trite to state that the kind of remedial help that is necessary depends upon the child's difficulties, but in fact this statement is really the most crucial one of all: for unless an accurate diagnosis is made of the child's learning problems in that the basic difficulties are established, the remedial programme which is initiated may fail because it is aimed at a comparatively less important or even an irrelevant aspect of the problem. For example, children are sometimes referred to educational psychologists as having difficulty in writing: perhaps being very slow, and forming almost illegible letters. It is not unknown to discover that the *real* cause of the poor writing is very poor spelling, in that the child has such difficulties in spelling that he is extremely slow because he doesn't know how to spell the words, and the illegibility is partly a cover for this fact. In this case it may be necessary to design a remedial programme which is aimed firstly at improving the spelling, and secondly at improving the writing itself: and it may well be necessary to delve still further initially, to try and establish why there is a spelling difficulty in order to choose the most effective way of teaching some basic rules for English spelling (and there *are* some basic rules, even if there are many exceptions).

In order to design a remedial programme, therefore, one must first establish what exactly is to be remedied, which means that not only must adequate tools for diagnosis be available but also a knowledge of how to use them. The term 'prescriptive teaching' has become very fashionable in the U.S.A.; this really implies the ultimate ideal for all education that was referred to at the outset of this chapter, in that an accurate assessment would be made of each child's actual strengths and weaknesses and then the teaching tailored to the child's individual requirements, so that, for example, a child with a very poor auditory memory would not be taught to read in the same way as a child with a very poor visual memory. It is necessary to admit in all honesty that present diagnostic tools are still crude, although in the past two decades there have been improvements. Some of the tests now available have been mentioned elsewhere: the Illinois Test of Psycholinguistic Abilities, for example, which was designed as just such a diagnostic tool to guide remedial teaching (see Chapter 20). Kirk and MacCarthy (1961) have this to say about the purpose of psychological testing:

> it is necessary to distinguish between testing for the purpose of classification and testing for the purpose of diagnosis. *Classification* testing has as its goal the assignment of the subject to a group, type or category. Tests which yield a global score, such as M.A. or I.Q. can be used for this purpose. *Diagnostic testing*, on the other hand, has as its goal the detection of specific abilities and

disabilities within the subject so that an educational or remedial programme can be initiated based on these findings.

Another test which is used in a similar manner as a diagnostic tool is the Frostig Developmental Test of Visual Perception (Frostig *et al.*, 1964). Tests which are predominantly used for classification can also be used diagnostically, as, for example, when the difference between Verbal and Performance Scale I.Q.s or the subtest patterns of the W.I.S.C. provide a basis of information as to the kinds of abilities in which children show varying strengths and weaknesses. Bannatyne (A.C.L.D., 1967) suggested that W.I.S.C. subtests could be divided into three broad categories which would be of value in diagnostic work: Conceptualizing Ability (Comprehension, Similarities and Vocabulary); Spatial Ability (Picture Completion, Block Design and Object Assembly); and Sequencing Ability (Digit Span, Picture Arrangement and Coding – or possibly Arithmetic in lieu of Picture Arrangement).

As well as these psychological tests of a broadly cognitive type, some more highly specialized than others, there are also various developmental tests which tap other functions and abilities, such as tests of gross and fine motor skills. Some of these straddle both medicine and psychology, in that paediatricians and neurologists also use them in a rather similar fashion. Psychologists in this country have been slower to use these tests than their European counterparts: examine, for instance, the range of developmental and motor tests in *Manuel pour l'Examen Psychologique de l'Enfant*, edited by Zazzo (1960). Since the upsurge of interest in the experience of bodily movement in the growing organism as a basis for the adequate development of visual perception, tests such as the Oseretsky (in one of its many revisions) or the Purdue Perceptual-Motor Survey (Roach and Kephart, 1966) have attracted much attention. Attainment tests have a place in the diagnostic battery fairly frequently: tests of reading ability (including accuracy, comprehension, and sometimes rate), tests of spelling and numeracy (though these last are still in general the most unsophisticated of all the attainment tests). Finally, there are the projective tests. Some experts suggest that some of these (i.e. the Rorschach) serve a useful purpose diagnostically in pointing to difficulties in perception as well as fulfilling the more widely known function of revealing basic personality traits and difficulties or aberrancies in the child's interaction with the environment. Whether or not the claims are justified, the tests are a possible addition to the diagnostic battery and in expert hands may give useful information.

However, having stated that an essential prerequisite for a remedial programme is first of all a clear diagnosis of the child's difficulties, it is necessary now to qualify this statement in that, given the crudity of some of the psychological tools available at present, it may not be possible initially to pinpoint the exact area of disability. In this case, to an even more important degree than in more clear-cut diagnosis, the teaching itself carries the burden of diagnosis in that the payoff from different approaches gives some indication as to where the difficulties lie; but some general idea at least of the area of difficulty must be available in order to establish the initial teaching techniques that are to be employed. Whether the preliminary diagnosis gives clear-cut or more general indications as to a child's difficulties, the remedial programme that is initiated has to remain flexible. Even children without specific difficulties do not learn at precisely the same rate and using identical strategies, and this is still more important to bear in mind where the child is in difficulties over learning.

To turn to the essential corollary of the diagnostic process – the remedial programme itself. Just as no two children are exactly alike, so presumably no two remedial programmes can be exactly alike, although there will be sufficient similarities between the difficulties of some children to make it possible to achieve some broad groupings. In this country by far the greatest provision has been made for children having difficulty in learning to read, because universal literacy is considered essential both for adequate participation in what schools have to offer and in a modern technological society. However, awareness is growing of the necessity for numeracy as well, and while the pressure for remedial help for children having difficulty with number work is not as great as for help for poor readers, there are signs that it is growing. This is partly a matter of outlook: it has always been much more socially acceptable to be 'not good at figures' than to be an inadequate reader – although spelling is another matter again! Most modern educationists would agree that education in its fullest sense is concerned with the development of the whole child rather than merely with progress in literacy and numeracy – that is, that the child should be given the opportunity to use and develop his growing body and mind in a variety of ways, to learn about his environment and to enrich his imagination, exploring the use of a variety of media which will make it possible for him to express and create his own impression and understanding of the world. Reading, writing and numbering are necessary tools in much of this process, but in their turn could be considered to be dependent on more basic skills such as perceptual and perceptual-motor abilities, and therefore it is towards these underlying skills that many remedial programmes are now directed, more in the U.S.A. than in the U.K. at present. Historically, the problem of the remediation of reading difficulties has been intertwined with the remediation of the underlying skills, in that as the reading process has been looked at more closely so the underlying skills have attracted greater attention. But interest in perceptual and perceptual-motor abilities has been increased also by the greater attention given to the learning problems of children who have been considered to be brain injured and some account of this development is necessary to the understanding of the use of certain techniques. As this should precede any discussion on the design of remedial reading programmes it is given forthwith.

III THE GROWTH OF INTEREST IN PERCEPTUAL DIFFICULTIES

The factors necessary for progress in learning to read and write have attracted attention for several decades; along with the study of every aspect of the reading process, they have accounted for many thousands of research papers and books. Betts (1946) suggested that the teaching of reading to beginners would be a less complex task if each child could meet *eighteen* previous requirements, including many visual and auditory perceptual abilities. Other authorities on the teaching

---

1. Immediate needs that require satisfaction through reading.
2. Sufficient prereading experiences to whet the reading appetite and to be aware of the significance of visual symbols.
3. A social adjustment sufficiently adequate to cope with the give-and-take situations in the classroom.
4. A chronological age which would have made possible a general development of the organism sufficient to cope with reading activities.
5. An interest in and good attitudes toward reading.
6. A level of mental maturity that would insure a reasonably rapid rate of learning.
7. A background of information pertinent to that which he is to read.
8. Language facility adequate to deal with direct and vicarious, or second-hand experience.
9. Ability to relate ideas accurately and rapidly.
10. A memory span that would insure competence in following directions and in relating experience pertinent to that which is being read.
11. Ability to hear sounds sufficiently well for normal communication.
12. Ability to make auditory discriminations sufficiently well to acquire phonic techniques for word recognition.
13. A level of visual efficiency sufficient to permit the rapid development of specific visual skills required in reading.
14. Ability to make visual discriminations sufficiently well to acquire reasonably rapid control over sight word and visual analysis techniques.
15. Ability to perceive differences in colour so that such words as 'red' and 'blue' represent phenomena within his experience and so that experiences gained from reading may be applied to work-book and art activities.
16. Motor control sufficiently developed to permit efficient eye movements, to facilitate the handling of books, and to make possible participation in construction and physical activities.
17. An integrated nervous system free from defects that would interfere with learning, such as speech disorders, confused dominance, and word blindness.
18. A general health status that promotes a feeling of well-being and an attitude of approach to, rather than withdrawal from, worthwhile learning activities.

TABLE 22.1
Prerequisites for reading (Betts, 1946).

---

of reading, such as Gates, Monroe, and Harrison have stressed all, or some of these perceptual factors also. Vernon (1957) in *Backwardness in Reading* gave a comprehensive outline of much of the research that has taken place, particularly on the relevance of necessary levels of visual and auditory perception. In the

U.S.A., Reading Readiness tests were one outcome of research into factors involved in success in learning to read, and these were administered routinely to large numbers of children on entry to school. Although these tests, or similar ones, have never been widely used in the United Kingdom, teachers of Infant's Reception classes have sometimes made their own estimates of the child's ability in skills comparable to those assessed by the Reading Readiness tests, with the same end in view: to discover if the child has developed a sufficient level of visual and auditory perceptual ability, *inter alia*, to be ready to begin learning to read.

In the 1930s and 1940s it was considered frequently that the perceptual skills necessary for adequate auditory and visual discrimination of symbols did not generally mature until about the age of six years, and this was possibly one reason for the much quoted dictum that the optimum period for starting to teach children to read was when they had attained a mental age of six. While exercises to encourage reading readiness were among the activities of many reception classes in Infant schools, few specific programmes were designed to remedy difficulties in, say, visual or auditory perception as assessed by tests or teachers – the stress was still on the role of maturation in development. The most popular method of teaching reading to young beginners was predominantly some variant of 'Look and Say' and perhaps for this method particularly the necessity for a minimum mental age of six years was especially relevant in so far as the demand on visual memory for symbols was concerned. Work during the Second World War on improving aircraft recognition by adults using the tachistoscope stimulated interest in improving children's recognition skills for letters and words using similar techniques, but the results were equivocal (Goins, 1958). By the 1960s, however, the climate of educational opinion had begun to change with regard not only to the optimum age, mental or otherwise, at which the teaching of reading could be started but also with regard to the methods used, and whether specific help should be given to children who showed developmental lags in the underlying perceptual skills. While Marion Monroe, for example, in her Reading Readiness test (1935) had given a list of suggestions of various ways in which teachers could help children develop the particular skills on which the different subtests showed them to have difficulties, Marianne Frostig, having designed and standardized with colleagues a Developmental Test of Visual Perception (1964) for children between the ages of about 3 and 9 years, suggested that children showing difficulty in any of the postulated five areas tested required specific remediation, possibly using a programme developed in her Center for Educational Therapy in Los Angeles. She suggested (Frostig and Horne, 1962) that the difficulties of many young children in learning to read arise from a lack of the basic perceptual abilities involved. Attempting to compensate for this lack helps in the learning process, not only from the point of view of developing the skill but because it rebuilds the childs' confidence, which is already shaken by the difficulties he experiences in many of the everyday activities of young children, due to this developmental lag.

The other educational development in the U.S.A. which has increased interest in perceptual – especially visual perceptual difficulties in children, and specific techniques for their remediation, has stemmed from the work of Strauss and colleagues on brain-injured children, which first made an impact on educationists and psychologists with the publication of *Psychopathology and Education of the Brain-Injured Child* by Strauss and Lehtinen (1947). Among the chief behavioural characteristics which, it was suggested, discriminated brain-injured children who presented as subnormal from 'genuine' mentally subnormal children (exogenous as compared with endogenous) was a difficulty in coping with figure-ground perception, whether in visual, auditory or tactile modalities. The particular relevance of the book to this present chapter arises more especially from the second part, in which Lehtinen described specific techniques for teaching the child with difficulties in figure-ground perception (as well as a possible combination of hyperactivity, perseveration, motor disinhibition, etc.). By using these specific techniques it was possible to educate more efficiently children who otherwise showed such a severe learning disability in certain areas that overall they presented as mentally subnormal, and functioned as such in many learning situations. While later research results by a variety of workers were equivocal in respect of the validity of the behavioural characteristics noted by Strauss *et al.* as an aid in diagnosing brain injury, nevertheless the impact of their work has been far reaching, especially in the field of special and remedial education. The possibility that some children who had been assessed as mentally subnormal had been, in a sense, mis-diagnosed, with the further implication that if they had been correctly diagnosed later management might have been different, was one which caused concern and required further exploration. The dangers of diagnosing brain injury on the basis of behavioural characteristics only, without supportive neurological evidence, were recognized. It was possible, of course, to postulate a minimum cerebral dysfunction, with supportive evidence from 'soft' signs, but gradually it has begun to be accepted that a diagnosis of brain damage, however minimal, is not the most relevant matter educationally. What *does* matter is the type of difficulty shown by the child, be it in figure-ground perception, distractability and hyperactivity, or perseveration, and what can be done to structure the situation so that it is possible for the child to learn. The stress has moved from the possibility of brain injury or dysfunction – which may be present according to various criteria – to the learning disability itself, and it is for the child with learning disability that many highly specialized educational programmes are coming into being. Many of these programmes make use of remedial material such as that of Frostig mentioned earlier; in Frostig's test, one of the five postulated areas of visual perception tested is figure-ground discrimination, and many of the remedial training activities are directed towards developing and strengthening this area. Since Frostig's remedial programme, many others have been published in the U.S.A., suggesting that a boom in special and remedial education is in progress, with an attendant boom in research, publications and teaching materials. The methods which

Lehtinen originally publicized were developed and taken further by Cruickshank and colleagues (1961) and one of the published remedial programmes in visual and visual-motor perception is by Miss Ruth Cheves, who trained many teachers of 'brain-injured children' in the 'Cruickshank' method (issued by Teaching Resources Inc., Education Service of New York Times, 334 Boylston Street, Boston, Mass. 02116). Among other collections of remedial material for visual-perceptual and perceptual-motor functions now published are some by leading workers and educationists from private schools which have become well known also in this particular area of educational therapy (issued by Teaching Resources Inc.): one is by Dubnoff and associates from the Dubnoff School in Los Angeles, another by Fairbanks and Robinson of the Vanguard School in Philadelphia.

The convergence of the two streams of interest in perceptual – especially visual perceptual – difficulties in children has meant that the child with difficulties in learning to read is being studied more closely, and from a wider point of view. His difficulties in learning to read may be one symptom of a general perceptual difficulty which also affects other areas of behaviour, and needs more than just the employment of a different method in the teaching of reading, although this may be necessary too. Questions will arise such as whether to postpone the teaching of reading until more basic skills are at adequate levels and to concentrate on the development of these, or whether to attempt to develop the basic skills concurrently while continuing the teaching of reading – bearing in mind that it has been demonstrated frequently through research that, although the level of visual perceptual abilities of the kind tested especially by pencil and paper tests does show some significant relationship with progress in learning to read, the correlation is by no means a perfect one (it is often about 0·4) and therefore many other factors are involved also. Furthermore, it has been observed that there are some children (girls with Turner's syndrome, see Money in A.C.L.D. report, 1967) who, while being able to read up to or above their age-expectancy level, show quite severe problems in space-form perception.

There has been a tendency when talking about the manifestation of perceptual difficulties to lump under this heading many types of behaviour which upon further examination may not reflect purely perceptual so much as perceptual-motor or visuo-motor difficulties. If perception is interpreted very broadly as recognition, then it is useful to try to separate not only levels of recognition but also to distinguish recognition from reproduction, and not to infer deficiencies in the former from the latter. For example, a transparent cube is the line-drawing stimulus in both the last item of Section Four of the Frostig Developmental Test of Visual perception (Position in Space) and the twenty-second item in the Beery Developmental Test of Visual-Motor Integration (Beery, 1967). In the Frostig test, the child has to find an exactly similar figure from the row of transparent cubes alongside the stimulus figure, whereas in the Beery test the child has to draw a copy of the figure. It may be that the child fails both these tasks, matching the stimulus in the Frostig test to another cube not exactly similar in that the lines are orientated differently, and in the Beery test producing a totally inadequate drawing perhaps of a rectangle within a square. If when being presented with the stimulus in either test the child makes a comment such as 'Oh, it's a glass box!' then presumably it is reasonable to suggest that his description would tally with that given by many other people and that therefore his perception of the figure as a whole is not aberrant. However, the fact that he is unable to choose the identical figure from among four others suggests that the awareness of certain more complex aspects of perception is lacking, in that although the other four choices are also 'boxes', only one is a box in the identical orientation of the stimulus figure. Young children under 5 years of age sometimes show the same type of unawareness of orientation when, on being shown a drawing of a row of say, ducks, in which one is in mirror-image, and asked to pick out the one that is different, will reply that they are all the same, and possibly for similar reasons classify together *b* and *d* where outlines are identical although orientation is different. On the other hand, the child who reproduces the drawing of the transparent cube as a rectangle within a square is not seeing the transparent cube in this manner but just draws it like this because he finds it difficult to organize the lines of his drawing so that they follow those of the stimulus figure correctly; and in fact the expected age level for a successful copy of this figure is higher than that for the matching of the figure to one of four alternatives in the Frostig test. Some children above seven years of age are apparently totally unable to copy the drawing of a diamond (7-year level Binet) but if offered an exact copy of the stimulus as well as their own unsatisfactory copy and other drawings such as a square and asked to say which is most like the stimulus will unhesitatingly choose the correct copy. It is useful when carrying out diagnostic testing for the purpose of remediation to check that in tests that are predominantly visuo-motor the child who fails at this level can match correctly if given a correct copy of the stimulus and alternatives (Meyer Taylor, 1959; Delany, 1966). In a similar manner, when assessing difficulties in auditory perception, careful attention must be paid to differences between input and output, because, as Johnson and Myklebust (1967) have pointed out, children with difficulties in understanding language present a different remedial problem from children whose output processes are affected, although speech resulting from both input and output handicaps may be impaired. Remedial programmes must be tailored also to different levels of difficulty in the input or output systems. Compare, for example, the Peabody Language development kit (Dunn and Smith, 1965) with remedial techniques developed by McGinnis or Lea (see Chapter 20).

IV REMEDIAL PROGRAMMES FOR BACKWARD AND NON-READERS

It is hoped that enough has been said to enable the inference to be made that there are many reasons why children have difficulty in learning to read. When asked to see a child who is a non-reader, or who is very slow in making progress, the educational psychologist in his interview with the child invariably administers an individual intelligence test (most often the Binet or the W.I.S.C. depending to some extent on age) and a test of reading ability. The intelligence test results are used firstly to answer the question as to whether the child's current intellectual level is adequate for the academic demands being made, and secondly to yield qualitative information about the weaknesses and strengths in the different types of task of which the intelligence test is composed. The reading test is usually a fairly comprehensive one which will give information about whether the child has any idea of how to tackle previously unseen material and the kinds of errors he makes, etc. Often other psychological tests are used also. On the basis of the information obtained, the educational psychologist is usually expected to give advice as to how the remedial programme for the child should be planned or occasionally to carry it out himself. Much will depend on the type of remedial provision available, whether individually with remedial tutors, in small groups in remedial reading classes outside the child's classroom or whether the classroom teacher herself is to attempt remediation.

Three prime considerations are of importance, then, in planning a remedial programme of this kind: (1) the deployment of resources; (2) the child's personality and 'intellectual' profile; and (3) a wide knowledge of available techniques and methods from which a teaching plan tailored to the particular child needs to be selected.

1 The deployment of resources

If enough remedial tutors are available to give comprehensive individual attention to each child, the question of how to share out available time does not arise. Given the size of the population of non-readers and backward readers, however, it is more usually a case of giving as much individual help as possible to the children with the severest problems and working in small groups alternating with occasional individual help where possible. Probably in the beginning stages of remediation a one-to-one situation is highly desirable for all children, as most of them will have experienced failure, and it is essential to establish a level at which the child is able to achieve success, and this is probably more easily and quickly done in individual teaching. The type and variety of remedial provision in the U.K. varies with different Local Education Authorities: there may be remedial teachers attached to the School Psychological Service, based on certain schools or centres to which the children are taken, or peripatetic remedial teachers who visit the different schools to take individual children or small groups. Many primary schools have their own special remedial teacher who works with individual children or groups throughout the school. In some areas a specialist teacher in remedial reading visits all schools acting as an adviser both to remedial teachers and classroom teachers. One interesting experiment on how best to deploy limited resources is that being undertaken by McCarthy at Hoffman Estates in Illinois (a fast-growing middle-class suburb of Chicago). Dr McCarthy has suggested (1966) that the problem of children who have a

z

learning disability (which would probably include difficulty in learning to read) is one which may be too great to be dealt with entirely by specialists attached to various educational services; the aim should be to help the classroom teacher to undertake some of the necessary remediation herself. Initially, a team of psychologists and psycho-educational diagnosticians (highly skilled teachers with advanced training in diagnostic and remedial techniques) make a detailed assessment of the child and his learning problems, the psychologists using predominantly psychological tests and the psycho-educational diagnosticians a variety of tests of attainment as well as certain more specifically psychological diagnostic tests such as the I.T.P.A. and the Frostig. After collation of information, a plan of remediation is decided upon, and the psycho-educational diagnostician starts this, visiting the school and possibly sharing the task with the resource room teacher (broadly speaking a resource room is one where special remedial and educational apparatus, etc., is available to teachers). The psycho-educational diagnostician discusses the progress of the remedial work with the child's own teacher and aims to enable the teacher to take over initially a small share of the teaching and then gradually more and more as she feels capable of doing so, always supporting, discussing and being ready to provide the necessary materials. Whether teachers in primary schools in the U.K. with classes of up to 40 children (sometimes more) would be physically capable of undertaking specialized remedial work for possibly 10% of the children in their classrooms, even with continuous support, is a matter for speculation.

2 The child's profile

Diagnostic testing has been considered already, but a good deal of information other than that from the psychological and attainment tests is necessary. Competent checks on the child's hearing and vision and general physical well-being, knowledge about home background and the incentive to read, and information about the child's previous educational history are relevant. Children who have been absent a great deal because of illness, or had many changes of teacher, or just poor teaching, may not have started learning to read for rather different reasons from those who have had every opportunity with regular and consistently competent teaching. As experienced psychologists are aware, the degree of difficulty in learning to read forms yet one more continuum from mild to very severe. There has been some argument as to whether among the severe cases of reading difficulty there is a particular condition described by various terms such as word-blindness, specific developmental dyslexia or specific language disability. It has been argued that this condition is not one extreme of the continuum but in a discrete category, and that because of the aetiology and the specific nature of the condition it requires separate consideration from all other cases of reading difficulty or disability as remedial techniques are highly specific. Recent reviews of the evidence for and against specific dyslexia lend support to the view that even this postulated specific condition may not be a single entity in that the extreme difficulties shown in interpreting printed material – decoding – and in reproducing words in writing – encoding – can be of various types and these types in their turn occur with developmental lags or disabilities of dissimilar pattern. While some severely dyslexic children (using dyslexia here in the sense merely of disability in reading) manifest visuo-spatial problems including finger agnosia and difficulty in right/left discrimination, other severely dyslexic children show developmental language retardation with qualities akin to various forms of dysphasia. This brings us back again to the question of relating the teaching to the diagnosis, in that these two kinds of specific dyslexia (and there may be further subdivisions) require different remedial plans for treatment.

3 Knowledge of techniques

All students training to be teachers of children in infant schools are told a fair amount about the teaching of reading. Some students training to teach children of junior age are also taught something about the teaching of reading, as it is realized increasingly that a fairly high proportion of children move from infant to junior classes without either having made a start in reading or being very much at the beginning stages. It is unusual for students training to be teachers of secondary children to be told how to teach reading as the assumption is made usually that by secondary school age all children are able to read. For those children who have not managed to learn to read the task of teaching them is generally taken over by remedial teachers, for by secondary age it is obvious that special help is required. The remedial teachers who undertake this work come either from the ranks of infant or possibly junior teachers who have experience of teaching reading, from special schools where the problem has always been more clearly seen and accepted, or have received extra training through advanced courses for experienced teachers. Possibly the widest knowledge of a variety of approaches is found among the remedial teachers, both of the *medium* (i.e. traditional orthography, i.t.a., etc.) and of the *method* (look and say, word-whole, sentence-whole, mixed, phonic, alphabetic, visual-auditory-kinaesthetic, etc.). In general, teachers of large classes of infants do not vary methods to suit individual children, and, reverting to Barsch's point quoted earlier about the curriculum model child, for the majority of children in the class this does not matter as they can possibly succeed without a highly individualized approach. Those who *do* need a different strategy, however, are unfortunately placed, and it is often these children for whom the remedial programmes are necessary later. It is worthy of comment that at a time when the initial approach to the teaching of reading is an 'interest' method relying strongly on look-and-say to begin with, that many remedial teachers seem to rely more generally on phonic methods for a breakthrough. Although it has been demonstrated that a change in approach of whatever kind seems to have a beneficial effect, it is possible that some form of phonic method is popular for remedial purposes because many of the children needing help are those with a poor visual memory for letter patterns and sequences who can however manage to memorize 26 individual letters with their more usual sounds, some rules governing changes in sound, and are able to use the context to help discover difficult words. In order to meet the needs of a wide range of problems in learning to read, then, a knowledge of a variety of techniques from which one or a combination of several can be chosen to suit a particular child's learning strategy is necessary, including, for children with extreme reading disability, some slow but highly structured and developed programme such as that of Gillingham and Stillman (1964). Miss Gillingham worked with Samuel Torrey Orton, psychiatrist and neurologist, in developing methods to teach word-blind or 'strephosymbolic' children – the latter term was coined by Orton himself (Orton, 1966). The Orton Society exists today to honour his memory and continue his work, drawing attention to the learning problems of severely dyslexic children and remedial techniques to overcome them. Another similar rather specific remedial method is that of the late Edith Norrie of the Word Blind Institute in Copenhagen (Norrie, 1960), and yet another rather slow 'last hope' method is that of Fernald (1943).

Of recent years more and more programmes for the teaching of reading have been produced, including schemes using aids to decoding, such as diacritical marks or colour codes. Where practice is necessary various self-correcting games or games that two children or more can play are available. Many remedial programmes for retarded or severely disabled readers include help for spelling difficulties, much of it in the form of reinforcing what has been learned in the area of recognition (decoding) by ensuring that it is accompanied by correct reproduction (encoding). There are some children, however, who while appearing to be able to read fairly competently, have a very great difficulty in spelling correctly. Again, different methods appear to work well with individual children: for some with poor visual but good auditory memory, the old-fashioned method of memorizing the spelling of a few words aloud daily, and then writing them down as they are spelled aloud seems to be the most helpful technique for ensuring that at least the more generally used words will be reproduced correctly; for others, a method such as Fernald's relying heavily on kinaesthetic memory accompanied eventually by both sounding out the words by syllables and the visual stimulus of the word simultaneously, is the most effective. Along with the stress on the 'interest' approach to the teaching of reading, relying heavily on look-and-say, has been a reluctance to teach children the alphabet, which rather hampers the rapid use of a dictionary to verify spellings by the older, uncertain speller. Finally, there is the problem of the older child or student who has learned to read, but is so slow that the assimilation of information through printed material is very painstaking; here again there are commercial programmes available in card form, and also various techniques using film projectors or tachistoscopes. The subject has been well covered by De Leeuw and De Leeuw (1965).

4 Evaluation of the success of the remedial reading programme

At the most obvious quantitative level, remedial reading programmes should be the simplest to evaluate by one clear index of success – progress in reading as measured by a test of reading ability. However, there are many qualitative factors which may be important but which are not so simple to measure such as changes in attitude towards reading and more general changes in self-regard and self-confidence. Even the quantitative index is not quite as simple as it appears when comparisons are attempted between the progress of different children or of different methods with the same child. What to one child with fairly severe problems may be enormous progress even if only of an increase in reading age of a few months may be less of an advance for another; the weighting of problems to allow for this would be highly subjective. When evaluating progress in the individual child, the increase by a year from a 6- to 7-year reading age may not be comparable with another year's increase from an 8- to 9-year reading age, because different skills may be required for the higher reading age. Successful remediation has also to be evaluated against the purpose for which the special tuition is given: for some children, it may be necessary to be content with what might be described as functional literacy – an ability to read the tabloid newspapers and to take in through the written word information which is communicated in that medium for the purposes of everyday living in a moderately literate technologically based community. For children with cultural and technological interests and abilities which normally would lead towards further education or training in some form, the pressures towards a high level of skill in reading are proportionately greater and the measure of a successful outcome may be correspondingly stiffer. If the aim is to enable children to participate in the educational mainstream, then presumably the ultimate measure of success is that they have sufficient reading skill to do so, other things being equal.

V PROGRAMMES FOR THE CHILD WITH LEARNING DISABILITY

Earlier in this chapter the movement in the U.S.A. towards the evolution of a category of handicapped child called the child with learning disability was described; it was stated that many of the remedial programmes now available were for the child with a learning disability whose handicap could be shown to be related to developmental lags, particularly in visual-perceptual and visuo-motor abilities. Special classes in some public (state) school systems are specifically for children with perceptual handicaps. As knowledge grows and diagnosis improves, however, perceptual handicaps are seen to be just one facet of a complex of disabilities; with older children it is not only perceptual but also cognitive factors that must be studied when planning remedial help. While the learning disability may be most noticeable in areas such as learning to read, and in arithmetic, it may influence the child's entire repertoire of responses to all kinds of situations which provide important learning experiences, although not necessarily academic and formal ones. The question must be raised here as to how the differential diagnosis is to be made between children whose learning problems are the result of intellectual subnormality and children whose difficulties arise from a learning disability. In fact, probably one more continuum is present, so that it is not easy to decide where a generally slower educational pace for the intellectually retarded child gives way to the specialized, perhaps more highly structured, techniques that may be needed for the child with a learning disability. This problem has barely arisen in the United Kingdom as yet, because there is very little formal educational provision for children with learning disabilities as such, although many teachers both in special schools and in remedial departments are groping towards some kind of differentiation. There are some private schools in the U.S.A. who have made a name for themselves as pace-setters in diagnosing and teaching children with learning disabilities; broadly speaking, they will accept as a child with a learning disability one whose intellectual profile, as assessed through a battery of psychological tests, is irregular (after discounting physical handicaps such as hearing loss or visual defect and severe emotional-social problems). In other words, provided the child has some subtest scores in the average range or above, he will be accepted as a pupil, even though other subtest scores are below, perhaps considerably below average. On this basis, an English educational psychologist can be forgiven for speculating as to how many children in E.S.N. schools in this country would qualify as children with a learning disability, bearing in mind that cultural and environmental factors will play a major role as well. Although overall I.Q. level is no longer such a firm guideline as it used to be in influencing placement in E.S.N. schools, old habits die hard and administrators particularly seem to find comfort in a firm number regardless of the averaging mechanism by which it was achieved. Schools and Centres in the U.S.A. specializing in educational therapy for the child with a learning disability use a variety of psychological and developmental assessment techniques in order to establish the child's profile and plan the remedial programme on its basis. One of the best documented and most comprehensive is that carried out at the Marianne Frostig Centre for Educational Therapy in Los Angeles, and it is useful to quote it here as an example of what is possible, given the expert knowledge and the facilities.

Dr Frostig lays great stress on the necessity for the educator to be familiar with the developmental sequences of the basic aspects of behaviour, and use this knowledge to ensure that attention is paid to lags in earlier developmental phases (sensory-motor, language and perceptual), thus helping the child to establish a firm foundation for cognitive and higher thought processes. Two main theoretical influences are evident in this approach: that of Piaget in relation to the stages of development and the interrelatedness of one stage with another, and that of Guilford in respect of the structure of intellect. Although a wide variety of diagnostic instruments may be used, four tests are basic to the planning of the educational programme. These are the Wepman Test of Auditory Discrimination (Wepman, 1958) the Frostig Developmental Test of Visual Perception, the W.I.S.C. and the I.T.P.A.

The W.I.S.C. is not used for children below 6½ years of age, the I.T.P.A. for children below 5 years or the Frostig for children below 4 years of age; although the tests are standardized for ages lower than these, they are considered less reliable at lower ages. Conversely, although the I.T.P.A. and Frostig tests have ceilings between 8 and 10 years of age they may be used with children above this age level to detect difficulties which result in the child functioning at a lower age level in these particular areas. The rationale for the choice of these tests and the way in which the information obtained is used are explained as follows by Frostig (1968):

A test summary sheet is made out for each child before his individual educational program is designed. *The Basic Test Results Sheet* bears the name and age of the child, and lists the four tests together with each of the subtests. A horizontal line divides the space in which the test scores are entered. The scores above the line are equal to or higher than the mean for the given age level, the scores below the line denote areas which require training. Slightly lowered scores, as for instance a standard score of nine on the W.I.S.C. or on the Frostig, are put above and close to the midline and circled. Space also is provided for an evaluation of the child's sensory-motor functions, and for any important additional information.

These four tests furnish us with a rough measure of the functions we aim to explore: visual perception (Frostig), auditory perception (Wepman), higher thought processes (W.I.S.C.), and language functions (I.T.P.A.). These tests do not reflect a clearcut division between these functions. The I.T.P.A., for example, taps thought processes, such as concept formation and memory functions. In fact, a survey of the four tests seems to indicate that Guilford's factors of the intellect at the six-year level studied by Orpet and Myers (1965) are well represented by the subtests.

Once this profile is established, along with information about the child's social and emotional development and the presence of factors such as distractability or hyperactivity, the educational therapist has a 'blueprint' to work from. As well as Frostig's own remedial programme for visual perception, which includes many suggestions in the Teacher's Guide for three-dimensional exercises which can precede and accompany the pencil-and-paper worksheets, other programmes are used to help remedy difficulties in individual aspects of psycholinguistic function as assessed by the I.T.P.A. and programmes such as that of Levi (1966) to aid in concept formation. Work appropriate to the older child's chronological age in communication skills and mathematics and in subjects such as geography and history is presented in a form in which it is possible for the child to learn. For example, for the older child who cannot yet read, information can be given verbally and the child can respond in similar fashion. If the information is tape-recorded, the child can have it repeated as often as necessary and can also follow any directions given to carry out various exercises involving responses other than writing. Subjects are presented also in a way which provides extra training in the basic skills that need developing. Frostig (1968) suggests that

> subjects which involve perception of spatial relationships are especially helpful. Geometry, geography, astronomy and biology are examples of content subjects, and spelling, writing, reading and arts and crafts are examples of skill subjects, which lend themselves to this purpose. . . . In geography, one can use drawing to scale, making road maps, and transposing information from a physical to a political map and vice versa. In astronomy, the children can be shown how to draw diagrams to illustrate the solar system and movements of the planets; drawing lines on star maps to outline constellations, and tracing the orbits of man-made satellites are excellent alternative exercises in spatial relationships.

With wide general interest in motor (or sensory-motor) functions as a basis for efficient perceptual learning, emphasis is placed increasingly on giving the kinds of motor experience that should lead to a better defined body-image; many types of exercises involving body movement, and eye movement, are used. The child's profile of abilities and attainments as shown on the Basic Test Results Sheet is under regular review and it is borne in mind continuously that the aim is to help the child to acquire the educational attainment necessary to enable him to take his place without undue stress at his age-grade level in an ordinary school. Presumably, the numbers of children returning successfully to the ordinary school system provide a more objective assessment of the entire programme.

For educationists there are many problems in making objective assessments of remedial work. One problem is an ethical one. One way of assessing efficiency of a programme is the use of a comparison group, whose members have attainments (or non-attainments) and difficulties similar to those shown by the experimental group, but who do not receive the specialized remedial help, and whose progress over a period of time can be compared with that of the children receiving the special help. However, this implies denying help to the comparison group perhaps over several months, and even if it is by no means certain that the special help is genuinely useful, many educationists would not feel justified in denying any form of help which might be beneficial. On the other hand, a different type of remediation could be attempted with the comparison group, but where two groups have similar patterns of difficulty and have been chosen for this purpose the various remedial programmes to be used will in all probability be similar. Thus it is not always easy to arrange controlled studies of treatment *versus* no-treatment, or treatment *versus* a different kind of treatment; yet without controlled studies it is difficult to assess the value of a particular remedial approach. To complicate the matter still further, no two children are exactly alike, and trying to achieve matched groups for intensive study from what are often relatively small populations is a researcher's nightmare.

The Frostig programme for the training of visual perception has been subjected to assessment in various research projects. The first use of it in this country (Tyson, 1963) during the course of a larger multi-disciplinary research sponsored by the Spastics Society (Abercrombie *et. al*, 1964) was with physically handicapped children who had been found to have severe visuo-motor difficulties. In this case, an attempt was made to conform to a reasonably strict research design. Four children were fairly well matched in pairs with four others for medical condition, degree of visuo-motor difficulty, and I.Q., but not exactly for age, sex or class in school (see Table 22.2).

Pair	Experimental	Control	Age	Medical Condition	I.Q.	Class
I	Boy		8-5	Diplegia	84	5
I		Girl	10-8	Diplegia	80	5
2	Girl		11-1	Hemiplegia	72	5
2		Girl	11-3	Hemiplegia	67	5
3	Girl		14-4	Diplegia	66	3
3		Boy	14-0	Diplegia	64	3
4	Boy		15-6	Hemiplegia	64	2
4		Girl	13-6	Hemiplegia	66	3

TABLE 22.2

Matching of experimental and control groups on Frostig
Training Programme (Tyson, 1963).

While the experimental children received remedial help using three-dimensional material and Frostig's workbooks (then in an experimental edition), each control child received more general help directed towards linguistic skills for exactly the same amount of time as his or her experimental pair. The pre- and post-programme testing and the remedial programme itself were carried out during the course of one school year. Evaluation of results was achieved in two ways. Firstly, by comparing each child's pre- and post-programme test results on a variety of psychological tests which included Block Design and Object Assembly from the W.I.S.C., adaptations by Zazzo and colleagues of the Bender Gestalt and Kohs Goldstein Blocks tests, the Goldstein Scheerer sticks test and the Frostig test. The Neale test of Reading Ability measuring accuracy and comprehension was also used. Secondly, evaluation was more general and subjective in that the children's progress in class and attitude to the school, other children, and learning tasks were observed continuously. Broadly speaking, the results of the testing suggested that the experimental children had, on average, improved on their earlier scores rather more than the control children, particularly the two younger children (statistically significant results rather better than the 5% level). Most of the children showed positive changes of some degree in the classroom and school situation also, but again it was the youngest experimental

z*

boy who showed the greatest progress in school work and increase in self-confidence. Other evaluations of the Frostig programme for perceptual training have been carried out in the U.S.A. and are reported by Frostiq *et al.* (1964). Similarly, various language programmes developed on the basis of the I.T.P.A. have been reported, including the well-known Peabody Language Development Kit (Dunn and Smith, 1965).

Before leaving remedial programmes for the child with a learning disability, it would be appropriate to mention some other approaches to the problem, although these are but a brief selection of the wealth of theory and material that is now being propounded and developed. The approach to the remediation of perceptual-motor difficulties through the motor bases of achievement is exemplified very clearly in the work of Kephart. While the assessment of the difficulties involves the use among other instruments of the Purdue Perceptual-Motor Survey (Roach and Kephart, 1966) a detailed plan for remediation is outlined in *The Slow Learner in the Classroom* (Kephart, 1960). Apparatus such as walking boards and balance boards are used for some of the motor training, and the chalkboard (blackboard) also figures prominently. There are many suggestions for the training of form perception using puzzles, stick figures, and pegboards.

A detailed account of a very comprehensive remedial programme for children with a variety of disabilities in language (including both receptive and expressive aspects), disorders of reading, written language or arithmetic, or non-verbal disorders of learning, is given by Johnson and Myklebust (1967). Diagnosis of the child's learning disability is painstaking, lengthy, and requires the professional contributions of many disciplines. Johnson and Myklebust consider that there are many types of learning disability

> but a basic underlying homogenity serves to unite and characterize this population. This homogeneity is derived from the fact that it is the neurology of learning that has been disrupted, thereby altering and determining the psychology by which these children learn. Unlike the mentally retarded, they have normal potential for learning; hence, the educational objectives differ; unlike those with deafness or blindness, they receive information through all sensory modalities. However, the brain dysfunction precludes organization and use of these sensations in the normal manner; they cannot learn in the usual way.

The special approach and techniques used with these children has been designated *clinical teaching* by the authors.

A very individual approach is that of the Institutes for the Achievement of Human Potential in Philadelphia, where the 'Doman-Delacato' method is taught to parents of children most of whom are diagnosed as having brain injury or neurological dysfunction. One of the theoretical bases of the approach is that ontogeny recapitulates phylogeny; the developing human organism has to progress correctly through a series of stages including the development of locomotion through crawling and creeping in a manner which elicits the appropriate reflexes. A malfunctioning human brain can 're-learn' these neuro-logical patterns if they are imposed on it, and therefore 'patterning' of the child who cannot do this voluntarily is part of the treatment. Occlusion of one eye to improve dominance and sidedness may be recommended, as also masking for short periods to force the child to re-breathe his exhalations, thus increasing carbon dioxide intake and making the lungs work harder, improving deep breathing. Methods for teaching reading on the lines propounded by Doman in *Teach Your Baby To Read* (1965) may be followed also. Evaluation of the success of the method has been a subject of considerable controversy in the U.S.A.: recently a long critique has appeared in the *Journal of the American Medical Association* (Freeman, 1967; Robbins, 1967).

VI REMEDIAL PROGRAMMES FOR THE 'CULTURALLY UNDER-PRIVILEGED'

As discussed by Dr Ravenette in Chapter 19, research findings on the effect on cognitive growth of the level of access to complex or simpler linguistic structures has had much to do with the changing climate of opinion on the educational needs of children from lower socio-economic levels. These educational programmes for preschool children particularly may be considered remedial in the sense that they are intended to provide *preventive* remediation, attempting to avert the likelihood of later school failure and large numbers of drop-outs from underprivileged groups in high school. In its earliest days, Operation Headstart in the U.S.A. was in many areas carried out chiefly in the long summer vacation, when schools stood empty and the supply of workers, both voluntary and paid, including teachers, was better. Most of the earlier programmes were of the 'enrichment' variety and based on good nursery school practices, but with experience and time to evaluate results, some variations and also entirely new approaches have emerged, particularly where the special programmes have been sponsored by University departments or colleges. Thus again the growth of a wealth of theory and practice has come about, as in the field of learning disability (and indeed there are many links between the two kinds of programme, and some cross-fertilization). Among other developments, two will be selected for mention here, because they embody points which may be of particular relevance when bearing the remedial aspect in mind. One of the main concerns in evaluation of the success of the programmes has been whether the children retain any gains made as measured by pre- and post-programme testing.

Probably the most controversial programme initiated for the preschool disadvantaged child is that described by Bereiter and Engelmann (1966) in *Teaching Disadvantaged Children in the Preschool*. Having studied the differences between a sample of disadvantaged Negro preschool children and children of members of the University of Illinois staff, particularly in language use, the teaching programme was directed specifically towards enabling the disadvantaged children to acquire those aspects of language which are more complex and abstract and which, it is argued, the usual nursery school approach may not achieve in the time available. A good deal of early teaching in this programme is directed towards enabling children to make statements about objects rather than using the slurred telegrammatic phrases which are common. Polar concepts are taught using these statements, i.e. 'this plate is big', 'this plate is small'. Then the concept of negation using 'not' is developed, e.g. 'this plate is not big', followed by the teaching of other linguistic concepts. Thus the teaching is structured in a manner by which children are helped to develop logical thinking using appropriate language. There is a good deal of drill, which is carried out in a forceful, lively, rather cheer-leader fashion. Evaluation of results has suggested that in the period since the programme was first instituted, the children who have been through it have retained their gains as measured on the Binet, I.T.P.A., etc., rather better than some of the more traditional pre-school enrichment programmes.

The Demonstration and Research Center for Early Education (DARCEE) at George Peabody College in Nashville, Tennessee, has been set up as the result of work over many years for culturally disadvantaged preschool children by Dr Susan Gray and colleagues. The methods and materials employed are described in *Before First Grade* (Gray *et al.*, 1966), but the project has been developing continuously and has diversified also, as results of earlier work have shown, for example, that control group children in frequent contact with experimental group children will benefit from the improvement in the experimental children, as will also younger brothers and sisters. Preschool classes are run in various parts of Nashville and suburbs, and the effect, in some cases, of making it a condition for accepting the child that the mother also attends part of the time, is being studied. Results are encouraging and many children seem to retain the gains they have made.

VII   BEHAVIOUR MODIFICATION TECHNIQUES AS PART OF REMEDIATION

Both Engelmann's preschool groups in Illinois and Gray's classes in Tennessee initially use some form of reward as reinforcement, gradually substituting tokens for exchange for the earlier more immediate rewards. In this respect, 'behaviour modification' techniques have become accepted practice in much of special and remedial education in the U.S.A., and are in isolated instances becoming accepted in the U.K. also. The practice of behaviour modification as derived from the theory of operant conditioning has been shown in many studies to achieve a valuable new dimension to thinking about teaching and learning. There is a danger, however, that in copying the ways in which pioneering educationists (such as some of those mentioned earlier) have employed behaviour modification techniques, that other workers in the field who are not very familiar with the theoretical basis will see in the techniques only the superficial concrete adjuncts. Bijou, a leading researcher in this field, has commented (1968):

The fact that academic and social behaviours are operants, and hence sensitive to consequent stimulation, has led many teachers and researchers to use indiscriminately, contrived contingencies such as tokens, M & Ms (Smarties), points, stars, etc. Such contrived reinforcers are not always necessary, and in many instances in which they have been used, they have not been meaningful to the child. That is to say, the child's behaviour was not strengthened by directly dispensing M & Ms to him, or by whatever else he received when he exchanged a collection of tokens or a sum of points for it. Contrived reinforcers are appropriate *only* when the reinforcers available to a teacher (confirmation, such as 'Yes, that's right'; indications of progress, such as charts; approval, like 'Fine work'; and so on) are not functional for a child. Furthermore, when contrived reinforcers are considered necessary, they should be programmed so that they arc gradually eliminated and replaced by the reinforcers which evolve from the activity learned.

It is necessary now to draw attention to different uses of the word 'programme'. So far it has been employed in the sense in which one definition of it occurs in the Penguin English Dictionary: 'agenda, list or summary of things to be done'. But many of the remedial programmes mentioned, in using the word 'programme' in their titles, carry overtones also of a more specific meaning connected with programmed instruction, and particularly linear programmes. In the strict sense in which Skinner uses the term, programming has emerged as part of a technology of teaching based on an analysis of behaviour in which the processes of operant conditioning are revealed as being important for human learning. To quote Skinner (1968):

> The application of operant conditioning to education is simple and direct. Teaching is the arrangement of contingencies of reinforcement under which students learn. They learn without teaching in their natural environments, but teachers arrange special contingencies which expedite learning, hastening the appearance of behaviour which would otherwise be acquired slowly or making sure of the appearance of behaviour which might otherwise never occur.

It is not the purpose of this chapter to describe the different programmes which Skinner differentiates in *The Technology of Teaching*, but to draw attention to the fact that the basic principles underlying these programmes can be used in remediation, particularly of what could be called in general problems of social behaviour. Examples of the application of the theory of operant conditioning in this manner can be found in the reports of Wolf, Mees and Risley (1964) and Wagner (1968). The 'engineered classroom', using the model of behaviour modification, has been developed also to help the child who is known (in California) as educationally handicapped or emotionally disturbed. In a co-operative project between the Santa Monica Unified School District and the University of California, Los Angeles, the Engineered Classroom has been developed to attempt to 'lengthen attention span, promote successful accomplishment of carefully graded tasks, and to provide a learning environment with rewards and structure for the child in accord with the principles of learning theory' (Hewett *et al.*, undated). See also *Exceptional Children* (March, 1967).

VIII THE 'HARDWARE' OF REMEDIATION

Mention of programmed instruction raises quite naturally the question of teaching machines and their place in a remedial programme. There is a wide range of hardware which can be employed, from the highly expensive E.R.E. (Edison Responsive Environment, or talking typewriter), to the home-made boxes which many remedial teachers contrive in order to present self-instructional material in an interesting manner. As has been stated frequently, one possible advantage of the use of the machine – apart from novelty – is that the arranging of the teaching plan – the programme – is a matter for tremendous care and teaches the teacher a lot about the logical structure of his material. Close attention must be given to the step-by-step sequence and this in itself is a salutory exercise, as any would-be teacher/programmer has discovered. When working individually with children, the good remedial teacher receives immediate feedback from the child so can alter his approach accordingly, returning to a simpler level at which the child is successful and attempting a different route to the same goal – acting, in fact, as an efficient branching programme. When for various reasons it is decided to design a programme for use with a machine instead, the conditions that must be fulfilled for a successful outcome impose a heavy task on the programmer; if this is carried out well the results can be gratifying.

In conclusion, one recurring fact appears to the writer to be the inescapable lesson to be drawn from this review of the plethora of methods, techniques, media, technology, that come under the general umbrella of remedial programmes. Because children are infinitely variable in physical constitution and behaviour, flexibility of approach based on a sound knowledge of how learning takes place is the essential ingredient in all teaching. Perhaps Skinner's (1968) thoughts on the subject of the Idols of the School are relevant. He discusses the Idol of the Good Teacher ('the belief that what a good teacher can do, any teacher can do') and the Idol of the Good Student ('the belief that what a good student can learn, any student can learn') and says 'It is possible that we shall progress more rapidly towards effective education by leaving the good teacher and the good student out of account altogether. They will not suffer, because they do not need our help. We may then devote ourselves to the discovery of practices which are appropriate to the remaining – what? – ninety-five percent of teachers and students'.

REFERENCES

ABERCROMBIE, M. L. J., GARDINER, P. A., HANSEN, E., JONCKHEERE, J. LINDON, R. L., SOLOMON, G. and TYSON, M. C. (1964) Visual, Perceptual and Visuomotor Impairments in Physically Handicapped Children. *Perceptual and Motor Skills, Monog. Supp.* 3-VI8.

BANNATYNE, A. D. (1967) The Etiology of Dyslexia and the Color Phonics System. *International Approach to Learning Disabilities of Children and Youth.* Selected papers of 1966 Annual Inter. Conf. Tulsa, Oklahoma: Association for Children with Learning Disabilities.

BARSCH, R. H. (1967) *Achieving Perceptual Motor Efficiency, Perceptual Motor Curriculum,* Vol. 1. Seattle, Washington: Special Child Pubs.

BEERY, K. E. (1967) *Visual Motor Integration.* Chicago: Follett.

BEREITER, C. and ENGELMANN, S. (1966). *Teaching Disadvantaged Children in the Preschool.* Englewood Cliffs, N.J.: Prentice-Hall.

BETTS, E. A. (1946) *Foundations of Reading Instruction.* New York: Amer. Book Co.

BIJOU, S. (1968) *Promoting Optimum Learning in Children.* Paper presented at 6th Inter. Study Group on Child Neurology and Cerebral Palsy, St Edmund Hall, Oxford. Sept. 1968.

CRUIKSHANK, W. M., BENTZEN, F. A., RATZEBURG, F. H. and TANNHAUSER, M. T. (1961) *A Teaching Method for Brain-Injured and Hyperactive Children.* Syracuse, N.Y.: Syracuse Univ. Press.

DELANY, F. I. (1966) *An Investigation into certain aspects of Visual and Visuo-Motor Perception in Children with Cerebral Palsy.* Unpub. Ph.D. thesis, Fordham Univ.

DE LEEUW, M. and DE LEEUW, E. (1965) *Read Better Read Faster.* Harmonds-worth, Middx.: Pelican Books.

DOMAN, G. (1965) *Teach Your Baby to Read.* London: Cape.

DUNN, L. and SMITH, J. (1965) Peabody Language Development Kit. Minnea-polis: American Guidance Service.

FERNALD, G. M. (1943) *Remedial Techniques in Basic School Subjects.* New York: McGraw-Hill.

FREEMAN, R. D. (1967) Controversy over 'Patterning' as a treatment for brain damage in children. *J. Am. Med. Assn.,* **202**, 5.

FROSTIG, M. (1968) Education for Children with Learning Disabilities. *Progress in Learning Disabilities,* Vol. 1. New York and London: Grune and Stratton.

FROSTIG, M. and HORNE, D. (1962) Assessment of Visual Perception and its Importance in Education. Los Angeles: A.A.M.D. *Education Reporter,* Vol. 2, No. 2.

FROSTIG, M., MASLOW, P., LEFEVER, D. W. and WHITTLESEY, J. R. B. (1964) The Marianne Frostig Development Test of Visual Perception, 1963 Standardization. *Perceptual and Motor Skills, Monog. Supp.,* 2-VI9.

GILLINGHAM, A. and STILLMAN, B. W. (1964) *Remedial Training for Children with Specific Disability in Reading, Spelling and Penmanship.* Cambridge, Mass.: Educators Pub. Service.

GOINS, J. T. (1958) *Visual Perceptual Abilities and Early Reading Progress.* Supp. Educ. Monog. No. 87. Univ. Chicago Press.

GRAY, S. W., KLAUS, R. A., MILLER, J. O. and FORRESTER, B. J. (1966) *Before*

First Grade. The Early Training Project for Disadvantaged Children. New York: Teachers College Press.

HEWETT, F. M., TAYLOR, F. D. and ARTUSO, A. A. (undated, probably 1967) *The Santa Monica Project. An Engineered Classroom for Educationally Handicapped Children.* Unpub. paper re Demonstration Grant OEG-4-7-062893-0377.

JOHNSON, D. J. and MYKLEBUST, H. R. (1967) *Learning Disabilities: Educational Principles and Practice.* New York and London: Grune and Stratton.

KEPHART, N. C. (1960) *The Slow Learner in the Classroom.* Columbus, Ohio: Merrill Books.

LEVI, A. (1966) Remedial techniques in disorders of concept formation. *J. Special Educ.,* **1.**

MCCARTHY, J. MCR. (1966 and earlier, undated) *A Public School Program of Remediation for Children with Severe Learning Disabilities.* Demonstration of Proposal submitted to the U.S. Commissioner of Education. Unpubl. papers.

MCCARTHY, J. J. and KIRK, S. A. (1961) *The Illinois Test of Psycholinguistic Abilities (Exper. Ed.).* Urbana, Ill.: Inst. for Research in Exceptional Children.

MEYER TAYLOR, E. (1959) *Psychological Appraisal of Children with Cerebral Defects.* Cambridge, Mass.: Harvard Univ. Press.

MONEY, J. (1967) The Laws of Constancy and Learning to Read. *International Approach to Learning Disabilities of Children and Youth.* Selected papers of 1966 Annual Inter. Conf. Tulsa, Oklahoma: Association for Children with Learning Disabilities.

MONROE, M. (1935) *Reading Aptitude Tests.* Houghton Mifflin.

NORRIE, E. (1960) Word Blindness in Denmark: its Neurological and Educational Aspects. *The Independent School Bulletin,* 1959-1969 (3): 8-12.

ORPET, R. and MYERS, C. (1965) *A Study of Eight Structure-of-Intellect Hypotheses in 6 year old Children.* Draft Report, N.I.M.H. Grant MHO8666-01.

ORTON, S. T. (1966) *Word Blindness in Schoolchildren* and other papers on Strephosymbolia (specific language disability – Dyslexia) (1925-1946). Compiled by J. L. Orton, Monog. No. 2. Pomfret, Conn: Orton Society Inc.

ROACH, E. G. and KEPHART, N. C. (1966) *The Purdue Perceptual-Motor Survey.* Columbus, Ohio: C.E. Merrill Books.

ROBBINS, M. P. (1967) Test of the Doman-Delacato Rationale with Retarded Readers. *J. Am. Med. Assn.,* **202,** No. 5.

SKINNER, B. F. (1968) *The Technology of Teaching.* New York: Appleton-Century-Crofts.

STRAUSS, A. A. and LEHTINEN, L. E. (1947) *Psychopathology and Education of the Brain Injured Child.* New York and London: Grune and Stratton.

TYSON, M. C. (1963) Pilot Study of Remedial Visuomotor Training. *Special Education,* **52,** No. 4.

VERNON, M. D. (1957) *Backwardness in Reading.* London: Cambridge Univ. Press.

WAGNER, M. K. (1968) A case of public masturbation treated by operant conditioning. *J. Child Psychol. & Psychiatry,* **9,** 61-65.

WEPMAN, J. (1958) *Wepman Test of Auditory Discrimination.* Chicago: Language Research Associates.

WOLF, M., RISLEY, T. and MEES, H. (1964) Application of operant conditioning procedures to the behaviour problems of an autistic child. *Behav. Res. & Therapy,* I.

ZAZZO, R. (1960) *Manuel pour l'examen Psychologique de l'enfant.* Neuchatel: Delachaux and Niestlé.

23

The assessment of cognitive processes: Piaget's approach

W. Mary Woodward

I INTRODUCTION

There has been a trend in recent years towards the experimental investigation of the single case, particularly in the clinical field (Shapiro, Chapter 21). The approach of Piaget provides one means by which this may be achieved, especially when children have learning difficulties. Over the past 50 years the application of intelligence tests in this situation has ensured that a more satisfactory educational recommendation has been made than would have been possible without them. But now a test finding is increasingly being regarded as a starting-point for further investigation, rather than as an end-result in itself. When such further inquiry is necessary, the techniques devised by Piaget and Inhelder are a means of exploring cognitive processes and concepts. Secondly, when, for some reason or other, conventional scales are inapplicable, these techniques may themselves be the starting-point.

To describe in detail the kinds of clinical problems to which the techniques can be applied and the theoretical assumptions underlying the approach, together with a discussion of the procedures of administration and problems of interpretation, would require something in the nature of a 'test manual'. All that can be achieved in a short chapter is to indicate the general features of the method and to discuss some of the questions that can be tackled with it.

Perhaps the approach can best be introduced by describing the writer's experience of problems met in clinical work and of attempts to meet them by means of techniques based on Piaget's approach. The first was that of assessing levels of intellectual function in young children who had severe or multiple physical handicaps or a marked behaviour disturbance that interfered with co-operation in the test situation. A second concerned assessment of the degree of subnormality in children with results outside a certain limit on a conventional test (e.g. −3 S.D.). Techniques based on Piaget's studies of sensori-motor development in the first 18 months of life were devised for these two problems. These techniques could be used for very young children or older retarded ones. Thirdly, some of the problems devised by Piaget and Inhelder for the investigation of children's concepts of number and space were used for severely subnormal children over the age of 11 years and for younger children with physical handicaps or emotional disturbance. This left a gap for the period between $1\frac{1}{2}$ and $4\frac{1}{2}$ or

695

5 years. Research was conducted (and is still in progress) on developments in this phase in normal and severely subnormal children. Investigations are now being carried out on the use of the approach with child guidance referrals when there is a severe learning difficulty that is not accounted for by limited intelligence. In these cases the aim is to investigate directly the concepts that are relevant to the learning difficulty.

In all these cases the aim was to obtain information that could be used to place the child in an appropriate learning situation, with a view to making a further assessment when the child had had the opportunity to learn in such a situation.

Adults for whom the techniques have been used are subnormal ones who may be rehabilitated to live in the community and the more severely subnormal who need supervision but nevertheless can work in an industrial unit. Information gained from the study of number concepts was used to indicate whether or not it was appropriate to teach the elementary number operations.

Finally, the behaviour of some children when tackling the problems has suggested that these techniques may be of value for the investigation of non-cognitive factors that interfere with learning.

This approach was first used in a clinical setting many years ago by Inhelder (1944) who studied concepts of quantity and equivalence in subnormal adults and children. She and Piaget (1947) later suggested that the 'diagnosis of thinking' was more useful for purposes of assessment than the I.Q. The present discussion is in the context of educational and clinical practice in this country, where standardized intelligence tests are considered to give useful information – a view not shared by Piaget and Inhelder.

In this chapter a description will be given of the kinds of techniques devised by Piaget and Inhelder, and suggestions will be made of ways of modifying them for clinical purposes. The procedures may validly be modified for such a purpose, but if there is such a radical departure from them that the necessary behavioural criteria for interpretation in accordance with Piaget's approach are not satisfied then that approach is not being applied and the procedures would best be given another name. The main features of the approach have thus been retained: these will be outlined before the specific procedures are discussed.

II MAIN FEATURES OF THE APPROACH

The techniques being discussed cannot be separated from Piaget's theory, though a detailed exposition of this theory will not be made. Readers who are not familiar with the work of the Geneva group will no doubt be daunted by the long list of publications, which is continually being extended. Apart from the difficult *Psychology of Intelligence* (1950), Piaget has not written a book summarizing his observations and theoretical interpretations; the first of his *Six Etudes de Psychologie* (1964) is a fairly comprehensive though brief, statement made nearly 30 years ago. A detailed account is available in Flavell's book (1963); this, however, goes into more detail about the logical aspects of the theory than most readers will require. In a more general discussion of experience and cognitive functioning in the context of an information-processing approach, Hunt (1961) devotes two long chapters to a description of Piaget's work. Brief outlines by the present writer can be found in Ellis (1963) in relation to mental subnormality, and in Howells (1965) in relation to child psychiatry. Brown (1965) includes a chapter on Piaget's approach in his book on social psychology. Accounts of the work outside Geneva can be found in Flavell (1963) and Hunt (1961). Studies of British children have been carried out by Lovell and others (1959, 1960, 1960, 1961, 1961, 1961, 1962, 1962), Lunzer (1960a, 1960b, 1965), Peel (1959) and Woodward (1959, 1961, 1962a, 1962b, 1963a).

A few words are in order about the history of the work at Geneva, since the name 'Piaget' still evokes in many psychologists the work of the twenties and early thirties, when children's concepts of the world, physical causality, etc., were investigated by means of questions about objects and events remote from their experience, and when the theoretical analysis was in terms of 'syncretism', 'nominal realism', etc. (Piaget, 1926, 1928a, 1928b, 1930).

The second phase of the work in Geneva includes Piaget's very detailed observations of the behaviour of his own children in infancy and the studies of various concepts in older children, by the observation of behaviour in problem-solving situations, sometimes followed up with questions. It is the work of the latter period which has most application to clinical problems, though some of the earlier work might well be worth looking at: it might be useful for instance to know whether a given child persisted in an animistic attitude when others had abandoned it – provided methods are used that avoid suggesting, in the form of the question, that inanimate objects might be alive; Russell and Dennis (1939) devised a standardized procedure for the study of animism. Work in *The Language and Thought of the Child* (Piaget, 1926) also suggests a basis for further study.

Although the work of a group of people for a period of 40 years cannot be adequately summarized in a few pages, a brief outline may help to orient the reader in the subsequent discussion of clinical applications. Piaget has postulated that cognitive development is a matter of a sequence of phases or periods which are characterized by a certain kind of behaviour pattern or thinking (schema). Each of the four major changes constitutes a new level of organization that develops out of the preceding one. These are listed below. The ages quoted are rough approximations only.

Periods of development	*Approximate ages*
Sensori-motor (6 substages)	Birth to $1\frac{1}{2}$ years
Pre-operational	
(*a*) Symbolic and pre-conceptual	$1\frac{1}{2}$ to $4\frac{1}{2}$ years
(*b*) Intuitive	4-$4\frac{1}{2}$ to $6\frac{1}{2}$-7 years
Concrete operational	$6\frac{1}{2}$-7 to 11-12 years
Formal operational	11 to 12 years upwards

Piaget distinguished six types of adaptive behaviour patterns in the sensori-motor period, the first being that of the reflexes of the first month. The next four are described in terms of the concept of the circular reaction: an action by chance produces or precedes an event which the child sees or hears, and the action is then repeated. The objects on which they are performed in the second substage of primary circular reactions are parts of the child's own body such as his hand; external objects are involved in the secondary circular reactions of the third substage (e.g. a rattle is shaken). In the next phase, two behaviour patterns of the third substage are co-ordinated in such a way that one is used as a means to carry out the other (e.g. a screen is knocked over in order that a toy behind it may be grasped). The fifth substage is that of tertiary circular reactions: the actions with the object are varied and so are the effects obtained by them, e.g. an object is banged successively on different surfaces, producing different sounds. Novel effects are thus produced. Problems of obtaining objects out of reach, on supports or attached to strings within reach, are solved in this substage: 'new means' are discovered. In the sixth substage, new means to solve problems are 'invented', or, in other words, there is solution of the type of problems used to study insightful problem-solving (e.g. using a stick in order to obtain a toy).

Piaget also investigated in this period the child's reactions when objects go out of the perceptual field (the development of the 'object concept'); of the child's behaviour with regard to the spatial relations between objects and to the causes of their movements; and of imitative behaviour. Developments in these respects correspond with developments in adaptive behaviour patterns. Piaget argues that the developments at the sixth substage imply central representative schemata. Thus the symbolic and pre-conceptual phase begins. The difference between this latter and the next phase is seen in a task such as that of copying a row of beads in the same order: success with this implies intuitive thinking in Piaget's terms.

The difference between intuitive and operational thinking is illustrated by Piaget's most often quoted findings on the lack of conservation of number, quantity, time, area, length, etc., in children under about 7 years. The children believe that a quantity has changed with a change in the spatial arrangement of the elements. Similarly, intuitive and operational thinking are distinguished by an understanding of seriation, part-whole relations and class-inclusion. Inhelder and Piaget (1958) define operation as 'actions which are not only internalized, but are also integrated with other actions to form general reversible systems'. By this they mean that thinking is no longer tied to the action involved. In action, red squares and green squares can be placed in two separate groups or they can be combined into one class of squares, but they cannot be both at the same time. Hence the child whose thinking is tied to action can conceive either of the two subclasses or of the general class, but not both at once. When the child can think of both, and pass from considering one to considering the other, Piaget describes his thinking as reversible. Similarly reversibility is shown when one element can be thought of as being in two different relations with other elements at one and the same time, as when an element in a series is at one and the same time more than those before it and less than those after it. A clear exposition of the concept of operation can be found in Lunzer's (1964) introduction to his translation of *The Early Growth of Logic*.

Putting in order of magnitude (serializing) and classifying (at least to two levels) are the main concrete operations. These operate on the information which is given, in contrast to the formal variety, which operate on the information that has already been operated on by concrete operations; namely they are second-order operations. Formal thinking is hypothetico-deductive, and it involves logical implication (if this, then that . . .). (For a discussion of formal operations see Lunzer, 1965.)

The value of this system for clinical work is that it is a sequence of development: what matters is the order in which developments occur, not the age at which they are attained. It is thus applicable to all children no matter how slowly or how quickly they develop. The point of the assessment, therefore, is to establish how far the child has progressed through the sequence and then to recommend an appropriate learning situation. This may be in a special remedial teaching group or in a given type of school. This will be discussed in a later section. First two general questions must be discussed. The first concerns the phases – or stages; the second is that of factors that influence this development.

Probably the most controversial (and possibly most misunderstood) of Piaget's concepts is that relating to stages of development. This question cannot be discussed in detail here, though it may be pointed out that what is involved is the *organization* of behaviour and central processes at successively higher levels, and that 'stage' or 'period of development' are merely descriptive terms. The 'plan' concept of Miller, Galanter and Pribram (1960) can very well be applied to this scheme (Woodward, 1967). Cognitive changes in the period that has been most studied by the Geneva group have also been found by Luria (1961) and White (1965), who summarizes the developmental changes in learning that take place in the 5- to 7-year period.

The really relevant question is to what the stages or categories refer – to specific concepts such as space, time, causality, number, etc., or to all the child's cognitive development for a period? Probably few would question the former on the basis of the present evidence; the latter is more arguable. The 'all' in any case means 'all the aspects selected for investigation' or – improbably – 'all the aspects I can think of'. Children certainly show different kinds of thinking (e.g. intuitive and concrete operational) for different concepts at the beginning of a new period. There is as yet no evidence of how long mixed types of thinking persist. Transitional periods are a focal point of interest for the investigation of the development of new schemata; their relevance for clinical assessment will be taken up in a later section.

The question of what variables influence development through the sequence involves a fundamental feature of Piaget's theory: that new schemata are acquired as the result of the child's learning through handling objects, and that the child is an active agent in this process. His views on the interaction of 'assimilation' and 'accommodation' in such acquisitions are very similar to current notions of feedback, as he himself recognizes (Piaget, 1953b). This stress on organism-environment interaction has of course a direct and important bearing on remedial and other educational programmes – though it is misapplied if the aim is to speed up the process, as if appropriate experiences were the only factor in development. Piaget has been misunderstood on this point, and he wrote a preface to the second edition of *The Psychology of Intelligence* (1950) stating that maturation was, of course, also a factor in this process (a misunderstanding of an opposite kind is made when it is assumed that Piaget's postulation of an orderly sequence of development implies that he thinks that maturation must be the only operative factor).

Social experiences, particularly through the medium of language, are obviously also important. It is, of course, people too who determine the amount and variety of objects that the child has to interact with – and indeed the culture determines whether the objects are only sticks and stones or are toys. Thus, when using Piaget's approach for assessment, as with any other method, the important question to ask is: what experiences has the child lacked?

III   THE TECHNIQUES

1 As used in the basic research in Geneva

In this section general points of procedure will be described; the next considers modifications for assessment. The basic aim may be illustrated by a comparison with the psycholinguists' approach to the study of language. Their concern is with the child's mastery of grammatical rules, not merely with whether he uses them when he speaks, since the usage may have resulted from imitation alone. Thus, means have to be devised in order to determine whether the child who, for instance, uses plurals has mastered the rule. In the same way the point of the Piaget and Inhelder methods of investigation is to find out whether the child has developed a particular pattern of action or thinking and to elicit behaviour in such a way as to find out.

It is *not* a matter merely of adopting a standard procedure for each problem, recording the child's response to it and stopping there. To know that the child lifted a cup and took the sweet or toy that he saw placed underneath it is insufficient; it is also insufficient to know that he says that two identical patterns of counters are no longer equivalent in quantity when one is disarranged. One wants to know whether or not he *lifted the cup in order to take the sweet*, and whether he believes that the quantities really *are* different, not merely that they *look* different, and moreover that he continues to think this despite the repeated experience of 'seeing' the corresponding patterns remade and disarranged. That a child pulls a piece of cloth towards him and thereby brings within his grasp an object that was out of his reach is inconclusive evidence that he has acquired the 'behaviour pattern of the support', namely that he draws the support towards him *in order* to obtain the object. It is necessary to exclude the possibility that the child grasped the support out of an interest in that and obtained the toy fortuitously. If the child looks at the toy as he moves the support, discards the latter as soon as the toy is in reach and then takes the toy, it would appear that that possibility is excluded. One of the checks that Piaget used gives more conclusive evidence: the object is placed on the further of two overlapping supports, and it is noted whether the child still pulls the nearer one when the toy does not move with it.

Similarly with the conservation problems, the child's statement about the equivalence of numbers of objects differently arranged, of two areas, continuous quantities, lengths, etc., is insufficient by itself. It is the reason *why* he believes they are equivalent that it is important to elicit. The first step is to establish with the child the equivalence of the balls of plasticine, or groups of counters, or amounts of water in identical glasses, of the length of two sticks, etc. The next step is to destroy the perceptual cues to the equivalence by rolling one ball into a different shape, disarranging the set of counters, pouring the contents of one glass into another of a different shape, pushing one stick along so that it is no longer directly below the other. If the child maintains a belief in the equivalence after these changes, the reason for his belief is requested. If he thinks the quantity, length, etc. changes with a change in shape or position, then the changed object or liquid is restored to its original position or container, then reshaped or poured again. The child is thus given repeated opportunities to correct his false beliefs. This is an essential point of all the procedures – to find out whether the child can correct an incorrect inference on the basis of further relevant experience. That this is a learning situation is not a disadvantage of the method; it is the whole point of it.

Regardless of whether the child develops a schema in the course of the trials, or whether he displayed it on the first trial, it is necessary to establish whether the schema is generalized to new instances. If the child does think lumps of plasticine of different shapes and liquids in differently shaped glasses are the same in amount (having seen the equivalence demonstrated previously), does he still think so for a further different shape and when one ball is broken up into two or four small pieces and when the contents of one glass are poured into two or four smaller ones, and when the sticks are pushed even further out of line or at right angles to each other, or broken up? If there is not such generalization of conservation, the child is only at a transitional point, and concrete operational schemata are not firmly established.

Some of the problems are designed to find out whether the child has an operational or only intuitive understanding of seriation and classification. For seriation it is not sufficient evidence of concrete operational thinking that the child places a set of 10 sticks in order of size without trial and error methods. His method of inserting a second intermediate set of sticks is more likely to reveal whether he realizes that each element has only one place in the series. It is even more conclusive, if the child is familiar with ordinal numbers, to disarrange the set of sticks, to select one, and ask the child what its ordinal position is. The behaviour of a child who does nothing except to say 'It might be fourth' is in contrast to that of a child who remakes the series up to the place of the stick in question.

So also with the distinction between intuitive and operational classification. The latter involves the understanding of 'class inclusion' (see section II). Some aspects of children's understanding of classification can be studied by giving them a sorting task, using, for example, a set of objects that vary in colour and form. Inhelder and Piaget (1964) point out that an understanding of the relation of subclasses to a general class that contains them is not fully revealed when children can sort such a group of objects into two classes by a consistent criterion, e.g. either of colour or of form. They had to devise additional problems in order to distinguish between operational and intuitive classifying.

If the child does not spontaneously make use of the materials that are necessary to solve a problem, it is permissible with these procedures to suggest that he might do so, in some such form as 'Can you make use of this?' or 'Would this help?' For example, in the study of the spontaneous use of materials for measuring, the child is required to build a tower of bricks the same height as a model, the latter being on a lower table, a solution by means of a one-to-one correspondence between the elements on the model and copy being ruled out by the material provided. If the child tries to use his own hand as a measuring instrument and ignores the sticks, etc., his attention can be drawn to them.

These various examples indicate that the aim is not only to 'test the limits' of the child's development but also to determine whether the schemata he has developed are firmly established. As well as testing his generalization to new instances, an attempt may be made to shake the child's belief, for example, in conservation of quantity, etc. Children with the conservations barely established can quickly be made doubtful, whereas others will not be shaken – and may even be scornful of the examiner for suggesting otherwise!

Even when something has clearly gone wrong, children with operational schemata behave differently from those with intuitive schemata. Smedslund (1961), for instance, having shown the child that two balls of plasticine made the pans of a balance level, surreptitiously removed a piece of plasticine from one ball while making it into a sausage shape; the two pieces of plasticine then no longer made the pans of the balance level, as they had before. Some children sought for an explanation of the event without resorting to non-conservation as an explanation, as others did very readily, the operational level in the latter thus being less consolidated. Whether the former children hit on the actual reason is of course irrelevant; that they search for one that is consonant with a belief in the conservation of quantity through a change in shape is the point.

A final general point on these procedures is that it is the classifications that are standard and the criteria for them that must be strictly adhered to: materials and procedures for eliciting the necessary behaviour for an unambiguous classification can – and often have to be – modified to suit particular circumstances.

Although the illustrative protocols of Piaget and Inhelder abound with descriptions of the methods that they use to check on their interpretations, and although it is possible to suggest others that have occurred to the writer in clinical situations, an exhaustive list of possible modifications to suit all likely contingencies obviously cannot be made; the psychologist using this approach has to be prepared to think up variations as the situation demands, namely to regard the method as one of experiment with a single case, rather than one of using a standardized test. Some possible modifications are suggested in the next section, together with clinical applications.

Suggestions which are made arise from the writer's experience with subnormal children and adults, including those who are physically handicapped, and with emotionally disturbed children. A selection of problems was made and modifications were introduced in the light of experience. When new clinical techniques are being devised, one person's experience is insufficient. What is needed is for several psychologists to exchange information after trying out the techniques with various kinds of children. It would be possible, for the information of readers interested in doing this, to append to this chapter a list of items of spontaneous behaviour recorded and of problems administered by the writer, but this would serve no useful purpose unless a detailed account of the criteria for classifying the behaviour were also given. The approach is not an item-inventory one: what the examiner needs to do is to be familiar with the system of classification and so to be able to recognize a secondary circular reaction when he sees one, although that particular one may not be on his list of items.

2 Practical applications and modifications of the techniques

(a) *The Sensori-motor Period*

This period extends from birth to about 18 months in normal infants and up to any age thereafter in subnormal children, depending on the rate of development. Piaget's observations for this period are reported in *The Origins of Intelligence* (1953a), *The Child's Construction of Reality* (1955a), and *Play, Dreams and Imitation in Childhood* (1951).

It is clear that all aspects of sensori-motor development that Piaget studied cannot be investigated in the clinical situation. Moreover, normal babies are rarely seen in the clinic: they present some behaviour which raises doubts about development or they are autistic, deaf or have cerebral palsy. This alone makes it difficult to administer all of a standard set of problems, as those who have tried to apply a developmental scale in these circumstances are well aware.

Furthermore, in the pre-verbal period of development, children who have neither a physical handicap nor a behaviour disturbance often tend to have a dominant interest which lasts for the whole of the session, or even a series of sessions; they apply the same behaviour pattern to all objects, even to ones that are not very appropriate. For example, some children put all small objects presented to them in and out of containers.

Techniques derived from Piaget's observations of the sensori-motor period can deal with the problem of an examiner who can observe only a limited sample of behaviour, for two reasons. One is that the 'experimental object' in problem-solving situations need not be standard. This object is used in problems for determining the level of 'object concept development' when the object is hidden and for problems of toys out of the child's reach, attached to strings, or standing on a support or near a stick. The important point is that the child should be maximally motivated to solve the problem. Hence the most useful experimental object is that in which the child shows most interest; this may be a sweet, a toy or the piece of string, bootlace or scrap of paper that the child arrived with. It is possible, with this technique, for the examiner to accommodate himself to the child's interests, instead of having to try to make the child take an interest in his standard equipment.

The second reason is that the aim is to classify the *type* of behaviour that the child shows. For this any problem that gives the opportunity for co-ordinating secondary schemata (substage IV), discovering new means (V) or inventing new means (VI) will do, and any problems that permit an unambiguous classification of the level of object concept development will suffice. Similarly, with the classification of manipulations of objects, any objects will do. The essential observation is what children do with them, in order that a distinction may be made between secondary and tertiary circular reactions. For example, when the child repetitively bangs a brick on something, what matters is whether he does so on the same surface each time and produces the same effect from it, or whether he varies the action and the sound by banging it successively on different surfaces. If the material can be varied it follows that the sensory channel used can be also, provided that the same types of behaviour pattern can be elicited.

Woodward (1959) devised techniques for use in research in the first instance, using a group of 147 severely subnormal children without physical handicaps; the procedures were later modified for use in clinical assessment, and thereby extended to children with all the varieties of sensory and motor handicap that are found in a subnormal population. The practice has been to determine first whether co-ordinations had been developed between vision and hearing, sucking and grasping (both of substage II) and between grasping and vision (substage III). The child's spontaneous behaviour with his hands and a variety of objects were observed and recorded for the classification of circular reactions (substages II to V). Problems were devised in order to elicit behaviour for classifying the adaptive behaviour patterns and object concept development into substages III to VI. Information on the child's actions in relation to spatial relations among objects and of the relation of one environmental event to another were obtained by observing spontaneous manipulations of objects (substages III to VI). Substage I was indicated by the absence of substage II behaviour. This is considered to be sufficient for an adequate assessment; a possible useful addition, in view of its role in language development, is the observation of imitative behaviour.

The classification of problem-solving behaviour clearly depends both on definite positive evidence of the presence of one kind of behaviour pattern and definite evidence of the absence of the next one up the scale. When such evidence has not been obtained one way or the other with the standard procedure, then modifications are necessary. All possible contingencies and modifications cannot be discussed here: a few will be mentioned by way of illustration.

One means of checking on the support problem has already been mentioned in section III, 1, namely, to use two overlapping supports. Similarly with the string problem: a second string in addition to the one attached to the object can be used.

For children with cerebral palsy, particularly those with athetosis, it has been found useful, before presenting a problem, to observe the movements in progress, and then to present the problem and observe whether the movements change. After the usual procedure of showing an attractive object to the child and placing an unattractive cover on it, the cover may then be presented alone, the attractive object not being shown and hidden under it. If the child makes movements towards the cover only when the attractive object is involved, the evidence is clear. In these cases clear evidence of an attempt to uncover the object is obviously sufficient, even though the motor handicap may prevent actual success. If children attempt to grasp the cover under both conditions there is no behaviour from which to make a definite inference.

With the object concept problems of the sixth stage it may be preferable for children with a motor handicap to rely only on the invisible displacement procedures. The usual procedure is to show an object and, while the child is looking, to cover it with five successive cups, cloths, etc. With the invisible displacement method, the child is shown a sweet or other small object which is then placed in the examiner's closed fist, which is held out to the child. When he has obtained it (stage V behaviour), the examiner places it or another object in his hand, but this time he puts his closed hand under a cloth and, without making a noise, releases the object (making sure, of course, that the child is looking) then removes his closed hand and offers it to the child, who, usually, looks inside it. The crucial point then is whether he does nothing more or looks under the cover. Again, in the case of children with a motor handicap, movements in the direction of the cover may be regarded as sufficient evidence for a stage VI classification. Information on the cognitive development of children with severe behaviour disturbances (see Woodward, 1960, 1963a for description) has been obtained by these techniques that could not be obtained otherwise. In some cases, however, two alternative hypotheses could explain the results. When children neither reach towards the cover, strings or support, nor towards the object that is out of reach, one hypothesis is that the child has not developed the stage V schemata; the other is that he is too inhibited to take the object when this has been hidden or put out of reach by an adult. There may be no alternative but to observe the child playing (if he plays!) in order to see whether he searches when he loses his toy. One check is to pretend to drop something accidentally on the object. Some very withdrawn children may not take any object offered, but if they find something else in the room that interests them, this can be used as the 'experimental object'. One autistic child observed by the writer was interested only in the electric light switch. When a cloth was dangled over it, he quickly whipped it aside.

With blind children, of course, visual presentation of problems is not possible, and as a consequence fewer problems can be administered. Nevertheless it is possible, unless the child also has a severe behaviour disturbance, to elicit behaviour in such a way as to obtain a classification for all the sensori-motor stages. For example, when the sighted child grasps an object he sees (instead of one that touches his hand) he is at the beginning of stage III. With blind children it may be a comparable co-ordination to grasp an object when it touches his arm, though this is an assumption that needs verifying. Provided that they are not also deaf, blind children form circular reactions when the effect is auditory, and in default of evidence from problems, it would seem advisable in these cases to base the classification on manipulative behaviour, bearing in mind that if the child is disturbed, it may not indicate his most advanced development.

Behaviour in the blind child that is comparable to the persistent searching of the sighted child for an object he has seen hidden, may be persistent searching when an object has touched his hand. This would indicate stage VI development. An alternative, with sighted children, for stage V object concept development, is that he lifts a cover and finds the object when a sound indicates its presence (the examiner makes it sound, without having first gone through the procedure of showing it). Blind children, at a certain point in development, put out their hands and grasp an object which makes a sound, whereas less advanced ones do not. Research may establish the correspondence between this action and the behaviour of the sighted children.

Although it is not a matter with this approach of ticking off all items on a list and adding up the score of 'successes', it is useful to have a list of possible behaviour that can be observed. In order to give opportunities for any type of secondary circular reaction to be evoked, it is necessary to provide a variety of objects that have a number of possibilities, such as things that can be shaken, banged, swung, moved by shaking a string and so on. Unless opportunities for manipulating objects in a variety of ways are extensive, behaviour patterns the child has acquired may not be manifested. The writer has observed that some children (S.S.N.) would, while seated, tap a taut string on the side of a table for long periods, thereby causing an object tied to it to rattle, but they did nothing with objects picked up. Equally children cannot show the behaviour of putting objects in and out of a hollow one unless a hollow object is supplied.

It may be asked how many examples of a given type of behaviour pattern are needed for a classification of the child's behaviour into one of the substages. A detailed discussion of this is beyond the reach of this chapter. It was found in Woodward's (1959) study referred to above that children who solved one problem of a given type usually solved the other. Equally, children who showed adaptive behaviour patterns of a given type shown in problem-solving in most cases showed the corresponding object concept development expected in terms of Piaget's classifications. The exceptions were extremely disturbed children.

Classifications of manipulative behaviour with hands and objects corresponded less closely with the classifications of problem-solving. Again many of the children with such discrepancies were those with severe behaviour disturbance: the manipulative behaviour was of a lower kind than the problem-solving behaviour. This was attributed to the differences in motivation involved in solving problems and in manipulating objects. In the former the child has to solve the problem in order to obtain an object; if he wants the object, he is motivated to attempt to solve the problem. The motivating conditions which lead infants to manipulate objects in order to produce sights and sounds from them appear to be a moderate or low state of arousal, namely a state of relaxation. Such is not the state of a hungry, tired, distressed or disturbed child.

In reporting results the writer is in favour of stating the classifications separately: those for adaptive behaviour patterns shown in problem-solving; those for object concept development and those for manipulative behaviour, though not separating circular reactions from behaviour relating to spatial and causal relations. If the information is being used to place the child in an appropriate learning situation, it is useful to state the most advanced type of manipulative behaviour and the most common kind. It has been found that experience in a training centre, for severely subnormal children at any rate, can bring up the manipulative behaviour to the level of the problem-solving behaviour. Thus recommendations for such placement are best made on the basis of the problem-solving behaviour.

A further question which might be raised is whether it is necessary to spend the time and effort to make this classification into the sensori-motor substages. The answer to this would appear to depend on the purpose for which the assessment is being made.

With the educational provision for children split as it is at present between the Education and Health authorities, the important distinction is between the S.S.N. and the E.S.N. or above. If the child is over 4 years old and his co-operation can be obtained, and if he fails the earliest items on the Stanford-Binet scale, it can quickly be established that he has an I.Q. below 50 – or outside −3 s.d. For some purposes this is sufficient. But educational facilities in training centres and hospital schools are not available for all children below this point. Hence there is a need to differentiate among them. In the writer's experience, development to the substage VI level is a clear indication for such education in a training centre or hospital school, at any rate up to a certain age; children who do not reach this development until the age of 8 or 9 years or more may be able to benefit from training, but they are too big to be in a class with children between 3 and 6 or 7 years. If places are available, it has also been found that children at the fifth sensori-motor substage, aged between 3 and $4\frac{1}{2}$ or 5 years, benefited from going to the hospital school, though if the home or the hospital ward is satisfactory, placement is probably less urgent. Children of 5 and 6 years at this level were experimentally placed in a hospital school, but when little progress was shown, these were excluded on the recommendation of the teaching staff. Additional research concerned with early training of the severely subnormal is needed.

Such a distinction is also needed when the assessment is used for research purposes. Since this aspect has been fully discussed elsewhere (Woodward, 1963b), it will not be entered into here.

In the case of the children who cannot be assessed by any other means, the important distinction is that between substage VI on the one hand and below it on the other. If substage VI has been attained, it can be pointed out to others in the report that this implies that other developments may be expected, e.g. language, imaginative play, drawing (Woodward and Stern, 1963). The development of substage VI might, for example, be used as a criterion for referring a child with a language defect to a speech therapist. In children of $1\frac{1}{2}$ to 2 years when all other evidence on the rate of development is lacking, or at best uncertain, through early autism or severe cerebral palsy (particularly if combined with deafness), the findings of substage VI development may very well indicate placement in a small, specialized unit, when otherwise the child might be regarded as severely subnormal and placed accordingly where education, even if it is available, will be inappropriate. The decision may affect the eventual development which the child attains. There are children at the moment in hospitals for the subnormal whose cognitive development is virtually unassessed (Mittler and Woodward, 1966). The description of a child as severely subnormal when his co-operation cannot be obtained is a comment on the techniques used by the examiner rather than a statement about the intelligence of the child.

There is, however, the question of age. Substage VI development in a child of 7 or 8 years would not mean very much, though in a child of $1\frac{1}{2}$ or 2 years, possibly $2\frac{1}{2}$ years, it could mean the possibility of more advanced development if the appropriate experiences were given. This is a question on which longitudinal research is necessary. The long-term follow-up of children placed in appropriate learning situations on the basis of this kind of assessment is likely to be of more value than age-norm data.

For children over the age of 2 years it is insufficient merely to know that they have reached the sixth sensori-motor substage. We wish to know how much further the child has proceeded in the pre-conceptual phase. This takes us on to consider the pre-operational and operational periods of development.

(b) *Pre-operational and Concrete Operational Thinking*
Piaget and Inhelder have paid relatively little attention to the period of development from $1\frac{1}{2}$ to $4\frac{1}{2}$ years, though they have devised many problems for investigating the change from intuitive to concrete-operationa schemata, for a variety

of concepts: number (Piaget, 1952), space (Piaget and Inhelder, 1956), geometry (Piaget, Inhelder and Szeminska, 1960), classification and seriation (Inhelder and Piaget, 1964), movement and speed (Piaget, 1946), time (Piaget, 1955b) and chance (Piaget and Inhelder, 1951). In only a few instances has the research extended down to children younger than 4 years. Children below this age have been used in the study of some spatial concepts (e.g. drawing, haptic perception, copying a spatial order) and in the study of classification.

Some of the problems devised for these studies can obviously be applied for assessment, but they reveal the limitations of the cognitive functions of preschool children compared with older children; we do not know what advances take place in this period. Woodward's (1967) research on this problem has not yet reached the stage where clinical applications can be made.

Choice of the problems for distinguishing between intuitive and concrete-operational thinking will obviously depend on the views of the particular psychologist. The specific problems a child presents (for example marked backwardness in number work or severe spatial disabilities) will clearly guide the selection – or indicate the area that is investigated more intensively. It may, nevertheless, be useful to discuss this question in the light of certain general principles.

The study of concepts of number, in both conservation and seriation aspects, seems an obvious choice. In view of Piaget's distinction between logico-arithmetical and spatio-temporal schemata, some exploration of spatial concepts and comparison with those of number is perhaps useful. To know something of the child's concepts of time may also be of value, though it is less easy to devise problems using simple equipment.

As mentioned earlier, some of the questions investigated in Piaget's earlier studies may yield interesting information. The question of animism and the attendant problem of method has already been raised. To find out about the child's knowledge of left and right relating to himself, another person and three objects is simply done (Piaget, 1928b). Another problem suggested by *Language and Thought* (1926) is that in which the child is given a simple problem to solve and then set the task of explaining to another child how he did it. (If another child is not available for this purpose, the examiner would do.) The explanations of younger children fail to take account of the other person's lack of knowledge of the object concerned, namely, they cannot put themselves in the situation of another person. If prior research established that the ability to do this corresponded with concrete-operational thinking and if emotionally disturbed children with this type of thinking were still egocentric in their explanations, this information would be of interest from the point of view of their social development, if not of their cognitive structures.

If it is desired to include something on general logical operations rather than limiting the inquiry to specific concepts, there are many suggestions in Inhelder and Piaget's *The Early Growth of Logic in the Child*, to use Lunzer's title for the translation (1964).

2 A

There are fewer situations that require the modification of the techniques for the classification of intuitive and concrete-operational thinking. This is because the child's co-operation is required, to listen to and carry out the instructions for the task, and, for some, to make verbal responses. Only the problems of the sensori-motor period can be given to otherwise 'unassessable' children. Some highly disturbed children can be given problems that do not require a verbal response. Since there is no question of timing the problems, the distractible children who keep interrupting their efforts by irrelevant chatter or wandering round the room can be assessed on the more 'performance' type of problem, and sometimes on those requiring a verbal response. If, however, problems whose solution required the use of 'intuitive' or 'concrete-operational' thinking were devised in such a way that no instructions were necessary, the techniques could be used for older children with severe behaviour disturbances.

Modifications required for blind children would be considerable, but there is no reason why suitable problems that required comparable operations for their solution should not be devised. These would, however, need to be developed by research before they could be applied clinically.

Problems of administration with cerebral palsied children arise only if the motor handicap is severe, and affecting both arms, or if there is associated deafness. Some problems are thereby eliminated, but with others the child can be asked to indicate what he would do if he could – which element he would take, etc. When the child is required to draw a straight line, as in the reference points problem (Piaget and Inhelder, 1956), he can instead be shown drawings of various alternatives and asked to choose.

Children with a speech defect require problems of a kind that elicit behaviour which is sufficient by itself for classificatory purposes. With some problems that investigate spatial concepts a verbal response is not required, e.g. copying the spatial order of rows or circular arrangements of elements, reproducing a model as it would be if seen from different viewpoints, using measuring instruments, constructing a spatial layout, making use of external reference points, etc.

The modifications with severely deaf children are obviously those of conveying the instruction by gesture, demonstration or other means. These are similar, though not entirely so, to those required for children or adults with extremely limited verbal development, to the level that occurs when children live their childhood in units of 50, with little contact with adults. The writer found that such problems as copying a spatial order could be conveyed by non-verbal means or simpler language to subnormal children and adults by pointing to the first element on the model and indicating that the subject was to select one like it from the array and put it on a rod, and so on. Then, when it was completed, the beads were taken off and a simple 'you do it' was sufficient for comprehension of the task. The task of putting a set of sticks in order could be conveyed by showing the subject a model on a card, which was then removed, or by carrying out the task without letting the subject see the method of selection. The instructions for some problems could not be put in simple enough words for understanding. However, those who could not understand the instructions for these problems performed at a pre-intuitive level on the tasks they could understand (Woodward, 1961).

When children of any level of intelligence have been deprived by a sensory defect or by a restricted environment of the necessary conditions for cognitive development, the results of this kind of assessment indicate the appropriate level of teaching. If there are marked discrepancies in the types of thinking shown for different concepts by either of the above groups of children, or by children with behaviour disturbances and learning difficulties, there are two alternative hypotheses to explain the results. One is that the more advanced kind of thinking has been developed only for certain concepts; the other is that general schemata of the more advanced kind have been acquired and, provided appropriate experiences are given, will quickly be extended to the concepts for which the less advanced type of thinking is shown. This is a question which needs follow-up research of children given appropriate remedial teaching in small groups.

Some of the problems devised for children are unsuitable for adults, when for instance the task is introduced as a game which is assumed to interest 5- to 6-year-old children. Instead of counters called 'sweets' and dolls and other toys, it seems desirable to present the problem as something the adult might encounter in real life and to use material, such as nuts and bolts, which they meet in their work in industrial units and jobs. Minor modifications can, however, be made with the material used for children: for example, instead of setting the task in the form of 'giving you and your friend the same number of sweets' or asking whether 'you and your friend have the same amount of lemonade to drink', the task can be set in the form of a mother having two children, and 'how can she give them the same number' – or 'has she done so . . .' (this form could be used for children, too). The kitchen and toolshed are also fruitful sources of problems. On the basis of results obtained with subnormal adults (Woodward, 1961), the writer takes the view that the finding of intuitive or concrete-operational thinking for number concepts is a better indicator than an intelligence test result of ability to master the simple number operations. Further research is needed to determine whether any level of thinking, in terms of Piaget's sequence, distinguishes, among subnormal adults, those who can learn to read and those who are limited to word-recognition.

The findings of this kind of investigation can be used in other ways for subnormal adults. In industrial units, for instance, the level of the adult's conceptual development can indicate the sort of job he can do, and the simpler operations that more complex jobs have to be broken into. If the adult can place a set of objects into a one-to-one correspondence with another set, but lacks understanding of the invariance of number, he can select given numbers of objects if he is given a piece of cardboard marked out with the appropriate number of squares, and is instructed to place one object in each square. He can also take one from each of a pile of objects (e.g. washer, bolt, nut) and put them in a bag. This job is, however, unsuitable for an individual who is unable to make a one-to-one correspondence between two sets of objects and the checker has to spend time putting in the missing one and taking out the redundant one. Such adults can, however, learn assembly jobs, involving a sequence of actions when the nature of the material (to be folded or fitted together) prevents such errors.

A further possible application to rehabilitation is suggested by the study of Stephens (1968), who is investigating the relation of operational and non-operational thinking to the maturity of social judgements and to actual conduct in a structured situation.

(c) *Formal Operational Thinking*

The problems devised by Inhelder and Piaget (1958) for distinguishing between less and more advanced operational thinking rely, for purposes of classification, on the child's actions to a greater extent than do some of those just discussed. One such problem is to present a horizontal bar with holes in it balanced on a pivot, to place a weight on one arm, and then to set the child the task of making the bar horizontal again by placing a weight on the other arm. He can be given first a weight of the same value and then others of different values. His actions can be observed and the placing of the weight recorded. Analysis of the successive placements will reveal whether the child uses what he observes of the effect of one action in order to guide the next, or whether his actions are random. The discovery of the inverse relation between weight and distance in a qualitative manner, achieved by trial and error, is classifiable as concrete operational thinking, though of an advanced kind. It can of course be determined whether the child has discovered the exact quantitative relation by setting him a different problem with different weights.

Another problem of this sort is the task of placing two rings of different diameters at such distances between a source of light and a screen that the shadows coincide.

Similarly when the child is asked to verify his proposed solution, his subsequent actions can be observed. One of Inhelder's problems, for instance, consists in presenting the child with five bottles containing colourless chemicals, three of which combine to produce one with a colour. The fourth neutralizes the colour and the fifth contains water. How the child goes about trying to produce the colour reveals whether he systematically tries each with the other, or proceeds haphazardly, and whether he combines only two, or goes on to combine three. If he proposes that the fifth contains water, since it produces no change, his verifying actions, such as getting water from a tap, are easily observable.

The disadvantage of some of these ingenious problems described in *The Growth of Logical Thinking* (Inhelder and Piaget, 1958) for the itinerant psychologist is that the materials are cumbersome. Different and more portable equipment can, however, test the same operations; for example an arrangement in which three elements combine to produce a result, a fourth reverses it and a fifth produces no change, could be achieved by buttons, a battery and a light bulb. The problem of balancing equal and unequal weights requires only a balance and a set of weights, and that of finding the law of floating bodies needs only a bowl of water, objects that sink and float, including some of the same material of different volumes, and a hollow measure of the same volume as some.

An apparent difficulty in the practical application of these problems is that they concern topics taught in secondary school science. Lovell (1961), however, reports that the children who found the principle could be distinguished from those who repeated parrot-like what they had been taught, without having a formal-operational understanding of the principle. Some other problems described in the books on concepts of space and geometry (Piaget and Inhelder, 1956; Piaget *et al.*, 1960) extend up to the formal level without involving school subjects.

(d) *The Investigation of Non-cognitive Factors*

The attention of the writer has been drawn, first in a clinical situation and then during research with normal 5-year-old children, to the possibility of using these techniques as a means of exploring some of the non-cognitive factors that interfere with learning. They can be used to get information about the child's reactions to making mistakes. The starting-point for teaching is an incorrect attempt by the learner; a child who made no errors would have no need of a teacher. If a child becomes upset on making them or is afraid to make them, he is in an emotional state that is not conducive to concentrating and learning.

In some of the techniques of Piaget and Inhelder only the investigator knows when the child is incorrect; with others both know it, as when the child is shown the model and his incorrect copy, before he makes another attempt. A child observed in a clinical setting began to show manneristic behaviour (glancing backwards with jerky head movements) at the point at which her attention was drawn to the discrepancies between her copy and the model (a row of coloured beads). Manneristic behaviour was absent during the next problem, a conservation one, when the examiner but not the child was aware of the incorrect inferences, but it occurred again during the next one, in the form of waving as if to someone outside the window and sweeping her hand on the table and scratching it. The problem was that of making two unequal groups of counters equal in number and the child carried out a series of trial and error actions by moving a few counters from one group to the other, saying 'I think that's right' and counting in order to find out. She thus found out about her errors herself. She eventually arrived at a difference of two (12 counters in one group and 14 in the other), and she twice moved over two before hitting on the solution of moving only one over. The manneristic behaviour occurred again at this point. The third problem was easier: groups of 8 and 12 counters were given. She moved over two but did not know whether it would be correct when she counted.

When she discovered it was, she exclaimed 'It is the same and I said I didn't know'. The scratching mannerism occurred here.

These three types of problem thus provide the opportunity to observe the behaviour of children when they make mistakes in three conditions: (1) when they have made an error and do not know that they have done so; (2) when they know that they have through the action of the examiner in drawing attention to it; (3) when they spontaneously see themselves that they have. Although the third condition is different from the second in its social aspects, the child's discovery of his error still occurs in a social situation, knowing that the adult is aware of it. A fourth variation, which can only be undertaken with a one-way screen, is to observe the child's behaviour when he discovers a mistake himself when he is alone. It would be interesting to compare autonomic changes and speed in arriving at a correct solution in these circumstances.

Further incidental observations were made in the course of a study of 5-year-old infant-school children. Some of these blushed on making mistakes; one or two others kept asking permission before they took any action 'Shall I take this one?', 'Shall I take them out?' (referring to incorrectly placed elements). Two others made very slow, small inhibited movements when they dealt with the material, and, once having placed an element, they did not remove it and try another in its place. (The typical behaviour of 5-year-old children with these problems – e.g. placing a set of sticks in order of size is to try one, remove it if it is wrong, try another, remove that, and so on until the correct one is found.) It could be postulated that to ask permission before doing something or to take as little action as possible is one way of avoiding mistakes. This behaviour has not been observed with younger, nursery-school children, who also attempted some of the same problems. They sometimes commented in an unconcerned way on making the same mistakes repeatedly, for example 'Oh, I done it again'. It is probably at the time of starting school that children meet for the first time, to any degree, the achievement pressures (from home or school or both) in relation to school learning that are a feature of Western culture.

These comments are made on the basis of incidental observations. Research may point to the further use of these techniques for the study of attitudes that interfere with learning. If so, the implications for the social aspect of a remedial teaching programme are as important as are the findings on cognitive development for *what* is taught.

IV CONCLUDING COMMENTS

In conclusion, the clinical applications of Piaget's approach may be summarized as follows: the direct investigation of certain concepts (e.g. of number and space) may be undertaken when children of any level of intelligence have learning difficulties, physical handicaps, or live in an unstimulating environment. The aim of this assessment is to place the child in a learning situation that is appropriate to his present level of development, with a view to making further assessments when he has had experiences and opportunities to learn from tasks designed to foster the development of the next level. Similar studies of subnormal adults provide useful information for remedial teachers and staff in industrial units.

In some instances information about cognitive development can be obtained by means of this approach when it cannot by any other. One reason for this is that the procedure can be modified to suit various contingencies, such as those that arise from severe or multiple physical handicaps or behaviour disturbance. Another reason is that the assessment is based on the type of behaviour pattern or of thinking; consequently it is not necessary to administer a standard set of items in its entirety. Further, the items are not timed. The application of the approach to this problem raises the need for long-term research on children assessed and placed by these techniques.

REFERENCES

BROWN, R. (1965) *Social Psychology*. New York: The Free Press; London: Collier-Macmillan.

ELLIS, N. (1963) *Handbook of Mental Deficiency*. New York: McGraw Hill.

FLAVELL, H. J. (1963) *The Developmental Psychology of Jean Piaget*. New Jersey: Van Nostrand.

HOWELLS, J. G. (1965) *Modern Perspective in Child Psychiatry*. Edinburgh: Oliver and Boyd.

HUNT, J. MCV. (1961) *Intelligence and Experience*. New York: Ronald.

INHELDER, BARBEL (1944) *Le Diagnostique du Raisonnement chez les Débiles Mentaux*. Neuchatel: Delachaux et Niestlé. English translation (1968). New York: John Day.

INHELDER, BARBEL and PIAGET, J. (1958) *The Growth of Logical Thinking from Childhood to Adolescence*. A. Parsons and S. Milgram (Trans.). London: Routledge.

INHELDER, BARBEL and PIAGET, J. (1964) *The Early Growth of Logic in the Child: Classification and Seriation*. E. A. Lunzer and D. Papert (Trans.). London: Routledge.

LOVELL, K. (1959) A follow-up study of some aspects of the work of Piaget and Inhelder on the child's conception of space. *Brit. J. Educ. Psychol.*, **29**, 104-117.

LOVELL, K. (1961) A follow-up study of Inhelder and Piaget's *The Growth of Logical Thinking*. *Brit. J. Psychol.*, **52**, 143-153.

LOVELL, K., HEALEY, D. and ROWLANDS, A. D. (1962) The growth of some geometrical concepts. *Child Developm.*, **33**, 751-767.

LOVELL, K., KELLETT, V. L. and MOORHOUSE, E. (1962) The growth of the concept of speed: a comparative study. *J. child. Psychol. Psychiat.*, **3**, 101-110.

LOVELL, K. and OGILVIE, E. (1960) A study of the concept of conservation of substance in the junior school child. *Brit. J. educ. Psychol.*, **30**, 109-118.

LOVELL, K. and OGILVIE, E. (1961a) The growth of the concept of volume in junior school children. *J. Child Psychol. Psychiat.*, **2**, 118-126.

LOVELL, K. and OGILVIE, E. (1961b) A study of the conservation of weight in junior school children. *Brit. J. educ. Psychol.*, **31**, 138-144.

LOVELL, K. and SLATER, A. (1960) The growth of the concept of time: a comparative study. *J. Child Psychol. Psychiat.*, **1**, 179-190.

LUNZER, E. A. (1960a) *Recent Studies in Britain based on the Work of Jean Piaget*. London: Nat. Found. Educ. Res. England Wales.

LUNZER, E. A. (1960b) Some points of Piagetian theory in the light of experimental criticism. *J. Child Psychol. Psychiat.*, **1**, 191-202.

LUNZER, E. A. (1964) Translator's introduction to Inhelder and Piaget's *The Early Growth of Logic in the Child*. London: Routledge.

LUNZER, E. A. (1965) Problems of formal reasoning in test situations. *In European Research in Cognitive Development. Monog. Soc. Res. Child Developm.*, **30**, 19-46.

LURIA, A. R. (1961) *The Role of Speech in the Regulation of Normal and Abnormal Behaviour*. Oxford. Pergamon Press.

MILLER, G. A., GALANTER, E. and PRIBRAM, K. H. (1960) *Plans and the Structure of Behaviour*. New York: Holt.

MITTLER, P. and WOODWARD, M. (1966) The education of children in hospitals for the subnormal: a survey of admissions. *Developm. Med. child Neurol.*, **3**, 16-25.

PEEL, E. A. (1959) Experimental examination of some of Piaget's schemata concerning the child's perception and thinking, and a discussion of their educational significance. *Brit. J. educ. Psychol.*, **29**, 89-103.

PIAGET, J. (1926) *The Language and Thought of the Child*. M. Warden (Trans.). London: Routledge.

PIAGET, J. (1928a) *The Child's Conception of the World*. T. Thomlinson and A. Thomlinson (Trans.). London: Routledge.

PIAGET, J. (1928b) *Judgement and Reasoning in the Child*. M. Warden (Trans.). London: Routledge.

PIAGET, J. (1930) *The Child's Conception of Physical Causality*. M. Gabain (Trans.). London: Routledge.

PIAGET, J. (1946) *Les Notions de Mouvement et de Vitesse chez L'enfant*. Paris: Presses Universitaires de France.

PIAGET, J. (1950) *The Psychology of Intelligence*. M. Piercy and D. E. Berlyne (Trans.). London: Routledge.

PIAGET, J. (1951) *Play, Dreams and Imitation in Childhood*. C. Gattegno and F. M. Hodgson (Trans.). London: Heinemann.

PIAGET, J. (1952) *The Child's Conception of Number*. C. Gattegno and F. M. Hodgson (Trans.). London: Routledge.

PIAGET, J. (1953a) *The Origins of Intelligence in the Child*. M. Cook (Trans.). London: Routledge.

PIAGET, J. (1953b) Structures operationnelles et cybernetique. *L'Année Psychologique*, **53**, 379-388.

PIAGET, J. (1955a) *The Construction of Reality in the Child*. M. Cook (Trans.). London: Routledge.

PIAGET, J. (1955b) The development of time concepts in the child. *In* HOCH, P. H. and ZUBIN, J. (Eds.) *Psycho-pathology of Childhood*. New York: Grune and Stratton.

PIAGET, J. (1964) *Six Études de Psychologie*. Geneva: Editions Gonthier.

PIAGET, J. and INHELDER, BARBEL (1947) Diagnosis of mental operations and theory of intelligence. *Amer. J. ment. Defic.*, **51**, 401-406.

PIAGET, J. and INHELDER, BARBEL (1951) *La Genèse de l'idée de Hasard chez l'enfant*. Paris: Presses Universitaires de France.

PIAGET, J. and INHELDER, B. (1956) *The Child's Conception of Space*. F. J. Langdon and J. L. Lunzer (Trans.). London: Routledge.

PIAGET, J., INHELDER, B. and SZEMINSKA, A. (1960) *The Child's Conception of Geometry*. E. A. Lunzer (Trans.). London: Routledge.

RUSSELL, R. W. and DENNIS, W. (1939) Studies of animism. I: A standardized procedure for the investigation of animism. *J. Genet. Psychol.*, **55**, 389-400.

SMEDSLUND, J. (1961) The acquisition of conservation of substance and weight in children. III: Extinction of weight acquired 'normally' and by means of empirical controls on a balance scale. *Scand. J. Psychol.*, **2**, 85-87.

STEPHENS, WILL BETH (1968) *The Development of Reasoning, Moral Judgement, and Moral Conduct in Normals and in Retardates*. Final Report, Vocational Rehabilitation Administration Project No. RD-2382-P. Philadelphia: Temple University. (In press.)

WHITE, S. H. (1965) Evidence for a hierarchical arrangement of learning processes. *Adv. Child Devel. Beh.*, **2**, 187-220.

WOODWARD, MARY (1959) The behaviour of idiots interpreted by Piaget's theory of sensori-motor development. *Brit. J. educ. Psychol.*, **29**, 60-71.

WOODWARD, MARY (1960) Early experiences and later social responses of severely sub-normal children. *Brit. J. med. Psychol.*, **33**, 123-132.

WOODWARD, MARY (1961) Concepts of number in the mentally subnormal studied by Piaget's method. *J. Child Psychol. Psychiat.*, **2**, 249-259.

WOODWARD, MARY (1962a) Concepts of space in the mentally subnormal studied by Piaget's method. *Brit. J. soc. clin. Psychol.*, **1**, 25-37.

WOODWARD, MARY (1962b) The application of Piaget's theory to the training of the subnormal. *J. ment. Subnormal*, **8**, 3-11.

WOODWARD, MARY (1963a) Early experiences and behaviour disorders in severely subnormal children. *Brit. J. soc. clin. Psychol.*, **2**, 174-184.

WOODWARD, MARY (1963b) The application of Piaget's theory to research in mental deficiency. *In* ELLIS, N. (Ed.) *Handbook of Mental Deficiency*. New York: McGraw-Hill.

2 A*

WOODWARD, MARY (1965) Piaget's theory. *In* HOWELLS, J. G. (Ed.) *Modern Perspectives in Child Psychiatry*. Edinburgh: Oliver and Boyd.

WOODWARD, MARY (1967) Plans and strategies in young children. *Bull. Brit. Psychol. Soc.*, **20**, 66.

WOODWARD, MARY and STERN, DIANA J. (1963) Developmental patterns of severely subnormal children. *Brit. J. educ. Psychol.*, **33**, 10-21.

24

Some problems in the construction
of individual intelligence tests

F. W. Warburton, T. F. Fitzpatrick, J. Ward and Mary Ritchie

I INTRODUCTION

Since January 1965 a research team at Manchester University has been engaged
on the construction of a new individual test of intelligence which, it is anticipated,
will eventually replace such tests as the Stanford-Binet and the various Wechsler
scales for clinical use with children. The proposed form of this test has been
described by Warburton (1966a, 1966b); its present stage of development is
designed to test the age range 5-12 (although some items are available from 2 to
15 years in order to accommodate dull 5-year-old and bright 12-year-old
children.) It consists of twelve subscales organized round six hypothetical
'factors' or special abilities. The material has been subjected to large-scale try-
out and work on the preparation of a final version for standardization is now in
progress.

The research was established after several years of preparatory work by a
special committee of the British Psychological Society; for as long ago as 1921
Sir Cyril Burt (1921) had written that to replace the Binet scales would require
a lifetime of researches; the considerable resources necessary for the various
revisions of the Binet and for the construction of the Wechsler scales gave an
indication of the magnitude of the task. It was predictable, therefore, that a wide
range of problems would be encountered. These may be seen as concerned with
two basic issues: (1) The construction of a scale of general mental capacity
or 'educability' adapted to British culture and standardized on a British population, and (2) The extension of the scale into a measure of special abilities.

It is obvious that the latter objective poses the main problem since most
of the requirements for the construction of a test of general ability could be
satisfied simply by the adaptation or restandardization of one of the tests in
current use.

II ITEM WRITING

Choice of a rationale. Most acceptable accounts of psychological research attempt
to give some justification of the procedure adopted in order to permit integration
of the results into a systematic theory. In this respect the constructors of
individual tests have been found seriously wanting for, although the empirical

value of their work is not seriously questioned, its place in a general theory of mental functioning has been difficult to assess owing to the lack of adequate rationales – cf. Littell (1960), Eysenck (1967) and Guilford (1967). Traditionally individual testing has been associated with the measurement of general intelligence – a concept which has been under consistent attack on the grounds that it is too vague to merit scientific status. Admittedly much of this criticism has been indirect in the sense that it has been linked with Spearman's *g* and the methodological issues surrounding factor analysis, but the need for developed rationales has met with little response from test constructors. Thus Terman (1916) offered no satisfactory definition of what he was trying to measure except to stress the primacy of conceptual thinking largely mediated by language; Wechsler (1958) took a global view of intelligence, acknowledging the importance of *g* and pointing to significant 'performance' elements in test performance. It might be said that neither of these has gone much further than Binet's (1905) original attempt to measure 'judgement' which he considered the most important among a hierarchy of diverse intelligences; and despite an early lead given by Burt (1921) reasoning items have been poorly represented in test content although their high *g* loading has been known for many years. The statement of an explicit rationale is thus an obvious step forward in the construction of a new test.

III   THE PRINCIPAL SOURCES OF EVIDENCE

In arriving at such a rationale the constructors have had to consider three principal sources of evidence: (1) psychometric work on the structure of human ability, (2) the rapidly accumulating knowledge of the nature and sequence of cognitive structures obtained from developmental psychology and (3) the vast experience of individual testing gained by clinicians and research workers over the last sixty years.

1 Psychometric factors

A major criticism of established tests is that they fail to sample the more important group factors or mental abilities identified in factor analytical research by such workers as Thurstone (1938), Burt (1949) and Cattell (1957). Almost all researchers in this field recognize the presence of such abilities; they differ, however, in the extent to which they regard them as related to one another, predictively useful, or indeed measurable at all. Of the many contemporary theorists, undoubtedly the most extreme position has been taken by Guilford (1967) whose 'Model of the Intellect' postulates no less than 120 abilities categorized by content process and product. It must be conceded that the model is very useful for the analysis of test content and, in focusing attention to neglected areas such as reasoning and fluency, he has performed a valuable service. However, despite the body of supportive evidence supplied, this is essentially an experimental approach, and Guilford's use of homogeneous populations together with an insistence on orthogonal factors rather restricts the generality of the model. McNemar (1964) called the model 'scatterbrained', and latterly Eysenck (1967) has observed that if this is the best model currently available then something has gone very wrong indeed.

It must be emphasized that the nature of individual testing calls for a comparatively simple factorial model; the groups studied are usually heterogeneous and the constraints of time and presentation are against the achievement of complex factorial profiles. A cautious but more realistic approach is suggested by the evidence for stable and predictively useful factors of the 'Primary Mental Ability' type advanced by Thurstone (1938).

The model of the present scale is based upon the assumption that intelligence is a composite of related mental abilities, some of which are more closely associated with learning – and consequently the prediction of scholastic attainment – than others. The same factors are included at each age level, although the nature of the test material changes radically.

Table 24.1 is based on the distinction between (1) the *content* of an item and (2) the main mental *process* involved. For example, the subject may be presented with a list of words and be asked to memorize and later recognize them. The content of these two tasks is the same (viz. words), but the mental processes of memory and recognition are different. Analogously, if we are asked to classify separate series of words and of shapes, the mental process of classification is the same in the two tasks, but the content (words and shapes) is different.

It is not difficult to draw up a list of types of content. The six categories below cover a very considerable proportion of the material in published tests:

   (i) shapes;
  (ii) symbols;
 (iii) numbers;
 (iv) objects (and pictures of objects);
  (v) words;
 (vi) sentences.

It is however, not easy to agree on a classification of types of mental process, partly because the number of categories included in the list depends on how detailed an examination is made of the nature of the mental processes involved. In Table 24.1 mental processes have been classified as follows:

    (i) perception;
   (ii) memorization;
  (iii) recognition;
  (iv) conceptualization;
   (v) convergent reasoning (classification);
  (vi) convergent reasoning (operational);
 (vii) divergent reasoning (creativity).

Mental process	Shapes	Symbols	Numbers	Objects	Words	Sentences
Perception	Perceptual speed (shapes) Gottschaldt	Perceptual speed (symbols), letter cancellation	Perceptual speed (numbers), number cancellation	Perceptual speed (objects)	Clerical tests, perceptual speed	Perceptual speed (sentences)
Memorization	Memory for designs	Memory for symbols	Memory for numbers	Memory for objects	Memory for words	Memory for sentences
Recognition		Symbol recognition	Number recognition	Recognition of objects	Word recognition	Sentence recognition
Conceptualization	Meaning of shapes	Meaning of symbols	Notation	Object assembly, pictorial identification	Vocabulary, names	Sentence completion scrambled sentences, information
Convergent reasoning (classificatory)	Matching, classifying and re-sorting figures	Symbol matching (classification of symbols)	Handling relative quantities, sets and subsets, matching number groups	Similarities of pictures, differences of pictures, picture classification	Differences, similarities, opposites, controlled association, word classification	Classification of sentences
Convergent reasoning (operational)	Completion, temporal integration, block designs, mazes, figure series, formboard, rotation, reflection, figure fitting	Symbol series	Inductive and deductive problems (both arithmetical and mathematical) number series, seriation	Bead chain, orientation, conservation, equivalence, seriation	Word series, word games, coding	True-false, comprehension, verbal induction, verbal deduction, syllogism, assumptions, relevance, logical tests
Divergent reasoning (creativity)	Design construction, Rorschach	New symbols	Number series (original)	New uses for objects, hidden objects	Novel uses for words, word lists, free association, suffixes, prefixes, word fluency	Essay, story making, fluency of ideas, unusual consequences, new proverbs.

TABLE 24.I

These seven processes combined with the six types of content above yield $7 \times 6 = 42$ categories of test. Table 24.1 presents types of mental test which fall into each of these 42 categories. A comprehensive intelligence test could be designed to cover all these categories. For practical reasons this was not possible in the case of the British Intelligence Scale, but the material can be classified according to a reduced model comprising all the content categories and all the mental processes except Perception and Memory, i.e. $5 \times 6 = 30$ types of test.

It would be possible by means of statistical techniques such as analysis of variance to separate out the influence of (1) different types of test content, (2) different types of mental process and, most importantly, (3) their conjoint effects and interactions.

The various classifications and cross-classifications of scores that would be afforded might prove valuable for diagnostic and predictive purpose in educational guidance and profiles of the children's performance might be drawn up according to some such scheme. This rationale would be heavily criticized by Gestalt theorists as too atomistic and it would no doubt have crippling limitations as an explanation of children's thinking in every day life, but some such analysis of the data nevertheless seems well worth carrying out, as the present Scale has a range of items that has rarely been obtained from a single (large) group of subjects.

The general notion of distinguishing between content and process is, of course, not new. Guilford's structure of the intellect (Guilford, 1967) puts forward certain modes of classification, two of which – Contents and Operations – closely resemble the contents and mental processes of the present model, as follows:

Guilford's 1967 Categories

Contents	*Operations*
Figural	Cognitive
Symbolic	Memory
Semantic	Divergent thinking
Behavioural	Convergent thinking
	Evaluation

(Guilford also puts forward a third category, viz. products, comprising units, classes, relations, systems, transformations, implications.) Similarly Eysenck (1953) distinguishes between:

Test Material	*Mental Process*
Verbal	Perception
Numerical	Memory
Spatial	Reasoning

(Eysenck also puts forward a third category, viz. quality, comprising speed and power.)

These two schemes are somewhat less detailed than the present model. The only substantive difference appears to be our omission of the content 'Behavioural' and the operation 'evaluation' put forward by Guilford. 'Behavioural' content is concerned with the information, essentially non-verbal, involved in human interactions, where awareness of the attitudes, moods, intentions, perceptions, thoughts, or other persons and of ourselves is important. This category was not included in the present model (although the Scale has a few items with behavioural content) since most of this type of material was considered to be more apposite to tests of temperament and personality than to intelligence scales. The other category excluded from the present scheme is the operation of 'evaluation' which is concerned with reaching decisions or making judgements concerning the goodness (correctness, suitability, adequacy, desirability) of information in terms of criteria of identity, consistency and goal satisfaction. It was not included as a separate mental process since the evaluative tests used by Guilford appear to rest mainly on other operations such as perception (perceptual speed, clerical aptitude), classification (similarity of proverbs), and convergent reasoning. Moreover, evaluation implies the use of non-cognitive criteria, e.g. notions of suitability, adequacy and desirability, which depend on cultural background rather than cognitive capacity.

Incidentally, Thurstone's classification of the 'primary mental abilities' into verbal ability (V), verbal fluency (W), numerical ability (N), spatial ability (S), perceptual ability (P), inductive reasoning (R) and memory (M) does not fit into the content/mental process model. For example, the distinction between numerical ability, spatial ability and verbal ability is drawn according to differences in content, i.e. between numbers, shapes and words and phrases, whereas the distinction between perceptual ability, inductive reasoning and memory is made between different types of mental process – each process involving the use of items of various content, i.e. words, symbols, numbers and shapes.

The same criticism may be made of the try-out form of the British Intelligence Scale, which is organized (at least for administration) into Thurstonian factors. Analysis of the results will show whether it is worth while to retain these categories, or whether it would be better to substitute other modes. The classification does not have to be vertical: alternative rationale might group the contents horizontally following the developmental stages suggested by Piaget (1950), and the feasibility of this has been carefully considered.

2 Developmental scales

The traditional intelligence scale is used in two ways, diagnostic and prognostic: first, to examine the child's present level of intellectual functioning and to relate this to his educational and social background and, secondly, to assess his intellectual *potential* and make appropriate recommendations about his future education. Yet none of the existing scales are based on any recognized theory of intellectual development. In the construction of traditional scales the designers have relied, perhaps too heavily, on empirical evidence for their results. The placement of items at a given age level has depended on that item meeting statistical requirements rather than psychological criteria. This does not imply that the constructors of the present scale have questioned orthodox methods of item analysis and test construction, but rather that they have also considered the psychological suitability of the items that have been included in terms of children's thinking.

Workers concerned with children's thinking such as Hamley (1936), Piaget (1950), Brunswick (1956), Dienes (1964) and Bruner (1966) have outlined developmental structures and mechanisms which should be taken into account in the construction of any new scale of intelligence. These models are derived from logical or mathematical sources. Their fundamental idea is that the quality of a person's thinking must be assessed against qualitative criteria. Within certain areas of ability, Mathematics or Languages for example, conventional operations and logical sequences can be readily discerned, but it is extremely difficult to extend these concepts to all types of ability and to write adequate test items.

Several theories of intellectual development have been examined in a search for items which will enable psychologists to relate their assessments systematically to educational practice and opportunities. Among these theories, that outlined by Piaget (1950) undoubtedly deserves the greatest attention. It has had an impact in a great variety of psychological and educational fields, and his experimental findings have been replicated in a wide range of circumstances. Piaget postulates the development of a structure which systematizes thinking in the child as he develops. This structure is, fundamentally, his knowledge of the world, developed by activity and changing with age and experience. It acts as a mediating link in the assimilation of, and subsequent accommodation to, new experiences. Assimilation is the incorporation of input into existing structures of knowledge. Accommodation, on the other hand, is the changing of existing structure to make it better adapted to the new condition. Thus the quality of adaptive behaviour is partly determined by the state of development of this scheme which stores organizations or 'strategies'. Considerable research work has already been carried out on the adaptive styles of children, in order to determine the quality of their cognitive skills at different ages. Table 24.2 outlines the principal Piagetian stages and states briefly the cognitive operations which appear to be available in the repertoire of the normally developing child.

An attempt has been made in the scale to test the child's understanding of concepts and operations by means of a series of questions which it is hoped will illustrate the Piagetian levels. Explanations are sought and scored differentially at two or three levels. Some of the items are, therefore, different from those found in the traditional scales. Earlier experiments have shown that the sequential ordering of the main Piagetian stages is the same for all children, but there is a considerable overlap between one content area and another. Nor has it been clearly demonstrated that skills or strategies available in the earlier stages of development remain available at a later stage. However, it seems likely that there

Stage	Age range	Cognitive skill characteristics
1. *Sensori-motor*	(0–2 years)	Gradual integration of reflex activity to develop motor habits in response to objects in the immediate environment. This leads to a sense of *object permanence* and crude concepts of space, time, causality and intentionality. There is a tendency to fixate on individual objects rather than the relations between objects. The child can begin to imitate visual and auditory models.
2. *Pre-operational* (i) Preconceptual	(2–7 years) (2–4 years)	Verbal symbols begin to be substituted for objects (naming). Imitation of language models in immediate environment leads to 'deferred imitation'. Tendency to fixate on single objects persists. This period is characterized by the use of *transductive logic*.
(ii) Intuitive thought	(4–7 years)	Can successfully decenter from one object to another but such decentering is successive and discrete. Errors are corrected by alternative guessing. Cannot 'conserve' by relating variables, or classify, or ordinate successfully. The earliest classification operations of sorting, numbering and relating start towards the close of this period. At this stage the child's thinking is irreversible, bound by the immediate perceptual field, as in conservation problems. The main features are the representation of objects and the growth of language.
3. *Operational* (i) Concrete operational thought	(7–11 years)	Uses concrete materials to carry out operations which have the properties of combinativity, reversibility, associativity and identity in a logical or mathematical sense. Capable of 'situation directed' thought and requires the materials and objects to reach a solution. Conservation skills are available. Well organized classificatory systems are available. The child can construct hierarchies.
(ii) Formal operational thought	(11–16 years)	Concrete reasoning skills become internalized. The child is capable of reflecting on operations, setting up hypotheses and testing them. He can begin to deal with logical relationships of identity, negation, reciprocity, and correlation. He readily uses the laws of logic or mathematics in dealing with implication, proportionality, permutations and combinations. The child can turn round on his schema and think about thought. The thought processes approximate more closely to formal logico-mathematical lattices.

TABLE 24.2

The main Piagetian stages of intellectual development and the operational skills that characterize them.

will be a fairly reliable step-wise development in at least two of the content areas we have selected, namely Number and Verbal ability. Because of their substantive nature, these areas of knowledge are built up systematically and develop more regularly in complexity as the body of knowledge increases.

A developmental scale would constitute an exciting departure from orthodox practice, but at present the evidence does not lead one to believe that such a model would possess sufficient stability to be used as the basis for a test of this nature. However, an obvious compromise exists since most factorists – cf. Burt (1954), Vernon (1960), and Guilford (1967) – would regard the work of the developmental psychologists, such as Piaget and Bruner, as complementary to a factorial model. A combined classification of test content is shown in Table 24.3 where, in addition to the factors, the areas of qualitative change in children's thinking are represented. Here Piaget's stages replace chronological age or, more relevantly, mental age on the vertical axis and form a second principle for the choice of items.

3 Clinical aspects

We also have to consider the clinical aspects of the test, and this introduces a fresh set of methodological problems. In the clinical situation everything has to justify itself not only in terms of discriminative power but also in terms of variety, clinical richness and ease of rapport. The main purpose of the test is to generate as many hypotheses as possible about the subject.

On the other hand, it would not be viable to categorize subscales according to types of clinical usefulness, since this would cut clean across the factorial structure and content of the tests. For instance, the division of the Memory subscale into auditory and visual memory tests has no obvious justification purely in terms of clinical practice.

Table 24.4 shows the main 'clinical dichotomies' for the six subscales – i.e., the crucial point that has to be borne in mind when evaluating the child's responses.

(a) *Work with Young Children*

Clinical aspects are particularly important at the lower end of the age scale. This arises largely from the need for clarification of the crucial stages through which the child passes. If successful tests for young children can be developed they will enable educational programmes to be evaluated more realistically and facilitate the early and accurate diagnosis of cases of mental or physical handicap. For these reasons, the construction of items for the younger children has been given particular attention in the construction of the present scale, despite the fact that building up cognitive profiles at these ages raises special difficulties.

Information from the previous literature which would aid in the construction of homogeneous scales is sparse. Despite the criticisms of multiple factorists such as Guilford (1967), the theory that ability in the young child is largely undifferentiated finds support among many psychologists – cf. Burt (1954).

Stage	Reasoning	Number	Verbal	Creativity	Memory	Spatial
2 (i) Pre-operational (conceptual)	Simple classification Tactile testing' Pattern completion	Counting Matching tasks	Picture vocabulary Double description	Naming objects (fluency) Creative play with blocks	Recognition of toys⌐ Imitation (digit span) Object memory	Imitation Matching Shapes
2 (ii) Pre-operational (intuitive)	Simple Matrices Inclusion classes Inductive problems Sorting	Conservation Various	Verbal classification Differences Similarities General knowledge	Controlled word association Pattern meaning Unusual uses Consequences	Recognition of designs Recall designs Object memory Sentence M. Sense of a passage	Block designs Matching involving reversals Copying tasks
3 Concrete operational	Sorting (several attributes) Logical multiplication (Matrices) Inference problems Induction (several variables)	Shapes	Definitions Social reasoning Similarities	As above, plus Number of synonyms Number of meanings	As above	Block designs Visualization of cubes Reversal and rotation of shapes
4 Formal operational	Matrices (sets and operations) Hypothesis testing (induction) Inference problems Propositional logic	Number bases Practical calculations	Abstract definitions Proverbs Harder similarities	As above	As above]	Block designs (three dimensional) Cube development three views of cube

TABLE 24.3

Moreover, non-cognitive influences such as Bayley's (1958) 'goal directed' factors must be borne in mind. There is, of course, a wealth of general observational data on the adaptive behaviour of young children in the work of Isaacs (1933), Gesell and Ilg (1946) and, particularly, Piaget (1950) leading to distinctive theories of child development. From the point of view of the test constructor,

Subscale	Tests	Clinical dichotomies
Verbal	Vocabulary Comprehension Information	Definition versus Identification
Reasoning	Induction Operational thinking Matrices	Verbal versus Non-verbal Reasoning Induction versus Deduction
Creativity	Creativity	Verbal versus Pictorial Fluency versus Originality
Memory	Auditory Visual	Recognition versus Recall
Number	Number	Numerical versus Conceptual
Spatial	Visual Spatial Block designs	Visual versus Visuo-motor (manipulative)

TABLE 24.4
Clinical dichotomies.

however, Bayley's (1958) work is perhaps the most relevant. She considers that three main factors operate constructively at the pre-school level. These are:

(i) a sensori-motor factor in the first year of life;
(ii) a factor related to persistence and goal directed behaviour which predominates in the second and third years; and
(iii) the factor she refers to as 'intelligence' which is not present until 8 months but eventually becomes dominant at 4 years. Bayley described it as the 'general basic and stable mental capacity that is found in children of school age and is characterized as the ability to learn and carry on abstract thinking'. These analyses have served as a basic rationale in the construction of items for young children in the present scale.

The linguistic aspects of testing are particularly important. Instructions must be very short in order to cater for the short span of attention and general distractability of young children, yet they should give all the information required by a child to give an adequate response; they must be capable of spontaneous and varied delivery so that a relaxed and informal atmosphere can be maintained. It is often found that the language used by young children in problem solving is idiosyncratic or culturally distinctive and that instructions entirely appropriate for adults do not necessarily evoke the correct response in children. It is desirable that concepts should be tested out in as many ways as possible, as children sometimes use original strategies; for example, it was found that a whole series of items on conservation and transitivity could be answered correctly simply by adopting a certain method of counting.

For young children the tester must have a wide variety of items at his disposal, almost all of which should be attractive to the subject, easily administered and readily scored; many items must be very easy, since the child's interest is sustained by success and continuous involvement in the task. These items facilitate clinical observation and enable the psychologist to base his judgements on actual behaviour.

The preschool years are a period of very rapid mental growth in which the feeling, exploring and manipulating of objects plays a large part in mental development. Thus, the Visual-Spatial and Operational Thinking scales are very important. The main difficulty is to find tasks and materials which are really attractive to the subject – no one can be more stubborn than a 3-year-old child who does not want to co-operate. Thus materials must be easy and pleasant to handle, attractive to the eye, robust enough to stand up to the rough treatment handed out to them by toddlers, and preferably washable. Whenever possible, toys have been made from gaily coloured plastic or perspex materials, which have the additional advantage of being reasonably light in weight.

As a general rule, toys and apparatus are more interesting to the child than pictures. Items based on pictures have caused an unforeseen number of difficulties. It is remarkable how often children interpret pictures of everyday objects in a completely new way, e.g. what to an adult is a perfectly obvious drawing of an eye is seen as a fish by some children. It is important to have uncluttered line-drawings with a minimum of detail. These experiences confirm Vernon's (1952) work on visual perception in children presented with simple outline drawings of animals and familiar household objects. Vernon found that these drawings were recognized correctly by 11% of 2-year-olds, 67% of 3-year-olds and 90% of 4-year-olds. However, if the drawings were made more complicated and were coloured, they were not identified until much later. It was found that when children were presented with a detailed scene they could not give even a partial interpretation of it until they were 7 years old, and they could not interpret it as a whole until about 11 years of age. Young children do not concentrate easily and it is necessary to present them with a constant flow of materials and apparatus, interspersing manipulative items with verbal tasks in an attempt to balance the various types of activity.

It is also important that the psychologist's test administration work should be kept to a minimum. Whenever possible, the same piece of apparatus has been used in different items – e.g. certain sets of pictures are used in both the comprehension and classification items.

(b) *Co-operation with Psychologists*

The opinion of clinicians about a test designed specifically for their use is paramount, since they will probably be using it most of their professional careers. They will have to be satisfied with each step in the administration of the test and with the scoring system. Several discussions have been held, therefore, with educational psychologists who were collaborating in the project. This led to considerable modification in the form and content of many of the items and sometimes major alterations to whole subscales. 'Workshops' and residential courses have been held for these psychologists, first to enable them to try out the items with children and then to meet for discussion, criticism and consideration of new items. The procedure helped in spotting badly worded and administratively cumbersome items. However, experience shows that many difficulties become evident only after an item has been used extensively over a period of weeks or months; very often the test constructor is seduced by a brilliant idea and does not see serious deficiencies in the procedure until he has used it a great deal. Those who took part in the preliminary discussions were drawn from all the ten regions in which the try-out was to be made. This training of psychologists did much to overcome some of the difficulties of standardizing the testing procedure and scoring of items.

The try-out sampling, will, in the end, have been carried out by a hundred or so trained psychologists working with children at various age levels. It might have been more desirable if each psychologist worked on all sections of every scale, but some degree of specialization was found necessary for practical reasons.

The reader may question our policy in using so many testers at this stage, but it was thought that the advantages clearly outweigh the disadvantages. It means that at the constructional stage of the research most of the items had already been modified by consultation with practising psychologists. The overall effect was to spread the testing load which exceeded 5,000 hours of testing time. The employment of a few full-time testers could have involved an undue waste of time in locating suitable subjects. L.E.A. psychologists, having a knowledge of local conditions, are more likely to find a more truly representative sample. Another disadvantage in using few testers, each working on large subsamples, is that they may have tended to take highly individual, efficient, but short cut methods to achieve their goals. It seems more likely that the method adopted led to testing being carried out under real-life conditions.

IV CONCLUSIONS

Ideally, therefore, the new test will permit the measurement of special abilities together with a qualitative assessment of the level of thinking achieved. It must be stressed, however, that this is a proposed rather than an attained factorial structure; if the factors are reproduced over most of the age range of the test then this will be a remarkable piece of test construction. On the other hand, if the test results do not follow the predicted pattern, then the heavy weight of reasoning items together with other items known to load high on *g* will nevertheless ensure a powerfully discriminative test. It is hoped, of course, that the subscales from which factors are derived will be long and strong enough to allow profile analysis, but even if this is not the case there should be sufficient representative items to give strong clinical hints as to the presence of special abilities.

REFERENCES

BAYLEY, N. (1958) Value and limitations of infant testing. *Children*, July-August.

BINET, A. and SIMON, T. (1905) Méthodes nouvelles pour le diagnostic du niveau intellectuel des anormaux. *L'Année Psychologique*, 11, 191-244.

BRUNER, J. S. et al. (1966) *Studies in Cognitive Growth*. New York: Wiley.

BRUNSWIK, F. (1956) *Perception and the Representative Design of Psychological Experiments*. Berkely, California: University of California Press.

BURT, C. L. (1921) *Mental and Scholastic Tests*. London: University of London Press.

BURT, C. L. (1949) Group factors analysis. *Brit. J. Psychol.* (Stat. Sec.), 3, 40-75.

BURT, C. L. (1954) Differentiation of intellectual ability. *Brit. J. educ. Psychol.*, 24, 76-90.

CATTELL, R. B. (1957) A universal index for psychological factors. *Psychologia*, 1, 74-85.

DIENES, Z. P. (1964) *Mathematics in the Primary School*. Melbourne: Hutchinson.

EYSENCK, H. J. (1953) *Uses and Abuses of Psychology*. London: Penguin Books.

EYSENCK, H. J. (1967) Intelligence assessment: a theoretical and experimental approach. *Brit. J. educ. Psychol.*, 37, 81-98.

GESELL, A. and ILG, F. L. (1946) *The Child from Five to Ten*. New York: Harper.

GUILFORD, J. P. (1967) *The Nature of Human Intelligence*. New York: McGraw Hill.

HAMLEY, H. R. (1936) Formal training: a critical survey of experimental work. *Brit. J. educ. Psychol.*, 6, 233-241.

ISAACS, S. (1933) *Social Development in Young Children*. London: Routledge.

LITTELL, W. M. (1960) The Wechsler Intelligence Test for Children. Review of a decade of research. *Psychol. Bull.*, 57, 149-60.

MCNEMAR, Q. (1964) Lost: Our Intelligence? Why? *Amer. J. Psychol.*, 19, 871-882.

PIAGET, J. (1950) *The Psychology of Intelligence*. London: Routledge and Kegan Paul.

TERMAN, L. (1916) *The Measurement of Intelligence*. Boston: Houghton Mifflin.

THURSTONE, L. L. (1938) *Primary Mental Abilities*. University of Chicago Press.

VERNON, M. D. (1952) *A Further Study of Visual Perception*. Cambridge: Cambridge University Press.

VERNON, P. E. (1960) *Intelligence and Attainment Tests.* London: University of London Press.

WARBURTON, F. W. (1966a) The construction of the new British Intelligence Scale. *Bull. Brit. Psychol. Soc.*, **19**, 59.

WARBURTON, F. W. (1966b) The construction of the new British Intelligence Scale: progress report. *Bull. Brit. Psychol. Soc.*, **19**, 68-70.

WECHSLER, D. (1958) *The Measurement and Appraisal of Adult Intelligence.* Baltimore: Wilkins.

25

Developments in automated testing systems

J. L. Gedye and E. Miller

I INTRODUCTION

Whilst we have no wish to belittle in any way the very real and impressive advances in psychological assessment which have taken place since the turn of the century, it is still fair to say that present techniques leave much to be desired. Many tests in current use in clinical and educational practice involve highly trained administrators in the expenditure of considerable amounts of time and effort for relatively low returns in terms of relevant and useful information. In this chapter we wish to outline, and to illustrate from our own experience, the tentative beginnings of the use of automated devices in psychometric testing, a development which may well contribute to the solution of some of the present difficulties in this field.

Automated testing is, of course, nothing new in psychology. Any visitor to a psychological laboratory is likely to see automatic equipment being used for both the programming and the recording of human and animal experiments. Similar equipment has been used for a long time in research in the applied fields. Automated devices for test administration have already been in use for some time for the administration of very limited forms of psychometric tests, particularly questionnaires. However, the development of automated systems such as the ESL ts 512, to be described later, which are capable of the automatic administration of a wide range of different tests would appear to be a new development, only paralleled by computer-based systems such as that described by Elithorn and Telford (1969). This chapter is particularly concerned with the rationale for the use of such systems in routine clinical practice and with their nature and future development. As the authors' experience is almost entirely confined to the clinical field the discussion will be directed towards automated testing in clinical psychology, but it is felt that the arguments developed in this chapter could be equally well applied to educational psychology and to other areas of applied psychology in which there is a need to assess people individually.

II BEHAVIOURAL TECHNOLOGY

We are becoming accustomed nowadays to having our attention drawn to the various implications of the current revolution in information handling technology. Indeed there is a real danger of our awareness being numbed and of our failing to recognize the urgent need for all those who may, before long, find themselves in the position of *users* of the new technology to start thinking through its implications for their own discipline. This is particularly true of the situation in the behavioural sciences, where the new technology has much to contribute.

One of the greatest obstacles to such thinking is lack of relevant practical experience. Our own experience with the ts 512 has shown that it can be very difficult to communicate the significance of one's work – even to those who stand to gain from it the most – without some kind of demonstration; although the existence of a working system of some kind, even if it is only a very simple one, can make all the difference between passive acceptance of a proposed system as theoretical possibility on the one hand, and active participation in the exploration of its practical implications on the other. Thus, we feel that the significance of the early developments we describe in this chapter is likely to lie not so much in their contribution to psychology, which is minimal, but in the fact that they may enable potential users of future systems to gain sufficient practical experience in advance of the new technology being generally available to allow them to adopt a constructive approach to the specification of future system requirements.

If our judgement in this matter is right, the above argument has important implications for the financial appraisal of the new techniques. It implies that we should consider, not so much the cost of assessments using currently available systems, such as the ts 512 – which are not intended for anything more than exploratory research by a limited number of workers – but rather the cost of comparable assessments using possible future systems that are known at the present time to be technologically feasible. It is, of course, notoriously difficult to estimate costs of this type, where there are many unknown factors that might need to be taken into account, and perhaps even more difficult to estimate cost-effectiveness when no agreed procedure for assigning a utility value to a clinical service exists at the present time. For our present purposes, it is sufficient to point out that recent calculations have indicated that, even under 'worst case' conditions, psychological assessments carried out as part of a service available from a clinical information utility, would be likely to cost much the same as current biochemical assessments using the latest automated equipment. This would seem to imply that unless one is prepared to countenance the adoption of different standards of expenditure on investigatory techniques in different branches of clinical practice, the cost of automated psychological assessments seems to be by no means prohibitive and, as will be illustrated later, may well be considerably less than it would be with current techniques.

It does not, therefore, seem reasonable to dismiss the possibility of automated psychometric assessment purely on financial grounds, although there is no doubt that the exploratory research that would have to precede the introduction of the type of clinical service referred to above would involve a greater scale of research expenditure in clinical psychology than it has enjoyed in the past. However, it does not follow that because a new approach is both technologically feasible and financially acceptable, it is therefore necessarily professionally desirable; and before going on to a description of an actual automated testing system it is necessary to devote some space to a discussion of some of the implications of current developments in behavioural technology for psychology in general and clinical psychology in particular.

At a time of rapid development in information handling technology, it is reasonable to expect corresponding advances in disciplines, such as psychology, which depend to an extent on information handling techniques. As each new technological advance opens up new possibilities, it is one of the responsibilities of the psychologist to explore these possibilities and to take advantage of the new opportunities they present.

Medawar (1967) has recently pointed out that 'no scientist is admired for failing in the attempt to solve problems that lie beyond his competence . . . research is . . . the art of the soluble'. One of the effects of the current growth of interest in the technical basis of psychology seems to be an increasing awareness amongst psychologists, particularly amongst those interested in the more practical branches of the subject, that the extent to which the range of problems they can usefully tackle at any one point in time is limited by the current state of behavioural technology.

It is very important to realize that psychology has a technical basis – in the past no less than in the future – and it is to be hoped that the technological developments referred to earlier will lead to a rather more balanced approach to the technical basis of psychology than has usually prevailed in the past. A consideration of the psychological implications of these developments leads us, firstly, to ask to what extent psychologists in the past have looked at certain aspects of behaviour, not so much because they were the things they most wanted to look at but because they were the only things they *could* look at, given the then current state of behavioural technology; and, secondly, to a critical reappraisal, in the light of these findings, of the psychology that has been inherited from previous generations. In the authors' opinion this re-evaluation could, in itself, make a significant contribution to the development of psychological science. Moreover, an increased awareness of the extent to which current practices are technically determined allows us to appreciate the implications of new developments more readily than would otherwise be possible.

Because many of the relevant new technical innovations may appear to psychologists to be of bewildering complexity, particularly in the early stages of their development when their essential nature may not be fully appreciated even by the responsible technologists themselves, there has very often, in the past, been an unfortunate tendency to equate technical and psychological simplicity on the one hand, and technical and psychological complexity on the other.

It is, perhaps, difficult, for the psychologist, to imagine a simpler situation than the collision of two particles, or a simpler experiment than arranging for such a collision to be observed; yet, if these particles be the elementary particles of the physicist, such an experiment may involve an investment in technical resources on a scale without parallel in the behavioural sciences. In this situation the physicist buys his experimental simplicity at the cost of technical complexity. At the same time, it must be pointed out that technical complexity is, in itself, no guarantee of experimental simplicity, and it must be admitted that it is sometimes all too easy to use technical skill to cover up a lack of thought – at least for a time.

But if it be accepted that there are pitfalls for the psychologist in technical complexity, there are probably even greater pitfalls (partly because the opportunities are more abundant) in technical simplicity. In clinical and educational psychology it is all too easy to fall into the trap of assuming that because a situation is technically simple – that, for example, because a test is easy to administer and easy to score – its results are capable of being understood within a simple conceptual framework. It may be technically simpler to administer a test under relatively uncontrolled conditions, but this is more likely to increase the complexity of the model needed to represent the results adequately than to simplify it – unless we give up altogether! It *may* be possible to buy psychological simplicity at the cost of some technical complexity, and if it *is* possible it may or may not be worth while, depending on circumstances. The two major types of problem confronting the behavioural technologist in this area are thus:

1. To decide, for any given behavioural situation, whether or not it is possible, at the particular point in time, given the state-of-the-art, to contribute to the achievement of psychological simplicity.
2. To decide, for any given behavioural situation, whether or not the benefits of investing in the currently available technology are such as to justify such an investment.

Miller (1968) has described two reasons for wishing to automate certain aspects of clinical psychological assessment. The first derives from the fact that many of the tests in common use in clinical psychology fall far short of desirable levels of reliability and validity. Whilst the usefulness of any test is based upon a large number of factors, of which reliability and validity are but two (Cronbach and Gleser, 1965) – and in some applied settings tests of surprisingly low levels of validity can be shown to be of use (Taylor and Russell, 1939) – it is in situations, as in clinical psychology, where it is necessary to assess and make decisions about individual cases that high levels of reliability and validity become essential rather than merely desirable. Reliability, in addition to being a prerequisite for validity, is also important in its own right in the common clinical situation of wishing to assess changes in behaviour by retesting after an interval of time.

The second reason given for automating testing is that, on the one hand, many tests in common use are time consuming to administer and score and, on the other, that there is a general shortage of psychologists to carry out this work. As automated testing can in many cases speed up the administration of tests and, especially as it reduces the psychologist's own direct involvement in testing, it should help to relieve this particular problem.

The routine nature of much day-to-day work in psychological assessment makes it particularly suitable for automation. Out of the vast possible repertoire of tests, most clinical psychologists seem to use a very restricted range of tests which are applied most routinely to most patients that they see. It is in just this sort of situation, where a limited range of operations are applied over and over again, that automation has so far proved to be most useful.

III · A DESCRIPTION OF AN AUTOMATED TESTING SYSTEM

We now move on to a description of an automated system with which we have both been associated. The system was developed over the period 1965-8 under the direction of one of us (J.L.G.) at the Unit for Research on Medical Applications of Psychology, University of Cambridge, with the support of a grant from the Medical Research Council for work on 'fundamental psychological problems relating to the development of automated guidance systems for use in the industrial rehabilitation of patients with brain damage'. It was made available commercially as the ESL ts 512, and several systems are currently in use in the United Kingdom.

Our reason for choosing to describe this system in some detail is not because we feel that it is in any way generally superior to other systems but because we feel that in the present context it is better to discuss a system with which we have been closely connected at all stages of development than one of which we have only second-hand knowledge. Our experience extends from the original conception through to the construction of development and production prototypes, and their subsequent evaluation in field trials under realistic clinical working conditions. We have also been in a position to discuss, in considerable depth, the problems of other workers who have been interested in using the system and this has given us valuable insights into many aspects of the whole field of automated testing.

As a system design the ts 512 was, in a sense, already obsolete before it reached the stage of commercial production. Nevertheless, although its useful days are numbered, we believe that it and other 'first-generation' systems have a vital role to play in the development of the techniques of the future, by helping potential users of future systems to gain valuable first-hand experience of automated techniques and thus equip themselves to formulate their requirements for the designers of future systems.

The ts 512 is a development from the primitive system described by Gedye (1967b), and consists of a programmable visual (or audiovisual) display (Gedye and Gaines, 1967) linked to a data-logger which produces a record in computer-compatible form.

The display is a modified ESL tm 1024 machine,* and its appearance in the testing situation is shown in Figure 25.1.

* The ESL tm 1024 is the commercial version of the programmable visual display device developed by Newman and Scantlebury (1967) at the National Physical

The illustration shows the tester's view of the ts 512 – based on the testing situation discussed in the text. Each trial begins with the exposure of a frame from a 35 mm program filmstrip, which is back-projected on to the 9-inch square screen to provide the patient's display. The illustration shows a typical 'matching-to-sample' format (see Fig. 25.7).

Below and in front of the display are two large square pushbuttons mounted separately. These buttons are raised above the surface of the response unit so that they can be felt easily; they are internally illuminable, being alight normally

FIGURE 25.1
Tester's view of test situation.

signifying that they are active, and they can carry visual markers for labelling purposes.

Each frame of the program requiring a response can be thought of as a request for a left or a right response from the patient, which is given by their pressing the left or right button accordingly. On each side of each program frame is a 10-bit coded instruction which can be read by the machine, and which specifies the direction of movement and the number of frames to be moved by the film transport mechanism. If the left button is pressed the left-sided instruction is followed, and if the right button is pressed the right-sided instruction is followed.

Laboratory, which has been used, amongst other things, as a teaching machine. The letters 'tm' are the initials of the words 'teaching machine' and the number 1024 (2^{10}) represents the number of frames directly addressable by a single instruction (± 512 (2^9)). In the designation ts 512, the letters 'ts' are the initials of the words 'testing system', and the number 512 indicates that 512 (2^9) frames (± 256) are addressable by a single instruction. In the ts 512, 2 bits (1 bit, from location 9, of each of the 2, 10-bit, coded instructions (see description of Fig. 25.1)) contribute to the generation of the first character of the data word (See description of Figs. 25.1 and 25.6). The tm 1024 modified in this way to function as the visual display unit of the ts 512 is referred to as the tm 512.

The logger has been designed primarily for use with 8-bit Teletypewriter equipment, the standard model using ASCII code (American Standard Code for Information Interchange). The termination of the presentation of each frame of the program causes an 8-character record word to be generated, the last 2 characters being typically used for Carriage Return/Line Feed to give an acceptable layout on the page printer. The other 6 characters are used for carrying information relating to the frame just presented. The first character is chosen from a set which includes START (9) and STOP (8) symbols, and eight symbols (0-7) defining the parameters of the response (left, right; correct,

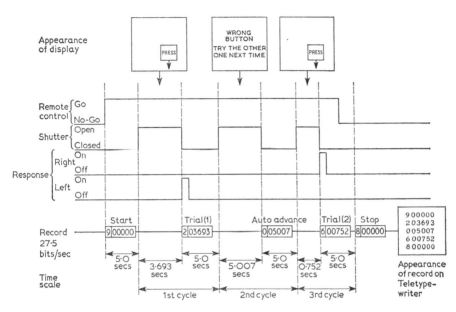

FIGURE 25.2
Details of operation cycle of ts 512 system.

incorrect; and so on); this information is also used for subsequent checking of tm 512 operation (see footnote on p. 739 and description of Fig. 25.6). The five characters 2-6 are typically used to record response time.

The logger may either drive a Teletypewriter direct, producing a print-out and a punched paper tape record; or its output may be recorded on an integral magnetic tape recorder for subsequent replay into a Teletypewriter, or sent on-line to the computer for immediate processing (see Fig. 25.3).

The operation of the system can best be understood by examining the structure of the operation cycle as illustrated in Figure 25.2.

The diagram shows the detailed time relationships of three operating cycles of the system, in which the subject is presented with a program frame demanding a right response, makes an incorrect left response, is presented with an auto-

2 B

advance frame (that is, a frame not requiring a response) giving knowledge of the result of the first trial, and is finally re-presented with the original frame, and this time makes a correct right response. The recording configuration is the typical one shown in Figure 25.3.

The squares at the top give the appearances of the program frames presented. The top line gives the state of the tester's remote control, the three lines below this the state of the shutter and the left and right response buttons (active only when shutter open) respectively, whilst the bottom line shows the successive stages of generation of the record (the final appearance of which is shown at the extreme right).

Before starting, the *tester* sets the film strip to the appropriate initial frame of the program, and operates the remote control to close the shutter of the visual display. When ready to start the test, the tester starts the tape-recorder and then operates the remote control to open the shutter. This action generates a 6-character data word 900000, the symbol 9 in the first position indicating 'start-of-test' and the 00000 that the 5-digit timer has been reset. When this data has been transferred serially to the tape, or 5 seconds has elapsed, whichever is the longer, the shutter opens and the response buttons become active (this gives a constant inter-trial period of 5 seconds for short inter-frame jumps). When the subject responds by pressing the left button, the data word 203693 is generated, the symbol 2 in the first position indicating an 'incorrect-left' response and the 03693 a response time of 3·693 seconds. When this has been transferred to the tape the first cycle is complete. The second cycle is an autoadvance frame (that is, it is exposed for a preset interval of approximately 5 seconds) and the third cycle the correct right response. While the data word generated by the second trial is being transferred to tape the tester operates the remote control to end the test, and this generates the data word 800000, the symbol 8 in the first position indicating 'end-of-test'. This is transferred to the tape at the end of the 5-second inter-trial delay.

Figure 25.3 shows the structure of the testing situation by indicating the various possible indirect communication links between the tester and the patient.

The interaction between the patient and the system is controlled by the program stored on film in the tm 512 in the manner indicated in the description of Figure 25.1. This interaction generates data which may be processed in a number of different ways according to the facilities available and the needs of the tester.

In the clinical research programme for which the system was developed the typical process which has been used is indicated by the heavy line. Data is recorded on magnetic tape at 27·5 pulses/second with a tape speed of $1\frac{7}{8}$ in./sec. The tape is replayed at $7\frac{1}{2}$ in./sec giving a 4:1 time compression, and a data rate of 110 pulses/second, to drive the Teletypewriter set and produce a print-out and punched paper tape. Edited tapes are batch processed to produce the type of results illustrated in Figures 25.8-25.11.

In addition, experience has been gained with all the other processing modes illustrated (these have included real-time situations in which the ts 512 has acted as a peripheral to the Cambridge University Mathematical Laboratory's 'Titan' multiaccess system, over both teleprinter and modem links). This experience has given valuable insights into the design requirements for future systems.

Clinical experience with the ts 512 system has to date been almost entirely confined to work on the assessment of learning ability in various groups of

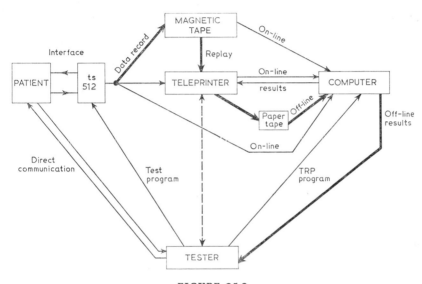

FIGURE 25.3
Information flow in the test situation.

geriatric patients (Gedye and Wedgwood, 1966), ranging from a group randomly selected from the community (Williamson, 1968, personal communication), through groups selected from geriatric day hospital and geriatric in-patient populations (Gedye and Wedgwood, to be published), to a group selected from a psycho-geriatric population (Neale, 1967, personal communication). In addition, pilot studies of groups of patients in a general rehabilitation unit, a recovery unit for severe head injuries and a mental subnormality hospital have recently been undertaken.

All the recent studies referred to above have used the second edition of the Pictorial Paired-Associate Learning Test (PPA-2) (Gedye, 1967a). The first edition of this test (PPA-1) (Gedye, 1965) has been described by Gedye (1967b) in some detail and readers are referred to this account for background information on the reasons underlying the choice of test and for a fuller account of the principles than can be given here. The second edition differs from the first in several ways, incorporating in its redesign much of the experience gained with PPA-1, but is organised on the same general lines.

The main idea underlying the design of PPA-1 and 2 was to present the subject with a series of lessons of graded difficulty, and to allow him to go on to a more difficult lesson only when he had demonstrated that he had mastered the preceding lesson. The structural unit of the program corresponding to the lesson is called the *filter*, and programs consist of a series of filters connected in series. The connections and functions of the filter are illustrated in Figure 25.4.

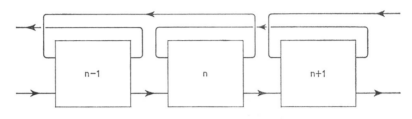

FIGURE 25.4
The connections and functions of the filter

The figure shows the connections and functions of the filter. Filter *n*, which is typical, has two incoming paths – one from a lower-level filter, *n*−1, and one from a higher-level filter, *n*+1; and two outgoing paths – one to the higher-level filter, and one to the lower-level filter. The only exceptions are the first and last filters in the program, which are naturally without lower and higher levels respectively, and the first filters of program blocks which have no lower level, acting as unidirectional gates.

The filters are designed so that once having arrived at a filter the pupil will stay there unless (1) he makes an error-free run, in which case he is promoted to a higher level; *or* (2) having made a mistake, he fails to correct it when instructed to do so, in which case he fails to *complete* the filter and is demoted to a lower level.

The filter can be regarded as a device for basing a binary decision (for example, whether to move on to a new filter or not) on the results of a series of binary decisions – in this case the responses to four successive frames. Our experience suggests that in this form it provides a powerful means of separating patients who have 'grasped the principle' of the task being presented from those who have not, even though the chance of successful completion by successive, independent, equiprobable, random binary choice is 1/16. Needless to say, the means for implementing the filter structure which are available on the ts 512 are extremely crude; for example, the lack of any response memory facility, apart from that inherent in the current frame address, necessarily leads to wasteful frame replication on the film strip. Nevertheless, this provides a good illustration of the way in which practical experience with a primitive system can highlight requirements for future systems.

The internal structure of the filter can be illustrated most easily by reference to Figures 25.5 and 25.6, which show filter 3,2 of PPA-2 in the form of a digraph structure and a list structure respectively (Harary, Norman and Cartwright, 1965).

It will be apparent from Figure 25.6 that the interconnections between frames of programs written for the ts 512 can be specified by numbering each frame on

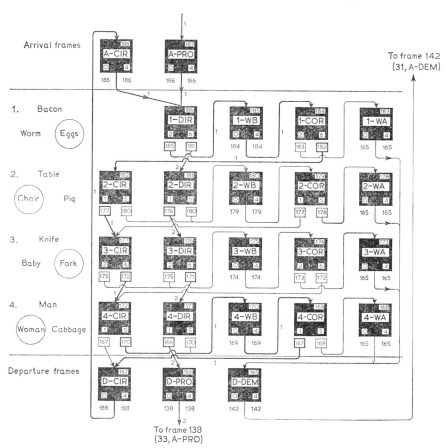

FIGURE 25.5
A digraph representation of the structure of a typical filter.

the film strip serially and listing the target frames for each frame in turn, according to whether a left or right response is made. Consequently, if the sequence of responses made by a pupil is known and if it is assumed that the machine has obeyed the instructions correctly, the pupil's path through the program can be reconstructed by reference to the list. It will be obvious that the weak point of this procedure is the assumption that the machine has obeyed the instructions correctly, which cannot be avoided as long as a relative address coding system of the above type is used. The procedure can, however, be made more acceptable by means of an error detection system.

The test result processing (TRP) program works on this principle and the procedure, together with the error-detection mechanism, is more fully explained in the description of Figure 25.6.

The diagram shows the structure of filter 3,2 of the Pictorial Paired-Associate Learning Test (PPA-2) in the form of a digraph.

Interpretation and Meaning of Frame Labels

Label	Interpretation	Meaning
1. Arrival Labels		
(stage A)		About to *start* current filter, following:
PRO	PROMOTION	Error-free completion of relevant lower-level filter
CIR	CIRCULATION	Non-error-free completion of current filter
DEM	DEMOTION	Failure to complete current or relevant higher-level filter
2. Transit Labels		
(stages 1-4)		In transit through current filter:
DIR	DIRECT	On direct route through filter, that is: 'no mistakes so far'
COR	CORRECTION	Re-presentation of a DIR or CIR frame to which a wrong response has just been made
CIR	CIRCULATION	On circulation route through filter, that is: 'at least one mistake so far'
3. Departure Labels		
(stage D)		Just *finished* current filter, following:
PRO	PROMOTION	Error-free completion of current filter
CIR	CIRCULATION	Non-error-free completion of current filter
DEM	DEMOTION	Failure to complete current filter

Each frame of the filter is represented by a square and two response buttons; the next frame to be visited, according to the response, is indicated by a directed line joining the response buttons to the frame. Autoadvance frames do not have response buttons.

The diagram is divided horizontally into three regions; the top and bottom regions contain arrival (A) and departure (D) frames. These are autoadvance frames carrying captions appropriate to the circumstances – promotion, circulation or demotion. The middle region contains the frames of the four stages of the filter itself; each stage has the picture frame format indicated on the left, the correct sample being ringed.

The middle region is divided into five columns containing 'circulation route' frames, 'direct route' frames, 'wrong button' frames, 'correction' frames and 'wrong again' frames respectively. In order to produce the list structure shown in Figure 25.6 the array is scanned from right to left starting at the bottom and working upwards, since at this point in the PPA-2 program the general direction of movement along the film strip is from right to left.

1	2-4			5-6		7-8	
Frame	Filter	Stage	Label	First Character		Next Frame	
				Left	Right	Left	Right
165	32	D	DEM	0	4	142	142
166	32	D	PRO	0	4	138	138
167	32	D	CIR	0	4	188	188
168	32	4	WA	0	4	165	165
169	32	4	COR	1	5	167	168
170	32	4	WB	0	.4	169	169
171	32	4	DIR	1	5	166	170
172	32	4	CIR	1	5	167	170
173	32	3	WA	0	4	165	165
174	32	3	COR	2	6	173	172
175	32	3	WB	0	4	174	174
176	32	3	DIR	2	6	175	171
177	32	3	CIR	2	6	175	172
178	32	2	WA	0	4	165	165
179	32	2	COR	1	5	177	178
180	32	2	WB	0	4	179	179
181	32	2	DIR	1	5	176	180
182	32	2	CIR	1	5	177	180
183	32	1	WA	0	4	165	165
184	32	1	COR	2	6	183	182
185	32	1	WB	0	4	184	184
186	32	1	DIR	2	6	185	181
187	32	A	PRO	0	4	186	186
188	32	A	CIR	0	4	186	186

FIGURE 25.6

A list representation of the structure of a typical filter.

The figure shows the structure of filter 3,2 of the Pictorial Paired-Associate Learning Test (PPA-2) in the form of a list. Each row of the list refers to one frame of the film strip and the entry in column 1 gives the serial number, or address, of the frame as it occurs on the film strip. It will be seen that filter 3,2 occupies frames 165-188.

Columns 2-4 give the filter number 3,2, of each frame together with the stage, A, 1-4 or D, and the label. Columns 5-6 give the first characters to be expected in the data word according to left and right responses. Columns 7-8 give the addresses of the next frames according to the response made.

The TRP program has access to a list of this type which describes the whole PPA-2 program. Given the address of the starting frame, for example 186, it reads the first character of the first data word following the start word (900000), say 2, and searches for this in columns 5 and 6; if it finds it in the left column, as in this example, it reads the address of the next frame in left address column (7), which in this case is 185, and jumps to this address to decode the next word.

If the TRP program finds that the first character of the data word does not appear in columns 5 or 6 it rejects the test data and prints a diagnostic message. In this way it is possible to detect an error, due to faulty film transport for example, within a few frames of its occurrence.

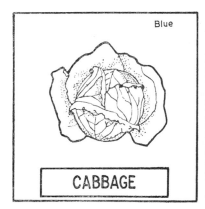

FIGURE 25.7
Example of 'matching-to-sample' program frame layout.

Given the filter as the basic constructional unit of the program, it was necessary to devise a means of teaching paired-associates. The method used was based on the work of Filby and Edwards (1963) (see also Gedye, 1967b) who used a 'matching-to-sample' method to teach form discrimination to aphasic patients. It can best be illustrated by means of an example; to teach the item-pair 'MAN-WOMAN', the program frame layout might be as shown in Figure 25.7.

The 'program frame' has three colour-coded 'picture-frames', each containing a labelled picture. At the top is the *sample* picture-frame and at the bottom are two *match* picture-frames. The left match picture-frame always has an orange background, while the right always has a blue background, and they appear on the screen directly above the left and right control buttons, which are similarly shaped and coloured and light up when the shutter of the machine opens to display the frame. This provides a highly compatible display-control relationship.

The sample picture-frame may have a blue (B) or orange (O) background according to the background colour of the picture-frame that contains the correct match, if the aim is to cue the response by colour, *or* it may have a grey background (G) if no cues are to be given. In the example shown, stage 4 of Filter 3,2, DIR, COR and CIR (PPA-2), the sample picture-frame, which contains the item 'MAN', is grey.

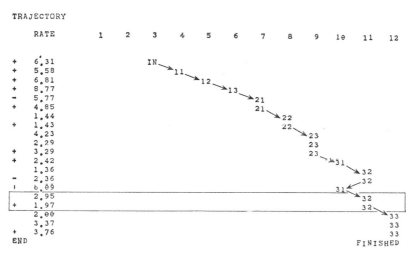

FIGURE 25.8
Example of print-out of test trajectory.

In order to illustrate the lines on which we have started to develop our TRP program, Figures 25.8-25.11 show the results of a test administered on 18th June 1968 in Dr J. Williamson's Geriatric Unit in Edinburgh. The patient was a woman of 68 (Unit number 183) who completed the program, but with less than maximum efficiency.

The general principle underlying the design of the TRP program has been to provide a means of information presentation which will allow the clinician requesting the assessment to get an overall picture of the results, even if he is not in a position to understand all the details. This allows him to ask further questions of the data and to enter into constructive discussion with the psychologist. This approach would seem to be typical of the relationship that exists between clinicians and investigatory specialists in other branches of medicine, but which has not, to date, been very prominent in the relationship between the clinician and the clinical psychologist. Whilst there are, no doubt.

2 B*

many reasons to account for this state of affairs in the past, it would seem that the automation of psychological assessment could do much to improve communication between the two professional groups. One of the most important reasons for desiring this is the fact that the clinician is in a unique position to spot connections between behavioural patterns revealed by the automated assessment on the one hand and features deriving from other modes of clinical investigation on the other; and this would seem, from our experience in geriatric assessment, to be a very fruitful approach for the future.

The first way in which the test results are displayed is in the form of a graph of level of achievement against number of completed filter cycles. This allows a general impression of the patient's performance to be seen at a glance.

The page is divided vertically into 12 regions corresponding to the 12 filters of the program ranked in order of difficulty. Each row corresponds to a completed

```
SEQUENCE

   3    4    5    6    7    7    8    8    9    9    9   10   11   11   10   11   11   12   12   12

MEAN CORRECT RATE     4.66


LAST CORRECT FILTER 33
SECS        412.19        RATE        3.76
TRIALS         90         MIN TRIALS            40
EFFICIENCY              0.44
```

FIGURE 25.9
Example of print-out of answers to anticipated questions.

filter cycle, the particular filter designation being printed in the appropriate column. Thus the first filter completed, the introductory filter is shown by an entry, IN, in column 3, the appropriate level of difficulty for this filter.

In the left-hand margin, under the heading RATE, the mean rate of response (mean reciprocal response time × 10) for the particular filter will be found. It will be seen that the rate for the introductory filter was 6·31 responses/dekasec. If the patient was promoted from a filter the rate value is prefixed by +, if the patient was required to repeat the filter there is no prefix and if the patient was demoted the rate value is prefixed by −.

It will be apparent that inspection of this trajectory may lead the tester to ask further questions. For example, he may wish to know more about the patient's performance in the cycles enclosed by the rectangle (16 and 17), when the patient was in Filter 3,2. This further information may be obtained from the test log (see Fig. 25.10).

(*Note.* In this figure the filter transitions have been emphasized by joining the filter designations with directed lines.)

After some experience with a particular test program has been gained it becomes possible to anticipate certain questions that the tester may wish to ask and to provide the answers routinely. The number of such questions must be kept as small as possible in the interests of easy assimilation of the results; too many questions would defeat this purpose. It is important to emphasize that the most suitable particular set of questions may depend very much on the tester's purpose, and that the discovery of suitable sets of questions for particular purposes may involve a considerable amount of research.

The questions answered in the sample of print-out illustrate some of the ways in which test results may be scrutinized, but they are not intended to be representative or exhaustive. First, under the subheading 'SEQUENCE' is the sequence of filter transitions coded by level of difficulty. By comparing sequences from two different tests it is possible to derive measures of similarity of the two trajectories, and such measures can be used as a basis of various pattern sorting

TRIAL	FILTER	STAGE	LABEL	RESPONSE	LATENCY	MEAN L.	RATE	MEAN R.	CUM TIME
67	32	1	DIR	* L	6.744		1.48		307.27
68	32	1	COR	R	2.181		4.59		309.45
69	32	2	CIR	L	7.961		1.26		317.41
70	32	3	CIR	R	3.804		2.63		321.22
71	32	4	CIR	* R	6.386		1.57		327.60
72	32	4	COR	L	1.617		6.18		329.22
						4.78		2.95	329.22
73	32	1	DIR	R	5.015		1.99		334.23
74	32	2	DIR	L	3.434		2.91		337.67
75	32	3	DIR	R	14.259		0.70		351.93
76	32	4	DIR	L	4.384		2.28		356.31
+						6.77		1.97	356.31

FIGURE 25.10
Example of part of print-out of test log.

and classification procedures. Next, 'MEAN CORRECT RATE', the mean rate of response for filter cycles leading to promotion, gives some measure of the patient's overall rate of response; 'LAST CORRECT FILTER' tells how far the patient got with the program; 'SECS' gives the total decision time taken, and 'TRIALS', the number of trials taken to get this far; 'MIN TRIALS' reminds the tester of the smallest number of trials that could have achieved this result, and 'EFFICIENCY' is a measure derived from these last two.

An important use for this type of derived information is for indexing in a Data Bank to allow searches to be made on the basis of various performance characteristics.

The test log gives a trial by trial account of the patient's performance from the first frame requiring a response to the last. Figure 25.10 shows the part of the log, trials 67-76, dealing with the two filter cycles referred to in the description of Figure 25.8.

The page is divided vertically into four main regions, which, reading from left to right, give information about the trial, the frame, the response, and the time scale respectively.

The first column gives the serial number of the trial, the first frame of the test being trial 1. The next three columns (2-3) identify the filter, the stage, and the route of the particular frame presented. The next five columns (5-9) give: the response made, left button (L) or right button (R), wrong responses being prefixed by an asterisk; the latency of the response to the nearest millisecond; the mean latency for the filter; the equivalent response rate in responses/dekasec.; and the mean response rate for the filter. The final column (10) gives the cumulative response time from trial 1, and allows records to be compared on a common time base.

It will be apparent that the information in this print-out allows the tester to reconstruct the patient's route through the program, and an example of such a reconstruction is shown in Figure 25.5, where the frame connections are labelled '1' and '2' to show the first and second cycles, respectively.

```
AUTOADVANCE EXPOSURES   56
MIN      4.724  MAX       4.804
MEAN     4.766  STD DEV   0.022
```

FIGURE 25.11
Example of print-out of quality control information.

An important aspect of automated testing is the possibility it offers of not only controlling the test situation more than would otherwise be possible, but of checking that such control has in fact been exerted. Such checking extends from the circumstances of the tester's demonstration on the one hand to the performance of the equipment itself on the other.

The figure shows the print-out of a check on the performance of the pre-set exposure control which operates in the autoadvance mode. A fault in the timer, for example, could be detected by inspection of these values.

The results shown in Figures 25.8-25.11 were all produced on the line-printer output of the computer running the TRP program. They could equally well have been produced on a Teletypewriter output shortly after the completion of the test if a real-time configuration of the system had been used, although this would be a rather slow process. In the future it is clear that some much faster way of interrogating the output of the TRP program on-line will be required. This could be by means of a cathode ray tube or similar display device, such as the ITT* 'Ferrodot' (soft copy); but it will almost certainly be necessary to obtain print-outs of selected pieces of information (hard copy) on request, so that the clinician can study these away from the information utility terminal.

At the present time it is difficult to be definite about future requirements, but it is hoped that the preceding account will have given the reader some idea of the ways in which current work with simple systems can help to clarify the picture.

* International Telephone and Telegraph Corporation.

IV SOME CHARACTERISTICS OF AUTOMATED TESTING

As will be seen from the description of the ts 512 system, work in this field is unfortunately only in its infancy. Most of the basic studies which could define and elaborate the strong points and weaknesses of automated testing still remain to be carried out. However, subject to the need to modify expressed opinions in the light of future findings, it is now possible to discuss in greater detail the general theoretical and practical characteristics of automated testing.

1 Objectivity and reliability

The main technical advantage of automated testing, from a psychometric point of view, is that it ensures an objective and standard presentation of test materials and recording of responses by a neutral 'examiner'. Those with any experience at all in the administration of psychological tests will know how difficult it is in practice to achieve standard administration and scoring, and research has shown the pervasive influence of the 'experimenter effect' (Kintz *et al.*, 1965). Of course, the 'experimenter effect' cannot be entirely excluded, as the attitudes and expectations induced in the subject by the tester on introducing the subject to the test situation are likely to affect the subject's responses to some degree. However, it is reasonable to suppose that automated testing will attentuate this undesirable source of bias to some extent.

A consequence of standard administration and scoring is that test reliability should be increased. Increased reliability should enable the construction of tests with improved validity, and also ensure that the repeated administration of tests in order to measure changes in the individual subject becomes a much more profitable activity than it is at present.

2 Advantages and limitations in test design

Devices such as the ts 512 are obviously going to affect the nature of tests used, as a large proportion of conventional tests will not easily transcribe into automated forms. At present it is easiest if the stimuli to be presented to the subject are visual, and the responses button presses, which necessitates the use of recognition-type items. However, neither of these present restrictions are unsurmountable. Even with the ts 512 an auditory 'slave' in the shape of a tape recorder which works in step with the testing device and delivers an appropriate auditory stimulus with each visual stimulus has been used experimentally. It is possible to get over the response limitations by getting the device to instruct the subject either to write down his response or to indicate it in some other way, but this loses some of the advantages which follow from the automatic production of a complete computer-compatible record. In this context it is worth mentioning the recent paper by Hill (1969), which draws attention to the possibilities opened up by the use of currently available limited vocabulary automatic speech recognition (ASR) devices as interfaces to systems like the ts 512.

A potentially powerful advantage in test design conferred by automated testing is that it permits the accurate recording of response latencies and, incidentally, the accurate timing of presentation of stimuli, should this be required, as in some learning and memory tests. The accurate recording of response latencies is carried out without the subject's awareness, unless he is specifically informed of this, and thus permits the easier use of the type of speed and level analysis advocated by Furneaux (1960).

A further characteristic of automated testing devices, as exemplified by the ts 512, relates to the fact that they are based on, or can function as, teaching machines. As a result they can be used to instruct the subject as to the nature of the test procedures involved and to ensure, by means of practice items, that the subject has in fact grasped the instructions before going on to the administration of the test items proper. This means that the whole testing procedure, at least for the types of testing suitable for automation, is taken over by the machine and hence not only are the items presented in a standard way, but the instructions are also standardized.

3 The use of computers

Although it is possible to have automated testing devices which would present results as 'raw scores' to be read from some kind of visual display, the production, by the testing device, of a computer compatible output (as in the ts 512) seems the best way of getting the maximum information from the results of testing. Not only can the computer be programmed to transcribe the data into raw scores and transform them into such derived measures as I.Q.s, and to present the results in various ways for easy assimilation, but further analyses of the data can also be made – such as tests of the reliability of differences between scores, or the comparison of test scores with established norms. In fact, it seems that it will, in the future, be possible to program the computer to analyse the results of several tests given to a subject, to make all the necessary comparisons with the results, and to write a report based on the findings for subsequent editing by the psychologist.

One problem frequently met with in the use of any psychological test is the generalizability of the norms from the population on which the test was standardized to that on which it is intended to use the test. With conventional tests it is always possible to re-standardize or to make adjustments in the norms, to take care of local population peculiarities where the test is to be used. This is very infrequently done, due presumably to the extremely heavy labour often involved. The use of a computer-based automated testing system would not, of course, eliminate this problem, but since it would provide a ready and easy means of storing data, it would make it a lot easier to solve, by allowing easier statistical evaluation of amassed data and the readjustment or updating of norms where necessary.

It is understandable that the use of computer-based systems may seem too futuristic for many practising psychologists in the National Health Service or elsewhere, but in view of the arguments put forward earlier, and the increasingly extended use of computers for other purposes, it seems unlikely that many psychologists will be without some kind of access to one within the near future. Many regional hospital boards, for example, have either acquired, or are acquiring, computers and there are now a number of commercial computer organizations supplying services to most parts of the United Kingdom, including on-line real-time facilities over telephone data links.

4 Practical considerations

The use of automated testing has a number of practical advantages. The administration of tests automatically is very speedy, at least for some types of test. We have, for example, administered both editions of the pictorial paired-associate learning test referred to earlier to geriatric patients, some of whom were very deteriorated and untestable by conventional methods, at rates of up to four subjects per hour or more. This is greatly in excess of the speed of administration of a conventional learning test, such as the Synonym Learning Test (Kendrick *et al.*, 1965), with similar patients. It is therefore likely that the amount of testing that it is possible to carry out with automated methods will, in many instances, prove greater than that possible by conventional methods. In addition, there is some indication that it may be possible to test very deteriorated patients by machine, where conventional testing would be impossible.

As an automated testing system can, as explained earlier, both instruct the subject in the test procedure and then administer the test items, the direct involvement of the tester in the actual testing situation can be reduced to operating the equipment and introducing the subject to the testing situation. This has the implications that the psychologist's skills are not necessary in the automated testing situation and that test technicians could carry out automated testing just as adequately. This would then release the psychologist for other things, and in particular could enable him to spend much more time with the patient to carry out functions which either cannot or should not be automated. At the same time it must be emphasized that our experience has shown that the automated testing situation can be a very rich source of behavioural material that can only be assessed by a skilled human observer, and that any investment of skilled time is amply repaid.

There are two main practical disadvantages of current automated testing systems like the ts 512. First, the current testing equipment, although transportable, is not readily moved around from place to place. Thus, it is necessary for subjects to come to a special testing room to be tested and more or less rules out the testing of individuals in their own homes, in wards, schools, and so on. However, this is not a fundamental limitation as it seems quite feasible to produce a truly transportable system. The second disadvantage of the current system is that with computer-based scoring it is desirable to accumulate as much data as possible before having it processed, and this causes delay. In addition, without real-time facilities, there is likely to be some delay, perhaps of the order of a few days, between testing and the results being available from the computer. Under the normal working conditions of most departments this delay is acceptable, but in certain situations it may not be. However, the current developments in computer utilities may do much to solve this problem.

5 Economic factors

As mentioned earlier, economic factors and the 'cost effectiveness' of psychological testing have received little attention from psychologists in the past. Nevertheless they are important, particularly in the context of automated testing, where it may be necessary to justify an initial high capital outlay on equipment or the renting of a terminal. The question of the economic feasibility of automated testing is likely to depend on the particular situation in which it is used. The writers have given some consideration to this problem and are convinced that it is possible to justify automated testing on economic grounds. Detailed calculations are inappropriate in this context but the general principles can be outlined.

With a system like the ts 512, which, it must be remembered, is a first generation system intended for experimental work, much of the expense of automated testing lies in the initial cost of the equipment, which, by currently accepted standards in clinical psychology in the United Kingdom, is considerable (but not when compared with other accepted medical equipment). By comparison, the initial outlay in the purchase of materials for conventional testing is trivial. Where conventional testing becomes expensive is in its administration. It requires the full time attention of a highly skilled, and therefore relatively highly paid, administrator, which makes the cost of administering most conventional tests quite substantial in terms of the tester's time alone. Added to this is the cost of the time involved in scoring and doing the comparisons and analysis of data which in automated testing are carried out by the computer. These factors make the day-to-day administration of automated tests much cheaper, given that automated testing is much less time consuming and only requires the partial attention of a much lower paid technician. The writers have estimated that within the usual conditions at present prevailing within the National Health Service a reasonably busy psychology department should be able to write off the initial capital cost of a system such as the ts 512 against the savings made in test administration within two years. A crucial factor is the amount of testing to be done; if this is large, automated testing is economical, but if it is slight this may not be so.

6 The psychologist's relationship with his patient

The substitution of a supposedly impersonal machine for the usually warm relationship between the tester and the person being tested is likely to worry some psychologists. The experience of the writers, whose joint experience extends to several hundred automated patient-tests, is that fears in this direction are nearly always unfounded and that the effects on the psychologist-patient relationship are either negligible or positive rather than negative. There are indications, particularly from experience with subnormal children, that it might be better to think of an automated system as having, from the patient's point of view, a simple personality, rather than no personality at all.

Subjects of all ages seem to take very well to automated testing, possibly because this is seen much more as a game rather than as a testing (that is, examination) type of situation. In addition the subject is not placed in the position of failing or of having to answer potentially embarrassing questions in a face-to-face situation. The psychologist is also relieved of the necessity of assuming the rather didactic role demanded by some conventional tests. The fact that the psychologist's time is not taken up in test administration means that the time saved can, if he so wishes, be spent in developing a relationship with the patient and in carrying out other less routine procedures. The acceptability of automated testing to geriatric patients is evidenced by the fact that of several who refused to be tested by the writers by conventional methods none objected to automated testing. There is nothing that ruins the psychologist-patient relationship more completely than the necessity to push a reluctant patient to do tests that he does not wish to do.

7 The likely role of automated testing

As in any other field, automated procedures are ideally suited to taking over routine work. In psychological assessment, therefore, automated testing is likely to play its most important role in the administration of frequently used test procedures. Such routine procedures could well include intelligence tests, learning tests and personality questionnaires. The relative speed and efficiency of automated testing, coupled with the fact that it does not necessarily require a qualified psychologist to operate the equipment and introduce the patient to it, means that routine screening tests applied to all admissions to an institution become a feasible proposition.

In addition to removing some of the routine work from the psychologist's shoulders, it is more than likely that automated testing will create new roles for itself. For example, medical consultations in many medical specialities involve the doctor in spending a considerable portion of his time with the patient in going through a standard series of questions about the patient's problem. Such questioning could well be carried out by the automated testing device before the patient actually meets the doctor (Edwards, 1968; Mayne, Weksel and Sholtz, 1968).

8 Research and developments needed

In the course of the present chapter a number of assertions have been made with regard to the likely advantages and characteristics of automated testing. Whilst the writers' experiences in the use of the ts 512 system bear these opinions out, it is obvious that much empirical research is required in order to demonstrate unequivocally that the expected advantages of automated testing do materialize in practice and to explore further the characteristics of automated testing. Two main, but interacting, areas of research are indicated.

First, there is a need to carry out experiments with existing equipment, such as the ts 512, in order to demonstrate that the expected increases in reliability of testing, work load capabilities, subject acceptability and type of patient accessible to testing do appear in practice. More important still, it is necessary to demonstrate that these improvements do lead to the increased clinical effectiveness of psychological assessment. Due to the high initial capital costs of automated testing, cost effectiveness studies should also be done in comparison with conventional forms of testing (in the writers' opinion this is a much neglected field of study with regard to conventional testing as much expensive time is often spent in psychological assessment in lengthy procedures of unknown validity).

It will be obvious that many of the characteristics of automated testing will interact with the type of hardware to be used and, therefore, research into the nature and optimal design of hardware will be required. Of course, it is possible that the type of hardware which gives optimal results with one type of patient will not be the same as that giving optimal results with another, and some degree of compromise will have to be involved. One of the reasons for the concern with geriatric patients in preliminary work in this field has been the belief that these subjects are amongst the most difficult to assess and that equipment which could be used adequately by them would therefore be usable by most other classes of patients. Much work in the area of hardware design needs to be done on such simple questions as the maximum number of response alternatives that different classes of patients can handle, the optimal type of stimulus displays, and so on. However, it is reasonable to hope that before really extensive work is carried out in hardware design, some attempts will be made to demonstrate that automated testing with currently available hardware can go at least some way towards realizing the benefits that we believe this new technique ought to display.

ACKNOWLEDGEMENTS

The work described in this chapter was started during J. L. Gedye's tenure of the Pinsent-Darwin Studentship in the Department of Medicine, University of Cambridge, and continued during his tenure of the University Lectureship in Psychopathology.

The development of the automated testing system was supported by a grant from the Medical Research Council, and its application to the assessment of senile mental changes by a grant from the Joint Committee on Clinical Research of the East Anglian Regional Hospital Board and the Board of Governors United Cambridge Hospitals.

The authors wish to acknowledge the advice and help of their former Cambridge colleagues C. J. Cheney, B. R. Gaines and S. H. Salter, who made substantial contributions to the early development of the automated testing system. C. J. Cheney was responsible for the design and construction of the development prototype ts 512, and for the implementation of the TRP software on the University Mathematical Laboratory's 'Titan' computer. Our thanks are due to Professor M. V. Wilkes, Director and Mr E. N. Mutch, Superintendent of Computing Services, University Mathematical Laboratory, Cambridge, for making the facilities of the 'Titan' multiaccess system available to the project.

REFERENCES

CRONBACH, L. J. and GLESER, G. C. (1965) *Psychological Tests and Personnel Decisions*. Urbana, Illinois: University of Illinois Press.

EDWARDS, D. A. W. (1968) Clinical analysis of dysphagia – steps towards automation and early diagnosis. *In Symposium on 'Carcinoma of the Oesophagus'*. 29th Annual General Meeting of the British Society of Gastroenterology, London.

ELITHORN, A. and TELFORD, A. (1969) Computer analysis of intellectual skills. *Int. J. Man-Machine Studies*. **1**, 189-209.

FILBY, Y. and EDWARDS, A. E. (1963) An application of automated-teaching methods to test and teach form discrimination to aphasics. *J. Programmed Instruction*, **2**, 25-33.

FURNEAUX, W. D. (1960) Intellectual abilities and problem solving behaviour. *In* EYSENCK, H. J. (Ed.) *Handbook of Abnormal Psychology*. London: Pitman.

GEDYE, J. L. (1965) A pictorial paired-associate learning test. First Edition (PPA-1). A program film-strip for the ts 512. London: Educational Systems Limited.

GEDYE, J. L. (1967a) A pictorial paired-associate learning test. Second Edition (PPA-2). A program film-strip for the ts 512. London: Educational Systems Limited.

GEDYE, J. L. (1967b) A teaching machine programme for use as a test of learning ability. *In* UNWIN, D. and LEEDHAM, J. (Eds.) *Aspects of Educational Technology*. London: Methuen.

GEDYE, J. L. and GAINES, B. R. (1967) Medical applications of programmable audio-visual displays. *Dig. VII int. Conf. med. biol. Engng. Stockholm*, p. 226.

GEDYE, J. L. and WEDGWOOD, J. (1966) Experience in the use of a teaching machine for the assessment of senile mental changes. *Proc. VII int. Congr. Gerontol. Vienna*, pp. 205-207.

HARARY, F., NORMAN, R. Z. and CARTWRIGHT, D. (1965) *Structural Models: An Introduction to the Theory of Directed Graphs*. New York: Wiley.

HILL, D. (1969) An ESOTerIC approach to some problems in automatic speech recognition. *Int. J. Man-Machine Studies*, **1**, 101-121.

KENDRICK, D. C., PARBOOSINGH, R. C. and POST, F. (1965) A synonym learning test for use with elderly psychiatric subjects. *Brit. J. soc. clin. Psychol.*, **4**, 63-71.

KINTZ, B. L., DELPRATO, D. J., METTEE, D. R., PERSONS, C. E. and SCHAPPE, R. H. (1965) The experimenter effect. *Psychol. Bull.*, **63**, 223-232.

MAYNE, J. G., WEKSEL, W. and SHOLTZ, P. N. (1968) Toward automating the medical history. *Mayo Clin. Proc.* **43**, 1-25.

MEDAWAR, P. B. (1967) *The Art of the Soluble*. London: Methuen.

MILLER, E. (1968) A case for automated clinical testing. *Bull. Brit. psychol. Soc.*, **21**, 75-78.

NEWMAN, E. A. and SCANTLEBURY, R. A. (1967) Teaching machines as intelligence amplifiers. National Physical Laboratory Report Auto 31. London.

TAYLOR, H. C. and RUSSELL, J. T. (1939) The relationship of validity coefficients to the practical effectiveness of tests in selection: discussion and tables. *J. appl. Psychol.*, **23**, 565-575.

26

Concepts and personality: Kelly and Osgood

D. Bannister

I INTRODUCTION

The development of methods for investigating an individual's general outlook, the language in which that outlook is expressed and the assumptions underlying it, has come relatively late to psychology. This may well be because two traditional creeds – behaviourism and reductionism – delayed the idea that conceptual analysis, in any form, could be a scientifically useful undertaking.

Behaviourism, in its radical form, discouraged any tendency to explore the viewpoint of the subject, since this would be to admit the relevance of 'subjective' material. Although in latter days the outlook of the individual was given some sort of status as an 'intervening variable' and self report in various forms was considered relevant material, such changes did not usually extend to acknowledging that the subject might have an overview as systematic and abstract as that of the psychologist, which might merit investigation.

The reductionist posture in psychology has always encouraged a concentration on what were thought to be simple and unitary behaviours and necessarily discouraged the investigation of conceptualization. 'Higher processes' are to be explained at some later date and, on the basis that there will be pie in the sky bye and bye, it is assumed that the sum total of fragmentary laboratory studies will add up, eventually, to an explanation of man.

Reductionism has come under formal attack as in Jessor (1958) and Popper (1963), but as a general postion it may have lost popularity less as a result of academic criticism and more as an outcome of sheer intellectual weariness with the *minutiae* of the traditional experiment.

Behaviourism has encountered many criticisms, but perhaps the most relevant for those interested in the development of studies of conceptualization has been the growing doubt as to who is to define the nature of the 'stimulus', the experimenter or the subject. Significant here has been the elaboration of the phenomenological view of behaviour (Combs and Snygg, 1949) which argues that all behaviour is determined by and pertinent to the perceptual field of the behaving organism. The 'perceptual field' of a person in this context was defined as the entire universe including himself *as it is experienced by* an individual. This kind of approach deprives the psychologist of his claim to subsume man within a deterministic science and burdens him with the task of theorizing about theorists and predicting predictors.

761

In brief, within psychology, the status of the subject has been slowly improving. From a drive dominated mass of habits, he is steadily ascending to the ranks of thinking men; he is moving out of the objective ghetto where organisms live into the lush residential suburbs hitherto reserved for psychologists and other scientists.

The two methods which most completely recognize that it is the subject who imposes significance on his environment were developed in the mid-1950s. These two strategies for exploring interpretative man are repertory grid method, as proposed by Kelly (1955) and the Semantic Differential, developed by Osgood, Suci and Tannenbaum (1957).

II GRID METHOD

Grid methods have been evolved as an integral part of the elaboration of personal construct theory. The theory is based on the assumption that all men may be thought of as scientists in the sense that each is concerned with the prediction and control of his environment. Each individual is seen as developing his own personal repertoire of bi-polar constructs by means of which he structures (interprets, conceptualizes) his world and seeks to anticipate events. These constructs are interrelated and organized into a system by means of which the individual codifies and gives meaning to his experience. Thus the psychology of personal constructs is very much concerned with the ways in which personal construct systems can be analysed and described and with accounting for the ways in which they develop and change. In terms of this framework an individual's 'personality' is his view of the world and personality assessment is essentially the evaluation and analysis of this view. Commentaries on and summaries of construct theory are available in Bannister (1962a), Sechrest (1963) and Kelly (1963 and 1969).

What follows is a description of some forms of grid technique, largely in operational terms. It must be stressed, however, that grid method is very closely related to personal construct theory and it is doubtful if it can effectively be used without careful consideration of the assumptions of the theory, since these are equally the assumptions underlying grid method.

Repertory grids are forms of sorting tests. They differ from conventional sorting tests in that there are no standard sorting materials or sorting categories (both can be supplied to or elicited from individual subjects in terms of the area under investigation), nor is there any standard single form of administration procedure. Their unique characteristics are:

1. What is measured is the relationship between the sorting categories (constructs, concepts, ideas) for the subject – not the 'correctness' of the sorts as such;
2. They are so designed that statistical techniques which are normally applied only to group data can be used to assess the performance of a single subject.

The assumption underlying many forms of repertory grid examination is that the psychological relationship between any two constructs, for a given subject, is reflected in the degree of statistical association between them when they are used as sorting categories by the subject. This rationale can be exemplified in an extreme case as follows.

If a subject nominates 40 people known personally to him, categorizes each in turn as *sincere* or *hypocritical* and then re-sorts them as *courageous* or *frightened*, we may find that, say, the 20 designated as *sincere* are also designated as *courageous* and the 20 designated as *hypocritical* are designated as *frightened*. We can then infer a high positive relationship (which can be assessed in terms of its binomial probability) between the constructs, *sincere-hypocritical* and *courageous-frightened* for that subject. Such a procedure treats the subject as a scientist in his own right and the analog of the psychologist who sets out, in the form of contingency tables, observations which exemplify hypothesized relationships.

The flexibility of repertory grid technique becomes apparent if we examine the aspects which can be varied in constructing any particular form of grid measure.

Elements

The elements are the 'objects' to be sorted by the subject. What they are will depend entirely upon the area of construing under investigation. For example, they may be people known personally to the subject, photographs of people unknown to him, the names of physical objects, lists of emotions, political parties, book titles, films and so forth. Examples of the different kinds of sorting material which can be used within grid format can be found in Carver (1967) who used films, Fransella and Adams (1965) who used named emotions and Bannister and Salmon (1966) who used the names of physical objects.

Constructs

A construct is a bipolar concept as defined in construct theory. In grid practice it often takes adjectival form and is used as a sorting category. Two major types of grids are extant – those in which the subject is required to use his constructs as pure dichotomies and allot the elements to one or the other pole (e.g. *black-white, bright-stupid*) or those in which he is required to use his constructs as scales and rank order his elements (*blackest to whitest, brightest to most stupid*). Although little used so far, rating scale forms of grid equally permit an analysis of construct interrelationships.

Constructs can either be elicited from the subject or supplied to him by the psychologist. One way of eliciting constructs is by the triadic method in which groups of three elements are placed before the subject who is then asked to suggest some important way in which two of them are alike and thereby different from the third. Thus if the elements of a particular grid are people known personally to the subject he might respond to the triad presented to him by saying that two of the people were *warm* and the other one was *cold*. Thus a construct (presumably one which he habitually uses to dimensionalize his interpersonal world) would have been elicited from him. With some subjects (particularly children) discussion of the subject's problems and views may reveal characteristic modes of construing which can then be embodied as grid constructs. Alternatively, constructs can be supplied by the psychologist in terms of specific hypotheses which he wishes to test or areas which he wants to examine. The latter procedure entails the assumption that the verbal labels supplied are meaningful to the subject – an assumption which is commonly enough made (e.g. in all questionnaires) but which involves risks all its own. At least in grid techniques, where the meaning (interrelationship) of constructs is precisely what we seek to measure, some quantified assessment of the sense conveyed by supplied verbal labels is possible.

It should be noted that the distinction between constructs and elements is a formal one and they can be transposed operationally in different forms of grid test. Kelly covers this theoretically by pointing out that any construct can be an element within the range of convenience of a superordinate construct. Equally in grid procedure the element *myself* can be converted into the construct *like myself in character* and the construct *intelligent-stupid* may appear in alternative grids (where the *elements* were characteristics of people) as the element *intelligence*.

1 Types of administration

Early repertory grid forms required the subject to say whether each of his elements belonged to the emergent or implicit (contrast) pole of each construct. For example, he might simply categorize all people to be judged as *friendly* or *snobbish* and then re-categorize them as *nervy* or *easy going* and so forth. Thus a matrix was constructed with the elements along the top and the constructs down the side and each cell in the matrix represented the intersect of construct and element. A tick might be used to signify that the element occupied the emergent pole of the construct and the cell could be left blank if the element occupied the implicit pole. On such a grid, the subject is, in effect, rating the elements on two point scales.

The degree of relationship between constructs in this type of dichotomous grid is expressed as a 'matching score'. This is derived by taking the two rows representing two constructs and counting the numbers of corresponding ticks and blanks. By chance one would expect half the cells to correspond and the degree of deviation from chance could be calculated and marked plus or minus to indicate whether the constructs were positively or negatively related. It should be noted that negative or positive relationship is a function of which way round the poles of the two constructs are placed in relation to each other. Each row of ticks or blanks can be regarded as a kind of operational definition of a construct given by the subject. Equally, each column of ticks or blanks is a kind of personality profile of the element as drawn up by the subject. Just as relationships between constructs can be calculated by scanning the *rows* for matches, so similarities and differences between people, as viewed by the subject, can be quantified by scanning the *columns* for the degree to which they match each other.

Statistically, difficulties are encountered in this form of grid if the subject is permitted to nominate as few or as many elements as he likes for each pole of the grid. This can result in heavily lopsided lines with either very few ticks or very few blanks and this in turn may give rise to misleading matching scores. This difficulty can be overcome by forcing the subject to divide his elements equally between the two poles of each construct, but the statistical problem is then

										Elements										Constructs
1	2	3	4	5	6	7	8	9	10	11	12	13	14	15	16	17	18	19	20	
x		x	x	x					x		x			x	x		x		x	1. *generous – mean*
x		x	x		x			x	x		x			x		x		x		2. *lazy – energetic*
x		x	x			x		x	x		x			x		x			x	3. *musical – tone deaf*
x			x	x	x	x	x			x			x			x			x	4. *going places – stick-in-the-muds* etc.

Matching Scores

Note: chance expectancy is 10 and the matchings can therefore, for convenience, be recorded as positive or negative deviations from chance level, e.g. $16 = +6$, $8 = -2$, $10 = 0$.

1-2	−4	2-3	−2	3-4	0
1-3	+4	2-4	−6		
1-4	+4				

TABLE 26.1
Split-half form

resolved at the cost of creating psychological difficulties for the subject and a degree of confusion about what the subject's test behaviour implies. The procedures involved in this kind of equal division grid technique are usually referred to as the split-half method and an example of part of a grid of this type is given above as Table 26.1 with matching scores (expressed as a deviation from chance) given below the table.

In later variations of grid method, subjects were asked to rank order their elements on the constructs and the 'matching score' was replaced by a 'relationship score'. This was derived by working out the Spearman *rhos* of the rank orders of the various pairs of constructs and then squaring each rho and multiplying it by 100 to give a 'variance in common' score. This latter procedure was adopted since correlations cannot be directly used as scores, being non-linear. This rank order type of grid yields greater variance (scores can range from plus 100 through zero to minus 100) and thus allows a grid test to be constructed with a far smaller number of elements. Eight or ten elements are sufficient for rank ordering purposes but at least 20 to 30 elements are needed if a valid matching score pattern is to be extracted from a dichotomous grid. There is considerable doubt as to whether the increase in variance using rank ordering systems represents any actual gain in meaningful measurement. A discussion of this point is available in Mair and Boyd (1967).

An example of part of a rank order grid is shown in Table 26.2 with relation-ship scores given immediately below the Table. Tables can be prepared which will considerably shorten the labour of calculating Spearman rhos for particular numbers of elements and an example of such a table is available in Bannister and Fransella (1967).

Elements										Constructs
1 2 3 4 5 6 7 8 9 10										
10 9 8 7 6 5 4 3 2 1										1. *artistic – philistine*
1 2 3 4 5 6 7 8 9 10										2. *intelligent – stupid*
1 2 8 7 6 5 4 3 9 10										3. *keep promises – let you down*

Note: here rank positions are entered in the body of the table. The resulting correlations (Spearman's rho) and relationship scores (variance in common $= \text{rho}^2 \times 100$ retaining sign) are shown below.

	rho		relationship score
1–2	−1·0	=	−100
1–3	−0·58	=	−34
2–3	+0·58	=	+34

TABLE 26.2
Rank order form

In Bannister and Mair (1968) there is a discussion of the rating form of grid administration. Here the subject is asked to rate each of his elements on a 7-point scale, the end points of the scale being anchored into the two poles of the construct. Relationships between constructs could then be derived by converting the ratings into split half dichotomous rows or converting them into rankings or calculating difference scores directly from the two sets of ratings which represent each pair of constructs. The advantage of this type of administration is that it allows the subject considerable freedom to express his construing in a natural and unforced manner. If, for example, elements for him are lopsidedly distributed on a particular construct, then he could reflect this in his ratings.

A contemporary difficulty in grid research is that little information is available as to whether or not these various methods of grid administration are equivalent in terms of the picture they yield of the subject's construct system. There has been a tendency to use them interchangeably on grounds of convenience, but although they have an underlying rationale in common, it would seem safer not to assume equivalence until the psychological effects on the subject of administrative variations have been thoroughly investigated.

2 Analysis of grids

The relationships between constructs as expressed by matching scores, Spearman *rhos* or other indices, are the basic data derived from grids in that they represent the network of linkages between constructs. However, they can be processed to give a variety of specific measures.

For example, comparisons can be made between a given set of relationships culled from one subject, and normative data from a number of subjects which can be assumed to represent the *mean* relationship between a set of constructs. Such comparisons might be a rough index of the degree of idiosyncrasy in the construct patterning of each individual subject.

A qualitative comparison can be made between a grid derived set of construct relationships and what the subject imagines his construct relationship to be, in terms of direct verbal report by him. The discrepancy between the two might be regarded as a measure of 'insight' although neither test scores or verbal statements need be regarded as absolute criteria of 'truth'.

Types of 'social agreement' and 'insight' measure are illustrated in Bannister (1962b). The consistency of grid relationship scores over time, or from one set of elements to another, can be calculated and this might be regarded as an index of the degree of stability of the subject's construct system. Stability, in this sense, can be measured either as a simple function of time or in relation to the impact of varying validational fortunes. As an example of the pervasive relationship between grid method and construct theory, the idea of the purposive function of constructs can be cited. In construct theory terms the network of relationships between constructs constitutes the implicit anticipations of the subject and each interlinkage represents a prediction. Thus, for an individual who links the construct *punctual-unpunctual* to the construct *trustworthy-untrustworthy*, there is an implicit prediction on his part that anyone who is *trustworthy* will turn up on time. Since constructs are not merely labels or categories but are implicit predictions, then any act of construing can have one of three outcomes. The construer can be validated: that is to say the elements (ensuing events) behave appropriately in terms of the pole of the construct in which he has construed them. He can be invalidated: the elements behave in terms of the *contrast* pole of the construct which he used to construe them. The ensuing events can turn out to be outside the range of convenience of the construct which he utilized, so that he was neither right nor wrong but merely irrelevant. The use of grid method as a measure of the way in which individuals change the structure and content of their construct systems in relation to varying validational fortunes is illustrated in Bannister (1963, 1965).

Given a matrix of interrelationships such as is yielded by a grid, various forms of cluster analysis can be applied and a number have been developed. Most notable of these is a form of Principle Component Analysis developed by Slater (1967) which yields a map of the segment of a construct system under consideration and shows the loading of elements upon constructs and of constructs upon elements. Obviously the use of cluster analysis methods is potentially related to the construct theory idea that constructs are hierarchically related into a system. However, the psychological significance which can be attached to the factors derived from sophisticated forms of mathematical analysis is still obscure.

3 Principles of grid construction

Since there is no grid test as such, but only a very broad and complex methodological approach, no specifications of the 'Manual of Instruction' variety can be presented. In constructing a grid, a psychologist is involved in all the problems he would face in any novel experimental undertaking. He must decide what would be appropriate material for the subject to sort, what type of administration is most suitable, what area of construing he wishes to make the focus of the grid, what kind of analysis he intends to make of grid data and in what form he will cast his hypotheses so that they are testable in grid terms. In short, to devise a grid is to design an experiment. Some of the broad considerations which have to be borne in mind are discussed below.

In any single grid all elements must be within the range of convenience of all constructs or the subject must be permitted to specify when he is faced by a range of convenience problem. Construct theory argues that all constructs have limited ranges of convenience – that is to say that there are certain elements to which each construct is entirely inapplicable. It is difficult, for example, to construe Christmas cards in terms of the construct *electronic-mechanical*, or brass bands in terms of the construct *odd-even*. To force a subject to dimensionalize elements in terms of constructs which are not (for him personally) applicable is to produce spurious low intercorrelations between the constructs and a distorted picture of the conceptual framework which the subject is using. It should not be assumed from the gross examples given that this is an easy mistake to avoid. For example, in individual grids it has been found that some subjects use the construct *attractive-unattractive* as a way of differentiating between women but as being entirely inapplicable to men. The position of such a construct for such a subject, within the hierarchy of constructs, could only be examined if the elements presented for sorting were entirely women. Pilot testing or pre-test interviewing of the subject about the way in which he applies his constructs should help to avoid this source of error but the possibility that it has occurred should always be borne in mind when examining grid results.

A related source of difficulty has to do with the contexts in which particular constructs are applied. For example, the construct *delicate-robust* may have one set of implications for a subject when it is utilized in the context of porcelain and quite other implications when it is applied within the context of people. Ideally, within a single grid, the subject should explicate his constructs with an unchanging context in view.

What is being examined in a grid investigation is the *personal* construct system of the subject. It must not be assumed that the subject's meaning for any verbal label is identical with that which would be given to it by the psychologist. For example, a subject from whom was elicited the construct *conservative* gave as its contrast pole *generous* – i.e. the construct *conservative* had to do with attitude to money and was not perhaps the more conventional *conservative-radical* political construct. The construct relationship scores themselves provide some safeguard here, in that if verbal labels are being used by the subject in their conventional sense, then the resulting construct relationships should prove to be approximately predictable in terms of 'conventional meaning'. The farther the psychologist moves from the original requirements of the role construct repertory test, the more cautious the interpretation of test results needs to be. In Kelly's original form the subject worked with a sample of people who were significant in his life (in terms of the role titles by which they had been elicited) and constructs were not only *elicited* but both poles of each construct were articulated. This is a substantially different situation from that obtaining in some current forms of grid examination in which the materials may be photographs of people unknown to the subject and constructs are supplied in the form of single adjectives.

Where possible, grid results should be predicted in advance of testing; the normal scientific habit of placing bets before the race is run should apply. It is unfortunately both an easy and a fascinating task to explain a set of construct relationships appearing out of a grid performance in terms of what one imagines to be the psychopathology of the subject. However, this is *post hoc* wisdom and it is naturally preferable to set out specific hypotheses which both guide the construction of the grid and which are directly tested by grid results. Granted, in some cases, it may be necessary to use the grid initially as a dragnet or screening technique in order to derive hypotheses which can then be tested on subsequent grids or in terms of ensuing behaviour.

4 Limitations of grid technique

Although grid method provides operational definitions for some of the tenets of construct theory, it is by no means adequate as an experimental expression of the total theory. Inevitably, grid procedures provide only a very inadequate sample of an individual's construct system and in quantifying it they grossly oversimplify it. That this is so has been sharply illustrated by the development of a new form of grid by Hinkle (1965). This he terms an Implication Grid.

In this type of grid, the subject is no longer asked to sort elements in terms of his constructs nor is the relationship between the constructs inferred from statistical ratios between judgements. Instead, the subject is asked directly and explicitly to index the implications of each of his constructs for the other constructs in the grid.

In Hinkle's main experiment each subject provided 20 constructs. The first 10 of these were elicited by the usual triadic method and the second 10 were elicited by a new procedure termed 'laddering'. Hinkle began by selecting a construct derived by the triadic method and asking the subject who had given it to state at which pole he would prefer to see himself. Thus if the construct was say *well dressed-badly dressed* the subject might say that he would prefer to see himself as *well dressed*. He would then be asked why he preferred to see himself as *well dressed* and might reply that he felt that in this way he would make a *good impression on people*. He would then be asked why he wished to make a *good impression on people* (note the implied contrast pole of the construct— making a *bad impression on people*) and he might reply that this would enable him to form *good inter-personal relationships*. Again he would be asked why he would prefer to form *good interpersonal relationships* and the answer might be that in this way he would *develop himself as a personality* and so forth. The argument here is that the interrogation procedure causes the subject to go upwards through his construct system towards more superordinate constructs. Hinkle is here arguing that laddering provides an operational definition of superordinacy/ subordinacy, as this construct is used in personal construct theory.

In the Implication grid proper, Hinkle asked his subjects to examine each pair of constructs in turn and to say whether one implied the other or was implied by it. Thus, a matrix of direct linkages between constructs was prepared for each subject.

Finally, the subject was given yet a further type of grid, termed a Resistance to Change Grid. The subject was presented with his constructs two at a time and was asked to say which he would prefer to change on, if he had to move from his preferred pole to the unpreferred pole on one of the constructs. For example, he might be faced with the problem of whether he would prefer to cease being *musical* (preferred) and become *unmusical* or whether he would prefer to move from *intelligent* (preferred) to *stupid*. In this way constructs were eventually rank ordered for each subject from those which were most resistant to change down to those on which the subject would most readily alter his polar position.

Experimentally, Hinkle showed that those constructs which have the greater number of implications (in terms of the subject's own indexing on the Implication grid) were those constructs which were derived by laddering rather than by the triad method and that they were equally those constructs most resistant to change. Apart from the theoretical interest of the experiment and the operational definitions it supplies for the construct of subordinate-superordinate, the procedures highlight some of the limitations of element sorting grid method.

For example, Hinkle in his general approach emphasized the variety of relationships which can exist between a pair of constructs. Consider, for example, two constructs such as *asleep-awake* and *sings musically-sings unmusically. Awake* implies neither pole of the second construct, but either pole of the second construct implies *awake* and is negatively implied by *asleep*. A variety of forms of implicative inter-relationship between constructs is possible, but in element sorting grids they have to be reflected in a simple index of association such as correlation coefficient or a matching score. Such simple indices of association can only reflect reciprocal relationships between constructs and must necessarily conceal or distort the complexities of actual construct sytems.

Additionally, examination of the grids of Hinkle's subjects showed interesting contradictions. For example, in Resistance to Change Grids (since then it has been found to be true of Implication Grids) intransitivity was evident. That is to say that the subject would prefer to remain fixed on A rather than B and on B rather than C, but would prefer to remain fixed on C rather than A. This is a logical, though not apparently a psychological, impossibility and is of considerable interest in that such contradictions may be the centres of psychological conflict and the foci of potential change. However, such difficulties and contradictions cannot manifest themselves in standard element sorting grids since the very mathematics of this type of grid *enforce* consistency.

Finally the whole of Hinkle's experimental work tends to stress the importance of the position of constructs in the hierarchical network. As yet there is no proven way in an element sorting grid of detecting the difference between superordinate and subordinate constructs, although there has been a tendency to assume that those which account for a greater amount of the variance in correlational terms may be more superordinate.

5 Evaluation

The value and potential of grid method is still uncertain but indications of its usefulness can be found in diverse studies such as those on schizophrenic thought disorder (Bannister, 1960 *et seq.*) and the studies by Landfield on threat (1955 *et seq.*). Experimental examinations of grid method as such are available in Mair (1966 *et seq.*). A detailed examination of grids studies in relation to construct theory and more traditional perspectives in psychology is available in Bannister and Mair (1968). The prime danger for the future development of grid techniques would seem to lie in the risk of distorting them by regarding them as simply an addition to standard techniques of psychological measurement. The most useful and significant aspects of grid method arise out of its relationship to construct theory and it is doubtful if its full potential will be realized if we ignore theoretical implications and simply recast grid method into the mould of orthodox test measures.

III SEMANTIC DIFFERENTIAL

Osgood *et al.* (1957, 1962) sketched out a theory of meaning within the general framework of learning theory. It was argued that 'words represent things because they produce in human organisms some replica of the actual behaviour towards these things as a meditation process'. Thus, in stimulus response terms, Osgood appears to be arguing that a word is a stimulus which produces a pattern of behaviour similar to that originally produced by the object which the word represents. This general approach has met with criticisms on the grounds that it is oversimplified (e.g. Carroll, 1959). In any case Osgood's further definition of meaning as a multi-dimensional space in which a particular word will be represented by a specific position seems to owe much more to the factor analytic method which he used to develop the Semantic Differential rather than to the learning theory explanation he gives for 'meaning'.

The Semantic Differential is derived from a series of factor analytic studies, but since these were fairly standard in design only a general description is given. In a typical experiment, say 100 subjects would be provided with booklets containing 50 descriptive 7 point scales, each end of each scale being named. These scales were originally chosen from a Thesaurus and might include items such as *rough-smooth, good-bad, large-small, beautiful-ugly, yellow-blue, hard-soft, sweet-sour, strong-weak, clean-dirty* and so forth. On each of these 7-point scales subjects were asked to rate a number of concepts such as *lady, boulder, sin, father, lake, symphony, Russian, feather, me* and so forth. Given 50 scales, 20 concepts and 100 subjects, a study would generate a 50 by 20 by 100 cube of data with each scale position being assigned a number 1-7 arbitrarily from left to right and each cell in this cube containing a number representing the judgement of a particular concept on a particular scale by a particular subject. Such data were summed over both subjects and concepts to generate an intercorrelational matrix of every scale with every other scale. The matrix was then factor analysed and the resulting factors labelled by examining the scales most highly loaded on them and speculatively determining their common aspect.

Such studies repeatedly produced what was termed an *evaluative* factor which usually accounted for about 35 % of the total variance and which is best defined by the scale *good-bad*. Other scales which loaded on this factor were *wise-foolish, beautiful-ugly, cruel-kind, successful-unsuccessful, true-false* and so forth. A second factor which usually accounted for about $7\frac{1}{2}$% of the total variance often emerged which was labelled *potency* since it was usually best defined by the *potent-impotent* scale and carried high loadings for scales such as *hard-soft, masculine-feminine, strong-weak*. A third factor of about equal strength to *potency* was labelled *activity* and this was usually best defined by the *active-passive* scale with loadings on *excitable-calm, fast-slow*, and so forth. Other factors emerged in each study but varied considerably from study to study and usually accounted for so little of the variance as to be of doubtful empirical value. It should be noted that the *evaluative* factor was by far the most stable in experimental terms, since in some studies the potency and activity factors would combine (being then labelled *dynamism*) or each would show loadings on scales which were normally related to the other factor.

These three factors were made the basis of the final measuring instrument and in practice Osgood's multi-dimensional semantic space turned out to be tri-dimensional.

1 The Semantic Differential in practice

In testing an individual or group with the Semantic Differential a number of scales are selected which, between them, will define the three major nomothetic dimensions of *evaluation, activity* and *potency*. Concepts are supplied to the subject which have particular relevance to the study in hand and the subjects are asked to rate each concept on each 7-point scale. Analysis of Semantic Differential data can be either in terms of specific ratings of concepts on scales or, if the purpose is to compare the meaning of two concepts or to compare two people for the way they rate the same concept, then a difference score is used. The precise score used is designated Dil and it is the total linear distance between the concepts in the semantic space defined by the three dimensions. The formula for Dil is:

$$\text{Dil} = \sqrt{\sum_{jd_{\imath\imath}}^{2}}$$

For example, the rating of two words X and Y by a single subject on the three concepts, a, b and c (which may be assumed to define the three major dimensions) may be as follows (the working out of the difference score is shown below):

```
          1    2    3    4    5    6    7
   a X:    :    :    :    Y :       :
   b   :    : X :       : Y :       :
   c   :    :    : X : Y :       :
```

$$\text{Dil} = \sqrt{(1-5)^2 \ + \ (3-5)^2 \ + \ (4-5)^2}$$
$$= \sqrt{16 \ \ \ + \ \ 4 \ \ \ + \ \ 1}$$
$$= \sqrt{21}$$
$$= \ \ 4.65$$

Difference scores may be compared (in the absence of normative data) with an expected zero if the words have completely the same meaning on these three dimensions and the expected 10·4 if the words have completely different and opposite meanings from each other.

Examples of the use of the Semantic Differential can be found in Osgood and Luria (1954). This paper describes the famous 'Eve' case of multiple personality, and demonstrates that the Semantic Differential can be regarded as a personality measure in its own right – a point of some theoretical interest.

There are a number of theoretical and practical problems which arise in

2 C

relation to the Semantic Differential, some of which have been discussed by writers such as Gulliksen (1958), Brown (1958) and others. They include the following.

The repeated finding of marked scale-concept interaction in the type of factor analytic data on which the Semantic Differential is based (see Dalziel, 1960) casts doubt on the legitimacy of the general pooling procedures which Osgood used to derive his basic dimensions. An example of such a scale-concept inter-action occurs in relation to the scale *deep-shallow* which loads on to the evaluative dimensions in terms of the concept sonar but not in terms of other concepts.

The assumption in the Semantic Differential that there are three major dimensions of meaning which are orthogonal to each other is based on the averaging of many individual protocols within which the dimensions may not, in fact, be orthogonal. Thus, a massive cancelling out effect may have taken place and this makes the use of three dimensions as a framework for viewing the meaning attached to terms by particular individuals a dubious venture. Experimental work relating to this possibility and utilizing both repertory grid and Semantic Differential techniques is reported in Fransella (1965).

On face inspection it seems possible that the Semantic Differential faces subjects with rather tricky psychological problems. For example, many may not find the opposites given for the scales true opposites from their point of view or equally they may face range of convenience problems such as were implied by Brown (1958) when he entitled an article critical of the Semantic Differential 'Is a boulder sweet or sour?'

2 Illustrative studies

The very considerable number of studies reported in the first decade of the Semantic Differential's existence suggest that the technique fits in well with the economics of experimental psychology and that a considerable demand exists for a measuring instrument with 'meaning' as its target. Three studies which illustrate the diversity of uses found for the Semantic Differential are cited below.

Warr and Knapper (1966) used the Semantic Differential in the field of interperson perception. They studied the general view taken of a stimulus person by subjects and the effect of communications about that person with particular biases. In their first experiment the person employed as the stimulus was a leading politician and their subjects were asked to rate him on twelve 9-point Semantic Differential scales. These were selected so that each of the three major factors was represented by 4 scales thus: *true-false, wise-foolish, sweet-sour, fair-unfair* (defining evaluation), *strong-weak, hard-soft, large-small, rugged-delicate* (defining potency) and *sharp-dull, hot-cold, active-passive, fast-slow* (defining activity). A week later each subject was presented with one of two narrative reports of a speech made by the politician. The two reports were drawn from national newspapers and differed in how favourably they reported the speech.

Subjects were asked to complete the Semantic Differential with exactly the same scales using as their concept the politician's *performance* in giving the speech. The two Semantic Differentials for each subject were then compared in order to calculate the differential effect of the two narrative reports. The effects *were* differential and on a number of scales one of the narrative reports had resulted in a more positive picture being generated. However, it is noteworthy that there remained a significant positive correlation between the two Semantic Differentials for each subject, indicating that if a subject holds the opinion that the stimulus person is a *wise* person, he tends to perceive his behaviour in accordance with the expectation that it will be relatively *wise*. The experiment was repeated using a different and politically opposed stimulus figure with broadly the same results. The experiment confirms the ease with which subjects can rate actual people on the Semantic Differential and shows it used in the context of a manipulative experiment with experimental intervention, as contrasted with its more frequent use in 'survey' contexts.

Hooper and Padden (1965) were interested in what they called the 'enduring perceptions' of nurses when working in a psychiatric milieu, and particularly those which relate to social discriminations. Their subjects were 11 nurses who had long experience on a particular therapeutic community ward. They were asked to complete a Semantic Differential which involved them in rating three concepts on fourteen 7-point scales. The three concepts were 'the social position of a Hillview nurse', 'the social position of a Hillview ward patient' and 'the social position of a Hillview ward doctor' (Hillview being the particular therapeutic community ward which was the focus of interest for the study). The scales were selected from polar adjectives known from previous studies to load on to the three major dimensions and to these were added *therapeutic-untherapeutic* and *well-ill*, which had been found to load on *potency* in a previous study. An initial comparison of mean ratings showed that while the 'social position' concepts of nurse and doctor did not differ significantly, the concept of patient differed significantly from both nurse and doctor. When the differences were broken down into their scale source, it was found that patients had been judged more towards the latter pole on the scales *well-ill* and *calm-excited*. A cluster analysis of the semantic ratings confirmed that the patient stereotype was one of 'disturbance or illness and not one of badness or unimportance'. A further breakdown of the ratings which discriminated between the long and short service nurse showed that the former rated the patient as rather more responsible, calmer and more active. In general the results were taken to confirm that the therapeutic community system had not entirely blurred distinctions between staff and patients but it had related them to treatment rather than to authority as such. The study illustrates how data from one Semantic Differential experiment can be carried forward as the basis for more elaborated studies, since it followed and related to a similar investigation by Talbot, Miller and White (1961). The use of a form of linkage analysis (McQuitty, 1957) demonstrates that the Semantic Differential user is in no sense dependent upon or limited to its original factor analytic base but can subject new Semantic Differential data to cluster analysis in its own right.

Brown (1964) used the Semantic Differential to investigate the intentions underlying changes in the titles of books when they were given a paperback edition following their original hardback presentation. He located eight books which had had their titles changed in this way and presented the 16 titles as concepts to be rated on 13 Semantic Differential scales which had been chosen to represent the three factors of evaluation, potency and activity. A comparison between the ratings given in dimensional terms to the original titles and the paperback titles showed a general shift which lowered the position of the books *evaluatively* and heightened them in terms of *potency*. Although these results can be interpreted in various ways, it is interesting to note that here Osgood's three dimensions provide the framework, and thereby the potential hypotheses, for explaining the intention of the publishers in making the title changes.

It is worthy of note that in these, as in many other studies, the psychologists making use of the Semantic Differential seem well content with its flexibility, particularly its capacity to accept many different types of concept for rating, but find it necessary to stress that what seems to be measured is 'connotative' (or 'metaphorical') meaning.

Future development of the Semantic Differential may hinge on the issue of whether to measure in terms of the nomothetic dimensions elucidated by Osgood or cluster analyse each new set of differential data in an attempt to picture its underlying axes afresh. In so far as the latter course is adopted grid and differential may well move closer since the grid involves the kind of matrix analysis for each individual's data that Osgood performed for large normative groups.

IV CONCLUSIONS

There are major differences, both of theory and practice, between grid method and the Semantic Differential, and Bannister and Mair (1968) have argued that they represent two sharply contrasting approaches within psychology as a discipline. Yet viewed from other angles they stand together in contrast to many traditional perspectives.

Both ignore the orthodox distinction between cognition and personality (a descendant of older lay dichotomies such as reason and will, thought and passion). Psychologists have accepted the kind of chapter heading theory of man which segments him into 'areas' and thereby delayed the development of any coherent theoretical framework in psychology. Thus there is a psychology of 'problem solving' that largely ignores man solving personal problems because that is 'personality' and problem solving is 'cognition'. There is a psychology of 'perception' which has to have 'person perception' added as quite a new concern and so forth. Both grid and Semantic Differential can be variously viewed as 'cognitive' or 'personality' measures because, in essence, they are neither. They stem from the notion of man as seeking to make sense of his world, not as bifurcated into 'cognition' and 'drive' – although Osgood's theory for the Semantic Differential bows uneasily to this polarity. The habit of bracketing together 'concepts' and 'personality' (as in the title of this essay) reflects the awareness that the methods here discussed deny the distinction and they may well outlive such fragmented thinking in psychology.

Grid and differential are alike in that they are methods not tests and they are thereby in conflict with much of psychology's psychometric history. The notion of the 'variable' and the 'continuum' has proved pervasive in psychology, although, as Kelly pointed out, there is not much you can do with a variable except to let it sit on its own continuum. The unitary test habit has been prolonged and rationalized by trait psychology (and under 'trait' can be included the intelligence test era) and the development of methodological approaches such as grid and Semantic Differential may well initiate a movement away from the tautology of traits. Additionally they challenge the psychologist to elaborate his explanations and experimental intentions since they do not supply him with set *continua* but require a series of design decisions.

Finally, both techniques rest on the assumption that man interprets events and sees meaning in them. They imply that man does more than 'behave': he attaches significance to his own behaviour and that of others. Moreover he does this systematically for both 'semantic space' and 'the personal construct system' are systematic networks and imply that man is, in Lynn's (1957) phrase, a manufacturer of theories. This picture of man as an interpreter of his universe puts him on a level with the psychologist who 'studies' him and pushes psychology as a science towards reflexivity in the manner prescribed by Oliver and Landfield (1963). It moves psychologists away from mimicry of 19th century physical scientists pondering the pre-determined behaviour of organisms, towards an attempt to predict men by understanding what they intend. The significance of grid and Semantic Differential as techniques of psychological exploration may lie as much in the shift in approach which they portend, as in their present empirical returns.

REFERENCES

BANNISTER, D. (1960) Conceptual structure in thought disordered schizophrenics. *J. Ment. Sci.*, **106**, 1230.

BANNISTER, D. (1962a) Personal Construct Theory: A summary and experimental paradigm. *Acta. Psychol.*, **20**, 2, 104.

BANNISTER, D. (1962b) The nature and measurement of schizophrenic thought disorder. *J. Ment. Sci.*, **108**, 825.

BANNISTER, D. (1963) The genesis of schizophrenic thought disorder: a serial invalidation hypothesis. *Brit. J. Psychiat.*, **109**, 680.

BANNISTER, D. (1965) The genesis of schizophrenic thought disorder: re-test of the serial invalidation hypothesis. *Brit. J. Psychiat.*, **111**, 377.

BANNISTER, D. and FRANSELLA, FAY (1967) *A Grid Test of Schizophrenic Thought Disorder: A Standard Clinical Test.* Barnstaple: Psychological Test Publications.

BANNISTER, D. and MAIR, J. M. M. (1968) *The Evaluation of Personal Constructs.* London and New York: Academic Press.

BANNISTER, D. and SALMON, P. (1966) Schizophrenic thought disorder: specific or diffuse? *Brit. J. med. Psychol.*, **39**, 215.

BROWN, R. W. (1958) Is a boulder sweet or sour? *Contemp. Psychol.*, **3**, (5), 113.

BROWN, W. P. (1964) The titles of paperback books. *Brit. J. Psychol.*, **55** (3), 365.

CARROLL, J. B. (1959) The measurement of meaning: a review. *Lang.*, **35** (1), 58.

CARVER, M. V. (1967) *The critical evaluation of films by repertory grid.* Unpub. Ph.D. Thesis, London Univ.

COMBS, A. W. and SNYGG, D. (1949) *Individual Behaviour.* New York: Harper and Brothers.

DALZIEL, F. R. (1960) *An experimental study of the concept of meaning.* Unpub· Ph.D. Thesis, Univ. of Aberdeen.

FRANSELLA, FAY (1965) *The effects of imposed rhythm and certain aspects of personality in the speech of stutterers.* Unpub. Ph.D. Thesis, Univ. of London.

FRANSELLA, FAY and ADAMS, B. (1965) An illustration of the use of repertory grid technique in a clinical setting. *Brit. J. soc. clin. Psychol.*, **5**, 51.

GULLIKSEN, H. (1958) How to make meaning more meaningful. *Contemp. Psychol.*, **3**, (5) 115.

HINKLE, D. N. (1965) *The change of personal constructs from the viewpoint of a theory of implications.* Unpub. Ph.D. Thesis, Ohio State University.

HOOPER, D. and PADDEN, D. (1965) Psychiatric roles and their meaning. *Brit. J. soc. clin. Psychol.*, **4** (1), 35.

JESSOR, R. (1958) The problem of reductionism in psychology. *Psych. Bull.*, **65** (3), 170.

KELLY, G. A., (1955) *The Psychology of Personal Constructs*, Vols. I and II. New York: Norton.

KELLY, G. A. (1963) *A Theory of Personality.* New York: Norton.

KELLY, G. A. (1969) *Clinical Psychology and Personality: the selected papers of George Kelly.* Ed. B. A. Maher. John Wiley and Sons: New York-London.

LANDFIELD, A. W. (1955) Self-predictive orientation and the movement interpretation of threat. *J. abn. soc. Psychol.*, **51**, 434.

LYNN, D. B. (1957) The organism as a manufacturer of theories. *Psych. Rep.*, **3**, 353.

MCQUITTY, L. L. (1957) Elementary linkage analysis for isolating orthogonal types and typal relevancies. *Educ. Psychol. Meas.*, **17**, 207.

MAIR, J. M. M. (1966) Prediction of grid scores. *Brit. J. Psychol.*, **57** (1 and 2), 187.

MAIR, J. M. M. and BOYD, P. R. (1967) A comparison of two grid forms. *Brit. J. soc. clin. Psychol.*, **6**, 220.

OLIVER, W. D. and LANDFIELD, A. W. (1963) Reflexivity: an unfaced issue of psychology. *J. indiv. Psychol.*, **29**, 187.

OSGOOD, C. E. (1962) Studies on the generality of affective meaning systems. *Am. Psychol.*, **17** (1), 10.

OSGOOD, C. E. and LURIA, Z. (1954) A blind analysis of a case of multiple personality using the semantic differential. *J. abnormal Soc. Psychol.*, **49**, 579.

OSGOOD, C. E., SUCI, G. J. and TANNENBAUM, P. H. (1957) *The Measurement of Meaning*. Urbana: Univ. of Ill. Press.

POPPER, K. R. (1963) *Conjectures and Refutations*. London: Routledge and Kegan Paul.

SECHREST, L. B. (1963) The psychology of personal constructs: George Kelly. *In* WEPMAN, J. M. and HEINE, R. W. (Eds.) *Concepts of Personality*. Chicago: Aldine.

SLATER, P. (1967) *Notes on Ingrid* 1967. Maudsley Hospital: Biometrics Unit.

TALBOT, E., MILLER, S. C. and WHITE, R. B. (1961) Some aspects of self conceptions and role demands in a therapeutic community. *J. abn. soc. Psychol.*, **63**, 338.

WARR, P. B. and KNAPPER, C. (1966) The role of expectancy and communication content in indirect person perception. *Brit. J. soc. clin. Psychol.*, **4** (1), 35.

27

Personality and illness

T. M. Caine

I INTRODUCTION

The work to be described in the present chapter has its roots and rationale in practical clinical problems. The research interest throughout has been in the refinement and systematization of observations concerning psychiatric patients rather than in the development of a general theory of psychology or psychopathology, and in relating these observations to concrete clinical questions frequently asked of clinical psychologists in their everyday work.

It is our conviction that knowledge cannot be pursued without classification. In the suggested framework of classification to be described, we have remained within the historical pyschiatric tradition, partly because of our respect for the acute and detailed clinical observations of the classical psychiatrists, but mainly because the questions asked of the clinical psychologist by his psychiatric colleagues in their professional work are likely to be formulated within this tradition. As Foulds, who has never underrated the value of clinical experience as a valid source of knowledge and hypotheses, writes:

> Clinical psychologists are fortunate in entering an area in which the subjects of their enquiries have been so thoroughly observed by their psychiatric colleagues. In no other branch of psychology are psychologists at such an advantage. It seems unduly optimistic to assume that general psychology has so much to offer that psychologists can, with scant regard for existing psychiatric knowledge, abruptly set up their experiments and produce meaningful results .... It would be surprising, and indeed disquieting, if the foundations of an experimental science of abnormal behaviour looked utterly different from what psychiatrists had always thought them to be. This is not to say that the roof may not eventually look different, meantime psychiatrists should bear the confirmation of their observations with benign resignation (Foulds, 1965).

In a further defence of this position it can be argued that at bottom general principles of judgement abstracted in science (and philosophy) are arrived at only through reflection upon particular judgements exercised in particular, practical situations, the dicta of Occam's razor and the hypothetico-deductive method notwithstanding. In addition, one might consider the role played by the scientist's own value judgements, biases, and personal assumptions in his choice of hypotheses and method of inquiry even in the more advanced physical

2 C*

sciences (Caine and Smail, 1969). From a more practical point of view, however, it can simply be remarked that abnormal and clinical psychology have not developed to the stage where precise, definitive experiments can be carried out in many important areas, even if they were ethically possible or the subject matter appropriate. Foulds (1965) has observed that the social sciences suffer from the handicap that the object of study answers back. Indeed, such a verbal response may be a condition of the experiment. There is no guarantee, however, that it is solely determined by our carefully defined *experimental* stimulus for as Klein (1958) has pointed out, even the rigorously controlled psychophysical experiment in which maximal accuracy is intended is not free of selective response. The subject's *report* of what he sees in a perceptual experiment is an active process of sifting and choosing among alternatives and this can hold true even in the compulsive world of the psychotic (Caine, 1966). From this point of view refinements of statistical analyses have quite outstripped the precision of our measuring instruments and our capacity to decide just what it is we are or should be observing. As Tukey (1962) has indicated, statistical refinements in research may take our attention away from the crudity of the basic data involved and are by no means substitutes for the common sense required in evaluating results (Bakan, 1966). It is true that certain assumptions, or hypotheses, have directed our observations – that hostility and guilt have something to do with mental breakdown, for example. It is also true, however, that these assumptions have derived from clinical observation and experience rather than from scientific experiment.

II HISTORICAL BACKGROUND

Some years ago Foulds found himself diagnosing hysteria on the basis of test results more frequently than his psychiatric colleagues cared to do on a clinical basis. Patients provisionally classified by psychiatrists as anxiety states or neurotic depressives were sent to the psychology department for diagnostic testing and duly returned as hysterics. Some weeks later the clinical picture seemed to confirm the test results. This occurred with sufficient regularity to suggest the possibility that the psychiatrists were initially concentrating on presenting *symptoms* whereas the psychological tests might be measuring the underlying *personality traits*. With some symptom relief following removal from environmental stress and drug treatments, certain dominant personality traits might re-emerge and influence the clinical diagnosis. In clinical work the term 'hysteria' is frequently used to cover a very wide range of psychological phenomena including the 'hysterical personality'. Chodoff and Lyons (1958), for example, list five ways in which the term 'hysteria' is currently used:

1. a particular kind of psychosomatic symptomatology called conversion hysteria or conversion reaction;
2. a psychoneurotic disorder characterized by phobias and/or certain anxiety manifestations – called anxiety hysteria;

3. a particular psychopathological pattern;
4. a pattern of behaviour habitually exhibited by people said to have hysterical personalities or hysterical characters;
5. a term of approbrium.

Slater (1965), considers that the term is used so loosely as to be virtually meaningless. A similar situation pertains for the diagnosis 'obsessional' (Sandler and Hazari, 1960). Foulds (1955) published a preliminary study of this problem in which some suggestive evidence was presented and the arguments concerning classification in *Personality and Personal Illness* (Foulds, 1965) were anticipated.

A notion that neurotics can be diagnosed in terms of both symptom complexes and personality trait constellations is not new although it is often ignored. A history of these concepts, together with a description of the conflicting theories concerning their respective aetiologies and relationship has been given elsewhere (Caine, 1965a). This review may be briefly summarized.

Pierre Janet is credited with the first attempt to dichotomize symptoms and personality traits in neurotics (Mackinnon, 1944). Symptoms were classified into hysteria and psychasthenia, personality traits into obsessoid and hysteroid. This distinction has been widely accepted by textbook writers although the term psychasthenia has become unfashionable and is usually replaced by anxiety state, depression or perhaps dysthymia. Among the writers who have accepted Janet's distinctions are Kretschmer (1926), Bowlby (1940), Lewis and Mapother (1941), Fenichel (1945), Curran and Guttman (1949), and Mayer-Gross, Slater and Roth (1954). It is therefore curious that most clinicians are disinclined to make a double classification of, say, 'hysteria in a hysteroid personality', 'hysteria in an obsessoid personality', 'dysthymia in a hysteroid personality', or 'dysthymia in an obsessoid personality'. All too frequently one encounters the single description 'anxiety state' or 'hysterical personality'. This is unfortunate, since such diagnoses undoubtedly contribute to the notoriously low reliability of psychiatric diagnosis within the neuroses, both from the point of view of agreement between diagnosticians and re-diagnosis by the same clinician.

At least three main schools of thought about the nature of the relationship between symptom complexes and trait constellations can be described. Janet himself represents the first school, which postulates that an underlying weakness of psychological synthesis produces both the symptoms and the traits. Both are evidence of an underlying psychopathology, a failure of personal synthesis and integration. In Janet's view the hysteric and hysterical personality share this condition with criminals and imbeciles. Fenichel (1945) agrees with Janet in that he feels that the respective character traits develop simultaneously with the symptoms, but he thinks that the development of the character structure may actually prevent the development of symptoms.

The second school considers that the symptoms are dependent on the traits: thus an obsessive-compulsive neurosis appears when the defensive thoughts and acts of the person of obsessoid personality become too pervasive and deviant

(Masserman, 1946; Noyes, 1954). For Reich (1949) there are only fluid transitions from compulsive symptoms to the corresponding personality traits; similarly Michaels and Porter (1949) consider that an obsessional neurosis is a pathological exaggeration of the normal character. Rapaport (1948) believes that an obsessional neurosis inevitably follows the breakdown of the obsessional character. Jung (1920), who may be said to belong to this second school, considers that the traits precede the illness and are more enduring; he quotes Binet who pointed out that 'the neurotic only accentuates and shows in relief the characteristic traits of his personality'.

Thus, for the second school, traits precede symptoms and are more enduring, but when symptoms do develop, they are an exacerbation of the pre-existing traits. This is regarded as a sufficient explanation of the form taken by the symptoms.

The present series of studies belongs to a third school which maintains that there is no *necessary* connection between symptoms and personality traits (Lewis and Mapother, 1941; Curran and Guttman, 1949; Mayer-Gross *et al.*, 1954; Chodoff and Lyons, 1958; Forrest, 1967; Rosenberg, 1967). On this view not all persons exhibiting obsessional or hysterical symptoms have the corresponding constellations of personality traits. Anxiety states and neurotic and psychotic depressives are more commonly associated with obsessoid personalities than are obsessive or compulsive states. Table 27.1 shows the incidence of association of symptom complex and personality type, as rated by psychiatrists, occurring in one study involving 68 successive admissions to a mental hospital (Foulds and Caine, 1958a).

Hysterics of hysteroid personality	16
Hysterics of obsessoid personality	4
Dysthymics of hysteroid personality	26
Dysthymics of obsessoid personality	22

TABLE 27.1

Thus the dysthymics were fairly evenly split between the hysteroid and obsessoid personalities. In their series of patients Slater and Slater (1944) found correlations of the following order between symptoms and traits:

Obsessional and compulsive symptoms and obsessoid personality	0·8
hysteria and hysteroid personality	0·5

In a later summary of research findings with regard to symptoms and personality, particularly in the field of genetics, Slater (1950) concluded that personality has a physical basis. Neurosis he considered to be the result of an interaction between personality and environment, with the environment playing an important part in precipitating the illness and even, to some extent, determining the nature and symptomatology. On the whole he maintained that 'the specific quality of the neurotic reaction is, however, principally derived from the personality'.

It can be argued, then, that although there is disagreement about the precise mechanisms involved in symptom formation in a personality type, systematic observation supports the view that symptom complexes and personality trait constellations can be distinguished clinically. Before much progress in this area can be expected, it seemed to us that an essential first step is a refinement and objectification of the relevant measuring instruments.

The following is a detailed list of the symptom syndromes and personality trait constellations which originally concerned us.

Dysthymia

Anxiety: palpitations, breathlessness, hand tremors, excessive perspiring, generalized anxiety, phobias, tension and insomnia.

Depression: loss of interest, suicidal thoughts, suicidal attempts, lack of energy, depression, poor concentration, poor memory, retardation, crying.

Obsessional states: distress from repetitive, pointless thoughts, excessive concern over cleanliness, compulsions and prohibitions.

Hysteria

Hysteria: No organic basis for, loss of use of some bodily part, loss of feeling in the skin, blurred vision, amnesia, preoccupation about physical health, fits, blackouts.

Personality trait constellations (dichotomized)

hysteroid	obsessoid
excessive display of emotions	scarcely any display of emotions
vivid daydreams which come to be half believed	complete inability to indulge in fanciful thinking
very frequent mood changes	mood tends to remain extremely constant
completely lacking in conscience	often conscience stricken
given to precipitate action	slow and undecided owing to weighing of pros and cons
childishly over-dependent	obstinately independent
careless and inaccurate	stickler for precision
emotions appear shallow	appears to feel things deeply
extreme desire to impress and gain attention	extremely self-effacing

---

TABLE 27.2
Symptom syndromes and personality trait constellations.

III THE PRESENT RESEARCHES

Following Foulds' pilot study (Foulds, 1955) our first attempts to measure these different aspects of psychological functioning were carried out at Runwell

Hospital in 1958 and 1959 (Foulds and Caine, 1958a, 1959a). In the first of these studies, 68 women neurotics between the ages 20 and 59 successively admitted to the hospital over a 14-month period were psychologically tested on a wide range of tests on admission and diagnosed clinically according to the double classification described. The psychiatric diagnosis, arrived at independently of test results, which was entered in the official records was accepted.

For the personality classification two psychiatrists independently rated the pre-morbid personality of subjects on a five-point Hysteroid-Obsessoid rating scale composed of the traits dichotomized as above.

The re-rating reliability correlation after an average interval of one month was 0·65. The inter-psychiatrist correlation was 0·67. In 14% of the cases on the initial personality rating, on which the classification was based, the two psychiatrists failed to agree on the category. A third rater was then used to decide the issue. The resulting distribution of cases is shown in Table 27.1.

The psychological tests employed were the Mill Hill Vocabulary Scale, the Progressive Matrices (1938), the Porteus Mazes, the Thematic Apperception Test, the Minnesota Multiphasic Personality Inventory, the Superiority-Inferiority Index and the Tapping Test.

The Mill Hill Vocabulary Scale and the Progressive Matrices intelligence test were included in the battery for obvious reasons and were given with their standard administration. Although the Matrices were untimed the time taken by the subject to complete each set was noted with her knowledge.

The Porteus Maze Test, involving the tracing through of an increasingly complex series of mazes, was chosen because Porteus (1942), Chapuis (1949) and Foulds (1951, 1952b) have emphasized the orectic factors involved in this psychomotor exercise. The ability to thread mazes is thought by Porteus to depend on such qualities as prudence, forethought and planning rather than simply on intelligence. In experimental work Foulds has found differences in the quality of performance between various diagnostic groups on an administration of the test designed to accentuate 'temperamental' differences. In his view a high proportion of psychoneurotic and psychotic subjects deviate markedly from the normal tempo in many diverse activities. Time taken to start tracing the mazes and total time taken were accordingly included in the scoring system. In addition the number of lines crossed, number of wrong directions taken, waviness of the pencil line and the number of times the pencil was lifted contrary to the administrative instructions were noted. A measure of distraction was devised in which the subject had to repeat numbers after the tester while tracing the mazes a second time. The distraction effect was calculated by taking the time taken on the second performance as a percentage of the time taken on the first performance.

In his initial studies using the Porteus Mazes Foulds found the following characteristic maze performances:

Hysterics (and psychopaths). Start without prolonged delay and then proceed rapidly. The pencil line is relatively smooth and even flowing but a large number of maze lines are crossed. They have a low score for lifted pencils since pencils are most frequently lifted at choice points and these subjects tend to hesitate rather less than others. Foulds interprets these findings as suggestive of impulsivity and carelessness. On entering a cul-de-sac they characteristically wheel about immediately; this is observed without obvious signs of tension such as an increase in the waviness or pressure of the line or lifting the pencil.

The dysthymic groups. Anxiety states. Start slowly and then work reasonably quickly but progress is jerky and accomplished only with a very tremulous line, which results in their crossing many lines. Foulds interprets this as an indication of their inability to make decisions.

Reactive (neurotic) depressives. The tempo is slow throughout, which enables them to avoid crossing an undue number of lines. Foulds feels that these subjects are slow to adjust to the total situation and therefore they tend to make frequent errors in the early stages and forget to heed the instructions about lifting the pencil. There is a slight tendency for depressives to proceed further up blocked roads than other subjects. They sometimes stop, say they have gone wrong and then continue further in the wrong direction, often making self-deprecatory remarks.

Obsessionals. Rather slow tempo throughout, with relative freedom from very gross errors of direction and few lifted pencils. They produce firm, straight lines down the centre of the channel with careful right-angled cornering. There are consequently very few crossed lines.

In his consideration of these results Foulds maintains that the main differentiation on the test, as far as the neuroses are concerned, is between hysterics on the one hand and anxiety states, reactive depressives and obsessionals on the other – i.e. the dysthymic group. Interestingly there is no significant difference between hysterics, psychopaths and normals.

The Thematic Apperception Test was included since an objective method of scoring had previously been devised by Foulds (1952b) and related to hysterics and dysthymics. As with the Porteus Maze Test, the *way* in which the T.A.T. was tackled by the subjects served as the basis of measuring differences. Thus Foulds found that hysterics start their stories more quickly than dysthymics and tell longer stories at a higher speed. Starting time, fluency (the number of words spoken per minute) and productivity (mean number of words per picture) were all used as diagnostic measures in this later investigation. Although Foulds had also found that the type of story recounted tended to differ for the two groups his method of scoring this remained very crude and the decision was taken to concentrate on the rating (by three judges) of *hostility* themes.

The Minnesota Multiphasic Personality Inventory seemed an obvious choice for the battery to determine both the relation between the clinical scales and the double clinical classification and to allocate Siegel's Hostility Scale (Siegel, 1956) as a symptom or a personality measure. Siegel's scale is drawn from the M.M.P.I. and consists, in the main, of some 50 miscellaneous items expressing outwardly directed hostility.

Two other lesser known tests were included since they looked promising. One of these was the Superiority-Inferiority Index (Foulds, 1958). This is a 'self-concept' type of test along the lines of Rosenzweig's Picture Frustration (P-F) Study (Rosenzweig, 1945) in which the subject must select the response, from four alternatives, that he would most likely make in a number of frustrating situations described by the test. In addition he must also decide what is the *ideal* response and also how *most people* might respond. Although the given alternatives can be classified under Rosenzweig's three types of extrapunitive, intropunitive and impunitive, the Superiority-Inferiority Index is essentially a measure of how close one approaches one's ideal of conduct *vis-à-vis* other people. A positive score, shown by a greater distance from the ideal of most people than of the self, indicates that the subject thinks he comes nearer to his conception of ideal conduct than most people. A negative score indicates that he feels relatively inferior. The Tapping Test (Eysenck, 1952) was included as a psychomotor test which might possibly have to do with outwardly directed energy. Subjects were simply asked to tap with a pencil as quickly as possible for 10 seconds. A transparent sheet marked off into 320 half-inch squares was placed over the protocol and the number of squares containing dots was counted. The scatter score used was the average of three trails.

The following test results were found to be associated with either diagnosis or personality:

Diagnostic measures
  (1) the distraction effect on Porteus Maze tracing time;
  (2) the difference between the Depression and Hypochondriasis scales on the M.M.P.I.;
  (3) the T.A.T. mean total words per story;
  (4) the number of squares entered on the tapping test.

Personality measures
  (1) the total time in seconds taken to trace the Porteus Mazes;
  (2) the 'lifted pencils' score on the Porteus Mazes;
  (3) the time taken to complete the Progressive Matrices;
  (4) Siegel's Hostility Scale;
  (5) the Superiority-Inferiority Index;
  (6) the summed scores on the M.M.P.I. clinical scales of Psychopathic Deviate, Hysteria, Psychasthenia and Schizophrenia.

In 60% of the cases the test classifications were in agreement with both the clinical diagnosis and the personality rating. Taken separately, there was a higher percentage of agreement – of the order of 78% for the psychiatric diagnosis and similarly for the personality rating.

The study was cross validated using a sample of male neurotics (Foulds and Caine, 1959a). The general approach was substantiated but although the same battery was used, with the exception of the introduction of an Intropunitive Scale derived from the M.M.P.I. (Foulds, Caine and Creasy, 1960), somewhat different measures were found to differentiate the groups.

Diagnostic measure
The summed scores on the M.M.P.I. Depression and Psychasthenia Scales.

Personality measures
(1) the time taken in minutes to do the Progressive Matrices;
(2) distraction effect on the Porteus Maze tracing time;
(3) the Intropunitive Scale.

That such sex differences have emerged is perhaps not surprising. Allowances were made for these in the standardization of the M.M.P.I. in America, for example, and the picture here is bound to be further confused by cultural differences. Porteus has himself recognized sex differences in Maze performance.

It is of considerable interest that a speed factor is associated with *personality* level in both men and women (time taken to do the Progressive Matrices and some timed aspects of the Porteus Mazes). Previous studies have associated speed with diagnosis. Himmelweit (1946) found that mental hospital patients diagnosed as hysterics preferred speed to accuracy, whereas those diagnosed as dysthymics preferred accuracy to speed when completing a battery of tests. No double classification as suggested here was made and one wonders if her sample contained only the so-called 'pure' cases of hysteroid hysterics and obsessoid dysthymics. Furneaux (1963) has reported abnormal slowness in psychotics on Nufferno Test GS/14E.36 when compared with normals and neurotics. Slowness was also found to be associated with academic failure. In this connection he quotes recent experimental work which 'strongly supports the hypothesis that the score which a person obtains when he is given marks for every correct answer in a problem solving test of the type which is used for measuring "intelligence", is a function of at least three relatively independent, but interacting, attributes which have been designated Speed, Accuracy and Continuance'. Continuance is defined as a personality factor in that 'a person who displays high C will continue to work at problems of high subjective difficulty for a longer time than will a person displaying low C. Under certain circumstances it is clear that Continuance will become synonymous with Persistence.' The hysteroid/obsessoid dimension seems clearly relevant here.

An interesting finding, reported by Vernon and Parry (1949), that recruits to the Armed Forces discharged on psychiatric grounds did particularly poorly on a timed test of spatial ability, prompted us to investigate neurotic performance on the N.I.I.P. Group Test 80A in relation to symptom and trait clusters (Foulds and Caine, 1958b). We found that there was no significant difference in spatial ability with respect to diagnosis but that persons of obsessoid personality omitted a significantly greater number of items and made fewer errors than did persons of hysteroid personality. We therefore suggested that in timed tests of ability it is possible that hysteroid persons may sacrifice their accuracy for speed and that obsessoids might do better given more time. Because she prefers accuracy to speed (the study was confined to women) the obsessoid woman will probably continue to work at problems of high subjective-difficulty for a longer time. Obsessoids should show higher Accuracy and Continuance but slower Speed than hysteroids on the Nufferno Tests. Scoring patterns on ability tests, related in this way to personality, would be an extremely useful adjunct to the assessment techniques of the occupational psychologist. A number of these points have recently been discussed by Eysenck (1967).

Before many of the problems raised could be tackled, however, it was necessary to simplify our measuring instruments. The psychological test battery was very time-consuming to administer and the rating scale measure of personality was of limited usefulness since in addition to the well known difficulties associated with ratings, one had to depend on outside observers who might seldom be readily available. We decided to concentrate on the questionnaire level in the first instance rather than embark on a more ambitious scheme involving psycho-motor or projective tests. The questionnaire type tests used in the initial battery had effectively discriminated at both the symptom and personality levels in both men and women although they had not been devised originally with this aim specifically in view. We felt that if we could devise questionnaires in which symptoms, attitudes and personality traits were kept relatively uncontaminated at the face validity level we might go some way in sharpening our discriminators. We considered that, apart from the empirical evidence, certain conceptual differences exist which justify the differentiation of these three levels of personality functioning. *Symptoms*, for example, are typically observed and experienced as stressful and as inhibiting normal adjustment, *personality traits* facilitate adjustment, and *attitudes* fall somewhere in between.

The differences have been tabulated as follows (Caine, 1965a):

Symptoms
  (1) experienced as stressful;
  (2) inhibit adjustment;
  (3) disrupt the normal continuity of behaviour;
  (4) experienced as alien to the personality;
  (5) relatively transient in nature;
  (6) may be idiosyncratic.

Traits
  (1) facilitate adjustment;
  (2) the 'how' of behaviour (McClelland, 1951);
  (3) dispositional;
  (4) may be constitutionally determined (Slater, 1950);
  (5) relatively persistent in nature;
  (6) universal in the population.

Attitudes
  (1) fall somewhere between symptoms and traits;
  (2) not experienced as alien to the personality;
  (3) do not represent a break in the normal continuity of behaviour;
  (4) are not the 'how' of behaviour but are motivational (Krech and Crutchfield, 1948);
  (5) may be learned rather than constitutionally determined;
  (6) have been described as enduring organizations of motivational, emotional, perceptual and cognitive processes (Krech and Crutchfield, 1948).

Similarly, in his discussion of *personality variables, personality types, symptoms, subjective and objective signs* and *syndromes*, Foulds (1965) argues that traits and attitudes can be distinguished from symptoms and signs of 'personal illness' by means of three criteria:

  1. Traits and attitudes are universal; symptoms are not.
  2. Traits and attitudes are relatively ego-syntonic; symptoms and signs are stressful, either to the patient or to his closest associates.
  3. Traits and attitudes, particularly the former, are relatively enduring.

A *personality variable* (he argues) may be regarded as a convenient abstraction of behavioural qualities which fall along a continuum differentiable from other such continua and which provide a distinguishable feature in personality in general. A personality type is a constellation of traits and attitudes which can be distinguished from other such constellations. On the other hand, a symptom may be viewed as a *change* in bodily or mental functioning which the subject reports because it is stressful to him. A subjective sign is a *change* in bodily or mental functioning which the patient reports, of the significance of which he is not aware, but which is indicative, to the skilled observer, of maladaptation. An objective sign is a *change* in bodily or mental functioning which the subject does not report, but which indicates maladaptation to the skilled observer (e.g. thought block). A syndrome is a constellation or cluster of symptoms and subjective and objective signs, which tends to occur rather commonly and which is distinguishable from other such clusters of signs and symptoms.

The difference between a trait and a symptom is a qualitative one. We all wash our hands. But the normal person, even of obsessoid personality, feels free to decide whether or not he will do so. The obsessional neurotic feels no such freedom and is distressed by his compulsion to do so or by an interference with his compulsion. Somewhat similar qualitative differences can be made between normal and neurotic anxiety.

It was therefore necessary to develop questionnaires related to the three levels of psychological functioning of symptom complexes, attitudes, and personality trait constellations. A full description of the measures constructed, together with normative and validative data, is to be found in *Personality and Personal Illness* (Foulds, 1965) and in the manuals published for use with the tests (Caine,

Foulds and Hope, 1967; Caine and Hope, 1967; Foulds and Hope, 1968). A short description of these measures and some of the published material concerning them will be in order here.

At the symptom level

The measure constructed at this level was the clinically administered Symptom-Sign Inventory (S.S.I.) questionnaire. We have argued that the main justification for constructing yet another diagnostic inventory for an already saturated and perhaps somewhat disillusioned market is precisely to include symptoms and signs of illness only and to exclude personality traits.

For example, the most widely used inventory – the Minnesota Multiphasic Personality Inventory – is something of a hotchpotch. The Hysteria scale is composed of what could well be regarded as personality traits and the Hypochondriasis scale contains what some clinicians regard as hysterical symptoms. McCall (1958) has broken down the Depression scale into items having face-validity for, apparent congruence with and apparent irrelevance to depression. Foulds and Caine (1959b) have broken the scale down into effective, functional, health and irrelevant items and split these where applicable into face-valid and congruent items. In relating these different classes of items to groups of mental patients (paranoids, melancholics, neurotic depressives and hysterics) they confirmed McCall's finding that items chosen from the D scale for face-validity differentiated better than items which were merely congruent with depression and that both these sets of items differentiated better than those which, clinically, appeared to be irrelevant. These investigations could well be extended to other scales within the M.M.P.I. and to other symptom or personality inventories and would appear to justify our approach based on clinical experience rather than on actuarial differentiation as far as this particular problem is concerned.

The possible advantages of the S.S.I. over the clinical interview can be enumerated. All S.S.I. questions must be put to all subjects, whereas in clinical interviewing only certain areas are likely to be covered. Some clinicians have a tendency, for example, to look for certain diagnostic phenomena and to diagnose certain conditions more frequently than their colleagues. Such selective attention and suggestion may be somewhat reduced under standard administrative conditions. The scales are quantitive and public and this facilitates replication studies. A standard method of selection of subjects is made possible and the scales lend themselves to large scale computer analyses.

There are, however, certain disadvantages. Although the S.S.I. may reduce the influence of suggestion, it can easily be faked. Since the *number* of symptoms complained about is of great importance in differentiating patients from normals, monosymptomatic subjects might well be misclassified. Similarly, in terms of severity of illness, one single symptom might well be more crippling or have more sinister implications than a number of superficial ones. Phasic illnesses are more difficult to identify without a case history. These objections might be overcome, to some extent, by supplementary observer ratings.

The S.S.I. was constructed from 80 items derived from various psychiatric textbooks, from general clinical experience and from the M.M.P.I. Ten symptoms commonly associated with each of the following eight Kraepelinian diagnostic categories were organized into scales of the 'true/false' type, on an *a priori* basis:

A. *'Anxiety state' scale*
1. Does your hand often shake when you try to do something?
2. Do you sweat very easily, even on cool days?
3. Do you suffer from palpitations or breathlessness?
4. Are there times when you feel anxious without knowing the reason?
5. Are you afraid of being in a wide-open space or in an enclosed space?
6. Are you afraid that you might be going insane?
7. Have you a pain, or feeling of tension, in the back of your neck?
8. Have you difficulty in getting off to sleep without sleeping pills?
9. Are you afraid of going out alone?
10. Have you any particular fear not already mentioned?

B. *'Neurotic depression' scale*
1. Do you cry rather easily?
2. Have you lost interest in almost everything?
3. Have you ever attempted to do away with yourself?
4. Is the simplest task too much of an effort?
5. Are you depressed because of some particular loss or disappointment?
6. Have you found it difficult to concentrate recently?
7. Does the future seem pointless?
8. Are you more absent-minded recently than you used to be?
9. Are you slower recently in everything you do than you used to be?
10. Do you ever seriously think of doing away with yourself because you are no longer able to cope with your difficulties?

C. *'Manic' scale*
1. Do you ever feel so confident and successful that there is nothing you can't achieve?
2. Do you ever become very excitedly happy at times for no special reason?
3. Are you ever so cheerful that you want to laugh and joke with *everyone*?
4. Are there times when exciting new ideas and schemes occur to you one after another?
5. Are you ever so full of pep and energy that you carry on doing things indefinitely?
6. Do you ever become so excited that your thoughts race ahead faster than you can express them?
7. Are you ever so cheerful that you want to wear lots of gay things, like button-holes, flowers, bright ties, jewellery, etc.?
8. When you get bored, do you ever like to stir up some excitement?

9. Do you ever feel so full of energy that you don't want to go to bed?
10. Are you a much more important person than most people seem to think?

D. '*Paranoid*' scale
1. Are people talking about you and criticising you through no fault of your own?
2. Have you an important mission to carry out?
3. Are there people who are trying to harm you through no fault of your own?
4. Is someone trying to poison you or make you ill in some way?
5. Have you some special power, ability or influence which is not recognized by other people?
6. Is someone, other than yourself, deliberately causing most of your troubles?
7. Are people plotting against you through no fault of your own?
8. Do you ever take strong action against an evil person for the sake of a principle?
9. Do you ever see someone do or say something which most people do not take much notice of, but which you know has a special meaning?
10. Can people read your thoughts and make you do things against your will by a sort of hypnotism?

E. '*Obsessional*' scale
1. Are you *distressed* by silly, pointless thoughts that keep coming into your mind against your will?
2. Are you *compelled* to think over abstract problems again and again until you can't leave them alone?
3. Are you *unnecessarily* careful in carrying out even simple everyday tasks, like folding up clothes, reading notices, etc.?
4. Are you unable to prevent yourself from doing pointless things – like tapping lamp-posts, touching things, counting windows, uttering phrases etc.?
5. Are you afraid you might do something seriously wrong against your will?
6. Do distressing thoughts about sex or religion come into your mind against your will?
7. Do you feel you have to check things again and again – like turning off taps or lights, shutting windows at night, etc. – although you know there is really no need to?
8. Have you an *unreasonable* fear that some careless act of yours might have very serious consequences?
9. Are you *excessively* concerned about cleanliness?
10. Do you have an uneasy feeling that if you don't do something in a certain order, or a certain number of times, something might go wrong?

F. '*Schizophrenia*' scale
1. Do you feel that there is some sort of barrier between you and other people so that you can't really understand them?

2. Do you ever see visions, or people, animals, or things around you that other people don't seem to see?
3. Do you often wonder who you really are?
4. Do you ever have very strange and peculiar experiences?
5. Do you think other people regard you as very odd?
6. Do you often feel puzzled, as if something has gone wrong either with you or with the world, without knowing just what it is?
7. Do you ever hear voices without knowing where they come from?
8. Do you feel that you cannot communicate with other people because you don't seem to be on the same wave-length?
9. Do you have very strange and peculiar thoughts at times?
10. Is there something unusual about your body – like one side being different from the other and meaning something different?

G. *'Hysteria' scale*
1. Do you ever lose the use of an arm or leg or face muscle?
2. Do you ever have fits or have difficulty in keeping your balance?
3. Do you ever completely lose your voice (except from a cold)?
4. Do you ever lose all feeling in any part of your skin, so that you would not be able to feel a pin-prick; or do you ever have burning or tingling sensations under your skin?
5. Do you ever have black-outs, dizzy spells, or faints?
6. Have you been in poor physical health during most of the past few years?
7. Do you often suffer from blurring of vision or any other difficulty with your sight which no one seems able to put right?
8. Are you often bothered with pains over your heart, in your chest, or in your back?
9. Do you ever do things in a dream-like state without remembering afterwards what you have been doing?
10. Are you worried about your physical health?

H. *'Melancholia' scale*
1. Are you worried about having said things that have injured others?
2. Are you an unworthy person in your own eyes?
3. Have you some bodily condition which you find disgusting?
4. Are you a condemned person because of your sins?
5. Are you troubled by waking in the early hours and being unable to get off to sleep again (without sleeping pills)?
6. Because of things you have done wrong, are people talking about you and criticizing you?
7. Are you ever so low in spirits that you just sit for hours on end?
8. Do you cause harm to people because of what you are?
9. Are you ever so worked up that you pace about the room wringing your hands?
10. Do you ever go to bed feeling you wouldn't care if you never woke up again?

Although these items were initially placed under the various diagnostic categories on an *a priori* basis, it was anticipated that standardization would proceed along the lines of that described by Foulds, Caine and Creasy (1960) in their analysis of the first version of the Hostility and Direction of Hostility scales (see below). Rather than attempting to construct a diagnostic inventory in which the same collection of items organized in fixed scales (or scale patterns) are used for all diagnostic comparisons, specific items are selected for specific comparisons. Ideally the diagnostic question asked of the psychology department should be framed 'Is this an anxiety state or is this hysteria?' Statistical analyses of the S.S.I. show that the best set of items to answer this question is A1, A4, A5, A9, C2, C4, D1, G6, G9. On the other hand, if the question posed is 'Is this an anxiety state or a neurotic depression?' the best set of items would be A1, A4, A9, C4, C5, C6, D8, E2, E5, E6, G3, B3, G6, H3, H7. By a process of elimination, of course, a diagnosis can be arrived at even if the psychologist has to start from *carte blanche*. It just takes a little longer.

Similar sets of items have been worked out to distinguish between normal and patient samples, between psychotics and neurotics, and between non-integrated and integrated psychotics, the latter consisting of paranoids and melancholics.

The results obtained from the inventory for 100 psychotics and 150 neurotics (women) show that the overall agreement with the clinical diagnosis was 62% in a main sample and 50% in a smaller additional sample of 68. In 8 and 13% respectively the S.S.I. diagnosis was uncertain and in 31 and 37% respectively the inventory and clinical diagnoses were at variance.

We felt that the inventory should be administered orally. Experience with self-administered tests of this kind led us to believe that many subjects, even of average intelligence or verbal ability and relatively emotionally undisturbed, had difficulty in grasping the precise meaning of many of the questions asked them and might often distort them to fit their own case. In addition, subjects varied considerably in their use of the '?' or 'cannot say' categories of response. In short, we felt that control over response sets might be better achieved by an oral administration which would give the psychologist an opportunity to understand what the subject thought he was responding to and why he chose that particular response. A number of guiding rules, with these sort of problems in mind, have been set out in the manual (Foulds and Hope, 1968).

The Personality Measure – the Hysteroid-Obsessoid Questionnaire (H.O.Q.)
It had been found in previous work that self-ratings on the hysteroid-obsessoid rating scale described above failed to distinguish between observer-rated hysteroids and obsessoids with sufficient accuracy to be of much practical value. The untrained subjects found the scale very difficult; the scale itself, as worded, carried value judgements and in any case it was too short for high reliability. To avoid these difficulties it was decided to construct a questionnaire of the true/false variety directed specifically at the areas covered by the rating scale which was extended to eleven traits. The two additional traits which were added were

concerned with enjoying being the centre of attention (hysteroid) *v.* preferring to stay in the background (obsessoid) and making superficial friendships (hysteroid) *v.* making deep, lasting friendships (obsessoid). Thus, for example, rating scale item 1 (excessive display of emotion *v.* scarcely any display of emotion) formed the basis of the following true/false questions:

1. I keep my feelings to myself.
2. I feel better after I've had a good row and got it off my chest.
3. I like to show people exactly how I feel about things.
4. I do not show my emotions in front of people.
5. I act out my feelings.

And rating scale item 2 (vivid day dreams *v.* inability to indulge in fanciful thinking):

1. I find it hard to think up stories.
2. I have a good imagination.
3. I can lead more than one life in my imagination.
4. I cannot completely lose myself in a book or story.
5. When watching a play I identify with the characters.

In this way 48 statements were compiled, each of which could be scored in a hysteroid or in an obsessoid direction; thus only one score is necessary in establishing a person's position on the dimension. In practice we have used only the total hysteroid score in all our studies. The test in full is given below:

The Hysteroid-Obsessoid Questionnaire
1. I find it hard to think up stories.
2. I like to wear eye-catching clothes.
3. I keep my feelings to myself.
4. I am slow in making up my mind about things because I weigh up all the pros and cons.
5. I am a moody sort of person, with lasting moods.
6. I have rigid standards I feel I should stick to.
7. When I am working I like a job which calls for speed rather than close attention to details.
8. I like to ask for other people's opinions and advice about myself.
9. I don't feel awkward when meeting people because I know how to behave.
10. I prefer to be popular with everyone than to have a few deep lasting friendships.
11. I cannot shake off my troubles easily even if I get the opportunity.
12. I have a good imagination.
13. I keep quiet at parties or meetings.
14. I feel better after I've had a good row and got it off my chest.

15. I am quick in sizing up people and situations.
16. My mood is easily changed by what happens around me.
17. My conscience seldom bothers me.
18. I keep a place for everything and everything in its place.
19. I'm rather lacking in the social graces.
20. I have the same friends now as I had years ago.
21. It pleases me to be the centre of a lively group.
22. I like to show people exactly how I feel about things.
23. The first impressions or reactions are usually the right ones in the end.
24. I do not mind if things turn out badly as long as I know I've done the right thing.
25. I can lead more than one life in my imagination.
26. I like discussing myself with other people.
27. I do not show my emotions in front of people.
28. When someone asks me a question I give a quick answer and look for the reasons later.
29. If I am not in the right mood for something it takes a lot to make me feel differently.
30. I usually get by without having to worry about whether I've done the right thing morally or not.
31. One can understand most things without having to go into all the details.
32. It is important to be fashionable in your opinions, clothes, etc.
33. My party manners are pretty good.
34. The only friends I make I keep.
35. If I happen to be upset about something it seems to carry over into all I do for a long time.
36. I cannot completely lose myself in a book or story.
37. I like to sit in the background or in an inconspicuous place at socials, meetings, etc.
38. I act out my feelings.
39. I wait until I am sure of all my facts before I make a decision.
40. I spend a good deal of time worrying about the rights and wrongs of conduct.
41. When going into a room or meeting someone for the first time I get a strong general impression first and only gradually take in the details.
42. When meeting people I haven't met before I usually feel I make a rather poor impression.
43. It upsets me to leave friends and make new ones even if I have to.
44. When watching a play I identify myself with the characters.
45. My feelings about things and towards other people seldom change.
46. I do not like taking a leading part in group activities.
47. Mistakes are usually made when people make snap decisions.
48. If two people find they disagree about things they shouldn't try to carry on being close friends.

Having constructed our questionnaire, it was decided to validate it against an outside criterion of observer ratings, using a form of the rating scale set out below:

Instructions: After each heading underline the words which give the best description.

1. *Day dreams, including wishful thinking.*   (*a*) seldom, (*b*) sometimes, (*c*) very often, (*d*) hardly ever, (*e*) often.

2. *Centre of attention.*   (*a*) sometimes dislikes, (*b*) hardly ever dislikes, (*c*) usually dislikes, (*d*) dislikes, (*e*) seldom dislikes.

3. *Displays emotions.*   (*a*) very often, (*b*) hardly ever, (*c*) often, (*d*) seldom, (*e*) sometimes.

4. *Makes decisions.*   (*a*) slowly, (*b*) quickly, (*c*) very quickly, (*d*) sometimes slowly, (*e*) very slowly.

5. *Moods change.*   (*a*) seldom, (*b*) very often, (*c*) sometimes, (*d*) often, (*e*) hardly ever.

6. *Personally concerned about rights and wrongs.*   (*a*) hardly ever, (*b*) often, (*c*) seldom, (*d*) very often, (*e*) sometimes.

7. *Concerned about details.*   (*a*) sometimes, (*b*) seldom, (*c*) hardly ever, (*d*) very often, (*e*) often.

8. *Depends upon opinion of others.*   (*a*) very often, (*b*) often, (*c*) sometimes, (*d*) seldom, (*e*) hardly ever.

9. *Expects to make a favourable impression.*   (*a*) very often, (*b*) often, (*c*) sometimes, (*d*) seldom, (*e*) hardly ever.

10. *Makes deep lasting friendships.*   (*a*) often, (*b*) very often, (*c*) hardly ever, (*d*) sometimes, (*e*) seldom.

11. *Feels things deeply.*   (*a*) hardly ever, (*b*) sometimes, (*c*) seldom, (*d*) very often, (*e*) often.

The bulk of the validation sample (76 cases) came from the neurosis unit at Claybury Hospital and the remainder (17 cases) from other units of the hospital. The patients completed the questionnaire shortly after admission and ratings were obtained on all patients from medical, nursing and occupational therapy staff after training in the use of the rating form. The number of raters per patient varied from 3 to 11 with a mean of 7·5. Ratings were usually completed towards the end of the second week after admission, when raters felt reasonably confident of making an accurate assessment.

An analysis of the internal consistency of the rating scale items showed that only 6 of the 11 original traits were being successfully differentiated for the groups by the raters, namely, attention seeking, emotional display, speed of decision, lability of affect, conscientiousness, and shallowness of affect. These six items formed the subsequent basis of the hysteroid-obsessoid rating allocation.

An analysis of the mean rating was computed and from this confidence limits were calculated. Despite the safeguards taken in the rating scheme these calculations showed that the dependability of the ratings was in question. Although this is a common and recognized weakness of ratings, a factorial experiment was carried out in an effort to improve the validation criterion. Five of the raters each rated 10 male and 10 female patients twice, with a 10-day interval between ratings, making a total of 200 ratings. An analysis of variance was carried out with raters, replication of ratings, and patients as the sources of variance. The between-rater, between patient, and rater/patient interaction variances were significant but the replications were not. The between raters variance was too small to be of practical significance and since the rater/patient interaction could not, in practice, be allowed for, it was included in the residual variance. The experiment was collapsed into a 5 (raters) × 20 (patients) factorial design. Estimates of the variance of the factors were made on the assumption of Model II of the analysis of variance (Snedecor, 1946). The variance of the raters was only 0·35, while that of the patients was 4·37. The error variance was 2·69.

One may conclude from the factorial experiment that the raters tended to show something of a bias in one direction or another but that this bias was too small to be worth correction, and that the raters differed frequently from each other in their individual classifications. The reliability of the mean rating of each patient (averaged over the five raters and measured by an intraclass correlation coefficient) was 0·92.

To establish the hysteroid or obsessoid rating classification the ratings for each patient were pooled, taking the total hysteroid score less the total obsessoid score as the allocation. This allocation yielded 65 obsessoids, 27 hysteroids, and 1 intermediate. The validation correlation coefficient between the HOQ and the rating classification was 0·68.

An improved validation study has been reported (Hope and Caine, 1968). In this study the H.O.Q. was completed by 20 patients, 10 men and 10 women, diagnosed as neurotic on the S.S.I. and admitted to the neurosis unit at Claybury Hospital. At the time of completing the questionnaire the patients were rated by three of the unit staff, who made their ratings independently. The same three nurses each rated all 20 patients on the 11-trait rating scale described above. As in the previous validation study care was taken in the training of the raters. In the unit concerned (a therapeutic community) there is continual interaction between patients and staff. All staff members are expected to act as therapeutic agents. The nurses and other staff members see patients individually, in formal groups, in ward meetings and at socials. Information is shared among the staff in frequent staff meetings and all members are expected to make some contribution regarding a patient's behaviour and reactions. The nurses are therefore in an unusually favoured position to assess a patient's personality.

In this study the calculation of a correlation between total score on H.O.Q. and the sum of all 11 rating scale traits, averaged over all three raters, yielded a coefficient of 0·72. This compares very closely with the coefficient of 0·68 in the initial validation study carried out in similar conditions. However, since this coefficient is only an approximation because of the differences among the means and variances of the 33 rating scales involved (11 traits rated by 3 raters), an improved criterion could be arrived at by the centring and standardizing of each rating scale separately for each rater. After such correction the validity coefficient rose to 0·78.

A number of reliability studies have been carried out. Thirty normal subjects retested after an interval of one year yielded a coefficient of 0·85 (Caine, 1965a). In the same study a sample of 62 neurotics tested on admission to hospital and retested after six weeks of intensive psychotherapy gave a value of 0·77. Retest correlations of a similar order have been reported for patients following treatment by Foulds (1965).

In the original validation study there was a small significant correlation with age ($r = 0.23$, $n = 93$) but this was not sustained in further studies of depressives and neurotics reported in the test manual. No significant association was found with verbal ability.

In general the empirical evidence is that the association of the H.O.Q. with symptom tests is minimal. Table 27.3 shows the order of the relationship with symptom measures as quoted in a number of our studies.

Subjects		N	Correlation	$p <$
Neurotics	Clinical diagnosis (hysteria or dysthymia)	86	0·28	0·05
	M.M.P.I. scales			
	Hs	77	−0·14	—
	D	77	−0·15	—
	Pt	77	−0·11	—
	Maudsley Personality Inventory			
	Neuroticism	53	−0·40	0·01
	Symptom Sign Inventory			
Psychotic Depr.	Personal illness scale	24	−0·43	0·05
		37	−0·19	—
Neurotics	S.S.I., Psychotic *v.* Neurotic	24	0·21	—
Psychotic Depr.	S.S.I., Psychic-Somatic	24	−0·42	0·05
Neurotics	S.S.I., Psychic-Somatic	60	0·18	—
'integrated' psychotics	S.S.I., Psychic-Somatic	40	−0·30	—
'non-integrated' psychotics	S.S.I., Psychic-Somatic	30	0·20	—

TABLE 27.3
Correlations of the Hysteroid/Obsessoid Questionnaire
with symptom measures.

It is clear that the H.O.Q. is more closely related to the validation criterion of personality traits than it is to either clinical diagnosis or to symptom measures. In addition, a number of studies show that, compared with other tests of symptoms and attitudes, the re-test correlations for the personality measures after treatment are higher (Caine, 1965a) and that mean differences for test and re-test scores are lower (Foulds, 1965).

Apart from the validation criteria, the highest measure of agreement with the H.O.Q. is with the extraversion 'E' scale of the Maudsley Personality Inventory. Correlations as high as $r = 0.84$ (Caine and Hawkins, 1963), and $r = 0.70$ (Caine and Hope, 1964) have been reported. This is encouraging since the two scales were constructed independently under quite different conditions and for different purposes. Eysenck (1959a) writes that the 'E' scale is a 'rough-and-ready' measure of Extraversion, composed of 24 questions 'carefully selected after lengthy item analyses and factor analyses'. The H.O.Q. was based on clinical observation and items constructed on a simple face validity basis. In this case there is striking agreement between the clinical and actuarial approaches, and there seems little doubt that the two scales are measuring some aspect of the total personality which is of a relatively permanent and enduring nature.

Although this may be true, the Eysenckian and Fouldsian systems of classification are not, in fact, interchangeable. Eysenck considers that 'the traditional psychiatric syndromes in the field of neurosis are generated by two factors, continua or dimensions, namely those of neuroticism and of extraversion-introversion' and he goes on, 'As Jung was the first to point out, hysteria is a syndrome typically found in the extraverted neurotic, psychasthenia is a syndrome typically found in the introverted neurotic'. He further suggests that dysthymia replaces the diagnosis psychasthenia. In his work Eysenck in fact equates introversion with dysthymia and extraversion with hysteria/psychopathy (Eysenck, 1957, p. 28, table VI). But Jung conceptualized a difference between extraversion and the hysterical character/hysteria and considered that there was an *association only* between them. In fact the hysteric could become introverted when the illness became fully established. Similarly in associating introversion with psychasthenia and dementia praecox there is a reversal in the developed illness. The 'precocious dement' is an extravert. Jung's concept of extraversion-introversion is a dynamic motivational one involving the direction of flow of psychical energy, libido, or interest. It does not refer to the 'how' of behaviour which defines the personality trait (McClelland, 1951). Eysenck makes no conceptual differences between the various aspects of psychological functioning that are being emphasized here. For example, he places more reliance on '*attitudes*' than on symptoms in hysterical symptom questionnaire construction and equates hysterical conversion symptoms, 'hysterical attitudes', hysterical personality and psychopathy in establishing extraversion criterion groups (Eysenck, 1959b). This validation procedure has been challenged by Foulds (1962, 1965), Ingham (1962) and Crookes and Hutt (1962) and replied to by Eysenck (1962).

Undoubtedly this confusion must have contributed to the proliferation of contradictory findings among experiments in which 'introverts' and 'extraverts' (usually hysterics and dysthymics) have been used as subjects, and despite arguments to the contrary, a statistical technique such as factor analysis cannot supply a complete and acceptable map of personality, nor, by itself, can it determine what aspects of psychological functioning we must classify and measure (Vernon, 1957).

In spite of evidence quoted above, Eysenck argues that his system preserves the distinction between personality and symptomatology (Eysenck, 1962). As Foulds (1965) points out, however, it preserves only the distinction between personality and such symptomatology as is common to all neurotics (i.e. between 'extraversion' and 'neuroticism'), but confuses the distinction between personality and such symptomatology as is specific to each of the neurotic groups (i.e. between extraversion and hysteria). It is in this respect that the fundamental difference lies between his approach and the one suggested here. Again, this is not a difference that can be resolved by factor analytic type solutions.

This is not simply an argument about the difficulties of defining extraversion-introversion (and/or hysteroidness-obsessoidness), although it is obvious that different authors and test constructors have different psychological processes in mind when they are considering the former dichotomy. For Eysenck (Eysenck and Claridge, 1962) extraversion and introversion are simply personality traits having something to do with sociability and speed of decision. He justifies the altering of Jung's original concepts on the grounds that his (Eysenck's) theory and method demand it. Nevertheless, Jung's original ideas are conceptually very useful and important in their own right and may yet prove measurable. Indeed, Briggs Myers (1962) has devised an index which she claims reflects whether a person is an extravert or an introvert 'in the sense intended by Jung, who coined the terms'. 'The extravert is orientated primarily to the outer world, and thus tends to focus his perception and judgement upon people and things. The introvert is orientated primarily to the inner world postulated in Jungian theory, and thus tends to focus his perception and judgement upon concepts and ideas.' It may well be that certain personality traits (or symptom complexes) are *associated* with the direction of psychical energy as Jung supposed. However, until this has been demonstrated it seems better to reserve extraversion-introversion for Jung's dynamic dimension and to use hysteroid-obsessoid for the dimension of personality traits measured by the H.O.Q. and the M.P.I. E scale (Caine and Hope, 1964). There is little controversy in the literature about the sorts of traits defining the hysteroid and obsessoid personality and these are directly observable. At the moment, extraversion and introversion can only be *inferred* from supposedly associated personality traits. It is unscientific to introduce a third, unidentifiable and controversial concept in an explanation of data when two traditional concepts referring to observable phenomena will do the job.

This conceptual confusion has practical implications. Thus Ingham and Robinson (1964) separated a group of patients diagnosed as hysterics into those with conversion hysteria and those with hysterical personality. The mean E score of the conversion hysterics was similar to that of the dysthymics while the hysterical personalities obtained an extraverted score. This suggests that psychiatrists are influenced by personality as well as symptoms in assigning a diagnosis, that the E scale is a measure of personality, and that extraverts and introverts should be the criterion groups for validating a measure of extraversion-introversion rather than hysterics and dysthymics, particularly when no double classification into symptoms and personality type is made.

The Caine and Hope study has confirmed that of Ingham and Robinson and has shown, in a group of 50 neurotic patients classified according to personality and diagnosis, that the E scale is a measure of personality and that, in this sample, it is not related to type of illness or to any interaction between personality and diagnosis.

These considerations throw some doubt about what conclusions should be drawn from studies employing the M.P.I. The sampling procedure which has been adopted in previous attempts to validate the M.P.I. has not always been clearly stated. It may be surmised that only clear-cut cases were selected and that such sampling maximized the number of obsessoid dysthymics and hysteroid hysterics, and minimized the number of hysteroid dysthymics and obsessoid hysterics. If a psychiatrist expects a hysteric to have a hysteroid personality (assuming he makes the distinction at all) he will hesitate to diagnose an obsessoid person as a hysteric and may classify him as 'diagnosis in doubt' or 'mixed neurosis' and the subject may be excluded from a validation study on the basis of psychiatric diagreement. One must conclude that the samples involved were selected samples and not typically representative of hysterics and dysthymics in general. Indeed, Hope (personal communication) found that in a sample of 169 neurotics, 37% were either obsessoid hysterics or hysteroid dysthymics. These findings cannot be dismissed by pointing to the unreliability of psychiatric diagnosis and by an insistence on the employment in experiments of only so called 'typical' cases. Experimental evidence supporting the distinctions being made here between symptoms and personality has recently been published by Kline (1967) with regard to obsessional illness and obsessoid personality. Kline analysed statistically scores obtained on the M.M.P.I., two tests of obsessoid personality traits and a test of obsessional symptoms and was able to conclude that his results unequivocally supported the symptom/trait dichotomy argued here.

Attitudes of hostility and guilt – the Hostility and Direction of Hostility Question-naire (H.D.H.Q.).

The third area of psychological functioning in which we were interested was that of attitudes, particularly of attitudes of hostility and guilt. As defined above, attitudes may be thought of as falling somewhere between symptoms and personality traits, although having characteristics that distinguish them. It will be seen that the ones with which we are concerned here are indeed related in some respects to the symptom level and in other respects to the personality trait level.

The selection of hostile and guilty attitudes for special study in work of this kind with mental patients needs little justification. Whatever their differences in other areas, psychiatrists, clinical psychologists and psychoanalysts are in general agreement about the importance for diagnosis and psychopathology of feelings of hostility and guilt, with the concomitant expression of extrapunitive and intropunitive attitudes. Freud conceived of aggression as an instinct which, in the extreme instance, may be turned outwards to destroy others or inwards to destroy ourselves. As Allport (1958) has pointed out, the tendency in Freud's writing is 'to consider aggression as a global, instinctive, steam boiler-like force. It is regarded as one of a small number of prime movers in life. It is ubiquitous, urgent, basically unavoidable.' This insistence on the importance of aggression for human motivation and action can be detected in a wide range of sources not necessarily subscribing to the psychoanalytic theory of its origins. Dollard, Miller, Doob, Mowrer and Sears (1944) regard aggression as an inevitable consequence of frustration. An aggressive reaction may be delayed, disguised, displaced or deflected from the immediate and logical goal but it is never destroyed. Their sympathies lie with Freud's earlier standpoint rather than with his later death-instinct theory and they quote McDougall (1923), James (1890) and Sumner and Keller (1927) in their support. Later authors who have dealt in this area include Buss (1961) and McKellar (1949), the latter having amassed a monumental bibliography on the general problem of human aggressiveness.

That individuals may develop a preferred way of expressing hostility (or a preferred defence mechanism in this respect) is a commonplace observation amongst those working with mental patients. But for the diagnostician, a measure of 'hostility' is not enough. The mode, the direction and the amount of its expression are the variables with which he must work, although what determines these factors in an individual is still a matter of conjecture. For despite the Freudian emphasis on the importance of a possible aggressive instinct, cultural pressures must play their part, as cultural anthropologists have reminded us.

But, however it may be in primitive societies or cultures other than our own, clinical observation of western tradition has established a connection between certain forms of mental disorder and the expression of varous aspects of hostility and guilt. For example, psychopaths are characterized by the tendency to 'act out' their hostility, paranoids by its projection and psychotic depressives by introjection.

The early series of studies in this connection, carried out at Runwell Hospital, represents an attempt to distinguish various aspects of hostility, to devise relevant measuring instruments and to determine more precisely their relation to psychiatric symptom complexes and personality trait constellations. A number of tests of extrapunitiveness and intropunitiveness were developed (Rosenzweig, 1945; Rosenzweig, Clarke, Garfield and Lehndorff, 1946) which included the Superiority-Inferiority Index (Foulds, 1958), a sentence building test (Caine, 1960, 1963, 1966, 1967) and the Hostility and Direction of Hostility Questionnaires (H.D.H.Q.) (Caine, 1960; Foulds, Caine and Creasey, 1960; Foulds, 1965; Caine, Foulds and Hope, 1967). It is the latter test which has been used as the attitude level measure in the set of tests comprising the Personality and Personal Illness Questionnaires.

2 D

The H.D.H.Q. is composed of items drawn from the M.M.P.I. and allocated to five subscales, three *extrapunitive* and two *intropunitive*. The three extrapunitive subscales are composed of an *acting out* hostility subscale, a *criticism of others*, and a *projected or delusional* hostility subscale. The two intropunitive subscales are composed of a *self-criticism* and a *guilt* subscale. The scales in full are reproduced below.

Acting Out Hostility (A.H.)

In school I was sometimes sent to the principal for misbehaving.
I don't blame anyone for trying to grab everything he can get in this world.
I easily become impatient with people.
I get mad easily and then get over it soon.
At times I feel like smashing things.
At times I feel like picking a fist fight with someone.
At times I have a strong urge to do something harmful or shocking.
Sometimes I feel as if I must injure either myself or someone else.
I can easily make other people afraid of me, and sometimes do for the fun of it.
Sometimes I enjoy hurting persons I love.
I sometimes tease animals.
I am too easily downed in an argument.
I get angry sometimes.

Criticism of Others (C.O.)

I have very few quarrels with members of my family.
Some of my family have habits that bother and annoy me very much.
I have at times stood in the way of people who were trying to do something, not because it amounted to much but because of the principle of the thing.
Most people make friends because friends are likely to be useful to them.
I do not blame a person for taking advantage of someone who lays himself open to it.
Most people are honest chiefly through fear of being caught.
I think most people would lie to get ahead.
I think nearly anyone would tell a lie to keep out of trouble.
When someone does me a wrong I feel I should pay him back if I can, just for the principle of the thing.
It is safer to trust nobody.
I have often found people jealous of my good ideas just because they had not thought of them first.
Some people are so bossy that I feel like doing the opposite of what they request, even though I know they are right.

Projected Delusional Hostility (P.H. or D.H.)

I have no enemies who really wish to harm me.
If people had not had it in for me I would have been much more successful.

Someone has it in for me.

I am sure I get a raw deal from life.

I believe I am being followed.

I commonly wonder what hidden reason another person may have for doing something nice for me.

I believe I am being plotted against.

Someone has been trying to rob me.

I know who is responsible for most of my troubles.

Self-Criticism (S.C.)

I seem to be about as capable and smart as most others around me.

I have often lost out on things because I couldn't make up my mind soon enough.

I usually expect to succeed in things I do.

Often I can't understand why I have been so cross and grouchy.

My hardest battles are with myself.

I have several times given up doing a thing because I thought too little of my ability.

I am too easily downed in an argument.

I have sometimes felt that difficulties were piling up so high that I could not overcome them.

I am certainly lacking in self-confidence.

I am entirely self-confident.

I shrink from facing a crisis or difficulty.

Guilt (G. or D.G.)

Much of the time I feel as if I have done something wrong or evil.

I believe my sins are unpardonable.

I have not lived the right kind of life.

I believe I am a condemned person.

I wish I could get over worrying about things I have said that may have injured other people's feelings.

At times I think I am no good at all.

I certainly feel useless at times.

In the original study (Foulds *et al.*, 1960) amongst men, psychopaths scored significantly higher on *acting out* hostility and on *criticism of others* than other clinical groups. On *projected hostility* their scores were exceeded (though not significantly) by melancholics and particularly by paranoid states. These groups differed significantly from the neurotic and normal samples employed. On *self-criticism*, obsessoid dysthymics scored significantly higher than all other groups and normals significantly lower. On the *guilt* scales, psychopaths and melancholics scored significantly higher than all others and hysterics and normals significantly lower.

Amongst women, psychopaths again scored higher than all other groups on *acting out* hostility and *criticism of others*. On *projected* hostility their score was exceeded by paranoid states, but both groups were significantly higher than the remainder. On *self-criticism* paranoid states and normals scored significantly lower than the rest. On the *guilt* scale, melancholics and psychopaths were the highest scorers and normals and obsessoid dysthymics the lowest.

Apart from the high delusional guilt score of the psychopaths, the clinical groups behaved as predicted, although not all differences were significant statistically. With regard to the *guilt* scale psychopaths may enjoy being thought of as wicked but they eschew the idea of being inadequate.

In a discriminant function analysis of the data, each of the five subscales contributed very considerably to the differentiation between the groups, and weighted subscale patterns are available for distinguishing between clinical groups for diagnostic purposes.

	A.H.	C.O.	P.H.	S.C.	G.	Total Hostility	Direction
Test-retest correlation	0·70	0·59	0·40	0·70	0·23	0·75	0·51
Test mean	3·73	3·07	0·60	3·00	1·00	11·40	−0·40
Re-test mean	3·33	3·30	0·20	2·70	0·70	10·23	−0·73

TABLE 27.4

Means and test-retest correlations of a sample of 30 normals re-tested
one year after initial testing (Caine, Foulds and Hope, 1967).

Hope (1963) has carried out an intensive statistical study of the H.D.H.Q. involving a principal components analysis of a considerably extended body of data. He concluded (1) that the *projected hostility, self-criticism* and the *guilt* subscales measure what they purport to measure, (2) that the *criticism of others* subscale is 'as likely as not to be measuring criticism of others' and, (3) that the '*acting out* subscale is measuring a variable which may tentatively be identified as "urge to act out hostility" '.

In the same study Hope found that the two principal components underlying the subscales were (1) amount of aggression as measured by the formula $AH + CO + PH + SG + G$ and (2) direction of hostility, represented by the formula $(2SC + G) − (AH + CO + PH)$, where AH is *acting out* hostility, CO is *criticism of others*, PH is *projected* hostility, SC is *self-criticism*, and G is *guilt*.

With regard to reliability, test/re-test correlations are available for a sample of 30 normal persons (15 men and 15 women) drawn from a number of voluntary societies within the community and from a firm specializing in the standardization of industrial designs who were tested and re-tested one year later. The means and correlations of this sample are shown in Table 27.4, taken from the test manual.

The battery was also administered to neurotic in-patients of a therapeutic community on four occasions – on admission, after six weeks of treatment, on discharge, and one year after discharge. On the last occasion patients were allotted to a success or failure group according to how they had responded to treatment. The test/re-test correlations are shown in Table 27.5 for the 41 patients who completed the battery on all four occasions. These correlations are associated with a very considerable linear fall in the scores of the patients who had responded to treatment (Caine, 1965b).

		A.H.	C.O.	P.H.	S.C.	G.	Total Hostility	Direction
Failure	A-S	0·94	0·73	0·83	0·35	0·40	0·85	0·68
	S-D	0·39	0·78	0·84	0·69	0·33	0·87	0·30
	D-Y	0·46	0·95	0·74	0·31	0·78	0·73	0·57
Success	A-S	0·43	0·47	−0·02	0·54	0·26	0·33	0·43
	S-D	0·43	0·52	0·29	0·30	0·41	0·44	0·30
	D-Y	0·47	0·42	0·20	0·78	0·65	0·50	0·72

TABLE 27.5

Test-retest correlations in a sample of neurotics tested on admission to hospital (A), six weeks after admission (S), on discharge (D) and one year after discharge (Y). The sample was split into those whose treatment was a failure ($n=9$) and those whose treatment was a success ($n=32$).

A number of studies have related the H.D.H.Q. to changes in psychiatric state. Neurotics (Caine, 1965b) and Depressives (Foulds, 1965; Mayo, 1966) show a drop in Hostility and a decrease in Intropunitiveness (direction) with improvement in their psychiatric condition. After partialling out psychiatric diagnosis, Foulds (1966) found that patients who claim to have mainly physical symptoms tend to score lower on Hostility than patients who claim to have mainly psychological symptoms. He also found that the average Hostility score of male prisoners in a Scottish prison who had volunteered to complete the questionnaire was 23 – a score which is more than one and a half standard deviations above the normal mean.

Amount of hostility expressed on the H.D.H.Q. was found by Hope (1963) to be correlated 0·27 with the neuroticism scale of the Maudsley Personality Inventory and −0·58 and −0·65 with the K score of the M.M.P.I. in two samples of neurotics. This latter finding was confirmed by Salmon (1965).

The K scale was introduced originally as a suppressor variable (Meehl and Hathaway, 1946) and has been variously described as a measure of test-taking attitude, a measure of acquiescence (King and Schiller, 1958), a measure of ego-strength (Sweetland and Quay, 1953) and a not very reliable measure of willingness to admit to feelings, thoughts, actions, etc., which are not socially and

2 D*

morally acceptable (Meehl and Hathaway, 1946; Fricke, 1956; Hope 1963). This fairly high correlation between the first component of the H.D.H.Q., or the Hostility score, and the K scale is artefactual in so far as both measures contain the same seven items scored in opposite directions.

Nevertheless, one may safely assume that response sets (selecting socially acceptable or socially desirable items, suppressing socially 'taboo' material, etc.) will be operating when subjects are completing the H.D.H.Q., and that they will operate most strongly in normal subjects when the material presented to them has little personal relevance. Edwards (1957) holds that 'social desirability' is a powerful, relatively all-pervasive influence in normal subjects in determining the response to personality inventories and Wiggins (1962) considers that it is the 'deviant' individuals who ascribe socially undesirable statements to themselves. These arguments are supported by the finding of the writer that subjects tended to suppress socially 'taboo' material in areas *not* related to their psychopathology

	H.D.H.Q. Total Hostility	Direction of Hostility
Personal illness	0·392*	−0·187
H.O.Q.	−0·017	0·408*
	* $p < 0.001$	

TABLE 27.6

Correlations between Total Hostility, Direction of Hostility, Personal Illness Scale and H.O.Q.

when responding to a sentence building test and that consistency of response between the questionnaire testing level and the sentence-building test level obtained only when the material involved was of pathological significance for the subject (Caine, 1963, 1966, 1967). The argument that to get meaningful results personally relevant test material must be presented to the subject can be extended to many types of test (Hutt, 1951, 1954; Smail, 1966; Caine and Smail, 1967). The 'cognitive attitude' theory of Klein and his co-workers is also of direct relevance in a discussion of response determinants of psychological tests (Klein and Schlesinger, 1949; Klein, 1950; Holzman and Klein, 1954; Klein, 1954, 1958) in that a subject's report of what he remembers, perceives and describes in psychological testing situations is determined by cognitive attitudes involving motivated, selective report.

Be that as it may, the Hostility score of the H.D.H.Q. has consistently been associated with the *symptom* level of personality function and the direction of hostility with the *personality* level. Foulds (1965), for example, has reported the following correlations (Table 27.6) between Total Hostility, Direction of Hostility, the Personal Illness scale of the S.S.I., and the H.O.Q. for a sample of 120 female mental patients, both psychotic and neurotic.

Direction of Hostility has been associated with *personality* in a number of studies, with hysteroids tending to direct their hostility outwards *vis-à-vis* obsessoids (Foulds and Caine, 1958a, 1959a; Hope, 1963; Caine, 1965a). The subjects in Hope's study were drawn from those described in the other published reports; his analysis of the data, however, was different.

Some practical applications of the test battery
The Personality and Personal Illness battery of tests is being applied to the practical task of assessing psychological change accompanying psychiatric treatment. It is argued that superficial treatments may well be expected to achieve test score changes at the symptom level but that the attitude and personality tests should be relatively unaffected. Intensive psychotherapy, on the other hand, should achieve attitude change at least. A pilot study of this hypothesis has been reported by Caine (1965b), which has now been extended extensively to include a comparative treatment group (Caine and Smail, 1969). This recent investigation (Caine and Smail, 1969) has reported results substantiating the predictions with regard to the psychotherapy group in comparison with a 'conventionally' treated sample. Significant changes were achieved at all levels in the psychotherapy group on follow up but not in the comparative sample. The evidence indicated that the H.O.Q. has the highest reliability of the tests in the battery and is the most resistant to change. The attitude tests, with one exception, fall between the personality and symptom measures in terms of reliability in the normal sample and in the neurotic sample, following treatment (Caine, 1965b).

Foulds (1965) has studied the test scores of 120 women made up of 20 of each of the following diagnostic groups: non-paranoid schizophrenics, paranoid states (including paranoid schizophrenics), melancholics, hysterics, anxiety states, and neurotic depressives, using the Personality and Personal Illness Questionnaires. The main findings were that those who scored high on the Non-integrated Psychotic *v.* Integrated Psychotic scale tended to have more non-specific symptoms on the S.S.I. and to have higher Hostility scores on the H.D.H.Q. Those who score high on the Psychotic *v.* Neurotic scale tended to have high total S.S.I. and Hostility scores. Those who score high on the Personal Illness *v.* Normal scale also tended to have high scores on the total S.S.I. and the H.D.H.Q. Hostility score. As noted above, hysteroidness of personality was associated with outwardly directed hostility. When improved and unimproved groups were compared on re-testing with their previous results, changes were more marked in the improved group on measures which tended to be closely associated with *symptoms* rather than with *personality*. This was taken as evidence that personality traits and attitudes are relatively more enduring than are the signs and symptoms of illness.

A further example of the value of the double classification system in terms of symptom complexes and personality trait constellations is to be found in the work of Vinoda on the personalities of attempted suicides (Vinoda, 1964, 1966). The H.D.H.Q. was found to be of direct relevance to the problem. At the *symptom* level attempted suicides were found to have higher total Hostility scores on the H.D.H.Q. than other psychiatric patients. At the *personality* level, predictably, within the attempted suicide group those whose hostility was more inwardly directed as measured by the H.D.H.Q. and those who were more obsessoid as measured by the H.O.Q. made the more serious suicide attempts.

IV CONCLUSIONS

In evaluating the published clinical and experimental evidence it seems fair to say that the distinction between symptoms and personality traits originally posited by Janet has been sustained in clinical practice and in research work. In view of the critical influence played by both these aspects of psychological functioning on the behaviour of patients there is no justification for the continued use of a single classification or diagnosis in terms of symptom complexes only. This is particularly true in research work where the composition of groups of subjects used must be precisely stated if results are to be duplicated.

There is little doubt that the double classification system has utility in a wide range of clinical problems. Its use in the evaluation of treatment results, in abilities testing and in other areas has been indicated. From this point of view, much previously published material relating test results to single psychiatric diagnoses might well be re-worked using a symptom *and* personality classification. This is true of Foulds' earlier work on the T.A.T. and the Porteus Mazes for example. The latter would be a particularly rewarding test to investigate since it could be used as a *personality* measure for illiterates, cross-cultural studies, and for children. As far as the latter are concerned, the mazes might go some way in establishing how early personality types can be identified and how persistent they subsequently prove to be. Before treatment programmes can be adequately evaluated along the lines suggested here, long-term studies of normal samples will be required to determine the vicissitudes of the various aspects of psychological functioning, particularly in relation to mental illness.

REFERENCES

ALLPORT, G. W. (1958) *The Nature of Prejudice*. New York: Doubleday and Co.

BAKAN, D. (1966) The test of significance in psychological research. *Psychol. Bull.*, **66**, 423-437.

BOWLBY, J. (1940) *Personality and Mental Illness*. London: Kegan Paul, Trench and Trubner.

BUSS, A. H. (1961) *The Psychology of Aggression*. New York: Wiley.

CAINE, T. M. (1960) The expression of hostility and guilt in melancholic and paranoid women. *J. consult. Psychol.*, **24**, 18-22.

CAINE, T. M. (1963) Response suppression in normal and psychotic groups. *Psychol. Rep.*, **12**, 942.

CAINE, T. M. (1965a) Obsessoid and Hysteroid components of personality. *In* FOULDS, G. A., *Personality and Personal Illness.* London: Tavistock Publications.

CAINE, T. M. (1965b) Changes in symptom, attitude, and trait measures among chronic neurotics in a therapeutic community. *In* FOULDS, G. A., *Personality and Personal Illness.* London: Tavistock Publications.

CAINE, T. M. (1966) Perceptual sensitization, response suppression and psychopathology. *Brit. J. Psychol.*, **57**, 301-306.

CAINE, T. M. (1967) Response consistency and testing levels. *Brit. J. soc. clin. Psychol.*, **6**, 38-42.

CAINE, T. M. and HAWKINS, L. G. (1963) Questionnaire measure of the hysteroid/obsessoid component of personality. *J. consult. Psychol.*, **27**, 206-209.

CAINE, T. M. and HOPE, K. (1964) Validation of the Maudsley Personality Inventory E scale. *Brit. J. Psychol.*, **55**, 447-452.

CAINE, T. M. and HOPE, K. (1967) *Manual of the Hysteroid-Obsessoid Questionnaire (H.O.Q.).* London: University of London Press.

CAINE, T. M. and SMAIL, D. J. (1967) Personal relevance and the choice of constructs for the repertory grid technique. *Brit. J. Psychiat.*, **113**, 517-520.

CAINE, T. M. and SMAIL, D. J. (1969) *The Treatment of Mental Illness: Science, Faith and the Therapeutic Personality*, pp. 102-132. London: University of London Press.

CAINE, T. M., FOULDS, G. A. and HOPE, K. (1967) *Manual of the Hostility and Direction of Hostility Questionnaire (H.D.H.Q.).* London: University of London Press.

CHAPUIS, F. (1949) *Le Test du Labyrinthe.* Berne: Hans Huber.

CHODOFF, P. and LYONS, M. D. (1958) Hysteria, the hysterical personality and 'hysterical' conversions. *Amer. J. Psychiat.*, **114**, 734-740.

CROOKES, T. G. and HUTT, S. J. (1963) Scores of psychotic patients on the Maudsley Personality Inventory. *J. consult. Psychol.*, **27**, 243.

CURRAN, D. and GUTTMAN, E. V. (1949) *Psychological Medicine.* Edinburgh: Livingstone.

DOLLARD, J., MILLER, N. E., DOOB, L. W., MOWRER, O. H. and SEARS, R. R. (1944) *Frustration and Aggression.* London: Kegan Paul.

EDWARDS, A. L. (1957) *The Social Desirability Variable in Personality Assessment and Research.* New York: Dryden.

EYSENCK, H. J. (1952) *The Scientific Study of Personality.* London: Routledge and Kegan Paul.

EYSENCK, H. J. (1957) *The Dynamics of Anxiety and Hysteria.* London: Routledge and Kegan Paul.

EYSENCK, H. J. (1959a) *Manual of the Maudsley Personality Inventory.* London: University of London Press.

EYSENCK, H. J. (1959b) *The Structure of Human Personality* (2nd Ed.). London: Methuen.

EYSENCK, H. J. (1962) Correspondence. *Brit. J. Psychol.*, **53**, 455.

EYSENCK, H. J. (1967) Intelligence assessment: a theoretical and experimental approach. *Brit. J. Educ. Psychol.*, **37**, Pt 1, 81-98.

EYSENCK, H. J. and CLARIDGE, G. (1962) The position of hysterics and dysthymics in a two-dimensional framework of personality description. *J. abnorm. soc. Psychol.*, **64**, 45-46.

FENICHEL, O. (1945) *The Psychoanalytic Theory of Neurosis*. New York: Norton.

FORREST, A. D. (1967) Diagnosis of hysterical personality. *Brit. J. med. Psychol.*, **40**, 65-78.

FOULDS, G. A. (1951) Temperamental differences in maze performance. Part I. *Brit. J. Psychol.*, **42**, 209-217.

FOULDS, G. A. (1952a) Temperamental differences in maze performance. Part II. *Brit. J. Psychol.*, **43**, 33-41.

FOULDS, G. A. (1952b) A method of scoring the T.A.T. applied to psycho-neurotics. *J. ment. Sci.*, **415**, 235-246.

FOULDS, G. A. (1955) Psychiatric syndromes and personality types. *Psychologische Forschung*, **25**, 65-78.

FOULDS, G. A. (1958) Superiority-inferiority index in relation to frustrating situations. *J. clin. Psychol.*, **14**, 163-166.

FOULDS, G. A. (1962) Correspondence. *Brit. J. Psychol.*, **53**, 456.

FOULDS, G. A. (1965) *Personality and Personal Illness*. London: Tavistock Publications.

FOULDS, G. A. (1966) Psychic-somatic symptoms and hostility. *Brit. J. soc. clin. Psychol.*, **5**, 185-189.

FOULDS, G. A. and CAINE, T. M. (1958a) Psychoneurotic symptom clusters, trait clusters and psychological tests. *J. ment. Sci.*, **104**, 722-731.

FOULDS, G. A. and CAINE, T. M. (1958b) Personality factors and performance on timed tests of ability. *Occ. Psychol.*, **32**, 102-105.

FOULDS, G. A. and CAINE, T. M. (1959a) Symptom clusters and personality types among psychoneurotic men compared with women. *J. ment. Sci.*, **105**, 469-475.

FOULDS, G. A. and CAINE, T. M. (1959b) The assessment of some symptoms and signs of depression in women. *J. ment. Sci.*, **105**, 182-189.

FOULDS, G. A., CAINE, T. M. and CREASY, M. A. (1960) Aspects of extra- and intro-punitive expression in mental illness. *J. ment. Sci.*, **106**, 599-610.

FOULDS, G. A. and HOPE, K. (1968) *Manual of the Symptom Sign Inventory*. London: University of London Press.

FRICKE, B. G. (1956) Response set as a suppressor variable in the O.A.I.S. and M.M.P.I. *J. consult. Psychol.*, **20**, 161-169.

FURNEAUX, W. D. (1963) *Manual of Nufferno Level Tests*. London: University of London Press.

HIMMELWEIT, H. T. (1946) Speed and accuracy of work as related to temperament. *Brit. J. Psychol.*, **36**, 132-144.

HOLZMAN, P. S. and KLEIN, G. S. (1954) Cognitive system-principles of levelling and sharpening: individual differences in assimilation effects in visual time-error. *J. Psychol.*, **37**, 105-122.

HOPE, K. (1963) *The Structure of Hostility among Normal and Neurotic Persons.* Unpublished Ph.D. thesis, University of London.

HOPE, K. and CAINE, T. M. (1968) The hysteroid obsessoid questionnaire: a new validation. *Brit. J. soc. clin. Psychol.*, 7, 210-215.

HUTT, M. L. (1951) The assessment of individual personality by projective tests: current problems. *J. proj. Tech.*, 15, 388-393.

HUTT, M. L. (1954) Towards an understanding of projective testing. *J. proj. Tech.*, 18, 197-201.

INGHAM, J. (1962) Correspondence. *Brit. J. Psychol.*, 53, 458.

INGHAM, J. G. and ROBINSON, J. O. (1964) Personality in the diagnosis of hysteria. *Brit. J. Psychol.*, 55, 276-84.

JAMES, WM. (1890) *Principles of Psychology*, Vol. II. London: Macmillan.

JUNG, C. G. (1920) *Collected Papers on Analytical Psychology.* London: Baillière Tindall and Cox.

KING, G. F. and SCHILLER, M. (1958) Note on ego-strength, defensiveness, and acquiescence. *Psychol., Rep.*, 4, 434.

KLEIN, G. S. (1950) The personal world through perception. *In* BLAKE, R. R. and RAMSAY, G. V. (Eds.) *Perception: an Approach to Personality.* New York: Ronald.

KLEIN, G. S. (1954) Need and regulation. *In* JONES, M. R. (Ed.) *Nebraska Symposium on Motivation*, Vol. 2. Lincoln, Nebr.: University Nebraska Press.

KLEIN, G. S. (1958) Cognitive control and motivation. *In* LINDZEY, G. (Ed.) *Assessment of Human Motives.* New York: Rinehart.

KLEIN, G. S. and SCHLESINGER, H. J. (1949) Where is the perceiver in perceptual theory? *J. Pers.*, 18, 32-47.

KLINE, P. (1967) Obsessional traits and emotional instability. *Brit. J. med. Psychol.*, 40, 153-157.

KRECH, D. and CRUTCHFIELD, R. S. (1948) *Theory and Problems of Social Psychology.* London: McGraw-Hill Book Co. Inc.

KRETSCHMER, E. (1926) Hysteria. *Nerv. and ment. Dis. Monogr.*, 44, New York.

LEWIS, A. J. and MAPOTHER, E. (1941) In *Price's Textbook of the Practice of Medicine.* London: Oxford University Press.

MCCALL, R. J. (1958) Face Validity in the D scale of the M.M.P.I. *J. clin. Psychol.*, 14, 1, 77-80.

MCCLELLAND, D. C. (1951) *Personality.* New York: Sloane.

MCDOUGALL, WM. (1923) *Outline of Psychology.* London: Methuen.

MCKELLAR, T. P. H. (1949) *A Psychological Study of Human Aggressiveness.* Unpublished Ph.D. thesis, University of London.

MACKINNON, D. W. (1944) The structure of personality. *In* HUNT, J. MCV. (Ed.) *Personality and the Behaviour Disorders*, Vol. I. New York: Ronald.

MASSERMAN, J. H. (1946) *Principles of Dynamic Psychiatry.* London and Philadelphia: Saunders.

MAYER-GROSS, W., SLATER, E. and ROTH, M. (1954) *Clinical Psychiatry* (2nd Ed., 1960). London: Cassell; Baltimore: Williams and Wilkins, 1955.

MAYO, P. R. (1966) Some psychological changes associated with improvement in depression. *Brit. J. soc. clin. Psychol.*, **6**, 63-68.

MEEHL, P. E. and HATHAWAY, S. R. (1946) The K factor as a suppressor variable in the Minnesota-Multiphasic Personality Inventory. *J. appl. Psychol.*, **30**, 525-564.

MICHAELS, J. J. and PORTER, R. T. (1949) Psychiatric and social implications of contrasts between psychopathic personality and obsessive-compulsive neurosis. *J. nerv. ment. Dis.*, **109**, 122.

MYERS, I. B. (1962) Manual. *The Myers-Briggs Type Indicator*. Princeton, N.J.: Educational Testing Service.

NOYES, A. P. (1954) *Modern Clinical Psychiatry*. London and Philadelphia: Saunders.

PORTEUS, S. D. (1942) *Qualitative Performance in the Maze Test*. Vineland, N.J.: Smith Printing House.

RAPAPORT, D. (1948) *Diagnostic Psychological Testing*, Vol. 2. Chicago Year Book.

REICH, W. (1949) *Character Analysis*. New York: Orgone Institute Press.

ROSENBERG, C. M. (1967) Personality and obsessional neurosis. *Brit. J. Psychiat.*, **113**, 471-477.

ROSENZWEIG, S. J. (1945) The picture-association method and its application in a study of reactions to frustration. *Char. & Pers.* **14**, 3-23.

ROSENZWEIG, S., CLARKE, H. J., GARFIELD, M. S. and LEHNDORFF, A. (1946) Scoring samples for the Rosenzweig Picture-Frustration study. *J. Psychol.*, **21**, 45-72.

SALMON, P. (1965) Foulds' punitiveness scales in relation to M.M.P.I. validation and diagnostic scales. *Brit. J. soc. clin. Psychol.*, **4**, 207-213.

SANDLER, J. and HAZARI, A. (1960) The 'obsessional': On the psychological classification of obsessional character traits and symptoms. *Brit. J. med. Psychol.*, **33**, 113-122.

SIEGEL, S. M. (1956) The relationship of hostility to authoritarianism. *J. abnorm. soc. Psychol.*, **52**, 368-372.

SLATER, E. (1950) *The genetical aspects of personality and neurosis*. Congrès internat. de psychiatrie, Paris, VI, Psychiatrie sociale, génétique et engénique.

SLATER, E. (1965) Diagnosis of hysteria. *Brit. med. J.* **1**, 1395.

SLATER, E. and SLATER, P. (1944) A heuristic theory of neurosis. *J. neurol. Psychiat.*, **7**, 49.

SMAIL, D. J. (1966) A multiple-choice version of the T.A.T. as a measure of aggression in psychiatric patients. *Brit. J. med. Psychol.*, **39**, 163-169.

SNEDECOR, G. W. (1946) *Statistical methods*. Ames, Iowa: Iowa State Coll. Press.

SUMNER, W. G. and KELLER, A. G. (1927) *The Science of Society*. New Haven: Yale University Press.

SWEETLAND, A. and QUAY, H. (1953) A note on the K scale of the Minnesota Multiphasic Personality Inventory. *J. consult. Psychol.*, **17**, 314-316.

TUKEY, J. W. (1962) The future of data analysis. *Annals of Mathematical Statistics*, **33**, 1-67.

VERNON, P. E. (1957) *Personality Tests and Assessments*. London: Methuen and Co. Ltd.

VERNON, P. E. and PARRY, J. B. (1949) *Personnel Selection in the British Forces*. London: University of London Press.

VINODA, K. S. (1964) *A Study of Personality Characteristics of Attempted Suicides*. Unpublished Ph.D. thesis, University of London.

VINODA, K. S. (1966) Personality characteristics of attempted suicides. *Brit. J. Psychiat.*, **112**, 1143-1150.

WIGGINS, J. S. (1962) Definitions of social desirability and acquiescence in personality inventories. *In* MESSICK, S. and ROSS, J. (Eds.) *Measurement in Personality and Cognition*. New York and London: Wiley.

P. J. Mittler

1 LINKING ASSESSMENT WITH TREATMENT

This book was conceived on the assumption that psychological assessment is at a turning-point in its evolution. In the past, psychologists have tended to confine themselves to assessment, and left others to incorporate (or ignore) their findings in whatever was done for the patient or client. The emphasis of the future will almost certainly lie on the psychologist using his own findings as a basis for helping the individual patient. Tests will always provide 'basic' information, but a change of emphasis in the aims and goals of psychological assessment is bound to effect a corresponding change in the nature of the assessment instruments used and in the whole assessment process.

The forging of an organic link between assessment and treatment is one of the most consistent themes of this book. It informs the introductory chapter by Jones, and it is described in detail by Shapiro, who has for some time been advocating the intensive experimental approach to the individual patient. Other psychologists, represented in this volume by Tyson and several others, are experimenting with a 'profile' approach to diagnostic testing, with the aim of making a more penetrating analysis of a child's cognitive assets and deficits than can be provided by the traditional intelligence tests.

There are several pertinent issues here. In the first place, the classical global test approach makes the assumption that constructs such as 'intelligence' and 'personality' are in themselves relevant in helping the individual patient; thus, if systematic information can be collected under these headings, it is assumed that this must be of value in treatment. But it frequently happens that the psychologist's findings play no significant part in deciding how an individual can be helped. Reports couched in the most general terms and confined to global descriptive statements about intelligence or personality are duly filed away, together with routine investigations such as skull X-ray, haemoglobin counts and urine analysis which are carried out for the sake of clinical thoroughness, and not because there is anything in the patient's symptoms or problems which specifically call for these investigations rather than for any others. The more relevant the psychologist's assessment, the more concerned with 'narrow bandwidth and high fidelity', to echo Jones's analogy, the richer the contribution that the psychologist can make to the patient. Diagnosis divorced from treatment is a mere intellectual exercise, and sometimes hardly that.

A second problem is raised by the nature of the generalizations which are involved in the translation of test information from the standardization group to the individual. This is, of course, a necessary procedure if one wants to place the individual on a 'brightness scale' in relation to the normative group in order to make relevant comparisons – e.g. in judging the probability of his success in some course of education or training. Even so, estimates of probability based on interpretation of test data carry a high (and sometimes known) risk of error; moreover, it is precisely in borderline cases that the psychologist's opinion is invoked, and it is here that the possibility of error is at its greatest. A psychologist is unlikely to be asked whether a child with an I.Q. of 65 should study medicine, or whether a man with a high introversion score should become a door-to-door salesman. It is in the borderline cases that one is confronted by the need to take other factors into account. Whether a child with a certain I.Q. has the abilities to take a particular training may depend not only on a proper interpretation of test information but on the extent to which other factors interact with his intellectual abilities – parental attitudes and environmental factors in general, appropriate motivation, etc. The psychologist may be best equipped to investigate intelligence, but is not necessarily better than any other observer in estimating the relevance and role of other variables, though these may be vital in affecting outcome. His scientific contribution can often only take the form of '*Other things being equal*, he has or has not the intellectual abilities required for this course'.

The implication here is obvious enough; there is an urgent need for psychologists to widen their assessment repertoire in order to incorporate into their findings information on a person's developmental history, experiences that have affected his development, home background, environmental variables, motivation, etc. The importance of these variables is richly attested in recent research – some references to which are available in chapters by Ravenette, Chazan and the editor – but very few attempts have been made to systematize the collection of information in a valid and reliable way, or to incorporate such variables in a prediction model.

A third point that arises concerns the doubts which some psychologists have felt about the scientific basis of working with the individual case. One aspect that is frequently mentioned concerns the validity of making a statement about an individual which is not based on a comparison of that individual with some normative group. Implicit in this attitude is often a doubt about the availability of statistical techniques to evaluate or even describe such work. Here again, both Shapiro's work, as well as much of the applied operant approach, indicates that these fears are largely unfounded. In operant work, for example, the individual is used as his own control in order to assess the effects of a particular 'treatment' on base-line behaviour.

II 'INDIVIDUAL DIFFERENCES' IN REAL LIFE

This work is of particular importance in the field of psychiatric or developmental disorders, whether in adults or children. Psychologists working with handicapped children do not need to be reminded that within each of the official categories of 'handicapped pupil' is to be found a vastly heterogeneous population, who, although having a common handicap, differ greatly within themselves. The earliest object lesson was learned by those who reported findings on 'brain-damaged' patients, who, it is now well realized, constitute a highly heterogeneous population who need to be examined in relation to the nature and extent of the 'damage', previous levels of functioning and a large number of other factors. The term 'brain damage' is now seen to be anything but a clinical entity (Meyer, 1960), but this is partly for the fortuitous reason that it does not correspond to a medically recognized disorder. (It may be noted parenthetically, however, that 'minimal brain damage' is replacing 'brain damage' as a focus of interest, even though it is much more difficult to recognize.) Other, more orthodox disorders, such as motor and sensory handicaps, although undoubtedly recognizable as a medically diagnosed handicap, are nevertheless extremely variable in their effects on individuals. Thus, two partially hearing children of the same age may have identical audiograms and I.Q.s, but be at quite different levels of language development, and respond quite differently to teaching, both in level and in type.

What is being called into question here is the validity of the medical model of classification in developmental and assessment psychology. The assumption of the medical model within which psychologists have worked for many years is that a medically diagnosed condition or syndrome necessarily has certain behavioural or psychological correlates. Thus, it is common for research reports to appear in which 'spastics' have been tested on a particular measure or compared with another nosological group, presumably on the assumption that this highly heterogeneous group is likely to have certain psychological characteristics in common, and that skilled research will reveal these to the patient researcher. To a certain extent, of course, this is a valid and fruitful procedure, at a particular stage in the development of knowledge about a disorder. It is useful and important to know, for example, that deaf children are normally distributed on non-verbal tests of intelligence, or that children with Down's Disease (mongolism) are likely to have particularly marked language difficulties. On the other hand, such generalizations may come to mask more than they reveal, and can at best provide no more than probabilistic statements in respect of a single individual. In clinical work, it is certainly necessary to be armed with generalizations derived from research, but these are only the starting-point of a more intensive assessment which is prepared to consider each person as an individual who may differ fundamentally from the tester's expectations.

Similar difficulties arise in experimental work when it becomes necessary to construct a 'control' group. The inclusion of a control group is generally regarded as an essential feature of scientific procedure, but its use involves many difficulties. In experimental work with the mentally subnormal, for example, it is common to find subnormals matched on 'mental age' with normals; thus, a group of subnormal adults with a mental age of 4 years may be matched with a 'control' group of nursery-school children who also have a mental age of 4. The two groups are then solemnly compared on a series of measures, such as short term memory, discrimination learning and the like. This procedure is obviously artificial, though in capable hands it has yielded findings which have been replicated.

To what extent, then, is it meaningful to use a control group in research on normative work with handicapped populations? In working with normal children, it is permissible to make certain assumptions about the nature of the comparison groups in terms not only of their age but also of their life experiences, social background, etc. While it may be reasonable to construct experimental and control groups by random allocation of normal children to one or other condition, the procedure may be less justified in the case of handicapped groups. *The more handicapped the child, the less comparable he is with any other child, no matter how perfectly matched in terms of his score on a series of measures.* Quite apart from the artificiality of matching older subnormals with younger normals, the handicapped child will be likely to have restricted experiences by virtue of his handicap; his opportunities for learning and acquiring skills will be different, and his social history and exposure to rewards is in many senses different from those likely to be experienced by the normal child. Even more important is the heterogeneity likely to be found within a handicapped group; in other words, the experimenter is confronted by the problem of individual differences.

In theory, the psychologist is interested in individual differences – they are his stock in trade, and whole sections of his undergraduate texts purport to deal with them. But in terms of research methods and experimental design, they present a formidable problem. Underwood (1964) is quoted by Jensen (1967) as referring to the I.D. sources of variance as 'pesky statistical problems' and from a recent conference at the University of Pittsburgh devoted entirely to individual differences in learning, it is clear that problems posed by the constructive use of individual differences in research have barely begun to be tackled, though some promising techniques and models were presented (Gagné, 1967). Nevertheless, there are still many psychologists who seriously think that the problem of individual differences in an experiment can be resolved by inspection of the standard deviation. Perhaps this notion is one of the more naïve legacies of experimental psychology to the abnormal field.

It is our contention that handicapped individuals do not fit easily into the traditional research designs favoured by experimental psychologists. To say this is not to make a woolly sentimental plea for the 'uniqueness of the individual' but to reiterate that in the heterogeneity of a handicapped population lies its strength. Instead of looking at the characteristics of groups, they force us to devise and refine our techniques of looking at the individual, since it is he who requires such professional skills as the psychologist has to offer.

III OPERANT WORK

One of the most promising approaches to the study of the individual case is along operant lines. Advances made by behaviour therapy are now well documented, and some of the early enthusiasm has given way to a more cautious and realistic appreciation of the potentialities and limitations of this approach. Far less known are the applied behaviouristic approaches to assessment and treatment which are now being widely applied in the United States. These cannot be easily summarized, though reference has already been made to the pioneering work of Bijou (Bijou and Baer, 1967) at Illinois, Sidman and Stoddard (1966) in Boston, and an active group in Kansas (Spradlin and Girardeau, 1966). In essence, applied operant methods partly resolve the problem of within group differences by using the individual as his own control and by systematic analyses of specific aspects of behaviour before, during and after the application of a particular procedure – e.g. reinforcing 'looking' behaviour, social co-operation, etc., and ignoring (as far as possible) deviant or unwanted behaviour. Whatever reservations may be entertained about these approaches, the weight of published evidence of their effectiveness is increasingly impressive. Their advantage lies not only in the partial solution of the problem of the artificial control group but in the link created between assessment and treatment. This is a worthy model for the clinical psychologist who sometimes wonders whether his test findings can really be of any value in the treatment (by others or by no one) of the patient whom he has just seen and may never see again.

A further advantage of the operant approach is that it enables the psychologist (temporarily, perhaps) to escape from the medical model of disorder. He should, of course, be aware of the useful generalizations which earlier generations of research workers have produced about the group that he is studying, but he is basically interested in the individual case, and in producing or reducing specific behaviours. The fact that his subject has Down's Disease or phenylketonuria will impose certain constraints on his expectations of the subject's learning ability within the experimental situation, but the extent of these constraints is largely an unknown factor, and should not influence him in anything other than the most general terms, since here again the information at the psychologist's disposal is in terms of probabilities. Thus, it is likely that his mongol patient will be relatively retarded in verbal tasks compared with matched normals, and care will therefore have to be taken in the presentation of instructions on a task designed to measure, say, visual scanning ability. But he need not necessarily make assumptions about his subject's verbal abilities, since the technique allows for training by shaping, by grading learning into small steps and by other methods (Millenson, 1967). In other words, the behaviour-orientated psychologist is not interested in assessment for assessment's sake – his motto has been characterized as 'Don't test – teach'. In case this might be thought to be rather an extreme viewpoint, it could be modified to 'Don't test without teaching'.

It has taken psychologists many years to learn that people differ not only in their scores on standardized intelligence and personality tests, but in many other ways too complex for their analytical and descriptive skills to encompass. While operant methods reduce much of the complexity of human behaviour, they inevitably rob it of its richness and subtlety. Yet there is no reason why behaviouristic approaches should necessarily run counter to other research strategies. The work of Piaget, Bruner and others interested in fundamental cognitive processes is in many ways complementary to that of the neo-Skinnerians. Indeed, either in isolation is in danger of artificiality. Both Piaget and Bruner have vitalized educational research, while the legacy of Skinner will in time be seen to lie in the pragmatic approach to the individual and his needs. One obvious limitation of operant methods, however, is that they are best suited for dealing with only one 'behaviour' at a time, and that this is uneconomical of human resources in terms of ordinary classroom practice. As against this, the method lends itself ideally to the home, and parents have been trained to apply operant principles with considerable success, not only in their own homes but also as helpers in school.

IV   NEED FOR NEW TECHNIQUES

The overriding need in applied psychology is for the development of a wider range of techniques – not only tests in the conventional sense but also better and more penetrating methods of analysis of a fuller body of data on individuals and groups. Several contributors have described work being done to develop new assessment techniques and have discussed their application to handicapped populations; there is also a corresponding need for more refined statistical methods; perhaps the most promising advances are multivariate methods of analysis (Cattell, 1966; Nunnally, 1967), including profile, pattern and various forms of cluster and discriminant analysis. Their advantage lies in allowing the psychologist to examine several variables and trends independently and to look at the variance within groups by going beyond standard deviations and classical analysis of variance.

It cannot be too strongly emphasized that new developments in applied psychology must be linked to the mainstream of general and experimental psychology. The speed of advance in applied psychology in recent years is most probably related to the fact that there has been much more exchange between 'pure' and 'applied' psychology – in fact the distinction between the two is now seen as blurred and artificial. The exchange of ideas has been facilitated by more movement of psychologists between and within fields. More experimental psychologists are working in applied settings and more applied (or ex-applied) psychologists are to be found working in academic departments of psychology, often still engaged in experimental clinical work. Prejudice based on ignorance is giving way to a more realistic awareness of the size of the contribution which psychology still has to make to the assessment and treatment of the handicapped.

V THE PSYCHOLOGIST IN SOCIETY

While the psychologist of the future is likely to make a much more effective contribution to the treatment of the individual case by becoming more directly involved with both the planning and execution of a therapeutic or training programme, he also has a wider social function. He is a member of a society just like anyone else, but one with professional training and skills which makes him potentially able to make an important contribution over and above the work that he does with individual patients. The psychologist has to educate as well as inform, to reform as well as educate. Obviously, he must proceed cautiously on the basis of evidence, but he should not shelter too long behind scientific caution or even behind his own clinical work by avoiding involvement with wider social issues. There is no reason why psychologists should not be a little bolder than at present in making politicians, policy makers and administrators more aware of their skills, and of research findings which are relevant to a particular area of public concern. Other professions are not always as reticent.

One example that might be given concerns the work of investigators such as Tizard who, together with associates from other disciplines, has been investigating the effect of different types of social organization on children in residential institutions (Tizard, 1964; Tizard *et al.*, 1966). They found that child care practices were related not so much to the size of the institution as to its social structure: the hospitals were 'hierarchical, overdepartmentalized and too highly centralized', and were 'task rather than child orientated', whereas the children's homes (both for mentally handicapped and normal children) were so organized as to delegate responsibility for most decisions to the child care staff, who had almost the same freedom of choice in 'making decisions as parents. Earlier, in the Brooklands experiment (1964), he had shown that severely subnormal children make faster verbal and social progress when looked after in small groups by child-care principles than a matched control group who remained in the institution.

Findings such as these are clearly of the greatest importance in affecting policy making at a time when more thought is being given to the residential care of handicapped children. Nevertheless, the psychologist who wishes to see some useful practical outcome from his research must expect to do more than publish his results in a learned journal, which is unlikely to be read by administrators. He must constantly confront them with findings, not only from his own research but from the relevant literature which he will know much better than most professional administrators.

Other examples could be taken from the work of Bowlby (1951) which has fundamentally affected children's hospitals, especially when reinforced by professionally inspired publicity, including the judicious use of mass media, and by parents' and lay organizations. Similarly, there is now a much greater awareness of the effect of institutional environments per se on the course of chronic mental and physical illnesses, though the effects of institutionalization are not easy to distinguish from the symptoms of chronic schizophrenia.

These are complex research problems, which have resulted in relatively few definite findings that can be confidently presented to administrators. Nevertheless, the trend of the evidence is in many cases discernible, and no psychologist can now afford to ignore the wider context within which he deploys his professional skills.

REFERENCES

BIJOU, S. W. and BAER, D. M. (Eds.) (1967) *Child Development: Readings in Experimental Analysis*. New York: Appleton-Century-Crofts.

BOWLBY, J. (1951) *Maternal Care and Mental Health*. Geneva: World Health Organization.

CATTELL, R. B. (1966) *Handbook of Multivariate Experimental Psychology*. Chicago: Rand McNally.

GAGNÉ, R. M. (Ed.) (1967) *Learning and Individual Differences*. Columbus, Ohio: Merrill.

JENSEN, A. R. (1967) Varieties of individual differences in learning. *In* GAGNÉ, R. (Ed.) *Learning and Individual Differences*. Columbus, Ohio: Merrill.

MEYER, V. (1960) Psychological effects of brain damage. *In* EYSENCK, H. J. (Ed.) *Handbook of Abnormal Psychology*. London: Pitman.

MILLENSON, J. R. (1967) *Principles of Behavioral Analysis*. New York and London: Macmillan.

NUNNALLY, J. C. (1967) *Psychometric Theory*. New York: McGraw-Hill.

SIDMAN, M. and STODDARD, L. T. (1966) Programming perception and learning for retarded children. *In* ELLIS, N. R. (Ed.) *International Review of Research in Mental Retardation*, 2. New York: Academic Press.

SPRADLIN, J. E. and GIRARDEAU, F. L. (1966) The behavior of moderately and severely retarded persons. *In* ELLIS, N. R. (Ed.) *International Review of Research in Mental Retardation*, 1. New York: Academic Press.

TIZARD, J. (1964) *Community Services for the Mentally Handicapped*. London: Oxford Univ. Press.

TIZARD, J., KING, R. D., RAYNES, N. V. and YULE, W. (1966) The care and treatment of subnormal children in residential institutions. In *What is Special Education?* London: Assocn for Special Education.

UNDERWOOD, B. J. (1964) Laboratory studies of verbal learning. *In* HILGARD, E. R. (Ed.) *Theories of Learning and Instruction*. Chicago: National Soc. for Study of Education. (Cited by Jensen, 1967.)

Author Index

Abel, G. L., 306
Abel, G. L. and Kinder, E. F., 292
Abercrombie, M. L. J., 395, 447, 458, 461, 685
Abt, L. E., 570
Achilles, E. M., 49, 54
Adams, B., 224, 763
Adcock, C. J., 32, 92, 93, 96, 113
Affleck, D. C. and Garfield, S. L., 221
Aita, J. A., 50
Ajuriaguerra, J. de, 265, 277, 280, 282
Albee, G. W., 47
Albitreccia, S. L., 459
Albrecht, R., 112
Alimena, B., 41
Al-Issa, I., 244, 246
Al-Issa, I. and Robertson, J. P. S., 244
Allen, R. M., 47, 51, 52
Allport, G. W., 83, 84, 85, 93, 95, 100, 101, 102, 805
Alper, A. E. and Horne, B. M., 300
Amatruda, C. S., 388, 501, 523
Ammons, R. B., 41, 488-9
Anastasi, A., 30, 34, 111, 474, 499, 549, 560-1, 567, 568
Anderson, L. D., 105, 568, 570
Andry, R. G., 564
Angelergues, R., 268, 276-7
Anthony, A. J., 351
Appell, M. J., 38
Arenberg, D., 324
Armitage, S. G. and Pearl, 40
Arnhoff, F. N., 89, 110
Arrigoni, G. and de Renzi, E., 281
Arthur, A. Z., 228
Ash, P., 89, 113-14, 159, 208, 209-10
Asher, H., 388, 585
Astrup, C., 213, 214
Ayllon, T. and Houghton, E., 253
Ayllon, T. and Michael, J., 303
Azrin, N. H., 223, 361

Babcock, H., 43, 44, 46, 49, 53, 59, 265, 379
Babcock, H. and Levy, L., 49
Bachelis, L., 42
Baer, D. M., 350, 823
Bain, A., 29
Baker, J. A., 329
Ball, R. S., 627
Baller, W. R., 292, 299
Balthaser, E. E., 52
Bannister, D., 60, 84, 100, 101, 102, 210, 225, 297-8, 762-3, 766-7, 771, 776
Bannister, D. and Fransella, F., 220
Bannister, D., Salmon, P. and Lieberman, D. M., 213
Barbigan, M. M., 212
Barclay, A., 296
Barnard, E. L., 491
Barnes, M. R. and Felterman, J. E., 50
Barnett, S. A., 358
Baroff, G. S., 293
Barr, B., 424
Barrett, A. M., 40, 41
Barrett, M. L., 450
Barry, J. R., 227, 383
Barry, J. R., Blyth, D. D. and Albrecht, R., 112
Barsch, R. H., 668
Bartlett, F. C., 169, 661, 663
Barton, R., 240
Basowitz, H., 177
Bass, B. M., 87, 101
Bass, B. M. and Berg, I. M., 100, 106, 107
Bateman, B., 629, 632
Bates, A., 433
Battersky, H. S., 60
Bauer, R. W. and Johnson, D. E., 44
Baughman, E. E., 111
Baumeister, A. A., 292, 351
Bax, M. and McKeith, R. M., 347

827

2E

Tindall, R. H., 549
Tischler, 615
Titaeva, M. A., 188
Tizard, J., 32, 113, 301, 305, 307, 361, 495, 505, 624, 825
Tizard, J. and O'Connor, N., 295
Tizard, J. and Venables, P. H., 59
Tobias, J. and Gorelick, J., 307
Tooth, G., 50
Town, C. H., 302
Tozer, A. H. D. and Larwood, H. J. C., 106
Trapp, C. E. and James, E. B., 47
Tregold, R. F. and Soddy, K., 290
Trembley, D. and O'Connor, J., 320
Trist, E., 50
Truax, C. B., 654
Trumbo, D., 114
Tubbs, V. K., 630-1
Tuddenham, R. D., 111
Tukey, J. W., 782
Tutko, T. A. and Spence, J. T., 248
Tversky, 9, 24
Tyson, M. C., 349, 685

Ucko, L. E., 571-2
Ullman, L. P., 226
Ulrich, L. and Trumbo, D., 114
Underwood, B. J., 224, 822
Uyeno, E., 55

Vail, D. J., 306
Van de Geer, J., 61
Van der Merwe, A. B., 182
Van Wagenen, M. J., 520
Vane, J. R., 502
Venables, P. H., 59, 116, 184, 187, 188, 215, 225, 595
Venables, P. H. and Martin, I., 178
Venables, P. H. and Wing, J. K., 183
Vernon, P. E., 33, 34, 84, 87, 90, 92, 94, 95, 96, 97, 100, 103, 107-8, 110-14, 159, 248, 345, 476, 483, 485, 486, 491, 503, 505, 549, 554, 555, 557, 568, 570, 575, 583, 596, 606, 650, 655, 672, 727, 803
Vernon, P. E. and Parry, J. B., 32, 114, 135, 789

Vignolo, L. A., 269
Villey, P., 379-81
Vincent, N. L., 102
Vinoda, K. S., 811
Vygotsky, L. S., 602

Wagner, E. E. and Hawver, D. A., 307, 689
Wales, R., 612-13
Walker, A., 551
Walker, J., 360
Walkey, F. A., 54
Wallace, S. R., 38, 100
Walsh, J. J., 112
Walster, E., 100
Walter, W. Grey, 189
Walton, D., 212, 216, 300, 508
Walton, D. and Black, D. A., 46, 53, 241, 244
Walton, R. E., 569
Warburton, F. W., 554, 719
Warner, J. S., 43
Warr, P. B., 774
Warren, S. A. and Kraus, M. J., 294
Warrington, E. K., 283
Warrington, E. K. and Weiskrantz, L., 266
Watson, L. S., 19, 85, 303, 304
Watts, A. F., 485, 487
Weale, R. A., 385
Webb, A. P., 38, 40, 47, 214
Wechsler, D., 31, 33, 37, 38, 39-40, 41-2, 43, 45, 49, 51, 52, 54, 55, 58, 250, 265, 294, 320, 328-9, 334, 348, 426, 499, 501, 530, 587, 647, 719
Wedell, K., 395-6
Wedgewood, J., 743
Weinstein, S. and Tenber, H. L., 263
Weisenberg, T. H. and McBride, K. L., 271
Weiskrantz, L., 266
Weitz, J., 100
Weksel, W., 757
Welder, D., 60
Welford, A. T., 58, 61, 322
Wellman, B. and Pegram, E. L., 358
Wells, E. L., 49
Wells, E. L. and Kelley, C. M., 45

General Index

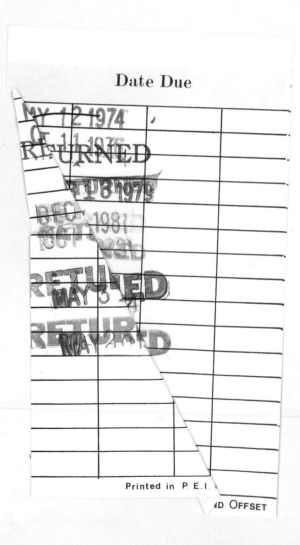

Date Due